*View*points

Authors
Robert Dawe
Margaret Iveson
Sharon Jeroski
Christel Kleitsch
Wendy Mathieu
Robin Pearson
Dirk Verhulst

Series Consultants
John Borovilos
Robert Dawe
Margaret Iveson
Wendy Mathieu
Dirk Verhulst

Publishing Consultant
Anthony Luengo

Assessment Consultant
Sharon Jeroski

PEARSON
Prentice
Hall

Toronto

National Library of Canada Cataloguing in Publication Data

Main entry under title:
Viewpoints 12

ISBN 0-13-092462-8 (bound)   ISBN 0-13-092450-4 (pbk.)

1. Readers (Secondary). I. Dawe, Robert T. (Robert Thomas), 1948– II. Mathieu, Wendy Lee, 1959–

PE1121.V55 2002   428.6   C2001-903519-5

ISBN 0-13-092462-8 (hardcover)   ISBN 0-13-092450-4 (paperback)
ISBN 0-13-039212-X (Trillium hardcover)   ISBN 0-13-039213-8 (Trillium paperback)

Publisher: Mark Cobham
Product Manager: Anita Borovilos
Managing Editor: Elynor Kagan
Project Manager: Anthony Luengo
Anthologist and Developmental Editor: Irene Cox
Production Editor: Angelie Kim
Text Researchers: Angelie Kim, Stephen Sanborn, Rebecca Vogan
Visuals Researchers: Krista Alexander, Angelie Kim
Contributing Writer: Laura Edlund
Copy Editor: Sarah Swartz
Proofreaders: Gail Copeland, Milena Mazzolin, Geri Savitz-Fine, Rebecca Vogan
Production Coordinator: Zane Kaneps
Art Direction: Zena Denchik
Cover Design: Jennifer Federico
Cover Image: Freeman Patterson/Masterfile
Interior Design: Zena Denchik
Page Layout: David Cheung Design Inc.
Permissions: Karen Hunter, Elizabeth Kelly, Michaele Sinko

5 TCP 09

Printed and bound in Canada

The publisher has taken every care to meet or exceed industry specifications for the manufacturing of textbooks. The spine and the endpapers of this sewn book have been reinforced with special fabric for extra binding strength. The cover is a premium, polymer-reinforced material designed to provide long life and withstand rugged use. Mylar gloss lamination has been applied for further durability.

Contents by Genre and Form

Preface. xviii

Acknowledgements xix

Invitation to Literature   2

The Word   *poem*
Pablo Neruda 4

Reading on "the Rez"   *memoir*
Tomson Highway 6

For the Love of Books   *memoir*
Rita Dove 7

Not a Boyhood Passion   *memoir*
Mordecai Richler 10

How Reading Changed My Life   *memoir*
Anna Quindlen 12

The Secret   *poem*
Denise Levertov 14

Invitation to Literature: Activities 15

Unit 1   Short Fiction   16

The Rocking-Horse Winner   *short story*
D.H. Lawrence 18

Write Me Sometime   *short story*
Taien Ng-Chan 36

Calgary from Sunnyside   *woodblock print*
Margaret Shelton 46

Outside Edges   *short story*
Ivan Dorin 48

Twisted Roots   *photograph*
Lyle McIntyre 60

The Shining Houses   *short story*
Alice Munro. 62

A Devoted Son   *short story*
Anita Desai 74

Magpies   *short story*
Thomas King 87

The Winner   *short story*
Barbara Kimenye 96

Windows   *short story*
Bernice Morgan 109

Easter at My Aunt's   *lithograph*
Christopher Pratt 118

War   *short story*
Timothy Findley 120

Peace and War   *short story*
Moacyr Scliar 138

The Spirit of Haida Gwaii   *sculpture*
Bill Reid 142

Mazes   *speculative fiction*
Ursula K. Le Guin 144

Was It a Dream?   *ghost story*
Guy de Maupassant 150

From **No Great Mischief**   *novel excerpt*
Alistair MacLeod 155

Unit Wrap-Up Activities 163

In-Depth: Universal Themes and Patterns   **164**

From The Archetypes of Literature   *literary criticism*
Northrop Frye 166

The Hero's Adventure   *interview*
Joseph Campbell with Bill Moyers 171

Ode to the West Wind   *poem*
Percy Bysshe Shelley 177

Araby *from* Dubliners   *short story*
James Joyce 181

Utopian Dreams   *book review*
Val Ross 188

Universal Themes and Patterns: Activities 193

Unit 2 Essays, Articles, and Media   194

Essays

Portrait of the Essay as a Warm Body   *expository essay*
Cynthia Ozick 196

Personal and Reflective Essays

Ka-Ching!   *personal essay*
Margaret Atwood 205

Afternoon of an American Boy   *personal essay*
E.B. White. 209

A Place to Stand On   *reflective essay*
Margaret Laurence. 216

Chameleons and Codas   *personal essay*
Patricia Conrad 224

Elegy in Stone   *reflective essay*
Steven Heighton 229

The Death of the Moth   *reflective essay*
Virginia Woolf 236

Biographical Essays

Guy Lafleur   *biographical essay*
Ken Dryden 242

My Mother's Blue Bowl   *biographical essay*
Alice Walker 251

Migrant Mother   *photograph*
Dorothea Lange 256

Expository and Analytical Essays

Of Youth and Age   *analytical essay*
Francis Bacon 258

Why I Write   *analytical essay*
George Orwell 263

The Not-So-Deadly Sin   *expository essay*
Barbara Kingsolver. 272

Call of the Weird   *expository essay*
Drew Hayden Taylor. 279

Argumentative and Persuasive Essays

A Modest Proposal   *persuasive essay*
Jonathan Swift 283

Get Beyond Babel   *argumentative essay*
Ken Wiwa 294

The Death of History Is Bunk   *persuasive essay*
Patrick Watson 300

Wanderers by Choice   *argumentative essay*
Eva Hoffman 306

Peace, Technology, and the Role of Ordinary People
speech
Ursula Franklin 313

Articles

Slide to Entropy   *newspaper column*
Kathleen Winter 323

Paradise, a Poet, and Promised Land   *magazine article*
George Elliott Clarke 327

Hockey Night in Port Hawkesbury   *magazine article*
Lynn Coady 331

The Sixth Flight   *magazine article*
Chantal Tranchemontagne 336

Buying Your Next Synthesizer   *tech-advice column*
Amin Bhatia 345

A Chat with Al Purdy   *interview*
Kate Climenhage 349

Ours by Design   *magazine feature article*
Alison Blackduck 354

Media

Look What I Found   *cartoon*
Marian Henley 364

Landscape with the Fall of Icarus   *painting*
Pieter Brueghel 366

Shower at Ohashi Bridge   *print*
Hiroshige Utagawa 368

The Poetry of Earth and Sky   *photo essay*
Courtney Milne with Ormond and Barbara Mitchell . . 370

Canada: A Virtual History   *newspaper feature article*
Ray Conlogue 380

Unzipped   *annotated graphic*
Anna Husarska 389

The Humpback of Notre Dame   *print advertisement*
Government of Newfoundland and Labrador 392

Morty Mania   *trade magazine article*
Judy Waytiuk 394

The Monkey's Paw   *magazine feature article*
Daniel Wood 403

Restoring Life on the Edge   *newspaper article*
Chris Rose 421

Unit Wrap-Up Activities 429

In-Depth: Media on Media   430

Aphorisms   *aphorisms*
Marshall McLuhan 431

The News   *analytical essay*
Neil Postman 434

Learning Without Lectures   *newspaper article*
Ann Rees 443

King Zog's Birthday   *radio script*
Bob Elliott and Ray Goulding 446

almost visible   *poem*
Kenneth J. Harvey 449

Media on Media: Activities 451

In-Depth: Argument and Persuasion   452

Effective Persuasion *from* Rhetoric   *argument*
Aristotle 454

Giant Database Is Ripe for Abuse   *newspaper editorial*
Edmonton Journal 456

**Let's Stop Being Hysterical, Shall We, and Start Selling
Water to Those Who Need It**   *opinion piece*
Lee Morrison 459

Our Water Sovereignty Is at Risk   *opinion piece*
Eric Reguly 463

From **Water** *non-fiction book excerpt*
Marq de Villiers 466

Poetry *poem*
Marianne Moore 473

Argument and Persuasion: Activities 475

Unit 3 P o e t r y   4 7 6

The Twentieth Century and Beyond

Engineers' Corner *light verse*
Wendy Cope 478

Is the Pathetic Fallacy True? *lyric*
Elizabeth Brewster 481

Evening *etching*
Mary Cassatt 484

Birch Bark *lyric*
Michael Ondaatje 486

vancouver–courtenay–calgary *free verse*
George Bowering 489

Prairie Flight *free verse*
Dorothy Livesay 492

Fern Hill *lyric*
Dylan Thomas 494

Amiri Baraka *photograph*
C. Daniel Dawson 498

The Committee to Upgrade Celestial Signs *shape poem*
Kurt Brown 500

The Heroes You Had as a Girl *free verse*
Bronwen Wallace 503

foremother *narrative*
Lillian Bouzane 507

to you who would wage war against me *dramatic monologue*
Kateri Akiwenzie-Damm 511

I, Icarus *free verse*
Alden Nowlan 515

Musée des Beaux Arts   *reflective verse*
W.H. Auden 518

People on the Bridge   *reflective verse*
Wislawa Szymborska 521

Progress   *free verse*
Emma LaRocque 524

Summer Night   *lyric*
Langston Hughes 527

The Love Song of J. Alfred Prufrock   *dramatic monologue*
T.S. Eliot 530

Afternoons & Coffeespoons   *song lyrics*
Brad Roberts of The Crash Test Dummies 539

The River   *lyric*
Derek Walcott 542

grammar poem   *shape poem*
Rita Wong 545

Traditions

Mu-lan   *ballad*
Anonymous 548

From **Beowulf**   *epic*
Anonymous, Translated by Seamus Heaney 553

From **The Canterbury Tales: General Prologue**   *narrative*
Geoffrey Chaucer 560

Sonnet 116   *sonnet*
William Shakespeare 570

A Poison Tree   *engraving*
William Blake 572

The Rime of the Ancient Mariner   *narrative*
Samuel Taylor Coleridge 574

O Can You Leave Your Native Land?   *quatrain*
Susanna Moodie 601

Dover Beach   *dramatic monologue*
Matthew Arnold 604

Because I Could Not Stop for Death—   *allegorical verse*
Emily Dickinson 608

Unit Wrap-Up Activities 611

Unit 4 Drama 612

A Marriage Proposal *stage play*
Anton Chekhov 614

Set Design for **The Foreigner** *set design*
Karen Schulz Gropman 634

From **Acoose: Man Standing Above Ground** *monologue*
Janice Acoose and Brenda Zeman 636

Film Location for Random Passage *film location*
CBC Television 640

Stop! *stage play*
Donna Lewis. 642

Dead Parrot *television script*
Monty Python 650

Unit Wrap-Up Activities. 655

In-Depth: Shakespeare 656

Invisible Genius: The Quiet Talent of Tanya Moiseiwitsch
magazine article
Therese Greenwood 658

From **Hamlet** *film script*
William Shakespeare and Kenneth Branagh 666

Shakespeare in the Cinema: A Film Directors' Symposium
symposium. 677

The Shakespearean Tragic Hero *literary criticism*
A.C. Bradley. 687

From **Strong Women Prevail in Shakespeare's Comedies**
literary criticism
Angela Pitt 692

Saloonio *short story*
Stephen Leacock 696

Shakespeare: Activities 700

Glossary 701

Another Viewpoint Index 714

Author Index 715

Credits. 716

Contents by Theme

Sense of Self

The Rocking-Horse Winner *18* ■ Outside Edges *48* ■ A Devoted Son *74* ■ War *120* ■ No Great Mischief *155* ■ The Hero's Adventure *171* ■ Araby *181* ■ Ka-Ching! *205* ■ Afternoon of an American Boy *209* ■ A Place to Stand On *216* ■ Chameleons and Codas *224* ■ My Mother's Blue Bowl *251* ■ Of Youth and Age *258* ■ Why I Write *263* ■ The Not-So-Deadly Sin *272* ■ Wanderers by Choice *306* ■ Paradise, a Poet, and Promised Land *327* ■ Hockey Night in Port Hawkesbury *331* ■ Is the Pathetic Fallacy True? *481* ■ Fern Hill *494* ■ The Heroes You Had as a Girl *503* ■ I, Icarus *515* ■ Summer Night *527* ■ The Love Song of J. Alfred Prufrock *530* ■ Afternoons & Coffeespoons *539* ■ grammar poem *545* ■ Stop! *642*

Personal Challenges

The Rocking-Horse Winner *18* ■ Outside Edges *48* ■ The Hero's Adventure *171* ■ Chameleons and Codas *224* ■ Wanderers by Choice *306* ■ The Sixth Flight *336* ■ Landscape with the Fall of Icarus *366* ■ Restoring Life on the Edge *421* ■ foremother *507* ■ I, Icarus *515* ■ The Canterbury Tales *560* ■ Acoose *636* ■ Hamlet *666*

Creating and Breaking Stereotypes

The Shining Houses *62* ■ Chameleons and Codas *224* ■ Elegy in Stone *229* ■ Call of the Weird *279* ■ Mu-lan *548*

Close Connections

The Rocking-Horse Winner *18* ■ Write Me Sometime *36* ■ Outside Edges *48* ■ A Devoted Son *74* ■ Magpies *87* ■ The Winner *96* ■ Windows *109* ■ Easter at My Aunt's *118* ■ War *120* ■ Was It a Dream? *150* ■ No Great Mischief *155* ■ Araby *181* ■ Afternoon of an American Boy *209* ■ A Place to Stand On *216* ■ Chameleons and Codas *224* ■ My Mother's Blue Bowl *251* ■ Look What I Found *364* ■ The Monkey's Paw *403* ■ Evening *484* ■ Birch Bark *486* ■ The Heroes You Had as a Girl *503* ■ foremother *507* ■ to you who would wage war against me *511*

■ The Love Song of J. Alfred Prufrock *530* ■ Sonnet 116 *570* ■ Dover Beach *604* ■ A Poison Tree *572* ■ A Marriage Proposal *614* ■ Hamlet *666*

Heroes and Rebels

The Archetypes of Literature *166* ■ The Hero's Adventure *171* ■ Elegy in Stone *229* ■ Guy Lafleur *242* ■ Amiri Baraka *498* ■ The Heroes You Had as a Girl *503* ■ foremother *507* ■ I, Icarus *515* ■ Mu-lan *548* ■ Beowulf *553* ■ The Canterbury Tales *560* ■ Acoose *636* ■ The Shakespearean Tragic Hero *687* ■ Strong Women Prevail *692*

Loss

A Devoted Son *74* ■ Magpies *87* ■ Was It a Dream? *150* ■ No Great Mischief *155* ■ The Archetypes of Literature *166* ■ The Death of the Moth *236* ■ Migrant Mother *256* ■ The Rime of the Ancient Mariner *574* ■ Because I Could Not Stop for Death— *608* ■ Hamlet *666*

Creativity

Calgary from Sunnyside *46* ■ Twisted Roots *60* ■ Easter at My Aunt's *118* ■ The Spirit of Haida Gwaii *142* ■ Portrait of the Essay *196* ■ A Place to Stand On *216* ■ Guy Lafleur *242* ■ Why I Write *263* ■ The Not-So-Deadly Sin *272* ■ Ours by Design *354* ■ Shower at Ohashi Bridge *368* ■ The Poetry of Earth and Sky *370* ■ Morty Mania *394* ■ Aphorisms *431* ■ Engineers' Corner *478* ■ Is the Pathetic Fallacy True? *481* ■ Evening *484* ■ Amiri Baraka *498* ■ People on the Bridge *521* ■ Progress *524* ■ *Set Design for* The Foreigner *634* ■ Invisible Genius *658* ■ Shakespeare in the Cinema *677*

Learning

A Devoted Son *74* ■ The Death of History Is Bunk *300* ■ Learning Without Lectures *443* ■ grammar poem *545* ■ Saloonio *696*

Work and Careers

Write Me Sometime *36* ■ Ka-Ching! *205* ■ Guy Lafleur *242* ■ Unzipped *389* ■ Morty Mania *394* ■ Engineers' Corner *478* ■ Prairie Flight *492* ■ Amiri Baraka *498* ■ *Set Design for* The Foreigner *634* ■ Invisible Genius *658*

Recreation

The Winner *96* ■ Guy Lafleur *242* ■ Hockey Night in Port Hawkesbury *331* ■ The Sixth Flight *336* ■ Buying Your Next Synthesizer *345*

Rights and Responsibilities

The Shining Houses *62* ■ Utopian Dreams *188* ■ Chameleons and Codas *224* ■ Why I Write *263* ■ A Modest Proposal *283* ■ The Death of History Is Bunk *300* ■ Peace, Technology *313* ■ Ours by Design *354* ■ Look What I Found *364* ■ Restoring Life on the Edge *421* ■ Giant Database Is Ripe for Abuse *456*

Nature and the Environment

Outside Edges *48* ■ Twisted Roots *60* ■ The Shining Houses *62* ■ Windows *109* ■ No Great Mischief *155* ■ The Archetypes of Literature *166* ■ Ode to the West Wind *177* ■ The Death of the Moth *236* ■ Peace, Technology *313* ■ Paradise, a Poet, and Promised Land *327* ■ Look What I Found *364* ■ The Poetry of Earth and Sky *370* ■ The Humpback of Notre Dame *392* ■ Restoring Life on the Edge *421* ■ Let's Stop Being Hysterical *459* ■ Our Water Sovereignty Is at Risk *463* ■ Water *466* ■ Is the Pathetic Fallacy True? *481* ■ Birch Bark *486* ■ vancouver–courtenay –calgary *489* ■ Prairie Flight *492* ■ Fern Hill *494* ■ Progress *524* ■ The River *542* ■ The Rime of the Ancient Mariner *574* ■ Dover Beach *604* ■ *Film Location for* Random Passage *640*

Science and Technology

Peace, Technology *313* ■ Buying Your Next Synthesizer *345* ■ Canada: A Virtual History *380* ■ The Monkey's Paw *403* ■ Aphorisms *431* ■ Learning Without Lectures *443* ■ Engineers' Corner *478*

Media

The Winner *96* ■ Canada: A Virtual History *380* ■ The Humpback of Notre Dame *392* ■ Morty Mania *394* ■ Aphorisms *431* ■ The News *434* ■ Learning Without Lectures *443* ■ King Zog's Birthday *446* ■ almost visible *449* ■ The Committee to Upgrade Celestial Signs *500* ■ Shakespeare in the Cinema *677*

Home and Exile

How Reading Changed My Life *12* ■ Calgary from Sunnyside *46* ■ Outside Edges *48* ■ Twisted Roots *60* ■ The Shining Houses *62* ■ Windows *109* ■ Easter at My Aunt's *118* ■ Peace and War *138* ■ Utopian Dreams *188* ■ A Place to Stand On *216* ■ Elegy in Stone *229* ■ Migrant Mother *256* ■ Wanderers by Choice *306* ■ Paradise, a Poet, and Promised Land *327* ■ The Poetry of Earth and Sky *370* ■ vancouver–courtenay–calgary *489* ■ Prairie Flight *492* ■ Fern Hill *494* ■ Summer Night *527* ■ The Love Song of J. Alfred Prufrock *530* ■ The River *542* ■ O Can You Leave Your Native Land? *601*

Aboriginal Cultures

Reading on "the Rez" *6* ■ Magpies *87* ■ The Spirit of Haida Gwaii *142* ■ Call of the Weird *279* ■ Ours by Design *354* ■ to you who would wage war against me *511* ■ Progress *524* ■ Acoose *636*

Canada

Reading on "the Rez" *6* ■ Not a Boyhood Passion *10* ■ Write Me Sometime *36* ■ Calgary from Sunnyside *46* ■ Outside Edges *48* ■ Twisted Roots *60* ■ The Shining Houses *62* ■ Magpies *87* ■ Windows *109* ■ Easter at My Aunt's *118* ■ War *120* ■ The Spirit of Haida Gwaii *142* ■ No Great Mischief *155* ■ The Archetypes of Literature *166* ■ Utopian Dreams *188* ■ Ka-Ching! *205* ■ A Place to Stand On *216* ■ Chameleons and Codas *224* ■ Elegy in Stone *229* ■ Guy Lafleur *242* ■ Call of the Weird *279* ■ Get Beyond Babel *294* ■ The Death of History Is Bunk *300* ■ Peace, Technology *313* ■ Slide to Entropy *323* ■ Paradise, a Poet, and Promised Land *327* ■ Hockey Night in Port Hawkesbury *331* ■ The Sixth Flight *336* ■ Buying Your Next Synthesizer *345* ■ A Chat with Al Purdy *349* ■ Ours by Design *354* ■ The Poetry of Earth and Sky *370* ■ Canada: A Virtual History *380* ■ The Humpback of Notre Dame *392* ■ Morty Mania *394* ■ The Monkey's Paw *403* ■ Restoring Life on the Edge *421* ■ Aphorisms *431* ■ Learning Without Lectures *443* ■ almost visible *449* ■ Giant Database Is Ripe for Abuse *456* ■ Let's Stop Being Hysterical *459* ■ Our Water Sovereignty Is at Risk *463* ■ Water *466* ■ Is the Pathetic Fallacy True? *481* ■ Birch Bark *486* ■ vancouver–courtenay–calgary *489* ■ Prairie Flight *492* ■ The Heroes You Had as a Girl *503* ■ foremother *507* ■ to you who would wage war against me *511* ■

I, Icarus *515* ■ Progress *524* ■ Afternoons & Coffeespoons *539* ■ grammar poem *545* ■ O Can You Leave Your Native Land? *601* ■ Acoose *636* ■ *Film Location for* Random Passage *640* ■ Stop! *642* ■ Invisible Genius *658* ■ Saloonio *696*

Caribbean

The River *542*

South America

The Word *4* ■ Peace and War *138*

Africa

The Winner *96* ■ Get Beyond Babel *294* ■ Water *466*

Europe

The Rocking-Horse Winner *18* ■ Was It a Dream? *150* ■ Ode to the West Wind *177* ■ Araby *181* ■ The Death of the Moth *236* ■ Of Youth and Age *258* ■ Why I Write *263* ■ A Modest Proposal *283* ■ Wanderers by Choice *306* ■ Landscape with the Fall of Icarus *366* ■ Effective Persuasion *454* ■ Engineers' Corner *478* ■ Fern Hill *494* ■ Musée des Beaux Arts *518* ■ People on the Bridge *521* ■ The Love Song of J. Alfred Prufrock *530* ■ Beowulf *553* ■ The Canterbury Tales *560* ■ Sonnet 116 *570* ■ A Poison Tree *572* ■ The Rime of the Ancient Mariner *574* ■ Dover Beach *604* ■ A Marriage Proposal *614* ■ Dead Parrot *650* ■ Hamlet *666* ■ Shakespeare in the Cinema *677* ■ The Shakespearean Tragic Hero *687* ■ Strong Women Prevail *692*

Asia

A Devoted Son *74* ■ Shower at Ohashi Bridge *368* ■ Birch Bark *486* ■ grammar poem *545* ■ Mu-lan *548*

Myth and Archetypes

The Rocking-Horse Winner *18* ■ Outside Edges *48* ■ The Spirit of Haida Gwaii *142* ■ The Archetypes of Literature *166* ■ The Hero's Adventure *171* ■ Araby *181* ■ Utopian Dreams *188* ■ Elegy in Stone *229* ■ Landscape with the Fall of Icarus *366* ■ The Committee to Upgrade

Celestial Signs *500* ■ I, Icarus *515* ■ Musée des Beaux Arts *518* ■ Mu-lan *548* ■ Because I Could Not Stop for Death— *608*

Oral Traditions and Language

The Word *4* ■ Reading on "the Rez" *6* ■ Magpies *87* ■ The Spirit of Haida Gwaii *142* ■ Chameleons and Codas *224* ■ Get Beyond Babel *294* ■ Effective Persuasion *454* ■ Birch Bark *486* ■ grammar poem *545* ■ Mu-lan *548* ■ Beowulf *553* ■ Shakespeare in the Cinema *677*

Reading and Writing

The Word *4* ■ Reading on "the Rez" *6* ■ For the Love of Books *7* ■ Not a Boyhood Passion *10* ■ How Reading Changed My Life *12* ■ The Secret *14* ■ Write Me Sometime *36* ■ Portrait of the Essay *196* ■ A Place to Stand On *216* ■ Why I Write *263* ■ The Not-So-Deadly Sin *272* ■ Paradise, a Poet, and Promised Land *327* ■ A Chat with Al Purdy *349* ■ The Poetry of Earth and Sky *370* ■ Poetry *473* ■ Engineers' Corner *478* ■ Evening *484* ■ Amiri Baraka *498*

Humour

Not a Boyhood Passion *10* ■ Magpies *87* ■ The Winner *96* ■ Was It a Dream? *150* ■ Ka-Ching! *205* ■ Afternoon of an American Boy *209* ■ The Not-So-Deadly Sin *272* ■ Call of the Weird *279* ■ Slide to Entropy *323* ■ Hockey Night in Port Hawkesbury *331* ■ Look What I Found *364* ■ King Zog's Birthday *446* ■ Engineers' Corner *478* ■ The Committee to Upgrade Celestial Signs *500* ■ A Marriage Proposal *614* ■ Stop! *642* ■ Dead Parrot *650* ■ Saloonio *696*

Parody and Satire

A Modest Proposal *283* ■ Poetry *473* ■ The Love Song of J. Alfred Prufrock *530* ■ Afternoons & Coffeespoons *539*

Mystery and Intrigue

The Secret *14* ■ Peace and War *138* ■ Mazes *144* ■ Was It a Dream? *150* ■ almost visible *449* ■ People on the Bridge *521* ■ The Rime of the Ancient Mariner *574* ■ Because I Could Not Stop for Death— *608*

Conflict and War

War *120* ■ Peace and War *138* ■ Elegy in Stone *229* ■ Peace, Technology *313* ■ Unzipped *389* ■ The News *434* ■ King Zog's Birthday *446* ■ to you who would wage war against me *511* ■ Musée des Beaux Arts *518* ■ Mu-lan *548* ■ Beowulf *553* ■ The Canterbury Tales *560* ■ A Poison Tree *572* ■ The Rime of the Ancient Mariner *574* ■ Dover Beach *604* ■ A Marriage Proposal *614* ■ Hamlet *666*

Ethical and Moral Questions

The Rocking-Horse Winner *18* ■ The Shining Houses *62* ■ A Devoted Son *74* ■ Peace and War *138* ■ Mazes *144* ■ The Archetypes of Literature *166* ■ The Hero's Adventure *171* ■ Araby *181* ■ Utopian Dreams *188* ■ Chameleons and Codas *224* ■ Elegy in Stone *229* ■ The Death of the Moth *236* ■ Why I Write *263* ■ A Modest Proposal *283* ■ Peace, Technology *313* ■ Ours by Design *354* ■ Look What I Found *364* ■ Landscape with the Fall of Icarus *366* ■ The Monkey's Paw *403* ■ Effective Persuasion *454* ■ Giant Database Is Ripe for Abuse *456* ■ to you who would wage war against me *511* ■ Musée des Beaux Arts *518* ■ People on the Bridge *521* ■ The Love Song of J. Alfred Prufrock *530* ■ A Poison Tree *572* ■ The Rime of the Ancient Mariner *574* ■ Dover Beach *604* ■ Hamlet *666* ■ The Shakespearean Tragic Hero *687*

Preface

The thinkers and dreamers gathered in this anthology—writers of fiction, essayists, poets, dramatists, literary critics, journalists, artists, photographers—all have one thing in common. They invite you to experience the world from their perspective. Their goal is to present their ideas to their audience in exciting, appealing, and thought-provoking ways. This is what the painter Edgar Degas meant when he said: "Art is not what you see but what you make others see." These outstanding works of literature and art will help you to see the world through the eyes of their creators, challenge you with their vision and insights, and stimulate you to formulate your own viewpoints.

Viewpoints 12 features a collection of compelling texts ranging from the traditional to the contemporary. The four main units are organized by genre—short fiction; essays, articles, and media; poetry; and drama. Interspersed among them are multi-genre "In-Depth" sections that explore Universal Themes and Patterns, Media on Media, Argument and Persuasion, and Shakespeare. Many styles and modes of writing are represented and numerous media texts are recreated in their original formats. The five essay sections provide a rich range of argument and reflection.

Each selection begins with an introduction that provides relevant background about the life and times of its creator, and ends with notes that offer information to enhance your understanding of the work. The activities at the end of each "In-Depth" section encourage your personal response to the text and challenge you to react critically as well as creatively through words and images. Many selections are followed by "Another Viewpoint," which broadens your perspective by examining the selection through a critical lens that might be historical, archetypal, or sociological. The wrap-up activities at the end of each unit make connections among the selections.

Without you, the reader, the words and images on these pages would have no purpose. By engaging with them, you bring the ideas they contain to life. Their example and inspiration will help you to understand and interpret the world around you as you consolidate the skills you have been building throughout your high-school years. This book will be a doorway to appreciating and enjoying literature in your post-secondary education and beyond.

Acknowledgements

The editors and publisher would like to thank all the reviewers of Prentice Hall Senior English.

Philip Allingham
Susan Balfe
Alice Barlow-Kedves
Jamie Bell
John Borovilos
Connie Bray
Danielle Brown
Mike Budd
Jane Burningham-Ernst
Terri Carleton
Scott Carter
Jackie Chambers
Annette Chiu
Carrie Collins
Mary Conway
Owen Davis
Dan DiGravio
Sandy Dobec
Janis Fertuck
Linda Ferworn
Barbara Fullerton
Ross Garnett
Margie Gartland
Gail Grant
Bryan Harrigan
Amanda Joseph
Myra Junyk
Gabriel Kampf
Michelle Kennedy
Diana Knight
Marty Kofsky
Lorne Kulak
Patricia Lachance

Gerd Laudenbach
Kathryn Lemmon
Elaine Leslie
Noël Lim
Cheryl Manny
Janie McTavish
Ian Mills
Yula Nouragas
Victoria Nutting
Adam Oberfrank
Keith Pearce
Larry Peters
Frank Petruzella
Louise Pivato
Sheila Powell
Peter Purcell
Judith Robinson
Tom Sbrocchi
Richard Schultz
Lawrence Smith
Sally Spofforth
Jim Stewart
Brian Switzer
Jean Szeles
Cornelia Wagner
Judy Wedeles
Darlene White
Stephen Willcock

Ian Esquivel, Media Consultant
Linda Laliberté, Equity and
    Aboriginal Consultant
Hari Lalla, Equity Consultant

The Library, 1960, *Jacob Lawrence*

What comes to mind when we talk about a *text*? Why does this concept matter? Every one of us is surrounded daily by books, magazines, television, CDs, DVDs, e-mail, the Internet, cell phone screens, billboards, virtual reality arcades—all of them texts. How do we sift through these texts and make sense of them? How do we sort out which ones are important to us? Texts contain words, images, sounds, textures, or a combination of all four. They may embody information that we need. Many texts hold a story or a narrative. These texts form *literature*, a body of work that communicates meaningful information and insights into ideas, culture, and history.

Literature is more than simply information; it is information with lasting significance, created because someone has a story to tell. As Ezra Pound said, "Literature is news that stays news." Literature is unique because it allows direct access into the mind of the person who created it. When you become engaged with a piece of literature, what began as a *writer* addressing a *reader* becomes a two-way conversation. As you react to the text with your own experiences, thoughts, and emotions, it becomes an invigorating exchange that engages your intellect and your imagination as you form your own meaning from the text in front of you. Literature is about ideas, but it is also about people. It broadens your understanding of human nature by giving you the opportunity to view life through the eyes of someone in a different time or place, or someone of a different gender, ethnicity, or age.

This anthology contains selections of many kinds. Some of the selections will entertain you. Some will challenge you, making you reconsider things you already know something about. This book contains texts that open up new worlds, introducing you to cultures that are new to you, as well as to people—real and imagined—who are leading remarkable lives. There are texts that will take you to places you've never been and ones that will transport you to distant times. There, long ago, you will recognize some things that are different, and much that is the same, about human beings and how they think, feel, and behave.

In this introductory section, you will experience poetry by the Chilean poet Pablo Neruda, who speaks of "the word" as something "in the blood," elemental, oral, and existing before words were ever written down. Tomson Highway, Rita Dove, Mordecai Richler, Anna Quindlen, and Denise Levertov will share their experiences with literature and articulate its power. As you read through this section, think of how works of literature, and texts in general, are part of your life. They were there when you were first read to and they will continue to exist for you in meaningful ways in your future.

The Word

Pablo Neruda

Translated by Alastair Reid

The word
was born in the blood,
grew in the dark body, beating,
and flew through the lips and the mouth.

Farther away and nearer
still, still it came
from dead fathers and from wandering races,
from lands that had returned to stone
weary of their poor tribes,
because when pain took to the roads   10
the settlements set out and arrived
and new lands and water reunited
to sow their word anew.

And so, this is the inheritance—
this is the wavelength which connects us
with the dead man and the dawn
of new beings not yet come to light.

Still the atmosphere quivers
with the initial word
dressed up   20
in terror and sighing.
It emerged
from the darkness
and until now there is no thunder
that rumbles yet with all the iron
of that word,

the first
word uttered—
perhaps it was only a ripple, a drop,
and yet its great cataract falls and falls.   30

Later on, the word fills with meaning.
It remained gravid and it filled up with lives.
Everything had to do with births and sounds—
affirmation, clarity, strength,
negation, destruction, death—
the verb took over all the power
and blended existence with essence
in the electricity of its beauty.

Human word, syllable, combination
of spread light and the fine art of the silversmith,   40
hereditary goblet which gathers
the communications of the blood—
here is where silence was gathered up
in the completeness of the human word
and, for human beings, not to speak is to die—
language extends even to the hair,
the mouth speaks without the lips moving—
all of a sudden the eyes are words.

I take the word and go over it
as though it were nothing more than a human shape,   50
its arrangements awe me and I find my way
through each variation in the spoken word—
I utter and I am and without speaking I approach
the limit of words and the silence.

I drink to the word, raising
a word or a shining cup,
in it I drink
the pure wine of language
or inexhaustible water,
maternal source of words,   60
and cup and water and wine
give rise to my song
because the verb is the source
and vivid life—it is blood,
blood which expresses its substance
and so implies its own unwinding—
words give glass-quality to glass, blood to blood,
and life to life itself.

*Born in 1904 in Chile, **Pablo Neruda** is generally considered to be one of the greatest poets who wrote in Spanish in the twentieth century. An avowed Marxist, he was very politically active and served his country as a professional diplomat in a number of countries. His work has been widely translated and was awarded the Nobel Prize in Literature in 1971. He died in 1973.*

Reading on "the Rez"
Tomson Highway

Well, you see, up where I was born and grew up—the wilds of northern Manitoba and the Territories, everybody born in tents, dogsleds, caribou herds, etc., Cree country to the hilt—there weren't any books. So I never grew up with those little kiddie books that all other kids did. Plus, English wasn't our language. Our version of books was "oral" storytelling sessions with elders, in the Cree language, fabulous, mystical, hilarious tales about the Trickster, mostly, and about other mythological beasts, creatures, and heroes. That was our world of magic.

By the time I got comfortably conversant with the English language, I was about fifteen years old. I just could never learn the damn thing before then.

So I remember reading the summer I was fifteen, late into at least three nights, back on "the Rez," a ratty old copy of Victor Hugo's *The Hunchback of Notre-Dame*. Really the first novel I ever read. And I couldn't stop. I remember that, back in those days, there was no electricity on the Rez so I read by the light of one candle until five in the morning, as I say, three nights in a row. I started wearing glasses the next year—and have ever since. So that's one way that book changed my life. Darn!

But I couldn't stop, because I was so enthralled by the tale. Just a plain, rollicking good yarn. I was amazed, more than anything else, at the skill, the magic, the spell that a really good storyteller wields. Ever since then, I've always wanted to be like Esmeralda when I grow up. Just kidding…

Tomson Highway was born in northwestern Manitoba in 1951 and spoke only Cree until he was six years old. He received degrees in English and music from the University of Western Ontario. An Aboriginal activist and writer, he is best known as a playwright. He has won several Dora Mavor Moore Awards for plays including The Rez Sisters *and* Dry Lips Oughta Move to Kapuskasing.

For the Love of Books

Rita Dove

When I am asked: "What made you want to be a writer?" my answer has always been: "Books." First and foremost, now, then, and always, I have been passionate about books. From the time I began to read, as a child, I loved to feel their heft in my hand and the warm spot caused by their intimate weight in my lap: I lived the crisp whisper of a page turning, the musky odour of old paper and the sharp inky whiff of new pages. Leather bindings sent me into ecstasy. I even loved to gaze at a closed book and daydream about the possibilities inside—it was like contemplating a genie's lamp. Of course, my favourite fairy tale was *A Thousand and One Nights*—imagine buying your life with stories!—and my favourite cartoons were those where animated characters popped out of books and partied while the unsuspecting humans slept. In books, I could travel anywhere, be anybody, understand worlds long past and imaginary colonies in the future. My idea of a bargain was to go to the public library, wander along the bookshelves, and emerge with a chin-high stack of books that were mine, all mine, for two weeks—free of charge!

What I remember most about long summer days is browsing the bookshelves in our solarium to see if there were any new additions. I grew up with those rows of books; I knew where each one was shelved and immediately spotted newcomers. And after months had gone by and there'd be no new books, I would think: Okay, I guess I'll try this one— and then discover that the very book I had been avoiding because of a drab cover or small print was actually a wonderful read. Louis Untermeyer's *Treasury of Best Loved Poems* had a sickeningly sweet lilac and gold cover and was forbiddingly thick, but I finally pulled it off the shelf and discovered a cornucopia of emotional and linguistic delights, from "The Ballad of Barbara Fritchie," which I adored for its sheer length and rather numbing rhymes, to Langston Hughes' dazzlingly syncopated "Dream Boogie." Then there was Shakespeare—daunting for many years because it was his entire oeuvre, in matching wine-red volumes that were so thick they looked more like oversized bouillon cubes than books, and yet it was that ponderous title—*The Complete Works of William Shakespeare*—that enticed me, because here was a lifetime's work—a lifetime!—in two compact, dense packages. I began with the long poem "The Rape of Lucrece"…I sampled a few sonnets, which I found beautiful but rather adult; and finally wandered into the plays— first *Romeo and Juliet*, then *Macbeth, Julius Caesar, A Midsummer Night's Dream, Twelfth Night*—enthralled by the language, by the fact that poetry was spinning the story. Of course I did not understand every single word, but I was too young to know that this was supposed to be difficult; besides, no one was waiting to test me on anything, so, free from pressure, I dove in.

Although I loved books, for a long time I had no aspirations to be a writer. The possibility was beyond my imagination. I liked to write, however—and on long summer days when I ran out of reading material or my legs had fallen asleep because I had been curled up on the couch for hours on end, I made up my own stories. Most were abandoned midway. Those that I did bring to a conclusion I neither showed to others nor considered saving.

My first piece of writing I thought enough of to keep was a novel called *Chaos*, which was about robots taking over the earth. I had just entered third or fourth grade; the novel had forty-three chapters, and each chapter was twenty lines or less because I used each week's spelling list as the basis for each chapter, and there were twenty words per list. In the course of the year I wrote one installment per week, and I never knew what was going to happen next—the words led me, not the other way around.

At that time I didn't think of writing as an activity people admitted doing. I had no living role models—a "real" writer was a long-dead white male, usually with a white beard to match. Much later, when I was in eleventh grade, my English teacher, Miss Oechsner, took me to a book-signing in a downtown hotel. She didn't ask me if I'd like to go— she asked my parents instead, signed me and a classmate (who is now a professor of literature) out of school one day, and took us to meet a writer. The writer was John Ciardi, a poet who also had translated Dante's *Divine Comedy*, which I had heard of, vaguely. At that moment I realized that writers were real people and how it was possible to write down a poem or story in the intimate sphere of one's own room and then share it with the world.

Born in Akron, Ohio, in 1952, the African American writer **Rita Dove** *is a renowned poet, novelist, short story writer, and educator. Among her many achievements, she was the poet laureate of the United States in 1993 and was awarded the Pulitzer Prize for Poetry in 1987.*

Not a Boyhood Passion

Mordecai Richler

Reading was not one of my boyhood passions. Girls, or rather the absence of girls, drove me to it. When I was thirteen years old, short for my age, more than somewhat pimply, I was terrified of girls. As far as I could make out, they were only attracted to boys who were tall or played for the school basketball team or at least shaved. Unable to qualify on all three counts, I resorted to subterfuge. I set out to call attention to myself by becoming a character. I acquired a pipe, which I chewed on ostentatiously, and made it my business to be seen everywhere, even at school basketball games, pretending to be absorbed by books of daunting significance: say, H.G. Wells' *The Outline of History*, or Paul de Kruif's *Microbe Hunters*, or John Gunther inside one continent or another. I rented these thought-provoking books for three cents a day from a neighbourhood lending library that was across the street from a bowling alley where I used to spot pins four nights a week.

O my God, I would not be thirteen again for anything. The sweetly scented girls of my dreams, wearing lipstick and tight sweaters and nylon stockings, would sail into the bowling alley holding hands with the boys from the basketball team. "Hi," they would call out, giggly, nudging each other, even as I bent over the pins: "How goes the reading?"

The two ladies who ran the lending library, possibly amused by my pretensions, tried to interest me in fiction.

"I want fact. I can't be bothered with *stories*," I protested, waving my pipe at them, affronted.

I knew what novels were, of course. I had read *Scaramouche*, by Rafael Sabatini, at school, as well as *Treasure Island* and some Ellery Queen and a couple of thumpers by G.A. Henty. Before that there had been *Action Comics, Captain Marvel, Batman*, and—for educational reasons—either *Bible Comics* or *Classic Comics*.

Novels, I knew, were mere romantic make-believe, not as bad as poetry, to be fair, but bad enough. Our high-school class master, a dedicated Scot, was foolish enough to try to interest us in poetry. A veteran of World War I, he told us that during the nightly bombardments on the Somme he had fixed a candle to his steel helmet so that he could read poetry in the trenches. A scruffy lot, we were not moved. Instead, we exchanged knowing winks behind that admirable man's back. Small wonder, we agreed, that he drove an ancient Austin and had ended up no better than a high-school teacher.

Bottle, Cup and Newspaper, 1912–13,
Pablo Picasso

My aunts consumed historical novels like pastries. My father read *Black Mask* and *True Detective.* My mother would read anything on a Jewish subject, preferably by I.J. Singer or Sholem Asch, though she would never forgive Asch for having written *The Nazarene,* never mind *Mary and the Apostle.* My older brother kept a novel, *Topper Takes a Trip,* secure under his mattress in the bedroom we shared, assuring me that it was placed at just such an angle on the springs that if it were moved so much as a millimetre in his absence he would know and bloody well make me pay for it.

I fell ill with a childhood disease, I no longer remember which, but one obviously meant as a rebuke for those girls in tight sweaters who continued to ignore me. Never mind, they would mourn at my funeral, burying me with my pipe. Too late they would say, "Boy, was he ever an intellectual!"

Novelist, journalist, scriptwriter, and essayist, **Mordecai Richler** *was born in Montreal in 1931, where he died in 2001. He first achieved* *international recognition with his 1959 novel* The Apprenticeship of Duddy Kravitz, *which was made into a film. Among his many awards are the Order of Canada, the Governor General's Award (twice), and the Giller Prize.*

How Reading Changed My Life

Anna Quindlen

My home was in that pleasant place outside Philadelphia, but I really lived somewhere else. I lived within the covers of books and those books were more real to me than any other thing in my life. One poem committed to memory in grade school survives in my mind. It is by Emily Dickinson: "There is no Frigate like a Book / To take us Lands away / Nor any coursers like a Page / Of prancing Poetry."

Perhaps only a truly discontented child can become as seduced by books as I was. Perhaps restlessness is a necessary corollary of devoted literacy. There was a club chair in our house, a big one, with curled arms and a square ottoman; it sat in one corner of the living room, catty-corner to the fireplace, with a barrel table next to it. In my mind I am always sprawled in it, reading with my skinny, scabby legs slung over one of its arms. "It's a beautiful day," my mother is saying; she said that always, often, autumn, spring, even when there was a fresh snowfall. "All your friends are outside." It was true; they always were. Sometimes I went out with them, coaxed into the street, out into the fields, down by the creek, by the lure of what I knew intuitively was normal childhood, by the promise of being what I knew instinctively was a normal child, one who lived, raucous, in the world.

I have clear memories of that sort of life, of lifting the rocks in the creek that trickled through Naylor's Run to search for crayfish, of laying pennies on the tracks of the trolley and running to fetch them, flattened, when the trolley had passed. But at base it was never any good. The best part of me was always at home, within some book that had been laid flat on the table to mark my place, its imaginary people waiting for me to return and bring them to life. That was where the real people were, the trees that moved in the wind, the still, dark waters. I won a bookmark in a spelling bee during that time with these words of Montaigne upon it in gold: "When I am reading a book, whether wise or silly, it seems to me to be alive and talking to me." I found that bookmark not long ago, at the bottom of a box, when my father was moving.

Years later I would come to discover, as Robinson Crusoe did when he found Man Friday, that I was not alone in that world or on that island. I would discover (through reading, naturally) that while I was sprawled, legs akimbo, in that chair with a book, Jamaica Kincaid was sitting in the glare of the Caribbean sun in Antigua reading in that same way that I did, as though she was starving and the book was bread. When she was grown-up, writing books herself, winning awards for her work, she talked in one of her memoirs of ignoring her little brother when she was supposed to be looking after him: "I liked reading a book much more than I liked looking after him."

While I was in that club chair with a book, Hazel Rochman and her husband were in South Africa, burying an old tin trunk heavy with hardcovers in the backyard, because the police might raid their house and search it for banned books. Rochman, who left Johannesburg for Chicago and became an editor for the American Library Association's *Booklist,* summed up the lessons learned from that night, about the power of reading, in a way I would have recognized even as a girl. "Reading makes immigrants of us all," she wrote years later. "It takes us away from home, but, most important, it finds homes for us everywhere."

Born in Philadelphia in 1953, **Anna Quindlen** *was a journalist with the* Washington Post *and the* New York Times *before becoming a full-time novelist. She won the Pulitzer Prize in 1992 for her journalism.*

The Secret

Denise Levertov

Two girls discover
the secret of life
in a sudden line of
poetry.

I who don't know the
secret wrote
the line. They
told me

(through a third person)
they had found it   10
but not what it was
not even

what line it was. No doubt
by now, more than a week
later, they have forgotten
the secret,

the line, the name of
the poem. I love them
for finding what
I can't find,   20

and for loving me
for the line I wrote,
and for forgetting it
so that

a thousand times, till death
finds them, they may
discover it again, in other
lines

in other
happenings. And for   30
wanting to know it,
for

assuming there is
such a secret, yes,
for that
most of all.

Poet and essayist **Denise Levertov** *was born in Ilford, England, in 1923. She worked as a nurse during World War II and moved to the United States in 1948 with her American husband. She published her first collection of poetry in 1946. Most of her writing from the late 1960s and 1970s focuses on political and social issues such as the Vietnam War and racial unrest in American cities. She died in 1997.*

Invitation to Literature: Activities

1. In a small group or as a class, discuss the ways in which literature affected the lives of the writers in this section. How do your own earlier and later experiences with literature compare with those described here?

2. Identify a world—fictional or factual—that one or more texts opened up for you. Describe the way in which this text or texts led you into this new world.

3. Think of an image combined with words that you are familiar with, such as an advertisement. To what extent does the image alone have an impact on you? To what extent do the words affect you? How do the image and words work together to convey a message?

1 short fiction

"The act of writing is the creation of something in the world that hasn't existed before in just this form, and while I'm engaged in it I am at a very high level of concentration, absorption, and joy."

— *Alice Walker*

"I find the world around me much more interesting than what I can come up with inside my own head. If you write just what you have experienced, you've only got about a book and a half in you."

— *Michael Ondaatje*

The Rocking-Horse Winner

D.H. Lawrence

David Herbert Lawrence was born into poverty in Nottinghamshire, England, in 1885. He attended university, where he began publishing poems and briefly worked as a teacher. Lawrence wrote novels, poetry, plays, travel books, and essays; he was also a painter. His work often featured themes of freedom, redemption, and tormented family relationships. When talking about writers, he said: "His art, if it be art, will tell you the truth of his day. And that is all that matters. Away with eternal truth." A controversial writer, he experienced the banning of several of his books. He died in France in 1930. "The Rocking-Horse Winner" explores class issues and the notion of luck. What does it mean to be a lucky person? To what extent do you think luck and success are the same?

There was a woman who was beautiful, who started with all the advantages, yet she had no luck. She married for love, and the love turned to dust. She had bonny children, yet she felt they had been thrust upon her, and she could not love them. They looked at her coldly, as if they were finding fault with her. And hurriedly she felt she must cover up some fault in herself. Yet what it was that she must cover up she never knew. Nevertheless, when her children were present, she always felt the centre of her heart go hard. This troubled her, and in her manner she was all the more gentle and anxious for her children, as if she loved them very much. Only she herself knew that at the centre of her heart was a hard little place that could not feel love, no, not for anybody. Everybody else said of her: "She is such a good mother. She adores her children." Only she herself, and her children themselves, knew it was not so. They read it in each other's eyes.

There were a boy and two little girls. They lived in a pleasant house, with a garden, and they had discreet servants, and felt themselves superior to anyone in the neighbourhood.

Although they lived in style, they felt always an anxiety in the house. There was never enough money. The mother had a small income, and the father had a small income, but not nearly enough for the social position which they had to keep up. The father went in to town to some office. But though he had good prospects, these prospects never materialized. There was always the grinding sense of the shortage of money, though the style was always kept up.

At last the mother said, "I will see if I can't make something." But she did not know where to begin. She racked her brains, and tried this thing and the other, but could not find anything successful. The failure made deep lines come into her face. Her children were growing up, they would have to go to school. There must be more money, there must be more money. The father, who was always very handsome and expensive in his tastes, seemed as if he never would be able to do anything worth doing. And the mother, who had a great belief in herself, did not succeed any better, and her tastes were just as expensive.

And so the house came to be haunted by the unspoken phrase: There must be more money! There must be more money! The children could hear it all the time, though nobody said it aloud. They heard it at Christmas, when the expensive and splendid toys filled the nursery. Behind the shining modern rocking horse, behind the smart doll's house, a voice would start whispering: "There must be more money! There must be more money!" And the children would stop playing, to listen for a moment. They would look into each other's eyes, to see if they had all heard. And each one saw in the eyes of the other two that they too had heard. "There must be more money! There must be more money!"

It came whispering from the springs of the still-swaying rocking horse, and even the horse, bending his wooden, champion head, heard it. The big doll, sitting so pink and smirking in her new pram, could hear it quite plainly, and seemed to be smirking all the more self-consciously because of it. The foolish puppy, too, that took the place of the Teddy bear, he was looking so extraordinarily foolish for no other reason but that he heard the secret whisper all over the house: "There must be more money!"

Yet nobody ever said it aloud. The whisper was everywhere, and therefore no one spoke it. Just as no one ever says: "We are breathing!" in spite of the fact that breath is coming and going all the time.

"Mother," said the boy Paul one day, "why don't we keep a car of our own? Why do we always use Uncle's, or else a taxi?"

"Because we're the poor members of the family," said the mother.

"But why are we, Mother?"

"Well—I suppose," she said slowly and bitterly, "it's because your father has no luck."

The boy was silent for some time.

"Is luck money, Mother?" he asked, rather timidly.

"No, Paul. Not quite. It's what causes you to have money."

"Oh!" said Paul vaguely. "I thought when Uncle Oscar said filthy lucker, it meant money."

"Filthy lucre does mean money," said the mother. "But it's lucre, not luck."

"Oh!" said the boy. "Then what is luck, Mother?"

"It's what causes you to have money. If you're lucky you have money. That's why it's better to be born lucky than rich. If you're rich, you may lose your money. But if you're lucky, you will always get more money."

"Oh! Will you? And is Father not lucky?"

"Very unlucky, I should say," she said bitterly.

The boy watched her with unsure eyes.

"Why?" he asked.

"I don't know. Nobody ever knows why one person is lucky and another unlucky."

"Don't they? Nobody at all? Does nobody know?"

"Perhaps God. But He never tells."

"He ought to, then. And aren't you lucky either, Mother?"

"I can't be, if I married an unlucky husband."

"But by yourself, aren't you?"

"I used to think I was, before I married. Now I think I am very unlucky indeed."

"Why?"

"Well—never mind! Perhaps I'm not really," she said.

The child looked at her, to see if she meant it. But he saw, by the lines of her mouth, that she was only trying to hide something from him.

"Well, anyhow," he said stoutly, "I'm a lucky person."

"Why?" said his mother, with a sudden laugh.

He stared at her. He didn't even know why he had said it.

"God told me," he asserted, brazening it out.

"I hope He did, dear!" she said, again with a laugh, but rather bitter.

"He did, Mother!"

"Excellent!" said the mother, using one of her husband's exclamations.

The boy saw she did not believe him; or rather, that she paid no attention to his assertions. This angered him somewhere, and made him want to compel her attention.

He went off by himself, vaguely, in a childish way, seeking for the clue to "luck." Absorbed, taking no heed of other people, he went about with a sort of stealth, seeking inwardly for luck. He wanted luck, he wanted it, he wanted it. When the two girls were playing dolls in the nursery, he would sit on his big rocking horse, charging madly into space, with a frenzy that made the little girls peer at him uneasily. Wildly the horse careered, the waving dark hair of the boy tossed, his eyes had a strange glare in them. The little girls dared not speak to him.

When he had ridden to the end of his mad little journey, he climbed down and stood in front of his rocking horse, staring fixedly into its lowered face. Its red mouth was slightly open, its big eye was wide and glassy-bright.

"Now!" he would silently command the snorting steed. "Now, take me to where there is luck! Now take me!"

And he would slash the horse on the neck with the little whip he had asked Uncle Oscar for. He knew the horse could take him to where there was luck, if only he forced it. So he would mount again, and start on his furious ride, hoping at last to get there. He knew he could get there.

"You'll break your horse, Paul!" said the nurse.

"He's always riding like that! I wish he'd leave off!" said his sister Joan.

But he only glared down on them in silence. Nurse gave him up. She could make nothing of him. Anyhow, he was growing beyond her.

One day his mother and his Uncle Oscar came in when he was on one of his furious rides. He did not speak to them.

"Hallo, you young jockey! Riding a winner?" said his uncle.

"Aren't you growing too big for a rocking horse? You're not a very little boy any longer, you know," said his mother.

But Paul only gave a blue glare from his big, rather close-set eyes. He would speak to nobody when he was in full tilt. His mother watched him with an anxious expression on her face.

At last he suddenly stopped forcing his horse into the mechanical gallop, and slid down.

"Well, I got there," he announced fiercely, his blue eyes still flaring, and his sturdy long legs straddling apart.

"Where did you get to?" asked his mother.

"Where I wanted to go," he flared back at her.

"That's right, son!" said Uncle Oscar. "Don't you stop till you get there. What's the horse's name?"

"He doesn't have a name," said the boy.

"Gets on without all right?" asked the uncle.

"Well, he has different names. He was called Sansovino last week."

"Sansovino, eh? Won the Ascot. How did you know his name?"

"He always talks about horse races with Bassett," said Joan.

The uncle was delighted to find that his small nephew was posted with all the racing news. Bassett, the young gardener, who had been wounded in the left foot in the war and had got his present job through Oscar Cresswell, whose batman he had been, was a perfect blade of the "turf." He lived in the racing events, and the small boy lived with him.

Oscar Cresswell got it all from Bassett.

"Master Paul comes and asks me, so I can't do more than tell him, sir," said Bassett, his face terribly serious, as if he were speaking of religious matters.

"And does he ever put anything on a horse he fancies?"

"Well—I don't want to give him away—he's a young sport, a fine sport, sir. Would you mind asking him himself? He sort of takes a pleasure in it, and perhaps he'd feel I was giving him away, sir, if you don't mind."

Bassett was serious as a church.

The uncle went back to his nephew, and took him off for a ride in the car.

"Say, Paul, old man, do you ever put anything on a horse?" the uncle asked.

The boy watched the handsome man closely.

"Why, do you think I oughtn't to?" he parried.

"Not a bit of it! I thought perhaps you might give me a tip for the Lincoln."

The car sped on into the country, going down to Uncle Oscar's place in Hampshire.

"Honour bright?" said the nephew.

"Honour bright, son!" said the uncle.

"Well, then, Daffodil."

"Daffodil! I doubt it, sonny. What about Mirza?"

"I only know the winner," said the boy. "That's Daffodil."

"Daffodil, eh?"

There was a pause. Daffodil was an obscure horse comparatively.

"Uncle!"

"Yes, son?"

"You won't let it go any further, will you? I promised Bassett."

"Bassett be damned, old man! What's he got to do with it?"

"We're partners. We've been partners from the first. Uncle, he lent me my first five shillings, which I lost. I promised him, honour bright, it was only between me and him; only you gave me that ten-shilling note I started winning with, so I thought you were lucky. You won't let it go any further, will you?"

The boy gazed at his uncle from those big, hot, blue eyes, set rather close together. The uncle stirred and laughed uneasily.

"Right you are, son! I'll keep your tip private. Daffodil, eh? How much are you putting on him?"

"All except twenty pounds," said the boy. "I keep that in reserve."

The uncle thought it a good joke.

"You keep twenty pounds in reserve, do you, you young romancer? What are you betting, then?"

"I'm betting three hundred," said the boy gravely. "But it's between you and me, Uncle Oscar! Honour bright?"

The uncle burst into a roar of laughter.

"It's between you and me all right, you young Nat Gould," he said, laughing. "But where's your three hundred?"

"Bassett keeps it for me. We're partners."

"You are, are you! And what is Bassett putting on Daffodil?"

"He won't go quite as high as I do, I expect. Perhaps he'll go a hundred and fifty."

"What, pennies?" laughed the uncle.

"Pounds," said the child, with a surprised look at his uncle. "Bassett keeps a bigger reserve than I do."

Between wonder and amusement Uncle Oscar was silent. He pursued the matter no further, but he determined to take his nephew with him to the Lincoln races.

"Now, son," he said, "I'm putting twenty on Mirza, and I'll put five for you on any horse you fancy. What's your pick?"

"Daffodil, Uncle."

"No, not the fiver on Daffodil!"

"I should if it was my own fiver," said the child.

"Good! Good! Right you are! A fiver for me and a fiver for you on Daffodil."

The child had never been to a race meeting before, and his eyes were blue fire. He pursed his mouth tight, and watched. A Frenchman just in front had put his money on Lancelot. Wild with excitement, he flayed his arms up and down, yelling "Lancelot! Lancelot!" in his French accent.

Daffodil came in first, Lancelot second, Mirza third. The child, flushed with eyes blazing, was curiously serene. His uncle brought him four five-pound notes, four to one.

"What am I to do with these?" he cried, waving them before the boy's eyes.

"I suppose we'll talk to Bassett," said the boy. "I expect I have fifteen hundred now; and twenty in reserve; and this twenty."

His uncle studied him for some moments.

"Look here, son!" he said. "You're not serious about Bassett and that fifteen hundred, are you?"

"Yes, I am. But it's between you and me, Uncle. Honour bright!"

"Honour bright all right, son! But I must talk to Bassett."

"If you'd like to be a partner, Uncle, with Bassett and me, we could all be partners. Only, you'd have to promise, honour bright, Uncle, not to let it go beyond us three. Bassett and I are lucky, and you must be lucky, because it was your ten shillings I started winning with…."

Uncle Oscar took both Bassett and Paul into Richmond Park for an afternoon, and there they talked.

"It's like this, you see, sir," Bassett said. "Master Paul would get me talking about racing events, spinning yarns, you know, sir. And he was always keen on knowing if I'd made or if I'd lost. It's about a year since, now, that I put five shillings on Blush of Dawn for him: and we lost. Then the luck turned, with that ten shillings he had from you: that we put on Singhalese. And since that time, it's been pretty steady, all things considering. What do you say, Master Paul?"

"We're all right when we're sure," said Paul. "It's when we're not quite sure that we go down."

"Oh, but we're careful then," said Bassett.

"But when are you sure?" smiled Uncle Oscar.

"It's Master Paul, sir," said Bassett, in a secret, religious voice. "It's as if he had it from heaven. Like Daffodil, now, for the Lincoln. That was as sure as eggs."

"Did you put anything on Daffodil?" asked Oscar Cresswell.

"Yes, sir. I made my bit."

"And my nephew?"

Bassett was obstinately silent, looking at Paul.

"I made twelve hundred, didn't I, Bassett? I told Uncle I was putting three hundred on Daffodil."

"That's right," said Bassett, nodding.

"But where's the money?" asked the uncle.

"I keep it safe locked up, sir. Master Paul he can have it any minute he likes to ask for it."

"What, fifteen hundred pounds?"

"And twenty! And forty, that is, with the twenty he made on the course."

"It's amazing!" said the uncle.

"If Master Paul offers you to be partners, sir, I would, if I were you: if you'll excuse me," said Bassett.

Oscar Cresswell thought about it.

"I'll see the money," he said.

They drove home again, and, sure enough, Bassett came round to the gardenhouse with fifteen hundred pounds in notes. The twenty pounds' reserve was left with Joe Glee, in the Turf Commission deposit.

"You see, it's all right, Uncle, when I'm sure! Then we go strong, for all we're worth. Don't we, Bassett?"

"We do that, Master Paul."

"And when are you sure?" said the uncle, laughing.

"Oh, well, sometimes I'm absolutely sure, like about Daffodil," said the boy; "and sometimes I have an idea; and sometimes I haven't even an idea, have I, Bassett? Then we're careful, because we mostly go down."

"You do, do you! And when you're sure, like about Daffodil, what makes you sure, sonny?"

"Oh, well, I don't know," said the boy uneasily. "I'm sure, you know, Uncle, that's all."

"It's as if he had it from heaven, sir," Bassett reiterated.

"I should say so!" said the uncle.

But he became a partner. And when the Leger was coming on, Paul was "sure" about Lively Spark, which was a quite inconsiderable horse. The boy insisted on putting a thousand on the horse, Bassett went for five hundred, and Oscar Cresswell two hundred. Lively Spark came in first, and the betting had been ten to one against him. Paul had made ten thousand.

"You see," he said, "I was absolutely sure of him."

Even Oscar Cresswell had cleared two thousand.

"Look here, son," he said, "this sort of thing makes me nervous."

"It needn't, Uncle! Perhaps I shan't be sure again for a long time."

"But what are you going to do with your money?" asked the uncle.

"Of course," said the boy, "I started it for Mother. She said she had no luck, because Father is unlucky, so I thought if I was lucky, it might stop whispering."

"What might stop whispering?"

"Our house. I hate our house for whispering."

"What does it whisper?"

"Why—why"—the boy fidgeted—"why, I don't know, But it's always short of money, you know, Uncle."

"I know it, son, I know it."

"You know people send Mother writs, don't you, Uncle?"

"I'm afraid I do," said the uncle.

"And then the house whispers, like people laughing at you behind your back. It's awful, that is! I thought if I was lucky—"

"You might stop it," added the uncle.

The boy watched him with big blue eyes, that had an uncanny cold fire in them, and he said never a word.

"Well, then!" said the uncle. "What are we doing?"

"I shouldn't like Mother to know I was lucky," said the boy.

"Why not, son?"

"She'd stop me."

"I don't think she would."

"Oh!"—and the boy writhed in an odd way—"I don't want her to know, Uncle."

"All right, son! We'll manage it without her knowing."

They managed it very easily. Paul, at the other's suggestion, handed over five thousand pounds to his uncle, who deposited it with the family lawyer, who was then to inform Paul's mother that a relative had put five thousand pounds into his hands, which sum was to be paid out a thousand pounds at a time, on the mother's birthday, for the next five years.

"So she'll have a birthday present of a thousand pounds for five successive years," said Uncle Oscar. "I hope it won't make it all the harder for her later."

Paul's mother had her birthday in November. The house had been "whispering" worse than ever lately, and, even in spite of his luck, Paul could not bear up against it. He was very anxious to see the effect of the birthday letter, telling his mother about the thousand pounds.

When there were no visitors, Paul now took his meals with his parents, as he was beyond the nursery control. His mother went into town nearly every day. She had discovered that she had an odd knack of sketching furs and dress materials, so she worked secretly in the studio of a friend who was the chief "artist" for the leading drapers. She drew the figures of ladies in furs and ladies in silk and sequins for the newspaper advertisements. This young woman artist earned several thousand pounds a year, but Paul's mother only made several hundreds, and she was again dissatisfied. She so wanted to be first in something, and she did not succeed, even in making sketches for drapery advertisements.

She was down to breakfast on the morning of her birthday. Paul watched her face as she read her letters. He knew the lawyer's letter. As his mother read it, her face hardened and became more expressionless. Then a cold, determined look came on her mouth. She hid the letter under the pile of others, and said not a word about it.

"Didn't you have anything nice in the post for your birthday, Mother?" asked Paul.

"Quite moderately nice," she said, her voice cold and absent.

She went away to town without saying more.

But in the afternoon Uncle Oscar appeared. He said Paul's mother had had a long interview with the lawyer, asking if the whole five thousand could not be advanced at once, as she was in debt.

"What do you think, Uncle?" said the boy.

"I leave it to you, son."

"Oh, let her have it, then! We can get some more with the other," said the boy.

"A bird in the hand is worth two in the bush, laddie!" said Uncle Oscar.

"But I'm sure to know for the Grand National; or the Lincolnshire; or else the Derby. I'm sure to know for one of them," said Paul.

So Uncle Oscar signed the agreement, and Paul's mother touched the whole five thousand. Then something very curious happened. The voices in the house suddenly went mad, like a chorus of frogs on a spring evening. There were certain new furnishings, and Paul had a tutor. He was really going to Eton, his father's school, in the following autumn. There were flowers in the winter, and blossoming of the luxury Paul's mother had been used to. And yet the voices in the house, behind the sprays of mimosa and almond blossom, and from under the piles of iridescent cushions, simply trilled and screamed in a sort of ecstasy: "There must be more money; Oh-h-h; there must be more money. Oh, now, now-w! Now-w-w—there must be more money!—more than ever! More than ever!"

It frightened Paul terribly. He studied away at his Latin and Greek with his tutor, but his intense hours were spent with Bassett. The Grand National had gone by: he had not "known," and had lost a hundred pounds. Summer was at hand. He was in agony for the Lincoln. But even for the Lincoln he didn't "know," and he lost fifty pounds. He became wild-eyed and strange, as if something were going to explode in him.

"Let it alone, son! Don't you bother about it!" urged Uncle Oscar. But it was as if the boy couldn't really hear what his uncle was saying.

"I've got to know for the Derby! I've got to know for the Derby," the child reiterated, his big blue eyes blazing with a sort of madness.

His mother noticed how overwrought he was.

"You'd better go to the seaside. Wouldn't you like to go now to the seaside, instead of waiting? I think you'd better," she said, looking down at him anxiously, her heart curiously heavy because of him.

But the child lifted his uncanny blue eyes.

"I couldn't possibly go before the Derby, Mother!" he said. "I couldn't possibly!"

"Why not?" she said, her voice becoming heavy when she was opposed. "Why not? You can still go from the seaside to see the Derby with your Uncle Oscar, if that's what you wish. No need for you to wait here. Besides, I think you care too much about these races. It's a bad sign. My family has been a gambling family, and you won't know till you grow up how much damage it has done. But it has done damage. I shall have to send Bassett away, and ask Uncle Oscar not to talk racing to you, unless you promise to be reasonable about it: go away to the seaside and forget it. You're all nerves!"

"I'll do what you like, Mother, so long as you don't send me away till after the Derby," the boy said.

"Send you away from where? Just from this house?"

"Yes," he said, gazing at her.

"Why, you curious child, what makes you care about this house so much, suddenly? I never knew you loved it."

He gazed at her without speaking. He had a secret within a secret, something he had not divulged, even to Bassett or to his Uncle Oscar.

But his mother, after standing undecided and a little bit sullen for some moments, said:

"Very well, then! Don't go to the seaside till after the Derby, if you don't wish it. But promise me you won't let your nerves go to pieces. Promise you won't think so much about horse racing and events, as you call them!"

"Oh, no," said the boy casually. "I won't think much about them, Mother. You needn't worry. I wouldn't worry, Mother, if I were you."

"If you were me and I were you," said his mother, "I wonder what we should do!"

"But you know you needn't worry, Mother, don't you?" the boy repeated.

"I should be awfully glad to know it," she said wearily.

"Oh, well, you can, you know. I mean, you ought to know you needn't worry," he insisted.

"Ought I? Then I'll see about it," she said.

Paul's secret of secrets was his wooden horse, that which had no name. Since he was emancipated from a nurse and a nursery governess, he had had his rocking horse removed to his own bedroom at the top of the house.

"Surely, you're too big for a rocking horse!" his mother had remonstrated.

"Well, you see, Mother, till I can have a real horse, I like to have some sort of animal about," had been his quaint answer.

"Do you feel he keeps you company?" she laughed.

"Oh, yes! He's very good, he always keeps me company, when I'm there," said Paul.

So the horse, rather shabby, stood in an arrested prance in the boy's bedroom.

The Derby was drawing near, and the boy grew more and more tense. He hardly heard what was spoken to him, he was very frail, and his eyes were really uncanny. His mother had sudden strange seizures of uneasiness about him. Sometimes, for half-an-hour, she would feel a sudden anxiety about him that was almost anguish. She wanted to rush to him at once, and know he was safe.

Two nights before the Derby, she was at a big party in town, when one of her rushes of anxiety about her boy, her firstborn, gripped her heart till she could hardly speak. She fought with the feeling, might and main, for she believed in common sense. But it was too strong. She had to leave the dance and go downstairs to telephone to the country. The children's nursery governess was terribly surprised and startled at being rung up in the night.

"Are the children all right, Miss Wilmot?"

"Oh, yes, they are quite all right."

"Master Paul? Is he all right?"

"He went to bed as right as a trivet. Shall I run up and look at him?"

"No," said Paul's mother reluctantly. "No! Don't trouble. It's all right. Don't sit up. We shall be home fairly soon." She did not want her son's privacy intruded upon.

"Very good," said the governess.

It was about one o'clock when Paul's mother and father drove up to their house. All was still. Paul's mother went to her room and slipped off her white fur cloak. She had told her maid not to wait up for her. She heard her husband downstairs, mixing a whisky and soda.

And then, because of the strange anxiety at her heart, she stole upstairs to her son's room. Noiselessly she went along the upper corridor. Was there a faint noise? What was it?

She stood, with arrested muscles, outside his door, listening. There was a strange, heavy, and yet not loud noise. Her heart stood still. It was a soundless noise, yet rushing and powerful. Something huge, in violent, hushed motion. What was it? What in God's name was it? She ought to know. She felt that she knew the noise. She knew what it was.

Yet she could not place it. She couldn't say what it was. And on and on it went, like a madness.

Softly, frozen with anxiety and fear, she turned the door handle.

The room was dark. Yet in the space near the window, she heard and saw something plunging to and fro. She gazed in fear and amazement.

Then suddenly she switched on the light, and saw her son, in his green pyjamas, madly surging on the rocking horse. The blaze of light suddenly lit him up, as he urged the wooden horse, and lit her up, as she stood, blonde, in her dress of pale green and crystal, in the doorway.

"Paul!" she cried. "Whatever are you doing?"

"It's Malabar!" he screamed, in a powerful, strange voice. "It's Malabar!"

His eyes blazed at her for one strange and senseless second, as he ceased urging his wooden horse. Then he fell with a crash to the ground, and she, all her tormented motherhood flooding upon her, rushed to gather him up.

But he was unconscious, and unconscious he remained, with some brain fever. He talked and tossed, and his mother sat stonily by his side.

"Malabar! It's Malabar! Bassett, Bassett, I know! It's Malabar!"

So the child cried, trying to get up and urge the rocking horse that gave him his inspiration.

"What does he mean by Malabar?" asked the heart-frozen mother.

"I don't know," said the father stonily.

"What does he mean by Malabar?" she asked her brother Oscar.

"It's one of the horses running for the Derby," was the answer.

And, in spite of himself, Oscar Cresswell spoke to Bassett, and himself put a thousand on Malabar; at fourteen to one.

The third day of the illness was critical; they were waiting for a change. The boy, with his rather long, curly hair, was tossing ceaselessly on the pillow. He neither slept nor regained consciousness, and his eyes were like blue stones. His mother sat, feeling her heart had gone, turned actually into a stone.

In the evening, Oscar Cresswell did not come, but Bassett sent a message saying could he come up for one moment, just one moment? Paul's mother was very angry at the intrusion, but on second thoughts she agreed. The boy was the same. Perhaps Bassett might bring him to consciousness.

The gardener, a shortish fellow with a little brown moustache, and sharp little brown eyes, tiptoed into the room, touched his imaginary cap to Paul's mother, and stole to the bedside, staring with glittering, smallish eyes at the tossing, dying child.

"Master Paul!" he whispered. "Master Paul! Malabar came in first all right, a clean win. I did as you told me. You've made over seventy thousand pounds, you have; you've got over eighty thousand. Malabar came in all right, Master Paul."

"Malabar! Malabar! Did I say Malabar, Mother? Did I say Malabar? Do you think I'm lucky, Mother? I knew Malabar, didn't I? Over eighty thousand pounds! I call that lucky, don't you, Mother? Over eighty thousand pounds! I knew, didn't I know I knew? Malabar came in all right. If I ride my horse till I'm sure, then I tell you, Bassett, you can go as high as you like. Did you go for all you were worth, Bassett?"

"I went a thousand on it, Master Paul."

"I never told you, Mother, that if I can ride my horse, and get there, then I'm absolutely sure—oh, absolutely! Mother, did I ever tell you? I am lucky!"

"No, you never did," said the mother.

But the boy died in the night.

And even as he lay dead, his mother heard her brother's voice saying to her: "My God, Hester, you're eighty-odd thousand to the good, and a poor devil of a son to the bad. But, poor devil, poor devil, he's best gone out of a life where he rides his rocking horse to find a winner."

Notes

Ascot a race course in Ascot, England, founded by Queen Anne in 1711. The first four-day annual Royal Meeting horse race took place there in 1768 and continues to this day. From this race course came the use of the word *ascot*, meaning a broad-necked scarf knotted so that one end lies flat against the other. This apparel was customarily worn by the upper-class spectators at Ascot.

batman an attendant who serves a military officer

blade of the "turf" a gambler on horse races

writs a written order issued by a court, stating that the addressee must legally either engage in or stop engaging in a specified act

Activities

1. Write a journal entry in which you first summarize the story. Next describe your responses to the characters and events at various points. Then develop two open-ended questions you are interested in discussing. Work with others in the class to develop a structured discussion around the group's questions. Afterward add one or two paragraphs to your journal entry, incorporating new insights or interpretations from your discussion.

2. Create a visual representation, such as a collage, collection of objects, or a sketch, that conveys the overall mood and theme of this story without including any of the characters. Reread the story closely, noting descriptions of objects and the physical setting. Then consider the mood, or *emotional setting*, of the story. Identify which objects, if any, might play a symbolic role in "The Rocking-Horse Winner" and include those in your visual. Display your work and invite others to comment on your interpretation.

3. "The Rocking-Horse Winner" is set in an upper middle-class home in England, early in the twentieth century. Choose a passage of dialogue that reflects this context, both in the language and speech patterns of the characters and in the values and beliefs that underlie their words. Then create a new version of the passage by rewriting the dialogue to reflect a contemporary context of your choice. Which elements of the story are specific to the context in which it was written? Which elements are universal?

Another Viewpoint: Archetypal Patterns

In literary traditions from various cultures, the horse has functioned as an omen of death and symbolized the transport of the soul. How might Paul's rides be interpreted as a journey of the soul to the "other world"? What does he gain from these journeys? Do research to learn more about symbolism connected both with the horse and with visits to another world beyond life. Then present an argument for or against this interpretation of "The Rocking-Horse Winner."

Storefronts, Jose Luis Ortiz

Write Me Sometime

Taien Ng-Chan

Taien Ng-Chan is a playwright, poet, editor, producer, and photographer, as well as a writer of fiction. Born in Vancouver in 1970, she is currently based in Montreal. Ng-Chan was a winner of the CBC New Voices Radio Drama Competition in 2000. She has also served as a contributing editor and Web site designer at *Matrix* magazine, as well as editor and producer of *Speakeasy*, a webzine. Ng-Chan has said, "I often find it painful to read my older writings, but there are certain pieces that work for me every time I read them, and that's when I think I've been successful." When have you considered your writing successful? What are some of the qualities of a piece of writing that make it a success?

Whenever I think of my father, I think of food. I think of the years we spent eating at McDonald's and the Old Spaghetti Factory and pizza parlours galore. From as far back as I can remember, I saw my dad only once a week, when he picked me up every Saturday afternoon to go out for lunch. I'd get to choose which restaurant we'd go to, and then he'd ask me about school, my mother and assorted things that I can't remember now. I was probably too busy eating. My mother did come along with us at first, mainly to keep an eye on me, but she eventually stopped because she didn't want to deal with my father. I don't blame her.

When I turned ten, my six-year-old half sister started joining our Saturday excursions. Suddenly, I had a weekend sibling, which was strange because I had always thought I was an only child. The three of us would argue about where to go for lunch, but as my sister liked the same things I did, it wouldn't take too long for us to decide. Every now and then we'd let Dad choose, but we knew he'd just want to go for dim sum, which we thought was boring.

I used to look forward to these Saturdays because I could eat anything I wanted. As I got older, we started going out for steak and seafood, but for the longest time, I just wanted pizza. My mother never made pizza, or even spaghetti. Sometimes she made pork chops or shepherd's pie or soya sauce chicken and rice, which I liked well enough. But I loved my pizza. Thin crust with extra sauce, sometimes ham and pineapple, sometimes all dressed but no olives. My dad and I were harsh pizza critics: the sauce had to be spicy, and the vegetables cut and arranged just right. An abundance of pineapple was a must, and the cheese had to pull away into long, thin strands between the slices. One particular restaurant failed abysmally to meet our standards and was forever dubbed "The Yucky House of Pizza," which we'd shout every time we drove past it.

After lunch, we'd go bowling, or to the dinosaur park at the zoo, or paddle boating at Prince's Island in the summer, or skating and tobogganing in the winter. Sometimes, Dad would take us to IKEA and spend an hour pretending to look at furniture while we jumped around in the room full of blue and red plastic balls. Other times, we'd go to the bakery at the mall and each pick out two slices of cake, plus a couple for my mom. Chocolate cheesecake, fruit tarts, danishes. We'd make a pot of tea and pretend to have a party. Then, just before dinnertime, my dad and my sister would go home.

The images I have in my head of these Saturdays are blurry, happy pictures that go with my dad's stories like illustrations. There was the time he ate two slices of a pizza and I ate the rest. I must have been only six or seven at the time, and I see myself sitting small in the corner of a restaurant booth with dark brown vinyl seats, a huge pizza in front of me. "The whole pizza!" my dad exclaims every time he brings up that story.

Or the time we went for spaghetti, and the top fell off the container as I was shaking out some parmesan over the spicy meat sauce, spilling a ton of cheese like a snowfall over the entire plate. That's the picture I have, me with the container still in my hand, the lid in the spaghetti. From then on, we made a great ritual of checking the lids every time.

If I could look just at these pictures, I'd think that my childhood was made up of fifty-two happy lunches a year. But somewhere along the way, I stopped looking forward to Saturdays. I'd listen to my sister talk about playing basketball with Dad after supper, or the way they both called grilled cheese sandwiches "grouchy" sandwiches. Or notice how my sister knew all the songs on the tape of Chinese opera that my dad liked to play in the car. It left me with the taste of something sharp and grey under my tongue, like a tiny piece of rock had slipped into my food. If I wasn't careful, I'd break my teeth on it. Once I told him not to bother coming any more, that I had lots of friends and needed more time to play with them. But I felt sad about it afterwards, remembering how his face had changed. After that, I seemed to go into automatic cheer whenever I saw him. Our Saturday lunch rituals continued right up until the time I moved out to go to university.

We live in different cities now, and I only see my father once or twice a year, when I come home to Calgary for Christmas or if he happens to come by Vancouver on business. I see my half sister even less, and I'm still apt to think of myself as an only child. I think she feels the same way, because we've never tried to stay in touch.

I don't know why I feel the need to keep in touch with my father, when he wasn't much more in my life than lunch once a week. But somehow I think that the lines have to be kept open. My mom thinks so too, oddly enough.

"Have you heard from your dad lately?" she says every time she phones. "What did he say? You should write him."

And I do write him. I write him longer letters than I write my friends. I write him about what I've been doing, how my classes are going, what projects I've been working on. I sent him the entire movie script that I had gotten funding to write, and the last essay I researched about the effects of Darwinism on Victorian literature. I tell him about newspaper articles I've been reading on the controversy over the age of the universe, and what I've been thinking about our last conversation on artificial intelligence.

My father, you see, is a scientist. More precisely, a geophysicist. When I was younger, he used to tell me he sat at a desk and drank lots of coffee for a living. When I found out that he flew all over the world to look at rocks and stuff, I wanted to be a scientist too. Or an artist. "A scientist or an artist, I haven't made up my mind yet," I used to tell people who asked what I wanted to be when I grew up. In my letters to my dad, I guess I try to be both.

He hardly ever writes back to me, but every so often he calls. Every time we talk, we say that we should write more often, get to know each other better. And then I won't hear from him for another year. I feel as if I'm trying to communicate with outer-space life-forms, my satellite dish sending out signals just in case.

The last time I saw my father was about a year ago, when he was in Vancouver for a business meeting. He called me just before noon and wanted to take me out for lunch. I had already eaten an avocado and tomato sandwich.

"That's okay," Dad said. "You can eat more!"

"Well, maybe we can go for a walk instead," I suggested. "We could go to Stanley Park."

"I can't do too much walking," he said. "I've been having a little trouble with my feet lately. Your dad's getting old, you know…"

"Oh, Dad, you're not getting old," I said, as cheerfully as I could. "We can do something else. Maybe we can go to the art gallery. Or what else do you want to see?"

"I don't have too much time," he said. "Why don't we go have lunch anyway? We can go a little later if you like."

So I gave up and let him take me out for lunch. We ended up at a trendy restaurant on Robson Street, since it was close by, and Dad tried to order me everything on the menu.

"How about an appetizer?" he said, poking his finger at the description of the liver pâté. "This sounds good. Or how about a salad? That's good for you. How are you eating these days? You should have some soup, too."

"I'm really not that hungry," I said. "I can't eat like I used to. What about you? What are you going to have?"

"I'm not too hungry either. I'll just have a beer," he said. I'd never seen him have a drink before. "Maybe we should've gone to the pub," I said jokingly.

The waiter came over and waited.

"I guess I'll have the spinach salad," I said, handing him my menu. "And a glass of white wine, please."

"I'll have a beer," Dad said. "Any kind."

The waiter nodded and smiled and went away. Dad looked at me funny for a second, probably because he'd never seen me drink before, either.

"Is that all you're having?" he said. "You should have an entrée. The veal looked very good."

"Veal…," I said, screwing up my nose. "Dad, I'm a vegetarian."

"Oh. That's right." He scratched his head.

I could see him wanting to debate the issue, just as he had when I first explained to him why I was a vegetarian. I was back in Calgary for Christmas. I hadn't seen my dad or my sister in quite a while, and we were about to go out for lunch when I told them the big news.

"So," he had said, "that means you don't eat meat any more." My sister looked at me as if I was crazy.

"What about chicken?" Dad asked. "Do you eat chicken? Seafood?"

"No, Dad, chickens aren't vegetables. Fish aren't vegetables either."

"What's your reason for not eating meat? It's not just because you have to kill animals, is it? After all, death is a part of life."

"I know. If you went out and killed your own animal and ate it, that'd be fine with me."

I had launched into the whole thing about battery cages and steroids and how you could feed the world with the grain that goes to feeding cows and how the rainforests of Brazil were being destroyed for hamburgers. Dad countered each point. We ended up discussing the impact individuals could make, and why Buddhists didn't eat meat. My sister just looked on.

Finally, Dad asked us what we wanted for lunch. My sister suggested pizza.

"Uh," I said, "actually, I don't eat pizza much any more. I try to stay away from dairy products. Hard to digest."

But there weren't too many places to go to in Calgary, so I compromised. "Wow," my sister said after lunch. "I never had a pizza without meat before."

When the waiter came back with our drinks and my spinach salad, there were bacon bits that I had to pick out. My dad watched me for a while and fiddled with his beer glass. Then he started what had become our usual routine.

"So," he began, "what do you think of what's been happening in the news lately?"

We had an ongoing discussion about politics and the economy and the state of the world—it gave us something to talk about. These talks always started and ended the same way. He would ask me what I thought about recent events, and then we would talk about the future, the need to adapt to change, the impact of technology. Dad always got very animated when talking about technology. I would bring up the need for human responsibility in science, and he would agree with me wholeheartedly. They were good conversations.

My father likes to debate things, to argue for the sake of argument. My mother said he had wanted to be a philosopher when he was young and idealistic. A lot like you, she said. That was when she first met him. That was before he decided there was no living to be made in philosophy and went into the oil industry.

"Arts," he said to me once, "are for the weekends." I told him then that I wanted to be a writer. "Journalism?" he said.

"No, writing," I said. "Stories and plays and stuff."

"Write for the newspapers," he said. "That's what you should do if you like writing."

I told him I would think about it.

But he never did ask me what I wrote about. And I never asked what he thought of the things I sent him, either. Except once, about the Darwin essay.

"Interesting," he said. "Very interesting. Why don't you write a book about the relationship between science and the arts?"

I said I might do that. And we haven't mentioned it since.

By the time I had finished my salad, Dad had convinced me to have dessert. I mulled over the menu, torn between the chocolate hazelnut torte and the blueberry apple flan.

"Aren't you going to have any?" I asked, hoping we could swap bites. Dad shook his head.

"Why don't you get both anyway?" he said. "After all, how often do you get to have lunch with your dad?"

I settled for the flan.

The rest of the lunch was spent in polite enquiry. We had run out of politics and technology, so I asked him how his work was, and how my sister was. He asked me how my work was, and how my mother was. She's fine, we both said. Things are going fine.

After I had finished eating, we walked up Robson Street. We passed chocolate shops and pizza joints, and every time I looked in the window of a store, Dad would ask me if I wanted anything. When we passed a frozen yogurt shop he wanted to buy a tub of frozen yogurt for me.

"Yogurt's very healthy," he said. "I want you to eat right."

"But I just ate."

"You can eat it later," he said. "You're a growing girl!"

"Not any more," I said. "I haven't grown an inch in years."

"Remember that time you ate a whole pizza?"

"I was seven years old, Dad."

"A whole pizza! How about getting some pizza now? You can bring it home for dinner."

"That's okay."

"You don't eat much any more. Are you getting enough protein? You have to be careful, being vegetarian."

I nodded and smiled. "Yes, Dad."

We went on like this all the way up the street, with Dad ducking into a store every now and then despite my protests. By the time we reached my apartment, my arms were laden with bags of food. I invited him in, but he said he had had only a couple of hours to spare.

"Write me sometime," he said. "Let me know if there's anything you need."

I closed the door behind him, my insides feeling forlorn and empty. I went into the kitchen to put the pizza in the fridge, the frozen yogurt in the freezer, the chocolate in the cupboard. But I didn't feel like eating again for days.

When I told my mother about Dad's visit, she wanted to know all the details. Where we ate, what we talked about, what he had bought me.

"Did he give you any spending money?" she said. "Well, he should have. He's your father. And he can afford it."

"I don't want him to," I said.

I could hear her clucking her tongue over the phone. "You're his *daughter*," she said. "You shouldn't even have to *ask*."

I haven't seen my father since that lunch, although he did call me a couple of weeks ago. I was out at the time. When I came home, I found my father's voice on my answering machine, sounding almost querulous. He said that he'd call back some other time. I called him a few days later. The phone rang twice before he picked it up.

"Hi, Dad," I said, only to be greeted enthusiastically with my sister's name. "Uh, no," I said. I felt almost apologetic. "It's your other daughter."

"Oh," Dad said. There was a moment's silence, then he cleared his throat. "You sound very much alike."

"Well," I said, as cheerfully as I could. "We are sisters, after all." The conversation went downhill from there.

"Are you in town?" my father asked.

"No, I just called to say hi. And to return your call."

"Ah," he said.

I asked him how his work was, and how my sister was; he asked me how my work was, and how my mother was. She's fine, we both said. Things are going fine.

Notes

dim sum traditional Chinese breakfast dish of steamed dumplings and pastry, filled with meat and vegetables

IKEA a Scandinavian furniture warehouse store, featuring "assemble-it-yourself" furniture displayed in room-like settings

Darwinism the theory of evolution first put forward by Charles Darwin in his book *On the Origin of Species* (1859); subsequently used as the basis for theories about social evolution in the Victorian era (1832–1901)

geophysicist a scientist who studies the physics of the earth

Activities

1. The story begins with the narrator's observation that "whenever I think of my father, I think of food." Explain how the changes in the relationship between the girl and her father are reflected in the changes in what, when, where, and under what circumstances they meet and eat.

2. The story concludes with these lines: "She's fine, we both said. Things are going fine." Find another point in the story where these lines are used. How does their repetition add to the pathos of the story? Explain the irony in these words.

3. The narrator is a creative writer and her father is a geophysicist. With a partner, locate a creative writer and scientist in your community. Interview each, specifically asking them in what ways their professions are similar to and different from other professions. In a short essay, use specific examples from the story to assess the extent to which you think the conflict between the girl and her father is the result of the differing perspectives of a writer and a scientist.

CALGARY FROM SUNNYSIDE

Margaret Shelton

About the Visual   Margaret Shelton was born in Bruce, Alberta, in 1915 and has spent most of her life in Calgary. As a young woman, she studied at Calgary's Provincial Institute of Technology and Art (now The Alberta College of Art and Design). Shelton has produced a large body of work that includes watercolours, prints, and drawings. *Calgary from Sunnyside* is a woodblock print, made by cutting a design in a block of wood and using ink to transfer the image to paper. In an artwork representing a familiar place, do you prefer the work to feature recognizable landmarks and reflect your mental images or would you rather have it offer a unique perspective? Why?

Activities

1. Record your first impression of *Calgary from Sunnyside* by jotting down the initial words that come to mind. Use your notes to write a dialogue journal entry to exchange with a partner. Read and respond to each other's writing. What factors in your own experiences and preferences affected your reactions?

2. In preparation for a class discussion, analyze some of the key visual elements and principles of design that Shelton has used in this print. How has she used contrast to emphasize parts of the picture? What texture and shapes has she used? What observation or "truth" about an urban landscape does the print convey?

woodblock print, 12 cm x 24.4 cm

Outside Edges

Ivan Dorin

Ivan Dorin lives in Calgary, Alberta. He is an earth scientist who has worked at the Royal Tyrrell Museum of Palaeontology in Drumheller, Alberta. He writes in his spare time and his stories have appeared in literary journals, including *Alberta Rebound* and *Vox*. "Outside Edges" explores a young man's goals and his relationship with his father. Think about a personal goal you had when you were young. Did you share your goal with anyone and, if so, what was that person's reaction? How did the goal change as you got older? What are some of the benefits of setting goals? Are there any drawbacks?

I always wanted my feelings for David to be understated, a tastefully drawn picture in a smooth-edged rectangular frame. I didn't want something too big for me to express. I didn't want to gush; to take endless rolls of baby pictures or display my kid's sports trophies for everyone to see. I was surprised at how difficult it was. I restrained myself constantly. I didn't just believe that my kid was special; that he could do anything he set his mind to. I *knew* it, and that made it even harder for me to find the right words. Once when he was seven, I was boring everyone at the supper table by talking about my latest real estate deal, so I asked David what he had learned in school that day. He said the teacher talked about Christopher Columbus and his four ships. I chewed over the names for a minute: Nina, Pinta, Santa Maria; Nina, Pinta, Santa Maria. Finally I swallowed.

"Are you sure about that? I thought Columbus had three ships."

"Well," he said expressionlessly, pausing to wash down his broccoli, "he started out with four, but one went off the edge."

He didn't crack a smile all through dinner. I started to think the world *was* flat before Columbus. My favourite line came when he was eight years old, on the way home from school.

"Daddy?"

"Uh huh?"

"When I grow up, I'm gonna skate across the country."

I started to smile, but that little face looked so determined. (If anyone could do it, you could.) "It's a big country."

"But people have run across it, haven't they? And skating's easier than running, once you get good. I'm sure I could skate faster than that Terry Fox guy. He had to run, and he had only one leg."

"He ran along the highway though. How would you skate on the highway?"

"I could have a Zamboni drive along in front of me."

No, I thought, the ice wouldn't be thick enough. Then I got this image of a convoy of Zambonis steaming down the Trans-Canada, past a signpost saying "Wawa 46," past some disconsolate hitchhikers ("Wawa's the armpit of Canada," I remember them saying. "If you get left there, you can be stranded for days") framed against the snow-covered pines. Then came David in his hockey gear, just far enough behind for the water to freeze in front of him, pausing from his shuffle to scoop a puck out of the ditch, deking out an invisible defender, and getting a breakaway on the Pacific.

I really shouldn't have laughed.

"Well, I could, couldn't I?"

(You bet. Will you let me drive the Zamboni?)

"I don't think the government would let you flood the highway. It wouldn't be safe."

"But I wouldn't need much. Just the part on the side."

"Not all the highways in this country are as good as ours, son. Some shoulders are just dirt and gravel. Others aren't even there at all."

"Oh."

"You just worry about skating across the rink for now, okay?"

"Yeah."

It was a long drive home. He hardly moved except when we crossed the Bow River, and he craned his neck for a better view. I wanted to rewind and start the conversation over somehow, but all I could think of was how simple it would be to have a son who just wanted to be a fireman. We didn't talk again until after supper.

"Where does the Bow River come from, Dad?"

"Somewhere in Banff, I guess."

"But where does it really start?"

I had to admit I didn't know. I found a road map, and we traced the thin blue line to Bow Lake, but he wasn't satisfied.

"Well, this is a road map of Alberta," I explained. "They can't show every little creek."

"Are there ones where they do have all the creeks on?"

"The University library has some, I think. I'm going there tomorrow, if you'd like to look at some."

"Really? Could I? Mum, guess what! Dad's taking me to the library tomorrow."

I expected him to forget about it overnight, but he didn't. I told him that I had my own work to do and he would have to be by himself part of the time, but he didn't mind. I think I helped him with the map index, so that he could find out which maps he wanted to look at. In hopes that his interest might lead him into real estate someday, I showed him how the township and range system worked. It was the last thing I ever told him about maps.

When I got home from work the next day, he was poring over a pair of brand new topographic maps. He had obtained the address of the government map office from the librarian at the University, dumped out his piggy bank and begged Marie to drive him there at lunchtime. "Look, Dad! We live at 51 degrees 2 minutes north, 114 degrees 5 minutes west. And here's where the Elbow River meets the Bow." He wasn't satisfied for long. For one thing, Calgary falls on a four-corner junction in the topographic system, and even at a scale of 1 to 250,000 or four miles to the inch, it takes four maps to show the whole city. He liked the 1 to 50,000 (1.24 inches to the mile) Calgary map best, but its edges frustrated him. There were always so many more hills and valleys and creeks just beyond the edge of the map. His allowance couldn't come in fast enough. His favourite map had a little tic-tac-toe style grid in the bottom right-hand corner, labelled "Index to adjoining sheets of National Topographic System," with Calgary in the middle. As his eye spiralled outward from our house, he wanted more and more to have those eight adjoining sheets. We didn't have a maid then; Marie paid him for doing chores around the house, and she said she'd never had it so good. One by one the maps came in: Dalroy, Dalemead, Priddis, Bragg Creek, Jumpingpound Creek, Wildcat Hills, Crossfield, Irricana.

His ninth birthday presented us with a dilemma. We weren't strapped for money, even then; there just weren't that many things he wanted. We'd bought him things like a bicycle and a baseball glove and a new hockey stick, and he hadn't touched some of his toys. As a last resort I asked him, rather sheepishly, if he'd like me to go to the map office with him and pick up a couple of maps for his birthday.

The map office had a large index map on one wall, dividing Canada into more than a hundred blocks arranged in north-south columns, with numbers increasing from east to west. The women at the desk greeted him by name, and asked all sorts of questions about him while he flipped through the sample maps of block 82.

"I don't really know what got him started," I told them. "He wanted to know about the Bow River first, and it just mushroomed from there." He closed the cover of block 82, and wandered from one sample pile to another, northward through Alberta, 83, 84, 85.

"How many maps per block?" I asked, eyeing the map on the wall.

"Sixteen, at 1:250,000 scale, A through P. Some blocks are mostly ocean. The 1:250,000 series covers the whole country with 917 sheets. Each of those is subdivided into sixteen 1:50,000 scale maps."

"My God. I'll be ruined."

We watched him move north through Saskatchewan. 72, 73, 74.

"Well, we have some extra maps. Sometimes we order too many, or they go out of print. Maybe he might be interested in those."

We expected a couple of rolls of maps sitting on a desk somewhere. He was intrigued at the prospect of getting some maps for free, of course, but wasn't prepared to be led around the counter and find rolls stacked three feet high. It was like seeing Anthony Henday climb one of thousands of ordinary prairie hills, reach the top with his eyes to the ground, and look up to see for the first time the blue and white wall of the Rockies spread before him.

Mackenzie Delta. "Ooh, look at all the *lakes*!" Spence Bay. "Look at how high the raised beaches are, Dad! That's where the ocean used to be. The ice is gone so the land is bouncing back now. See? It came up 400 feet here." Tammarvi River. "Why do the lakes and rivers all run the same way, Dad? And they're so straight." Tanquary Fiord. "This part goes all the way across the map. I bet the whole thing would run from here to Lethbridge." Azure River. "The glacier goes all the way down to 5,200 feet. They must get tons of snow there." We must have been there for a couple of hours at least, rolling and unrolling the maps. It astounded him that such treasures could remain unclaimed. We had time to examine only a few maps closely; we had all we could carry by the time we were finished. Then he turned to the clerk and asked, as if opening his last Christmas present, "Is that all?"

"We order maps all the time," she smiled. "If you check back in a couple of months, we'll probably have some more."

He was content to leave then. We were partway out the door when I stopped.

"What is it, Dad?"

"Well, uh, haven't we forgotten something?"

"What?"

"Your birthday present."

"Oh."

"We don't have to, now I mean—"

"No, that's okay, Dad." He put on his best smile for me. "I know some I really want." He turned back to the index map on the wall. "This one," he said, pointing just west of Lake Superior. Then he took a step west. "And this one," just west of Calgary. 52B, Quetico, and 82N, Golden. There was no hesitation; no implication that he was just being kind. But after that, it seemed that he was happiest with his maps for company, and there was nothing more I could give him.

Sometimes I thought about that day in the car, and would imagine us on skating expeditions. Once I saw some figure skaters drawing circles on the ice with scribes, telescoping metal rods with screws at both ends and foldout handles. As I watched, I began to see myself and David at the bottom of a frozen waterfall. I stood on the bank with a duffel bag, awaiting his instructions like a surgical caddy as he scanned what I thought would be a portage.

"Hmmn," he said, frowning in concentration, "I'll need the figure skates for this one." I passed the skates to him efficiently. He changed out of his hockey skates without taking his eyes off the curtain of ice, stood up and held out his right hand, palm upward.

"Scribe," he said solemnly.

"Scribe," I answered, passing it to him.

"Other scribe."

"Other scribe."

He skated to the bottom of the waterfall, rechecked his route, and then drove one skate, toe pick first, into the vertical ice face. Then he extended the scribes to full length, stuck them into the ice above, and shortened them as he climbed. At first, he looked as if he were being pulled upward by two thin metal caterpillars, but as he climbed higher, he used them less and less. His toes turned outward too; with each step, he put more weight on the blades. Then his skates began to slide upward a little more with each step, and as he approached the top, I realized that he wasn't climbing anymore. And I wanted to tell him, hold on, I'll just run up and throw down a rope for you.

Sipanok Channel, Oskikebuk Lake, Ne-Parle-Pas Rapids, Potter Landing. He kept the index maps beside his bed and coloured them in, one square at a time, as his pile of maps grew thicker and thicker. He never folded them, and rolled them up only for transport. When the older kids were still at home, we went on Sunday drives to Moraine Lake (the one on the back of the $20 bill), and he studied the route in keen anticipation. But when we reached the turnoff just below Lake Louise, he always wanted me to avoid the familiar left-hand route. "Can't we go toward Field this time, Dad? Just a few miles?" Sure, I told him. Today Field, tomorrow Japan. (If I went everywhere I wanted to go with you, we'd never get home.) Eventually, he stopped mentioning that stretch of road directly. He talked intermittently about the sights to be seen just across the border in Yoho: Takakkaw Falls, Emerald Lake, Lake O'Hara, the Natural Bridge. We never had quite enough time. I had to draw the line somewhere.

Nova Zembia Island, Sabine Peninsula, Coral Harbour, Laredo Sound. As a teenager, David didn't put up posters of rock singers or women in wet T-shirts. When he found enough adjoining maps, he wallpapered the ceiling and walls of his room with them. He cut away the white borders and fitted the edges together, so that his room became a chunk of northwestern Ontario. I always closed his door when we had company. It wasn't the maps themselves that bothered me, but the way I was forced to look at them. I felt distanced and suffocated at the same time, as if part of the globe had been turned inside out.

Pointe Louis XIV, Cape Krusenstern, Queen Maud Gulf, Sault Ste. Marie. His supply network extended across the country: friends and relatives, retiring geologists, oil companies, librarians, someone who knew someone in the Ottawa map office. The maps filled his room, overflowed into the basement and attic, formed isolated blocks, lines and checkerboard patterns that grew and filled and reached toward each other across the vast jigsaw puzzle. By the time he graduated from high school, the gaps on the 1:250,000 index map had become lonely outposts in an expanse of pencil crayon, but he was more interested in completing his 1:50,000 collection. I tried to get him to tell me why, but he only said, "I'd map the country at one to one if I could."

He left home to go to university, got a student loan and a place just big enough for him and his maps. He worked in the map office during the summer. I felt more at ease after he moved out; the further apart we were, the more I enjoyed the reunions.

Smoky Falls, Grinnell Glacier, Tute Inlet, Swift Current, Lac Mesgouez, Washahigan Lake. The summers flew by; he graduated and got a job at the main map office in Ottawa. He came home for Christmas, without a wife or girlfriend, and always made one visit to the map office. He told me about how more of the Arctic was being mapped at 1:50,000, and that the whole country would probably be covered soon. I told him about my plans to make West Edmonton Mall look like the corner grocery store. I wanted to build sort of a Disneyland North and call it Western Canada Mall. Each year Marie, the other "kids" and I had a few more plans drawn up. By the time David was 32, we had the land and were ready to break ground. We were still unsatisfied about the skating facilities, though. We wanted them bigger and better than those at West Edmonton Mall, and indoors, but that was all we could agree on. David listened to us argue over turkey. After dinner, he brought me a piece of paper with an irregular triangle shape drawn on it in pencil.

"It should be about 350 feet across, this way. The other directions would be a little less. It would probably be the biggest indoor ice surface in the world. What do you think? Could you do it?"

"Well, sure we could do it. That's about the right size. But why the shape?"

"Well, it's Canada, of course. One unit of ice for every 50,000 of Canada."

I said it would be too expensive to hire people to cut and assemble all those maps, and we wouldn't be able to get the right plastic to cover them, and even with uncoloured ice, we'd have to keep replacing it to keep it transparent, and maybe the maps should be displayed some other way. "No!" he said. "This isn't just the biggest map in the world, of the most glaciated country in the world, with the largest area of fresh water in the world, and most of the largest lakes. It's fur and fish and floating logs and Toller Cranston and Gaetan Boucher and Gordie Howe and voyageurs and cold and people who are supposed to know how to make love in a canoe! If you can't skate on it, it's not Canadian."

The rest of the family eventually convinced me. I guess I really wanted to be convinced. But I held out until David had gone back to Ottawa.

Port aux Basques, Kananaskis Lakes, Seymour Arm, Pipmuacan Reservoir, Snowbird Lake, Lac la Ronge, Trois Rivières, Kiyiu Lake, Carcajou Canyon. When he came home the next Christmas, he looked like he hadn't slept in days. He didn't say hi or anything, just walked straight across the carpet and handed me the index map, worn and starting to curl up at the corners. I saw nothing but coloured pencil.

"That's great," I said. "Amazing. Should I arrange for a truck to have them moved?"

He looked at me as if I had slapped him. Then he turned and walked back out the door.

I went and sat in his old room. Somehow, I'd never arranged to have the maps taken down. I looked at that tangle of lakes, rivers and muskeg for I don't know how long, squinting, running my fingers along the lines. I even got a stepladder to get a closer look at the ones on the ceiling. Then I saw a faint pencil line. It followed the Nipigon River upstream from Lake Superior to Lake Nipigon, then went up the Little Jackfish River past the Summit Control Dam to the Ogoki Reservoir, west and south up the Ogoki River, Allan Water, Brightsand River and Wowing River to Wowing Lake, along a tiny creek into McCausland Lake, down the McCausland River and then down the English River. The line crossed two drainage divides without ever leaving the water.

I looked at the coloured index map again. My eyes followed the English and Winnipeg rivers to Lake Winnipeg, then followed the Saskatchewan, South Saskatchewan and Bow rivers. Just west of Lake Louise, there was a tiny blank rectangle.

I went to the map office and tried to buy him a copy, but the clerk wouldn't accept money. "I'll take care of it," she said. "I'd be honoured. Just tell him who it's from." I thanked her, and then drove west. Below Lake Louise, near the map's eastern edge. I turned right and took the old highway toward Field. I stopped at the Continental Divide, where the map showed a creek on the Alberta side, gradually flowing closer to the border, and ending in an arrow. I puffed uphill through the snow and found the creek, or creeks. The main stream divided; half flowed to Hudson Bay, and half to the Pacific. And I saw him eight years old again, in his hockey jersey, with one skate on each frozen branch. See, Dad? I told you I could do it.

When I got back, he was waiting for me. "I talked to Francine at the map office," I said, passing him the map. "She wants you to have this." He didn't say anything. I coughed and continued. "Funny thing about maps. The more you look at them, the less you need them." I paused again. "I often thought about you skating across the country, but each time, it seemed to get easier for you. I guess I figured that all you really had to do was put on your skates." (I'm sorry.) "I'm sorry I didn't tell you before."

It wasn't an instant reconciliation. We did make one trip to the Divide, though. We also spent a lot of hours at the construction site, quietly watching the edges of the maps merge and spread in a great carpet from east to west.

David would have made a great real estate developer. We filled Hudson Bay in with blue paper, but our tenants had other ideas. Everybody from furriers to fast food chains wanted to locate there. One guy wanted to rename his franchise Hudson Bay Hot Dogs and had already drawn up an advertising campaign, with Sir John Franklin's last expedition abandoning their ships in open water and trekking across the frozen tundra to sample his wares. Finally I got tired of refusing offers and had a 30-foot tall NOT FOR SALE sign erected in the middle of the Bay. David just beamed when he saw it. When the offers finally stopped, we decided to leave it there.

On opening day, the ice cover was still being completed. The Mayor and Miss Calgary and thousands of people waited outside with the ribbon and scissors as the workmen finished. Then they cleared the place, and David and I sat down on a bench just east of St. John's to put on our skates. He had chosen speed skates for the occasion, and he was finished lacing them before I was done with my hockey skates. He stood at the last edge, much as one climber might pause to allow the other to reach the summit with him.

"No, that's okay," I said, "you go ahead. I'll catch up."

He smiled then, and skated smoothly over the forests and hills of Newfoundland, leaning over and swinging one arm. I watched his strides grow longer as he sailed over Québec, and then finished tying my skates. When I looked up again, he was gone. I followed the offset herringbone pattern of his traces over James Bay and Lake Winnipeg, across the prairies and the mountains, to a final thin line. There was no wobble or curve to that trace, no second trace beside it, no telltale line of snow. He hadn't slowed down or even broken stride as he glided over South Moresby Island and off the edge of the Pacific. But it was only by knowing exactly where to look, getting down on my hands and knees, and placing my head sideways on the ice, that I could trace the faint lines across the concrete and out the door.

Notes

Terry Fox a young runner, recovering from the loss of his leg due to cancer, who decided to run across Canada to raise money for cancer research. At the age of 21, he began his "Marathon of Hope" at St. John's, Newfoundland, on April 12, 1980, but was forced to abandon his run on September 1 in Thunder Bay, Ontario, when cancer had spread to his lungs. He died in 1981. Thousands of people continue to participate in an annual fundraising run held in his memory.

Zamboni a machine used by a driver to prepare and clean the ice surface in a skating arena

National Topographic System an agency developed by the Canadian federal government in the 1920s to provide detailed maps of Canada for military, geological, and aeronautical uses, among others. Full map coverage of Canada was not completed until the 1990s.

West Edmonton Mall the world's largest shopping mall, located in the suburbs of Edmonton. It contains over 800 stores, including eleven major department stores, seven amusement parks, twenty-five salt water aquariums, nineteen movie theatres, and an NHL-sized rink.

Sir John Franklin an arctic explorer who charted much of Canada's arctic seaboard. He died tragically in 1847 when his ships, the Erebus and the Terror, became locked in the frozen ice. The surviving crew members tried to trek southward, but all perished.

Activities

1. This is a story about hopes, dreams, and the determination to make them come true. What is David's goal? Why is it important to him? What obstacles must he overcome to reach his goal? In what ways do people help him along the way? How does his personal goal eventually become a vision shared with others?

2. In writing this story, Dorin has made frequent use of proper nouns. In a language handbook, look up the differences between the following kinds of nouns: proper and common, specific and general, concrete and abstract. Have a class discussion about ways in which language is more vivid and descriptive when a writer uses proper, specific, and concrete nouns instead of nouns that are common, general, and abstract. Find examples from the story that demonstrate this.

3. Find a detailed map of Canada and make a copy of it. On your copy, locate as many of the places mentioned in the story as possible. Connect them with a pencil, trying to follow the route David used to "skate" across Canada. Imagine that David kept a diary as he crossed the country. Write an entry for a journal that he might have written while skating through *your* part of the country. Include in your description the places and people that he might have encountered along the way.

Another Viewpoint: Archetypal Patterns

Locate a reference book on mythology, such as *The Hero with a Thousand Faces* by Joseph Campbell, and do research on myths that depict the quests of heroes or heroines. What patterns emerge that are characteristic of each of these quests? What do these myths reveal to us about patterns of personal growth and development? In what ways does "Outside Edges" follow the archetypal pattern of quest myths?

TWISTED ROOTS

Lyle McIntyre

About the Visual   Lyle McIntyre was born in Huntsville, Ontario, in 1937. McIntyre began his photographic career in 1971. His work has been published in international photographic magazines and he has won numerous awards, including the Canadian Professional Photographer of the Year Award in 1986. McIntyre describes his love of photography this way: "Photography allows me to see and feel without being disturbed, to drink in nature, and to escape the everyday." What locations have inspired you to take landscape photographs? How would you describe your results? What are the challenges of capturing natural beauty through landscape photography?

Activities

1. Photographer Bill Brandt wrote: "We look at a thing and think we have seen it and yet what we see is only what our prejudices tell us should be seen, or what our desires want to see. Very rarely are we able to free our minds of thought and emotions and just see for the simple pleasure of seeing, and so long as we fail to do this, so long will the essence of things be hidden from us." Discuss the meaning of Brandt's words and then consider your response to *Twisted Roots* in terms of *thought*, *emotions*, and *essence*.

2. Lyle McIntyre has said that he works in black and white because he feels it can "communicate texture, mood, and depth to a greater degree." Write a paragraph in which you analyze which of these three elements contributes most to the impact of *Twisted Roots*. In your writing, consider the photographer's purpose in creating this image.

1992, black-and-white print

The Shining Houses

Alice Munro

Alice Munro, one of Canada's most distinguished writers, was born in Huron County, Ontario, in 1931. Her stories frequently appear in prestigious international publications such as *The New Yorker*, *The Atlantic Monthly*, and *The Paris Review* and have been translated into many languages. Munro has won many prizes, including three Governor General's Awards and the Giller Prize. Praised for being able to "create an entire life in a page," she has a keen eye for domestic detail and has said, "I know I get excited by ordinary things." To what extent are people's homes an extension of themselves? What dangers are there in stereotyping people by the appearance or location of their homes?

Mary sat on the back steps of Mrs. Fullerton's house, talking—or really listening—to Mrs. Fullerton, who sold her eggs. She had come in to pay the egg money, on her way to Edith's Debbie's birthday party. Mrs. Fullerton did not pay calls herself and she did not invite them, but, once a business pretext was established, she liked to talk. And Mary found herself exploring her neighbour's life as she had once explored the lives of grandmothers and aunts—by pretending to know less than she did, asking for some story she had heard before; this way, remembered episodes emerged each time with slight differences of content, meaning, colour, yet with a pure reality that usually attaches to things which are at least part legend. She had almost forgotten that there are people whose lives can be seen like this. She did not talk to many old people any more. Most of the people she knew had lives like her own, in which things were not sorted out yet, and it is not certain if this thing, or that, should be taken seriously. Mrs. Fullerton had no doubts or questions of this kind. How was it possible, for instance, not to take seriously the broad blithe back of Mr. Fullerton, disappearing down the road on a summer day, not to return?

"I didn't know that," said Mary. "I always thought Mr. Fullerton was dead."

"He's no more dead than I am," said Mrs. Fullerton, sitting up straight. A bold Plymouth Rock walked across the bottom step and Mary's little boy, Danny, got up to give rather cautious chase. "He's just gone off on his travels, that's what he is. May of gone up north, may of gone to the States, I don't know. But he's not dead. I would of felt it. He's not old neither, you know, not old like I am. He was my second husband, he was younger. I never made any secret of it. I had this place and raised my children and buried my first husband, before ever Mr. Fullerton came upon the scene. Why, one time down in the post office we was standing together by the wicket and I went over to put a letter in the box and left my bag behind me, and Mr. Fullerton turns to go after me and the girl calls to him, she says, here, your mother's left her purse!"

Mary smiled, answering Mrs. Fullerton's high-pitched and not trustful laughter. Mrs. Fullerton was old, as she had said—older than you might think, seeing her hair still fuzzy and black, her clothes slatternly-gay, dime-store brooches pinned to her ravelling sweater. Her eyes showed it, black as plums, with a soft inanimate sheen; things sank into them and they never changed. The life in her face was all in the nose and mouth, which were always twitching, fluttering, drawing tight grimace-lines down her cheeks. When she came around every Friday on her egg deliveries her hair was curled, her blouse held together by a bunch of cotton flowers, her mouth painted, a spidery and ferocious line of red; she would not show herself to her new neighbours in any sad old-womanish disarray.

"Thought I was his mother," she said. "I didn't care. I had a good laugh. But what I was telling you," she said, "a day in summer, he was off work. He had the ladder up and he was picking me the cherries off of my black-cherry tree. I came out to hang my clothes and there was this man I never seen before in my life, taking the pail of cherries my husband hands down to him. Helping himself, too, not backward, he sat down and ate cherries out of my pail. Who's that, I said to my husband, and he says, just a fellow passing. If he's a friend of yours, I said, he's welcome to stay for supper. What are you talking about, he says, I never seen him before. So I never said another thing. Mr. Fullerton went and talked to him, eating my cherries I intended for a pie, but that man would talk to anybody, tramp, Jehovah's Witness, anybody—that didn't need to mean anything.

"And half an hour after that fellow went off," she said, "Mr. Fullerton comes out in his brown jacket and his hat on. I have to meet a man downtown. How long will you be, I said. Oh, not long. So off he goes down the road, down to where the old tram went—we was all in the bush then—and something made me look after him. He must be hot in that coat, I said. And that's when I knew he wasn't coming back. Yet I couldn't've expected it, he liked it here. He was talking about putting chinchillas in the back yard. What's in a man's mind even when you're liv-ing with him you will never know."

"Was it long ago?" said Mary.

"Twelve years. My boys wanted me to sell then and go and live in rooms. But I said no. I had my hens and a nanny goat too at that time. More or less a pet. I had a pet coon too for a while, used to feed him chewing gum. Well, I said, husbands maybe come and go, but a place you've lived fifty years is something else. Making a joke of it with my fam-ily. Besides, I thought, if Mr. Fullerton was to come back, he'd come back here, not knowing where else to go. Of course he'd hardly know where to find me, the way it's changed now. But I always had the idea he might of suffered a loss of memory and it might come back. That has happened.

"I'm not complaining. Sometimes it seems to me about as reason-able a man should go as stay. I don't mind changes, either, that helps out my egg business. But this baby-sitting. All the time one or the other is asking me about baby-sitting. I tell them I got my own house to sit in and I raised my share of children."

Mary, remembering the birthday party, got up and called to her little boy. "I thought I might offer my black cherries for sale next summer," Mrs. Fullerton said. "Come and pick your own and they're fifty cents a box. I can't risk my old bones up a ladder no more."

"That's too much," Mary said, smiling. "They're cheaper than that at the supermarket." Mrs. Fullerton already hated the supermarket for lowering the price of eggs. Mary shook out her last cigarette and left it with her, saying she had another package in her purse. Mrs. Fullerton was fond of a cigarette but would not accept one unless you took her by surprise. Baby-sitting would pay for them, Mary thought. At the same time she was rather pleased with Mrs. Fullerton for being so unaccommodating. When Mary came out of this place, she always felt as if she were passing through barricades. The house and its surroundings were so self-sufficient, with their complicated and seemingly unalterable layout of vegetables and flower beds, apple and cherry trees, wired chicken-run, berry patch and wooden walks, woodpile, a great many roughly built dark little sheds, for hens or rabbits or a goat. Here was no open or straightforward plan, no order that an outsider could understand; yet what was haphazard time had made final. The place had become fixed, impregnable, all its accumulations necessary, until it seemed that even the washtubs, mops, couch springs and stacks of old police magazines on the back porch were there to stay.

Mary and Danny walked down the road that had been called, in Mrs. Fullerton's time, Wicks Road, but was now marked on the maps of the subdivision as Heather Drive. The name of the subdivision was Garden Place, and its streets were named for flowers. On either side of the road the earth was raw; the ditches were running full. Planks were laid across the open ditches, planks approached the doors of the newest houses. The new, white and shining houses, set side by side in long rows in the wound of the earth. She always thought of them as white houses, though of course they were not entirely white. They were stucco and siding, and only the stucco was white; the siding was painted in shades of blue, pink, green and yellow, all fresh and vivid colours. Last year, just at this time, in March, the bulldozers had come in to clear away the brush and second-growth and great trees of the mountain forest; in a little while the houses were going up among the boulders, the huge torn stumps, the unimaginable upheavals of that earth. The houses were frail at first, skeletons of new wood standing up in the dusk of the cold spring days. But the roofs went on, black and green, blue and red, and the stucco, the siding; the windows were put in, and plastered with signs that said, Murry's Glass, French's Hardwood Floors; it could be seen that the houses were real. People who would live in them came out and tramped around in the mud on Sundays. They were for people like Mary and her husband and their child, with not much money but expectations of more; Garden Place was already put down, in the minds of people who understood addresses, as less luxurious than Pine Hills but more desirable than Wellington Park. The bathrooms were beautiful, with three-part mirrors, ceramic tile, and coloured plumbing. The cupboards in the kitchen were light birch or mahogany, and there were copper lighting fixtures there and in the dining ells. Brick planters, matching the fireplaces, separated the living rooms and halls. The rooms were all large and light and the basements dry, and all this soundness and excellence seemed to be clearly, proudly indicated on the face of each house—those ingenuously similar houses that looked calmly out at each other, all the way down the street.

Today, since it was Saturday, all the men were out working around their houses. They were digging drainage ditches and making rockeries and clearing off and burning torn branches and brush. They worked with competitive violence and energy, all this being new to them; they were not men who made their livings by physical work. All day Saturday and Sunday they worked like this, so that in a year or two there should be green terraces, rock walls, shapely flower beds and ornamental shrubs. The earth must be heavy to dig now; it had been raining last night and this morning. But the day was brightening; the clouds had broken, revealing a long thin triangle of sky, its blue still cold and delicate, a winter colour. Behind the houses on one side of the road were pine trees, their ponderous symmetry not much stirred by any wind. These were to be cut down any day now, to make room for a shopping centre, which had been promised when the houses were sold.

And under the structure of this new subdivision, there was still something else to be seen; that was the old city, the old wilderness city that had lain on the side of the mountain. It had to be called a city because there were tramlines running into the woods, the houses had numbers and there were all the public buildings of a city, down by the water. But houses like Mrs. Fullerton's had been separated from each other by uncut forest and a jungle of wild blackberry and salmonberry bushes; these surviving houses, with thick smoke coming out of their chimneys, walls unpainted and patched and showing different degrees of age and darkening, rough sheds and stacked wood and compost heaps and grey board fences around them—these appeared every so often among the large new houses of Mimosa and Marigold and Heather Drive—dark, enclosed, expressing something like savagery in their disorder and the steep, unmatched angles of roofs and lean-tos; not possible on these streets, but there.

* * *

"What are they saying," said Edith, putting on more coffee. She was surrounded in her kitchen by the ruins of the birthday party—cake and moulded jellies and cookies with animal faces. A balloon rolled underfoot. The children had been fed, had posed for flash cameras and endured the birthday games; now they were playing in the back bedrooms and the basement, while their parents had coffee. "What are they saying in there?" said Edith.

"I wasn't listening," Mary said, holding the empty cream pitcher in her hand. She went to the sink window. The rent in the clouds had been torn wide open and the sun was shining. The house seemed too hot.

"Mrs. Fullerton's house," said Edith, hurrying back to the living-room. Mary knew what they were talking about. Her neighbours' conversation, otherwise not troubling, might at any moment snag itself on this subject and eddy menacingly in familiar circles of complaint, causing her to look despairingly out of windows, or down into her lap, trying to find some wonderful explanatory word to bring it to a stop; she did not succeed. She had to go back; they were waiting for cream.

A dozen neighbourhood women sat around the living room, absently holding the balloons they had been given by their children. Because the children on the street were so young, and also because any gathering-together of the people who lived there was considered a healthy thing in itself, most birthday parties were attended by mothers as well as children. Women who saw each other every day met now in earrings, nylons and skirts, with their hair fixed and faces applied. Some of the men were there too—Steve, who was Edith's husband, and others he had invited in for beer; they were all in their work clothes. The subject just introduced was one of the few on which male and female interest came together.

"I tell you what I'd do if I was next door to it," Steve said, beaming good-naturedly in expectation of laughter. "I'd send my kids over there to play with matches."

"Oh, funny," Edith said. "It's past joking. You joke, I try to do something. I even phoned the Municipal Hall."

"What did they say?" said Mary Lou Ross.

"Well I said couldn't they get her to paint it, at least, or pull down some of the shacks, and they said no they couldn't. I said I thought there must be some kind of ordinance applied to people like that and they said they knew how I *felt* and they were very *sorry*—"

"But no?"

"But no."

"But what about the chickens, I thought—"

"Oh, they wouldn't let you or me keep chickens, but she has some special dispensation about that too, I forgot how it goes."

"I'm going to stop buying them," Janie Inger said. "The supermarket's cheaper and who cares that much about fresh? And my God, the smell. I said to Carl I knew we were coming to the sticks but I somehow didn't picture us next door to a barnyard."

"Across the street is worse than next door. It makes me wonder why we ever bothered with a picture window, whenever anybody comes to see us I want to draw the drapes so they won't see what's across from us."

"Okay, okay," Steve said, cutting heavily through these female voices. "What Carl and I started out to tell you was that, if we can work this lane deal, she has got to go. It's simple and it's legal. That's the beauty of it."

"What lane deal?"

"We are getting to that. Carl and I been cooking this for a couple of weeks, but we didn't like to say anything in case it didn't work out. Take it, Carl."

"Well she's on the lane allowance, that's all," Carl said. He was a real estate salesman, stocky, earnest, successful. "I had an idea it might be that way, so I went down to the Municipal Hall and looked it up."

"What does that mean, dear?" said Janie, casual, wifely.

"This is it," Carl said. "There's an allowance for a lane, there always has been, the idea being if the area ever got built up they would put a lane through. But they never thought that would happen, people just built where they liked. She's got part of her house and half a dozen shacks sitting right where the lane has to go through. So what we do now, we get the municipality to put through a lane. We need a lane anyway. Then she has to get out. It's the law."

"It's the law," said Steve, radiating admiration. "What a smart boy. These real estate operators are smart boys."

"Does she get anything?" said Mary Lou. "I'm sick of looking at it and all but I don't want to see anybody in the poorhouse."

"Oh, she'll get paid. More than it's worth. Look, it's to her advantage. She'll get paid for it, and she couldn't sell it, she couldn't give it away."

Mary set her coffee cup down before she spoke and hoped her voice would sound all right, not emotional or scared. "But remember she's been here a long time," she said. "She was here before most of us were born." She was trying desperately to think of other words, words more sound and reasonable than these; she could not expose to this positive tide any notion that they might think flimsy and romantic, or she would destroy her argument. But she had no argument. She could try all night and never find any words to stand up to their words, which came at her now invincibly from all sides: *shack, eyesore, filth, property, value.*

"Do you honestly think that people who let their property get so rundown have that much claim to our consideration?" Janie said, feeling her husband's plan was being attacked.

"She's been here forty years, now we're here," Carl said. "So it goes. And whether you realize it or not, just standing there that house is bringing down the resale value of every house on this street. I'm in the business, I know."

And these were joined by other voices; it did not matter much what they said as long as they were full of self-assertion and anger. That was their strength, proof of their adulthood, of themselves and their seriousness. The spirit of anger rose among them, bearing up their young voices, sweeping them together as on a flood of intoxication, and they admired each other in this new behaviour as property-owners as people admire each other for being drunk.

•　•　•

"We might as well get everybody now," Steve said. "Save going around to so many places."

It was supper time, getting dark out. Everybody was preparing to go home, mothers buttoning their children's coats, children clutching, without much delight, their balloons and whistles and paper baskets full of jelly beans. They had stopped fighting, almost stopped noticing each other; the party had disintegrated. The adults too had grown calmer and felt tired.

"Edith! Edith, have you got a pen?"

Edith brought a pen and they spread the petition for the lane, which Carl had drawn up, on the dining-room table, clearing away the paper plates with smears of dried ice cream. People began to sign mechanically as they said goodbye. Steve was still scowling slightly; Carl stood with one hand on the paper, businesslike, but proud. Mary knelt on the floor and struggled with Danny's zipper. She got up and put on her own coat, smoothed her hair, put on her gloves and took them off again. When she could not think of anything else to do she walked past the dining-room table on her way to the door. Carl held out the pen.

"I can't sign that," she said. Her face flushed up, at once, her voice was trembling. Steve touched her shoulder.

"What's the matter, honey?"

"I don't think we have the right. We haven't the right."

"Mary, don't you care how things look? You live here too."

"No, I—I don't care." Oh, wasn't it strange, how in your

imagination, when you stood up for something, your voice rang, people started, abashed; but in real life they all smiled in rather a special way and you saw that what you had really done was serve yourself up as a conversational delight for the next coffee party.

"Don't worry, Mary, she's got money in the bank," Janie said. "She must have. I asked her to baby-sit for me once and she practically spit in my face. She isn't exactly a charming old lady, you know."

"I know she isn't a charming old lady," Mary said.

Steve's hand still rested on her shoulder. "Hey what do you think we are, a bunch of ogres?"

"Nobody wants to turn her out just for the fun of it," Carl said. "It's unfortunate. We all know that. But we have to think of the community."

"Yes," said Mary. But she put her hands in the pockets of her coat and turned to say thank you to Edith, thank you for the birthday party. It occurred to her that they were right, for themselves, for whatever it was they had to be. And Mrs. Fullerton was old, she had dead eyes, nothing could touch her. Mary went out and walked with Danny up the street. She saw the curtains being drawn across living-room windows; cascades of flowers, of leaves, of geometrical designs, shut off these rooms from the night. Outside it was quite dark, the white houses were growing dim, the clouds breaking and breaking, and smoke blowing from Mrs. Fullerton's chimney. The pattern of Garden Place, so assertive in the daytime, seemed to shrink at night into the raw black mountainside.

*   *   *

The voices in the living room have blown away, Mary thought. If they would blow away and their plans be forgotten, if one thing could be left alone. But these are people who win, and they are good people; they want homes for their children, they help each other when there is trouble, they plan a community—saying that word as if they found a modern and well-proportioned magic in it, and no possibility anywhere of a mistake.

There is nothing you can do at present but put your hands in your pockets and keep a disaffected heart.

Notes

Plymouth Rock in this instance, refers to a breed of hen; named after the place in Massachusetts where the Pilgrims from England are said to have first set foot on North American soil after disembarking from *The Mayflower* ship

Jehovah's Witness a member of a religious Christian sect. Members of this sect canvass door-to-door as witnesses for their faith.

Activities

1. Create a two-column chart. In the first column, record three quotations that you believe are central to the story. In the second column, explain the context and significance of each. With a group, compare and discuss your choices.

2. In a group, consider characterization by discussing the motivation of the "people who win" in this story: Why is Mrs. Fullerton's house so important to them? What underlying beliefs and values are revealed in their words and behaviour? Do you agree with Mary that "they are good people"? To what extent does Alice Munro offer a fair and balanced portrait of these characters?

3. Work with a group to create a script for a dramatization of a scene that might result from the conflicts in "The Shining Houses." Before presenting, prepare an audience-response form to collect feedback about your production. Afterward, have your group evaluate both your collaborative skills and the quality of your presentation.

Another Viewpoint: Culture

Consider the following statement: "The main character in 'The Shining Houses' is a quintessential Canadian character—she would not exist in any other culture." To what extent do you agree with this statement? Make a "top ten" list of Canadian characters in fiction—characters who represent something essential about Canada and who would not be "at home" in any other context. Be prepared to defend your choices.

A Devoted Son

Anita Desai

Anita Desai was born in India, in 1937, to a German mother and a Bengali father. She attended Delhi University, where she studied English literature. Although her family spoke German at home and Hindi to their friends, she has always written in English. Desai published her first story in a children's magazine at the age of nine. She published her first book in 1963. A recent novel, *Fasting, Feasting*, was published in 2000. Desai has received a number of international awards and has been short-listed for the prestigious Booker Prize three times. What are some frequent causes of tensions within families? Do these causes change at different stages of life? As parents age, to what extent do power and control shift from parents to their children?

When the results appeared in the morning papers, Rakesh scanned them, barefoot and in his pyjamas, at the garden gate, then went up the steps to the veranda where his father sat sipping his morning tea and bowed down to touch his feet.

"A first division, son?" his father asked, beaming, reaching for the papers.

"At the top of the list, Papa," Rakesh murmured, as if awed. "First in the country."

Bedlam broke loose then. The family whooped and danced. The whole day long visitors streamed into the small yellow house at the end of the road, to congratulate the parents of this *Wunderkind*, to slap Rakesh on the back and fill the house and garden with the sounds and colours of a festival. There were garlands and *halwa*, party clothes and gifts (enough fountain pens to last years, even a watch or two), nerves and temper and joy, all in a multicoloured whirl of pride and great shining vistas newly opened: Rakesh was the first son in the family to receive an education, so much had been sacrificed in order to send him to school and then medical college, and at last the fruits of their sacrifice had arrived, golden and glorious.

To everyone who came to say, "*Mubarak, Varma-ji,* your son has brought you glory," the father said, "Yes, and do you know what is the first thing he did when he saw the results this morning? He came and touched my feet. He bowed down and touched my feet." This moved many of the women in the crowd so much that they were seen to raise the ends of their saris and dab at their tears while the men reached out for the betel leaves and sweetmeats that were offered around on trays and shook their heads in wonder and approval of such exemplary filial behaviour. "One does not often see such behaviour in sons any more," they all agreed, a little enviously perhaps. Leaving the house, some of the women said, sniffing, "At least on such an occasion they might have served pure *ghee* sweets," and some of the men said, "Don't you think old Varma was giving himself airs? He needn't think we don't remember that he comes from the vegetable market himself, his father used to sell vegetables, and he has never seen the inside of a school." But there was more envy than rancour in their voices and it was, of course, inevitable— not every son in that shabby little colony at the edge of the city was destined to shine as Rakesh shone, and who knew that better than the parents themselves?

And that was only the beginning, the first step in a great, sweeping ascent to the radiant heights of fame and fortune. The thesis he wrote for his M.D. brought Rakesh still greater glory, if only in select medical circles. He won a scholarship. He went to the U.S.A. (that was what his father learnt to call it and taught the whole family to say—not America, which was what the ignorant neighbours called it, but, with a grand familiarity, "the U.S.A.") where he pursued his career in the most prestigious of all hospitals and won encomiums from his American colleagues which were relayed to his admiring and glowing family. What was more, he came *back*, he actually returned to that small yellow house in the once-new but increasingly shabby colony, right at the end of the road where the rubbish vans tipped out their stinking contents for pigs to nose in and rag-pickers to build their shacks on, all steaming and smoking just outside the neat wire fences and well-tended gardens. To this Rakesh returned and the first thing he did on entering the house was to slip out of the embraces of his sisters and brothers and bow down and touch his father's feet.

As for his mother, she gloated chiefly over the strange fact that he had not married in America, had not brought home a foreign wife as all her neighbours had warned her he would, for wasn't that what all Indian boys went abroad for? Instead, he agreed, almost without argument, to marry a girl she had picked out for him in her own village, the daughter of a childhood friend, a plump and uneducated girl, it was true, but so old-fashioned, so placid, so complaisant that she slipped into the household and settled in like a charm, seemingly too lazy and too good-natured to even try and make Rakesh leave home and set up independently, as any other girl might have done. What was more, she was pretty—really pretty, in a plump, pudding way that only gave way to fat—soft, spreading fat, like warm wax—after the birth of their first baby, a son, and then what did it matter?

For some years Rakesh worked in the city hospital, quickly rising to the top of the administrative organization, and was made a director before he left to set up his own clinic. He took his parents in his car— a new, sky-blue Ambassador with a rear window full of stickers and charms revolving on strings—to see the clinic when it was built, and the large sign-board over the door on which his name was printed in letters of red, with a row of degrees and qualifications to follow it like so many little black slaves of the regent. Thereafter his fame seemed to grow just a little dimmer—or maybe it was only that everyone in town had grown accustomed to it at last—but it was also the beginning of his fortune for he now became known not only as the best but also the richest doctor in town.

However, all this was not accomplished in the wink of an eye. Naturally not. It was the achievement of a lifetime and it took up Rakesh's whole life. At the time he set up his clinic his father had grown into an old man and retired from his post at the kerosene dealer's depot at which he had worked for forty years, and his mother died soon after, giving up the ghost with a sigh that sounded positively happy, for it was her own son who ministered to her in her last illness and who sat pressing her feet at the last moment—such a son as few women had borne.

For it had to be admitted—and the most unsuccessful and most rancorous of neighbours eventually did so—that Rakesh was not only a devoted son and a miraculously good-natured man who contrived somehow to obey his parents and humour his wife and show concern equally for his children and his patients, but there was actually a brain inside this beautifully polished and formed body of good manners and kind nature and, in between ministering to his family and playing host to many friends and coaxing them all into feeling happy and grateful and content, he had actually trained his hands as well and emerged an excellent doctor, a really fine surgeon. How one man—and a man born to illiterate parents, his father having worked for a kerosene dealer and his mother having spent her life in a kitchen—had achieved, combined and conducted such a medley of virtues, no one could fathom, but all acknowledged his talent and skill.

It was a strange fact, however, that talent and skill, if displayed for too long, cease to dazzle. It came to pass that the most admiring of all eyes eventually faded and no longer blinked at his glory. Having retired from work and having lost his wife, the old father very quickly went to pieces, as they say. He developed so many complaints and fell ill so frequently and with such mysterious diseases that even his son could no longer make out when it was something of significance and when it was merely a peevish whim. He sat huddled on his string bed most of the day and developed an exasperating habit of stretching out suddenly and lying absolutely still, allowing the whole family to fly around him in a flap, wailing and weeping, and then suddenly sitting up, stiff and gaunt, and spitting out a big gob of betel juice as if to mock their behaviour.

He did this once too often: there had been a big party in the house, a birthday party for the youngest son, and the celebrations had to be suddenly hushed, covered up and hustled out of the way when the daughter-in-law discovered, or thought she discovered, that the old man stretched out from end to end of his string bed had lost his pulse; the party broke up, dissolved, even turned into a band of mourners, when the old man sat up and the distraught daughter-in-law received a gob of red spittle right on the hem of her new organza sari. After that no one much cared if he sat up cross-legged on his bed, hawking and spitting, or lay down flat and turned grey as a corpse. Except, of course, for that pearl amongst pearls, his son Rakesh.

It was Rakesh who brought him his morning tea, not in one of the china cups from which the rest of the family drank, but in the old man's favourite brass tumbler, and sat at the edge of his bed, comfortable and relaxed with the string of his pyjamas dangling out from under his fine lawn night-shirt, and discussed or, rather, read out the morning news to his father. It made no difference to him that his father made no response apart from spitting. It was Rakesh, too, who on returning from the clinic in the evening, persuaded the old man to come out of his room, as bare and desolate as a cell, and take the evening air out in the garden, beautifully arranging the pillows and bolsters on the divan in the corner of the open veranda. On summer nights he saw to it that the servants carried the old man's bed onto the lawn and himself helped his father down the steps and onto the bed, soothing him and settling him down for a night under the stars.

All this was very gratifying for the old man. What was not so grat-ifying was that he even undertook to supervise his father's diet. One day when the father was really sick, having ordered his daughter-in-law to make him a dish of *soojie halwa* and eaten it with a saucerful of cream, Rakesh marched into the room, not with his usual respectful step but with the confident and rather contemptuous stride of the famous doctor, and declared, "No more *halwa* for you, Papa. We must be sensible, at your age. If you must have something sweet, Veena will cook you a little *kheer*, that's light, just a little rice and milk. But nothing fried, nothing rich. We can't have this happening again."

The old man who had been lying stretched out on his bed, weak and feeble after a day's illness, gave a start at the very sound, the tone of these words. He opened his eyes—rather, they fell open with shock—and he stared at his son with disbelief that darkened quickly to reproach. A son who actually refused his father the food he craved? No, it was unheard of, it was incredible. But Rakesh had turned his back to him and was cleaning up the litter of bottles and packets on the medicine shelf and did not notice while Veena slipped silently out of the room with a little smirk that only the old man saw, and hated.

Halwa was only the first item to be crossed off the old man's diet. One delicacy after the other went—everything fried to begin with, then everything sweet, and eventually everything, everything the old man enjoyed. The meals that arrived for him on the shining stainless steel tray twice a day were frugal to say the least—dry bread, boiled lentils, boiled vegetables and, if there were a bit of chicken or fish, that was boiled too. If he called for another helping—in a cracked voice that quavered theatrically—Rakesh himself would come to the door, gaze at him sadly and shake his head, saying, "Now, Papa, we must be careful, we can't risk another illness, you know," and although the daughter-in-law kept tactfully out of the way, the old man could just see her smirk sliding merrily through the air. He tried to bribe his grandchildren into buying him sweets (and how he missed his wife now, that generous, indulgent and illiterate cook), whispering, "Here's fifty *paise*" as he stuffed the coins into a tight, hot fist. "Run down to the shop at the crossroads and buy me thirty *paise* worth of *jalebis*, and you can spend the remaining twenty *paise* on yourself. Eh? Understand? Will you do that?" He got away with it once or twice but then was found out, the conspirator was scolded by his father and smacked by his mother and Rakesh came storming into the room, almost tearing his hair as he shouted through compressed lips, "Now, Papa, are you trying to turn my little son into a liar? Quite apart from spoiling your own stomach, you are spoiling him as well—you are encouraging him to lie to his own parents. You should have heard the lies he told his mother when she saw him bringing back those *jalebis* wrapped up in filthy newspaper. I don't allow anyone in my house to buy sweets in the bazaar, Papa, surely you know that. There's cholera in the city, typhoid, gastro-enteritis—I see these cases daily in the hospital, how can I allow my own family to run such risks?" The old man sighed and lay down in the corpse position. But that worried no one any longer.

There was only one pleasure left the old man now (his son's early morning visits and readings from the newspaper could no longer be called that) and those were visits from elderly neighbours. These were not frequent as his contemporaries were mostly as decrepit and helpless as he and few could walk the length of the road to visit him any more. Old Bhatia, next door, however, who was still spry enough to refuse, adamantly, to bathe in the tiled bathroom indoors and to insist on carrying out his brass mug and towel, in all seasons and usually at impossible hours, into the yard and bathe noisily under the garden tap, would look over the hedge to see if Varma were out on his veranda and would call to him and talk while he wrapped his *dhoti* about him and dried the sparse hair on his head, shivering with enjoyable exaggeration. Of course these conversations, bawled across the hedge by two rather deaf old men conscious of having their entire households overhearing them, were not very satisfactory but Bhatia occasionally came out of his yard, walked down the bit of road and came in at Varma's gate to collapse onto the stone plinth built under the temple tree. If Rakesh were at home he would help his father down the steps into the garden and arrange him on his night bed under the tree and leave the two old men to chew betel leaves and discuss the ills of their individual bodies with combined passion.

"At least you have a doctor in the house to look after you," sighed Bhatia, having vividly described his martyrdom to piles.

"Look after me?" cried Varma, his voice cracking like an ancient clay jar. "He—he does not even give me enough to eat."

"What?" said Bhatia, the white hairs in his ears twitching. "Doesn't give you enough to eat? Your own son?"

"My own son. If I ask him for one more piece of bread, he says no, Papa, I weighed out the *ata* myself and I can't allow you to have more than two hundred grammes of cereal a day. He *weighs* the food he gives me, Bhatia—he has scales to weigh it on. That is what it has come to."

"Never," murmured Bhatia in disbelief. "Is it possible, even in this evil age, for a son to refuse his father food?"

"Let me tell you," Varma whispered eagerly. "Today the family was having fried fish—I could smell it. I called to my daughter-in-law to bring me a piece. She came to the door and said No…"

"Said No?" It was Bhatia's voice that cracked. A *drongo* shot out of the tree and sped away. "*No?*"

"No, she said no, Rakesh has ordered her to give me nothing fried. No butter, he says, no oil—"

"No butter? No oil? How does he expect his father to *live*?"

Old Varma nodded with melancholy triumph. "That is how he treats me—after I have brought him up, given him an education, made him a great doctor. Great doctor! This is the way great doctors treat their fathers, Bhatia," for the son's sterling personality and character now underwent a curious sea change. Outwardly all might be the same but the interpretation had altered: his masterly efficiency was nothing but cold heartlessness, his authority was only tyranny in disguise.

There was cold comfort in complaining to neighbours and, on such a miserable diet, Varma found himself slipping, weakening and soon becoming a genuinely sick man. Powders and pills and mixtures were not only brought in when dealing with a crisis like an upset stomach but became a regular part of his diet—became his diet, complained Varma, supplanting the natural foods he craved. There were pills to regulate his bowel movements, pills to bring down his blood pressure, pills to deal with his arthritis and, eventually, pills to keep his heart beating. In between there were panicky rushes to the hospital, some humiliating experiences with the stomach pump and enema, which left him frightened and helpless. He cried easily, shrivelling up on his bed, but if he complained of a pain or even a vague, grey fear in the night, Rakesh would simply open another bottle of pills and force him to take one. "I have my duty to you, Papa," he said when his father begged to be let off.

"Let me be," Varma begged, turning his face away from the pills on the outstretched hand. "Let me die. It would be better. I do not want to live only to eat your medicines."

"Papa, be reasonable."

"I leave that to you," the father cried with sudden spirit. "Let me alone, let me die now, I cannot live like this."

"Lying all day on his pillows, fed every few hours by his daughter-in-law's own hands, visited by every member of his family daily—and then he says he does not want to live 'like this,'" Rakesh was heard to say, laughing, to someone outside the door.

"Deprived of food," screamed the old man on the bed, "his wishes ignored, taunted by his daughter-in-law, laughed at by his grandchildren—*that* is how I live." But he was very old and weak and all anyone heard was an incoherent croak, some expressive grunts and cries of genuine pain. Only once, when old Bhatia had come to see him and they sat together under the temple tree, they heard him cry, "God is calling me— and they won't let me go."

The quantities of vitamins and tonics he was made to take were not altogether useless. They kept him alive and even gave him a kind of strength that made him hang on long after he ceased to wish to hang on. It was as though he were straining at a rope, trying to break it, and it would not break, it was still strong. He only hurt himself, trying.

In the evening, that summer, the servants would come into his cell, grip his bed, one at each end, and carry it out to the veranda, there setting it down with a thump that jarred every tooth in his head. In answer to his agonized complaints they said the Doctor Sahib had told them he must take the evening air and the evening air they would make him take—thump. Then Veena, that smiling, hypocritical pudding in a rustling sari, would appear and pile up the pillows under his head till he was propped up stiffly into a sitting position that made his head swim and his back ache. "Let me lie down," he begged. "I can't sit up any more."

"Try, Papa, Rakesh said you can if you try," she said, and drifted away to the other end of the veranda where her transistor radio vibrated to the lovesick tunes from the cinema that she listened to all day.

So there he sat, like some stiff corpse, terrified, gazing out on the lawn where his grandsons played cricket, in danger of getting one of their hard-spun balls in his eye, and at the gate that opened onto the dusty and rubbish-heaped lane but still bore, proudly, a newly touched-up signboard that bore his son's name and qualifications, his own name having vanished from the gate long ago.

At last the sky-blue Ambassador arrived, the cricket game broke up in haste, the car drove in smartly and the doctor, the great doctor, all in white, stepped out. Someone ran up to take his bag from him, others to escort him up the steps. "Will you have tea?" his wife called, turning down the transistor set, "or a Coca Cola? Shall I fry you some *samosas*?" But he did not reply or even glance in her direction. Ever a devoted son, he went first to the corner where his father sat gazing, stricken, at some undefined spot in the dusty yellow air that swam before him. He did not turn his head to look at his son. But he stopped gobbling air with his uncontrolled lips and set his jaw as hard as a sick and very old man could set it.

"Papa," his son said, tenderly, sitting down on the edge of the bed and reaching out to press his feet.

Old Varma tucked his feet under him, out of the way, and continued to gaze stubbornly into the yellow air of the summer evening.

"Papa, I'm home."

Varma's hand jerked suddenly, in a sharp, derisive movement, but he did not speak.

"How are you feeling, Papa?"

Then Varma turned and looked at his son. His face was so out of control, and all in pieces, that the multitude of expressions that crossed it could not make up a whole and convey to the famous man exactly what his father thought of him, his skill, his art.

"I'm dying," he croaked. "Let me die, I tell you."

"Papa, you're joking," his son smiled at him, lovingly. "I've brought you a new tonic to make you feel better. You must take it, it will make you feel stronger again. Here it is. Promise me you will take it regularly, Papa."

Varma's mouth worked as hard as though he still had a gob of betel in it (his supply of betel had been cut off years ago). Then he spat out some words, as sharp and bitter as poison, into his son's face. "Keep your tonic—I want none—I want none—I won't take any more of—of your medicines. None. Never," and he swept the bottle out of his son's hand with a wave of his own, suddenly grand, suddenly effective.

His son jumped, for the bottle was smashed and thick brown syrup had splashed up, staining his white trousers. His wife let out a cry and came running. All around the old man was hubbub once again, noise, attention.

He gave one push to the pillows at his back and dislodged them so he could sink down on his back, quite flat again. He closed his eyes and pointed his chin at the ceiling, like some dire prophet, groaning, "God is calling me—now let me go."

Notes

first division the highest level of achievement in a high school based on the British academic model

Wunderkind a person who achieves great success while very young; from the Old High German *wuntar*, meaning "wonder," and from the German *kind*, meaning "child"

halwa a popular Indian dessert

ghee clarified butter, a common ingredient in Indian cooking

little black slaves of the regent a reference to enslaved servants of the regent or viceroy, the representative of the British crown. Viceroys ruled India from the seventeenth century until the country's independence in 1947. The slave trade, mainly of African peoples, was abolished in the British Empire in 1807.

betel juice juice of a leaf that is chewed with parings of the areca nut

lawn linen or cotton fabric; from the Middle English word *laun*, which is probably a reference to Laon, a city in northern France

soojie halwa a dessert made with semolina

kheer a rice pudding

paise a coin equal to one-hundredth of a rupee, the main monetary unit in South Asian countries such as India, Pakistan, and Sri Lanka; a Hindi word, originally from the Sanskrit word *rūpya*, meaning "wrought silver"

jalebis pretzel-shaped sweets that are fried to a golden crisp and soaked in saffron syrup

dhoti a loincloth worn as ceremonial dress by male Hindus

ata corn flour

drongo a type of blackbird

samosas triangular fried pastries with meat or vegetable filling; a word in the Persian and Urdu languages

Activities

1. Write a journal response in which you describe your feelings toward Rakesh and his father as the story progressed. Did your feelings remain consistent or did they change? Which character did you most identify with at the beginning, middle, and end of the story? How might your own experiences have shaped your reactions to these characters?

2. Discuss the title of the story. Do you think that Desai intends it to be interpreted literally or ironically? How does the title contribute to the meaning and the theme? With whom—the "devoted son" or the father—do the author's sympathies seem to lie?

3. Desai has commented that she is more influenced by poets than by fiction writers: "Poets use language in a way I would like to emulate. I would like to achieve that gravity, compression, the intensity of their language." Find a passage in "A Devoted Son" where Desai's language reflects the intensity and imagery of poetry. Write a short analysis of the style in the passage you have selected. What do you notice about the diction, sentence structure, and use of literary devices? Next, use Desai's passage as a model for a short piece of descriptive writing in which you try to achieve the same precision and intensity of language.

Another Viewpoint: Culture

In a recent interview, Anita Desai commented that "Indians manage to slip back and forth between the modern world and ancient world, the Indian world and the Western world, with a great ease, without feeling any strain." If possible, find several people of South Asian descent in your community and interview them about whether Desai's statement is true for them. Then consider how the dualities represented in her quotation are reflected in "A Devoted Son."

Magpies

Thomas King

Thomas King is an award-winning novelist, short story writer, children's writer, scriptwriter, and photographer. Born in California, in 1943, of Greek and Cherokee descent, he has spent much of his adult life in Canada, first teaching at the University of Lethbridge for ten years, and more recently at the University of Guelph. His first novel, *Medicine River,* was published in 1990 and became a television movie. King has twice been nominated for the Governor General's Award, was runner-up for the 1991 Commonwealth Writer's Prize, and won the Canadian Authors Association Award for Fiction. Central to "Magpies" is the act of making a promise. When you make a promise, how far will you go to keep it? How do you feel and behave when you have difficulty keeping your word?

This one is about Granny. Reserve story. Everyone knows this story. Wilma knows it. Ambrose knows it. My friend, Napioa. Lionel James. Billy Frank knows it, too. Billy Frank hears this story in Calgary. He hears it three times. Maybe six. Boy, he tells me, here comes that story again.

Sometimes this story is about Wilma. Some people tell it so Ambrose is all over the place. The way I tell it is this way and I tell it this way all the time.

Sometimes I tell you about those Magpies first. With those noses. Good noses, those ones. Magpies talk all the time, you know. Good gossips, those. Hahahahaha. Good jokes, too. Sometimes I start that way.

Okay. Here comes that story again.

Granny falls and hurts her leg. So, that leg is pink. Then it looks blue. Another time it is black. Yellow for a long time. That leg. Granny's leg.

Granny looks at that leg and thinks about dying. So she talks about falling over dead. When that Granny starts talking about being dead, Wilma says no, no, no. That is just a bruise. Yellow bruise. Those ones are okay.

Granny talks to everyone she see about dying. I'm going to die, she says to me and I say yes, that's right. Old people know these things. It happens. Maybe that blood thing. Maybe cigarettes. Maybe a truck. Maybe that bottle. Granny likes to talk of dying. I'm going to be dead real soon, she says. Going to rot and nobody comes by but those birds tell all those stories and laugh.

Watch those Magpies, that old woman tells Ambrose. You see them?

Sure, says Ambrose.

They smell death, she says. Isn't that right?

Yes, I says, that's true.

Those ones take the eyes first, she says, soft parts. Nice round parts they like first. Ripe. That's why you got to wrap them tight.

That's right, I says.

You listening, Ambrose? That old Granny shake Ambrose so he is awake. They smell death, those birds, like you smell chokecherries on the boil. When I die, they'll come to me like that.

You can count on me, says Ambrose.

I'm going to die, then, Granny tells me, and I says okay.

Wilma takes that old woman to the hospital to see two, maybe five white doctors. They took at the leg. They look at that leg again. They do it some more times, too. Ummmm, ummmm, ummmm. That way. In the mouth. They don't dance. They don't sing. They think they talking to Granny. Ummmm, ummmm, ummmm.

Granny says to me there are good places to die. River is a good one. Coulees is okay, too. Maybe a mountain. Bad places, too, she says. Grocery store. Shopping mall. Movie show. Hospital.

That hospital is one bad place to die. See-po-aah-loo. See-po-aah-loo is like a hole. In the ground. See-po-aah-loo is one old word. Where you put stew bones. Where you put old things that are broke. Where you put old things that smell bad. Where you put beer cans. Coffee grounds. Fish guts. Milk cartons. Newspapers. Tractor oil. That black dog Walter Turnbull hit with his truck. Everything you don't want people to see. You put them there. See-po-aah-loo.

Then you cover it up. Go someplace else.

Hospital.

Those doctors tell Granny, ummmm, ummmm, ummmm. Maybe you better stay here. One day. Four days. Maybe we see something. Ummmm, ummmm, ummmm. Ambrose says Whites go to that hospital to get a new nose. Get good breasts. Fix up that old butt. Haul out things you don't need no more. Ambrose tells me that. Fix you up. Like a car. Run better. Ummmm, ummmm, ummmm.

Those ones don't fool Granny. I can tell you that.

That Granny nod her head. Look at that floor. Look at that door. Shuffle her feet. Like a Round dance. Ho-ho-ho-ho, that one dances out of See-po-aah-loo. Don't want to be in no hole, she says.

God loves you, Granny, Wilma says. Good woman, that Wilma. Loves Granny. Fixes her food. Washes her clothes. Wilma is mostly Catholic in the middle. Knows about dying. Reads those papers you get from church. In that wood pocket. Near that water.

When God takes you, Momma, you'll be real happy. This is how Wilma talks. Dead is okay, Wilma says. That God fellow just waiting for you. Good to see you. Howdy-do.

Don't put me in that grave, See-po-aah-loo, Granny tell Wilma.

Garbage hole.

Hospital.

One word. You see?

Yes, says Wilma, that's the modern way. You need a priest. He can make it clean.

Holes are cold, Granny says.

God will keep you warm, Wilma says.

So, Granny finds Ambrose.

Ambrose is a big man. Big chest. Big legs. Big head. Friendly man that Ambrose. Have a joke. Have a story. Always thinking about things to do. Going to fix this thing. Going to fix that thing. Granny finds Ambrose. You fix this thing for me, she says. Yes, that one says, I will do it. You can count on me.

Granny brings that boy to my house. Ho, I says, you got your big boy with you. Yes, she says, we come to see you, talk with you. Sit down, I says. Coffee is here. Tea, too. Sit down and eat some food.

You must talk to my big boy, Granny says. Tell him the way. Show him how to do this thing. You listen to this old one, Granny says. You can count on me, Ambrose says.

Granny squeeze her eyes. You be here when I die. You tell Wilma how to do this thing. You look out for me, take care of me, my big boy.

You can count on me.

I'm counting on you, says Granny. In that cottonwood at Heavyshield's cabin. Aoo-lee-sth. That's the one. Other ways that hole will get me and I'll come back.

You can count on me.

That leg get better. Granny's leg. But Granny dies anyway. Later. Not right now. Two, maybe four years. Maybe more. She falls over dead then. Like that. It is finished.

Ambrose is not there when Granny dies. Someone says he is in Edmonton at those meetings. Someone says, no, he is in Toronto. Someone says he is across the line. Wilma sniff her nose this way and that one sniff her nose that way. We can't wait for that Ambrose maybe come along. We going to do this thing right, Wilma says. We going to do this thing now.

So they get a priest.

So they put Granny in a box.

So they stick Granny in the church.

So they throw her in a hole.

Just like that. Pretty quick. They put her in that hole before Ambrose comes home. Everyone stands there. Ho ho ho ho. All of them feel bad, Granny in that hole. Wilma cries, too. Smack her hands and says, that's okay now. Everything is done now. It is finished.

Aoh-quwee.

That's the end of the story.

No, I was just fooling.

There's more.

Stick around.

Okay. Ambrose comes home. Everyone figures out this part, Ambrose comes home. No smile. No happy joke. Momma is with God, Wilma says. She's happy. Nothing for you to do.

I gave her this promise, Ambrose says, and I says, yes, that's right.

Keep your promise in your pocket, Wilma says. Momma don't need that promise. Everything is pretty good. God's got her.

God don't live in a hole, says Ambrose.

God is everywhere, says Wilma.

Those two talk like that. One day, maybe two, three weeks. Talk about God. Talk about that promise. You make lots of promises, Wilma says. Those things are easy for you to make. They fall out of your mouth like spit. Everybody got three or four of them.

That part is true. I can tell you that. Ambrose is generous with those things. Those promises. I help you chop wood for winter, Ambrose tells my friend Napioa. Fix that truck for you, he says to Billy Frank. Going to dig that ditch tomorrow, he tells his uncle.

You can count on me.

Keep that promise in your pocket, Wilma tells that one.

Ambrose comes to my house. Ho, he says, we got to fix that window. Yes, I says, it is broke alright. Maybe I'll bring some tools out next week, he says. Yes, I says, that would be good.

That Ambrose sits down and starts to cry. Hoo hoo hoo hoo. Like that. That big boy cries like that. Sit down, I says. Have some tea.

You got to help me, he says. Sure, I says. I can do that.

Granny's in that hole, he says. She's going to come back. You got to help me do this thing. We got to get her out and do it right. Put her in that tree. Heavyshield's tree. In the mountains. Like she said.

Boy, I says, lots of work that. They put her in pretty deep. Way down there. With that God fellow.

I can dig her up, Ambrose says. You don't have to do anything. I'll dig her up and get you and you can tell me how to do this thing. Got to keep that promise.

Okay, I says.

So.

That Ambrose gets everything we need. Wilma watches him and sniffs with her nose. Tonight I'm going to do it, Ambrose says. But he doesn't. Flat tire, he says.

Tonight I'm going to do it, that one tells me. But he doesn't. No moon.

Tonight I'm going to do it. That big boy has one good memory. But he doesn't do it then, either. Got the flu.

Ambrose gets a skin and he keeps that skin in the back of his truck. Green. Getting to smell, I think. Maybe not. Those Magpies hang around that truck. What you got in that truck, Wilma says. Nothing, says Ambrose. Just some stuff.

But you know, he does it. That big boy comes to my house early in the morning. With his truck. With that skin. With Granny sewed up in that skin. Just like I said. Ho, I says, you got that Granny. Yes, says Ambrose, I dig her up last night. Now we can do it right.

So we do. Ambrose drives that truck with Granny sewed up in the skin to Heavyshield's cabin and that good boy climbs that tree and that one drags Granny up that tree with a rope. High. On those skinny branches. Near the sun. He puts that old woman. Then he climbs down. There, he says, and smacks his hands together. That does it.

I make some tea. Ambrose sits on the ground, watches Granny in the tree. Pretty soon he is asleep.

Let's see what happens.

Well, pretty quick those Magpies come along and look in that tree. And they fly in that tree. And they sit in that tree. Talking. They sit on that hide has Granny hid inside and talk to her. Hello. Nice day.

Then that sun comes down. Into the tree. With those birds. With Granny. Ho, that sun says, what we got here? Granny and a bunch of Magpies. That's right, I says.

Then that big dust ball comes along, right up to the house. Heavyshield's place. Rolls into the yard.

Then Wilma gets out.

Then the RCMP gets out.

Then Benny Goodrunner, tribal policeman, gets out.

Out of that dust ball.

Boy, those birds are some fast talkers.

Where's Granny, Wilma says. Where's Ambrose? She says that, too. Where's Ambrose Standing Bull, RCMP says. Benny don't say nothing. He just stand there. Look embarrassed.

Ambrose wakes up. Wilma sees him wake up. There he is, she says. There is that criminal. There is that thief. Then she uses words I don't understand.

Ambrose stands right up. I'm just doing what Granny asked. Nothing wrong with that.

That RCMP got his bright uniform on. Body-stealing is against the law, he says.

This is reserve land, Ambrose says.

Benny's going to arrest you, Ambrose, says Wilma. Going to put you in jail for digging up Granny.

Lots of Magpies in the tree now. They just listening. All ears.

Wilma looks in that tree. She sees those birds. She sees that sun. She sees that hide. He's already stuck her in that tree. We got to bring her down.

RCMP man looks at Wilma and looks at Benny. Wilma looks at Benny. Ambrose looks at Benny. Maybe you boys want some tea, I says. Nice evening. Maybe you want to sit and have some tea.

No time for tea, old one, Wilma says in our language. My mother's in that tree. We got to get her down.

So. Benny is the one. Have to climb that tree. All the way. So, he starts up. Those birds stop walking on Granny and watch Benny. Ambrose watches Benny. Wilma watches Benny. RCMP man watches Benny. That Benny is a rodeo man, rides those bulls. Strong legs, that one. He climbs all the way to Granny. Then he sits down. On a limb. Like those birds. Hey, he says, I can see the river. Real good view.

Look for Granny, says that Wilma.

Leave her alone, says Ambrose.

Boy, those Magpies are jumping around in that tree. Dancing. Choosing sides. Singing songs. Telling jokes.

Milk carton comes out of that tree.

Peach can comes out of that tree.

Bottle of Wesson cooking oil comes down. Empty.

Carburetor.

Magazine.

Hey, says Benny. Granny's not here. She's not in this skin. She's gone. Nothing here but garbage. Benny comes down that tree.

Everybody looks at Ambrose.

Must be magic, says Ambrose and he walks into that cabin and closes the door.

Wilma stands up straight and she looks at that RCMP man. Benny has his clothes all dirty. That RCMP is mostly clean. Nothing but garbage in that tree, Benny says. Alright, says Wilma. She gets back in the truck, that one. Benny gets in that truck. RCMP gets in that truck.

Boy, pretty exciting.

That sun gets down behind the mountain. Ambrose comes out of that house, says, everybody gone? Yes, I says. Good trick, that one, he says. Yes, I says, that one had me fooled. My shovel broke, says Ambrose. I'm going to get her tonight. Nobody will see me this time. I would have got her that other time but my shovel broke. You got a shovel I can borrow? Sure, I say, you can use my good shovel.

You watch, says Ambrose. This is my plan. Benny saw that bag of garbage. So now I get Granny and put her up there. Take that garbage down and put Granny in that tree like I promise. No one will look there again. That's my plan.

That's a good plan, I says. That should fool them. Good thing you got some of that garbage out of the ground.

You got to promise me you won't tell anyone about my plan, Ambrose says. Watch out for those birds, I says. They told Wilma about your bag of garbage, I bet. They got good ears, those ones. You got to sing that song so they can't hear. So they won't remember. You know that song?

No, say Ambrose. You better listen then, I says. Otherwise those birds will tell everyone what your plan is. So I show Ambrose the song and he sings it pretty good, that boy. And he borrows my shovel. My good shovel. And I don't see him for a long time. And I don't see Wilma either. And I don't tell Ambrose's plan.

But I know what happened.

But I can't tell.

I promised.

You can count on me.

Activities

1. In discussing contemporary Aboriginal literature, Thomas King has identified two frequently recurring themes: a sense of community and the oral tradition. How are these two themes reflected in "Magpies"? What other themes are central to this story?

2. With a partner, use a literary reference guide to develop working definitions for the terms *reliable narrator* and *unreliable narrator*. Prepare to write an analytical essay on narration in "Magpies" by developing a profile of the narrator. Consider from whose point of view the story is told. What information does the story provide about this narrator and about his or her relationship to characters and events? Create a thesis statement in which you take a position on whether this narrator is reliable or unreliable. When writing your essay, use definition and detailed evidence to support your thesis.

3. Work with a small group to present this story as readers' theatre. Identify the roles you will need to include and decide how you will incorporate the narrator's part. Explore various ways of staging the reading and of focusing audience attention on the speaker. Develop an audience reaction sheet. After the performance, write a group self-evaluation based on feedback from the audience, as well as your own analysis of your performance.

Another Viewpoint: Culture

It has been observed that the focus on good and evil that often appears in Western and other literatures is commonly replaced in Native literature with a focus on balance and harmony. Discuss this perspective in relation to "Magpies" and at least two other works by Aboriginal authors.

Dialogue, 1991, Nuwa Wamala Nnyanzi

The Winner

Barbara Kimenye

Barbara Kimenye was born in 1940, in Buganda, the former kingdom of East Africa on the north shore of Lake Victoria, now part of Uganda. In Africa, she worked as private secretary for the government of Buganda. She was also a newspaper journalist and columnist in Kenya. In 1974, she moved to London, England, and became a social worker. She is well known for her children's books and has published story collections dealing with the everyday lives of Ugandans. Many African writers, like Kimenye, choose to write in English in order to reach a wider audience. Others write only in African languages because they believe that their culture and values are best carried by their own language. What might some of the disadvantages and advantages be of writing in a "second" language?

When Pius Ndawula won the football pools, overnight he seemed to become the most popular man in Buganda. Hosts of relatives converged upon him from the four corners of the kingdom: cousins and nephews, nieces and uncles, of whose existence he had never before been aware, turned up in Kalasanda by the busload, together with crowds of individuals who, despite their downtrodden appearance, assured Pius that they and they alone were capable of seeing that his money was properly invested—preferably in their own particular businesses! Also lurking around Pius's unpretentious mud hut were newspaper reporters, slick young men weighed down with cameras and sporting loud checked caps or trilbies set at conspicuously jaunty angles, and serious young men from Radio Uganda who were anxious to record Pius's delight at his astonishing luck for the edification of the Uganda listening public.

The rest of Kalasanda were so taken by surprise that they could only call and briefly congratulate Pius before being elbowed out of the way by his more garrulous relations. All, that is to say, except Pius's greatest friend Salongo, the custodian of the Ssabalangira's tomb. He came and planted himself firmly in the house, and nobody attempted to move him. Almost blind, and very lame, he had tottered out with the aid of a stout stick. Just to see him arrive had caused a minor sensation in the village, for he hadn't left the tomb for years. But recognizing at last a chance to house Ssabalangira's remains in a state befitting his former glory made the slow, tortuous journey worthwhile to Salongo.

Nantondo hung about long enough to have her picture taken with Pius. Or rather, she managed to slip beside him just as the cameras clicked, and so it was that every Uganda newspaper, on the following day, carried a front-page photograph of "Mr. Pius Ndawula and his happy wife," a caption that caused Pius to shake with rage and threaten legal proceedings, but over which Nantondo gloated as she proudly showed it to everybody she visited.

"Tell us, Mr. Ndawula, what do you intend to do with all the money you have won…?"

"Tell us, Mr. Ndawula, how often have you completed pools coupons…?"

"Tell us…Tell us…Tell us…"

Pius's head was reeling under this bombardment of questions, and he was even more confused by Salongo's constant nudging and muttered advice to "Say nothing!" Nor did the relatives make things easier. Their persistent clamouring for his attention, and the way they kept shoving their children under his nose, made it impossible for him to think, let alone talk.

It isn't at all easy, when you have lived for sixty-five years in complete obscurity, to adjust yourself in a matter of hours to the role of a celebrity, and the strain was beginning to tell.

Behind the hut—Pius had no proper kitchen—gallons of tea were being boiled, whilst several of the female cousins were employed in ruthlessly hacking down the bunches of *matoke* from his meagre plantains to cook food for everybody. One woman—she had introduced herself as Cousin Sarah—discovered Pius's hidden store of banana beer, and dished it out to all and sundry as though it were her own. Pius had become very wary of Cousin Sarah. He didn't like the way in which she kept loudly remarking that he needed a woman about the place, and he was even more seriously alarmed when suddenly Salongo gave him a painful dig in the ribs and muttered, "You'll have to watch that one—she's a sticker!"

Everybody who came wanted to see the telegram that announced Pius's win. When it had arrived at the Ggombolola Headquarters—the postal address of everyone residing within a radius of fifteen miles—Musisi had brought it out personally, delighted to be the bearer of such good tidings. At Pius's request he had gone straightaway to tell Salongo, and then back to his office to send an acknowledgement on behalf of Pius to the pools firm, leaving the old man to dream rosy dreams. An extension of his small coffee *shamba,* a new roof on his house—or maybe an entirely new house—concrete blocks this time, with a veranda perhaps. Then there were hens. Salongo and he had always said there was money in hens these days, now that the women ate eggs and chicken; not that either of them agreed with the practice. Say what you liked, women who ate chicken and eggs were fairly asking to be infertile! That woman welfare officer who came around snooping occasionally tried to say it was all nonsense, that chicken meat and eggs made bigger and better babies. Well, they might look bigger and better, but nobody could deny that they were fewer! Which only goes to show.

But news spreads fast in Africa—perhaps the newspapers have contacts in the pools offices. Anyway, before the telegram had even reached Pius, announcements were appearing in the local newspapers, and Pius was still quietly lost in his private dreams when the first batch of visitors arrived. At first he was at a loss to understand what was happening. People he hadn't seen for years and only recognized with difficulty fell upon him with cries of joy. "Cousin Pius, the family are delighted!" "Cousin Pius, why have you not visited us all this time?"

Pius was pleased to see his nearest and dearest gathered around him. It warmed his old heart once more to find himself in the bosom of his family, and he welcomed them effusively. The second crowd to arrive were no less well received, but there was a marked coolness on the part of their forerunners.

However, as time had gone by and the flood of strange faces had gained momentum, Pius's *shamba* had come to resemble a political meeting. All to be seen from the door of the house was a turbulent sea of white *kanzus* and brilliant *busutis,* and the house itself was full of people and tobacco smoke.

The precious telegram was passed from hand to hand until it was reduced to a limp fragment of paper with the lettering partly obliterated: not that it mattered very much, for only a few members of the company could read English.

"Now, Mr. Ndawula, we are ready to take the recording." The speaker was a slight young man wearing a checked shirt. "I shall ask you a few questions, and you simply answer me in your normal voice." Pius looked at the leather box with its two revolving spools, and licked his lips. "Say nothing!" came a hoarse whisper from Salongo. The young man steadfastly ignored him, and went ahead in his best BBC manner. "Well, Mr. Ndawula, first of all let me congratulate you on your winning the pools. Would you like to tell our listeners what it feels like suddenly to find yourself rich?" There was an uncomfortable pause, during which Pius stared mesmerized at the racing spools and the young man tried frantically to span the gap by asking, "I mean, have you any plans for the future?" Pius swallowed audibly, and opened his mouth to say something, but shut it again when Salongo growled, "Tell him nothing!"

The young man snapped off the machine, shaking his head in exasperation. "Look here, sir, all I want you to do is to say something—I'm not asking you to make a speech! Now, I'll tell you what. I shall ask you again what it feels like suddenly to come into money, and you say something like 'It was a wonderful surprise, and naturally I feel very pleased'— and will you ask your friend not to interrupt! Got it? Okay, off we go!"

The machine was again switched on, and the man brightly put his question, "Now, Mr. Ndawula, what does it feel like to win the pools?"

Pius swallowed, then quickly chanted in a voice all off key, "It was a wonderful surprise and naturally I feel very happy and will you ask your friend not to interrupt!" The young man nearly wept. This happened to be his first assignment as a radio interviewer, and it looked like it would be his last. He switched off the machine and mourned his lustreless future, groaning. At that moment Cousin Sarah caught his eye. "Perhaps I can help you," she said. "I am Mr. Ndawula's cousin." She made this pronouncement in a manner that suggested Pius had no others. The young man brightened considerably. "Well, madam, if you could tell me something about Mr. Ndawula's plans, I would be most grateful." Cousin Sarah folded her arms across her imposing bosom, and when the machine again started up, she was off. Yes, Mr. Ndawula was very happy about the money. No, she didn't think he had any definite plans on how to spend it—with all these people about he didn't have time to think. Yes, Mr. Ndawula lived completely alone, but she was prepared to stay and look after him for as long as he needed her. Here a significant glance passed between the other women in the room, who clicked their teeth and let out long "Eeeeeeehs!" of incredulity. Yes, she believed she was Mr. Ndawula's nearest living relative by marriage…

Pius listened to her confident aplomb with growing horror, while Salongo frantically nudged him and whispered, "There! What did I tell you! That woman's a sticker!"

Around three in the afternoon, *matoke* and tea were served, the *matoke* on wide fresh plantain leaves, since Pius owned only three plates, and the tea in anything handy—tin cans, old jars, etc.—because he was short of cups too. Pius ate very little, but he was glad of the tea. He had shaken hands with so many people that his arm ached, and he was tired of the chatter and the comings and goings in his house of all these strangers. Most of all he was tired of Cousin Sarah, who insisted on treating him like an idiot invalid. She kept everybody else at bay, as far as she possibly could, and when one woman plonked a sticky fat baby on his lap, Cousin Sarah dragged the child away as though it were infectious. Naturally, a few cross words were exchanged between Sarah and the fond mother, but by this time Pius was past caring.

Yosefu Mukasa and Kibuka called in the early evening, when some of the relatives were departing with effusive promises to come again tomorrow. They were both alarmed at the weariness they saw on Pius's face. The old man looked utterly worn out, his skin grey and sickly. Also, they were a bit taken aback by the presence of Cousin Sarah, who pressed them to take tea and behaved in every respect as though she were mistress of the house. "I believe my late husband knew you very well, sir," she told Yosefu. "He used to be a Miruka chief in Buyaga County. His name was Kivumbi." "Ah, yes," Yosefu replied, "I remember Kivumbi very well indeed. We often hunted together. I was sorry to hear of his death. He was a good man." Cousin Sarah shrugged her shoulders. "Yes, he was a good man. But what the Lord giveth, He also taketh away." Thus was the late Kivumbi dismissed from the conversation.

Hearing all this enabled Pius to define the exact relationship between himself and Cousin Sarah, and even by Kiganda standards it was virtually nonexistent, for the late Kivumbi had been the stepson of one of Pius's cousins.

"Your stroke of luck seems to have exhausted you, Pius," Kibuka remarked, when he and Yosefu were seated on the rough wooden chairs brought forth by Cousin Sarah.

Salongo glared at the world in general and snarled, "Of course he is exhausted! Who wouldn't be with all these scavengers collected to pick his bones?" Pius hushed him as one would a child. "No, no, Salongo. It is quite natural that my family should gather round me at a time like this. Only I fear I am perhaps a little too old for all this excitement."

Salongo spat expertly through the open doorway, narrowly missing a group of guests who were preparing to bed down, and said, "That woman doesn't think he's too old. She's out to catch him. I've seen her type elsewhere!"

Yosefu's mouth quirked with amusement at the thought that "elsewhere" could only mean the Ssabalangira's tomb, which Salongo had guarded for the better part of his adult life. "Well, she's a fine woman," he remarked. "But see here, Pius," he went on, "don't be offended by my proposal, but wouldn't it be better if you came and stayed with us at Mutunda for tonight? Miriamu would love to have you, and you look as though you need a good night's rest, which you wouldn't get here—those relatives of yours outside are preparing a fire and are ready to dance the night away!"

"I think that's a wonderful idea!" said Cousin Sarah, bouncing in to remove the tea cups. "You go with Mr. Mukasa, Cousin Pius. The change will do you as much good as the rest. And don't worry about your home—I shall stay here and look after things." Pius hesitated. "Well, I think I shall be all right here—I don't like to give Miriamu any extra work...." Salongo muttered, "Go to Yosefu's. You don't want to be left alone in the house with that woman—there's no knowing what she might get up to...!" "I'll pack a few things for you, Pius," announced Cousin Sarah and bustled off before anything more could be said, pausing only long enough to give Salongo a look that was meant to wither him on the spot.

So Pius found himself being driven away to Mutunda in Yosefu's car, enjoying the pleasant sensation of not having to bother about a thing. Salongo too had been given a lift to as near the tomb as the car could travel, and his wizened old face was contorted into an irregular smile, for Pius had promised to help him build a new house for the Ssabalangira. For him the day had been well spent, despite Cousin Sarah.

Pius spent an enjoyable evening with the Mukasas. They had a well-cooked supper, followed by a glass of cold beer as they sat back and listened to the local news on the radio. Pius had so far relaxed as to tell the Mukasas modestly that he had been interviewed by Radio Uganda that morning, and when Radio Newsreel was announced they waited breathlessly to hear his voice. But instead of Pius, Cousin Sarah came booming over the air. Until that moment the old man had completely forgotten the incident of the tape recording. In fact, he had almost forgotten Cousin Sarah. Now it all came back to him with a shiver of apprehension. Salongo was right. That woman did mean business! It was a chilling thought. However, it didn't cause him to lose any sleep. He slept like a cherub, as if he hadn't a care in the world.

Because he looked so refreshed in the morning, Miriamu insisted on keeping him at Mutunda for another day. "I know you feel better, but after seeing you yesterday, I think a little holiday with us will do you good. Go home tomorrow, when the excitement has died down a bit," she advised.

Soon after lunch, as Pius was taking a nap in a chair on the veranda, Musisi drove up in the Land Rover, with Cousin Sarah by his side. Miriamu came out to greet them, barely disguising her curiosity about the formidable woman about whom she had heard so much. The two women sized each other up and decided to be friends.

Meanwhile, Musisi approached the old man. "Sit down, son." Pius waved him to a chair at his side. "Miriamu feeds me so well it's all I can do to keep awake."

"I am glad you are having a rest, sir." Musisi fumbled in the pocket of his jacket. "There is another telegram for you. Shall I read it?" The old man sat up expectantly and said, "If you'll be so kind."

Musisi first read the telegram in silence, then he looked at Pius and commented, "Well, sir, I'm afraid it isn't good news."

"Not good news? Has somebody died?"

Musisi smiled. "Well, no. It isn't really as bad as that. The thing is, the pools firm say that owing to an unfortunate oversight they omitted to add, in the first telegram, that the prize money is to be shared among three hundred other people."

Pius was stunned. Eventually he murmured, "Tell me, how much does that mean I shall get?"

"Three hundred into seventeen thousand pounds won't give you much over a thousand shillings."

To Musisi's astonishment, Pius sat back and chuckled. "More than a thousand shillings!" he said. "Why, that's a lot of money!"

"But it's not, when you expected so much more!"

"I agree. And yet, son, what would I have done with all those thousands of pounds? I am getting past the age when I need a lot."

Miriamu brought a mat onto the veranda and she and Cousin Sarah made themselves comfortable near the men. "What a disappointment!" cried Miriamu, but Cousin Sarah sniffed and said, "I agree with Cousin Pius. He wouldn't know what to do with seventeen thousand pounds, and the family would be hanging round his neck forevermore!"

At mention of Pius's family, Musisi frowned. "I should warn you, sir, those relatives of yours have made a terrific mess of your *shamba*—

your plantains have been stripped—and Mrs. Kivumbi here," nodding at Sarah, "was only just in time to prevent them digging up your sweet potatoes!"

"Yes, Cousin Pius," added Sarah. "It will take us some time to put the *shamba* back in order. They've trodden down a whole bed of young beans."

"Oh, dear," said Pius weakly. "This is dreadful news."

"Don't worry. They will soon disappear when I tell them there is no money, and then I shall send for a couple of my grandsons to come and help us do some replanting." Pius could not help but admire the way Sarah took things in her stride.

Musisi rose from his chair. "I'm afraid I can't stay any longer, so I will go now and help Cousin Sarah clear the crowd, and see you tomorrow to take you home." He and Sarah climbed back into the Land Rover and Sarah waved energetically until the vehicle was out of sight.

"Your cousin is a fine woman," Miriamu told Pius, before going indoors. Pius merely grunted, but for some odd reason he felt the remark to be a compliment to himself.

All was quiet at Pius's home when Musisi brought him home next day. He saw at once that his *shamba* was well nigh wrecked, but his drooping spirits quickly revived when Sarah placed a mug of steaming tea before him, and sat on a mat at his feet, explaining optimistically how matters could be remedied. Bit by bit he began telling her what he planned to do with the prize money, ending with, "Of course, I shan't be able to do everything now, especially since I promised Salongo something for the tomb."

Sarah poured some more tea and said, "Well, I think the roof should have priority. I noticed last night that there are several leaks. And whilst we're about it, it would be a good idea to build another room on and a small outside kitchen. Mud and wattle is cheap enough, and then the whole place can be plastered. You can still go ahead and extend your coffee. And as for hens, well, I have six good layers at home, as well as a fine cockerel. I'll bring them over!"

Pius looked at her in silence for a long time. She is a fine looking woman, he thought, and that blue *busuti* suits her. Nobody would ever take her for a grandmother—but why is she so anxious to throw herself at me?

"You sound as if you are planning to come and live here," he said at last, trying hard to sound casual.

Sarah turned to face him and replied, "Cousin Pius, I shall be very frank with you. Six months ago my youngest son got married and brought his wife to live with me. She's a very nice girl, but somehow I can't get used to having another woman in the house. My other son is in Kampala, and although I know I would be welcome there, he too has a wife, and three children, so if I went there I wouldn't be any better off. When I saw that bit about you in the paper, I suddenly remembered—although I don't expect you to—how you were at my wedding and so helpful to everybody. Well, I thought to myself, here is somebody who needs a good housekeeper, who needs somebody to keep the leeches off, now that he has come into money. I came along right away to take a look at you, and I can see I did the right thing. You do need me." She hesitated for a moment, and then said, "Only you might prefer to stay alone...I'm so used to having my own way, I never thought about that before."

Pius cleared his throat. "You're a very impetuous woman," was all he could find to say.

A week later, Pius wandered out to the tomb and found Salongo busily polishing the Ssabalangira's weapons. "I thought you were dead," growled the custodian, "it is so long since you came here—but then, this tomb thrives on neglect. Nobody cares that one of Buganda's greatest men lies here."

"I have been rather busy," murmured Pius. "But I didn't forget my promise to you. Here! I've brought you a hundred shillings, and I only wish it could have been more. At least it will buy a few cement blocks."

Salongo took the money and looked at it as if it were crawling with lice. Grudgingly he thanked Pius and then remarked, "Of course, you will find life more expensive now that you are keeping a woman in the house."

"I suppose Nantondo told you," Pius smiled sheepishly.

"Does it matter who told me?" the custodian replied. "Anyway, never say I didn't warn you. Next thing she'll want will be a ring marriage!"

Pius gave an uncertain laugh. "As a matter of fact, one of the reasons I came up here was to invite you to the wedding—it's next month."

Salongo carefully laid down the spear he was rubbing upon a piece of clean barkcloth and stared at his friend as if he had suddenly grown another head. "What a fool you are! And all this stems from your scribbling noughts and crosses on a bit of squared paper! I knew it would bring no good! At your age you ought to have more sense. Well, all I can advise is that you run while you still have the chance!"

For a moment Pius was full of misgivings. Was he, after all, behaving like a fool? Then he thought of Sarah, and the wonders she had worked with his house and his *shamba* in the short time they had been together. He felt reassured. "Well, I'm getting married, and I expect to see you at both the church and the reception, and if you don't appear, I shall want to know the reason why!" He was secretly delighted at the note of authority in his voice, and Salongo's face was the picture of astonishment. "All right," he mumbled, "I shall try and come. Before you go, cut a bunch of bananas to take back to your good lady, and there might be some cabbage ready at the back. I suppose I've got to hand it to her! She's the real winner!"

Notes

Buganda a state in southern Uganda

garrulous talkative in a tedious, rambling manner; from the Latin word *garrulus*, meaning "chatter"

Ssabalangira refers to any revered man in Uganda who is deceased

matoke a Ugandan food staple; cooked green bananas usually served with a meat sauce

kanzu a robe worn by some East African men

busuti a long cloak

shamba a garden with fruits and vegetables

aplomb confident composure or self-assurance

Activities

1. Choose several passages in the story that you found particularly engaging and explain in a few sentences why each appeals to you. Share your thoughts with the class and come up with a co-operative list of the positive features of "The Winner." Name other literary works you have read which have similar characteristics. If you disliked the story, be prepared to explain why.

2. Why do you think Kimenye chose to conclude the story with a scene between Pius and Salongo? In a group, make a list of other moments either within the story or beyond the story that could also serve as appropriate endings. Select an ending from your list which you think would be most effective and write it. Which ending do you prefer, yours or the author's? Explain.

3. Locate and read reviews of children's books in a number of newspapers and on the Internet, and analyze their content and style. Then find and read several children's books by either Barbara Kimenye or other writers of African origin. Write a review of one of these books, using the reviews you read as models.

Windows

Bernice Morgan

Bernice Morgan was born in St. John's, Newfoundland, in 1935. She is a writer of short stories, plays, and novels. Her novel *Random Passage* and its sequel, *Waiting for Time*, were made into a CBC television mini-series; a production photograph of the filming appears on page 641 of this anthology. A book of her short stories, *The Topography of Love*, was published in 2000. Morgan has also worked for many years in public relations, first with Memorial University of Newfoundland, and later with the Newfoundland Teachers Association. Morgan's fiction often depicts the plight of immigrant individuals and families who settled in Canada. What major challenges do immigrants face in a new country? What are some of the ways they deal with them?

One morning in late winter, Leah Levitawitz opened her eyes on the sure knowledge that she was dying. Dawn did not waken her, for dawn never came to this room, only a pale greenish light that slithered down from the roof of the old house and along the dripping mouldy wall of the warehouse next door. It must have been the cold that woke her; it seeped in around the sagging sills and loose clapboards, the damp cold of late winter that cut through the threadbare blankets and even penetrated Leah's old tweed coat.

Leah checked down the length of her thin body. "Strange," she thought, "I don't feel any worse than I did yesterday...how can I be so sure this is it?"

Brain, heart, arms and legs seemed to be functioning as usual—sluggish but still in working order. In a little while she would get up, dress and go, very slowly, down the rickety steps to the kitchen. But not yet. Leah could hear the screams of her grandchildren and the tired, peevish voice of her son's wife. Leah burrowed down, pulling the old coat up over her yellow-grey hair. She would wait, as she always did, until they had gone, maybe Ruth would go out too, then she could creep down and have her drop of tea in peace. Leah closed her eyes against the dingy green light of the room and set herself to wait.

To wait, and to think about this new knowledge of death that had come from somewhere in the night. This dying, it must have been going on for a long time, she realized. Strange that it hadn't come to her before to put a name to it! She'd always thought of death as something that pounced upon you when you were least expecting it—like it had pounced down on Mikail twenty years ago, shoving him off that little piece of steel and smashing him like an egg on the concrete. Dead...the papers said, or deceased—it sounded like one quick, single act, but it wasn't going to be, not for her anyway. For her death would not pounce but come creeping, creeping, inch by inch—like a cat creeping toward its prey.

Leah wondered when it had started—when Mikail died? Probably, but it was a long way off then. Now it felt much closer. She remembered waking on the morning after he died, waking and not knowing, and then, knowing—and the terrible emptiness. Yes that must have been the beginning.

But in those years she hadn't the time to notice, she'd been too busy, getting coal and firewood, mitts and shoes—all the things that had to somehow be gotten before little children turned into men and women. And the lying—Leah remembered all the lying she'd done, when you had no money you bartered in lies, and she'd lied to everyone. To the landlord, "The Welfare man was here and said he'd have this place condemned if you didn't fix that roof." To the grocer, "I'm expecting a cheque from my brother, it should have been here yesterday, in the meantime I'll have to charge one or two things." To the teachers, "Sam is such a careless boy...he lost his gym shoes on the way to school the first day...I'll get him another pair the first chance I get."

She'd even lied to the children, "The winter's almost over now, things are always easier in the summer. Maybe this year we can all go on a little vacation, to a farm maybe, wouldn't it be nice to go to a farm?"

They had never gone to the farm. Leah wondered if all her lies lay piled up somewhere waiting to be displayed at some day of reckoning. Well, she didn't care…they had been necessary. Thank God it was behind her, all five of the children were raised and none of them had ended up in jail like some she'd known. Jack was the worst off and married to a woman who would rather whine than work, there wasn't much chance of his ever being any richer.

"Why do I stay with them?" she asked herself the question for the thousandth time and for the thousandth time replied with the automatic answer, "Because they need my pension." Only this morning she forced herself to stop and admit there was another reason, another answer to why she slept in this miserable room and listened to Ruth's whining day after day.

Three years ago when she had been notified that her old apartment building was being demolished, Jack had said, "Better come over and stop with us, Ma." None of the others had asked her to come with them.

Leah knew she got on Ruth's nerves, look how she was always trying to get her out of the house…"Aw Ma, go on over and visit your friend Mrs. Palaskine, you haven't been over there once this year." Or, "Ma, for God's sake go out somewheres…let Jack drop ya off at the park and you can take your time comin' back."

Take your time; that was funny.

Half asleep now, Leah's thoughts slipped back to her own childhood on a farm in Estonia. Someone told her that Estonia didn't exist any more, but of course that was nonsense, a country didn't disappear. They might call it a different name but it was still the same country.

It had been cold there, too, but she and her sisters had slept in a bed built against the side of the chimney. Sometimes in the morning the bricks were still warm with the heat of yesterday's fires.

The farm had been poor. "I haven't made much progress," Leah mused, "born poor and dying poor." There had been a few years, first when she and Mikail were married, when she'd thought that they might make it, might get ahead enough to own something, even a piece of land perhaps. She hadn't missed the farm in those years, it was only later, later when all the hope was gone that she'd begun to lie awake remembering how beautiful Estonia had been. The pattern of green leaves against a blue sky, the amber glow of firelight on stone walls, fields of wheat and girls in red kerchiefs cutting it…if Estonia still existed, then those things must exist also. Canada was a big country, Leah knew, she'd heard it often on the radio. There were probably trees and open fields, rivers and hills in Canada too…but she'd never seen them.

Leah dozed, the flicker of leaves in sunshine making dream pictures inside her closed eyes.

A noise, like a cannon ripping a city apart, tore across her room, jerking her awake and sitting. The noise kept up, it filled her head, the room, the house, the world. Dear God—could this be death? Leah felt her heart pounding and even in the chill of the room, sweat beaded around her neck. Then the noise stopped for a minute and she heard men shouting and trucks…it wasn't what she'd thought.

"Oh Lord, how foolish am I?" Leah eased her thin legs over the edge of the bed and pushed her feet into sagging carpet slippers. By the time she'd reached the window the noise had started again, but of course she couldn't see anything, only the wet slimy walls of the old warehouse that she'd been looking at for three years. "Digging up the street, someone's pipes froze again more than likely!" Well, now that she was up she'd better get dressed. The room felt even colder. "Will I live to see the end of winter?" she wondered.

In the kitchen a naked bulb hung from a twisted black cord. The kitchen window also faced the warehouse and the bulb was kept burning all day. Its hard, yellow glare revealed every grease mark on the motley wallpaper, every chip in the rust-coloured sink, it shone unmercifully on Ruth's tired face and unkempt hair.

The two women did not talk. Leah shuffled about getting a cup of tea and toasting a slice of bread on a fork over the coal fire. One thing Ruth did, she made good bread. Leah sniffed with pleasure as the edges of the bread turned golden brown.

Ruth stood at the sink listlessly washing dishes, her head tilted toward the radio. Ruth filled her days with second-hand drama. Leah watched the younger woman shaking her head over some unwise decision the radio character had made. "They're more real to her than I am—than any of us are."

Then the radio sputtered and the sobbing voice of the forsaken heroine disappeared under a barrage of sound.

"Oh damn, now I'll never know how it comes out! It's that darn machine they're workin' the street with."

Radio listening was a necessary background for dish washing. Ruth dried her hands and untied her apron.

"Look Ma, I'm goin' down town, the kids won't be home to lunch— you fix yourself something and I'll be back around four."

Being careful not to let her pleasure show, Leah nodded and turned the toast over on the fork.

It took Ruth only a minute in front of the cracked mirror to slash a red line across her mouth and button her lint-covered black coat. She started to leave, then stuck her head in the kitchen door to ask, "Anything you want?"

Leah shook her head and grunted negatively. As if she'd let that nit-wit shop for her! But Ruth always asked. She enjoyed shopping and spread the necessary purchases of socks, shoes and underwear over as many trips to the stores as possible.

You'd hardly notice the noise once you got used to it. Leah carefully carried her tea and toast over to the stove and sat with her feet in the oven. The old rocker was the only thing in the house that she owned. Ruth said she was always tripping over it but Leah was glad she'd held onto it. Leah sipped her tea and rocked. She wished she had some knitting— maybe she should have told Ruth to get her wool and needles. She could knit a bright wool afghan for her bed...but no, it would take too long, too long to finish.

It was nice to sit here with the warm stove and the warm tea, if only the light wasn't so bright! Carefully Leah set the thick cup down on the back of the stove, she got up slowly and turned off the terrible light. There! That was so much better, how she hated that light! Now the kitchen was almost dark, the pleasant glow of the fire softened the harsh look of poverty.

The noise wasn't really so bad, much more bearable than the radio. Leah began thinking once more about death, turning the idea over, getting used to it. She rocked and dozed.

The crash of glass and an icy wind at her back woke her. The entire window had smashed in, frame and all. Leah stood facing the broken glass and waited for something else to happen…this time she was more curious than frightened. What in the world was going on out there?

Two men appeared in the window wearing those yellow hats that look like mixing bowls. They were young, frightened and embarrassed. Leah could hardly keep from smiling. A voice behind the two young men shouted, "What the Hell you two doin'?" An older man with a clip board in his hand appeared. The young men blushed and stammered something about the lever of the crane.

"Honest to God I don't know where they get the jokers they send down to me these days—how the Hell did the lever slip? The same if you'd killed this old dame here! Look Missus," the big man stuck his head in the broken window, "we'll be through here in about two hours. How about if we nail a piece of plywood to keep the weather out and then I'll have someone come over and fix the window?"

Leah nodded, the heads disappeared and a few minutes later the hole was covered with a sheet of wood. Leah sighed, sorry the excitement had ended so soon. She looked at the splinters of glass and wood on the floor and wondered if she'd sweep them up. No, it was really too much trouble, she decided. Leah gave the fire one poke and settled down in the rocker again.

It was nice and quite comfortable but this time Leah couldn't sleep—the noises outside kept intruding. What in the world were they doing anyway? The house shook and on the back of the stove her cup rattled. If this kept on the house would fall down around her ears. There would be a nice fast death! Leah decided she wouldn't really mind…the city would have to pay Jack and Ruth for all the things that got broken. Except her of course. There wouldn't be any need to pay for her.

What would she get herself for lunch? She wasn't hungry but it gave her something to think about. She'd seen Ruth stick a package of sausages out in the back porch. Leah was fond of sausage, maybe she'd fry a few, but no—they always gave her heartburn and besides she'd have a greasy pan to scrub. Maybe she'd get herself an egg—that young public health nurse who came by was always askin' her if she'd had an egg—she'd never liked eggs. She couldn't bear thinkin' about what they really were— ah well, she'd have an egg today, boiled, that way there'd be no pot to wash!

The fire seemed to be dying. She got up and took a look at it— might just as well burn those pieces of window frame. As Leah stuffed the rotten wood into the stove she listened. The noises outside seemed to be different, the pounding had stopped.

"Maybe I'll just take a nip out and see what they're doin'."

Then she remembered she'd left her coat upstairs on her bed. It was too much trouble to climb the steep steps. Leah was just about to settle down in her rocker again when she noticed Jack's old army parka hanging on the kitchen door. She pulled it on, it was big and bulky, the sleeves covered her hands and it hung down to her knees—but it was warm. Near the front door there was a pair of children's rubber boots. Leah sat on the bottom stair and pulled them on over her slippers— she'd always been proud of her little feet.

It wasn't really as cold as she'd expected. Leah hobbled around the corner of the house. She stopped in amazement. The corner lot next door was empty! Just one big empty space, not a sign of the old warehouse remained! Two tractors were smoothing over the black earth.

Leah stood and watched them and marvelled. "Now wasn't that something!" She looked at the house, at the plywood-covered kitchen window and at her own bedroom window above it. They would be able to see right down the street! Sunlight would come in. And look what they were doin' now. Leah watched as cranes gently lifted two trees and set them down into holes. There'd be grass too, no doubt, they'd be just like rich people, with a garden of their own. Maybe the city would plant flowers, tulips perhaps, yes, tulips first, then petunias and later big orange coloured chrysanthemums…and the leaves would turn on the trees…Leah sighed. Maybe she could make a little plot of her own over by the kitchen window—surely no one would mind that. Maybe the children could help her, they probably couldn't tell one flower from another, or maybe they could. She didn't really know much about her grandchildren.

Watching the men plant the trees and lost in thoughts of how the land ("the land" was what her father had always called any open space) would look when summer came, Leah didn't realize someone was speaking to her until the big man touched her sleeve.

"Look Missus—you the lady in that house—where we broke the window?"

Leah nodded.

"Well I've just written down the measurements of that window and two carpenters will be over to repair it later. I wonder if you can tell me what kind of window it was. Did it have small panes of glass or what?"

Leah remembered the windows in the farmhouse in Estonia, they'd opened out from the middle—lovely on a summer's day to unlatch your window and look out across the land!

Leah cleared her throat. "Well it was a very unusual window…"

The big man had never seen a window like it. Leah had to draw a picture of the window on his yellow paper.

"Well, well," he studied the sketch, "seems to me it was plainer than that…I haven't seen a window like that…not for forty years! We'd have to get it custom made—" He looked at the house again. "The other windows aren't like that." The man fixed a skeptical look at the old woman in the army parka. "You sure it was that kind of window?"

With all the dignity she could muster Leah stared right back at him.

"It certainly was, young man! I had it copied especially from my old home in Estonia."

The words came out strong and clear—much better than she had feared. The man blinked and nodded.

"And just make sure there's a little latch in the middle." Leah waved him off with a regal hand—it was the first lie she'd told in years; it gave her a heady feeling to know she could still do it so well.

Leah took one more long look at the trees, to make sure they were being properly planted, and turned back to the house—she thought she'd fry the sausages after all, what was a little heartburn for something you liked! After lunch she'd walk over to see her friend Mrs. Palaskine. Mrs. Palaskine always got all the free seed catalogues. They could talk about what to do with the land this year!

Activities

1. In a class discussion about "Windows," explore to what extent you think Morgan's gender influenced her depiction of the main character. Consider, as well, to what extent you think your gender affects your response to the character.

2. Consider the use of symbolism in this story by identifying one or more objects that Morgan uses symbolically in "Windows." Write a thesis statement in which you explain how the symbolic use of the object you have identified contributes to the overall theme of the story. Then write an analytical essay in which you use detailed examples to make connections and illustrate your thesis. Have a partner evaluate to what extent the examples in your essay provide evidence to support your viewpoint.

3. With the class, discuss the implications of Morgan's decision to write this story from the third-person point of view. Include in your discussion how the point of view affects the tone. Then, with a partner, select a page of the story and rewrite it from the first-person point of view. Compare what you have written with Morgan's original. Share your adaptation with the class, and discuss the advantages and disadvantages of using one point of view over the other.

Another Viewpoint: Society

Many writers have focused on older adults, the process of aging, and "ageism," which is discrimination based on age. As a class, recall stories, poems, or songs you have encountered about older people at the point in their life Shakespeare described as "the time of yellow leaf." Discuss some different perspectives you have garnered either from your readings or actual experience with older adults.

EASTER AT MY AUNT'S

Christopher Pratt

About the Visual   Christopher Pratt was born in St. John's, Newfoundland, in 1935, and still lives in the province. He studied fine art at the Glasgow School of Art in Scotland and at Mount Allison University in New Brunswick, where he worked with Alex Colville. Pratt works in numerous media, including oil paint, watercolour, silk-screening, lithography, and collage. He has been appointed both a companion and an officer of the Order of Canada. Pratt often depicts features of buildings in his work. Why might an artist choose to focus on everyday, constructed objects, such as a door or a set of stairs? Do you think some subjects are more valid than others as the focal point of an artist's work?

Activities

1. Draw a sketch or write a journal entry describing in detail a special scene you remember from your past. Include any objects, colours, sounds, or smells that set in motion a sequence of associative memories.

2. Christopher Pratt's first studies at university were in engineering. Examine closely the style of Pratt's lithograph. What makes this lithograph a work of art rather than an engineer's drawing?

1985, lithograph, 39.5 cm x 51 cm

War

Timothy Findley

Timothy Findley was born in Toronto, in 1930. He worked as an actor early in his career, appearing on stages in North America, including Stratford, as well as in Europe. He has written for television and the stage, and his novel *The Wars* won the Governor General's Award for Fiction in 1977. Another novel, *Not Wanted on the Voyage,* and his first work of non-fiction, *Inside Memory: Pages for a Writer's Notebook,* both won Canadian Authors Association Awards. Some of the dialogue in this story appears in the form of a dramatic work, in which each character speaks without any narrative context. What are some of the differences between the use of dialogue in a work of fiction and its use in a dramatic work?

That's my dad in the middle. We were just kids then, Bud on the right and me on the left. That was taken just before my dad went into the army.

Some day that was.

It was a Saturday, two years ago. August, 1940. I can remember I had to blow my nose just before that and I had to use my dad's hankie because mine had a worm in it that I was saving. I can't remember why; I mean, why I was saving that worm, but I can remember why I had to blow my nose, all right. That was because I'd had a long time crying. Not exactly because my dad was going away or anything—it was mostly because I'd done something.

I'll tell you what in a minute, but I just want to say this first. I was ten years old then and it was sort of the end of summer. When we went back to school I was going into the fifth grade and that was pretty important, especially for me because I'd skipped grade four. Right now I can't even remember grade five except that I didn't like it. I should have gone to grade four. In grade five everyone was a genius and there was a boy called Allan McKenzie.

Anyway, now that you know how old I was and what grade I was into, I can tell you the rest.

It was the summer the war broke out and I went to stay with my friend, Arthur Robertson. Looking back on it, Arthur seems a pretty silly name for Arthur Robertson because he was so small. But he was a nice kid and his dad had the most enormous summer cottage you've ever seen. In Muskoka, too.

It was like those houses they have in the movies in Beverly Hills. Windows a mile long—pine trees outside and then a lake and then a red canoe tied up with a yellow rope. There was an Indian, too, who sold little boxes made of birch-bark and porcupine quills. Arthur Robertson and I used to sit in the red canoe and this Indian would take us for a ride out to the raft and back. Then we'd go and tell Mrs. Robertson or the cook or someone how nice he was and he'd stand behind us and smile as though he didn't understand English and then they'd have to buy a box from him. He certainly was smart, that Indian, because it worked about four times. Then one day they caught on and hid the canoe.

Anyway, that's the sort of thing we did. And we swam too, and I remember a book that Arthur Robertson's nurse read to us. It was about dogs.

Then I had to go away because I'd only been invited for two weeks. I went on to this farm where the family took us every summer when we were children. Bud was already there, and his friend, Teddy Hartley.

I didn't like Teddy Hartley. It was because he had a space between his teeth and he used to spit through it. Once I saw him spit two-and-a-half yards. Bud paced it out. And then he used to whistle through it, too, that space, and it was the kind of whistling that nearly made your ears bleed. That was what I didn't like. But it didn't really matter, because he was Bud's friend, not mine.

So I went by train and Mr. and Mrs. Currie met me in their truck. It was their farm.

Mrs. Currie got me into the front with her while Mr. Currie put my stuff in the back.

"Your mum and dad aren't here, dear, but they'll be up tomorrow. Buddy is here—and his friend."

Grownups were always calling Bud "Buddy." It was all wrong.

I didn't care too much about my parents not being there, except that I'd brought them each one of those birch-bark boxes. Inside my mother's there was a set of red stones I'd picked out from where we swam. I thought maybe she'd make a necklace out of them. In my dad's there was an old golf ball, because he played golf. I guess you'd have to say I stole it, because I didn't tell anyone I had it—but it was just lying there on a shelf in Mr. Robertson's boathouse, and he never played golf. At least I never saw him.

I had these boxes on my lap because I'd thought my mum and dad would be there to meet me, but now that they weren't I put them into the glove compartment of the truck.

We drove to the farm.

Bud and Teddy were riding on the gate, and they waved when we drove past. I couldn't see too well because of the dust but I could hear them shouting. It was something about my dad. I didn't really hear exactly what it was they said, but Mrs. Currie went white as a sheet and said: "Be quiet," to Bud.

Then we were there and the truck stopped. We went inside.

And now—this is where it begins.

After supper, the evening I arrived at the Curries' farm, my brother Bud and his friend Teddy Hartley and I all sat on the front porch. In a hammock.

This is the conversation we had.

BUD: (to me) Are you all right? Did you have a good time at Arthur Robertson's place? Did you swim?

ME: (to Bud) Yes.

TEDDY HARTLEY: I've got a feeling I don't like Arthur Robertson. Do I know him?

BUD: Kid at school. Neil's age. (He said that as if it were dirty to be my age.)

TEDDY HARTLEY: Thin kid? Very small?

BUD: Thin and small—brainy type. Hey, Neil, have you seen Ted spit?

ME: Yes—I have.

TEDDY HARTLEY: When did you see me spit? (Indignant as hell) I never spat for you.

ME: Yes, you did. About three months ago. We were still in school. Bud—he did too, and you walked it out, too, didn't you?

BUD: I don't know.

TEDDY HARTLEY: I never spat for you yet! Never!

ME: Two yards and a half.

TEDDY HARTLEY: Can't have been me. I spit four.

ME: Four YARDS!!

TEDDY HARTLEY: Certainly.

BUD: Go ahead and show him. Over the rail.

TEDDY HARTLEY: (Standing up) Okay. Look, Neil...Now watch...Come on, WATCH!!

ME: All right—I'm watching. (Teddy Hartley spat. It was three yards-and-a-half by Bud's feet. I saw Bud mark it myself.)

BUD: Three yards and a half a foot.

TEDDY HARTLEY: Four yards. (Maybe his feet were smaller or something.)

BUD: Three-and-foot. Three and one foot. No, no. A *half*-a-one. Of a foot.

TEDDY HARTLEY: Four.

BUD: Three!

TEDDY HARTLEY: Four! Four! Four!

BUD: Three! One-two-three-and-a-half-a-foot!

TEDDY HARTLEY: My dad showed me. It's four! He showed me, and he knows. My dad knows. He's a mathematical teacher—yes, yes, yes, he showed me how to count a yard. I saw him do it. And he knows, my dad!!

BUD: You dad's a crazy man. It's three yards and a half a foot.

TEDDY HARTLEY: (All red in the face and screaming) You called my dad a nut! You called my dad a crazy-man-nut-meg! Take it back, you. Bud Cable, you take that back.

BUD: You dad is a matha-nut-ical nutmeg tree.

TEDDY HARTLEY: Then your dad's a…your dad's a…your dad's an Insane!

BUD: Our dad's joined the army.

* * *

That was how I found out.

They went on talking like that for a long time. I got up and left. I started talking to myself, which is a habit I have.

"Joined the army? Joined the army? Joined the ARMY! Our dad?"

Our dad was a salesman. I used to go to his office and watch him selling things over the phone sometimes. I always used to look for what it was, but I guess they didn't keep it around the office. Maybe they hid it somewhere. Maybe it was too expensive to just leave lying around. But whatever it was, I knew it was important, and so that was one thing that bothered me when Bud said about the army—because I knew that in the army they wouldn't let my dad sit and sell things over any old phone—because in the army you always went in a trench and got hurt or killed. I knew that because my dad had told me himself when my uncle died. My uncle was his brother in the first war, who got hit in his stomach and he died from it a long time afterwards. Long enough, anyway, for me to have known him. He was always in a big white bed, and he gave us candies from a glass jar. That was all I knew—except that it was because of being in the army that he died. His name was Uncle Frank.

So those were the first two things I thought of: my dad not being able to sell anything any more—and then Uncle Frank.

But then it really got bad, because I suddenly remembered that my dad had promised to teach me how to skate that year. He was going to make a rink too, in the back yard. But if he had to go off to some old trench in France, then he'd be too far away. Soldiers always went in trenches—and trenches were always in France. I remember that.

Well, I don't know. Maybe I just couldn't forgive him. He hadn't even told me. He didn't even write it in his letter that he'd sent me at Arthur Robertson's. But he'd told Bud—he'd told Bud, but I was the one he'd promised to show how to skate. And I'd had it all planned how I'd really surprise my dad and turn out to be a skating champion and everything, and now he wouldn't even be there to see.

All because he had to go and sit in some trench.

·   ·   ·

I don't know how I got there, but I ended up in the barn. I was in the hayloft and I didn't even hear them, I guess. They were looking all over the place for me, because it started to get dark.

I don't know whether you're afraid of the dark, but I'll tell you right now, I am. At least, I am if I have to move around in it. If I can just sit still, then I'm all right. At least, if you sit still you know where you are—but if you move around, then you don't know where you are. And that's awful. You never know what you're going to step on next and I always thought it would be a duck. I don't like ducks—especially in the dark or if you stepped on them.

Anyway, I was in that hayloft in the barn and I heard them calling out—"Neil, Neil"—and "Where are you?" But I made up my mind right then I wasn't going to answer. For one thing, if I did, then I'd have to go down to them in the dark—and maybe I'd step on something. And for another, I didn't really want to see anyone anyway.

It was then that I got this idea about my father. I thought that maybe if I stayed hidden for long enough, then he wouldn't join the army. Don't ask me why—right now I couldn't tell you that—but in those days it made sense. If I hid then he wouldn't go away. Maybe it would be because he'd stay looking for me or something.

The trouble was that my dad wasn't even there that night, and that meant that I either had to wait in the hayloft till he came the next day— or else that I had to go down now, and then hide again tomorrow. I decided to stay where I was because there were some ducks at the bottom of the ladder. I couldn't see them but I could tell they were there.

I stayed there all night. I slept most of the time. Every once in a while they'd wake me up by calling out "Neil! Neil!"—but I never answered.

I never knew a night that was so long, except maybe once when I was in the hospital. When I slept I seemed to sleep for a long time, but it never came to morning. They kept waking me up but it was never time.

Then it was.

I saw that morning through a hole in the roof of the hayloft. The sunlight came in through cracks between the boards and it was all dusty; the sunlight, I mean.

They were up pretty early that morning, even for farmers. There seemed to be a lot more people than I remembered—and there were two or three cars and a truck I'd never seen before, too. And I saw Mrs. Currie holding on to Bud with one hand and Teddy Hartley with the other. I remembered thinking, "If I was down there, how could she hold on to me if she's only got two hands and Bud and Teddy Hartley to look after?" And I thought that right then she must be pretty glad I wasn't around.

I wondered what they were all doing. Mr. Currie was standing in the middle of a lot of men and he kept pointing out the scenery around the farm. I imagined what he was saying. There was a big woods behind the house and a cherry and plum-tree orchard that would be good to point out to his friends. I could tell they were his friends from the way they were listening. What I couldn't figure out was why they were up so early—and why they had Bud and Teddy Hartley up, too.

Then there was a police car. I suppose it came from Orillia or somewhere. That was the biggest town near where the farm was. Orillia.

When the policemen got out of their car, they went up to Mr. Currie. There were four of them. They all talked for quite a long time and then everyone started going out in all directions. It looked to me as though Bud and Teddy Hartley wanted to go, too, but Mrs. Currie made them go in the house. She practically had to drag Bud. It looked as if he was crying and I wondered why he should do that.

Then one of the policemen came into the barn. He was all alone. I stayed very quiet, because I wasn't going to let anything keep me from going through with my plan about my dad. Not even a policeman.

He urinated against the wall inside the door. It was sort of funny, because he kept turning around to make sure no one saw him, and he didn't know I was there. Then he did up his pants and stood in the middle of the floor under the haylofts.

"Hey! Neil!"

That was the policeman.

He said it so suddenly that it scared me. I nearly fell off from where I was, it scared me so much. And I guess maybe he saw me, because he started right up the ladder at me.

"How did you know my name?"

I said that in a whisper.

"They told me."

"Oh."

"Have you been here all night?"

"Yes."

"Don't you realize that everyone has been looking for you all over the place? Nobody's even been to sleep."

That sort of frightened me—but it was all right, because he smiled when he said it.

Then he stuck his head out of this window that was there to let the air in (so that the barn wouldn't catch on fire)—and he yelled down, "He's all right—I've found him! He's up here."

And I said: "What did you go and do that for? Now you've ruined everything."

He smiled again and said, "I had to stop them all going off to look for you. Now,"—as he sat down beside me—"do you want to tell me what it is you're doing up here?"

"No."

I think that sort of set him back a couple of years, because he didn't say anything for a minute—except "Oh."

Then I thought maybe I had to have something to tell the others anyway, so I might as well make it up for him right now.

"I fell asleep," I said.

"When—last night?"

"Yes."

I looked at him. I wondered if I could trust a guy who did that against walls, when all you had to do was go in the house.

"Why did you come up here in the first place?" he said.

I decided I could trust him because I remembered once when I did the same thing. Against the wall.

So I told him.

"I want to hide on my dad," I said.

"Why do you want to do that? And besides, Mrs. Currie said your parents weren't even here."

"Yes, but he's coming today."

"But why hide on him? Don't you like him, or something?"

"Sure I do," I said.

I thought about it.

"But he's...he's...Do you know if it's true, my dad's joined the army?"

"I dunno. Maybe. There's a war on, you know."

"Well, that's why I hid."

But he laughed.

"Is that why you hid? Because of the war?"

"Because of my dad."

"You don't need to hide because of the war—the Germans aren't coming over here, you know."

"But it's not that. It's my dad." I could have told you he wouldn't understand.

I was trying to think of what to say next when Mrs. Currie came into the barn. She stood down below.

"Is he up there, officer? Is he all right?"

"Yes, ma'am, I've got him. He's fine."

"Neil dear, what happened? Why don't you come down and tell us what happened to you?"

Then I decided that I'd really go all out. I had to, because I could tell they weren't going to—it was just obvious that these people weren't going to understand me and take my story about my dad and the army and everything.

"Somebody chased me."

The policeman looked sort of shocked and I could hear Mrs. Currie take in her breath.

"Somebody chased you, eh?"

"Yes."

"Who?"

I had to think fast.

"Some man. But he's gone now."

I thought I'd better say he was gone, so that they wouldn't start worrying.

"Officer, why don't you bring him down here? Then we can talk."

"All right, ma'am. Come on, Neil, we'll go down and have some breakfast."

They didn't seem to believe me about that man I made up.

We went over to the ladder.

I looked down. A lot of hay stuck out so that I couldn't see the floor.

"Are there any ducks down there?"

"No, dear, you can come down—it's all right."

She was lying, though. There was a great big duck right next to her. I think it's awfully silly to tell a lie like that. I mean, if the duck is standing right there it doesn't even make sense, does it?

But I went down anyway and she made the duck go away.

When we went out, the policeman held my hand. His hand had some sweat on it but it was a nice hand, with hair on the back. I liked that. My dad didn't have that on his hand.

Then we ate breakfast with all those people who'd come to look for me. At least, *they* ate. I just sat.

After breakfast, Mr. and Mrs. Currie took me upstairs to the sitting-room. It was upstairs because the kitchen was in the cellar.

All I remember about that was a vase that had a potted plant in it. This vase was made of putty and into the putty Mrs. Currie had stuck all kinds of stones and pennies and old bits of glass and things. You could look at this for hours and never see the same kind of stone or glass twice. I don't remember the plant.

All I remember about what they said was that they told me I should never do it again. That routine.

Then they told me my mother and my dad would be up that day around lunch time.

What they were really sore about was losing their sleep, and then all those people coming. I was sorry about that—but you can't very well go down and make an announcement about it, so I didn't.

•   •   •

At twelve o'clock I went and sat in Mr. Currie's truck. It was in the barn. I took out those two boxes I'd put in the glove compartment and looked at them. I tried to figure out what my dad would do with an old box like that in the army. And he'd probably never play another game of golf as long as he lived. Not in the army, anyway. Maybe he'd use the box for his bullets or something.

Then I counted the red stones I was going to give my mother. I kept seeing them around her neck and how pretty they'd be. She had a dress they'd be just perfect with. Blue. The only thing I was worried about was how to get a hole in them so you could put them on a string. There wasn't much sense in having beads without a string—not if you were going to wear them, anyway—or your mother was.

And it was then that they came.

I heard their car drive up outside and I went and looked from behind the barn door. My father wasn't wearing a uniform yet like I'd thought he would be. I began to think maybe he really didn't want me to know about it. I mean, he hadn't written or anything, and now he was just wearing an old blazer and some grey pants. It made me remember.

I went back and sat down in the truck again. I didn't know what to do. I just sat there with those stones in my hand.

Then I heard someone shout, "Neil!"

I went and looked. Mr. and Mrs. Currie were standing with my parents by the car—and I saw Bud come running out of the house, and then Teddy Hartley. Teddy Hartley sort of hung back, though. He was the kind of person who's only polite if there are grownups around him.

He sure knew how to pull the wool over their eyes, because he'd even combed his hair. Wild-root-cream-oil-Charlie.

Then I noticed that they were talking very seriously and my mother put her hand above her eyes and looked around. I guess she was looking for me. Then my dad started toward the barn.

I went and hid behind the truck. I wasn't quite sure yet what I was going to do, but I certainly wasn't going to go up and throw my arms around his neck or anything.

"Neil. Are you in there, son?"

My dad spoke that very quietly. Then I heard the door being pushed open, and some chicken had to get out of the way, because I heard it making that awful noise chickens make when you surprise them doing something. They sure can get excited over nothing—chickens.

I took a quick look behind me. There was a door there that led into the part of the barn where the haylofts were and where I'd been all night. I decided to make a dash for it. But I had to ward off my father first—and so I threw that stone.

I suppose I'll have to admit that I meant to hit him. It wouldn't be much sense if I tried to fool you about that. I wanted to hit him because when I stood up behind the truck and saw him then I suddenly got mad. I thought about how he hadn't written me, or anything.

It hit him on the hand.

He turned right around because he wasn't sure what it was or where it came from. And before I ran, I just caught a glimpse of his face. He'd seen me and he sure looked peculiar. I guess that now I'll never forget his face and how he looked at me right then. I think it was that he looked as though he might cry or something. But I knew he wouldn't do that, because he never did.

Then I ran.

From the loft I watched them in the yard. My dad was rubbing his hands together and I guess maybe where I'd hit him it was pretty sore. My mother took off her handkerchief that she had round her neck and put it on his hand. Then I guess he'd told them what I'd done, because this time they all started toward the barn.

I didn't know what to do then. I counted out the stones I had left and there were about fifteen of them. There was the golf ball, too.

I didn't want to throw stones at all of them. I certainly didn't want to hit my mother—and I hoped that they wouldn't send her in first. I thought then how I'd be all right if they sent in Teddy Hartley first. I didn't mind the thought of throwing at him, I'll tell you that much.

But my dad came first.

I had a good view of where he came from. He came in through the part where the truck was parked, because I guess he thought I was still there. And then he came on into the part where I was now—in the hayloft.

He stood by the door.

"Neil."

I wasn't saying anything. I sat very still.

"Neil."

I could only just see his head and shoulders—the rest of him was hidden by the edge of the loft.

"Neil, aren't you even going to explain what you're angry about?"

I thought for a minute and then I didn't answer him after all. I looked at him, though. He looked worried.

"What do you want us to do?"

I sat still.

"Neil?"

Since I didn't answer, he started back out the door—I guess to talk to my mother or someone.

I hit his back with another stone. I had to make sure he knew I was there.

He turned around at me.

"Neil, what's the matter? I want to know what's the matter."

He almost fooled me, but not quite. I thought that perhaps he really didn't know for a minute—but after taking a look at him I decided that he did know, all right. I mean, there he was in that blue blazer and everything—just as if he hadn't joined the army at all.

So I threw again and this time it really hit him in the face.

He didn't do anything—he just stood there. It really scared me. Then my mother came in, but he made her go back.

I thought about my rink, and how I wouldn't have it. I thought about being in the fifth grade that year and how I'd skipped from grade three. And I thought about the Indian who'd sold those boxes that I had down in the truck.

"Neil—I'm going to come up."

You could tell he really would, too, from his voice.

I got the golf ball ready.

To get to me he had to disappear for a minute while he crossed under the loft and then when he climbed the ladder. I decided to change my place while he was out of sight. I began to think that was pretty clever and that maybe I'd be pretty good at that war stuff myself. Field Marshal Cable.

I put myself into a little trench of hay and piled some up in front of me. When my dad came up over the top of the ladder, he wouldn't even see me and then I'd have a good chance to aim at him.

The funny thing was that at that moment I'd forgotten why I was against him. I got so mixed up in all that Field Marshal stuff that I really forgot all about my dad and the army and everything. I was just trying to figure out how I could get him before he saw me—and that was all.

I got further down in the hay and then he was there.

He was out of breath and his face was all sweaty, and where I'd hit him there was blood. And then he put his hand with my mother's hankie up to his face to wipe it. And he sort of bit it (the handkerchief). It was as if he was confused or something. I remember thinking he looked then just like I'd felt my face go when Bud had said our dad had joined the army. You know how you look around with your eyes from side to side as though maybe you'll find the answer to it somewhere near you? You never do find it, but you always look anyway, just in case.

Anyway, that's how he was just then, and it sort of threw me. I had that feeling again that maybe he didn't know what this was all about. But then, he had to know, didn't he? Because he'd done it.

I had the golf ball ready in my right hand and one of those stones in the other. He walked toward me.

I missed with the golf ball and got him with the stone.

And he fell down. He really fell down. He didn't say anything—he didn't even say "ouch," like I would have—he just fell down.

In the hay.

I didn't go out just yet. I sat and looked at him. And I listened. Nothing.

Do you know, there wasn't a sound in that whole place? It was as if everything had stopped because they knew what had happened.

My dad just lay there and we waited for what would happen next. It was me.

I mean, I made the first noise.

I said: "Dad?"

But nobody answered—not even my mother.

So I said it louder. "*Dad?*"

It was just as if they'd all gone away and left me with him, all alone.

He sure looked strange lying there—so quiet and everything. I didn't know what to do.

"Dad?"

I went over on my hands and knees.

Then suddenly they all came in. I just did what I thought of first. I guess it was because they scared me—coming like that when it was so quiet.

I got all the stones out of my pockets and threw them, one by one, as they came through the door. I stood up to do it. I saw them all running through the door, and I threw every stone, even at my mother.

And then I fell down. I fell down beside my dad and pushed him over on his back because he'd fallen on his stomach. It was like he was asleep.

They came up then and I don't remember much of that. Somebody picked me up, and there was the smell of perfume and my eyes hurt and I got something in my throat and nearly choked to death and I could hear a lot of talking. And somebody was whispering, too. And then I felt myself being carried down and there was the smell of oil and gasoline and some chickens had to be got out of the way again and then there was sunlight.

Then my mother just sat with me, and I guess I cried for a long time. In the cherry and plum-tree orchard—and she seemed to understand because she said that he would tell me all about it and that he hadn't written me because he didn't want to scare me when I was all alone at Arthur Robertson's.

And then Bud came.

My mother said that he should go away for a while. But he said: "I brought something" and she said: "What is it, then?" and now I remember where I got that worm in my handkerchief that I told you about.

It was from Bud.

He said to me that if I wanted to, he'd take me fishing on the lake just before the sun went down. He said that was a good time. And he gave me that worm because he'd found it.

So my mother took it and put it in my hankie and Bud looked at me for a minute and then went away.

The worst part was when I saw my dad again.

My mother took me to the place where he was sitting in the sun and we just watched each other for a long time.

Then he said: "Neil, your mother wants to take our picture because I'm going away tomorrow to Ottawa for a couple of weeks, and she thought I'd like a picture to take with me."

He lit a cigarette and then he said: "I would, too, you know, like that picture."

And I sort of said: "All right."

So they called to Bud, and my mother went to get her camera.

But before Bud came and before my mother got back, we were alone for about ten hours. It was awful.

I couldn't think of anything and I guess he couldn't, either. I had a good look at him, though.

He looked just like he does right there in that picture. You can see where the stone hit him on his right cheek—and the one that knocked him out is the one over the eye.

Right then the thing never got settled. Not in words, anyway. I was still thinking about that rink and everything—and my dad hadn't said anything about the army yet.

I wish I hadn't done it. Thrown those stones and everything. It wasn't his fault he had to go.

For another thing, I was sorry about the stones because I knew I wouldn't find any more like them—but I did throw them, and that's that.

They both got those little boxes, though—I made sure of that. And in one there was a string of red beads from Orillia and in the other there was a photograph.

There still is.

Notes

Muskoka a cottage and resort region in Ontario, approximately 200 km north of Toronto

Indian term originally used for First Nations peoples by European colonialists who thought they had landed in India when they arrived in North America. Today, a small number of First Nations do refer to themselves as Indians, but the most accurate term for Aboriginal people generally is First Nations, Native, or indigenous people.

Wild-root-cream-oil-Charlie a greasy cream that many young men used at the time to slick down unruly hair

Field Marshal traditionally, an officer of a very high rank in the British army

Activities

1. Reread the story, focusing specifically on the way in which Findley has captured the thoughts and feelings of a twelve-year-old boy who is looking back on events that happened when he was ten years old. Focus particularly on the explanations and interpretations that the narrator at the age of twelve offers for things he said and did at age ten. In what ways does the older version of the narrator understand more fully the significance of the events described in the story?

2. Find examples of vocabulary, expressions, and syntax in the story that are typical of a young person. What are some features of language that are used unconventionally to imitate the direct speech of a young person whose use of language is still developing?

3. At one point in his story, the narrator switches from normal narrative conventions to a dramatic version of a conversation held by the three boys. This part of the selection is set up more as a play than as a story. Explain how effectively this scene works as a piece of drama. Pick another episode in the story that would work well as a dramatic scene and rewrite it using the example provided by Findley as a model. Remember to make the dialogue specific to each character's personality. Prepare an oral or taped reading of your scene.

Another Viewpoint: Society

With a group of approximately six students, plan a symposium on the subject of war. Have each student select and read or view a work that focuses on war, such as the novel *All Quiet on the Western Front* (1929) by German author Erich Maria Remarque, paintings by Canadian designated "war artists" Frederick Varley or Molly Lamb Bobak, the non-fiction book *The Guns of August* (1962) by American author Barbara Tuchman, poetry by the British writer Wilfred Owen, or the American film *The Thin Red Line* (Fox Pictures, 2000). During your symposium, have each student articulate the impressions of and ideas about war evident in each text. Then explore some of the following questions: What characteristics are common to all wars, regardless of the era or location? How has war changed over the centuries? Is war today more dangerous than wars of previous eras? How does war affect the daily life of civil society? Can war ever be eradicated?

Peace and War

Moacyr Scliar

Translated by Tricia Feeney

Moacyr Scliar, born in 1937, is one of Brazil's most distinguished writers, and the most recognized voice of Brazilian-Jewish literature. He graduated from medical school and has written several short story collections, beginning with *The Carnival of the Animals*, in 1968. He writes in Portuguese, the official language of Brazil. Many of his stories have been translated into English and other languages. Scliar has been the recipient of many prizes, including the Guimaraes Rosa Prize. Scliar's recent novels focus on some of Brazil's famous historical figures. His work has been described as "magical and powerful." To what extent do you expect stories to be "magical" in the sense of taking you beyond the world and ideas that are familiar to you? How would you describe the relationship between fiction and reality in general?

I was late for the war; I had to take a taxi. A setback: with the recent fare increase, it was an unforeseen and unwelcome expense, a blow to my budget. Nevertheless, I arrived just in time to clock on, thereby avoiding greater problems. There was a long queue next to the clocking-on machine: I wasn't the only laggard. There was Walter, my trench colleague, grumbling: he'd had to take a taxi too. We were neighbours and we had entered the war almost at the same time. On the second Thursday of every month we caught the bus from the corner of the street, to take part in the hostilities.

"I'm fed up with this business," said Walter.

"So am I," I replied.

Sighing, we punched our cards and headed for the administration shed where the cloakroom had temporarily (more than fifteen years ago) been installed.

"Late today?" asked the youth in charge of the cloakroom.

We didn't bother to reply. We took the keys to our lockers. We quickly changed our clothes, putting on our old campaign uniforms, collected our rifles and ammunition (twenty cartridges) and made our way to the front line.

The setting for the conflict was open country, on the outskirts of the city. The battlefield was fenced off with barbed wire posted with signboards: WAR, KEEP OUT. An unnecessary warning: few people came there to that place of cottages and summer retreats.

We, the soldiers, occupied a trench almost two kilometres long. An enemy, whom we never saw, was about one kilometre away, also entrenched. The ground between the two trenches was strewn with debris: wrecked armoured cars and tanks mingled with the bones of horses, a reminder of a time when the struggle had been fierce. Now the conflict had entered a stable phase—a holding operation, in the words of our commander. Battles no longer occurred. The only piece of advice they gave us was not to get out of the trench. A problem for me: my younger son wanted an empty shell cartridge, which I had not been able to obtain. The boy kept asking for it; I could do nothing.

We went down into the trench, Walter and I. The place was not altogether uncomfortable. We had tables, chairs, a small stove, cooking utensils, not to mention a record-player and a portable TV. I suggested a game of cards.

"Later," he said. He was examining his rifle with a furrowed brow and an air of annoyance.

"This lousy thing doesn't work any more," he announced.

"Well," I said, "it's over fifteen years old, it's already given all it had to give." And I offered him my weapon. At that moment we heard a crack and the whine of a bullet over our heads.

"That was close," I said.

"Those idiots," grumbled Walter. "One of these days they'll end up hurting someone." He took my weapon, stood up and fired two shots into the air.

"Let that be a warning to you," he shouted, and sat down again. An orderly appeared, with a cordless telephone: "Your wife, Mr. Walter."

"The devil take her!" he exclaimed. "Even here she won't leave me in peace." He picked up the phone.

"Hello! Yes, it's me. I'm fine. Of course I'm fine. No, nothing's happened to me, I've already told you I'm fine. I know you get nervous, but there's no need. Everything's all right. I'm well wrapped up, it's not raining. Did you hear? Everything's fine. No need to apologize. I understand. Bye bye."

"What a pain that woman is," he said, handing the telephone back to the orderly. I said nothing. I too had a problem with my wife, but a different one: she didn't believe that we were at war. She suspected I spent the day in a motel. I would have liked to explain to her what sort of war this was, but to tell the truth I didn't know. No one did. It was a very confusing thing; so much so that a commission had been set up to study the situation. The chairman of the commission came to visit us from time to time, and complained about the car he'd been given for his tours of inspection: an old banger, according to him. For reasons of economy they refused to change it.

All was quiet on the front that morning; one of us fired a shot, those on the other side replied, and that was it. At midday they served lunch. Green salad, roast meat and Greek rice, followed by a tasteless pudding.

"This is getting worse and worse," complained Walter. The orderly asked him if he thought he was in a restaurant, or what. Walter didn't reply.

We lay down for our afternoon nap and slept peacefully. When we awoke, night was falling.

"I think I'll be off now," I said to Walter. He couldn't come with me: he was on duty that night. I went to the cloakroom, changed my clothes.

"How was the war?" the cheeky youth asked.

"Fine," I replied, "just fine." I called into admin to collect my cheque from a sour-faced official. I signed the three copies of the receipt. I got to the bus stop in plenty of time.

At home, my wife was waiting for me in her leotard. I'm ready, she said, drily. I went to the bedroom and put on my kit. We went into the study, climbed on to our ergometric bicycles.

"Where were we, then?" I asked.

"You never seem to know," she replied. She picked up the map, studied it for a moment and said: "Bisceglie, on the Adriatic coast."

We began to pedal furiously. Two hours later, when we stopped, we were near Molfetta, still on the Adriatic. We're hoping to do Italy in a year. After that, we'll see. I don't like to make long-term plans; because of the war, naturally, but even more because keeping the future unknown is a source of permanent excitement.

Notes

clock on to sign in to work

Bisceglie, Molfetta Italian towns on the Adriatic Sea

Activities

1. Write a short response to the story, focusing on your first reactions. If you were describing this story to a friend, what key points would you include? What connections can you make between this story and other works you have viewed or read?

2. In a group, discuss this story's meaning and theme. To what extent could this story be described as a parable? If you consider it to be a parable, what does the story represent? Be prepared to defend your interpretation by providing convincing evidence and sound reasoning.

3. Scliar provides a detailed description of the setting in which the conflict is taking place. Reread the story, recording specific descriptive details that contribute to vivid visual images. Use this information to create a visual representation of the setting using a medium of your choice. Compare your representation with those of other students. How did this activity enhance or change your interpretation of the story?

THE SPIRIT OF HAIDA GWAII

Bill Reid

About the Visual   One of Canada's most renowned artists, Bill Reid was born in Victoria, British Columbia, in 1920 into the Haida First Nation. During his life, he received an impressive list of honours, including the Lifetime National Aboriginal Achievement Award. He died in 1998. *The Spirit of Haida Gwaii* is located in the Canadian Embassy in Washington, D.C. Reid said that his sculpture made no political or artistic statement: he only wanted to thank the mythical Haida figures, depicted in the canoe, who had given his life meaning. How might a political statement be different from an artistic one? In what ways might mythical figures contribute to a person's meaning of life?

Activities

1. As you view the photograph of *The Spirit of Haida Gwaii*, list every item you see, beginning with whatever first catches your eye. Without using any evaluative language, make your list of items as descriptive and detailed as possible, including the shapes, lines, and forms, and the position and juxtaposition of the sculpture's parts. Share your list with others in the class.

2. In *The Spirit of Haida Gwaii*, Reid has packed many figures into a confined space. This compression of energies is an underlying principle of Haida art. What mood or feeling does this "containment" produce? How might the impact of the piece change if the canoe were larger or if there were fewer passengers?

1991, black bronze, L. 6 m x H. 3.5 m

Mazes

Ursula K. Le Guin

Ursula K. Le Guin was born in Berkeley, California, in 1929. Her father was a renowned anthropologist and her mother a writer. She attended Harvard University and Columbia University. Her first published work appeared in 1962. Le Guin is celebrated primarily for her writing in the fields of science fiction and fantasy. Among her awards are five HUGOS, five Nebulas, and the National Book Award. Le Guin, who is also a poet and essayist, has said, "I don't write stories to make a point or push opinions. In fact, usually I write a story and only find out what I was thinking or telling...when I read it afterwards." What types of writing benefit from planning? Is there a type of writing that benefits from a stream-of-consciousness approach and, if so, why?

I have tried hard to use my wits and keep up my courage, but I know now that I will not be able to withstand the torture any longer. My perceptions of time are confused, but I think it has been several days since I realized I could no longer keep my emotions under aesthetic control, and now the physical breakdown is also nearly complete. I cannot accomplish any of the greater motions. I cannot speak. Breathing, in this heavy foreign air, grows more difficult. When the paralysis reaches my chest I shall die: probably tonight.

The alien's cruelty is refined, yet irrational. If it intended all along to starve me, why not simply withhold food? But instead of that it gave me plenty of food, mountains of food, all the greenbud leaves I could possibly want. Only they were not fresh. They had been picked; they were dead; the element that makes them digestible to us was gone, and one might as well eat gravel. Yet there they were, with all the scent and shape of greenbud, irresistible to my craving appetite. Not at first, of course. I told myself, I am not a child, to eat picked leaves! But the belly gets the better of the mind. After a while it seemed better to be chewing something, anything, that might still the pain and craving in the gut. So I ate, and ate, and starved. It is a relief, now, to be so weak I cannot eat.

The same elaborately perverse cruelty marks all its behaviour. And the worst thing of all is just the one I welcomed with such relief and delight at first: the maze. I was badly disoriented at first, after the trapping, being handled by a giant, being dropped into a prison; and this place around the prison is disorienting, spatially disquieting, the strange, smooth, curved wall-ceiling is of an alien substance and its lines are meaningless to me. So when I was taken up and put down, amidst all this strangeness, in a maze, a recognizable, even familiar maze, it was a moment of strength and hope after great distress. It seemed pretty clear that I had been put in the maze as a kind of test or investigation, that a fast approach toward communication was being attempted. I tried to co-operate in every way. But it was not possible to believe for very long that the creature's purpose was to achieve communication.

It is intelligent, highly intelligent, that is clear from a thousand evidences. We are both intelligent creatures, we are both maze-builders: surely it would be quite easy to learn to talk together! If that were what the alien wanted. But it is not. I do not know what kind of mazes it builds for itself. The ones it made for me were instruments of torture.

The mazes were, as I said, of basically familiar types, though the walls were of that foreign material much colder and smoother than packed clay. The alien left a pile of picked leaves in one extremity of each maze, I do not know why; it may be a ritual or superstition. The first maze it put me in was babyishly short and simple. Nothing expressive or even interesting could be worked out from it. The second, however, was a kind of simple version of the Ungated Affirmation, quite adequate for the reassuring outreaching statement I wanted to make. And the last, the long maze, with seven corridors and nineteen connections, lent itself surprisingly well to the Maluvian mode, and indeed to almost all the New Expressionist techniques. Adaptations had to be made to the alien spatial understanding, but a certain quality of creativity arose precisely from the adaptations. I worked hard at the problem of that maze, planning all night long, re-imagining the lines and spaces, the feints and pauses, the erratic, unfamiliar, and yet beautiful course of the True Run. Next day when I was placed in the long maze and the alien began to observe, I performed the Eighth Maluvian in its entirety.

It was not a polished performance. I was nervous, and the spatio-temporal parameters were only approximate. But the Eighth Maluvian survives the crudest performance in the poorest maze. The evolutions in the ninth encatenation, where the "cloud" theme recurs so strangely transposed into the ancient spiralling motif, are indestructibly beautiful. I have seen them performed by a very old person, so old and stiff-jointed that he could only suggest the movements, hint at them, a shadow-gesture, a dim reflection of the themes: and all who watched were inexpressibly moved. There is no nobler statement of our being. Performing, I myself was carried away by the power of the motions and forgot that I was a prisoner, forgot the alien eyes watching me; I transcended the errors of the maze and my own weakness, and danced the Eighth Maluvian as I have never danced it before.

When it was done, the alien picked me up and set me down in the first maze—the short one, the maze for little children who have not yet learned how to talk.

Was the humiliation deliberate? Now that it is all past, I see that there is no way to know. But it remains very hard to ascribe its behaviour to ignorance.

After all, it is not blind. It has eyes, recognizable eyes. They are enough like our eyes that it must see somewhat as we do. It has a mouth, four legs, can move bipedally, has grasping hands, etc.; for all its gigantism and strange looks, it seems less fundamentally different from us, physically, than a fish. And yet, fish school and dance and, in their own stupid way, communicate! The alien has never once attempted to talk with me. It has been with me, watched me, touched me, handled me, for days: but all its motions have been purposeful, not communicative. It is evidently a solitary creature, totally self-absorbed.

This would go far to explain its cruelty.

I noticed early that from time to time it would move its curious horizontal mouth in a series of fairly delicate, repetitive gestures, a little like someone eating. At first I thought it was jeering at me; then I wondered if it was trying to urge me to eat the indigestible fodder; then I wondered if it could be communicating *labially*. It seemed a limited and unhandy language for one so well provided with hands, feet, limbs, flexible spine, and all; but that would be like the creature's perversity, I thought. I studied its lip-motions and tried hard to imitate them. It did not respond. It stared at me briefly and then went away.

In fact, the only indubitable *response* I ever got from it was on a pitifully low level of interpersonal aesthetics. It was tormenting me with knob-pushing, as it did once a day. I had endured this grotesque routine pretty patiently for the first several days. If I pushed one knob I got a nasty sensation in my feet, if I pushed a second I got a nasty pellet of dried-up food, if I pushed a third I got nothing whatever. Obviously, to demonstrate my intelligence I was to push the third knob. But it appeared that my intelligence irritated my captor, because it removed the neutral knob after the second day. I could not imagine what it was trying to establish or accomplish, except the fact that I was its prisoner and a great deal smaller than it. When I tried to leave the knobs, it forced me physically to return. I must sit there pushing knobs for it, receiving punishment from one and mockery from the other. The deliberate outrageousness of the situation, the insufferable heaviness and thickness of this air, the feeling of being forever watched yet never understood, all combined to drive me into a condition for which we have no description at all. The nearest thing I can suggest is the last interlude of the Ten Gate Dream, when all the feintways are closed and the dance narrows in and in until it bursts terribly into the vertical. I cannot say what I felt, but it was a little like that. If I got my feet stung once more, or got pelted once more with a lump of rotten food, I would go vertical forever... I took the knobs off the wall (they came off with a sharp tug, like flowerbuds), laid them in the middle of the floor, and defecated on them.

The alien took me up at once and returned to my prison. It had got the message, and had acted on it. But how unbelievably primitive the message had had to be! And the next day, it put me back in the knob room, and there were the knobs as good as new, and I was to choose alternate punishments for its amusement... Until then I had told myself that the creature was alien, therefore incomprehensible and uncomprehending, perhaps not intelligent in the same manner as we, and so on. But since then I have known that, though all that may remain true, it is also unmistakably and grossly cruel.

When it put me into the baby maze yesterday, I could not move. The power of speech was all but gone (I am dancing this, of course, in my mind; "the best maze is the mind," the old proverb goes) and I simply crouched there, silent. After a while it took me out again, gently enough. There is the ultimate perversity of its behaviour: it has never once touched me cruelly.

It set me down in the prison, locked the gate, and filled up the trough with inedible food. Then it stood two-legged, looking at me for a while.

Its face is very mobile, but if it speaks with its face I cannot understand it, that is too foreign a language. And its body is always covered with bulky, binding mats, like an old widower who has taken the Vow of Silence. But I had become accustomed to its great size, and to the angular character of its limb-positions, which at first had seemed to be saying a steady stream of incoherent and mispronounced phrases, a horrible nonsense-dance like the motions of an imbecile, until I realized that they were strictly purposive movements. Now I saw something a little beyond that, in its position. There were no words, yet there was communication. I saw, as it stood watching me, a clear signification of angry sadness—as clear as the Sembrian Stance. There was the same lax immobility, the bentness, the assertion of defeat. Never a word came clear, and yet it told me that it was filled with resentment, pity, impatience, and frustration. It told me it was sick of torturing me, and wanted me to help it. I am sure I understood it. I tried to answer. I tried to say, "What is it you want of me? Only tell me what it is you want." But I was too weak to speak clearly, and it did not understand. It has never understood.

And now I have to die. No doubt it will come in to watch me die; but it will not understand the dance I dance in dying.

Notes

aesthetic related to beauty and good taste; from the Greek word *aisthetikos*, meaning "of sense perception"

perverse persistent in going against what is expected or considered to be right

feint a false movement intended to deceive the viewer; from the Old French *feindre*, meaning "to feign"

parameter a limit or boundary

motif a recurring element or theme in an artistic or literary work; originally a French word meaning "motive"

labially using the lips

indubitable unquestionable, without a doubt

feintways false passages or parts

Activities

1. In your journal, make a list of issues about human nature and interaction with alien beings that are raised in this story. What is your response to Le Guin's views on these subjects? Share your ideas with the class. After the discussion, make notes on aspects of speaking and listening which you find difficult. Then list strategies for improving your performance.

2. What does the narrator reveal about the captor? Reread the story, noting passages where the captor's behaviour and attitudes are described. How does the author's use of irony affect your response to these descriptions?

3. Why do you think Le Guin chose not to provide a physical description of the alien narrator in the story? Imagine that you have been given the task of creating an illustration for "Mazes." What medium and visual style will you choose? How can you balance the author's style with your need to represent the content? In a group, present and discuss your illustrations. Assess the choices you made in your illustration and consider how its impact might be strengthened.

Was It a Dream?

Guy de Maupassant

Translated by Marjorie Laurie

Guy de Maupassant is considered to be the greatest French writer of short stories. He was born in 1850 in Normandy, studied law in Paris, served in the army during the Franco-Prussian War, and worked as a civil servant. De Maupassant's productivity was remarkable: three hundred stories, six novels, three travel books, and one volume of verse. His writing is characterized by strong, naturalistic language and keen observations of human life. He died at the age of forty-three in Paris, in 1893. In your opinion, is tragic love or fulfilled love a better subject for a story? What examples of each type can you provide to explain your choice?

I had loved her madly!

Yesterday I returned to Paris, and when I saw my room again—our room, our bed, our furniture, everything that remains of the life of a human being after death—I was seized by such a violent attack of fresh grief that I felt like opening the window and throwing myself out into the street. I could not remain between these walls which had sheltered her, which retained a thousand atoms of her, of her skin and of her breath. I took up my hat to make my escape, and just as I reached the door I passed the large mirror in the hall, which she had put there so that she might look at herself every day from head to foot as she went out, from her little boots to her bonnet.

I stopped short in front of that looking glass in which she had so often been reflected—so often, so often, that it must have retained her reflection. I was standing there trembling, with my eyes fixed on the glass—on that flat, profound, empty glass—which had contained her entirely and had possessed her as much as I. I felt as if I loved that glass. I touched it; it was cold. Sorrowful mirror, burning mirror, horrible mirror, to make men suffer such torments! Happy is the man whose heart forgets everything that it has contained.

I went out without knowing it toward the cemetery. I found her simple grave, a white marble cross, with these few words:

She loved, was loved, and died.

She is there below. I sobbed with my forehead on the ground, and I stopped there for a long time. Then I saw it was getting dark, and a strange, mad wish, the wish of a despairing lover, seized me. I wished to pass the night in weeping on her grave. But I should be seen and driven out. How was I to manage? I was cunning and got up and began to roam that city of the dead. I walked and walked. How small this city is in comparison with the city in which we live. And yet how much more numerous the dead are than the living. We need high houses, wide streets, and much room. And for all the generations of the dead, there is scarcely anything. The earth takes them back. Adieu!

At the end of the cemetery, I was in its oldest part, where the crosses themselves are decayed. It is full of untended roses, of strong and dark cypress trees—a sad and beautiful garden.

I was perfectly alone. So I crouched under a green tree and hid myself amid the thick and sombre branches.

When it was quite dark, I left my refuge and began to walk softly. I wandered about for a long time, but could not find her tomb again. I went on with extended arms, knocking against the tombs with my hands, my feet, my knees, my chest, even with my head, without being able to find her. I groped about like a blind man; I felt the stones, the crosses, the iron railings, and the wreaths of faded flowers. I read the names with my fingers. I could not find her again!

There was no moon. What a night! I was horribly frightened in those narrow paths between two rows of graves. I sat down on one of them, for I could not walk any longer; my knees were so weak. I could hear my heart beat! And I heard something else as well. What? A confused, nameless noise. Was the noise in my head, in the impenetrable night, or beneath the mysterious earth? I looked all around me: I was paralyzed with terror, cold with fright, ready to shout out, ready to die.

Suddenly it seemed to me that the slab of marble on which I was sitting was moving. As if it were being raised. With a bound I sprang onto the neighbouring tomb, and I distinctly saw the stone which I had just quitted rise upright. Then the dead person appeared, pushing the stone back with its bent back. I saw it quite clearly, although the night was so dark. On the cross I could read:

> Here lies Jacques Olivant,
> who died at the age of fifty-one.
> He loved his family,
> was kind and honourable,
> and died in the grace of the Lord.

The dead man also read what was inscribed on the tombstone; then he picked up a stone off the path, a little, pointed stone, and began to scrape the letters carefully. He slowly effaced them, and with the hollows of his eyes he looked at the place where they had been engraved. Then, with the tip of the bone that had been his forefinger, he wrote in luminous letters:

> Here reposes Jacques Olivant,
> who died at the age of fifty-one.
> He hastened his father's death by his unkindness, as
> he wished to inherit his fortune;
> he tortured his wife,
> tormented his children,
> deceived his neighbours,
> robbed everyone he could,
> and died wretched.

When he had finished writing, the dead man stood motionless, looking at his work. On turning around, I saw that all the graves were open, that all the dead had emerged, and that all had effaced the lines inscribed on their gravestones by their relations, substituting the truth instead. And I saw that all had been tormentors of their neighbours—malicious, dishonest, hypocrites, liars, rogues; that they had stolen, deceived, performed every disgraceful, every abominable action, these good fathers, these faithful wives, these devoted sons, these chaste daughters, these honest tradesmen. They were all writing at the same time, on the threshold of their eternal abode, the truth, the terrible and the holy truth, of which everybody was ignorant, or pretended to be ignorant while they were alive.

I thought that *she* also must have written something on her tombstone; and now, running without any fear, I went toward her, sure that I should find her immediately. I recognized her at once without seeing her face, and on the marble cross where shortly before I had read:

> She loved, was loved, and died.

I now saw:

> Having gone out in the rain one day
> in order to deceive her lover,
> she caught cold and died.

It appears they found me at daybreak, lying on the grave, unconscious.

Activities

1. With a group, reflect on the different ways of interpreting the title of the story. Which one do you think best fits the story? What answer would you give to this interpretation of the title? Consider what the author's purpose might have been in choosing an ambiguous title. Keep notes during your discussion and share your ideas with the rest of the class.

2. Author Henry James wrote that de Maupassant's axiom seemed to be "that you produce the effect of truth better by painting people from the outside than from the inside." Consider how this statement applies to "Was It a Dream?" Discuss the notion of *truth* as it is depicted in the story.

3. Imagine the scene that might take place in this narrative when a police officer and a cemetery groundskeeper awaken the narrator in the morning. Work in groups of three to write and then act out this conversation for the class. Have your classmates assess your work in terms of how effectively you use dialogue to reveal character.

Another Viewpoint: Literary Modes and Forms

Guy de Maupassant is considered a key figure in the development of the short story as a literary form. Using a variety of primary and secondary sources, write a research essay on the history of the short story as a genre. Be sure to cite specific writers from a variety of cultures as examples.

From

No Great Mischief

Alistair MacLeod

Alistair MacLeod was born in North Battleford, Saskatchewan, in 1936. As a child, he moved with his family to Nova Scotia, and he has been linked with the landscape and the people of Cape Breton ever since. Known primarily as a writer of short fiction, MacLeod wrote his first novel, *No Great Mischief*, to great acclaim when he was in his sixties. It won the prestigious international IMPAC Award in 2001, as well as the Trillium Prize in 2000. MacLeod's fiction explores individual Maritimers against a timeless backdrop of universal human nature. Does all literature contain "universal messages"? Whether you agree or not, do you think a requirement of good fiction should be that it include a message or meaning that can be applied to all of humanity?

My twin sister and I were the youngest children in our family, and we were three on March 28 when it was decided that we would spend the night with our grandparents.

After he returned from naval service in the war, my father had applied for the position of lightkeeper on the island which seemed almost to float in the channel about a mile and half from the town which faced the sea. He had long been familiar with boats and the sea and, after passing the examination, was informed in a very formal letter that the job was his. He and my mother were overjoyed because it meant they would not have to go away, and the job reeked of security, which was what they wanted after the disruption of the years of war. The older generation was highly enthusiastic as well. "That island will stay there for a damn long time," said Grandpa appreciatively, although he later apparently sniffed, "Any fool can look after a lighthouse. It is not like being responsible for a *whole* hospital."

On the morning of March 28, which was the beginning of a weekend, my parents and their six children and their dog walked ashore across the ice. Their older sons, who were sixteen, fifteen, and fourteen, apparently took turns carrying my sister and me upon their shoulders, stopping every so often to take off their mitts and rub our faces so that our cheeks would not become so cold as to be frozen without our realizing it. Our father, accompanied by our brother Colin, who was eleven, walked ahead of us, testing the ice from time to time with a long pole, although there did not seem much need to do so for he had "bushed" the ice some two months earlier, meaning he had placed spruce trees upright in the snow and ice to serve as a sort of road guide for winter travellers.

During the coldest days of winter, the so-called "dog days," the ice became amazingly solid. It was a combination of drift ice from the region of the eastern Arctic and "made" ice which resulted from the freezing of the local channel. In extremely cold winters if the ice was smooth, it was possible to move freely from the island to the mainland and back again. One could walk, or skate, or fashion an iceboat which would skim and veer with cutting dangerous speed across the stinging surface. People would venture out on the ice with cars and trucks, and on one or two weekends there would be horse races to the delight of all. The sharpshod horses would pull light sleighs or even summer sulkies as they sped around yet another track staked out by temporary spruce. At the conclusion of their races, their owners would hurry to cover them with blankets as the perspiration on their coats began to turn to frost. They seemed almost, for a few brief moments, to be horses who had prematurely aged before the eyes of those who watched them, their coats of black and brown turning to a fragile white. White horses frozen on a field of ice and snow.

My parents welcomed the winter ice because it allowed them to do many practical things that were more difficult to accomplish in the summer. They could truck their supplies over the ice without the difficulty of first hauling everything to the wharf and then trying to load it on the boat which swayed below and then, after sporting it across to the island, having to hoist it up out of the boat to the wharf's cap and then again having to transport it up the cliff to the promontory where the lighthouse stood. They took coal and wood across in the winter, and walked and traded animals, leading them by their halters across the treacherous and temporary bridge.

Also in the winter their social life improved, as unexpected visitors crossed to see them, bringing rum and beer and fiddles and accordions. All of them staying up all night, singing songs and dancing and playing cards and telling stories, while out on the ice the seals moaned and cried and the ice itself thundered and snapped and sometimes groaned, forced by the pressures of the tides and currents, running unabated and unseen beneath the cold white surface. Sometimes the men would go outside to urinate and when they would return the others would ask, "*De chuala?*" "What did you hear?" "Nothing," they would say. "*Cha chuala sion.*" "Nothing, only the sound of the ice."

On March 28 there was a lot for my family to do. My older brothers were going to visit their cousins in the country—those who still lived in the old *Calum Ruadh* houses neighbouring the spot which my grandparents had left when they became people of the town. If they could get a ride they were going to spend the weekend there. Even if they could not get a ride, they were planning to walk, saying that ten miles on the inland sheltered roads would not be as cold as a mile and a half straight across the ice. My parents were planning to cash my father's cheque, which they hoped my grandparents had picked up at the post office, and my brother Colin was looking forward to his new parka, which my mother had shrewdly ordered from the Eaton's sale catalogue when such heavy winter garments were reduced by the coming promise of spring. He had been hoping for it since before Christmas. My sister and I were looking forward to the visit with our grandparents, who always made a great to-do about us and always told us how smart we were to make such a great journey from such a far and distant place. And the dog knew where she was going too, picking her way across the ice carefully and sometimes stopping to gnaw off the balls of snow and ice which formed between the delicate pads of her hardened paws.

Everything went well and the sun shone brightly as we journeyed forth together, walking first upon the ice so we could later walk upon the land.

In the late afternoon, the sun still shone, and there was no wind but it began to get very cold, the kind of deceptive cold that can fool those who confuse the shining of the winter sun with warmth. Relatives visiting my grandparents' house said that my brothers had arrived at their destination and would not be coming back until, perhaps, the next day.

My parents distributed their purchases into haversacks, which were always at my grandparents' house, and which they used for carrying supplies upon their backs. Because my parents' backs would be burdened and because my brothers were not there, it was decided that my sister and I would "spend the night" and that our brothers would take us back to the island when they returned. It was suggested that Colin also might stay, but he was insistent that he go, so that he might test the long-anticipated warmth of the new parka. When they left, the sun was still shining, although it had begun to decline, and they took two storm lanterns which might serve as lights or signs and signals for the last part of the trip. My mother carried one and Colin the other, while my father grasped the ice pole in his hand. When they set out, they first had to walk about a mile along the shore until they reached the appropriate place to "get on" the ice and then they started across, following the route of the spruce trees which my father had set out.

Everyone could see their three dark forms and the smaller one of the dog outlined upon the whiteness over which they travelled. By the time they were halfway across, it was dusk and out there on the ice they lit their lanterns, and that too was seen from the shore. And then they continued on their way. Then the lanterns seemed to waver and almost to dance wildly, and one described an arc in what was now the darkness and then was still. Grandpa watched for almost a minute to be sure of what he was seeing and then he shouted to my grandmother, "There is something wrong out on the ice. There is only one light and it is not moving."

My grandmother came quickly to the window. "Perhaps they stopped," she said. "Perhaps they're resting. Perhaps they had to adjust their packs. Perhaps they had to relieve themselves."

"But there is only one light," said Grandpa, "and it is not moving at all."

"Perhaps that's it," said Grandma hopefully. "The other light blew out and they're trying to get it started."

My sister and I were playing on the kitchen floor with Grandma's cutlery. We were playing "store," taking turns buying the spoons and knives and forks from each other with a supply of pennies from a jar Grandma kept in her lower cupboard for emergencies.

"The light is still not moving," said Grandpa and he began hurriedly to pull on his winter clothes and boots, even as the phone began ringing. "The light is not moving. The light is not moving," the voices said. "They're in trouble out on the ice."

And then the voices spoke in the hurriedness of exchange: "Take a rope." "Take some ice poles." "Take a blanket that we can use as a stretcher." "Take brandy." "We will meet you at the corner. Don't start across without us."

"I have just bought all his spoons and knives," said my sister proudly from the kitchen floor, "and I still have all these pennies left."

"Good for you," said Grandma. "A penny saved is a penny earned."

When they were partway to the shore, their lights picked up the dog's eyes, and she ran to Grandpa when he called to her in Gaelic, and she leaped up to his chest and his outstretched arms and licked his face even as he threw his mitts from his hands so he could bury them deep within the fur upon her back,

"She was coming to get us," he said. "They've gone under."

"Not under," someone said. "Perhaps down but not under."

"I think under," said Grandpa. "She was under, anyway. She's soaked to the spine. She's smart and she's a good swimmer and she's got a heavy, layered coat. If she just went down, she'd be down and up in a second but she's too wet for that. She must have gone down, and then the current carried her under the ice and she had to swim back to the hole to get herself back out."

They went out on the ice in single file, the string of their moving lights seeming almost like a kind of Christmas decoration; each light moving to the rhythm of the man who walked and carried it in his hand.

They followed the tracks and walked towards the light which remained permanent in the ice. As they neared it, they realized it was sitting on the ice, sitting upright by itself and not held by any hand. The tracks continued until they came to the open water, and then there were no more.

Years later, my sister and I were in Grade XI and the teacher was talking to the class about Wordsworth and, as an example, was reading to us from the poem entitled "Lucy Gray." When she came to the latter lines, both my sister and I started simultaneously and looked towards each other, as if in the old, but new to us, we had stumbled upon the familiar experience:

"They followed from the snowy bank
Those footmarks, one by one,
Into the middle of the plank;
And further there were none!"

"And further there were none!" But on March 28 we were tiring of our game of store and putting the cutlery away as our grandmother prepared to ready us for bed while glancing anxiously through the window.

Out on the ice the dog began to whine when they came near the open water, and the first men in the line lay on their stomachs, each holding the feet of the man before him, so that they might form a type of human chain with their weight distributed more evenly than if they remained standing. But it was of no use, for other than the light there was nothing, and the ice seemed solid right up to the edge of the dark and sloshing void.

There was nothing for the men to do but wonder. Beyond the crater, the rows of spruce trees marched on in ordered single file in much the same way that they led up to the spot of their interruption. It was thought that perhaps only one tree had gone down and under. The section of the ice that had gone was not large, but as my grandfather said, "It was more than big enough for us."

The tide was going out when they vanished, leaving nothing but a lantern—perhaps tossed on to the ice by a sinking hand and miraculously landing upright and continuing to glow, or perhaps, set down after its arc, wildly but carefully by a hand which sought to reach another.

The men performed a sort of vigil out on the ice, keeping the hole broken open with their ice poles and waiting for the tide to run its course. And in the early hours of the morning when the tide was in its change, my brother Colin surfaced in one of those half-expected uncertainties known only to those who watch the sea. The white fur hood of his parka broke the surface and the half-frozen men who were crouched like patient Inuit around the hole shouted to one another, and reached for him with their poles. They thought that he had not been a great distance under, or that his clothes had snagged beneath the ice; and they thought that, perhaps, since he was not bearing a backpack, he had not been so heavily burdened and, perhaps, the new material in his parka possessed flotation qualities that had buoyed him to the top. His eyes were open and the drawstrings of his hood were still neatly tied and tucked beside his throat in the familiar manner that my mother always used.

My parents were not found that day, or the next, or in the days or months that followed.

Notes

drift ice a piece of ice carried along by water currents

sulkies a two-wheeled, single-person vehicle pulled by a horse, which is used in trotting races

Calum Ruadh a Gaelic phrase meaning "the red Calum," which is the nickname for a character in the novel *No Great Mischief*, from which this excerpt is taken

Activities

1. What emotional response do you think the author intends his narrative to elicit from his audience? By what means does he invoke this emotional response in his readers? What lasting impression, if any, will you take away from this narrative?

2. MacLeod has said about his writing, "I like to give the impression that I am telling the story rather than writing the story." Reread the excerpt to see to what extent this statement applies to this excerpt from *No Great Mischief*. Locate at least three sentences or passages which have the feel of oral storytelling. Write two or three sentences explaining each of your choices. Share your ideas with your classmates and then discuss any advantages and disadvantages of this style of writing.

3. Imagine that this narrative will be read aloud on the radio and it is your job to select accompanying music. Locate three or more appropriate vocal or instrumental selections to be played as an introduction, interlude, and fade-out to the reading. Prepare a verbal pitch you would present to the producer of the program, explaining how your musical choices would contribute to the listeners' enjoyment and understanding of the narrative.

Another Viewpoint: Culture

Many prominent Canadian writers and literary critics, such as Margaret Atwood in her book *Survival: A Thematic Guide to Canadian Literature* (1972), have noted that a central preoccupation and symbol in Canadian texts has been survival. With the class, discuss different ways in which the concept of survival is manifested: What circumstances are people surviving? Then read Alistair Macleod's entire novel *No Great Mischief* and compare it with other instances in Canadian literature in which individuals survive—or do not survive—their circumstances. Have a group discussion on which characteristics of Canadian culture contribute to a focus on survival.

wrap-up
short fiction

1. Write a formal comparative essay in which you discuss the treatment of the same or a similar theme in two of the stories in this unit. Have a classmate review a complete draft of your essay to help you strengthen its content and improve its organization. Ask your classmate to evaluate such features of the draft as a clear thesis statement, logical connections between key ideas, and the reinforcement of arguments through the use of compelling evidence.

2. Identify two or three stories in this unit that you think have strong poetic qualities. Outline in a chart what those poetic qualities are and how the stories you have selected exemplify them. Present your thoughts to the class. In a panel discussion, compare your choice of stories and ideas with those of two other classmates who have participated in this activity. In your presentation and subsequent discussion, be sure to include and accurately use pertinent academic and theoretical concepts and language.

3. On your own or with a partner, choose a story in this unit that made a strong impression on you. Next, use the Internet to do research on how to form and run a reading group. Write a two- to three-page guide for creating a reading group to explore this story. In it, provide specific questions for a group discussion and include concise background on the author and his or her work as it relates to the questions you have devised. Use a desktop publishing program to write, format, and publish your guide, adding appropriate graphics to enhance your publication.

4. Work with a group to create a radio play script for characters from at least two of the stories in this unit. In discussing and preparing your script, assign roles within your group, such as a director, researchers to scan stories and recommend characters, actors to perform the radio play, and technicians to take charge of background music and sound effects. Audiotape your play and present it to the class. In a post-presentation discussion, elicit feedback from your classmates on the strengths of your performance and areas for improvement.

Contrasting, often opposing, cosmic and moral forces (such as light and dark, virtue and vice) are common in many mythological and belief systems. In Hindu mythology, Durga is one of the manifestations of the goddess Devi. A many-armed warrior seated on a tiger, Durga represents benevolence. Here, Durga battles the monster Mahisha, a colossal water-buffalo, representing the forces of malevolence.

Can you remember watching a movie or reading a story and thinking, "The same thing has happened to me"? Maybe an event in a book or film reminded you of an incident in the life of someone you know or of another story you have come across. Narratives, regardless of their literary forms or specific historical or cultural contexts, spring from themes or patterns that are universal. These themes and patterns—such as self-discovery, love, and the cycles of days and seasons—are known as *archetypes*. Archetypes are truthful, essential prototypes of characters or events that provide a blueprint for the individual experiences that make up real life. Archetypes can be considered a reflection of what has been called the *collective unconscious*, a shared body of knowledge, assumptions, and interpretations that an entire culture holds, sometimes without even being aware of it. An archetypal approach to literature reveals recurring patterns and themes in myths, folklore, literature, and art—even in cultures widely separated by time and space.

Some archetypes express the way in which individuals experience the world—in roles such as the hero, rebel, or star-crossed lover. Other archetypes explore the situations in which we find ourselves and the journeys we undertake—such as initiation, loss of innocence, or death of a loved one. Part of what gives literature its power and primacy is the way it attracts its reader by creating interest on multiple levels. When we immerse ourselves in texts, we experience these archetypal patterns, universal themes, and literary modes and consciously or unconsciously integrate them into our lives.

This In-Depth includes a variety of selections that highlight such archetypal patterns and concepts as duty, passage of seasons, and utopia. Excerpts from Northrop Frye's classic essay "The Archetypes of Literature" describe the archetypes and patterns prevalent in narratives. In an interview, Joseph Campbell talks about heroes in mythology. The short story "Araby" by James Joyce, with its quest motif, follows the structure of a medieval romance. The poem "Ode to the West Wind" by Percy Bysshe Shelley and "Utopian Dreams," a book review by Val Ross, contain many of the ideals about rebirth and new beginnings also associated with the literary mode of romance. As you explore this section, consider ways in which universal themes and patterns create ties and common understanding in communities and cultures that you know. (To find related activities on archetypal patterns and literary modes and forms, see the references in the Another Viewpoint Index on page 714.)

From The Archetypes of Literature

Northrop Frye

Canadian literary critic Northrop Frye was born in Sherbrooke, Quebec, in 1912, and he spent the formative years of his life in Moncton, New Brunswick. In the history of Canadian scholarship, Frye has emerged as perhaps the most prominent figure. From 1939 until his death in 1991, he was based at Victoria College, University of Toronto, where he taught English and served as an administrator. Frye's authoritative study of the poetry of William Blake, *Fearful Symmetry* (1947), is considered a classic critical work. His synopsis of the principles and techniques of literary criticism, *Anatomy of Criticism* (1957), was his first work to win him international prominence. He won the Governor General's Award for Nonfiction in 1986 for *Northrop Frye on Shakespeare*. In the following two excerpts from his essay "The Archetypes of Literature," first published in 1951, Frye lays out some of the broader categories and modes by which texts can be classified. In order to show how texts work, he concentrates on the recurrent structures that might be described as *natural*. In this essay, Frye wrote, "All literary genres are derived from the quest myth." What do you know about the quest myth? Based on your own reading experience, do you agree or disagree with Frye's comment, and why?

[Frye, in this first excerpt from "The Archetypes of Literature," outlines four phases in the cycles of the day, the year, and human life. The quest hero and "subordinate characters" in literature, in his view, are bounded by these phases. The main literary modes—romance, comedy, tragedy, and satire—also reflect these phases.]

1. The dawn, spring, and birth phase. Myths of the birth of the hero, of revival and resurrection, of creation and (because the four phases are a cycle) of the defeat of the powers of darkness, winter, and death. Subordinate characters: the father and the mother. The archetype of romance and of most dithyrambic and rhapsodic poetry.

2. The zenith, summer, and marriage or triumph phase. Myths of apotheosis, of the sacred marriage, and of entering into Paradise. Subordinate characters: the companion and the bride. The archetype of comedy, pastoral, and idyll.

3. The sunset, autumn, and death phase. Myths of fall, of the dying god, of violent death and sacrifice and of the isolation of the hero. Subordinate characters: the traitor and the siren. The archetype of tragedy and elegy.

4. The darkness, winter, and dissolution phase. Myths of the triumph of these powers; myths of floods and the return of chaos, of the defeat of the hero, and Götterdämmerung myths. Subordinate characters: the ogre and the witch. The archetype of satire.

[In this second excerpt, Frye identifies archetypal communities, images, and characters that spring from the comic and tragic "visions" of the world.]

1. In the comic vision the *human* world is a community, or a hero who represents the wish-fulfillment of the reader. The archetype of images of symposium, communion, order, friendship, and love. In the tragic vision the human world is a tyranny or anarchy, or an individual or isolated man, the

leader with his back to his followers, the bullying giant of romance, the deserted or betrayed hero. Marriage or some equivalent consummation belongs to the comic vision; the harlot, witch, and other varieties of Jung's "terrible mother" belongs to the tragic one. All divine, heroic, angelic, or other superhuman communities follow the human pattern.

2. In the comic vision the *animal* world is a community of domesticated animals, usually a flock of sheep, or a lamb, or one of the gentler birds, usually a dove. The archetype of pastoral images. In the tragic vision the animal world is seen in terms of beasts and birds of prey, wolves, vultures, serpents, dragons, and the like.

3. In the comic vision the *vegetable* world is a garden, grove, or park, or a tree of life, or a rose or lotus. The archetype of Arcadian images, such as that of Marvell's green world or of Shakespeare's forest comedies. In the tragic vision it is a sinister forest like the one in *Comus* or at the opening of the *Inferno,* or a heath or wilderness, or a tree of death.

4. In the comic vision the *mineral* world is a city, or one building or temple, or one stone, normally a glowing precious stone—in fact the whole comic series, especially the tree, can be conceived as luminous or fiery. The archetype of geometrical images: the "starlit dome" belongs here. In the tragic vision the mineral world is seen in terms of deserts, rocks, and ruins, or of sinister geometrical images like the cross.

5. In the comic vision the *unformed* world is a river, traditionally fourfold, which influenced the Renaissance image of the temperate body with its four humours. In the tragic vision this world usually becomes the sea, as the narrative myth of dissolution is so often a flood myth. The combination of the sea and beast images gives us the leviathan and similar water-monsters.

and patterns

Notes

etiological having to do with the study of the cause, origin, or reason for something

dithyrambic an irregular or frenzied poetic expression; from the ancient Greek *dithurambos*, an impassioned hymn and dance held in honour of the god Dionysus

apotheosis glory, exaltation, ultimate achievement

Götterdämmerung myths narratives that deal with the turbulent end to an institution or a ruler's regime

Jung refers to Carl Jung (1875–1961). Originally a student of Sigmund Freud, this Swiss psychiatrist founded analytical psychology; Jung studied the links between myths, archetypes, and psychology, and he pioneered such concepts as "the collective unconscious."

Arcadian related to a pastoral paradise, the home of song-loving shepherds; in Greek mythology, Arcadia is the home of Pan, god of flocks and herds

Shakespeare's forest comedies refers to those romantic comedies by William Shakespeare, such as *A Midsummer Night's Dream* and *As You Like It*, in which characters move from the normal world of conflict and trouble into a "green world" in which these troubles are magically resolved

Marvell a reference to Andrew Marvell (1621–1678), an English metaphysical poet; his poems often contain have idyllic pastoral themes

starlit dome a reference to the following lines in the poem "Byzantium" by W.B. Yeats, in which he contrasts a spiritual, unchanging world with the ever-changing physical human world: "A startlit or moonlit dome disdains / All that man is, / All mere complexities, / The fury and mire of human veins."

four humours refers to what the Ancient Greeks believed were the four chief fluids of the body (blood, phlegm, yellow bile, and black bile) that were thought to determine a person's physical and mental qualities.

Comus a pastoral entertainment written by John Milton about the confrontation between good and evil

Inferno part one of three of *The Divine Comedy* by Italian poet Dante Alighieri (1265–1321), which is an allegorical journey through Hell.

leviathan a mythical, monstrous sea creature

There are common, or archetypal, traits in mythical figures revered by different cultures. This sculpture in the garden of the Versailles Palace in France depicts the figure of Diana from Roman mythology, who was goddess of the hunt and the protector of nature. The goddess Artemis in Ancient Greek mythology is identified with Diana. In Africa, in parts of Nigeria and Benin formerly known as Dahomey, people honoured a deity of the hunt named Age. To protect hunters, the Nago and Yoruba peoples of West Africa looked to Ogun, who corresponds with the deity Ogoun in the mythology of the Caribbean country of Haiti. For the Tlaxcalan indigenous people of Mexico, the god of hunting, Mixcoatl, took the form of a "cloud serpent."

The Hero's Adventure

Joseph Campbell with Bill Moyers

Joseph Campbell, an American writer on mythology and comparative religion, was born in New York City in 1904. Campbell received his master's degree in English and comparative literature from Columbia University in 1927 before pursuing post-graduate studies in Arthurian legends at the Universities of Paris and Munich. His predominant argument was that the world's mythologies, ritual practices, folk traditions, and major religions share certain symbolic themes, motifs, and patterns of behaviour. Campbell died in 1987. Bill Moyers was born in Oklahoma in 1934. He began his journalism career at age 16 as a cub reporter in Texas. During his thirty years in the media, Moyers has received numerous prizes, including over thirty Emmy Awards. Five of Moyers' books based on his television series have become best sellers, including *Joseph Campbell and the Power of Myth*, from which this interview excerpt is taken. Consider your definition of a hero and how it relates to Campbell's. How do his characteristics of a hero compare with your own? Based on Campbell's definition and criteria of heroes, what examples of heroes can you name?

Moyers: Why are there so many stories of the hero in mythology?

Campbell: Because that's what's worth writing about. Even in popular novels, the main character is a hero or heroine who has found or done something beyond the normal range of achievement and experience. A hero is someone who has given his or her life to something bigger than oneself.

Moyers: So in all of these cultures, whatever the local costume the hero might be wearing, what is the deed?

Campbell: Well, there are two types of deed. One is the physical deed, in which the hero performs a courageous act in battle or saves a life. The other kind is the spiritual deed, in which the hero learns to experience the supernormal range of human spiritual life and then comes back with a message.

The usual hero adventure begins with someone from whom something has been taken, or who feels there's something lacking in the normal experiences available or permitted to the members of his society. This person then takes off on a series of adventures beyond the ordinary, either to uncover what has been lost or to discover some life-giving elixir. It's usually a cycle, a going and a returning.

But the structure and something of the spiritual sense of this adventure can be seen already anticipated in the puberty or initiation rituals of early tribal societies, through which a child is compelled to give up its childhood and become an adult—to die, you might say, to its infantile personality and psyche and come back as a responsible adult. This is a fundamental psychological transformation that everyone has to undergo. We are in childhood in a condition of dependency under someone's protection and supervision for some fourteen to twenty-one years—and if you're going on for your Ph.D., this may continue to perhaps thirty-five. You are in no way a self-responsible, free agent, but an obedient dependent, expecting and receiving punishments and rewards. To evolve out of this position of psychological immaturity to the courage of self-responsibility and assurance requires a death and a resurrection. That's the basic motif of the universal hero's journey—leaving one condition and finding the source of life to bring you forth into a richer or mature condition.

Moyers: So even if we happen not to be heroes in the grand sense of redeeming society, we still have to take that journey inside ourselves spiritually and psychologically.

Campbell: That's right. Otto Rank in his important little book *The Myth of the Birth of the Hero* declares that everyone is a hero in birth, when he undergoes a tremendous psychological as well as physical transformation from the condition of a little water creature living in a realm of amniotic fluid into an air-breathing mammal which ultimately will be standing. That's an enormous transformation, and had it been consciously undertaken, it would have been, indeed, a heroic act. And there was a heroic act on the mother's part, as well, who had brought this all about.

Moyers: Then heroes are not all men?

Campbell: Oh, no. The male usually has the more conspicuous role, just because of the conditions of life. He is out there in the world, and the woman is in the home. But among the Aztecs, for example, who had a number of heavens to which people's souls would be assigned according to the conditions of their death, the heaven for warriors killed in battle was the same for mothers who died in childbirth. Giving birth is definitely a heroic deed, in that it is the giving over of oneself to the life of another.

Moyers: Don't you think we've lost that truth in this society of ours, where it's deemed more heroic to go out into the world and make a lot of money than it is to raise children?

Campbell: Making money gets more advertisement. You know the old saying: if a dog bites a man, that's not a story, but if a man bites a dog, you've got a story there. So the thing that happens and happens and happens, no matter how heroic it may be, is not news. Motherhood has lost its novelty, you might say.

Moyers: That's a wonderful image, though—the mother as hero.

Campbell: It has always seemed so to me. That's something I learned from reading these myths.

Moyers: It's a journey—you have to move out of the known, conventional safety of your life to undertake this.

Campbell: You have to be transformed from a maiden to a mother. That's a big change, involving many dangers.

Moyers: And when you come back from your journey, with the child, you've brought something for the world.

Campbell: Not only that, you've got a life job ahead of you. Otto Rank makes the point that there is a world of people who think that their heroic act in being born qualifies them for the respect and support of their whole community.

Moyers: But there's still a journey to be taken after that.

Campbell: There's a large journey to be taken, of many trials.

Moyers: What's the significance of the trials, and tests, and ordeals of the hero?

Campbell: If you want to put it in terms of intentions, the trials are designed to see to it that the intending hero should be really a hero. Is he really a match for this task? Can he overcome the dangers? Does he have the courage, the knowledge, the capacity, to enable him to serve?

• • •

Campbell: If you realize what the real problem is—losing yourself, giving yourself to some higher end, or to another—you realize that this itself is the ultimate trial. When we quit thinking primarily about ourselves and our own self-preservation, we undergo a truly heroic transformation of consciousness.

And what all the myths have to deal with is transformations of consciousness of one kind or another. You have been thinking one way, you now have to think a different way.

Moyers: How is consciousness transformed?

Campbell: Either by the trials themselves or by illuminating revelations. Trials and revelations are what it's all about.

Moyers: Isn't there a moment of redemption in all of these stories? The woman is saved from the dragon, the city is spared from obliteration, the hero is snatched from danger in the nick of time.

Campbell: Well, yes. There would be no hero deed unless there were an achievement. We can have the hero who fails, but he's usually represented as a kind of clown, someone pretending to more than he can achieve.

•   •   •

Moyers: Does your study of mythology lead you to conclude that a single human quest, a standard pattern of human aspiration and thought, constitutes for all humankind something that we have in common, whether we lived a million years ago or will live a thousand years from now?

Campbell: There's a certain type of myth which one might call the vision quest, going in quest of a boon, a vision, which has the same form in every mythology. That is the thing that I tried to present in the first book I wrote, *The Hero with a Thousand Faces*. All these different mythologies give us the same essential quest. You leave the world that you're in and go into a depth or into a distance or up to a height. There you come to what was missing in your consciousness in the world you formerly inhabited. Then comes the problem either of staying with that, and letting the world drop off, or returning with that boon and trying to hold on to it as you move back into your social world again. That's not an easy thing to do.

Moyers: So the hero goes *for* something, he doesn't just go along for the ride, he's not simply an adventurer?

Campbell: There are both kinds of heroes, some that choose to undertake the journey and some that don't. In one kind of adventure, the hero sets out responsibly and intentionally to perform the deed. For instance, Odysseus' son Telemachus was told by Athena, "Go find your father." That father quest is a major hero adventure for young people. That is the adventure of finding what your career is, what your nature is, what your source is. You undertake that intentionally. Or there is the legend of the Sumerian sky goddess, Inanna, who descended into the underworld and underwent death to bring her beloved back to life.

Then there are adventures into which you are thrown—for example, being drafted into the army. You didn't intend it, but you're in now.

You've undergone a death and resurrection, you've put on a uniform, and you're another creature.

One kind of hero that often appears in Celtic myths is the princely hunter, who has followed the lure of a deer into a range of forest that he has never been in before. The animal there undergoes a transformation, becoming the Queen of the Faerie Hills, or something of that kind. This is a type of adventure in which the hero has no idea what he is doing but suddenly finds himself in a transformed realm.

Moyers: Is the adventurer who takes that kind of trip a hero in the mythological sense?

Campbell: Yes, because he is always ready for it. In these stories, the adventure that the hero is ready for is the one he gets. The adventure is symbolically a manifestation of his character. Even the landscape and the conditions of the environment match his readiness.

Notes

elixir a substance or medicine thought to have the power to cure all ills or to provide a person with eternal life

Aztecs an Aboriginal people traditionally from central Mexico and noted for their rich civilization

Odysseus a mythical Greek hero who was the king of Ithaca and leader of the Greeks in the Trojan War; he returned home after ten years of wandering

Telemachus in Greek mythology, son of Odysseus and Penelope who helped kill Penelope's suitors

Athena the Greek goddess of wisdom, warfare, and the practical arts

Sumerian a reference to a fourth millennium BCE civilization based in Mesopotamia, between the Tigris and Euphrates rivers, in today's Iraq

Ode to the West Wind

Percy Bysshe Shelley

Born in 1792, Percy Bysshe Shelley was a poet whose work represented the sense of freedom, individualism, and search for truth and beauty that characterized the Romantic Movement in English life and literature. He was married to Mary Wollstonecraft Godwin, who later, as Mary Shelley, wrote the novel *Frankenstein*. In 1818, Shelley and his spouse settled permanently in Italy, where many of his most famous poems were written. In 1822, just before his thirtieth birthday, Shelley drowned in a storm while sailing the Mediterranean. Nature, for Romantic poets such as Shelley and Coleridge, contains forces that speak powerfully to fundamental aspects of human experience. What are some of the forces in nature that resonate in this way? Which forces are a powerful inspiration for poets with whom you are familiar? In what ways are you aware of and feel the power of the natural world?

I

O wild West Wind, thou breath of Autumn's being,
Thou, from whose unseen presence the leaves dead
Are driven, like ghosts from an enchanter fleeing,

Yellow, and black, and pale, and hectic red,
Pestilence-stricken multitudes: O Thou,
Who chariotest to their dark wintry bed

The winged seeds, where they lie cold and low,
Each like a corpse within its grave, until
Thine azure sister of the Spring shall blow

Her clarion o'er the dreaming earth, and fill
(Driving sweet buds like flocks to feed in air)
With living hues and odours plain and hill:

Wild Spirit, which art moving everywhere;
Destroyer and Preserver; hear, O hear!

II

Thou on whose stream, 'mid the steep sky's commotion,
Loose clouds like Earth's decaying leaves are shed,
Shook from the tangled boughs of Heaven and Ocean,

Angels of rain and lightning: there are spread
On the blue surface of thine aery surge,
Like the bright hair uplifted from the head

Of some fierce Maenad, even from the dim verge
Of the horizon to the zenith's height,
The locks of the approaching storm. Thou Dirge

Of the dying year, to which this closing night
Will be the dome of a vast sepulchre,
Vaulted with all thy congregated might

Of vapours, from whose solid atmosphere
Black rain and fire and hail will burst: O hear!

III

Thou who didst waken from his summer dreams
The blue Mediterranean, where he lay,
Lulled by the coil of his chrystalline streams,

Beside a pumice isle in Baiæ's bay,
And saw in sleep old palaces and towers
Quivering within the wave's intenser day,

All overgrown with azure moss and flowers
So sweet, the sense faints picturing them! Thou
For whose path the Atlantic's level powers

Cleave themselves into chasms, while far below
The sea-blooms and the oozy woods which wear
The sapless foliage of the ocean, know

Thy voice, and suddenly grow grey with fear,
And tremble and despoil themselves: O hear!

IV

If I were a dead leaf thou mightest bear;
If I were a swift cloud to fly with thee;
A wave to pant beneath thy power, and share

The impulse of thy strength, only less free
Than thou, O Uncontrollable! If even
I were as in my boyhood, and could be

The comrade of thy wanderings over Heaven,
As then, when to outstrip thy skiey speed
Scarce seemed a vision; I would ne'er have striven

As thus with thee in prayer in my sore need.
Oh! lift me as a wave, a leaf, a cloud!
I fall upon the thorns of life! I bleed!

A heavy weight of hours has chained and bowed
One too like thee: tameless, and swift, and proud.

V

Make me thy lyre, even as the forest is:
What if my leaves are falling like its own!
The tumult of thy mighty harmonies

Will take from both a deep, autumnal tone,
Sweet though in sadness. Be thou, Spirit fierce,
My spirit! Be thou me, impetuous one!

Drive my dead thoughts over the universe
Like withered leaves to quicken a new birth!
And, by the incantation of this verse,

Scatter, as from an unextinguished hearth
Ashes and sparks, my words among mankind!
Be through my lips to unawakened Earth

The trumpet of a prophecy! O Wind,
If Winter comes, can Spring be far behind?

Notes

hectic feverish

Thine azure...Spring Here, Shelley refers to the springtime's reviving wind.

clarion in this instance, a high-pitched trumpet; an Old French word originating from the medieval Latin word *clario*, meaning "clear"

angels in this instance, means messengers or harbingers

Maenad a female devoted to the worship of Dionysus (also known as
Bacchus), the Greek god of wine and vegetation

vapours clouds

chrystalline streams the currents that flow into the Mediterranean Sea

pumice isle an island formed from porous volcanic stone

Baiæ's bay the site west of Naples, Italy, where villas were erected by
Roman emperors

lyre in this instance, the Aeolian lyre, or wind harp, that responds to the wind
with musical chords; a common Romantic image for the response of the
human mind to the forces of nature

trumpet of a prophecy an allusion to the last trumpet of the apocalypse as
described in the Book of Revelation in the Bible

Araby

from Dubliners

James Joyce

A major figure in twentieth-century literature, James Joyce was born in Dublin, Ireland, in 1882. After the age of twenty, Joyce spent nearly his entire life away from Ireland, but he never stopped writing about his homeland. His first book, *Dubliners* (1907), was followed by his experimental masterpieces *Portrait of the Artist as a Young Man* (1916), *Ulysses* (1922), and *Finnegans Wake* (1939). He died in 1941. It has been observed that Joyce's narratives—no matter how daring in their use of literary forms—remain grounded in universal themes and patterns. How might you go about identifying such themes and patterns in a modern work? How would what you have discovered affect your reading of the work?

North Richmond Street, being blind, was a quiet street except at the hour when the Christian Brothers' School set the boys free. An uninhabited house of two storeys stood at the blind end, detached from its neighbours in a square ground. The other houses of the street, conscious of decent lives within them, gazed at one another with brown imperturbable faces.

The former tenant of our house, a priest, had died in the back drawing-room. Air, musty from having been long enclosed, hung in all the rooms, and the waste room behind the kitchen was littered with old useless papers. Among these I found a few paper-covered books, the pages of which were curled and damp: *The Abbot,* by Walter Scott,

The Devout Communicant and *The Memoirs of Vidocq.* I liked the last best because its leaves were yellow. The wild garden behind the house contained a central apple-tree and a few straggling bushes under one of which I found the late tenant's rusty bicycle-pump. He had been a very charitable priest; in his will he had left all his money to institutions and the furniture of his house to his sister.

When the short days of winter came dusk fell before we had well eaten our dinners. When we met in the street the houses had grown sombre. The space of sky above us was the colour of ever-changing violet and towards it the lamps of the street lifted their feeble lanterns. The cold air stung us and we played till our bodies glowed. Our shouts echoed in the silent street. The career of our play brought us through the dark muddy lanes behind the houses where we ran the gantlet of the rough tribes from the cottages, to the back doors of the dark dripping gardens where odours arose from the ashpits, to the dark odorous stables where a coachman smoothed and combed the horse or shook music from the buckled harness. When we returned to the street light from the kitchen windows had filled the areas. If my uncle was seen turning the corner we hid in the shadow until we had seen him safely housed. Or if Mangan's sister came out on the doorstep to call her brother in to his tea we watched her from our shadow peer up and down the street. We waited to see whether she would remain or go in and, if she remained, we left our shadow and walked up to Mangan's steps resignedly. She was waiting for us, her figure defined by the light from the half-opened door. Her brother always teased her before he obeyed and I stood by the railings looking at her. Her dress swung as she moved her body and the soft rope of her hair tossed from side to side.

Every morning I lay on the floor in the front parlour watching her door. The blind was pulled down to within an inch of the sash so that I could not be seen. When she came out on the doorstep my heart leaped. I ran to the hall, seized my books and followed her. I kept her brown figure always in my eye and, when we came near the point at which our ways diverged, I quickened my pace and passed her. This happened morning after morning. I had never spoken to her, except for a few casual words, and yet her name was like a summons to all my foolish blood.

Her image accompanied me even in places the most hostile to romance. On Saturday evenings when my aunt went marketing I had to go to carry some of the parcels. We walked through the flaring streets, jostled by drunken men and bargaining women, amid the curses of labourers, the shrill litanies of shop-boys who stood on guard by the barrels of pigs' cheeks, the nasal chanting of street-singers, who sang a *come-all-you* about O'Donovan Rossa, or a ballad about the troubles in our native land. These noises converged in a single sensation of life for me: I imagined that I bore my chalice safely through a throng of foes. Her name sprang to my lips at moments in strange prayers and praises which I myself did not understand. My eyes were often full of tears (I could not tell why) and at times a flood from my heart seemed to pour itself out into my bosom. I thought little of the future. I did not know whether I would ever speak to her or not or, if I spoke to her, how I could tell her of my confused adoration. But my body was like a harp and her words and gestures were like fingers running upon the wires.

One evening I went into the back drawing-room in which the priest had died. It was a dark rainy evening and there was no sound in the house. Through one of the broken panes I heard the rain impinge upon the earth, the fine incessant needles of water playing in the sodden beds. Some distant lamp or lighted window gleamed below me. I was thankful that I could see so little. All my senses seemed to desire to veil themselves and, feeling that I was about to slip from them, I pressed the palms of my hands together until they trembled, murmuring: *O love! O love!* many times.

At last she spoke to me. When she addressed the first words to me I was so confused that I did not know what to answer. She asked me was I going to *Araby*. I forgot whether I answered yes or no. It would be a splendid bazaar, she said; she would love to go.

—And why can't you? I asked.

While she spoke she turned a silver bracelet round and round her wrist. She could not go, she said, because there would be a retreat that week in her convent. Her brother and two other boys were fighting for their caps and I was alone at the railings. She held one of the spikes, bowing her head towards me. The light from the lamp opposite our door caught the white curve of her neck, lit up her hair that rested there and, falling, lit up the hand upon the railing. It fell over one side of her dress and caught the white border of a petticoat, just visible as she stood at ease.

—It's well for you, she said.

—If I go, I said, I will bring you something.

What innumerable follies laid waste my waking and sleeping thoughts after that evening! I wished to annihilate the tedious intervening days. I chafed against the work of school. At night in my bedroom and by day in the classroom her image came between me and the page I strove to read. The syllables of the word *Araby* were called to me through the silence in which my soul luxuriated and cast an Eastern enchantment over me. I asked for leave to go to the bazaar on Saturday night. My aunt was surprised and hoped it was not some Freemason affair. I answered few questions in class. I watched my master's face pass from amiability to sternness; he hoped I was not beginning to idle. I could not call my wandering thoughts together. I had hardly any patience with the serious work of life which, now that it stood between me and my desire, seemed to me child's play, ugly monotonous child's play.

On Saturday morning I reminded my uncle that I wished to go to the bazaar in the evening. He was fussing at the hallstand, looking for the hat-brush, and answered me curtly:

—Yes, boy, I know.

As he was in the hall I could not go into the front parlour and lie at the window. I left the house in bad humour and walked slowly towards the school. The air was pitilessly raw and already my heart misgave me.

When I came home to dinner my uncle had not yet been home. Still it was early. I sat staring at the clock for some time and, when its ticking began to irritate me, I left the room. I mounted the staircase and gained the upper part of the house. The high cold empty gloomy rooms liberated me and I went from room to room singing. From the front window I saw my companions playing below in the street. Their cries reached me weakened and indistinct and, leaning my forehead against the cool glass, I looked over at the dark house where she lived. I may have stood there for an hour, seeing nothing but the brown-clad figure cast by my imagination, touched discreetly by the lamplight at the curved neck, at the hand upon the railings and at the border below the dress.

When I came downstairs again I found Mrs Mercer sitting at the fire. She was an old garrulous woman, a pawnbroker's widow, who collected used stamps for some pious purpose. I had to endure the gossip of the tea-table. The meal was prolonged beyond an hour and still my uncle did not come. Mrs Mercer stood up to go: she was sorry she couldn't wait any longer, but it was after eight o'clock and she did not like to be out late, as the night air was bad for her. When she had gone I began to walk up and down the room, clenching my fists. My aunt said:

—I'm afraid you may put off your bazaar for this night of Our Lord.

At nine o'clock I heard my uncle's latchkey in the hall-door. I heard him talking to himself and heard the hall-stand rocking when it had received the weight of his overcoat. I could interpret these signs. When he was midway through his dinner I asked him to give me the money to go to the bazaar. He had forgotten.

—The people are in bed and after their first sleep now, he said.

I did not smile. My aunt said to him energetically:

—Can't you give him the money and let him go? You've kept him late enough as it is.

My uncle said he was very sorry he had forgotten. He said he believed in the old saying: *All work and no play makes Jack a dull boy.* He asked me where I was going and, when I had told him a second time, he asked me did I know *The Arab's Farewell to His Steed.* When I left the kitchen he was about to recite the opening lines of the piece to my aunt.

I held a florin tightly in my hand as I strode down Buckingham Street towards the station. The sight of the streets thronged with buyers and glaring with gas recalled to me the purpose of my journey. I took my seat in a third-class carriage of a deserted train. After an intolerable delay the train moved out of the station slowly. It crept onward among ruinous houses and over the twinkling river. At Westland Row Station a crowd of people pressed to the carriage doors; but the porters moved them back, saying that it was a special train for the bazaar. I remained alone in the bare carriage. In a few minutes the train drew up beside an improvised wooden platform. I passed out on to the road and saw by the lighted dial of a clock that it was ten minutes to ten. In front of me was a large building which displayed the magical name.

I could not find any sixpenny entrance and, fearing that the bazaar would be closed, I passed in quickly through a turnstile, handing a shilling to a weary-looking man. I found myself in a big hall girdled at half its height by a gallery. Nearly all the stalls were closed and the greater part of the hall was in darkness. I recognized a silence like that which pervades a church after a service. I walked into the centre of the bazaar timidly. A few people were gathered about the stalls which were still open. Before a curtain, over which the words *Café Chantant* were written in coloured lamps, two men were counting money on a salver. I listened to the fall of the coins.

Remembering with difficulty why I had come I went over to one of the stalls and examined porcelain vases and flowered tea-sets. At the door of the stall a young lady was talking and laughing with two young gentlemen. I remarked their English accents and listened vaguely to their conversation.

—O, I never said such a thing!

—O, but you did!

—O, but I didn't!

—Didn't she say that?

—Yes. I heard her.

—O, there's a…fib!

Observing me the young lady came over and asked me did I wish to buy anything. The tone of her voice was not encouraging; she seemed to have spoken to me out of a sense of duty. I looked humbly at the great jars that stood like eastern guards at either side of the dark entrance to the stall and murmured:

—No, thank you.

The young lady changed the position of one of the vases and went back to the two young men. They began to talk of the same subject. Once or twice the young lady glanced at me over her shoulder.

I lingered before her stall, though I knew my stay was useless, to make my interest in her wares seem the more real. Then I turned away slowly and walked down the middle of the bazaar. I allowed the two pennies to fall against the sixpence in my pocket. I heard a voice call from one end of the gallery that the light was out. The upper part of the hall was now completely dark.

Gazing up into the darkness I saw myself as a creature driven and derided by vanity; and my eyes burned with anguish and anger.

Notes

blind a dead-end street

The Abbot, The Devout Communicant, The Memoirs of Vidocq respectively, a popular historical romance by Sir Walter Scott, a Roman Catholic religious manual, and the memoirs of the chief of the French detective force

Mangan the surname of the Irish poet James Clarence Mangan, who was much admired by James Joyce

litanies prayers consisting of supplications by the Christian clergy and fixed responses by the congregation; from the medieval Latin word *letania*, meaning "entreaty"

come-all-you about O'Donovan Rossa a topical song that began "Come all you gallant Irishmen..." about the popular Irish leader Jeremiah O'Donovan (1831–1915), who was jailed by the British for inciting rebellion

the troubles the long-standing conflict in Northern Ireland between the Irish Catholics and the Irish Protestants; the latter are supported by the British armed forces

chalice the cup in which the wine of the Christian Eucharist is consecrated; from the Latin word *calix*, meaning "cup"

Freemason a Protestant fraternal organization that is unpopular with Irish Catholics

The Arab's Farewell to His Steed a popular sentimental poem by Caroline Norton

salver a tray for serving food or beverages; from the Spanish *salvar*, meaning "to save" or alternately "to taste food to detect poison"

Utopian Dreams

Val Ross

Val Ross was born in London, Ontario, in 1950. She worked at *Maclean's* magazine from 1979 to 1987, completing her tenure there as arts editor. For much of the 1990s, she covered books and magazines as a publishing editor at *The Globe and Mail*. In "Utopian Dreams," Ross reviews John Carey's *The Faber Book of Utopias,* a collection of utopian visions from across eras and cultures. What do you think causes people to experience dreams of utopia? What historical figures can you think of who have had views of a utopian society? What historical and world events resulted from these views or from other people trying to put into practice the utopian views of these people?

A worm gnaws at the blueprint of almost every social scheme that sets out to maximize human potential and human happiness. That worm— sometimes it destroys the entire blueprint—is the question of responsibility for Utopian dirt. Countless hippie communes came apart a generation ago in squabbles over who would clean the john and wash the encrusted dinner dishes.

In Plato's *The Republic* and Thomas More's *Utopia,* the dirty work is handled by slaves—one of the many reasons why those pioneering utopian thinkers' plans have dated so badly. In Aldous Huxley's dystopian *Brave New World* (1934), state hatcheries breed workers called "Deltas" who are stupid enough to accept scutwork happily. Alas, Huxley's hatcheries inflict terrible collateral damage on such concepts as motherhood, individual love, and human dignity. In Kurt Vonnegut's *Player Piano* (1952), machines do almost everything—leaving the human population unemployed, feeling useless, and prone to substance abuse, family breakdown, and violence.

This 1929 British poster uses a medical procedure of the time as a metaphor for what the Conservative and Unionist Party promised to do for constituents. Known as sun-ray treatment, a person would sit under an ultra-violet lamp to receive "artificial sunlight." This was thought to help everything from tuberculosis and allergies to skin ulcers and hair loss. The poster, with its promises of a glowing future, couples centuries-old utopian themes with techniques of modern political propaganda.

Those who invent schemes to promote human happiness must sooner or later wade into the offal matter of dirty work. But few have come up with solutions that neither oppress one segment of the population nor dislocate the role of useful work in human society. Of the 101 writers from Plato to Vonnegut anthologized in the fascinating, provocative, and idiosyncratic new *Faber Book of Utopias*, one of the few to have mused fruitfully on this issue is the French utopian writer Charles Fourier (1772–1837).

In Fourier's communal, egalitarian communities—groups of precisely 1,620 people he called Phalanxes—he dreamed that everyone would achieve happiness by doing only the jobs they were most suited to. Fourier imagined that people who rejoiced in heavy exertion (the "industrial athletes") would go off to build canals while more reflective souls would head for the looms and beehives.

It would be no different when it came to cleaning latrines; Fourier reasoned that the filthiest jobs would be done by those people who actually enjoy mucking around in filth—children, especially little boys. He proposed organizing these latrine cleaners into "a kind of half-savage legion" known as "Little Hordes." Each Little Horde would have its own slang, its own uniforms, and its own dwarf ponies to ride upon. Hauling poop would be a grand game.

Fourier's utopia is one of the more amiable visions in *The Faber Book of Utopias*, an inventory of more than 2,000 years of imaginary societies, broken dreams, strange hopes, and cautionary tales. Editor John Carey, author of *The Intellectuals and the Masses* and Merton Professor of English at Oxford, opens with an anonymous Egyptian, circa 1500 BCE, conjuring up "an island of the spirit, full of every good thing," and ranges through dreamers as varied as Ovid, Robert Owen, and Hitler.

The term "Utopia," invented by More in 1516, means "no place." As Carey notes, that makes his a book of nowheres. And that's a good thing. Many of the visions meant to be positive (eu-topian, as in euphoric) are instead actively repugnant.

Pious sadism informs the vision of the early Christian Tertullian, who imagined Heaven as a place where he would be eternally entertained by the torture of infidels; Hitler's utopian dream was of a Ukraine populated only by Teutonic races. "To count as a utopia, an imaginary place must be an expression of desire," Carey writes. But because our fellow humans have such dark desires, one of his book's clearest messages is that one person's utopia is another's dystopia.

Each vision reflects the anxieties of its age. Carey's earliest selections are fixated on food; they are about lands of eternal spring and fruitful abundance. Plato, Plutarch, Tacitus, and the utopias of 2,000 years ago are of societies (the Republic, the Germanic, and the Spartan) that are admirable because of their rigorous promotion of virtuous males.

Dreamers from the Renaissance on ponder how to organize society so as to minimize desires associated with wealth (More and Voltaire both invent worlds where gold is so common that no one covets it). By the early 20th century, dystopias abound, suggesting that world war sapped the optimism of the dreaming classes. More recent inventors of utopias regain a hopeful practicality.

One is the upbeat Michio Kaku, professor of theoretical physics at City University of New York. Kaku predicts that within the next couple of centuries, ubiquitous computers will give us smart homes, smart cars, and smart refrigerators, all monitoring and responding to our needs. ("Rather like living inside a Disney movie," Carey writes in his introductory note to Kaku, "where inanimate objects offer advice and crack jokes.")

Carey's witty and learned introductions—or justifications—for each selection are among the book's best and most informative passages. His introduction to the writings of H.G. Wells makes no effort to conceal his disgust at Wells' racism (he disdained "black, brown, yellow and dirty-white" peoples) and his embrace of eugenics. In *Anticipations* (1901), Wells wrote that the über-men of his "New Republic" would not be squeamish about "the merciful obliteration of weak and silly and pointless things"—notions that Carey terms "chilling."

While appalled by secular utopias from the likes of Wells and Hitler, Carey likewise has little enthusiasm for religious utopias. He hasn't bothered to include St. Augustine or selections from communities such as the Shakers. Instead, he has made room for some peripheral (if enjoyable) material from English literature such as Rupert Brooke's poem *Heaven*, which imagines a fishy utopia of "paradisal grubs, unfading moths, immortal flies," and Joseph Conrad's version of merchant navy life as paradise (a selection from *Youth*).

I'm not sure what Brooke and Conrad are doing in here. But I have no problem with a passage from Julian Barnes' *A History of the World in 10 1/2 Chapters*, in which the narrator goes to Heaven, eats a perfect bacon-and-egg breakfast, and learns that everything is available in Heaven, including God, *if one wants it to be*. This selection is delicious and ultimately terrifying.

Perhaps the editor's idiosyncratic choices for his book are precisely the point. Carey defines utopia as a place of desire, so it is only fitting that his anthology of utopias consists of whatever he desired to put in.

I thank him for including Oscar Wilde. Wilde's not as imaginative as Fourier when it comes to apportioning ugly jobs. ("Man is made for something better than disturbing dirt. All work of that kind should be done by a machine.") But he is very clear about the point of utopias. "A map of the world that does not include Utopia is not even worth glancing at, for it leaves out the one country at which Humanity is always landing," Wilde wrote in 1891. "And when Humanity lands there it looks out, and, seeing a better country, sets sail. Progress is the realization of Utopias."

Notes

egalitarian the belief in human equality with respect to one's social, economic, and political rights and privileges

Tertullian a Carthaginian theologian (circa 160–230 CE) who formed his own separate sect within the Christian church

Teutonic of or relating to the Germanic peoples

eugenics the highly controversial study of the attempt to hereditarily "improve" the human race by controlled, selective breeding

St. Augustine Aurelius Augustine (354–430 CE) is considered to be one of the most prominent Roman Catholic priests in history. His book *Confessions* is a classic of Christian theology.

Shakers an American religious sect which believed in the coming of an ideal society and which practised celibacy and lived a very disciplined communal lifestyle; popularly known today for their furniture and household design

Universal Themes and Patterns: Activities

1. With a partner, choose a universal theme or archetypal pattern and create a list of works of literature, movies, television programs, songs, videos, comics, magazines, illustrations, and advertisements that make use of your chosen theme or pattern. Then use text, sound, illustrations, photographs, and other visual images to create a multimedia presentation showing the enduring presence and impact of this universal theme or archetypal pattern in society.

2. In Northrop Frye's analysis of the literary mode of romance, he examines how romance reflects the phases of spring and birth. The romantic mode generally deals with such topics as humanity's quest for an ideal; the desire to return to nature; and the search for truth, beauty, goodness, and a better world. In a class presentation, outline and discuss how recurrent images, individual words, phrases, and figurative expressions in "Ode to the West Wind" and "Utopian Dreams" reflect the essentials and ideals of romance as outlined by Frye.

3. With a partner, do research to create a working definition of the term *dystopia*. Then locate and view a film that deals with either a utopian vision, such as *Animal Farm* (Turner Network Television, 2000), or a dystopian vision such as *1984* (Virgin Productions, 1984) or *Fahrenheit 451* (Image Entertainment, 2000). Write a review of the film for a mass-circulation newspaper audience. Include in your review the following features: a synopsis of the plot (without spoiling the ending); an explanation of how the film reflects a universal theme or archetypal pattern; and an evaluation of the effectiveness and quality of its cinematic techniques and their impact on viewers. Exchange draft reviews with a partner and ask for suggestions to improve your style and content.

4. Both Northrop Frye and Joseph Campbell emphasize the importance of the quest theme in literature. Does the importance of this feature extend to non-western literature? Choose a culture that is non-western, such as North American Aboriginal or South Asian. Then research a variety of primary and secondary print and non-print sources to determine the main characteristics of its oral and written literature. Write a formal essay in which you discuss the extent to which the quest theme applies to the literature of this culture. Be sure to integrate researched information into your essay, such as quotations from secondary sources.

2 essays, articles, and media

The contemplation of things as they are, without substitution or imposture, without error or confusion, is in itself a nobler thing than a whole harvest of invention.

— *Francis Bacon*

If you want a slice of life, look out the window. An artist has to look out that window, isolate one or two suggestive things, and embroider them together with poetry and fabrication, to create a revelation.

— *Barbara Kingsolver*

Portrait of the Essay as a Warm Body

Cynthia Ozick

Cynthia Ozick was born in New York in 1928. A writer of fiction, non-fiction, and drama, she has received numerous literary awards, including Guggenheim and National Endowment for the Arts fellowships. She has written several collections of essays, including *Quarrel and Quantary,* published in 2000. "Portrait of the Essay as a Warm Body" first appeared in *The Atlantic Monthly,* then became the introduction to *Best American Essays of 1998.* Ozick has said, "All good stories are honest and most good essays are not." What makes a good essay? What purposes and audiences do you associate with essays? In what ways can forms of non-fiction, such as essays and memoirs, be considered "literature"?

An essay is a thing of the imagination. If there is information in an essay, it is by-the-by, and if there is an opinion in it, you need not trust it for the long run. A genuine essay has no educational, polemical, or sociopolitical use; it is the movement of a free mind at play. Though it is written in prose, it is closer in kind to poetry than to any other form. Like a poem, a genuine essay is made out of language and character and mood and temperament and pluck and chance.

And if I speak of a genuine essay, it is because fakes abound. Here the old-fashioned term poetaster may apply, if only obliquely. As the poetaster is to the poet—a lesser aspirant—so the article is to the essay:

a look-alike knock-off guaranteed not to wear well. An article is gossip. An essay is reflection and insight. An article has the temporary advantage of social heat—what's hot out there right now. An essay's heat is interior. An article is timely, topical, engaged in the issues and personalities of the moment; it is likely to be stale within the month. In five years it will have acquired the quaint aura of a rotary phone. An article is Siamese-twinned to its date of birth. An essay defies its date of birth, and ours too.

A small historical experiment. Who are the classical essayists who come at once to mind? Montaigne, obviously. Among the nineteenth-century English masters, the long row of Hazlitt, Lamb, De Quincey, Stevenson, Carlyle, Ruskin, Newman, Martineau, Arnold. Of the Americans, Emerson. It may be argued that nowadays these are read only by specialists and literature majors, and by the latter only when they are compelled to. However accurate the claim, it is irrelevant to the experiment, which has to do with beginnings and their disclosures. Here, then, are some introductory passages:

> One of the pleasantest things in the world is going on a journey; but I like to go by myself. I can enjoy society in a room; but out of doors, nature is company enough for me. I am then never less alone than when alone.
> —William Hazlitt, "On Going on a Journey"

> To go into solitude, a man needs to retire as much from his chamber as from society. I am not solitary whilst I read and write, though nobody is with me. But if a man would be alone, let him look at the stars.
> —Ralph Waldo Emerson, "Nature"

> The human species, according to the best theory I can form of it, is composed of two distinct races, the men who borrow, and the men who lend.
> —Charles Lamb, "The Two Races of Men"

The future of poetry is immense, because in poetry, where it is worthy of its high destinies, our race, as times goes on, will find an ever and surer stay. There is not a creed which is not shaken, not an accredited dogma which is not shown to be questionable, not a received tradition which does not threaten to dissolve.... But for poetry, the idea is everything; the rest is a world of illusion, of divine illusion.

—Matthew Arnold, "The Study of Poetry"

The changes wrought by death are in themselves so sharp and final, and so terrible and melancholy in their consequences, that the thing stands alone in man's experience, and has no parallel upon earth. It outdoes all other accidents because it is the last of them. Sometimes it leaps suddenly upon its victims, like a Thug; sometimes it lays a regular siege and creeps upon their citadel during a score of years. And when the business is done, there is a sore havoc made in other people's lives, and a pin knocked out by which many subsidiary friendships hung together.

—Robert Louis Stevenson, "Aes Triplex"

It is recorded of some people, as of Alexander the Great, that their sweat, in consequence of some rare and extraordinary constitution, emitted a sweet odor, the cause of which Plutarch and others investigated. But the nature of most bodies is the opposite, and at their best they are free from smell. Even the purest breath has nothing more excellent than to be without offensive odor, like that of very healthy children.

— Michel de Montaigne, "Of Smells"

What might such a little anthology of opening sentences reveal? First, that language differs from one era to the next: there are touches of archaism here, if only in punctuation and cadence. Second, that splendid minds may contradict each other (outdoors, Hazlitt never feels alone; Emerson urges the opposite). Third, that the theme of an essay can be anything under the sun, however trivial (the smell of sweat) or crushing (the thought that we must die). Fourth, that the essay is a consistently recognizable and venerable—or call it ancient—form. In English: Addison and Steele in the eighteenth century, Bacon and Browne in the seventeenth, Lyly in the sixteenth, Bede in the seventh. And what of the biblical Koheleth—Ecclesiastes—who may be the oldest essayist reflecting on one of the oldest subjects: world-weariness?

So the essay is ancient and various: but this is a commonplace. There is something else, and it is more striking yet—the essay's power. By "power" I mean precisely the capacity to do what force always does: coerce assent. Never mind that the shape and intent of any essay is against coercion or suasion, or that the essay neither proposes nor purposes to get you to think like its author. A genuine essay is not a doctrinaire tract or a propaganda effort or a broadside. Thomas Paine's "Common Sense" and Émile Zola's "J'Accuse" are heroic landmark writings; but to call them essays, though they may resemble the form, is to misunderstand. The essay is not meant for the barricades; it is a stroll through someone's mazy mind. All the same, the essay turns out to be a force for agreement. It co-opts agreement; it courts agreement; it seduces agreement. For the brief hour we give to it, we are sure to fall into surrender and conviction. And this will occur even if we are intrinsically roused to resistance.

To illustrate: I may not be persuaded by Emersonianism as an ideology, but Emerson—his voice, his language, his music—persuades me. When we look for superlatives, not for nothing do we speak of "commanding" or "compelling" prose. If I am a skeptical rationalist or an advanced biochemist, I may regard (or discard) the idea of the soul as no better than a puff of warm vapour. But here is Emerson on the soul: "When it breathes through [man's] intellect, it is genius; when it breathes through his will, it is virtue; when it flows through his affection, it is love." And then—well, I am in thrall, I am possessed; I believe.

The novel has its own claims on surrender. It suspends our participation in the society we ordinarily live in, so that—for the time we are reading—we forget it utterly. But the essay does not allow us to forget our usual sensations and opinions; it does something even more potent: it makes us deny them. The authority of a masterly essayist—the authority of sublime language and intimate observation—is absolute. When I am with Hazlitt, I know no greater companion than nature. When I am with Emerson, I know no greater solitude than nature.

And what is most odd about the essay's power to lure us into its lair is how it goes about this work. We feel it when a political journalist comes after us with a point of view—we feel it the way the cat is wary of the dog. A polemic is a herald, complete with feathered hat and trumpet. A tract can be a trap. A magazine article generally has the scent of so-much-per-word. What is certain is that all of these are more or less in the position of a lepidopterist with his net: they mean to catch and skewer. They are focused on prey—i.e., us. The genuine essay, by contrast, never thinks of us; the genuine essay may be the most self-centred (the politer word would be subjective) arena for human thought ever devised.

Or else, though still not having you and me in mind (unless as an exemplum of common folly), it is not self-centred at all. When I was a child, I discovered in the public library a book that enchanted me then, and the idea of which has enchanted me for life. I have no recollection either of the title or of the writer—and anyhow very young readers rarely take note of authors; stories are simply and magically *there*. The characters included, as I remember them, three or four children and a delightful relation who is a storyteller, and the scheme was this: each child calls out a story element—most often an object—and the storyteller gathers up whatever is supplied (blue boots, a river, a fairy, a pencil box) and makes out of these random, unlikely, and disparate offerings a tale both logical and surprising. An essay, it seems to me, may be similarly constructed—if so deliberate a term applies. The essayist, let us say, unexpectedly stumbles over a pair of old blue boots in a corner of the garage, and this reminds her of when she last wore them—twenty years ago, on a trip to Paris, where on the banks of the Seine she stopped to watch an old fellow sketching, with a box of coloured pencils at his side. The pencil wiggling over his sheet is a greyish pink, which reflects the threads of sunset pulling westward in the sky, like the reins of a fairy cart...and so on. The mind meanders, slipping from one impression to another, from reality to memory to dreamscape and back again.

In the same way Montaigne, in our sample, when contemplating the unpleasantness of sweat, ends with the pure breath of children. Or Stevenson, starting out with mortality, speaks first of ambush, then of war, and finally of a displaced pin. No one is freer than the essayist—free to leap out in any direction, to hop from thought to thought, to begin with the finish and finish with the middle, or to eschew beginning and end and keep only a middle. The marvel of it is that out of this apparent causelessness, out of this scattering of idiosyncratic seeing and telling, a coherent world is made. It is coherent because, after all, an essayist must be an artist, and every artist, whatever the means, arrives at a sound and singular imaginative frame—or call it, on a minor scale, a cosmogony.

And it is into this frame, this work of art, that we tumble like tar babies, and are held fast. What holds us there? The authority of a voice, yes; the pleasure—sometimes the anxiety—of a new idea, an untried angle, a snatch of reminiscence, bliss displayed or shock conveyed. An essay can be the product of intellect or memory, lightheartedness or gloom, well-being or disgruntlement. But always there is a certain quietude, on occasion a kind of detachment. Rage and revenge, I think, belong to fiction. The essay is cooler than that. Because it so often engages in acts of memory, and despite its gladder or more antic incarnations, the essay is by and large a serene or melancholic form. It mimics that low electric hum, sometimes rising to resemble actual speech, that all human beings carry inside their heads—a vibration, garrulous if somewhat indistinct, that never leaves us while we wake. It is the hum of perpetual noticing: the configuration of someone's eyelid or tooth, the veins on a hand, a wisp of string caught on a twig, some words your fourth-grade teacher said, so long ago, about the rain, the look of an awning, a sidewalk, a bit of cheese left on a plate. All day long this inescapable hum drums on, recalling one thing and another, and pointing out this and this and this. Legend has it that Titus, emperor of Rome, went mad because of the buzzing of a gnat that made its home in his ear; and presumably the gnat, flying out into the great world and then returning to her nest, whispered what she had seen and felt and learned there. But an essayist is more resourceful than an emperor, and can be relieved of this interior noise, if only for the time it takes to record its murmurings. To seize the hum and set it down for others to hear is the essayist's genius.

It is a genius bound to leisure, and even to luxury, if luxury is measured in hours. The essay's limits can be found in its own reflective nature. Poems have been wrested from the inferno of catastrophe or war, and battlefield letters too: these are the spontaneous bursts and burnings that danger excites. But the meditative temperateness of an essay requires a desk and a chair, a musing and a mooning, a connection to a civilized surround; even when the subject itself is a wilderness of lions and tigers, mulling is the way of it. An essay is a fireside thing, not a conflagration or a safari.

This may be why, when we ask who the essayists are, it turns out—though novelists may now and then write essays—that true essayists rarely write novels. Essayists are a species of metaphysician: they are inquisitive—also analytic—about the least grain of being. Novelists go about the strenuous business of marrying and burying their people, or else they send them to sea, or to Africa, or (at the least) out of town. Essayists in their stillness ponder love and death. It is probably an illusion that men are essayists more often than women (especially since women's essays have in the past frequently assumed the form of unpublished correspondence). And here I should, I suppose, add a note about maleness and femaleness as a literary issue—what is popularly termed "gender," as if men and women were French or German tables and sofas. I *should* add such a note; it is the fashion, or, rather, the current expectation or obligation—but there is nothing to say about any of it. Essays are written by men. Essays are written by women. That is the long and the short of it. John Updike, in a genially confident discourse on maleness ("The Disposable Rocket"), takes the view—though he admits to admixture—that the "male sense of space must differ from that of the female, who has such an interesting, active, and significant inner space. The space that interests men is outer." Except, let it be observed, when men write essays: since it is only inner space—interesting, active, significant—that can conceive and nourish the contemplative essay. The "ideal female body," Updike adds, "curves around the centres of repose," and no phrase could better describe the shape of the ideal essay—yet women are no fitter as essayists than men. In promoting the felt salience of sex, Updike nevertheless drives home an essayist's point. Essays, unlike novels, emerge from the sensations of the self. Fiction creeps into foreign bodies; the novelist can inhabit not only a sex not his own, but also beetles and noses and hunger artists and nomads and beasts; while the essay is, as we say, personal.

And here is an irony. Though I have been intent on distinguishing the marrow of the essay from the marrow of fiction, I confess I have been trying all along, in a subliminal way, to speak of the essay as if it—or she—were a character in a novel or a play: moody, fickle, given on a whim to changing her clothes, or the subject; sometimes obstinate, with a mind of her own; or hazy and light; never predictable. I mean for her to be dressed—and addressed—as we would Becky Sharp, or Ophelia, or Elizabeth Bennet, or Mrs. Ramsay, or Mrs. Wilcox, or even Hester Prynne. Put it that it is pointless to say (as I have done repeatedly, disliking it every moment) "the essay," "an essay." The essay—an essay—is not an abstraction; she may have recognizable contours, but she is highly coloured and individuated; she is not a type. She is too fluid, too elusive, to be a category. She may be bold, she may be diffident, she may rely on beauty, or on cleverness, on eros or exotica. Whatever her story, she is the protagonist, the secret self's personification. When we knock on her door, she opens to us, she is a presence in the doorway, she leads us from room to room; then why should we not call her "she"? She may be privately indifferent to us, but she is anything but unwelcoming. Above all, she is not a hidden principle or a thesis or a construct: she is *there*, a living voice. She takes us in.

Notes

poetaster a paltry or inferior poet

lepidopterist a person who studies or collects butterflies

cosmogony in the strictest sense, an explanation, study, or model of the origin of the universe; here, a reference to an artist providing a coherent, imaginative universe in his or her works

tar babies in this instance, a difficult problem, especially one that is only aggravated by attempts to solve it; specifically, an allusion to the book *Brer Rabbit* by J.C. Harris (1848–1908), in which this phrase had a controversial and derogatory meaning

admixture a combination, especially of disparate elements

Becky Sharp, Ophelia, Elizabeth Bennet, Mrs. Ramsay, Mrs. Wilcox, Hester Prynne female characters from the following well-known literary works, respectively: *Vanity Fair* by William Thackeray, *Hamlet* by William Shakespeare, *Pride and Prejudice* by Jane Austen, *To the Lighthouse* by Virginia Woolf, *Howard's End* by E.M. Forster, and *The Scarlet Letter* by Nathaniel Hawthorne

Activities

1. Comment on the effectiveness of the title. To what extent does it engage the reader's interest? How well does it reflect the approach and theme of the essay? How effectively does Ozick use personification in the title to convey her theme?

2. Reread the essay, paying particular attention to the rhythm and cadence of the language. Choose two paragraphs that seem particularly effective and analyze the syntax. How does Ozick use techniques such as parallelism, repetition, variations in sentence length and type, inverted syntax, and sentence fragments to create particular effects?

3. Ozick has strong views about the nature and purpose of an essay. Think about a specific type of literature, art, music, sport, or other activity that is important to you. Write a personal essay on this subject with a clearly stated thesis, and use some of the techniques and stylistic devices of Ozick's essay. You may want to title your work, "Portrait of __ as __." In revising your essay, pay particular attention to your syntax. Then invite a peer editor to comment on your sentence variety and your use of techniques such as subordination, parallelism, and repetition.

Ka-Ching!

Margaret Atwood

Internationally acclaimed author Margaret Atwood was born in Ottawa, Ontario, in 1939. She received a bachelor's degree from the University of Toronto in 1961 and a master's degree from Harvard University in 1962. Since the mid-1960s, Atwood has received continuous critical acclaim for more than thirty books of fiction, poetry, essays, literary criticism, and children's literature. She is the recipient of dozens of awards, including most of the major literary prizes in Canada, as well as many from around the world, including the British Booker Prize in 2000 for her novel *The Blind Assassin*. Atwood is known for her careful craftsmanship, her precision with language, her erudition, and her stinging wit. In "Ka-Ching!" Atwood wittily describes her first job. What was your first job? What did you learn from it? Which skills required for that job are necessary for all your future jobs?

I'll pass over the mini-jobs of adolescence—the summer-camp stints that were more like getting paid for having fun. I'll pass over, too, the self-created pin-money generators—the puppet shows put on for kids at office Christmas parties, the serigraph posters turned out on the ping-pong table—and turn to my first real job. By "real job," I mean one that had nothing to do with friends of my parents or parents of my friends but was obtained in the adult manner, by looking through the ads in newspapers and going in to be interviewed—one for which I was entirely unsuited, and that I wouldn't have done except for the money. I was surprised when I got it, underpaid while doing it, and frustrated in the performance of it, and these qualities have remained linked, for me, to the ominous word "job."

The year was 1962, the place was Toronto. It was summer, and I was faced with the necessity of earning the difference between my scholarship for the next year and what it would cost me to live. The job was in the coffee shop of a small hotel on Avenue Road; it is now in the process of being torn down, but at that time it was a clean, well-lighted place, with booths along one side and a counter—possibly marble—down the other. The booths were served by a waitressing pro who lipsticked outside the lines, and who thought I was a mutant. My job would be serving things at the counter—coffee I would pour, toast I would create from bread, milkshakes I would whip up in the obstetrical stainless-steel device provided. ("Easy as pie," I was told.) I would also be running the customers' money through the cash register—an opaque machine with buttons to be pushed, little drawers that shot in and out, and a neurotic system of locks.

I said I had never worked a cash register before. This delighted the manager, a plump, unctuous character out of some novel I hadn't yet read. He said the cash register, too, was easy as pie, and I would catch on to it in no time, as I was a smart girl with an M.A. He said I should go and get myself a white dress.

I didn't know what he meant by "white dress." I bought the first thing I could find on sale, a nylon afternoon number with daisies appliquéd onto the bodice. The waitress told me this would not do: I needed a dress like her *uniform.* ("How dense can you be?" I overheard her saying.) I got the uniform, but I had to go through the first day in my nylon daisies.

This first humiliation set the tone. The coffee was easy enough—I just had to keep the Bunn filled—and the milkshakes were possible; few people wanted them anyway. The sandwiches and deep-fried shrimp were made at the back: all I had to do was order them over the intercom and bin the leftovers.

But the cash register was perverse. Its drawers would pop open for no reason, or it would ring eerily when I swore I was nowhere near it; or it would lock itself shut, and the queue of customers waiting to pay would lengthen and scowl as I wrestled and sweated. I kept expecting to be fired for incompetence, but the manager chortled more than ever. Occasionally, he would bring some man in a suit to view me. "She's got an M.A.," he would say, in a proud but pitying voice, and the two of them would stare at me and shake their heads.

An ex-boyfriend discovered my place of employment, and would also come to stare and shake his head, ordering a single coffee, taking an hour to drink it, leaving me a sardonic nickel tip. The Greek short-order cook decided I would be the perfect up-front woman for the restaurant he wanted to open: he would marry me and do the cooking, I would speak English to the clientele and work—was he mad?—the cash register. He divulged his bank balance, and demanded to meet my father so the two of them could close the deal. When I declined, he took to phoning me over the intercom to whisper blandishments, and to plying me with deep-fried shrimp. A girl as scrawny as myself, he pointed out, was unlikely to get such a good offer again.

Then the Shriners hit town, took over the hotel, and began calling for buckets of ice, or for doctors because they'd had heart attacks: too much tricycle-riding in the hot sun was felling them in herds. I couldn't handle the responsibility, the cash register had betrayed me once too often, and the short-order cook was beginning to sing Frank Sinatra songs to me. I gave notice.

Only when I'd quit did the manager reveal his true stratagem: they'd wanted someone as inept as me because they suspected their real cashier of skimming the accounts, a procedure I was obviously too ignorant to ever figure out. "Too stunned," as the waitress put it. She was on the cashier's side, and had me fingered as a stoolie all along.

Notes

serigraph a print made by the process of silk-screening, a stencil method in which a design is imposed on a screen of silk or other fine mesh material. Blank areas are coated with an impermeable substance and ink is forced through the mesh onto the printing surface.

ominous menacing; something related to an omen foreshadowing trouble

obstetrical related to the branch of medicine dealing with childbirth

unctuous characterized by exaggerated or insincere earnestness; something that feels oily or soapy when touched, greasy

appliquéd fabric that has been stitched onto another fabric as an ornament

perverse determinedly going against what is right; wayward or difficult to get along with

sardonic mocking, bitter, or scornful

blandishments cajoling, flattering compliments

stratagem a method that is formulated and executed to achieve a specific goal; originally referred to as a trick devised to deceive the enemy

stoolie a person acting as a decoy or informer, such as one who is a spy for the police; sometimes referred to as a "stool pigeon"

Activities

1. List all of the details that Atwood reveals about herself in the essay, from both the perspective of her past and her perspective at the time she wrote this essay. What, according to Atwood, are her strengths and weaknesses? Which are stated overtly and which are implied? How can you tell that Atwood is looking back with some nostalgia at a past experience?

2. With a partner, use the glossary in this anthology and other reference tools to create a working definition of the term *irony*. Then reread the essay and identify each time Atwood uses irony in this essay. Have a class discussion in which you explore questions such as the following: What is the tone of this essay and in which ways has the author's use of irony contributed to it? Is there a relationship between Atwood's subject matter in this essay and her decision to use irony? What are the differences between irony, satire, and parody? Are any elements of satire or parody used in this essay?

3. With a partner, use the Internet to identify and do research on any specific field of study in a master's degree program at a university. Then choose a job that is unrelated to this field of study and do research on that occupation. With your partner, write a comedic script for two people in which a master's program student does not have the appropriate skills to fulfill the job requirements. With your partner, act out your script to a group and invite their feedback on what elements of the script and the performance enhance the humour of your production.

Afternoon of an American Boy

E.B. White

Elwyn Brooks White was born in Mount Vernon, New York, in 1899. He is best known as a humourist and commentator on contemporary culture. After working on a newspaper, he became a contributing editor of the weekly magazine *The New Yorker*, writing the column "The Talk of the Town." White also wrote poetry and two children's books which have become classics: *Charlotte's Web* (1942) and *Stuart Little* (1945). He died in 1985. One critic wrote that "E.B. White is able to draw attention, in particular, to those ordinary or transitory things and imbue them with new meanings." In "Afternoon of an American Boy," he recollects his first date. What feelings do you have about dating? What anxieties do you have about first dates? What amusing possibilities do first dates hold?

When I was in my teens, I lived in Mount Vernon, in the same block with J. Parnell Thomas, who grew up to become chairman of the House Committee on Un-American Activities. I lived on the corner of Summit and East Sidney, at No. 101 Summit Avenue, and Parnell lived four or five doors north of us on the same side of the avenue, in the house the Diefendorfs used to live in.

Parnell was not a playmate of mine, as he was a few years older, but I used to greet him as he walked by our house on his way to and from the depot. He was a good-looking young man, rather quiet and shy. Seeing him, I would call "Hello, Parnell!" and he would smile and say "Hello, Elwyn!" and walk on. Once I remember dashing out of our yard on roller skates and executing a rink turn in front of Parnell, to show off, and he said, "Well! Quite an artist, aren't you?" I remember the words. I was delighted at praise from an older man and sped away along the flagstone sidewalk, dodging the cracks I knew so well.

The thing that made Parnell a special man in my eyes in those days was not his handsome appearance and friendly manner but his sister. Her name was Eileen. She was my age and she was a quiet, nice-looking girl. She never came over to my yard to play, and I never went over there, and, considering that we lived so near each other, we were remarkably uncommunicative; nevertheless, she was the girl I singled out, at one point, to be of special interest to me. Being of special interest to me involved practically nothing on a girl's part—it simply meant that she was under constant surveillance. On my own part, it meant that I suffered an astonishing disintegration when I walked by her house, from embarrassment, fright, and the knowledge that I was in enchanted territory.

In the matter of girls, I was different from most boys of my age. I admired girls a lot, but they terrified me. I did not feel that I possessed the peculiar gifts or accomplishments that girls liked in their male companions—the ability to dance, to play football, to cut up a bit in public, to smoke, and to make small talk. I couldn't do any of these things successfully, and seldom tried. Instead, I stuck with the accomplishments I was sure of: I rode my bicycle sitting backward on the handle bars, I made up poems, I played selections from "Aïda" on the piano. In winter, I tended goal in the hockey games on the frozen pond in the Dell. None of these tricks counted much with girls. In the four years I was in the Mount Vernon High School, I never went to a school dance and I never took a girl to a drugstore for a soda or to the Westchester Playhouse or to Proctor's. I wanted to do these things but did not have the nerve. What I finally did manage to do, however, and what is the subject of this memoir, was far brassier, far gaudier. As an exhibit of teenage courage and ineptitude, it never fails to amaze me in retrospect. I am not even sure it wasn't un-American.

My bashfulness and backwardness annoyed my older sister very much, and at about the period of which I am writing she began making strong efforts to stir me up. She was convinced that I was in a rut, socially, and she found me a drag in her own social life, which was brisk. She kept trying to throw me with girls, but I always bounced. And whenever she saw a chance she would start the phonograph and grab me, and we would go charging around the parlour in the toils of the one-step, she gripping me as in a death struggle, and I hurling her finally away from me through greater strength. I was a skinny kid but my muscles were hard, and it would have taken an unusually powerful woman to have held me long in the attitude of the dance.

One day, through a set of circumstances I have forgotten, my sister managed to work me into an afternoon engagement she had with some others in New York. To me, at that time, New York was a wonderland largely unexplored. I had been to the Hippodrome a couple of times with my father, and to the Hudson-Fulton Celebration, and to a few matinees, but New York, except as a setting for extravaganzas, was unknown. My sister had heard tales of tea-dancing at the Plaza Hotel. She and a girlfriend of hers and another fellow and myself went there to give it a try. The expedition struck me as a slick piece of arrangement on her part. I was the junior member of the group and had been roped in, I imagine to give symmetry to the occasion. Or perhaps Mother had forbidden my sister to go at all unless another member of the family was along. Whether I was there for symmetry or for decency I can't really remember, but I was there.

The spectacle was a revelation to me. However repulsive the idea of dancing was, I was filled with amazement at the setup. Here were tables where a fellow could sit so close to the dance floor that he was practically on it. And you could order cinnamon toast and from the safety of your chair observe girls and men in close embrace, singing along, the music playing while you ate the toast, and the dancers so near to you that they almost brushed the things off your table as they jogged by. I was impressed. Dancing or no dancing, this was certainly high life, and I knew I was witnessing a scene miles and miles ahead of anything that took place in Mount Vernon. I had never seen anything like it, and a ferment must have begun working in me that afternoon.

Incredible as it seems to me now, I formed the idea of asking Parnell's sister Eileen to accompany me to a tea dance at the Plaza. The plan shaped up in my mind as an expedition of unparalleled worldliness, calculated to stun even the most blasé girl. The fact that I didn't know how to dance must have been a powerful deterrent, but not powerful enough to stop me. As I look back on the affair, it's hard to credit my own memory, and I sometimes wonder if, in fact, the whole business isn't some dream that has gradually gained the status of actuality. A boy with any sense, wishing to become better acquainted with a girl who was "of special interest," would have cut out for himself a more modest assignment to start with—a soda date or a movie date—something within reasonable limits. Not me. I apparently became obsessed with the notion of taking Eileen to the Plaza and not to any darned old drugstore. I had learned the location of the Plaza, and just knowing how to get to it gave me a feeling of confidence. I had learned about cinnamon toast, so I felt able to cope with the waiter when he came along. And I banked heavily on the general splendour of the surroundings and the extreme sophistication of the function to carry the day, I guess.

I was three days getting up nerve to make the phone call. Meantime, I worked out everything in the greatest detail. I heeled myself with a safe amount of money. I looked up trains. I overhauled my clothes and assembled an outfit I believed would meet the test. Then, one night at six o'clock, when Mother and Father went downstairs to dinner, I lingered upstairs and entered the big closet off my bedroom where the wall phone was. There I stood for several minutes, trembling, my hand on the receiver, which hung upside down on the hook. (In our family, the receiver always hung upside down, with the big end up.)

I had rehearsed my first line and my second line. I planned to say, "Hello, can I please speak to Eileen?" Then, when she came to the phone, I planned to say, "Hello, Eileen, this is Elwyn White." From there on, I figured I could ad-lib it.

At last, I picked up the receiver and gave the number. As I had suspected, Eileen's mother answered.

"Can I please speak to Eileen?" I asked, in a low troubled voice.

"Just a minute," said her mother. Then, on second thought, she asked, "Who is it, please?"

"It's Elwyn," I said.

She left the phone, and after quite a while Eileen's voice said "Hello, Elwyn." This threw my second line out of whack, but I stuck to it doggedly.

"Hello, Eileen, this is Elwyn White," I said.

In no time at all I laid the proposition before her. She seemed dazed and asked me to wait a minute. I assume she went into a huddle with her mother. Finally, she said yes, she would like to go tea-dancing with me at the Plaza, and I said fine, I would call for her at quarter past three on Thursday afternoon, or whatever afternoon it was—I've forgotten.

I do not know now, and of course did not know then, just how great was the mental and physical torture Eileen went through that day, but the incident stacks up as a sort of unintentional un-American activity, for which I was solely responsible. It all went off as scheduled: the stately walk to the depot; the solemn train ride, during which we sat staring shyly into the seat in front of us; the difficult walk from Grand Central across Forty-second to Fifth, with pedestrians clipping us and cutting in between us; the bus ride to Fifty-ninth Street; then the Plaza itself, and the cinnamon toast, and the music, and the excitement. The thundering quality of the occasion must have delivered a mental shock to me, deadening my recollection, for I have only the dimmest memory of leading Eileen onto the dance floor to execute two or three unspeakable rounds, in which I vainly tried to adapt my violent sister-and-brother wrestling act into something graceful and appropriate. It must have been awful. And at six o'clock, emerging, I gave no thought to any further entertainment, such as dinner in town. I simply herded Eileen back all the long, dreary way to Mount Vernon and deposited her, a few minutes after seven, on an empty stomach, at her home. Even if I had attempted to dine her, I don't believe it would have been possible; the emotional strain of the afternoon had caused me to perspire uninterruptedly, and any restaurant would have been justified in rejecting me solely on the ground that I was too moist.

Over the intervening years (all thirty-five of them), I've often felt guilty about my afternoon at the Plaza, and a few years ago, during Parnell's investigation of writers, my feeling sometimes took the form of a guilt sequence in which I imagined myself on the stand, in the committee room, being questioned. It went something like this:

PARNELL: Have you ever written for the screen, Mr. White?

ME: No, sir.

PARNELL: Have you ever been, or are you now, a member of the Screen Writers' Guild?

ME: No, sir.

PARNELL: Have you ever been, or are you now, a member of the Communist Party?

ME: No, sir.

Then, in this imaginary guilt sequence of mine, Parnell digs deep and comes up with the big question, calculated to throw me.

PARNELL: Do you recall an afternoon, along about the middle of the second decade of this century, when you took my sister to the Plaza Hotel for tea under the grossly misleading and false pretext that you knew how to dance?

And as my reply comes weakly, "Yes, sir," I hear the murmur run through the committee room and see reporters bending over their notebooks, scribbling hard. In my dread, I am again seated with Eileen at the edge of the dance floor, frightened, stunned, and happy—in my ears the intoxicating drumbeat of the dance, in my throat the dry, bittersweet taste of cinnamon.

I don't know about the guilt, really. I guess a good many girls might say that an excursion such as the one I conducted Eileen on belongs in the un-American category. But there must be millions of aging males now slipping into their anecdotage, who recall their Willie Baxter period with affection, and who remember some similar journey into ineptitude, in that precious, brief moment in life before love's pages, through constant reference, had become dog-eared, and before its narrative, through sheer competence, had lost the first, wild sense of derring-do.

Notes

Aïda a popular nineteenth-century opera by Italian composer Giuseppe Verdi (1813–1901)

Hippodrome a sports arena used for horse shows

blasé exhibiting detachment due to a cynical worldliness

anecdotage the telling of anecdotes, which are accounts of interesting or humorous events; in this instance, a pun on the word "dotage"

Willie Baxter a character in *Seventeen,* an American novel popular in the 1940s, by Booth Tarkington. Baxter was a teenager determined to persuade everyone, including himself, that he was an authentic, full-grown man.

derring-do daring or reckless action

Activities

1. Reread "Afternoon of an American Boy" and find all the references White makes to being "American" or "un-American." What does he mean when he uses the term "un-American"? What underlying comment is he making?

2. White's writing style has been described in the following way: "educated vocabulary, evocative phrasing, specific images, embedded insights, and unexpected wording." Find examples from this essay to support each description. Share your findings with a group.

3. Interview several people of both genders, including peers and adults, about their recollections of first dates. Use this information to write an analysis of the experience of first dates in which you draw on the experiences of E.B. White, your interviewees, and yourself.

A Place to Stand On

Margaret Laurence

Margaret Laurence was born in Neepawa, Manitoba, in 1926. After studying English literature at Winnipeg's United College, she worked as a reporter for the *Winnipeg Citizen*. She lived the beginning of her adult life in England and Africa, eventually settling in Lakefield, Ontario. Laurence is best known for her Manawaka series of books which includes *The Stone Angel* (1964) and *The Diviners* (1974). She also published children's stories, essays, and memoirs. Laurence received many honours, including two Governor General's Literary Awards for Fiction. She was also a fervent social activist. She died in 1987. Laurence's experiences of growing up in Manitoba and living in Africa are important elements in her writing. To what extent do you think place is important in fiction? In what ways have the places where you grew up influenced your development?

> *The creative writer perceives his world once and for all in childhood and adolescence, and his whole career is an effort to illustrate his private world in terms of the great public world we all share.*
>
> —*Graham Greene*, Collected Essays

I believe that Graham Greene is right in this statement. It does not mean that the individual does not change after adolescence. On the contrary, it underlines the necessity for change. For the writer, one way of discovering oneself, of changing from the patterns of childhood and adolescence to those of adulthood, is through the explorations inherent in the writing itself. In the case of a great many writers, this exploration at some point—and perhaps at all points—involves an attempt to understand one's background and one's past, sometimes even a more distant past which one has not personally experienced.

This sort of exploration can be clearly seen in the works of contemporary African writers, many of whom recreate their people's past in novels and plays in order to recover a sense of themselves, an identity and a feeling of value from which they were separated by two or three generations of colonialism and missionizing. They have found it necessary, in other words, to come to terms with their ancestors and their gods in order to be able to accept the past and be at peace with the dead, without being stifled or threatened by that past.

Oddly enough, it was only several years ago, when I began doing some research into contemporary Nigerian writing and its background, that I began to see how much my own writing had followed the same pattern—the attempt to assimilate the past, partly in order to be freed from it, partly in order to try to understand myself and perhaps others of my generation, through seeing where we had come from.

I was fortunate in going to Africa when I did—in my early twenties—because for some years I was so fascinated by the African scene that I was prevented from writing an autobiographical first novel. I don't say there is anything wrong in autobiographical novels, but it would not have been the right thing for me—my view of the prairie town from which I had come was still too prejudiced and distorted by closeness. I had to get farther away from it before I could begin to see it. Also, as it turned out ultimately, the kind of novel which I can best handle is one in which the fictional characters are very definitely *themselves*, not me, the kind of novel in which I can feel a deep sense of connection with the main character without a total identification which for me would prevent a necessary distancing.

I always knew that one day I would have to stop writing about Africa and go back to my own people, my own place of belonging, but when I began to do this, I was extremely nervous about the outcome. I did not consciously choose any particular time in history, or any particular characters. The reverse seemed to be true. The character of Hagar in *The Stone Angel* seemed almost to choose me. Later, though, I recognized that in some way, not at all consciously understood by me at the time, I had had to begin approaching my background and my past through my grandparents' generation, the generation of pioneers of Scots-Presbyterian origin, who had been among the first to people the town I called Manawaka. This was where my own roots began. Other past generations of my father's family had lived in Scotland, but for me, my people's real past—my own real past—was not connected except distantly with Scotland; indeed, this was true for Hagar as well, for she was born in Manawaka.

The name Manawaka is an invented one, but it had been in my mind since I was about seventeen or eighteen, when I first began to think about writing something set in a prairie town. Manawaka is not my hometown of Neepawa—it has elements of Neepawa, especially in some of the descriptions of places, such as the cemetery on the hill or the Wachakwa valley through which ran the small brown river which was the river of my childhood. In almost every way, however, Manawaka was not so much any one prairie town as an amalgam of many prairie towns. Most of all, I like to think, it is simply itself, a town of the mind, my own private world, as Graham Greene says, which one hopes will ultimately relate to the outer world which we all share.

When one thinks of the influence of a place on one's writing, two aspects come to mind. First, the physical presence of the place itself—its geography, its appearance. Second, the people. For me, the second aspect of environment is the most important, although in everything I have written which is set in Canada, whether or not actually set in Manitoba, somewhere some of my memories of the physical appearance of the prairies come in. I had, as a child and as an adolescent, ambiguous feelings about the prairies. I still have them, although they no longer bother me. I wanted then to get out of the small town and go far away, and yet I felt the protectiveness of that atmosphere, too. I felt the loneliness and the isolation of the land itself, and yet I always considered southern Manitoba to be very beautiful, and I still do. I doubt if I will ever live there again, but those poplar bluffs and the blackness of that soil and the way in which the sky is open from one side of the horizon to the other—these are things I will carry inside my skull for as long as I live, with the vividness of recall that only our first home can have for us.

Nevertheless, the people were more important than the place. Hagar in *The Stone Angel* was not drawn from life, but she incorporates many of the qualities of my grandparents' generation. Her speech is their speech, and her gods their gods. I think I never recognized until I wrote that novel just how mixed my own feelings were toward that whole generation of pioneers—how difficult they were to live with, how authoritarian, how unbending, how afraid to show love, many of them, and how willing to show anger. And yet, they had inhabited a wilderness and made it fruitful. They were, in the end, great survivors, and for that I love and value them.

The final exploration of this aspect of my background came when I wrote—over the past six or seven years—*A Bird in the House,* a number of short stories set in Manawaka and based upon my childhood and my childhood family, the only semi-autobiographical fiction I have ever written. I did not realize until I had finished the final story in the series how much all these stories are dominated by the figure of my maternal grandfather, who came of Irish Protestant stock. Perhaps it was through writing these stories that I finally came to see my grandfather not only as the repressive authoritarian figure from my childhood, but also as a boy who had to leave school in Ontario when he was about twelve, after his father's death, and who as a young man went to Manitoba by sternwheeler and walked the fifty miles from Winnipeg to Portage la Prairie, where he settled for some years before moving to Neepawa. He was a very hard man in many ways, but he had had a very hard life. I don't think I knew any of this, really knew it, until I had finished those stories. I don't think I ever knew, either, until that moment how much I owed to him. One sentence, near the end of the final story, may show what I mean: "I had feared and fought the old man, yet he proclaimed himself in my veins."

My writing, then, has been my own attempt to come to terms with the past. I see this process as the gradual one of freeing oneself from the stultifying aspect of the past, while at the same time beginning to see its true value—which, in the case of my own people (by which I mean the total community, not just my particular family), was a determination to survive against whatever odds.

The theme of survival—not just physical survival, but the preservation of some human dignity and in the end some human warmth and ability to reach out and touch others—this is, I have come to think, an almost inevitable theme for a writer such as I, who came from a Scots-Irish background of stern values and hard work and puritanism, and who grew up during the drought and depression of the thirties and then the war.

This theme runs through two of my novels other than *The Stone Angel* (in which it is, of course, the dominant theme). In *A Jest of God* and *The Fire-Dwellers*, both Rachel and Stacey are in their very different ways threatened by the past and by the various inadequacies each feels in herself. In the end, and again in their very different ways and out of their very different dilemmas, each finds within herself an ability to survive—not just to go on living, but to change and to move into new areas of life. Neither book is optimistic. Optimism in this world seems impossible to me. But in each novel there is some hope, and that is a different thing entirely.

If Graham Greene is right—as I think he is—in his belief that a writer's career is "an effort to illustrate his private world in terms of the great public world we all share," then I think it is understandable that so much of my writing relates to the kind of prairie town in which I was born and in which I first began to be aware of myself. Writing, for me, has to be set firmly in some soil, some place, some outer and inner territory which might be described in anthropological terms as "cultural background." But I do not believe that this kind of writing needs therefore to be parochial. If Hagar in *The Stone Angel* has any meaning, it is the same as that of an old woman anywhere, having to deal with the reality of dying. On the other hand, she is not an old woman anywhere. She is very much a person who belongs in the same kind of prairie Scots-Presbyterian background as I do, and it was, of course, people like Hagar who created that background, with all its flaws and its strengths. In a poem entitled *Roblin Mills, Circa 1842*, Al Purdy said:

They had their being once
and left a place to stand on

They did indeed, and this is the place we are standing on, for better and for worse.

I remember saying once, three or four years ago, that I felt I had written myself out of that prairie town. I know better now. My future writing may not be set in that town—and indeed, my novel, *The Fire-Dwellers*, was set in Vancouver. I may not always write fiction set in Canada. But somewhere, perhaps in the memories of some characters, Manawaka will probably always be there, simply because whatever I am was shaped and formed in that sort of place, and my way of seeing, however much it may have changed over the years, remains in some enduring way that of a small-town prairie person.

Notes

Graham Greene renowned English novelist (1904–1991), who explored social and moral issues in novels often set in foreign countries

research into contemporary Nigerian writing a reference to *Long Drums and Cannons* (1968), Laurence's study of Nigerian literature

Roblin Mills, circa 1842 a reference to Al Purdy's poem about a pioneer settlement near Belleville in southern Ontario

Activities

1. In this essay, Laurence discusses the role of place in writing. She suggests that, for her, place has two characteristics: the physical environment and the people who inhabit it. Explain the ways in which Laurence felt ambivalent about the prairie community in which she grew up and about the people who lived there. Compare her feelings about people and places from her past with your own experience.

2. Prepare an analysis of the structure Laurence uses in this essay. Begin by selecting five major paragraphs. For each, reread the opening sentence. What is the main topic of the paragraph? What details in the paragraph support and develop the topic? How are the topics of individual paragraphs connected to the main topic and thesis of her paper?

3. In this essay, Margaret Laurence refers to several of the books she has written. Make a list in your journal of each title and record what she tells her readers about each book in this essay. Locate and read one of the books and prepare a book review of it. Focus your review on Laurence's use of physical space and the people who inhabit it.

Another Viewpoint: Society

The early part of Laurence's career was spent in Africa. Several of her early books were set in Africa or dealt with African issues. In this essay, Laurence suggests that, in her view, contemporary African writers "recreate their people's past in novels and plays in order to recover a sense of themselves, an identity and a feeling of value from which they were separated by two or three generations of colonialism and missionizing." Find an example of contemporary African fiction and assess to what extent Laurence's observation is accurate.

Chameleons and Codas

Patricia Conrad

Patricia Conrad lives in Calgary, Alberta. In this selection, Conrad chronicles her experiences growing up as a child of deaf parents. In our society, we are aware that sometimes hearing-impaired people are treated insensitively, whether intentionally or not, by the hearing world. What are some examples of insensitivity to which the children of deaf adults might be subjected? What strategies do you think could help facilitate respect between the non-hearing and the hearing worlds?

What I know of life and people, I learned as I juggled two worlds and two languages. As a hearing daughter born to deaf parents in rural Alberta, I lived at the crossroads of two cultures, a foreigner on the fringes of both. I had the ability to hear, so how could I understand the deaf experience? Yet I was never truly "hearing" either; a piece of my heart remained staunchly "deaf." So I became a chameleon, changing my colour as I shifted from one world to the other.

Sound had little meaning for Mom and Dad; he had been deaf since birth and she lost her hearing at the age of six because of illness. Their world was visual, not auditory, their conversations signed rather than spoken. Their language (American Sign Language, or ASL) became ours too; we "talked" with our hands and "listened" with our eyes. My siblings and I, all hearing, had licence to shout, sing, or yodel at will. No one told us to be quiet. We lived near a busy highway, with semi-trailer trucks roaring by at all hours. My parents were oblivious to the din, and we kids were so used to it we just tuned it out. My siblings and I squabbled without parental intervention, and learned the hard way to resolve our conflicts—with little finesse, alas; usually it boiled down to who yelled the loudest or gave up first.

Although sound was meaningless, sight and touch were vital to my parents. Vibration got us kids in trouble more than once. We dared not race down the stairway while Dad was napping; the shudder of the floor woke him instantly.

Like most deaf folk, my parents relied on visual and tactile cues to get each other's attention, stomping on the floor or flicking the light switch. We kids did the same, or else tapped a shoulder. We learned early that such deaf cultural norms are taboo in the hearing world. Foot-stomping is too loud, light-flashing too rude, and touching people (even a shoulder tap) too intimate.

At school, I excelled in my classes because it seemed the hearing thing to do, and besides, didn't it prove my parents' aptitude for raising us? I was a social dud but impressed my teachers.

Only when my two worlds collided did my chameleon soul falter, for how can one be two colours at once? Whenever my parents signed in public, curious onlookers stared, fascinated by their splendid expressions and fluttering hands. I grew fiercely protective, scowling at the oglers or blocking their view. I like to think I terrorized the bejesus out of some, though I cannot say for certain they noticed me at all.

Before the days of professional interpreters, TTYs (telephones with print displays), and enlightened attitudes, my siblings and I talked for our parents, relayed phone messages, and became their communication link to the hearing world. I took on the task of enlightening the insensitive, although results were variable. Many had not learned the "yelling the loudest or giving up first" method of conflict resolution. Others were not as bent on their own enlightenment as I was.

"Hey, is your mom deaf and dumb?" a classmate asked me once. Resisting the urge to respond in kind ("Hey, did your mom raise you to be hearing and thoughtless?"), I shot back: "She's deaf, but she's not dumb!" Hardly eloquent, but it addled him enough that he backed off.

My father, too, was saddled with "disabled" and "handicapped" stereotypes. "Can your daddy *drive*?" a stranger asked, incredulous, as Dad and I strode toward our car one day. It perplexed me when adults knew so little. (I was chest-high to my father and a half-dozen years shy of driving age. Just who did this guy think was about to take the wheel?) "Yes," I blurted, an answer so profound it surely bowled him over.

Indeed, my parents' disability was not their deafness, but people's attitudes toward it. At home, and with deaf friends (or anyone who used ASL), they conversed easily and fluently. With others, they wrote notes; both my parents carried notepads and pens everywhere. Dad especially was a master of mime, and would act out anything, even at the risk of looking ridiculous.

"Was it different, having deaf parents?" people ask. Different than what? It was the only life I knew, as normal to me as anyone else's is to them—and as precious.

Good parenting doesn't require functional ears; nor does good loving. We had plenty of both. Daddy was a farmer, a sociable fellow who loved teasing and rambunctious play with his kids. Mom was more shy and more reserved around people, but I adored her; she was the most unselfish being I ever knew. Mama's single-minded goal in life was to raise us well and release us to the world equipped with all we'd need, plus a healthy dose of common sense. She succeeded admirably.

As I grew into adulthood, I fretted that I would one day be forced to choose between my two worlds, and what good is a chameleon with only one colour? So I opted for careers that would keep me in both: teaching deaf students, freelance interpreting, and teaching interpreter trainees.

Today adults like me are labelled CODAs, an acronym for "children of deaf adults." But I prefer the deeper meaning of the word coda: an independent, concluding musical passage. Even a diehard chameleon yearns to one day find her own niche, and combine the best of both worlds into a multicoloured melody that is hers alone.

What I learned of life and people, chameleons and codas, I gained from two diverse communities. Growing up with deaf parents taught me resiliency, compassion in the face of ignorance, and the value of human diversity. In viewing the world from more than one angle, I learned to cherish my parents' gift to me: fluency in two languages, understanding of two cultures, access to two worlds—and the tools to create an independent coda with my own unique rhythm.

Now, if you'll excuse me, I believe my music's playing...

Activities

1. The author says, "Indeed, my parents' disability was not their deafness, but people's attitudes toward it." In a small group, identify and discuss what you think Conrad's purpose is in writing this selection. What led you to your conclusions? How effectively do you think Conrad has achieved her purpose for writing? Share your group's ideas with other groups in the class.

2. The author refers to herself as a chameleon and a coda. Review the essay to identify each occurrence of the two metaphors. What is the effect of her use of each metaphor? How does her use of these two metaphors relate to her main idea or theme?

3. Hearing-impaired people and their friends and families use ways other than voice to communicate with each other. Use the Internet and other sources to conduct some research about sign language, handspeak, finger spelling, and any other forms of communication used by hearing-impaired people. Prepare the text for a radio or television broadcast in which you describe the key features of these non-verbal communication systems.

Another Viewpoint: Society

Consider the following statement by the author: "I learned to cherish my parents' gift to me: fluency in two languages, understanding of two cultures, access to two worlds." If possible, contact some people in your community who are the children or siblings of hearing-impaired adults and interview them about whether Conrad's statement reflects their experiences. What are some of the characteristics of the culture of hearing-impaired people and their children? How is it different from that of people in the hearing world? Compare your findings with those of other students who conducted interviews.

Elegy in Stone

Steven Heighton

Steven Heighton was born in Toronto, Ontario, in 1961. Heighton studied at Queen's University in Kingston, Ontario, the city he subsequently made his home. He is a writer of poetry, essays, and fiction. Heighton was awarded the Gerald Lampert Prize and received a gold medal for fiction at the National Magazine Awards. His book of poems *The Ecstasy of Skeptics* (1995) was a finalist for the Governor General's Literary Award. In this selection, Heighton describes his visit to the war memorial at Vimy Ridge in France. Consider the war memorial in your community or another one you have visited. What objects, words, and other features are included in this memorial? If you were designing a war memorial, which features would you include and which would you leave out? What impact would you expect these features to have on visitors to the memorial?

Vimy Ridge, April 1992

The park's entrance—a border crossing, really—was modest enough: a small sign you could easily miss if you were driving past. But we were on foot. And though it turned out to be a much longer walk than we'd expected, it was a good place to walk, the fields along the road billowing with mustard, wheat, and poppies, the oaks and maples fragrant with new growth. We could be in Canada, I thought—then remembered that, for official purposes, we were.

The wind as we neared the ridge grew chilly, the sky grey.

Before long the road passed through a forest of natural growth and entered an old plantation of white pines, thick and towering, a spacious colonnade receding in the gloom. Fences appeared along the road, then signs warning us not to walk among the trees where sheep foraged above grassed-in trenches, shell holes, unexploded mines. In the blue-green, stained-glass light of the forest, the near-silence was eerie, solemn, as in the cathedral at Arras.

Finally we heard voices, saw a file of parked cars ahead through the trees, and came out at the main exhibit site of the park, some distance below the monument that crowns Vimy Ridge. Here, in 1917, from a line of trenches now preserved in concrete and filled daily with French tourists, the Canadian troops had launched their attack. Preserved like-wise is the first obstacle they had met: the front-line German trench, barely a grenade's throw away. This whites-of-their-eyes proximity sur-prised us and made stories of verbal fraternization between the lines—of back and forth banter in broken English and German—all the more plausible, and poignant.

A few years after the end of the First World War the government of France gave Canada a sizable chunk of the cratered, barren terrain around Vimy Ridge, where 20,000 Canadians fell before the ridge was finally taken on 12 April 1917. Today many Canadian visitors to France pass the memorial park en route to Arras or Lille without realizing the site is officially a small piece of Canada. Though "plot" might be a better word, for although the trenches where Canadian and Allied soldiers lived and died during their siege have healed over, the fields are scarred with ceme-teries and the woodlots filled with unmarked graves.

We'd arrived the night before in nearby Arras, finding a hotel and visiting the town's medieval cathedral. The hotel manager had elabo-rately regretted that we hadn't come two weeks earlier, on Easter Monday, when French President François Mitterrand, and Prime Minister Brian Mulroney and a handful of Vimy veterans had arrived for the seventy-fifth anniversary of the ridge's fall. I told the manager that I'd read about the ceremony back home, but felt the park was probably best experienced without the crowds and fanfare of an official visit. I could have said more but didn't trust my French enough to try explaining how disturbed

I'd been by photographs of those heads of state and their aides beaming glibly among the hunched veterans, whose nation-building sacrifice was clearly far from the politicians' minds.

Nation-building sacrifice sounds far too much like the kind of pious, pushy rhetoric I've learned to mistrust and fear, yet for years the bloody achievement of the Canadians on Vimy Ridge did stand, like the ridge itself, as a landmark, a high point around which the idea of a distinct Canadian identity could form.

"*C'est magnifique*," the manager told us when we explained we wanted to go. "*Magnifique*."

At the park's main exhibit site we went into a small, undistinguished brick building to see about a tour of the tunnel system under the trenches. The young guides, in Parks Canada uniforms, explained that we'd just missed the tour and unfortunately would have to wait for the next. But as we turned and went outside to confer, they must have noticed the small Canadian flag sewn onto my backpack, because one of them came out after us and beckoned us toward the tunnels. "You should have told us you're Canadian," he said with a soft Manitoba-French accent. "We don't get all that many."

The low-ceilinged, labyrinthine "subways"—where men ate and slept before the attack and couriers ran with their messages and sappers set charges under the German lines—have been carefully restored, but more or less unembellished. The impression, as above in the trenches, was sobering. I was relieved that this sad, clammy underworld had not been brightened up into some gaudy monument to Our Glorious Past; I was relieved that it still looked, and felt, like a tomb. It reminded me of the tunnels of the besieged Huguenots under the cathedral in Arras.

It was good to get back up into the daylight. We agreed to meet Mario and the other guides for a beer that night in town.

We followed the road up the last part of the ridge to the monument, wind blowing over the bare fields in a steady barrage. Seventy-five years before, the Canadians had advanced at dawn through driving sleet and snow, and now, nearing the exposed crown of the ridge, we could see how weather of that intensity must be quite common. The monument stands atop Hill 145, the Canadians' final objective and the highest point for miles around—but on the morning of the attack it must have been invisible through the snow and the timed barrage behind which the men were advancing.

Before the hilltop and the monument came in sight I'd felt uneasy, recalling the many monuments I had seen that stylized or made over the true face of war so as to safeguard an ideology, to comply with aesthetic conventions, or to make life easier for the recruiters of future wars. But as we neared the monument—two enormous white limestone pillars that meet at the base to form a kind of elongated U—I was impressed. And, as before, relieved. I'd first become anxious when the hotel keeper had told us to expect something "magnifique," but now I saw that in a sense he was right, for here was something magnificent in its simplicity, its solemnity, its understatement. And brilliant in its implication, because the pillars did not quite form a triumphant V, as you might expect, but a shape uncannily resembling the sights mounted on machine guns of the First World War—the kind that claimed tens of thousands of Canadian lives in the war and several thousand on the morning of the attack.

I don't believe such resemblances can be assigned to chance. An artist's hand is always guided in large part by the subconscious. I don't know whether the architect of the Vimy monument was ever asked about his intentions, conscious or subconscious, but in a sense they're no longer the point; unlike so many other old monuments, Walter Seymour Allward's is strikingly modern because of the way it surpasses, or second-guesses, all conventional intent.

We drew closer. Our feeling that this monolith was more a cenotaph, a vast elegy in stone instead of petrified hot air, grew stronger. And with it a feeling of pride. But a kind of pride very different, I think, from the tribal, intolerant swagger so many monuments have been built to inspire. A shy pride in our country's awkwardness at blowing its own horn—because sooner or later every country that does blow its own horn, with flamboyance, starts looking for somebody else to outblow. A pride in our reluctance—our seeming inability—to canonize brave, scared, betrayed adolescents as bearded heroes of mythic dimension, larger than life. Unreal.

And the monument is a cenotaph: we find its base inscribed with the names of the 11,285 Canadians whose final resting place is unknown. Blown to pieces. Lost in the mud, or buried anonymously in the graveyards below the ridge. The parade of names marches on and on, a kind of elegy whose heartbreaking syllables are English- and French-Canadian, Ojibway, Ukrainian, Dutch, German, Italian, Japanese…

Many are the names of our own distant relations.

The figures carved on and around the monument, though dated in style, are not blowing trumpets or beating breasts or drums. They seem instead to grieve. We round the monument and the Douai Plain fans out below us: another figure, much larger, cloaked, stands apart at the edge of the monument overlooking the plain. Behind her a sparsely worded inscription, in English and French, tells of the ridge's fall.

The figure, we will learn later that night, is Canada, "mourning her lost sons."

Tonight in Arras we'll learn other things as well from the Canadian guides we meet for a beer. That the whole park is planted with shrubs and trees from Canada. That 11,285 pines were planted after the war for every lost man whose name appears on the monument. That the prime minister's Easter visit was indeed a grand and lavish affair—everything the monument itself is not—but that the old soldiers on display carried themselves with dignity and a quiet, inconspicuous pride. And it's that feeling we end up coming back to toward the end of the night when the drinks have made us a bit more open and, I suppose, sentimental. Because we learn that these young expatriates have all felt just as we have about the austerity of the Vimy monument—and, by implication, the Canadian tendency to downplay the "heroism" of our achievements, to refuse to idealize, poeticize, and thus censor an obscene, man-made reality.

Or am I wrong to offer Canada these drunken toasts on a virtue that's largely a matter of historical and political necessity? Perhaps what I'm trying to say is that Canadians are lucky to have been spared, so far, that sense of collective power combined with intense tribal identity that makes every imperial nation so arrogant, competitive, and brutal. And as our friends guide us back to our hotel, I wonder if Canadians will ever stop berating themselves for not believing—as too many other nations have believed, and keep on believing—that they're better than others, that they're the chosen, the elect, the Greatest Nation on Earth, with God on their side.

"Make sure to let people back home know about the memorial," Mario calls out as we enter our hotel. And I reflect that a visit to the monument and the many battlefields around it might help convince some Canadians that there are worse things than uncertainty and under-statement.

And if the monument doesn't convince them, or the battlefields, then surely the graveyards will. In the park or within walking distance lie thirty cemeteries where the remains of over 7,000 Canadians are buried. They are peaceful places, conscientiously tended. Flowers bloom over every grave. Many are poppies. The paint on the crosses is fresh, a daz-zling white in the April sun. Here, no doubt, many of the boys whose names appear on the monument are actually buried, beneath long files of anonymous crosses, or stones ranked like chairs in a vast, deserted cathedral. Another endless parade, this time of the nameless—though here and there we do find stones inscribed with a name, an age. David Mahon, 1901–1917. IN MEMORY OF OUR DEAR AND ONLY CHILD.

We recite the words aloud, but this time the feeling they inspire has little to do with pride. The huge limestone gunsight looms above us on the ridge as we enter yet another aisle, and read, yet again:

A SOLDIER OF THE GREAT WAR

A Canadian Regiment

Known Unto God

Notes

Huguenots French Protestants who, during the sixteenth and seventeenth centuries, were in frequent conflict with French Catholics. Because of continued persecution, many Huguenots immigrated to foreign countries, including Canada; from a combination of the Old High German word *eid*, meaning "oath" and *ginōz*, meaning "companion"

Activities

1. The Battle of Vimy Ridge has been described as a defining moment in Canadian history. What did you learn from this essay about the battle itself, Canada's role in it, and the significance of the battle for Canada and its allies?

2. Steven Heighton wrote this essay when he was a young man. In what ways might this essay have been different in style and content if it had been written by someone older? Include examples from the essay to support your interpretation.

3. Interview someone who has experienced war first-hand. Use the results of your interview and those of other students in the class to prepare a commemorative booklet that could be used on Remembrance Day. Help edit each other's writing by focusing on elements of style that make the experiences as vivid as possible for the readers.

Another Viewpoint: Archetypal Patterns

In his essay, Heighton makes the observation that "an artist's hand is always guided in large part by the subconscious." This statement is an expression of the psychoanalytic approach to art and literature that emphasizes the role of the unconscious in the creative process. Take a second look at the essay. To what extent do you think Heighton's own unconscious influenced the style and content of this essay? Provide evidence from the text to support your observations.

The Death of the Moth

Virginia Woolf

Virginia Woolf, one of the most important writers of the twentieth century, was born in London, England, in 1882. Woolf received little formal education. However, she had an inquiring mind and educated herself by reading from her father's library. After his death, she moved to the London neighbourhood known as Bloomsbury and was part of a brilliant circle of writers and intellectuals known as the Bloomsbury Group. Woolf's best-known novels include *Mrs. Dalloway* (1925) and *To the Lighthouse* (1927). Together with her husband, Leonard Woolf, she established and ran Hogarth Press, which published some of the most innovative literature of the day. Virginia Woolf died in 1941. In some religious or ethical systems, the death of a creature such as a moth is considered to be as significant as the death of a person. What is your response to this idea?

Moths that fly by day are not properly to be called moths; they do not excite that pleasant sense of dark autumn nights and ivy-blossom which the commonest yellow-underwing asleep in the shadow of the curtain never fails to rouse in us. They are hybrid creatures, neither gay like butterflies nor sombre like their own species. Nevertheless the present specimen, with his narrow hay-coloured wings, fringed with a tassel of the same colour, seemed to be content with life. It was a pleasant morning, mid-September, mild, benignant, yet with a keener breath than that of the summer months. The plow was already scoring the field opposite

◀ *Virginia Woolf, 1902, George Charles Beresford*

the window, and where the share had been, the earth was pressed flat and gleamed with moisture. Such vigour came rolling in from the fields and the down beyond that it was difficult to keep the eyes strictly turned upon the book. The rooks too were keeping one of their annual festivities; soaring round the treetops until it looked as if a vast net with thousands of black knots in it had been cast up into the air; which, after a few moments, sank slowly down upon the trees until every twig seemed to have a knot at the end of it. Then, suddenly, the net would be thrown into the air again in a wider circle this time, with the utmost clamour and vociferation, as though to be thrown into the air and settle slowly down upon the treetops were a tremendously exciting experience.

The same energy which inspired the rooks, the ploughmen, the horses, and even, it seemed, the lean bare-backed downs, sent the moth fluttering from side to side of his square of the windowpane. One could not help watching him. One was, indeed, conscious of a queer feeling of pity for him. The possibilities of pleasure seemed that morning so enormous and so various that to have only a moth's part in life, and a day moth's at that, appeared a hard fate, and his zest in enjoying his meagre opportunities to the full, pathetic. He flew vigorously to one corner of his compartment, and, after waiting there a second, flew across to the other. What remained for him but to fly to a third corner and then to a fourth? That was all he could do, in spite of the size of the downs, the width of the sky, the far-off smoke of houses, and the romantic voice, now and then, of a steamer out at sea. What he could do he did. Watching him, it seemed as if a fibre, very thin but pure, of the enormous energy of the world had been thrust into his frail and diminutive body. As often as he crossed the pane, I could fancy that a thread of vital light became visible. He was little or nothing but life.

Yet, because he was so small, and so simple a form of the energy that was rolling in at the open window and driving its way through so many narrow and intricate corridors in my own brain and in those of other human beings, there was something marvellous as well as pathetic about him. It was as if someone had taken a tiny bead of pure life and decking it as lightly as possible with down and feathers, had set it dancing and zigzagging to show us the true nature of life. Thus displayed one could not get over the strangeness of it. One is apt to forget all about life, seeing it humped and bossed and garnished and cumbered so that it has to move with the greatest circumspection and dignity. Again, the thought of all that life might have been had he been born in any other shape caused one to view his simple activities with a kind of pity.

After a time, tired by his dancing apparently, he settled on the window ledge in the sun, and, the queer spectacle being at an end, I forgot about him. Then, looking up, my eye was caught by him. He was trying to resume his dancing, but seemed either so stiff or so awkward that he could only flutter to the bottom of the windowpane; and when he tried to fly across it he failed. Being intent on other matters I watched these futile attempts for a time without thinking, unconsciously waiting for him to resume his flight, as one waits for a machine, that has stopped momentarily, to start again without considering the reason of its failure. After perhaps a seventh attempt he slipped from the wooden ledge and fell, fluttering his wings, on to his back on the windowsill. The helplessness of his attitude roused me. It flashed upon me that he was in difficulties; he could no longer raise himself; his legs struggled vainly. But, as I stretched out a pencil, meaning to help him to right himself, it came over me that the failure and awkwardness were the approach of death. I laid the pencil down again.

The legs agitated themselves once more. I looked as if for the enemy against which he struggled. I looked out of doors. What had happened there? Presumably it was midday, and work in the fields had stopped. Stillness and quiet had replaced the previous animation. The birds had taken themselves off to feed in the brooks. The horses stood still. Yet the power was there all the same, massed outside, indifferent, impersonal, not attending to anything in particular. Somehow it was opposed to the little hay-coloured moth. It was useless to try to do anything. One could only watch the extraordinary efforts made by those tiny legs against an oncoming doom which could, had it chosen, have submerged an entire city, not merely a city, but masses of human beings; nothing, I knew, had any chance against death. Nevertheless after a pause of exhaustion the legs fluttered again. It was superb, this last protest, and so frantic that he succeeded at last in righting himself. One's sympathies, of course, were all on the side of life. Also, when there was nobody to care or to know, this gigantic effort on the part of an insignificant little moth, against a power of such magnitude, to retain what no one else valued or desired to keep, moved one strangely. Again, somehow, one saw life, a pure bead. I lifted the pencil again, useless though I knew it to be. But even as I did so, the unmistakable tokens of death showed themselves. The body relaxed, and instantly grew stiff. The struggle was over. The insignificant little creature now knew death. As I looked at the dead moth, this minute wayside triumph of so great a force over so mean an antagonist filled me with wonder. Just as life had been strange a few minutes before, so death was now as strange. The moth having righted himself now lay most decently and uncomplainingly composed. O yes, he seemed to say, death is stronger than I am.

Notes

benignant mild and serene

share in this instance, the blade of a plough

down in this instance, an undulating, treeless upland

rooks European and Asiatic crows with a hoarse chirp

vociferation loud, insistent, unpleasant noise

bossed embossed, ornamented

garnished decorated, embellished

cumbered hindered, burdened

circumspection cautiousness, prudence

wayside along the way

mean in this instance, unimposing or insignificant

Activities

1. According to the American philosopher and essayist Henry David Thoreau, "There is no such thing as pure *objective* observation. For your observation to be interesting—to be significant—it must be *subjective*." Discuss "The Death of the Moth" in terms of this quotation. In what sense, if any, would you say that this essay is significant to you? Explain.

2. State in your own words the thesis of this essay. Create an outline or diagram showing how the essay is structured. How is time used in this essay? How does the author move back and forth between the external world and a reflective contemplation of it?

3. On the Internet or at your library, locate a copy of Virginia Woolf's *Monday or Tuesday*, a book of early short stories representative of the *stream-of-consciousness* style of writing. Scan the book to find a story that interests you and read it. Then write an essay analyzing the use and effectiveness of stream-of-consciousness.

Another Viewpoint: Critical Approaches

Using the Internet and other resources, research the Bloomsbury Group to which Virginia Woolf belonged. Who were the other members of the group and for which works are they best known? What were the commonalities in their approach to life and literature? Present the results of your investigation in a research essay or class presentation.

Guy Lafleur

Ken Dryden

Ken Dryden was born in Islington, Ontario, in 1947. During the 1970s, he was the all-star goaltender with the Montreal Canadiens. In his rookie year, Dryden won the Calder Trophy; he also won the Vezina Trophy five times as the league's top goaltender. He sat out the 1974–75 NHL season to finish his law degree. A member of both the Hockey and the Sports halls of fame, Dryden has continued to find success as a lawyer, writer, sports commentator, lecturer, consultant, and, most recently, as the president and general manager of the Toronto Maple Leafs. He is the author of several books, including *The Game* (1983), which was nominated for a Governor General's Literary Award. What is it about professional athletes that appeals to us? Some people think that it is important for well-known athletes to act as role models in their personal conduct, while others argue that we should simply judge them on their athletic ability. What is your opinion?

The Forum is disturbingly empty: just a few players sit quietly cocooned away in a dressing room; twenty-five or thirty staff work in distant upstairs offices; throughout the rest of its vast insides a few dozen men are busy washing, painting, fixing, tidying things up. There is one other person. Entering the corridor to the dressing room, I hear muffled, reverberating sounds from the ice, and before I can see who it is, I know it's Lafleur. Like a kid on a backyard rink, he skates by himself many

◀ *Guy Lafleur*

minutes before anyone joins him, shooting pucks easily off the boards, watching them rebound, moving skates and gloved hands wherever his inventive instincts direct them to go. Here, far from the expedience of a game, away from defenders and linemates who shackle him to their banal predictability, alone with his virtuoso skills, it is his time to create.

The Italians have a phrase, *inventa la partita.* Translated, it means to "invent the game." A phrase often used by soccer coaches and journalists, it is now, more often than not, used as a lament. For in watching modern players with polished but plastic skills, they wonder at the passing of soccer *genius*—Pelé, di Stefano, Puskas—players whose minds and bodies in not so rare moments created something unfound in coaching manuals, a new and continuously changing game for others to aspire to.

It is a loss they explain many ways. In the name of team play, there is no time or place for individual virtuosity, they say; it is a game now taken over by coaches, by technocrats and autocrats who empty players' minds to control their bodies, reprogramming them with X's and O's, driving them to greater *efficiency* and *work rate,* to move *systems* faster, to move games faster, until achieving mindless pace. Others fix blame more on the other side: on smothering defences played with the same technical sophistication, efficiency, and work rate, but in the nature of defence, easier to play. Still others argue it is the professional sports culture itself which says that games are not won on good plays, but by others' mistakes, where the safe and sure survive, and the creative and not-so-sure may not.

But a few link it to a different kind of cultural change, the loss of what they call "street soccer": the mindless hours spent with a ball next to your feet, walking with it as if with a family pet, to school, to a store, or anywhere, playing with it, learning new things about it and about yourself, in time, as with any good companion, developing an *understanding.* In a much less busy time undivided by TV, rock music, or the clutter of modern lessons, it was a child's diversion from having nothing else to do. And, appearances to the contrary, it was creative diversion. But now, with more to do, and with a sophisticated, competitive society pressing on the younger and younger the need for training and skills, its time has run out. Soccer has moved away from the streets and playgrounds to soccer fields, from impromptu games to uniforms and referees, from any time to specific, scheduled time; it has become an *activity* like anything else, organized and maximized, done right or not at all. It has become something to be taught and learned, then tested in games; the answer at the back of the book, the one and only answer. So other time, time not spent with teams in practices or games, deemed wasteful and inefficient, has become time not spent at soccer.

Recently, in Hungary, a survey was conducted asking soccer players from 1910 to the present how much each practised a day. The answer, on a gradually shrinking scale, was three hours early in the century to eight minutes a day today. Though long memories can forget, and inflate what they don't forget, if the absolute figures are doubtful, the point is nonetheless valid. Today, except in the barrios of Latin America, in parts of Africa and Asia, "street soccer" is dead, and many would argue that with it has gone much of soccer's creative opportunity.

When Guy Lafleur was five years old, his father built a small rink in the backyard of their home in Thurso, Quebec. After school and on weekends, the rink was crowded with Lafleur and his friends, but on weekdays, rushing through lunch before returning to school, it was his alone for half an hour or more. A few years later, anxious for more ice time, on Saturday and Sunday mornings he would sneak in the back door of the local arena, finding his way unseen through the engine room, under the seats, and onto the ice. There, from 7:30 until just before the manager awakened about 11, he played alone; then quickly left. Though he was soon discovered, as the manager was also coach of his team, Lafleur was allowed to continue, by himself, and then a few years later with some of his friends.

There is nothing unique to this story; only its details differ from many others like it. But because it's about Lafleur it is notable. At the time, there were thousands like him across Canada on other noon-hour rinks, in other local arenas, doing the same. It was when he got older and nothing changed that his story became special. For as others in the whirl of more games, more practices, more off-ice diversions, more travel, and everything else gave up solitary time as boring and unnecessary, Lafleur did not. When he moved to Quebec City at fourteen to play for the Remparts, the ice at the big Colisée was unavailable at other times, so he began arriving early for the team's 6 p.m. practices, going on the ice at 5, more than thirty minutes before any of his teammates joined him. Now, many years later, the story unchanged, it seems more and more remarkable to us. In clichéd observation some would say it is a case of the great and dedicated superstar who is first on the ice, last off. But he is not. When practice ends, Lafleur leaves, and ten or twelve others remain behind, skating and shooting with Ruel. But every day we're in Montreal, at 11 a.m., an hour before Bowman steps from the dressing room as signal for practice to begin, Lafleur goes onto the ice with a bucket of pucks to be alone.

Not long ago, thinking of the generations of Canadians who learned hockey on rivers and ponds, I collected my skates and with two friends drove up the Gatineau River north of Ottawa. We didn't know it at the time, but the ice conditions we found were rare, duplicated only a few times the previous decade. The combination of a sudden thaw and freezing rain in the days before had melted winter-high snow, and with temperatures dropping rapidly overnight, the river was left with miles of smooth glare ice. Growing up in the suburbs of a large city, I had played on a river only once before, and then as a goalie. On this day, I came to the Gatineau to find what a river of ice and a solitary feeling might mean to a game.

We spread ourselves rinks apart, breaking into river-wide openings for passes that sometimes connected, and other times sent us hundreds of feet after what we had missed. Against the wind or with it, the sun glaring in our eyes or at our backs, we skated for more than three hours, periodically tired, continuously renewed. The next day I went back again, this time alone. Before I got bored with myself an hour or two later, with no one watching and nothing to distract me, loose and daring, joyously free, I tried things I had never tried before, my hands and feet discovering new patterns and directions, and came away feeling as if something was finally clear.

The Canadian game of hockey was weaned on long northern winters uncluttered by things to do. It grew up on ponds and rivers, in big open spaces, unorganized, often solitary, only occasionally moved into arenas for practices or games. In recent generations, that has changed. Canadians have moved from farms and towns to cities and suburbs; they've discovered skis, snowmobiles, and southern vacations; they've civilized winter and moved it indoors. A game we once played on rivers and ponds, later on streets and driveways and in backyards, we now play in arenas, in full team uniform, with coaches and referees, or to an ever-increasing extent we don't play at all. For, once a game is organized, unorganized games seem a wasteful use of time; and once a game moves indoors, it won't move outdoors again. Hockey has become suburbanized, and as part of our suburban middle-class culture, it has changed.

Put in uniform at six or seven, by the time a boy reaches the NHL, he is a veteran of close to 1,000 games—30-minute games, later 32-, then 45-, finally 60-minute games, played more than twice a week, more than seventy times a year between late September and late March. It is more games from a younger age, over a longer season than ever before. But it is less hockey than ever before. For, every time a twelve-year-old boy plays a 30-minute game, sharing the ice with teammates, he plays only about ten minutes. And ten minutes a game, anticipated and prepared for all day, travelled to and from, dressed and undressed for, means ten minutes of hockey a day, more than two days a week, more than seventy days a hockey season. And every day that a twelve-year-old plays only ten minutes, he doesn't play two hours on a backyard rink, or longer on school or playground rinks during weekends and holidays.

It all has to do with the way we look at free time. Constantly preoccupied with time and keeping ourselves busy (we have come to answer the ritual question "How are you?" with what we apparently equate with good health, "Busy"), we treat non-school, non-sleeping, or non-eating time, unbudgeted free time, with suspicion and no little fear. For, while it may offer opportunity to learn and do new things, we worry that the time we once spent reading, kicking a ball, or mindlessly coddling a puck might be used destructively, in front of TV, or "getting into trouble" in endless ways. So we organize free time, scheduling it into lessons—ballet, piano, French—into organizations, teams, and clubs, fragmenting it into impossible-to-be-bored segments, creating in ourselves a mental metabolism geared to moving on, making free time distinctly unfree.

It is in free time that the special player develops, not in the competitive experience of games, in hour-long practices once a week, in mechanical devotion to packaged, processed, coaching-manual, hockey-school skills. For while skills are necessary, setting out as they do the limits of anything, more is needed to transform those skills into something special. Mostly it is time—unencumbered, unhurried, time of a different quality, more time, time to find wrong answers to find a few that are right; time to find your own right answers; time for skills to be practised to set higher limits, to settle and assimilate and become fully and completely yours, to organize and combine with other skills comfortably and easily in some uniquely personal way, then to be set loose, trusted, to find new instinctive directions to take, to create.

But without such time a player is like a student cramming for exams. His skills are like answers memorized by his body, specific, limited to what is expected, random and separate, with no overviews to organize and bring them together. And for those times when more is demanded, when new unexpected circumstances come up, when answers are asked for things you've never learned, when you must intuit and piece together what you already know to find new answers, memorizing isn't enough. It's the difference between knowledge and understanding, between a super-achiever and a wise old man. And it's the difference between a modern suburban player and a player like Lafleur.

For a special player has spent time with his game. On backyard rinks, in local arenas, in time alone and with others, time without short-cuts, he has seen many things, he has done many things, he has *experienced* the game. He understands it. There is *scope* and *culture* in his game. He is not a born player. What he has is not a gift, random and other-worldly, and unearned. There is surely something in his genetic makeup that allows him to be great, but just as surely there are others like him who fall short. He is, instead, *a natural.*

"Muscle memory" is a phrase physiologists sometimes use. It means that for many movements we make, our muscles move with no message from the brain telling them to move, that stored in the muscles is a learned capacity to move a certain way, and, given stimulus from the spinal cord, they move that way. We see a note on a sheet of music, our fingers move; no thought, no direction, and because one step of the transaction is eliminated—the information-message loop through the brain—we move faster as well.

When first learning a game, a player thinks through every step of what he's doing, needing to direct his body the way he wants it to go. With practice, with repetition, movements get memorized, speeding up, growing surer, gradually becoming part of the muscle's memory. The great player, having seen and done more things, more different and personal things, has in his muscles the memory of more notes, more combinations and patterns of notes, played in more different ways. Faced with a situation, his body responds. Faced with something more, something new, it finds an answer he didn't know was there. He *invents the game.*

Listen to a great player describe what he does. Ask Lafleur or Orr, ask Reggie Jackson or Julius Erving what makes them special, and you will get back something frustratingly unrewarding. They are inarticulate jocks, we decide, but in fact they can know no better than we do. For ask yourself how you walk, how your fingers move on a piano keyboard, how you do any number of things you have made routine, and you will know why. Stepping outside yourself you can think about it and decide what *must* happen, but you possess no inside story, no great insight unavailable to those who watch. Such movement comes literally from your body, bypassing your brain, leaving few subjective hints behind. Your legs, your fingers move, that's all you know. So if you want to know what makes Orr or Lafleur special, watch their bodies, fluent and articulate, let them explain. They know.

When I watch a modern suburban player, I feel the same as I do when I hear Donnie Osmond or René Simard sing a love song. I hear a skilful voice, I see closed eyes and pleading outstretched fingers, but I hear and see only fourteen-year-old boys who can't tell me anything.

Hockey has left the river and will never return. But like the "street," like an "ivory tower," the river is less a physical place than an *attitude,* a metaphor for unstructured, unorganized time alone. And if the game no longer needs the place, it needs the attitude. It is the rare player like Lafleur who reminds us.

Notes

Pelé, di Stefano, Puskas refers to three star soccer players of the twentieth century: the Brazilian "Pelé" whose real name is Edson Arantes do Nascimento; the Argentinian Alfredo di Stefano; and the Hungarian Ferenc Puskas

Bobby Orr a hockey defenceman, born in Parry Sound, Ontario, in 1948, who spent his career with the Boston Bruins

Reggie Jackson Pennsylvania-born star baseball player for the Oakland Athletics and the New York Yankees; nicknamed "Mr. October" for his tremendous performances in numerous World Series championships

Julius Erving a star basketball player with the New York Knicks during the 1970s

René Simard Québécois singer who began his career as a child soprano and became a well-known Canadian pop singer in the 1970s

Activities

1. According to Dryden, a major "cultural change" in recent years has resulted in the loss of the special environment that nurtured the growth of athletes such as Guy Lafleur. What features of Canadian culture and hockey culture fostered the development of Lafleur? What has changed in how athletes are developed in today's society? Based on your experience as a sports player or spectator, do you agree with Dryden's assessment?

2. In your notebook, write down the topic of each paragraph in this selection. Then organize the entries in your list into three to five major categories. What do you notice about the organizational pattern that Dryden uses in his profile of Guy Lafleur? How has he connected the various elements into a coherent, unified whole? How does the organization of the essay contribute to Dryden's theme and the persuasiveness of his argument?

3. With a group, use Dryden's profile to prepare a list of elements for an effective biographical sketch. Then watch a television program or film based on the biography of a famous person. Using the criteria you developed, assess the quality of the biography. Prepare a brief report on the effectiveness of the format, structure, and style used in the biography.

My Mother's Blue Bowl

Alice Walker

Alice Walker was born in Georgia in 1944. She studied at Spellman College in Georgia and Sarah Lawrence College in New York. A passionate social activist in the American civil rights movement, Walker has taught literature and women's studies at various American universities. In 1974, Walker received the prestigious Guggenheim Fellowship. In 1983, her novel *The Color Purple* won the Pulitzer Prize and the American Book Award. Walker's writing often draws on her experiences growing up as an African-American in the South. What fiction and non-fiction selections have you read that create powerful pictures of the author's childhood? To what extent do you draw on your own childhood memories when you are generating ideas for a piece of writing?

Visitors to my house are often served food—soup, potatoes, rice—in a large blue stoneware bowl, noticeably chipped at the rim. It is perhaps the most precious thing I own. It was given to me by my mother in her last healthy days. The days before a massive stroke laid her low and left her almost speechless. Those days when to visit her was to be drawn into a serene cocoon of memories and present-day musings and to rest there, in temporary retreat from the rest of the world, as if still an infant, nodding and secure at her breast.

For much of her life my mother longed, passionately longed, for a decent house. One with a yard that did not have to be cleared with an axe.

One with a roof that kept out the rain. One with floors that you could not fall through. She longed for a beautiful house of wood or stone. Or of red brick, like the houses her many sisters and their husbands had. When I was thirteen she found such a house. Green-shuttered, white-walled. Breezy. With a lawn and a hedge and giant pecan trees. A porch swing. There her gardens flourished in spite of the shade, as did her youngest daughter, for whom she sacrificed her life doing hard labour in someone else's house, in order to afford peace and prettiness for her child, to whose grateful embrace she returned each night.

But, curiously, the minute I left home, at seventeen, to attend college, she abandoned the dream house and moved into the projects. Into a small, tight apartment of few breezes, in which I was never to feel comfortable, but that she declared suited her "to a T." I took solace in the fact that it was at least hugged by spacious lawn on one side, and by forest, out the back door, and that its isolated position at the end of the street meant she would have a measure of privacy.

Her move into the projects—the best housing poor black people in the South ever had, she would occasionally declare, even as my father struggled to adjust to the cramped rooms and hard, unforgiving qualities of brick—was, I now understand, a step in the direction of divestiture, lightening her load, permitting her worldly possessions to dwindle in significance and, well before she herself would turn to spirit, roll away from her.

She owned little, in fact. A bed, a dresser, some chairs. A set of living-room furniture. A set of kitchen furniture. A bed and wardrobe (given to her years before, when I was a teenager, by one of her more prosperous sisters). Her flowers: everywhere, inside the house and outside. Planted in anything she managed to get her green hands on, including old suitcases and abandoned shoes. She recycled everything, effortlessly. And gradually she had only a small amount of stuff—mostly stuff her children gave her: nightgowns, perfume, a microwave—to recycle or to use.

Each time I visited her I marvelled at the modesty of her desires. She appeared to have hardly any, beyond a thirst for a Pepsi-Cola or a hunger for a piece of fried chicken or fish. On every visit I noticed that more and more of what I remembered of her possessions seemed to be missing. One day I commented on this.

Taking a deep breath, sighing, and following both with a beaming big smile, which lit up her face, the room, and my heart, she said: Yes, it's all going. I don't need it anymore. If there's anything you want, take it when you leave; it might not be here when you come back.

The dishes my mother and father used daily had come from my house; I had sent them years before when I moved from Mississippi to New York. Neither the plates nor the silver matched entirely, but it was all beautiful in her eyes. There were numerous paper items, used in the microwave, and stacks of plastic plates and cups, used by the scores of children from the neighbourhood who continued throughout her life to come and go. But there was nothing there for me to want.

One day, however, looking for a jar into which to pour leftover iced tea, I found myself probing deep into the wilderness of the overstuffed, airless pantry. Into the land of the old-fashioned, the outmoded, the outdated. The humble and the obsolete. There was a smoothing iron, a churn. A butter press. And two large bowls.

One was cream and rose with a blue stripe. The other was a deep, vivid blue.

May I have this bowl, Mama, I asked, looking at her and at the blue bowl with delight.

You can have both of them, she said, barely acknowledging them, and continuing to put leftover food away.

I held the bowls on my lap for the rest of the evening, while she watched a TV program about cops and criminals that I found too horrifying to follow.

Before leaving the room I kissed her on the forehead and asked if I could get anything for her from the kitchen; then I went off to bed. The striped bowl I placed on a chair beside the door, so I could look at it from where I lay. The blue bowl I placed in the bed with me.

In giving me these gifts, my mother had done a number of astonishing things, in her typically offhand way. She had taught me a lesson about letting go of possessions—easily, without emphasis or regret—and she had given me a symbol of what she herself represented in my life.

For the blue bowl especially was a cauldron of memories. Of cold, harsh, wintry days, when my brothers and sister and I trudged home from school burdened down by the silence and frigidity of our long trek from the main road, down the hill to our shabby-looking house. More rundown than any of our classmates' houses. In winter my mother's riotous flowers would be absent, and the shack stood revealed for what it was. A grey, decaying, too small barrack meant to house the itinerant tenant workers on a prosperous white man's farm.

Slogging through sleet and wind to the sagging front door, thankful that our house was too far from the road to be seen clearly from the school bus, I always felt a wave of embarrassment and misery. But then I would open the door. And there inside would be my mother's winter flowers: a glowing fire in the fireplace, colourful handmade quilts on all our beds, paintings and drawings of flowers and fruits and, yes, of Jesus, given to her by who knows whom—and, most of all, there in the centre of the rough-hewn table, which in the tiny kitchen almost touched the rusty wood-burning stove, stood the big blue bowl, full of whatever was the most tasty thing on earth.

There was my mother herself. Glowing. Her teeth sparkling. Her eyes twinkling. As if she lived in a castle and her favourite princes and princesses had just dropped by to visit.

The blue bowl stood there, seemingly full forever, no matter how deeply or rapaciously we dipped, as if it had no bottom. And she dipped up soup. Dipped up lima beans. Dipped up stew. Forked out potatoes. Spooned out rice and peas and corn. And in the light and warmth that was *Her*, we dined.

Thank you, Mama.

Activities

1. Write a response to this essay by recording your initial impressions of the text. Then make connections between this essay and objects or relationships in your own life. Compare your responses with those of your classmates. To what extent did your own experiences, values, and perspectives influence your interpretation?

2. Choose a passage of approximately five to eight sentences that strikes you as particularly powerful. Analyze each sentence, considering its length and whether its type is simple, compound, complex, fragment, or run-on. Write a short passage on a topic of your choice in which you mimic the sentences you analyzed. Share your insights and conclusions about Walker's use of syntax in a class or group discussion.

3. Write an autobiographical essay in which you reflect on an object, place, or activity that symbolizes an important relationship with someone in your life. In developing your essay, use Walker's essay as a model in weaving together exposition, description, and narration in order to convey the nature and importance of the relationship. Invite a partner to react to the structure and style of your first draft. Then revise your essay to strengthen the organization and deepen the impact of the language.

Another Viewpoint: Society

Alice Walker identifies the American writers Flannery O'Connor and Zora Neale Hurston as key influences on her writing. Research the connections among these three women writers from the American South. To what extent did the society of the American South in the twentieth century contribute to these writers' visions?

Migrant Mother

Dorothea Lange

About the Visual   Dorothea Lange was born in Hoboken, New Jersey, in 1895. After high school, she decided to train as a photographer, despite never having used a camera before. She began her professional career in 1918 when she opened a portrait studio in San Francisco. By the 1930s, however, Lange took her camera to the streets to record the plight of people of the Depression era. In 1935, she was hired by the Farm Security Administration (FSA); her task was to document families leaving their devastated farms in the dust bowl of the American Midwest in a migration to California in search of work. Lange died in 1965. She called the camera "an instrument that teaches people to see without a camera." What might she have meant by this statement? To what extent is the statement paradoxical?

Activities

1. This photograph was taken in the United States during the Great Depression. Record your initial response to the photograph—your thoughts, feelings, questions, and associations. Share your response with the class and note the similarities and differences in your classmates' reactions. How do you account for them?

2. Discuss how the perspective, scale, and composition of this photograph contribute to its impact. Consider, for example, how the following changes would affect the picture: increasing or decreasing the distance between the camera and the subject, showing more of the background or only the face of the mother, or taking the picture from a lower or a higher angle.

1936, black-and-white print

Two Heads, 15th or 16th century, Leonardo da Vinci

Of Youth and Age

Francis Bacon

Sir Francis Bacon was born in London, England, in 1561, and died in 1626. He studied law at Cambridge University, travelled through Europe, and returned to England to serve in the English court. Bacon made significant contributions to Renaissance thought and culture through his scientific and political writings, especially *The Advancement of Learning* and the *Novum Organum* (New Instrument of Learning). In the latter, he emphasized the importance of what has become the modern scientific method. Often called the first English essayist, Bacon wrote with wit and style about such diverse topics as marriage, truth, education, travel, beauty, revenge, riches, and friendship. What are some of the outstanding characteristics of the young and the old? Why are young people often in conflict with their elders? What can the two groups learn from each other?

A man that is young in years may be old in hours, if he have lost no time. But that happeneth rarely. Generally, youth is like the first cogitations, not so wise as the second. For there is a youth in thoughts as well as in ages. And yet the invention of young men is more lively than that of old, and imaginations stream into their minds better, and as it were more divinely. Natures that have much heat, and great and violent desires and perturbations, are not ripe for action till they have passed the meridian of their years: as it was with Julius Caesar, and Septimius Severus. Of the latter of whom it is said, *Juventutem egit erroribus, imo furoribus, plenam,* and yet he was the ablest emperor, almost, of all the list. But reposed natures may do well in youth. As it is seen in Augustus Caesar, Cosmus,

Duke of Florence, Gaston de Foix, and others. On the other side, heat and vivacity in age is an excellent composition for business. Young men are fitter to invent than to judge, fitter for execution than for counsel, and fitter for new projects than for settled business. For the experience of age, in things that fall within the compass of it, directeth them, but in new things abuseth them. The errors of young men are the ruin of business; but the errors of aged men amount but to this, that more might have been done, or sooner. Young men, in the conduct and manage of actions, embrace more than they can hold; stir more than they can quiet; fly to the end, without consideration of the means and degrees; pursue some few principles which they have chanced upon absurdly; care not to innovate, which draws unknown inconveniences; use extreme remedies at first; and, that which doubleth all errors, will not acknowledge or retract them; like an unready horse that will neither stop nor turn. Men of age object too much, consult too long, adventure too little, repent too soon, and seldom drive business home to the full period, but content themselves with a mediocrity of success. Certainly it is good to compound employments of both; for that will be good for the present, because the virtues of either age may correct the defects of both; and good for succession, that young men may be learners while men in age are actors; and, lastly, good for extern accidents, because authority followeth old men, and favour and popularity youth. But for the moral part, perhaps youth will have the preeminence, as age hath for the politic. A certain rabbin, upon the text, *Your young men shall see visions, and your old men shall dream dreams*, inferreth that young men are admitted nearer to God than old, because vision is a clearer revelation than a dream. And certainly, the more a man drinketh of the world, the more it intoxicateth; and age doth profit rather in the powers of understanding than in the virtues of the will and affections. There be some have an over-early ripeness in their years, which fadeth betimes. These are, first, such as have brittle wits, the edge whereof is soon turned; such as was Hermogenes the rhetorician, whose books are exceeding subtle, who afterward waxed stupid. A second sort is of those that have some natural dispositions which have better grace in youth than in age, such as is a fluent and luxuriant speech, which becomes youth well, but not age: so Tully saith of Hortensius, *Idem manebat, neque idem docebat.* The third is of such as take too high a strain at the first, and are magnanimous more than tract of years can uphold. As was Scipio Africanus, of whom Livy saith in effect, *Ultima primis cedebant.*

Notes

Juventutem egit erroribus, imo furoribus, plenam from *The Life of Severus* by the Roman writer Spartianus; translated from the Latin as "He passed a youth full of folly, or rather of madness"

Cosmus, Duke of Florence refers to the historical figure Cosimo de'Medici

Gaston de Foix King Louis XII of France's nephew, who died at the battle of Ravenna in 1512

Hermogenes Greek rhetorician of the second century CE, who is said to have lost his memory at the age of twenty-five

Tully refers to the Roman philosopher and orator Cicero, who lived in the first century BCE

Hortensius Roman orator, at one time a rival of Cicero

Idem manebat, neque idem docebat translated from the Latin as "He remained the same when the same style no longer became him"

tract in this instance, length

Scipio Africanus Roman general who died in 183 BCE. According to some historians, Scipio was more suited to war than to the peaceful times of his later years.

Ultima primis cedebant translated from the Latin as "His last actions were not equal to his first"

Activities

1. In your notebook, make two lists. One list should feature the characteristics of "youth," according to Bacon, and the other the characteristics of "age." Beside each characteristic, mark whether you agree or disagree. Compare your responses with those of others in the class. Have a small group or whole class debate on the advantages and disadvantages of both youth and age.

2. Bacon did not divide his essays into paragraphs. Using what you know about the principles of paragraph organization, divide "Of Youth and Age" into paragraphs. In a small group, compare and discuss the reasons for your decisions. With the group, try to come to a consensus about the placement of paragraph divisions and present your decisions to the class.

3. Many of the references that Bacon uses in this essay may be obscure to the modern reader. The notes following the essay provide information on the sources cited by Bacon. Check these sources and evaluate the extent to which the allusions enrich or obscure the meaning of Bacon's essay for contemporary readers.

Another Viewpoint: Critical Approaches

Sir Francis Bacon was an important political and cultural figure in the era known as the Renaissance in Europe. Do research about the Renaissance and Bacon's life. Write an essay in which you explain how the circumstances and values of the Renaissance period might have influenced Bacon as he was writing this essay.

Why I Write

George Orwell

Generally considered to be one of the major essayists of the twenti-eth century, George Orwell was born Eric Arthur Blair in 1903 in what was then British-ruled India. He was educated in England and, after graduation, served in Burma with the Indian Imperial Police. Among his best-known works are *Burmese Days*, the story of his police career; *Homage to Catalonia,* a record of his involvement in the Spanish Civil War; *Animal Farm*, an allegory about the failure of Russian socialism under Stalin; and *Nineteen Eighty-Four* (1948), his portrayal of life under totalitarian rule in the future. Orwell died in 1950. In this essay, Orwell tells his readers that a writer's "subject mat-ter will be determined by the age he lives in." What do you think he means by this? Do you agree with him? Why or why not? What are some of the major issues that affect writers today?

From a very early age, perhaps the age of five or six, I knew that when I grew up I should be a writer. Between the ages of about seventeen and twenty-four I tried to abandon this idea, but I did so with the con-sciousness that I was outraging my true nature and that sooner or later I should have to settle down and write books.

I was the middle child of three, but there was a gap of five years on either side, and I barely saw my father before I was eight. For this and other reasons I was somewhat lonely, and I soon developed disagreeable mannerisms which made me unpopular throughout my schooldays. I had the lonely child's habit of making up stories and holding conver-sations with imaginary persons, and I think from the very start my literary ambitions were mixed up with the feeling of being isolated and undervalued. I knew that I had a facility with words and a power of facing unpleasant facts, and I felt that this created a sort of private world in which I could get my own back for my failure in everyday life. Nevertheless the volume of serious—i.e. seriously intended—writing which I produced all through my childhood and boyhood would not amount to half a dozen pages. I wrote my first poem at the age of four or five, my mother taking it down to dictation. I cannot remember anything about it except that it was about a tiger and the tiger had 'chair-like teeth'—a good enough phrase, but I fancy the poem was a plagiarism of Blake's 'Tiger, Tiger'. At eleven when the war of 1914–18 broke out, I wrote a patriotic poem which was printed in the local newspaper, as was another, two years later, on the death of Kitchener. From time to time, when I was a bit older, I wrote bad and usually unfinished 'nature poems' in the Georgian style. I also, about twice, attempted a short story which was a ghastly failure. That was the total of the would-be serious work that I actually set down on paper during all those years.

However, throughout this time I did in a sense engage in literary activities. To begin with there was the made-to-order stuff which I produced quickly, easily and without much pleasure to myself. Apart from school work, I wrote *vers d'occasion*, semi-comic poems which I could turn out at what now seems to me astonishing speed—at fourteen I wrote a whole rhyming play, in imitation of Aristophanes, in about a week—and helped to edit school magazines, both printed and in manuscript. These magazines were the most pitiful burlesque stuff that you could imagine, and I took far less trouble with them than I now would with the cheapest journalism. But side by side with all this, for fifteen years or more, I was carrying out a literary exercise of a quite different kind: this was the making up of a continuous 'story' about myself, a sort of diary existing only in the mind. I believe this is a common habit of children and adolescents. As a very small child I used to imagine that I was, say, Robin Hood, and picture myself as the hero of thrilling adventures, but quite soon my 'story' ceased to be narcissistic in a crude way and became more and more a mere description of what I was doing and the things I saw. For minutes at a time this kind of thing would be running through my head: 'He pushed the door open and entered the room. A yellow beam of sunlight, filtering through the muslin curtains, slanted on to the table, where a matchbox, half open, lay beside the inkpot. With his right hand in his pocket he moved across to the window. Down in the street a tortoiseshell cat was chasing a dead leaf,' etc., etc. This habit continued till I was about twenty-five, right through my non-literary years. Although I had to search, and did search, for the right words, I seemed to be making this descriptive effort almost against my will, under a kind of compulsion from outside. The 'story' must, I suppose, have reflected the styles of the various writers I admired at different ages, but so far as I remember it always had the same meticulous descriptive quality.

When I was about sixteen I suddenly discovered the joy of mere words, i.e. the sounds and associations of words. The lines from *Paradise Lost*—

So hee with difficulty and labour hard
Moved on: with difficulty and labour hee,

which do not now seem to me so very wonderful, sent shivers down my backbone; and the spelling 'hee' for 'he' was an added pleasure. As for the need to describe things, I knew all about it already. So it is clear what kind of books I wanted to write, in so far as I could be said to want to write books at that time, I wanted to write enormous naturalistic novels with unhappy endings, full of detailed descriptions and arresting similes, and also full of purple passages in which words were used partly for the sake of their sound. And in fact my first completed novel, *Burmese Days*, which I wrote when I was thirty but projected much earlier, is rather that kind of book.

I give all this background information because I do not think one can assess a writer's motives without knowing something of his early development. His subject matter will be determined by the age he lives in—at least this is true in tumultuous, revolutionary ages like our own—but before he ever begins to write he will have acquired an emotional attitude from which he will never completely escape. It is his job, no doubt, to discipline his temperament and avoid getting stuck at some immature stage, or in some perverse mood: but if he escapes from his early influences altogether, he will have killed his impulse to write. Putting aside the need to earn a living, I think there are four great motives for writing, at any rate for writing prose. They exist in different degrees in every writer, and in any one writer the proportions will vary from time to time, according to the atmosphere in which he is living. They are:

(i) *Sheer egoism.* Desire to seem clever, to be talked about, to be remembered after death, to get your own back on grown-ups who snubbed you in childhood, etc., etc. It is humbug to pretend that this is not a motive, and a strong one. Writers share this characteristic with scientists, artists, politicians, lawyers, soldiers, successful business men— in short, with the whole top crust of humanity. The great mass of human beings are not acutely selfish. After the age of about thirty they abandon individual ambition—in many cases, indeed, they almost abandon the sense of being individuals at all—and live chiefly for others, or are simply smothered under drudgery. But there is also the minority of gifted, wilful people who are determined to live their own lives to the end, and writers belong in this class. Serious writers, I should say, are on the whole more vain and self-centred than journalists, though less interested in money.

(ii) *Aesthetic enthusiasm.* Perception of beauty in the external world, or, on the other hand, in words and their right arrangement. Pleasure in the impact of one sound on another, in the firmness of good prose or the rhythm of a good story. Desire to share an experience which one feels is valuable and ought not to be missed. The aesthetic motive is very feeble in a lot of writers, but even a pamphleteer or a writer of text-books will have pet words and phrases which appeal to him for non-utilitarian reasons; or he may feel strongly about typography, width of margins, etc. Above the level of a railway guide, no book is quite free from aesthetic considerations.

(iii) *Historical impulse.* Desire to see things as they are, to find out true facts and store them up for the use of posterity.

(iv) *Political purpose*—using the word 'political' in the widest possible sense. Desire to push the world in a certain direction, to alter other people's idea of the kind of society that they should strive after. Once again, no book is genuinely free from political bias. The opinion that art should have nothing to do with politics is itself a political attitude.

It can be seen how these various impulses must war against one another, and how they must fluctuate from person to person and from time to time. By nature—taking your 'nature' to be the state you have attained when you are first adult—I am a person in whom the first three motives would outweigh the fourth. In a peaceful age I might have written ornate or merely descriptive books, and might have remained almost unaware of my political loyalties. As it is I have been forced into becoming a sort of pamphleteer. First I spent five years in an unsuitable profession (the Indian Imperial Police, in Burma), and then I underwent poverty and the sense of failure. This increased my natural hatred of authority and made me for the first time fully aware of the existence of the working classes, and the job in Burma had given me some understanding of the nature of imperialism: but these experiences were not enough to give me an accurate political orientation. Then came Hitler, the Spanish civil war, etc. By the end of 1935 I had still failed to reach a firm decision. I remember a little poem that I wrote at that date, expressing my dilemma:

> A happy vicar I might have been
> Two hundred years ago
> To preach upon eternal doom
> And watch my walnuts grow;
>
> But born, alas, in an evil time,
> I missed that pleasant haven,
> For the hair has grown on my upper lip
> And the clergy are all clean-shaven.
>
> And later still the times were good,
> We were so easy to please,
> We rocked our troubled thoughts to sleep
> On the bosoms of the trees.

All ignorant we dared to own
The joys we now dissemble;
The greenfinch on the apple bough
Could make my enemies tremble.

But girls' bellies and apricots,
Roach in a shaded stream,
Horses, ducks in flight at dawn,
All these are a dream.

It is forbidden to dream again;
We maim our joys or hide them;
Horses are made of chromium steel
And little fat men shall ride them.

I am the worm who never turned,
The eunuch without a harem;
Between the priest and the commissar
I walk like Eugene Aram;

And the commissar is telling my fortune
While the radio plays,
But the priest has promised an Austin Seven,
For Duggie always pays.

I dreamed I dwelt in marble halls,
And woke to find it true;
I wasn't born for an age like this;
Was Smith? Was Jones? Were you?

The Spanish war and other events in 1936–7 turned the scale and thereafter I knew where I stood. Every line of serious work that I have written since 1936 has been written, directly or indirectly, *against*
totalitarianism and *for* democratic socialism, as I understand it. It seems
to me nonsense, in a period like our own, to think that one can avoid

writing of such subjects. Everyone writes of them in one guise or another. It is simply a question of which side one takes and what approach one follows. And the more one is conscious of one's political bias, the more chance one has of acting politically without sacrificing one's aesthetic and intellectual integrity.

What I have most wanted to do throughout the past ten years is to make political writing into an art. My starting point is always a feeling of partisanship, a sense of injustice. When I sit down to write a book, I do not say to myself, 'I am going to produce a work of art'. I write it because there is some lie that I want to expose, some fact to which I want to draw attention, and my initial concern is to get a hearing. But I could not do the work of writing a book, or even a long magazine article, if it were not also an aesthetic experience. Anyone who cares to examine my work will see that even when it is downright propaganda it contains much that a full-time politician would consider irrelevant. I am not able, and I do not want, completely to abandon the world-view that I acquired in childhood. So long as I remain alive and well I shall continue to feel strongly about prose style, to love the surface of the earth, and to take pleasure in solid objects and scraps of useless information. It is no use trying to suppress that side of myself. The job is to reconcile my ingrained likes and dislikes with the essentially public, non-individual activities that this age forces on all of us.

It is not easy. It raises problems of construction and of language, and it raises in a new way the problem of truthfulness. Let me give just one example of the cruder kind of difficulty that arises. My book about the Spanish Civil War, *Homage to Catalonia,* is, of course, a frankly political book, but in the main it is written with a certain detachment and regard for form. I did try very hard in it to tell the whole truth without violating my literary instincts. But among other things it contains a long chapter full of newspaper quotations and the like, defending the Trotskyists who were accused of plotting with Franco. Clearly such a chapter, which after a year or two would lose its interest for any ordinary reader, must ruin the book. A critic whom I respect read me a lecture about it. 'Why did you put in all that stuff?' he said. 'You've turned what might have been a good book into journalism.' I happened to know, what very few people in England had been allowed to know, that innocent men were being falsely accused. If I had not been angry about that I should never have written the book.

In one form or another this problem comes up again. The problem of language is subtler and would take too long to discuss. I will only say that of late years I have tried to write less picturesquely and more exactly. In any case I find that by the time you have perfected any style of writing, you have always outgrown it. *Animal Farm* was the first book in which I tried, with full consciousness of what I was doing, to fuse political purpose and artistic purpose into one whole. I have not written a novel for seven years, but I hope to write another fairly soon. It is bound to be a failure, every book is a failure, but I do know with some clarity what kind of book I want to write.

Looking back through the last page or two, I see that I have made it appear as though my motives in writing were wholly public-spirited. I don't want to leave that as the final impression. All writers are vain, selfish, and lazy, and at the very bottom of their motives there lies a mystery. Writing a book is a horrible, exhausting struggle, like a long bout of some painful illness. One would never undertake such a thing if one were not driven on by some demon whom one can neither resist nor understand. For all one knows that demon is simply the same instinct that makes a baby squall for attention. And yet it is also true that one can write nothing readable unless one constantly struggles to efface one's own personality. Good prose is like a window pane. I cannot say with certainty which of my motives are the strongest, but I know which of them deserve to be followed. And looking back through my work, I see that it is invariably where I lacked a *political* purpose that I wrote lifeless books and was betrayed into purple passages, sentences without meaning, decorative adjectives and humbug generally.

Notes

Kitchener Lord Kitchener, much decorated and honoured British administrator and soldier, famous for campaigns in Egypt and South Africa

Vers d'occasion public poetry inspired by historically or socially significant events

Spanish Civil War In 1936, a group of generals, led by Francisco Franco and supported by fascist governments in Italy and Germany, revolted against Republican government forces. Despite popular support by people from many different nationalities who came to Spain to fight with Republicans against fascism, Franco became the dictator of a totalitarian Spanish state in 1939.

Activities

1. In this analytical essay, George Orwell explains his development as a writer. The author discusses key stages in his personal and professional life and the characteristics of his writing at each stage. In your notebook, describe the characteristics of the stages discussed by Orwell, as well as the personal, political, and historical events that influenced him at each stage.

2. The essay is organized chronologically. Prepare a timeline for Orwell's biography, based on the information provided in the article. Include events from both Orwell's personal life and contemporary historical events. Within the existing chronological structure, what other organizational patterns does Orwell use? Use your timeline to make a schematic plan, incorporating the major topics and subtopics found in Orwell's essay. Assess the effectiveness of the combination of various organizational structures used by Orwell in this essay.

3. Write your own analytical, autobiographical essay using Orwell's as a model. Begin by creating a personal timeline of key dates and events in your life. Using on-line or published yearbooks, write down important historical, political, and cultural events that parallel those in your life. Weave the personal and historical events together as Orwell has done in this essay.

Another Viewpoint: Critical Approaches

Orwell suggests in this essay that it is difficult for a writer to separate himself or herself from the political, historical, and cultural context in which a novel or any work of art is created. Some literary critics agree with this view. Others suggest that a work of art should be treated as a self-contained object and that we do not need to go outside of the text to understand it. What do you think would be Orwell's reply to such critics? Which side do you think is correct? Use examples from your own reading to support your argument.

The Not-So-Deadly Sin

Barbara Kingsolver

Barbara Kingsolver was born in Kentucky in 1955. At university in Indiana, she studied both science and creative writing and, after graduation, she worked as a science writer at the University of Arizona. Her articles have been published in many journals. She is also a well-known fiction writer, especially for the international best-seller *The Poisonwood Bible*. To Kingsolver, writing is in part a form of political activism. She has written that in her twenties she "began to understand how a person could write about the problems of the world in a compelling and beautiful way." She has said that writing should "improve on" real life. To what extent do you think that writing can reflect real life? How can writing improve on real life? Are some forms of writing better at depicting real life and others better at improving it? If so, why?

Write a non-fiction book, and be prepared for the legion of readers who are going to doubt your facts. But write a novel, and get ready for the world to assume every word is true.

Whenever I am queried about my fiction, if people want to know something in particular they nearly always want to know the same thing: How much is autobiographical? Did it all really happen, in exactly that way? Was my childhood like that? Which character is me? Commonly people don't ask, they just assume. I get letters of sympathy for the loss of my sister (the heroine of one of my novels lost her sister) and my father (ditto, same novel). Since one of my characters adopted a Cherokee child, I get advice about cross-cultural adoptions. And so on.

My sister and parents are alive and well, thanks. I don't have an adopted child. The mute waif named Turtle who appears in two of my novels is the polar opposite of my own Camille—a sunny, blonde child who spoke her first word at eight months and hasn't stopped talking since. At the time I invented Turtle, I had no child at all. Mine came later, and I didn't find her in a car, as happened in *The Bean Trees.* Mine was harder to produce. I never use my own family and friends as the basis of fictional characters, mainly because I would like them to remain my family and friends. And secondarily, because I believe the purpose of art is not to photocopy life but distill it, learn from it, improve on it, embroider tiny distinct pieces of it into something insightful and entirely new. As Marc Chagall said, "Great art picks up where nature ends."

I know, in real life, many fascinating people; every one of them has limits on what she or he can be talked into. Most, in fact, will ask for my recommendations on their love lives or vacation plans, then reliably do the opposite. When I'm writing a story, I can't mess around with that kind of free spirit. I need characters I can count on to do what I say—take on a foundling baby rather than call the police; fall in love with my self-effacing heroine rather than the sturdy, good-looking divor-cée down the street; pursue a passion for cockfighting, then give it all up at a lover's request; die for honour; own up to guilt. What's more, they must do it all *convincingly.* That means they have to be carrying in their psyches all the right motives—the exact combination of past experi-ences that will lead them to their appointment with my contrived epiphany. Trying to graft a plot onto the real-life history of anyone I actually know, including myself, would be as fruitless as lashing a cit-rus branch onto the trunk of an apple tree. It would look improbable. It would wither and die. Better to plant a seed in the good dirt of imagi-nation. Grow a whole story from scratch.

Most people readily acknowledge the difference between life and art. Why, then, do so many artists keep answering the same question again and again? No, none of those characters is me. It's not my life, I made it up. Yes, *all of it!* Strangers' assumptions about deaths in my fam-ily and the like, odd as this might seem, have caused us some genuine pain. How I wish my art could stand apart from us, carrying no more suggestions about my private life than the work of, say, a stonemason or a tree surgeon. I was raised to be polite, but sometimes I'm inclined to get cranky and bark about this: Give us writers a little credit, will you? We're not just keeping a diary here, we're inventing! Why can't you believe we're capable of making up a story from scratch? Of stringing together a long, elaborate *lie,* for heaven's sake?

When it's put that way, it dawns on me that this may be the snag— the part about lying. In the book-jacket photos I look like a decent girl, and decent girls don't lie. That social axiom runs deep, possibly deeper than any other. The first important moral value we teach our children, after "don't hit your sister," is the difference between fantasy and truth. Trying to pass off one for the other is a punishable infraction, and a lesson that sticks for life. Whether or not we are perfectly honest in adulthood, we *should* be, and we know that on a visceral level. So visceral, in fact, a machine measuring heart rate and palm perspiration can fairly reliably detect a lie. We don't even have to think about it. Our hearts know.

So I suppose I should be relieved when people presume my stories are built around a wholesome veracity. They're saying, in effect, "You don't *look* like a sociopath." And it's true, I'm not; I pay my taxes and don't litter. Track down any grade-school teacher who knew me in childhood and she'll swear I was a goodie two-shoes even back then.

But ask my mother, and she'll tell you I always had a little trouble with the boundaries of truth. As the aerospace engineers say, I pushed the envelope. As a small child I gave my family regular updates on the white horse wearing a hat that lived in the closet. When I was slightly older, family vacations offered me the delightful opportunity to hang out alone in campground restrooms, intimating to strangers that I came from a foreign country and didn't comprehend English, or plumbing. When I got old enough to use public transportation by myself, my sport was to entertain other passengers with melodramatic personal histories that occurred to me on the spot. I was a nineteen-year-old cello virtuoso running away from my dreadful seventy-year-old husband; or I had a brain tumour, and was determined to see every state in the union by Greyhound in the remaining two months of my life; or I was a French anthropologist working with a team that had just uncovered the real cradle of human origins in a surprising but as-yet-undisclosable location. Oh, how my fellow passengers' eyes would light up. People two rows ahead of me would put down their paperbacks, sling an elbow over the back of the seat, and ride all the rest of the way to Indianapolis backward, asking questions. I probably registered an increased heart rate and sweaty palms, but I couldn't stop myself. I strove for new heights in perjury, trying to see how absurd a yarn I could spin before some matron would finally frown at me over her specs and say, "Now really, dear."

No one ever did. I concluded that people want pretty desperately to be entertained, especially on long bus rides through flat midwestern cornfields.

For me, it was more than a pastime. It was the fulfillment of my own longing to reach through the fences that circumscribed my young life, and taste other pastures. Through my tales I discovered not exactly myself but all the selves I might have been—the ones I feared, the ones I hoped for, and the ones I'd never know. None of them was me. Each of them was a beckoning path into the woods of what might have been.

Eventually I found a socially acceptable outlet for my depravity. Now I spend hours each day, year after year, sitting at my desk with a wicked smirk on my face, making up whopping, four-hundred-page lies. Oh, what a life.

I do want to state for the record that I no longer have any inclination toward real dishonesty; I don't bear false witness to strangers or to friends. And I check my laces obsessively when serving the journalist's or essayist's trade. So my mother isn't to blame—she did, evidently, teach me to know true from false. I gather I was just born with an excess of story, the way another poor child might come into this world with extra fingers on each hand. My imagination had more figment in it than my life could contain, so some of it leaked out here and there. As I've matured, I've learned to control the damage.

I don't believe I'm extraordinary on this account. Every one of us, I think, is born with an excess of story. Listen quietly to a group of toddlers at play: the lies will swarm around their heads, thick as a tribe of bright butterflies, flickering gracefully from one child to another, until they notice a grown-up has come into the room—and in a sudden rush of wings the lies will vanish into air.

A little bit sad, isn't it? If you look it up, you'll find lying was never registered as one of the seven deadly sins. (Pride—an anemic sin if you ask me—is on that list, and so is gluttony, and of all things, sloth. But not lying.) Yet, in the age of evidence and reason, it has gotten such a very bad name. When so many smart, lively people keep insisting to me that all my stories must be true, I begin to suspect they can't quite get their minds around the notion of pure fabrication.

I want to tell them: Stop a minute, right where you are. Relax your shoulders, shake your head and spine like a dog shaking off cold water. Tell that imperious voice in your head to be still, then close your eyes, and tap the well. Find the lie you are longing to tell. It's in there. When you manage to wrestle that first one out, a whole flood may gush out behind it. Take them up in your hands, drink their clarity, write them down in a secret book. Tell them to your children behind the golden door of "Once upon a time." Choose one chair at your dinner table, give it to a different family member each night, and declare it "the liar's seat."

Or take a long bus trip through the cornfields. You may find a new career.

Notes

Marc Chagall a renowned Russian painter (1889–1985) noted for his dream-like, fanciful imagery; his influences included Jewish mysticism and the art-work of the French Post-Impressionists and Picasso

seven deadly sins a reference to the most severe sins according to the Judeo-Christian tradition as documented in the Bible, identified as pride, avarice, lust, anger, sloth, gluttony, and envy

Activities

1. In this essay, although Kingsolver calls stories "lies" and "fabrications," in what sense are fictional narratives "true"? What reasons does Kingsolver give for people's fascination with stories? If stories are lies, what is their purpose? Have a class discussion in which you identify some of the truths in fictional stories you have read.

2. Find what you think is Kingsolver's thesis statement for this essay. Explain how Kingsolver uses personal anecdotes, humour, emotional appeal, and logical reasoning to make her arguments convincing to the reader. Write an alternative thesis statement that captures the subject of the essay and Kingsolver's tone.

3. Use Kingsolver's suggestion about declaring a chair as a "liar's seat" for a class improvisation activity. Take turns or ask for volunteers to sit in the "liar's seat." Open the flood gates of your imagination and begin to tell a fictional "chain" story. On a pre-arranged signal, have different students assume the "liar's seat" and take up the story where the previous narrator left off. Use some of the lies that Kingsolver told to fellow passengers on the bus as story starters.

Call of the Weird

Drew Hayden Taylor

Drew Hayden Taylor was born at the Curve Lake Reserve near Peterborough, Ontario, in 1962. Taylor is a writer of non-fiction, fiction, plays, and television and film scripts. His plays have received numerous awards, including the Chalmers Award. Taylor has written that "storytelling, in my opinion, should always be a mysterious process; otherwise there goes much of the fun. If we know where the stories come from, then the journey to where they end might seem a little less magical." In this essay, Taylor explores cultural assumptions and misunderstandings. Can you think of a time when someone made inaccurate assumptions about your cultural background? What are some of the dangers of making assumptions about others based on their background?

When I first read the job description for the position of Artistic Director of Native Earth Performing Arts, Toronto's only professional Native theatre company, I don't remember coming across any paragraph or subsection anywhere on the page requiring me to become the "oracle of the Aboriginal trivia."

On any given day, questions of unusual and frequently surreal nature are posed to me and the other intelligent, though often puzzled, members of the office. The number of times I've seen heads, with telephones attached, shaking in amazement, makes me wonder about the logical processes of people's minds.

We are a theatre company. That is what we do. We produce plays by and about Native people. Check it out, it's in our mandate. We'll fax it to you if you don't believe us. The majority of questions that Bell Canada sends our way are not within our realm of expertise. While one of our functions as a theatre company is to educate the public, that does not mean one at a time, about obscure issues, while our other work waits. We have lives too, you know.

Our beleaguered office staff has put together a collection of some of the more…interesting…inquiries to come through our office in recent months.

I'm trying to find Sam Ke-something or other. I really don't know how to pronounce his last name. Do you know where I can find him? Or, *I'm trying to locate a Bob Whitecloud of the Sioux tribe in the States. I heard he might be in Canada. Can you tell me how to get in touch with him?*

It's a little known fact that Native Earth Performing Arts is the focal point for all Native people in North America. The one million or so people claiming some sort of Aboriginal ancestry all pass through our doors at one point or another. That's why we have to replace our carpets at least four times a year.

Do all the seats face the stage?

I guess you can call us slaves to conformity. We did try having the seats face the back of the theatre but audience reaction, shall we say, was not that favourable.

Hi, I'm wondering if you can help me. I'm to locate an Apache wedding prayer.

I checked. Sorry, no Apaches in our office, married or not. I did however manage to find a Mohawk secret handshake.

I'm with a casting company for a movie. I'm looking for a Native man, tall and lean with long dark hair and presence. Preferably he should be in his early 30s. And yes, he has to look very striking.

Yeah, most of the women in my office are looking for him too. What do you want me to do about it? The line starts behind them.

I'm phoning from Edinburgh, Scotland. I'm doing research on Native people in the 1930s. Can you send me information?

There were none. I have it on good authority all Native people were killed off in the late 1800s. But in the latter part of this century, due to an overabundance of bureaucrats in Ottawa, the federal government decided to create a new department to employ these people. So the Department of Indian Affairs was created with no Indians. Through secret DNA experiments, a new race of Native people was created at a clandestine location known as…Algonquin Park.

I'm Herman —— from Germany. I'm looking for people of the Bear clan. My last name means bear in German. Do you know any or can you help me find the Bear clan?

Sorry, we have yet to update our database and cross-reference our membership, actors, directors, stage managers, and others by clan affiliation. We're awaiting the software to come out for Windows.

We're an organization of men against men who commit violence against women. We want to know if you guys could provide any ceremonies or spiritual things of that nature that would help us with healing and matters like that.

While that is a noble cause, we are not "Ceremonies 'R' Us," or "have medicine pouch, will travel."

Do you know where I can get my hands on some Inuit throat singers?

As a Native organization, we do not condone violence against the Inuit.

In all fairness and honesty, we do try to be as polite and helpful as possible, and pass callers on to the appropriate organizations. But we are in the business of making art, not making a Native trivial pursuit game. But it makes me wonder if the Mirvishes ever get calls asking, "There's this Jewish song I keep hearing. Hava-something. You wouldn't happen to know the full title and who sang it, would you?"

Notes

Native Earth Performing Arts an arts organization based in Toronto that produces and promotes Aboriginal theatrical works

Mirvishes the father and son team of Ed and David Mirvish, businessmen who have been influential in the development and presentation of theatre in Canada and who own the Royal Alexandra Theatre, among others, in Toronto

Activities

1. Have a class discussion on the title of this essay. To what work of literature does it allude? Explain the purpose of the literary allusion in the title and how Taylor's title prepares us for the content, style, and tone of the essay.

2. Use the glossary in this anthology and other reference tools to review the meaning of the term *irony*. Prepare to write an analytical essay by finding examples of irony in Taylor's essay. Create a thesis statement in which you explain the impact of Taylor's use of irony on his audience. When writing your essay, use the method of *cause and effect* to explore and assess how Taylor uses this literary device to instruct his readers and persuade them to change their attitudes.

3. Working with a partner, pick one of the questions and answers from Taylor's essay and use it as the basis for a humorous improvised skit. In your skit, reconstruct the entire conversation that could have taken place. Record your skit or perform it for another pair. Afterward, have the pair evaluate how successful both the content and the style of your skit were in using humour to inform, entertain, and educate.

Another Viewpoint: Culture

Discuss whether or not you think this type of irony would be appropriate if it had been written by someone with a non-Native background. Do research into the issue of voice appropriation. Then participate in a class discussion in which you explore and analyze the arguments that form the basis of this issue.

A Modest Proposal

For Preventing the Children of Poor People in Ireland from Being
a Burden to Their Parents or Country, and for Making Them
Beneficial to the Public

Jonathan Swift

Jonathan Swift, one of the most renowned satirists in world literature,
is best known for his novel *Gulliver's Travels*. Although he spent a
great deal of his life in England, Swift was born in Ireland in 1667,
where he died in 1745. He was an Anglican priest, but often chastised
the Church for religious complacency. Though Swift began by writing poetry, he turned increasingly to satire and social commentary, frequently about the plight of the Irish, who were experiencing extreme
poverty and famine. What responsibility do writers have to comment
on social issues and injustices? To what extent can they affect public opinion and government policy? Why do you think writers are
often among the first people imprisoned by totalitarian regimes?

It is a melancholy object to those who walk through this great town or
travel in the country, when they see the streets, the roads, and cabin
doors, crowded with beggars of the female sex, followed by three, four,
or six children, all in rags and importuning every passenger for an alms.
These mothers, instead of being able to work for their honest livelihood,
are forced to employ all their time in strolling to beg sustenance for
their helpless infants, who, as they grow up, either turn thieves for want
of work, or leave their dear native country to fight for the Pretender in
Spain, or sell themselves to the Barbadoes.

I think it is agreed by all parties that this prodigious number of children in the arms, or on the backs, or at the heels of their mothers, and frequently of their fathers, is in the present deplorable state of the kingdom a very great additional grievance; and therefore whoever could find out a fair, cheap, and easy method of making these children sound, useful members of the commonwealth would deserve so well of the public as to have his statue set up for a preserver of the nation.

But my intention is very far from being confined to provide only for the children of professed beggars; it is of a much greater extent, and shall take in the whole number of infants at a certain age who are born of parents in effect as little able to support them as those who demand our charity in the streets.

As to my own part, having turned my thoughts for many years upon this important subject, and maturely weighed the several schemes of other projectors, I have always found them grossly mistaken in their computation. It is true, a child just dropped from its dam may be supported by her milk for a solar year, with little other nourishment; at most not above the value of two shillings, which the mother may certainly get, or the value in scraps, by her lawful occupation of begging; and it is exactly at one year old that I propose to provide for them in such a manner as instead of being a charge upon their parents or the parish, or wanting food and raiment for the rest of their lives, they shall on the contrary contribute to the feeding, and partly to the clothing, of many thousands....

The number of souls in this kingdom being usually reckoned one million and a half, of these I calculate there may be about two hundred thousand couple whose wives are breeders; from which number I subtract thirty thousand couples who are able to maintain their own children, although I apprehend there cannot be so many under the present distresses of the kingdom; but this being granted, there will remain an hundred and seventy thousand breeders. I again subtract fifty thousand for those women who miscarry, or whose children die by accident or disease within the year. There only remain an hundred and twenty thousand children of poor parents annually born. The question therefore is, how this number shall be reared and provided for, which, as I have already said, under the present situation of affairs, is utterly impossible by all the methods hitherto proposed. For we can neither employ them in handicraft or agriculture; we neither build houses (I mean in the country) nor cultivate land. They can very seldom pick up a livelihood by stealing till they arrive at six years old, except where they are of towardly parts; although I confess they learn the rudiments much earlier, during which time they can however be looked upon only as probationers, as I have been informed by a principal gentleman in the county of Cavan, who protested to me that he never knew above one or two instances under the ages of six, even in a part of the kingdom so renowned for the quickest proficiency in that art.

I am assured by our merchants that a boy or a girl before twelve years old is no salable commodity; and even when they come to this age they will not yield above three pounds, or three pounds and half a crown at most on the Exchange; which cannot turn to account either to the parents or the kingdom, the charge of nutriment and rags having been at least four times that value.

I shall now therefore humbly propose my own thoughts, which I hope will not be liable to the least objection.

I have been assured by a very knowing American of my acquaintance in London, that a young healthy child well nursed is at a year old a most delicious, nourishing, and wholesome food, whether stewed, roasted, baked, or boiled; and I make no doubt that it will equally serve in a fricassee or a ragout.

I do therefore humbly offer it to public consideration that of the hundred and twenty thousand children, already computed, twenty thousand may be reserved for breed, whereof only one fourth part to be males, which is more than we allow to sheep, black cattle, or swine; and my reason is that these children are seldom the fruits of marriage, a circumstance not much regarded by our savages, therefore one male will be sufficient to serve four females. That the remaining hundred thousand may at a year old be offered in sale to the persons of quality and fortune through the kingdom, always advising the mother to let them suck plentifully in the last month, so as to render them plump and fat for a good table. A child will make two dishes at an entertainment for friends;

and when the family dines alone, the fore or hind quarter will make a reasonable dish, and seasoned with a little pepper or salt will be very good boiled on the fourth day, especially in winter.

I have reckoned upon a medium that a child just born will weigh twelve pounds, and in a solar year if tolerably nursed increaseth to twenty-eight pounds.

I grant this food will be somewhat dear, and therefore very proper for landlords, who, as they have already devoured most of the parents, seem to have the best title to the children.

Infant's flesh will be in season throughout the year, but more plentiful in March, and a little before and after. For we are told by a grave author, an eminent French physician, that fish being a prolific diet, there are more children born in Roman Catholic countries about nine months after Lent than at any other season; therefore, reckoning a year after Lent, the markets will be more glutted than usual, because the number of popish infants is at least three to one in this kingdom; and therefore it will have one other collateral advantage, by lessening the number of Papists among us.

I have already computed the charge of nursing a beggar's child (in which list I reckon all cottagers, labourers, and four fifths of the farmers) to be about two shillings per annum, rags included; and I believe no gentleman would repine to give ten shillings for the carcass of a good fat child, which, as I have said, will make four dishes of excellent nutritive meat, when he hath only some particular friend or his own family to dine with him. Thus the squire will learn to be a good landlord, and grow popular among the tenants; the mother will have eight shillings net profit, and be fit for the work till she produces another child.

Those who are more thrifty (as I must confess the times require) may flay the carcass; the skin of which artificially dressed will make admirable gloves for ladies, and summer boots for fine gentlemen.

As to our city of Dublin, shambles may be appointed for this purpose in the most convenient parts of it, and butchers we may be assured will not be wanting; although I rather recommend buying the children alive, and dressing them hot from the knife as we do roasting pigs.

A very worthy person, a true lover of his country, and whose virtues I highly esteem, was lately pleased in discoursing on this matter to offer a refinement upon my scheme. He said that many gentlemen of this kingdom, having of late destroyed their deer, he conceived that the want of venison might be well supplied by the bodies of young lads and maidens, not exceeding fourteen years of age nor under twelve, so great a number of both sexes in every county being now ready to starve for want of work and service; and these to be disposed of by their parents, if alive, or otherwise by their nearest relations. But with due deference to so excellent a friend and so deserving a patriot, I cannot be altogether in his sentiments; for as to the males, my American acquaintance assured me from frequent experience that their flesh was generally tough and lean, like that of our schoolboys, by continual exercise, and their taste disagreeable; and to fatten them would not answer the charge. Then as to the females, it would, I think with humble submission, be a loss to the public, because they soon would become breeders themselves; and besides, it is not improbable that some scrupulous people might be apt to censure such a practice (although indeed very unjustly) as a little bordering upon cruelty; which I confess, hath always been with me the strongest objection against any project, how well soever intended.

But in order to justify my friend, he confessed that this expedient was put into his head by the famous Psalmanazar, a native of the island Formosa, who came from thence to London above twenty years ago, and in conversation told my friend that in his country when any young person happened to be put to death, the executioner sold the carcass to persons of quality as a prime dainty; and that in his time the body of a plump girl of fifteen, who was crucified for an attempt to poison the emperor, was sold to his Imperial Majesty's prime minister of state, and other great mandarins of the court, in joints from the gibbet, at four hundred crowns. Neither indeed can I deny that if the same use were made of several plump young girls in this town, who without one single groat to their fortunes cannot stir abroad without a chair, and appear at the playhouse and assemblies in foreign fineries which they never will pay for, the kingdom would not be the worse.

Some persons of a desponding spirit are in great concern about that vast number of poor people who are aged, diseased, or maimed, and I have been desired to employ my thoughts what course may be taken to ease the nation of so grievous an encumbrance. But I am not in the least pain upon that matter, because it is very well known that they are every day dying and rotting by cold and famine, and filth and vermin, as fast as can be reasonably expected. And as to the younger labourers, they are now in almost as hopeful a condition. They cannot get work, and consequently pine away for want of nourishment to a degree that if at any time they are accidentally hired to common labour, they have not strength to perform it; and thus the country and themselves are happily delivered from the evils to come.

I have too long digressed, and therefore shall return to my subject. I think the advantages by the proposal which I have made are obvious and many, as well as of the highest importance.

For first, as I have already observed, it would greatly lessen the number of Papists, with whom we are yearly overrun, being the principal breeders of the nation as well as our most dangerous enemies; and who stay at home on purpose to deliver the kingdom to the Pretender, hoping to take their advantage by the absence of so many good Protestants, who have chosen rather to leave their country than stay at home and pay tithes against their conscience to an Episcopal curate.

Secondly, the poorer tenants will have something valuable of their own, which by law may be made liable to distress, and help to pay their landlord's rent, their corn and cattle being already seized and money a thing unknown.

Thirdly, whereas the maintenance of an hundred thousand children, from two years old and upwards, cannot be computed at less than ten shillings a piece per annum, the nation's stock will be thereby increased fifty thousand pounds per annum, besides the profit of a new dish introduced to the tables of all gentlemen of fortune in the kingdom who have any refinement in taste. And the money will circulate among ourselves, the goods being entirely of our own growth and manufacture.

Fourthly, the constant breeders, besides the gain of eight shillings sterling per annum by the sale of their children, will be rid of the charge of maintaining them after the first year.

Fifthly, this food would likewise bring great custom to taverns, where the vintners will certainly be so prudent as to procure the best receipts for dressing it to perfection, and consequently have their houses frequented by all the fine gentlemen, who justly value themselves upon their knowledge in good eating; and a skilful cook, who understands how to oblige his guests, will contrive to make it as expensive as they please.

Sixthly, this would be a great inducement to marriage, which all wise nations have either encouraged by rewards or enforced by laws and penalties. It would increase the care and tenderness of mothers toward their children, when they were sure of a settlement for life to the poor babes, provided in some sort by the public, to their annual profit instead of expense. We should see an honest emulation among the married women, which of them could bring the fattest child to the market. Men would become as fond of their wives during the time of their pregnancy as they are now of their mares in foal, their cows in calf, or sows when they are ready to farrow; nor offer to beat or kick them (as is too frequent a practice) for fear of a miscarriage.

Many other advantages might be enumerated. For instance, the addition of some thousand carcasses in our exportation of barrelled beef, the propagation of swine's flesh, and improvement in the art of making good bacon, so much wanted among us by the great destruction of pigs, too frequent at our tables, which are no way comparable in taste or magnificence to a well-grown, fat, yearling child, which roasted whole will make a considerable figure at a lord mayor's feast or any other public entertainment. But this and many others I omit, being studious of brevity.

Supposing that one thousand families in this city would be constant customers for infants' flesh, besides others who might have it at merry meetings, particularly weddings and christenings, I compute that Dublin would take off annually about twenty thousand carcasses, and the rest of the kingdom (where probably they will be sold somewhat cheaper) the remaining eighty thousand.

I can think of no one objection that will probably be raised against this proposal, unless it should be urged that the number of people will be thereby much lessened in the kingdom. This I freely own, and it was indeed one principal design in offering it to the world. I desire the reader will observe, that I calculate my remedy for this one individual kingdom of Ireland and for no other that ever was, is, or I think ever can be upon earth. Therefore let no man talk to me of other expedients: of taxing our absentees at five shillings a pound: of using neither clothes nor household furniture except what is of our own growth and manufacture: of utterly rejecting the materials and instruments that promote foreign luxury: of curing the expensiveness of pride, vanity, idleness, and gaming in our women: of introducing a vein of parsimony, prudence, and temperance: of learning to love our country, in the want of which we differ even from Laplanders and the inhabitants of Topinamboo: of quitting our animosities and factions,... of being a little cautious not to sell our country and conscience for nothing: of teaching landlords to have at least one degree of mercy toward their tenants: lastly, of putting a spirit of honesty, industry, and skill into our shopkeepers; who, if a resolution could now be taken to buy only our native goods, would immediately unite to cheat and exact upon us in the price, the measure, and the goodness, nor could ever yet be brought to make one fair proposal of just dealing, though often and earnestly invited to it.

Therefore I repeat, let no man talk to me of these and the like expedients, till he hath at least some glimpse of hope that there will ever be some hearty and sincere attempt to put them in practice.

But as to myself, having been wearied out for many years with offering vain, idle, visionary thoughts, and at length utterly despairing of success, I fortunately fell upon this proposal, which, as it is wholly new, so it hath something solid and real, of no expense and little trouble, full in our own power, and whereby we can incur no danger in disobliging

England. For this kind of commodity will not bear exportation, the flesh being of too tender a consistence to admit a long continuance in salt, although perhaps I could name a country which would be glad to eat up our whole nation without it.

After all, I am not so violently bent upon my own opinion as to reject any offer proposed by wise men, which shall be found equally innocent, cheap, easy, and effectual. But before something of that kind shall be advanced in contradiction to my scheme, and offering a better, I desire the author or authors will be pleased maturely to consider two points. First, as things now stand, how they will be able to find food and raiment for an hundred thousand useless mouths and backs. And secondly, there being a round million of creatures in human figure throughout this kingdom, whose sole subsistence put into a common stock would leave them in debt two millions of pounds sterling, adding those who are beggars by profession to the bulk of farmers, cottagers, and labourers, with their wives and children who are beggars in effect; I desire those politicians who dislike my overture, and may perhaps be so bold to attempt an answer, that they will first ask the parents of these mortals whether they would not at this day think it a great happiness to have been sold for food at a year old in the manner I prescribe, and thereby have avoided such a perpetual sense of misfortunes as they have since gone through by the oppression of landlords, the impossibility of paying rent without money or trade, the want of common sustenance, with neither house nor clothes to cover them from the inclemencies of the weather, and the most inevitable prospect of entailing the like or greater miseries upon their breed forever.

I profess, in the sincerity of my heart, that I have not the least personal interest in endeavouring to promote this necessary work, having no other motive than the public good of my country, by advancing our trade, providing for infants, relieving the poor, and giving some pleasure to the rich. I have no children by which I can propose to get a single penny; the youngest being nine years old, and my wife past childbearing.

Notes

the Pretender in Spain James Stuart, son of James I, who claimed the English throne in 1688, but was unsuccessful and continued to live in exile in Spain. A Roman Catholic, he was supported by the Scottish and Irish.

sell themselves to the Barbadoes work as indentured servants in the Caribbean, especially the island of Barbados

raiment clothing

apprehend understand

towardly parts advanced readiness to learn

probationers in training to be thieves

popish, Papists Roman Catholics

cottagers tenant farmers

repine to be discontented

artificially in this instance, skilfully

shambles slaughterhouses

Psalmanazar George Psalmanazar (circa 1679–1763) was an English literary imposter whose real name is not known. Born and educated in France, he was able without detection to invent a complete "Formosan" language and teach this language at Oxford University. In 1706, he was forced to repudiate his claims.

mandarins high public officials; from the Sanskrit word *mantrin*, meaning "counsellor"

gibbet gallows where people were hanged; from the Old French word *gibet*, a diminutive of the word *gibe*, meaning "club"

groat small sum of money

Papists...deliver the kingdom to the Pretender Most Roman Catholics supported James Stuart in his struggle to become king of England.

custom in this instance, business

receipts a synonym for the word *recipes*

Activities

1. In point form, outline the speaker's "modest proposal" and several reasons presented to support it. Then record your personal reactions: How did you react when you first realized what is being proposed? At what point did you realize that the proposal is satirical?

2. Swift's essay "A Modest Proposal" is carefully structured in its beginning (paragraphs 1–7), middle (paragraphs 8–19), and end (paragraphs 20–37). Read the essay and outline the following: which aspects of his topic Swift presents in each section; the methods of development Swift uses to make his argument; and the inclusion of Swift's personal motives and values. Share your observations in a small group.

3. Write your own "modest proposal" to draw attention to a current injustice, cruelty, or folly. After you have completed a first draft, revise your draft to make sure that your thesis is clearly stated and developed, and to enhance the effectiveness of your style.

Another Viewpoint: Literary Modes and Forms

Satire is designed to expose human weaknesses and follies, often with the purpose of stimulating intellectual and social reform. Satirists look at the disparity between the ideal and the reality of individuals, institutions, or practices. In an analytical essay, explore which injustices Swift is denouncing, which particular elements of satire are evident, and which "ideal" conditions Swift is hoping to achieve by his proposal.

Tower of Babel, 1928, M.C. Escher

Get Beyond Babel

Ken Wiwa

Ken Wiwa was born in Lagos, Nigeria, in 1968. Educated in England, Wiwa became a journalist. He was thrust into the spotlight when his father, Ken Saro-Wiwa, was arrested and sentenced to death in Nigeria for his efforts to protect human rights and the environment. Though the son had previously distanced himself from his father's political activities, he led the public campaign to save his father's life. Despite worldwide outcry, Ken Saro-Wiwa was executed in 1995. Today, Ken Wiwa lives and writes in Toronto. In 2000, he published a memoir, *In the Shadow of a Saint: A Son's Journey to Understand His Father's Legacy*. Many individuals and organizations work to protect our physical environment. Threats to our cultural environments also exist. How can a culture be threatened? Do you think we should have the same level of concern for endangered languages and cultures as we do for endangered species?

Earlier this week I received compelling evidence that I am doomed to extinction. According to figures released by the Worldwatch Institute, half of the world's 6,800 languages face annihilation; that's because they are spoken by fewer than 2,500 people. Here in Canada, only three of 50 aboriginal languages may survive the coming cultural Armageddon. Lurking in the reaction to this news, I suspect, is the fear that we will end up speaking English in some monocultural flatland called "Disney."

There is an impassioned school of thought that says that unless we take active steps to preserve our "cultural diversity"—read "languages"—the human race is in danger. When we lose a language, these doomsday prophets say, we lose its knowledge base and worldview; this, they assure us, impoverishes us all.

As a member of an indigenous people, and as someone actively concerned about the fate of my culture, I used to subscribe to this view. I'd soak up the arguments of philologists and writers I admired warning about the implications of losing our languages. I bought all these arguments. Then I started examining my own community's experience.

I am Ogoni. We number an estimated 500,000, and speak six mutually unintelligible dialects—languages, by now—on an overpopulated but fertile floodplain in southern Nigeria. The Ogoni languages and culture are threatened by Nigeria's socioeconomic realities. Our environment has been compromised by aggressive and irresponsible oil exploration. Unemployment, inadequate health care, and neglect by the country's rulers have ripped out my community's heart.

The young, the energetic, and the ambitious have no option but to leave in search of better opportunities. The community is left in the care of the old and the infirm. A whole generation of Ogoni is growing up elsewhere, speaking English, forgetting our languages, exiled from our villages and our traditions. When the elders die, they take our traditions, our folk tales, our myths, our history, and our cultural memories with them. As we say in Africa, "When an old man dies it is like a library has been burned down."

Which is why I started looking into Ogoni history, thinking about my language, trying to shoehorn our myths and folk tales into a compelling story to keep them alive for another generation. But the more I study our history, especially the way our culture and our language has evolved, the more I suspect that those of us who have set out with the intention of reviving a culture by fixing it in time and space may actually be doing more harm than good.

Take the development of my language. According to one of our creation myths, the original Ogoni settlement was at a place called Nama. Here the first Ogoni people cleared the surrounding forest, left one tree standing, and established our roots. Over time our community grew, and people migrated westward into the rain forests until there were 128 villages in Ogoni. Because these settlements were isolated, the language altered subtly. If you go to Ogoni today you can still hear the effects. In the eastern villages we speak a different dialect from the villages on the western fringes.

The point I am making here is that language is in constant flux. To fix it in a particular time and place is to arrest the movement and vitality that shape a language's evolution. The more I examine the way my language has evolved, the more I believe that the best a language can do in response is to go with the flow. As far as I know, no Ogoni language has a word for "computer," but we do say *faa-bu-yon* (car of the sky)— or airplane.

Unless we make a huge effort to open up the language and the culture to embrace our experience of contact with other cultures and the modem world, we will always be vulnerable. To say that is not to diminish the past or our culture, but to acknowledge a simple truth: indigenous peoples must not turn inward and cling to nostalgia for sustenance. Though we look back, we must always go forward.

For me, that's the great poetic insight in Gabriel García Márquez's novel, *One Hundred Years of Solitude.* The community of Macondo begins amid vibrant energy, but ossifies into a parochialism trapped in a cycle of self-repeating prophecies that refuse to embrace or even acknowledge the passage of time. When Marquez delivers his verdict on Macondo (races condemned to 100 years of solitude do not get a second chance), it seems to me to be a warning to all the language curators and conservationists working to preserve our cultures in some cultural museum.

It is a warning that the guardians of the French language, the Académie française, might heed. Once French was the international language of the world; thanks to the Académie's fastidious custody, it is becoming inflexible. English, on the other hand, has rarely been as neurotic about its purity. Most English words are borrowed from other languages; little Anglo-Saxon survives. Only an incurable romantic would attempt to revive Old English for general use. No, English has evolved, absorbed, and adapted. Open to foreign influence, it borrows unashamedly. That's why English has more than 500,000 words in its vocabulary, while French has little more than 100,000.

For me the rise and pre-eminence of English is an example to all cultures about how a language survives and thrives. When Julius Caesar invaded Britain 2,000 years ago, English did not exist. Fifteen hundred years later, Shakespeare had a potential audience of only five million English-speakers. Over the next 400 years, English would come to be spoken by more than one billion people. According to *The Story of English* (by Robert McCrum and Robert MacNeil), English is now "more widely scattered, more widely spoken than any other language has ever been."

Thanks to its versatility, shameless habit of appropriation, and the violence and aggression of its people, English is now the *lingua franca* of the world. What is more remarkable is that despite its mongrel nature, the English worldview has persisted. Through all the mutations and adaptations it has still managed to service and protect a small island's place in the world.

The English people and the English language have survived by picking up influences and adapting words from dead languages, like Latin and ancient Greek, and grafting elements from their worldviews, religions, and philosophies onto the English trunk.

English is both a lesson and an obstacle to the development of other languages and cultures. Which is why it strikes me that to lament the death of languages and to prescribe a solution that freezes language in time is to condemn a culture and a language to certain extinction.

If cultural diversity is so vital to our survival as a race, we must understand how languages work over time. After all, it only took English 400 years to achieve its current status. Who is to say that in another 500 years English will not go the same way as Greek, Latin, or French? There is one more lesson that leaps out from my reading of the story of English. It is this: languages and cultures don't die—they just get absorbed into something else.

Notes

Babel a biblical city where construction of a tower ended when builders could not understand each other's language

Worldwatch Institute a non-profit public policy research organization that collects and analyzes cross-disciplinary information about global environmental issues

Armageddon a huge battle resulting in the total defeat of one side; a reference, in the New Testament, to a battle between good and evil before the day of judgment; from the Hebrew words *har megiddon*, meaning "the hill of Megiddo"

Académie française a French literary academy whose mission is to "protect the purity" of the French language.

lingua franca any combination of languages which two people who do not speak the same language use to communicate with each other; refers, specifically, to a mixture of Italian, French, Greek, Turkish, Arabic, and other languages formerly spoken on the eastern Mediterranean coast

Activities

1. Write an informal response to this essay, in which you describe and react to its context. Consider questions such as the following: From what social and cultural perspective or context is Wiwa writing? How does your social and cultural perspective affect your reaction to his essay?

2. Meet in groups of three to analyze and discuss the organization and persuasive strategies Wiwa uses. Assign each person one of the following sections of the essay: paragraphs 1–6, 7–11, or 12–16. Have each person make a chart that documents his or her paragraphs' topic, purpose, rhetorical devices, and persuasive strategies. Meet to share and discuss your analyses. As a group, evaluate the effectiveness of the organization and persuasive strategies Wiwa has used.

3. Do research to identify other views and data related to the issue of endangered languages in Canada and elsewhere. Organize a class debate on one of the following resolutions: a) Endangered languages should be preserved; b) Preserving a language is not an essential part of preserving a culture. Invite feedback on the effectiveness of the arguments presented.

The Death of History Is Bunk

Patrick Watson

Patrick Watson was born in Toronto in 1929. He has worked as an actor, producer, director, and writer. He has hosted such documentary television programs as *This Hour Has Seven Days*, *The Watson Report*, *Live from the Lincoln Center* and *The Canadians*. His *Witness to Yesterday* television series featured encounters with great figures from the past. From 1989 to 1994, he was the chairman of the CBC. In 1998, he was appointed to the position of commissioning editor for History Television. Some people are concerned about the extent to which people are familiar with the history of their own country. Do you think Canadians and citizens from other countries know enough about Canadian history? What stands out in your memory about the Canadian history you have studied in school? What do you think are the best ways to teach Canadian history?

It is fashionable to deplore the fact that few Canadian schools teach Canadian history. The hand-wringers whimper that young Canadians don't know about Canada's first prime minister, or the date of Confederation, or the meaning of Vimy Ridge.

The assumption is that naming events and memorizing dates make for good citizenship and a wise life. Garbage! If the disappearance of history from high-school curriculums means that the kind of classes I suffered as a kid are gone for good, then bravo. The new generations have been spared the mind-paralyzing waste we were forced to endure, copying from the blackboard lists of dates, of battles, of kings and other dignitaries, of the passing of legislation. If we could reproduce those vacuous details in a quiz, we passed—we had "done history."

But such an approach has not disappeared from the minds of those who write books about who killed Canadian history. In 2000, author Rudyard Griffiths wrote in the *Globe and Mail* that history means "defining events."

"To deny students…a coherent education in the history of Canada is to shut them out of the National Conversation," he wrote. If readers are unable to equate the Charlottetown Conference with Confederation, "they are ill-equipped to gauge the veracity of the claim that Charlottetown was, indeed, a defining moment."

Hello? I cannot equate the Charlottetown Conference with Confederation! And if anybody tells me they can I will soon lose interest in them as conversational partners.

It is a thin theory of history that "equates" a conference with the complex and endless activities that flow therefrom. The Canadian Confederation got a name and some marching orders at Charlottetown, yes. But would it not be more enlightening to know that was done in the salons and backrooms and bedrooms and dining rooms and rectories and bars where the real thinking and compromises took place—before and after being brought to the long table in the big room with the high, arched windows?

To think that Charlottetown defined Confederation is to leave out a catalogue of later events of massive impact, such as the genocide of the European Jews, the Russian Revolution, the telephone, rural electrification, Marquis wheat, urban tramways, free public schools, Italian restaurants, American movies, and television. These are only a few transforming forces that have spoken more to the texture of the civil society we are trying to build than did one conference, however much a crossroads, a century and a third ago.

There are, of course, moments that change our compass bearing sufficiently that we can determine a measure of definition in them. But the Canadians who continuously reshape our society are the class president who sticks up for a principle, the poet or novelist, designer, painter, candidate for town council, fundraiser, creative restaurateur, or the comic who says, "The separatist movement is the glue that holds Canada together." These people remake our nation not by redefining Canada, but by tinkering with it.

That's what writer Evan Solomon says makes us what we are: our tinkering. The Americans like to define. They started with a Declaration of Independence and followed with a Bill of Rights and a Constitution. So now when things go wrong, they scratch their historical heads and ask, "What did the Founding Fathers intend?"

Canadians don't do that. We say, "Well, the old buggy won't run on these new roads with those worn tires; let's see if we can figure out a better way." We are not overwhelmed by guilt or a sense of failure when it's time to fix things.

History contains, but is not made up of great events, defining moments, crucial institutions. History, like art and music, begins locally and grows outward as its students grow in their capacity to look at a larger world. The first historical question is, "Mommy, where did I come from?" In a sense it is the only important question. The exploration of history is a rewarding activity only if it produces meaning out of the chaos of experience. Then, if we find meaning that we can share with others, we become engaged with those others. That engagement will be the beginning of citizenship. Citizenship does not begin with preachings about defining moments, whether Charlottetown or John A. Macdonald or Vimy Ridge.

Travelling the country to the heritage fairs that have emerged from the Heritage Project of Charles Bronfman's CRB Foundation, I have seen Canadian children come back from a foray into the local community, their eyes glistening with the joy of having discovered meaning by doing local history.

In a small city in the B.C. interior I met a 12-year-old girl who, curious about her French surname, tracked it back through the generations. She found not only a lot of ancient photographs and clippings, but ultimately the actual parchment that carried the signature of the Sovereign, appointing her great-great-great-grandfather as the first French-speaking judge of the superior court of Quebec. Do I have to spell out what that search meant in terms of history? Of meaning? Of engagement with her society? And of pride and satisfaction in the completion of a self-initiated search? She owns that piece of history. She knows, existentially, what doing history means and that it is not memorizing the dates of battles or the names of prime ministers.

At the Summerside heritage fair, two 11-year-olds wondered aloud to each other what all those old rusted bits of farm machinery were that lay half-buried in the fence rows—"Hey, Dad, what is that stuff?" Dad didn't know. So they asked some elderly farmers. One of these found an old Massey-Harris catalogue. Another had a friend with a front-end loader who agreed to lift some of this stuff out of the ground so they could see it better. And with that kind of help, those two boys put together a display in a hangar at the old Summerside base of part of the past of Prince Edward Island that nobody else knew.

Perhaps some day a girl in Kelowna or a couple of boys in Summerside will want to fit some of the things they have learned into a larger context. Perhaps they will stumble, in a novel or a play or a book or a film, over the fact that Canada refused asylum to refugees from the Holocaust, and that changing that attitude radically changed the country. Perhaps their inquiries will go elsewhere: to the reason why a certain stream runs red and murky, not clear and sweet; or to the puzzle behind a group who demand that a certain prayer be made formally part of the school day, or what a man meant about the state and the bedrooms of the nation.

But however far their inquiries go, no amount of classroom time, or fretting about the legacy of Charlottetown, can approach what those kids discovered when they found a meaningful answer to an apparently trivial question.

So if we genuinely care about how history impinges upon citizenship (that is, our collective search for a civil society), let us fret less about what is catalogued in the curriculum, and more about how to stimulate the young inquiring mind.

There is a hunger for narrative about our past. History Television here in Canada has had a steady growth in viewership in its four years of life, 64 per cent last year alone. Those heritage fairs, which began in Winnipeg eight years ago with a few hundred kids, last year found more than 100,000 young Canadians doing research projects and writing playlets and producing historical videos. Across Canada, playwrights are attracting enthusiastic audiences to history on the stage, much of it very local in setting, if not in significance.

Hollywood continues to love movies on historical subjects; they win Oscars and other international awards. Millions of kids are playing historical computer games. CTV's broadcast of *Nuremberg* this month averaged two million viewers a night. Even CBC Television, as committed to ratings and the sale of advertising as any other aggressive network, has committed tens of millions of dollars and some 30 hours of documentary television to its *Canada: A People's History.*

History isn't dead; we are making it every day, and it is making us.

Notes

Vimy Ridge battle fought from April 9–14, 1917, during World War I, in which 3,598 Canadians were killed. It was the first time that Canadians attacked as a united group. Despite the large number of casualties, they swept the German soldiers off the ridge and their success created a strong sense of achievement and national pride.

Charlottetown Conference Held in September 1864, this conference set Confederation in motion. The Maritime legislatures had planned the conference to discuss a union of the Maritime provinces, but representatives from the rest of Canada asked to attend. There delegates agreed on an outline for what would become the new country of Canada.

Marquis wheat a hybrid variety of wheat produced by Canadians Percy and Charles Saunders at the end of the nineteenth century. Its early maturation greatly extended the area where wheat could be grown.

Activities

1. In this essay, Patrick Watson holds a strong position on the teaching of history. In your notebook, describe what kind of teacher you think Watson would make. Would you like to be a student in his class? What is your response to the types of learning activities he suggests?

2. In a three-column chart, prepare an analysis of the techniques that Watson uses to persuade his readers. In the first column, list the techniques Watson uses to appeal to reason, emotion, authority, and to ethics, beliefs, values. In the second column, write an example of each technique from the essay. In the third column, write a sentence of your own that illustrates effective use of the technique. Then list each fact or example he uses to illustrate his argument.

3. Patrick Watson has served as the commissioning editor for History Television. In this capacity, the commissioning editor receives submissions and makes decisions about the kinds of programs that will be broadcast on this specialty channel. In small groups, brainstorm some ideas that you think would make effective and interesting programming for History Television. Include suggestions that would have particular appeal for high-school students of history. You may want to send your best ideas via e-mail to a history television channel.

Wanderers by Choice

Eva Hoffman

Eva Hoffman was born in Krakow, Poland, in 1945, the child of Holocaust survivors. When she was thirteen, the family immigrated to Vancouver. At age nineteen, Hoffman moved to the United States and eventually became an editor and writer for the *New York Times*. She has written widely on political and cultural subjects and has received many grants and awards, including a Guggenheim Fellowship. Think of someone you know who has travelled extensively. What are the benefits and the challenges of travel? Would you ever consider living in another country? If so, what appeals to you about this prospect? What challenges might you face?

Exile was once the worst punishment. Now it's a glamorous adventure.

Since Adam and Eve left the Garden of Eden, is there anyone who does not, in some way, feel like an exile? We feel ejected from our first homes and landscapes, from our first romance, from our authentic self. An ideal sense of belonging, of attuning with others and ourselves, eludes us.

Historically, the symbolic meaning and experience of exile have changed. In medieval Europe, it was the worst punishment possible, because people's identities were defined by their role and place in society. This implied a highly charged concept of home—although home did not necessarily mean birthplace. For medieval clerics, it was the city that housed the papal seat. Jews nurtured a powerful idea of home that existed on two levels: the real communities they inhabited and "Israel," which became an imaginative centre from which they derived their essential identity.

In recent years, great shifts in the political and social landscape have affected the very notion of exile. Cross-cultural movement has become the norm, which means that leaving one's native country is not as dramatic or traumatic as it used to be. The ease of travel and communication, combined with the looser borders, gives rise to endless crisscrossing streams of wanderers and guest workers, nomadic adventurers and international drifters. Many are driven by harsh circumstance, but the element of choice is there for most.

People who leave the former Soviet Union nowadays are likely to be economic migrants or Mafia tax dodgers rather than dissidents expelled by ruthless state power. One Bengali village has a tradition of long migrations: many men leave for years or even decades, but always intend to return. They are not powerless victims of globalization; smart young men choose different countries for the economic advantages they offer. Almost all go back, a bit richer and more important in the eyes of their fellow villagers.

The *Herald Tribune* recently characterized the increasing number of American expatriates in Europe: "They are the Americans abroad, and their number is soaring in a time when travel is unblinkingly routine, communications easy and instant, and telecommuting a serious option. They are abroad in a world where they can watch the Super Bowl live from a Moscow sports bar or send an e-mail from an Internet café in Prague."

We all recognize these basic features of our new, fast-changing social landscape. Whether or not we have left, we know how easy it is to leave. We know that we live in a global village, although the village is virtual indeed—dependent not on locality but on the detachment of knowledge, action, information, and identity from a specific place. We have become less spacebound.

Exile used to be considered difficult. It involves dislocation, disorientation, self-division. But today we have come to value exactly those qualities of experience that exile demands—uncertainty, displacement, fragmented identity. Within this framework, exile becomes sexy and glamorous. Nomadism and diasporism have become fashionable terms in intellectual debate. Not only actual exile is at stake, but also how we situate ourselves in the world.

My emigration took place during the Cold War, though not in the worst Stalinist years. I happened to be a young, unwilling emigrant, yanked from my happy childhood. I felt the loss of my first homeland acutely, fuelled by the sense that this departure was irrevocable. Poland was suddenly unreachable, and I felt as if I were being taken out of life itself.

Like so many emigrants, I was in effect without language. To lose an internal language is to slide into an inarticulate darkness where we become alien to ourselves; to lose the ability to describe the world is to render the world a bit less vivid. It takes time before a new language begins to inhabit us deeply, to enter the fabric of our psyches and express who we are.

As with language, so with culture: how much incoherence we risk if we fall out of its matrix. We know that cultures differ in customs, food, religions, social arrangements. What takes longer to understand is that each culture has subliminal values and beliefs. They inform our most intimate assumptions and perceptions, our sense of beauty, of acceptable distances between people, or notions of pleasure and pain. On that fundamental level, a culture gives form and focus to our mental and emotional lives. We are nothing more—or less—than an encoded memory of our heritage.

Real dislocation, the loss of all familiar external and internal parameters, is not glamorous or cool. It is an upheaval in the deep material of the self.

Exile, however, gives perspective, making every emigrant an anthropologist and relativist. To have a deep experience of two cultures is to know that no culture is absolute, to discover that the seemingly natural aspects of our identities and social reality can be arranged, shaped, or articulated in another way. Biculturalism has its pleasures—the relish of sharpened insight, the savviness of skepticism—and they can become addictive.

These virtues have serious defects. The addiction may be too seductive; as a psychological choice, being in exile may become not only too arduous but also too easy. The exile lives in a story in which one's past becomes radically different from the present. The lost homeland, sequestered in the imagination as a mythic, static realm, can be idealized or demonized, or become a space of projections and fantasies.

In our habitually diasporic and nomadic world, the playing field has changed. When all borders are crossable and all boundaries permeable, it is harder to imagine an idyllic realm or a permanent enemy. This situation is initially confusing, yet its merits are easily discernible. We move not only between places but also between cultures with grace and ease. We are less shocked by prevailing assumptions, less prone to absolute assertions. The literature of this new nomadism, represented by Salman Rushdie, is full of multiple cultural references colliding and colluding in robust, vital play. This is a vision of exile as comedy rather than despair.

But I wonder if, in our world of easy come, easy go, of sliding among places and meanings without alighting on any of them for very long, we don't lose an internal focus and certain strengths that come from gathering experiences and accumulating understanding, from placing ourselves squarely where we are and living in a shared framework. I wonder if, in trying to exist in barely perceivable spaces, or conceiving of experience as movement between discrete dots on a horizontal map, we don't risk what the novelist Milan Kundera calls "the unbearable lightness of being." It is the illness that comes upon unanchored people, those who travel perpetually to new moments and sensations and to whom no internal feeling is more important than another.

Among nomads, exile loses its charge because there is no place from which one can be expelled, no powerful notion of home. Indeed, now we are less likely to say that all fiction is homesickness than to say that all homesickness is fiction—that home never was what it was cracked up to be, the haven of safety and affection we imagine. Instead, we conceive of home mostly as a site of enclosure and closure, of narrow-mindedness and nationalism. There are two kinds of homes: the home of our childhood and origin, which is a given, and the home of our adulthood, which is achieved only through hard-earned, patient choice, the labour of understanding and gradual arrival.

In a parable about the founder of the Jewish Hasidic movement, thieves tell the Baal Shem Tov about a network of underground corridors that leads directly from Poland to Palestine and offer to take him there. With great difficulty, they walk through the tunnels more than halfway to their destination. Then, suddenly, the Baal Shem Tov sees before him "a flaming sword, turning this way and that," and decides to turn back.

On one level this parable shows the Baal Shem Tov's ambivalence about going to Palestine. On another, its unconscious, compressed message may be that we can't steal into paradise, or take a shortcut to the tree of life. Of course, the parable also suggests something about the fear of approaching our object of desire and finding ourselves in paradise— which may then turn out to be an ordinary garden, needing weeding, tilling, and watering.

To be sure, it takes long, strenuous work to find terrain of safety or significance or love. And it may often be easier to live in exile with a fantasy of paradise than to suffer the ambiguities and compromises of cultivating actual, earthly places. And yet, if we do not create home structures for ourselves, we risk exile that we do not even recognize as banishment. And, paradoxically, if we do not acknowledge the possibility and pain of expulsion, then we will not know that somewhere a tree of life—if we labour hard enough to approach it—can yield fruits of meaning after all.

Notes

clerics members of the clergy, such as priests or ministers

papal seat the residence of the Pope of the Roman Catholic Church, located in Rome, Italy

diasporism dispersal of people away from their homeland; from the Greek words *dia*, meaning "through," and *speirein*, meaning "to scatter or sow"

Cold War the struggle for power and prestige between the Western powers and the Communist bloc from the end of World War II to about 1990

Stalinist policies associated with Joseph Stalin, the leader of the Soviet Union from 1924 to 1953; marked by terror and authoritarianism

psyches in this instance, souls

matrix the object or place where something originates; from the Latin word *mater*, meaning "mother"

sequestered isolated, set apart

colluding conspiring or plotting with others

Milan Kundera a renowned novelist, born in Czechoslovakia, who settled in France for political reasons and had his Czech citizenship revoked by the Communist regime

Jewish Hasidic movement Founded in Poland in the eighteenth century, this branch of Judaism stresses joyous religious expression through song and dance.

Baal Shem Tov in Hebrew, the Master of the Good Name; the name given to the founder of the modern Hasidic movement, Israel ben Eliezer, whose life was the subject of many tales

Activities

1. Write a letter to the editor of a hypothetical magazine in which this article might appear. Before you begin, select a number of magazines and study the content and style of their letters to the editor. Using these letters as a model for your own, express your response to the author's ideas.

2. Discuss the rhetorical strategies the author employs in "Wanderers by Choice." Identify, for example, the effective use of narrative, description, analogy, and cause and effect. With a partner, reread some recent pieces of your own writing and consider how incorporating these strategies would strengthen your work.

3. Recall a time when you experienced some of the thoughts and emotions the author describes in this essay. Write a narrative essay in which you explore this incident in your life. How did your experience change your understanding of yourself or of the world? Read your work aloud in order to ensure that your punctuation contributes to the clarity of your text.

Peace, Technology, and the Role of Ordinary People

Ursula Franklin

Ursula Franklin was born in Munich, Germany, in 1921. She studied at the Technical University of Berlin in Germany and did postdoctoral work at the University of Toronto. Franklin is a world-renowned expert in the structure of metals and alloys. She pioneered the development of archaeometry, the science of applying the modern techniques of materials analysis to archaeology. In 1984, Franklin became the first woman to be named a full university professor at the University of Toronto. Franklin has helped to develop Canadian science policy through the Science Council of Canada and the Natural Sciences and Engineering Research Council of Canada. She has worked tirelessly to educate scientists and society on the impact of technology upon our quality of life and our survival. Her many honours include a Governor General's Award in 1991 and Companion of the Order of Canada in 1992. In this speech, she outlines the transformation of war from the time of the Cold War to what she believes is now a war for global market power. What does peace mean to you? What conditions must exist in order for world peace to exist?

What I would like to do tonight is to look at what has happened to the concerns about peace and science since 1989 when John and Lois Dove so tragically left us. I want to do it by looking at the three corners that encompass this field of concern: one is peace, the second is technology, and the third is the role of ordinary people in the search for peace.

In 1989 it looked as if our concerns for peace were coming to some resolution. It looked as if there might be peace because the end of the Cold War appeared to be in sight; the quest for peace in some way was going to be, if not completely successful, at least substantially advanced.

The general quest for peace can be seen as the set of questions that makes us think: how do we get from here to a world in which there is, to use a term that Kenneth Boulding favoured, stable peace?

We know that peace means the presence of justice, and the absence of fear, as well as the absence of war—war both as a threat and as a reality. It appeared in 1989 that there might be a chance to get closer to that goal of stable peace. Our dream of getting there seemed closer to realization.

The peace we pray and work for is not a commodity, but the consequence of a just ordering of society. Thus there are essential political, human, and economic components that make peace possible. What would become possible through stable peace is the prevalence of justice, compassion, and fairness and with it the absence of fear.

Unfortunately, the sphere of our own reality has changed very drastically since 1989, mostly for the worse, even though our activities in the quest for peace have not diminished. The global political realities have changed in a very strange way. All who had hoped that, with the end of the Cold War, some of the developments that we had pressed for would come to pass were deeply saddened by the turn of events.

There had been, for instance, the expectation that money that used to be spent on the arms race would become available to meet human needs. In other words, there was the hope for a peace dividend. We expected there would be more money for teaching and research, for arresting environmental deterioration, for building institutions of peace and international co-operation. Once the burden of the arms race would be lightened or lifted, we thought, a very different set of priorities for the use of public funds would emerge. Why did this not happen? The end of the Cold War did not rechannel resources into peace, the environment, or unmet human needs. Instead of the promised peace dividend, we got a displacement of war, rather than an abolition of war. The displacement of war occurred essentially on two levels. On the first level, war as the old shooting reality is still painfully present in Bosnia, Chechnya, and many other places in the world.

But in addition to the replacement of the threat of war between the big powers by war among smaller states, we have witnessed another form of the displacement of war: its displacement into the economic sphere. As part of these developments we have seen significant transmutations of the social institution of war. War has been updated with a set of modern instruments to assist in the struggle for global commercial hegemony.

Economic competition and conflict have taken on the very characteristics of active, slaughtering warfare—from propaganda and scapegoating to the loss of lives, displacement of populations, and the destruction of natural and built environments. These events put the peace movement again in the position of having to struggle against the arrogance and ignorance of power, against impending destruction, occupation, and conquest.

Instead of enjoying a peace dividend, we see in our own country cutbacks and layoffs. We see neglect and degradation of scholarship, of the civil environment, and of nature. The so-called job crisis, the automation of work and human tasks, is on the most profound level a war against people. The new policies of rationalization and globalization of alliances and trade agreements are part and parcel of the type of threat system that the peace movement has tried to expose and fight at least for the past four decades.

In spite of the end of the Cold War, neither the mentality nor the practitioners of the threat system have disappeared. On the contrary, the threat system is growing internationally and nationally. What we have seen at the end of the Cold War was not, as one might have hoped for in 1989, a decrease in the incidence of war. What happened, I hold, is that war has been transposed into another key.

Just as music can be transposed into another key, I would like to put to you the thought that war, in addition to its continuing presence in terms of armed struggle and the preparation for armed conflict (complete with arms sales and attendant profits) has undergone a social and political transposition into a new key. We, as peace people, need to understand, explain, and confront the new transposition, the new mutation of the social institution of war.

At this point you well may ask: How come? What happened? Surely, with the end of the Cold War, the justification and the stated reason for an arms race ended (remember, there was an evil empire, justifying everything from Star Wars to stealth bombers). Why did the major world power not convert to peace? Why did the co-operative and constructive developments we had hoped for not come about? In order to come to grips with these questions, let us reflect for a moment on the nature of the transposition of war into a new key and on the new instruments that are now playing the old tunes.

First, anyone wanting to make war needs an enemy. In the new war context one may ask: Who is the enemy? Where is the enemy? In looking for an answer, it will be necessary to give some special attention to the recent manifestation of modern technologies. Let's start with a definition of technology. From my point of view, technology is best defined as practice, i.e., "the way things are done around here."

Current practice, of course, includes machines and devices, computers and every form of network and machinery. Yet all these instrumentalities are embedded in something larger, which is why I find helpful the definition of technology as "the way things are done around here." Clearly, the way things are done today is not necessarily the way things were done in the past nor the way things will be done in the future. Thus this definition of technology lets us keep determinism and fatalism at bay.

Citizen advocacy has often involved discussions of technology, critiques of the way things were done—as well as what was being done. Technological changes have frequently brought groups within society face to face with the need to influence decision-making and regulations in areas that suddenly affected everyone's daily lives—be it the testing of nuclear weapons, the pollution of air or water, or the depiction of violence on television. The subject and thrust of citizen interventions can be a sensitive barometer indicating incipient changes in social and political relationships.

What then should be the themes of citizen interventions in the mid-'90s, particularly those involving the work for peace? I am convinced that it is necessary to refocus the citizens' perspectives and priorities as well as to scrutinize the role technology played in the transition from the Cold War world to the present post–Cold War relations.

In the Massey Lectures on "The Real World of Technology" I tried to illustrate the relationships between the development of military technologies and economic policies of national governments. I said then that there are two distinct tasks for any state that wishes to use military production as an infrastructure for the advancement of technology and employment: (1) the state has to assure the flow of money to the military-industrial complex, and (2) the state has to assure at the same time the ongoing presence of an enemy who can justify massive outlays of public funds for research, development, and procurement of instruments and infrastructures of "defence."

The designated enemy must warrant the development of the most advanced technological devices. The enemy must be cunning, threatening, and just barely beatable by novel, truly ingenious, and heroic technologies. And I added then (it was 1989) that it will be interesting to see how Western "defence" infrastructures respond to the possibility that internal changes in the Soviet Union could eliminate its role as the designated enemy.

I ventured the thought that the social and political needs for an enemy might be so deeply entrenched in the real world of technology, as we know it, that new enemies would have to appear relatively speedily, so that the existing technological power structure could be maintained. Even then I was afraid that there could be a turning inward of the war machine. One has to remember that, after all, the enemy does not have to be the government or the citizens of a foreign state. There is a lot of scope, as well as historical precedence, for pursuing the enemy within.

Unfortunately, it seems that this turning inward of the war machine was what happened when "the evil empire" collapsed. The West's technological infrastructures were not dismantled but continued to be used. Their new use, I would suggest to you, is a new form of war (i.e., the transposition I spoke about earlier) that is now called globalization and global competition.

In other words, the technological tools of control and conquest are now serving their old functions in a new key, thus creating a new form of war. The new battlefields are "the markets," though not pleasant local markets like the St. Lawrence Market or the Kensington Market, where real people sell and buy, chat, and get to know each other.

The new markets are the stock and currency markets, the faceless markets of electronic transactions. The responses of these markets have become significant indicators of the supposed well-being of people and nations. How the stock and money markets react to elections and referenda appears to be much more meaningful to governments than the so-called will of the people. It is, of course, not new that wars are being fought for access to resources, for the enhancement of commerce and trade. What is new, in terms of the transmutation of war itself, is that the battlefields are no longer territorial. There is no physical ground involved that may be "ours" or "theirs."

What the technologies of forty years of war-making have achieved is to make territory immaterial, just as intercontinental ballistic missiles have made national boundaries immaterial and neutrality irrelevant. The development that we witness now is an internally consistent extension of the extraterritoriality in modern weapons developments.

The full arsenal of the publicly financed technologies of war— from operations research to computer systems, from satellites to space communications and integrated networks—has become the instrument of a new transposed war for global commercial power.

You may well ask, "If what we experience today is indeed a war without national boundaries and defined territories, who is the enemy? Where is the enemy?"

Let me give you my response first, and then my arguments—which you may or may not consider valid. In the war of global competition the enemy are people—not the people, meaning a particular class, group, or nationality, but all those people who look at community, at work, at nature, and at other human beings as sources of meaning and interaction and not as commodities.

Whatever cannot be merely bought and sold, whatever cannot be expressed in terms of money and gain/loss transactions, stands in the way of "the market" and is enemy territory to be occupied, transformed, and conquered. Whatever work can be done by machines or devices, will be done by machines or devices, rather than by people, who become surplus; they have to be "laid off"—put aside like dirty dishes, sent away to someone else—the nightmare of ethnic cleansing in a technological transposition.

Let me now restate my interpretation of the current scene, because I would like to come to the third strand of my argument: the question of the role of ordinary people. I hold that in the new form of transposed war there is no longer a clear distinction between "them" and "us"—a distinction that passports might define. The new enemy territory that is being attacked is the territory of non-market forces and its inhabitants.

It is every area that is informed by concerns other than the market considerations of buying and selling and profiting. The new battlefields are in those territories, physical as well as mental, that are the home of the common good, of art, of friendship and scholarship, of whatever is held in common and cannot be cut up into private parcels of property. This realm and those who care for it contain the main targets and enemies of the new war.

It may be that I am wrong in my interpretation and I would be most happy if this were so. Yet I feel compelled to make this argument and urge you to talk about these thoughts. It is imperative that we not close our eyes to what is going on in our country and in many other countries.

From a historical peace perspective we are in the middle of a market-driven war on the common good. Wherever human beings see themselves neither as buyers nor sellers, as customers nor clients, but feel that their values, their vitality, and their sustenance comes out of a collectivity of interests, a community of shared experiences, their lives may be under attack. The attack can be subtle or neighbourly. It is not always clear and overt. Yet for the peace movement, this face of war must become as unacceptable as the old face of war.

When we began the work for peace as the Voice of Women we tried to speak to women across the globe about the future of all our children. We must now speak about the new war in the same manner. We must ask each other: what about the common good, the care of the environment? What kind of work will there be for our children? What is happening to the human community? In what way can we make cause with other ordinary people of this world in a concerted resistance against the new war?

You may ask how we can refocus the new peace approach, when many of the old problems are still so much with us. There are still nuclear weapons and their testing, land mines, arms sales, and weapons development.

The new developments, however, are so much embedded in the old, both technologically and politically, that both can and should be addressed together. We need to analyze as clearly as possible the market ideology as war, identify its destructiveness as well as its immorality, and protest its practice by our country and with our money.

Surely, the commandment "thou shall not kill" does not apply only to those who use guns or bombs. Peace is a most pressing issue to engage all of us who wish to use Camus' words—to be neither victim nor executioner.

Notes

John and Lois Dove so tragically left us John Dove was a professor of chemistry at the University of Toronto, and his wife Lois Dove was an accomplished biochemist; they were also committed peace activists. When they were killed in an automobile accident in Botswana, their friends and colleagues established an annual event in their honour at University College, University of Toronto.

Cold War from 1945 to 1990, the state of tension and military rivalry between the United States and the USSR, which stopped short of full-scale war

Kenneth Boulding (1910–1993) a renowned American economist and social scientist who worried about humanity's ability to survive the challenges of the modern world

transmutations transformations

hegemony the dominance of one state over others; from the Greek word *hēgēmon*, meaning "leader"

globalization the process of making something worldwide in scope or application

determinism the philosophical belief that every act, event, and decision is the result of antecedents that are independent of human will

fatalism the belief that events in the world are predetermined and unalterable

incipient beginning to exist or to appear

Massey Lectures Each year, CBC Radio and Massey College in Toronto invite one of the world's leading thinkers to deliver five one-hour talks, on a subject of current interest, at the University of Toronto. In 1989, Ursula Franklin spoke on "The Real World of Technology."

ballistic missile a projectile that takes on a free-falling flight path after an internally guided, self-powered ascent

ethnic cleansing the removal of an ethnic group from a society by expulsion or killing

Camus Albert Camus (1913–1960), a French existentialist who won the Nobel Prize for literature in 1957

Activities

1. Reread Franklin's speech and compare and contrast her message with your own experiences and beliefs. Use your findings to create a thesis statement for a personal essay that will explain in which ways you agree and in which ways you disagree with the ideas Franklin presents. When writing your essay, use detailed examples to illustrate the similarities and differences between Franklin's point of view and your own. Include an explanation of the ways in which you questioned Franklin's assertions and reasoning, rather than simply accepting the ideas you read.

2. Ursula Franklin draws an analogy between war and music. Identify, explain, and evaluate her use of this analogy in making her point. Is the analogy developed well enough to have a significant effect on the reader? How does her analogy support the thesis of her speech?

3. In this speech, delivered by Franklin in 1996, she proposes that the "new" war that has evolved since the Cold War is the war for global commercial power. She says the enemy of globalization comprises "those people who look at community, at work, at nature, and at other human beings as sources of meaning and interaction and not as commodities." Work in a group to do research on globalization in the twenty-first century. To what extent does her argument apply to key world events that have occurred since 1996? Are there ways in which her argument no longer applies or have events since 1996 further bolstered her point of view? Share your ideas in a class discussion.

Another Viewpoint: History

Locate some reference materials on the Cold War and do research into this time in world history. What countries were involved in the Cold War? What conditions created the Cold War? What conditions emerged as a result of it? What literary works reflect the Cold War and in what ways do they do so? How did this historical event affect other countries that were not directly involved? How and why did the Cold War finally come to an end?

Slide to Entropy

Kathleen Winter

Kathleen Winter was born in Corbridge, England, in 1960, and immigrated with her family to Newfoundland at the age of eight. Winter is a researcher and writer whose poetry, short stories, and essays have been published in numerous Canadian periodicals. Her novella *Where Is Mario?* was published in 1987 and her personal journal, *The Necklace of Occasional Dreams*, appeared in 1996. Winter writes a weekly column entitled "Naturally" in the St. John's newspaper *The Telegram*, in which she comments on life and just about anything. "Slide to Entropy" provides readers with a humorous account of the writer's change in lifestyle in middle age. What prevents people from eating nutritionally sound foods all of the time? Why might people's eating habits either improve or deteriorate during the course of their lives?

I don't know how long I've been railing against entropy. It could be since an Australian clairvoyant—the youth hostels were full of them in my travelling days—took one look at me and pronounced I'd end up spending all my time reading trash pulp fiction.

Oh no, my dear, I said inwardly. You will find me continuing my studies with Beaudelaire, with Anaïs Nin and Katherine Mansfield. Perhaps with luck I might even move on to de Maupassant and Shakespeare. I kept my guard up, not only against pulp novels, but against all that goes with them. Lounging around eating family packs of cheesies watching daytime soaps, ending up at bingo instead of yoga, forgetting to buy soy milk and putting Carnation in your tea…. All of a sudden, though, last week my guard came down.

West Indies sarong

It started in Dominion, where I go because they have wholewheat couscous and organic brown rice cereal. My hand bypassed these staples my family loves to see me come home with, and it grabbed canned chili with meatballs and a club-sized pack of white English muffins and a bottle of mustard pickles.

I was just in the store to get away from my kids for a while, not really to buy groceries. I do that sometimes to look at exotic peppers from the West Indies and imagine myself there in a sarong. This time I looked at cans, cans, cans and thought, imagine, you have only to scoot the can opener around them and you have ravioli or Alphagettis without peeling a thing.

At the checkout I did not leaf through Country Living or the antiques magazines but went straight for a two-inch thick No. 1 best-seller with embossed red foil letters, and I bought it.

Two days later and 39 pages into a bunch of stereotyped characters who I'm enjoying very much, I blame our last camping trip. My friend said I could read any book I wanted in her cabin. Over the detective novels and Archie comics I chose a murder mystery featuring a writerly old woman sleuth. It was the thin edge of the wedge. Beaudelaire and brown rice, you are finished.

Every day I discover more advantages to letting down my guard. You cannot read Beaudelaire if you have youngsters hanging off you and jumping on you and demanding glasses of milk and new things to put in their bookbags. But you can do these things and read a No. 1 best-seller. God knows, maybe one can do these things and write one—isn't that a thought. But that's getting too ambitious. That's raising the old guard. Better to let it stay down and just enjoy. Enjoyment is what the slide to entropy is all about, and why hadn't I figured it out before?

Fake cheese dip

Because I had not read the choice of TV programs one can get with a satellite dish. I have now. My husband, coincidentally, brought the flyer home the day I found out about crackers that come with their own little vat of fake cheese dip. Until now, the only thing we've watched with our brown rice has been the news on the one channel we get.

Life is suddenly careening toward entropy and I like it. This is middle age. This is mellowing out. This is the time my children cry out, "Mommy, what's got into you? You're getting to be so much fun."

Fun? Uh-oh, what's that? The anti-entropy alert slides up the back of my head and I come to my senses and boil a pot of rice. I tell myself we can eat it with fresh legumes in a sauce of herbs from the kitchen garden, but I am lying. I know I'm going to open up that can of meatball chili and eat it while I peruse the channel combinations to see if we can get one that has Martha Stewart, "Beverly Hillbillies" reruns, and "Days of Our Lives" in succession on a weekday afternoon...

Notes

entropy the scientific term for an inevitable and steady deterioration of a system; a transformation

clairvoyant a person who can purportedly see what cannot be perceived by the senses, such as events in distant places or events in the future; from the French words *clair*, meaning "clear," and *voir*, meaning "to see"

Charles Beaudelaire (1821–1867) a French Romantic poet

Anaïs Nin (1903–1977) an American author best known for her diaries

Katherine Mansfield (1888–1923) New Zealand's most renowned writer of fiction

Guy de Maupassant (1850–1893) considered to be the greatest French short story writer

Carnation the brand name of a type of canned, evaporated milk

Dominion the brand name of a chain of supermarkets throughout Canada

Activities

1. Use the glossary in this anthology, a dictionary, and other reference tools to create working definitions of the terms *mood* and *tone*. What are the differences between these two concepts? With a partner, discuss whether the tone and mood of this piece are the same or different and why. What feelings do the tone and mood of the piece evoke in you?

2. Write a few well-developed paragraphs in which you answer the following questions: Why does Winter use humour in this selection? What techniques of humour does she use? How does humour contribute to what her purpose might be in writing the piece? What is her thesis? Under what circumstances would you choose to use humour to make a point?

3. Create a single-frame cartoon or a multiple-frame cartoon strip to illustrate Winter's point. Make sure that you maintain her theme and tone. Share your completed cartoon with a classmate and ask for feedback on how effectively you reflected the theme and tone of Winter's work. Based on the feedback you receive, make any revisions you think will improve your cartoon's effectiveness.

Paradise, a Poet, and Promised Land

George Elliott Clarke

George Elliott Clarke was born in the Black Loyalist community of
Windsor Plains, Nova Scotia, in 1960 and grew up in Halifax. A poet,
journalist, and political activist, Clarke is a seventh generation
Africadian. He earned his B.A. from the University of Waterloo, an
M.A. from Dalhousie University, and a Ph.D. in English from Queen's
University. His poetry, written in a lyrical style, intentionally alludes to
his Black Loyalist heritage. In 1998, Clarke received the esteemed
Portia White Prize for what has been called his "influential and
resounding Maritime voice," and in 2001 he won the Governor
General's Literary Award for *Execution Poems*. This article explores
Clarke's understanding of a "sense of place" and "promised land."
What place would you consider to be your paradise, your promised
land? On what land do you "feel whole"?

Postcard images of Nova Scotia accent either the granite slag-heap coast-
line of Peggy's Cove or Cape Breton's cliff-hugging Cabot Trail. But
when I was a "coloured" kid growing up in Halifax's rough-and-tum-
ble North End (all pavement and smashed glass and malice-eyed cops and
pink-faced drunks), I felt immeasurably blessed. I knew that, 40 minutes
away by car, bus, or train, there was a grassy apple-blossomed paradise,
the "Gateway to the Annapolis Valley," the town of Windsor. Just southeast of it was Three Mile Plains, a black Eden where my mother's parents
lived.

Three Mile Plains is also—ecumenically—"Five Mile Plains" and "Windsor Plains." Not flat, it's several loping kilometres of rolling slope upon which folks farm, raise cows and horses, and allow hay to explode skyward.

My mother's people—American slaves liberated by the British during the War of 1812—arrived in coastal Nova Scotia in 1813. A generation later, they moved inland, perhaps to join a larger black community, to Three Mile Plains. There, blacks were granted too little land—deliberately—to become farmers. So they toiled in gypsum quarries and in white people's homes to eke out livings. Some of them, including my maternal relatives, intermarried with the Mi'kmaq. They also erected a church, Windsor Plains (African) United Baptist, and attended the segregated (until 1956) one-room Three Mile Plains School.

Acadia University reported in 1965 that most Three Mile Plains adults had only an elementary-school education. However, my mother, Geraldine Elizabeth Johnson, graduated from teachers' college and my father, Bill Clarke, is a self-taught polymath, so when I was born in 1960 (my mother matching my initials to her own), they ensured that I received the best public education available.

My formal schooling was gilded by visits to unpaved Green Street, which bisects Three Mile Plains, and my grandparents' two-storey, white wooden house—with ocean-sounding conch-shell doorstops and a veranda—and what seemed an expansive, dandelioned, and willow-treed sloping front lawn. I loved their antique wood stove and the smells of burning wood crackling in the blue dawns and the Sunday supper riches from their garden: carrots, cucumbers, lettuce, cabbage, potatoes. They even had a pear tree and a crabapple tree. The cheek-by-jowl woods, approached via tall fields of hay, sprouted trickily thorny blackberry and raspberry bushes along their fringe and brandished hazelnut bushes among pine, birch, spruce, alder, and maple trees. A footpath plunged and twisted through the woods down to the iron tracks that bore freight and passengers through the valley, the train horns blaring *whoo, whoo* as they trundled past us, leaving a fragrant—to a child—whiff of diesel fuel in the air.

I was a bookish boy. I thrilled to know that the Mi'kmaq deity, Glooscap, presided over Blomidon—only some 30 km west—and that Henry Wadsworth Longfellow's tragic Acadian heroine, Evangeline, had wept, Ruth-like, amid the "unalien" marsh of Grand Pré. I adored a memorial at Hantsport to William Hall, the third Canadian—and first black—to win the Victoria Cross. I knew that English Canada's first great writer, Thomas Chandler Haliburton, had lived near Windsor's Shakespeareanly named Avon River. For me, the intense, infernal beauty of Three Mile Plains and the Annapolis Valley is a fount of emotional history and heart-startling poetry: "Arcadia." I'd begun to craft poetry—unmusicked "songs"—when I was 15, and Three Mile Plains was their locus. The day I became incontrovertibly, irremediably a poet was February 12, 1977, my 17th birthday, when my mother and I drove to Three Mile Plains on a sunny, frigid, snowy morning. That day, as I trudged up and down hilly, white-dusted Green Street, I drafted in my head a poem, my first attempt to sing a black *and* Nova Scotian—an *Africadian*—consciousness. With my breath hanging clear in front of me, I claimed my Afro-Mi'kmaq heritage. I was standing on land that has always made *us* feel whole.

When my mother passed away last August, my two brothers and I inherited her Three Mile Plains property. Walking there, I feel as though I'm traversing a little northern fragment of Africa. Promised land.

Notes

Eden the first home of Adam and Eve in the Old Testament of the Bible

War of 1812 a war declared by the United States against Great Britain in June 1812. The United States attacked Upper and Lower Canadas, incorrectly assuming that the settlers who lived there would readily secede to the Americans. At the end of 1814, British and American negotiators agreed to return to the status quo of 1811.

Mi'kmaq the First Nation people centred primarily in Nova Scotia, New Brunswick, Prince Edward Island, and the Gaspé Peninsula of Québec

Henry Wadsworth Longfellow an American writer (1824–1884) best known for his narrative poem *Evangeline: A Tale of Acadie* (1847)

Victoria Cross a bronze Maltese cross given by Canada and Britain as their highest military award

Activities

1. Listen carefully as your teacher or a classmate performs an oral reading of this selection. Allow the author's words to create images in your mind. Afterward, share with your class your most vivid mental pictures. Discuss how Clarke uses details, words, phrases, and writing techniques to create strong imagery for his readers.

2. Discuss with a partner what you consider to be the mood of "Paradise, a Poet, and Promised Land" and discuss ways in which Clarke formulates this mood. Consider what an opposite mood to Clarke's would be. With a partner, create a collage that reflects the mood of the article and a second collage that reflects the opposite mood. Consider how you can use composition in your collages to further emphasize each mood. After completing your collages, share them with your classmates. Can they identify the mood you intended in each collage?

3. Write a personal essay about an important association you have with a particular place. Make your writing powerful by including the following in your personal essay: a subjective, first-person point of view; a unifying mood; personal anecdotes and flashbacks; strong imagery and vivid sensory details; and stylistic devices such as parallelism, repetition, and varied sentence lengths. Share your essay with a group of classmates. Ask them to comment on how you used descriptive details to evoke a sense of place.

Another Viewpoint: History

Although the American slaves who came to Canada were liberated by the British during the War of 1812, they still encountered discrimination and differential treatment. Clarke mentions one example of how blacks were granted land, but too little of it to become viable farmers. With a group of your classmates, complete some research on the discriminatory social and economic conditions faced by Africadians in the Maritimes in the years following the War of 1812 to the present time. Present a summary of your research in the form of an illustrated timeline.

Hockey Night in Port Hawkesbury

Lynn Coady

Lynn Coady was born in Sydney, Nova Scotia, in 1970. She was adopted into a large Cape Breton family and raised in Port Hawkesbury and the Margaree Valley of Nova Scotia. Coady writes novels, plays, screenplays, and short stories, as well as non-fiction. Her novel *Strange Heaven* was nominated for the Governor General's Literary Award and won Coady the Canadian Authors Association/Air Canada Award for the most promising writer in Canada. It is a *coming-of-age* novel that reveals how growing up in any culture is universally difficult. Think of some coming-of-age novels, stories, or movies that you are familiar with. What difficult aspects of growing up are dealt with in these narratives? In your opinion, how realistic are these accounts and to what extent do they reflect your own experiences? Why do you think this genre is so popular?

My hometown's hockey team was called the Port Hawkesbury Pirates. Their colours were maroon and white and they had a fierce pirate's-head eyepatch emblazoned in the centre of their jerseys. Their greatest rivals were the Antigonish Bulldogs. I remember one particular playoff where the entire town was mobilized against the mainland village of Antigonish. My dad owned the Dairy Queen, and used its towering sign to denigrate everything about our neighbours on the other side of the causeway. *Ho ho Shebo,* he used to have up there, to the befuddlement of tourists looking for a deal on Brazier Burgers. Shebo was the name of the opposing team's coach. It was a chant the town liked to use whenever our team was ahead. Another day it was *Port Hawkesbury Pirates versus the Antigonish Poodles.* I thought that up. Dad was tickled, and thrilled me by enshrining it beneath the DQ logo for a whole two weeks.

I went to the big game with my dad. I was attired in a Port Hawkesbury Pirates jacket zipped up over a Pirates jersey. Perched on my head was a Pirates cap. Clutched in my hand, a Go Pirates pennant. I loved everything about that night. Listening to Dad holler the most eloquent of personal insults at the nefarious Shebo, the guffaws of the surrounding adults. A woman swaddled head to toe in fox-fur cursing a blue streak like I had never heard. The hard benches. My brother's hand-me-down long johns bunching underneath my clothes. The insane excitement all around me such as I had never experienced in that town before or after.

But I can't relate to you a single thing about the actual game. Because I didn't understand a goddamn thing that was going on. When the crowd screamed, I screamed. When the crowd booed, I booed. When the crowd threatened to disembowel the referee, I too became a mindless, homicidal maniac. I was having the time of my life. But when the actual game was going on, and the crowd sat in rapt awe, this is approximately what was going on in my head:

Guy skating, guy skating, guy skating. Another guy. Skate, skate, skate. Guy from other team. Skate, skate. Who has it now?

Oh. Fat guy. Skating, skating…

There you have, summed up, my eternally ambivalent relationship with the game of hockey and everything it represents. And it represents a lot, let's not kid ourselves. To grow up anywhere in small-town Canada is to grow up with the conviction that hockey is, if not the only thing that matters, one of the things that definitely matters most. In memories of my family, my town, my youth, hockey is always front and centre. My dad coached, and my two older brothers played. Hockey-related pictures, trophies, plaques galore adorn my parents' home.

As a teenager, I was not permitted to be off in my room "sulking" when a Leafs game was on. It was a sacred time that I was expected to participate in, like when we said the rosary. Dad and the boys would eat chips with dip, drink pop, yell and bounce up and down in their seats. My mother would commandeer the couch and sneak in little naps between goals and intermission, when she would play Ron McLean to Dad's Don Cherry. A Toronto game is the only thing I have ever seen my father stay up past 11 for. I would sit at the very back of the living room with a selection of magazines on the table beside me.

You think I am not aware of what I sound like: Miss Priss, brimming with lofty notions and a hearty disdain for anything involving protective cups. "Really, faw-tha, another Leafs game? Can't you see I'm reading Joyce? If only we had an alternative cinema, I'd be so out of here." But it's not true. I was an adolescent, remember, and even more than screening the occasional Fassbinder film, what I really wanted was to fit in. Hockey wasn't merely my dad's trip. It was everybody's. People spoke hockey, do you see? It was like a club, or a religion, and if you understood it, everybody else could understand you. You made sense to them. You fit.

Here are some terms and expressions I don't understand to this day.

Blue line.

Sudden death.

De-*fense*! De-*fense*! (I know what the word means, but why do people yell it over and over again?)

And what's with the octopi?

I have alternated my whole life from a fierce resentment of hockey to a wistful longing I can't quite put my finger on. The resentment is simple enough. It comes from having the overriding importance of hockey burned into me my entire life while at the same time understanding that someone like me (female) should never expect to have anything to do with such a vastly significant phenomenon. It comes from the fact that were I to admit this to any of my brothers they would assume I had not received enough oxygen to my brain as a baby.

So off I went into the world of books and English departments, where nary a taint of hockey fever could be felt—or so I thought. (Bill Gaston's newest novel is about a former pro-hockey player who becomes an English undergrad. The comedy writes itself.) Imagine my chagrin when I discovered that my own patron saint of Maritime Lit despised such stuffy havens for precisely the reason I sought them out. In *Hockey Dreams*, a veritable hymn to the gods of the rink, David Adams Richards tells of a variety of literary snotties who think it terribly impish to root for the Russians because "Wayne Gretzky's just so Canadian." Then there is the woman from Penguin Books who becomes awfully confused when Richards and a Czech writer strike up an animated conversation about the (Pittsburgh) Penguins. That would be me, I can't help but think. Desperately veering the conversation toward Kafka, praying no one discovered my pathetic ignorance about what really mattered—who made the big save, who got the most assists.

But what confounds me even more is how much I relate to this book. I understand, whether I want to or not. It is not so much the games Richards is remembering, but the way his friends floated in their oversized jerseys, the smell of wet wool, sub-zero Saturdays gathered around *Hockey Night in Canada*. The feeling. Throughout the book, Richards struggles to explain the unexplainable, the mystery of hockey. There are those who understand and those who will never understand, he intimates. I know what he means, because I am both.

So that wistful longing makes sense, I suppose, when I look back on that Pirates versus Bulldogs game. I grew up with the understanding that hockey was all-important, hockey players were gods, and to be a hockey fan was to enter into some kind of enchanted circle that bestowed instant community and good fellowship upon you. That's what I was feeling that night. I was sitting on the Port Hawkesbury side of the rink, *our* rink, screaming for *our* team, on behalf of *our* town. I was 12 years old, sexually invisible, my days of artsy alienation far off in the inconceivable future. For a moment, I belonged. Because of hockey.

Notes

Ron McLean, Don Cherry Canadian television hockey commentators

Joyce James Joyce (1882–1941), the groundbreaking Irish writer whose works include the novels *Ulysses* (1922) and *Finnegans Wake* (1939)

Fassbinder Rainer Werner Fassbinder (1945–1982), a German film director-writer

Bill Gaston award-winning Canadian author of novels, short fiction, and poetry

chagrin feeling of humiliation based on miscalculation or failure

David Adams Richards leading Maritime writer (born in 1950) whose prizes include the Governor General's Literary Award for his novel *Nights Below Station Street*

Kafka Franz Kafka (1883–1924), a Czech writer whose work centred on the problematic existence of humanity in the modern era

Activities

1. Lynn Coady describes her relationship with the game of hockey as "ambivalent." Trace how this ambivalence is documented in the article. What thoughts and feelings about hockey did the article provoke in you? Did the article provide you with any insights into why hockey can be so important to life in a small community?

2. For what kind of audience has this article been written? What assumptions do you think Coady makes regarding her readers' ages, educational and cultural backgrounds, values and attitudes, and knowledge about hockey? How does her language and syntax reflect her relationship with her audience?

3. Write a personal essay in which you explore an aspect of yourself that sets you apart from other members of your family. Begin your essay with an episode that clearly illustrates the issue you will be examining. Speculate on how this "difference" might affect your future relationship with various family members. Make a recording of yourself reading your essay. Listen to it to determine whether you have maintained a consistent tone and style throughout. Make any necessary revisions to improve the effectiveness of your written essay.

The Sixth Flight

Chantal Tranchemontagne

Chantal Tranchemontagne was born in Cornwall, Ontario, in 1973. As a child, her parents taught her that travel, exploration, and adventure were the keys to a well-rounded education. She received a B.A. from the University of Guelph in Ontario. She then drove across Canada with friends, after which she moved on a monthly basis throughout western Canada, working in a variety of jobs, including as a construction worker, restaurant server, stonemason, and librarian's assistant. Tranchemontagne received a graduate diploma in journalism from Concordia University in Montreal, where she currently works as a freelance writer. Why do you think the idea of human-powered flight has fascinated people for so many centuries? Do you think there will be a time in the near future when individual flying machines will come into use? Consider how the automobile changed the world and speculate on the ramifications of such flying machines.

The birdman emerged from the river, his wetsuit glistening in the early evening sun. He caught me by surprise, but I wasn't averse to a little company, as I'd only recently brought my rusty '82 Toyota pickup to a shuddering halt after a two-year post-university circumnavigation of Alberta and British Columbia. I was just about as beat up and burnt out as my truck, and had begun squatting on the Birkenhead River, just outside of the Mt. Currie Reserve in the Coastal Mountains, 40 kilometres north of Whistler. I had rigged a 10-metre square tarp as a roof,

◀ *Hanging from the rafters, Chantal Tranchemontagne practises turning manoeuvres* and set up an apartment: my tent became a cozy bedroom; a lugged-in couch swathed in mosquito netting made a fine living room; a stone firepit with cooking grills functioned as a kitchen; and a solar shower perched precariously in a tree provided the final luxury—hot water, on sunny days at least. It wasn't Frank Lloyd Wright, but my simple dwelling came with a river view and a skylight that filled each night with more stars than a city dweller would see in a lifetime.

Homestead in place, I made plans to explore the region by foot, raft, bike, and maybe even skis. The last thing I expected was an aerial view of my adopted habitat, but a chance encounter with Jim the Birdman changed all that.

It seemed I had chosen a prime spot for finding warm uprisings of air—the phenomena that drove human fliers wild with delight. Despite his watery entrance, the Birdman was first and foremost a paraglider. I offered him a beer, and my education in the philosophy, history, mechanics, meteorology, and gadgetry of paragliding began almost immediately. Thermals are critical for keeping the rectangular parachute aloft, but almost as crucial was getting the chute and equipment up high enough to launch. I thought that behind the Birdman's friendliness was my charming personality. I took it in stride when I found out he was just a guy looking for a ride.

And of course he wasn't alone. Paragliding is relatively new. Just a decade ago, only five or so pioneers soared above the steep, treed valleys of the Mackenzie Basin. I arrived in the middle of a mini-boom in the sport. Up to 40 paragliders roamed the logging access roads looking for a lift to one of several launch sites around the valley, most located in old clearcuts.

That summer, I became a chauffeur for Jim, his paragliding cronies, and their gear. My limousine was an abused 4x4, cab window smashed by a windblown tree, body scratched and torn from windfall, and chassis dented by boulders on rough lumber roads. On my first fare, I wrestled the steering wheel, my foot constantly slipping off the clutch. After 30 minutes of violent bouncing and rocking, we reached the end of the road. By then, I was so sore and stiff that I was more than ready to rediscover the beauty of hiking.

We walked down a steep trail to the launch site, a 20-square-metre forest clearing that had been raked and meticulously scoured to remove any debris that could snag a paraglider line. Three windsocks blew high in second-growth fir trees and several pieces of flagging tape flapped haphazardly from twigs stuck in the ground and out of the way. They were sacrosanct: these wind indicators determined the pilots' fate.

During these jarring rides and long waits in mountain meadows, my enlightenment continued. I learned that paragliders delicately juggle many variables. There's only one constant—what goes up, must come down—but how far, when, and where are decided by Mother Nature.

At night I would retreat to the tranquillity of my isolated campsite, but my charges knew to find me every morning enjoying a Montreal-style bagel at the Pony Espresso coffee house in Pemberton. I wasn't the only one to watch and learn. Newer pilots, fresh from paragliding school at Whistler or drawn here from Vancouver or abroad, showed up at launch sites to watch experienced pilots take off.

I got used to the technical banter on the weather, especially as we waited on mountainsides for a gust of wind. To lift the wing, just the right amount of breeze is required. Optimism permeated the hours whiled away playing hacky sack. I soon realized that the fliers' eagerness consisted of 90 per cent hope. Still, the remaining ingredient—the 10 per cent of actual meteorological knowledge—was essential. I learned that cold creeping shadows on the south side of the valley pushed warm winds up the north ridge to where we sat at the Mackenzie launch site. These wondrous updrafts were the invitation to take off into smooth, buoyant air.

I realized that to survive the summer without destroying my back, I would have to learn to fly off this mountain, otherwise I would remain the designated driver. I watched as Jim and his cohorts set up and laid out the wing. All joking and small talk ceased as they checked strings for tangles, pulled on the bulky harness, and clipped into the glider. Like a newborn gosling I was imprinted with the first thing I saw: Safety is paramount, check and double-check every detail before takeoff.

The takeoffs were a sight unto themselves. The pilots would run down a slight slope, straining against the harness to lift the wing out of the dirt. The running was almost Monty Pythonesque as the chute arched and lifted slowly behind them. Just as they disappeared below the brim of the hill, the wind caught the paragliders and lifted them miraculously off their feet.

All Earth-like encumbrances disappeared. Each paraglider became a human bird. Every successful launch contained the same miracle of freedom. And every drive down the launch road reaffirmed my conviction. I must begin to fly.

The weeks passed, and I lived, ate, and slept to the soothing gurgle of the Birkenhead River. I met new people, often from different parts of the globe. I climbed crags from Squamish to the Swiss Cheese Wall in Whistler and kayaked the lively Birk in my own backyard. Even the dreaded drive up to the Mackenzie launch was made tolerable as I gradually came to assist in more launches. I was no sucker for punishment; I knew I was getting a free education, one that might cost top dollar at a school. But what really kept me keen was wanting to get a taste of what the posse of pilots were obsessed with—flying with the birds. "Zenlike," they said. "A natural high." "Nothing is the same after you've been to 3,000 metres." My new-found friends would try, but fail, to nail the right description. I wasn't the obsessive type, but I knew that before the fall pulled me back East to work and school, I would have to try to launch.

I observed the surefire signs of flight addiction in others. I saw the excitement of first-time pilots on their early flights, the awe as their skills grew, and finally the obsession and addiction with the paragliding high. At this stage, another clue to their obsession was the gadgetry. The truly addicted spent small fortunes on radios, variometers (which show speed, ascent, and altitude), and Global Positioning Systems.

One bright morning I was getting ready to hike to a nearby peak when the Birdman showed up. By this time I could read the signs of a great flying day. Morning sun, puffy cumulus clouds, light wind. "Will you drive us to the launch?" The trip up was getting old, but Jim knew how to push the right buttons. "A couple of more times," he egged me on, "and you'll be able to soar with the birds, too." We clambered into the 4x4.

Today, I fly high. My first five attempts were unspectacular, but I did manage to get off the ground, at least. First a 60-metre scramble, then I tried a few short jaunts from the 500-metre Mackenzie launch. These flights were tense, scary, and thrilling affairs. On the morning of my sixth flight, a late August breeze brought hints of summer's demise. Our ride was via helicopter to the launch—south-facing and on the same range as Mackenzie. We congregated at Pemberton Helicopters at 10:00 a.m., and met with local pilot, John Goats. The 15-minute flight was a treat—no hiking or back-wrenching ride—just a motorized bird's-eye view of peaks and patchwork fields. We circled above turquoise Tenquille Lake and dropped into an alpine meadow blanketed with flowering white and purple lupines. The helicopter slid away, leaving us gulping in fresh, cool mountain air.

We tied flagging tape to twigs to serve as primitive wind meters. All signs indicated a beautiful day. The wind was blowing gently up-slope and the sun was beaming onto the cliffs below, creating rock-released thermals. Earlier in the summer I had seen paragliders play above these cliffs, now it was my turn. If my first five tries had taught me anything, it was not to be too scared to enjoy the view. Still, I was a little frightened. But mostly, I was excited.

My friend Ty laid out his wing. He performed his safety check, tested his radio, and with a final wave, he was off, hooting and hollering with glee above us. My little brother was visiting, and was to try a tandem flight with Robert, a charismatic pilot and the owner of Whistler Paragliding. They went next, and I snapped some photos to send back to our mom. The duo started running. The takeoff looked a little awkward, what with both of them tethered together. But once they were in the air, they looked comfortable.

After a few more launches by more experienced pilots, it was finally my turn. I was still more excited than nervous, but kept my butterflies in check by mentally going through the launching motions. After my safety check, I looked back at Jim for the signal. The wind picked up slightly and I started to run, straining to get my wing off the ground. There were 37 cells to inflate on my paraglider, and each seemed to be working extra hard to pull me back. I felt the wing swinging to the right and tried to bring it back to centre. It didn't work. Instead of risking a serious accident, I pulled down on the steering toggles and flared the wing back to the ground. It dragged me a few feet through the dirt but that, even with the inconvenience of setting up again, was small compared with a crash and a hospital stay. I bunched up the wing and walked back uphill. Jim reassured me that aborting was the right move. I reset, ran, and this time the launch was perfect.

There is a common misconception that paragliders are extreme athletes or worse, crazy thrill-seekers. But suspended above the Mackenzie Basin, I could only think it was everyone else who was crazy for not trying this at least once. The ground was speckled with barns that looked like tiny Lego blocks. The grand, glacial Lillooet River looked like a stream. But the mountains looked ever so huge. I circled to gain attitude, then headed out toward the valley and caught thermals that lifted me 150 metres, like an elevator. From this height I could see the Miller Creek Glacier, Mount Overseer, and the Pemberton ice cap. The air was smooth and the nervousness from my previous flights was gone: it was time to play. Again I caught a thermal: higher, further, faster. Without realizing it I had moved from excitement to awe. Although this was longer than I had ever flown, I couldn't even consider landing. I was having too much fun.

Forty glorious minutes later, 40 kilometres away from the launch site, and from a height of 1,700 metres, I began to descend. I targeted a farmer's field to land in—no growing crops, no cattle, no freshly plowed fields, just a nice, safe, grassy field.

Despite the perfect landing zone, I was still concerned. An old, beat up, black Chevy truck was creeping its way along a dirt road on the perimeter of the field. Some landowners are known to chase off paragliders, or worse, demand payment in the form of a case of beer. Although Pemberton residents are mostly friendly, more than one flyer has a story to say about a rough welcome. For now, however, there was no time for distractions. I focused on my well-choreographed routine: stand up in the harness, flare the wing to slow down, and when the feet touch the ground, run like hell.

It should have been simple, but I miscalculated the wind direction and landed with it behind me. I was going faster than I'd hoped. My legs couldn't keep up with the wing, and instead of a gentle landing, my feet planted hard, my knees buckled, and I became intimate with good old B.C. soil. After a few seconds of mild shock, I extracted my face from the ground, dirty but unharmed.

I was staring at a pair of worn boots less than a foot away from where I lay. I stood up quickly, expecting a reprimand. The man introduced himself as Grandpa Ronayne, a potato farmer whose family had been in the Pemberton Valley since the late 1800s. His overalls were permanently stained with dirt (not unlike my face), his straw hat held together by duct tape. But instead of a scolding, his wrinkled face broke into a smile, and soon he was talking weather like only a farmer can. "And what about that turkey vulture," he asked. I looked at him quizzically and he lifted his finger to the sky. There, above us, a large, red-headed bird was soaring, wings stretched out, unmoving. "He's been stalking you for a while," said Grandpa Ronayne.

From the earliest times, humans have strived to soar with the birds. I, too, had dreamt about flying alongside a majestic eagle. A vulture would have to do, I thought. In fact, my dream had come true on my first real flight, but I had been too busy enjoying the view to realize it. Suddenly, it seemed easier to understand why some people get obsessed with paragliding.

Notes

squatting in this instance, occupying land without the permission of the owner

Frank Lloyd Wright American architect (1869–1959) who revolutionized building design and techniques

paraglider a non-motorized, foot-launched inflatable wing constructed of rip-stop nylon from which the pilot is suspended in a sitting position by Kevlar lines

thermals rising currents of warm air

chassis the supporting frame of an automobile

sacrosanct sacred or holy

Monty Pythonesque referring to the "silly walks" performed by members of the British comedy troupe Monty Python's Flying Circus

Global Positioning System a network of satellites emitting precisely timed signals which a receiver anywhere on Earth can use to fix its exact position

rock-released thermals bubbles of hot air (created when rocks are heated by the sun), which rise through the surrounding air

Birkenhead River, Mt. Currie Reserve, Coastal Mountains, Whistler, Mackenzie Basin, Pemberton, Squamish, Swiss Cheese Wall, Tenquille Lake, Lillooet River, Miller Creek Glacier, Mount Overseer locations in southwestern British Columbia

Activities

1. Why do you think people engage in highly risky activities, such as paragliding, mountain climbing, or sky diving? Do extreme sports like these appeal to you? What insights did you gain from this article about the author's reasons for taking up paragliding and how the experience affected her?

2. In a group, study a number of feature articles in magazines, making note of the elements they contain. Then skim "The Sixth Flight," making notes on design features you would incorporate into a fully-formatted design of this article. With the group, come to a consensus on such decisions as the following: the choice and placement of colour; typeface; type size; visuals; and pull-quotes. Create a deck for the article and use paper to create a rough layout of your design. Present your layout to another group.

3. Locate and read the poem "High Flight," written in September 1941 by John Gillespie Magee Jr., a nineteen-year-old Spitfire pilot who was training to serve in World War II with the Royal Canadian Air Force. Paraphrase the experiences and emotions Magee describes. Discuss the relationship between the poet's response to the experience of flight and those of Chantal Tranchemontagne and her acquaintances. How do the historical era and circumstances in which these accounts were written explain the differences in style and spiritual perspective?

Buying Your Next Synthesizer

Amin Bhatia

Composer Amin Bhatia was born in London, England, in 1961. He immigrated to Canada and now lives in Toronto. Bhatia has been writing, recording, and programming music for twenty years. Bhatia has said that he originally wanted to work with an orchestra, but pragmatism led him to the synthesizer. Because early synthesizers could only play one note at a time, Bhatia was forced to learn how each instrument of the orchestra worked in order to simulate and record it properly. He now uses real instruments in his writing, but his days with a Roland sequencer and a Minimoog have given him insight into arranging and orchestration for real players. He scores music for film and television, as well as doing sound design for clients such as MuchMusic. "Buying Your Next Synthesizer" is an example of an expository article which explains how a buyer can "audition" a new synthesizer. What kinds of research do you engage in before purchasing an electronic item? What kinds of information sources are available to consumers for this research? How much influence do first-hand accounts or testimonials have in your purchasing decisions?

In response to phone calls and e-mails I've had from other musicians in the community I've put together a short guide to help you when you buy your next synthesizer.

I must begin with the bad news that it's going to take you weeks, not hours, to get up and running. Yes, it is amazing technology, and yes, it claims to make you a star overnight. But if you've bought that new synthesizer on the belief that you'll be making music with an instant orchestra within a few hours, then sit down and have a good cry now. As wonderful as this technology is, there are very few brochures or salespeople that have the guts to tell you that it's going to take some time to get it right!

Think about how many years it takes to master an acoustic instrument. A synthesizer studio is a group of instruments, each one with a whole new set of freedoms and restrictions. The freedom is that any instrument is capable of hundreds of unique and exciting sounds. The restriction is that the technical and sonic structure of each synthesizer has nothing in common with another one. You'll have to learn each synthesizer in your studio, one at a time before you can take it into battle on your next project. If this were a live player that you'd never heard of, would you trust him or her with a solo at your next recording date without even an audition? Same thing.

And yes you should read the manual, no matter how badly it's written. It's your only clue to what the manufacturers were thinking when they built the thing. When you open the box, take the manual out first and read through it somewhere else, ideally over a weekend. Then when you come back, you'll have a peripheral idea of its workings as well as a general idea of where to find something in the manual.

In getting to know your new instrument you have to start with its existing sounds. A major fallacy is the instrument's display that tells you what sound you are playing. Unlike looking at a real player who holds an oboe in his hands, the synth patch display that says "oboe" is no guarantee that you're going to hear a convincing simulation. Synth technology is a combination of waveforms or digital data programmed by technicians and while some are amazing, some are downright awful. One might dial up "English horn" or even "bagpipe" and come up with an oboe sound that actually sounds more convincing.

So, ignore the display and use your ear. Go through your new synthesizer patch by patch and make note of the sounds that truly inspire you. Play with each sound for a long time (have your MIDI sequencer running to capture that musical idea too) and try the sound in different registers and different dynamics. Also decide where it would be placed in an ensemble situation. Is it a distant sound, akin to muted strings? Or a small but pointed solo sound that would perform the same function of a flute double for violins? Any ensemble skills you have, whether orchestrating or playing in a band, are valuable here. Thinking in terms of layers now will help you blend these instruments later.

Now rename your sound. Give it a practical name that relates to its timbre, e.g., "metallic piano" or "breathy flute." Patch names like "Itz Kool" or "Angela's Pad" serve no useful purpose and you should rename these patches to something more useful. If your synthesizer has ROM presets only (non-rewritable memory) then you won't be able to rewrite the patches. In this case use a notepad or a database to log your favourite sounds and their memory location.

This auditioning exercise is crucial because it allows you to get to know the personality of the instrument and helps you instinctively write for it. This also allows you to give the instrument your own unique trademark since you've chosen the sounds that appeal to you. Just as in acoustic writing, it's not the sound, but how you blend that sound with others, that will make or break a good arrangement. In time you'll start editing patch parameters and actually change and create new sounds.

After the above exercise you can then consider taking your new synth into battle with the rest of your toys and tricks on your next gig. Don't do it before. How many times have we had a friend call us over to "check this out," only to be greeted with malfunctions and "that's funny, it never did that before…Oh I know…nope that's not it…just give me a minute…"

Time is precious. Use it and your new gear well.

Notes

synthesizer an electronic instrument, often played with a keyboard, combining simple waveforms to produce more complex sounds

acoustic an instrument that does not feature electronically modified sound

sonic of or relating to audible sound

peripheral relating to an outside boundary or outer surface

oboe a slender woodwind instrument that uses a double reed to produce a humming sound similar to that of a bagpipe

MIDI sequencer a standard for representing sound in a form that a computer can understand

timbre the distinctive tone of an instrument

Activities

1. In a group, discuss what you know about how synthesizers work. How is each track of a synthesizer different from a "real" player of the instrument it recreates? What are the advantages and disadvantages of using synthesizers to perform music? With which performers or bands who use synthesizers are you familiar? What makes a musician a good synthesizer performer? Access print and non-print resources to flesh out your understanding of this modern musical instrument.

2. Bhatia identifies several ideas for getting started with a new synthesizer. With a partner, review the article to identify all the tips he suggests. Create a checklist of tips. Then review the career section of a number of newspapers to acquaint yourself with the format and language used in employment ads. Use your checklist to write a job advertisement for a synthesizer salesperson.

3. Choose a topic on which you could give advice. It might be on how to make something, or how to write something, or how to perform a particular skill. Make notes on the stages you go through to complete the activity, including any problems that might be encountered during the process. Then write an expository article about your topic using process analysis to help you organize and explain the stages. Exchange work with a classmate and evaluate the article's clarity and coherence. Make any revisions your partner suggests that will improve the organization and effectiveness of your piece.

A Chat with Al Purdy

Kate Climenhage

Kate Climenhage was born in Brockville, Ontario, in 1976, and grew up in the neighbouring town of Orono. She received a bachelor's degree in literature from the University of Guelph in 2000. Climenhage, who is both a writer and a photographer, was still a teenager when she was asked by *IN2PRINT* magazine to conduct this interview with Canadian poet Al Purdy. Born in Wooler, Ontario, in 1918, Al Purdy is one of Canada's most respected poets. Although known primarily as a poet, Purdy wrote radio and television plays, book reviews, travel essays, and magazine articles. Purdy, who won two Governor General's Literary Awards for Poetry, died in 2000. Kate Climenhage had the opportunity to interview one of her childhood idols. If you could interview a person of your choice, who would it be and why? What approach would you take in the interview and what would you hope to learn?

Who were the first poets you read?

I was in first year of high school and it was the poetry we were taught then—Bliss Carman, Charles G.D. Roberts—the Canadian poets. You know, the usual array.

I was rather taken with Bliss Carman at the time—something I should be ashamed to admit now (laugh) but I'm not. I can still remember some of them. "Make me over Mother April when the sap begins to stir." They were rhyming and metric and very different from mine.

Many years later I was hypnotized by Dylan Thomas. I imitated Dylan Thomas for a long time. D.H. Lawrence was probably the strongest influence of anybody. Strangely enough, Lawrence is not paid much attention as a poet but only as a novelist or an essayist. *Lady Chatterley's Lover* was so sensational that it takes away attention from his poems. As far as I'm concerned, his poems are groundbreaking.

There have been other influences of course.

I think Layton influenced me: he loosened the language up quite a bit. Other than that there were no people who ever took me in hand and said, "You write like this." Some people do have those exemplars or teachers, mentors.

Do you think that's a good thing?

I don't know. From my own experience, I think you can learn all you want to from books and from your own curiosity—if you want, if you're really interested. To read a fine poem, a really good poem, is to learn something. It's to learn what the guy or the woman who wrote it knew when they wrote it. You can see the tricks that are used. You see everything else about that writer because he put it in that poem. I've done that and learned from other people. And, of course, you learn from life itself.

Do you think that starting out metrically and in a tight form helped you to develop?

Well, I think that a little stupidity helps a great deal. When you start out writing poems, the reason you write is you think, "Look at me, Ma, how great I am, how wonderful I am." You want to show off. I did the same thing and I thought it was wonderful. After a while I came to the conclusion that it wasn't so wonderful. You come to a kind of a plateau in your life, and you look at what you've done and it ain't so hot. So, you look for other exemplars, other models if you like, and you find 'em and then you move again. You can, anyway. I did. And I kept doing it. I kept moving. So, I don't think it ever ends because you never stop, at least as long as you're not quite senile, you keep on going.

Metred forms are very tough to break away from—you get too much in the habit. I wrote in metre for years as in my first published book: "I saw the milkweed float away, to curtsy, climb and hover, and seek among the crowded hills, another warmer lover." Well, that's crap.

Free verse is much harder than metric. If you write in metrics, the metre makes you remember. It's much harder to write something that is not metred and rhymed. I've got passages without metre or rhyme that I think are better than anything—*And women with such a glow it makes their background vanish.* That's one of them. You get these lines in your mind. If you're writing in rhyme you're trying to fit them in to make them rhyme. You use inversions, you revert the normal sequence of grammar.

Well, you can see the way I feel but if you want to write in metre, why you go ahead and write in metre. But the thing is you've got to say something and it's not so easy. You'd think it's easy; it's easy to write anything down but to make it mean something is something else.

What kind of discipline does it take to be a writer?

Oh God, I don't know. I have no idea. I wrote when I was interested in something. I never did sit down to write poems every day at a certain time. I think that's pretty silly. You write when you have something in your mind that says *this is a poem.* You're on the lookout for something. Your mind knows when you come to something that will make a poem. I knew an Australian poet who said that a poet should stay stupid— that was his way of phrasing it.

Keep your mind open. For instance, within the last five years, I had four or five people die that I knew quite well. In fact I was very fond of them; they were friends, or more than friends. I thought about the things about them that would make a poem and I just wrote the poem. That's the last poem I've written. It's just sort of an elegy for them, if you like.

I heard you reading at the Albion Hotel in Guelph, Ontario. You said something like, "I know no one here knows any of my stuff so I'm just going to read what I want." I was wondering if you actually think that of the younger generation or if it was just tongue-in-cheek...

When you go to a town that you've not read at before you take it for granted that people have never heard you read and that you're not very familiar to them. I always like that but it's always a challenge. I think it's a lot of fun to get up there before an audience and get them, uh, let's say, eating out of the palm of your hand (laughs). You know you're a stranger to most of them and I think it's a lot of fun. It's an ego trip of course: I used to deny that I liked it because I didn't like the idea of an ego trip. But I don't mind a bit, it's fun.

I'm not afflicted with nerves. At the so-called tribute at Harbourfront [1996 Toronto Harbourfront International Reading Series] it got me. I recited "Necropsy of Love," just about the only poem of mine I can remember. All those people applauding and I felt quite emotional. This affected my voice adversely. Very difficult to read when it affects your voice like that.

What advice would you give to young writers?

When I was a writer-in-residence at University of Western Ontario there were a lot of people come in and all they wanted was to be told that their stuff was good. I asked one of them—I remember particularly— "What do you read?" He said he didn't read; he didn't want to be influenced. That is absolute crap because that's what you *do* want to be—you want to be influenced. There's nobody who's going to stop you from writing poems. It isn't a matter of making a decision—I am now going to be a poet. I'm going to write. You wanna write, you write. *Who's stopping you?* Your mother's not going to stop you. She's glad to get you out of her hair.

People ask, "Should I give up everything else to write great poems?" The only answer I can give them is there's nobody stopping you. It isn't even a matter of decision. I do believe that if you're writing prose and you intend to write a novel it is very difficult if you're working at some job. But poems? Lord, I wrote all the time I worked in factories. No matter what you're doing you can write poems.

If I had to give anybody any advice it would be never go into a business with your in-laws.

Notes

Bliss Carman and Sir Charles G.D. Roberts Carman (1861–1929) and Roberts (1860–1943) were two of a group of Canadian poets known as the Confederation Poets who wrote lyrical romantic verse inspired by the Canadian landscape. Also included in the group were Archibald Lampman (1861–1899) and Duncan Campbell Scott (1862–1947).

Activities

1. In a small group, discuss the following questions: Why did Purdy write? How did Purdy's writing change over the course of his career? How does this interview reveal qualities about Purdy both as a person and as a writer?

2. The title of this selection, "A Chat with Al Purdy," suggests an informal, casual tone. Look again at the language used by Purdy in answering the questions. What particular elements are typical of oral speech? Refer to specific words, phrases, aspects of grammar, syntax, and usage to prove that the language is conversational rather than formal. Next, find at least one example of each of the following: sentence fragments, interjections, unconventional usage, colloquial language, slang, unconventional spelling, contractions, and run-on sentences. Use your examples to draw conclusions about the differences between oral language and written language.

3. In the interview, Purdy names poets who influenced his development as a writer: Bliss Carman, Charles G.D. Roberts, Dylan Thomas, D.H. Lawrence, and Irving Layton. Research at least one poem by each of these poets. Then locate and read more of Purdy's poetry and write an analytical essay in which you identify similarities in the content and style of the work of these six poets. Be sure to include evidence from the poems in your analysis.

Ours by Design

Alison Blackduck

Alison Blackduck was born in Inuvik, Northwest Territories, in 1975. In 2000, Blackduck completed her undergraduate degree in communication studies at Concordia University. While still at university, she began writing freelance articles. She became a reporter for the *Nunatsiaq News* in Iqaluit, Nunavut, and worked at the CBC North's Inuvik bureau. Blackduck's writing has appeared in such publications as the *Globe and Mail*, the *Gazette*, and *Up Here* magazine, and she is a regular columnist for the *Toronto Star*. Blackduck wrote this article because, as she said, "The amauti, a symbol of traditional Inuit garment design, is being threatened with exploitation. Inuit are seeking a way to protect it as intellectual property. They're hoping to clear the way for other indigenous groups as they go." A very complex, controversial issue in our contemporary world is how we protect cultures, while at the same time creating an atmosphere for them to co-exist. Under what circumstances should we accommodate transformations to culture? What are some of the ways we, as a society, can reconcile the need to recognize, respect, and protect cultures with the need to accept the inevitable adaptations of cultures?

Robbie Watt credits the amauti—the jacket-like garment most Inuit women use to carry their infants and toddlers—for making him the person he is today.

◀ *Young Mother Skipping, 1992, Mary Pudlat*

"It was my home, it was my bed," says Watt, president of Avataq Cultural Institute, an organization mandated to protect and promote Inuit culture in Nunavik (Northern Quebec).

"The amauti was my everything; I didn't want to be anywhere else... It's the same for all Inuit, male and female."

In a way, his recollections of an infancy spent snuggled in the warmth and security of his mother's amauti is an expression of his gratitude toward Inuit women for their integral contribution to Inuit identity. It's also an acknowledgement of the debt all Inuit owe to women for their ingenuity and hard work.

Watt is in Rankin Inlet, Nunavut, for a workshop hosted by Pauktuutit, the Inuit women's association which represents all Inuit women living in Canada. The workshop's focus is to develop a strategy to protect the intellectual property of the Inuit people at a regional, national, and international level. The participants also hope other indigenous people will benefit from their work.

"No other organization is doing what we're doing—not the AFN [the Assembly of First Nations], not the Métis National Council. They're looking at us as pioneering this work," says Veronica Dewar, president of Pauktuutit.

The people who have travelled from across Nunavut and Nunavik for this workshop are using the amauti design as a test case. They feel the design has been threatened in recent years by non-Inuit commercial interests. If the women can find a way to protect this unique Inuit innovation from being exploited for mass profit without their permission, they should be able to apply it to other Inuit designs, like the kayak, or commodities such as Inuit knowledge of the therapeutic benefits of particular plants, herbs, and flowers. Writers and artists are covered by copyright, inventors apply for patents, companies have trademarks—surely a people can protect their collective knowledge.

"So much of our Inuit culture needs protecting," says Rankin Inlet's Bernadette Dean, social development coordinator for the Kivalliq Inuit Association. "Look at what countries around the world have done with the kayak," she continues. "To my knowledge, not one red penny has been given to the Inuit...to me, it's a form of exploitation."

In October 1999, the New York fashion designer Donna Karan sent her global design director, Bonnie Young, to several western Arctic communities to purchase items such as handmade seal-skin clothing, beaded jackets, and knitted fur clothing. The purpose was to gather things Karan could use to help inspire her Fall 2000 collection.

Young reportedly bought a tuilli—a beaded amauti—from Pangnirtung, kamiks, fur garments, and garments knitted from musk-ox hair at a store in Yellowknife. Was Karan planning to acknowledge the source of her inspiration? Nobody knows. Despite calls from numerous Canadian reporters, neither Karan nor Young would comment publicly on the buying trip.

The lack of acknowledgement for use of another's ideas is the problem. Those ideas are called intellectual property, ideas that are new and result from human creativity and entrepreneurship. Knowledge wasn't considered a commodity until the invention of the printing press in the fifteenth century, says Barry Mandelker, who holds a master of laws in intellectual property. With the advent of mass-produced books like the Bible, and pamphlets printed and sold by publishers, the general public began perceiving abstract knowledge as having a concrete monetary value.

Even then, the concept of the right to protect and to profit from one's ideas didn't arise immediately. "Shakespeare and Milton didn't have copyright," Mandelker says. "The first [intellectual property] legislation in the world wasn't enacted until 1710—the Statute of Anne, which was named after the British monarch of the day."

Almost two centuries passed before international lawmakers legislated the Berne Convention for the Protection of Literary and Artistic Works, in 1886. Its aim was to advance capitalistic ideals like the preeminence of individual rights over collective rights, stimulate market growth through promoting and rewarding human innovation, and spur industrial competition.

The Berne Convention, which has been revised several times, wasn't only about money. Peoples' demands for effective intellectual property legislation were also based on then-radical notions of rights and fairness, and ensuring that people and their work were managed in a fair and just manner by authorities and their fellow citizens. These notions were born of a time marked indelibly by the French and American revolutions, and the American Bill of Rights, whose first amendment protects freedom of speech and of the press.

Today, protection of intellectual property is used mostly for economic gain and influence. "Major corporations file and receive thousands of patents every year," says Mandelker. "Often it's not about protecting new innovations, it's about protecting their market position and intimidating their competitors."

But the economic gain and influence offered by such laws are what many indigenous people are seeking. It would give them some measure of control over what's left of their cultural identity after centuries of colonization displaced them from their traditional lands and alienated them, leading to widespread poverty and few means to access economic opportunity.

Intellectual property rights for indigenous peoples is a hot topic around the world these days. In Canada, Mandelker and another intellectual property specialist were hired just a year ago by the federal government, Mandelker as a copyright policy analyst and the other with Industry Canada. It's a move they say reflects the increasing interest in and awareness of the conundrums surrounding intellectual property, which is still a relatively new legal concept.

In Canada, a 1999 government publication called Intellectual Property and Aboriginal People stipulates that to be protected, intellectual property "must be new, novel, original, or distinctive." The paper acknowledges these criteria can be tricky to determine, and indicates that intellectual property must have "utility," be "fixed," or be "used" in order to be protected.

The paper also describes the mechanisms in place to protect those ideas. Patents protect new technological products and processes. Copyrights protect original literary, artistic, dramatic, or musical works and computer software when they are expressed or fixed in a material form. Industrial designs protect the shape, pattern, or ornamentation applied to a manufactured product. Trademarks safeguard words, symbols, or pictures used to distinguish goods or services of an individual or organization from those of others in the marketplace. None of these lasts forever except the trademark, as long as the trademark holder renews it every 15 years.

These avenues of protection, however, don't quite fit the concept of protecting the intellectual property of a people. Pauktuutit, the Inuit women's association, has discovered this through four years of trying to find a way to protect the amauti design on behalf of Inuit women.

Pauktuutit has applied established international intellectual property legislation and it's trying to be creative with newer legislation like the United Nations Convention on Biological Diversity. The convention wasn't intended to protect intellectual property: its focus was to protect global biodiversity, conserve the environment, and ensure benefits arising from the use of genetic resources are shared fairly. But the wording of one of its articles has led many indigenous people to argue that section protects not only their knowledge of their environment but also their culture.

On the whole, however, Pauktuutit finds the existing legislation and mechanisms too time-specific and too narrow in scope. Copyright, for example, remains in effect only until 50 years after the death of the producer, at which time the work enters the public domain. This means anybody can use it without acknowledging the original producer or paying royalties for its use. That's not good enough, says Pauktuutit's Dewar. She says Inuit want their ideas and innovations to be protected in perpetuity for all Inuit, not just a few individuals or those represented by certain organizations.

The other constraint of current legislation is its narrow scope. Intellectual property protection applies to individual producers or organizations, and what's considered worthy of protection by international treaties like the Berne Convention is limited.

Where does the amauti fit in the existing legal framework?

Inuit have been using the amauti design for generations, so the design is neither original nor new. Even if it were discovered who developed that first amauti, Inuit have used the design for so long that legal experts would likely categorize it as belonging in the public domain. The same problem may apply to the kayak design, which has long been insinuated into the global cultural mainstream through mass production. Since it has been used for many generations, is it too considered "public domain"?

Of all available options—trademark, copyright, patent among them—Pauktuutit has concluded that an Inuit trademark is probably best-suited for identifying the physical manifestation of Inuit ideas. Robbie Watt of the Avataq Cultural Institute agrees trademark protection could work. However, he says, it should be amended in form and content to reflect the cultural reality of not only Inuit but other indigenous people, too. He suggests a Cultural Property, or CP, symbol similar to the ™ used to distinguish trademarks.

"We've come to a stumbling block," Watt said at the workshop. "Legally, we need a definition, but if all we want is meaningful recognition of our creations, maybe a special trademark would work."

A CP or other trademark would identify all products created by and through the application of indigenous peoples' knowledge. The Canadian government has employed a similar strategy for more than 30 years with its trademarked igloo design to identify "Canadian Eskimo art." However, that strategy is out of date, say intellectual property specialists like Mandelker. Besides, the igloo trademark doesn't apply to all indigenous people. Pauktuutit's directors want to design a solution that's inclusive.

How do Inuit women at the grassroots define the issue? Sewers like Rhoda Karetak of Arviat, Susan Avingaq from Igloolik, and Kugluktuk's Alice Anablak say that if an Inuk makes an anorak emblazoned with a copyrighted logo like the Toronto Maple Leaf insignia for her child, that's an acceptable use of another entity's design.

If the woman then decides to mass-produce the anoraks and sell them for profit, however, that's a problem. It would lead undoubtedly to National Hockey League lawyers sending her cease-and-desist orders and threatening a lawsuit if she didn't comply. In other words, the women believe that personal use inspired by another's knowledge is acceptable. Exploiting that knowledge for commercial gain is not.

World leaders are listening to what indigenous people have to say about the lack of legal protection their knowledge receives. "I just returned from an international UN conference on protecting traditional knowledge and folklore," Mandelker says. "Right now, every nation in the world is working on this."

Interest in indigenous peoples' views has as much to do with the fact that intellectual property protection as a whole has emerged as a hot topic in legal, government, and social justice circles over the past few years. But Article 8 (j) of the United Nations' Convention on Biological Diversity, which went into effect in 1993, is shining the spotlight on this particular issue.

This article states the traditional knowledge of indigenous people should be used only with the approval of the holders of such knowledge, and only if they also profit from the application of their knowledge. It also stipulates that each signatory must respect, promote, and preserve the traditional knowledge and activities of indigenous people and local communities.

However, the protection the article offers is limited at best. The Convention on Biological Diversity wasn't created as intellectual property legislation. However, says copyright expert Mandelker, "Once the treaty was ratified, indigenous people who were worried about the misappropriation of their knowledge focused on that aspect of the relationship between intellectual property rights and traditional knowledge."

One of the convention's objectives was to address emerging issues like genetic information and biotechnology. The United Nations wanted to ensure the fair and equitable distribution of benefits arising from the use of genetic resources, including acknowledging the source of genetic material and sharing benefits with that source.

One interesting development is that the treaty is now being associated with everything from cutting-edge technology—such as genetic sequencing—to age-old technology such as traditional Inuit clothing designs that are a reflection of cultural expression.

For the Inuit in the midst of the intellectual property discussion, finding a creative way to protect the amauti design as intellectual property is a priority. For people like Robbie Watt, the amauti is bound inextricably with Inuit identity. For people such as Pauktuutit president Veronica Dewar, international recognition of Inuit intellectual property is a human right.

"Our crafts are being exploited," Dewar says. "Inuit are real, we have feelings, and our knowledge is ours."

Notes

indigenous refers to those parts of nature, such as particular plants, animals, or ethnicities of people, in a specific region that originated in that region; from the Latin word *indigena*, meaning "native"

integral significant part of something that cannot be taken away from the whole; something required for completeness

collective referring to a group as one entity

misappropriation to take something from someone that is rightfully that person's, or to use it wrongly, as in exploitation

Activities

1. Have a class discussion in which you explore the following questions: What are some of the purposes of copyright laws? What is meant by "intellectual property" and "public domain"? What are today's trademarks, copyrights, and patents each designed to protect? What procedures might be required to protect the traditional arts of indigenous peoples from exploitation?

2. In a small group, select six to eight sequential paragraphs in this article. In a chart entitled "facts," list every fact that appears in the passage you have chosen. In a second chart entitled "opinions," list every opinion that appears in the passage. Beside each item in your "facts" list, make notes in point form on how credible each fact is and what makes it either credible or not. Beside each item in your "opinions" list, make notes in point form on how persuasive each opinion is to you, and how surrounding information influences whether or not it is persuasive. Present your information to the class and elicit feedback on your conclusions.

3. Working in small groups, select an Aboriginal community and do research on some of its inventions and practices. Choose one invention or practice and outline requirements you would have if you were creating a cultural property trademark for this item or practice. Develop a rationale and a defence of your proposal. Present your proposal to the class and get feedback on the thoroughness and persuasiveness of your argument.

Another Viewpoint: Society

With a group, identify an important technology-related copyright issue. State the issue in the form of a resolution for a class debate. Conduct the debate, videotaping it if possible to help identify strengths and areas for improvement in your presentation.

About the Visual   Marian Henley was born in Dallas, Texas, in 1954. She has been a full-time cartoonist since her weekly comic strip "Maxine!" debuted in 1981. Other cartoons by Henley have appeared in publications such as *MAD* magazine. She published her first book, *Maxine!*, in 1987. In 1989, she produced and starred in three short live-action videos based on "Maxine!" which have appeared on MTV. She also published a short fiction book called *Smile* in 1991. *Laughing Gas*, a twenty-year collection of "Maxine!" strips, appeared in May 2002. What subjects can be more effectively illustrated in a cartoon than in writing? Why do you think comic strips aimed at children are sometimes more appealing than standard books? How are cartoons aimed at adults different from those intended for children?

Activities

1. Put yourself in this picture by imagining the beach environment where these two characters are situated. In a journal entry, write what you might notice in this type of setting. List all the sensory details, both beautiful and messy, that you can imagine finding on a beach.

2. Consider the gender of each character. Do you think that Henley has engaged in any gender stereotyping in this cartoon? Why or why not? With a partner, create six to eight more frames for this cartoon. In your cartoon, maintain and extend the characterizations of the two people that Henley has created. Then post your cartoons in the classroom and discuss with your partner the similarities and differences among your classmates' work.

1989

Landscape with the Fall of Icarus

About the Visual   Pieter Brueghel, who historians believe lived from 1525 to 1569, was a Flemish painter who worked most of his life in what is now Belgium. After being apprenticed to a leading artist in the city of Antwerp, he travelled to Italy to continue his studies. In his work, he celebrated peasant life and also produced paintings on religious and mythological themes. This painting focuses on a Greek legend, in which Daedalus and his son Icarus escape from the island of Crete using wings of wax and bird feathers. Icarus disregards his father's warning not to fly too close to the sun; his wings melt and he falls into the sea and drowns. Why do you think artists over the centuries have been moved to paint and sculpt so many works based on mythological and religious themes? To what extent do you think these subjects might continue to occupy artists in centuries to come?

Activities

1. What does the portrayal of Icarus in the painting tell you about Brueghel's feelings toward Icarus? If you were an artist, which moment in the story of Icarus and Daedalus would you represent in a painting? Explain your choice.

2. One critic has suggested that the perspective of the painting—looking at the landscape and action from above—indicates that the audience is sharing Daedalus' horrified vision of the tragedy rather than observing an objective portrayal of the scene. Explain whether or not you agree. How does the painting's perspective, or angle of view, affect your understanding of the picture and your emotional response to it?

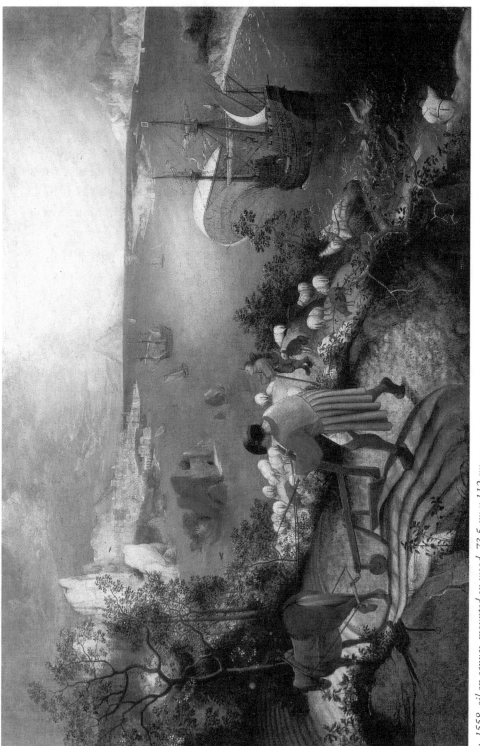

c. 1558, oil on canvas, mounted on wood, 73.5 cm x 112 cm

About the Visual   Hiroshige Utagawa was born in the city of Edo, now Tokyo, in 1797. Hiroshige won recognition as a landscape artist, especially for the two print series *One Hundred Famous Views of Edo* and *Fifty-three Stations of the Tokaido*, which are considered his masterpieces. It has been said of Hiroshige that "he captured, in a poetic, gentle way that all could understand, the ordinary person's experience of the Japanese landscape...." He died in 1858. What main features of any society are typically expressed in its most popular art form? Why do you think that the art of different cultures is so varied? Do you believe that these differences are more pronounced today than they were one or two centuries ago or that the differences have diminished? Why?

Activities

1. *Shower at Ohashi Bridge* is considered one of the most outstanding of Hiroshige's landscape works. Choose three elements of this picture that you think contribute most to this assessment of the work. Write several sentences about each element and then share your thoughts with the class. After your discussion, consider how your classmates' ideas contributed to your appreciation of the work.

2. *Shower at Ohashi Bridge* is part of Hiroshige's series *One Hundred Famous Views of Edo.* With the class, brainstorm a list of famous views or settings in the community where you live. Choose one of the views on your list and create a painting or drawing of it in the style of Hiroshige. Present your work to a group of classmates and explain the stylistic and content choices you made.

19th century, nishiki-e print ▶

The Poetry of Earth and Sky

Photographer Courtney Milne was born in Saskatoon, Saskatchewan, in 1943. Milne received formal training in photography and has two master's degrees, one in psychology and the other in journalism and mass communication. Since 1975, he has been a freelance photographer, concentrating on nature and landscape. Milne has taken over 420,000 exposures in over thirty-five countries across seven continents. Ormond Mitchell, son of W.O. Mitchell, was born in Edmonton, Alberta, in 1943. His spouse, Barbara Mitchell, was born in Saskatoon in 1944. They both grew up in High River, Alberta. They lived in western Canada before moving to England, where each received a doctorate degree in English literature. Both teach at Trent University in Peterborough, Ontario. Do you believe that the landscape in which people grow up influences their personality and how they view the world? Why or why not? To what degree, if any, does the landscape of your community influence your life?

Notes

litmus literally, a blue powder derived from lichens used in paper form as a test for chemical acidity or basicity; in this instance, used metaphorically to mean investigating or experimenting; from the Old Norse words *litr*, meaning "colour" or "dye," and *mosi*, meaning "moss" or "bog"

minimalist related to a movement of abstract art, consisting of simple geometric forms

wolf willow a North American shrub found especially on the prairies

Activities

1. In the last sentence of the essay, the authors describe W.O. Mitchell's skill in appealing to his readers' senses, particularly the sense of sight. Do you think there is any contradiction in illustrating Mitchell's words with photographs? Why or why not?

2. Choose three photographs from this essay in which pattern is an important element. Explain how the focus on pattern enhances the impact of each photograph. Take your own photographs in which you emphasize the patterns you discover in both the natural and constructed environment.

Photography by Courtney Milne
Text by Ormond Mitchell and Barbara Mitchell

The Poetry
of Earth and Sky

Half a century after the writing of Who Has Seen the Wind,

Courtney Milne's images capture the timeless elements

of W.O. Mitchell's prose: the drama of cloudscape, the

seasonal extremes, the promise of harvest, the geometry

of land and sky

W.O. Mitchell was born in 1914 in Weyburn, Saskatchewan. As a child, he absorbed the wide spaces of the prairie, its dramatic shifts of light and shadow, its straight lines, and its salient signs of life and death. For the rest of his life, he was marked by this landscape, emotionally and even, it seemed, physically. His face was as transparently expressive as a field of wheat, bright and mobile in the wind, but as easily transformed by the shadow of the clouds. His tousled hair always looked as wild as the prairie grasses. One of his school chums described him as having "no side." What he meant was that W.O. had a guilelessness that invited immediate friendship, an openness as wide as the prairie itself. There was nothing restrained about him; he was down-to-earth and irrever-ent. But he also had a darker streak—a profound sense of mortality and the passing of things taught to him early on the prairies.

Now and as a child I walked out here to ultimate emptiness, and gazed to no sight destination at all. Here was the
melodramatic part of the earth's skin that had stained me
during my litmus years, fixing my inner and outer perspective, dictating the terms of the fragile identity contract I
would have with myself for the rest of my life.

— *How I Spent My Summer Holidays*

"It's going to storm, Sammy," shouted Brian.

A tumbleweed bounding past the boy and the old man
caught itself against the strands of the fence, then,
released, went rolling on its way. An unnatural dusk that
had grown over the whole prairie made Brian strain his

eyes to see through the spreading darkness of dust licked
up by the wind in its course across the land. His ears were
filled with the sound of the wind, singing fierce and lost
and lonely, rising and rising again, shearing high and higher
still, singing vibrance in a void forever and forever wild.

— *Who Has Seen the Wind*

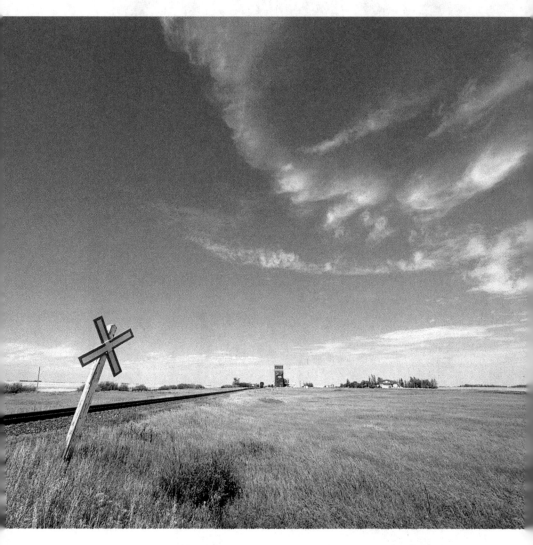

Who Has Seen the Wind opens with one of the most recognizable
lines in Canadian literature: "Here was the least common denominator
of nature, the skeleton requirements simply, of land and sky—
Saskatchewan prairie." The mathematical metaphor not only catches
the visual image of a landscape reduced to the bare minimum of sky,
horizonline, and land, it also suggests the skeletal destiny of humans.
The novel depicts Brian's quest for answers to the basic, "skeleton"
questions about birth and death. Visually precise and metaphorically
suggestive though it is to Canadian eyes, this first line of the novel was

considered dull and boring by W.O.'s American editor. When asked to remove it, W.O. argued that it expressed the "bareness of the prairie itself" and that it must stay in. There was, he thought, a distinction to be made between bareness and dullness. What W.O. saw was that the ultimate emptiness of the prairie was also melodramatic.

And for sensitive eyes and ears, there is variety in the seasonal changes to prairie, in its cloudscapes, in its wind voices. W.O.'s sensibility, his philosophy of being, his aesthetics were all informed by this minimalist landscape, which trained him to look closely and to listen acutely. In *Who Has Seen the Wind*, he celebrates prairie landscape in rich, lyrical prose and explores the growth of this way of seeing in his child protagonist, Brian. He called the prairie, and later the foothills, his "grass tower": "I had a grass tower childhood in the Saskatchewan prairies. Now I value the opportunity to stand still, to stare, to listen. You can do these things well in a grass tower. The listening is particularly important to a writer."

Looking up at sky and looking down at earth, "you're in a world," says the kid in *Jake and the Kid*, and "she's your own world." As a young boy, W.O., along with his friends, had the whole prairie around Weyburn as their world, their grass tower.

They hunted gophers, dug caves, and swam in the Souris River— more a slow-moving creek with cattails spearing its mud banks—or skated on it in winter. The prairie sharpened his senses, and his prose is rich with what he called sensuous fragments: the "stitching sound of grasshoppers," the "faint honey scent of wolf willow," the "escargot taste and smell" of the Souris, the meadowlark's "sudden bright notes splintering stillness." Even the no sound of a hot mid-August noon is captured: "She was kind of numb out there, like the prairie bumped its funny bone." Like Joseph Conrad, one of his literary heroes, W.O. believed that the writer must appeal to his readers' senses, must strive through image and rhythm to make us touch, hear, smell, taste—above all, to make us "see" our world.

Canada: A Virtual History

Journalist Ray Conlogue was born in Toronto in 1949. Conlogue received a bachelor's degree in English literature and a master's degree in drama from the University of Toronto. From 1980 to 1991, he was the theatre critic for the *Globe and Mail*. Conlogue won a National Newspaper Award for theatre criticism in 1986. This newspaper feature article describes a television production about Canadian history. In what ways do you think filmed productions of historical periods should be realistic? What kinds of "poetic licence" do you think writers and directors can take when recreating a historical drama?

Notes

Iroquois term that refers to a confederation of five Aboriginal nations that originally inhabited the northern part of New York State

Captain James Cook explorer, navigator, and map-maker who charted part of the Gaspé and helped prepare the map that enabled James Wolfe's armada to navigate the St. Lawrence River

Plains of Abraham the site of the battle for Quebec in September 1759 between the British forces led by James Wolfe and the French forces led by Montcalm, both of whom were mortally wounded in the battle

Louis Riel (1844–1885) Métis leader, founder of Manitoba, and the central figure in the Northwest Rebellion

Montagnais Aboriginal people living in the eastern and northern portions of the Quebec-Labrador peninsula

Activities

1. In one column of a chart, describe three visuals referred to in the article. Beside each description, explain how it was created. Assess the effectiveness of the techniques for the viewer.

2. Analyze the characteristics of a newspaper feature article, using this selection as a model. Then assess the effectiveness of this article using the criteria you have developed. Focus on the use of elements such as the following: a "hook" at the beginning to capture the reader's interest, the use of a journalist's "W5H" (Who, What, Where, When, Why, and How), detailed examples, background information, and interviews with experts.

Canada:
A virtual history

CBC had a relatively paltry $25 million to bring the story of our nation to life, writes **Ray Conlogue**, so it used some ambitious digital magic to take us back in time

"**M**ake the meteorite warmer and slower, please!"

This, if you can believe Steve Dutcheshen, was a typical director's request to CBC-TV's special-effects department during the creation of *Canada: A People's History*. Four new episodes of the 16-part, $25-million series are airing this month and producer Mark Starowicz has given the go-ahead to show how the magic was done.

The first half of the series, running from prehistory through early settlement and up to Confederation, is mostly about the prephotographic era. To get visuals of the British fleet attacking Quebec in 1763, or of Iroquois torturing French missionaries, it was necessary to generate the images by a variety of clever techniques. One involved filming actors climbing stepladders, then shrinking down the footage so they could "seem" to be working the sails on a 5-foot museum model of a warship. Another called on computers to create a huge village of native teepees out of film footage of a single teepee "which, on top of it all, was too narrow," says Roger Hupman, an effects director. "We had to make it twice as wide, which means each teepee has the same wrinkles twice."

Not to mention slowing down a meteorite, changing daytime footage of a steam locomotive to night-time, and, says Dutcheshen, "my favourite instruction of all: 'Keep the French bodies, the heads haven't arrived yet.'"

How to recreate the past with special-effects computers

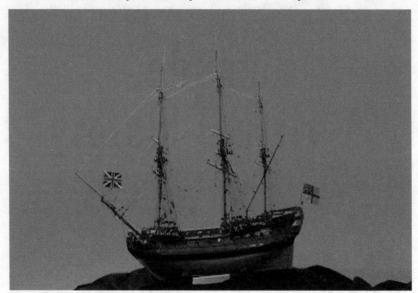

The challenge: Create the illusion that British ships are attacking Quebec. **Step 1:** A five-foot-long model is filmed in various positions against a neutral backdrop, making it easy for artists to remove the background later.

Step 2: Current footage of Quebec City is altered to remove any buildings constructed after the attack of 1759, such as the landmark Chateau Frontenac, from the skyline. Clouds are added for dramatic effect.

Step 3: Superimpose various ship shots on the background to create the illusion of many vessels. Artists change colour of ships to fit background and add reflections and shadows.

Now, this may seem unnecessarily complicated to those who have kept up with developments in Hollywood. When the producers of *Titanic* wanted to recreate the doomed liner racing through the ocean, they built their own museum-quality "model" (14 metres, the length of many houses), and then used prototype high-power computers to create an ocean for it to slice through—binary point by binary point—likewise calling up the throngs of passengers from the cyber-ether.

But the *Titanic* team had 100 million bucks (U.S.), and the CBC didn't. Although the 30-hour series's $25-million (Cdn) budget had the usual right-wing critics choking in indignation (waste of taxpayers' dollars, splut, splut), it works out to less than $1-million per hour—about what the average U.S. sitcom costs.

That had consequences. Take eighteenth-century warships, for example. Even with a bank of shiny new effects computers, the CBC simply didn't have the gigabytes, or the time, to generate an image of a warship. The Royal Ontario Museum kindly let them film a magnificent, fully detailed 5-foot model of a period British battleship, which the new computers were then able to duplicate many times over (the whole British fleet bearing down on Quebec in the summer of 1759 is in fact the same ship, promiscuously cloned).

"And," says series executive producer Mark Starowicz, "when you have a close-up of a prow cutting through water with a crew hanging off the bow, the ship you see is actually the Endeavour." A CBC crew captured footage of the working replica of Capt. James Cook's ship (based in Sydney, Australia) off the North American east coast.

By such devious devices was a vanished world recreated. And yet, despite his exacting passion for accuracy, and the knowledge that video clips from the series would be "freeze-framed in Canadian classrooms" for decades to come, Starowicz knew that compromises would have to be made.

"Take the battle of the Plains of Abraham," he says. "In the real event, the muskets sounded like popcorn popping and there was

so much smoke the soldiers couldn't even find the battle after the third volley." A far cry from the clear vistas of soldiers on the TV screen, and the satisfying thunder of musket volleys.

Starowicz considers it a triumph that CBC spent as much on current-generation graphic compositing computers as it did. And, remembering all the jibes he endured about how young viewers would not be interested in "musty" history, it is an additional sweet pleasure that "the graphic compositing department is full of kids with green hair."

One of them, a twentysomething named Jennifer Vuckovic (who has, as it happens, alarmingly jet-black hair), was responsible for creating the celebratory ball which marked the signing of the British North America Act in 1867. "It's what I call rotoscope hell," she says, recalling that the director of photography who oversaw the original filming of a small group of actors dancing in period costume, "didn't realize we'd need a middle layer of dancers to fill the historic ballroom we were using."

The trick here is that the costumed actors were filmed against a

A rope trick that didn't work

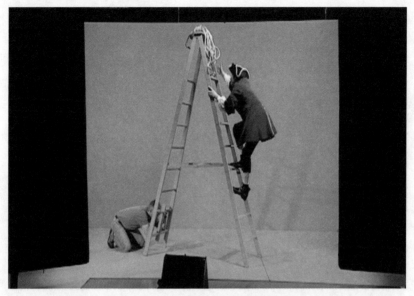

The challenge: Have sailors climb ropes on ships to make static model boats look more realistic. **The problem:** Actors in costume were shot against a neutral background climbing ladders to simulate the effect of climbing ropes. However, when these images were shrunk and superimposed on the ship footage, the effect was unconvincing and was dropped.

neutral background in Toronto, and later superimposed on the historic ballroom located in Prince Edward Island. Fair enough—it saves travel expenses—but why not just film a whole lot of actors in the first place? "The costumes cost a fortune," replies Vuckovic.

Instead, she created the "middle layer" of dancers out of the existing footage, picking one here, one there, shrinking them to the appropriate size, and setting them spinning in the background of dancers who are—are you still with me?—themselves. "But they're rearranged and smaller, and we're real sure that nobody has noticed," says Vuckovic. The feat, however, required her to sit in front of a rotoscope camera for two weeks, rolling the film backward and forward a few frames at a time until the job was done. "It's worse than carpal tunnel syndrome," she says morosely, before rushing off to meet friends at a club.

Dutcheshen, a Manitoba native who studied fine arts in Winnipeg

And filling the ballroom with dancers

THE
INTERCOLONIAL
RAILROAD

The challenge: Create a ballroom full of dancers with a limited number of actors wearing expensive costumes.

Step 1: Film many sequences of a small group of dancers in various positions in front of a neutral backdrop, some in the foreground, some in the background.

and design at the Ontario College of Art, feels that much of his team's work was about pictorial design. Actors supposedly dining on a train were actually shot in a studio, with footage of countryside racing past being projected on a train-window cut-out behind them. The result looked miserably fake until Dutcheshen's team created reflections of the actors' faces and wineglasses in the window glass. "As a fine artist, I found a lot of it came down to painting

skills. I had to know which details would make it look real."

And it was with a pang that I learned that the Confederation-era locomotive steaming off toward the horizon in one episode was in fact lifted from the 1974 CBC series *The National Dream.* The locomotive was originally shot moving through rocky Ontario countryside by day, and Roger Hupman demonstrates the painfully tricky business of generating a new setting for it—the

Step 2: Combine the various sequences digitally. If viewers look closely, they can see the same actors in different parts of the room at the same time.

Prairies by night—as demanded by the script. Why not just shoot such a train again? Here's the answer that causes the pang: "*The National Dream* was shot when such a train could be found."

The team is rightly proud that it managed to weave material from so many sources, in so many media—real and virtual—into a convincing on-screen result. And their commitment to historic truth was obsessive. In a War of 1812 scene they realized that a U.S. general had been filmed in a brick fort at a time when forts were actually wooden palisades. It wasn't hard to computer-brush in a wooden palisade, but there were gaps between the logs where you should have seen the general's brass buttons.

"So we put them in, and it's pretty good," says Dutcheshen, "except that when he moves, his buttons don't."

But you didn't notice, did you? Not the first time, anyway.

Getting it right

At the other extreme from computer legerdemain is the rock-solid reality of what is called "materials history." In *Canada: A People's History*, the Native war paint was made from coloured clay and the chiefs' armour from plaited reeds, exactly as they would have been centuries ago. "The reed armour looks bizarre," says Peter Twist, "but it worked against arrows."

Twist, an engineer by training, became a builder of museum displays and Parks Canada installations out of a passion for history. Asked by CBC to help out on one episode of *A People's History*, he soon became a fixture. He was the one who found out what caps and badges were worn by the Midland battalion which fought Louis Riel, and that the French cannoneers on the Plains of Abraham wore red coats. He fully expected to see them stuck in blue coats, like the French infantry, in order to avoid confusion with the red coats of the British, "but to my amazement the CBC was absolutely rigorous about historical accuracy." This contrasts with U.S. films he's worked on where the "historical sensitivity is laughable."

In Ontario-based episodes, Twist also advised on Native history, which sometimes caused friction with Natives certain they knew their culture better than he did. "But a lot of Natives' impressions of their culture have been corrupted by Buffalo Bill shows and so on," says Twist. "So I'd have to say, 'No, you [your ancestors] didn't dress like that, they dressed like this.'"

He emphasizes that most Natives who participated "built up trust in us; they liked what was happening."

In the Quebec shoots, Native adviser Marco Bacon, a Montagnais from Lac Saint-Jean, was in charge of historic accuracy. Not surprisingly, he sees the issue differently. White advisers, he says, find it hard to accept "when we try to validate things through oral tradition. And it's true that many of our rituals were condemned and people were afraid to practise them. But they remembered them and told their children. That's why a Native can disagree with a historian. The historian presumes, but the Native can feel in his bones whether something is right or not."

Bacon worked for many years as a film actor, playing Native roles that were "more folklore than authentic. I found if I was going to argue with a director, I needed authoritative facts to change his manner of seeing things." He became a self-taught researcher, and willingly used any European documents he could find. Today he laments the paucity of documentation of his own people, the Montagnais. "They weren't taken back to Europe like the Iroquois."

Bacon and Twist both agree that there were dark spots where no information exists, and here it was necessary to guess. "You try not to overdo it, or imagine too much," says Bacon.

"We'd take a best guess," says Twist. "A film isn't like a book, you can't leave a black box. When guessing, we'd go with the mundane."

And both agree that the world hasn't necessarily caught up with what the CBC was trying to do. Some U.S. reviewers, says Twist, "were horrified by our sympathetic treatment of the Natives. They didn't like it that we quoted, say, an American who survived a native massacre of his shipmates and wrote that Americans like him had it coming to them. One of the things I liked about this series was that we could not change a word or sentence of an original document."

Anna Husarska was born and raised in Warsaw, Poland, studied in France, and now uses New York as her home base. She has worked as a journalist and translator since 1979, contributing to publications such as *The Buenos Aires Herald*, *The New Republic*, *The New Yorker*, *The Washington Post*, and *The Wall Street Journal*. Husarska's facility for languages—she writes in five languages, speaks six languages fluently, and has working knowledge of three additional languages—has been invaluable in her work. Husarska has covered civil wars and other conflicts in Central America, Central Europe, the Middle East, and Southeast Asia. In this selection, Husarska explains how she prepares for her assignments. What challenges—to their mobility, research and communications capabilities, ethics, and psyche—do journalists reporting on conflicts in other countries have to deal with? What do you imagine would be the rewards of such work?

Notes

infrastructure the system of public works in a country, such as telephone and train service

flak jacket a bullet-proof jacket worn in a war zone

fonctionnaire de l'aventure a government official or civil servant

Activities

1. To many people, working as a foreign correspondent is an appealing job involving travel and adventure. Write a short report explaining how the information in this annotated graphic might influence a person's understanding of this career. Look up each of the places and nationalities listed within it and cite specific information from the selection to support your ideas. In your conclusion, reflect on your own suitability for and your interest in this kind of work.

2. Construct a character analysis of Anna Husarska, using information from "Unzipped." In your analysis, consider what she says as well as the tone she creates. How might her attitudes have been formed by the situations in which she has worked over the years? Ask a classmate to read your work and provide feedback on how you might rephrase passages or combine sentences to improve the clarity of your writing.

Unzipped

What's inside the travel bag of a foreign correspondent on the go?

After I get the call, I start packing and turn on the short-wave radio to find out who hates whom where I am heading, and perhaps the reason why they kill each other. To communicate from countries with inefficient infrastructures, I take my satellite phone [1]; the problem is, if the security police are efficient they'll confiscate it.

I take a whole bunch of plug adapters [2] and a good pair of alligator

Maps, country surveys, and posters of war criminals come in handy [7]. I write in notebooks [8] that fit in my back pocket and last for six months—if my handwriting's not too big and the war not too intensive. I carry CDs [9] with dictionaries and encyclopedias—they make my copy look intelligent. And of course, a book [10], perhaps about a former conflict, just for a change?

The basic survival kit is really simple: compass, Mag-Lite, Swiss Army knife, Leatherman all-purpose tool [11]. Cash [12] is crucial—most countries-at-war don't take credit cards—and I stuff it in a variety of places; in Somalia, $2,000 cash cushioned each of my running shoes.

A black, 100 per cent polyester skirt [13] that never wrinkles goes on every trip. For Muslim (or potentially Muslim) countries I always have a head scarf [14].

As for toiletries: reduce, reduce, reduce, which means small, concentrated quantities of shampoo, washing powder, and cream [15]. I take *chancletas* [16], the awful flip-flops that I bought in Tajikistan. They are the only thing that G. (the man who waits for my return) really insists I wear—he fears an infection. I fear for other things that I'll catch and often put a flak jacket in my backpack. And always, always some coffee [17], Cuban if possible, for a kick-start before facing more atrocities—another day at the office for what my friend calls *fonctionnaire de l'aventure*.

clips [3] so I can plug in wherever I am. And of course I include my laptop [4], whose hard drive is the closest thing to home.

I need credentials, business cards, and clippings of previous coverage [5]. I usually take a big sign stating my profession [6], but I am not sure it keeps the snipers away.

The Humpback of Notre Dame

About the Visual   Between 1993 and 1998, the Government of Newfoundland and Labrador's Department of Tourism, Culture and Recreation conceived and initiated an award-winning advertising campaign to entice visitors to the province. This "Imagine That" campaign grew to eight print advertisements, including the ad depicted here, posters, billboards, television commercials, and a postcard mail campaign. These advertisements were circulated throughout Canada and numerous other countries. The campaign had a forty per cent *conversion rate*, meaning that forty per cent of the people who saw the advertisements and then called to inquire actually visited the province. Not calculated in the conversion rate were those people who saw the ad and went to the province without calling. This advertisement contains not just a reference to a site on the northeast coast of Newfoundland, Notre Dame Bay, but a literary allusion as well. What are the purpose and contribution of literary allusions? If a viewer or reader is not aware of the allusion, is the impact of the phrase lost? Why or why not?

Activities

1. In a class discussion, share information and impressions of various provinces you have visited in Canada. If you have never visited Newfoundland and Labrador, would the advertisement "The Humpback of Notre Dame" entice you to visit there? Why or why not? What is the main impression of Newfoundland and Labrador you get from the advertisement? Does the ad successfully appeal to your wishes, attitudes, values, or lifestyle?

2. The first purpose of print advertisements is to catch and hold viewers' eyes and attention. In an essay, explore to what extent this advertisement uses the following attention-grabbing techniques in either illustration or text: a catchy title or headline; hyperbole and tongue-in-cheek humour; parallel structure and repetition; juxtaposition; symbolism; size, style, and placement of typeface or font.

Morty Mania

Judy Waytiuk was born in Winnipeg, Manitoba, in 1950. For over thirty years, Waytiuk has worked as a reporter, commentator, documentarian, producer, and anchor in the media of newspaper, radio, and television. From 1987 to 1994, she was head of television news and current affairs programming for Global Television's Winnipeg affiliate. Her articles have appeared in publications including *Chatelaine* and the *National Post*. In "Morty Mania," she profiles Manitoba's very successful MTS advertising campaign. In what ways have specific advertisements influenced your view of a particular product or service? Can you think of ads that had a negative impact on you, rather than the intended positive one? If so, what was it about those ads that repelled you?

Notes

anthropomorphism attributing human characteristics to animals or inanimate objects, or personality to an animal or a god; from the Greek words *anthrōpos*, meaning "human being," and *morphē*, meaning "form"

self-deprecating refers to humorously negative remarks a person has made about herself or himself

Huns generally, a disparaging term referring to barbarous, uncivilized people; historically, refers to members of a nomadic, pastoral people who invaded Europe in the fourth and fifth centuries CE and were defeated in 455 CE

Activities

1. In a two-column chart, list on the left all the advertising campaigns you remember that were appealing to you. On the right, list all of the advertising campaigns you remember because they were ridiculous or offensive to you. Below, list the features of these advertisements that made them either appealing or offensive. Compare your list with that of a partner to see which, if any, features appear on both lists. Discuss reasons for your choices.

2. In small groups, analyze the features of the two advertisements depicted here, considering the target audience and the need to which the ad is appealing; the product or service being promoted; design elements such as use of colour, typeface, and layout; and the underlying values that are espoused through the ads.

morty
mania

Judy Waytiuk

how Manitoba's

MTS turned a

lovable bison

into a pop-cult

phenomenon that

ranks among the

top 1 per cent in

ad recall

THE MOST RELIABLE SUPPORT IN MANITOBA.

With MTS, all your business needs are backed up with an incomparable level of support and service. From local, long distance and wireless, to high-speed Internet, telephone systems, equipment and data applications, we have technicians province-wide to ensure your business never misses a beat. To speak to someone who knows what they're talking about, call your MTS sales representative or 225-5687 (CALLMTS) toll-free today.

mts.mb.ca

MTS BUSINESS
All your needs. In one place.

MTS

Morty the Manitoba Telecom Services bison and his wry, shaggy friends and relations have stolen the hearts of Manitobans even more effectively than Molson's Joe and his "I AM Canadian" rant fired up Canadians a year ago. Joe was a one-spot wonder, while the MTS campaign, now into its second year, has turned into a Manitoba mania.

The developers of the campaign say it took luck, a maintenance man, creative brilliance, and agonizing corporate rethinking—

"THE MAINTENANCE GUY DISCREETLY SUGGESTED THAT THE BISON MIGHT BE A MORE APPROPRIATE ANIMAL."

without which none of the other factors would have come into play. So was it worth it to MTS?

Jack Riediger, the telco's Winnipeg-based advertising and marketing services manager, never dreamed a campaign could do this well. "We're benchmarking this stuff against things like the 'I AM Canadian' campaign," he says. "Our overall advertising recall is well over 80 per cent, and that's very high. Last quarter we said the problem is we'll never be able to improve on it, and it just keeps getting better."

Paul Millen, senior vice-president at Ipsos-ASI in Toronto, an advertising research company, offers further figures to show just how remarkably well this campaign is working. "In overall recall, we track over 1,500 campaigns in Canada, and this is in the top 1 per cent," he says. "We work with most of the major advertisers across the country, and this is one of the most successful campaigns I've ever been associated with."

Manitobans traded MTS bison paper cut-out Christmas tree ornaments as gifts last year. Bison Beanie Babies are hot items. Kids wanted bison costumes at Halloween, and they trade bison knock-knock jokes while waiting at bus stops. At the Fort Whyte Nature Centre outside Winnipeg, a flyer advertising a lecture series on bison leads off "Contrary to the popular television commercials, today's bison do not talk, laugh, wear sweaters, or surf the Internet."

Bison are this province's animal symbol. They're everywhere—stuffed in museums, bronze-sculpted in the legislature, painted on the province's crest and flag, served on restaurant menus, and alive and kicking in herds in parks and nature centres.

And anthropomorphism has always been "a popular and effective vehicle—Spuds Mackenzie, the Hamm's bear, Exxon and Esso with their tiger in your tank, Qantas and the koala bear," points out Rob Warren, director of the Asper Centre for Entrepreneurship at the University of Manitoba. "People like animals, especially animals that are somehow warm and cuddly. And even though bison are big animals, they look very docile and huggable."

Aside from MTS, only Ensis Growth Fund, a Manitoba government-sponsored investment fund, has used bison in an ad campaign—as a thundering backdrop herd on a projection screen while the CEO drones on about growth opportunities.

"KIDS WANT BISON COSTUMES AT HALLOWEEN, AND THEY TRADE BISON JOKES WHILE WAITING AT BUS STOPS."

"It's not creative at all," sniffs Warren, who thinks part of the reason for MTS's success is that, for a heady change, "here's somebody standing up with one of our major symbols, and making something of it. Manitobans are usually so self-deprecating, and this is a direct descendant of the Joe 'I AM Canadian' thing, on a local level." Besides, he adds, the MTS campaign is by far the best-executed, most creative stuff in a market where the advertising humour benchmark is Nick Hill, discount furniture baron, "talking about number-one son leaving the sofa-making machine on too long."

Morty arrived on the scene in October 1999, with a spot selling long-distance services. Manitobans ran to their TV sets when Morty bellowed "WHAT?" in response to another bison yelling "We stampede AT TWO!" "Gesundheit," the monosyllabic Morty finally shouted back—a tad irritably.

Manitoba chuckled, and fell in love.

Since then, Morty's been seen painted with a stylized fluorescent red lightning streak while bopping (in a dignified manner) to a vaguely heavy-metal guitar riff. That spot sold high-speed Internet service. Cellphones wearing tiny bison horns promote the company's cellular service, as do "backup bison" twitching their skinny tails, in perfect digitized unison, to the beat of a white-bread Motown bison soloist singing "My mamma tol' me, yuh bettuh shop around."

Simon Cameron, VP associate creative director at Cossette Communication-Marketing in Vancouver, hatched the campaign with associate CD John Edmonds. "When a new ad comes on television, viewers will call someone in from the kitchen to see it," observes Cameron. "People are actively waiting for the next execution to appear." Cossette has churned out more than three dozen bison TV playlets in the last 16 months, and they remain Manitoba's hottest ads.

"IT'S NOT ABOUT A LOGO OR AN AD— IT'S ABOUT THE EXPERIENCE ONE HAS WITH A PARTICULAR BRAND."

MTS is understandably delighted, but how'd it happen? Cameron thinks "it's one of those things where there are so many small, tiny reasons why it works. I think, in broad strokes, that having the freedom to use humour in the message goes a long way."

The humour is deft, and is the first reason cited by both observers and creators for the campaign's popularity. But the real root of its success lies in the reasons that this warm, funny bent was finally chosen by a company with a long tradition of straight-up slice-of-life advertising.

MTS had been a provincial Crown corporation for most of its history. In the late '90s, the company went public at the same time deregulation opened the floodgates to hard-nosed, aggressive competition. MTS president and CEO Bill Fraser was trying to pull diverse corporate segments together into a clean whole as he ran defence against invading telco Huns.

The public, meanwhile, viewed MTS as conservative, stuffy, stodgy, and old—a deadly reputation when young people form the bulk of the burgeoning market for newfangled forms of communication, MTS's major business-growth areas.

On the upside, says Riediger, it was considered "homegrown. We could be trusted. People felt we were part of the family, and a secure supplier."

Impact Research, Cossette Communications Group's research arm, did a marketing audit inside and outside the company, while Peter Drummond, managing director of Geyser Branding, also in Montreal, steered the MTS reinvention project from the strategic perspective. Reinvention, says Drummond, "takes incredible vision, incredible commitment from the top. Sometimes it requires organizational change, behavioural change, reorganization across a number of sectors. Not all companies can go as deep as we're talking about, but it's a matter of trying to close the gap as much as possible."

He's talking about the gap between what the company is and how it perceives itself—and what the public sees through ads and experiences through direct contact. "Look at all the great brands out there, whether Disney, Harley-Davidson, or Virgin. They consider the brand an integral part of the experience," Drummond points out. "It's not about a logo, it's not about an ad, but it's about the experience that one has with that brand."

At the same time, MTS had strained its existing agency beyond capacity. "We literally were choking the last agency we had, [the Winnipeg office of] Palmer Jarvis," says Riediger. "We would throw a couple of campaigns at them and deadlines would start falling, and we just had so much volume to do. And there wasn't any agency [in Manitoba] that was any bigger."

Besides, although MTS spends more than 70 per cent of its ad budget inside the province, Manitoba is not a creative genius hotbed. "Let's face it," Riediger says, "if you're a top creative talent, you're going to be looking in bigger markets to be working." So a new agency, the Vancouver office

of Cossette, came on the scene just as MTS realized "we were taking ourselves far too seriously in our advertising."

In their Vancouver office in mid-1999, Cameron and Edmonds had settled on prairie dogs as the new MTS symbol, and were kicking around potential creative. "The maintenance guy, who's from Winnipeg, was doing something in our office," recalls Cameron. "Once he got interested in what we were doing, he discreetly suggested the bison might be a more appropriate animal."

Hmmm, the two thought. "It's just such a deeply entrenched icon that it was almost too obvious," says Edmonds now. There were some at MTS who worried "talking bison might be seen as goofy, and we didn't want to be perceived as goofy," Riediger remembers. But the chance was taken, and brand linkage has been "hugely successful. You see a bison, you know it's MTS. There's no question. Pretty much all the dimensions have strengthened: people's regard for the brand, do we have the best advertising, will we compete successfully in the future?"

As for where Morty and all his

bison buddies go next, "if we manage this thing carefully, I can't imagine it taking a downturn in the near future. Where we take it next, I'm not really too concerned about that," says Riediger. "We determine what the message has to be, then let the creative guys tell us whether the creative platform can take the message. And we haven't run across anything yet that the creative platform couldn't support."

Still, there is one fly in the ointment. "People are remembering the commercial but not the product," Warren observes.

He's right, and MTS knows it. Riediger wants better product recall. "The challenge in the campaign is to make sure the creative doesn't overpower the message," he says. "For the most, we're either at norms or slightly above norms." And, concedes Millen, product recall "is an area we've targeted as a priority for improvement."

Exactly how MTS will do so hasn't been figured out yet. But Morty's chewing on the problem…

Daniel Wood was born in Newton, Massachusetts, in 1943. He moved to Canada in 1969, as a conscientious objector to the Vietnam War, and has been based in Vancouver ever since. Both a writer and a photographer, Wood is the author of over fifteen books and scores of magazine articles for which he has received dozens of awards. For more than twenty years, he has taught writing at the University of British Columbia and Simon Fraser University. "The Monkey's Paw" explores highly complex and controversial issues about scientific subjects. When exploring a scientific subject, for which qualities do you look to give you confidence about the validity of information? Why is it so important that information be as complete as possible and not simply correct? What occurs when facts are accurate, but critical information is missing from an argument?

Notes

nature-versus-nurture dichotomy two mutually exclusive theories of the origin of human behaviour, one holding that behaviour is innate (nature), the other that behaviour is learned (nurture)

paradigm a philosophical or theoretical framework on which ideas are based

epidemiology the branch of medicine that deals with the control of disease; from the Greek words *epidēmia*, meaning "prevalence of disease," and *logos*, meaning "speech" or "reason"

spectre an image that haunts the mind

mitigate to lessen the effect of something

cryptology the deciphering of messages written in code; from the Greek words *kruptos*, meaning "hidden," and *logos*, meaning "speech" or "reason"

Brave New World a satirical novel by Aldous Huxley, which paints a grim picture of a future in which human embryos are grown in bottles and conditioned to collectivism and passivity

eugenics the highly controversial belief that the human race can be "improved" by selective breeding

determinism the belief that human action is not free, but determined by preceding events or natural laws

proclivities tendencies toward particular actions or habits

tabula rasa a term in psychology suggesting that humans are born as "blank slates" and are completely shaped by their environment; from the Latin, meaning "blank slate"

Human Genome Project an effort to identify all thirty thousand or more genes in human DNA and to deal with issues related to human genetics

sword of Damocles a symbol of anxiety; from the Greek legend in which Damocles, a fourth-century BCE courtier, praised the happiness of Dionysus, the ruler of Syracuse. Dionysus then hung a sword by a single hair and had it dangle over Damocles' head to symbolize the precariousness of happiness.

IMF abbreviation for International Monetary Fund, an agency of the United Nations that purchases foreign currencies in order to discharge international debt and stabilize exchange rates

terra incognita from the Latin, meaning "unknown territory"

Activities

1. In the course of this article, the author and the people he interviews pose many controversial questions. Choose the question that interests you the most and explore your thoughts on it in a journal entry. Share and discuss your ideas with your classmates.

2. The title of the article alludes to the classic story "The Monkey's Paw" by W.W. Jacobs, as well as to the Laurie Anderson song "Monkey's Paw." Use the Internet to obtain copies of these works. Write an essay in which you examine the thematic links between the article, the story, and the song. Reflect on Wood's purpose in choosing this title.

3. In his conclusion, the author implies that he believes cloning human beings is a less serious action than manipulating human genes. As a class, discuss these issues and frame a resolution for a debate. Do research to locate facts and knowledgeable opinions to support the position you take on the resolution. After the debate, assess your performance as a speaker and consider how you might work to improve your skills for future debates.

Daniel Wood

The Monkey's Paw

The scientific study of twins is

revealing fascinating links

between genes and human

behaviour. In this hall of mirrors,

the reflections are becoming

increasingly disturbing.

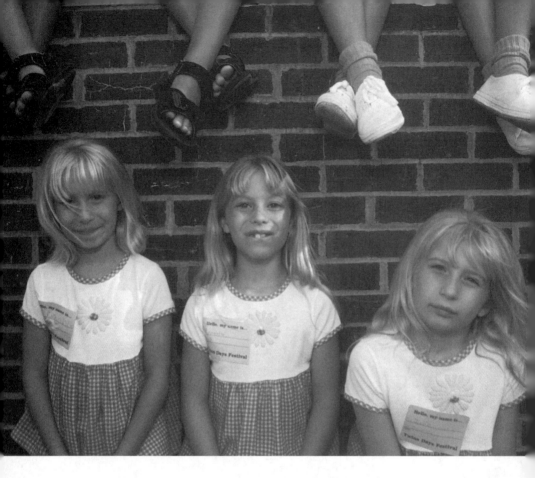

As the morning sun clears the highest branches of the elms in Twinsburg, Ohio, it reveals an utterly bizarre scene, for snaking beneath the trees in the town square are lines of perfectly matched sets of twins, triplets, and quadruplets—some 2,660 sets of them in all—each set dressed exactly alike. A stranger catches me gawking and whispers, "It's like Noah's Ark!" There are overweight twins dressed as Holstein cows, blond triplets in geometric-print micro-minis, bonneted baby quadruplets in comically elongated strollers. The head of each line converges on a cluster of bunting-wrapped fire engines, impatient baton twirlers, crepe-draped floats, fez-topped Shriners, and roving television cameras. It's impossible not to stare. It's impossible not to smile.

Here, for example, are identical twins Doug and Phil Malm,

41, of Moscow, Idaho, who met identical twins Jena and Jill, 31, at the Twinsburg Twins Days Festival in 1991, proposed to them on the festival stage in 1992, were married on the same stage in 1993, and have since spent, they tell me, every single day together, all four living in the same house, sharing bank accounts and holidays and toiletries. Here are bachelors John and Bill Reiff, 68, riding a rusty tandem bicycle and sporting Minnesota Twins baseball caps. They are looking, they say, for some twins to marry. Here are the Holland twins, Margaret and Louise, who have dressed alike—unfailingly—for 90 years. Here are identical twins Patti Carter and Carmen Smith, 38, from Windsor, Ontario, who developed their own language as youngsters and today wear matching pink toe and fingernail polish. "There's no line between us," says Patti. "We understand what each other thinks and why we're thinking it."

At 9:15 a.m., the fire engines begin wailing, a latter-day Noah shouts into his megaphone, and the lines go marching two by two up Ravenna Road, heading for the Twins Days' festivities. The road is lined with thousands of grin-ning onlookers, among them dozens of scientists and researchers who have come to Twinsburg to study twins. Twins are a unique example of genetic inheritance—they can tell us which characteristics are learned and which are part of our genetic code. Researchers have known this for a century, but what the new generation of scientists is discovering has turned everything previously thought about human psychology and behaviour on its head.

On the wall of Tony Vernon's office at the University of Western Ontario, in London, are a half-dozen photos of previous Twinsburg celebrants, including one of 2,800 matched pairs staring up at the camera with the words "Where's Waldo?" scrawled across their faces. Vernon, a 48-year-old professor of psychology, is one of scores of twins researchers worldwide who are investigating the strange realm of behavioural genetics. Based on his study of 500 twin sets, he is asking a very controversial question: How do our genes determine our behaviour?

Most mammals can produce dizygotic, or fraternal, twins, which are the result of the simultaneous fertilization of two different eggs.

Twins research has removed the old dichotomy between nature and nurture. It's not a dichotomy — it's both.

As do any pair of siblings, fraternal twins share 50 per cent of their genes. Humans and armadillos, however, also have the ability to produce monozygotic twins, one fertilized egg splitting into identical halves at a very early stage of development. Monozygotic twins are, in fact, natural clones, identical down to their genes.

In the past two decades, twins studies have become hugely popular. The Scandinavians have massive twins registers that go back generations. In England, the United States, Australia, and Canada, there are several ongoing studies involving almost 50,000 sets of twins.

Vernon compares fraternal and identical twins in two ways. First, since identical twins are 100 per cent the same, any differences in their responses to Vernon's questions about their behaviour point to areas least affected by genetic encoding. Analyses of his survey reveal clear patterns of high or low genetic influence. Second, by comparing responses from identical twins with those from fraternal twins, he can assess which characteristics are inherited and which are environmental—the old nature-versus-nurture dichotomy. A decade ago, behavioural psychologists thought all behaviour was the result of learned responses to specific childhood experiences. Not any more.

"The old idea that behaviour is all nurturing is gone," says Vernon. "It's a paradigm change. There's not a single personality characteristic that doesn't show some genetic basis."

Every twins researcher is finding the same thing, he says: political views, alcoholism, marital choices, altruism, religious beliefs, attitudes toward sex—everything, even intelligence quotient (IQ), can be an inherited trait. "Want a smart, blond, blue-eyed, Aryan kid?" asks Vernon. He pauses to make sure his words have sunk in and then sighs. "The ramifications are enormous. With cloning increasingly easy, we'll have the means to change human evolution."

Halfway around the planet from London, 48-year-old Nick Martin, a professor of genetic epidemiology at Brisbane's Queensland Institute of Medical Research, sits atop one of the world's largest twins registries: 27,000 pairs of Australian twins. Since he's been collecting data for 20 years and comparing the survey results from a pool of 7,000 sets of adults, he can statistically assess with accuracy the genetic versus the non-genetic influences affecting human intelligence and personality traits.

In an early study, Martin showed that 80 per cent of the variation in IQ among twins was genetic. The results scared him. "Twenty years ago," he says, "to even breathe IQ and genes in the same sentence was to invite a raging controversy. You'd be called a Nazi. The nature/nurture question was no joke. But we found so many things that were genetically influenced, it was getting boring: we wanted to find something that wasn't genetic. Surely, we thought, social attitudes were completely determined by culture."

To test the hypothesis that 100 per cent of our social attitudes is the result of nurturing, Martin and his associates looked at twins' attitudes toward capital punishment, divorce, voting, sexual attraction, and religion. To their astonishment, they found that on average, only 50 per cent of the variation in those attitudes is determined by culture: the other 50 per cent is genetic. They also found that 65 per cent of the variation in predisposition to alcoholism in both men and women is genetically heritable. Even more surprising, they found virtually no correlation between family environment and the development of children's behaviour. It is as though parenting hardly matters.

Martin is well aware of the profound implications of what he's saying. He knows that the spectre of eugenics and racism and ethnic purity lurks behind his findings, but he reassures me that the direction of modern research is simply to locate places in the 70,000-gene human genetic code that influence disease, depression, or addiction in order to better understand the interaction of genes and the environment. The goal, he assures me, is to develop new therapies, new drugs (drug companies are avidly funding twins research), and new microsurgical techniques to mitigate or eliminate the detrimental genetic defects, not to open the door to genetic manipulation.

In North America, the number of multiple births is increasing exponentially, largely due to the widespread use of fertility drugs. Since 1973, the rate that women are having twins has doubled and the level of greater-numbered multiple births has increased sevenfold.

I feel uneasy, however. Today it may be merely cryptology—decoding the secret genetic messages—but what about the future? What about altering people's behaviour or IQ? Martin's research confounds deeply held views about the malleability of human nature, the role of society in improving disadvantaged people's lives, as well as religious and ethical notions of free will and equality.

"Where's this twins research leading?" I ask.

"People see *Brave New World* scenarios," he says. "Critics are afraid we're going to turn humans into frogs. I'm not going to pooh-pooh that: there are big ethical challenges ahead. But the '60s idea that there's an equality baseline in humans is wrong. There's no such thing as equality. We're affected by genetic variation. Why shouldn't people triumph over genetic adversity? If you're short, you can wear high heels. And if enough people want blond, blue-eyed babies, what's the danger?"

Part of the answer lies in looking at how science got to the point of considering the genetic manipulation of human beings. It is a curious detour in the path of this story, for the road back in the mirror world of twins is as convoluted as the road ahead.

Twins research began 125 years ago, when British scientist Francis Galton, a cousin of Charles Darwin, founded behavioural genetics with his work on the role heredity plays in intelligence, personality, and class. He invented the word *eugenics*, from the Greek word for "well-born," to propose a solution to the problems, as he saw them then, of reproduction among the unfit, the colonial underclass, and the mentally handicapped: control their reproductivity. By the turn of the century, many socialists and early feminists, including a

Amazingly, identical twins reared apart are *more* likely to share major life events than are identical twins reared together.

number of prominent Canadians, were avowed supporters of eugenics. They believed that the betterment of civilization would be brought about by enforced family planning, selective sterilization, and the state regulation of reproductive rights. By the 1930s, several Canadian provinces and more than half the American states had eugenics laws.

By then, however, the centre for twins research was Frankfurt, Germany, and the man in charge was Dr. Josef Mengele. Within a few years, Mengele and his assistants were patrolling the station platform at Auschwitz, shouting "Twins? Twins?" to the disembarking prisoners, hoping to make use of Jewish twins in his research into the genetics of creating a master race. He gathered 3,000 twins at Auschwitz, first cloistering them as human guinea pigs before systematically destroying them. Only 157 of the twins survived.

For the next decade, behavioural genetics and twins studies more or less ceased, tainted by the association with the Holocaust. In their place rose a belief in environmental determinism led by Harvard University psychologist B.F. Skinner, who argued that it was conditioning—nurture—that shaped human destiny. With good education and progressive legislation, Skinner argued, the constraints of poverty or class could be erased. People would be able to realize their nascent potential. Undesirable inherited traits could be conditioned out, socially acceptable ones conditioned in.

Then University of Minnesota psychologist Thomas Bouchard, now 61, began looking at the genetics of twins behaviour. Amid accusations of being a Nazi sympathizer, Bouchard pointed back toward genes, toward nature, as the determining factor in human personality. The pendulum had begun to swing again.

Bouchard's interest in genetic heritability had begun 19 years earlier, after his chance encounter with Jim Springer and Jim Lewis, both then 39 and both from Ohio. They were the rarest of twins and most prized by researchers: identical twins who had been separated at birth, were raised in different families, and had grown to adulthood completely unaware of each other's existence. Their nature was the same, but their nurturing was not. What Bouchard learned from them, and from the 135 sets of raised-apart twins he went on to study, opened the lid to a genetic Pandora's box.

When Jim Lewis finally found his twin brother, Jim Springer, after years of searching through court records, he knew their unwed mother had put them up for adoption shortly after giving birth. When the two first met, Lewis describes it as "like looking into a mirror." For starters, both had the same first name. They were physically identical. But when they got talking, the similarities were astounding. Both had childhood dogs named Toy. Both had been nail-biters and fretful sleepers. Both had migraines. Both had married first wives named Linda, second wives named Betty. Lewis named his first son James Allen; Springer named his James Alan. For years, they both had taken holidays on the same Florida beach. They both drank Miller Lite, smoked Salem cigarettes, loved stock car racing, disliked baseball, left regular love notes to their wives, made doll furniture in their basements, and had added circular white benches around the trees in their backyards.

When Bouchard ran them through what has become his standard 50 hours of testing—involving a 15,000-item questionnaire series, physical measurements, psychiatric interviews, and videotaping—the "Jim Twins" became even more bizarre. Their IQs, habits, facial expressions, brainwaves, heartbeats, and handwriting were nearly identical. As Jim Lewis puts it, "In all the tests we took, it looked like one person had taken them twice."

Bouchard was staggered. His findings contradicted his own most fundamental belief as a social psychologist: that almost all psychological traits were environmentally shaped. For further research, he established the Minnesota Center for Twin and

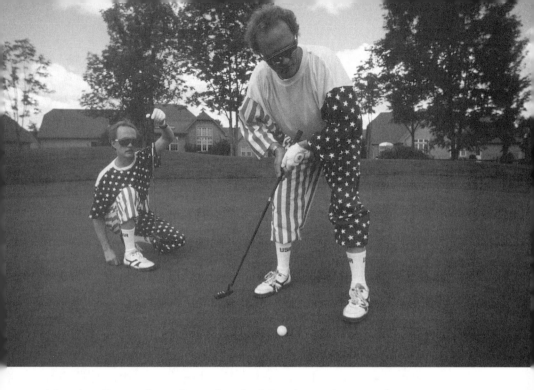

Adoption Research—where else but in the Twin Cities of Minneapolis and St. Paul—and the project soon collected data on 8,000 sets of twins. He now knows that in many traits, identical twins raised apart are as alike as those raised together. In fact, identical twins, unlike fraternal twins, become more identical over time.

Bouchard's twins tests show that genetic factors account for 66 per cent of the variance in intelligence, 60 per cent for heritability of social attitudes, and 50 per cent for religiosity and personality.

What everyone finds incomprehensible is that studies of identical pairs like the Jim twins also show that twins reared apart are more likely to share major life events than are identical twins reared together. The twins for whom Twinsburg, Ohio, was named, for example, lived apart but died on the same day from the same illness at the age of 57. Since events have no DNA, such twin events are inexplicable. The only explanation that fits is a source of much scientific discussion: human experience may actually be shaped by genetic proclivities. In other words, nature and nurture are linked forces, shaping each other.

"How this happens, we don't know!" booms Bouchard. "We haven't the vaguest idea! We don't know how genes assemble the brain or how the brain assembles experiences."

My own brain boggles: can the mind assemble experiences in such a way as to influence their outcome?

Every discussion I have with identical twins in Twinsburg suggests that they aren't quite like the rest of us. Although most twins don't dress alike except at Twinsburg and don't share the same home like the Malms, they do testify to a depth of connectedness that as a single, I find hard to fathom. Take the Windsor, Ontario, twins, Patti Carter and Carmen Smith. Their twinness, they tell me, is a source of immense security. Although they have different jobs and different weights, they are each other's best friend, they talk on the telephone at least once a day, and they take their holidays together. Others, such as the identical Richmond twins from Aurora, Illinois, have no identity outside their twinness. At the Twinsburg Wiener Roast (two hot dogs, two bags of potato chips, and a package of twin Hostess Twinkies each), LaVelda and LaVona, 65, tell me that they dated 13 sets of twins before finding identical twins Arthur and Alwin Richmond in 1973. At their wedding, most of the bridesmaids, the organists, and the wedding-cake figurines were all twins. There were 30 more sets among the guests. To celebrate the marriage, they went to their first Twinsburg Twins Days together. The four then lived in the same house, sharing everything from meals to toothpaste. And, Alwin tells me, the three have "struggled" since the death of Arthur 11 years ago. "Losing an identical twin," he says, "is like losing half yourself." As he speaks, he is wearing a metre-high Egyptian-style headpiece covered with scores of photographs of the two couples.

Twinning varies widely from race to race. On average, only 6 pairs of twins per 1,000 births occur in Japan, 20 per 1,000 in North America, and 45 per 1,000 in Nigeria. The Yoruba tribe of Nigeria, who eat estrogen-rich yams, average 90 sets of twins per 1,000, the highest rate on earth.

Once Bouchard published his findings, others, seeing the implications of his research, wanted Twinsburg twins for their own studies, and before long, behavioural geneticists, clinical psychologists, and medical researchers were flocking annually to Ohio, soliciting volunteers and mailing out surveys to thousands of far-flung twins.

When John Livesley, a University of British Columbia (UBC) professor of psychiatry, heard about Bouchard's work, he realized that twins would be invaluable in finding the root causes of certain personality pathologies: such things as depression, phobias, compulsions, and violence. "Twins," he says, "are nature's perfect experiment. Twins research can define the architecture of personality. We're looking at the basis of human nature."

Working with psychologist Kerry Jang, Livesley is studying the questionnaire results from more than 1,000 sets of Canadian twins, who responded to 3,000 statements, such as: "I like to squash flies." "Frightening thoughts sometimes come into my head." "I follow the same route when I go someplace." As he runs through the statistical tabulations for me, showing the heritability in percentages of various components that define a behaviour such as callousness, his voice becomes animated.

"Look at this!" he keeps repeating, pointing to anomalies in the figures. "This is very exciting!"

He explains, for example, that the figures show certain elements of callous, psychopathic behaviour are strongly genetic and therefore not amenable to traditional clinical treatment. They are, to use the old saying, bred in the bone. But other aspects of callousness—those that show a low genetic heritability—appear to be affected primarily by environmental forces and are therefore more likely to respond to therapy.

Overall, like other twins research, the UBC Twin Project has found that 50 per cent of personality is genetic (nature) and 50 per cent is environmental (nurture). But the genetic components of many types of behaviours vary. Phobias, for example, display a 20 per cent heritability; nicotine addiction shows a 70 per cent heritability.

It is clear from these figures that in many areas, people have a genetic proclivity toward certain behaviours. These are not inevitable, but they are inclinations that may be heightened or diminished by surrounding events. "Your personality," says Livesley, "alters the way you see the world. If you're an optimist, you see the world through rose-coloured glasses. If you're a pessimist, it's grey. Genetics shapes the environment you select, and it shapes the way you perceive it."

It also appears that some elements of personality vary between the sexes. In the UBC sample, compulsiveness, suspicion, and violence showed a strong heritability in males, but not in females. Submissiveness was heritable only among females. Furthermore, some elements of personality—modesty, self-discipline—appeared to be entirely the result of nurturing.

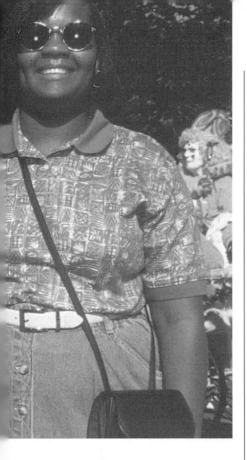

"People used to quote [English philosopher John] Locke," says Livesley. "The brain is a *tabula rasa*. But clearly, it's not." What emerges from these findings is that the brain is a slate that comes with writing scribbled all over it. "We used to think we could change those basic traits. We can't. We know now the basic personality is fixed. What twins research has done is remove the old dichotomy between nature and nurture. It's not a dichotomy; it's both."

This is a refrain I hear repeated again and again. Gradually I find myself succumbing to the barrage of data from dozens of twins research projects around the world. Stockholm, Minneapolis, Brisbane, Vancouver, London, Twinsburg…for every human behaviour, the heritability statistics are remarkable. Something geneticist Kenneth Kendler tells me sets my mind reeling. Kendler is one of the researchers working with the data of the Virginia 30,000, a massive American study involving 7,000 pairs of twins and their families.

"Heritability is only the beginning for understanding humans," he says. "We're on the coast of a huge, unknown continent, and we've found the mouths of some rivers. We've only started to chart the geography of human behaviour and intelligence."

Kendler notes that by the year 2003, the Human Genome Project will have identified the entire 70,000-gene human genetic code. "Then," he says. "Then!" His voice rises, his finger points to the ceiling, but he doesn't finish the sentence. In the ensuing silence, I imagine a genetic sword of Damocles hanging over the heads of twenty-first-century humankind. I know that once we have identified every gene in the code, it is a small step to choosing which ones we want in our body or our family or our country and which ones we don't.

"Is that what you mean?" I ask Kendler.

"Talk to Plomin," he says.

That's what they all tell me. Robert Plomin is the genial deputy director of the Kings College Social Genetics and Developmental Psychiatry Research Centre in London, England. He has been investigating twins for medical research since the early 1970s. He tells me that molecular genetics used to concentrate on finding which chromosome is associated with each of the 1,000 single-gene disorders, such as cystic fibrosis, which affect only 2 per cent of humankind, and has begun to explore the complex, multiple-gene field of human behaviour. Metaphorically speaking, he is switching his attention from single stars to whole constellations. Plomin's goal is to bridge 1980s behavioural genetics twins research with twenty-first-century molecular genetics. We have the technology. And he has focused on that dangerous bugaboo, intelligence.

In particular, the genetics of IQ.

With data from 15,000 pairs of British twins, Plomin has found a 75 per cent correlation between genes and early childhood language development disorders. After correlating that with studies of American 13-year-olds—kids with identifiable, genius-level IQs and kids with average IQs—he has found the precise sites, the "genetic markers," as he calls them, that show a difference between high and average IQ. Each of the three chromosomes, he explains, may account for only a 2 per cent increase in IQ. There are many more to be found. But he will find them. Soon.

"Intelligence is not one thing," he says, "not one gene. It's not like catching a whale. It's more like catching little fish, one by one. IQ is the sum of a lot of behaviours. In three to five years," he goes on, echoing Kendler's words, "we'll be postgenomic. We'll have the human genetic code down. At that point, we'll have to figure out exactly how the different genes affect IQ."

Plomin, too, talks mainly about using this information to develop better treatments for disorders. His voice is calm and rational.

> "We're on the coast of a huge, unknown continent, and we've only started to chart the geography of human behaviour and intelligence."

Nonetheless, I find myself wondering if I'm just naive, or whether someone, somewhere, won't soon be exploring pathways that humans can take to enhance intelligence genetically.

On the Internet, for example, there is a Web site called Future Generations. Whoever maintains it admits that it is politically incorrect in its mission statement: 1. Intelligence is highly heritable; 2. The least intelligent are having the most children worldwide; and 3. Without reversing this trend, civilization will decline.

The future, it seems, could begin very soon to resemble the past. The difference between enforced sterilization, as preached in the 1930s, and whole populations rendered genetically asexual is, after all, essentially technological. My guide to that possible future is Charles Crawford, an evolutionary psychologist at British Columbia's Simon Fraser University. He's a legendary synthesizer and visionary and, it seems somehow appropriate to me, is legally blind. His mind encompasses several million years of human behaviour, from modern primate research to Neanderthal studies to the development of civilizations to twentieth-century behavioural genetics research. And he believes that current twins studies are a watershed event.

"With Bouchard, with the Jim twins," he says, "it's bizarre, almost frightening. We don't understand what it means. Livesley and Jang at UBC say the same thing: the power of genes. We're floundering because it's all so astounding."

"What about Plomin?" I ask.

"Plomin's work raises the issue of eugenics," says Crawford. "It takes us back a hundred years. In evolution, the message is always: nothing comes free. We're wealthy now in North America and Europe; we can afford to be kind.

But in 25, 50 years? When our society's in decline, and we're going to the IMF for bailouts? When the Chinese are doing well? Then the issues the twins projects are beginning to raise may come back to haunt us. Do we abort babies with gene X or Y or Z?"

Crawford shrugs. "That's when we'll have to come to terms with some fundamental questions," he says. "I'm glad I'll be dead by then."

At Chasers, a crowded nightclub just outside Twinsburg, Ohio, the Twins Days parade, the wiener roast, the look-alike competitions, the talent show, the T-shirt sales, and even the scientific testing are history. I'm sitting with 250 sets of identically dressed twins, all of them drinking and dancing. The music is loud, the voices are raised, and the ambience is dim. Two by two, male twins are putting the hustle on female twins. It seems as if everyone has safely boarded Noah's Ark and is doing exactly what the Boss intended. Except me: the doomed dodo. Phil Malm sees my hang-dog expression and shouts in my ear, "It's a place where you feel out of place."

The world record for the number of children produced by one woman goes to an eighteenth-century Russian who had 16 pairs of twins, 7 sets of triplets, and 4 sets of quadruplets. Altogether, she had 69 children.

I nod. I do. The song that comes to my mind is Laurie Anderson's "Monkey's Paw": *But Nature's got rules / and Nature's got laws, / And if you cross her look out! / It's the monkey's paw.*

The words seem eerily apt in light of what I've learned about twins research. We are at the threshold of a new world. What will happen when we have charted the entire geography of human behaviour and intelligence? Will we take the small step from cloning sheep to cloning human beings? Or the bigger step from removing a gene responsible for a genetic disorder to inserting one that makes us more intelligent or vote a certain way? The continent rising before us is almost entirely *terra incognita*, marked in my mind by the snaking twin helix of DNA and the traditional cartographer's warning: Here be dragons.

Restoring Life on the Edge

Chris Rose was born in Vancouver, British Columbia, in 1950. He is a reporter with the *Vancouver Sun* newspaper. This article highlights the Living By Water project, which aims to rejuvenate shorelines by changing people's attitudes about how to maintain their shoreline properties. Newspapers and other information sources are filled with daily reports on environmental issues. How do you assess these reports? In order to judge their importance and reliability, what kinds of questions do you ask yourself as you read or view these reports?

Notes

riparian of, on, or relating to the banks of a natural body or course of water

roughshod treat with brutal force; from the practice in which horses are shod with horseshoes that have projecting nails or points to prevent slipping

covenants binding agreements

septic refers to a sewage disposal system in which waste is decomposed by an aerobic bacteria

epiphany an understanding or perception of something through a sudden intuitive realization

biodiversity biological variety

Activities

1. Before reading the article, what were your views about the ideal shoreline and waterfront property? To what extent did your views change as a result of reading this selection? Why did your views either change or remain the same?

2. This article contains very specific, illuminating detail. With a partner, reread the article and in your notebook write down every sentence that is general rather than specific. Read these sentences in sequence and compare the style, tone, and impact of the new passage with the original article. Then choose an environmental topic of particular interest to you. With your partner, write down any general ideas about it that you can think of. Do research to locate specific details about your topic and use them to write your own expository article.

Restoring life on the edge

Chris Rose

From a small Interior lake to the Strait of Georgia, the Living by Water project aims to rejuvenate shorelines by changing attitudes and allowing nature another chance.

GARDOM LAKE—At first glance, the waterfront here seems unkempt. Rotting logs are scattered about, vegetation grows close to the shoreline, the tiny beach is hidden in the reeds, and the floating dock isn't much wider than a city sidewalk.

There is no concrete boat launch, no asphalt parking lot, no homes crammed against the water's edge, and no perfectly manicured lawn so often associated with the good life, and those lucky enough to own riparian properties.

But that's just fine with Sarah Kipp and Clive Callaway, owners of this property on a spring-fed lake 541 m above sea level. They eagerly predict the untidy beauty of natural vegetation and a reclaimed shoreline teeming with animal life are a sign of good things to come.

Their property—complete with bulrushes, cattails, duck down, mud, and a rich collage of decomposing foliage—is at the forefront of a new campaign to restore shorelines and help heal the environment.

UNSPOILED: *Sarah Kipp on a part of the Gardom Lake shoreline that has been left natural. Photo: Ian Smith, Vancouver Sun*

Kipp and Callaway note that a generous buffer zone of plants between the houses and the shore helps cleanse the air and filter the water—some of which will eventually make its way 480 km southwest to Vancouver via Shuswap Lake, the South Thompson, and the Fraser River.

As Kipp says, in reference to the estimated 2.6 million people living near the Strait of Georgia, "we all live downstream of something."

And that "something" is what

Kipp and Callaway are trying to change.

They contend that few waterfront dwellers realize how they are degrading their piece of shoreline—along with their emotional and financial investment—by allowing unchecked urban attitudes to run roughshod over nature.

"Together we make a huge impact," says Callaway, adding that watching their waterfront become healthy again has taken on spiritual overtones.

"We love to look at it, we love to hear it, we love to experience it. Every Canadian who's spent time by the water's edge would probably agree with us. It's an exciting place, it's alive, it's vibrant."

"We see the shoreline as a ribbon of life."

That's where their non-profit Living By Water Project, with its gentle philosophy of heightened environmental awareness, comes in.

Kipp, who has a master of arts degree specializing in geography from the University of Alberta, and Callaway, who has a master of environmental design degree from the University of Calgary, bought a seasonal fishing lodge here on 4.5 hectares when they decided to leave the big city 12 years ago.

"We had a dream to change our lifestyle—to live in semi-wilderness, out of the rat race—and do something useful for the environment," Callaway, 55, says.

He and Kipp, 49, became entranced by Gardom Lake, situated on a rolling height of land between the Shuswap and the Okanagan, and 17 km southeast of Salmon Arm.

"It is so special," he adds. "We've just come to love living on the edge."

For about eight years they tried to run the lodge, which had a number of cabins on it, as an environment teaching centre but it increasingly became difficult to raise money, sustain the workload, and operate it year-round.

They eventually sold off some of their property and voluntarily put "conservation covenants" on the remaining three hectares to protect the natural features of the shoreline. Except for the small communal wharf and tiny beach shared by the seven owners, no other development along the 185 m of communal shoreline was allowed.

Little by little, by trial and error, Kipp and Callaway accumulated a wealth of knowledge about their shoreline.

They learned everything they never wanted to know about septic systems, water tables, setbacks, infiltration, evaporation. They were told that the elegant European willows planted decades ago along their portion of the lake should be replaced with native willows and dogwoods, which let more light onto the shore, which in turn provides a healthier habitat for fish, birds, insects, and turtles.

They began to realize that humans—even well-meaning humans—can cause as much damage to the environment as greedy industry and nearsighted government policy. They learned that bulrushes eat heavy metals, and that wild grasses are more beneficial than an attractive lawn. They were shocked to understand that "non-point source pollution" was a scientific way of saying that all

sorts of tiny, non-traceable human excesses can account for a problem of gigantic proportions.

The epiphany they experienced suggested waterfront dwellers quit trying to triumph over nature and instead live in harmony with the plants and animals that naturally gravitate to shorelines.

"Basically we see the shoreline as a ribbon of life," said Callaway, noting Environment Canada describes riparian areas as one of the most productive ecological zones on Earth.

Three years ago, armed with freshly acquired insights, Kipp and Callaway decided that if they could be re-educated about their little bit of paradise, so could others.

They came up with the idea of the Living By Water Project, which they hope will make people reassess how they mistreat shorelines on rivers, lakes, wetlands, and the ocean, negatively affecting water quality and degrading wildlife habitat.

Calling the project "a new fashion statement," Callaway says he and Kipp want it to become as pervasive in the next decade as recycling's blue box campaign has become since it began in the 1980s.

Their first big break came when they approached the Federation of B.C. Naturalists to help in fundraising. Deciding the idea of promoting a healthier waterfront lifestyle would appeal to ordinary citizens, the federation signed on, and became the lead partner for the project.

Tiny, non-traceable human excesses can account for a problem of gigantic proportions.

Federation president Anne Murray said her 5,500-member organization became involved two years ago because the project's message helps promote biodiversity from the edges of small Interior lakes to shorelines surrounding the Strait of Georgia.

"How waterfront residents behave with their little bit of property can add up to great results," Murray, a Delta resident, said. "Everybody gets worked up about forests [but] people don't always think of shorelines."

She noted that while riparian zones are incredibly important habitat, they are also extremely vulnerable—especially because so many people try to tame nature instead of allowing it to flourish.

Murray added shorelines and their rich nutrients have to be protected because that is where so much of the food chain begins.

"It's both a ribbon of life and a nursery of life. I think we're only just beginning to understand that as a society."

Some of Kipp and Callaway's research has already been implemented by the Adams Lake Indian Band near Chase because of concerns about unprecedented development on Shuswap Lake and declining water quality.

Greg Witzky, fisheries manager for the 600-member band, said Kipp and Callaway were recently hired to talk to non-Native lakeshore leaseholders about how to reverse shoreline degradation.

"We learned a lot of people wanted to protect the foreshore but they didn't know how to go about it," Witzky recalled. "People were really responsive in a positive manner. They wanted more information on how to protect their little shoreline."

As a result of that response, Witzky said, the band has since presented about 1,700 non-Natives who own land along Shuswap Lake with information packages on how to better protect the foreshore for fish habitat.

"If the fish are healthy, you can pretty well say that the whole lake is healthy too," Witzky said, adding what goes into the water near Chase eventually makes its way downstream to the coast.

Callaway says similar organizations in all the other provinces are now involved in the project, and he hopes the three territories will soon be included.

A major component of the project, which will be unveiled across Canada over the next two years, is a handbook about B.C. waterfront-living that Callaway and Kipp are now completing. It is expected to be published in the spring of 2000.

Editions dealing with other regions of the country, also written by Callaway and Kipp, will follow. Callaway expects about 125,000 copies of the handbook will be sold nationally in the next five years.

At least 5,000 copies of the 128-page book—titled *On the Living Edge*—will initially be printed. The handbook is full of tips designed to help first-time buyers of waterfront property and people who already reside along a shoreline.

The tips include choosing the proper type of detergent to use in the home and explanations about why not to cut the lawn too close to the edge of the water. There is also information on how to replant a natural shoreline and make sure the septic system is working properly.

The untidy beauty of natural vegetation is a sign of good things to come.

Coastal dwellers with access to a sewer system can learn how to deflect water running off roads and driveways into little ponds to reduce erosion and help keep pollutants out of the ocean. Other sections address hobby farmers and boaters.

Subsidized by five key sponsors, the book will likely cost about $6. The project has about 30 sponsors across Canada ranging from public and private foundations to various government departments.

More than $600,000 has already been raised nationally—about one-third from millennium funds. Callaway estimates an equal amount has been raised through donated time. He, Kipp, and two assistants are now working full time on the project and receiving funding managed by the federation of naturalists.

The project will be formally launched in Vancouver toward the end of January.

In addition to the book, the project will promote next September as "shoreline celebration and restoration month" and use artists, scientists, and community volunteers to bring attention to waterfront protection.

The project will also host a national children's poster competition in February, a touring theatre production in B.C. in August, and an instructional video by the end of next year. There are also plans for a travelling exhibition to demonstrate the values and functions of shorelines and a home-site visitation program will likely begin in B.C. next fall.

Callaway says it is important people realize that altering their shorelines isn't always expensive or difficult. Most changes to existing properties can be brought about incrementally, he said, while new developments can be planned with nature in mind before any building is started.

"It can be very, very simple—it's as simple as leaving it alone. They can be complicated but in many, many cases very simple actions can result in great improvements. So much of it is about changing habit and behaviour."

wrap-up
essays, articles, and media

1. Choose an essay in this unit that focuses on a problem affecting one or more people. Reread it carefully in preparation for writing an analytical essay about the problem addressed. Research what your audience needs to know about your subject. In your essay, clearly identify the problem, explain how it affects people, and outline the steps to your solution. Remain objective in your approach. Have a classmate read a draft of your essay and comment on its logic, clarity, and objectivity. Make any necessary revisions.

2. Create a glossary of academic and technical terms that appear in selections in this unit. For each of your entries, provide a precise, clear definition of the word or term and a sample sentence that includes it, both in your own words; a detailed outline of its origins and roots; and the page number in the anthology where it appears. Include a bibliography of the sources to which you referred in creating your glossary.

3. Develop a plan for a Web site that would provide information related to a topic of interest triggered by a selection in this unit. Think about how you will organize and synthesize your information. Your site plan should cover the purpose of your site, an annotated table of contents, a flowchart that illustrates the internal and external links you will include, a description of the navigation bar, and a list and brief description of visuals that will appear. As appropriate, provide rough sketches of the features of the site as part of your plan.

4. Work with a partner. After looking at several travel brochures or travel-related CD-ROMs, develop a checklist of criteria for developing an effective travel brochure or multimedia travel presentation. Use your checklist to help you create a brochure or multimedia presentation that will make people want to visit one of the settings depicted in a selection from this unit. Locate effective photographs and other visuals and arrange the visuals and the text into an order that makes sense. Review and revise your draft or multimedia script. Use a word-processing or desktop publishing program to create your brochure or deliver your multimedia presentation to the class.

In the morning, it might be a radio alarm clock that wakes you up. Then, perhaps you head to the computer to check your e-mail or to go to a favourite site. You may grab the remote to check out today's weather on television. Later, you wander into the kitchen to get some breakfast and find that a family member has the section of the newspaper that you want. Face-to-face communication is about to begin. Now take yourself back to humanity's early days, when the only form of communication was face-to-face. Through conversation, story-telling, and song, humans shared news or gossip, learned or taught a skill, and made a friend or an enemy. From then to now, methods of communication have expanded exponentially by means of print and electronic sources. Throughout history, those people who have communicated skilfully, decoded messages, and manipulated information in all its various forms have had social power. That is why contemporary theories of literacy go beyond the ability to read and write and include such concepts as *visual literacy* and

media literacy. Your fluency in each medium—how well you understand such components as its internal language, its codes, conventions, formats, production requirements, and economic realities—as well as the ability to create your own media products allows you, as media expert Paolo Friere has said, to "read the world."

This In-Depth will offer insights about media both through its content and its various forms. Marshall McLuhan's "Aphorisms" touches on a range of topics and kick-starts your explorations. An essay by Neil Postman challenges you to deconstruct television and print news. A newspaper article by Ann Rees looks at on-line, *virtual* classrooms. A radio script by Bob Elliott and Ray Goulding takes a comic look at television news production. And a poem by Kenneth J. Harvey touches on a more personal connection between the specific medium of television and a person. As you gain a stronger understanding of the media that permeate our lives, you will have the insight and power to make the media work for you.

Aphorisms

Marshall McLuhan

A pioneer who revolutionized communications theory, Herbert Marshall McLuhan was born in Edmonton, Alberta, in 1911. As a professor of English at the University of Toronto, his seminal studies of the effects of mass media on thought and behaviour brought him international fame in the 1960s. His books include *Understanding Media* (1964). He died in 1980. McLuhan's aphorisms have been described as catchy, succinct, and deceptively simple. What is the purpose of an aphorism? Are there universal characteristics of aphorisms? If so, what are they?

My father decided in the sixties that he would try as much as he could to present his ideas in an aphoristic style. Aphorisms, as Francis Bacon said, are incomplete, a bit like cartoons. They are not filled-out essay writing that is highly compressed. The aphorism is a poetic form that calls for a lot of participation on the part of the reader. You have to chew on an aphorism and work with it for a while before you understand it fully. A good aphorism could keep you busy for a week—kicking it around, playing with it, exploring it, taking it apart to see what you can get out of it. And applying it here, there, and everywhere. My father deliberately chose this form of statement because he wanted to teach, not tell or entertain. He said, "For instruction, you use incomplete knowledge so people can fill things in—they can round it out and fill it in with their own experience." If what you want to do is simply to tell people something, then by all means spell it out in the connected essay. But if you want to teach, you don't do that. There's no participation in just telling: that's simply for consumers—they sit there and swallow it, or not. But the aphoristic style gives you the opportunity to get a dialogue going, to engage people in the process of discovery.

—Eric McLuhan

I don't explain—I explore.

Unlike previous environmental changes, the electric media constitute a total and near instantaneous transformation of culture, values, and attitudes.

Under instant circuitry, nothing is remote in time or in space. It's now.

Since the telegraph and radio the globe has contracted, spatially, into a single large village. Tribalism is our only resource since the electromagnetic discovery.

In the eighties, as we transfer our whole being to the
data bank, privacy will become
a ghost or echo of its former
self and what remains of community will disappear.

**Everybody at the speed of light tends to
become a nobody.**

The three-year-old standing
up in his playpen in front of
the TV sees as much of the
adult world as anybody.

In the electric age the connection in narrative and art is
omitted, as in the telegraph press. There is no storyline
in modern art or news—just a dateline. There is no past
or future, just an inclusive present.

At present, TV is a service only during a crisis.

PEOPLE NEVER REMEMBER BUT THE
COMPUTER NEVER FORGETS.

The News

Neil Postman

Neil Postman is a communications theorist, critic, educator, and essayist who was born in New York City. He received his doctorate
from Columbia University. Postman has taught at New York University
for over three decades, where he has served as the chair of Media
Ecology and of the Department of Communication, Arts, and Sciences.
This department focuses on how symbols are organized to convey
meaning, how communication affects cultural institutions, and how
new media affects education. He is the author of more than a dozen
books, including *Amusing Ourselves to Death: Public Discourse in
the Age of Show Business* (1986) and *Building a Bridge to the
Eighteenth Century: Ideas from the Past that Can Improve Our Future*
(1999). What are some of the differences between print, radio, and television news? Do you think that one medium is better suited to reporting on the news than others? Why or why not?

The whole problem with news on television comes down to this: all the
words uttered in an hour of news coverage could be printed on one page
of a newspaper. And the world cannot be understood in one page. Of
course, there is a compensation: television offers pictures, and the pictures
move. It is often said that moving pictures are a kind of language in
themselves, and there is a good deal of truth in this. But the language of
pictures differs radically from oral and written language, and the differences are crucial for understanding television news.

To begin with, the grammar of pictures is weak in communicating
past-ness and present-ness. When terrorists want to prove to the world
that their kidnap victims are still alive, they photograph them holding a
copy of a recent newspaper. The dateline on the newspaper provides the
proof that the photograph was taken on or after that date. Without the

help of the written word, film and videotape cannot portray temporal dimensions with any precision. Consider a film clip showing an aircraft carrier at sea. One might be able to identify the ship as Soviet or American, but there would be no way of telling where in the world the carrier was, where it was headed, or when the pictures were taken. It is only through language—words spoken over the pictures or reproduced in them—that the image of the aircraft carrier takes on meaning as a portrayal of a specific event.

Still, it is possible to enjoy the image of the carrier for its own sake. One might find the hugeness of the vessel interesting; it signifies military power on the move. There is a certain drama in watching the planes come in at high speeds and skid to a stop on the deck. Suppose the ship were burning: that would be even more interesting. This leads to a second point about the language of pictures. The grammar of moving pictures favours images that change. That is why violence and destruction find their way onto television so often. When something is destroyed violently its constitution is altered in a highly visible way: hence the entrancing power of fire. Fire gives visual form to the ideas of consumption, disappearance, death—the thing which is burned is actually taken away by fire. It is at this very basic level that fires make a good subject for television news. Something was here, now it's gone, and the change is recorded on film.

Earthquakes and typhoons have the same power: before the viewer's eyes the world is taken apart. If a television viewer has relatives in Mexico City and an earthquake occurs there, then she may take an interest in the images of destruction as a report from a specific place and time. That is, she may look to television news for information about an important event. But film of an earthquake can still be interesting if the viewer cares nothing about the event itself. Which is only to say that there is another way of participating in the news—as a spectator who desires to be entertained. Actually to see buildings topple is exciting, no matter where the buildings are. The world turns to dust before our eyes.

Those who produce television news in America know that their medium favours images that move. That is why they despise "talking heads," people who simply appear in front of a camera and speak. When talking heads appear on television, there is nothing to record or document, no change in process. In the cinema the situation is somewhat different. On a movie screen, close-ups of a good actor speaking dramatically can sometimes be interesting to watch. When Clint Eastwood narrows his eyes and challenges his rival to shoot first, the spectator sees the cool rage of the Eastwood character take visual form, and the narrowing of the eyes is dramatic. But much of the effect of this small movement depends on the size of the movie screen and the darkness of the theatre, which make Eastwood and his every action "larger than life."

The television screen is smaller than life. It occupies about 15 per cent of the viewer's visual field (compared to about 70 per cent for the movie screen). It is not set in a darkened theatre closed off from the world but in the viewer's ordinary living space. This means that visual changes must be more extreme and more dramatic to be interesting on television. A narrowing of the eyes will not do. A car crash, an earthquake, a burning factory are much better.

With these principles in mind, let us examine more closely the structure of a typical newscast. In America, almost all news shows begin with music, the tone of which suggests important events about to unfold. (Beethoven's Fifth Symphony would be entirely appropriate.) The music is very important, for it equates the news with various forms of drama and ritual—the opera, for example, or a wedding procession—in which musical themes underscore the meaning of the event. Music takes us immediately into the realm of the symbolic, a world that is not to be taken literally. After all, when events unfold in the real world, they do so without musical accompaniment. More symbolism follows. The sound of teletype machines can be heard in the studio, not because it is impossible to screen this noise out, but because the sound is a kind of music in itself. It tells us that data are pouring in from all corners of the globe, a sensation reinforced by the world map in the background (or clocks noting the time on different continents).

Already, then, before a single news item is introduced, a great deal has been communicated. We know that we are in the presence of a symbolic event, a form of theatre in which the day's events are to be dramatized. This theatre takes the entire globe as its subject, although it may look at the world from the perspective of a single nation. A certain tension is present, like the atmosphere in a theatre just before the curtain goes up. The tension is represented by the music, the staccato beat of the teletype machines, and the sight of news-workers scurrying around typing reports and answering phones. As a technical matter, it would be no problem to build a set in which the newsroom staff remained off camera, invisible to the viewer, but an important theatrical effect would be lost. By being busy on camera, the workers help communicate urgency about the events at hand, which it is suggested are changing so rapidly that constant revision of the news is necessary.

The staff in the background also helps signal the importance of the person in the centre, the anchorman (or -woman) "in command" of both the staff and the news. The anchorman plays the role of host. He welcomes us to the newscast and welcomes us back from the different locations we visit during filmed reports. His voice, appearance, and manner establish the mood of the broadcast. It would be unthinkable for the anchor to be ugly, or a nervous sort who could not complete a sentence. Viewers must be able to believe in the anchor as a person of authority and skill, a person who would not panic in a crisis—someone to trust.

This belief is based not on knowledge of the anchorman's character or achievements as a journalist, but on his presentation of self while on the air. Does he look the part of a trusted man? Does he speak firmly and clearly? Does he have a warm smile? Does he project confidence without seeming arrogant? The value the anchor must communicate above all else is control. He must be in control of himself, his voice, his emotions. He must know what is coming next in the broadcast, and he must move smoothly and confidently from segment to segment. Again, it would be unthinkable for the anchor to break down and weep over a story, or laugh uncontrollably on camera, no matter how "human" these responses may be.

Many other features of the newscast help the anchor to establish the impression of control. These are usually equated with professionalism in broadcasting. They include such things as graphics that tell the viewer what is being shown, or maps and charts that suddenly appear on the screen and disappear on cue, or the orderly progression from story to story, starting with the most important events first. They also include the absence of gaps or "dead time" during the broadcast, even the simple fact that the news starts and ends at a certain hour. These common features are thought of as purely technical matters, which a professional crew handles as a matter of course. But they are also symbols of a dominant theme of television news: the imposition of an orderly world—called "the news"—upon the disorderly flow of events.

While the form of a news broadcast emphasizes tidiness and control, its content can best be described as chaotic. Because time is so precious on television, because the nature of the medium favours dynamic visual images, and because the pressures of a commercial structure require the news to hold its audience above all else, there is rarely any attempt to explain issues in depth or place events in their proper context. The news moves nervously from a warehouse fire to a court decision, from a guerrilla war to a World Cup match, the quality of the film often determining the length of the story. Certain stories show up only because they offer dramatic pictures. Bleachers collapse in South America: hundreds of people are crushed—a perfect television news story, for the cameras can record the face of disaster in all its anguish. Back in Washington, a new budget is approved by Congress. Here there is nothing to photograph because a budget is not a physical event; it is a document full of language and numbers. So the producers of the news will show a photo of the document itself, focusing on the cover where it says: "Budget of the United States of America." Or sometimes they will send a camera crew to the government printing plant where copies of the budget are produced. That evening, while the contents of the budget are summarized by a voice-over, the viewer sees stacks of documents being loaded into boxes at the government printing plant. Then a few of the budget's more important provisions will be flashed on the screen in written form, but this is such a time-consuming process—using television as a printed page—that the producers keep it to a minimum. In short, the budget is not televisable, and for that reason its time on the news must be brief. The bleacher collapse will get more minutes that evening.

With priorities of this sort, it is almost impossible for the news to offer an adequate account of important events. Indeed, it is the trivial event that is often best suited for television coverage. This is such a commonplace that no one even bothers to challenge it. Walter Cronkite, a revered figure in television and anchorman of the CBS Evening News for many years, has acknowledged several times that television cannot be relied on to inform the citizens of a democratic nation. Unless they also read newspapers and magazines, television viewers are helpless to understand their world, Cronkite has said. No one at CBS has ever disagreed with his conclusion, other than to say, "We do the best we can."

Of course, it is a tendency of journalism in general to concentrate on the surface of events rather than underlying conditions; this is as true for the newspaper as it is for the newscast. But several features of television undermine whatever efforts journalists may make to give sense to the world. One is that a television broadcast is a series of events that occur in sequence, and the sequence is the same for all viewers. This is not true for a newspaper page, which displays many items simultaneously, allowing readers to choose the order in which they read them. If a newspaper reader wants only a summary of the latest tax bill, he can read the headline and the first paragraph of an article, and if he wants more, he can keep reading. In a sense, then, everyone reads a different newspaper, for no two readers will read (or ignore) the same items.

But all television viewers see the same broadcast. They have no choices. A report is either in the broadcast or out, which means that anything which is of narrow interest is unlikely to be included. As NBC News executive Reuven Frank once explained:

> A newspaper, for example, can easily afford to print an item of conceivable interest to only a fraction of its readers. A television news program must be put together with the assumption that each item will be of some interest to everyone that watches. Every time a newspaper includes a feature, which will attract a specialized group, it can assume it is adding at least a little bit to its circulation. To the degree a

television news program includes an item of this sort...it must assume that its audience will diminish.

The need to "include everyone," an identifying feature of commercial television in all its forms, prevents journalists from offering lengthy or complex explanations, or from tracing the sequence of events leading up to today's headlines. One of the ironies of political life in modern democracies is that many problems which concern the "general welfare" are of interest only to specialized groups. Arms control, for example, is an issue that literally concerns everyone in the world, and yet the language of arms control and the complexity of the subject are so daunting that only a minority of people can actually follow the issue from week to week and month to month. If it wants to act responsibly, a newspaper can at least make available more information about arms control than most people want. But commercial television cannot afford to do so.

This illustrates an important point in the psychology of television's appeal. Many of the items in newspapers and magazines are not, in a strict sense, demanded by a majority of readers. They are there because some readers *might* be interested or because the editors think their readers *should* be interested. On commercial television, "might" and "should" are not the relevant words. The producers attempt to make sure that "each item will be of some interest to everyone that watches," as Reuven Frank put it. What this means is that a newspaper or magazine can challenge its audience in a way that television cannot. Print media have the luxury of suggesting or inviting interest, whereas television must always concern itself with conforming to existing interests. In a way, television is more strictly responsive to the demands of its huge audience. But there is one demand it cannot meet: the desire to be challenged, to be told "this is worth attending to," to be surprised by what one thought would not be of interest.

Another severe limitation on television is time. There is simply not enough of it. The evening news programs at CBS, NBC, and ABC all run for thirty minutes, eight of which are taken up by commercials. No one believes that twenty-two minutes for the day's news is adequate. For years news executives at ABC, NBC, and CBS have suggested that the news be expanded to one hour. But by tradition the half-hour after the national evening news is given over to the hundreds of local affiliate stations around the country to use as they see fit. They have found it a very profitable time to broadcast game shows or half-hour situation comedies, and they are reluctant to give up the income they derive from these programs.

The evening news produced by the three networks is profitable for both the networks and the local stations. The local stations are paid a fee by the network to broadcast the network news, and they profit from this fee since the news—produced by the network—costs them nothing. It is likely that they would also make money from a one-hour newscast, but not as much, they judge, as they do from the game shows and comedies they now schedule.

The result is that the evening news must try to do what cannot reasonably be done: give a decent account of the day's events in twenty-two minutes. What the viewer gets instead is a series of impressions, many of them purely visual, most of them unconnected to each other or to any sense of a history unfolding. Taken together, they suggest a world that is fundamentally ungovernable, where events do not arise out of historical conditions but rather explode from the heavens in a series of disasters that suggest a permanent state of crisis. It is this crisis—highly visual, ahistorical, and unsolvable—which the evening news presents as theatre every evening.

The audience for this theatre is offered a contradictory pair of responses. On the one hand, it is reassured by the smooth presentation of the news itself, especially the firm voice and steady gaze of the trusty anchorman. Newscasts frequently end with a "human-interest story," often with a sentimental or comic touch. Example: a little girl in Chicago writes Gorbachev a letter, and he answers her, saying that he and President Reagan are trying to work out their differences. This item reassures viewers that all is well, leaders are in command, we can still communicate with each other, and so on. But—and now we come to the other hand—the rest of the broadcast has told a different story. It has shown the audience a world that is out of control and incomprehensible, full of violence, disaster, and suffering. Whatever authority the anchorman may project through his steady manner is undermined by the terror inspired by the news itself.

This is where television news is at its most radical—not in giving publicity to radical causes, but in producing the impression of an ungovernable world. And it produces this impression not because the people who work in television are leftists or anarchists. The anarchy in television news is a direct result of the commercial structure of broadcasting, which introduces into news judgments a single-mindedness more powerful than any ideology: the overwhelming need to keep people watching.

Notes

Beethoven's Fifth Symphony a triumphant instrumental piece of music written by Ludwig van Beethoven (1770–1827), often recognized for its suspenseful "da-da-da-dum" opening

teletype machines electromechanical typewriters that transmit and receive messages coded in electrical signals carried by telegraph or telephone wires. These machines have become virtually obsolete since the onset of the use of the Internet and fax machines in the 1980s.

Congress the national legislative body of the United States, composed of the Senate and the House of Representatives

Gorbachev Mikhail Gorbachev, born in 1931, was the general secretary of the USSR's Communist Party (1985–1991) and the Soviet Union's president (1989–1991).

President Reagan Ronald Reagan, born in 1911, was the fortieth president of the United States, serving two terms from 1981 to 1989.

leftists believers and supporters of the ideology of the political left, which usually advocates liberal or radical measures to effect egalitarian change

anarchists proponents of anarchy, the absence of all forms of government. More generally, anarchy refers to political disorder or the absence of a cohesive principle.

Learning Without Lectures

Ann Rees

Ann Rees was born in Cardiff, Wales, in 1952. She immigrated to Canada with her family at the age of five, moving to Cold Lake, Alberta. She has lived in many communities in Saskatchewan, Alberta, and British Columbia. For over two decades, Rees has been an investigative journalist in Vancouver with the *Province* newspaper, where she focuses on special projects and longer, in-depth investigations. Rees has said that, in terms of the journalist's "W5H" (Who, What, When, Where, Why, and How), her work is most focused on the "why" part. This article appeared in the *Province* on June 6, 2001. How does Rees' use of language reflect the timeliness of newpapers? How does the information she provides suit the needs of the target audience?

Tammy Mooney is on the cutting edge of education in B.C.'s first high-tech university.

The 33-year-old enrolled in the first class at the two-year-old Technical University of B.C. in Surrey.

"It is a risk and a challenge, but I have no regrets whatsoever," said Mooney, who is working toward a bachelor of science degree in management and technology.

What makes Tech B.C. so different is that there are no traditional lectures.

Students are required to read the lecture material on-line.

"We don't listen to our professor talk," said Mooncy, who is also student council president.

In many ways the courses are similar to a traditional correspondence course, but with a significant difference.

Students have regular tutorials with their professors and fellow students in which they discuss what they have read and "fill in the gaps" in their understanding of the material.

"It requires a lot of self-discipline and time-management," said Mooney, who already holds an e-commerce certificate.

But the computer labs, which the professors attend, are "very interactive and we ask a lot of questions." Students also have access to professors during office hours and by e-mail and phone.

Chat rooms are also a popular venue for students working on the many teamwork assignments.

Mooney would like professors to participate in some of the chat rooms so that instruction can be more immediately interactive.

"There is always a lag time with e-mail," she said.

Math is the only course students believe would benefit from traditional live or videotaped instruction, rather than being taught through on-line instruction.

"We found, as students, that anything that is mathematics-based, you need to watch your professor as they are going through the examples in math," said Mooney. "Streaming video would work fine."

Tech B.C.'s enrolment is scheduled to double this fall from 200 to 400 students, who will be housed in temporary quarters at Surrey Place Mall.

By the time a permanent facility is completed in 2003, enrolment will be 1,600, according to Jane Fee, associate vice-president of Tech B.C.

She believes the entirely on-line—as opposed to lecture-based—approach to teaching is a first in North America.

Which is why Tech B.C. refers to its students as learners.

"Basically, the old notion of a teacher is someone who imparts education and a student as someone who receives it," Fee explained. "A learner is someone who is more actively involved in the process."

The on-line program frees professors from lecture time to allow more time with the learners.

"Most of the time, when the students are in a situation where they are with a faculty member, it is relatively small groups compared [with] what you would find elsewhere," said Fee.

The labs tend to comprise groups of four to 12 students.

Tech B.C. will introduce third-year courses this fall and a fourth year next fall.

At the end of four years, students will graduate with a bachelor of science in information technology, management and technology or interactive arts.

The university will offer a master's and Ph.D. this fall.

The university is well equipped with up-to-date computer equipment, but since students do much of their work at home, they also require up-to-date home computers, said Mooney.

King Zog's Birthday

Bob Elliott and Ray Goulding

Bob Elliott and Ray Goulding teamed up in 1946 at the radio station WHDH in Boston, Massachusetts, where Elliott had a morning show and Goulding read the news. From their radio program, *Matinee with Bob and Ray*, they turned to writing television scripts and screen-plays and created a Broadway show, *The Two and Only.* In the late 1970s, their radio program was revived on National Public Radio. As humourists, they are best known for their memorable characters. What makes a protest rally memorable or newsworthy? What are some examples of recent protests that you have seen on television newscasts? What were the issues and how did the demonstrators show their opinions?

BOB: It's been said that some news might never occur if there were no microphones or television cameras to cover it; that events are often staged by pressure groups just to get some free air time. Editors can't know in advance whether a story is going to be real news—or just a media event. That was our problem when we handed out this assignment to reporter Artie Schermerhorn...

SCHERMERHORN: Here outside Oakdale Park we're awaiting the big protest rally that Albanian monarchists have scheduled for King Zog's birthday. This gentleman is one of the demonstrators...

DEMONSTRATOR: I don't think I should say anything before the others get here. Could you come back later?

SCHERMERHORN: No, I'm sorry. Your people were supposed to be staging a huge demonstration here an hour ago.

DEMONSTRATOR: Well, the others are coming over from Jersey in Bruno's Datsun. And you know us Albanians. We're always late.

SCHERMERHORN: Well, at least, tell us the purpose of this big protest you plan to stage—once the others get here.

DEMONSTRATOR: We're all of Albanian descent. And every year, we get together on King Zog's birthday and reminisce about the good old times.

SCHERMERHORN: And then you stage a demonstration in favour of restoring the monarchy. Is that it?

DEMONSTRATOR: No. Then we usually play pinochle. But this year we decided to try for some TV coverage. Only the guy in your newsroom said he wouldn't send a film crew out just to show us playing pinochle.

SCHERMERHORN: You really don't need to go into…

DEMONSTRATOR: He said it would only be visual if we got the whole mob together with picket signs. Then maybe the police would come and we'd have a pitched battle and…

SCHERMERHORN: Did our editor know that your whole membership could get into one car when he suggested that?

DEMONSTRATOR: I don't believe any specific numbers were mentioned—no.

SCHERMERHORN: I see. Well, now that you've gotten us down here, would you please pick up your sign and walk around with it?

DEMONSTRATOR: I'd feel kind of foolish doing it alone. Couldn't we wait till we're on the air?

SCHERMERHORN: We're on the air, fellah.

DEMONSTRATOR: Oh, gosh. This is a real shame. Without the other guys here it may look like our group doesn't have much popular support.

SCHERMERHORN: I imagine it may look that way!

DEMONSTRATOR: Could you position your cameraman farther over, so I'll seem like a bigger crowd? You know, like the others are all standing behind me?

SCHERMERHORN: Look, Buster—I had a choice of two assignments today. And the one I turned down was a big ecology rally.

DEMONSTRATOR: Well, I wouldn't worry. Those people demonstrate at least once a week.

SCHERMERHORN: But today they were having Robert Redford. He was scheduled to do a sit-in next to a barrel of toxic chemical waste.

DEMONSTRATOR: I'm afraid you're a little naive. I hear they always promise Robert Redford—but he usually doesn't even know about it.

SCHERMERHORN: Well, his name still draws a crowd. But I passed it up for you.

DEMONSTRATOR: And you won't be sorry. After all, there's nothing visual about a sit-in. For TV, you want people moving around. *(He picks up sign and starts walking in a small circle)* Up the monarchy! Albania for Albanians! Long live the monarchy!

SCHERMERHORN: And there you have it—the action at this moment from the potentially explosive rally at Oakdale Park. Now this is Artie Schermerhorn sending it back to our studio.

Notes

King Zog Ahmed Bey Zogu (1895–1961), a politician who was Albania's premier (1922–1924), its president (1925–1928), and king (1928–1939). When Italy invaded Albania in 1939, Zog went into exile and later abdicated the throne (1946).

Jersey a nickname for New Jersey, a state in the United States on the Hudson River where it feeds into the Atlantic Ocean; its northern part is across the river from Manhattan and the Bronx in New York City

pinochle a card game played by two to four persons using a special deck of forty-eight cards

Robert Redford an American movie actor and director, born in 1937, whose watershed role was in *Butch Cassidy and the Sundance Kid* (1969). He starred in films such as *All the President's Men* (1976) and *Out of Africa* (1986).

almost visible

Kenneth J. Harvey

Kenneth J. Harvey was born in St. John's, Newfoundland, in 1962, and has lived in that province for much of his life. He writes poetry, fiction, and essays and has published thirteen books. Harvey was nominated for the Commonwealth Writers Prize and the Chapters/Books in Canada First Novel Award. His opinion pieces have appeared in newspapers across Canada. He is the founder of the ReLit Awards, which honours books produced by independent literary publishers in Canada. Harvey has been writer-in-residence at the University of New Brunswick and at Memorial University in Newfoundland. He has said, "I wrote 'almost visible' many years ago. In fact, I couldn't have been much older than a grade twelve student at the time." What is your relationship to television? What role does television play in your life?

almost visible

he was almost
visible
thin
pale
fading
in and out
of conversation
speech;
an irregular
flickering
(a loose connection)
his eyes
folding
half-shut
moving
like the current
of a timeless
tv
a ghost
of neon
blinking
in and out
of dreams
holding himself
between words
and then slipping
fading
almost visible

Media on Media: Activities

1. When Marshall McLuhan first spoke of a single *global village*—in which time and space disappear and everyone, regardless of physical location, is connected simultaneously through electronic media—the Internet was used only by the military and academics and the Web did not even exist. Make a multimedia presentation in which you explore how the Web fulfills McLuhan's vision of a global village.

2. Locate a videotape of a television news program from ten or more years ago. Carefully watch it, as well as a current television news program. Write a commentary for a radio broadcast in which you compare the two news samples, offering reasons for the ways in which TV news has either changed or stayed the same. Make sure that you have a clearly stated thesis and that you use a comparative report structure to pique the interest of your listeners.

3. Imagine that you have just voted in your first federal or provincial election. In the weeks preceding the election, you researched the candidates, parties, and issues, but you find that the media does not answer all your questions and, at times, provides biased coverage. Set yourself the task of helping thirteen- to sixteen-year-olds read and view the news critically, identify bias, and recognize the differences between explicit and implicit messages. In a group, plan, script, and tape a video to achieve this goal. Keep an ongoing diary of choices you make during the production process to help you assess your overall effectiveness.

4. In a group, research and evaluate possibilities for post-secondary education provided by technology, such as Internet distance-learning or instructional videos. Analyze the various options for technological learning you discover by defining each option and considering its applications and implications. Be sure to evaluate these options in light of your experiences at school and your goals for the future. As a group, present your findings in one of two ways: as an oral or multimedia presentation with a well-developed thesis; or as a dramatic or comic presentation based on a prepared script.

Arguments and persuasion are all around us. We find them in television commercials, billboards, radio spots, Internet screens, company logos, and letters to the editor. They exist in places as diverse as television commentaries, resumés, telemarketing calls, designer labels, flyers, annual reports, political speeches, and T-shirts. When we use the word *argument*, we often mean a quarrel or dispute. The term *persuasion* may bring to mind an infomercial's attempt to manipulate us into buying something we don't need. In fact, the ability to develop and sustain thoughtful arguments—and to use those arguments to persuade people to take action—is essential not only to our academic career, but to our working and personal lives as well.

Let's say that a classmate has an opinion about something and wants to formulate an argument. She creates her argument by proving her point of view through the *choice* and *arrangement* of ideas, evidence, and language. The main purpose of her argument is not necessarily to change others' opinions, but to lay out a detailed position. Once she has determined her thesis, she supports it by presenting numerous credible facts, anecdotes, and up-to-date statistics to convince her audience of the validity of her thesis. To help strengthen her argument, she can use an organizing principle such as classification, comparison and contrast, or cause and effect. She also needs to be able to anticipate and refute potential counter-arguments. She must avoid potential bias and ensure that her argument is not distorted by any personal prejudices she may hold on the topic. As she thinks through her argument, she may find that discussing it and writing about it will help her to make her argument more precise.

Persuasion takes argumentation one step further. It uses an argument as the basis for urging people to alter their thinking or behaviour. Generally, persuasion reflects an emotional commitment on the part of the writer, artist, or speaker and appeals to the audience's human needs, emotions, and values.

This In-Depth introduces you to what Aristotle had to say about the techniques of persuasion. You will also read a newspaper editorial that examines the issue of privacy of information. Three opinion pieces are offered exploring one issue: the sale of a natural resource. And you'll read a poem that presents an argument about poetry. As you read through this section, remember that the ability to reflect deeply on an issue and to successfully articulate thoughts in oral or written forms is an invaluable skill. (For related selections, turn to the argumentative and persuasive essays section on pages 283–322 of this anthology.)

Effective Persuasion

from Rhetoric

Aristotle

Translated by W. Rhys Roberts

Renowned philosopher and scholar Aristotle was born in Stagirus, Greece, in 384 BCE. In 367 BCE, he went to Athens to study at Plato's academy. There, he served as the tutor of Alexander the Great and founded the famed Lyceum school. Aristotle's teachings cover a vast array of subjects, including logic, ethics, biology, physics, psychology, astronomy, rhetoric, poetry, and politics. As a philosopher, scholar, and scientist, Aristotle has had an extensive and profound influence on many fields of study. The following excerpts are from *Rhetoric*, his study of the art and technique of eloquence. In this text, he argues for the middle ground between two conflicting contemporary positions, one supporting the importance of content, the other the importance of style. Aristotle believed in the importance of both. How are these two elements different from each other? In what ways are both elements important?

...we must be able to employ persuasion, just as strict reasoning can be employed, on opposite sides of a question, not in order that we may in practice employ it in both ways (for we must not make people believe what is wrong), but in order that we may see clearly what the facts are, and that, if another man argues unfairly, we on our part may be able to confute him. —*from Book 1, Part 1*

A statement is persuasive and credible either because it is directly self-evident or because it appears to be proved from other statements that are so. In either case it is persuasive because there is somebody whom it persuades. —*from Book 1, Part 2*

Of the modes of persuasion furnished by the spoken word there are three kinds. The first kind depends on the personal character of the speaker; the second on putting the audience into a certain frame of mind; the third on the proof, or apparent proof, provided by the words of the speech itself. Persuasion is achieved by the speaker's personal character when the speech is so spoken as to make us think him credible. We believe good men more fully and more readily than others: this is true generally whatever the question is, and absolutely true where exact certainty is impossible and opinions are divided. This kind of persuasion, like the others, should be achieved by what the speaker says, not by what people think of this character before he begins to speak. It is not true, as some writers assume in their treatises on rhetoric, that the personal goodness revealed by the speaker contributes nothing to his power of persuasion; on the contrary, his character may almost be called the most effective means of persuasion he possesses. Secondly, persuasion may come through the hearers, when the speech stirs their emotions. Our judgments when we are pleased and friendly are not the same as when we are pained and hostile. It is toward producing these effects, as we maintain, that present-day writers on rhetoric direct the whole of their efforts.... Thirdly, persuasion is effected through the speech itself when we have proved a truth or an apparent truth by means of the persuasive arguments suitable to the case in question.

There are, then, these three means of effecting persuasion. The man who is to be in command of them must, it is clear, be able (1) to reason logically, (2) to understand human character and goodness in their various forms, and (3) to understand the emotions—that is, to name them and describe them, to know their causes and the way in which they are excited.... —*from Book 1, Part 2*

Notes

rhetoric the study of the art of effective speaking and writing; in this case, also the title of Aristotle's study of the effective use of oral and written language. In contemporary culture, the term *rhetoric* has developed a negative connotation through the implication that rhetoric is the artificial, even misleading, use of language.

Giant Database Is Ripe for Abuse

Edmonton Journal

This editorial appeared in the *Edmonton Journal* on May 18, 2000. It was written in response to the release of an annual report by Bruce Phillips, the federal privacy commissioner at the time. In his report, Phillips warns about the potential abuse of a huge database, called the Longitudinal Labour Force File, which was continuously compiled and maintained by Human Resources Development Canada (HRDC), a department of the federal government. The writer of the editorial echoes Phillips' concern and argues in favour of immediate action to ensure the privacy of Canadian citizens. Subsequent to Phillips' report, the database was dismantled by Jane Stewart, federal minister responsible for the HRDC. Are you worried about the potential abuse of the accumulation of personal information in computer databases and, if so, why? Who might be especially concerned about this practice and who might promote it?

Just because you're paranoid doesn't mean the government hasn't compiled a detailed dossier of personal information about you in its computers.

In fact, Human Resources Development Canada has dossiers on almost 34 million Canadians all in one single, huge database—quite a feat considering there are only 30 million people in this country. But because HRDC never purges the database, it has accumulated files on the dead as well as the living.

In his latest report to government, federal privacy commissioner Bruce Phillips not only points out the surprising existence of this database—despite assurances from previous privacy commissioners that no such single information bank existed—but he also highlights the deep concerns it raises for the privacy of Canadians.

The HRDC database contains information gleaned from a wide range of other federal departments—information from tax returns, which are supposed to be used only by Canada Customs and Revenue, details of social and income security programs from Health and Welfare Canada, information on unemployment insurance and employment programs from Employment and Immigration, to name just a few. And HRDC, in its continuing quest to compile still more information, is considering expanding the database to include further details about student loans, pensions, and old age security.

The information is used primarily for research and program analysis, a benign enough purpose. It may be turned over to provincial governments or to private sector firms or universities under research contracts to government.

Such a huge stockpile of personal information has clear benefits for bureaucrats and researchers, who undoubtedly have no malevolent intent. Nonetheless, the potential for breach of privacy, whether through unintentional error or outside infiltration, is disturbing.

As Phillips points out, the sheer volume of information alone—up to 2,000 elements on a single individual—is cause for concern, particularly when the vast majority of Canadians don't know this information is being collected about them, or cross-referenced with other personal details. There are few legal restrictions on how the information is used, unlike at Statistics Canada, for example, which operates under strict legislation. And the files are never purged. "Without an end, the temptation is to subject everyone to unrelenting information surveillance," Phillips says.

The simple existence of a single, huge database leaves it ripe for abuse. Who knows what some future government or individual might deem beneficial to extract from this mountain of information? Phillips raises the spectre of information being used to make decisions or predictions about individuals, or being retrieved in an unforeseen way, such as by ethnic origin or disability.

Perhaps most disturbing, though, is the department's apparent lack of interest in addressing these privacy issues. Phillips' office first raised the concerns almost two years ago, but HRDC officials have been slow to respond. While they have addressed some of the security issues, they have been less willing to tackle the privacy concerns.

Certainly there are benefits to having an extensive research database to mine, but they do not outweigh the potential risks to individual privacy.

While we cannot turn back the technological clock to a pre-computer, pre-Internet age when access to such information would have been far more limited, we can put safeguards in place to protect its privacy.

These could include separating the information into a number of different databases, as Phillips recommends, and establishing strict rules on the kind of information collected and the way in which it is used.

Let's Stop Being Hysterical, Shall We, and Start Selling Water to Those Who Need It

Lee Morrison

Lee Morrison was born in Vidora, Saskatchewan, in 1932. A former member of parliament, he is a geological engineer who has worked in the mining industry for a variety of companies. Since retiring from politics, he has written for a range of publications, including the *Calgary Sun, Regina Leader Post, Ottawa Citizen, Calgary Herald*, and *Toronto Star*. He currently resides in Eastend, Saskatchewan. This opinion piece was originally published in *Report*, a news magazine. As the title suggests, Morrison takes a controversial position on the issue of selling our water. Before reading the selection, what suppositions can you make about its content and tone from its title? Do you think this title is effective for an opinion piece? Why or why not?

There are encouraging signs that the dog-in-the-manger nationalism barring Canadian bulk water exports may slowly be giving way to common sense. The Liberal government of Newfoundland is poised to permit sales from Gisborne Lake on the island's south shore, and Jean Chrétien is sending mixed but somewhat favourable signals about the federal position.

In spite of furious howling by the xenophobic Council of Canadians and its NDP political arm, and tut-tutting by the increasingly politically correct Canadian Alliance, there is a reasonable chance that this previously unmentionable subject will soon receive serious consideration.

With 0.5% of the world's population, Canada is blessed with 20% of the earth's fresh water, including 9% of the renewable supply. We mismanage it, pollute it, and waste it, but won't even consider exporting it to eager buyers in the U.S., Asia, and the Middle East. A lot of nonsense has been written about water being too precious to sell—the very blood in the veins of Mother Earth, etc. Certainly, it is one of life's necessities, but so is the food that we buy and sell every day. Food, lumber, and bulk water are all renewable resources, but we export only the first two, because water is somehow "sacred." Meanwhile, we merrily dispose of precious, non-renewable natural gas. When it's gone, our lives will be much less comfortable, but we'll still have 20 times the water we need. Oh joy!

There are three possible ways to export water: on a small scale, in bottles, which we do now; by sea, in supertankers, which has quite recently become economically feasible; and by massive inter-basin transfers via systems of canals and pipelines that are technically possible, but too astronomically costly and environmentally questionable to merit serious consideration.

There is a myth that Canada would be "obliged" under the North American Free Trade Agreement (NAFTA) to permit inter-basin transfers if any bulk water exports were allowed, but nothing in the agreement inhibits the rights of provinces to manage their resources. NAFTA requires only that domestic and foreign entrepreneurs be treated equally and that contracts be honoured. Provinces would continue to decide what water could be tapped, at what rate, under what conditions, and for what price—just as they do now with oil.

Proponents of a total export ban tend to damage their credibility by resorting to exaggerated propaganda and misrepresentation. In 1998, Ontario issued a permit to a private company to ship water from Lake Superior to Asia. After a protest orchestrated by the Council of Canadians, the permit was cancelled. The council, in a fundraising letter headed "They're coming to take our water," proclaimed, "This country came within a whisker of selling as much as 600 million litres of our precious water each year." Oh my. It left unexplained that this is less than one-eighth of 1% of the amount that Lake Superior loses to evaporation on one hot summer's day, or about one-fifth of what the greater

Chicago area daily draws from Lake Michigan. Nonetheless, the letter probably raised a wad of money from the gullible.

Much has been made of the fact that only 1% of Great Lakes water is renewed annually. That equates to 121 cubic kilometres of new water in Lake Superior alone; enough to fill about 600,000 very large tankers which, tied bow to stern, would encircle the earth five times. In a recent press release, Alliance deputy House Leader Cheryl Gallant raised alarm about the Great Lakes question. Like most MPs, her grasp of mathematics is apparently limited to counting the votes that may be gained by appealing to public prejudice and misinformation.

In any event, shipping Great Lakes water, in even modest quantities, isn't an attractive proposition. Ontarians drink the stuff, but its quality isn't great, so why ship it halfway around the world? Besides, the very large tankers needed to make shipment economically attractive can't pass through the canal system from the sea. Finally, it is boundary water, which raises legal questions.

The provinces with the brightest prospects for selling water are Newfoundland and British Columbia. Both have easily accessible unpolluted sources, with no jurisdictional problems.

In British Columbia, 1.3 billion cubic metres of fresh water (enough to fill seven thousand 200,000 ton tankers) reaches the sea every day. There are dozens of streams from which water of exceptionally high quality could be loaded into tankers for shipment anywhere in the world, especially to southern California.

How much could fresh, clean, easily accessible water be worth? I pay almost 1/5 of a cent per litre for the foul-tasting discharge from my household taps. Sparkling mountain water should be worth substantially more, but instead of encouraging market development, British Columbia has banned large-scale exports. Meanwhile, neighbouring Alaska has granted a long-term export licence to a Canadian company negotiating possible sales to far-away Singapore.

Ultimately, the price of bulk water will be determined, as it should be, by competition among suppliers and by the benchmark price of desalinated water, which is currently about 1/4 to 1/3 cent per litre. Desalination, however, has its shortcomings. The product is generally inferior to fresh water, and a desalination plant, unlike a supertanker, can't be economically used only during a drought and sent elsewhere when water is plentiful. The town of Santa Barbara, California, learned that economic lesson the hard way in the 1990s.

With aggressive private sector marketing, British Columbia and Newfoundland could ultimately earn billions of dollars in royalties by exporting tiny fractions of their liquid wealth. The petty obstructiveness of those who would rather see it all spill into the sea than sell a little to those who need it is not only mean-spirited, it is masochistic. By spitefully refusing to market an abundant renewable resource, they deprive Canadians of economic benefits far into the future. It's time to grow up.

Notes

dog-in-the-manger a person who selfishly withholds from others something useless to himself; from "The Fable of the Dog" (one of *Aesop's Fables*) in which the dog prevents an ox from eating hay which he himself does not want

Council of Canadians a public interest group founded in 1985, dedicated to the development of policies that encourage Canadian economic, political, social, and cultural sovereignty

North American Free Trade Agreement (NAFTA) a trade and investment liberalization arrangement signed by Canada, the United States, and Mexico; it came into effect on January 1, 1994, and extended and superseded the Canada–United States Free Trade Agreement of 1989

desalination the process of removing salt from sea water

Our Water Sovereignty Is at Risk

Eric Reguly

Eric Reguly was born in Vancouver, British Columbia, in 1957. He earned a B.A. in English and French literature and a master's degree in journalism from the University of Western Ontario. Reguly's many articles have been published in a range of publications, including the London *Times*, the *Financial Post* in New York and London, the *Financial Times* of Canada, *Alberta Report* magazine, and the *London* (Ontario) *Free Press*. He has also served as host for "ROB-TV" (Report on Business Television). The following opinion piece was originally published in the *Globe and Mail* where he regularly comments on a variety of issues in his column "To the Point." This piece presents a point of view opposite to the one written by Lee Morrison, which precedes it. When examining two sides of an issue in two separate texts, what similarities might you expect? What kinds of differences in the two texts might you encounter?

A CBC documentary called *Captured Rain*, broadcast in December 2000, examined the emotionally charged issue of bulk water exports and left little doubt that the United States eventually will get as much Canadian water as it wants. The documentary didn't elicit an iota of interest among the ruling Liberals and was barely mentioned in the press.

A week later, the U.S. Interior Department published the results of an extensive, two-year study on the effects of global warming on water. Among other things, it warned of vanishing mountain snowpacks and a hotter and drier South. It too was widely ignored, even though the Interior Department is hardly a partisan observer of climate change.

Add the conclusions of the CBC documentary to the conclusions of the U.S. government report and you've got a scenario that, you would think, would nudge Canadian bulk water exports back on to the political agenda. But no. Water exports were a hot topic last year, when a U.S. company sued the federal government for water it agreed to buy but never got. This year, water, except for the Walkerton tragedy, received about as much publicity as Canadian mutton exports to Kazakhstan. There is no federal-provincial water accord. Bill C-15, the legislation that would have amended the International Boundary Waters Treaty Act to prohibit the bulk removal of boundary waters (notably the Great Lakes) is dead. There is no national ban on bulk water exports. Canada's environment minister, David Anderson, showed early promise but has been a dud on water, the one resource that most Canadians seem willing to protect.

Water could go the way of so many of Canada's resources and industries. Not so many years ago, light manufacturing, such as appliance making, was a big Canadian industry. It has all but disappeared. In the 1980s, Canada gave up any notion of energy sovereignty when it signed the free-trade agreement with the United States. Canadian water sovereignty may be next, if it hasn't gone already.

The American case for importing water grows by the day. In the U.S. Southwest, especially California, lack of water is cited as the biggest impediment to the state's economic growth. The current power crisis in California and the Northwest is partly a result of the shortage of water needed to power hydroelectric generators. Groundwater supplies in the Midwest, where much of the world's grain is produced, are at critically short levels. Population growth in the Sun Belt states is putting enormous pressure on existing supplies. There are millions of pools to fill, lawns to water, and cars to wash. The demand for water from thirsty states and countries is so great that the governors of the eight Great Lakes states this month called for a binding agreement with Canada by 2004 to protect the lakes from excessive withdrawals.

The water issue came to the forefront last year when two export schemes came to national attention. The first came from California's Sun Belt Water, which wanted to import water by tanker from British

Columbia to moisten the southern California landscape. The plan failed when the B.C. government slapped a moratorium on bulk water exports. Sun Belt retaliated by suing Ottawa for $10.5-billion under NAFTA's investment provisions, on the grounds that provinces are not allowed to halt the free trade of goods. The second came from Nova Group, which somehow secured an Ontario licence to siphon water from Lake Superior and export it by tanker to Asia. When the news broke, everyone from Canadian nationalists to governors of the Great Lakes states went berserk and the licence was revoked.

Threats to Canadian water would not exist if Canadian politicians specifically excluded water from NAFTA's trade list. It wasn't, which means there is little doubt that bulk water exports, once they start, will become a commercial good whose international sale comes under NAFTA protection. One possible way around this is to use environmental law to make water invulnerable to trade challenges. This too hasn't happened.

In the end, of course, it's all about business. As long as the United States is willing to pay for Canadian water, ways probably will be found to provide it. But until an environmentally sound export structure is found, why open the floodgates and take the risk that they can't be closed? Better yet, why not impose a national bulk water export ban and force industry to come to water instead of the other way around? Think of the jobs it would create as water becomes scarcer and scarcer in the United States and factories move north.

Notes

U.S. Interior Department refers to the U.S. Department of the Interior, which is the United States federal government's principal conservation agency. Its mandate is to serve as a steward for the approximately 437 million acres of public lands in the United States and for the natural and cultural resources connected with these lands.

Walkerton tragedy In May 2000, in the town of Walkerton, Ontario, a number of residents became ill and some died, as a result of deadly E. coli bacteria that contaminated the town's water supply.

Kazakhstan a country in central Asia

free-trade agreement a bilateral free-trade deal between Canada and the United States, enacted on January 1989 after almost three years of negotiations

Great Lake states refers to the eight states in the United States which touch on the Great Lakes: Illinois, Indiana, Michigan, Minnesota, New York, Ohio, Pennsylvania, and Wisconsin

NAFTA acronym for the North American Free Trade Agreement, a trade and investment liberalization arrangement signed by Canada, the United States, and Mexico; it came into effect on January 1, 1994, and extended and superseded the Canada–United States Free Trade Agreement of 1989

From Water

Marq de Villiers

Marq de Villiers was born in Bloemfontein, South Africa, in 1940. He currently resides in Lunenberg, Nova Scotia. A former editor and publisher of *Toronto Life*, he is currently the editorial director for *Where Magazine International*. *Water*, from which the following updated afterword was taken, was first published in Canada and won the 1998 Governor General's Literary Award for Nonfiction. It has since been published widely in other countries and translated into nine languages. He has published several other books on exploration, history, politics, and travel. His latest book, *Sahara* (to be published in 2002), is about the natural history of the Sahara region. In this selection, de Villiers considers both sides of the argument on the issue of the sale of water. What tone appeals to you when you are reading or listening to an argumentative essay? Do you believe certain tones are more effective in an argument than others, or does it depend on the subject matter and purpose of the piece? Why?

I'd always considered the export debate to be ludicrous, and in the last year or so most of the applications for corporate export licences have quietly faded from view. This is partly because of the politics, of course. Brian Tobin in Newfoundland robustly declared himself categorically against any water exports; Ottawa followed suit with a more equivocal ban. But politics wasn't the real reason. The exporting of water, in reality, simply made no business sense. The only real customers for Canadian water are the southern Californians and the arid states of the Colorado basin down to High Plains, Texas; the most optimistic business projections for delivering water to customers came in at about $2 a ton, and that figure depended on a number of more or less implausible assumptions. Set that against the fact that in August 1999 Tampa Bay Water in Florida announced it had hired a consortium to build a new reverse-osmosis desal plant that would produce 25 million gallons of fresh water a day, at a declared cost of 45 cents a ton. At second glance, the economics didn't seem quite as rosy—over the life of the plant, the water would cost better than $2 a ton, but this is still better than most other sources. The economics were possible because Tampa Bay is less naturally saline than the Gulf of Mexico and because the plant would be built next door to a major power plant that would supply it with cheap electricity. Nevertheless, the price was such that it attracted a delegation from Singapore, which was planning a 36-million-gallons-a-day plant—at an average cost of nearly $8 a ton. It simply reinforced what I had been telling interviewers for the better part of a year: if I had any money to invest (a vain hope), I'd sink it into desal research and not into the illusory business of exporting water.

As for privatization...the anti-corporatist lobby groups were vociferous in their opposition to turning any water delivery or purification systems over to private enterprise: bafflingly, their main argument seemed to be that since water was part of the global commons it should therefore not "belong" to anyone, which rather missed the point that it was the delivery of the commodity, not the commodity itself, that was at issue. The other argument revolved around pricing, and there were dozens of stories circulating that private water companies had boosted prices beyond the reach of the poor and had even cut off some of the truly indigent altogether. Most of these stories proved, on examination, to be false. In this all-or-nothing debate, the notion that public authorities could suitably regulate private companies seems hardly to have emerged. It's true there were problems, but the real argument, in most of the world without adequate water, was not whether the rich would benefit from private water supplies but whether there would be any water deliveries at all: strapped Third World governments were in no position to repair their crumbling infrastructure or to extend it to the relentlessly expanding slums in the new megacities. I have made the point, in the past, that even studies by NGOs suspicious of private enterprise had found baseless the notion that ending water subsidies would boost prices beyond the reach of the poor. And then a World Water Forum in The Hague early in 2000 declared forthrightly, and correctly, that without privatization, water matters would get steadily worse. It was, the meeting said, privatization or nothing, and the ideological debate was therefore, at this stage, pointless.

Some people have told me that they found an incongruity between my gloomy recounting of the world's water woes, and my "relatively" optimistic final chapter. Yet I continue to believe that, serious as the world's water problems are, they are not without solution. There is enough water for everyone; we just need the political will and therefore the money to do what we already know needs to be done. For example, in Boston, among other places, proper pricing has forced through conservationist measures with relatively little pain; proper use of market forces and a true cost-accounting of polluters (so that they can therefore pay their real share of the necessary cleanup) are not pie-in-the-sky economics but sensible business practice.

My environmentalist friends also distrust my reliance on technology; among many of them there is an almost Luddite suspicion of technological solutions. I, on the other hand, think sophisticated engineering can be usefully combined with a conservationist ethic to provide solutions that can be arrived at in no other way. It's true, as some have pointed out, that were we to provide cheap and energy-efficient desalination of seawater, one of the net results would be to encourage even more growth in places where, ecologically speaking, it shouldn't happen, such as in the deserts of the southwestern United States. This is the same argument that has brought home to traffic engineers that adding a lane to a freeway never alleviated traffic congestion, but only encourages more cars onto the roads. So in a way, I agree. But I never said that water woes can be solved in isolation from other human-caused problems.

It all, in the end, comes back to the engine that drives all environmental problems—the astonishing growth in human populations. Meanwhile, people are dying of contaminated water. If engineers can save them, they should be enabled to do so.

For Canada, which is so water-rich, what is the proper course? What, in this welter of conflicting assumptions and rapidly changing hydrological realities, should a Canadian water policy seek to achieve?

In my view, all water policy-making should follow three imperatives:

- Water should be priced to mandate thrifty use (that is, it should be priced for conservation).
- Water users should be obligated to maintain the water that passes through their systems in as pristine a state as possible and should be penalized for not doing so.
- Unsustainable withdrawals from water systems should be prohibited.

All three of these have practical implications for Canadian users of water and, if they are used to govern bulk sales of water to others, will allow those sales to do the minimum amount of damage—and at the same time neatly bypass NAFTA's Chapter 11, which seeks to prevent nations differentiating between domestic and foreign investors—the notion that you can't sell at one price to the locals and at another to foreigners.

Even if Canada has plenty of water, it makes no sense to waste it. There are hundreds of communities in Canada that still don't meter water usage. The town in which I now live, Lunenburg in Nova Scotia, charges a flat annual rate and allows me to use as much as I please. It is no surprise that communities where water is measured and charged for use less water than those that don't. The Americans can be worse than we can, but sometimes they're better, too.

As I've said above, the idea that this penalizes the poor and makes manufacturing more expensive is wrong. American industrial users use much less water than Chinese ones, for example, because their technology is more advanced, and so charging more for water in the end has the beneficial result of winnowing out older and less efficient factories. And as for the poor…in most countries it is the rich who benefit from the current subsidies, since they use more water and are more likely to be connected to the grid in the first place.

And there is no reason why there has to be a single-tier pricing system. For example, I would suggest a three-tier system similar to the one in the south of France. This could consist of a very low price (yes, a subsidized price) for basic human uses like sanitation and drinking. Fifty litres per person per day is usually sufficient for these purposes. After that, charge more for uses that include, say, watering the garden. And charge the earth if someone wants to fill a swimming pool. Apart from the obvious advantages such a system would have on consumption habits, there is a peripheral benefit: for Canadians, it would have a substantial inhibiting effect on foreign bulk sales.

Why? Obviously, the Americans have enough water for basic sanitation and for simple household uses; therefore, any water they import could—should—be charged at the highest rate, perfectly legitimately, under NAFTA. Call it, say, $6 a ton. At that price, only a few very desperate customers would buy, and the amount of water being shifted would be minimal. Alternatively, if the country decides it wants a small water export industry, adjust the pricing accordingly. It's important to note that this is not a tax or a subsidy or a fee but a price—this is free marketeering at work. We, the nominal "owners" of the water, would simply be charging customers what they would be willing to pay.

The second policy imperative is to insist that water users leave the water they use in as pristine a state as they found it. That is, either don't change the water, or pay for its restoration. This has several benefits. It will focus public perception on the parlous state of our waterways. It will force industry to be more technologically sophisticated—or pay the price. And it will, at last, help to regulate agricultural uses of pesticides and herbicides.

Industry, of course, will squeal. They will maintain that the added costs would be ruinous to their competitiveness. They will seek to label the charge a "tax" when it is nothing of the sort. We should pay no attention to this. The argument has the same weight as the notion a hundred years ago that forbidding the use of child labour would drive businesses into bankruptcy. Ignore it.

The third necessary component of a national water policy is a flat-out prohibition of unsustainable withdrawals from drainage basins, and of unsustainable transfers from one basin to another. Of course, definitions of what is "sustainable" will sustain the lawyers for years to come, but the policy is nevertheless right. It will effectively put an end to the grandiose notions that have so stimulated visionary engineers over the years (the notion, for example, to turn Hudson Bay into a fresh water lake and divert its rivers southwards).

Megaprojects aren't the only reason to prohibit water transfers. We also need them to prevent the small-scale draining of wetlands and "swamps" and floodplains for "development," changes that damage water tables and exaggerate natural hazards such as floods or droughts. Such a prohibition would help us remember what water is, a substance fundamental to human life and society. We all need to be reminded, from time to time, of the deeper implications of that ecologists' motto that "we're all downstream."

Notes

Brian Tobin Born in Newfoundland, Tobin became a federal member of parliament in 1980, at the age of 26. In 1996, he resigned to become the premier of Newfoundland, an office he held until 2000, when he returned to federal politics to become a cabinet minister in the Liberal party's majority government.

reverse-osmosis desal the movement of fresh water through a semi-permeable membrane when pressure is applied to a solution (such as sea-water) on one side of it

indigent impoverished, destitute

Third World a term referring to developing countries; originally coined in the context of the United States as the "First World" and the Soviet Union as the "Second World"; currently considered pejorative because it implies developing countries are less important than developed countries

NGOs the abbreviation for non-governmental agencies; generally refers to an agency which provides a social service, but is neither created nor funded by a government

The Hague refers to The Hague Tribunal, an international institution, founded in the Netherlands in 1899, which judges international legal cases and proposes nominees to the International Court of Justice

Luddite originally, referred to a member of a group of workers who engaged in riots (1811–1816), destroying machinery that threatened to eliminate jobs; in contemporary usage, refers to any person who shuns technology and believes that society is better off without its reliance on technology

pristine in this instance, remaining free from dirt or bacteria; clean

NAFTA acronym for the North American Free Trade Agreement, a trade and investment liberalization arrangement signed by Canada, the United States, and Mexico; it came into effect on January 1, 1994, and extended and superseded the Canada–United States Free Trade Agreement of 1989

wetlands a lowland area, such as a marsh or swamp, that is saturated with moisture and contains a delicate ecosystem

floodplains plains bordering a river that are made up of soil deposited by flooding

Poetry

Marianne Moore

Marianne Moore was born near St. Louis, Missouri, in 1887, and educated at Bryn Mawr College in Pennsylvania. After graduation, she taught business at Carlisle Indian School, worked as a librarian in New York, and edited *The Dial*, a poetry magazine. Her early poems attracted serious attention. T.S. Eliot described her poems as "part of the body of endurable poetry written in our time." Another of her contemporaries, Randall Jarrell, described her poetry as having "the lacy mathematical extravagance of a snowflake." In 1951, her *Collected Poems* won all the top prizes for that year: the National Book Award, the Bollinger Prize, and the Pulitzer Prize. She died in 1972. The following poem begins with a rather surprising comment about poetry, but continues with some thoughtful insights into the nature of poetry. What do you think is the value of poetry? Which poems have been particularly meaningful to you?

I, too, dislike it: there are things that are important beyond all this fiddle.
　Reading it, however, with a perfect contempt for it, one discovers in
　it after all, a place for the genuine.
　　Hands that can grasp, eyes
　　that can dilate, hair that can rise
　　　if it must, these things are important not because a

high-sounding interpretation can be put upon them but because they are
　useful. When they become so derivative as to become unintelligible,
　the same thing may be said for all of us, that we
　　do not admire what
　　we cannot understand: the bat
　　　holding on upside down or in quest of something to

eat, elephants pushing, a wild horse taking a roll, a tireless wolf under
   a tree, the immovable critic twitching his skin like a horse that feels
         a flea, the base-
   ball fan, the statistician—
      nor is it valid
         to discriminate against "business documents and

schoolbooks"; all these phenomena are important. One must make a
         distinction
      however: when dragged into prominence by half poets, the result is
         not poetry,
   nor till the poets among us can be
      "literalists of
      the imagination"—above
         insolence and triviality and can present

for inspection, "imaginary gardens with real toads in them," shall we have
   it. In the meantime, if you demand on the one hand,
   the raw material of poetry in
      all its rawness and
      that which is on the other hand
         genuine, then you are interested in poetry.

Notes

"business documents and schoolbooks" Moore, herself, provided a note
for this reference in the poem. She quotes from a section from the diary
of the Russian writer Leo Tolstoy (1828–1910), in which he considers the
difference between poetry and prose: "Where the boundary between prose
and poetry lies, I shall never be able to understand. The question is raised in
manuals of style, yet the answer to it lies beyond me. Poetry is verse: prose
is not verse. Or else poetry is everything with the exception of business
documents and school books."

"literalists of the imagination" Here, Moore refers to a passage from the
book *Ideas of Good and Evil* (1903) by the English writer W.B. Yeats
(1865–1939), in which he talks about the deficiencies of the Romantic poet

William Blake (1757–1827): "The limitation of his view was from the very intensity of his vision; he was a too literal realist of imagination, as others are of nature; and because he believed that the figures seen by the mind's eye, when exalted by inspiration, were 'eternal existences,' symbols of divine essences, he hated every grace of style that obscured their lineaments."

Argument and Persuasion: Activities

1. Write an argumentative essay in which you present your position on the issue of the sale of water by Canada to other countries. Use the selections in this unit as your sources. Be sure to include a clearly stated thesis, an effective organizational structure, well-reasoned and persuasive arguments, convincing supporting information, a thoughtful conclusion, and accurate documentation.

2. On your own or with a partner, locate a sample of two or three print or Internet newsletters published by special interest groups. Analyze the various techniques used in the newsletters to make the groups' arguments and to persuade readers. In your analysis, consider features or elements such as methods of development (for example, cause and effect); use of rhetorical devices (for example, analogy); and the actual design or layout of the newsletter (for example, use of boldface and highlighted quotations). Present your analysis orally or in a written report to the class, using graphic organizers and visual aids as appropriate.

3. Choose a topic of urgent local, provincial, or national interest for a formal class debate. Working with a group, formulate a resolution for the debate, choose two teams, and appoint a moderator and two judges. Ensure that all participants are clear on their respective roles and on the criteria and procedural rules for a formal debate. At the end of the debate, the judges, in consultation with the moderator, will make an oral presentation to the class, identifying the strengths and weaknesses of each team's arguments.

4. Work with a group to prepare a documentary video on an issue related to the topic of water. As sources, use the selections provided in this unit, as well as material available in your school resource centre and through the Internet. In your production, demonstrate the ways in which video can be used to argue a position and persuade viewers of the need to take action. During the production process, keep ongoing notes on your choices to help you reflect on and increase the effectiveness of your process and final product.

3 poetry

I wrote when I was interested in something, I never did sit down to write poems at a certain time. I think that's pretty silly. You write when you have something in your mind that says "this is a poem."

— *Al Purdy*

Writing for me is a puzzle, the working out of a puzzle. I have to find the right word, the right line, the right sentence all the time.

— *Dionne Brand*

Engineers' Corner

Wendy Cope

Wendy Cope, who was born in Erith, Kent, England, in 1945, is known for her humorous poetry. "Engineers' Corner" is from her book *Making Cocoa for Kingsley Amis* (1986), in which she includes parodies of writers she admires. Cope, who studied literature at Oxford University, contends that humorous poetry can convey a serious message: "I believe that a humorous poem can also be 'serious,' deeply felt, and say something that matters." She has received numerous awards, including the American Academy of Arts and Letters Award for Light Verse in 1995. How do countries decide which of their citizens should be honoured with statues and other commemorative hallmarks, such as stamps or holidays? How important are writers and artists to their countries? What other groups might deserve special honours and why?

Engineers' Corner

Why isn't there an Engineers' Corner in Westminster Abbey? In Britain
we've always made more fuss of a ballad than a blueprint.... How many
schoolchildren dream of becoming great engineers?
— Advertisement placed in The Times *by the Engineering Council*

We make more fuss of ballads than of blueprints—
That's why so many poets end up rich,
While engineers scrape by in cheerless garrets.
Who needs a bridge or dam? Who needs a ditch?

Whereas the person who can write a sonnet
Has got it made. It's always been the way,
For everybody knows that we need poems
And everybody reads them every day.

Yes, life is hard if you choose engineering—
You're sure to need another job as well;   10
You'll have to plan your projects in the evenings
Instead of going out. It must be hell.

While well-heeled poets ride around in Daimlers,
You'll burn the midnight oil to earn a crust,
With no hope of a statue in the Abbey,
With no hope, even, of a modest bust.

No wonder small boys dream of writing couplets
And spurn the bike, the lorry and the train.
There's far too much encouragement for poets—
That's why this country's going down the drain.   20

Notes

Westminster Abbey a cathedral in London, England, built between 1045 and approximately 1400 CE in the English gothic style. It is where the monarchs of the United Kingdom are crowned and is the burial place of the country's leading poets, in a section called "Poets' Corner."

The Times a newspaper based in London, England

Daimler a type of luxury car

bust a sculpture of a person's head, shoulders, and chest

Activities

1. Reread the advertisement at the beginning of this poem, in which the British Engineering Council conducts a campaign to bring public attention to the contributions of engineers and to recruit young people into the profession. With a partner, consider the explicit or literal meaning of the advertisement. Next consider what implicit message it conveys. To what extent do you agree with the implicit message?

2. Do research to create a working definition of the term *verbal irony*. Then create a two-column chart. In one column, summarize the literal meaning of each stanza. In the second column, record the key idea you believe Cope intends to convey in each stanza. Create a thesis statement for an analytical essay in which you explore and evaluate Cope's use of verbal irony. In your essay, contrast the differences between the literal and the intended meaning, speculate on Cope's purpose, and evaluate how effectively Cope has achieved her purpose.

Is the Pathetic Fallacy True?

Elizabeth Brewster

Elizabeth Brewster was born in Chipman, New Brunswick, in 1922. She has lived in Ontario, Alberta, British Columbia, Saskatchewan, England, and the United States. From 1972 until her retirement in 1992, she taught in the Department of English at the University of Saskatchewan. Brewster has been the recipient of numerous prizes for her poetry and has been awarded several honorary degrees. She is the author of twenty-two books—poetry, short stories, and novels— as well as being a founding member of the literary journal *Fiddlehead* and a lifetime member of the League of Canadian Poets. Based on your own experience, how would you explain the phrase "a sense of wonder"? Why do you think this sense either increases or decreases as you grow older?

Is the Pathetic Fallacy True?

When I was a child
the stones were living.
Hot under my hand, they felt like flesh,
and sands slipped through my fingers
with a caress.

Yes, everything was alive:

the clumsy, roaring wind
stepped on the flounced pink dress
of the apple-tree,
tearing it to shreds   10

the puffed cheeks of clouds

the brook with its pebbled tongue
and the hoarse old grave old sea
its gravelly song

and earth itself
a brown warm girl
turning and tanning in the sun.

All false, all wrong,
somebody told me:
Winds are not lovers,   20
clumsy or gentle.
There's no blood
in stones,
no tears in water.

Nevertheless
sometimes lately when I touch a chair or table
I think I feel atoms stir
under my fingers

and at night in dreams I hear
the small remote voices of grains of dust   30
or the inaudible whispers of stars

as they will speak to me some time
when I lie with the living grass above me
and the wind my old lover
singing me to sleep

and to wake

Notes

pathetic fallacy the act of attributing human emotions or characteristics
to inanimate objects or to nature

Activities

1. Elizabeth Brewster begins her poem by asking a question in the title.
Paraphrase the title "Is the Pathetic Fallacy True?" restating the poet's central question in your own words. With a classmate, discuss how the poem
relates to your paraphrase of its title.

2. In a class presentation, explore the relationship in "Is the Pathetic Fallacy
True?" between Brewster's use of personification and her focus on the
topic of the pathetic fallacy.

EVENING

Mary Cassatt

About the Visual Mary Cassatt was born in 1844, in Allegheny City, Pennsylvania, now part of Pittsburgh. She attended the Pennsylvania Academy of Fine Arts and later continued her studies in Europe. In 1874, she settled in Paris, where she came under the influence of the French painter Edgar Degas, who invited her to join the Impressionist group of artists. Cassatt adopted the Impressionist technique of applying paint rapidly from a bright palette. An exhibition of Japanese prints inspired her to begin printmaking. She also practised the art of etching. What characteristics, if any, do poetry and visual works of art have in common? How does your response to works of art compare with your response to poetry?

Activities

1. Cassatt has been praised for her ability to create "the joyous quietude, the tranquil simplicity of an interior." Discuss the impact of *Evening* in terms of this statement. Record your response to the works in your journal and then share responses in a small group.

2. Mary Cassatt's work often expresses the bond between women and their children. The models who sat for *Evening* were Cassatt's own mother and sister. By what means does Cassatt articulate the close relationship between her adult sister and her mother in this work? In your answer, consider factors such as composition and the use of lighting.

1879/80, soft-ground etching and aquatint on cream laid paper, 20 cm x 22 cm

Birch Bark

Michael Ondaatje

Canadian novelist, poet, and filmmaker Michael Ondaatje was born in Sri Lanka (then known as Ceylon) in 1943. After studying in England, Ondaatje immigrated to Canada in 1962; today he lives in Toronto. Ondaatje, who published his first book of poetry in 1967, has received two Governor General's Literary Awards for poetry. In 1992, he received the prestigious Booker Prize for his novel *The English Patient,* subsequently made into an Academy Award-winning film. Recent books include *Handwriting,* a book of poetry, and *Anil's Ghost,* a novel set in Sri Lanka that was co-winner of the Giller Prize in 2000. Ondaatje's work—which often blends fact and fiction, poetry and prose, and personal and political issues—is characterized by strong images. He has said that his writing is less influenced by books than by other art forms, such as music and painting. In what ways do other art forms influence your writings? Would art forms primarily influence your creative writing, or might they have an impact on your non-fiction writing as well?

Birch Bark

(for George Whalley)

An hour after the storm on Birch Lake
the island bristles. Rock. Leaves still falling.
At this time, in the hour after lightning
we release the canoes.
Silence of water
purer than the silence of rock.
A paddle touches itself. We move
over blind mercury, feel the muscle
within the river, the blade
weave in dark water.   10

Now each casual word is precisely chosen
passed from bow to stern, as if
leaning back to pass a canteen.
There are echoes, repercussions of water.
We are in absolute landscape,
among names that fold in onto themselves.

To circle the island means witnessing
the blue grey dust of a heron
released out of the trees.
So the dialogue slides   20
nothing more than friendship
an old song we break into
not needing all the words.

We are past naming the country.
The reflections are never there
without us, without the exhaustion
of water and trees after storm.

Notes

George Whalley a Canadian literary critic, translator, and author of books, including *Poetic Process* (1973)

Birch Lake a lake in northern Ontario, approximately 100 km north of Red Lake, partially accessible only by bush plane. The area is a ruggedly beautiful terrain of lakes and timberland.

mercury a liquid metallic chemical compound, known colloquially as quicksilver. The chemical symbol for mercury (Hg) is derived from the Greek word *hydrargyros*, meaning "water silver."

Activities

1. The author uses the five senses to communicate his experiences in this poem. Create a five-column chart, labelling each column with one of the senses. In your chart, list every word or image in the poem that falls into one of your five categories. In a small group, compare your findings. Have a class discussion by answering questions such as: Which sense did the author evoke most often in this poem? Which sensory detail do you find most effective and why? In what ways would the poem be different if it evoked only one of the senses?

2. Like many poems, the meaning of "Birch Bark" appears to exist on several levels—literal and figurative, conscious and unconscious. The different levels of meaning are partially created through Ondaatje's use of personification. In a small group, list every instance of personification that occurs in the poem. Have a group discussion on the following: To what extent does this poem explore the relationship between humans and nature? To what extent is it about the nature of friendship? With your group, use chart paper to create a graphic organizer such as a Venn diagram to document some of the poem's themes. Under each general theme that you list, provide images or phrases from the poem that contribute to that theme. Share your findings with the class.

vancouver–courtenay–calgary

George Bowering

Born in the Okanagan Valley of British Columbia in 1935, George Bowering has made the landscape and people of western Canada a major focus of his poetry and fiction. He has published dozens of books and taught at universities in Alberta, Quebec, and British Columbia. Bowering once said, "When I started writing, I wanted mainly to be a sports writer who 'committed poetry' from time to time." A major figure in contemporary Canadian literature, Bowering has won two Governor General's Awards, one in 1969 for poetry, the other in 1980 for fiction. One critic wrote that "Bowering calls on the language and cadence of common speech; a witty sense of play animates his vision in all his poetic works." What places have had the most impact on you as an individual? What features of the landscape were particularly important to you as a child, and why? In what ways did the people who lived there influence you?

vancouver–courtenay–calgary

The ocean
is the last thing
to think of
leaving Vancouver

to the Island
offshore up to Sunshine
Coast where shells
sprout out of the water

like eggs in chicken nests
pluckt, eaten all   10
in an hour.
A thing taken

for granted this time
of year. But
think: next year
we will live across

the Rockies: earth
will be the largest concern.
A thin trickle of water
cuts thru cow country mud.   20

Shrimp sells for
three dollars a pound;
sunshine is dry with
wide white mountain clouds.

The plains
are ever present
to the eye
looking back, smooth as water.

Notes

Sunshine Coast refers to an 86 km stretch of mainland coast that begins just north of Vancouver in British Columbia

Activities

1. In this poem, Bowering uses words and phrases to evoke strong emotions about places on opposite sides of the Rocky Mountains. For the narrator, what emotions are associated with the places described in the poem? Which place do you think the narrator prefers? Use specific references to the poem to support your response.

2. Early in his career, Bowering was strongly influenced by developments in modern American poetry that used plain, concrete language, avoiding abstraction and the excessive use of similes and metaphors. Examine the language Bowering uses in this poem and assess the extent to which it exhibits these characteristics while still evoking powerful feelings. What parts of speech are predominant in the poem? Why do you think the poet has chosen these parts of speech?

Prairie Flight

Dorothy Livesay

Dorothy Livesay was born in Winnipeg, Manitoba, in 1909. Livesay's father was a journalist and author who was the first general manager of the Canadian Press. Her mother was a poet of distinction and a translator of poetry from Ukrainian into English. Livesay attended the University of British Columbia, the University of Toronto, and the Sorbonne in Paris. Livesay lived at various times in British Columbia, New Brunswick, and Alberta. She was a founding member of the League of Canadian Poets and won numerous awards for her poetry, including two Governor General's Awards, in 1944 and in 1947. Livesay became an officer of the Order of Canada in 1987. She died in 1996. Livesay's early poetry deals with issues of women's rights and international peace, as well as the plight of the aged. Her later poems tend to reflect more personal and intimate emotions and reflections. Do you prefer poetry that is highly personal or poetry that deals with contemporary issues? Do you think one of these approaches is more valuable than the other? If so, why?

Prairie Flight

In Canada
no need for abstract painters.
Farmers have shaped
with their hands, their boots, their horses' hooves
last, with tractors
a bright geometry imposed
on buffalo bones

Staring at land
only for wheat and hay
with the curled rivers and lakes
sore thumbs
right in their way
those silent carvers of the land
send messages they never see.

Activities

1. Have a class discussion about how Livesay uses free verse to fuse the form and the meaning of her poem. In your discussion, refer to the poem's speech-like rhythm, the natural, easy-flowing word order, the variations of line length according to the importance of ideas, and the control of shorter and longer pauses.

2. Livesay ends her first stanza with the lines "a bright geometry imposed / on buffalo bones." In several paragraphs, discuss the effectiveness of these lines in terms of their descriptive power, their use of alliteration, and the historical context to which they refer.

Fern Hill

Dylan Thomas

Dylan Thomas was born in Swansea, Wales, in 1914. The son of an English schoolmaster, Thomas never learned the Welsh language. At the age of twenty, he moved to London and published his first collection of poems. During his lifetime, Thomas produced books of poetry, essays, stories, radio plays, and film scripts. Thomas' poetry, which was influenced by the intricate patterns of sound and meaning of the English poet Gerard Manley Hopkins, was seen as a reaction against the classicism of the poet W.H. Auden. An international literary star during his lifetime, he died in 1953. Thomas' passion, his arresting imagery, and his bold experiments with language have ensured him a permanent place in the pantheon of best-loved twentieth-century poets. Would you say that the majority of poets espouse an optimistic or a pessimistic view of life? To what extent do you think this attitude reflects the attitude of the general public?

Fern Hill

Now as I was young and easy under the apple boughs
About the lilting house and happy as the grass was green,
   The night above the dingle starry,
     Time let me hail and climb
   Golden in the heydays of his eyes,
And honoured among wagons I was prince of the apple towns
And once below a time I lordly had the trees and leaves
     Trail with daisies and barley
   Down the rivers of the windfall light.

And as I was green and carefree, famous among the barns   10
About the happy yard and singing as the farm was home,
   In the sun that is young once only,
     Time let me play and be
   Golden in the mercy of his means,
And green and golden I was huntsman and herdsman, the calves
Sang to my horn, the foxes on the hills barked clear and cold,
     And the sabbath rang slowly
   In the pebbles of the holy streams.

All the sun long it was running, it was lovely, the hay
Fields high as the house, the tunes from the chimneys, it was air   20
   And playing, lovely and watery
     And fire green as grass.
   And nightly under the simple stars
As I rode to sleep the owls were bearing the farm away,
All the moon long I heard, blessed among stables, the nightjars
   Flying with the ricks, and the horses
     Flashing into the dark.

And then to awake, and the farm, like a wanderer white
With the dew, come back, the cock on his shoulder: it was all
   Shining, it was Adam and maiden, 30
     The sky gathered again
   And the sun grew round that very day.
So it must have been after the birth of the simple light
In the first, spinning place, the spellbound horses walking warm
   Out of the whinnying green stable
     On to the fields of praise.

And honoured among foxes and pheasants by the gay house
Under the new made clouds and happy as the heart was long,
   In the sun born over and over,
     I ran my heedless ways, 40
   My wishes raced through the house high hay
And nothing I cared, at my sky blue trades, that time allows
In all his tuneful turning so few and such morning songs
   Before the children green and golden
     Follow him out of grace,

Nothing I cared, in the lamb white days, that time would take me
Up to the swallow thronged loft by the shadow of my hand,
   In the moon that is always rising,
     Nor that riding to sleep
   I should hear him fly with the high fields 50
And wake to the farm forever fled from the childless land.
Oh as I was young and easy in the mercy of his means,
     Time held me green and dying
   Though I sang in my chains like the sea.

Notes

Fern Hill the farm of Ann Jones, Dylan Thomas' aunt, where he spent his summer holidays as a boy

dingle a small, wooded valley; from the Middle English *dell*, meaning a hollow

hail to call out an enthusiastic greeting

heydays the period of one's life in which one experiences the greatest vigour or prosperity; possibly of Germanic origin, perhaps from the low German *heidi* or *heida*, an exclamation of joy

windfall a fruit brought down by the wind

night-jars medium-sized nocturnal birds such as whippoorwills or nighthawks; also called goatsuckers

ricks stacks of hay in the open air

Adam and maiden Adam and Eve in the Garden of Eden as described in the Book of Genesis in the Bible

Activities

1. Do you think that Dylan Thomas' purpose in writing this poem was celebratory or cautionary? Based on your response, how would you express either its celebratory or cautionary view of time? To what extent do the poet's ideas fit in with your own experiences and observations?

2. How would you describe the predominant tone in the first stanza of "Fern Hill"? Contrast this with the tone of the last three lines of the poem. Go through the poem stanza by stanza, identifying words and images that foreshadow the emotional closure which Thomas voices at the end. Do you think the poet has managed to successfully integrate the innocent joy of the child with the mature resignation of the adult, without invalidating either one? Explain.

Amiri Baraka

C. Daniel Dawson

About the Visual   The subject of this portrait is the writer Amiri Baraka, born LeRoi Jones in 1934. Baraka was educated at Howard University and became part of the 1950s "beat" scene in New York's Greenwich Village. The assassination of activist Malcolm X in 1965 led Baraka to distance himself from white culture. He dropped his Western name and adopted black nationalist views, which he later abandoned for Marxism. Today Baraka continues his work as a writer, speaker, and activist for African-American causes. The photographer of this portrait, C. Daniel Dawson, was born in 1944 and studied at Columbia University. Dawson is an award-winning African-American photographer and filmmaker. Why do you think an intentional portrait of a person might reveal either more or less than a candid snapshot of the same person?

Activities

1. Write a poem in which you respond to some aspect of this photograph. For example, you might focus on its mood, its subject, the emotion you discover within the photograph, or the emotion it elicits from you. Have a partner read a polished version of your poem to provide feedback on the consistency of your tone. Make revisions to strengthen your work. Share your poem with the class.

2. According to the American photographer Robert Llewellyn, "Every photograph you make is a self-portrait." What do you think the portrait of Amiri Baraka reveals about C. Daniel Dawson? Consider the choices Dawson made in terms of subject, props, mood, medium, lighting, and composition.

c. 1970, gelatin silver print ▶

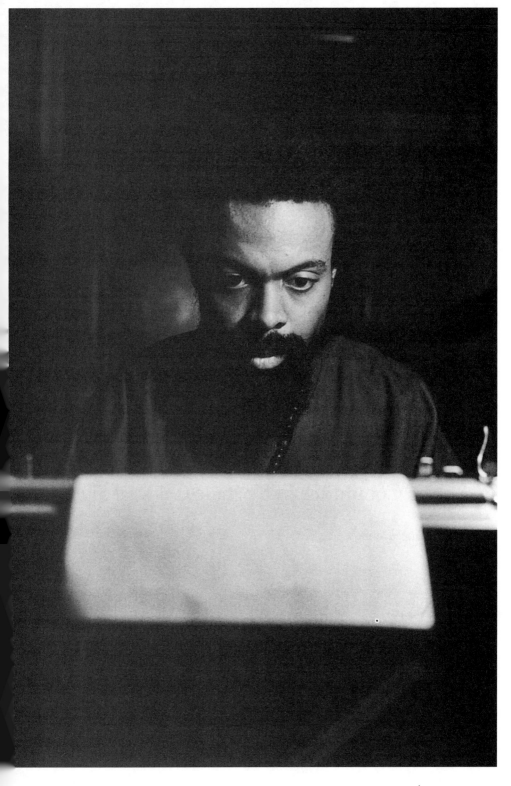

The Committee to Upgrade Celestial Signs

Kurt Brown

Kurt Brown was born in Brooklyn, New York, in 1944. He attended the University of Connecticut. For many years, he lived in Aspen, Colorado, where he founded the Aspen Writers' Conference. Brown has edited several books of poetry, and he published his own first collection, *Return of the Prodigals*, in 1999. Why do you think people are fascinated by the patterns that stars form in the night sky? What human impulse caused the ancient Greeks and other civilizations to connect these patterns to their myths and heroes?

The Committee to Upgrade Celestial Signs

> meets once a year
> > to re-evaluate old myths
> > > that spangle heaven:
> > > Taurus,   Draco,
> Perseus,
> > Boötes…
> outdated in their Greek shining.

Quickly renamed,
                    they are reconfigured into modern shapes
                         —cluster by cluster—
              Guitaris Major,   Double Arches,
      Empire State Building,
                              Bottle of Coke...
Each fall,
                the firmament glitters like a new marquee,
                   a hit parade of celebrities
                                     to correspond
         with the season's upcoming shows:
                where Cepheus glittered—
                         the visage of an actress
                                      shines;
      Libra morphs into the body
                              of a reigning hunk;
          the Pleiades burn all night—
                             divas in a female rock group.
Trained over centuries
                   to forget the past
entire populations suffer
                        from cultural
                            amnesia
                   catalyzed by constant change—
"This is NOW!"
                a favorite bumper sticker shouts,
         and
             "Welcome to the Interactive Cosmos!"
Constellations rise and fall,
                      brief as ads
                            that flash across the blank screen
                                of heaven.

Computers work around the clock
                    to thread stars
                                into relevant patterns
      while last year's icons
                    fade
                      like the memory
    Of someone's face
                before cosmetic surgery.
At last
        the Committee votes on current choices,
                      having sifted
      through a copious Printout
                of Possible Skies:
Hands go up around the table
                    as they nod and smile—
      with the stroke of a finger
                the Zodiac is realigned
    against the infinite blackness behind the stars.

Notes

Taurus, Draco, Perseus, Boötes, Cepheus, Libra, Pleiades constellations of stars, named after figures in Greek mythology

Activities

1. Make a list of key characteristics of contemporary life that Brown highlights in this poem. Choose three that you feel are key to the poem. Around each concept, cluster relevant words and phrases from the poem and form your own associations around each concept. In small groups, compare your clusters and create a statement about the meaning and theme of the poem.

2. Write an essay in which you analyze and assess the style of the poem based on its diction, syntax, and literary devices. Consider the effect of these choices on such elements as tone and theme, and evaluate the impact of these choices.

The Heroes You Had as a Girl

Bronwen Wallace

Bronwen Wallace was a poet, short story writer, essayist, and film-maker. She was born in 1945 in Kingston, Ontario. She attended Queen's University, then moved to Windsor where she became a social activist, focusing on issues concerning the working class and women. After seven years, she moved back to Kingston, where she taught at St. Lawrence College and Queen's University and made documentary films. Wallace received the National Magazine Award, the Pat Lowther Award, and the Du Maurier Award for Poetry. Wallace died in 1989. Who comes to mind when you consider the heroes you had when you were a child? What might those heroes reveal about you at that time? Who are some of your heroes today and what qualities do they have in common with your earlier heroes?

The Heroes You Had as a Girl

The heroes you had as a girl
were always three grades ahead of you
taller than the boys in your own class
taller even than your brothers
and the layers of muscle ripening
under their thin shirts their jeans
made your palms itch
for something you didn't know how to explain
but wanted to   sitting with your girlfriends
in the hot dry grass   10
at the edge of the parking-lot
where all day Saturday they worked on their cars
hunched over the greasy mysteries of their engines
occasionally raising their heads
their eyes flicking
to where you were included
as part of the landscape

Sundays they practised more dangerous manoeuvres
till your eyes stung with the smell
of oil and burning rubber   20
and once they built arches of flaming
orange crates   you remember them spinning
through the air when one car missed
remember the screams that burned your throat
before you realized no-one was hurt
your voices fluttering like foolish birds
on the wild currents of their laughter

and now twenty years later the hero
who drove that car returns as unexpectedly
as the memory and just as out of place   30
you watch him study a display of bathroom fixtures
in the hardware department of Simpsons-Sears
he's grown fat and balding
and you think how easy it would be
to walk right over tap him
on the shoulder say *hello*
remember me   and if he didn't
you could laugh it off
at least you've kept your figure
that's not what stops you now   40
though something does
and as he walks away
you can feel the dry grass biting
the backs of your legs   the uncomfortable
angle of your knees as you sat just so
practising your own dangerous manoeuvres
not being noticed   not noticing
the other girls   forgetting their names
the shapes of their faces reddening in the sun
(though you remember those burning arches   50
your throat tightening again around those foolish screams,
you think you could explain it now
and that's what stops you
knowing you want nothing less
than for him to turn
peel off his shirt to show you
burn scars on his chest
and in the sullen landscape of his eyes
you want the faces of those girls
your own among them burning   60
brighter than any fire

Activities

1. In a letter, Bronwen Wallace once expressed concern that women's writing was often discounted as "personal" rather than "universal." Consider to whom this poem is addressed. Why do you think Wallace chose to use the second-person point of view? Meet with a small group to discuss whether this is a poem about human experience or one woman's personal story. Try to come to consensus on your conclusions. Report to the class, providing evidence for your interpretation.

2. With a group, present a readers' theatre performance of the poem. Decide what meaning you want to convey to your listeners and explore various ways of reading in order to create the effects you want. After your performance, write an independent analysis of what you learned about the meaning and style of the poem through your reading.

Another Viewpoint: Critical Approaches

Gender criticism examines how gender identity influences both the creation and the reception of literary works. In your view, to what extent, if any, do male and female writers differ in their choice of subject or in their perspective? Formulate a thesis to explain whether you think that women are more likely to create works that interest other women and whether the same can be said of men. When you read or view a story, to what extent are you aware of the gender of the author? In what ways might your gender influence the way in which you read a work of literature?

foremother

Lillian Bouzane

Lillian Bouzane was born in Little Bay NDB, Newfoundland, in 1932. A writer of fiction, non-fiction, and poetry, she has received many literary prizes, including Government of Newfoundland and Labrador Arts and Letters Awards for both fiction and non-fiction. In 1999, she published *In the Hands of the Living God*, a novel that recounts the story of John Cabot, and his discovery of Newfoundland, through the eyes of his wife, Mathye Cabot of Venice. The novel is written in the form of letters and diary entries. "Foremother" recounts selected events from the life of the narrator's great-grandmother. How is life different for women today than for their great-grandmothers? When you think of women in Canada in the 1800s, what images come to mind?

foremother

my great-grandmother watched her husband
wash overboard
in a Labrador gale
just one more fishing skipper lost
in the Strait of Belle Isle
nobody noticed

she was a grieving woman
until the merchant at Quirpon
moved to short-change her by fifty quintal
on the fish from their last voyage   10
with a scorn she bothered to show
she ordered the catch reloaded
took the wheel herself
and set her course for the next harbour
where she sold it at a neat profit

steeling her nerve
she raised her flag to full staff
and sailed into her home port
the priest came to see her
to admonish and comfort   20
she gave him good whiskey
with a glint in her eye
that said "don't meddle with me"
he didn't

each year thereafter
she made two voyages to the Labrador Coast
spring and summer
hired for hands only bedlamer boys
kept her name clear
took one trip to Boston each year   30
left the children behind
with orders to say to the neighbours
"don't meddle with my mother's good name"
they obeyed her

when she was fifty
and had fourteen schooners in her name
she married again
a man half her age
she made him her bookkeeper/bartender
he was good at both   40
she got ten winters out of him
she said so herself

once she sailed her flagship
to Montreal to buy a dress
her only purchase
when the Duke's son came
to plant a tree
and settle other matters of State
she danced the night through with him
at the government ball   50
he walked her down to the harbour
they sat on her quarter-deck 'til dawn
drinking port and singing bawdy songs
it was said he asked her to marry him
it was said she turned him down
she already had more ships than he

before the bank crash of 1894
she liquidated her assets
bought gold
lived another ten years to be ninety   60
to the consternation of her sons
and the delight of her daughters
who loved her
and got her money
they passed it on to my mother
who educated my five sisters and me
with what was left of it

I, her offspring, thrice removed
write this poem in praise of her
and tell only half I know   70

Notes

Strait of Belle Isle a body of water separating the island of Newfoundland
from Labrador

fifty quintal approximately 2,300 kg; from the Old French word *quintal* and
the medieval Latin word *quintalen*; originally from the Arabic word *qintār*

thrice removed three generations later

Activities

1. Choose a scene from this poem that is particularly rich in descriptive
details, and represent it in a visual form, such as a sketch, web, map, or
word cluster. Use a line from the poem as a caption. Compare your choice
and representation with those of other students. Which scenes were most
often chosen and why?

2. Analyze and assess the effectiveness of the free-verse form that Bouzane
has chosen for this poem. Next, consider how Bouzane has created imagery
and to what effect she has used repetition. Be prepared to explain and support your analysis in a class discussion.

Another Viewpoint: Critical Approaches

In a small group, use dictionaries, other reference materials, and the Internet
to research the term *feminism*, and try to reach consensus on a working
definition of this term. Once you have refined your definition, have a class discussion on whether this poem is or is not a "feminist" poem.

to you who would wage war against me

Kateri Akiwenzie-Damm

Born in Toronto in 1965, Kateri Akiwenzie-Damm is Anishnaabe of mixed ancestry from the Chippewas of Nawash First Nation. Akiwenzie-Damm received a master's degree in English literature from the University of Ottawa. She credits her grandmother with providing her with the inspiration to become a writer. Akiwenzie-Damm, who has published numerous collections of poetry and fiction, is deeply committed to promoting the work of indigenous writers, not only from Canada but other countries as well. In 1999, she established NiSHin Productions, an indigenous performing arts production company. She lives and works on the Cape Croker Reserve on the Saugeen Peninsula near Wiarton, Ontario. This poem explores a relationship. When you interact with someone, how do you try to figure out what that person is really thinking and feeling? How might a person try to hide his or her true thoughts and feelings from you?

to you who would wage war against me

i

there are many lines
you have not traced on my palms
still
you think you know me

when i speak
you nod knowingly
as if
you've already read my mind
and are only politely acknowledging
the confirmation of my spoken words   10

ii

but you cannot possibly know
what i've been contemplating
these days

my head is full of blood
but you show no fear
and i do not trust my hands
they look to me like stones

you do not cower when i approach
though i feel like a runaway train
and i can hear your voice cool and steady   20
while my brain screams profanities
into the air around your ears

our past has given you no reason
to be afraid
but still i am surprised you cannot see
the danger burning brightly in my eyes
the fire i am struggling to control

iii

as i sit stewing in the kitchen's false light
with tears my daughter
comes to me   30
frightened by what she cannot see
afraid tonight to sleep
i hold her in my arms
singing soft words of comfort
feeling her heart quickly
beating against my chest
knowing before i can think that
i have forgiven us
for our stupid little wars

knowing in that incandescent light   40
that anger will never move me
as delicately as she has moved me
this night

Notes

incandescent artificial light produced by a hot, glowing filament

Activities

1. The title of the poem refers to a nameless "you" and "me." Look closely at the poem for clues about the personalities of the two people referred to by the pronouns in the title. By reading between the lines, what can you conclude about the personalities of the two individuals, the conflict between them, and how they react to each other? Be sure to support your observations with references to the poem.

2. The poem deals with two powerful contrasting emotions, anger and love. What words and images does the writer use to convey the intensity of these emotions? What is the significance of the narrator's observation that "anger will never move me / as delicately as she has moved me / this night"? In the end, why does the narrator's concern and love for her daughter move her more than anger? In general, which of the two emotions do you think is stronger? Explain your choice.

Another Viewpoint: Culture

Consider the extent to which Akiwenzie-Damm's cultural background adds another possible level of meaning to this poem. Is it culturally significant that the "you" and "me" remain unidentified? Who else could be referred to by these generic pronouns? Use the Internet to research information on Kateri Akiwenzie-Damm. Then, in an analytical essay, use what you discover about the author as the basis for your interpretation of the poem.

I, Icarus

Alden Nowlan

Alden Nowlan was born in Windsor, Nova Scotia, in 1933. A remark-ably prolific writer, he published twenty-four books. Although his formal education ended at grade five, Nowlan became a successful journalist, story writer, playwright, and novelist. In 1967, he was the recipient of the Governor General's Award for his book *Bread, Wine and Salt*. Throughout his career, Nowlan gained notoriety for fic-tionalizing his own life. About his writing, he said, "I write for the same reason that I'm six-feet three-inches tall: I can't do anything about it." One critic wrote that Nowlan's work is "rich in regional sensibility and in affection for ordinary people, but connected—by Nowlan's intelligence, temperament, and reading—to a literary world far beyond folk culture." Nowlan became well known for this ability to combine the views of ordinary people and events with a sense of the mystery of life. To what extent do you think literature deals with the mysteries of human life?

I, Icarus

There was a time when I could fly. I swear it.
Perhaps, if I think hard for a moment, I can even tell you the year.
My room was on the ground floor at the rear of the house.
My bed faced a window.
Night after night I lay on my bed and willed myself to fly.
It was hard work, I can tell you.
Sometimes I lay perfectly still for an hour before I felt
       my body rising from the bed.
I rose slowly, slowly until I floated three or four feet
       above the floor.
Then, with a kind of swimming motion, I propelled myself
       toward the window.
Outside, I rose higher and higher, above the pasture fence,
       above the clothesline, above the dark, haunted trees
       beyond the pasture.
And, all the time, I heard the music of flutes.
It seemed the wind made this music.
And sometimes there were voices singing.

Notes

Icarus refers to the story of Daedalus and Icarus. According to this Greek legend, Daedalus was the architect of the elaborate labyrinth that housed the Minotaur in Crete. Daedalus helped the hero Theseus escape from the labyrinth after he had been imprisoned there by the king of Crete. As punishment, Daedalus and his son, Icarus, were themselves placed in the labyrinth. Determined to escape, Daedalus made a pair of wings for himself and one for his son. Before taking off, Daedalus cautioned his son about flying too close to the sun, but Icarus disobeyed his father. The heat of the sun melted the wax that held the feathers together and Icarus dropped into the sea and drowned.

Activities

1. Reread the poem, looking specifically at the words and images Nowlan uses to describe the experience of flight. Why does he say that willing himself to fly was "hard work"? Why is his flight limited to "three or four feet above the floor" at first? How and why does the nature of his flight change once he leaves the house? Why are the trees below him "dark" and "haunted"? How do you explain the music he hears?

2. In literature, the source of an allusion—a direct or indirect reference in one work to another work or to a historical person or event—is often mythological or religious. Use reference materials to investigate the links in this poem to Icarus and to Aeolian harps. How does the allusion to Icarus enhance the experience described by the narrator? How does the allusion to Aeolian harps enrich the meaning of the last three lines of the poem? Can you detect other allusions in the poem?

Another Viewpoint: Archetypal Patterns

Many human situations, such as the idealism or rebelliousness of youth, are inherently similar and can be analyzed as archetypes. The psychologist Carl Jung suggested that the meaning of the Icarus myth is related to the idealism of youth, which often leads to over-confidence. He warns us that "the human ego can be exalted to experience godlike attributes, but only at the cost of over-reaching itself and falling to disaster." In a well-developed paragraph, consider the extent to which Jung's observation is demonstrated in Nowlan's poem.

Musée des Beaux Arts

W.H. Auden

Wystan Hugh Auden was born in 1907, in York, England. Auden was interested primarily in science and at first intended to be a mining engineer, but by 1922 he had discovered his vocation as a poet. His first volume of poetry was published in 1930. The brilliance and originality of his work brought him a wide readership and much praise from critics. As well as writing poetry, Auden collaborated on plays and on travel books that focused on countries such as China and Iceland. He also wrote opera libretti, working with renowned twentieth-century composers including Benjamin Britten and Igor Stravinsky. In his works, he addressed social, political, and religious issues. In 1939, he moved to the United States, where he won the Pulitzer Prize for *The Age of Anxiety* in 1948. Auden eventually returned to England, where he died in 1973. "Musée des Beaux Arts" is a poem Auden wrote in response to a painting by Pieter Brueghel entitled *Landscape with the Fall of Icarus*, which appears on page 367 of this anthology. The poem explores how humans react when disasters occur to others. When you see news reports of wars and natural disasters, to what extent do you feel a sense of personal obligation toward the people involved? How active a role do you think Canada should take in solving problems in other countries?

Musée des Beaux Arts

About suffering they were never wrong,
The Old Masters: how well they understood
Its human position; how it takes place
While someone else is eating or opening a window or just walking
    dully along;
How, when the aged are reverently, passionately waiting
For the miraculous birth, there always must be
Children who did not specially want it to happen, skating
On a pond at the edge of the wood:
They never forgot
That even the dreadful martyrdom must run its course   10
Anyhow in a corner, some untidy spot
Where the dogs go on with their doggy life and the torturer's horse
Scratches its innocent behind on a tree.

In Brueghel's Icarus, for instance: how everything turns away
Quite leisurely from the disaster; the ploughman may
Have heard the splash, the forsaken cry,
But for him it was not an important failure; the sun shone
As it had to on the white legs disappearing into the green
Water; and the expensive delicate ship that must have seen
Something amazing, a boy falling out of the sky,   20
Had somewhere to get to and sailed calmly on.

Notes

Musée des Beaux Arts an art museum in Brussels, Belgium, where Brueghel's *Landscape with the Fall of Icarus* can be found

Old Masters distinguished European painters of the fifteenth through seventeenth centuries whose works have become recognized as masterpieces. Among the Old Masters are Botticelli, Da Vinci, Michelangelo, Raphael, Titian, Bosch, Holbein, Brueghel, El Greco, Rubens, Velázquez, and Rembrandt.

miraculous birth the birth of Christ to the Virgin Mary and her husband Joseph, as recorded in the New Testament of the Bible

dreadful martyrdom the death of Christ on the cross. In Christianity, Christ is believed to have sacrificed himself to save humanity.

Brueghel Pieter Brueghel the Elder, a Flemish painter of the sixteenth century noted for landscapes and scenes in the lives of ordinary people; also spelled Bruegel and Breughel

Icarus In the Greek legend, Daedalus and his son Icarus escape from the island of Crete using wings of wax and bird feathers. Icarus disregards his father's warning not to fly too close to the sun; his wings melt and he falls into the sea.

Activities

1. In the legend of Icarus and Daedalus, as told by the Roman poet Ovid (43 BCE–17 CE), the plowman, the shepherd, and the angler witnessed with amazement the fall of Icarus from the sky. How is Auden's poem a meditation on the difference between the original story and Brueghel's version of it? In general, what do you think influences varied interpretations of an event?

2. Auden combines allusions to Christianity and Greek mythology in this poem. Discuss the connections he makes between the "miraculous birth," "the dreadful martyrdom," and the story of Icarus and Daedalus. How do these allusions contribute to an understanding of the poem?

People on the Bridge

Wislawa Szymborska

Translated by Joanna Trzeciak

Wislawa Szymborska was born in Konik, Poland, in 1923. In 1952, she joined the Communist Party, but later repudiated her membership and disclaimed the work she published during her tenure in the Party. Szymborska, whose poetry has been translated into many languages, has written only 200 poems, in part because she discards much of what she writes. She received the Nobel Prize in Literature in 1996. In her acceptance speech, Szymborska said, "Inspiration is not the exclusive privilege of poets or artists generally. Inspiration visits all those who've consciously chosen their calling and do their job with love and imagination. Difficulties and setbacks never quell their curiosity." This poem was inspired by a Japanese print, *Sudden Shower at Ohashi Bridge* by Hiroshige Utagawa, which appears on page 369 of this anthology. When you look at a print or a painting, to what extent do you speculate about the story behind the picture or the fate of the people who are illustrated? Are you more inclined to project yourself into the scene or to view it with detached objectivity?

People on the Bridge

Strange planet and strange people on it.
They yield to time, but don't want to recognize time.
They have their ways of expressing resistance.
They make pictures such as this:

Nothing remarkable at first glance.
One can see water,
one riverbank,
a narrow boat strenuously moving upstream,
a bridge over the water,
and people on the bridge.   10
They are clearly picking up the pace,
as rain starts lashing down from a dark cloud.

The point is, nothing happens further.
The cloud changes neither shape nor color.
The rain neither subsides nor surges.
The boat moves without moving.
The people on the bridge run
exactly where they ran before.

It is hard to get by without commentary:
This is not at all an innocent picture.   20
Time's been stopped here,
its laws no longer consulted.
It's been denied impact on the course of events,
disregarded and dishonored.

Thanks to a rebel,
one Hiroshige Utagawa
(a being who, by the way,
passed away, as is proper, long ago),
time stumbled and fell.

Perhaps it is merely a prank without much meaning,   30
a whim on the scale of just a few galaxies,
but just in case,
let's add what happens next:

For generations it has been considered in good taste
to hold this painting in high esteem,
to praise it and be greatly moved by it.

For some, even that is not enough.
They hear the patter of rain,
feel the chill of raindrops on necks and shoulders,
they look at the bridge and the people on it   40
as if they saw themselves there,
in that never-ending race
along the endless road, to be traveled for eternity
and they have the audacity to believe
that it is real.

Notes

Hiroshige Utagawa a Japanese artist (1797–1858) from the Edo period in
Japan

Activities

1. Paraphrase each stanza of the poem. Then write a response in which
you react to the theme and ideas of the poem. Comment on connections you
made to your own experiences or to other literary works.

2. Use an authoritative literary reference guide to locate and record definitions of *poetry* and *prose*. Create a two-column chart, labelled "poetic
characteristics" and "prose characteristics." Analyze the poem carefully,
recording in the appropriate columns the features that are poetic and those
that are prosaic. Then create a thesis statement in which you state how
effectively these two characteristics work together to create a unified poem.

Another Viewpoint: Literary Modes and Forms

Both this poem and "Musée des Beaux Arts" by W.H. Auden, which appears
on page 518 of this anthology, can be classified as reflective verse. Reflective
literature often poses essential questions, searches for universal truths, and
expresses profound themes regarding humanity's existence. Discuss in
which ways each of these poems is reflective, and to what extent the way
in which each poem relates to a specific work of art contributes to its reflective nature.

Progress

Emma LaRocque

Emma LaRocque was born in 1949 in Big Bay, Alberta. A Plains Cree Métis by birth, she is currently a professor of Native Studies at the University of Manitoba. LaRocque began publishing essays, social commentaries, and research articles in 1971. She describes herself as a "closet poet" and has published only a handful of poems in literary journals and collections. In the preface to *Writing the Circle*, LaRocque says, "Writing is the art of bringing to birth the human condition in thought form." She has reflected optimistically on the struggle of Native women writers, saying, "To be a Native writer of some consciousness is to be in a lonely place. Happily, our isolation is about to come apart at the seams." When you think of "progress," what words, ideas, and images come to mind? To what extent are these associations positive and optimistic? Which negative aspects of progress are of concern to you?

Progress

Earth poet
So busy
weaving
            magic
into words

so busy
placing
            patterns
quilting
            stars
so busy
making
            the sun
dance
so busy
singing
            your songs
in circles
so busy
tipping
            moons
in dreams

Earth poet
so busy
touching
            the land
scape
mad modern man
must make me
look at
cold steel spires
stealing earth and sun
            dance.

Activities

1. In a group, discuss the significance of the poem's title. What "progress" is represented in the poem? How does the repetition of the words "so busy" relate to the title? How does the title contribute to the meaning of the poem? Try to reach consensus on these questions and justify your answers in a class discussion.

2. Free verse uses the simple rhythms of everyday speech. Poet W.H. Auden said that a poet needs an "infallible ear" to determine where the lines should end. Enter the text of the poem into a word-processing file and experiment with different line lengths and breaks. How effective are LaRocque's original choices? How does the form of this poem help to convey the meaning? Did you find another line arrangement you preferred?

Summer Night

Langston Hughes

Langston Hughes was born in Joplin, Missouri, in 1902, and grew up there and in Illinois. After high school, he briefly attended university and travelled to Mexico, Europe, and Africa, before completing his studies. In 1924, he moved to Harlem in New York City, where he became a key figure in the "Harlem Renaissance" cultural movement. A prolific writer, Hughes wrote poetry, humorous sketches, social-protest essays, children's books, short story collections, novels, and twenty plays. He is best known for his portrayals of African-American life in the United States, as well as his connection to the world of jazz and blues music, which influenced his writing. Hughes received many awards, including Guggenheim and Rosenwald Fellowships. He died in 1967. What specific memories do you associate with summer nights? In what ways do the physical aspects of summer, in the country or city, contribute to a particular memory you have?

Summer Night

The sounds
Of the Harlem night
Drop one by one into stillness.
The last player-piano is closed.
The last victrola ceases with the
"Jazz Boy Blues."
The last crying baby sleeps
And the night becomes
Still as a whispering heartbeat.
I toss   10
Without rest in the darkness,
Weary as the tired night,
My soul
Empty as the silence,
Empty with a vague,
Aching emptiness,
Desiring,
Needing someone,
Something.

I toss without rest   20
In the darkness
Until the new dawn,
Wan and pale,
Descends like a white mist
Into the court-yard.

Notes

player-piano a piano that is fitted with an apparatus that allows it to play songs automatically by pulling down the required keys from the inside, giving the appearance of a "phantom" player

victrola a record player manufactured in the 1920s

Activities

1. Read the poem aloud with a partner, paying particular attention to the sounds and images. What mood does the poem convey? What images stand out in your mind? How do the line breaks and the language of the poem help to create these effects?

2. Langston Hughes is often called the "jazz poet." Do research into the jazz of the 1920s. Next, on the Internet, locate an early jazz recording, preferably from the 1920s or 1930s. Alternate listening to the recording with rereading the poem. After you have listened to the music several times, create a Venn diagram or write an essay comparing Hughes' poem to the jazz music you heard.

Another Viewpoint: Critical Approaches

Biographical criticism explores how knowledge of an author's life and background can illuminate our understanding of her or his writing. One literary critic has written that "Hughes refused to differentiate between his personal experience and the common experience of black America." Research biographical information on Langston Hughes. Consider to what extent you think "Summer Night" is a poem of black America. In a literary research essay, explain whether your interpretation of Hughes' poems is enhanced by connecting Hughes' life with the life he wrote about in his poetry. Make sure that your interpretation includes a carefully formulated and clearly stated thesis.

The Love Song of J. Alfred Prufrock

T.S. Eliot

A major figure in twentieth-century literature, T.S. Eliot was born in St. Louis, Missouri, in 1888. He earned a master's degree from Harvard University, then studied literature and philosophy in France and Germany. He eventually settled in England shortly after the outbreak of World War I, where he came under the influence of the poet Ezra Pound, who assisted in the publication of Eliot's work. In 1922, he published his poem "The Wasteland," generally considered one of the most influential poetic works of the twentieth century. In addition to poetry, Eliot wrote numerous successful plays and works of literary criticism. His book of light verse *Old Possum's Book of Practical Cats* was turned into the immensely popular musical *Cats* by Andrew Lloyd Webber. Eliot, who died in 1965, helped create the modernist style of blending references to the classics with mundane realism, and expressing this blend in majestic language which seems to mock the subject. "The Love Song of J. Alfred Prufrock" was written while Eliot was still a college student at Harvard and is often considered the first modernist poem. What are some of the subjects you would expect a college or university student to write about? What do you think would be a typical student's attitude to these subjects?

◀ *Les Escaliers de Montmartre, 1936, Gilberte Brassai*

The Love Song of J. Alfred Prufrock

S'io credesse che mia risposta fosse
A persona che mai tornasse al mondo,
Questa fiamma staria senza piu scosse.
Ma perciocche giammai di questo fondo
Non torno vivo alcun, s'i'odo il vero,
Senza tema d'infamia ti rispondo.

Let us go then, you and I,
When the evening is spread out against the sky
Like a patient etherized upon a table;
Let us go, through certain half-deserted streets,
The muttering retreats
Of restless nights in one-night cheap hotels
And sawdust restaurants with oyster shells:
Streets that follow like a tedious argument
Of insidious intent
To lead you to an overwhelming question...   10
Oh, do not ask, "What is it?"
Let us go and make our visit.

In the room the women come and go
Talking of Michelangelo.

The yellow fog that rubs its back upon the windowpanes,
The yellow smoke that rubs its muzzle on the windowpanes
Licked its tongue into the corners of the evening,
Lingered upon the pools that stand in drains,
Let fall upon its back the soot that falls from chimneys,
Slipped by the terrace, made a sudden leap,   20
And seeing that it was a soft October night,
Curled once about the house, and fell asleep.

And indeed there will be time
For the yellow smoke that slides along the street,
Rubbing its back upon the windowpanes;
There will be time, there will be time
To prepare a face to meet the faces that you meet;
There will be time to murder and create,
And time for all the works and days of hands
That lift and drop a question on your plate;   30
Time for you and time for me,
And time yet for a hundred indecisions,
And for a hundred visions and revisions,
Before the taking of a toast and tea.

    In the room the women come and go
Talking of Michelangelo.

    And indeed there will be time
To wonder, "Do I dare?" and, "Do I dare?"
Time to turn back and descend the stair,
With a bald spot in the middle of my hair—   40
(They will say: "How his hair is growing thin!")
My morning coat, my collar mounting firmly to the chin,
My necktie rich and modest, but asserted by a simple pin—
(They will say: "But how his arms and legs are thin!")
Do I dare
Disturb the universe?
In a minute there is time
For decisions and revisions which a minute will reverse.

    For I have known them all already, known them all—
Have known the evenings, mornings, afternoons,   50
I have measured out my life with coffee spoons;
I know the voices dying with a dying fall
Beneath the music from a farther room.
    So how should I presume?

And I have known the eyes already, known them all—
The eyes that fix you in a formulated phrase,
And when I am formulated, sprawling on a pin,
When I am pinned and wriggling on the wall,
Then how should I begin
To spit out all the butt-ends of my days and ways?   60
    And how should I presume?

    And I have known the arms already, known them all—
Arms that are braceleted and white and bare
(But in the lamplight, downed with light brown hair!)
Is it perfume from a dress
That makes me so digress?
Arms that lie along a table, or wrap about a shawl.
    And should I then presume?
    And how should I begin?

                    . . .

    Shall I say, I have gone at dusk through narrow streets   70
And watched the smoke that rises from the pipes
Of lonely men in shirt-sleeves, leaning out of windows?...

    I should have been a pair of ragged claws
Scuttling across the floors of silent seas.

                    . . .

    And the afternoon, the evening, sleeps so peacefully!
Smoothed by long fingers,
Asleep…tired…or it malingers,
Stretched on the floor, here beside you and me.
Should I, after tea and cakes and ices,
Have the strength to force the moment to its crisis?   80
But though I have wept and fasted, wept and prayed,
Though I have seen my head (grown slightly bald)
            brought in upon a platter,

I am no prophet—and here's no great matter;
I have seen the moment of my greatness flicker,
And I have seen the eternal Footman hold my coat, and snicker,
And in short, I was afraid.

And would it have been worth it, after all,
After the cups, the marmalade, the tea,
Among the porcelain, among some talk of you and me,
Would it have been worth while,   90
To have bitten off the matter with a smile,
To have squeezed the universe into a ball
To roll it toward some overwhelming question,
To say: "I am Lazarus, come from the dead,
Come back to tell you all, I shall tell you all"—
If one, settling a pillow by her head,
    Should say: "That is not what I meant at all.
    That is not it, at all."

And would it have been worth it, after all,
Would it have been worth while,   100
After the sunsets and the dooryards and the sprinkled streets,
After the novels, after the teacups, after the skirts that trail along the
    floor—
And this, and so much more?—
It is impossible to say just what I mean!
But as if a magic lantern threw the nerves in patterns on a screen:
Would it have been worth while
If one, settling a pillow or throwing off a shawl,
And turning toward the window, should say:
    "That is not it at all,
    That is not what I meant, at all."   110

                        . . .

No! I am not Prince Hamlet, nor was meant to be;
Am an attendant lord, one that will do
To swell a progress, start a scene or two,
Advise the prince; no doubt, an easy tool,
Deferential, glad to be of use,
Politic, cautious, and meticulous;
Full of high sentence, but a bit obtuse;
At times, indeed, almost ridiculous—
Almost, at times, the Fool.

    I grow old...I grow old...   120
I shall wear the bottoms of my trousers rolled.

    Shall I part my hair behind? Do I dare to eat a peach?
I shall wear white flannel trousers, and walk upon the beach.
I have heard the mermaids singing, each to each.

I do not think that they will sing to me.

I have seen them riding seaward on the waves
Combing the white hair of the waves blown back
When the wind blows the water white and black.

We have lingered in the chambers of the sea
By sea-girls wreathed with seaweed red and brown   130
Till human voices wake us, and we drown.

Notes

S'io credesse...ti rispondo This Italian epigraph is a quotation from *The Inferno* by the Italian writer Dante Alighieri (1265–1321). It is translated into English as: "If I thought that my reply would be to one who would ever return to the world, this flame would stay without further movement; but, since no one has ever returned alive from this depth, if what I hear is true, I answer without fear of infamy" (*Inferno*, 27, lines 61–66). Here, Guido da Montefeltro, enclosed in the flames of hell for being a false counsellor during his life on Earth, tells Dante about the shame of his evil life, because he believes that Dante, like all damned souls, will never return to Earth to report it.

And indeed there will be time a reference to a line from Andrew Marvell's poem "To His Coy Mistress": "Had we but world enough, and time..."

And time for all the works and days of hands a reference to "Works and Days," a poem about the farming year by Hesiod, Greek poet of the eighth century BCE

I know the voices dying with a dying fall a reference to a line in Duke Orsino's speech in Shakespeare's *Twelfth Night* (1.1.4): "That strain again! It had a dying fall"

I should have been a pair of ragged claws a reference to Hamlet's comment to Polonius: "For you yourself, sir, should be old as I am, if, like a crab, you could go backward" (2.2.205–6)

Though I have seen my head (grown slightly bald) brought in upon a platter a reference to the biblical story of John the Baptist in Mark 6.17–28 and Matthew 14.3–11

To have squeezed the universe into a ball a reference to part of Marvell's poem "To His Coy Mistress": "Let us roll all our strength and all / Our sweetness up into one ball, / and tear our pleasures with rough strife / Thorough the iron gates of life"

"I am Lazarus, come from the dead" a reference to the biblical story of Lazarus in Luke 16.19–31 and John 11.1–44

Almost, at times, the Fool a reference from Elizabethan drama to the role of the fool, who functions both as a clown and as a teacher of his social superiors

I have heard the mermaids singing a reference to a line in John Donne's poem "Go and Catch a Falling Star": "Teach me to hear mermaids singing," considered an impossibility

Activities

1. The poem is written in the form of a dramatic monologue that presents the thoughts and feelings of a single character. What do you learn about J. Alfred Prufrock from his monologue? What are his likes, dislikes, concerns, fears, and anxieties? How does he relate to others? What kind of person do you think he is?

2. When first published, this poem was the source of much bewilderment. Reasons for this confusion included Eliot's deliberate elimination of the connectives and transitions between passages, his frequent allusions to other works of literature, and his extremely ironic tone. In groups, analyze and assess Eliot's use of these features in the poem.

Another Viewpoint: Critical Approaches

On the Internet and elsewhere, research the terms *modernism* and *postmodernism* as they apply to literature. When did the terms first appear and how were they used? Are they still used in the same way? What literary works from a variety of countries reflect these concepts and how do they do so? Present the results of your research in a class presentation or as a research essay.

Afternoons & Coffeespoons

Brad Roberts of The Crash Test Dummies

Since 1988, Brad Roberts has been the lead singer and songwriter of the Canadian band The Crash Test Dummies. Roberts was born in Winnipeg, Manitoba, in 1964. He was studying for a master's degree in literature and philosophy when he left the University of Winnipeg to form his band. The release of their first album, *The Ghosts That Haunt Me* (1991), produced the hit "Superman's Song." This international success was followed by the best-selling album *God Shuffled His Feet* (1993), which included the hit "Mmm, Mmm, Mmm" as well as the song "Afternoons & Coffeespoons." In reviewing this album, a music critic in the *Globe and Mail* wrote, "Roberts' voice, a resonant baritone, sets him apart from most pop singers, [as do] his equally distinctive songs, which dare to address substantial ideas with penetrating wit." Notable awards for the band include a Juno in 1991 for Group of the Year and three U.S. Grammy Awards, including Best New Artist. What is your impression of the music and words of the songs you have heard by The Crash Test Dummies? What makes the songs different from those of typical rock bands?

Afternoons & Coffeespoons

There's a breeze that makes my breathing not so easy ——▶ old age.
I've had my lungs checked out with X rays
I've smelled the hospital hallways

Someday I'll have a disappearing hairline ——▶ shaved head/old age?
Someday I'll wear pyjamas in the daytime ——▶ hospital clothing/care- less?

Times when the day is like a play by Sartre ⎰ mood
When it seems a bookburning's in perfect order— ⎱ swings.
I gave the doctor my description
I tried to stick to my prescriptions

Someday I'll have a disappearing hairline   10
Someday I'll wear pyjamas in the daytime

Afternoons will be measured out
Measured out, measured with ◁
Coffeespoons and T.S. Eliot

Maybe if I could do a play-by-playback
I could change the test results that I will get back ⎰ cancer?
I've watched the summer evenings pass by
I've heard the rattle in my bronchi...

Someday I'll have a disappearing hairline   20
Someday I'll wear pyjamas in the daytime

Afternoons will be measured out
Measured out, measured with
Coffeespoons and T.S. Eliot

Notes

Sartre a reference to Jean-Paul Sartre (1905–1980), the French novelist, playwright, essayist, and leader of the philosophical movement known as *existentialism*

Activities

1. Look closely at the lyrics of "Afternoons & Coffeespoons." Identify those words and phrases that allude to "The Love Song of J. Alfred Prufrock." What do you think Roberts is trying to say about existence? How do the references to Eliot's poem reinforce his thoughts and feelings? In what ways are Roberts' lyrics similar in style to Eliot's poem? In what ways do Roberts' lyrics speak to a contemporary audience?

2. Like Eliot, Roberts makes use of striking and unusual images. Analyze and explain some of the similes and metaphors that you find in the lyrics. Assess how well you think they capture the songwriter's meaning.

The River

Derek Walcott

Derek Walcott was born on the island of St. Lucia in 1930. Considered by many to be the most important Caribbean poet and dramatist writing in English, he was awarded the Nobel Prize in Literature in 1992. Walcott has published over twenty volumes of poetry and more than twenty-five plays. As a writer, his primary aim has been to create literature that remains true to Caribbean life and traditions. A dominant theme in his work is the region's fusion of indigenous, African, Asian, and European cultures. To what extent do you think literature should be closely connected to the region and culture in which it was created? What obligation do writers have to deal with the important issues of their time and native place?

The River

was one, once;
reduced by circumstance
the Council tends it. Once

it could roar through town,
foul-mouthed, brown-muscled, brazenly
drunk, a raucous country-bookie,

but lately it has grown
too footloose for this settlement
of shacks, rechristened a city;

its strength wasted on gutters,   10
it never understood the age,
what progress meant,

so its clear, brown integument
shrivelled, its tongue stutters
through the official language,

it surrenders its gutturals
to the stern, stone Victorian bridge;
reclaimed, it dies a little

daily, it crawls towards a sea
curdled with oil-slick, its force   20
thins like the peasantry,

it idles like those resinous
wrinkled woodsmen, the country
reek still on them, hoarse

with municipal argument,
who, falling suddenly silent
on wire-bright afternoons, reflect

on mornings when a torrent
roared down their gorges, and
no one gave a damn what the words meant.   30

Notes

country-bookie eastern and southern Caribbean dialect term for "country bumpkin"

integument a natural covering, such as skin, rind, or husk

gutturals sounds or letters produced in the throat

stern Victorian bridge a reference to a bridge that crosses the river, likely built in the architectural style of Victorian England

resinous like a resin, a sticky substance formed in and oozing from trees

Activities

1. In this poem, Walcott personifies the river of the past and of the present, using contrasting words and images. With a partner, explore the significance of this contrast. What do you think has caused the changes between the past and the present? What impact do the changes have on the reader? How does the poet feel about these changes?

2. In his acceptance speech for the Nobel Prize, Walcott discussed the similarity between the culture of the Caribbean islands and the process of making poems: "Antillean art is this restoration of our shattered histories, our shards of vocabulary, our archipelago becoming a synonym for pieces broken off the original content. And this is the exact process of making poetry, or what should be called not its 'making' but its remaking." In what ways has Walcott demonstrated this process of "remaking" in both the content and style of "The River"?

Another Viewpoint: Society

Consider this viewpoint: "Poems about nature always express a concern, at times only implicit, about the state of the natural environment." Choose two or three poems about nature. To what extent do you think the writers of these poems are expressing a concern about the environment? To what extent do you think they are using nature as a backdrop to express ideas about human experience?

grammar poem

Rita Wong

Rita Wong was born in 1968 in Calgary, Alberta, where she grew up. She has worked as an archivist, a teacher of English as a second language, and a coordinator for the Alberta/Northwest Territories Network of Immigrant Women. Her writing has appeared in many literary magazines and in an anthology entitled *monkeypuzzle* (1998). Wong was the recipient of the 1998 Asian Canadian Writers' Workshop Emerging Writer Award for Poetry. In 2002, she received her doctoral degree from Simon Fraser University. Many people equate grammar with a dull, frustrating discipline. What is your working definition of *grammar* and what do you predict about a poem entitled "grammar poem"? What qualities of grammar have the potential to make it an interesting subject?

grammar poem

write around the absence, she said, show
its existence
demonstrate   *this is*
its contours   *the sound of*
how it   *my chinese tongue*
tastes   *whispering:* nei tou
where   gnaw ma? *no*
its edges   *tones can*
fall   *survive this*
hard   *alphabet*
on my stuttering tongue, how its tones &
              pictograms get flattened out by the
                   steamroller of the english language,
live   its etymology of
half-submerged   assimilation
in the salty home of   tramples budding
my mother tongue,   memory into sawdusty
shallows   stereotypes, regimented capitals,
                 arrogant nouns & more nouns,
              punctuated by subservient descriptors.
         grammar is the dust on the streets waiting to be washed off
by immigrant cleaners or blown into your eyes by the wind. grammar
is the invisible net in the air, holding your words in place. grammar,
like wealth, belongs in the hands of the people who produce it.

Notes

tones different pitches used in a tonal language in which one word can be expressed several ways to mean very different things

pictograms written words presented as characters or graphics, such as those used in the Cantonese, Mandarin, and Japanese languages; alternatively, hieroglyphics used in the ancient Egyptian language. These are all in contrast to languages, such as Phoenician, Latin, and English, which use an alphabet.

etymology the origin and history of a word or of words, often presented in dictionaries, between the pronunciation and the definition of a word; from the Greek words *etumon*, meaning "the true sense of a word," and *logia*, meaning "study of or dealing with"

assimilation the process of taking over and incorporating into its own

Activities

1. With a partner, take turns reading the poem aloud. As you read, tell your partner what you are thinking as your eyes follow the words. Afterward, discuss how this "think-aloud" exercise gave you insight into your reading. Discuss any sections that were confusing to you. Share your insights with another pair by asking three questions about the poem.

2. In a group, copy out all the metaphors for language that you find in the poem. Have a class discussion on the use of these metaphors in the poem. Then choose a literary technique that interests you, such as personification or irony, and create your own shape poem.

Another Viewpoint: Critical Approaches

Post-colonial literary theory examines issues of imperialism and nationality. Do research into the meaning of the terms *post-colonial* and *imperialism*. What messages do you find in "grammar poem" that could be considered post-colonial? Explain whether or not you agree with the messages you have identified. Then, in a brief critical analysis, select four consecutive lines and analyze them from the perspective of the "politics" of language.

Hua Mu-lan, 1995, Lu Yanguang

Mu-lan

Anonymous

Translated by Hans H. Frankel

Folk ballads are narrative poems that have been orally transmitted among ordinary people, either through recitation or song. "Mu-lan," also known as "The Ballad of Mu-lan," was composed between 500 and 600 CE and tells a story set during a military campaign between Mu-lan's people, the Hsien-pi of what is now northern China, and their enemies, the nomadic Jou-jan. The poem would have been written down by a member of the court or the literati. The original Chinese poem comprises sixty-two lines, each of which consists generally of five Chinese "characters," or written symbols. This original poem was written in the form of Chinese poetry known as "yüeh-fu." This form was derived from folk songs, which usually were narrative poems accompanied by music. The poem was expanded into a novel near the end of China's late Ming Dynasty (1368–1644 CE). What kinds of stories get told in your own family year after year? Which of your family stories have been passed down from previous generations? How do you explain your family's interest in these stories?

Mu-lan

Tsiek tsiek and again *tsiek tsiek*,
Mu-lan weaves, facing the door.
You don't hear the shuttle's sound,
You only hear Daughter's sighs.
They ask Daughter who's in her heart,
They ask Daughter who's on her mind.
"No one is in Daughter's heart,
No one is on Daughter's mind.
Last night I saw the draft posters,
The Khan is calling many troops,   10
The army list is in twelve scrolls,
On every scroll there's Father's name.
Father has no grown-up son,
Mu-lan has no elder brother.
I want to buy a saddle and horse,
And serve in the army in Father's place."

In the East Market she buys a spirited horse,
In the West Market she buys a saddle,
In the South Market she buys a bridle,
In the North Market she buys a long whip.   20
At dawn she takes leave of Father and Mother,
In the evening camps on the Yellow River's bank.
She doesn't hear the sound of Father and Mother calling,
She only hears the Yellow River's flowing water cry *tsien tsien*.

At dawn she takes leave of the Yellow River,
In the evening she arrives at Black Mountain.
She doesn't hear the sound of Father and Mother calling,
She only hears Mount Yen's nomad horses cry *tsiu tsiu*.
She goes ten thousand miles on the business of war,
She crosses passes and mountains like flying.   30
Northern gusts carry the rattle of army pots,

Chilly light shines on iron armor.
Generals die in a hundred battles,
Stout soldiers return after ten years.

On her return she sees the Son of Heaven,
The Son of Heaven sits in the Splendid Hall.
He gives out promotions in twelve ranks
And prizes of a hundred thousand and more.
The Khan asks her what she desires.
"Mu-lan has no use for a minister's post.   40
I wish to ride a swift mount
To take me back to my home."

When Father and Mother hear Daughter is coming
They go outside the wall to meet her, leaning on each other.
When Younger Sister hears Elder Sister is coming
She fixes her rouge, facing the door.
When Little Brother hears Elder Sister is coming
He whets the knife, quick quick, for pig and sheep.
"I open the door to my east chamber,
I sit on my couch in the west room,   50
I take off my wartime gown
And put on my old-time clothes."
Facing the window she fixes her cloudlike hair,
Hanging up a mirror she dabs on yellow flower-powder.
She goes out the door and sees her comrades.
Her comrades are all amazed and perplexed.
Traveling together for twelve years
They didn't know Mu-lan was a girl.
"The he-hare's feet go hop and skip,
The she-hare's eyes are muddled and fuddled.   60
Two hares running side by side close to the ground,
How can they tell if I am he or she?"

Notes

Khan the provincial lord

Yellow River the second largest river in China, nearly 5,000 km long

Mount Yen's nomad horses the enemy cavalry

stout brave, bold, strong

Splendid Hall the most important temple of the ancient Chinese rulers

Son of Heaven the Emperor

yellow flower-powder yellow make-up, commonly used by nomadic women of Northern China to powder their foreheads

Activities

1. Mu-lan's military exploits are merely hinted at in the poem. Do you think this omission is meant to stimulate the reader to imagine the details of the battles? Or does it suggest that the essence of the poem lies elsewhere? Discuss your response to the poem in terms of its content and focus.

2. The Chinese version of "Mu-lan" has neither punctuation nor personal pronouns. The division of the poem into verses is also at the translator's discretion. With this in mind, enter the text of "Mu-lan" into a word-processing file and experiment with punctuation, pronouns, and verse divisions until you have a version that expresses the poem as you'd like it to be read. Exchange and discuss alternative versions in a group.

From
Beowulf

Anonymous

Translated by Seamus Heaney

Composed at some point between the eighth and tenth centuries CE, *Beowulf* is the oldest surviving poem written in Old English, a linguistic predecessor of modern English. An epic poem of more than 3,000 lines, *Beowulf* contains fictional (and probably some factual) events that occurred in the sixth century CE in the Germanic regions of Northern Europe. *Beowulf* is the story of the exploits and character of a renowned Scandinavian warrior and hero who travels across the sea to the land of the Danes to help the Danish King Hrothgar rid his country of a monster called Grendel. After battles with Grendel and Grendel's mother, Beowulf returns to his homeland, Geatland, where he rules as king for fifty years. The section below occurs before Beowulf's battle with Grendel. It is taken from a 1999 translation by Seamus Heaney, an Irish poet born in 1939 in Northern Ireland. Heaney is the recipient of numerous awards, including the Nobel Prize in Literature in 1995 and the Whitbread Book of the Year Award for this translation of *Beowulf*. What comes to mind when you read or hear the word *hero*? In what ways is a hero today similar to one from the distant past?

Beowulf and the Dragon, 1932, Rockwell Kent

From Beowulf

When he heard about Grendel, Hygelac's thane
was on home ground, over in Geatland.
There was no one else like him alive.
In his day, he was the mightiest man on earth,
high-born and powerful. He ordered a boat
that would ply the waves. He announced his plan:
to sail the swan's road and search out that king,
the famous prince who needed defenders.
Nobody tried to keep him from going,
no elder denied him, dear as he was to them. 10
Instead, they inspected omens and spurred
his ambition to go, whilst he moved about
like the leader he was, enlisting men,
the best he could find; with fourteen others
the warrior boarded the boat as captain,
a canny pilot along coast and currents.
Time went by, the boat was on water,
in close under the cliffs.
Men climbed eagerly up the gangplank,
sand churned in surf, warriors loaded 20
a cargo of weapons, shining war-gear
in the vessel's hold, then heaved out,
away with a will in their wood-weathered ship.
Over the waves, with the wind behind her
and foam at her neck, she flew like a bird
until her curved prow had covered the distance
and on the following day, at the due hour,
those seafarers sighted land,
sunlit cliffs, sheer crags
and looming headlands, the landfall they sought. 30

It was the end of their voyage and the Geats vaulted
over the side, out on to the sand,
and moored their ship. There was a clash of mail
and a thresh of gear. They thanked God
for that easy crossing on a calm sea.

When the watchman on the wall, the Shieldings' lookout
whose job it was to guard the sea-cliffs,
saw shields glittering on the gangplank
and battle-equipment being unloaded
he had to find out who and what   40
the arrivals were. So he rode to the shore,
this horseman of Hrothgar's, and challenged them
in formal terms, flourishing his spear:

"What kind of men are you who arrive
rigged out for combat in coats of mail,
sailing here over the sea-lanes
in your steep-hulled boat? I have been stationed
as lookout on this coast for a long time.
My job is to watch the waves for raiders,
any danger to the Danish shore.   50
Never before has a force under arms
disembarked so openly—not bothering to ask
if the sentries allowed them safe passage
or the clan had consented. Nor have I seen
a mightier man-at-arms on this earth
than the one standing here: unless I am mistaken,
he is truly noble. This is no mere
hanger-on in a hero's armour.
So now, before you fare inland
as interlopers, I have to be informed   60
about who you are and where you hail from.
Outsiders from across the water,
I say it again: the sooner you tell
where you come from and why, the better."

The leader of the troop unlocked his word-hoard;
the distinguished one delivered this answer:
"We belong by birth to the Geat people
and owe allegiance to Lord Hygelac.
In his day, my father was a famous man,
a noble warrior-lord named Ecgtheow.   70
He outlasted many a long winter
and went on his way. All over the world
men wise in counsel continue to remember him.
We come in good faith to find your lord
and nation's shield, the son of Halfdane.
Give us the right advice and direction.
We have arrived here on a great errand
to the lord of the Danes, and I believe therefore
there should be nothing hidden or withheld between us.
So tell us if what we have heard is true   80
about this threat, whatever it is,
this danger abroad in the dark nights,
this corpse-maker mongering death
in the Shieldings' country. I come to proffer
my wholehearted help and counsel.
I can show the wise Hrothgar a way
to defeat his enemy and find respite—
if any respite is to reach him, ever.
I can calm the turmoil and terror in his mind.
Otherwise, he must endure woes   90
and live with grief for as long as his hall
stands at the horizon, on its high ground."

Undaunted, sitting astride his horse,
the coast-guard answered, "Anyone with gumption
and a sharp mind will take the measure
of two things: what's said and what's done.

I believe what you have told me: that you are a troop
loyal to our king. So come ahead
with your arms and your gear, and I will guide you.
What's more, I'll order my own comrades
on their word of honour to watch your boat
down there on the strand—keep her safe
in her fresh tar, until the time comes
for her curved prow to preen on the waves
and bear this hero back to Geatland.
May one so valiant and venturesome
come unharmed through the clash of battle."

Notes

Beowulf the son of King Hygelac's sister. Foremost among the Geat warriors, Beowulf hears the story of Grendel from a sea captain who visits King Hygelac's hall.

Grendel a night stalker, the "Death shadow," a troll-like creature who makes his lair among the sea inlets and coastal marshes. This monster, who hates all humans and all joy, hears the music and laughter from King Hrothgar's mead hall and comes each night, killing the best of the King's thanes. No sword could cut this monster's hide. No Danish champion could be found with the strength to subdue this creature.

Hygelac King of the Geats, uncle to Beowulf

Geatland a geographic area; in modern times southern Sweden

swan's road this phrase means "the sea"; it is an example of the Old English and Old Norse poetic technique known as a "kenning," in which a compound word is used instead of a single noun to mean one thing: other examples are "oar-steed" for a ship and "whale's road" for the sea

Shieldings the Danes

Hrothgar a great warrior and king of the Danes

Ecgtheow Beowulf's father. As a young man, Ecgtheow was embroiled in a blood feud and killed a man. He and his young wife had to leave Geatland and found a loyal friend in the Danish King Hrothgar. Beowulf was born at the Danish Court. It was King Hrothgar who paid compensation to the family of the man Ecgtheow had killed, thus allowing Ecgtheow and his family to return to Geatland. When Beowulf, as a young man, heard of King Hrothgar's trouble with the monster Grendel, he felt an obligation to help this friend and repay his father's debt to the Danish king.

Halfdane King Hrothgar's father

Hrothgar's hall the great mead hall of Hrothgar. The hall was called Heorot, the Hart, because great antlers of a stag graced its gable. The size and magnificence of the hall were known far and wide. Ironically, instead of a place of joy and celebrations, the great hall became a place of terror because of Grendel's attacks.

Activities

1. What impression of Beowulf are you left with after reading this exerpt? In a journal entry, describe the warrior by referring to what others say about him and what he himself says in the passage. In your entry, consider what you were able to predict about the Anglo-Saxon ideal of a hero. Does Beowulf seem like a war-monger or a peace-maker?

2. Find a definition of epic poetry and discuss some of the elements and characteristics of that form evident in this excerpt from *Beowulf*. Describe what you were able to predict from this passage in terms of the themes in *Beowulf* that pertain to all epic poems.

Another Viewpoint: Society

The events in *Beowulf* could be compared with current strife-torn political situations. Complete some research on contemporary wars, their causes, and their aftermaths. Is there some universal message that endures in this epic poem to address the feuding and anguish that exist in many areas of the world today? Present the findings of your research as a multimedia presentation to your class.

Ellesmere manuscript, c. 1410

From

The Canterbury Tales: General Prologue

Geoffrey Chaucer

Translated into modern English by Nevill Coghill

Geoffrey Chaucer, the most important writer of Middle English, is believed to have been born in London, England, circa 1340. At the age of seventeen, he became a page at court and was associated with the royal household for the rest of his life, both as a business person and a poet. In 1359, Chaucer served in the English army during its invasion of France, where he was captured and held for ransom. He was given a life pension in 1367 and went on diplomatic missions to France and Italy. On one trip to Italy, he discovered the works of Dante, Boccaccio, and Petrarch, which greatly influenced his own writing. Chaucer worked on his masterpiece *The Canterbury Tales* from 1387 until his death in 1400. He was buried in the Poets' Corner of Westminster Abbey, where a monument was erected to him in 1555. *The Canterbury Tales*, which comprises 17,000 lines, consists of stories told by pilgrims travelling to the shrine of Saint Thomas Becket in Canterbury Cathedral. In this excerpt, Chaucer's original Middle English text appears on the left-hand pages, with the modern English translation on the facing, right-hand pages. It is interesting to note that, starting at line 57, each Middle English line of verse cannot necessarily be translated into one line in modern English; therefore, the remaining lines of this excerpt do not have a one-to-one correspondence. What other "on-the-road" narratives have you come across in print or on the screen? What elements do these narratives share? How are these elements used to achieve specific effects on the reader or viewer?

From The Canterbury Tales: General Prologue

Middle
English

Here bygynneth the Book of the Tales of Caunterbury.

    Whan that Aprill with his shoures soote
The droghte of March hath perced to the roote,
And bathed every veyne in swich licour
Of which vertu engendred is the flour;
Whan Zephirus eek with his sweete breeth
Inspired hath in every holt and heeth
The tendre croppes, and the yonge sonne
Hath in the Ram his halfe cours yronne,
And smale foweles maken melodye,
That slepen al the nyght with open eye—   10
So priketh hem nature in hir corages—
Thanne longen folk to goon on pilgrimages,
And palmeres for to seken straunge strondes,
To ferne halwes, kowthe in sondry londes;
And specially from every shires ende
Of Engelond to Caunterbury they wende,
The hooly blisful martir for to seke
That hem hath holpen whan that they were seeke.
    Bifil that in that seson on a day
In Southwerk at the Tabard as I lay   20
Redy to wenden on my pilgrymage
To Caunterbury with ful devout corage,
At nyght was come into that hostelrye
Wel nyne and twenty in a compaignye
Of sondry folk, by aventure yfalle
In felaweship, and pilgrimes were they alle,
That toward Caunterbury wolden ryde.
The chambres and the stables weren wyde,
And wel we weren esed atte beste.

Here begins the Book of the Tales of Canterbury.

Modern
English

When in April the sweet showers fall
And pierce the drought of March to the root, and all
The veins are bathed in liquor of such power
As brings about the engendering of the flower,
When also Zephyrus with his sweet breath
Exhales an air in every grove and heath
Upon the tender shoots, and the young sun
His half-course in the sign of the Ram has run
And the small fowl are making melody
That sleep away the night with open eye   10
(So nature pricks them and their heart engages)
Then people long to go on pilgrimages
And palmers long to seek the stranger strands
Of far-off saints, hallowed in sundry lands,
And specially, from every shire's end
Of England, down to Canterbury they wend
To seek the holy blissful martyr, quick
To give his help to them when they were sick.

It happened in that season that one day
In Southwark, at The Tabard, as I lay   20
Ready to go on pilgrimage and start
For Canterbury, most devout at heart,
At night there came into that hostelry
Some nine and twenty in a company
Of sundry folk happening then to fall
In fellowship, and they were pilgrims all
That towards Canterbury meant to ride.
The rooms and stables of the inn were wide;
They made us easy, all was of the best.

And shortly, whan the sonne was to reste,   30
So hadde I spoken with hem everichon
That I was of hir felaweship anon,
And made forward erly for to ryse,
To take oure wey ther as I yow devyse.
    But nathelees, whil I have tyme and space,
Er that I ferther in this tale pace,
Me thynketh it acordaunt to resoun
To telle yow al the condicioun
Of ech of hem, so as it semed me,
And whiche they weren, and of what degree,   40
And eek in what array that they were inne;
And at a knyght than wol I first bigynne.

THE KNYGHT

    A KNYGHT ther was, and that a worthy man,
That fro the tyme that he first bigan
To riden out, he loved chivalrie,
Trouthe and honour, fredom and curteisie.
Ful worthy was he in his lordes werre,
And therto hadde he riden, no man ferre,
As wel in cristendom as in hethenesse,
And evere honoured for his worthynesse.   50
    At Alisaundre he was whan it was wonne.
Ful ofte tyme he hadde the bord bigonne
Aboven alle nacions in Pruce.
In Lettow hadde he reysed and in Ruce,
No Cristen man so ofte of his degree.
In Gernade at the seege eek hadde he be
Of Algezir, and riden in Belmarye.
At Lyeys was he and at Satalye,
Whan they were wonne; and in the Grete See
At many a noble armee hadde he be.   60

And, briefly, when the sun had gone to rest, 30
I'd spoken to them all upon the trip
And was soon one with them in fellowship,
Pledged to rise early and to take the way
To Canterbury, as you heard me say.
    But none the less, while I have time and space,
Before my story takes a further pace,
It seems a reasonable thing to say
What their condition was, the full array
Of each of them, as it appeared to me,
According to profession and degree,   40
And what apparel they were riding in;
And at a Knight I therefore will begin.

THE KNIGHT

    There was a Knight, a most distinguished man,
Who from the day on which he first began
To ride abroad had followed chivalry,
Truth, honour, generousness and courtesy.
He had done nobly in his sovereign's war
And ridden into battle, no man more,
As well in Christian as in heathen places,
And ever honoured for his noble graces.   50
When we took Alexandria, he was there.
He often sat at table in the chair
Of honour, above all nations, when in Prussia.
In Lithuania he had ridden, and Russia,
No Christian man so often, of his rank.
When, in Granada, Algeciras sank
Under assault, he had been there, and in
North Africa, raiding Benamarin;
In Anatolia he had been as well
And fought when Ayas and Attalia fell,   60

At mortal batailles hadde he been fiftene,
And foughten for oure feith at Tramyssene
In lystes thries, and ay slayn his foo.
This ilke worthy knyght hadde been also
Somtyme with the lord of Palatye
Agayn another hethen in Turkye;
And everemoore he hadde a sovereyn prys.
And though that he were worthy, he was wys,
And of his port as meeke as is a mayde.
He nevere yet no vileynye ne sayde   70
In al his lyf unto no maner wight.
He was a verray, parfit gentil knyght.
　　But for to tellen yow of his array,
His hors weren goode, but he was nat gay.
Of fustian he wered a gypoun
Al bismotered with his habergeoun,
For he was late ycome from his viage,
And wente for to doon his pilgrymage.

For all along the Mediterranean coast
He had embarked with many a noble host.
In fifteen mortal battles he had been
And jousted for our faith at Tramissene
Thrice in the lists, and always killed his man.
This same distinguished knight had led the van
Once with the Bey of Balat, doing work
For him against another heathen Turk;
He was of sovereign value in all eyes.
And though so much distinguished, he was wise   70
And in his bearing modest as a maid.
He never yet a boorish thing had said
In all his life to any, come what might;
He was a true, a perfect gentle-knight.
    Speaking of his equipment, he possessed
Fine horses, but he was not gaily dressed.
He wore a fustian tunic stained and dark
With smudges where his armour had left mark;
Just home from service, he had joined our ranks
To do his pilgrimage and render thanks.   80

Notes

liquor a potent liquid

engendering bringing about; giving rise to

Zephyrus the god or personification of the West Wind in classical mythology

heath a flat, open area of wasteland

Ram the astrological sign of Aries

pricks awakens, incites

palmers pilgrims returning from the Holy Land, wearing a cross of palm branches

stranger strands foreign shores

sundry various; from the Old English word *syndrig*, meaning "separate"

shire a group of counties in England, such as Devonshire and Hampshire

wend go, travel

the holy, blissful martyr Saint Thomas Becket, an English bishop who was murdered and buried in Canterbury Cathedral

Southwark a town across from London on the Thames River

The Tabard the Tabard Inn

array clothing

degree social rank

Alexandria a city in northern Egypt, captured by Christians in 1365

Prussia an area of northeastern Europe, conquered by the Teutonic Knights in the thirteenth century

Granada a state in Spain

Algeciras a city in Granada, Spain

Benamarin a Moorish kingdom in North Africa

Anatolia the Asian part of Turkey

Ayas, Attalia cities in Asia Minor, captured by the Crusaders in 1361 and 1367, respectively

Tramissene a Moorish kingdom in North Africa

Bey of Balat the lord of a city in Asia Minor

sovereign great

fustian made of sturdy cotton and linen fabric; originally referring to cloth from El Fostat, a district of Cairo, Egypt

Activities

1. Reread the first eleven lines of the poem and discuss them in a group. What might Chaucer's reasons have been for writing opening lines filled with references common to love lyrics of his time? What symbolic parallel between spring awakening and setting off on a pilgrimage might the author be suggesting? How do these lines "set up" what follows?

2. Discuss Chaucer's method of characterizing the Knight. What does Chaucer's description reveal about his own values and the values of his society? Given the historical context of this work and its courtly audience, why is it not surprising that the author focuses on the "full array" of the pilgrims, their "profession and degree, / And what apparel they were riding in"?

Another Viewpoint: Literary Modes and Forms

Geoffrey Chaucer wrote his works at the end of the medieval era. In small groups, choose a medieval romance, such as one of the King Arthur legends, the story of Tristan and Isolde (with various spellings such as Isolt and Isolde), or the story of Sir Gawain and the Green Knight, and complete some research on it. Find out some background information. Present your findings to the class, outlining the key characteristics of your text. Then discuss with the class the following: in what way was the medieval romance well suited to the medieval era? What variations on these romances do we find in contemporary literature?

Sonnet 116

William Shakespeare

William Shakespeare was born in 1564 in Stratford-upon-Avon, England. Shakespeare's 154 sonnets, which were printed in 1609, were probably written in the 1590s. They are considered the most personal works by Shakespeare, who died on his birthday in 1616, at the age of fifty-two. Why do you think that love is the most celebrated emotion in poetry, song, and story? Does the majority of literature with which you are familiar present a realistic or an idealized picture of love?

Sonnet 116

Let me not to the marriage of true minds
Admit impediments; love is not love
Which alters when it alteration finds,
Or bends with the remover to remove.
O no, it is an ever-fixed mark
That looks on tempests and is never shaken;
It is the star to every wand'ring bark,
Whose worth's unknown, although his highth be taken.
Love's not Time's fool, though rosy lips and cheeks
Within his bending sickle's compass come;
Love alters not with his brief hours and weeks,
But bears it out even to the edge of doom.
    If this be error and upon me proved,
    I never writ, nor no man ever loved.

Notes

impediments in this instance, bars or hindrances to a legal marriage

the remover one who changes his mind or position

ever-fixed mark a mark on land used by mariners to fix their position at sea; for example, a church steeple or high cliff

the star in this instance, the North Star

wand'ring bark a ship or boat that has lost its way

highth be taken measuring the elevation of stars above the horizon for purposes of navigation

fool plaything; alternatively, a court jester

sickle an implement consisting of a curved metal blade attached to a short wooden handle. Death is often portrayed as carrying a sickle.

compass the circular range of a sickle, cutting down grass

bears survives

doom death or Judgment Day

upon against

Activities

1. Shakespeare often uses the couplet at the end of a sonnet to summarize the ideas he has developed in the preceding twelve lines. Is this true of "Sonnet 116"? If not, what do you think is the function of this couplet in relation to the rest of the sonnet?

2. Go through the sonnet, making note of all the verbs, adjectives, and nouns that are repeated two or more times. (If the same root word is used, count it as a repetition.) Consider what other synonyms could have been used. Why, in each case, do you think Shakespeare chose to repeat the same word? Assess how this study of the sonnet's diction has contributed to your understanding of the poet's style.

Another Viewpoint: Literary Modes and Forms

Research the poetic form known as the *sonnet*, investigating the characteristics of the Italian (Petrarchan) and the English (Shakespearean) sonnet. Comment on the rhyme, rhythm, and structure of each form. Then demonstrate how Shakespeare's use of the conventional structure and organization of the English sonnet contributes to the theme and the coherence of "Sonnet 116."

A POISON TREE

William Blake

About the Visual   William Blake was born in 1757, in London, England. Although he received little formal education, he became an avid reader of Latin and Greek classical literature and the Bible. As a fifteen-year-old, Blake was apprenticed to an engraver and later set up his own engraving business. Blake engraved his poems on illustrated backgrounds, so that they looked like handwriting rather than type. He died in 1827. This poem is about anger. How well are you able to hide your feelings when you are angry? To what extent do you think that it is better to express rather than repress feelings such as anger? What do you think are acceptable and unacceptable methods of expressing anger?

Activities

1. In virtually every culture, trees have symbolic significance. With the class, make a list of everything you can think of that a tree might symbolize. In a discussion, explore which of these symbols have positive associations and which have negative ones.

2. Read the poem aloud several times, considering how the form of this poem enhances the meaning. Describe the following features, giving specific examples and reasons for how they affect your interpretation and reaction to the poem: rhyme scheme, rhythm and metre, organization into stanzas, language, and syntax.

1794, copperplate engraving, 16 x 14 cm ▶

A POISON TREE.

I was angry with my friend ;
I told my wrath, my wrath did end.
I was angry with my foe :
I told it not. my wrath did grow.

And I waterd it in fears,
Night & morning with my tears :
And I sunned it with smiles,
And with soft deceitful wiles.

And it grew both day and night,
Till it bore an apple bright.
And my foe beheld it shine,
And he knew that it was mine.

And into my garden stole,
When the night had veild the pole ;
In the morning glad I see ;
My foe outstretchd beneath the tree.

The Watersnakes Appear, 1877, Gustave Doré

The Rime of the Ancient Mariner

Samuel Taylor Coleridge

Poet, critic, and philosopher Samuel Taylor Coleridge was born in 1772. Although he was a brilliant scholar, he dropped out of university and joined the cavalry. By 1797, Coleridge had become a close friend of William Wordsworth, with whom he published *Lyrical Ballads,* in which "The Rime of the Ancient Mariner" first appeared. This collection of poetry is generally considered the beginning of the English Romantic Movement. Later, Coleridge published *Biographia Literaria*, the most significant book of criticism of its time. He died in London in 1834. How important is it to consider people's intentions when judging their acts? Why does or doesn't it matter whether someone behaves maliciously or thoughtlessly, if the consequences are the same?

The Rime of the Ancient Mariner

Facile credo, plures esse Naturas invisibiles quam visibiles in rerum universitate. Sed horum omnium familiam quis nobis enarrabit? et gradus et cognationes et discrimina et singulorum munera? Quid agunt? quae loca habitant? Horum rerum notitiam semper ambivit ingenium humanum, nunquam attigit. Juvat, interea, non diffiteor, quandoque in animo, tanquam in tabula, majoris et melioris mundi imaginem contemplari: ne mens assuefacta hodiernae vitae minutiis se contrahat nimis, et tota subsidat in pusillas cogitationes. Sed veritati interea invigilandum est, modusque servandus, ut certa ab incertis, diem a nocte, distinguamus. (T. Burnet, *Archaeol. Phil.*)

ARGUMENT

How a ship, having first sailed to the Equator, was driven by storms to the cold Country towards the South Pole; how the Ancient Mariner cruelly and in contempt of the laws of hospitality killed a Seabird and how he was followed by many and strange Judgments: and in what manner he came back to his own Country.

PART I

An ancient Mariner meeteth three Gallants bidden to a wedding feast, and detaineth one.

It is an ancient Mariner,
And he stoppeth one of three.
—"By thy long gray beard and glittering eye,
Now wherefore stopp'st thou me?

The Bridegroom's doors are opened wide,
And I am next of kin;
The guests are met, the feast is set:
May'st hear the merry din."

He holds him with his skinny hand,
"There was a ship," quoth he.   10
"Hold off! unhand me, graybeard loon!"
Eftsoons his hand dropt he.

He holds him with his glittering eye—
The Wedding-Guest stood still,
And listens like a three years' child:
The Mariner hath his will.

The Wedding-Guest sat on a stone;
He cannot choose but hear;
And thus spake on that ancient man,
The bright-eyed Mariner.   20

"The ship was cheered, the harbour cleared,
Merrily did we drop
Below the kirk, below the hill,
Below the lighthouse top.

The Sun came up upon the left,
Out of the sea came he!
And he shone bright, and on the right
Went down into the sea.

Higher and higher every day,
Till over the mast at noon—"   30
The Wedding-Guest here beat his breast,
For he heard the loud bassoon.

The bride hath paced into the hall,
Red as a rose is she;
Nodding their heads before her goes
The merry minstrelsy.

The Wedding-Guest he beat his breast,
Yet he cannot choose but hear;
And thus spake on that ancient man,
The bright-eyed Mariner.   40

The ship driven by a
storm toward the
South Pole.

"And now the STORM-BLAST came, and he
Was tyrannous and strong;
He struck with his o'ertaking wings,
And chased us south along.

With sloping masts and dipping prow,
As who pursued with yell and blow
Still treads the shadow of his foe,
And forward bends his head,
The ship drove fast, loud roared the blast,
And southward aye we fled.   50

And now there came both mist and snow,
And it grew wondrous cold:
And ice, mast-high, came floating by,
As green as emerald.

The land of ice, and of
fearful sounds where
no living thing was to
be seen.

And through the drifts the snowy clifts
Did send a dismal sheen:
Nor shapes of men nor beasts we ken—
The ice was all between.

The ice was here, the ice was there,
The ice was all around: 60
It cracked and growled, and roared and howled,
Like noises in a swound!

Till a great sea bird,
called the Albatross,
came through the
snow-fog, and was
received with great joy
and hospitality.

At length did cross an Albatross,
Thorough the fog it came;
As if it had been a Christian soul,
We hailed it in God's name.

It ate the food it ne'er had eat,
And round and round it flew.
The ice did split with a thunder-fit;
The helmsman steered us through!   70

And lo! the Albatross proveth a bird of good omen, and followeth the ship as it returned northward through fog and floating ice.

And a good south wind sprung up behind;
The Albatross did follow,
And every day, for food or play,
Came to the mariners' hollo!

In mist or cloud, on mast or shroud,
It perched for vespers nine;
Whiles all the night, through fog-smoke white,
Glimmered the white Moon-shine."

The ancient Mariner inhospitably killeth the pious bird of good omen.

"God save thee, ancient Mariner!
From the fiends, that plague thee thus!—   80
Why look'st thou so?"—With my cross-bow
I shot the ALBATROSS.

PART II

The Sun now rose upon the right:
Out of the sea came he,
Still hid in mist, and on the left
Went down into the sea.

And the good south wind still blew behind,
But no sweet bird did follow,
Nor any day for food or play
Came to the mariners' hollo!   90

And I had done a hellish thing,
And it would work 'em woe:
For all averred, I had killed the bird
That made the breeze to blow.
Ah wretch! said they, the bird to slay,
That made the breeze to blow!

Nor dim nor red, like God's own head,
The glorious Sun uprist:
Then all averred, I had killed the bird
That brought the fog and mist.   100
'Twas right, said they, such birds to slay,
That bring the fog and mist.

The fair breeze blew, the white foam flew,
The furrow followed free;
We were the first that ever burst
Into that silent sea.

Down dropped the breeze, the sails dropped down,
'Twas sad as sad could be;
And we did speak only to break
The silence of the sea!   110

All in a hot and copper sky,
The bloody Sun, at noon,
Right up above the mast did stand,
No bigger than the Moon.

Day after day, day after day,
We stuck, nor breath nor motion;
As idle as a painted ship
Upon a painted ocean.

Water, water, everywhere,
And all the boards did shrink;   120
Water, water, everywhere,
Nor any drop to drink.

The very deep did rot: O Christ!
That ever this should be!
Yea, slimy things did crawl with legs
Upon the slimy sea.

About, about, in reel and rout
The death-fires danced at night;
The water, like a witch's oils,
Burnt green, and blue and white.   130

A Spirit had followed
them; one of the
invisible inhabitants of
this planet, neither
departed souls nor
angels; concerning
whom the learned Jew,
Josephus, and the
Platonic
Constantinopolitan,
Michael Psellus, may
be consulted. They are
very numerous, and
there is no climate or
element without one
or more.

And some in dreams assurèd were
Of the Spirit that plagued us so;
Nine fathom deep he had followed us
From the land of mist and snow.

And every tongue, through utter drought,
Was withered at the root;
We could not speak, no more than if
We had been choked with soot.

The shipmates, in their
sore distress, would
fain throw the whole
guilt on the ancient
Mariner: in sign
whereof they hang the
dead sea bird round his
neck.

Ah! well-a-day! what evil looks
Had I from old and young!   140
Instead of the cross, the Albatross
About my neck was hung.

Part III

There passed a weary time. Each throat
Was parched, and glazed each eye.
A weary time! a weary time!
How glazed each weary eye,
When looking westward, I beheld
A something in the sky.

At first it seemed a little speck,
And then it seemed a mist;   150
It moved and moved, and took at last
A certain shape, I wist.

A speck, a mist, a shape, I wist!
And still it neared and neared:
As if it dodged a water-sprite,
It plunged and tacked and veered.

With throats unslaked, with black lips baked,
We could nor laugh nor wail;
Through utter drought all dumb we stood!
I bit my arm, I sucked the blood,   160
And cried, A sail! a sail!

With throats unslaked, with black lips baked,
Agape they heard me call:
Gramercy! they for joy did grin,
And all at once their breath drew in,
As they were drinking all.

See! see! (I cried) she tacks no more!
Hither to work us weal;
Without a breeze, without a tide,
She steadies with upright keel!   170

The ancient Mariner beholdeth a sign in the element afar off.

At its nearer approach, it seemeth him to be a ship; and at a dear ransom he freeth his speech from the bonds of thirst.

A flash of joy;

And horror follows. For can it be a ship that comes onward without wind or tide?

The western wave was all aflame.
The day was well nigh done!
Almost upon the western wave
Rested the broad bright Sun;
When that strange shape drove suddenly
Betwixt us and the Sun.

It seemeth him but the
skeleton of a ship.

And straight the Sun was flecked with bars,
(Heaven's Mother send us grace!)
As if through a dungeon-grate he peered
With broad and burning face.   180

And its ribs are seen as
bars on the face of the
setting Sun.

Alas! (thought I, and my heart beat loud)
How fast she nears and nears!
Are those *her* sails that glance in the Sun,
Like restless gossameres?

The Specter-Woman
and her Deathmate,
and no other on board
the skeleton ship.

Are those *her* ribs through which the Sun
Did peer, as through a grate?
And is that Woman all her crew?
Is that a DEATH? and are there two?
Is DEATH that woman's mate?

Like vessel, like crew!

Her lips were red, *her* looks were free,   190
Her locks were yellow as gold:
Her skin was as white as leprosy,
The Night-mare LIFE-IN-DEATH was she,
Who thicks man's blood with cold.

Death and Life-in-
Death have diced for
the ship's crew, and
she (the latter)
winneth the ancient
Mariner.

The naked hulk alongside came,
And the twain were casting dice;
"The game is done! I've won! I've won!"
Quoth she, and whistles thrice.

No twilight within the
courts of the Sun.

The Sun's rim dips; the stars rush out:
At one stride comes the dark;   200
With far-heard whisper, o'er the sea,
Off shot the spectre-bark.

At the rising of the
Moon,

We listened and looked sideways up!
Fear at my heart, as at a cup,
My life-blood seemed to sip!
The stars were dim, and thick the night,
The steersman's face by his lamp gleamed white;
From the sails the dew did drip—
Till clomb above the eastern bar
The hornèd Moon, with one bright star   210
Within the nether tip.

One after another,

One after one, by the star-dogged Moon,
Too quick for groan or sigh,
Each turned his face with a ghastly pang,
And cursed me with his eye.

His shipmates drop
down dead.

Four times fifty living men,
(And I heard nor sigh nor groan)
With heavy thump, a lifeless lump,
They dropped down one by one.

But Life-in-Death
begins her work on the
ancient Mariner.

The souls did from their bodies fly—   220
They fled to bliss or woe!
And every soul, it passed me by,
Like the whizz of my cross-bow!

Part IV

The Wedding-Guest
feareth that a Spirit is
talking to him;

"I fear thee, ancient Mariner!
I fear thy skinny hand!
And thou art long, and lank, and brown,
As is the ribbed sea-sand.

I fear thee and thy glittering eye,
And thy skinny hand, so brown."—
Fear not, fear not, thou Wedding-Guest! 230
This body dropped not down.

But the ancient
Mariner assureth him
of his bodily life, and
proceedeth to relate his
horrible penance.

Alone, alone, all, all alone,
Alone on a wide wide sea!
And never a saint took pity on
My soul in agony.

He despiseth the
creatures of the calm,

The many men, so beautiful!
And they all dead did lie:
And a thousand thousand slimy things
Lived on; and so did I.

And envieth that they
should live, and so
many lie dead.

I looked upon the rotting sea, 240
And drew my eyes away;
I looked upon the rotting deck,
And there the dead men lay.

I looked to heaven, and tried to pray;
But or ever a prayer had gushed,
A wicked whisper came, and made
My heart as dry as dust.

I closed my lids, and kept them close,
And the balls like pulses beat;
For the sky and the sea, and the sea and the sky 250
Lay like a load on my weary eye,
And the dead were at my feet.

But the curse liveth for
him in the eye of the
dead men.

The cold sweat melted from their limbs,
Nor rot nor reek did they:
The look with which they looked on me
Had never passed away.

An orphan's curse would drag to hell
A spirit from on high;
But oh! more horrible than that
Is the curse in a dead man's eye!   260
Seven days, seven nights, I saw that curse,
And yet I could not die.

In his loneliness and
fixedness he yearneth
towards the journeying
Moon, and the stars
that still sojourn, yet
still move onward; and
everywhere the blue
sky belongs to them,
and is their appointed
rest, and their native
country and their own
natural homes,
which they enter
unannounced, as lords
that are certainly
expected and yet there
is a silent joy at their
arrival.

The moving Moon went up the sky,
And no where did abide:
Softly she was going up,
And a star or two beside—

Her beams bemocked the sultry main,
Like April hoar-frost spread;
But where the ship's huge shadow lay,
The charmèd water burnt alway   270
A still and awful red.

By the light of the
Moon he beholdeth
God's creatures of the
great calm.

Beyond the shadow of the ship,
I watched the watersnakes:
They moved in tracks of shining white,
And when they reared, the elfish light
Fell off in hoary flakes.

Within the shadow of the ship
I watched their rich attire:
Blue, glossy green, and velvet black,
They coiled and swam; and every track   280
Was a flash of golden fire.

Their beauty and their
happiness.

O happy living things! no tongue
Their beauty might declare:
A spring of love gushed from my heart,

He blesseth them in
his heart.

And I blessed them unaware:
Sure my kind saint took pity on me,
And I blessed them unaware.

The spell begins to break.

The self-same moment I could pray;
And from my neck so free
The Albatross fell off, and sank   290
Like lead into the sea.

PART V

Oh sleep! it is a gentle thing,
Beloved from pole to pole!
To Mary Queen the praise be given!
She sent the gentle sleep from Heaven,
That slid into my soul.

By grace of the holy Mother, the ancient Mariner is refreshed with rain

The silly buckets on the deck,
That had so long remained,
I dreamt that they were filled with dew;
And when I awoke, it rained.   300

My lips were wet, my throat was cold,
My garments all were dank;
Sure I had drunken in my dreams,
And still my body drank.

I moved, and could not feel my limbs:
I was so light—almost
I thought that I had died in sleep,
And was a blessèd ghost.

He heareth sounds and seeth strange sights and commotions in the sky and the element.

And soon I heard a roaring wind:
It did not come anear;   310
But with its sound it shook the sails,
That were so thin and sere.

The upper air burst into life!
And a hundred fire-flags sheen,
To and fro they were hurried about!
And to and fro, and in and out,
The wan stars danced between.

And the coming wind did roar more loud,
And the sails did sigh like sedge;
And the rain poured down from one black cloud; 320
The Moon was at its edge.

The thick black cloud was cleft, and still
The Moon was at its side:
Like waters shot from some high crag,
The lightning fell with never a jag,
A river steep and wide.

The bodies of the
ship's crew are
inspirited, and the ship
moves on;
The loud wind never reached the ship,
Yet now the ship moved on!
Beneath the lightning and the Moon
The dead men gave a groan.
                                        330

They groaned, they stirred, they all uprose,
Nor spake, nor moved their eyes;
It had been strange, even in a dream,
To have seen those dead men rise.

The helmsman steered, the ship moved on;
Yet never a breeze up-blew;
The mariners all 'gan work the ropes,
Where they were wont to do;
They raised their limbs like lifeless tools—
We were a ghastly crew.
                                        340

The body of my brother's son
Stood by me, knee to knee:
The body and I pulled at one rope,
But he said nought to me.

But not by the souls of
the men, nor by
demons of earth or
middle air, but by a
blessed troop of
angelic spirits, sent
down by the
invocation of the
guardian saint.

"I fear thee, ancient Mariner!"
Be calm, thou Wedding-Guest!
'Twas not those souls that fled in pain,
Which to their corses came again,
But a troop of spirits blest:

For when it dawned—they dropped their arms,   350
And clustered round the mast;
Sweet sounds rose slowly through their mouths,
And from their bodies passed.

Around, around, flew each sweet sound,
Then darted to the Sun;
Slowly the sounds came back again,
Now mixed, now one by one.

Sometimes a-dropping from the sky
I heard the sky-lark sing;
Sometimes all little birds that are,   360
How they seemed to fill the sea and air
With their sweet jargoning!

And now 'twas like all instruments,
Now like a lonely flute;
And now it is an angel's song,
That makes the heavens be mute.

It ceased; yet still the sails made on
A pleasant noise till noon,
A noise like of a hidden brook
In the leafy month of June,   370
That to the sleeping woods all night
Singeth a quiet tune.

Till noon we quietly sailed on,
Yet never a breeze did breathe:
Slowly and smoothly went the ship,
Moved onward from beneath.

The lonesome Spirit
from the South Pole
carries on the ship as
far as the Line, in obe-
dience to the angelic
troop, but still
requireth vengeance.

Under the keel nine fathom deep,
From the land of mist and snow,
The spirit slid: and it was he
That made the ship to go.   380
The sails at noon left off their tune,
And the ship stood still also.

The Sun, right up above the mast,
Had fixed her to the ocean:
But in a minute she 'gan stir,
With a short uneasy motion—
Backwards and forwards half her length
With a short uneasy motion.

Then like a pawing horse let go,
She made a sudden bound: 390
It flung the blood into my head,
And I fell down in a swound.

The Polar Spirit's fel-
low demons, the invis-
ible inhabitants of the
element, take part in
his wrong; and two of
them relate, one to the
other, that penance
long and heavy for the
ancient Mariner hath
been accorded to the
Polar Spirit, who
returneth southward.

How long in that same fit I lay,
I have not to declare;
But ere my living life returned,
I heard and in my soul discerned
Two voices in the air.

"Is it he?" quoth one, "Is this the man?
By him who died on cross,
With his cruel bow he laid full low   400
The harmless Albatross.

The spirit who bideth by himself
In the land of mist and snow,
He loved the bird that loved the man
Who shot him with his bow."

The other was a softer voice,
As soft as honeydew:
Quoth he, "The man hath penance done,
And penance more will do."

PART VI

FIRST VOICE
"But tell me, tell me! speak again,   410
Thy soft response renewing—
What makes that ship drive on so fast?
What is the ocean doing?"

SECOND VOICE
"Still as a slave before his lord,
The ocean hath no blast;
His great bright eye most silently
Up to the Moon is cast—

If he may know which way to go;
For she guides him smooth or grim.
See, brother, see! how graciously   420
She looketh down on him."

The Mariner hath
been cast into a trance;
for the angelic power
causeth the vessel to
drive northward faster
than human life could
endure.

FIRST VOICE
"But why drives on that ship so fast,
Without or wave or wind?"

SECOND VOICE
"The air is cut away before,
And closes from behind.

Fly, brother, fly! more high, more high!
Or we shall be belated:
For slow and slow that ship will go,
When the Mariner's trance is abated."

The supernatural motion is retarded; the Mariner awakes, and his penance begins anew.

I woke, and we were sailing on   430
As in a gentle weather:
'Twas night, calm night, the moon was high;
The dead men stood together.

All stood together on the deck,
For a charnel-dungeon fitter:
All fixed on me their stony eyes,
That in the Moon did glitter.

The pang, the curse, with which they died,
Had never passed away:
I could not draw my eyes from theirs,   440
Nor turn them up to pray.

The curse is finally expiated.

And now this spell was snapped: once more
I viewed the ocean green,
And looked far forth, yet little saw
Of what had else been seen—

Like one, that on a lonesome road
Doth walk in fear and dread,
And having once turned round walks on,
And turns no more his head;
Because he knows, a frightful fiend   450
Doth close behind him tread.

But soon there breathed a wind on me,
Nor sound nor motion made:
Its path was not upon the sea,
In ripple or in shade.

It raised my hair, it fanned my cheek
Like a meadow-gale of spring—
It mingled strangely with my fears,
Yet it felt like a welcoming.

Swiftly, swiftly flew the ship,   460
Yet she sailed softly too:
Sweetly, sweetly blew the breeze—
On me alone it blew.

And the ancient
Mariner beholdeth his
native country.

Oh! dream of joy! is this indeed
The lighthouse top I see?
Is this the hill? is this the kirk?
Is this mine own countree?

We drifted o'er the harbour bar,
And I with sobs did pray—
O let me be awake, my God!   470
Or let me sleep alway.

The harbour bay was clear as glass,
So smoothly it was strewn!
And on the bay, the moonlight lay,
And the shadow of the Moon.

The rock shone bright, the kirk no less,
That stands above the rock:
The moonlight steeped in silentness
The steady weathercock.

And the bay was white with silent light,   480
Till rising from the same,
The angelic spirits
leave the dead bodies,
Full many shapes, that shadows were,
In crimson colours came.

And appear in their own forms of light.

A little distance from the prow
Those crimson shadows were:
I turned my eyes upon the deck—
Oh, Christ! what saw I there!

Each corse lay flat, lifeless and flat,
And, by the holy rood!
A man all light, a seraph man,   490
On every corse there stood.

This seraph band, each waved his hand:
It was a heavenly sight!
They stood as signals to the land,
Each one a lovely light;

This seraph band, each waved his hand,
No voice did they impart—
No voice; but oh! the silence sank
Like music on my heart.

But soon I heard the dash of oars,   500
I heard the Pilot's cheer;
My head was turned perforce away
And I saw a boat appear.

The Pilot and the Pilot's boy,
I heard them coming fast:
Dear Lord in Heaven! it was a joy
The dead men could not blast.

I saw a third—I heard his voice:
It is the Hermit good!
He singeth loud his godly hymns   510
That he makes in the wood.
He'll shrieve my soul, he'll wash away
The Albatross's blood.

PART VII

The Hermit of the
Wood,

This Hermit good lives in that wood
Which slopes down to the sea.
How loudly his sweet voice he rears!
He loves to talk with marineres
That come from a far countree.

He kneels at morn, and noon, and eve—
He hath a cushion plump: 520
It is the moss that wholly hides
The rotted old oak-stump.

The skiff-boat neared: I heard them talk,
"Why, this is strange, I trow!
Where are those lights so many and fair,
That signal made but now?"

Approacheth the ship
with wonder.

"Strange, by my faith!" the Hermit said—
"And they answered not our cheer!
The planks looked warped! and see those sails,
How thin they are and sere!   530
I never saw aught like to them,
Unless perchance it were

Brown skeletons of leaves that lag
My forest-brook along;
When the ivy tod is heavy with snow,
And the owlet whoops to the wolf below,
That eats the she-wolf's young."

"Dear Lord! it hath a fiendish look,"
(The Pilot made reply)
"I am a-feared"—"Push on, push on!"   540
Said the Hermit cheerily.

The boat came closer to the ship,
But I nor spake nor stirred;
The boat came close beneath the ship,
And straight a sound was heard.

Under the water it rumbled on,
Still louder and more dread:
It reached the ship, it split the bay;
The ship went down like lead.

Stunned by that loud and dreadful sound,   550
Which sky and ocean smote,
Like one that hath been seven days drowned
My body lay afloat;
But swift as dreams, myself I found
Within the Pilot's boat.

Upon the whirl, where sank the ship,
The boat spun round and round;
And all was still, save that the hill
Was telling of the sound.

I moved my lips—the Pilot shrieked   560
And fell down in a fit;
The holy Hermit raised his eyes,
And prayed where he did sit.

I took the oars: the Pilot's boy,
Who now doth crazy go,
Laughed loud and long, and all the while
His eyes went to and fro.
"Ha! ha!" quoth he, "full plain I see,
The Devil knows how to row."

And now, all in my own countree, 570
I stood on the firm land!
The Hermit stepped forth from the boat,
And scarcely he could stand.

The ancient Mariner
earnestly entreateth the
Hermit to shrieve him;
and the penance of life
falls on him.

"O shrieve me, shrieve me, holy man!"
The Hermit crossed his brow.
"Say quick," quoth he, "I bid thee say—
What manner of man art thou?"

Forthwith this frame of mine was wrenched
With a woeful agony,
Which forced me to begin my tale; 580
And then it left me free.

And ever and anon
throughout his future
life an agony
constraineth him to
travel from land to
land;

Since then, at an uncertain hour,
That agony returns:
And till my ghastly tale is told,
This heart within me burns.

I pass, like night, from land to land;
I have strange power of speech;
That moment that his face I see,
I know the man that must hear me:
To him my tale I teach. 590

What loud uproar bursts from that door!
The wedding-guests are there:
But in the garden-bower the bride
And bride-maids singing are:
And hark the little vesper bell,
Which biddeth me to prayer!

O Wedding-Guest! this soul hath been
Alone on a wide wide sea:
So lonely 'twas, that God himself
Scarce seemèd there to be.   600

O sweeter than the marriage feast,
'Tis sweeter far to me,
To walk together to the kirk
With a goodly company!—

To walk together to the kirk,
And all together pray,
While each to his great Father bends,
Old men, and babes, and loving friends
And youths and maidens gay!

And to teach, by his own example, love and reverence to all things that God made and loveth.

Farewell, farewell! but this I tell   610
To thee, thou Wedding-Guest!
He prayeth well, who loveth well
Both man and bird and beast.

He prayeth best, who loveth best
All things both great and small;
For the dear God who loveth us,
He made and loveth all.

The Mariner, whose eye is bright,
Whose beard with age is hoar,
Is gone: and now the Wedding-Guest   620
Turned from the bridegroom's door.

He went like one that hath been stunned,
And is of sense forlorn:
A sadder and a wiser man,
He rose the morrow morn.

Notes

Facile credo... "I readily believe that there are more invisible than visible Natures in the universe. But who will explain for us the family of all these beings, and the ranks and relations and distinguishing features and functions of each? What do they do? What places do they inhabit? The human mind has always sought the knowledge of these things, but never attained it. Meanwhile I do not deny that it is helpful sometimes to contemplate in the mind, as on a tablet, the image of a greater and better world, lest the intellect, habituated to the petty things of daily life, narrow itself and sink wholly into trivial thoughts. But at the same time we must be watchful for the truth and keep a sense of proportion, so that we may distinguish the certain from the uncertain, day from night." Adapted by Coleridge from Thomas Burnet, *Archaeologiae Philosophicae* (1692)

eftsoons a straight path

kirk a church

swound swoon

uprist arose

wist knew; from the Old English *witan*

gramercy an expression meaning "great thanks"; from the French phrase *grand-merci*

weal benefit; from the Old English word *wela*

hoary grey or white

silly lowly, harmless

sheen shone

sedge rush-like plants that grow around lakes and streams

corses corpses

jargoning warbling

rood the Christian cross; from the Old English word *rod*

shrieve to set free from sin; from the Old English word *scrifan*, meaning "to impose as a penance"; originally from the Latin word *scribere*, meaning "to write"

tod a bushy clump

crossed his brow refers to gesticulating to make the sign of the Christian cross

Activities

1. Divide a page into three columns. On your first reading of the poem, pause at the end of each section to paraphrase, question, and react. In the first column, write a point-form summary of the section; in the second, record at least two questions about the events, ideas, and language; and in the third, note your reaction to the section. Discuss your notes with a partner.

2. "The Rime of the Ancient Mariner" is a ballad, the oldest form of poetry. Choose three or four verses of the poem that are particularly appealing to your ear and analyze the rhyme scheme, metre, and stanzas. Write a short parody that follows the same form. Share your parodies, considering the following questions: How does the form of the poem enhance the meaning? What features of the form and style of this poem make it easy to memorize short excerpts? Why do you think this poem is one of the most quoted and parodied poems in the English language?

Another Viewpoint: History

During the eighteenth century, the British Empire expanded, as British explorers colonized other countries and merchants engaged in the slave trade. The British public was fascinated by tales of perilous voyages and exotic discoveries. Keeping this context in mind, reread the poem as a story of unfortunate exploration, paying particular attention to the geographical and topographical description. How does Coleridge depict travel and exploration? What might the ghost ship symbolize?

O Can You Leave Your Native Land?

Susanna Moodie

Susanna Moodie was born in 1803, in Suffolk, England, into an afflu-ent family. When her father died in 1818, Moodie and her sisters began to write books for children and romantic novels, in part to earn money. In 1832, she and her husband immigrated to Canada along with her sister, Catharine Parr Trail. Moodie's stories of pio-neer life near Cobourg, Ontario, including *Roughing It in the Bush* (1852) and *Life in the Clearings* (1854), provided a realistic reflection of wilderness living in stark contrast to the glowing reports usually given to potential immigrants to Canada by English land agents. This poem, which explores the topic of immigration to Canada, was writ-ten as song lyrics. Moodie has been commended for her fascination with differences in character, her considerable psychological insight, and a generous measure of wit and playfulness in her writing. Have you or your parents or friends immigrated to Canada from another country? If so, what were the first impressions of this country? What were some of the difficulties encountered and how were they dealt with?

O Can You Leave Your Native Land?

(For Music.)

O can you leave your native land,
      An exile's bride to be;
Your mother's home and cheerful hearth
      To tempt the main with me—
Across the wide and stormy sea
      To trace our foaming track,
And know the wave that heaves us on
      Will never bear us back?

And can you in Canadian wood
      With me the harvest bind,   10
Nor feel one lingering sad regret
      For all you leave behind!
Can those dear hands, unused to toil,
      The woodman's wants supply,
Nor shrink beneath the chilly blast
      When wintry storms are nigh?

Amid the shades of forests dark,
      Our loved isle will appear
An Eden, whose delicious bloom
      Will make the wild more drear—   20
And you in solitude will weep
      O'er scenes belov'd in vain,
And pine away your life to view
      Once more your native plain!

Then pause, dear girl, ere those fond lips
    Your wanderer's fate decide;
My spirit spurns the selfish wish—
    You must not be my bride—
But oh, that smile—those tearful eyes
    My firmer purpose move—   30
Our hearts are one—and we will dare
    All perils thus to love.

Activities

1. From whose point of view is this poem written and to whom is it addressed? How does the narrator describe life in the "Canadian wood"? How does this description contrast with that of life in the "native land"?

2. Reread the poem with a particular focus on the language used by the author. Make a list of words, phrases, and spellings that are typical of nineteenth-century language and style. Rewrite the poem using contemporary language and idioms.

Another Viewpoint: Culture

Margaret Atwood wrote a book of poetry in response to Moodie's writing; she called it *The Journals of Susanna Moodie*. In the afterword, Atwood makes the following observation: "What struck me most about [Susanna Moodie's] personality was the way in which it reflects many of the obsessions still with us." Consider the extent to which this poem contains some of the same "obsessions" that contemporary Canadians experience.

Dover Beach

Matthew Arnold

Born in 1822, Matthew Arnold was a major figure in Victorian England. Educated at Oxford University, he later had a great impact on the English education system as an inspector of schools. He was also a professor at Oxford, where he became a well-known literary critic who believed that objective literary criticism was essential to the welfare of a nation. Like many of his contemporaries, he struggled with the growing tension between science and religion during his era, which contributed to a sense of pessimism and spiritual isolation within his culture. Arnold died in 1888. To what extent do scenes in nature, such as an ocean, a forest, or a flock of birds, prompt you to reflect on your own life situation? What scenes are most likely to create a reflective mood for you and why?

◀ *Cliffs of Dover*

Dover Beach

The sea is calm tonight.
The tide is full, the moon lies fair
Upon the straits—on the French coast the light
Gleams and is gone; the cliffs of England stand,
Glimmering and vast, out in the tranquil bay.
Come to the window, sweet is the night air!
Only, from the long line of spray
Where the sea meets the moon-blanched land,
Listen! you hear the grating roar
Of pebbles which the waves draw back, and fling,   10
At their return, up the high strand,
Begin, and cease, and then again begin,
With tremulous cadence slow, and bring
The eternal note of sadness in.

Sophocles long ago
Heard it on the Aegean, and it brought
Into his mind the turbid ebb and flow
Of human misery; we
Find also in the sound a thought,
Hearing it by this distant northern sea.   20

The Sea of Faith
Was once, too, at the full, and round earth's shore
Lay like the folds of a bright girdle furled.
But now I only hear
Its melancholy, long, withdrawing roar,
Retreating, to the breath
Of the night wind, down the vast edges drear
And naked shingles of the world.

Ah, love, let us be true
To one another! for the world, which seems   30
To lie before us like a land of dreams,
So various, so beautiful, so new,
Hath really neither joy, nor love, nor light,
Nor certitude, nor peace, nor help for pain;
And we are here as on a darkling plain
Swept with confused alarms of struggle and flight,
Where ignorant armies clash by night.

Notes

Sophocles long ago heard it on the Aegean Sophocles (495–406 BCE)
wrote about the powerlessness of human beings against fate. Two of his
best-known tragic figures are Antigone and Oedipus. Some critics see a
direct parallel between this poem and lines 583 to 591 of Sophocles' play
Antigone.

shingles beaches covered with pebbles or small stones

Activities

1. What view of the world is depicted in this poem by Matthew Arnold?
Which feelings is Arnold exploring? How does his view compare with your
feelings and ideas about the future?

2. "Dover Beach" is a dramatic monologue. How does this form contribute
to the poem's mood and theme? Try revising the poem to eliminate the first-
and second-person references. How does this change the impact of the
poem? Compare and justify your answers in a small group, challenging and
building on each other's ideas.

Another Viewpoint: History

Some critics approach literature by stressing the relationship of literature
to its historical period. To a great extent, "Dover Beach" reflects the intellectual
and social world of the Victorian era. Conduct some research on the tension between science and religion during the Victorian period of English history. Use this information to set this poem in a historical context. Then
discuss in what ways placing a text in its context can either enhance or dis-
tort the understanding of a literary work.

Because I Could Not Stop for Death—

Emily Dickinson

Emily Dickinson was born in 1830 in Amherst, Massachusetts. As a young adult, she began to withdraw from the world. By her forties, she refused to leave her house altogether, though she was an avid letter-writer. Dickinson wrote poetry beginning in her childhood and, after her death in 1886, nearly 2,000 poems were found in her house. The years of Dickinson's greatest poetic output, about 800 poems, coincided with the American Civil War. In terms of her use of metre, her major influences were the English hymn writer Isaac Watts, William Shakespeare, and the King James Version of the Bible. Critic Carl Van Doren wrote that Emily Dickinson "did not so much cut her poems to the bone as leave them as they were, without adding the customary flesh. Her work approaches poetry's irreducible minimum, which is poetry's immortal part." Initially regarded as an eccentric minor voice, Dickinson is recognized today as one of America's greatest poets. What is appealing or unappealing about minimalist poetry? With which other minimalist poets are you familiar and how do their works compare with Dickinson's?

Because I Could Not Stop for Death—

Because I could not stop for Death—
He kindly stopped for me—
The Carriage held but just Ourselves—
And Immortality.

We slowly drove—He knew no haste
And I had put away
My labor and my leisure too,
For His Civility—

We passed the School, where Children strove
At Recess—in the Ring—   10
We passed the Fields of Gazing Grain—
We passed the Setting Sun—

Or rather—He passed Us—
The Dews drew quivering and chill—
For only Gossamer, my Gown—
My Tippet—only Tulle—

We paused before a House that seemed
A Swelling of the Ground—
The Roof was scarcely visible—
The Cornice—in the Ground—   20

Since then—'tis Centuries—and yet
Feels shorter than the Day
I first surmised the Horses Heads
Were toward Eternity—

Notes

gossamer light, insubstantial fabric; alternatively, filmy substance like cobwebs

tippet a woman's cape or wrap

tulle sheer material often used for veils

cornice the molded, projecting horizontal piece which crowns the top of an architectural composition

surmised inferred

Activities

1. Consider the following possibilities: Is Dickinson's primary intent in this poem to give expression to the hope for immortality or to describe the experience of living with the knowledge of death? Do you have another interpretation of the poet's purpose? Support your idea with references to the poem. What is your response to the poem's central theme?

2. One critic has identified the tone of the poem as "sad thoughtfulness, languor, and repressed terror." What passages do you think led to this evaluation? What other words would you use to describe the tone? Which elements of diction contribute to the tone?

Another Viewpoint: Archetypal Patterns

Analyze the archetypal patterns of birth, time, and death in Emily Dickinson's poem and compare your findings with the treatment of these patterns in Dylan Thomas' "Fern Hill" on page 494 of this anthology. Use your analyses to write a comparative essay in which you focus on the dominant recurring images in each poem.

wrap-up
poetry

1. Choose a poem from this unit to read aloud or tape-record for a small group. Write an introduction to the poem in which you provide a rationale for your choice, including what impressed you most about the poem and how you think it gains meaning by being read aloud and listened to. Rehearse reading your introduction and the poem. Present it to the group and elicit feedback about the persuasiveness of your rationale and the effectiveness of your reading.

2. In a small group, select the three poems in this unit that you think most effectively link an abstract concept with a concrete image. In a four-column chart (using the headings "Title," "Concept," "Concrete Image," and "Technique," respectively), record details about your choices. Then select three other written or visual forms, such as a short story, film, or advertisement. As a group, do research to track down one example of each form you selected in which an abstract concept is linked with a concrete image. Add these examples to your chart. Present your results to the class for discussion.

3. Poetry in the twentieth century was noted for a number of *movements*, particular approaches to writing verse that shared common techniques and conceptual frameworks. Using print and non-print resources, research one of these movements. Write a formal essay in which you describe and analyze the main ideas and characteristics of the movement, using specific examples from your research and, if applicable, from this anthology. As you revise your work, pay particular attention to clarity of expression, the effectiveness of your style, and the proper citation and integration of researched information.

4. Suppose that you and a group of your classmates want to start a student poetry magazine at your school. With your group, plan a proposal that will convince school administrators to allow you to publish this magazine and to allocate start-up funds for your endeavour. Brainstorm with your group to identify the focus and goal of your magazine and write a concise statement of purpose. Research the costs associated with your project to demonstrate that you have carefully considered all facets of your proposal. Itemize the costs in order to justify the expenses needed to produce the magazine. Use a word-processing and spreadsheet program to produce your final proposal.

4 drama

Drama should have for its subject a single action, whole and complete, with a beginning, a middle, and an end. It will thus resemble a living organism in all its unity, and produce the pleasure proper to it.

— *Aristotle*

When you work in the theatre there's a special joy and wonder when you see all the parts that make up a play come together with an audience to create an event of transcendence. It's a kind of miracle.

— *Sharon Pollock*

A Marriage Proposal

Anton Chekhov

Translated by Theodore Hoffman

Anton Chekhov was born in Taganrog, Russia, in 1860, the grandson of a serf. Chekhov attended medical school in Moscow. By the time he began practising medicine in 1894, he was already publishing short stories and humorous sketches. He published his first play, *Ivanov,* in 1887. From then until his death in 1904, he wrote an impressive body of stories and plays, while continuing to work as a doctor. Chekhov is often described as a *realist*. His writing portrays tragicomic characteristics of ordinary people and events. He emphasizes internal drama, characterization, and mood, rather than plot. He once commented, "Any idiot can face a crisis; it is this day-to-day living that wears you out." To what extent do you agree with Chekhov's comment that daily life is more challenging than a crisis? Do you prefer literature and entertainment that deals with small events in people's lives or with larger-than-life characters engaged in enormous struggles? Why?

Characters

CHUBUKOV—*a wealthy, middle-aged gentleman who owns an estate in nineteenth-century Russia*

NATALIA—*his daughter, an unmarried woman ready to take a husband*

LOMOV—*a neighbour gentleman, a neurotic bachelor of thirty-five*

(CHUBUKOV'S *mansion—the living room.* LOMOV *enters, formally dressed in evening jacket, white gloves, top hat. He is nervous from the start.*)

CHUBUKOV: *(Rising)* Well, look who's here! Ivan Vassilevitch! *(Shakes his hand warmly)* What a surprise, old man! How are you?

LOMOV: Oh, not too bad. And you?

CHUBUKOV: Oh, we manage, we manage. Do sit down, please. You know, you've been neglecting your neighbours, my dear fellow. It's been ages. Say, why the formal dress? Tails, gloves, and so forth. Where's the funeral, my boy? Where are you headed?

LOMOV: Oh, nowhere. I mean, here; just to see you, my dear Stepan Stepanovitch.

CHUBUKOV: Then why the full dress, old boy? It's not New Year's, and so forth.

LOMOV: Well, you see, it's like this. I have come here, my dear Stepan Stepanovitch, to bother you with a request. More than once, or twice, or more than that, it has been my privilege to apply to you for assistance in things, and you've always, well, responded. I mean, well, you have. Yes. Excuse me, I'm getting all mixed up. May I have a glass of water, my dear Stepan Stepanovitch? *(Drinks)*

CHUBUKOV: *(Aside)* Wants to borrow some money. Not a chance! *(Aloud)* What can I do for you my dear friend?

LOMOV:	Well, you see, my dear Stepanitch…Excuse me, I mean Stepan my Dearovitch…No, I mean, I get all confused, as you can see. To make a long story short, you're the only one who can help me. Of course, I don't deserve it, and there's no reason why I should expect you to, and all that.
CHUBUKOV:	Stop beating around the bush! Out with it!
LOMOV:	In just a minute. I mean, now, right now. The truth is, I have come to ask the hand…I mean, your daughter, Natalia Stepanovna, I, I want to marry her!
CHUBUKOV:	*(Overjoyed)* Great heavens! Ivan Vassilevitch! Say it again!
LOMOV:	I have come humbly to ask for the hand…
CHUBUKOV:	*(Interrupting)* You're a prince! I'm overwhelmed, delighted, and so forth. Yes, indeed, and all that!

(Hugs and kisses LOMOV)

This is just what I've been hoping for. It's my fondest dream come true. *(Sheds a tear)* And, you know, I've always looked upon you, my boy, as if you were my own son. May God grant to both of you His Mercy and His Love, and so forth. Oh, I have been wishing for this…But why am I being so idiotic? It's just that I'm off my rocker with joy, my boy! Completely off my rocker! Oh, with all my soul I'm…I'll go get Natalia, and so forth.

LOMOV:	*(Deeply moved)* Dear Stepan Stepanovitch, do you think she'll agree?
CHUBUKOV:	Why, of course, old friend. Great heavens! As if she wouldn't! Why she's crazy for you! Good God! Like a lovesick cat, and so forth. Be right back. *(Leaves)*

LOMOV:	God, it's cold. I'm gooseflesh all over, as if I had to take a test. But the main thing is, to make up my mind, and keep it that way. I mean, if I take time out to think, or if I hesitate, or talk about it, or have ideals, or wait for real love, well, I'll just never get married! Brrrr, it's cold! Natalia Stepanovna is an excellent housekeeper. She's not too bad looking. She's had a good education. What more could I ask? Nothing. I'm so nervous, my ears are buzzing. *(Drinks)* Besides, I've just got to get married. I'm thirty-five already. It's sort of a critical age. I've got to settle down and lead a regular life. I mean, I'm always getting palpitations, and I'm nervous, and I get upset so easy. Look, my lips are quivering, and my eyebrow's twitching. The worst thing is the night. Sleeping. I get into bed, doze off, and, suddenly, something inside me jumps. First my head snaps, and then my shoulder blade, and I roll out of bed like a lunatic and try to walk it off. Then I try to go back to sleep, but, as soon as I do, something jumps again! Twenty times a night, sometimes...

(NATALIA STEPANOVNA enters)

NATALIA:	Oh, it's only you. All Papa said was: "Go inside, there's a merchant come to collect his goods." How do you do, Ivan Vassilevitch?
LOMOV:	How do you do, dear Natalia Stepanovna?
NATALIA:	Excuse my apron, and not being dressed. We're shelling peas. You haven't been around lately. Oh, do sit down. *(They do)* Would you like some lunch?
LOMOV:	No thanks, I had some.

NATALIA:	Well, then smoke if you want. *(He doesn't)* The weather's nice today…but yesterday, it was so wet the workmen couldn't get a thing done. Have you got much hay in? I felt so greedy I had a whole field done, but now I'm not sure I was right. With the rain it could rot, couldn't it? I should have waited. But why are you so dressed up? Is there a dance or something? Of course, I must say you look splendid, but…Well, tell me, why are you so dressed up?
LOMOV:	*(Excited)* Well, you see, my dear Natalia Stepanovna, the truth is, I made up my mind to ask you to…well, to, listen to me. Of course, it'll probably surprise you and even maybe make you angry, but… *(Aside)* God, it's cold in here!
NATALIA:	Why, what do you mean? *(A pause)* Well?
LOMOV:	I'll try to get it over with. I mean, you know, my dear Natalia Stepanovna that I've known, since childhood, even, known, and had the privilege of knowing, your family. My late aunt, and her husband, who, as you know, left me my estate, they always had the greatest respect for your father and your late mother. The Lomovs and the Chubukovs have always been very friendly, you might even say affectionate. And, of course, you know, our land borders on each other's. My Oxen Meadows touch your birch grove…
NATALIA:	I hate to interrupt you, my dear Ivan Vassilevitch, but you said: "my Oxen Meadows." Do you really think they're yours?
LOMOV:	Why of course they're mine.
NATALIA:	What do you mean? The Oxen Meadows are ours, not yours!

LOMOV:	Oh, no, my dear Natalia Stepanovna, they're mine.
NATALIA:	Well, this is the first I've heard about it! Where did you get that idea?
LOMOV:	Where? Why, I mean the Oxen Meadows that are wedged between your birches and the marsh.
NATALIA:	Yes, of course, they're ours.
LOMOV:	Oh, no, you're wrong, my dear Natalia Stepanovna, they're mine.
NATALIA:	Now, come, Ivan Vassilevitch! How long have they been yours?
LOMOV:	How long? Why, as long as I can remember!
NATALIA:	Well, really, you can't expect me to believe that!
LOMOV:	But, you can see for yourself in the deed, my dear Natalia Stepanovna. Of course, there was once a dispute about them, but everyone knows they're mine now. There's nothing to argue about. There was a time when my aunt's grandmother let your father's grandfather's peasants use the land, but they were supposed to bake bricks for her in return. Naturally, after a few years they began to act as if they owned it, but the real truth is…
NATALIA:	That has nothing to do with the case! Both my grandfather and my great-grandfather said that their land went as far as the marsh, which means that the Meadows are ours! There's nothing whatever to argue about. It's foolish.
LOMOV:	But I can show you the deed, Natalia Stepanovna.
NATALIA:	You're just making fun of me…Great Heavens! Here we have the land for hundreds of years, and suddenly you try to tell us it isn't ours. What's wrong with you,

	Ivan Vassilevitch? Those meadows aren't even fifteen acres, and they're not worth three hundred rubles, but I just can't stand unfairness! I just can't stand unfairness!
LOMOV:	But, you must listen to me. Your father's grandfather's peasants, as I've already tried to tell you, they were supposed to bake bricks for my aunt's grandmother. And my aunt's grandmother, why, she wanted to be nice to them…
NATALIA:	It's just nonsense, this whole business about aunts and grandfathers and grandmothers. The Meadows are ours! That's all there is to it!
LOMOV:	They're mine!
NATALIA:	Ours! You can go on talking for two days, and you can put on fifteen evening coats and twenty pairs of gloves, but I tell you they're ours, ours, ours!
LOMOV:	Natalia Stepanovna, I don't want the Meadows! I'm just acting on principle. If you want, I'll give them to you.
NATALIA:	I'll give them to *you*! Because they're ours! And that's all there is to it! And if I may say so, your behaviour, my dear Ivan Vassilevitch, is very strange. Until now, we've always considered you a good neighbour, even a friend. After all, last year we lent you our threshing machine, even though it meant putting off our own threshing until November. And here you are treating us like a pack of gypsies. Giving me my own land, indeed! Really! Why that's not being a good neighbour. It's sheer impudence, that's what it is…
LOMOV:	Oh, so you think I'm just a land-grabber? My dear lady, I've never grabbed anybody's land in my whole life, and no one's going to accuse me of doing it now!

(Quickly walks over to the pitcher and drinks some more water)
The Oxen Meadows are mine!

NATALIA: That's a lie. They're ours!

LOMOV: Mine!

NATALIA: A lie! I'll prove it. I'll send my mowers out there today!

LOMOV: What?

NATALIA: My mowers will mow it today!

LOMOV: I'll kick them out!

NATALIA: You just dare!

LOMOV: *(Clutching his heart)* The Oxen Meadows are mine! Do you understand? Mine!

NATALIA: Please don't shout! You can shout all you want in your own house, but here I must ask you to control yourself.

LOMOV: If my heart wasn't palpitating the way it is, if my insides weren't jumping like mad, I wouldn't talk to you so calmly. *(Yelling)* The Oxen Meadows are mine!

NATALIA: Ours!

LOMOV: Mine!

NATALIA: Ours!

LOMOV: Mine!

(Enter CHUBUKOV*)*

CHUBUKOV: What's going on? Why all the shouting?

NATALIA: Papa, will you please inform this gentleman who owns the Oxen Meadows, he or we?

CHUBUKOV: *(To* LOMOV*)* Why, they're ours, old fellow.

Lomov:	But how can they be yours, my dear Stepan Stepanovitch? Be fair. Perhaps my aunt's grandmother did let your grandfather's peasants work the land, and maybe they did get so used to it that they acted as if it was their own, but…
Chubukov:	Oh, no, no…my dear boy. You forget something. The reason the peasants didn't pay your aunt's grandmother, and so forth, was that the land was disputed, even then. Since then it's been settled. Why, everyone knows it's ours.
Lomov:	I can prove it's mine.
Chubukov:	You can't prove a thing, old boy.
Lomov:	Yes I can!
Chubukov:	My dear lad, why yell like that? Yelling doesn't prove a thing. Look, I'm not after anything of yours, just as I don't intend to give up anything of mine. Why should I? Besides, if you're going to keep arguing about it, I'd just as soon give the land to the peasants, so there!
Lomov:	There's nothing! Where do you get the right to give away someone else's property?
Chubukov:	I certainly ought to know if I have the right or not. And you had better realize it, because, my dear young man, I am not used to being spoken to in that tone of voice, and so forth. Besides which, my dear young man, I am twice as old as you are, and I ask you to speak to me without getting yourself into such a tizzy, and so forth!
Lomov:	Do you think I'm a fool? First you call my property yours, and then you expect me to keep calm and polite! Good neighbours don't act like that, my dear Stepan Stepanovitch. You're no neighbour, you're a land grabber!

CHUBUKOV:	What was that? What did you say?
NATALIA:	Papa, send the mowers out to the meadows at once!
CHUBUKOV:	What did you say, sir?
NATALIA:	The Oxen Meadows are ours, and we'll never give them up, never, never, never, never!
LOMOV:	We'll see about that. I'll go to court. I'll show you!
CHUBUKOV:	Go to court? Well, go to court, and so forth! I know you, just waiting for a chance to go to court, and so forth. You pettifogging shyster, you! All of your family is like that. The whole bunch of them!
LOMOV:	You leave my family out of this! The Lomovs have always been honourable, upstanding people, and not a one of them was ever tried for embezzlement, like your grandfather was.
CHUBUKOV:	The Lomovs are a pack of lunatics, the whole bunch of them!
NATALIA:	The whole bunch!
CHUBUKOV:	Your grandfather was a drunkard, and what about your other aunt, the one who ran away with the architect? And so forth.
NATALIA:	And so forth!
LOMOV:	Your mother was a hunchback! *(Clutches at his heart)* Oh, I've got a stitch in my side...My head's whirling...Help! Water!
CHUBUKOV:	Your father was a rum-soaked gambler.
NATALIA:	And your aunt was queen of the scandalmongers!
LOMOV:	My left foot's paralyzed. You're a plotter...Oh, my heart. It's an open secret that in the last elections you brib...I'm seeing stars! Where's my hat?

NATALIA:	It's a low, mean, spiteful…
CHUBUKOV:	And you're a two-faced, malicious schemer!
LOMOV:	Here's my hat…Oh, my heart…Where's the door? How do I get out of here?…Oh, I think I'm going to die…My foot's numb. *(Goes)*
CHUBUKOV:	*(Following him)* And don't you ever set foot in my house again!
NATALIA:	Go to court, indeed! We'll see about that!

*(*LOMOV *staggers out)*

CHUBUKOV:	The devil with him! *(Gets a drink, walks back and forth excited)*
NATALIA:	What a rascal! How can you trust your neighbours after an incident like that?
CHUBUKOV:	The villain! The scarecrow!
NATALIA:	He's a monster! First he tries to steal our land, and then he has the nerve to yell at you.
CHUBUKOV:	Yes, and that turnip, that stupid rooster, has the gall to make a proposal. Some proposal!
NATALIA:	What proposal?
CHUBUKOV:	Why, he came to propose to you.
NATALIA:	To propose? To me? Why didn't you tell me before?
CHUBUKOV:	So he gets all dressed up in his formal clothes. That stuffed sausage, that dried-up cabbage!
NATALIA:	To propose to me? Ohhhh! *(Falls into a chair and starts wailing)* Bring him back! Back! Go get him! Bring him back! Ohhhh!
CHUBUKOV:	Bring who back?
NATALIA:	Hurry up, hurry up! I'm sick. Get him! *(Complete hysterics)*

CHUBUKOV:	What for? *(To her)* What's the matter with you? *(Clutches his head)* Oh, what a fool I am! I'll shoot myself! I'll hang myself! I ruined her chances!
NATALIA:	I'm dying. Get him!
CHUBUKOV:	All right, all right, right away! Only don't yell! *(He runs out)*
NATALIA:	What are they doing to me? Get him! Bring him back! Bring him back!

(A pause. CHUBUKOV *runs in)*

CHUBUKOV:	He's coming, and so forth, the snake. Oof! You talk to him. I'm not in the mood.
NATALIA:	*(Wailing)* Bring him back! Bring him back!
CHUBUKOV:	*(Yelling)* I told you, he's coming! Oh Lord, what agony to be the father of a grown-up daughter. I'll cut my throat some day, I swear I will. *(To her)* We cursed him, we insulted him, abused him, kicked him out, and now...because you, you...
NATALIA:	Me? It was all your fault!
CHUBUKOV:	My fault? What do you mean my fau...?

*(*LOMOV *appears in the doorway)*

Talk to him yourself!

(Goes out. LOMOV *enters, exhausted)*

LOMOV:	What palpitations! My heart! And my foot's absolutely asleep. Something keeps giving me a stitch in the side...
NATALIA:	You must forgive us, Ivan Vassilevitch. We all got too excited. I remember now. The Oxen Meadows are yours.
LOMOV:	My heart's beating something awful. My Meadows. My eyebrows, they're both twitching!

NATALIA:	Yes, the Meadows are all yours, yes, yours. Do sit down. *(They sit)* We were wrong, of course.
LOMOV:	I argued on principle. My land isn't worth so much to me, but the principle…
NATALIA:	Oh, yes, of course, the principle, that's what counts. But let's change the subject.
LOMOV:	Besides, I have evidence. You see, my aunt's grandmother let your father's grandfather's peasants use the land…
NATALIA:	Yes, yes, yes, but forget all that. *(Aside)* I wish I knew how to get him going. *(Aloud)* Are you going to start hunting soon?
LOMOV:	After the harvest I'll try for grouse. But oh, my dear Natalia Stepanovna, have you heard about the bad luck I've had? You know my dog, Guess? He's gone lame.
NATALIA:	What a pity. Why?
LOMOV:	I don't know. He must have twisted his leg, or got in a fight, or something. *(Sighs)* My best dog, to say nothing of the cost. I paid Mironov 125 rubles for him.
NATALIA:	That was too high, Ivan Vassilevitch.
LOMOV:	I think it was quite cheap. He's a first-class dog.
NATALIA:	Why Papa only paid eighty-five rubles for Squeezer, and he's much better than Guess.
LOMOV:	Squeezer better than Guess! What an idea! *(Laughs)* Squeezer better than Guess!
NATALIA:	Of course he's better. He may still be too young but on points and pedigree, he's a better dog even than any Volchanetsky owns.
LOMOV:	Excuse me, Natalia Stepanovna, but you're forgetting he's overshot, and overshot dogs are bad hunters.

NATALIA:	Oh, so he's overshot, is he? Well this is the first time I've heard about it.
LOMOV:	Believe me, his lower jaw is shorter than his upper.
NATALIA:	You've measured them?
LOMOV:	Yes. He's all right for pointing, but if you want him to retrieve…
NATALIA:	In the first place, our Squeezer is a thoroughbred, the son of Harness and Chisel, while your mutt doesn't even have a pedigree. He's as old and worn out as a pedlar's horse.
LOMOV:	He may be old, but I wouldn't take five Squeezers for him. How can you argue? Guess is a dog, Squeezer's a laugh. Anyone you can name has a dog like Squeezer hanging around somewhere. They're under every bush. If he only cost twenty-five rubles you got cheated.
NATALIA:	The devil is in you today, Ivan Vassilevitch! You want to contradict everything. First you pretend the Oxen Meadows are yours, and now you say Guess is better than Squeezer. People should say what they really mean, and you know Squeezer is a hundred times better than Guess. Why say he isn't?
LOMOV:	So, you think I'm a fool or a blind man, Natalia Stepanovna! Once and for all, Squeezer is overshot!
NATALIA:	He is not!
LOMOV:	He is so!
NATALIA:	He is not!
LOMOV:	Why shout, my dear lady?
NATALIA:	Why talk such nonsense? It's terrible. Your Guess is old enough to be buried, and you compare him with Squeezer!

LOMOV:	I'm sorry, I can't go on. My heart…it's palpitating!
NATALIA:	I've always noticed that the hunters who argue most don't know a thing.
LOMOV:	Please! Be quiet a moment. My heart's falling apart… *(Shouts)* Shut up!
NATALIA:	I'm not going to shut up until you admit that Squeezer's a hundred times better than Guess.
LOMOV:	A hundred times worse! His head…My eyes…shoulder…
NATALIA:	Guess is half-dead already!
LOMOV:	*(Weeping)* Shut up! My heart's exploding!
NATALIA:	I won't shut up!

(CHUBUKOV comes in)

CHUBUKOV:	What's the trouble now?
NATALIA:	Papa, will you please tell us which is the better dog, his Guess or our Squeezer?
LOMOV:	Stepan Stepanovitch, I implore you to tell me just one thing. Is your Squeezer overshot or not? Yes or no?
CHUBUKOV:	Well what if he is? He's still the best dog in the neighbourhood, and so forth.
LOMOV:	Oh, but isn't my dog, Guess, better? Really?
CHUBUKOV:	Don't get yourself so fraught up, old man. Of course, your dog has his good points—thoroughbred, firm on his feet, well-sprung ribs, and so forth. But, my dear fellow, you've got to admit he has two defects; he's old and he's short in the muzzle.
LOMOV:	Short in the muzzle? Oh, my heart! Let's look at the facts! On the Marusinsky hunt my dog ran neck and neck with the Count's, while Squeezer was a mile behind them…

CHUBUKOV:	That's because the Count's groom hit him with a whip.
LOMOV:	And he was right, too! We were fox hunting; what was your dog chasing sheep for?
CHUBUKOV:	That's a lie! Look, I'm going to lose my temper… *(Controlling himself)* my dear friend, so let's stop arguing, for that reason alone. You're only arguing because we're all jealous of somebody else's dog. Who can help it? As soon as you realize some dog is better than yours, in this case our dog, you start in with this and that, and the next thing you know—pure jealousy! I remember the whole business.
LOMOV:	I remember too!
CHUBUKOV:	*(Mimicking)* "I remember too!" What do you remember?
LOMOV:	My heart…my foot's asleep…I can't…
NATALIA:	*(Mimicking)* "My heart…my foot's asleep." What kind of a hunter are you? You should be hunting cockroaches in the kitchen, not foxes. "My heart!"
CHUBUKOV:	Yes, what kind of a hunter are you anyway? You should be sitting at home with your palpitations, not tracking down animals. You don't hunt anyhow. You just go out to argue with people and interfere with their dogs, and so forth. For God's sake, let's change the subject before I lose my temper. Anyway, you're just not a hunter.
LOMOV:	But you, you're a hunter? Ha! You only go hunting to get in good with the Count, and to plot, and intrigue, and scheme…Oh, my heart! You're a schemer, that's what!
CHUBUKOV:	What's that? Me a schemer? *(Shouting)* Shut up!
LOMOV:	A schemer!
CHUBUKOV:	You infant! You puppy!
LOMOV:	You old rat! You hawk!

CHUBUKOV: You shut up, or I'll shoot you down like a partridge! You idiot!

LOMOV: Everyone knows that—oh, my heart—that your wife used to beat you…Oh, my feet…my head…I'm seeing stars…I'm going to faint! *(He drops into an armchair)* Quick, a doctor! *(Faints)*

CHUBUKOV: *(Going on, oblivious)* Baby! Weakling! Idiot! I'm getting sick. *(Drinks water)* Me! I'm sick!

NATALIA: What kind of a hunter are you? You can't even sit on a horse! *(To her father)* Papa, what's the matter with him? Look, Papa! *(Screaming)* Ivan Vassilevitch! He's dead.

CHUBUKOV: I'm choking, I can't breathe…Give me air.

NATALIA: He's dead! *(Pulling* LOMOV's *sleeve)* Ivan Vassilevitch! Ivan Vassilevitch! What have you done to me? He's dead!

(She falls into an armchair. Screaming hysterically)
A doctor! A doctor! A doctor!

CHUBUKOV: Ohhhh…What's the matter? What happened?

NATALIA: *(Wailing)* He's dead! He's dead!

CHUBUKOV: Who's dead? *(Looks at* LOMOV*)* My God, he is! Quick! Water! A doctor!

(Puts glass to LOMOV's *lips)*
Here, drink this! Can't drink it—he must be dead, and so forth…Oh what a miserable life! Why don't I shoot myself? I should have cut my throat long ago! What am I waiting for? Give me a knife! Give me a pistol!

*(*LOMOV *stirs)*
Look, he's coming to. Here, drink some water. That's it.

LOMOV: I'm seeing stars…misty…Where am I?

CHUBUKOV:	Just you hurry up and get married, and then the devil with you! She accepted.

(Puts LOMOV's *hand in* NATALIA's*)*

	She accepts and so forth! I give you my blessing, and so forth! Only leave me in peace!
LOMOV:	*(Getting up)* Huh? What? Who?
CHUBUKOV:	She accepts! Well! Kiss her, damn you!
NATALIA:	He's alive! Yes, yes, I accept.
CHUBUKOV:	Kiss each other!
LOMOV:	Huh? Kiss? Kiss who? *(They kiss)* That's nice. I mean, excuse me, what happened? Oh, now I get it…my heart…those stars…I'm very happy, Natalia Stepanovna. *(Kisses her hand)* My foot's asleep.
NATALIA:	I…I'm happy too.
CHUBUKOV:	What a load off my shoulders! Whew!
NATALIA:	Well, now maybe you'll admit that Squeezer is better than Guess?
LOMOV:	Worse!
NATALIA:	Better!
CHUBUKOV:	What a way to enter matrimonial bliss! Let's have some champagne!
LOMOV:	He's worse!
NATALIA:	Better! Better, better, better, better!
CHUBUKOV:	*(Trying to shout her down)* Champagne! Bring some champagne! Champagne! Champagne!

Notes

formal dress, full dress clothing for either gender that is considered suitable for a formal occasion

tails short for a tailcoat, which is a formal man's jacket with an elongated back

gooseflesh a person's skin that has become rough, like that of a plucked goose, from cold or fright

lunatic an extremely foolish person; originally used as a derogatory term for a person who suffers from severe mental illness

rubles the standard monetary unit in Russia, divided into a hundred kopeks; from the Russian word *rublĭ*, meaning a "piece" cut from a silver bar

threshing machine the machine used for the process of beating out or separating grains or seeds from the stalk or another part of a plant, such as husks from cobs of corn

pack of gypsies in modern times, has come to refer to people who are inclined to a nomadic, unconventional way of life; originally referred to a nomadic ethnic group who migrated to Europe from northern India in the fourteenth century and who were persecuted in subsequent centuries for being "foreigners" outside the community

pettifogging quibbling over trivia

shyster a person who uses unethical, unscrupulous business practices

embezzlement someone who takes for one's own use such valuables as money in violation of a trust

hunchback an antiquated, derogatory term for a person whose back is hunched due to an abnormal curvature of the upper spine

devil in this instance, refers to a wicked person

Activities

1. In the style of a newspaper advice columnist, write short letters of advice to each of the three main characters in this play. Briefly summarize each character's "problem." Then outline a course of action that will help each character resolve the conflict and achieve his or her goals. Shape the content, style, and tone of your advice according to the context of a farming community in nineteenth-century Russia.

2. Choose a character in the play to analyze. Reread the play carefully and, in a character web or outline, record key characteristics and supporting evidence. Meet with two other students who have analyzed the same character to compare and discuss your notes. Choose one member of your group to be the "actor," while the other two serve as acting coaches. Discuss how the character should look, sound, and act. Have the actor practise reading her or his lines, while the coaches offer advice and support. As a class, present a dramatic reading of the play with actors from various groups taking turns in the roles. After the reading, discuss as a class: How were various actors' interpretations of the same character similar and different? What advice would the class offer an actor preparing for each of the roles?

3. Chekhov wrote this play in 1888. With a partner, consider Chekhov's purpose in writing this play and who his audience might have been. Discuss such questions as the following: What are you able to infer about audiences of his time? What does the play reveal about audience expectations for gender roles in 1888? How might Chekhov have wanted his audience to react? Does the play have a message or purpose other than to amuse the audience? What strategies did he use to engage the audience and to accomplish his purpose? Formulate a thesis statement that puts forward your interpretation of Chekhov's audience and his purpose. Select and organize examples from the play to support your thesis and incorporate them into an analytical essay.

SET DESIGN FOR
The Foreigner
Karen Schulz Gropman

About the Visual   Karen Schulz Gropman was born in Racine, Wisconsin, in 1951. She began her career as a theatrical set decorator and has been the art director on many feature films, including *The Cider House Rules* (1999) and *The Shipping News* (2001). Schulz Gropman designed this set for Larry Shue's play *The Foreigner* for the Astor Place Theatre in New York. The very small stage and auditorium of this theatre explain the odd shape and angles of her ground plan. When this production moved to a theatre in Chicago, Schulz Gropman had to adapt the set to accommodate that stage's wide thrust. Can you think of an unconventional space in your community that would be an interesting place in which to produce a play? If so, what play would you stage and why?

Activities

1. Look at the photograph of the set; then examine the ground plan. To what extent does referring to the photograph of the set help you to decipher the ground plan? Identify the similarities and the differences between the two.

2. In a group, obtain a number of plays and locate the descriptions of the stage setting at the beginning of the first scene. Read aloud and discuss the settings to familiarize yourself with their content and form. Then, together as a group, select a short story that you think would lend itself to being dramatized. Work by yourself to write a description of the stage setting. Discuss your ideas with the group.

From

Acoose: Man Standing Above Ground

Janice Acoose and Brenda Zeman

Janice Acoose was born in Broadview, Saskatchewan, in 1954. Her father was a member of the Saulteaux First Nation on the Sakimay Reserve and her mother was a Métis from Marival. She is also the granddaughter of the renowned runner Paul Acoose. She received a doctorate in English literature from the University of Saskatchewan. Acoose is a professor of indigenous literature, a distinguished scholar, journalist, scriptwriter, and producer. She was Saskatchewan's first Native Affairs columnist for the *Saskatoon Star Phoenix*. Brenda Zeman was born in Saskatoon, Saskatchewan, in 1951. She received a bachelor of science degree in anthropology from McMaster University in Ontario. Zeman received a teacher's certificate in 1977 from the University of Toronto, where she was a professional track-and-field athlete with the Toronto Tigers. She earned a master's degree in cultural anthropology from California State University at Long Beach. Zeman has said, "Athletes make good actors, because both professions excel at performance. In fact, I don't perceive many differences between sport and art." Both Acoose and Zeman have talked about writing as a mission. Do you believe that writers have the power to change the world in any way? Do they have a responsibility to do so? What kinds of writers do you think are the most influential? If you were to become a professional writer, what genre of writing would you pursue?

JANICE: Running has always been a tradition in my family. It was thoughts of my mooshum that inspired me as I first played with the idea of becoming a runner myself. Finally one day I thought, Janice Acoose, you are the granddaughter of Paul Acoose, one of the great long-distance runners, so what are you doing? Get out there and run. It's in your blood! *(Street sounds, birds. She begins to run.)*

I remember that first morning I went out to run. It was a warm day in March. The last of winter's cold was disappearing. It reminded me of another such morning a long time ago, the first time I met my mooshum. *(Street cross-fades to sound of powwow drums, singing.)* My dad told us we were going to the reserve to a powwow. You know, coming from the city, the only knowledge I had of my people were images I had seen in movies, rough and wild-looking creatures. When we drove through the gate I saw a number of tents set up. There were children and dogs running about. Almost immediately my dad's face broke out in a wide grin. And then I saw this man coming toward us. The sound of bells tinkled from his moccasins as they softly struck the ground. His face was painted up and he wore a bonnet of feathers. "Grandfather?" I said. And I remember him replying, "Noosisim, I'm your mooshum. You call me mooshum." *(Street traffic, running, come up again.)*

My memories were interrupted by city traffic that squeezed me to the outer limits of the road, like I was an intruder. So I turned around and started jogging toward open country.

My mooshum always hated cars. He would never ride in them. He walked everywhere.

I remember the first time I discovered he was a runner. A moonyaw, or a whiteman, had come out to the reserve to paint his picture. I asked him why that man was there. He motioned for me to sit down beside him and then he began to tell me his story. He talked about his father, Old Samuel Acoose, and his grandfather, Quewich, both famous runners. He told me of places he had raced in, places that seemed like they were on the other side of the world, like Madison Square Garden in New York City, Vancouver and Winnipeg. As he talked, the age disappeared and he looked strong and proud.

I reminded myself that I have a long way to go to achieve the kind of inner strength he had, and I turned and headed for home. As I ran I thought of how he must have felt when he returned home from racing. He was a hero, a world-class runner. But on the reserve, every aspect of his life was controlled by an Indian Agent.

My mooshum was a proud man, rich in the knowledge of his culture, yet prohibited by law from carrying on the traditions of his grandfathers. I can still hear him proudly speaking of the rain dance and the joy he felt as a grass dancer. But I also remember the Sunday ritual, when he would worship the Christian god. Rather than hold his head high in pride as he did when he spoke of the rain dance, he hung his head as he entered the house of worship.

Anger came over me as I remembered the way he was treated. But almost as soon as it came, it was gone.

I thought of the years when I watched my grandparents grow old. My kookum bedridden with illness, my mooshum always by her side. When she slept, he would sit with us kids, him in the middle and us all around. He told us then about the strengths and the beliefs of our people, the Saulteaux. He tried to teach us our language and instill values within us by telling us stories. I remember one thing he told me, "Never throw your hair away when you comb it." He said your hair is your strength. He reached into his pocket and showed me a little white bear. He told me he kept his and my kookum's hair and always wrapped it around the white bear. This always kept them safe. Then he put it back in the pocket closest to his heart.

My kookum and mooshum were two unique spirits. Their home on the reserve was a special meeting place for all my cousins, aunts and uncles. That special feeling isn't there anymore.

As I got to the last part of my run I slowed down to a walk, so I could cool down. Because of all the running, my legs were numb and my feet felt as though they weren't touching the ground! It was then I finally *really* understood my grandfather's name—Acoose, "Man Standing Above Ground."

Notes

mooshum grandfather

noosisim granddaughter

Madison Square Garden a sports and entertainment complex in New York City

Indian Agent historically, the representative of the government who lived on First Nations reserves and was in charge of many aspects of reserve life

rain dance a dance that honours rain and its importance to the nation

grass dancer a dancer whose job is to flatten the grass in the arena before a powwow; the "grass" also refers to the braids of sweetgrass tied to the dancer's belt.

kookum grandmother

Saulteaux a branch of the Ojibwa First Nation that lives in western Ontario and eastern Manitoba

Activities

1. What was your response to the voice and character of the speaker, Janice? To what extent do you think the identity of Janice, the monologuist, overlaps with Janice Acoose, the playwright, and Janice Acoose, the granddaughter of Paul Acoose? To what extent do Acoose's three roles lend authenticity to the work? What else do you think the playwrights might have had in mind when they made this choice of speaker?

2. Examine the structure of this monologue. How is it organized? Consider how the playwrights have balanced elements from the past and the present; dialogue and narrative; reflection and description. How has the content of the speech been shaped by its dramatic purpose?

3. Dramatize the life of a historical character, friend, or family member in a short radio play. You may want to obtain a copy of a complete, one-act radio play to use as a model for your own work. Prepare a taped performance of your play and present it to a group. Invite feedback on how effectively you employed the technical tools of radio drama, such as sound effects, music, and narrative bridges, to strengthen your play's impact.

FILM LOCATION FOR
Random Passage
CBC Television

Random Passage is a CBC television film based on two novels by Bernice Morgan, whose story "Windows" appears on pages 109–117 of this anthology. This film, set in the early nineteenth century and shot in 2000, depicts the life of fictional character Mary Bundle from her indenture in England to her new pioneer life in St. John's and Cape Random, Newfoundland. In the photograph, the film's director, John N. Smith, who is seated, watches as a camera operator films a scene in which a boat in the distance slowly approaches the shores of Cape Random. If you were selecting locations for a film, what requirements would you have for an indoor set and for an outdoor set? Are there features of a location that are essential for all film sets, regardless of subject matter?

Activities

1. Still photography captures a moment in time. What are some of the elements this photograph reveals about the moment in time in which it was taken? Are you able to surmise anything about the atmosphere of the film set from this photograph? If someone looked at this photograph a hundred years from now, which features would reflect the culture and the era in which this film was created?

2. Consider what role in the filmmaking process the woman seated in the foreground of the photograph might have. Then, adopting the tone of a professional person in her work environment, write, present, and evaluate a dramatic monologue in the voice of this woman.

2000, black-and-white print ▶

Stop!

Donna Lewis

Donna Lewis was born in Winnipeg, Manitoba, in 1963 and grew up in nearby Sperling. She received a bachelor's degree from the University of Manitoba in 1984. Lewis is a film and stage actor and a playwright. She taught acting at the Manitoba Theatre for Young People, and has been a teacher of English as a Second Language and of yoga. Lewis has also collaborated on the writing of plays, including *How Do You Do?* which was produced by the Prairie Theatre Alliance of Manitoba. In *Stop!* Lewis uses humour to explore the practice of meditation. When a writer explores a subject in a humorous way, do you think the main purpose is to "make fun of" the subject, or can there be other reasons for doing so? If so, what are some of the results achieved by taking a lighter approach to a subject?

Characters

A Meditator

Three Actors: One, Two, Three, personifying thoughts.

Setting

An empty stage.

(A MEDITATOR sits on stage listening to a meditation tape.)

TAPED VOICE: The idea of meditation is to quiet the mind… To bring about a stillness, a peaceful state, free from the confusion of your constant daily thoughts. Sit quietly and comfortably. Breathe deeply… Relax and breathe… Thoughts will come marching in.

(Enter ONE, TWO, THREE. They stand just behind the MEDITATOR who expresses facially and physically what they are saying at times, while at other times is rather perplexed by what is being said.)

But don't let them control you. After all, who's in the driver's seat?

(MEDITATOR points to self questioningly.)

You are! Now relax. And pay attention to your breath.

(MEDITATOR takes a deep breath. Throughout the play, the actors can use deep breathing where appropriate for laughs or poignancy.)

ONE: I hope I'm not offending anyone.

THREE: Buy breath mints, toothpaste, chewing gum. Eat less garlic.

ONE: It's just that sometimes it's like I'm rotting inside. As if the food just goes into my gut and just sits there.

THREE: Have that looked at.

ONE: What do they give you for rotting insides anyway? He'll probably tell me the rotting thing is all in my mind…just some crazy thought. Maybe he'll give me one of those pills that just has sugar in it. What do you call those again?

THREE: Pla-ce-bo, Latin for "I shall please."

ONE: They can give you pills to fix anything. They have this chemical called digitalis. I hear it regulates your heartbeat. It makes your heart normal.

Two:	Boomboomboomboomboomboomboomboom. Boomboom… Boomboom… Boomboom.
One:	Nowadays you have to do this—*(Makes quotation sign with hands.)*—when you say the word "normal." And then you have to say "if there is such a thing."
Three:	Normal is a relative term.
Two:	My relative's dog had a heart murmur. It had this extra part to its heartbeat. Kinda like boom boom chh. Boom boom chh. She said it didn't affect him except that he would never be able to fly. I mean in an airplane, the "normal" way.
One:	Before you go getting a dog, they say you really should be able to take care of your houseplants. Then, when you can manage the plants and the pets, then you are ready to have a baby.
Three:	Water the plants. Feed the dog. Have a baby.
Two:	I remember when I was a baby.
One:	I'm sure babies can see what you are like inside. I've noticed that some babies really seem to like me. They smile and laugh.

*(*Two *smiles and laughs.)*

But then there are other babies who really don't like me at all. In fact whenever I am near them, they start screaming.

*(*Two *screams.* Meditator *covers ears.)*

What if I had one of those babies. One that didn't like me. One that hated me. It'd be awful.

Three:	It is unfair to bring a child into this world. Water the plants. Feed the dog. Eat a healthy breakfast.
One:	I caught a glimpse of myself in the toaster this morning. Scary.

THREE:	Breakfast—the most important meal of the day. Start the day off right!
ONE:	My face looked all distorted in the front of the toaster. The top of my head lined up perfectly with the top of the toaster. Toast, toast, toast, I'm thinking about toast. Then all of a sudden the toast comes popping out of the toaster just like it was popping out of the top of my head. My thoughts came right out of my head. Pow! A couple of Tylenol and back to bed.
TWO:	I remember when I was little. I used to stare into the big stainless steel tea kettle. It was round, so whatever was close up to the round, protruding part looked really big, but whatever was further away looked really small. I'd stand back and put my hand out in front, right near the kettle, and my hand would be gigantic and the rest of me would be miniature and I'd say in a deep voice, "Stop!"
THREE:	*(Sings.)* "Stop in the name of love, before you break my heart."
TWO:	It was a lot of fun until I burned my hand on the boiling kettle. I feel like my hand can remember that last "stop!"
THREE:	*(Sings.)* "Think it o–o–ver."
ONE:	If only my palm reader were able to speak English. He studies my hand and then looks up at me and says, "Afraid, so afraid. Why? Why so afraid?" Then he says, "You are so so lucky."
THREE:	Buy a lottery ticket. Mail *Reader's Digest* Sweepstakes. Say a prayer to Saint Jude, patron saint of hopeless causes. Be more positive.
ONE:	So was it like this, "You are *so so* lucky!" or "You are so-so lucky"? *(Makes a hand gesture meaning "sort of.")* Hmmm.

THREE:	*(Sings.)* "Think it o–o–ver. Think it o–o–ver."
TWO:	Our family's pretty lucky. When I was a baby, a world traveller came to work for my dad at harvest time and one night he snuck away in the middle of the night without taking one of his suitcases. He didn't say anything—if he'd be back for it, or what was in it or anything... The suitcase...filled with treasures from the Orient?... Or dirty socks and underwear?
ONE:	So lucky. So so lucky. So-so lucky.
TWO:	The suitcase has always been there, ever since I can remember and nobody's looked inside. It isn't even locked. I snapped the latch open one day but it had this safety catch that kept it from flying open. I wanted to see what was inside but some deep voice in me said "stop." What if I brought bad luck to my family?
THREE:	*(Sings softly.)* "Stop before you tear us apart. Think it o–o–ver."
TWO:	Still, you gotta wonder what's in there—what you're missing... Now it's kept up in the attic.
THREE:	Out of sight, out of mind.
ONE:	That time the door-to-door vacuum salesman vacuumed my head in a demonstration, man, did that machine pick up a lot of dirt. My guests and I could not believe the dust and lint that was sucked from my head.
THREE:	Cleanliness is next to godliness.
ONE:	Now I shampoo as often as I can. Not being obsessive about it or anything. But...
TWO:	Still, you gotta wonder what's in there—what you're missing...
ONE:	It's the same with germs. They say we have the germ of pneumonia inside us all the time. They say our thoughts

can make us sick or well. Each one of us has pneumonia right this very second, but we might not know it. *(TWO starts coughing.)* Only if you start showing the symptoms does it become...apparent.

Two: Still, you gotta wonder what's in there—what you are missing...I used to play hide-and-go-seek. I'd hide so well no one could find me, and after a while they'd stop wondering where I was, start playing something else, and forget that I was missing.

ONE: That woman in the paper. She was about my age. She sure had something inside her.

THREE: *(Speaks as though reading a news report.)* "We do not know whether there is a danger that she will spontaneously combust again. We've consulted with experts on this and they have no idea. We're hoping that it was a one-time response to a horrible situation and we are trying to calm her fears about this."

ONE: She was just walking home and somebody jumped her. Boom! She burst into flames. She had all that fire inside her, just kind of smouldering. Nobody even knew. Not even her. Certainly not her assailant or he would have thought twice.

THREE: One. Two. Never mind.

ONE: The woman survived and is now in hospital with third-degree burns to her entire body. Reporters say her burns are minor compared to her trauma of discovering she was capable of so much fire.

THREE: *(Sings.)* "I don't want to set the world on fire. I just want to start a flame in your heart."

Two: My heart skipped a beat. Boomboom...Boom. Boomboom. Still, you gotta wonder what's in there. What's missing.

ONE:	Who's to say what could reignite her… Or me, for instance.
THREE:	A dirty look. One too many questions at the border. A simple phrase, "Let's just be friends."
TWO:	I remember the black-and-white days of Laurel and Hardy. They'd be in a small room with a package that was actually an uninflated life raft, and they'd end up pulling a plug or pushing a button, or doing something unintentional like that. And that tiniest gesture set off the process and the life raft would become enormous in no time. It was like the thing had all this "space" in it all along. The air had always been there; it just needed to be triggered.
THREE:	Emotions are in the body. They are in the body.
TWO:	I feel so big inside. So very big. And there's so many trigger points…so many safety valves… Still, you gotta wonder what's inside.
ONE:	Things like that really make you stop and think.
TWO:	Stop!
ONE:	I'm not sure what to think, but I can't stop thinking about it.
THREE:	Come to a complete stop. Count to three. One… Two… Three. Three-way stop. Always yield the right of way. Driving is a privilege, not a right.

ONE, TWO, and THREE: *(Together.)* Who's in the driver's seat?

MEDITATOR: I am! *(Puts hand out in front.) Stop!*

(The end.)

Notes

meditation the practice of focusing the mind through contemplation. This mental exercise has been a central component of many world religions and, in the twentieth century, a secular form was popularized as a means of reducing stress.

Activities

1. If you were the costume designer for this play, how would you dress the characters? Record your ideas in your journal and then discuss them in a group. After your discussion, reflect on the various approaches to costuming within your group and decide which of them you would choose if you were staging the play.

2. How has the author used diction and syntax to differentiate among characters One, Two, and Three? Reread the speeches by each character independent of their context and make notes on their distinctive styles and tones. By what other means does the author distinguish the characters from each other? Discuss and compare your ideas in a group.

3. If you could turn the three dominant aspects of your personality into characters, what would they be like? Imagine a conversation among these characters in a setting of your choice and write a play modelled on *Stop!* Before writing your script, make notes on the various directions the dialogue will take and identify the climax toward which you are moving. Present a dramatic reading of your play to your class.

Another Viewpoint: Critical Approaches

Psychological literary criticism often examines the author and the author's writings in the framework of Freudian psychology. Freudians divide the personality into three functional parts: id, ego, and superego. Look up these terms in several reference books and create your own definition for each. Consider which of the play's characters—One, Two, or Three—might represent the id, the ego, and the superego, respectively. How does this way of approaching the characters affect your thinking about the play?

Dead Parrot

Monty Python

Monty Python, a group of six British writers and performers, was formed in 1969 to create a comedy show for British television, *Monty Python's Flying Circus*. The result was a half-hour compilation of live sketches combined with some animation. Between 1969 and 1972, forty-five episodes of this extremely popular show were produced. The troupe also created several movies, including *And Now for Something Completely Different* (1972) and *Monty Python and the Holy Grail* (1975). To what extent is your sense of humour similar to or different from that of your friends? Are you more likely to laugh at physical comedy or a witty exchange of words? Why?

ANIMATION: including dancing Botticelli Venus, which links to pet shop. MR. PRALINE *walks into the shop carrying a dead parrot in a cage. He walks to counter where* SHOPKEEPER *tries to hide below cash register.*

PRALINE:	Hello, I wish to register a complaint... Hello? Miss?
SHOPKEEPER:	What do you mean, miss?
PRALINE:	Oh, I'm sorry, I have a cold. I wish to make a complaint.
SHOPKEEPER:	Sorry, we're closing for lunch.
PRALINE:	Never mind that, my lad, I wish to complain about this parrot that I purchased not half an hour ago from this very boutique.
SHOPKEEPER:	Oh yes, the Norwegian Blue. What's wrong with it?

PRALINE: I'll tell you what's wrong with it. It's dead, that's what's wrong with it.

SHOPKEEPER: No, no, it's resting, look!

PRALINE: Look, my lad, I know a dead parrot when I see one and I'm looking at one right now.

SHOPKEEPER: No, no sir, it's not dead. It's resting.

PRALINE: Resting?

SHOPKEEPER: Yeah, remarkable bird the Norwegian Blue, beautiful plumage, innit?

PRALINE: The plumage don't enter into it—it's stone dead.

SHOPKEEPER: No, no—it's just resting.

PRALINE: All right then, if it's resting I'll wake it up. *(shouts into cage)* Hello Polly! I've got a nice cuttlefish for you when you wake up, Polly Parrot!

SHOPKEEPER: *(jogging cage)* There, it moved.

PRALINE: No, he didn't. That was you pushing the cage.

SHOPKEEPER: I did not.

PRALINE: Yes, you did. *(takes parrot out of cage, shouts)* Hello Polly, Polly. *(bangs it against counter)* Polly Parrot, wake up, Polly. *(throws it in the air and lets it fall to the floor)* Now that's what I call a dead parrot.

SHOPKEEPER: No, no, it's stunned.

PRALINE: Look, my lad, I've had just about enough of this. That parrot is definitely deceased. And when I bought it not half an hour ago, you assured me that its lack of movement was due to it being tired and shagged out after a long squawk.

SHOPKEEPER: It's probably pining for the fiords.

PRALINE:	Pining for the fiords, what kind of talk is that? Look, why did it fall flat on its back the moment I got it home?
SHOPKEEPER:	The Norwegian Blue prefers kipping on its back. Beautiful bird, lovely plumage.
PRALINE:	Look, I took the liberty of examining that parrot, and I discovered that the only reason that it had been sitting on its perch in the first place was that it had been nailed there.
SHOPKEEPER:	Well, of course it was nailed there. Otherwise it would muscle up to those bars and voom.
PRALINE:	Look, matey *(picks up parrot),* this parrot wouldn't voom if I put four thousand volts through it. It's bleeding demised.
SHOPKEEPER:	It's not, it's pining.
PRALINE:	It's not pining, it's passed on. This parrot is no more. It has ceased to be. It's expired and gone to meet its maker. This is a late parrot. It's a stiff. Bereft of life, it rests in peace. If you hadn't nailed it to the perch, it would be pushing up the daisies. It's rung down the curtain and joined the choir invisible. This is an ex-parrot.
SHOPKEEPER:	Well, I'd better replace it then.

Notes

innit a slang expression meaning "isn't it"

shagged out a slang expression meaning "exhausted"

pining yearning; from the Old English *pīnian,* meaning "to cause to suffer"

kipping a slang expression meaning "sleeping"

Activities

1. Write a short personal response to this selection. What elements appeal or do not appeal to you? Meet with a small group to compare your reactions and identify the comedic techniques used in the script. Are there common social, cultural, personality, or demographic attributes that affect the reactions of group members? To what extent do these factors affect your response to other forms of comedy? Present your conclusions to the class.

2. Comedy relies on the actors' use of their voices and their movements, as well the words they speak. Make a copy of the script. Work with a small group to experiment with ways of delivering the lines by focusing on volume, pitch, facial expressions, physical movements, and timing. Then insert stage directions into the script. Present the script as a readers' theatre and compare the choices you made with those of other groups. If possible, view a videotape of the original Monty Python sketch and consider the extent to which their delivery enhanced the material.

3. View several episodes of a comedy show. Write an essay analyzing the intended audience and the underlying values reflected in the material. Make connections with the social or historical context in which the programs appeared. You may choose recent episodes of a program such as *The Royal Canadian Air Farce* or *This Hour Has Twenty-Two Minutes*, or videotapes and reruns of programs such as *SCTV* or *Monty Python's Flying Circus*.

Another Viewpoint: Literary Modes and Forms

The literary mode of comedy has a rich history and tradition. Do research into this mode by focusing on such conventions of traditional comedy as the use of stock characters and situations, bombastic language, and slapstick. Then write an analytical essay in which you consider to what extent "Dead Parrot" falls within the tradition of a classic literary comedy.

wrap-up
drama

1. Use the Internet or other sources to identify some well-known stage plays that have been adapted as television or feature films. Choose a film video that is easily accessible to you and find its script. Read the play and then watch the film, taking detailed notes on how the play has been interpreted on camera. Write a review that presents a strong argument for why you would or would not recommend the film. Use the Internet to look up reviews of other play adaptations for ideas on what you might include.

2. Choose one character from a dramatic work in this unit or from a story in the short fiction unit. Write and then present a monologue in which the character you have chosen reflects on her or his life ten years later. Maintain a consistent point of view in your portrayal by accurately reflecting what the character would see, know, and feel, and how he or she would speak. Rehearse your monologue aloud to yourself. Tape-record and replay it to determine whether it sounds like the voice of your chosen character. Present the monologue to your classmates and get their feedback on its effectiveness.

3. With a small group, select one or more scenes from a dramatic work in this unit, and, on chart paper, outline a plan for its set design. Be sure your plan contains the following: a clear statement of the rationale for your design, a description of the physical space you will use, rough sketches of the set, and a description of each element of the design, such as backdrops and props. Present your plan to the class and elicit their feedback on your rationale and design choices.

4. Work with a partner. Choose a dramatic selection in this anthology to convert from one dramatic form into another—for example, from a stage play into a radio play. Before you begin, study samples of the two forms you have chosen. Note the main script conventions of these forms, such as dialogue format, directions for actors' movements, use of props and sound effects, choice of camera shots, and set descriptions. Create a checklist of these conventions. Share your list with a small group and make revisions based on feedback. With your partner, write the script for your adaptation, carefully reviewing the revised checklist to make sure you have observed the conventions you identified.

Who was William Shakespeare? Today Shakespeare is considered more than just a brilliant writer from another era. Through his works, Shakespeare continues to have an influence throughout the world. In fact, his extraordinary talent has led scholars to question whether just one person of Shakespeare's background could have accomplished so many achievements. His very identity has been debated. We do know that there was a William Shakespeare who was born in Stratford-upon-Avon, England, in 1564. As a young man, he moved to London to become an actor and playwright. By 1590, he was active on the London stage. Over the next decade, he wrote such plays as *Romeo and Juliet* (1595), *A Midsummer Night's Dream* (1596), and *Julius Caesar* (1599). In 1599, Shakespeare's company, the Lord Chamberlain's Men, built their own theatre, The Globe, on the south bank of the river Thames. Works such as *Hamlet*, *King Lear*, and *Macbeth* were premiered there in the early seventeenth century.

Shakespeare's literary output was prodigious. His impact on cultural history and on the English language itself is inestimable. Many individual works of literature, contemporary drama, music and opera, dance, film, fine art, and non-fiction, and even such commercial media works as advertisements, have been inspired by or based on Shakespeare's work or contain allusions to it. At times, when Shakespeare could not come up with a suitable word, he invented one. Many of these invented words have remained within the modern English language. Phrases from his plays, such as "To be or not to be," have become very familiar. The depth with which Shakespeare's writing embodies human life and passion—our fears, hopes, frustrations, aspirations, secrets, victories, and defeats—can at times be breathtaking.

This In-Depth explores the pervasiveness of Shakespeare's influence. Included is a profile of a costume designer from the Stratford Festival in Ontario, who has created her own works of art for numerous Shakespearean play productions. An excerpt from Kenneth Branagh's screenplay of *Hamlet* allows us to experience how a screenwriter adapts an original play to bring it to life on screen. The question-and-answer format of a filmmakers' symposium offers insights by renowned film directors into their interpretations of Shakespeare's work. Examples of literary criticism—a classic segment on tragedy by A.C. Bradley and a contemporary take on comedy by Angela Pitt—allow us to enter the vibrant discipline of Shakespearean scholarship. And an anecdotal story by Stephen Leacock pokes fun at the discipline of Shakespearean criticism. As you explore some ways in which, centuries after his death, William Shakespeare continues to shape our lives, consider how other writers have had an impact on both your thinking and your decisions.

A print of a seventeenth century black-and-white engraving from a frontispiece to a published collection of Shakespeare's plays. The portrait of William Shakespeare is by Martin Droeshout.

Invisible Genius:
The Quiet Talent of Tanya Moiseiwitsch

Therese Greenwood

Therese Greenwood was born in 1962 on Wolfe Island, Ontario, one of the Thousand Islands near the city of Kingston. She holds a master's degree in journalism, has worked as a reporter, editor, and journalism professor, and is a regular correspondent for CBC Radio. She has also written historical fiction set in the Kingston area. This article, which appeared in the *Kingston Whig-Standard* magazine, describes the brilliance of Tanya Moiseiwitsch, a theatrical costume designer. What do you think are the responsibilities of a costume designer when designing the clothing for characters in a play? What do the clothes you wear suggest to others about yourself? How can clothes be symbolic of specific characteristics of society?

At first glance, it seems strange that the Stratford Festival's exhibition of theatre designs by Tanya Moiseiwitsch should contain only one letter of praise from a major theatrical figure. The exhibition, after all, celebrates a 40-year association between the festival and a woman whom many theatre experts consider the world's premier designer. Somewhere, one feels sure, there must be a trunk packed with letters from the world's greatest theatrical personalities, all testifying to her talents. For Tanya Moiseiwitsch has rubbed shoulders with such people as Sir Alec Guinness, Dame Edith Evans, James Mason, Vanessa Redgrave, and Sir Ralph Richardson—costuming many of them during her work at Stratford, where she designed 29 productions including both of the festival's inaugural shows in 1953.

Surprising, then, that the exhibition at the Gallery Stratford features only one testimonial, written by Sir Laurence Olivier 20 years ago for an earlier exhibition of her work? Not really. For in fact the absence of rave reviews from celebrities is a reflection of the personality of Tanya Moiseiwitsch, an artist who was able to command all the beauty and power of the theatre without placing herself at centre stage. Indeed, it is that very ability that has made her one of the world's best designers.

"I've yet to see a designer who has bettered her," says Ronald Bryden, theatre critic and drama professor at the University of Toronto. "There are designers who are more noticeable, who make a big splash on stage. She's the only one who's too good to make the splash."

Laurence Olivier would have agreed. "Tanya Moiseiwitsch is a very wonderful designer," he wrote in his letter. "Painters are not usually so successful in so completely disguising themselves and sinking their personalities into each project as if it was the first solution they had ever found. Her voice, though excessively quiet, one might say—her manner so retiring one feared she would disappear through the wall—was always marvellously assertive and solution-finding in its own quiet way."

Ms. Moiseiwitsch, now retired from the theatre, retains her unfailing modesty. She evades questions about the impact her designs have had on Stratford and theatre in Canada by praising someone else: the curators, the actors who wore the costumes, Tyrone Guthrie. She apologizes for sounding "too serious" or a "bit solemn." She asks an interviewer if they may sit in another part of the building so she might avoid the sound of her own voice being played back to her on the videotaped interview that plays on an endless loop in one part of the exhibition.

Yet her genteel sensitivity also has an air of theatricality. It is not theatricality in the vulgar sense of striking a grandiose pose, but in the sense that certain secrets must be preserved if the theatre is to maintain its magic. Now, as she makes her annual visit to Stratford as a member of the audience, she refrains from making technical comments on the productions, determined to maintain the confederacy of silence that sustains the magic of the theatre.

"I do see that it's all so stimulating and I see the work that goes into it," she says. "I suppose anybody who's worked in the theatre sees that. But the audience isn't supposed to know that. I think a certain air of mystery should be preserved and the audience must find things out for themselves."

Helping to maintain the theatre's aura of mystery, making her brilliant contribution disappear into the overall production, is a hallmark of Moiseiwitsch design, says Mr. Bryden. Her costumes are never so flashy that they detract from the performers and always fortify the foundations of the production.

"They are never so obtrusive that they take away from the actors. She never uses a strong colour that jumps out at you. She provides the kind of clothing design that assists a director in saying that this is the central figure, these are the subordinate characters.

"She's a great researcher," says Mr. Bryden, pointing to her ability to assemble details from paintings, sculptures, and other artistic sources that give her costumes historical accuracy. If a director casts a play in the seventeenth century, Mr. Bryden says, Ms. Moiseiwitsch will not use a colour that paintings suggest had not then been invented.

"If you know your classical art, you can look at your references and you can see from some of her notes how she went around assembling her costumes from little bits of details she sketches and then uses in her designs."

Bearing out these observations are the questions carefully printed on some of the exhibition's sketches, asking "How does this fasten, hooks or eyes?" On another, of a man wearing a birdlike mask, is the note "Beak held antiseptics during the plague of 1665."

But Ms. Moiseiwitsch's greatest achievement, says Mr. Bryden, is her ability to conceive a costume as it will appear on stage, that is, as a three-dimensional product that, as an extension of the actor, will be required to physically occupy space.

"This is her great quality: she thinks in spatial terms," he says. "The clothes are always structural rather than pictorial. She doesn't choose colours that will make the costume look like an oil painting. She chooses materials that fall in structural folds. The costumes always look like sculpture rather than paintings."

The Stratford exhibition of Ms. Moiseiwitsch's work succeeds in recreating this impression by presenting her designs on faceless dummies. (The placards list the actors who wore the costumes to help the viewer envision a familiar face amid the material.) The impression is enhanced by posing the costumes on reconstructed portions of the festival's famous thrust stage designed by Ms. Moiseiwitsch and Tyrone Guthrie.

The construction of the thrust stage created the need for a designer who could think in spatial terms—and, indeed, was responsible for the initial success of the festival. It was the organizing committee's assurance that he would be allowed to construct a stage of his own design that ultimately lured the famous London director Tyrone Guthrie to the small Ontario town that dreamed of operating a world-class Shakespeare festival.

Guthrie had long argued that Shakespeare's works were not well suited to the "picture frame" proscenium stages common to most theatres. He felt that this type of stage, originally designed for performances of opera, isolated the audience from the performers and fostered the impression that the theatre was only an illusion. He championed the concept of a "thrust" stage, which literally thrusts out into the viewing area and is surrounded on three sides by the audience, allowing one scene to flow into the next without the obstruction of a curtain or scenery changes.

When the founders of the Stratford Festival gave Guthrie carte blanche to build his stage, it was natural that he ask Tanya Moiseiwitsch to take the ideas from his head and transform them into a working model. As World War II was drawing to a close, Guthrie had chosen Ms. Moiseiwitsch to work with him at the newly expanded Old Vic in Liverpool. By 1953, she had already designed more than 50 productions at Dublin's Abbey Theatre, 150 productions at the Oxford Playhouse, and productions at the Old Vic in Liverpool, Bristol, and London. Most importantly she shared his belief in the thrust stage.

"Miss Moiseiwitsch and I, who are old collaborators, had long dreamed of such a stage as was now to come into being," he wrote in his autobiography.

Writing in *The Oxford Companion to the Canadian Theatre*, Mr. Bryden sums up the effect of a platform that still dominates the style of the festival's productions:

> The novel thrust stage that Guthrie and Moiseiwitsch de-signed tried to recreate the original style of Shakespearean performance. It rescued the actor from painted scenery and re-stored the primacy of the spoken word. With the general shape and features of the Elizabethan platform stage, sur-rounded on three sides by an auditorium reminiscent of clas-sical Greece, the stage also encouraged spectacle and movement, characteristics Guthrie exploited to the full as one colourful scene flowed smoothly into the next with a constant swirl of lavish costumes, eye-catching properties, and waving banners.

These eye-catching costumes and properties, necessary to create instant impressions of time, place, and mood, are essential, notes Mr. Bryden. "Guthrie said about the stage that she designed for him that it would need to be very richly furnished, that since they weren't going to have any scenery, costumes would have to do the work of the scenery." And, he adds, with the audience seated so much closer to the stage, props and costumes must look more authentic in order to bear up under closer scrutiny.

Most importantly, the thrust stage gives more "space" to actors, so that they are not seen within a frame, like pictures, but like sculptures oc-cupying a three-dimensional space. This means it is important for a de-signer to think in terms of the space the actors—and their costumes—will occupy. It is a concept that Tanya Moiseiwitsch understood completely, and her grasp of it is perhaps best illustrated in this exhibition by one of the most magnificent pieces of her work, the coronation robe from the 1953 production of *Richard III* starring Alec Guinness.

Ms. Moiseiwitsch, predictably, credits Tyrone Guthrie with deciding that as Alec Guinness, weighed down by 40 yards of heavy red velvet, made the long, slow trek to his throne, his costume would telegraph a message to the audience.

"By the time he got to the throne," she says, "the whole of the stage was covered in red velvet. And that wasn't just showing-off-costume time. That was Guthrie. The thought behind it was, to get to the throne he had killed a lot of people, and this was an ocean of blood that he was carrying as a burden on his shoulders. Did everybody know what they were meant to think? No, absolutely not. But that was the thought behind it."

But the impression of this scene was much stronger than Ms. Moiseiwitsch allows, according to Ronald Bryden, who says that theatregoers still remember the scene and how a talented actor made use of this extraordinary prop.

"He used the whole stage. The cloak was designed to just about cover the entire stage," says Mr. Bryden. "Then, I'm told, Guinness turned around and walked on the velvet and it was as if he was saying, 'This is my kingdom and I can now enjoy it.' It was this feeling of royalty in space and he was taking advantage of it. Not many designers would think of that."

This careful thought, this ability to contribute to the pageantry of Shakespeare without upstaging the performer, is Ms. Moiseiwitsch's legacy to the theatre that influences how most Canadians view classical theatre. Also, the Stratford stage—since remodelled several times to incorporate minor modifications made under her supervision—has continued to define the type of performance staged at the festival. And its lavish costuming, although threatened by budgetary constraints, continues to measure up to the best in the world.

"She set a standard at Stratford," says Mr. Bryden, pointing out that from the beginning she insisted on professional standards, bringing in a staff of specialists and painstakingly training locals to carry out her designs. "Gradually all of that got built into Stratford, so that the wardrobe and properties department is superlative, one of the best in the world."

Although today's designers live up to her standards, they don't always live up to Ms. Moiseiwitsch's self-effacing approach. "Sometimes they swamp the stage and overwhelm the production," says Mr. Bryden. It is an error Ms. Moiseiwitsch never committed.

Looking over her designs, Ms. Moiseiwitsch can voice no regrets. She says she wouldn't change a thing. "If I could do it over again, I would refuse. You don't go and try to wipe up any kind of spilled milk. Just let it lie. That's the beauty of the theatre. Usually it's in people's memories rather than anything visible."

That has been Tanya Moiseiwitsch's true talent: the ability to remain invisible, her individual brilliance devoted to making others live in the memory of theatregoers.

Notes

Sir Alec Guinness, Dame Edith Evans, James Mason, Vanessa Redgrave, and Sir Ralph Richardson renowned stage and screen actors of the twentieth century

Stratford a city in Ontario, the site of the Stratford Festival of Canada; North America's largest repertory theatre, presenting the works of William Shakespeare and other playwrights

Sir Laurence Olivier (1907–1989) a renowned British actor, producer, and director, who won the Best Actor Academy Award for *Hamlet* (1948)

Plague of 1665 the London plague, also known as the Black Death, a highly contagious bacterial infection that reached epidemic proportions, killing over 100,000 people in and around London, England

"picture frame" proscenium stage a stage with an arch at the front, creating a visual frame for the theatrical audience

carte blanche unrestricted power or authority; a French-language phrase meaning literally "blank paper"

Richard III in this instance, the popular historical tragedy written by Shakespeare in 1594

Shakespeare was instrumental in building the Globe Theatre, which he described in the chorus of his play Henry V as a "wooden O." The centre of the Globe was open-air, but its perimeter had a roof over the stage and galleries. The theatre's thrust stage had no curtain and jutted from the rear wall into an open, unroofed yard that accommodated about 800 groundlings, or members of the standing audience. When the house was full, approximately 1,500 spectators sat in the galleries. By all accounts, the audiences at the Globe were very vocal and participatory, calling back to the actors and throwing objects onto the stage if they were displeased.

From

Hamlet

William Shakespeare and Kenneth Branagh

Actor, director, producer, and writer Kenneth Branagh was born in Belfast, Northern Ireland, in 1960. He studied at the Royal Academy of Dramatic Arts and joined the Royal Shakespeare Company at the age of twenty-three. In 1988, he left that company to form his own, the Renaissance Theatre Company. Often credited with creating a popular movie audience for Shakespeare, Branagh has developed and starred in a number of film adaptations of the bard's plays, including *Henry V* (1989) and *Hamlet* (1996). This excerpt, from Branagh's screenplay, corresponds to Act I, Scene 2 of *Hamlet*. In it, Hamlet has returned home to find that his father is dead and his Uncle Claudius has become both his stepfather and the new king. How might a screenplay script of a Shakespearean work differ from the original play? In what ways might these differences affect how you approach your reading of a screenplay script?

Cut to:
Interior/State Hall Day
A glorious procession of the new KING CLAUDIUS: *and his* QUEEN GERTRUDE. *We move with them into a packed gathering of smiling Courtiers and Commoners. The men are crisp, sexy. The military cut—all dashing clothes and hair. The women's clothes colourful, gloriously textured, shapely and flesh-revealing.*

> *They walk from the enormous doors through rows of bleachers. It's like the House of Commons. Everyone stands. The guard of honour salutes.*

CLAUDIUS *in full military regalia. Severe cropped hair, brushed back, standing to attention atop a striking face that bears a crisp beard.* GERTRUDE, *complete with veil and generous bosom on show, also trim and vigorous. This irresistibly sexy, confident couple reach the throne. They face their Audience of bright festive colours and supportive faces.*

The King begins to speak. Measured, compassionate, intelligent. All listen attentively, particularly the Prime Minister, POLONIUS, *his son* LAERTES, *and his beautiful daughter* OPHELIA.

CLAUDIUS
Though yet of Hamlet our dear brother's death
The memory be green, and that it us befitted
To bear our hearts in grief, and our whole Kingdom
To be contracted in one brow of woe,
Yet so far hath discretion fought with nature
That we with wisest sorrow think on him
Together with remembrance of ourselves.
> *Moist eyes. A man of genuine compassion.*

CLAUDIUS *(continuing)*
Therefore our sometime sister, now our Queen
> *She, also moved, emotions very close to the surface.*

CLAUDIUS *(continuing)*
Th' imperial jointress of this warlike state,
Have we as 'twere with a defeated joy,
With one auspicious and one dropping eye,
With mirth in funeral and with dirge in marriage,
In equal scale weighing delight and dole,
Taken to wife.
> *(He kisses her hand.)*
Nor have we herein barred
Your better wisdoms, which have freely gone
With this affair along. For all, our thanks.
> *Slow, then quickening and intense applause. He overrides this reaction with his clearly genuine gratitude to this court. Now to business and*

a serious public policy statement for a worried nation. MARCELLUS *is not alone in his fears.*

CLAUDIUS *(continuing)*
Now follows that you know young Fortinbras,
Holding a weak supposal of our worth,
Or thinking by our late dear brother's death
Our state to be disjoint and out of frame,
Co-leaguèd with the dream of his advantage,
He hath not failed to pester us with message
    An Attendant gives him a paper.
Importing the surrender of those lands
Lost by his father, with all bonds of law,
To our most valiant brother.
    He tears up the paper. There is a gasp from the CROWD, *then applause. He's playing them well.*
So much for him.
    Now, tougher still. He's into Norman Schwarzkopf mode. There will be no messing with the Danish King. He plays it out confidently to the gallery, taking another paper.

CLAUDIUS *(continuing)*
Now for ourself, and for this time of meeting,
Thus much the business is: we have here writ
To Norway, uncle of young Fortinbras—
    Cut to:
    Interior/Bedroom Night (Flashback)
    We see the wizened, frightened old man.

CLAUDIUS V/O
Who, impotent and bed-rid, scarcely hears
Of this his nephew's purpose—to suppress
    The face grows dark. We see the surly young FORTINBRAS, *tearing up the map.*

CLAUDIUS V/O
His further gait herein, in that the levies,
The lists, and full proportions are all made
Out of his subject;

> *Cut to:*
> *Interior/State Hall Day (Real time)*

CLAUDIUS
and we here dispatch
You, good Cornelius, and you, Voltemand,

> *The two wise men, also in military garb, move to the throne.*

CLAUDIUS
For bearers of this greeting to old Norway,
Giving to you no further personal power
To business with the King more than the scope
Of these dilated articles allow.
Farewell, and let your haste commend your duty.

> VOLTEMAND *takes the papers.*

VOLTEMAND
In that, and all things, will we show our duty.

CLAUDIUS
We doubt it nothing, heartily farewell.

> *The* AUDIENCE *applauds. No hysteria this time, but all are quietly
> impressed by this statesmanship. Time now to turn on the charm with
> the young aristocrats. Also a good show for the ladies, who crane their
> necks on the balconies to see which of the bright young things around
> the throne will be indulged with a public favour.*

CLAUDIUS
And now, Laertes, what's the news with you?
You told us of some suit.

> *A darkly handsome young man steps forward. In the uniform of a
> cadet.*

CLAUDIUS *(continuing)*
What is't, Laertes?
You cannot speak of reason to the Dane
And lose your voice. What wouldst thou beg, Laertes,
That shall not be my offer, not thy asking?
The head is not more native to the heart,
The hand more instrumental to the mouth,
Than is the throne of Denmark to thy father.

> *He turns to* POLONIUS, *once again letting the court know how the power structure stands. Then on with a smile.*

CLAUDIUS *(continuing)*
What wouldst thou have, Laertes?

LAERTES *(nervous)*
My dread lord,
Your leave and favour to return to France,

> *Knowing looks from around the court. The phrase "sowing wild oats" comes to people's minds.* LAERTES *responds quickly.*

LAERTES
From whence, though willingly I came to Denmark
To show my duty in your coronation,
Yet now I must confess, that duty done,
My thoughts and wishes bend again towards France
And bow them to your gracious leave and pardon.

> *The King teases it out for a moment.*

CLAUDIUS
Have you your father's leave? What says Polonius?

> *Dad joins in with the gentle ribbing.*

POLONIUS
He hath, my lord, wrung from me my slow leave
By laboursome petition and at last
Upon his will I sealed my hard consent.
I do beseech you give him leave to go.

CLAUDIUS *steps down to* LAERTES.

CLAUDIUS
Take thy fair hour, Laertes. Time be thine,
And thy best graces spend it at thy will.
> *As the* AUDIENCE *applauds, the Camera tracks slowly past them and comes to a halt under the right hand balcony. There at the other end of the hall is a black silhouette of a man. We make an abrupt Cut. The humorous applause that has greeted* LAERTES' *departure is stopped by a big Close-up on* CLAUDIUS *and his firm tone.*

CLAUDIUS *(continuing)*
But note, my cousin Hamlet, and my son—
> *We make another abrupt Cut back to the lonely figure behind the bleachers.*

HAMLET
A little more than kin, and less than kind.

CLAUDIUS
How is it that the clouds still hang on you?
> *From* CLAUDIUS' *POV we see* HAMLET *move forward and sit down.*

HAMLET
Not so, my lord, I am too much in the sun.
> *We see reaction on the* AUDIENCE'*s faces. This is embarrassing. The* QUEEN *moves away from the throne and we see her and her son in profile 2-shot. She attempts intimacy. This should not be public.*

GERTRUDE
Good Hamlet, cast thy nighted colour off,
And let thine eye look like a friend on Denmark.
Do not for ever with thy vailèd lids
Seek for thy noble father in the dust.
Thou know'st 'tis common—all that lives must die,
Passing through nature to eternity.

HAMLET

Ay, madam, it is common.

GERTRUDE

If it be,
Why seems it so particular with thee?

> *In his shocked reaction he raises his voice, so that the* CROWD *can almost hear the hissed reproaches that he shoots at her grief-free demeanour.*

HAMLET

Seems, madam? Nay, it is. I know not "seems."
'Tis not alone my inky cloak, good mother
Nor customary suits of solemn black,
Nor windy suspiration of forced breath,
No, nor the fruitful river in the eye,
Nor the dejected haviour of the visage,
Together with all forms, moods, shapes of grief
That can denote me truly. These indeed "seem,"
For they are actions that a man might play;
But I have that within which passeth show—
These but the trappings and the suits of woe.

> *There are whispers now through the* CROWD. *They're witnessing a scene that should take place behind closed doors.* CLAUDIUS *has had enough. Time for action.*

CLAUDIUS

'Tis sweet and commendable in your nature, Hamlet,

> *He goes toward the Prince bringing in the* CROWD *with his voice. This will now be a very public conversation.*

CLAUDIUS *(continuing)*

To give these mourning duties to your father;
But you must know your father lost a father;
That father lost, lost his; and the survivor bound
In filial obligation for some term
To do obsequious sorrow. But to persevere

In obstinate condolement is a course
Of impious stubbornness, 'tis unmanly grief,
It shows a will most incorrect to heaven,

> *As* CLAUDIUS *gives this rough lecture, he directs his injunctions to the physically immobile Prince. The great gallery of Courtiers behind, packed to the rafters. The power and strength of the King's position chillingly clear.*

CLAUDIUS *(continuing)*
A heart unfortified, a mind impatient.
An understanding simple and unschooled;
For what we know must be, and is as common
As any the most vulgar thing to sense,
Why should we in our peevish opposition
Take it to heart? Fie, 'tis a fault to heaven,
A fault against the dead, a fault to nature.
To reason most absurd, whose common theme
Is death of fathers, and who still hath cried
From the first corpse till he that died today,
"This must be so."

> CLAUDIUS *puts his arm around* HAMLET. *An invasion of intimacy.*

CLAUDIUS *(continuing)*
We pray you throw to earth
This unprevailing woe, and think of us
As of a father; for let the world take note

> *He drags* HAMLET *out onto the dais and produces the next information with a great Churchillian flourish.* HAMLET *eventually will be King—* CLAUDIUS *has nominated him here and now—all is well. The* CROWD *respond.*

CLAUDIUS *(continuing)*
You are the most immediate to our throne,

> *Huge applause from the* CROWD.

CLAUDIUS *(continuing)*
And with no less nobility of love

Than that which dearest father bears his son
Do I impart towards you.
> *Now, the atmosphere changes.*

CLAUDIUS *(continuing)*
For your intent
In going back to school in Wittenberg,
> *The great issue comes up.* LAERTES, OPHELIA, GERTRUDE *all wanting to see* HAMLET *take his rightful place.*

CLAUDIUS *(continuing)*
It is most retrograde to our desire,
And we beseech you bend you to remain
Here in the cheer and comfort of our eye,
Our chiefest courtier, cousin, and our son.
> *Quiet again. The* AUDIENCE *straining to overhear.*

GERTRUDE
Let not thy mother lose her prayers, Hamlet.
I pray thee stay with us, go not to Wittenberg.
> *We see* HAMLET'S *crushed body language. The sense of a head bowed. Nevertheless he is a Prince and this is clear in the manner of his reply.*

HAMLET
I shall in all my best obey you, madam.

CLAUDIUS
Why, 'tis a loving and a fair reply.
Be as ourself in Denmark.
(To GERTRUDE*)* Madam, come.
> *He takes her hand and moves to the front of the Dais. They effectively mask* HAMLET *from the Court. Peace is restored. Finally neither foreign upstarts nor truculent nephews have thrown this new King off balance, at this formal opening of his new parliament. He is intimate with her now. Happily letting the Court share their obvious intoxication with each other.*

CLAUDIUS

This gentle and unforced accord of Hamlet
Sits smiling to my heart; in grace whereof,
No jocund health that Denmark drinks today
But the great cannon to the clouds shall tell,
And the King's rouse the heavens shall bruit again,
Re-speaking earthly thunder.

> *Confetti begins to fall.*

CLAUDIUS

Come, away.

> *Cheers, trumpets. The Royal Couple race out like the hungry newlyweds they are. The happy* CROWD *chase them like a drunken wedding party. The huge hall empties almost by magic. We see the end doors shut and then we see* HAMLET *still standing at the throne. His body collapses, leaning on the arms of the throne. As we hear him start to speak we move slowly around him.*

HAMLET

O that this too too solid flesh would melt,
Thaw and resolve itself into a dew,
Or that the Everlasting had not fixed
His canon 'gainst self-slaughter! O God, O God,
How weary, stale, flat, and unprofitable
Seem to me all the uses of this world!
Fie on't, ah fie, fie! 'Tis an unweeded garden
That grows to seed; things rank and gross in nature
Possess it merely. That it should come to this—

> *The Camera moves with* HAMLET *down the hall.*

HAMLET *(continuing)*

But two months dead—nay, not so much, not two—
So excellent a King, that was to this
Hyperion to a satyr, so loving to my mother
That he might not beteem the winds of heaven
Visit her face too roughly! Heaven and earth,

Must I remember? Why, she would hang on him
As if increase of appetite had grown
By what it fed on, and yet within a month—
Let me not think on't; frailty, thy name is woman—
>   *He turns to face away from the door.*

HAMLET *(continuing)*
A little month, or ere those shoes were old
With which she followed my poor father's body,
Like Niobe, all tears, why she, even she—
O God, a beast that wants discourse of reason
Would have mourned longer!—married with mine uncle,
My father's brother, but no more like my father
Than I to Hercules, within a month,
Ere yet the salt of most unrighteous tears
Had left the flushing in her gallèd eyes,
She married. O most wicked speed, to post
With such dexterity to incestuous sheets!
>   *He looks back down the almost empty state hall. We see the melan-*
>   *cholic profile of a young man in black military cadet uniform, flaxen*
>   *hair and a single tear trailing down a face more used to smiles.*

Notes

Norman Schwarzkopf the American general who was the allied commander during the Persian Gulf War (1990–91)

V/O the abbreviation for *voice-over,* a narration or commentary in a filmed work in which the viewer does not see the speaker, who is off-camera

Churchillian flourish a grand gesture; reference to Sir Winston Churchill, British prime minister during World War II, much praised for his heroic leadership and skills as an orator

Hyperion a Titan in classical Greek mythology

satyr a mythical creature that is half-human and half-goat

Niobe a character in Greek mythology who, while weeping for her slain children, is turned into a stone from which her tears continue to flow

Shakespeare in the Cinema: A Film Directors' Symposium

On December 15, 1998, the magazine editors of *Cineaste* posed several questions about cinematic adaptations of Shakespeare's plays to noted film directors Sir Peter Hall (*A Midsummer Night's Dream*, 1968), Richard Loncraine (*Richard III*, 1995), Baz Luhrmann (*William Shakespeare's Romeo + Juliet*, 1996), Trevor Nunn (*Twelfth Night*, 1996), Oliver Parker (*Othello*, 1995), Roman Polanski (*Macbeth*, 1971), and Franco Zeffirelli (*The Taming of the Shrew*, 1967; *Romeo and Juliet*, 1968; and *Hamlet*, 1990). Their intent was to gain insights into the aesthetic considerations and working methods of film directors who have adapted Shakespeare for the cinema. What is the role of a film director in the making of a movie? What do you think are the most typical modifications filmmakers make when adapting a Shakespearean play for film, and why are they made?

It is almost always necessary to make cuts and other changes in the text when cinematically adapting a Shakespeare play. What is your own philosophy or strategy for making cuts, for updating antiquarian or obscure words, or for rewriting or rearranging scenes?

Richard Loncraine: If you're making a Shakespeare film for a contemporary audience, you have to make sure that they don't get bored. Shakespeare wrote *Richard III* about 400 years ago, when people were used to words. They didn't have much visual stimulus, there was no set design, there was no television, there was no cinema obviously, so words were crucial. In our telling of the story, we have everything from special effects, to scored music and exciting imagery. We can communicate with pictures an awful lot of what Shakespeare expressed with words. I do believe that you can cut the text. Shakespeare's plays were almost never put on in their full-text form.

Baz Luhrmann: Our philosophy in adapting *Romeo and Juliet* for the screen was to reveal Shakespeare's lyrical, romantic, sweet, sexy, musical, violent, rude, rough, rowdy, rambunctious storytelling through his richly invented language. Consequently, our specific strategy was to avoid changing or adding words. We were adamant that we should maintain the colour and taste of the actual words even to the extent of the "thee" and "thou."

Setting the story in the contemporary world of urban gangs allowed us to put Shakespeare's inventive usage to work as a dexterous and ornate street rap. This game allowed us to justify all words even when the actual meaning was not immediately apparent.

Where we took significant liberty was in restructuring and cutting. We felt it was important to serve Shakespeare's ultimate goal of strong storytelling. He had to arrest the attention of a very noisy, disparate, savage yet honest audience not unlike at your local cinema. To facilitate this he used all the devices at his disposal: the clash of lowbrow comedy with high tragedy, the use of popular song (pop music), etc. Similarly, we developed a specific cinematic language for Romeo and Juliet that transformed all of these devices into cinematic equivalents in order to achieve the same goal with our noisy, disparate, savage yet honest audience.

Oliver Parker: I don't have a strategy regarding cuts. I'm sure it would vary according to the particular piece and my vision of it. To present the plays in their entirety would be a disservice to Shakespeare. I'm sure if he were alive today, he'd be radically reworking the text for a new medium, and would most likely want to direct it. His plays are colossal things, open to infinite interpretation. I'm interested in remaining true to the spirit, not to the text, of plays.

Roman Polanski: I'm definitely not for rewriting scenes, unless there's really a possibility of making them clearer by some minute change. There is so much literature written by so many scholars that, in certain cases, they have it all ready for you. If a change helps the clarity and does not spoil the verse, you may in some cases do that.

Cuts definitely have to be made, just because of length. You may also rearrange the text sometimes, film it in a different sequence, without harming the play—in fact, you can sometimes help it. The plays were written for the stage and had to take into account the rigidity of that format. The stage just doesn't allow you to tell your story in the way you would necessarily want to tell it, whereas the film allows you to tell it in any way. If there is some kind of retrospective narration, for example, you can use a flashback, which you cannot on the stage.

Franco Zeffirelli: Anything created in another medium, like a novel or a play, has to accept certain rules when it migrates into the formidable medium of cinema—the length of the film, the language of images, and so on. I cannot think of one novel or play that has been transposed entirely—apart from an exception like Branagh's *Hamlet*—because otherwise your film would last five hours. Adaptation is therefore inevitable, a necessity that no one can escape.

What is your view of the proper presentation of Shakespeare's verse in a film? Should it be delivered differently on screen than on the stage? Do you attempt to preserve the poetic and musical quality of the blank verse, or do you think it's more important for the actors to achieve a more naturalistic delivery that will not seem so alien to the ears of contemporary moviegoers, most of whom are not theatregoers?

Sir Peter Hall: The verse has to be underplayed. One of the problems about Shakespeare on screen is that he wrote for an intimate theatre, in which one could both shout and whisper, and that vocal range is part of the Shakespeare experience. If you shout in a film you look like an old ham. So half the Shakespeare dynamic range vocally goes out the window as soon as you put it on screen.

As for the musical quality of the blank verse, those are external judgments. I don't think that you can speak poetically or speak musically. You can speak with sense, with wit, and with a concrete imagination, and if you don't you're a rotten old Shakespearean ham. I detect at the back of your questions a feeling that film acting needs to be real whereas Shakespeare acting needs to be false, and that is not true.

Baz Luhrmann: One of the great things about Shakespeare's text is its musicality and rhythm. The fact is the actors learn so much about what they are doing and saying from the rhythm itself. I do believe that this rhythm should, where possible, be maintained. As far as the way in which it's delivered, again it is whatever works for a particular situation. There is no reason why an actor cannot deliver the line in a natural style while maintaining the underlying metre.

Trevor Nunn: It seems to me that the camera requires work of actors that is quite fundamentally untheatrical and unstylized. It requires actors to be as truthful as is conceivably possible. The camera is associated with eavesdropping on the real event. Consequently, what is said in front of the camera needs to convey to the cinema audience the sense that it has not been written, that the language of the screen is being invented by the character in the situation spontaneously at that moment. We must not be aware of the writer.

Oliver Parker: Shakespeare's verse is a gift to the actor. It contains great insights into the character and is an astonishing channel for emotions. Iambic pentameters have a rhythm very close to normal speech. On screen there is the opportunity to make it sound even more natural, to be even more intimate. At the same time, I find the language stylistically liberating. It challenges you to find an equivalent cinematic style.

Is it important for a director of a Shakespearean film to be knowledgeable about the history, the culture, and the cosmology of the Elizabethan world in which Shakespeare wrote his plays?

Sir Peter Hall: I think it helps, but it's much more important for him to have an imaginative response to Shakespeare's images. I don't mean his verbal images, but the image of the whole play.

Baz Luhrmann: As with any story, if you don't understand the world in which the text was generated and if you don't have an absolute, totally and utterly thorough understanding of the history, culture, and cosmology of everything about that world, then you are interpreting the text in a vacuum.

Trevor Nunn: I was taught as a young teenager by a teacher, with whom I had something bordering on idolatry, who read Shakespeare plays with us and who expanded the texts. So, from that age, I've been consumed with a desire to find out more about Shakespeare, to learn everything about his language, his vocabulary, his slang, the words he invented, the dramaturgy that he invented, things that didn't exist before Shakespeare. I can't think of starting on any of the plays without wanting to consult all of that background knowledge, and that's regardless of saying, "I concluded that I want to change the imagery of the play and set it in the nineteenth century." Every particle of its original intention needs to be understood because surely the intention of the contemporary production is to find ways of releasing the original intention more potently to an audience in our own age. I might need to represent the work differently in order to do that, but I must know everything about its original force, if I'm going to undertake that. I don't believe that one can ever say that ignorance is bliss.

Oliver Parker: Important, yes. Essential, no. It depends on the particular vision of the director and how close it is to the original play.

Franco Zeffirelli: I think it's essential, for Shakespeare, or for any great author you're dealing with. You study a lot about him, what came before, what happened around him. You can't just jump in and expect to know how a character behaves in a historical context without knowing that historical context.

What is your view of filming historically updated versions of Shakespeare's plays as opposed to period presentations?

Sir Peter Hall: Well, none of us know what "period" means, any more than we know what "update" means. Shakespeare put chimney pots and docks in Rome; it didn't bother him, he didn't know they didn't have them. I think every Shakespeare play or film has to have its own visual world, and if it makes you think, "Daddy, why are they talking about swords?" when actually all they've got is pistols, then it's rubbish. But you can't be period accurate, that's antiquarian and boring.

Richard Loncraine: I think both are valid, both have their place. Shakespeare never performed his plays in period costume, they were played in whatever actors turned up on the day in, so Shakespeare obviously didn't think it was that important, and neither do I.

Baz Luhrmann: Having directed Shakespeare in theatre, opera, and film, it's never been a question of, is there a right or a wrong method. One must simply address an audience at a particular moment in time and attempt to reveal the greater richness of the particular idea or story. Whether you do an unbelievably accurate Elizabethan version, performed on a bare stage, in the middle of the day to four thousand mostly drunk punters, with the female roles played by adolescent boys in drag and spoken in a virtually incomprehensible accent, or any other interpretation, it is correct if it reveals the heart of the story and engages and awakens the audience to the material.

Trevor Nunn: I'm all in favour of people taking a different approach to visual imagery in contemporary production, be it in the theatre or the cinema. Often what happens when strong conceptual lines are taken with Shakespeare is that things come alive in very unexpected ways and that's much more commendable than the inept version that sets out to take the play at face value.

Oliver Parker: I respect the desire to update the plays, especially when the intention is to connect with a wider audience. I don't think, though, that it necessarily makes it more relevant. Sometimes it seems just a gimmick. But when it's done wittily and thoroughly, it can be terrific. Baz Luhrmann's *Romeo + Juliet* is a case in point. I found it passionate and poignant and hugely accessible.

Roman Polanski: I absolutely hate those updated versions, I'm allergic to them. I think that Shakespeare can indeed be played like jazz—you know, there are no other directions than "enter" and "exit" or "is slain" or whatever—so you can act it and stage it any way you want, but what's the point of updating it? That's a cacophony. If filmmakers fear Shakespeare is antiquated, then leave him alone; they should look for different material.

Franco Zeffirelli: As I've said, I don't think dressing the characters in modern costumes has any advantage. When I did *Romeo and Juliet*, I did it period, but after a few minutes the audience forgot that the story took place in Verona four or five hundred years ago, and that people were dressed in a certain way. They were engaged immediately through their identification with characters they came to love. When you have the power of a character that surpasses contemporary dressing up and other references, I don't think you need to make that effort. Actually, it might misfire.

Producing a Shakespearean film is usually referred to as "popularizing" Shakespeare for a mass movie-going audience. What is your view? What sort of compromises does such "popularization" involve?

Sir Peter Hall: The fact that a lot of people are aware of *Romeo and Juliet* because of Baz's film doesn't mean, when they go to see the play of *Romeo and Juliet*, that they won't be woefully disappointed, because it's nothing like the film. I think that popularization is valuable but we shouldn't kid ourselves that it's the real thing. I'm a purist because I believe that a great artist deserves to be respected and not cut to hell.

Richard Loncraine: Shakespeare didn't write plays to be stuck in drawers or that no one went to see; he wrote them for a mass audience. He had no amplification, so with more than about five hundred people, no one could hear what the hell was going on, but if Shakespeare could have had loudspeakers he would have played to audiences in the thousands. Compromise by doing Shakespeare on film? Not at all. I think it's probably a strength. There are certainly things you have to adapt. In *Richard III*, Richard doesn't even get killed on stage. He's killed off stage and someone comes in and says, "The king is dead." Well, you certainly can't do that with a film audience, they would tear you apart. So Shakespeare certainly has to be adapted for the screen, but if you respect the man's writing and you approach it as if he is the one doing the adapting—I mean, try to think of what Shakespeare would have done—you probably won't go far wrong.

Baz Luhrmann: It is almost embarrassing to me when people start talking about Shakespeare as if his intention was not to be popular or as if he was a storyteller, playwright, poet, and actor who was not interested in the widest possible audience. Do we think Shakespeare would be turning in his grave because he beat Sylvester Stallone at the opening weekend of *Romeo and Juliet*? I don't think so.

Are we trying to say that a man who had to play to four thousand punters a day and to every kind of person from the street sweeper to the Queen of England wouldn't be interested in being successful in the multiplexes? At what time was Shakespeare only interested in playing to a small elite? I don't understand that notion. It seems the antithesis of everything Shakespeare stood for is to treat his text as high culture.

Trevor Nunn: There is this pressure, partly from film production companies and partly one's own knowledge and instincts. You want your film to play to the widest possible audience, and yet you want to be able to hold your head up amongst Shakespeare scholars and not to have to say, "I deliberately abandoned all my beliefs for that period of time," or "I wittingly vulgarized this bit of material for commercial considerations."

Shakespeare was an extraordinary example of a writer who discovered the going form. There was this huge creative energy in him, a sheer appetite for creation, and he chose the theatre. He didn't choose prose, he didn't choose long narrative poetry, he chose the theatre because it seemed to him to be the going form, where the excitement was. That was where people who could write were suddenly congregating, and where there was this huge burst of activity. I think the going form changes from age to age, and it's not an accident that in the nineteenth century, it was the novel, and the greatest writers became novelists and the less great writers continued to struggle with the theatre. There's obviously a sense in which the cinema is now the going form, and I'm convinced that, were he alive today, Shakespeare would be gravitating toward cinema.

Oliver Parker: I applaud the desire to popularize Shakespeare, to introduce him to a mass audience to prove the stories, characters, and language can be extremely entertaining and accessible. What makes him such a genius is the many layers to his work, his ability to be insightful, moving, and profound, while entertaining at the same time. Given that so many people now regard him as the province of academics, I think it is important to reclaim him as a popular artist. I don't think this need debase him. The point is to encourage people into their seats, and, as he was a shareholder in the Globe Theatre, I'm sure he would sympathize.

Roman Polanski: Whether you refer to it this way or not, it's a fact, not a matter of opinion. Certainly more people have seen Olivier's film of *Hamlet* than have seen theatrical productions of it. Whether a film adaptation of Shakespeare requires compromises depends on the standing of a director who can oppose the influence of the habitual committee that is asking him to make it for the lowest common denominator. When I shot *Macbeth*, I didn't compromise in any way. Whatever changes we made were based on research, and, as for the illustration, you can illustrate certain things in such a way that you do not need to replace antiquated words, because they become clear by the visual context or through acting.

Franco Zeffirelli: There is a preconceived attitude—Shakespeare, oh my God!—but there is also a big reward when you present a classical story straightforward, and you don't try to be literally modern with it, because people will respond. You must do everything possible to grab the audience, but convincing the audience that they are revisiting a great classic under the proper conditions is an effort we should make.

Notes

symposium a meeting or conference at which several experts discuss a topic and put forward their opinions on a subject

iambic pentameter a rhythmic pattern in poetry of ten syllables per line that comprise five beats known as *metrical feet*; each foot consists of an unstressed (short) syllable followed by a stressed (long) syllable

cosmology the study of the nature of the universe, including its origin, structure, and space-time relationships

punters a British slang term for people who bet at the racetrack

Peter Ustinov as Lear in a Stratford Festival production of King Lear, *1979*

The Shakespearean Tragic Hero

A.C. Bradley

Andrew Cecil Bradley, born in Cheltenham, England, in 1851, is considered to be the pre-eminent Shakespearean scholar of the late nineteenth and early twentieth centuries. He attended Oxford University and later held a professorship there and at the University of Liverpool and the University of Glasgow. Bradley died in 1935. This selection comes from his book *Shakespearean Tragedy* (1904), which is recognized as a classic of twentieth-century Shakespearean criticism. His work presents a psychological analysis of Shakespeare's characters, in which he deals with these characters almost as if they were real people. How would you define the word *tragedy*? What is a tragic hero? Why do you think readers like to read tragedies? What are we able to learn from reading or viewing tragedies?

Let us now turn from the "action" to the central figure in it; and, ignoring the characteristics which distinguish the heroes from one another, let us ask whether they have any common qualities which appear to be essential to the tragic effect.

One they certainly have. They are exceptional beings.... The hero, with Shakespeare, is a person of high degree or of public importance, and his actions or sufferings are of an unusual kind. But this is not all. His nature also is exceptional, and generally raises him in some respect much above the average level of humanity. This does not mean that he is an eccentric or a paragon. Shakespeare never drew monstrosities of virtue; some of his heroes are far from being "good"; and if he drew eccentrics he gave them a subordinate position in the plot. His tragic characters are made of the stuff we find within ourselves and within the persons who surround them. But, by an intensification of the life which they share with others, they are raised above them; and the greatest are raised so far that, if we fully realize all that is implied in their words and actions, we become conscious that in real life we have known scarcely anyone resembling them. Some, like Hamlet...have genius. Others, like...Lear, Macbeth...are built on the grand scale; and desire, passion, or will attains in them a terrible force. In almost all we observe a marked one-sidedness, a predisposition in some particular direction; a total incapacity, in certain circumstances, of resisting the force which draws in this direction; a fatal tendency to identify the whole being with one interest, object, passion, or habit of mind. This, it would seem, is, for Shakespeare, the fundamental tragic trait.... It is a fatal gift, but it carries with it a touch of greatness; and when there is joined to it nobility of mind, or genius, or immense force, we realize the full power and reach of the soul, and the conflict in which it engages acquires that magnitude which stirs not only sympathy and pity, but admiration, terror, and awe....

In the circumstances where we see the hero placed, his tragic trait, which is also his greatness, is fatal to him. To meet these circumstances something is required which a smaller man might have given, but which the hero cannot give. He errs, by action or omission; and his error, joining with other causes, brings on him ruin....

The tragic hero with Shakespeare, then, need not be "good," though generally he is "good" and therefore at once wins sympathy in his error. But it is necessary that he should have so much of greatness that in his error and fall we may be vividly conscious of the possibilities of human nature. Hence, in the first place, a Shakespearean tragedy is never, like some miscalled tragedies, depressing. No one ever closes the book with the feeling that man is a poor mean creature. He may be wretched and he may be awful, but he is not small. His lot may be heart-rending and mysterious, but it is not contemptible. The most confirmed of cynics ceases to be a cynic while he reads these plays. And with this greatness of the tragic hero (which is not always confined to him) is connected, secondly, what I venture to describe as the centre of the tragic impression.

This central feeling is the impression of waste. With Shakespeare, at any rate, the pity and fear which are stirred by the tragic story seem to unite with, and even to merge in, a profound sense of sadness and mystery, which is due to this impression of waste. "What a piece of work is man," we cry; "so much more beautiful and so much more terrible than we knew! Why should he be so if this beauty and greatness only tortures itself and throws itself away?" We seem to have before us a type of the mystery of the whole world, the tragic fact which extends far beyond the limits of tragedy…. Tragedy…forces the mystery upon us, and it makes us realize so vividly the worth of that which is wasted…. In this tragic world, then, where individuals, however they may be and however decisive their actions may appear, are so evidently not the ultimate power, what is this power?…

The ultimate power in the tragic world is a moral order. Let us…speak simply of good and evil. Let us understand by these words, primarily, moral good and evil, but also everything else in human beings which we take to be excellent or the reverse. Let us understand the statement that the ultimate power or order is "moral" to mean that it does not show itself indifferent to good and evil, or equally favourable or unfavourable to both, but shows itself akin to good and alien from evil. And, understanding the statement thus, let us ask what grounds it has in the tragic fact as presented by Shakespeare.

Here…I choose only two or three [grounds] out of many. And the most important is this. In Shakespearean tragedy the main source of the convulsion which produces suffering and death is never good…. The main source, on the contrary, is in every case evil; and, what is more (though this seems to have been little noticed), it is in almost every case evil in the fullest sense, not mere imperfection but plain moral evil. The love of Romeo and Juliet conducts them to death only because of the senseless hatred of their houses. Guilty ambition, seconded by diabolic malice and issuing in murder, opens the action in *Macbeth*. Iago is the main source of the convulsion in *Othello*; Goneril, Regan, and Edmund in *King Lear*. Even when this plain moral evil is not the obviously prime source within the play, it lies behind it: the situation with which Hamlet has to deal has been formed by adultery and murder…. And the inference is obvious. If it is chiefly evil that violently disturbs the order of the world, this order cannot be friendly to evil or indifferent between evil and good, any more than a body which is convulsed by poison is friendly to it or indifferent to the distinction between poison and food.

Again, if we confine our attention to the hero, and to those cases where the gross and palpable evil is not in him but elsewhere, we find that the comparatively innocent hero still shows some marked imperfection or defect—irresolution, precipitancy, pride, credulousness, excessive simplicity, excessive susceptibility to sexual emotions, and the like. These defects or imperfections are certainly, in the wide sense of the word, evil, and they contribute decisively to the conflict and catastrophe. And the inference is again obvious. The ultimate power which shows itself disturbed by this evil and reacts against it, must have a nature alien to it. Indeed its reaction is so vehement and "relentless" that it would seem to be bent on nothing short of good in perfection, and to be ruthless in its demand for it.

To this must be added another fact, or another aspect of the same fact. Evil exhibits itself everywhere as something negative, barren, weakening, destructive, a principle of death. It isolates, disunites, and tends to annihilate not only its opposite but itself. That which keeps the evil man prosperous, makes him succeed, even permits him to exist, is the good in him (I do not mean only the obviously "moral" good). When the evil in him masters the good and has its way, it destroys other people through him, but it also destroys him. At the close of the struggle he has vanished, and has left behind him nothing that can stand. What remains is a family, a city, a country, exhausted, pale, and feeble, but alive through the principle of good which animates it; and within it, individuals who, if they have not the brilliance or greatness of the tragic character, still have won our respect and confidence. And the inference would seem clear. If existence in an order depends on good, and if the presence of evil is hostile to such existence, the inner being or soul of this order must be akin to good.

These are aspects of the tragic world at least as clearly marked as those which, taken alone, suggest the idea of fate. And the idea which they in their turn, when taken alone, may suggest, is that of an order which does not indeed award "poetic justice," but which reacts through the necessity of its own "moral" nature both against attacks made upon it and against failure to conform to it. Tragedy, on this view, is the exhibition of that convulsive reaction; and the fact that the spectacle does not leave us rebellious or desperate is due to a more or less distinct impression that the tragic suffering and death arise from collision, not with a fate or blank power, but with a moral power, a power akin to all that we admire and revere in the characters themselves. This perception produces something like a feeling of acquiescence in the catastrophe, though it neither leads us to pass judgment on the characters nor diminishes the pity, the fear, and the sense of waste, which their struggle, suffering, and fall evoke. And, finally, this view seems quite able to do justice to those aspects of the tragic fact which give rise to the idea of fate. They would appear as various expressions of the fact that the moral order acts not capriciously or like a human being, but from the necessity of its nature, or, if we prefer the phrase, by general laws—a necessity or law which of course knows no exception and is as "ruthless" as fate....

Thus we are left at last with an idea showing two sides or aspects which we can neither separate nor reconcile. The whole or order against which the individual part shows itself powerless seems to be animated by a passion for perfection: we cannot otherwise explain its behaviour toward evil. Yet it appears to engender this evil within itself, and in its effort to overcome and expel it it is agonized with pain, and driven to mutilate its own substance and to lose not only evil but priceless good. That this idea, though very different from the idea of a blank fate, is no solution of the riddle of life is obvious; but why should we expect it to be such a solution? Shakespeare was not attempting to justify the ways of God to men, or to show the universe as a Divine Comedy. He was writing tragedy, and tragedy would not be tragedy if it were not a painful mystery.... We remain confronted with the inexplicable fact, or the no less inexplicable appearance, of a world travailing for perfection, but bringing to birth, together with glorious good, an evil which it is able to overcome only by self-torture and self-waste. And this fact or appearance is tragedy.

Notes

paragon a model of excellence or perfection

poetic justice an outcome in which vice is punished and virtue rewarded, often in an ironic manner

Divine Comedy a classic poem by the Italian Dante Alighieri, written from 1306 to 1321, that chronicles the main character's journey through hell, to Mount Purgatory, and finally into heaven

From

Strong Women Prevail in Shakespeare's Comedies

Angela Pitt

Angela Pitt was born in Aylesbury, Buckinghamshire, England, in 1946. She holds degrees in English from the University of London and the University of Ottawa, as well as a master's degree in archaeology from Oslo University in Norway. In the following selection, she explores the role of women in Shakespeare's comedies.

By the end of the fifth century BCE, the word *comedy* came to describe a play that was distinct from tragedy. In tragedy, the protagonist is seen to be a superior or special person in society, whereas the protagonist in comedy finds fulfillment within the existing society. A key attribute of the mode of comedy is that it always has a "happy ending." Regardless of the seriousness of the problems and situations depicted, the audience knows that everything will be joyfully resolved.

Comedy generally contains two other key characteristics. First, comedy occurs when specific events and characters of a play challenge basic assumptions about society. Traditional comic writers pit humanity's excesses, frauds, hypocrisies, and follies against a background of normality. Second, comedy often involves the suspension of the natural laws of logic and probability. Therefore, actions do not have the consequences they would have in real life. Often normal expectations are reversed.

Shakespeare wrote his comedies between 1594 and 1603. He is probably best known for his romantic comedies, such as *As You Like It* and *A Midsummer Night's Dream*, in which an idealized heroine and hero overcome impediments to be united. In romantic comedies, characters leave the troubled real world to enter a pastoral, magical world in which problems dissolve. Shakespeare also wrote comedies of manners, including *Love's Labours Lost* and *Much Ado About Nothing*, in which the intrigue between sophisticated gentlemen and ladies relies to a great extent on witty repartee. In such comedies as *The Taming of the Shrew* and *The Merry Wives of Windsor*, Shakespeare uses elements of farce. These plays have hilarious physical scenes filled with exaggerated caricatures, slapstick, and sight gags.

Note the title of Pitt's essay. Why might Shakespeare have cast women as strong characters in his comedies, but not necessarily in his tragedies? From what you know of Shakespeare's comedies, do you think his purpose in writing them was primarily to please the audience? Why or why not?

If the dark realm of Shakespeare's tragedies is essentially men's territory, pride of place in the bright panorama of his comedies must surely belong to the women. Set alongside vivacious heroines...their male counterparts pale into insignificance. The character of Beatrice, indeed, has such force and charm that interest in her eventually takes over the play, despite the fact that her fate is not an important aspect of the original plot.

Why should the women leap into prominence? One reason may be that Shakespeare found their traditional attributes of modesty, intuition, and high-spiritedness highly suitable material for his comedies, and in varying blends and degrees, all his comic heroines have these characteristics. They never go beyond the bounds of what an Elizabethan audience would have found acceptable in a woman: it is rather that Shakespeare exalts the positive, rather than the negative traits. Any women that go against prevailing conventions are redeemed by the end of the play. Thus Katharina in *The Taming of the Shrew* is forced to give in to Petruchio's will, and Helena's unfeminine pursuit of Bertram is justified by the fact that he had failed to recognize her true worth; once he does so, she is submissive.

Another reason is that Shakespeare tacitly accepts the medieval idea of a hierarchy of nature in which woman is second to man. This means that the high seriousness of tragedy, with its intense focus on the fate of the individual, is an unsatisfactory setting for all but a very few women, and even these have their destinies inescapably intertwined with those of the tragic heroes. Comedy, on the other hand, allows for a broader, more detached view of society and a lighter tone. Although moral issues are not excluded (*The Merchant of Venice* is very much concerned with the contrast between material and spiritual wealth, as well as the nature of justice), we do not become anxious or painfully involved with the characters and, as the play progresses, hints are given that everything will turn out all right in the end. The characters themselves are frequently capricious, willing to compromise, and although they may well have faults, these do not inspire *fear* in the audience, as would be the case in tragedy. The plots too are full of twists and turns, surprises and coincidences. Until the final scene makes everything clear, no decision is incapable of being changed or reversed.

The forces of charm and whimsy are so strong in his comedies as to offer a further strong indication as to why Shakespeare favoured women characters for the leading roles. His choice was not a foregone conclusion, for other Elizabethan writers of comedy—notably Ben Jonson—let men dominate the stage as in tragedy. In the sixteenth century there were two traditions of dramatic comedy. One was the satirical revelation of human errors, played out so that the audience laughed to see their own follies so skilfully exposed. The other was to use as a setting some upset, sadness, or problem that is subsequently resolved happily. Jonson wrote in the first, more hard-hitting tradition, where we laugh *at* the characters; Shakespeare in the second where we laugh *with* them. The hallmark of Shakespeare's comedies is consequently the move toward reconciliation and a restoration of order by the correct understanding of the original problem. Unlike the tragedies, which insist that chaos can be averted only by the elimination of those swept up in the catastrophe, the comedies show that problems can be solved and sorrows overcome if the situation is properly understood by those involved in it. Although we laugh at comedy, its purpose is as realistic and serious as that of tragedy: comedy shows us that happiness results from being able to face problems and put them into a balanced perspective; tragedy shows that misery and death result when dilemmas loom so large as to blot out all other aspects of life. As with the tragedies it is impossible to impose a strict formula on the construction of the comedies beyond the pattern mentioned above: that they all begin with the characters perplexed or threatened, but end happily. This general definition serves to embrace the eleven usually termed "comedies" by editors and the five "last plays."

The agents of happiness and order in Shakespeare's comedies are the heroines, and their function is therefore of supreme importance. Not only do the women have the leading roles but also they are more numerous than in the other types of plays. They cover a wide range of types and classes: a queen, a countess, princesses, dukes' daughters, a doctor's daughter, merchants' daughters, ladies-in-waiting, servants, shepherdesses, a goat-girl, nuns, and prostitutes. This rich variety gives tremendous scope for contrasts and comparisons among the women themselves, as well as between men and women. With the exception of *The Tempest*, in which Miranda is the only woman, the other comedies present women as foils to each other. At its best, use of this device not only results in the idiosyncrasies of speech and behaviour, which make the heroines so very alive and credible, but also allows Shakespeare to reveal many subtle facets of their natures....

Notes

comedy derived from the Greek word *kōmōidia*, which originally referred to a comic singer or to a celebratory song and dance performed by a chorus in a play

tragedies in this instance, refers to Shakespeare's plays that portray calamitous events, often containing a main character who has a fatal flaw that results in an unhappy ending

Beatrice a witty female character in Shakespeare's comedy *Much Ado About Nothing*

Elizabethan the time period between the mid-1500s and the early 1600s when Great Britain was ruled by Queen Elizabeth I (1533–1603)

medieval relating or belonging to the middle ages, an era in European history dating from 476 to 1453 CE

Ben Jonson an English actor and writer (1572–1637), whose best-known play is *Volpone* (1606)

foils characters who, through contrast to the main characters, either underscore or enhance the traits of the protagonists

Saloonio

Stephen Leacock

Born in Swanmore, England, in 1869, Stephen Leacock immigrated to Canada in 1876 and grew up near Lake Simcoe, Ontario. He attended Upper Canada College, the University of Toronto, and the University of Chicago, studying political science and economics and teaching these subjects at McGill University from 1903 until his retirement in 1936. Leacock was a prolific writer of humorous fiction, literary essays, and articles on social issues, politics, and other subjects. He won the Governor General's Award for Nonfiction in 1937. He died in

Leacock was a master of the short sketch or extended anecdote and his writing exhibits a strong oral characteristic. Have you encountered a short story before that takes the form of an anecdotal
sketch? If so, what was the piece about and why do you think the
writer chose this form?

They say that young men fresh from college are pretty positive about
what they know. But from my own experience of life, I should say that
if you take a comfortable, elderly man who hasn't been near a college
for about twenty years, who has been pretty liberally fed and dined ever
since, who measures about fifty inches around the circumference, and has
a complexion like a cranberry by candlelight, you will find that there is
a degree of absolute certainty about what he thinks he knows that will put
any young man to shame. I am specially convinced of this from the case
of my friend Colonel Hogshead, a portly, choleric gentleman who made
a fortune in cattle-trade out in Wyoming and who, in his later days, has
acquired a chronic idea that the plays of Shakespeare are the one subject
upon which he is most qualified to speak personally.

He came across me the other evening as I was sitting by the fire
in the club sitting room looking over the leaves of *The Merchant of
Venice*, and began to hold forth to me about the book.

"*Merchant of Venice*, eh? There's a play for you, sir! There's genius!
Wonderful, sir, wonderful! You take the characters in that play and where
will you find anything like them? You take Antonio, take Sherlock, take
Saloonio—"

"Saloonio, Colonel?" I interposed mildly, "aren't you making a
mistake? There's a Bassanio and a Salanio in the play, but I don't think
there's a Saloonio, is there?"

For a moment Colonel Hogshead's eye became misty with doubt,
but he was not the man to admit himself in error:

"Tut, tut! young man," he said with a frown, "don't skim through
your books in that way. No Saloonio? Why, of course there's a Saloonio!"

"But I tell you, Colonel," I rejoined. "I've just been reading the
play and studying it, and I know there's no such character—"

"Nonsense, sir, nonsense!" said the Colonel, "why he comes in all through; don't tell me, young man, I've read that play myself. Yes, and seen it played, too, out in Wyoming, before you were born, by fellers, sir, that could act. No Saloonio, indeed! why, who is it that is Antonio's friend all through and won't leave him when Bassoonio turns against him? Who rescues Clarissa from Sherlock, and steals the casket of flesh from the Prince of Aragon? Who shouts at the Prince of Morocco, 'Out, out, you damned candlestick'? Who loads up the jury in the trial scene and fixes the doge? No Saloonio! By gad! in my opinion, he's the most important character in the play—"

"Colonel Hogshead," I said very firmly, "there isn't any Saloonio and you know it."

But the old man had got fairly started on whatever dim recollection had given birth to Saloonio; the character seemed to grow more and more luminous in the Colonel's mind, and he continued with increasing animation:

"I'll just tell you what Saloonio is: he's a type. Shakespeare means him to embody the type of the perfect Italian gentleman. He's an idea, that's what he is, he's a symbol, he's a unit—"

Meanwhile I had been searching among the leaves of the play. "Look here," I said, "here's the list of the Dramatis Personae. There's no Saloonio there."

But this didn't dismay the Colonel one atom. "Why, of course there isn't," he said. "You don't suppose you'd find Saloonio there! That's the whole art of it! That's Shakespeare! That's the whole gist of it! He's kept clean out of the Personae—gives him scope, gives him a free hand, makes him more of a type than ever. Oh, it's a subtle thing, sir, the dramatic art!" continued the Colonel, subsiding into quiet reflection; "it takes a feller quite a time to get right into Shakespeare's mind and see what he's at all the time."

I began to see that there was no use in arguing any further with the old man. I left him with the idea that the lapse of a little time would soften his views on Saloonio. But I had not reckoned on the way in which old men hang on to a thing. Colonel Hogshead quite took up

Saloonio. From that time on Saloonio became the theme of his constant conversation. He was never tired of discussing the character of Saloonio, the wonderful art of the dramatist in creating him, Saloonio's relation to the modern life, Saloonio's attitude toward women, the ethical significance of Saloonio, Saloonio as compared with Hamlet, Hamlet as compared with Saloonio—and so on, endlessly. And the more he looked into Saloonio, the more he saw in him.

Saloonio seemed inexhaustible. There were new sides to him—new phases at every turn. The Colonel even read over the play, and finding no mention of Saloonio's name in it, he swore that the books were not the same books they had had out in Wyoming; that the whole part had been cut clean out to suit the book to the infernal public schools, Saloonio's language being—at any rate, as the Colonel quoted it—undoubtedly a trifle free. Then the Colonel took to annotating his book at the side with such remarks as, "Enter Saloonio," or "A tucket sounds; enter Saloonio, on the arm of the Prince of Morocco." When there was no reasonable excuse for bringing Saloonio on the stage the Colonel swore that he was concealed behind the arras, or feasting within with the doge.

But he got satisfaction at last. He had found that there was nobody in our part of the country who knew how to put a play of Shakespeare on the stage, and took a trip to New York to see Sir Henry Irving and Miss Terry do the play. The Colonel sat and listened all through with his face just beaming with satisfaction, and when the curtain fell at the close of Irving's grand presentation of the play, he stood up in his seat and cheered and yelled to his friends: "That's it! That's him! Didn't you see that man that came on the stage all the time and sort of put the whole play through, though you couldn't understand a word he said? Well, that's him! That's Saloonio!"

Notes

The Merchant of Venice a tragicomedy written by William Shakespeare in 1596

doge the elected chief magistrate of the former republics of Venice and Genoa; from the Latin word *dux*, meaning "leader"

Dramatis Personae a list of the characters or actors in a drama; a Latin phrase meaning "people in the drama"

tucket a fanfare on a trumpet; from the Middle English word *tukken*, meaning "to beat a drum"

arras a tapestry wall hanging or curtain; named after a city in northeastern France well known in medieval times for the manufacture of tapestries

Shakespeare: Activities

1. Some selections in this In-Depth deal with Shakespeare's relevance to today's world. Which specific issues related to relevance do these selections raise? Review the selections and, in the left-hand column of a chart, list any challenges raised about studying or staging Shakespeare today. In the right-hand column, list any solutions to these problems that the selections contain. To what extent do you agree with the solutions presented?

2. Choose a Shakespearean tragedy or comedy that you know well. How is its setting described in the original text? If you were creating a stage or film production of the play with a modern setting, what particular places would you use? What kind of costuming would you provide? Explain your decisions to the class in an oral presentation. Organize your material coherently, providing evidence for your decisions and using visual aids for support.

3. Working with a group, choose a scene from any Shakespearean play. Discuss the pros and cons of performing the scene live versus on videotape. Based on your discussion, decide which method you will pursue. Assign roles and create a brief list of the criteria you consider necessary for a good performance. Distribute your list to your classmates and present the scene to them. Collect your classmates' responses to the criteria and compare their views with your group's own assessment of the performance.

4. Write a research essay with a clearly stated thesis in which you discuss the similarities and differences between Shakespearean comedy and tragedy. Choose an example of each mode, read each play carefully, and do the research required to understand the nature and main characteristics of Shakespearean comedy and tragedy.

Glossary

act A major division in a dramatic work, larger than a **scene** or episode.

adaptation Any work that recreates or redevelops another work in a different medium (e.g., a film based on a novel, a television show based on a comic strip).

allegory A story with a literal surface meaning and a second deeper, usually moral, meaning; traditionally involves **personification** (e.g., in Dickinson's poem "Because I Could Not Stop for Death—," such objects, events, and ideas as the sun, death, and immortality have been personified into characters).

alliteration The repetition of the same sound *at the beginning of* nearby words (e.g., "Landscape-lover, lord of language"—Tennyson).

allusion A direct or indirect reference in one work to another work or to a historical person, place, or event. The essay title "Get Beyond Babel" by Ken Wiwa contains a *direct* allusion to the biblical town and story of Babel (now thought to be Babylon), where construction of a tower was halted when workers could not understand each other's language. The song title "Afternoons & Coffeespoons" by The Crash Test Dummies contains an *indirect* allusion to T.S. Eliot's poem "The Love Song of J. Alfred Prufrock." Though it does not contain the name of a person, place, or event, the title alludes to Eliot's lines: "For I have known them all already, known them all— / Have known the evenings, mornings, afternoons, / I have measured out my life with coffee spoons."

analogy A comparison based on partial similarity for the purpose of making something clearer or more powerful (e.g., comparing a telecommunications system to a spider web).

anecdote A brief story about a single humorous or interesting event (e.g., Stephen Leacock's short story "Saloonio" consists of one anecdote).

antagonist A **character** who is the **protagonist**'s main opponent.

anti-hero A **character** who is the **protagonist** of a narrative and is also obviously unheroic, or lacking typical qualities of a **hero**, but for whom an author might arouse sympathy or influence us to alter our view of his or her circumstances.

antithesis A rhetorical device that contrasts ideas that are opposite or at least very different; sometimes **parallelism** is used to heighten the contrast. In general use, something is said to be the antithesis, or direct opposite, of something else.

aphorism A brief, memorable, and often witty statement of truth or principle (e.g., Hippocrates' "Life is short, art is long, opportunity fleeting, experimenting dangerous, reasoning difficult" or George Eliot's "The happiest women, like the happiest nations, have no history").

archetypal criticism A critical approach to literature that seeks to find and understand the purpose of **archetypes** within literature. These archetypes may be themes, such as love; characterizations, such as the hero; or patterns, such as death and rebirth. Archetypal criticism draws on the works of the psychoanalyst Carl Jung, literary critic Northrop Frye, and others. Unlike **psychoanalytic** critics, archetypal critics such as Frye do not attempt to explain why archetypes exist.

archetype Something that represents the essential elements of its category or class of things; Greek for "original pattern" from which all copies are made, a prototype. Certain themes of human life (e.g., love, loss), character types (e.g., the rebel, the wise elder), animals (e.g., snake), and patterns (e.g., the quest, the descent into the underworld) are considered to be archetypal, forming a part of the collective unconscious (the sum of society's inherited mental images). For example, a character in a TV series who continuously changes careers might be said to be the archetypal "seeker."

aside A **monologue** in which a **character** speaks directly to the audience as though unheard by the other characters onstage. Often it is expressed in a "stage whisper," which is a loud whisper meant to be heard by the audience.

assonance The repetition of the same or similar vowel sounds *within* nearby words for musical effect (e.g., the three sounds repeated in "The *bows* glided *down*, and the coast/ **Blackened** with birds took a **last** look/ **At** his **thrashing** hair and whale-blue eyes;/ The <u>trodden</u> town **rang** its <u>cobbles</u> for luck" from "Ballad of the Long-Legged Bait" by Dylan Thomas).

atmosphere See **mood**.

autobiography A person's story of his or her own life. While a memoir generally contains selective recollections in no particular sequence, an autobiography generally tries to present a chronological view of one's own life, giving proportional weight to all events. A work by a person based on his or her life can be described as autobiographical, but see **biographical fallacy**.

ballad A **narrative poem** about common events and people, which in the Western tradition typically has four-line **stanzas** and a **refrain**; generally, ballads originate as songs passed by word of mouth, so their creators are unknown. The term is also used broadly to mean romantic songs.

bias Language or a thought that contains a prejudice (an inaccurate, irrational, usually negative perception) against something or someone. Bias within a text can exist when information essential to an accurate depiction of a subject has been omitted, thereby prejudicing the unwitting reader's understanding of the subject.

biographical fallacy The unwarranted interpretation of a work (e.g., a novel) based primarily on knowledge of the author's life; literally, the falsehood that a writer's work is necessarily biographical. Proponents of **New Criticism** in particular reject what they consider to be biographical fallacy in favour of viewing a work as self-contained.

biography The story of a person's life as told by another. A brief biography is often called a profile.

blank verse A type of unrhymed verse that closely resembles everyday conversation, is usually written in **iambic pentameter**, and is used in some **epics**, **lyric poems**, and drama (e.g., by Shakespeare).

byline The line near the beginning of a news or magazine article that provides the writer's name.

camera angle The relative height or position from which the camera films the subject, e.g., high (from above), low (from below), straight/flat (from the same height), etc.

caption A brief explanation or title given for a photograph, cartoon, chart, or other graphic. Some publications (e.g., a chemistry text) might use both title and explanatory captions.

caricature The depiction of a flat, one-dimensional **character**, who is often a comic, absurd, or grotesque exaggeration of characteristics. In a cartoon caricature, a person's distinguishing physical features are exaggerated.

catharsis The experience of a vicarious purification or relief. Aristotle defined tragedy as "incidents arousing pity and fear, wherewith to accomplish the catharsis of such emotions." In Aristotle's view, witnessing a tragic play provided the audience with a sort of instructive purification.

cause-and-effect organization The arrangement of ideas and information (e.g., in an essay) according to causes and effects, actions and their outcomes, or states of being and their impact (e.g., the effect of a trauma on a survivor's day-to-day habits).

character One of the people in a story, either in fiction or drama. The person may be a specific type of character, such as a **stock character, protagonist, antagonist, foil, hero,** or **anti-hero.**

characterization The techniques used to portray or describe a **character** (e.g., in a novel, through the character's **dialogue,** actions and interactions, thoughts, or through direct description).

chorus In song lyrics, the **refrain** or repeated phrases or lines. In drama, particularly Greek drama, one or more **characters** who narrate or comment on the action of the drama or voice a character's thoughts.

chronological organization The arrangement of ideas and information (e.g., in a **biography**) based on the sequential order of events (e.g., beginning with events from the subject's childhood, followed by the teen years, followed by early adulthood, etc.).

cinquain A **stanza** of five lines.

classification The arrangement of elements into classes, categories, or groups (e.g., folk tales classified according to their countries of origin; within each of these categories, they might be further classified according to era or purpose).

cliché An overused, time-worn phrase or description generally considered to be ineffective and therefore avoided. Certain uses of both **diction** and **characterization** can be considered *clichéd.*

climax In a **plot,** the height of the tension in the **conflict.** The turning point in the plot, sometimes called the *crisis.*

colloquial language Words, phrases, and expressions used in ordinary everyday, familiar conversation. **Informal language** that is typically relaxed and plain rather than formal and literary.

comedy A drama that may include misfortunes, but ends happily, intending to entertain, but sometimes also to educate or persuade. Types of comedy include **parody, physical comedy,** and **satire.**

comparison A consideration or description of two or more things in which similarities are identified.

conflict The central struggle or problem of a narrative, which moves the **plot** forward and motivates the **protagonist.**

connotation An implied meaning of a word or phrase that can be derived from association or frequent use. The connotation extends beyond the **denotation** of the word or phrase, providing additional meaning (e.g., the denotation of *independent* is "self-governing and free from the influence, guidance, or control of others or self-reliant, not relying on others for support"; its connotation in a letter of application, for example, would be "self-directed," "not requiring close supervision," and "able to complete tasks alone").

context In general, the surroundings or circumstances of something. In print, it refers to any element related to communication that influences the creation of a text or the understanding and interpretation of it. These elements include the purpose, the intended audience, and the circumstances including time, place, and cultural and gender issues. Examples include the words appearing before and after a phrase, the imagined world that a fiction author creates, and the cultural setting in which a writer works.

copy The text of an advertisement or, in magazines and newspapers, the matter to be printed. Thus, an advertisement can be said to consist of art and copy, created by art directors and copywriters.

couplet A pair of lines in a poem, one after the other, with rhyming ends; also known as a **rhyming couplet** (e.g., "In these deep solitudes and awful *cells*, / Where heavenly-pensive contemplation *dwells*, / And ever-musing melancholy *reigns*, / What means this tumult in a vestal's *veins?*" from "Eloisa to Abelard" by Alexander Pope).

critical approach A method or manner in which to describe, interpret, and evaluate a work such as a novel, dramatic performance, or television series, often based in a belief about the role or worth of works in the same class (e.g., **New Criticism**'s belief that each poem is self-contained and worthy, in itself, of close reading). See **archetypal criticism, cultural criticism, feminist criticism, New Criticism, New Historicism, poststructuralism, psychoanalytic criticism, reader-response criticism,** and **structuralism**. See also **literary analysis**.

cultural criticism A recent movement in criticism that is interdisciplinary by extending the range of examined texts beyond just the literary works themselves to objects or practices that can be interpreted as representative of a culture's beliefs, values, laws, etc. Practitioners of cultural criticism view a text in relation to the dominant or competing ideologies (belief systems) of the time and place in which the text was written. Works are therefore considered in light of their historical and cultural contexts (e.g., Joseph Conrad's *Heart of Darkness* may be read in terms of practices of European imperialists, race relations in Africa, or the economic history of ivory). Cultural criticism is related to *cultural studies* and shares some interests with **feminist criticism, New Historicism,** and Marxist criticism.

debate A formal or informal setting in which two or more participants discuss or argue two conflicting sides of an issue, question, or topic, with one side arguing for a particular belief or resolution and the other arguing against it.

deck In a periodical publication, a sentence or short paragraph of text explaining (and following) the **headline**, or title, of an article, thereby acting like a subtitle. It is often used to catch the reader's attention, drawing the reader into a text through the use of a dramatic, controversial, or humorous statement.

deconstructionism An approach to literary criticism that emphasizes rhetoric and the self-reference of language. See **poststructuralism**.

definition A statement of what a word or phrase means, especially in a specific **context** (e.g., a discussion of an immunization plan might require first giving definitions of *epidemiology, adverse effects, risk-benefit analysis, contra-indications, auto-immune diseases*).

denotation A literal dictionary meaning of a word or phrase (e.g., a heart as the chambered, muscular organ that pumps blood).

dénouement In a **plot**, the story's end or conclusion; also called the resolution.

description A style of writing that creates images of people, places, and objects using carefully observed, expressed, and arranged details. These details are perceived by the five senses. Description can range from objective, scientific details to subjective and impressionistic perceptions.

dialect A way of speaking or a variation on a specific language that is unique to a particular social or cultural group or to a specific region.

dialogue The conversation of two or more **characters** involving an exchange of ideas or information.

diction The choice of words and phrases by a writer or speaker.

dramatic irony A type of irony based on a situation that contrasts what a character perceives with what the audience and one or more of the other characters knows to be true (for example, a mother in a play believes her son has forgotten her birthday, whereas the audience knows that her son plans to wait until late in the day to give his mother a card and present).

dramatic monologue A poem in which the speaker addresses an unseen, silent listener. This form is related to the **soliloquy**.

elegy Traditionally, a formal poem that is a solemn meditation, written as a lament for the death of a particular person.

empathy The act of mentally identifying with a person or object, as a way of relating to and comprehending it fully (e.g., knowing a character's struggle because it echoes one's own); from the German term *Einfühlung* meaning "feeling into." In general use, sympathy is considered to be compassion, while empathy is the response to a shared or the *sense* of a shared feeling or condition.

epic A type of **narrative poem**, long and about historic or legendary people; like a legend but not prose (e.g., Virgil's *Aeneid*). In modern usage, the idea of an epic can extend beyond a poem to refer to such popular media as a film, for example.

epigram Originally (in ancient Greece) an inscription on a monument or statue, but now a short, witty statement in prose or verse. Coleridge defined it as "A dwarfish whole, / Its body brevity, and wit its soul."

epilogue A closing or concluding section of a drama.

essay development The manner in which an essay is organized, how it unfolds for the reader. Methods to develop an essay include **cause-and-effect organization**, **comparison** or contrast, **chronological organization**, spatial organization, and **classification**.

euphemism A vague, indirect term with a positive connotation, used instead of a more precise or blunt term that may offend or frighten (e.g., describing someone who has died as having "passed away" or "gone to a better place").

exposition A **style** of writing that is systematically explanatory and communicates information, primarily factual (e.g., an expository essay).

farce An obvious, unsubtle comedic drama that uses exaggeration, caricature, improbable and ludicrous happenings, absurd pretences, and physical slapstick to evoke laughter. In contemporary drama, farce is often used in television sitcoms.

feminist criticism Literary criticism based on feminist theories. It considers texts with the knowledge that societies treat men and women inequitably. Feminist criticism will analyze texts in light of patriarchal (male-dominated) cultural institutions, phallocentric (male-centred) language, masculine and feminine **stereotypes**, and the unequal treatment of male and female writers. Practitioners make use of key concepts from other approaches, such as **psychoanalytic criticism**, Marxist criticism, **cultural criticism**, and **deconstructionism**. Feminist criticism developed primarily in the 1960s and 1970s, although it is evident in earlier works as well (e.g., by Virginia Woolf).

figurative language Language that uses figures of speech, such as **simile**, **personification**, and **alliteration** to create **imagery** (e.g., "Like a student skimming reference books in a print-based library, Internet search engines systematically scour the Internet to scan site contents or summaries, flag and stockpile possibilities, and then evaluate and rank them. The effect is the same as that of someone choosing clothes for a date: a heap of clothes that won't make it out the door in a pile under those hung up for closer scrutiny.").

first-person point of view Storytelling in which one **character** of the story serves as the storyteller/**narrator**, telling the narrative from his or her **point of view**. One indication of first-person point of view is that at some point in the text, the speaker refers to herself or himself through such words as "I," "me," "my," "mine," "we," "our," or "us."

flashback A device used to depict events of the past (e.g., a biographical essay about a musician that focuses on the subject in adulthood and offers brief anecdotes about earlier performances).

foil A **character**, usually minor, who contrasts with and therefore sheds light on the **protagonist**.

foreshadowing A literary device in which a hint is provided about events that will occur later in the work (e.g., a crop that unexpectedly flourishes might foreshadow a character's personal growth against the odds).

form Broadly, the shape of a communication (e.g., one form of non-fiction is the **biography**; one form of poetry is the **ode**; one form of business communication is the sales letter). With literary texts, **genre**s are the larger divisions and forms are the smaller divisions.

formal language Language that is appropriate, polite and respectful in tone, and rigorously follows conventions. It might be used, for example, in a letter of application, in a research paper, or between strangers introduced at a school ceremony.

formalism See **New Criticism**.

free verse Poetry that follows natural speech **rhythm**s and has no regular pattern of line length, **rhyme**, or rhythm.

genre A type or class of literary texts (e.g., the novel) within which there are categories or **form**s (e.g., historical novel, speculative fiction, fantasy). Broadly, genre means any type or class. It can refer, for example, to media products (e.g., sitcoms, reality-based TV shows) and formal speeches (e.g., sales presentations, eulogies).

graphics Pictorial representations or other visual images (e.g., illustration, bar graph). On a Web site, for example, all that is seen can be categorized as either text or graphics.

haiku A traditional Japanese verse **form** consisting of three lines, of which the first line is five syllables, the second is seven syllables, and the third is five syllables.

head A short form for **heading** or **headline**.

heading The title for a section of a text. It is used to introduce a section of text, indicating the topic and offsetting it from other sections.

headline The title of an article in a periodical publication, sometimes called the **head**. Most often used to refer to the title of a news story, intended to both summarize the article and draw in the reader. It is sometimes followed by a **deck**.

hero A **character** who is the **protagonist** and also heroic, demonstrated by such characteristics as bravery and loyalty. Not all protagonists are heroes.

hyperbole Intended exaggeration, a device often used to create **irony**, humour, or dramatic effect.

iambic pentameter In poetry, a pattern of ten syllables (five **metrical feet**) per line, each foot (pair) beginning with an unstressed (ˇ), and ending with a stressed (ʹ) syllable.

idiom A form of expression, usually a phrase, in which the figurative meaning is different from the literal one (e.g., "neither here nor there" means "it doesn't matter" or "as fit as a fiddle" means "in trim, excellent shape"). Some idioms are so appealing that they become overused and therefore **clichés**.

imagery The collected images that exist in a text. These images include "mental pictures" and any other sensory perceptions that have been created in a text through its use of language. Imagery can be created through words or groups of words that evoke images that are visual (sight), auditory (hearing), tactile (touch), olfactory (taste), gustatory (smell), and kinesthetic (movement). Imagery can be descriptive (literal) or suggestive (metaphorical).

informal language Language that is familiar, intimate, casual, and sometimes includes slang terms or other **colloquial language**.

irony A literary device involving contrast; a discrepancy between the expected and the actual state of affairs. The most common type is verbal irony, a method of expression in which the actual meaning intended by a speaker is different from (and often opposite to) what she or he expresses. One famous example is the opening sentence of Jane Austen's *Pride and Prejudice*: "It is a truth universally acknowledged that a single man in possession of a good fortune must be in want of a wife."

juxtaposition The practice of placing two elements in a text side by side for the specific purpose of creating an effect through their association. Although the two items are not explicitly compared and contrasted, their proximity creates a contrast for the reader.

literary analysis A critical response to a literary text in the form of critical essay or oral commentary. It includes a thorough interpretation of the work. Such analysis may be based in a variety of critical approaches or movements, e.g., **archetypal criticism, cultural criticism, feminist criticism, New Criticism, New Historicism, poststructuralism, psychoanalytic criticism, reader-response criticism,** and **structuralism.**

logical fallacy A falsehood or misunderstanding based on flawed reasoning.

lyric poem A subjective, emotional poem with musical roots that may use **rhythm** or **rhyme** to evoke a reflective, introspective mood. Forms include **odes** and **sonnets**.

malapropism A ridiculous misuse of words, especially through confusing words that sound somewhat alike. From the French words *mal à propos*, meaning "out of place." A character in British playwright Richard Sheridan's comedy *The Rivals* (1775), noted for her speech blunders, was named Mrs. Malaprop; at one point, she is thinking of an alligator when she describes someone as being "as headstrong as an allegory on the banks of the Nile."

mass media Media that reaches a very large audience.

melodrama A sentimental drama using unrealistic **characters** and **plot** created primarily to appeal to emotions. Like a **farce** in **style**, but not humorous.

metaphor An implied **comparison** that (unlike a **simile**) does not use *like* or *as* (e.g., Walt Whitman's metaphor for grass in *Song of Myself*: "the beautiful uncut hair of graves"). The comparison connects two or more usually unlike things that have something in common (grass and hair).

metre The pattern of **rhythm** (stressed and unstressed syllables in poetry) measured and categorized in **metrical feet**.

metrical feet The units of stressed ($\prime$) and unstressed ($\smile$) syllables. A way of examining **metre** and identifying the feet according to type and number (e.g., **iambic pentameter**).

Middle English The language spoken and written in England from about the time of the Norman conquest (1066 CE) to the mid-fifteenth century. In contrast to **Old English**, it had a weaker and more regular inflectional system and incorporated many French and Latin words from Norman French, which was spoken in England by the ruling class after the conquest. *The Canterbury Tales, Piers Plowman,* and *Sir Gawain and the Green Knight* are surviving examples.

mode In literature, a manner, kind, method, or way of writing that brings with it certain expected customs and conventions (e.g., precise use of detail in descriptive writing, the tragic flaw in **tragedy**, the happy ending in **comedy**, the idealism in romance).

monologue In drama, a speech spoken by one **character** (e.g., a **soliloquy**, an **aside**).

mood The prevailing feeling created in or by a work, also known as the *atmosphere.*

motif An element (type of incident, device, or formula) that occurs frequently in literature and other artistic works (e.g., a child whose parents' absence or deaths leave the child unprotected and needing to fend for himself or herself). Also, a recurring image, character, or pattern of words that forms a dominant idea in one work (part of the **theme**) can be called a motif (or *Leitmotif,* German for "guiding motif"). For example, in Virginia Woolf's *Mrs. Dalloway,* a motif is the sound of clocks striking.

myth A story that involves supernatural beings or powers, that explains some aspect of nature (e.g., how the world began or the changing of the seasons) or of the human condition (e.g., romantic love, greed) *and* is part of a culture's mythology (its system of stories, often **archetypes**, passed down through generations).

narration A **style** of writing that incorporates **plot** to relay events over time by telling a story.

narrative poem A poem that tells a story (e.g., **ballad**, **epic**).

narrator The storyteller in narrative writing; a function of the **point of view**. Types include first-person, **omniscient**, and limited omniscient.

New Criticism A movement in literary criticism that proposes close reading and textual analysis of the text itself. It is referred to as "New" because it operates contrary to the previously favoured focus on the author's biography (see **biographical fallacy**), the historical **context**, and the perceived parallels between these and the text. Practitioners focus on both the "external form" (e.g., **ballad**, **ode**) and the "internal forms" (e.g., structure, repetition, patterns of figurative language, paradoxes). These practitioners reject consideration of the author's intention and the affect on the reader as illegitimate (thus coined *intentional fallacy* and *affective fallacy*). The movement is also referred to as *formalism.*

New Historicism A range of critical practices that examine works in their cultural and historical **context**s. Practitioners of this critical movement developed it by examining a wide range of texts such as newspapers, advertisements, popular music, historical accounts, poetry, novels, and diaries. Practitioners believe that works cannot be viewed in isolation from history and culture. A reading of a work must take into account its intention, **genre**, *and* historical situation. This approach developed in reaction to both **New Criticism** and **structuralism**.

octave A **stanza** of eight lines.

ode A **lyric poem**, typically long and formal, with a complex structure, created to offer praise to a person or location.

Old English The language of the Anglo-Saxon peoples in England spoken from the mid-fifth century CE to soon after the Norman conquest in 1066 CE, at which time the language of England changed to **Middle English**. Because it dates from the first invasion of the British Isles by the continental Angles, Saxons, and Jutes, Old English is Germanic and highly inflected. "The Dream of the Rood" and the **epic** *Beowulf* are surviving examples.

omniscient narrator An all-seeing, all-knowing storyteller/**narrator** who is "outside" the **characters**; one type of third-person narrator.

onomatopoeia A device in which a word imitates the sound it represents (e.g., the *hum* of the computer, the *twitter* of sparrows, the *boom* of a building's collapse).

oral tradition A custom or long-held practice of composing and transmitting works orally; using the spoken word to create and communicate narratives.

oxymoron A device that combines contradictory words for dramatic effect (e.g., wise fool, living death, deafening silence).

page layout The physical arrangement of the text and graphics content of a page, such as a newspaper, magazine, Web site, or book (e.g., the size of type, text running in one or more columns, the placement of graphics).

parable A brief folk tale or narrative that functions as an **analogy** in order to teach an *implied* moral or lesson.

paradox An apparent contradiction or absurdity that is somehow true (e.g., "There are no errors on this page, except this one.").

parallelism Similar constructions or treatments placed side by side, for effect (e.g., grammatical parallelism in "Early in the novel, the character Piers did…. In the fifth chapter, he did…. At the climax, in the seventh chapter, he did….").

parody A humorous, exaggerated imitation of a work, **style**, or person.

pathetic fallacy A technique of attributing inanimate objects, especially parts of nature, with human feelings and capacities (e.g., flowers that are blooming with joy). It is often used in poetry and is less formal than **personification**.

pathos The quality (e.g., in a novel or play) that evokes pity, sorrow, or tenderness; the Greek word for "suffering" or "feeling."

personification A technique in which inanimate objects or concepts are given human qualities, form, or actions (e.g., "The moon is no door. It is a face in its own right, / White as a knuckle and terribly upset. / It drags the sea after it like a dark crime…" from Sylvia Plath's "The Moon and Yew Tree").

persuasion A **style** of writing that attempts to convince the audience either to act in a certain way or to adopt a certain opinion, perspective, viewpoint, or belief.

physical comedy Performed **comedy**, such as slapstick, that depends on physical jokes (e.g., one **character** making faces behind another's back) more than verbal wit or other intellectual stimulation. It typically involves unsubtle, boisterous, clownish behaviour, and so is often part of a **farce**.

plain language Clear, straightforward communication that is intended to be read by the broadest audience, uses concrete and familiar words, avoids using (or explains) jargon, and is organized for easy comprehension.

plot The series of connected actions and events in a story that includes rising (or intensified) action, **conflict**, **climax**, falling action, and a **dénouement** (or resolution).

point of view The perspective and **voice** from which information and impressions are conveyed—either physical (from a tower, from within the grass) or psychological (e.g., from that of a police officer, from that of a robber)—which, in fiction, is determined by the choice of the **narrator**. See **first-person point of view, second-person point of view,** and **third-person point of view.** See also **visual point of view.**

poststructuralism Refers to a critical approach to language, literature, and culture that questions or criticizes **structuralism**. Like structuralists, poststructuralists rely on close readings of texts; however, poststructuralists believe that language is inherently unstable in meaning and the meaning of a text is ultimately indecipherable. The best-known poststructuralist approach is deconstructionism. Poststructuralism is often associated with **cultural**, Marxist, **feminist**, and **psychoanalytic criticism**.

précis As an action, to precisely summarize a text in writing. The resulting text is also called a précis.

prologue An opening section of a drama, a kind of introduction.

props Objects appearing in the action of a drama and used to perform or enhance it. Props, short for *properties*, include such items as furniture or common household objects.

protagonist The narrative's main **character**.

proverb A brief, familiar saying that expresses a general truth (e.g., "We cannot step twice in the same river" or "When you want a drink of milk, you don't buy the cow"). Some proverbs are the morals of fables.

psychoanalytic criticism Literary criticism grounded in the psychoanalytic theory of the founder of psychoanalysis, Sigmund Freud (1856–1939). Practitioners attempt to psychoanalyze the author's unconscious desires, the reader's responses, and the characters in the work. The last approach involves examining the text for **symbol**s and psychological complexes. In addition to Freud, key figures are psychiatrist Carl Jung (noteworthy for his exploration of **archetype**s) and, most recently, Jacques Lacan.

pun A play on words using a word with two meanings, two words of similar meanings, or words that are similarly spelled or pronounced (e.g., in *Romeo and Juliet,* Mercutio saying as he dies, "Ask for me tomorrow and you shall find me a grave man").

quatrain A **stanza** of four lines.

reader-response criticism A critical approach that shifts the emphasis to the reader from the text or the work's author and **context**. This approach focuses on the individual reader's evolving response to the text. The reader, to a great extent, "creates" the meaning of the text and therefore there is no one correct meaning. Reader-response criticism has some basis in **deconstructionism** and disputes **New Criticism**'s notions of the text as a self-sufficient object.

refrain A phrase, a line, or lines repeated in a poem. In song lyrics, these are often called the **chorus**.

review An evaluation of another work (e.g., stage play, movie, novel) in essay or report **form** or a report on a product (e.g., a consumer report).

rhetorical question A question asked to promote thought and reflection, and for dramatic effect, not to elicit an answer.

rhyme The sound effect of words that have, or end with, the same or similar sounds. Poetry that has a strong rhyming quality may be called rhyme.

rhyme scheme The pattern of **rhyme**d line-endings in a **stanza** or entire poem, as usually indicated by letters of the alphabet. For example, a common rhyme scheme for a **quatrain** is *abab*, in which the first and third lines rhyme, as do the second and fourth. An example from "Let No Charitable Hope" by Elinor Wylie: "I was, being human, borne alone/ I am, being woman, hard beset;/ I live by squeezing from a stone/ The little nourishment I get."

rhyming couplet A pair of successive lines in a poem, grouped to accentuate the unit of thought, that have the same **metre** and rhyming ends. Also known as a **couplet**.

rhythm The sound effect of stressed (accented) and unstressed (unaccented) syllables. The pattern of rhythm is called the **metre**. It sets the beat and tempo of a poem.

romance In medieval literature, this was a verse narrative originally written in Old French or Provençal (both were "Romance" languages), which recounted the marvellous adventures of a hero of chivalry. Such medieval romances fall into three main cycles: the Arthurian, based upon the life of King Arthur; those which retell the life and deeds of Charlemagne and his most celebrated Paladin; and those devoted to the exploits of Alexander the Great.

sarcasm Language, often ironic, that is bitter or hurtful toward others. The **connotation** of sarcastic comments or phrases are distinct from their **denotation**. Often the explicit meaning is more positive, but a sneering tone or expression reveals a negative **subtext**.

satire A **form** that uses **irony**, ridicule, or **sarcasm** to expose human flaws.

scene A division within a dramatic work, usually within an **act**. Typically, a scene takes place in only one specific place and unit of time.

second-person point of view A text in which the writer refers directly to the reader(s) as "you" (or an implied "you," as in "read and analyze this text"), and does not ever refer back to the writer.

sestet A **stanza** of six lines.

set design The plan and construction for the area in which a drama takes place (e.g., a political suspense film's imitation White House, a stage play's backdrops and furniture).

setting The place and time—"where" and "when"—of a **narrative**.

sidebar A short article, often boxed, appearing beside another article, typically to supplement or provide background information for the larger, main article.

simile A definitely stated **comparison** that (unlike a **metaphor**) uses "like" or "as" in its construction (e.g., Wordsworth's "I wandered lonely as a cloud" or a software manual's "Use this e-mail program like a filter, to sort and prioritize your messages").

soliloquy A **monologue**, often long, in which the lone **character** expresses his or her thoughts and feelings.

sonnet A **lyric poem** with fourteen lines, sometimes written in **iambic pentameter**. The major types of sonnet are the Italian (Petrarchan) and the English (Shakespearean).

sound effects Any sounds other than speech or music made in a movie, stage play, etc. (e.g., footsteps of a **character** running, rumbles of a volcano erupting, the screech of airplane brakes). Sound effects are imitative and made artificially.

sound track The recorded sounds of a film; any part of this made available for sale (e.g., the recording of a song written to accompany part of a movie).

special effects Illusions created for film, television, or the stage using camera work, **props**, lighting, or computers (e.g., a woman flying out of her body, computer-generated dinosaurs, a man sawn in half).

specialized terms Words or phrases arising from or using the precise meanings of a particular field of study, work, etc. (e.g., *formalism* in literary studies, *tone colour* in music, *portico* in architecture, and *prohibition* in law).

stage An area in which actors perform, arranged for the best presentation to the audience. Types include the *proscenium stage* (a raised platform with a large, square arch at the stage edge that frames the acting area for the audience), the *thrust stage* (a stage with an extended platform that juts into the audience's area; also called the Shakespearean or Elizabethan stage), the *platform stage* (an informal raised stage, such as a parade float), and the *arena stage* (an open area at floor level that is surrounded by raised, bleacher-like seating; sometimes called theatre in the round, even if the space is not round).

stage directions In scripts, text that outlines performance requirements or suggestions (e.g., instructions to say a line angrily or to enter from stage right).

stanza A grouping of successive lines in a poem, separated on the page from other stanzas above and below it by a blank space.

stereotype A type of flat **character**, who is one-dimensional and lacks complexity, often reflecting some **bias** on the part of the person who created it.

stock character A type of flat **character**, whom the audience will immediately recognize, who serves a familiar function.

storyboard One of a sequence of pictures (sometimes with writing) used to outline or plan, for example, the shot-by-shot narrative of a TV commercial or film.

structuralism A method of intellectual inquiry (used in the study of language, literature, anthropology, etc.) based on the belief that structuring is an innate part of all human behaviour. Proponents focus on **form**, structure, and patterns of literary language and works, not their cultural **context** or an author's **biography**.

style An individual's manner of expression. In writing, style is the result of the choices the writer makes regarding such elements as **diction**, sentence structure, and **figurative language**. Style also expresses the writer's personality and way of thinking.

subhead A short form for **subheading**.

subheading A secondary or subordinate heading, title, etc., within a text (e.g., titled subsections of a proposal or research paper); also called **subhead**.

subplot A secondary course of action in a narrative. Subplots serve such purposes as providing humour in a **tragedy**, rounding out minor **characters**, or helping to tie up loose ends.

subtext In a text, a hidden meaning that is not explicit.

summary A brief account; a condensation of a work's content. Sometimes called a **synopsis**.

suspense Increasing tension in a narrative, caused by uncertainty and excitement about the conclusion that generally springs from the narrative's **conflict**.

symbol Something that represents or stands for something else (e.g., a heart shape for love, a forked road for a choice to be made). Symbolism is many symbols collectively. Symbolic language includes **figurative language** (e.g., **metaphor**, **personification**) that is metaphorical, not literal, which creates a work's **imagery**.

synopsis A brief outline, **summary**, or general account (e.g., a synopsis of a **plot**).

syntax The arrangement of words to form phrases and sentences.

tableau A "frozen" moment in a drama, in which the performers freeze in position, motionless and soundless.

tanka Considered the most important form of poetry in Japan, the tanka was invented circa 700 CE, before the **haiku** form. A tanka requires thirty-one syllables and is divided into five lines broken into the following syllables: 5-7-5-7-7. Generally, tanka poems lyrically crystallize a moment or occasion.

target audience The chosen or intended readers, viewers, or listeners (e.g., of a speech); usually a distinct demographic group.

terza rima A verse **form** consisting of tercets (three-line **stanzas**) in which the second line of a stanza sets the **rhyme** for the first line of the next stanza. Thus the **rhyme scheme** is *aba bcb cdc ded efe* etc., ending with a **rhyming couplet**. It is an effective rhyme scheme for long **narrative poems** and was invented by Dante Alighieri and used most famously in his *Divine Comedy*.

theme The central insight, idea, focus, or message of a work (especially fiction), stated indirectly or directly (e.g., the theme of jealousy in Shakespeare's *Othello*).

thesis The main idea of a work of non-fiction writing. A thesis is focused and is developed with the use of examples and evidence. A thesis is usually stated directly in a **thesis statement**.

thesis statement The **thesis** provided by the writer of a text explicitly in one or several sentences of that text.

third-person point of view Written text in which the writer never refers either to himself/herself, or directly to the reader as "you." The position from which such a text is written.

tone In a text, the creator's attitude to the subject or audience as conveyed through elements of that text. In writing, the author's tone is often conveyed through **diction** and **style**. In spoken communication, the speaker's tone can be conveyed through her or his diction, volume, pitch, and body language. In visual representations, the artist's tone can be conveyed through the choice of subject matter, medium, technique, **visual composition**, emphasis, and balance.

tragedy Traditionally, a drama that focuses on the downfall of the **protagonist** (due to a character flaw or a mistake) and ends unhappily. In the traditional tragedy, the protagonist is of high social status (e.g., a prince, a goddess), but in contemporary tragedy is often an ordinary person. In current usage, tragedy might refer broadly to events, or works including events, that are catastrophic and that seem horribly unjust or preventable.

tragic hero The heroic **protagonist** of a **tragedy**.

tragicomedy A drama that combines aspects of **tragedy** and **comedy**.

usage The customary established or common manner of using words, phrases, and expressions in a way that is not yet reflected in dictionaries (e.g., as with computer terminology or with teen slang) *or* a writer's particular choice, when an option exists, in the use of a word, phrase, or expression.

visual composition The artistic arrangement of parts in the whole visual work; the way in which parts are combined and related. For example, Hiroshige Utagawa's *Shower at Ohashi Bridge* shows a bridge with people walking over it placed diagonally in the foreground, an expanse of river and a boat in the middle ground, a shore in the background, and drenching rain over the whole.

visual point of view The position from which something is viewed; the actual, physical or imagined standpoint. For example, a painter might paint the subject for the viewer to see as though from below, from above, from a bird's-eye view (aerial), from a worm's-eye view, from outside, from inside, or as in Pieter Brueghel's *Landscape with the Fall of Icarus,* from a field far from the figure falling from the sky.

visual scale Proper proportion; proportional representation of actual objects in a visual work. The relative size of objects in a visual work (e.g., in a painting, the representation of two buildings, one near and one far, or the foreshortening of a male subject's arm stretched forward).

voice Broadly, the personality of the speaker or persona (or the author) coming through in a work, created through the combination of **diction, point of view,** and **tone.** Narrowly defined, voice can be described as active (e.g., I made a mistake) or passive (e.g., Mistakes were made).

voice over Narration (e.g., in film) in which the speaker is not seen.

Another Viewpoint Index

**Another Viewpoint:
Archetypal Patterns**

The Rocking-Horse Winner 35

Outside Edges 59

Elegy in Stone 235

I, Icarus 517

Because I Could Not Stop for
Death— 610

**Another Viewpoint:
Critical Approaches**

The Death of the Moth 241

Of Youth and Age 262

Why I Write 271

The Heroes You Had as a Girl 506

foremother 510

Summer Night 529

The Love Song of J. Alfred Prufrock
538

grammar poem 547

Stop! 649

**Another Viewpoint:
Culture**

The Shining Houses 73

A Devoted Son 86

Magpies 95

No Great Mischief 162

Call of the Weird 282

to you who would wage war against
me 514

O Can You Leave Your Native Land?
603

**Another Viewpoint:
History**

Peace, Technology 322

Paradise, a Poet, and Promised Land
330

The Rime of the Ancient Mariner 600

Dover Beach 607

**Another Viewpoint:
Literary Modes and
Forms**

Was It a Dream? 154

A Modest Proposal 293

People on the Bridge 523

The Canterbury Tales 569

Sonnet 116 571

Dead Parrot 654

**Another Viewpoint:
Society**

Windows 117

War 137

A Place to Stand On 223

Chameleons and Codas 228

My Mother's Blue Bowl 255

Ours by Design 363

The River 544

Beowulf 559

Author Index

Acoose, Janice 636
Akiwenzie Damm, Kateri 511
Aristotle 454
Arnold, Matthew 605
Atwood, Margaret 205
Auden, W.H. 518

Bacon, Francis 259
Bhatia, Amin 345
Blackduck, Alison 355
Blake, William 572
Bouzane, Lillian 507
Bowering, George 489
Bradley, A.C. 687
Branagh, Kenneth 666
Brewster, Elizabeth 481
Brown, Kurt 500
Brueghel, Pieter 366

Campbell, Joseph 171
Cassatt, Mary 484
CBC Television 640
Chaucer, Geoffrey 561
Chekhov, Anton 614
Clarke, George Elliott 327
Climenhage, Kate 349
Coady, Lynn 331
Coleridge, Samuel Taylor 575
Conlogue, Ray 380
Conrad, Patricia 225
Cope, Wendy 478

Dawson, C. Daniel 498
Desai, Anita 75
de Villiers, Marq 466
Dickinson, Emily 608
Dorin, Ivan 48
Dove, Rita 7
Dryden, Ken 243

Edmonton Journal 456
Eliot, T.S. 531
Elliott, Bob 446

Findley, Timothy 120
Franklin, Ursula 313
Frye, Northrop 166

Goulding, Ray 446
Government of Newfoundland and Labrador 392
Greenwood, Therese 658

Harvey, Kenneth J. 449
Heaney, Seamus 553
Heighton, Steven 229
Henley, Marian 364
Highway, Tomson 6
Hiroshige Utagawa 368
Hoffman, Eva 307
Hughes, Langston 527
Husarska, Anna 389

Joyce, James 181

Kimenye, Barbara 97
King, Thomas 87
Kingsolver, Barbara 273

Lange, Dorothea 256
LaRocque, Emma 524
Laurence, Margaret 217
Lawrence, D.H. 18
Leacock, Stephen 696
Le Guin, Ursula K. 144
Levertov, Denise 14
Lewis, Donna 642
Livesay, Dorothy 492

MacLeod, Alistair 155
Maupassant, Guy de 150
McIntyre, Lyle 60
McLuhan, Marshall 431
Milne, Courtney 370
Mitchell, Barbara 370
Mitchell, Ormond 370
Monty Python 651
Moodie, Susanna 601
Moore, Marianne 473
Morgan, Bernice 109
Morrison, Lee 459
Moyers, Bill 171
Munro, Alice 63

Neruda, Pablo 4
Ng-Chan, Taien 37
Nowlan, Alden 515

Ondaatje, Michael 486
Orwell, George 263
Ozick, Cynthia 196

Pitt, Angela 692
Postman, Neil 434
Pratt, Christopher 118
Purdy, Al 349

Quindlen, Anna 12

Rees, Ann 443
Reguly, Eric 463
Reid, Bill 142
Richler, Mordecai 10
Roberts, Brad (The Crash Test Dummies) 539
Rose, Chris 421
Ross, Val 188

Schulz Gropman, Karen 634
Scliar, Moacyr 138
Shakespeare, William 570, 656–700
Shelley, Percy Bysshe 177
Shelton, Margaret 46
Swift, Jonathan 283
Szymborska, Wislawa 521

Taylor, Drew Hayden 279
Thomas, Dylan 494
Tranchemontagne, Chantal 337

Walcott, Derek 542
Walker, Alice 251
Wallace, Bronwen 503
Watson, Patrick 300
Waytiuk, Judy 394
White, E.B. 209
Winter, Kathleen 323
Wiwa, Ken 295
Wong, Rita 545
Wood, Daniel 403
Woolf, Virginia 237

Zeman, Brenda 636

Credits

Every reasonable effort has been made to find copyright holders of the material in this anthology. The publisher would be pleased to have any errors brought to its attention.

Literary Credits

p. 4 Translation © Alastair Reid; **p. 6** From *Everybody's Favourites: Canadians Talk About Books That Changed Their Lives,* Penguin Books Canada Ltd., 1997. Copyright © Tomson Highway; **p. 7** "For the Love of Books" from *Selected Poems,* Pantheon Books, © 1993 by Rita Dove. Reprinted by permission of the author; **p. 10** From *Everybody's Favourites: Canadians Talk About Books That Changed Their Lives,* Penguin Books Canada Ltd., 1997. Copyright © Mordecai Richler; **p. 12** From *How Reading Changed My Life* by Anna Quindlen, copyright © 1998 by Anna Quindlen. Used by permission of Ballantine Books, a division of Random House, Inc.; **p. 14** "The Secret" by Denise Levertov, from *Poems 1960–1967* copyright © 1974 by Denise Levertov/Reprinted by permission of New Directions Publishing Corp.; **p. 18** Used by permission of Laurence Pollinger Limited and the Estate of Frieda Lawrence Ravagli; **p. 37** With permission of the author; **p. 48** Copyright © Ivan Dorin; **p. 63** "Shining Houses" by Alice Munro from *Dance of the Happy Shades* © 1968, Ryerson Press. Used by permission of McGraw-Hill Ryerson; **p. 75** Copyright © 1978, Anita Desai. Reproduced by permission of the author c/o Rogers, Coleridge & White Ltd., 20 Powis Mews, London W11 1JN; **p. 87** Used by permission of HarperCollins Canada; **p. 97** "The Winner" from *Kalasanda.* Copyright © 1965 by Barbara Kimenye. Used by permission of East African Educational Publishers, Kenya; **p. 109** Bernice Morgan is the author of the novels *Random Passage* and *Waiting for Time* and a short story collection *The Topography of Love.* Used by permission of the author; **p. 120** From *Dinner Along the Amazon* by Timothy Findley. Copyright © 1984 by Pebble Productions Inc. Reprinted by permission of Penguin Books Canada Limited; **p. 138** "Paz e guerra" in: Moacyr Scliar: "Contos reunidos," Companhia das Letras, 1995 © 1995 by Moacyr Scliar. Translation by Patricia Feeney. Used by permission of the author and translator; **p. 144** Copyright © 1975 by Ursula K. Le Guin; first appeared in *Epoch*; from *Buffalo Gals and Other Animal Presences*; reprinted by permission of the author and the author's agents, the Virginia Kidd Agency, Inc.; **p. 155** *No Great Mischief* by Alistair MacLeod. Used by permission of McClelland & Stewart Ltd. *The Canadian Publishers*; **p. 166** Excerpts from "The Archtypes of Literature." First published in *The Kenyon Review*—Winter 1951, OS Vol. XIII, No. 1, Copyright *The Kenyon Review*; **p. 171** From *The Power of Myth* by Joseph Campbell & Bill Moyers, copyright © 1988 by Apostrophe S Productions, Inc. and Bill Moyers and Alfred Van der Marck Editions, Inc., for itself and the estate of Joseph Campbell. Used by permission of Doubleday, a division of Random House, Inc.; **p. 181** "Araby", *Dubliners* reproduced with the permission of the Estate of James Joyce; © copyright, Estate of James Joyce (1967); **p. 188** Reprinted with permission from *The Globe and Mail*; **p. 196** "Portrait of the Essay as a Warm Body" by Cynthia Ozick, from *The Best American Essays 1988.* Copyright © 1988 by Cynthia Ozick. Reprinted by permission of Houghton Mifflin Company. All rights reserved; **p. 205** Copyright © O.W. Toad, 2001; **p. 209** All lines from "Afternoon of an American Boy" from *Essays of E.B. White* by E.B. White. Copyright 1947 by E.B. White. Originally appeared in *The New Yorker.* Reprinted by permission of HarperCollins Publishers Inc.; **p. 217** *Heart of a Stranger* by Margaret Laurence. Used by permission of McClelland & Stewart Ltd. *The Canadian Publishers*; **p. 225** Used by permission of Patricia Conrad. First appeared in *The Globe and Mail,* July 10, 2000; **p. 229** "Elegy in Stone" from *The Admen Move on Lhasa* copyright © 1997 by Steven Heighton. Reprinted by permission of Stoddart Publishing Co. Ltd.; **p. 243** From *The Game: A Reflective and Thought-Provoking Look at a Life in Hockey,* 3rd Edition. Copyright © Ken Dryden, 1983, 1993, 1999. Reprinted by permission of Macmillan Canada, an imprint of CDG Books Canada, Inc.; **p. 251** "My Mother's Blue Bowl" published in *Anything We Love Can Be Saved: A Writer's Activism,* copyright 1997. Used by permission of Wendy Weil's Agency Inc.; **p. 263** *Why I Write* (Copyright © George Orwell 1953) and reproduced by permission of A.M. Heath & Co. Ltd. on behalf of Bill Hamilton as the Literary Executor of the Estate of the Late Sonia Brownell

Reprinted with permission of the author; **p. 550** "Mu-lan" published in *The Flowering Plum and the Palace Lady, Interpretations of Chinese Poetry.* Translation by Hans H. Frankel. Used by permission of Yale University Press, © 1976; **p. 555** From *Beowulf,* translated by Seamus Heaney. Copyright © 2000 by Seamus Heaney. Used by permission of W. W. Norton & Company, Inc.; **p. 560** Middle English excerpt edited by John H. Fisher; **p. 561** Modern English excerpt translated by Nevill Coghill. Reproduced with permission of Curtis Brown Group Ltd., London, on behalf of the Estate of Nevill Coghill © Nevill Coghill 1951; **p. 614** From *The Brute and Other Farces* by Anton Chekhov, edited by Eric Bentley, translated by Theodore Hoffman. Applause Theatre Book Publishers, 1985. © 1958 by Eric Bentley for collection; **p. 636** Prof. Janice Acoose: citizen of the Sakimay Saulteaux First Nation and Marival Métis Community; **p. 642** Used by permission of Donna Lewis, author and performer of various Sleeping Beauty Cabaret Monologues; **p. 651** Used by permission of Methuen Publishing Ltd., London; **p. 658** Courtesy of *The Kingston Whig Standard*; **p. 666** Printed by permission of Kenneth Branagh Ltd.; **p. 677** Used by permission of *Cineaste Magazine*; **p. 692** Used by permission of Angela Pitt.

Visual Credits

p. 2 Jacob Lawrence, Smithsonian American Art Museum, Washington, DC/Art Resource, New York; **p. 11** Pablo Picasso, *Bottle, Cup and Newspaper* 1912–1913. © Estate of Pablo Picasso (Paris)/SODRAC (Montréal) 2001; **p. 16** Ryuichi Sato/Photonica; **p. 36** Corbis/Jose Luis Ortiz; **p. 47** Margaret Shelton, *Calgary from Sunnyside* (undated), Woodcut, 5/100, Carleton University Art Gallery: The Frank H. Underhill Memorial Collection of Block Prints, 1998; **p. 61** Lyle McIntyre; **p. 62** Nikolaevich/Photonica; **p. 74** Hugh Sitton/Getty Images/Stone; **p. 96** Design "Dialogue" by Nuwa Wamala Nnyanzi www.nnyanziart.com; **p. 119** Ned Pratt; **p. 143** © Ulli Steltzer, photographer from *The Black Canoe,* Douglas & McIntyre, Vancouver; **p. 164** Copyright Victoria & Albert Museum, London/Art Resource, NY; **p. 170** CORBIS/Gian Berto Vanni; **p. 189** Poster published by The National Union of Conservative and Unionist Assoc., London, 1929/Bridgeman; **p. 194** Neil Leslie/Photonica; **p. 216** Kathy Warinner; **p. 224** Gord Wiebe; **p. 236** By courtesy of the National Portrait Gallery, London; **p. 242** London Life-Portnoy Hockey Hall of Fame; **p. 257** Dorothea Lange/CORBIS; **p. 258** © Scala/Art Resource, NY; **p. 272** Chuck Rancorn; **p. 294** M.C. Escher's Tower of Babel © 2001 Cordon Art B.V.—Baarn—Holland. All rights reserved; **p. 306** Eva Rubinstein/Photonica; **p. 336** Marty McLennan; **p. 354** Reproduced with the permission of The West Baffin Eskimo Co-operative, Cape Dorset Nunavut; **p. 365** Maxine! Comix. Reprinted by permission of the artist; **p. 367** Painting by Pieter Breugel the Elder courtesy of Bridgeman Art Library; **p. 369** Painting by Utagawa Hiroshige. Courtesy of Magma Photo; **pp. 371–79** Courtney Milne; **pp. 382–387** Used by permission of CBC; **pp. 390–91** Jozef Bury. Published in *Saturday Night* magazine, August 12, 2000; **p. 393** Compliments of Newfoundland and Labrador Tourism Advertising Campaign 1993–1999, Target Marketing; **pp. 395–400** Used by permission of MTS; **p. 405** Holly Harris/Getty Images/Stone; **pp. 406, 413, 416–17** Jeff Speed Photographer; **p. 408** © Dorling Kindersley; **p. 411** UHB Trust/Getty Images/Stone; **p. 414 left** PhotoDisc; **p. 414 right** Firstlight; **p. 415 left** Roger Wright/Getty Images/Stone; **p. 415 right** Rob Gage/FPG; **p. 419** © Dorling Kindersley; **p. 423** Ian Smith/*Vancouver Sun*; **p. 443** Cameron Cardow; **p. 452** Malcolm Mayes; **p. 476** Joseph Squillante/Photonica; **p. 485** Mary Cassatt, American, 1884–1926, Evening, 1879/80, soft-ground etching and aquatint on cream laid paper, 19.7 x 22.1 cm. The Albert H. Wolf Memorial Collection, 1938.33. Photograph © 2001, The Art Institute of Chicago, All Rights Reserved; **p. 499** C. Daniel Dawson; **p. 530** Used by permission of Madame Gilberte Brassai; **p. 548** Excerpt from *100 Celebrated Chinese Women* published by Asiapac Books www.asiapacbooks.com; **p. 554** Rockwell Kent/Granger; **p. 560** Ellesmere Manuscript, Canterbury Tales, Chaucer/Bridgeman; **p. 573** Used by permission of Rare Books and Special Collections, Princeton University; **p. 574** The Watersnakes Appear, scene from *The Rime of the Ancient Mariner* by S.T. Coleridge 1877 engraving. Collection Kharbine-Tapabor, Paris France/Bridgeman; **p. 604** E.O. Hoppé/CORBIS; **p. 612** Gen Nishino/Getty Images/Stone; **p. 635** Karen Schulz Gropman—set designer; **p. 641** Photo by Justin Hall, provided by Passage Films Inc.; **p. 650** Everett Collection/Magma Photo; **p. 657** Historical Picture Archive/CORBIS; **p. 686** Scene from the 1979 Stratford Festival production of King Lear by William Shakespeare. Directed by Robin Phillips. Designed by Daphne Dare with with l–r: Gregory Wanless as Officer to Cordelia, Rod Beattie as Doctor, John Lambert as Officer, Jim McQueen as Kent, Peter Ustinov as King Lear and Ingrid Blekys as Cordelia. Photograph by Robert C. Ragsdale. Courtesy of the Stratford Festival Archives.

William Mulholland
and the
Rise of Los Angeles

William Mulholland

and the

Rise of Los Angeles

Catherine Mulholland

UNIVERSITY OF CALIFORNIA PRESS
Berkeley · Los Angeles · London

University of California Press
Berkeley and Los Angeles, California

University of California Press, Ltd.
London, England

© 2000 by the Regents of the University
of California

Library of Congress Cataloging-in-Publication Data

Mulholland, Catherine.

   William Mulholland and the rise of
Los Angeles / Catherine Mulholland.

      p.   cm.

   Includes bibliographical references and index.

   ISBN 0-520-21724-1 (alk. paper).

     1. Water-supply—California—Los Angeles—
History.   2. Mulholland, William, 1855–1935.
   3. Engineers—California—Los Angeles—
Biography.   I. Title.
   HD4464.L7 M85   2000
   979.4'9404'092—dc21   99-048289
   [B]   CIP

Manufactured in the United States of America

09 08 07 06 05 04 03 02 01 00

10 9 8 7 6 5 4 3 2 1

The paper used in this publication meets the minimum requirements of ANSI/NISO Z39.48-1992
(R 1997) (Permanence of Paper).

Chapter 24 contains material previously published
in modified form as "Mulholland and the St.
Francis Dam," in *The St. Francis Dam Disaster
Revisited,* edited by Doyce B. Nunis, Jr. (Los
Angeles and Ventura: Historical Society of Southern
California and Ventura County Museum of History
and Art, 1995).

*To the memory of
Richard Perry Mulholland
(1925–1992), the Chief's
only grandson*

A story that was the subject of every variety of misrepresentation, not only by those who then lived but likewise in succeeding times: so true is it that all transactions of preeminent importance are wrapt in doubt and obscurity; while some hold for certain facts the most precarious hearsays, others turn facts into falsehood; and both are exaggerated by posterity.

Robert Graves, *I, Claudius*

Contents

List of Illustrations   xi

Preface   xiii

Acknowledgments   xix

1. The Long Journey from Dublin to Los Angeles, 1855–1876   3

2. The City of Angels, 1877   14

3. The Private Water Company and Its Owners, 1878–1879   23

4. Advancing in the Water Business, 1880–1886   30

5. The New Superintendent, 1887–1892   38

6. Water Plots and Politics, 1893–1895   48

7. The Years of Mayor Eaton, 1898–1900   61

8. The City's Victory over the "Grand Monopoly," 1901–1902   75

9. New Regime for a Booming Town, 1903–1904   88

10. Desperate Remedies in a Dry Season, 1904   100

11. A Plan Revealed, 1905   112

12. Preparations for an Aqueduct and a Trip to Washington,
    D.C., 1906   126

13. The Big Job Begins, 1907   141

14. The Chief and the General, 1908   159

15. Building the Aqueduct: The Best Year, 1909   171

16. Troubles and Interruptions, 1910   183

17. Aqueduct Progress and Political Fireworks, 1911   196

18. The Investigation, 1912   209

19. The Completion of the Aqueduct, 1913   228

20. After the Aqueduct, 1914–1919   249

21. A Stormy Decade Begins, 1920–1923   265

22. Boulder Dam and Dynamite, 1924   282

23. More Dynamite, 1925–1927   299

24. The Saint Francis Dam Disaster and After, 1928–1935   319

    Afterword   333

    Notes   335

    Bibliography   385

    Index   393

Illustrations

William Mulholland, 1916   *frontispiece*

plates follow page 136

MAPS

1. Waterworks structures, Elysian Park area   50
2. Los Angeles Aqueduct and adjacent territory
   with divisions, 1908   143
3. Profile of Los Angeles Aqueduct   155
4. Annexations to the City of Los Angeles, 1899–1944   217
5. Greater Los Angeles, 1925   267
6. Southern California water supply, 1925   269
7. Major water distribution facilities, City of Los Angeles   332

Preface

Los Angeles . . . No ordinary rules
explain its past growth or set limits
to its future expansion. It has been,
and will be, a law unto itself.

WILLIAM E. SMYTHE,
The Conquest of Arid America

A HISTORIC DISPUTE

William Mulholland presided over the creation of a water system that changed forever the course of Southern California history, and in so doing he became the focus of a controversy that has never died. When Los Angeles went water hunting and laid claim to the waters of the Owens River over two hundred miles away, its actions so conflicted with competing interests that they gave rise to a struggle of mythic proportions. Reading the varying accounts of this action reminds one of the classic paradox *All Cretans are liars, said the man from Crete*. Who lies? Does everyone lie or does everyone one tell the truth? Even if the dead could be brought back, could they tell us what we want to know? Writers who have scrutinized the same public documents, official records, and private correspondence have arrived at contrary conclusions, so the existing literature on the story of Los Angeles's water is not only voluminous but also often dissonant.

When I began research for this work in 1989, four books on the subject especially deserved serious consideration, each offering different yet valuable versions of the water story. The important pioneer effort was *The Water Seekers* (1950), by Remi Nadeau, a highly readable work that subsequent scholarship has somewhat superseded. *Water and Politics: A Study of Water Policies and Administration in the Development of Los Angeles* (1953), by Vincent Ostrom, is probably the best and most precise single survey of the subject but tends to be impersonal in its treatment of the individuals involved in the story. *Vision or Villainy: Origins of the Owens Valley–Los Angeles Water Controversy* (1981), by Abraham Hoffman, is a fair-minded and thorough work, especially valuable for its examination of the roles J. B. Lippincott and the Reclamation Service played in the Owens Valley saga. The fourth, *Water and Power* (1982), by William Kahrl (editor of the estimable *California Water Atlas*), while containing a wealth of documentation, technical information, and a valuable bibliography, is also full of inaccuracies and, because of its unremittingly jaundiced view of Los Angeles and its water seekers, ultimately proves to be a polemic masquerading as a scholarly study. *Water and Power* has been influential, however, in subsequent works that have relied and elaborated on Kahrl's views: *Cadillac Desert* (1986), a screed by Marc Reisner on the evils of water development in the West; *Western Times and Water Wars* (1992), by John Walton, a study of Owens Valley that is somewhat in the manner of the *Annales* school of French historiography as found in LeRoy Ladurie's *Montaillou* and that describes the purported injustice inflicted by large governmental power over a small region; and *The Lost Frontier* (1994), by John Sauder, an inquiry into the agricultural losses sustained in Owens Valley because of Los Angeles's water development. Although none of the authors of this latter group is as extreme as the popular Western writer Wallace Stegner, who wrote that he considered building a dam evidence of original sin, each reflects the fin de siècle skepticism toward large water projects along with a disapproval of Los Angeles and a resolute bias favoring Owens Valley. The inclination to side with the underdog is powerful and humane but also risks committing what Bertrand Russell called "the fallacy of the superior virtue of the oppressed." Even the objective scholar-historian Norris Hundley has described Los Angeles as "the West's most notorious water hustler" in *Water and the West* (1975), and in his extensive overview of California water history, *The Great Thirst* (1992), he trivializes the building of the Owens Valley Aqueduct under a pejorative chapter heading, "The Owens Valley Caper." These works' contentions have helped create public perceptions such as a woman recently voiced at an environmental conference I attended when she fairly shouted, "Mulholland was no engineer. All he did was take a few pipes up north and run water down and help make some men rich," or such as a recent news article expressed when it described "the shadowy fiddling that sucked Owens Valley water into Los Angeles." In these versions, Mulholland emerges as an antihero rather than an admired bringer of water. As one of his nieces once ruefully remarked, "The Greeks beat the Trojans, but now, after three thousand years, it is a greater compliment to be called a Trojan."

In fact, the whole thrust of the Los Angeles enterprise looked to the future. Just as Caesar did not look back to Alexander for his model of a Roman empire but anticipated as a model a kind of city-state existing in Rome's own peripheries and provinces, so the leaders of an expanding Los Angeles looked to extend boundaries in order to create a new kind of city. What, after all, made this venture more reprehensible than those undertaken by other American cities that had gone distances to find water: New York to Croton, Boston to Lake Winnipesaukee, and San Francisco to the Tuolumne River in the Sierra Nevada mountain range? Who still rails against the New York Catskill project, which in its construction bought and drowned ten towns and villages, removed three thousand dead from thirty-two cemeteries, relocated eleven miles of rail track, and built ten highway bridges? Furthermore, the New York project was simply a water delivery system, while the Owens River project was to produce electrical energy as well, making it at the time not only a municipally owned utility but also one of the most valuable commercial enterprises in the United States.

SOURCES AND THE ROLE OF THE PRESS

Newspapers, the "diaries of history," have been a rich source for the present work. Because the *Los Angeles Times* has outlived its former competitors, files of those defunct papers must now be sought in selected libraries where, in many cases, they exist only in incomplete runs. While the chief creators of the *Times,* General Harrison Gray Otis and Harry Chandler, enjoy enormous fame in the city's history, few trails of glory follow Colonel J. J. Ayers, Major Horace Bell, Manchester Boddy, Edward Dickson, Edwin T. Earl, J. D. Lynch, and Benjamin C. Truman. Yet all once either owned, published, and/or edited successful and influential newspapers in Los Angeles with editorial slants that are sometimes today overlooked or forgotten. Especially among journalists and popular historians, this imbalance has led to an inflation of the roles of Otis and Chandler as city-makers out of all proportion to the facts. Without in any way minimizing these powerful men's impact on the city's history, I have tried to introduce other opinion-molders who played roles in building the City of Los Angeles.

One must keep alert, however, to journalist Mark Sullivan's caveat that "a newspaper, as respects its fundamental character, is one of the least permanent of institutions . . . it can change ownership overnight," and that "even though it remain in the same ownership, its character, point of view, and policy may be altered by a change in the owner's interests, by his necessity for borrowing money, or otherwise" (*Our Times*, vol. 2, pp. 228–29). A new editor, or even a change in the post of managing-editor, can switch the emphasis upon the coverage of certain subjects. Otis's *Times*, for example, considered the leading booster for building the aqueduct and creating a municipal water system, became, under the later aegis of Harry Chandler, an implacable foe of the Boulder Dam project and the expansion of municipal power. Hearst's *Examiner* also reversed itself, beginning as an editorial foe of the aqueduct and ending as its champion, as well as later supporting Boulder Dam and the municipal ownership of water and power.

Archival papers of civic leaders and engineers also proved helpful because they document many of the interconnections between business interests and the water story of Los Angeles. Mulholland's friendship with Henry O'Melveny and Charles Dwight Willard was further demonstrated in their papers and journals, while those of political leaders John R. Haynes and Meyer Lissner augment the public record of their relationships during the rise of progressivism in Los Angeles and California.

ANOTHER VOICE ON THE SUBJECT

Biographies of engineers are scarce since they must deal with technical matters often beyond the ken of historian or biographer. Because the public and administrative life of an engineer tends to overshadow the private, it becomes the biographer's duty to render that public side in vivid, yet accurate, style. Aside from memoirs written soon after his death by close associates (engineers J. B. Lippincott and Harvey Van Norman), the first attempt at a biography of William Mulholland was a monograph, *William Mulholland: A Forgotten Forefather* (1976), by Robert Matson. Written for a master's degree at the University of the Pacific, it derives mostly from secondary materials and is only a partial account of the engineer's life. *Rivers in the Desert* (1993), by Margaret Leslie Davis, purports to be a "major biography" but is not. Mulholland's first fifty years remain unexplored, while accounts of his private and domestic life rely on hearsay and public records of marriage, divorce, and probate. Marred by many minor factual errors, the work demonstrates little depth of understanding about the complexity of the water story.

For background and information to supplement personal knowledge of the years when Mulholland was an anonymous figure in Los Angeles (1878–1904), I turned to city council proceedings, Department of Water and Power records, and reminiscences of Mulholland's early employees and associates. Only scanty information remains from the years 1888 to 1902, when he headed the private water company that ran the city's system. With records either lost or destroyed, the *Times* here proved valuable, as it provided the most detailed coverage of city council meetings during those years, when the official proceedings tended to be skeletal. Family scrapbooks, papers, and reminiscences were also useful, but especially helpful were Mulholland's office files (1902–1928) from the Los Angeles Water Department, which only in recent years have been discovered, catalogued, and made available.

This work is not only a biography of William Mulholland but also an account of how a small pueblo in a semiarid basin was able to secure the water and power that allowed it to grow into a major city. It describes the many associates—some heroic, some not—who worked in this epic endeavor. Because the water story remains the founding myth of modern Los Angeles, this work also calls into question many current versions of the so-called Owens Valley controversy. Was there really rape and betrayal by the city's leaders? Was the entire building of the Owens Valley Aqueduct the result of a conspiracy among Los Angeles capitalists to acquire water in order to develop for speculation their holdings in the San Fernando Valley? Who were the chief enemies of the city's water seekers? Also discussed are the developments leading to the building of Boulder Dam and, finally, the major disaster of the Saint Francis Dam (1928), which ended Mulholland's career.

The epigraph by Tacitus from Robert Graves's *I, Claudius* underscores the problems inherent in telling this story, with which in a sense I have lived all my life and which even now may be disbelieved, so fixed in some minds is the certainty of what transpired that nothing would alter their opinion. As the subject's granddaughter, my objectivity will be questioned. To answer that, I turn again to Tacitus, who almost two thousand years ago wrote of the profoundly divided opinions of those who were "bitterly alienated" by an event and those who were "deeply committed" to it: "But whereas the reader can easily discount the bias of the time-serving historian, detraction and spite find a ready audience.

Adulation bears the ugly taint of subservience, but malice gives the false impression of being independent." When the Chinese general Chou en Lai was asked in the 1950s what he thought had been the French Revolution's impact on western Europe, he replied that it was too soon to tell. Without insisting on Chou's long view, I would suggest that if there is to be a last word on this saga, it is yet to come. I also believe that diverse voices should continue to be heard, and I hope that mine will be among them.

Acknowledgments

Help comes from many people in a work such as this, with debts owed to librarians and archivists of special collections throughout California. Foremost of value have been materials from the Los Angeles Department of Water and Power, with special thanks to Elizabeth Wimmer, retired public affairs officer, who led me to obscure items of interest when I first began my research. Later, Paul Soifer and Tom Connors, archivists of the Records Center of the LADWP, were also most helpful, as was Linda M. Colton, former principal civil engineering drafting technician, who helped prepare the maps in this book.

Hynda L. Rudd, records management officer, and Robert B. Freeman, archivist, were generous and helpful in availing me of old city council records in the City Archives of Los Angeles.

I also extend my gratitude to the following libraries and their staffs:
    Bancroft Library, University of California, Berkeley
    Delmar Oviatt Library, California State University, Northridge
    Huntington Library, San Marino
    Los Angeles County Library, San Fernando
    Los Angeles Public Library
    National Library, Dublin, Ireland
    Research Library, University of California, Los Angeles
    Stanford University Libraries, Department of Special Collections
    Water Resources Center, University of California, Berkeley

Thanks also to Thomas F. Andrews, executive director of the Historical Society of Southern California, who encouraged me to continue my work at a time when it seemed a forlorn hope, and to author, scholar, and editor Doyce B. Nunis, Jr., who heartened me with the publication of my article on Mulholland and the Saint Francis Dam in *The St. Francis Dam Disaster Revisited* (1995).

In the later stages of my work, new acquaintances took time out from their busy lives to give invaluable time and effort on my behalf. To them I give sincerest thanks:

Steven P. Erie, professor of political science at U.C., San Diego, whose own work on the rise and growth of Los Angeles has spurred me to complete my own, has been of immeasurable help with sage counsel, friendship, and as a final boon, an introduction to William Deverell for a final paving of the way to publication.

William Deverell, associate professor of history at the California Institute of Technology, performed the great service of vetting the manuscript, making significant editorial comments, and recommending it to the University of California Press.

I owe a great debt to engineer Robert V. Phillips, whose knowledge of western water matters is encyclopedic and whose friendship I prize. His father, James E. Phillips, a close associate of both Mulholland and his successor, Harvey Van Norman, was in charge of the water affairs of the Aqueduct Division of the Los Angeles Department of Water and Power from 1928 until his death in 1940. The younger Phillips, after years as an engineer of the Owens Valley Division of the Aqueduct at Independence, served as general manager and chief engineer of the Los Angeles Department of Water and Power from 1972 to 1975 and as a member of the management board of the Navajo Tribal Utility Authority (an enterprise of the Navajo Nation) from 1976 to 1993. Not only did Phillips vet my manuscript and offer advice and information on technical matters of engineering and hydrology, as a longtime dweller in Owens Valley, he provided valuable insights into aspects of the controversy there.

I am grateful to J. David Rogers, civil and geological engineer, founder of his own consulting firms (Geolith Consultants and Rogers/Pacific), and part-time faculty member of the Department of Civil Engineering at U.C., Berkeley. His research and writings on the complexities of dam construction, especially his studies of the Saint Francis Dam failure, have not only shed new light on an old engineering controversy but also illustrate the importance of maintaining a questioning mind towards problematic events. Some have chosen to attack him for what they construe as his vindication of Mulholland, but as he has written, "historical truth is much more interesting, and more complicated, than the legend."

Thanks also go to those of my family, especially cousin Lillian Sloan Macedo, who dug into their trunks, records, and memories for items that shed light on the subject, and to my former husband, Gerard T. Hurley, for his editorial advice and assistance.

A special salute goes to my sister-in-law, Katherine Powell Mulholland. Her love and generosity can never be repaid.

My godson, Frank Ditto, made such a prodigious contribution as mentor and guide into the intricacies of word processing, computer use, and manuscript preparation that a mere expression of thanks seems barely adequate.

And finally, my thanks to California history editor Monica McCormick, who has helped see this project through to completion.

William Mulholland
and the
Rise of Los Angeles

CHAPTER 1

The Long Journey from Dublin to Los Angeles

1855–1876

A NOTABLE LIFE

Of those civil servants who helped develop the modern metropolis of Los Angeles in the early twentieth century, the most prominent was William Mulholland (1855–1935). For over forty years spanning the administrations of nineteen mayors, Mulholland was a central force in the creation of a municipally owned water and power system that allowed a small, otiose western outpost to swell to outsized proportions. As a self-taught and inventive engineer, he became the creator of a project that ranked in magnitude and daring with the Panama Canal.

A pen-and-ink cartoon of Mulholland drawn in 1902, about the time the City of Los Angeles had at last regained control of its domestic water supply from the private company to which it had foolishly leased its pueblo water rights thirty years earlier, portrays a sturdy man in work clothes planted in front of a pump and water trough with two buckets labeled "City Water" at his feet. By then, Mulholland had worked for that private company for twenty-four years, having advanced from anonymous ditch tender in 1878 to superintendent of the works in 1886, a position he continued to hold under the new municipal management. "When the city bought back its water, it bought me too," he later remarked. The authority of his stance and stern gaze leaves no doubt that he is indeed the keeper of the well, and at the height of his power and vigor, he was exactly that: the overseer and caretaker of water for Los Angeles. He brought fame (and some say ignominy) to the City of Los

Angeles when, in 1913, as chief engineer of the great Owens River Aqueduct, he delivered to the city from 233 miles away its first abundant water supply. When the University of California at Berkeley honored him with an honorary doctorate degree the following year, the inscription on the diploma read, *"Percussit saxa et duxit flumina ad terram sitientum"* (He broke the rocks and brought the river to the thirsty land). Upon the aqueduct's completion—after years of struggle and heroic labor to create this engineering marvel—Mulholland stood amidst the cheers of the crowd, and over the roar of the waters cascading down the spillway north of San Fernando, he uttered briefly and memorably, "There it is. Take it."

Not only did that moment become legendary in the city's modern history, but it also created a controversy that has never died. When *Life* magazine's fall 1990 special issue included Mulholland among the one hundred people who had most influenced American history in the twentieth century ("The engineer moved a river and made the desert bloom."), a New York journalist was quick to snipe, in an amusing instance of East Coast parochialism, that Mulholland's presence on the list seemed "a bit strained" and that it probably constituted "a sop to the hinterlands."[1]

Mulholland was to live amid political conflict and controversy into his seventies. Then while he was actively planning and campaigning for the expansion of the city's water supply from the Colorado River, a dam that he had approved failed and killed over four hundred people, thus drowning his career in the wake of the worst man-made disaster in California's history.

This saga deserves renewed scrutiny, as in recent years the popular media, relying upon old rumors and hearsay, have increasingly presented this water story as a tabloid yarn of water thievery and crooked land deals. One fictional and melodramatic movie, *Chinatown* (1979), has come to be regarded by the uninformed as a kind of documentary work on the history of Los Angeles, while others who hold the city in disdain see the film as a clever parable on the greed and ambition of an upstart town. In a May 1, 1991, article on city water systems, the *New York Times* saw fit to cite Los Angeles as a horrible example of overexploitation of resources. To substantiate its case, the *Times* egregiously cited *Chinatown* as the work "which chronicles how the city seized control" of water to which it had no right.

Three years after Mulholland's death, newspaperman John Russell McCarthy wrote of him, "He had little pity, much strength, great ambition. There is no one else in sight, past or present, whom Los Angeles is more likely to remember." And so, loved or hated, Mulholland remains important to the history of Los Angeles and Southern California, his status recalling historian Carl Becker's evaluation of Martin Luther: "The Protestant may love Luther, the Catholic may hate him, but they would agree that Luther is important for the Reformation." Whether cherished or reviled, Mulholland endures at least as a potent figure in the history of his adopted city.[2]

A NOTE ON THE PRIVATE LIFE

William Mulholland was a fine-featured, handsome man, who, although a shade under six feet, always gave the impression of being taller because of his straight-backed, commanding presence and the penetrating gaze of his blue eyes. He had enormous energy, got by on little sleep, and remained vigorous until the Saint Francis Dam disaster eroded his spirit and health. His greatest assets—and doubtless a key to his success in public life—were a ready wit and an ability to get along with men.

Mulholland's private life seldom impinged upon his public affairs. In 1890, at the age of thirty-five, he married Lillie Ferguson, then twenty-one. They remained devoted and compatible until the home-loving and retiring Lillie died of cancer in 1915. She bore seven children, five of whom survived to adulthood. The oldest, Rose Ellen (1891–1977), kept house for her father until his death, and although his domestic life amid children, relatives, and in-laws was sometimes turbulent, it rarely distracted him from work. His second daughter, Lucile (1896–1968), expressed it best when asked about her father at the time of the aqueduct's completion. "Father?" she laughed. "You mean that man who sometimes eats dinner with us."

The city's growth and change, which Mulholland had helped to create, also destroyed most of the landmarks of his private life. By the 1960s, his former family dwellings had disappeared, as had the ranch in the San Fernando Valley whose land he had purchased and which his oldest son, Perry (1892–1962), had cultivated. The Boyle Heights home at Sixth and Cummings, where the family had lived from 1894 to 1920, was bulldozed to make way for the Santa Ana Freeway, while his later home at 426 South Saint Andrews Place was razed for an apartment building. At the end of the twentieth century, the only habitation that remains is the house of his nineteenth-century childhood in Dublin, Ireland.

ORIGINS AND ANCESTORS

Mulholland was the second son of Hugh and Ellen (Deakers) Mulholland, born in Belfast, Ireland, on September 11, 1855. Although Mulholland's parents were Dubliners, his father, a mail guard, was stationed in the north when the first three children were born: Thomas (1853) and William (1855) in Belfast, Hugh Patrick (1856) in Derry. By 1860, the family had settled permanently in Dublin, five years after the end of the Great Famine, which had left Ireland a dispirited and depleted land. Mulholland later displayed little nostalgia for his native land, and when asked at the height of his career if he would not like to take a trip back to the old country, he snapped that he never wanted to see the "damned island" again.

His parents were of the newly emerging Catholic lower middle class, which had been pushed off the tenant farms of their ancestors and crowded into the cities. Since the early eighteenth century, Mulhollands had lived in northeastern Ireland, midway between Belfast and Dublin in Counties Meath and Louth, tenant farmers on the vast lands of the viscount Massarene. William's grandfather Patrick Mulholland had been born in 1798, the year of the French invasion of Ireland; his father, Hugh, born in 1827, came into the world during the first of the horrific famines that afflicted Ireland for the next forty years.[3]

Because an Irishman then was allowed to vote only if he had twenty acres, and because Patrick, a farmer in Colinbeg, had ended up through inheritance with only seven acres and a house, he and his sons were disenfranchised. Hugh, as the seventh and youngest son of a man who owned only seven acres, was at best without great expectations, and therefore had to cast about for a means of survival. Lord Massarene required his tenants to serve in the militia (Home Guard), and if a young man demonstrated ability and dependability he could advance to the position of a guard on the coaches that Massarene ran between Derry and Dublin. By this process, Hugh Mulholland worked his way into a position as a mail guard with the Royal British Mail. As there was no civil service until 1855, the only way to attain such employment was by nomination. Once nominated, one was assured of serving for the rest of one's life.

In his later public life, William Mulholland tended to couch his father's employment in general terms: "connected with the Government mail," he would say, as if he perceived something *infra dig* about his father's work. Yet in those desperate days in Ireland, a guard job with the

Royal Mail would have been a coveted post that offered a good living and some prestige, the term *royal* being not meaningless in Victorian Ireland. Long waiting lists were customary for this position, which demanded that a man be under thirty years of age and that he must pass a test on the three R's. That Hugh qualified for such a post also indicates his literacy, which was not to be assumed in his era, when 47 percent of persons ages five and up in Ireland could neither read nor write.[4]

A famous superintendent of mail coaches, Thomas Hasker, kept a voluminous record of his career and was said to have loved his guards as a great commander loves his soldiers; indeed, in the entire development of the Royal Mail service, the key men were the mail guards. "Everything depended on their integrity," Hasker wrote, "their loyalty, their tireless zeal in the discharge of their very arduous duties, their hardihood of body as well as of mind." These same admirable qualities that enabled Hugh Mulholland to survive and prosper in Victorian Ireland also produced in him a rectitude and hardness of character that ultimately drove two of his sons a world away. *Cherchez le père* may well be the watchword for the character of William Mulholland, as an interesting parallel suggests itself between a father and son who each, in different times and worlds apart, demonstrated similar abilities and behaviors as trusted employees of public agencies.[5]

In old age, Mulholland told certain questioners that he had no recollection of his mother, who had died when he was seven, but to his children he sometimes spoke of her, remembering that her wit, lively nature, and love of song had been an antidote to his father's grim seriousness. A monument to this bright-spirited young woman stands in Glasnevin, the famous Dublin Catholic cemetery built under the direction of the great emancipator, Daniel O'Connell, and immortalized by James Joyce in the Hades episode of *Ulysses*. Inscribed on the granite stele are the words "Erected by Hugh Mulholland in memory of his beloved wife—Ellen. Aged 28 years who died 18th September, 1862." Grave records further reveal that also buried in the plot with her are two infant daughters, six other members of the extended family, and later, Hugh.

Ellen Deakers had been to America as a girl before she returned to Ireland to marry Hugh Mulholland. Family lore has it that she grew so homesick for Ireland (and Hugh) that her father allowed her to return. Although no record has been found, their marriage occurred sometime between 1850 and 1852. Ellen's brother, Richard Deakers, Jr., however, remained in America and prospered in his father's draper's business in Pittsburgh during and after the Civil War. Because of Richard, two of

Ellen's sons, William and Hugh Patrick Mulholland, would one day find their way to Pittsburgh and ultimately to California.

A DUBLIN BOYHOOD

Willie Mulholland grew up in postfamine Victorian Dublin, a dispirited, shabby provincial capital, notorious for its slums, drinking, wenching, and political and religious contentions. Yet in this benighted place, within a few miles of each other, grew three little boys, all destined to become remarkable men. The most privileged, and one year older than young Mulholland, was Oscar Wilde, who lived in central Dublin on upper-class Merrion Square with parents who were both stars in the Anglo-Irish social firmament: his father, a prominent physician, and his mother, a poet and keeper of a literary salon. In a meaner part of town in a rented house on Synge Street, with a drunken father who made life seem hopeless for his stoic wife and their three small children, dwelled the youngest of the three (a year younger than Willie), George Bernard Shaw, enduring what he later called his "devil of a childhood." The coincidence of the three not only illustrates that talent can arise anywhere but also suggests that the Dublin environment, for all its shabbiness, was vibrant. Throughout the starving years, although Ireland's population declined by 20 percent, Dublin's increased by 9 percent, with 250,000 people living in the city proper and another 50,000 better-off inhabitants in the suburbs. (Dublin's growth was the result of rural depopulation as tenants of small holdings were forced off the land; farms from one to five acres declined from 182,000 in 1845 to 62,000 in 1910.)[6]

Sickness and death pervaded Willie Mulholland's childhood home. Consumption took two baby girls and then Ellen herself shortly after the birth of a sixth child, leaving Hugh, at thirty-three, a widower with four motherless boys, the youngest an infant of a few months and the oldest not yet ten. The impact of these losses upon the seven-year-old Willie is unknowable. On the evidence, he must simply have repressed much of what he felt and turned to his brothers and schoolmates for whatever companionship and warmth they could offer. His propensity for male friendships must have derived from that time when he lost the women of his family and, given the male-dominated Victorian world he lived in, perhaps concluded that it was safer to invest his time in those who did not seem to go under so easily.

At the time of their mother's death, the oldest boys, Thomas and Willie, were in their second year at the O'Connell School run by the Christian

Brothers on North Richmond Street, only a short walk from their home. Today the Christian Brothers Schools are honored for playing a leading role in the Irish Revival and are recognized for providing elite training to the urban poor of nineteenth-century Ireland. A chief justice of Ireland who attended during the same years as the Mulholland boys later wrote that "the school course contained comparatively few subjects, but they were well and efficiently taught." Willie left the O'Connell School before completing the full course of instruction, but while there he worked through three readers, four levels of grammar, four of geography, and being most advanced in arithmetic, had achieved six levels by the time he left the school.[7] The reasons for his leaving are not clear and are certainly murkier than those of James Joyce, who, a generation later, attended the same school—and was ashamed to admit it—as his devotion to the Jesuits was so powerful that he considered the Christian Brothers mere drones by comparison. "Paddy Stink and Mickey Mud," his class-conscious father, John Joyce, had dubbed two teachers there. Willie's chief memory (at least, the one he chose to tell his own children) was of the day, when almost ten, he joined his schoolmates at a special school assembly and heard the father superior tell them that a terrible tragedy had just befallen the world. In America, President Abraham Lincoln had been assassinated and they must all bow heads and pray for his soul.

Of greater immediate impact on young Willie than Lincoln's death, however, was the arrival of a stepmother. In 1865, after three years as a widower, thirty-six-year-old Hugh married Jane Smith, aged thirty, in Drogheda, where her sisters lived, wives of sea captains. By all accounts, Jane Smith tried to be a good mother to her stepsons, but as she herself was pregnant the next year with her first child (a daughter, Mary, born in 1867), followed by two sons (Joseph, 1869, and Michael, 1871), her attention never could have been fully focused upon the lively older boys, who were out of the house at school during the day and accustomed to a degree of independence. Tom, the oldest, eventually became a conforming son who followed his father into the postal service and at the time of his death from consumption at thirty-eight in 1891 was still unmarried and living at home with his widowed stepmother. Willie and Hugh Patrick, however, were another story. Only eleven months apart, they were almost like twins in their closeness, although family members who recalled them in later years always spoke of Willie as if he were much older and more dominating than Hugh. Described as "a pair of Dublin jackeens"—city kids who ran the streets with their buddies—they became the rebels of the family. At fourteen, Willie ran off to sea for the first time after a severe beating from his father because of bad marks at school (by then he probably was attending a national school, although all records are lost). He returned home and after a brief period of study entered the British Merchant Marine at fifteen. The following year, the father enrolled Hugh Patrick, then also fifteen, into the British Navy.

FOUR YEARS BEFORE THE MAST AND WESTWARD HO!

Although much of Dublin in the 1860s was decrepit, life on the waterfront was energetic and vital, with its port being developed into one of the best-run harbors in Europe. Between 1860 and 1914, over 38 million tons of debris were dredged from the Liffey, while docks, berths, and the new Alexandra Basin were added to the existing facilities. Irishmen such as John Wigham were pioneers in introducing gaslight to lighthouses and illuminating buoys. The famous Bailey light with its 9,000 candlepower, revolving lens, and gaslight that produced flashes in groups became the model on all the world's coasts. These matters, rather than Latin declensions or the Celtic Revival, were what excited the imagination of Willie Mulholland. Although surrounded by political tension and unrest (the 1860s saw the rise of the Sinn Fein movement), he dreamed of neither academic achievement nor Irish independence but rather of going to sea at a moment in the nineteenth century when, with the supremacy and protection of the Royal Navy, Britain possessed the largest merchant fleet in the world.[8]

After four years at sea, Willie would later enliven many a night circle in California construction camps and in the high Sierras with his tales of seafaring days on a three-masted, full-rigged merchantman, the *Glenifer*. Those yarns have vanished with the smoke of the long-dead campfires, and only meager accounts remain of his nineteen Atlantic crossings to various ports in North America and the West Indies and his eventual promotion to navigating officer of the vessel.[9]

Life at sea initially must have suited the young and enthusiastic Mulholland. Freed from the strictures of family, church, and a crowded household, he did not find the cramped confines of ship life as punishing as might a youth from a more solitary or privileged environment. By now, he had developed a propensity for inner solitude that he would retain for the rest of his life. Long before Joyce had articulated his youthful intention of employing "silence, exile, and cunning," Willie Mulholland, without saying so, had pursued such a course. He retained a lifelong love of the sea but at the end of four years concluded the sailor's life "would get him nowhere in a material way." After sailing into New York City on June 9, 1874, Willie returned to shore with a sense of pride in having survived the nautical experience and in having deepened his understanding of life and men amid the motley crews of the fo'c'sle.

In his first summer in America, Willie found work on a vessel in the Great Lakes and later cherished the memory of its Irish captain, who noticed him on deck one night as he stood at the rail and whistled a tune. Remarking that he had not heard that air since leaving Ireland, the captain made friendly talk with his young crewman, who would always remember how the encounter had eased his loneliness in a strange land.

In the winter of 1874–75, Mulholland worked in a lumber camp in Manistee, Michigan, where a logging accident altered his life and left him permanently appalled by the reckless deforestation he had witnessed. The mishap landed him in a camp hospital with an injured leg that developed erysipelas (a streptococcal infection). From his bed, he overheard doctors mention gangrene and the probable need to amputate the limb, so he bolted and somehow made his way to Cincinnati. There, at the age of twenty, weak and barely alive from his recent illness, having only a few dollars left and too proud to let any of his family know of his plight, he reached the lowest point of his young life. "Why bother?" he wondered. Ahead he saw nothing but endless years of grinding work with no reward. As he wandered the streets in this hopeless state, he suddenly heard a choir of clear-voiced boy sopranos singing the *Gloria in Excelsis* in a nearby church and felt a surge of hope and renewed courage. He entered the church and spent an hour in prayer and meditation as the suicidal mood passed and his zest for life returned.

Willie next became attached to an itinerant mechanic with a team, who drove through the country sharpening scissors and repairing clocks. He later told his daughter, Rose, that he grew so fond of the gypsy life that he had to force himself to give it up and follow the urge to do something worthwhile with his life.

During Willie's *Wanderjahr,* Hugh Patrick, having learned that his brother had left the sea, followed suit and upon reaching American shores jumped ship. As one of the family later explained his desertion from the British Navy, "Hugh got over into some American port, and he ejected himself." Somehow the brothers found each other and made their way to the Pittsburgh home of their American uncle, Richard Deakers, who never forgot the day in the autumn of 1875 when Willie and Hugh "just showed up on the doorstep."

The Mulholland boys had landed on a prosperous threshold, for the

Deakers family in all ways qualified as "lace curtain Irish," living as they did in the Hazelwood section of Pittsburgh in a pleasant home with a cook and servants. Uncle Richard was well established as a Pittsburgh dry goods merchant and husband of Catherine Thorpe, a native of Ireland, who, by all accounts, was the abiding genius of the family business. Her few surviving letters indicate that she was a highly competent lady concerned with maintaining order, proprieties, and good appearances. Devout Catholics, she and Richard had eight children, and they now charitably welcomed their two stray nephews from Ireland.

For almost two years, cousins Willie and Hugh stayed at the Deakers home and worked at their uncle's dry goods store. Events took an ominous turn, however, when another relative remembered only as "Uncle Hobson" showed up on the Deakers doorstep carrying tuberculosis. Soon some of the Deakers children were presenting symptoms of the disease, and by 1875 two had died. As three of Catherine's brothers had been ranching in San Diego County since 1868, the family made the wrenching decision to leave the city where they were so well established and join the throng of health-seekers who had begun crowding into certain areas of California to the extent that historian Hubert Howe Bancroft worried that they had introduced a weakness into "our exceptionally youthful and hardy community by an increasing proportion of delicate women and children."[10]

The journey was a disaster. While Richard stayed behind to close business, the other Deakerses followed medical advice that the Panama or Horn routes were best during the cold months and booked passage on a large, three-decked vessel, the *Crescent City* of Liverpool, which sailed out of New York Harbor on December 9, 1876. Its passengers included not only Catherine Deakers, her six surviving children, and Uncle Hobson, but two stowaways, Willie and Hugh Mulholland. Shortly before reaching Colón, however, the pair were caught and dumped at the Isthmus of Panama. Probably because they lacked the twenty-five dollars in gold to pay for the train ride to Balboa, they were forced to hike the forty-seven miles across the isthmus. (As an old man Mulholland rather grandly glossed this over, once declaring, "I would walk that far today to make twenty-five dollars.") Once on the west side, they signed on to a Peruvian man-of-war headed for Acapulco. From there they found another ship that took them to San Francisco. Ashore, they bought two horses and made their way southward to find the Deakers family in Los Angeles.

When at last they reached the pueblo, they learned that the voyage had continued to be ill-fated for their Aunt Catherine. Two more of her children, already weak with consumption, contracted typhoid and died on shipboard. When the ship from Panama had finally made port at Santa Monica, one of the younger Deakers children, fourteen-year-old Ella, looked about, caught her first glimpse of Los Angeles, and was aghast. It was, she later said, a place "where nothing looked like anything."

CHAPTER 2

The City of Angels

1877

A PUEBLO OF 9,000 SOULS

Ella Deakers was not the first to find Los Angeles unprepossessing. "A queer little Spanish town," young author Margaret Collier Graham reported to her parents in Keokuk, Iowa, shortly after she arrived in Los Angeles in 1876 with her consumptive husband. "There is not much to say of this wonderful city of the Angels," she wrote. "We have been walking around nearly all day through the narrow streets full of strange Spanish and Chinese faces, passing long rows of low adobe houses swarming with dusky children and reeking with foreign odors." Yet beyond the "squalor and nastiness," she also saw "groves of green trees, orange, fig, walnut, and acres of grape vines."[1]

What greeted the Mulholland brothers when they rode into town in January 1877, in addition to depression, drought, and their relatives' straitened circumstances, was a settlement in the grip of a smallpox epidemic. By February 9, fifty-three cases had been reported, the majority in the "Spanish quarter," where resistance to receiving the new Jenner vaccine was high. The editor of the *Los Angeles Daily Star* called for the ouster of the city's health officer, charging incompetence, while also offering readers such health tips as the claim that because Jews did not eat pork, they were less subject to bilious attacks and, therefore, less apt to suffer from smallpox. By May, after the city had spent $21,000 to fight the disease, including funds for the Sisters of Charity to maintain one of the pest houses, the epidemic subsided.[2]

Willie and Hugh had arrived in Southern California at the end of its first thirty years of American rule, as the Anglos gained dominion over the Spanish-Mexican colonizers and landholders. Only five months earlier, in September 1876, the Southern Pacific Railroad had connected Los Angeles from the north to the rest of the world. With the arrival of the railroad, Major Horace Bell, old-time scout, soldier, and owner-editor of the caustic *Porcupine*, had anticipated a new civility after the preceding lawless years' culmination in the ghastly 1871 Chinese Massacre in Nigger Alley, during which Chinatown was sacked, many were shot, and twenty Chinese hanged. When western correspondent J. Ross Browne wrote in *Harper's Weekly* about a visit to Los Angeles in the 1860s, he had described the social tone as one in which men discussed manhunting as a sporting activity: "Why, you would sit at the breakfast table of the Queen of the Angels and hear the question of going out to shoot men as commonly discussed as would be duck shooting in any other country. At dinner the question would be, 'Well, how many did they shoot today? Who was hanged?'" As Major Bell later observed, "It was barbarism gone to seed. The decent minority—for there was such a group of nonentities—wondered when and where it would all end." He fervently believed that "the day the whistle of the first S. P. locomotive was heard in Los Angeles, civilization started on the upgrade."[3]

Even with the railroad, however, Los Angeles was not much in the 1870s. Its population was 9,000, and its biggest local excitement one January day featured a bucking bronco from the Wells Fargo office at First and Spring that, after breaking the tongue on an old rattletrap wagon parked near the courthouse steps, proceeded to kick the vehicle to smithereens. As a crowd collected to watch, a local reporter noted, "it was the most fun for the boys since Christmas." The city council was spending its best efforts on a long debate over the need to drain the frog pond at Second and Olive. Because of the current drought, the streets were being sprinkled at night, so that when the council, which sat in night sessions, complained of the noise and nuisance, one editor noted that it was because "the rumble of carts disturbs the sleep of our councilmen, who can sit longer and talk more than any municipal body in the U. S., for they do not believe that brevity is the soul of wit."[4]

With relish and colorful rhetoric newsmen chronicled the day, paying special attention to crime and punishment. Stealing a ham could earn a man thirty days on the chain gang, as could chronic public drunkenness ("afflicted with intemperance" was one description). Red-light houses abounded, and their occupants were variously described as ladies of the night, nymphs of the pavement, or when a more genteel or discreet tone seemed indicated, *nymphes du pave.*

The mention of water—or lack of it—was frequent, and fire was always a menace. A house at Twelfth and Olive burned down because no water was in reach for the fire wagon. Brush fires and smoke in the San Gabriel and Cahuenga foothills were not uncommon summer sights, and in September 1878, a fire on the Kester Ranch (part of present-day Van Nuys) in the San Fernando Valley burned between two and three thousand acres of wheat.

Los Angeles's heterogeneous nature was already apparent. A Chinese funeral—CELESTIAL FUNERAL EXTRAORDINARY—caused one reporter to muse in cross-cultural allusions, "A Chinese High Muck-a-Muck Speeded Across the River Styx—The Dead March in Saul Struggling with the Cacophony of a Chinese Band." The pueblo celebrated Mexican independence with a parade and grand ball attended by Carrillos and del Valles at about the same time that General John Charles Frémont was in town on his way to Arizona and General William Tecumseh Sherman made a station stop on the train en route to San Francisco. Dominating these picturesque groups, however, was a rising class of Anglo-Yankee settlers and entrepreneurs bent on bringing into the American mainstream this town sometimes derisively referred to as the Queen of the Cow Counties. They believed in progress, and a new technology always excited their interest, as when a leading local citizen, L. M. Holt, purchased a model of Mr. Edison's latest invention, the phonograph, and invited friends to the Odd Fellows hall for a public demonstration. There, grown men sang such ditties as "Mary Had a Little Lamb" into a mouthpiece and produced a cylinder that afterwards could be played back, reproducing the sound of their voices to the wonderment and delight of all.[5]

This jumble of types and styles, mingling visions of the future with a touch of the romantic past, appealed to young men of ambition and dreams. Mulholland was attracted to the local lore of the pueblo; the tales of the notorious *bandido* Tiburcio Vasquez, who had been captured only two years before; and the exotic intrigues of Chinatown, with its opium dens and gambling parlors presided over by the mysterious men with queues. In spite of the troubled times, Los Angeles's overall mood was optimistic, as newspapers expressed the boosterism of a small town straining for a grander destiny. In a few years that boosterism would materialize in Los Angeles's first great land boom.

FIRST DAYS IN A WESTERN OUTPOST

As an old man, Mulholland remembered the pueblo with affection. It was "so attractive to me that it at once became something about which my whole scheme of life was woven, I loved it so much." But he probably came closer to the mark years earlier, in 1907, when he told a reporter, "After a month ashore I decided I had enough, and so started for San Pedro to find a ship. On the way down there a man who was driving a well offered me a job and I took it." The man who stopped the decamping Mulholland was Manuel Dominguez, grandson of the original grantee to Rancho San Pedro, one of the great Spanish land grants. Hired to dig artesian wells with a hand drill near the recently founded town of Compton, Mulholland later claimed that "the first well I helped to drive changed the whole course of my life. When we were about six hundred feet down we struck a tree. A little further down we brought up some fossils. These things fired my curiosity. I wanted to know how they got there and so I got hold of Joseph LeConte's book on the geology of this country. Right there I decided to become an engineer."

First, however, William and his brother Hugh went gold-seeking in Arizona Territory. Ignoring all reports of Indian uprisings in 1877–78 and amid rising hostility among the southern Arizona Apaches under Victorio and Geronimo, the two Irish greenhorns traveled to Ehrenberg, northeast of Yuma, where placer finds had been reported. To raise money for purchasing outfits, they found casual employment on the steamboats along the Colorado River, thus introducing Mulholland to the river that would one day figure so large in his history. In the midst of their unrewarded efforts, United States troops rode through Ehrenberg warning that Geronimo might be on the warpath. Needing no further encouragement, the two hightailed it back to Los Angeles. Years later, Mulholland told a reporter, "I went to Arizona prospecting—a very dangerous business at the time. There were a great many hostile Indians about . . . it was one of those cases where presence of mind was best secured by absence of body."[6]

LEARNING THE WATER BUSINESS

During his apprentice years, Mulholland became familiar with the various water projects that had been undertaken in Los Angeles over the twenty years before his arrival. Today near the plaza at the north end of

Olvera Street lies a line of diagonally set brick that marks the old water course of the Zanja Madre (Mother Ditch) that made life possible in the early pueblo. Surrounded now by paved streets crowded with automobiles and draped overhead with power lines that clutter the often smoggy skyline, the original town center struggles to survive as a last vestige of the Spanish-Mexican days, and a seeker must negotiate crowded aisles of curio booths and candle shops in order to look down on the spot where precious water once flowed from the Los Angeles River. To find the source of the Zanja Madre's water, however, one must leave Olvera Street and go north past New Chinatown along North Broadway to the freight yards of the Southern Pacific Railroad Company. There, east of the rail yard, lies the Los Angeles River, today a concrete flood channel but once a stream that Mulholland called "the most valuable asset of the municipality."[7]

The Spanish crown had granted the pueblo ownership and control of its water, and one of the first tasks of the original settlers *(los pobladores)* in 1781 had been to create the Zanja Madre with communal labor for both domestic use and irrigation. Although by the end of the nineteenth century, most of the zanjas had been moved underground, in earlier times, they had been an integral part of the landscape. John S. Hittell described them in *The Resources of California* (1863): "most of them have a body of water three feet wide and a foot deep running at a speed of five miles per hour. They carry water from the river to the gardens and are absolutely necessary to secure the growth of the vines and the many fruit trees." By the time Mulholland arrived, nine tributary zanjas flowed from the Mother Ditch to provide irrigation water to various districts of the city, while a private water company controlled water for domestic use. Although both irrigation and domestic uses drew their water from a common source—the Los Angeles River—their histories are intertwined but distinct.[8]

The zanjas—a distinctive and picturesque feature of the old pueblo often rhapsodized by travel writers who hearkened back to biblical images of oases in the desert—eventually outlived their usefulness in an expanding urban scene. By the opening years of the twentieth century, when the city had over 100,000 inhabitants, the zanjas, after 121 years of service, had nearly all been covered, piped, and converted to city water mains. Thus, early in his tenure as the city's water superintendent, William Mulholland reported to the board of water commissioners in 1903 that "the *zanja* system has made its usual poor showing for the year." Citing receipts of $5,809.75 and expenditures for upkeep of $8,537.15, he recommended abandoning the system, which was done in the following year.

In the Spanish-Mexican era, water-tending had always been a municipal effort, with each family at first making a communal contribution of labor. As the settlement grew, however, local government took over its management to assure an adequate water supply for both domestic use and the irrigation of crops in the semiarid land. The *zanjero* (water steward) was to become as important a figure as the *alcalde* (mayor). Although the Americans introduced their form of municipal government with mayor and city council, they retained the Spanish-Mexican practice of appointing a zanjero just as the *ayuntamiento* had done. (*Zanjero* was officially anglicized to *water overseer* in 1881.) Americans quickly demonstrated their capitalistic tendencies with various attempts to gain ownership of the city's water supply, along with its land. Major Horace Bell, who cast a sardonic eye on life in the pueblo in those transitional years of the 1850s and 1860s, described a convenient arrangement whereby the mayor and the council, after granting a contract in currency for excavating a ditch to expand the growing town's water system, would in reality pay the contractor with municipal acreage. In his gratitude, the contractor would then kick back a fraction thereof to the mayor and each member of the council. So flagrant was this practice that at one city council hearing, George Hansen—a civil engineer and pioneer of 1850, then serving as county surveyor—hung up for study certain tract maps, across each of which he had boldly inscribed with red ink, "This tract stolen when B—was mayor"; "This tract stolen when C—was mayor"; and finally on the largest of all, encompassing thousands of acres, he named the current mayor: "This tract stolen when Joel H. Turner was mayor."[9]

In the first years of American occupation and up to 1868, several private ventures into the management and distribution of domestic water were attempted and failed. Most conspicuous and ambitious were those of Prudent Beaudry, who, along with partners Dr. John Griffin and Solomon Lazard, in March 1868 helped finance the new Canal and Reservoir Company, which was to advance his real estate dreams. Beaudry, once described as prim and Napoleonic, was a French Canadian from Quebec, reputed to have made and lost several fortunes. He had been in San Francisco during the Gold Rush and came to Los Angeles in the 1850s. After prospering with his brother, Victor, as a smelter in the silver strike at Cerro Gordo, Beaudry bought quantities of real estate to subdivide and develop, as he envisioned hillside homes on the dry empty hills north and northwest of the city. He called his arid tract Bellevue Terrace, and he prevailed upon the city to grant additional land for building a dam in the barren chaparral hills west and northwest of Figueroa on the site of today's Echo Park.

Until then the city's water systems had involved only the central district around the plaza and along the river to the south, much of which was really river bottomland. Beaudry's new dam would allow the city to grow westward, an idea that many of the old-time conservative residents found farfetched, but to which the "intrepid Beaudry," as one of his associates called him, gave his full support. Thus, Beaudry became the power behind the Los Angeles Canal and Reservoir Company, to which the city granted a portion of land on March 23, 1868.

The president of the new Canal and Reservoir Company was the engineer and former county surveyor George Hansen. His previously mentioned sarcasm notwithstanding, Hansen was considered a man of integrity as well as an able engineer. The company bought the old Feliz Ditch and the water rights of the Feliz Rancho, which took its water from the Los Angeles River about six miles northwest of the city. The company planned to improve and widen the ditch and then run the water by creating a canyon through the hill by either a cut or tunnel so that the flow would debouch onto the plain and thence into a dam of stone concrete. The course followed along what is today Glendale Boulevard, cut through where Silver Lake Reservoir now stands, and from there emptied into a dam at the site of present-day Echo Park. This dam, also called Reservoir No. 4, had an extension ditch down to approximately where the Bonaventure Hotel stands today at Fifth and Figueroa. Because the water dropped 78 feet from the dam to the ditch, the Barnard brothers, who had been brick makers, conceived the idea of building a wool mill on the site to take advantage of the power and thus created the first industrial manufacturing plant in the City of Los Angeles.

Having successfully made one water deal with the city, Beaudry, Griffin, and Lazard nearly succeeded in wresting away all rights from the municipality when they proposed to the city council a complicated fifty-year lease that in reality would have resulted in the eventual sale of the waterworks and the stripping of the city's right or authority to fix or control water rates. At that time the sentiment against municipal ownership ran strong in the city council. One member argued, "Cities and towns can never manage enterprises of that nature as economically as individuals can, and besides, it is a continual source of annoyance and is made a political hobby." After a tie vote, the president of the council broke the deadlock with his vote favoring the lease. Mayor Don Cristobal Aguilar vetoed the ordinance, however, for he was a native Californian who knew what the water would always mean to the city. Although his veto saved the city's water rights, it did not end the matter, for the trio came back with a proposition for a thirty-year lease at $1,500 a year. This new proposition still included promises to fulfill such conditions of the earlier scheme as installing hydrants at downtown street crossings, providing free water in the city's public buildings, and constructing in the plaza an ornamental fountain that was to cost not less than $1,000.[10]

Although other interested parties offered proposals, the council was stacked in favor of the trio and committed what Mulholland would later call an act of "civil idiocy" by railroading through the infamous thirty-year lease. Charges of favoritism and political pull flew as two members of the city council who voted for the lease, William H. Perry and A. J. King, soon became members of the water company's board of trustees, formed immediately after the lease was secured. Griffin, Lazard, and Beaudry now incorporated this new entity, which would control the city's domestic water supply under the name of the Los Angeles City Water Company. For this plum, they paid the bargain rent of $1,500 a year, while the politicians who had signed away their city's water rights for the next third of a century congratulated themselves on having exorcised the specter of municipal ownership. Only Mayor Aguilar mitigated the situation by insisting, before reluctantly signing the agreement, that the mayor and the council would retain the right to regulate water rates. Thus the city was not stripped entirely of its power to manage its most vital resource, although the wrangle with the company over rates became an annual council event.

The lease ultimately proved a cheat to the city, for as the private company prospered and the value of its resource grew more precious, services did not always increase accordingly and the works fell into "a woefully inefficient condition," remembered Mulholland, who also recalled the politicking that resulted as each side manipulated for an advantage. "The fat earnings also proved an attractive lure to the politicians who promptly invoked the power delegated to municipal legislative bodies by the constitution of 1879 to regulate rates. This power was freely used to extort all sorts of contributions from the Company to the last year of its existence."[11]

Within two years of obtaining the lease, the company had maneuvered the city into a rent reduction so that for the next three decades it paid $400 a year, or a little over $33 a month, for all the water it wanted from the Los Angeles River. This absurdity came about when, after waiting two years for the company to fulfill its side of the bargain and remove

an abandoned reservoir from the plaza and build the long-awaited fountain, the council got up enough ginger to request that the work be done
pronto, only to be unpleasantly answered by the company's attorney with
a threat of lawsuit if the city persisted in its demands. Cowed, the council supinely agreed to reduce the annual rent to $400 a year if the com-
pany would deliver on its promise. Happy in its windfall, the company
at last tore down the old brick reservoir, landscaped the plaza, and erected
the long-promised fountain.[12]

The water company next built the Buena Vista Reservoir with a 378-
foot elevation to replace an earlier one northeast of the Catholic cemetery and in 1875 set out to improve the system by laying a twenty-two-
inch iron main from a point near the Buena Vista Bridge down to Main
and First Streets. The partners also pursued independent projects. Griffin
and his partner, John Downey, a former governor of California and now
president of the Los Angeles Water Company, expanded the domestic
water service on their tract in East Los Angeles (today, Lincoln Heights).
Meanwhile, the tireless Prudent Beaudry continued to develop his hill
lands to the west at his own expense, grading and installing streets, laying lines, pumping water and building two reservoirs, for which he was
said to have spent the then staggering sum of $95,000.[13]

When Beaudry became mayor of Los Angeles in 1875, he remained
determined to see his hillside developments succeed. Undaunted by
drought and depression, he proclaimed with the voice of the ultimate
booster, "I intend to spend money and keep on spending money in improvements and grading streets until this locality meets the attention it
deserves, and it will not be long, I assure you." He then built another,
even larger reservoir with a 5-million-gallon capacity on Angelino Heights.
Also called Beaudry's High Reservoir, it was a basin excavated in solid
rock with an elevation of 596 feet. This completed the series of reservoirs built for the various water systems in place when William Mulholland took his first job with the Los Angeles Water Company in the spring
of 1878.[14]

CHAPTER 3

The Private Water Company and Its Owners

1878–1879

THE IRISH APPRENTICE

When William Mulholland began his job with the Los Angeles Water Company as a deputy zanjero, he tended the main supply ditch from Crystal Springs, then the chief source of the city's domestic water supply. Paid $1.50 a day and housed in what he once described as "a shack near the Old Sycamore Tree" (the latter then a historic landmark in early deeds and records), he settled in for two years of work and study that were to lead to his career as a hydraulic engineer. The locale remained important to him. Visiting as an old man over fifty years later (after the Saint Francis Dam disaster had ended his career), he pointed out a sturdy oak to a young woman then writing a graduate thesis on the domestic water system of Los Angeles. After telling her how he had rescued it as a tiny three-inch seedling about to fall into the ditch he was digging, he approached and, apparently moved by the memory of that life-affirming act, reached out, "touched it lovingly and looking at it, said half to himself, 'I saved its life once. I wonder if it is conscious of my presence today?'" The old Chief's closest friends and associates later acknowledged his affinity for the place when they chose it as the appropriate site for the William Mulholland Memorial Fountain, erected in his honor by the City of Los Angeles in 1940 and restored and rededicated in 1996.[1]

In that shack by the river, he had, for the first time in his life, a place of his own. There, after a day of clearing brush and debris, removing dead animals from the stream, and keeping the flow in proper channels, he began the studies that ultimately led to his fame as a hydraulic engineer. Although the nearby Los Angeles River was no mighty stream such as one associates with great cities, it was, as Mulholland remembered affectionately, "a beautiful limpid little stream with willows on its banks." Originating in the western foothills of the San Fernando Valley thirty miles from the plaza and fed by the waters of the Tujunga Wash, its watershed covered about 500 square miles, and without it no city ever would have arisen.

Mulholland worked between the west bank of the river and the canal owned by the water company. The river supplied irrigation water to the zanjas and so came under the control of the city zanjero, while the channel, or main supply ditch, fed the city's domestic water system and belonged to the private company. Thus, the two groups of workers under different jurisdictions inevitably came together, sometimes in harmony but often in conflict. Although the waters of the main supply ditch flowed from Crystal Springs, contention over their source led to a great conflict between the city and the water company after the company contended that the city could not claim the springs, as they did not arise from the Los Angeles River. The controversy and legal arguments over Crystal Springs grew labyrinthine through the years and culminated in a memorable 1898 court case that concluded in the city's favor.

Crystal Springs was on the Los Feliz Rancho, six or seven miles northwest of the city's plaza. Today commemorated by Crystal Springs Drive, which runs through the golfing grounds of Griffith Park, the property had been purchased by the Los Angeles Water Company from the Feliz estate in 1868, after it had secured its thirty-year lease from the city. Formerly called the Feliz Springs, it was a marshy tract of slightly over fourteen acres south of an elbow bend where the Los Angeles River begins its southerly course through the city towards the sea. Judge Benjamin Eaton (brother-in-law of Dr. John Griffin), who earlier had superintended construction when the Canal and Reservoir Company bought the old Feliz Ditch and the water rights of the Feliz Rancho, once testified in court that the springs then "consisted of a body of water surrounded by tules" that trickled down to the river. After paying $8,000 for the property and christening it Crystal Springs, the new owners formed an auxiliary company called Crystal Springs Land and Water Company. They promptly declared it private, not city, property and proceeded to build a canal to carry water to a ravine in today's Elysian Park, where they built the Buena Vista Dam in 1868–1869.[2]

By July 1878, only months after Mulholland had been on his new job, a deputy zanjero was assigned to guard the river because parties were stealing water on the Feliz Ranch. By October, the city received a favorable judgment in the state supreme court, which ruled against the removal of water from the Los Angeles River by Leon Baldwin, the first American owner of the Feliz lands. This did not end the problem, however, for in the summer of 1879, Mulholland's second year on the river, the city council's zanja committee toured up the river and discovered three heads of water in use on the Feliz Rancho and three more on the Corralitos lands of Andrew Glassell, owner of a part of Rancho San Rafael on the river's east bank. (A head was in theory one hundred miner's inches, but because a miner's inch varies according to local agreement, Mulholland once archly described a head of water as all that the user could manage to take.) The city ran the water back into the river and placed guards on the ditches, but the guards were driven off, and the problem remained. Only years of court cases would finally settle the issue in the city's favor, but all that summer along the river where Mulholland worked and lived, the deputy zanjeros kept an alert watch for water thieves. They were authorized to arrest anyone taking water who could not produce a permit from the city.[3]

That same year, Reservoir No. 4 (Beaudry's High Dam, also called the Woolen Ditch Dam—today's Echo Park Lake) flooded part of the city when the embankment broke along the line of the exhaust tunnel. It released a flood that poured south to Agricultural Park (present campus of the University of Southern California) and east to Main and Spring Streets. No deaths occurred, and although property and crop damage was extensive, the greatest loss was the water itself, as fears arose of a possible water famine in the coming hot, dry summer. Two months after the flood, Mulholland was engaged in frantic efforts to repair and reopen a broken water line that threatened to shut off the city's supply. On June 10, a break in the canal and reservoir ditch flooded and clogged the main supply ditch. Although Buena Vista Dam was fortunately full at the time, all consumers of city water were warned to use it moderately for two or three days. These mishaps, however, were simply minor precursors of those that lay ahead as the city began to boom.

WATER BOSSES AND CITIZENS

For all its local power and ability to stir controversy, the Los Angeles Water Company was small, even for a town of only 10,000. Its owners may have been among the wealthiest in the community, but when Mulholland started work, the entire personnel consisted of fewer than a dozen people: Superintendent Fred Eaton; Assistant Superintendent Tom Burns; Burns's assistant, Thomas Brooks; a crew of four laborers; and two ditch and reservoir tenders. Eaton and Burns received salaries of $100.00 a month; the rest were paid $1.50 for a ten-hour day. The young superintendent was the son of builder Benjamin Eaton and the nephew by marriage of owner John Griffin. Being well connected to the management, he enjoyed the privilege of taking outside engineering work, so that he spent only about half his time with the company. The business office was near the plaza, and the working equipment was minimal. Brooks remembered that in the early 1880s the company had only two horses and two light one-horse spring wagons, two crude moisture-tapping "crows," some water buckets, and a few hand-operated "San Jose" pumps. The city's zanja department was equally rickety if one is to judge from a contemporary news item that reported the zanjeros failed to work one day because all the shovels were broken; in January 1882, the zanjero likewise reported to the city council that he had thirty-three broken shovels that needed to be replaced.[4]

Although Mulholland as a deputy zanjero was only a digger and tender of ditches, the city zanjero, or water overseer, ranked next in importance to the alcalde. Indeed, the zanjero's salary was larger than the mayor's, a precedent that stands to this day. When Mulholland went to work for the private water company, the city zanjero was Don Cristobal Aguilar, three-time mayor of Los Angeles (1866, 1868, and 1871), who in 1868 had vetoed the ordinance that would have handed over the city's water rights forever to private ownership.

Taking over from Aguilar in 1881 was Charles N. Jenkins, a crusty veteran who had been one of the only two men from Los Angeles to fight in the Union Army during the Civil War. After capture and a long imprisonment in Andersonville, he had returned to a Los Angeles so violently pro-Southern that he was forced to hide on San Clemente Island until some of the postwar hatreds died down. (Major Horace Bell, the other Union soldier from Los Angeles, claimed the pueblo had been so ardently pro-Confederate that "at the close of the Rebellion it was the most vindictive, uncompromising community in the United States.") Charlie Jenkins, hot-tempered and combative, was city zanjero from 1880 to 1886. Thus, during the years of his apprenticeship, Mulholland became familiar with the clashes between Jenkins and water company workers. Thomas Brooks, in charge of constructing water mains for the company, remembered that once as he had stood in a ditch inspecting the work,

Jenkins rode up and without preamble demanded that Brooks fire two men who, Jenkins felt, were interfering with city plans. When Brooks refused, Jenkins pulled a knife from his belt and demanded that Brooks come out of the ditch so that he could cut out his heart. When Brooks still refused, Jenkins simply pulled around and rode off.

Although Jenkins was of Southern California's vanishing old lawless Anglo world (his brother, William, a member of the Rangers, had been with the posse that brought down Joaquin Murrieta), and although he kept the city council anxious with his demands, he also improved and modernized the city's zanjas and wrote a city directive prescribing much more stringent duties for the deputy zanjero. Shortly after his appointment in 1881, the *Los Angeles Herald* noted that "The new Zanjero, Mr. Charles Jenkins, is giving great satisfaction . . . not only keeping the water supply of the East side up to the requisite standard, but he is actually selling water to the profit of the city. We note with pleasure any departure in the direction of swelling the city's revenues." Jenkins's reign represented the high point of the zanja system, for with the land boom of the 1880s, agricultural land was increasingly sold for commercial and residential use.[5]

Citizen complaints about water were constant, and "warm and nasty" and "so offensive to the taste and smell, as to be not only undrinkable, but positively nauseating" are only a sample. Stories one summer circulated that "a man had been drowned in the reservoir and that the water had become tainted by the putrid carcass allowed to remain there." Then variations of the story appeared: it was a cow, a horse, a sheep; two drowned "Chinamen," then a Chinaman and a horse, then two Chinamen and an Indian; finally, an Indian and a mule. Next, a leading physician of the town opined that "the offensive effluvia was nothing less than that emanating from decomposed human remains," for "he had smelled that smell on several occasions, and knew whereof he spoke." It would be good not to drink the water, he warned, lest there appear a vast amount of diarrhea and typhoid fever.[6]

Finally, William J. Broderick, the collector of the water company, explained that the water from the mains had been shut off to make necessary repairs. When the supply had been turned on again, the rush of water had stirred up the offensive slimy sediment that had been collecting in the old pipes for a long time past. With repairs completed and a steady supply of water back in the pipes, he assured, the troubles should end. Two nights later, however, the "City Water Company got a handling without gloves in the Council," and a committee of three councilmen along with the health officer were delegated to look into the matter. Investigations and debates continued for three months until October, when the board of health announced that the reservoir of the Los Angeles Water Company was "in as good condition as it can be kept."

Among the water company's owners were some of the leading capitalists in Los Angeles. (Some called them the political bosses of the city.) According to Thomas Brooks, they took a personal interest and active role in management but insisted that they receive a good return on every dollar spent for improvements. Mulholland's later opinion, however, was that because they all were men of large means and property, "the business of the water works was but a mere incident to them."[7]

The first to have a direct hand in shaping Mulholland's destiny was William Hayes Perry (1832–1906), president of the water company. Perry's life seemed to embody the wisdom of Horace Greeley's advice, "Go west, young man." The son of Michigan pioneers and a carpenter by training, in 1853 Perry joined a wagon party of about fifty, which included Colonel William Welles Hollister, of Santa Barbara, who was bringing a large band of stock to the Coast. Bedraggled and broke when he reached Los Angeles in 1854, Perry began work as a cabinetmaker but shortly advanced his affairs by opening a furniture store and factory, which in a few years, with the addition of new partners, prospered. By 1873, the firm of Perry, Woodworth & Co. was a leading dealer in lumber, hardware, and building supplies as Perry's acquisitions increased: timber lands, lumber mills, shipping vessels, and spur tracks to railroads. He became a president and director of banks and of gas and oil companies. (In 1867 he had received the first franchise to supply gas for the city after agreeing to furnish free gas for lamps to illuminate the principal crossings on Main Street.) With his endless business connections and social involvements, Perry epitomized a laissez-faire capitalist of the Gilded Age.[8]

The story has often been told how Perry, as he made his rounds of the waterworks, spied a worker vigorously clearing weeds and debris along the zanja that led to the reservoir at Elysian Park. Calling out "What are you doing?" he received a rude "None of your damn business" from the young worker, who continued shoveling. After Perry had flicked his reins and ridden on, a fellow worker informed the rude laborer, Mulholland, that the departing man was president of the water company. Prepared to be fired, Mulholland headed for the office to turn in his time but instead was advanced to foreman of the work crew. For the next twenty-four years, Perry remained Mulholland's boss, although the man who proved most significant in Mulholland's career was his immediate superior, the superintendent and engineer of the water company, Fred Eaton.

AN ENGINEERING FRIEND

Although the friendship and later discord between Frederick Eaton and William Mulholland has become notorious, perhaps the most remarkable aspect of their relationship is that they should ever have met at all. Not only were they born oceans and continents apart, their backgrounds and social standing were equally diverse. Almost exact contemporaries, they were born within days in September 1855, but whereas Mulholland was born to obscure Dubliners, Eaton came from the top drawer of pioneer Los Angeles society and was surrounded throughout his childhood by a family of strong, enterprising men and accomplished women. His father, Benjamin S. Eaton, attorney, engineer, newspaperman, and superior court judge in Los Angeles County (1865), was also one of the founders and promoters of the Indiana Colony that evolved into the City of Pasadena. His mother, Helena Hayes, was one of the sisters of Benjamin J. Hayes, the noted jurist and judge who presided over land cases during the transition from Mexican to American rule and whose writings and diaries have been invaluable in reconstructing much about that period of California history. At the time of Fred's birth, Helena's sister, Louisa Hayes, had become the first woman teacher in the Los Angeles public schools. She subsequently married the enterprising Dr. J. S. Griffin, who, in addition to his medical practice and ownership in the water company, was superintendent of schools and an associate of the senior Eaton in the development of early Pasadena.[9]

Eaton claimed that his serious interest in engineering began only after his marriage in 1875, but he had begun his apprenticeship at fifteen under Charles E. Miles, the first engineer for the Los Angeles Water Company. Miles, called Prince Charlie by his associates and later referred to as the father of the water system, was an able hydraulic engineer who, in 1868, had built the small earth dam known as the Buena Vista Reservoir for the water company in the hills of present-day Elysian Park. From that water storage site, a pipeline 7,730 feet long ran down Buena Vista Street (now North Broadway), over Short Street (now Sunset Boulevard), to First and Main Streets. As the first cast iron pipe to be laid in Los Angeles, the project was innovative in its departure from the traditional open ditch or Spanish zanja. By 1880, both Fred Eaton and Bill Mulholland would find themselves at work on expansions of Miles's projects.[10]

Advancing in the Water Business

1880–1886

Mulholland's promotion in 1880 moved him from his shack near the river to another rude dwelling west of North Broadway in the hills of what is today Elysian Park (approximately the present site of the Buena Vista Power Station). He was to be in charge of a crew laying an extension of twenty-two-inch pipe parallel to the west bank of the river to the toe of the Buena Vista Reservoir, which, under Fred Eaton, was undergoing one of its several enlargements. Living alone and largely indifferent to creature comforts, Mulholland possessed minimal housekeeping skills and would later recall that the place "looked like the devil." His only heat was a smoky stove that his uncle, Roderick Deakers, rigged up for him. The tree-planting urges persisted, however, as out of his own pocket he paid for and planted more than a thousand saplings, as well as cultivating seedlings in salmon cans whose original contents had comprised a main staple of his diet. Around the site of the Buena Vista Reservoir he set out eucalyptus, palm, willow, and live oak, some of which still live over a century later on land now used as a park and picnic grounds.[1]

While Mulholland laid pipe during the summer of 1880, Fred Eaton went off with his father for three weeks on an expedition whose findings would one day alter the history of Southern California—and ultimately, some would say, that of the entire state. During the drought of the late 1870s, Benjamin Eaton had become concerned about water for his vineyards in Pasadena. Aware that cattlemen in the south took their herds north during the summer to Owens Valley, where water was abundant,

Eaton decided to investigate. The scouting party included his sons, Fred and the younger George, along with two friends, Ed Mosher and J. H. Campbell, the latter a lad of thirteen who as an adult would serve as both city clerk and then city treasurer of Pasadena. Almost fifty years later, Campbell spoke of the three weeks he had spent with the Eatons in the Sierras. Judge Eaton, he remembered, took "measurements of water on all the streams, even going high into the mountains." His son Fred Eaton would one day make profound use of what he observed with his father that summer.[2]

Throughout the 1880s, the increasing urbanization and anglicizing of Los Angeles dictated changes in the local water system. In 1881, the city council adopted the words *ditch* and *water overseer* to replace *zanja* and *zanjero* in the interests of easier pronunciation for English-speaking people. What did not change, however, were the continuing water complaints from the city's almost 12,000 residents. (The 1880 census reported 11,128 inhabitants.) "There exist small fish about the size of the aphis in the liquid which the City Water Company palms off for drinking water," began a typical grievance. Chronic dissatisfaction with a company perceived to be indifferent to the public interest would lead eventually to public ownership of the waterworks. That lay years ahead, but in his weekly *Porcupine,* Major Horace Bell would claim that in 1882 he had been the first to advocate "a municipal water system under the ownership and control of the people themselves." In 1884, certain members of the city council pressed for the forfeiture of the water company's franchise, but to no avail.[3]

Eaton and Mulholland in the first blush of their acquaintance must have stimulated each other's engineering passions, as their early years at the water company constituted a sort of on-the-job technical institute. Not only did these two intelligent young men of such divergent backgrounds work together in dealing with immediate problems in the field; they also discussed theoretical matters along with the latest events in hydraulic engineering. They would not have been indifferent, for example, to the announcement in the local press on January 7, 1882, that the largest aqueduct in the world—New York's 40¼-mile-long Croton Aqueduct— had just been completed at a cost of $12 million. In contrast, Eaton and Mulholland struggled with a small-town water system that seemed always to be on the brink of collapse.

When work on Buena Vista was completed four years later, Eaton was about to leave the water company and Mulholland had already left to pursue other ventures (one was a junket with his brother, Hugh, to Washington State, "to study rivers"), so that neither was present in August 1884, when a group of city fathers inspected the newly enlarged works. In its improved state the reservoir was now surrounded by a 14-foot-thick wall of cement and stone, some of the largest of which weighed 2,000 pounds. Surrounding the outside of the wall was a ditch or moat to catch any overflow from the dam, while walks planned as a scenic promenade around the dam offered panoramic views of the city and surrounding hills. Although assured for the time being of an adequate water supply, the city could never take its water for granted, as warnings soon appeared in the papers admonishing users of company water to guard against "unnecessary waste in water closets" and to sprinkle their grounds only between 6:00 A.M. and 8:00 A.M. and between 6:00 P.M. and 8:00 P.M.[4]

Mulholland's move to the Buena Vista area in 1880 not only represented an advancement (and a salary increase from $50 to $65 a month), but also brought him closer to downtown and the public library. A dedicated reader, Mulholland once pronounced, "Damn a man who doesn't read books." His granddaughter, Lillian Sloan Macedo, never forgot his rebuke when he came upon her as a child playing jacks on the sidewalk with a little friend. "Aren't there any good books in the house that you girls could be reading?" he wanted to know. Mary Foy, the city's first librarian, remembered him as "one studious young man" who had once taken out and then renewed for many months "an enormous volume on water power development which nobody else ever wanted to read."[5]

Mulholland's desire to get ahead is evident in his joining with Eaton in 1881 to become officers of Los Angeles Lodge No. 35, International Order of Odd Fellows. Such a group provided not only sociability but also access to the men who controlled civic and business affairs. For as open and free-wheeling as Los Angeles may have seemed, its prosperous new American arrivals from the East and Midwest carried with them class and caste distinctions to which a young Irish immigrant worker would have been sensitive. A visiting journalist in March 1882 artlessly revealed the increasing assumptions of Anglo superiority in this remote provincial community when he first described Los Angeles as bustling, crowded, and full of "strangely different" sights: the old Spanish town with its one-story adobes, "simply a portion of the old Aztec empire left in the centre of a progressive town of our great republic"; the Chinese quarters, "a little chip from China"; and the Frenchmen, the Germans, the Jews, and the Indians, "gathered here for health, or pleasure or profit." But, he confessed, he breathed freer as he entered on Fort Street (now Broadway), "the beautiful, new and refined Anglo-Saxon part of the town with its fine architecture, its well-kept lawns, its evergreen trees."[6]

CIVIC DISCONTENT AND COMPANY DERELICTION

Mulholland's move to the Buena Vista area in 1880 also increased his contact with the water company's staff and directors, a handful of men who not only enjoyed a camaraderie at work but also seem always to have closed ranks when embattled by the frequent public attacks and complaints aimed at their performance. In all his years with the company, Mulholland kept a discreet public silence about his employers. Only after the city took over in 1902 did he voice critical comments, for as he once told his nephew and namesake, William B. Mulholland, "When you go to work for somebody, you do *his* work for him."[7]

Tom Brooks, who came to work for the water company in 1883 during one of Mulholland's absences, found the system somewhat primitive. To lay pipes, men simply lowered them with ropes into the trenches; only as the decade came to an end did more sophisticated equipment such as cranes, tripods, power pumps, cutting or welding torches, and dry-tapping machines begin to appear. Brooks described directors reluctant to make important improvements if doing so meant incurring heavy indebtedness, while he and three laborers struggled to keep the water flowing to customers: "They insisted that every dollar spent must show a return of 100 cents." "Some job!" he once laconically remarked as he went on to explain that in those days a man had to love water and unexpected shower baths if he wished to tap into a cast iron main to insert one-inch or smaller pipe for the purpose of providing a water service. The only equipment for the job was "a rather crude affair known as a 'crow' or 'the old man' which was chained to the main about to be tapped while a special drill and reamer produced an opening with the correct taper" for the corporation cock (the part that connected the service pipe to the main). The trick was to withdraw the drill under full main pressure and drive in the corporation cock without getting oneself and everyone in the neighborhood soaked. Because one needed a hand as steady as a surgeon's to do the job well, and even then, because there could be no guarantee, nearby storekeepers and occupants of rooms in line with the water were warned to close doors and windows while pedestrians were alerted to beware of a soaking.

The water company seemed to pay little heed to public relations, as when it announced in May 1879 that it would charge extra for any household with a bathtub. The city health officer quickly protested the fee to the city council, arguing that bathing should be encouraged in the city. The company was constantly laggard in its responsibilities to install fire hydrants and supply water free of charge to public schools, city hospitals, and jails. At one point the company even balked at paying for the water that the fire company used to put out blazes. In the matter of street sprinkling, the city and the company fought a long court battle over who should pay for the water used to lay the dust in the streets. Nor was this an inconsiderable matter, as dust was the smog of that era. In 1884 a disgruntled real estate man reported to his hometown paper in Marshalltown, Iowa, that Los Angeles was the most lied about city on the Coast and that its inhabitants lived for seven months of the year in so much dust that "they can't see. . . . As to water," he wrote, "it is controlled by a few and you must pay just what they have a mind to ask." The *Evening Express*, then owned in part by members of the water company, indignantly described the critic as a failed real estate salesman who was "too honest to work and too lazy to steal."[8]

Water company representatives never failed to attend the city council's ritual of establishing new water rates at the beginning of each year, and at the least hint of a rate reduction or demand for increased services, they bleated holy poverty. In 1882, for example, the council announced reductions that the company declared unacceptable, claiming to have expended $400,000 up to this time, to have declared no dividend for the past three years, and not to have paid salaries to the president and officers. After two years of court battles, the state supreme court ruled in favor of the city, but the company promptly appealed, and the wrangling continued.[9]

While this debate proceeded in the courts and work advanced on the Buena Vista Reservoir, a landslide in 1882 destroyed a flume at the north end of Pearl Street (today, Figueroa), so that Eaton had to begin excavating a new tunnel that would connect the main supply ditch from Crystal Springs to the Buena Vista Reservoir. A *Times* editorial worried that the city "has created a good part of its debt by its water system, having spent probably $200,000 on the whole" to produce works "of an ephemeral character as yet." It concluded with the hope that something more substantial than the present trenches and wooden flumes would appear. With a promise to continue its water mains out to Washington Street, the water company began laying a four-inch cast iron main from Seventh and Main to the southern line. As the area south of Washington was then largely fruit orchards and vineyards supplied with irrigation water from the zanjas, the new line proved adequate for domestic purposes for the next few years.[10]

A BRIEF LEAVE OF ABSENCE

Because the city looked forward to a transcontinental train connection, hopes stirred in 1884 for better times, as notices of new land developments increased along with booster talk about rising values. Heavy rains and flooding in the winter and spring of 1883–1884 provided plenty of jobs repairing damages to the city. Rainfall of 38.18 inches added up to the wettest period in the history of recorded rainfall in Los Angeles, whose annual average was less than 15 inches. One old-timer remembered that every bridge except the one at Aliso Street was swept away, along with from thirty to fifty houses at the southern end of the city. Many lives were lost, and rail service between San Francisco and Los Angeles stopped for six days after the track washed out in the San Fernando Valley.[11]

When Mulholland returned from his sojourn in Washington State, he and Fred Eaton attempted unsuccessfully to contract independent jobs with the city. Next, with another associate, D. McGregor (who later worked on the Owens Valley Aqueduct), Mulholland submitted a proposal to clean the cave in the Zanja Madre Tunnel and "repair and re-timber it in a substantial manner." This time the city awarded a contract on October 14, 1884, requiring that the job be completed by December 14. With final bills handed to the city on December 2, Mulholland returned to the water company on December 20 as foreman of a large crew of laborers working on a ditch and flume connecting to the Buena Vista Reservoir. One surviving company record book indicates that the workforce varied between twenty-eight and eighty men during the six months that the job continued. For a ten-hour, six-day week, the crew received $2 a day, while Mulholland received $3, or $72 a month.[12]

Shortly thereafter, in a dispute with Perry in early 1885, Eaton walked out on his job as superintendent of the water company. The following year he became the city surveyor and engineer at a salary of $200 a month. With the boom of the 1880s under way, he and his father also began to profit from increasing sales of their holdings in Pasadena. Perry replaced Eaton with W. J. Kelley, whom Brooks later described as "more of an office man than an engineer."

ON THE SESPE

Mulholland remained on the water company payroll until September 1885, when he left for a job in Ventura County that kept him away from the city for the next eight months. Perry and associates had engaged him and another engineer, Philip (Phil) Wintz, to design and lay out a system of irrigation ditches for the Sespe Land and Water Company, which was to supply water and power to the embryonic town site of Fillmore. Wintz, a young Virginian recently employed by the water company, became a lifelong associate and would one day be in charge of building the Hai-wee Dam on the Owens River Aqueduct. As the Sespe Land and Water Company's location in the Santa Clara Valley was fifty-two miles from Los Angeles with only one train running daily, the men remained there from late spring to the end of summer 1886. They grew to love the beauty of the area along the Santa Clara River with its background of rugged mountains and picturesque ranchos. Probably in payment for services, the men acquired approximately twenty acres each, on which they planted orange trees along Sespe Creek. (Mulholland would hold his Sespe land until 1903 or 1904, when he sold because of water scarcity.) Ironically, although this area would one day figure in the greatest tragedy of Mulholland's life, his original work on the Sespe has endured. As late as 1966, a Fillmore rancher reported that the routes Mulholland and Wintz laid out for irrigation lines were still in use. Perry's group also hired Mulholland to study the Sespe River's potential to provide power. He concluded that it would never be a feasible source of power because of its "fitful and unreliable" stream flow.[13]

When Mulholland returned to town in midsummer 1886, the water company was in the midst of a major overhaul of its Crystal Springs system. As the land by the river had become increasingly settled and culti-vated, especially near its bend by Griffith Park, the banks had eroded and the water become progressively silted. Where the stream had once run clear, it was now clouded and often foul tasting, "a by-word of reproach" among the citizenry. At a cost of $100,000, the company was about to build a closed-conduit system 27,000 feet long and able to deliver about ten mil-lion gallons of water to the city every twenty-four hours. The three-by-four-foot conduit, beginning at the eastern edge of Griffith Park and ex-tending to Dayton Avenue, was to be constructed of "butt-cut redwood—all carefully selected—the finest uniform quality of this kind of timber ever used in a similar undertaking on this coast," ran the company boast.[14]

Devised by local civil and hydraulic engineer J. P. Culver, the plan was not without its critics. Eaton's opposition to the use of wooden pipe may have led to his leaving the water company, for years later, in a pamphlet written for a 1905 Oakland sewer bond election, he harked back to 1886, when he had "watched the construction of a wooden conduit by the LA City Water Co., which I had formerly advised against, and observed its gradual decay thereafter, rendering the conduit entirely useless in less than ten years." Mulholland, awarded the contract to oversee the tricky flume and tunnel-building section, was to write in the same pamphlet that the timbers, lined with Portland cement and covered with earth to insure transporting the water in the cleanest possible circumstances, were giving trouble within three years of its completion and "in less than ten years had to be abandoned altogether."[15]

Shortly after beginning the project, the water company, for reasons unknown, took over Mulholland's contract and retained him as general foreman. At a time when labor organizations were struggling to break the contract system and obtain an eight-hour day, the company crews rotated on ten-hour day and night shifts so they could complete the difficult task by winter. Living in the camp with a crew of almost ninety men, Mulholland earned $5 a day while the company charged him $2.50 a day for board.

While working on this job, Mulholland became a naturalized American citizen in October 1886. When he registered to vote for the first time in November, he gave his occupation as contractor and his address as Sepulveda (then a section on the west bank of the Los Angeles River south of Mission Street). The job was also memorable because of the arrival of two tough, roistering Irish workingmen, Pat Harkins and Handsome Brady. Mulholland in aftertimes enjoyed recalling a payday when the paymaster had tossed down two silver dollars to Harkins as he completed his ten hours in the muddy ditch. As Harkins caught and flung them aloft again, he shouted to Brady, "To hell with Poverty! Tell the old lady to get out the big pot."

As work on this project wound down, fate intervened to secure Mulholland a job that, in a sense, became his for life. In November, during a recreational weekend at Santa Monica, Superintendent Kelly dropped dead of a heart attack. Perry first offered Assistant Superintendent Brooks the position, but Brooks, then twenty-four and feeling his lack of experience, suggested that Mulholland at thirty-one might be better suited. Perry offered, was accepted, and at the end of 1886, Bill Mulholland became superintendent of the waterworks.

CHAPTER 5

The New Superintendent

1887–1892

BOOM TIMES AND WASHOUTS

Mulholland's advancement to superintendent of the water company coincided with the city's first land boom, which, though brief, was dramatic. The population of Los Angeles bounded from 11,000 to 50,000 in less than three years as large areas of heretofore unoccupied land were promoted and established as town sites and new communities. With the upheaval, the need for public services became acute, so Mulholland and Eaton, the two chiefly responsible for maintaining the city's mains and drains, must at times have felt that they were the busiest men in the expanding town.

Heavy rains fell during Mulholland's first months as superintendent, and although rainfall for the entire season proved normal (14.05 inches), downpours in February did almost as much damage as those that had fallen in 1883–1884. Streets flooded, bridges went out, and water from the Big Tujunga Wash roared into the Los Angeles River, destroying the railroad bridge east of San Fernando. Rumors arose that Reservoir No. 4 north of Temple Street was about to break as it had six years before. Although the reservoir held, to avert a panic, police were sent out to assure neighboring dwellers that they were safe. The city remained isolated for several days and suffered extensive damage. For a time, bridge washouts completely cut off Boyle Heights.[1]

Serving his second year as city surveyor, Eaton had to deal with problems not only of sewage and sanitation but also those of reordering the growing city's infrastructure, such as grading and recontouring streets in the hilly downtown areas and replacing bridges that had been lost in the flood. Controversy encircled him through most of the year, beginning in March when he had to defend himself against the charge that he had made false statements to the mayor and the council as to the cost of bids to replace the destroyed Kuhrts Street Bridge, where Main Street extended east across the river. Suggestions that he had colluded with a low bidder for his own profit drew a spirited self-defense from Eaton, who denounced "ignorant men who will attempt to bring disgrace upon a man hitherto having the confidence and respect of his fellow-citizens." Ultimately, the council found no blame in the matter, or as a *Times* reporter skeptically commented, "And you are right, and we are right, and all is right as right can be."[2]

Eaton spent much of the remainder of the year making plans and surveys for an enlargement of the city sewerage that would involve expenditures of over a million dollars and that, under the name of the Eaton Plan, was presented for consideration to the city council in September. In November, a reporter caught up with Eaton on his return from an expedition to scout a route for the Salt Lake and Los Angeles Railroad, which would come into the city through the Arroyo Seco. Asked about his sewer plans, Eaton said they were still under consideration but stressed that "the situation is getting serious," for in the Vernon district surplus sewage was overflowing the land. Before leaving office at the end of the year, Eaton also revealed that his predecessor, George C. Knox, had taken thousands of dollars' worth of maps made during his term of office, along with field books containing notes of his surveys. Eaton asserted that no one who worked for a salary with the city had a right to help himself to such property. Eaton announced that he would not seek a reappointment to the post and that he already had engagements for the coming year.[3]

Meanwhile that summer, citizens once more had complained of too many fish in their water pipes and of dust and inadequate street sprinkling because the foot-dragging water company had failed again to install the hydrants that the council had ordered it to provide. The company finally did comply, so that by the end of the year, Mayor William Workman expressed satisfaction with the streets' condition. Other vexations confronted Mulholland in his first year as superintendent as several terrible fires had resulted in heavy property loss because the water company's mains had been too small to supply enough water to extinguish the conflagrations. As it became incumbent upon the company to enlarge the system, Mulholland found himself supervising the placement of increasingly large pipelines into the most heavily populated areas of the city.

At the end of 1887, most of the vineyards and orchards in the city having been subdivided so that zanjas were no longer much needed for irrigation, Mayor Workman called for a system of filtration and improved piping. He optimistically believed enough water was available "to supply a city of over a million people if it is properly handled. . . . We are blessed," he concluded, "with an abundance of water in Los Angeles, but the condition of some of it when it comes to the houses for domestic use is the reverse of tempting."[4]

EATON HAS A FAILURE

At the beginning of 1888, while Mulholland was still installing the pipeline on Buena Vista Street, Fred Eaton left the city to work on one of his engagements. During the boom years, no piece of Southern California seemed impossible to develop, so in 1887, in the remote scenic northwest corner of the San Fernando Valley on land formerly owned by Benjamin F. Porter, arose yet one more town site, this one bearing the idyllic name of Chatsworth Park. The promoters, George F. Crow and a group called the San Fernando Valley Water Company, predicted a glorious future for this beautiful but isolated area by the Santa Susana Mountains and announced grandiose plans for one of the "largest systems of waterworks in this part of the State." Eaton was to oversee building a series of reservoirs that would catch the overflow from a main dam in Brown's Canyon, through which, the promoters falsely claimed, flowed the headwaters of the Los Angeles River. A year after the completion of Eaton's first reservoir, however, the dream went a-glimmering. Not only did the boom end, but on December 24, 1889, after heavy rains, Eaton's dam washed out. Because the area was unpopulated, the damage was not catastrophic except to the builders' hopes.[5]

MULHOLLAND MOVES UP

At the beginning of 1888, during the laying of the 22-inch pipeline on Buena Vista Street, Mulholland lived nearby and alone in digs at 103 Buena Vista. When he registered to vote that year, he stated that he was superintendent of the city water company and for the first time identified himself as a civil engineer. Not all of his job demands, however, were of an engineering nature. On May 11, 1888, he was summoned to the Buena

Vista Reservoir to recover the body of a young woman whose life in California had turned bitter. Boys out hunting had seen her walk up to the reservoir, place her hat, wrap, and satchel on the ground, climb the stone wall of the dam, and jump. While the others ran off for help, one of the boys leaped in to save her, but she struggled so violently that he failed. With rope and grappling irons, Mulholland and the dam keeper retrieved the corpse from the water.[6]

The boom proved profitable to the water company, for on March 8, 1888, its directors called a meeting of stockholders to consider "the propriety of increasing the capital to $1,240,000, divided into 2,400 shares." A week later came word that the company would build new headquarters, and on Saturday, May 26, the old overcrowded office building north of the plaza was vacated as everything and everybody connected to the domestic waterworks moved to a new, two-storied brick and stone building at the corner of Alameda and Marchessault Streets.[7]

Said to have cost $11,000, the new building had a ground floor that comprised a workshop and storage area for pipes and equipment. From an entrance on Marchessault, a winding stone stairway climbed to the second floor and opened into a reception room, "well-lighted and comfortably arranged," separated from the main office by "a large carved window of pitch-pine." The main office contained desks for the clerical staff, while one wide door led off to a room for Chief Clerk S. B. Caswell's special use. All the interior fixtures were of polished pitch-pine, neat but not gaudy. In addition to a directors' boardroom upstairs, there were sleeping rooms for the superintendent and the company foreman. In effect, Mulholland and Brooks were house mates and, moreover, were never away from the job. One reporter explained, "Hitherto, when any accident occurred during the night, it was a matter of extreme difficulty to procure the company's workmen to repair the damage, but the presence of the superintendent and the foreman upon the premises at night renders it now a matter of less difficulty to attend to any damage and have it at once remedied, though it occur in the dead of night."[8]

Mulholland now lived as if back on shipboard, with round-the-clock interruptions to sleep. This may have proven no great hardship, however, as his children remembered that he never seemed to need much sleep. He was a lifelong catnapper who could doze off in a car or train for fifteen or twenty minutes and awaken fully refreshed and alert. He claimed to have acquired this ability on watches at sea, and it was to serve him in good stead during the years of aqueduct construction when he traveled constantly and arduously between Los Angeles and Owens Valley.

Out of that brief period when Mulholland and Brooks shared living quarters, they forged a lifelong friendship, for both men stayed with the water company to the end of their working days. At the time of his retirement in 1938, Brooks had been with the city's water system for fifty-five years. Associates said that Tom Brooks never took a vacation in his life, and once, as he and Mulholland watched some laborers work on a ditch, Brooks remarked that the men were growing old, to which Mulholland replied, "Yes. They got old working for you." One of the few who knew Mulholland well in his early years with the water company, Brooks later remembered that when they first met, "Bill Mulholland's library consisted chiefly of Fanning's Treatise on Hydraulics, Trautwine's Engineer's Pocket Book, Kent's Mechanical Engineer's Pocket Book, a Geometry, a Trigonometry, and Shakespeare's Works." He was also, Brooks remembered, "very fond of Grand Opera."[9]

MARRIAGE AND A GOLD WATCH

Within two years, however, Mulholland moved on to a new living arrangement, for in 1890, he married. Also that year he received a gold watch from a grateful water company for services beyond the call of duty when he had braved the torrential rains of Christmas week, 1889–1890, to save the city's water supply. During the downpours, the Los Angeles River had changed its course and broken the water connections at Crystal Springs; or as company president Perry explained, "The Los Angeles River got on a tear, cut a new channel through an alfalfa patch, and came rushing down upon the brick conduit then forming the head of the system with such force that it was knocked into a cocked hat." The water brought with it such an accumulation of sand and detritus that it filled the conduit until only a small opening "about as big as your arm" remained. If it had closed completely, no water would have flowed to the city, and so the morning before Christmas 1889, "William Mulholland, superintendent of the company, jumped out of bed when the alarm was given, . . . and he didn't get a chance to undress and go to bed like a Christian for four days; but he got the conduit open, and the city was not without its regular supply of water for a minute." Perry estimated that in two hours' time, the damage had amounted to $100,000, adding, "I did not know but that the city would have to go back to water carts for its supply."[10]

Two weeks before he was awarded his gold watch at a company din-

ner, Mulholland married Lillie Ferguson. They had met when he was overseeing a major project across the river from her father's farm in the summer of 1889. With a crew of one hundred men and several foremen, he
had begun laying percolation pipes at Crystal Springs in an effort to improve and increase the water supply for a growing population that now
consumed the equivalent of the Buena Vista Reservoir's contents every
two days in summer and every three in winter.[11] Rather than travel back
and forth to office headquarters, Mulholland had moved out to the work
camp near a new tract development called Ivanhoe. Ivanhoe was a product of the boom, when tracts and town sites sprang up like weeds and
wildflowers in spring. Perhaps James Slauson caught the spirit of the times
best. When asked why he was laying out a town site in the Azusa district amid boulders, cactus, and dry wash, Slauson replied, "If it's not
good for a town it isn't good for anything."

Lillie Ferguson lived with her family in neighboring Kenilworth,
which, like Ivanhoe, was on Los Feliz lands, the general location today
identified by surviving street names taken from the novels of Sir Walter
Scott: Waverly, Rowena, Locksley, Kenilworth, and Ivanhoe. Rowena
Reservoir (northwest of Silver Lake Reservoir) also remains a landmark
of Ivanhoe. Kenilworth stretched to the northwest over the hills and
looked down on the banks of the Los Angeles River. Among those who
had purchased land there was Mulholland's future father-in-law, James
Ferguson, a farmer and former hotel keeper from northern Michigan.
Ferguson's ten acres lay north of present-day Griffith Park and bordered
the Crystal Springs Land and Water Company's main supply ditch, where
percolation pipes were to be laid. When the company wished to situate
a correct surveying line and needed to drill a hole slanted toward a certain point, that point proved to be on James Ferguson's land. Seeking
permission to enter the property, Mulholland one day knocked at Ferguson's front door and was met by his twenty-one-year-old daughter,
Lillie. She later told her daughters that the first time she saw Mulholland, she knew that they would marry.[12]

The courtship was brief, and the nuptials took place on a warm and
cloudless day in the Fergusons' home on Thursday, July 3, 1890. When
the job at Crystal Springs was completed, the newlyweds moved to their
first "official" home at 914 Buena Vista (today, North Broadway), where
they remained for the next three years and where their first three children
were born: Rose Ellen (1891), William Perry (1892), and Thomas Ferguson (1894).

THE AMBITIONS OF EATON

The nineties saw Fred Eaton's ascendancy in civic affairs. By the end of
the decade, while William Mulholland remained a little-noted local figure,
Eaton had become mayor of Los Angeles (1899–1900). Aside from their
shared capacity for hard work and commitment to the engineering profession, the two men differed in ways that reflected their distinct backgrounds and paternal influences: Eaton's father was a California entrepreneur and civic booster driven by the competitive urge to strive and
win, whereas Mulholland's was an Irish public servant who had suppressed his spontaneity and individuality in the service of an inimical ruling order. By the time Mulholland married at almost thirty-five, Eaton
had been a husband for fifteen years and was the father of two adolescent children. He moreover maintained a full calendar of social, business, and civic activities among the leading lights of the town. On account of the lack of documentation, much about Eaton's character is
uncertain and perhaps will remain so. Existing contemporary accounts
suggest that, in addition to his outstanding engineering and business abilities, Eaton was an indefatigable go-getter and joiner. Except for the arts,
no aspect of civic life escaped his participation at one time or another.
He held city office as engineer and surveyor; he was active in real estate,
land, and water development; he served with the first volunteer fire
brigade; and he worked on committees for such events as the city's Fourth
of July celebrations and the formal opening of the Broadway Market. In
1890, he participated in the founding of the National Bank of California in Los Angeles, whose directors included associates from his water
and transportation ventures.[13]

Nor was he averse to frivolity, as a reporter once noted that "Fred
Eaton, in his trips to Santa Monica, devotes himself to showing bathers
a new trick in the waves. He has not ventured to try and instruct any of
his lady friends . . . as it is the marine equivalent of standing on your head
on horseback." Although he had been a Democrat when Mulholland first
met him, he later became an active Republican, even serving on the committee that greeted President Benjamin Harrison on his visit to the city
in April 1891. Earlier, in July 1890, he had been among the organizers
of the annual roundup and picnic of the Union League Club (a center of
Republican power), at what was then called San Juan-by-the-Sea, two
miles from Mission San Juan Capistrano on the oceanfront lands of Don
Marco Forster and Judge Richard Egan. The two-day revelry of important and wealthy Republican loyalists included such jollities as yacht

races, swimming, games, and feasts with a Mexican flavor. The menus featured barbecue, or "cabeza tatemada, hecho al gusto de Don Marco Forster," along with enchiladas, chile con carne, frijoles guisado, chiles rellenos, cerveza y vino tinto. The invitation also included the caveat, "if you expect to retire, take your blankets, and if this is your month to bathe furnish your own towels."[14]

Eaton was also involved in transportation schemes, including the promotion of an electric railway system for the city, which was rapidly outgrowing its horse-drawn car lines. He had participated earlier in a cable car company that failed and, while still city surveyor, had also played a role in gaining the Los Angeles, Salt Lake and Atlantic Railway's franchise for a right of way through the city via the Arroyo Seco. Partly impeded by economic hard times, none of these efforts succeeded until 1895, when Moses Hazeltine Sherman came to town from Arizona Territory with his partner, Eli Clark, and secured loans of $15 million dollars from Chicago capitalists to establish a successful electric rail system, the Pacific Electric Railway. When Henry Huntington later purchased the system, it evolved into the efficient interurban network of trolleys that today are happily remembered, not to say sentimentalized, as the Big Red Cars.[15]

Promotion and boosting were in Eaton's blood. A disciple of his father and uncles, between engagements of planning and building local dams, sewers, and rail lines, he planned land developments. On his wife's and mother-in-law's inherited property at Spring and Second Streets, he designed and built a commercial building, the Burdick Block, at a cost of $140,000. During the boom, he subdivided the Buena Vista Tract south of Chavez Ravine and immediately southeast of today's Dodger Stadium, and he surveyed and platted downtown tracts.[16]

A MENTOR FOR MULHOLLAND

While Fred Eaton pursued his hectic career in the 1890s, William Mulholland, apart from his newfound domestic life, could be said to have earned an advanced degree in engineering when, in August 1891, he patented a device utilizing wave force to generate power. He also acquired skills in business administration and political science, as he either witnessed or participated in the struggles and intrigues among the City of Los Angeles and rival private interests over who would control the waters of the Los Angeles River after the Los Angeles Water Company's lease expired in 1898. As he planned and oversaw the city's waterworks, he became privy to the company's business maneuvers, some of which flaunted such egregious unbridled laissez-faire capitalism that they called out for the pen of a Mark Twain, an Ambrose Bierce, or at the least, an O. Henry.

William Perry's influence was immense in the 1880s and '90s, when the notion of conflict of interest seemed a matter of indifference. At one point, he was both president of the water company and a member of the city council's water committee, the latter committee setting water rates for the very company of which he was president.

By this time most of the old Spanish-Mexican *hacendados* and rancheros were in decline, and many of the early Anglos of the pueblo were losing influence as the city filled with newcomers who were generally white, midwestern, and Protestant. During what journalist Phil Townsend Hanna called the Middle Nordic Period, old-timer Major Horace Bell, who had been a vibrant force in the legal and journalistic life of Los Angeles after the Civil War, grew increasingly disenchanted with his beloved Southern California. In the 1880s he had turned over the editorship of his lively weekly, *The Porcupine,* to his oldest son, Charles. It soon fell into decline, as Charles, a notorious boozer and womanizer, lacked his father's discipline and devotion to the job. The major himself became increasingly irrelevant in his hometown as he continued to engage in the old ways of the pueblo: drinking, roistering, challenging enemies to duels, and engaging in cantankerous litigations. Meanwhile, his sons provided scandal for the local press with their escapades of drunkenness, gambling, drug use, disorder, and in one instance, embezzlement. Although Bell was only two years older than Perry (and would outlive him by ten), he seemed to be from an earlier epoch—that of the freebooting, freethinking frontiersman—while Perry exemplified the entrepreneurial and acquisitive spirit of the Gilded Age.

Mulholland, a generation younger than either and shaped in another country, belonged to a new breed who believed that science and reason held the best hope for mankind. Though he may have shared with Bell a tart tongue and sometimes sardonic outlook on human folly, he nevertheless had cast his lot with entrepreneurs like Perry and Eaton. Eaton was Mulholland's colleague and instructor in engineering matters, but when it came to city politics and business, William H. Perry had also been a mentor.

By 1890, Perry and Mulholland had sustained a twelve-year relationship as employer and employee, but in spite of their bonhomie on the job—Tom Brooks remembered that many of the old water company's

board of directors meetings consisted largely of Mulholland's entertaining the assemblage with yarns of his seafaring days—a social chasm
yawned between the two. Perry, after all, was of the city's elite. His Pearl
Street home was the setting for frequent soirees and musicales that featured the singing talents of his daughter, Mamie, and for lavish parties
for the younger daughter, Florence, all of which were faithfully reported
in the newspapers. Into this social sphere Mulholland and his wife were
not to enter.[17]

CHAPTER 6

Water Plots and Politics

1893–1895

EXPANSIONIST MANEUVERS

Los Angeles's determination to grow in the 1890s led not only to the creation of a harbor through annexation of land adjoining the sea and the development of an efficient interurban transportation system but also to the laying of a groundwork for a water system that everyone hoped would provide an ample supply for a burgeoning population. Not surprisingly, the decade produced critical legal battles and decisions that arose from the city's struggle to maintain its rights to the waters of the Los Angeles River. Of one major and complicated water suit in the 1890s—*City of Los Angeles v. the Los Angeles Water Company*—a reporter once wrote, "The kaleidoscopic character of the city's water litigation becomes more pronounced with every step taken by either of the parties involved. Just when by persistent effort some faint conception of the case is formed by the ordinary intelligent layman a new turn or twist is given, and the status of the case in some of its parts or in whole affords new ground for speculation." Mulholland, who would testify in many of the cases, later wrote that the "bitterly contested" lawsuits ultimately "produced a compendium of facts that covers every phase of the subject that could possibly be gleaned either directly by observation or by theoretical inference."[1]

Much of the controversy in the 1890s concerned a crucial elbow bend of the Los Angeles River into which major feeder streams converged and flowed to the city from the San Fernando Valley, the Tujunga Wash, and the Coastal Basin. South of that bend and east of today's Crystal Springs

Drive in Griffith Park, on November 5, 1886, the water company established a new works on a few acres of marshy land and called its latest business entity the Crystal Springs Land and Water Company. The parent company then bought the new enterprise for a dollar and proceeded to assert that the underground waters of Crystal Springs did not come from the river but from springs discovered on its wetlands, thus declaring itself free from any claims the city might make upon the waters. The city had anticipated this maneuver, however, and in July 1886 had instructed Eaton, then city surveyor, to determine if the source of Crystal Springs waters were not the result of percolation from the river. Meanwhile, the water company proceeded to award Mulholland, now back from the Sespe and acting as an independent contractor, the job of building a tunnel and flume for the Crystal Springs project.[2]

Not until November 1891 did the City of Los Angeles bring suit against the Crystal Springs Company, enjoining it from making use of river water and asking damages of $225,000 for the water it had taken from the river during the past three years (1888–1891). The suit dragged through the decade until finally resolved in favor of the city in 1898 after a notable trial at which Eaton and Mulholland testified on opposing sides. This was, however, only one of many conflicts in which city and private interests struggled to gain control of water resources, especially after the boom had attracted a swarm of land speculators and fortune seekers, some quick to see the desirability of controlling the white gold of water in a semiarid land.

During the boom of the eighties, the corporate owners of the City Water Company and Crystal Springs decided to acquire some lesser systems. Shortly after they bought the Garvanza, or Arroyo Seco, works from Ralph Rogers in 1888, however, the boom died, and their expansion ceased until 1891, when they bought from Henry Hazard the East Side Springs Water Company, which delivered water east of the river and to Brooklyn Heights. Eventually they acquired the Highland Water Company servicing Highland Park; the Citizens' Water Company, headed by M. L. Wicks, which distributed water (badly!) to the hilly district northwest of Temple and Figueroa; and the Mountain Water Company, east of Brooklyn Heights. By the end of 1891, the Los Angeles City Water Company controlled almost all the city's domestic water supply.[3]

While the City Water Company—or the Grand Monopoly, as Horace Bell liked to call it in his *Porcupine*—was buying up local water plants and doing battle with the city council and the citizenry over water rates and services, local newspapers campaigned for municipal ownership of

1. Toma, or dam, for old ditch system
2. Zanja Madre, main ditch to plaza
3. Low-level gravity tunnel to supply Zanja Madre, used in 1879
4. Buena Vista Reservoir, built 1870
5. Tunnel for first eleven-inch outlet pipe from Buena Vista Reservoir
6. East Side Reservoir, built 1873, abandoned about 1887
7. Main supply ditch to Buena Vista Reservoir, used until about 1894
8. Tunnel constructed 1882 to carry supply-ditch water back of a landslide, abandoned 1894
9. Tunnel constructed 1887 for thirty-inch outlet pipe from reservoir
10. Buena Vista pumping plant, originally built 1893
11. Buena Vista inlet tunnel, constructed about 1894
12. Branch of tunnel, constructed 1929
13. Narrows infiltration gallery, started 1902
14. Pipe tunnel under railroad, built 1910
15. Elysian Reservoir, built 1903
16. Elysian Reservoir inlet tunnel, built 1908
17. High-gravity thirty-inch steel conduit to Elysian Reservoir, built 1908
18. Outlet tunnel, built 1910
19. New gate tunnel, built 1910
20. Landslide of November 1937

Map 1. Waterworks structures, Elysian Park area, showing waterworks structures dating from Zanja Madre days to 1937 (from Thomas Brooks, assisted by Laurance E. Goit, *Notes on Los Angeles Water Supply,* September 1938).

water. One reported in the spring of 1890 that not only was water scarce in some of the downtown public buildings but that during afternoons and evenings the upper portions of City Hall had no water at all. By summer, crowds demonstrated to protest the bad water service, so that the city, after much debate, decided not to wait for the termination of the water company's lease in 1898 but asked at the end of 1891 for a statement of the extent of the company's plant and the price for which it would be willing to sell.[4]

This decision set off a curious episode of intrigue and apparent collusion between the water company and parties from out of town. In response to the city's proposal, President Perry promptly replied that although he would have to consult with his board of directors and other stockholders before establishing an exact amount, he himself figured the price of the properties at $2.5 million. Debate ensued, with many feeling the figure too high. But the city's desire to take control of its water grew, along with the fear that the water company might sell its property to another private company (which it had every right to do). Thus, under a new management, it might manage to delay the city's resumption of control for perhaps another fifty years.[5]

The fear proved well founded, for in January 1892, one day after a court decision had defeated the city's attempt to annul the franchise of the Citizens' Water Company, a letter in the *Los Angeles Times* attacked the water company. Singling out Fred Eaton for special opprobrium (Eaton was advocating public ownership while at the same time developing downtown commercial real estate on behalf of his father-in-law, Horace Burdick), the letter claimed the poor were overcharged "to pay for water used to put out fires in buildings owned by rich landlords and to sprinkle the broad streets in front of their business blocks and their acres of residence grounds." This apparently populist attack against Eaton (and municipal ownership) proved to be, however, not the work of a reformer but rather of a promoter and front man, J. H. "Jayhawker" Woodard, for a pair of Indianapolis investors said to be interested in buying the water company. Although ostensibly having no connection with the city's insiders, as the drama played out, it proved to be an attempted preemptive buy on behalf of the water company.[6]

With the threat of the water company's sale, the city council decided the time had come to build its own waterworks, but both a judge and a United States district attorney warned that although under its contract with the water company the city could lay pipes in the streets, it could not carry water in them for sale to the people. Judge J. A. Anderson also reiterated the doctrine of riparian rights to the council: "Now, what is it you own? Water in the river was never owned by anybody. You can't get a title to water as it flows in the river. It is like the wild animal. It has to be captured before you can get a title to the water." The city was also advised that it could take only that river water that flowed within the city limits and, moreover, that the water company owned all the percolated water it had developed, that is, Crystal Springs. The city was counseled to find a group of capitalists who would form an omnibus corporation to buy out all existing water plants, unite them into one, and then turn over all to the city for operation. Water rates would then be established that could enable the city to pay off its bonded indebtedness for such a venture.[7]

In the midst of this debate, the water company sprang its surprise by announcing that the plant was to be sold to the syndicate fronted by the Indianapolis businessmen and their advance man, Jayhawker Woodard. Negotiations had taken place in San Francisco with the president of the Wells Fargo Nevada Bank, I. W. Hellman. Although Hellman had left Los Angeles in 1890 to join the bank, he still retained his ties to the city and remained one of the major stockholders of the City Water Company. According to the announcement, the buyers had made a first payment of $500,000 on the purchase price of $2.5 million that Perry had so readily quoted to the city a year before. Assurances followed that there was to be no change in management, as "Mr. Perry, Mr. Mott and Mr. Broderick have all shown themselves so capable." Suspecting corporate jugglery, the *Los Angeles Herald* suggested that the City Water Company was using the deal as a screen in order to produce a side company similar to Crystal Springs.[8]

In the municipal election of November 1892, voters approved a bond measure for building their own water system at a cost of $526,000. Then, just as the city was about to issue and sell water bonds for its new project in the spring of 1893, another eastern syndicate announced it was ready to buy the water company. This suspected water company ploy to circumvent the city's intentions was foiled, however, by the bad economic conditions of 1893, a year of national depression that resulted in hard times and a series of disastrous bank failures in Los Angeles. (I. W. Hellman personally bailed out the recently formed Farmers' and Merchants' Bank when he arrived on the afternoon train from San Francisco with $500,000 in sacks of gold coin aboard.)[9]

The Indianapolis gentlemen arrived in September to inspect their newly purchased water company. Within a week, they told the city that they were willing to reduce their previous sale price of $3.5 million to $3.3 million. Saying they could accept nothing less, they then took the train out of town, followed by Woodard, who, once home, boasted to the *Indianapolis Journal* that he had made $15,000 by bringing off the sale of the Los Angeles waterworks while his clients stood to clear $750,000 on the deal. When this story got back to the West Coast and reached the ears of the councilmen who were studying how to place an accurate valuation on the waterworks, certain members erupted. After declaring that "the people of this city are not fools," one recommended that further parley be cut off and that the city get busy again planning its own system.[10]

Under the direction of City Engineer Henry Dockweiler, a thorough inventory was being made of the water company's holdings, especially the amount of pipeline in the streets of the city, for which there was no written record. The city reached its own estimate of the value of the waterworks at $1,490,882.50, which the Indianapolis group rejected, asserting that in the event it should acquire the property, it did not wish to sell to the city. Then, abruptly, S. H. Mott, secretary of the water company, wrote that its property was not currently on the market and, moreover, challenged the city's inventory, especially in the matter of the waters at Crystal Springs. Thus, the city lost its round with the water company, but at least had been spared the expense of buying an overpriced water system.[11]

Amid this conniving, the city also found itself in another lengthy struggle that became noted as the Hooker and Pomeroy case, important because after a six-year lawsuit, the state supreme court in 1899 found in the city's favor and granted paramount rights of the waters of the Los Angeles River to the pueblo over those of private riparian owners. The case originated in the early 1890s when the city, planning to create its own water system, had turned to lands on the Providencia Rancho Company (today Glendale) as the site for a system of filtration pipes and head works. Head works for the water company were already in place on the south bank of the river on the Los Feliz side (about where Traveltown stands today in Griffith Park). In fact, much of the city's water was already being taken from the Providencia side, for the water company had for several years paid the landowners there $5 a day for the right to use their supply ditch. Now, however, the city wanted to purchase the land in question, so, early in 1893, just as the water company seemed about to be "sold" to the Indianapolis investors, the Providencia landowners, J. D. Hooker and A. E. Pomeroy, granted the city an option to buy 400 acres for $30,000. (The final purchase was 315 acres.) The president of the council thought the price too high and said the land was not worth it, but he was told that it was not land the city was after; it was water. Then a member mentioned that he had heard that Pomeroy had told someone he would sell the 400 acres for $15,000. The president next recommended condemnation, while another member pointed out that such a lengthy proceeding would leave them for several more years at the mercy of the water company. A judicial bombshell put an end to this dickering when word came from Sacramento that the bonds they had counted on to pay for their waterworks had been declared invalid. When Hooker and Pomeroy showed up in City Hall to arrange the sale for $30,000, the officials regretfully had to reveal that they lacked the money to pay for the deed. Four city banks would shut their doors two weeks later, and feeling that the alarming financial panic left them no other choice, the council turned to condemnation proceedings that would take the rest of the decade to resolve.[12]

During the depressed mid-nineties and amid political, financial, and municipal wrangling and maneuvering, not to say chicanery, Mulholland was overseeing the installation of a new pumping plant west of the Buena Vista Street Bridge. Once the pipes were laid, the plant was to bring relief to the distressed and water-deprived hill districts, where water shortages and stoppages had been a constant source of complaint under the disgraceful management of the Citizens' Water Company. One irate citizen described the hills as dotted with the charred remains of houses that had burned down because no water was available to fight the fires. Another long-suffering soul, a laboring man as he described himself, wrote that he lived west of Bunker Hill, and for the past four years had been unable to obtain a drop of water from 6:00 A.M. to 10:00 P.M. He had been forced to collect it in tubs and barrels during the early morning for use through the day. But, he noted, the bill collector was always on hand for payment, water or no water. *The Porcupine* had also fulminated against the Citizens' Water Company, claiming that the water the city delivered to irrigators was better than the water that Citizens' gave to humans. *The Porcupine* branded the former owners as robbers of the citizens, who had to use water containing remnants of "decaying animal and vegetable matter—pieces an inch or more long of fish, bugs and half-decayed weeds!"[13]

By May 1893, with two large gangs of men laying pipe, Mulholland promised that the work would be completed in thirty days and that water delivery would then increase from half a million to two million gallons a day. Three days later, Prudent Beaudry, the man who had first looked to the hills northwest of the plaza and dreamed of building homes there, the pioneer developer and builder of water systems, died unexpectedly of a stroke at the age of seventy-four. For thirty years he had been a force in civic affairs, twice mayor and one of the organizers of the water company. The *Times* remarked, "Only those who have lived in Los Angeles many years can form an idea of how great a debt the city owes to this unobtrusive, quietly energetic man."[14]

SATISFYING THE CITY'S THIRST

In December 1892, Mulholland first appeared as an expert witness in *Vernon Irrigation Company v. City of Los Angeles,* an important suit in the court of Judge Shaw, who would hear many of the water suits of this period. Along with old-timers Antonio Coronel, J. W. Potts, and E. H. Dalton, he testified for the city in a case that, although not notable at the time, became important because it established that one must be within the city limits to enjoy the use of river water, a ruling that consequently invited annexations to the city and thereby accelerated the expansion of the Los Angeles city limits into a vast and at times unwieldy municipality.[15]

The case concerned an irrigation and water company developed in the boom settlement of Vernon by two landowners, John A. Pirtle and George Hanna. Active players in many later water deals of the era, both in Hollywood and the San Fernando Valley (where a street bears Hanna's name), both had come to Southern California in 1887. Pirtle, a bond dealer from Arkansas, owned citrus land in Vernon, while Hanna, from Aurora, Illinois, had, after a few land deals, turned to the water business. The two charged that the city violated their riparian rights, because, being downriver, they did not receive a fair amount of water; that is, the upstream defendants took more than their share.[16]

Judge Lucien Shaw rendered his opinion six months after the suit began, reaffirming the city's control of its river water: "the city has the power to acquire and own a water supply for its inhabitants; that in the exercise of this power it has acquired and owns all the water flowing in the river and also the water caused to flow by the levees; that this is not an unreasonably large supply; that even if it were, the plaintiff has no right to raise the question, and that, being the owner of the water, it has power to sell such portion of it as may, from time to time, be in excess of its present needs. It follows that the plaintiff has no right to any relief against the city." The plaintiffs appealed, but five years later, in 1895, the California Supreme Court established that the city could not sell water for irrigation to extra-municipal lands as it had done in the past, nor did the recipients of that water have any right to it either.[17]

Perhaps anticipating an adverse decision and understanding that their case did not include the question of upper riparian rights, Pirtle and Hanna next embarked on another scheme to acquire waters upstream from the city via the Tujunga Wash for a development in the Cahuenga Valley. Had they succeeded, both men would have realized fortune and power, for they planned to capture the waters of the Los Angeles River before they flowed down to the city. Calling themselves the Cahuenga Mining and Water Company and using the subterfuge of wishing to activate an old mine that never had produced much gold but did have artesian waters in its hills, they intended to build a four-foot tunnel to tap those waters, whose source was probably percolation from the Los Angeles River. Confident that this new supply was safe from the demands of the city, the company reorganized, called itself the West Los Angeles Water Company, and quietly set about creating a new and independent system to supply the arid districts of Cahuenga Pass, Hollywood, and Sawtelle, where the soldiers' home had recently located.[18]

The project escaped notice until late 1895 when the water flowing into Los Angeles was observed to be unusually muddy. A city council investigation revealed that a water project had materialized twelve miles northwest of the city, evidently carried on in great secrecy by Pirtle, who with forty men and at a cost of $8,000, had, at the end of a tunnel or ditch, built down a steep slope an inverted flume with a dirt bottom to provide a continuous flow to a holding dam below. The dam had broken and its water and dirt had flowed into the river, thus producing the telltale flow of muddy water toward the city. At first, the city council was not unduly alarmed, as the water project fell outside its municipal jurisdiction. But the council's attitude became less casual when it discovered that Pirtle's men, while constructing a pipeline for their system, had undermined the city's main water supply ditch, which provided all the irrigating water the city used in city parks, cemeteries, and East Los Angeles. Deciding that things had gone too far, the council instructed the city attorney to order the deputy water overseer in charge of the ditch to quit work. The deputy water overseer refused; the chief of police was called in; and with more than a little drama, shortly before Christmas on December 19, at eight in the evening, two mounted police officers rode ten miles up the river road to call an official halt to the proceedings. The legal action over what came to be known as the Pirtle Cut eventually reaffirmed and expanded the city's right not only to the underground waters of the Los Angeles River but also to those of the Tujunga Wash. Eventually, in 1904, Hanna sold the West Los Angeles Water Company to the city.[19]

Heightened interest in water plots sometimes led to absurd conclusions, as when, not long after the discovery of Pirtle and Hanna's project in the Cahuenga hills, a reporter thought he had uncovered another "peculiar piece of work" when he found about two hundred men boring a tunnel into the hill south of the water company's gatehouse (today, Glendale Boulevard). He noted that the tunnel was egg shaped, like the tunnels of the outfall sewer, and that the shafts were being sunk in a westerly direction. This suggested to him that the line might be headed toward the Cahuenga Valley. To add to his speculation, he reported sightings of "Mr. Mulholland, superintendent of the City Water Company, and Mr. Hawgood, engineer for the same company," and inferred that they must be connected with the work.[20]

The intrigue vanished, however, when the water company announced that because of the city's growth, especially in the southwest, it was constructing a new pipeline and reservoir to fill the need. Beginning at the Crystal Springs just north of Riverside Drive and Hyperion Avenue, workers dug a 4,785-foot-long tunnel southwesterly through the Ivanhoe hills. The water then would flow beneath a short, recently christened Reservoir Street into the new Bellevue Dam. Built in a deep ravine at what was then the western edge of the city at Lucile and Bellevue Avenues on land the company had recently purchased especially for that purpose (Lot 1, Block 33, Hancock's Survey), the new dam had a high-water elevation of 386 feet and would hold 40 million gallons of water, three times the capacity of any other in the system. Its outlet pipe of 30-inch cast iron ran down Hoover Street to Seventh Street, and on from there in 20-inch pipe to Seventh and Broadway. Completed on March 24, 1895, the system supplied the fine new homes rising on Figueroa and Adams Streets with water for their gardens and great expanses of lawn. The company hoped this new project would satisfy the city's thirst for a long time to come, but skeptics saw it as yet another of the water company's moves to create a separate project in the Crystal Springs mode, thus enabling it to continue to sell private water once its lease had expired.[21]

A PILLAR OF SOCIETY

On the morning of August 17, 1895, William Mulholland took a day off from water plots and complications to join three hundred other guests on a special train with six coaches that pulled out of the Arcade Depot in Los Angeles for a swift trip to Rancho La Puente. There, their host, the popular William "Uncle Billy" Rowland, was to entertain with a bull's head breakfast, or, as it was described on a souvenir photograph of the occasion, *El Almuerzo de la Cabeza Tatemada* (The Lunch of the Roasted Head). Rowland, famed as the sheriff who led the posse that ran down the bandit Tiburcio Vasquez, was holding a traditional mortgage-burning party in the manner of the old rancho days, when after the crops were in and the banks paid off, the ranchero celebrated with a barbecue for his friends. On this occasion the guests comprised the leaders of Los Angeles. Juan Bandini, Reginaldo del Valle, Juan R. Ramirez, and Ygnacio Sepulveda mingled with H. W. Hellman, John Kenealy, William Workman, and William Llewellyn. In attendance were bankers, attorneys, merchants, manufacturers, and newspaper owners and editors, including Major Horace Bell, Colonels Harrison Gray Otis and J. J. Ayers, and old Major Ben Truman of the recently defunct *Star*. In a memorable day of feasting, drinking, and speechmaking, United States senator Stephen M. White acted as toastmaster, while Major Bell and state senator Reginaldo del Valle reminisced about the old days, and California governor Edwin C. Markham spoke on "The New California."

Mulholland's presence signaled his successful climb in eighteen years from obscurity to a recognized position in the community. Although not given to saving mementos, he kept his copy of the souvenir photograph taken that day when the assemblage had stretched out on the ground after the meal—a field of sated males caught for posterity as they stared towards the camera. Garbed in black, with a black hat on his lap and propped on one arm, he lounges in the front row, yet his rough-hewn visage suggests that he was a man of many cares. With three years remaining before the water company's lease expired, he faced an uncertain future as well as a present difficulty. Only later did he publicly acknowledge some of the problems he faced at that time with the wealthy owners of the company, who, he believed, because of their many other holdings and interests, found the waterworks but "a mere incident." He remembered how even the most makeshift of improvements required "most insistent efforts" on his part as superintendent to win approval. This proved especially exasperating, he said, in the last years before the lease expired, when any proposals for additions or improvements were evaded or denied because of the impending termination. Just one example was the endless bickering over hydrants used for both fire fighting and street sprinkling, as city and company each insisted the other should pay for water and costs. Yet Mulholland also found remarkable the tenacity with which the original stockholders held on to their investment. They had become old, he said, which had "had the disadvantage of excluding new blood which might have redeemed it from the effect of the parsimonious and timid policy of its later years."[22]

Politics also vexed Mulholland, as he heard certain "ambitious office seekers," who at that time tried to make political capital out of their views on water by proposing "all kinds of anarchistic remedies such as paralleling the pipe system or forcibly preventing the Company from taking water from the river . . . even to the act of confiscation pure and simple." Added to his list of aggravations was one of the last great fights over water rates in February 1896, when the water supply committee in the city council recommended a 33.33 percent reduction in water rates. The reporter covering the story remarked that the proposal gave the council an opportunity "for some rare 'grandstand playing,' and afforded divers and sundry City Solons occasion for an unusual display of councilmanic buffoonery." To combat that "insatiable octopus," the private water company, the city fathers unanimously adopted a 50 percent rate reduction. The water company promptly sued and, after two years of battle, won a judgment against the city in June 1898; but it was a token victory only, for a month later the company's lease expired and water revenues to the company stopped.[23]

When Mulholland joined the town leaders at Uncle Billy Rowland's gathering, he had not yet gone on record in favor of a municipally owned waterworks. As superintendent of the private works, he held his cards close to his vest and acted on his conviction that "If you go to work for somebody, you do *his* work for him." In the years of contention ahead, however, he became persuaded that the city must own its water system. For, as he once jestingly related, from his reading of history he had found that "in the progress of civilization the duty of supplying cities with water was assumed as a public work second only in importance to the defense of the country." He recalled from Scripture that Hezekiah, king of Judah from 717 to 688 B.C., had been a pioneer in constructing a system of waterworks to bring water into Jerusalem: "He made the pool and the conduit and brought the water into the city. He stopped the upper water course of Gihon and brought it straight down to the west side of the City of David, and Hezekiah prospered in all his works." Then Mulholland added that after diligent search he had failed "to find any mention of the dividends paid by this early enterprise," and so concluded that "we may infer that the works were public, for public officials are guiltless of paying dividends—except in the indirect way of good service—if it so happens that they are good servants."[24]

The road that led to Mulholland's becoming a good public servant was long and tortuous. Years later, Lincoln Steffens in his *Autobiography* described a meeting he once arranged with business and civic leaders of Los Angeles in order to argue his thesis that whatever they might otherwise believe would alleviate graft, they should "want, at the least, the public ownership of all public utilities and natural resources." (This would have been at a 1907 meeting with members of the progressive Municipal League.) In the question and answer period after his address, when someone asked "if the public operation of utilities would not put them into politics," Steffens replied:

> To answer that, I turned to William Mulholland, the popular, highly respected engineer, who was the manager of the city's water system. He had been the manager when the water company was a private corporation, and it was notorious that he was then a very active and efficient politician. Everybody in that room knew that Mr. Mulholland had said over and over again that the change from private to public operation had got him and the business out of politics. When I passed the question of politics to him he did not have to answer. The whole company burst into laughter.[25]

CHAPTER 7

The Years of Mayor Eaton

1898–1900

TROUBLES FOR THE GRAND MONOPOLY

At no time did Mulholland better demonstrate his ability to maneuver around the shoals of politics and water issues than in the closing years of the nineteenth century, when he found himself caught between private sympathy for a publicly owned system and public loyalty to his employer, the private company. Although popular sentiment seemed to favor public ownership, the community's primary desire was for "a water system which shall give pure and abundant water at fair prices." The private company defended its performance with occasional propaganda pieces claiming that it provided water at rates 50 percent less than any city on the Pacific Coast, yet critics, especially Fred Eaton, thought the company inadequate and laggard in initiating improvements. Moreover, in an era when trusts and monopolies were coming under increasing attack, the private company's links to California's major economic octopus, the Southern Pacific Railroad, influenced the public perception of "the Water Ring" as a political menace, insofar as it could influence nominations in both political parties.[1]

When no agreement emerged in the months before the expiration of the thirty-year lease, the prospect of arbitration loomed. The final resolution depended heavily, however, on the outcome of the Crystal Springs case, which would determine the source of the water-bearing lands the private company claimed as part of its improvements and for which it must receive remuneration from the city under the terms of the lease.

While the Crystal Springs Company claimed waters developed on its lands at and adjacent to Crystal Springs, the City of Los Angeles argued that the waters were legally part of the Los Angeles River, which belonged to the municipality. Of the many litigations over water rights to the Los Angeles River, none proved more troublesome than this. For Mulholland, who was often on the hot seat testifying for the company, it became a byword for any snarled, complex, and intractable situation. By the time it ended, the public had heard a veritable history of Los Angeles water projects since the American occupation.

Among the experts testifying in court were engineers who one day would work together under Mulholland's direction on the Owens River Aqueduct. Their diverse and often contradictory testimony about some-times arcane questions of hydrology, hydrography, and engineering lingo (terms such as *plane of saturation, miner's inch, flow velocity,* and *watershed area*) sometimes led to the impression that expert opinion depended a good deal on who had hired the expert. When Mulholland conceded under questioning that the origin of the waters in the infiltration pipes he had installed at Crystal Springs remained "a mystery to him," a reporter who for weeks had been following the testimony, "replete with technicalities of verbiage and of fact," found the testimony interesting simply because it could be easily understood. When the court set May 31 as the date for final arguments to begin, the same reporter commented that he found the city's case "detailed and specific," the water company's "somewhat hazy." Yet he acknowledged that when engineers so highly regarded throughout California arrived at diametrically opposed conclusions, then the layman was indeed thrown into a state of confusion.[2]

Water issues were briefly pushed into the background when, on April 19, 1898, the United States declared war against Spain over Cuba ("Remember the Maine"). The national popularity of this conflict, with its overtones of imperialism and jingoism, infused the Far West, and when Admiral George Dewey defeated the Spanish fleet at Manila on May 1, the Los Angeles Board of Public Works promptly requested that Don Pio Street be renamed Dewey Street. On the seventeenth, the name of the last Mexican governor of Alta California, Pio Pico, was swept away for America's latest military idol. Local patriots also cheered when at the end of the month, on May 27, President McKinley elevated the founder and owner of the *Los Angeles Times,* Colonel Harrison Gray Otis, to the rank of brigadier general of the volunteers. As Otis sailed off to active service in the Philippines, he named his son-in-law, Harry Chandler, to act as the *Times*'s general manager in his absence.[3]

Amid this martial enthusiasm, the Crystal Springs trial reconvened for final arguments at the end of May. In the intervening weeks, the city council had demanded that the water company provide a detailed description of its property and its relation to the Crystal Springs Land and Water Company. The water company then indicated its willingness to sell to the city but warned that to provide a detailed description of the property would require time and labor beyond reason. Moreover, prior to 1891, records of pipe laying had simply not been kept. Just as the city seemed willing to accept a less comprehensive cataloging of the company's property, a court decision denied the city's authority to regulate water rates. Although this finding came too late to be of much benefit, the company nevertheless sued the city for over $150,000 in lost revenue from unfairly low water rates.[4]

Subsequent negotiations broke down, and when the long-awaited date arrived for the expiration of the hated lease, instead of dancing in the streets, spectators crowded council chambers before eight o'clock in the morning to learn the outcome of a transaction that had grown so crucial to the city's future. By nine o'clock, when all council members had arrived, the galleries and seats were packed as property owners, stockholders, and the curious met to see the city offer $1.3 million for the waterworks. The water company's attorneys and directors appeared in full array, along with its superintendent, mistakenly identified in the *Times* as "John Mulholland." The city made its offer, the company declined it, and the council commenced arbitration.[5]

TWO FRIENDS DIVERGE

By the end of summer, as the fall municipal election neared, Fred Eaton's name was bruited for a possible place on the Republican ticket for mayor. The *Times*, which had once attacked Eaton's engineering skills in his plans for an outfall sewer, now declared that "his personal popularity would render him a strong nominee." Moreover, with Eaton's long-standing record of support for municipal ownership of water—an important plank in the local Republican platform—he was seen as the man of the hour. At the convention, he received the sole nomination and was approved by acclamation as three or four hundred delegates rose and cheered their native son. He made a gracious acceptance speech, thanked his fellow party members for the magnificent honor they had bestowed upon him, and promised to do well for the city. "I have been among you all my life," he continued. "My occupation during the active part of my career has brought me among the people, and I have at all times been open to their criticism."[6]

The *Times* was ecstatic over Eaton's nomination and threw its full editorial weight behind his campaign. Water was to be the central issue. The Republicans painted the Democrats as tools of the water ring, and Eaton warned citizens against bondage to a company that thought nothing of spending $100,000 to bribe councilmen. Not, he quickly noted, that the entire council could be bribed; he simply wished to indicate that out of the company's great income (reckoned at about $425,000 a year), it could easily expend $100,000. After citing the dire example of San Francisco, held in thrall to the private Spring Valley Water Company, he noted his own refusal to accept positions with the Pomeroy-Hooker or West End Water Companies, saying he preferred "to stand by the people's interests." His opponents attempted a weak last-minute attack, accusing him of overcharging the city with a high professional consultation fee in the Crystal Springs case. When the sum was revealed to be a modest $50, however, that issue quickly disappeared, and Eaton soared ahead with promises of municipal water and more schools.[7]

Arbitration hearings on the water question began during the campaign. While Eaton was on the hustings attacking the water company and its corrupt political influence in the city, Mulholland sat in a city council chamber reciting to the arbitration board in painstaking detail "the size and character of the various pipes of the system, the dates on which they were laid and the character of the soil in which they were placed." (The previous June, he had been asked to draw up a complete inventory and description of the company's holdings, which included more than three hundred miles of pipe and five hundred hydrants, along with pumping stations and machinery.) The material, complained a reporter, "was composed of minutiae of little public interest," but one associate later recalled the occasion as a demonstration of Mulholland's prodigious memory. According to J. B. Lippincott, after Mulholland had presented the inventory as an oral recollection, the arbitration board asked for two hundred places to be dug up in order to verify his accuracy. When all two hundred pipes agreed in every particular with Mulholland's account, the board accepted his inventory.

During six weeks of drilling on the witness stand, Mulholland earned a reputation for probity and fair-mindedness, willing to flout even the opinions of his employer's attorneys. At one point, when a controversy broke out over whether the valuation of pipe could best be established by its age or its appearance, Mulholland disagreed with company attorney Stephen M. White's opinion that more depended on its appearance than on its age. Neither age nor appearance, countered Mulholland, was as important in fixing the pipe's value as the condition of the soil in which it had been placed. As this scrutiny of the water system dragged on, a company attorney, after an exhausting cross-examination of one witness, turned to Mulholland and whispered, "What else shall I ask him?" Mulholland replied, "Ask him where he got the red necktie he's wearing."[8]

A NEW MAYOR ATTEMPTS REFORM

On December 6, 1898, after the normal amount of political mudslinging, Fred Eaton became mayor of Los Angeles. The year ended with optimism and hope that the depressed times of the 1890s might be ending. Merchants reported record volumes of business, with shoppers in the stores until almost midnight on Christmas Eve, while attorney Henry O'Melveny noted that it was the "warmest and dryest Christmas Los Angeles has known since I have been here."[9]

Although portents had augured well for Eaton's success, he would bow out after his first term, never again to run for public office. (His popular Democratic predecessor, Meredith "Pinky" Snyder, was swept back into office, where he remained until the end of 1904.) Eaton had professed progressive ambitions for the city, and besides his strong desire for a new city charter, municipally owned water, more schools, and an improved library, he also wanted slot machines outlawed (especially the nickel slots in saloons, which he felt unfairly robbed workingmen of their hard-earned money). He was in favor of open hours for saloons, but thought women and girls should be banned from the back rooms. He proposed to accomplish this by sealing all back doors and using only the front for arrivals and departures. He was no more than a man of his time in his conviction that "the presence of women in saloons is a constant factor in promoting vice and immorality, and serves to lead astray the young." Yet he also proved gallant to the *nymphes du pave,* and at one point championed several ladies of dubious reputation against a police officer accused of maltreating them. In public works, he wanted better public access to the parks, a larger police force, and a more efficient fire department. In short, he prescribed for his city of one hundred thousand souls what many regarded as an exemplary program for its improvement. To those who saw former mayor Snyder as a tool of the saloon and gambling interests as well as a cozy buddy of the police, Eaton seemed the necessary antidote.[10]

Eaton encountered heavy sledding when he attempted to regulate the saloon business and gambling. His rows with the police and the police commission continued throughout his two years in office, although with other commissions he enjoyed more harmonious relations that were often productive and constructive. Especially congenial were his associations with the board of health, for as men with a shared faith in the scientific method, they escaped many of the political and moral disagreements inherent in the problematic fields of police, crime, and vice. Eaton moreover had the good sense to retain the health officer who, except for two years in 1895 and 1896, served from 1893 to 1911: the forceful Luther Milton Powers, M.D. A Democrat, Powers nonetheless transcended party considerations, and mayors of both parties chose him as the guardian angel of the city's health. Among those who learned valuable lessons from the esteemed Dr. Powers was William Mulholland, for Powers became his family physician and treated his children through bouts of diphtheria and typhoid. Mulholland's notions of hygiene could be rather cavalier. He told his sons on camping trips to drink the water "if you can still cut it with a knife," and they remembered how, when coming upon a stream, he would crouch down, push aside the pond scum, scoop a sample into his palm, and after a reflective sip, nod and tell them, "It's all right." In a Los Angeles that had been lax, not to say ignorant and derelict, in matters of hygiene, Powers advanced the relatively new science of public health. His years of service constituted a major contribution to the betterment of the city's sanitation and hygiene at the turn of the century.[11]

ENGINEERS DISAGREE

Drought was a specter during Eaton's two years in office. The combined rainfall for those two seasons yielded only 13½ inches. In spite of all his desire and efforts to create a municipally owned water system, he did not achieve that goal during his administration, even though he led a successful $2,090,000 bond campaign for the purchase and improvement of a city waterworks. (The water company's machinations later frustrated that hope.) His disillusionment with the interminable lawsuits and joustings with the private company probably determined his eventual withdrawal from the city as the water arbitration hearings dragged on.

Eaton and Mulholland, although ostensibly in opposing camps, had frequent occasions to parley. A few days after Eaton took office, Mulholland requested and was granted a conference that took place in the mayor's private office with the city auditor. They discussed the long-standing and unresolved question of repairs to fire hydrants, most of which had been damaged by certain careless drivers of the city's sprinkling carts. After haggling with several councilmen who joined them, they reached a compromise in which the city agreed to pay half the cost of repairs. Two weeks later, at a water arbitration hearing, they disagreed over the capacity of Buena Vista Reservoir at the time the company began to enlarge it. Mulholland thought it was 3 million gallons, while Eaton, basing his figure on a chart he remembered having seen when he was superintendent of the company, claimed it was 5 million.[12]

In the spring of 1899, Mulholland appeared almost daily before the arbitration board to testify on such matters as the value of pipe or the cost of trenching, until at last in May, the board filed its report, which placed the water company's value at $1,183,591.42. The high estimate, from company engineer Harry Hawgood, was $2,467,778.00; the low, from City Engineer J. Henry Dockweiler, was $1,071,034.00; Mulholland's was $2,182,891.00. When the third arbitrator (the water company's representative) refused to sign, the arbitration failed, and the city decided to proceed with plans to build its own system, which Mulholland later described as a folly.[13]

At this time a favorable decision from the state supreme court on the Pomeroy and Hooker case allowed the city to advance its condemnation proceedings for building its own headworks. Since spring, concerned with lack of rainfall, City Engineer Frank L. Olmstead and engineer-hydrographers Joseph B. Lippincott and O. K. Parker had been taking measurements along the river north of Crystal Springs, in part to discover if tunneling by the secretive West Side Water Company had affected the river supply below. When the city council began to complain of too many requests for payments for water measurements, especially after Olmstead proposed a trek to the Big and Little Tujunga Canyons, he strongly defended the expense. He warned that farmers in the San Fernando Valley were already "milking the river," which could run dry. Already a delegation of farmers south of the city (among them, John A. Pirtle of the Pirtle Cut) had requested permission to begin pumping underground water because too little surface water was reaching them for irrigation.[14]

The city's struggle to secure control of its water system from the private water company became its stone of Sisyphus, for with each push ahead, a setback seemed to follow. As Eaton awaited what he expected to be a happy ruling from the arbitration board, he was dashed by a supreme court decision declaring that the water company in fact had a contract with the city and not simply a lease; that the city must pay a fair valuation on the plant; and that the monies held in receivership must be released to the company. Elated, the company's attorney declared that with revenues available again, the company could begin to make improvements.[15]

In the hot dry month of July, Los Angeles hosted the annual session of the American Forestry Service, noteworthy not only because it was the national body's first meeting in the West but because among the leading authorities on forestry, hydrography, and irrigation in attendance were two men who would play important roles in the city's water history: Gifford Pinchot, then United States forester and future secretary of the interior under Theodore Roosevelt; and Frederick H. Newell, United States hydrographer. Newell lectured on "The Reclamation of Arid Public Lands," and when asked about the water prospects for Southern California, replied, "I have been surprised at what has been done in Southern California since I was here last, some two or three years ago, in the development of water from underground sources." A notable local representative, J. B. Lippincott, spoke not of his current hydrographic activities but of his experiences with the National Geological Survey in the Bitterroot Forest Reserve in 1897. He concluded with a hard-hitting attack against the timber interests and "the reckless liberality of the timber laws."[16]

During the conference, on Saturday, July 22, a series of earthquakes shook the city. A week later, apparently unconnected with the earthquakes, a washout in the city's main supply tunnel cut all flow of water to the city's reservoirs. At a point just south of Kenilworth and a quarter of a mile from the water company's gatehouse, the water flooded down the hillside, across the road, and into a disused air shaft that led to the main supply tunnel of the Crystal Springs Water Company. The force of the water with its accumulated tons of rock and earth smashed and choked the walls of the tunnel and also washed away the nearby power flume.

Mulholland rushed to the scene with a force of men. Arriving at six o'clock in the evening, they spent the night clearing debris and tons of sticky mud. As he often did in such emergencies, Mulholland was quick to assure the public that water would be available again soon, asking them only to refrain from watering their gardens. Mayor Eaton immediately announced suspension of all street sprinkling, and although the reservoirs had been full at the time of the break, Mulholland still cautioned that "Los Angeles uses 20,000,000 gallons of water a day. Of this, 2,500,000 gallons is used on the streets, and at least 5,000,000 more for sprinkling the lawns and gardens of the city." No sooner had he dismissed the damage as "a mere bagatelle" than more of the tunnel caved in.[17]

Crews worked day and night to repair the power ditch and get water running in order to turn a Pelton wheel used for pumping irrigation water into the Zanja Madre, which in the emergency was to be diverted to Buena Vista Reservoir for domestic use. In the meantime, the supply ditch was not so quickly restored because of a labor shortage. Unemployment was still high, but many jobless had fled the city in midsummer to work on the outlying ranches; one aide reported having to spend a night ransacking cheap lodging houses looking for men.[18]

In this crisis, the city and the water company laid aside their differences. The water company furnished the city with forty-inch steel pipe to repair the supply ditch so that its flow could continue into the Echo Park line. The company also helped with the pipe's installation, which involved anchoring it to the side of the hill over timber supports. As the ditch lay almost directly above the company's damaged tunnel, the men had to take care that the new installation would not interfere with repairing the tunnel. For the first time since Christmas 1889, when he had kept the channel open during a flood, Mulholland received press notice for his efforts in preserving the water supply.[19]

A week after the break, Eaton began to campaign for passage in August of the $2,090,000 bond issue to acquire a municipal water system. Although city officials were enthusiastic, they feared apathy among the general public, so on August 13, Eaton issued a general proclamation notifying the public of the election and urging them to vote. On election eve, only a disappointing few hundred turned out for a probond rally at Hazard's Pavilion, but among the speakers were Eaton and Lippincott, who paid tribute to the arbitrators' work and argued that municipalities that owned their water supplies offered rates generally 43 percent lower than those supplied by private companies. The city attorney also singled out Mulholland for his "spirit of fairness in submitting evidence" during arbitration, recalling that in some instances, when the city engineer's estimates had been too high, Mulholland had suggested their reduction. The recently organized and progressive Committee of One Hundred worked to get out the largest vote ever cast in Los Angeles at a special election. With a two-thirds vote needed for passage, it carried every precinct in the city seven to one (7,179 for and 973 against). With victory assured, Eaton left that night for San Francisco to witness the California troops' arrival from the Philippines.[20]

Jubilation was short-lived, however, for the water company filed a suit to disallow the value of the waterworks established in the arbitration hearings. Then came word from the East that a pamphlet was circulating in financial circles stating that on account of the various pending lawsuits, the city's water and school bonds would be held up on legal technicalities for several years. (Rumor had it that the pamphlet had been prepared by a "large railroad"—the Southern Pacific?) Eaton called a series of secret meetings to plan strategies for a counterattack, but so serious was the impact of these attacks that the city decided to retain the services of a leading New York bond attorney to continue the struggle. A year later when Eaton left office, the matter would still be unresolved.[21]

THE CITY RENEWS ITS WATER CLAIMS

Eaton's second year as mayor began with a disaster when on January 23, 1900, the roof at the west end of the Third Street Tunnel caved in. Of the fifteen men buried, three died and twelve survived. One of the dead was the city inspector, who had been on an inspection tour when the tunnel gave way. The coroner's inquest refused to fix responsibility for the event, but City Engineer Frank L. Olmstead later blamed what he called the vicious system of contract work, whereby public officials granted contracts solely on the basis of low bid. Eaton, who at the time of the disaster was in the midst of a clash with the police commission, had little to say on the matter, but as a veteran of the contract system probably would not have criticized it as harshly as the younger Olmstead. The council of labor moved upon the city fathers with demands for improved supervision and worker safety, and although promises and assurances were forthcoming, little of real consequence occurred.[22]

Eaton increasingly focused on the water question. In February, just a week before the deadline for setting customer water rates, he proposed that the city council begin construction of a municipal headworks and cut water rates by one-third. In a subsequent hearing before the water supply committee, a large gathering of attorneys, water company representatives, and interested parties such as members of the Lodging House Association, who were disputing the water company's method of billing, listened to the company's attorney argue for higher rates based on the prospects of a dry year. Next, Mulholland explained why the company thought its rates should be raised. Water supplies were low after two dry seasons, and because the outlook was for another dry year (which proved correct, for the season's total finally came to a meager 7.91 inches), the company would have to install a new pumping plant costing from

$35,000 to $50,000. This would include pumping stations at three different points on the river, with operating expenses at about $2,000 a month. Because the hurriedly built installations would be somewhat insubstantial, Mulholland added that they would not add notably to the company's property.[23]

As Mulholland was answering questions about the seasonal variations in water use and specifying the proposed new installations' locations, Eaton entered the room and interrupted him by asking why the water company did not put the pumping stations on city lands. That question went unanswered as Councilman Charles Toll next wondered whether the Los Angeles City Water Company or the Crystal Springs Water Company would make the improvements. Mulholland replied that he did not know and repeated that the installation would be temporary, therefore adding little to the value of either plant. Two weeks later, after Eaton and Lippincott had returned from a day up the river investigating reports that riparian owners were using more water than allowed or necessary for irrigation of their ranches, they also announced that the water company, instead of using the total flow from its water supply, was allowing millions of gallons of currently unneeded water to go to waste. Eaton then refuted Mulholland: "The Mayor does not believe the contention of the company as to the necessity for, or the cost of, pumping the water into the reservoirs during the coming summer."[24]

Eaton continued the exploratory trips up the river accompanied by Lippincott and Thomas H. Means, a soil expert from the Department of Agriculture in Washington, D.C., who had been sent out to examine soils with the aim of perfecting a system for reclaiming alkali lands. As Means's mission involved examining water supplies of various districts to establish salt contents and as the findings might provide evidence to support their fight for municipal water, Eaton and Lippincott were eager to assist him. If, for example, the samples from various parts of the San Fernando Valley agreed and it became evident that the water was all from the same watershed, they could trace the source of the city's water supply to the very head of the valley, and "mark a distinct line along which the water of the river first flowed before entering the river or coming to the surface."[25]

In April, Eaton received the heartening news that the Supreme Court of the United States had refused to consider the Crystal Springs Water Company's attempt to quiet title to what it claimed to be its waters. After three years in litigation, the highest court in the land held that the federal government had no jurisdiction over the case. Now the city could renew its claims, but another roadblock loomed in May, when the water company enjoined the city from fixing water rates. In June, Eaton announced that the Supreme Court decision freed the city from its obligation to pay the water company for water used to irrigate the parks and public lands.[26]

As the deadlock continued, the summer of 1900 advanced dry and rainless. The Democrats chose as their mayoral candidate Meredith P. Snyder, while the Republicans nominated the current president of the city council, Herman Silver. As the water rate case dragged on in circuit court, a small and curious news item appeared. The mayor was showing off a new knife to admiring friends as he explained that he had invested in it for purposes of "offense and defense in view of his approaching trip into the Sierra Nevada Mountains on a hunting expedition." The hunting party proved special, however, as Eaton's companions were United States hydrographer Frederick H. Newell, Assistant Hydrographer J. B. Lippincott, and one Dr. F. T. Hicknell. Expected to join them later in the week was William Mulholland, engineer for the Los Angeles City Water Company. The group planned to go by train to Fresno and then, by stage, to follow the Kings River Valley to the top of the divide and over into the San Joaquin Valley. As the article explained, "The party will inspect the reservoir sites in these two valleys now being surveyed by the United States Government." It described Newell and Lippincott as "personally interested in the work," while Eaton and Mulholland were interested "on scientific grounds."[27]

When Eaton returned to town at the end of August, he was greeted with the news that the city had just lost its rate fight against the water company. The judge had upheld the thirty-year contract in a sixty-page typewritten document that boiled down to the conclusion that the city's case was without merit. As September grew hotter and drier, Eaton ominously predicted that within a few years Los Angeles might have to do without the man-made lakes in its parks. In a semitropical climate, he explained, large amounts of water were needed to keep the supply sanitary. He found the daily per capita consumption of 230 gallons of water "surprising, if not alarming," and joked that "if cleanliness is next to godliness, then the City of the Angels must occupy a high place in the scale of municipal virtue." He warned, however, that if the population increased by another hundred thousand, something would have to be done. With dwindling supplies, water would be needed for domestic purposes, and it would be up to the people themselves to practice strict economies in its use. He then set about planning the headworks filtration gallery on the Pomeroy and Hooker lands.[28]

In his last month as mayor and a week after McKinley defeated Bryan for the presidency of the United States, the rains came to Los Angeles. Attorney O'Melveny, who conscientiously kept rainfall records, noted on November 21 and 22, "Magnificent rain. Streetcar service stopped. Grandest rain in ten years. Everyone happy. San Gabriel River beyond measurement." There had been nothing like it since 1891, and fortunately, because the city prudently had cleared the riverbed of brush and debris in the early fall, there was no repetition of the damaging flood of 1884 when such an accumulation had checked the flow and created havoc in the city. Even so, flooding occurred. One two-story house on South Flower collapsed after its basement filled with eleven feet of water, while over in Mulholland's Boyle Heights neighborhood, Hollenbeck Park was inundated when its lake overflowed and covered lawns and flowers with mud. Some of the exotic birds drowned in the submerged aviary, and two blocks from the Mulholland home, stinking slime pools of stagnant water filled with the overflow from a break in a zanja. Yet at year's end the rains were heralded as a harbinger of good times.[29]

AN EX-MAYOR GOES "UP THE RIVER"

In January 1900, Fred Eaton devoted his departing message to his fellow Angelenos entirely to the subject of city water, past, present, and future. He chastised his foes, chiefly the officers and stockholders of the Los Angeles City Water Company and the Crystal Springs Land and Water Company. He praised those of his fellow citizens who had demonstrated their faith in a municipal system by voting for water bonds that were now also in contention because of certain obstructionists. He remained positive in his conviction that the city ultimately would prevail in its fight to own its own waterworks. Next day, as he cleared his office of books, maps, and files, a group of deputies and officers showed up and, with a gracious speech from City Engineer Olmstead, presented their outgoing mayor with a pair of small binoculars equipped with three lenses so that they were equal in power to larger field glasses. Touched, Eaton said that when he was alone upon the desert and beneath the panoply of the heavens on some of the engineering tours he planned, the gift would remind him of the last day he spent in City Hall. Leaving, he dropped a clue to his future plans by saying that he did not intend to let his interest in the water question lapse, but that this time, it would be in his own interest and not the city's.[30]

Too little is known of Fred Eaton to draw a dogmatic conclusion about his character. His early idealism seems to have given way to acquisitiveness, yet one also senses that he was largely honorable in intent. One also feels that his undoubted intelligence and ability were accompanied by a certain hauteur, perhaps not surprising in one who was something of a princeling in this western realm. Success had come to Eaton early, and he projected a presumption of rightness that came from being well-born and assured of a secure place in life. Scarcely mentioned during his mayoralty was the fact of his drinking, about which the newspapers maintained a discreet silence. Only several years afterwards, during a time of domestic troubles, was mention made. "During his political life he was somewhat addicted to the cup that cheers . . . ," wrote a reporter at the time of Eaton's divorce in 1903. Fred Eaton should have been one of the bright stars in the history of the city. Yet in his last months in office, he seemed to recede from view, so that by the time the Republicans convened to nominate a new candidate for mayor, he had disappeared. There were few public statements of appreciation or farewell, and the *Los Angeles Times*, which had been his chief booster, said nothing either by way of praise or blame. When one reporter found the mayor's office closed at City Hall and was told he was "up the river" and was further informed that the city engineer and attorney were also "up the river," he mused that "this practice has become so prevalent that it might make a fitting subject for inquiry by the Committee of Safety that is supposed to have taken in hand all the disorders in municipal affairs."[31]

The City's Victory over the "Grand Monopoly"

1901–1902

LAWSUITS AND "CARPING SPIRITS"

At the beginning of 1901, the city was snarled in thirty lawsuits growing out of its struggle for municipal water control. One alone consisted of 10,000 typewritten pages. The cost of all these litigations was draining the city's coffers at a time of economic slump, and in May the council ordered a retrenchment of all city expenses. In the following months, the city and the water company engaged in a kind of high-stakes poker game that called for alertness and skill with each new deal. When a local group called the Mountain Water Company suddenly surfaced with a request for a franchise to lay pipe and supply "pure, soft mountain water" to the city from a source in the San Gabriel Forest Reserve, City Attorney William B. Mathews was at first taken aback. He knew nothing of such a development and wondered if it were not some shrewd new trick of the water company that would involve the city in further legal strife and turmoil. As this mystery remained for the moment unresolved, the city council began to debate whether it should not at last try to settle quickly with the Los Angeles City Water Company.[1]

The city at this point had a $30,000 deficit in its cash fund, and the finance committee, seeking means to cut expenses, recommended a compromise with the water company. In the ensuing debate, attorney Mathews spoke out for a continued fight: "Don't give up the ship—fight on," he exhorted. "You will never get anything out of the water company until you knock it out with a court decree." After a lively debate dur-

ing a day in executive session, the entire council emerged with its decision to attempt a compromise with the water company. The company
answered that it desired to cooperate, but when it announced its price
of $2,275,000, the city fathers' howls could be heard all the way to
Catalina Island.[2]

With its population now over 100,000, the city made increasing demands on its water sources. By April 1901, the river was lower than it
had been at the same time the year before, partly because the ground,
dried by three arid years, had absorbed a great deal of the flow, but also,
charged the city zanjero, because the water company, asserting its first
rights to the water, had now taken the lion's share into its Crystal Springs
system. If the zanjas lacked water to supply irrigators, then the city would
lose much-needed revenue from this source. (Water then sold outside the
city for $5.00 a head for a twelve-hour day run and $2.50 for a night
run; within the city, it cost $4.00 and $2.00 for the same time periods.)
The zanjero wanted the private company to insist that its customers use
water more economically, so that farmers and truck gardeners would not
suffer a water famine in the coming summer.[3]

At the end of June, with hot dry days ahead, another setback hit the
city. A court ruling declared that the water bonds passed during Mayor
Eaton's term were invalid and, therefore, could not be issued or sold.
Mathews, a determined champion of municipal control, decided, even at
a time of near penury in the treasury, to use the water-bond sinking fund
for an appeal to the state supreme court. The council, caught in a dilemma
and not even sure of the legality of using the water-bond money for a lawsuit, decided on July 12 to put out another feeler and offered the water
company $2 million for its works (a provisional offer, as the whole mat-
ter had to go before the voters and be decided by ballot). Wonderfully,
the water company answered a week later, on July 29, that if the voters
were willing, it would accept the $2 million proposal. Mulholland, who
had acted as an important mediator during these negotiations, later recalled how he had been summoned to chief stockholder I. W. Hellman's
summer home in Lake Tahoe. There, the two held lengthy conferences
during which Mulholland urged Hellman to accept the offer because he
feared the growing public discontent would harm the water company. He
would later partially defend the private water company when he remembered how, for years, "the shibboleth of every self-seeking politician was
confiscation of the works or at the very best with the more moderate ones,
gross misrepresentations as to their value and exaggerated statements of
their net earnings." In 1904, as Pasadena's civic leaders contemplated mu-

nicipal ownership, Mulholland warned them to avoid overly harsh criticism of existing private plants, explaining that "the growth of towns is generally straggling and irregular and it would require the gift of prophecy on the part of an engineer to foresee the direction in which a town may extend most; hence the oft-seeming inaptness in pipe system designs of but a few years existence in growing towns." Stressing that excessive reproaches could interfere with "a just and businesslike appraisement," he added, "I was through that mill and it ground exceeding fine in the last years of my employment with the old Los Angeles Water Co. We found that the carping spirit that prompted it served to protract the controversy for a long period to the great disadvantage of both sides. In such matters we must expect to pay for at least some bone with the meat." He echoed these sentiments a year later during a speech before the Sunset Club, declaring that when the city's progress had been "vitally jeopardized," it required "a few wise heads" to engineer "an arrangement of compromise that settled the whole matter by the city agreeing to pay this sum of Two Million Dollars for the works."[4]

A small but obdurate group opposed the deal, largely on the grounds that the water company's price was too high. Proponents of the purchase argued, however, that the eventual legal costs of pursuing their cause would ultimately outweigh the current asking price. Moreover, they pointed out that this sale would include the long-disputed Crystal Springs installation. The majority in city council approved the buy and set about to draw up a compromise stipulation for the purchase of the waterworks as well as to draft an ordinance declaring its public necessity.[5]

With a bond election set for August 28, news items calculated to sway opinion began to appear. Less than two weeks before the election the city fathers sprang their own surprise with the revelation that on August 15, for $33,250, the city had secretly purchased 310 acres of water-bearing land in the Tujunga Wash adjoining the Pomeroy and Hooker lands. Eaton, Lippincott, and the others, it turned out, had made all those trips upriver for more than water measurements. This stratagem was to be repeated on a grander scale when Los Angeles made its giant reach for water in the Owens Valley. To secure options without arousing suspicion (and thereby causing owners to raise their price), two of the city's water attorneys had used as a front one of their clients, Don Antonio Lopez, purported to be the head of a Cuban syndicate interested in founding a colony in Southern California. After the farmers had sold and the land had gone into escrow, Don Antonio Lopez signed over the deeds to the City of Los Angeles. Perhaps because the newly acquired land lay near the headworks of the West Side Water Company and thus provided leverage against that company with which the city was in litigation, those opposing the water bonds failed to object, focusing instead solely on the private water company's sale price. At the time, no one questioned the morality of this subterfuge or its possible effect upon the farmers and owners who had sold. The deal was thoroughly publicized, and the mayor and the city attorney expressed their pleasure at the plan's success.[6]

The bond contest was spirited. Proponents made much of the fact that once the city had purchased the waterworks, it not only would see an end to all litigation with the old water company but would also own the Crystal Springs system. Above all, the city would enjoy the company's revenues, which W. H. Perry had declared to be $33,000 a month. On the eve of the election, a straw vote among the Merchants and Manufacturers Association yielded 230 for the bonds, 7 against, and 3 undecided. The opposition were few but vocal and used every legal means at hand to fight the proposal. The front man for this group of propertied and professional men with mingled motives was S. A. Waldron, a former deputy city assessor and now a schoolteacher whose father, David V. Waldron, was, according to contemporary Boyle Workman, a "chronic objector" and leading opponent of municipal ownership. While some bond foes doubtless wanted to continue litigation because they were honestly indignant over the $2 million price for the water company, most, like Waldron, seem to have acted out of self-interest. One opposing owner of a large acreage in the south end of town, who had long used only zanja water for a mere $2 a month, would pay much more under the city's management. The West Side Water Company also fought the purchase, while a vicious rumor circulated that agents were at work to influence black voters against the bonds. To what end, no one could say.[7]

To convince labor to vote against the bonds, a flier, or "dodger," as they were then called, circulated on the eve of election with language that would become familiar in future Los Angeles water debates. Titled "The Water Steal," it asked such inflammatory questions as "Why should the city donate $1,000,000 to the millionaires who own the water company? Give the million dollars to the laborers and mechanics instead of to the millionaires. VOTE AGAINST THIS STEAL!" The flier was not from labor, however, which already had tepidly endorsed the purchase in its official publication, the *Union Labor News*, presenting the choice as one between two evils: either paying too much for the waterworks or being bled under the present system. As with an aching tooth, the journal declared, "the sooner it's out the better." Both the American Federation of

Labor and the Socialist Party gave full support, but the portrayal of labor as victim to a water steal that would profit only the wealthy endured beyond this first municipal water contest.[8]

Voter turnout was light, and when many of the customary layabouts proved absent from the precincts, one old hand explained, "The water company and nobody else ain't passin' out no dough. So what's the use of the boys to get out and hustle the vote?" The final, unhustled, result favored the bonds five to one (6,284 for, 1,267 against), and the city at long last had its waterworks. Mayor Snyder immediately set off on a long-delayed summer vacation, and as he left, was congratulated by a well-wisher from San Francisco, who declared that he hoped his city, in its upcoming $25 million bond election, would follow the example of Los Angeles. After the official canvass of the vote, the president of the city council called out as he bid good-bye to his colleagues for the Labor Day weekend, "Don't forget that the city begins to make $1,000 a day next Sunday."[9]

MISADVENTURES IN BOND PEDDLING

The following week President William McKinley was shot while attending the Pan American Exposition in Buffalo, New York. He lingered until mid-September, when his death was tolled in Los Angeles by "Old Tom," the two-ton fire bell at City Hall. As the hushed city listened to its familiar tones—one stroke for each of the dead president's fifty-eight years—Theodore Roosevelt entered the White House. The twentieth century in America was now to begin in earnest, especially in Los Angeles, where the new president would play a fateful role.

Before the city could savor complete ownership of its waterworks, however, it had to sell the bonds, which turned out to entail as much conflict and drama as the election and also marked the beginning of attorney William B. Mathews's lifetime dedication to the city and the cause of municipal ownership. At first the bonds did not sell, and when the city discovered that on the first day of the sale the Waldron group had issued a printed notice warning prospective bond buyers of an impending suit against the bonds, certain infuriated councilmen suggested that a lynching should be in order. A *Los Angeles Times* cartoon portrayed Waldron as "his satanic majesty, Waldron the dummy," while a more reasoned response came from John M. Elliott, president of the First National Bank, a director of the private water company, and soon to be among the first city water commissioners. The diplomatic Elliott suggested that business conditions in the East, "and the consequent heavy demand for money, is partly the reason why the bonds were not sold." He dismissed the Waldron litigation as little more than a nuisance.[10]

When at last word came that buyers had been found, the pair who came to be known as "the two Billies" (City Attorney "Billy" Mathews and Treasurer "Uncle Billy" Workman) embarked on their bond-selling mission, which was to keep them in the East for two troublesome months. Their hopes rose and fell as bondbuyers materialized and defaulted. When a buyer was finally secured, they became so fearful of another monkey wrench from the Waldron crowd that they went immediately to the Guaranty Trust Company of New York, where Workman, as city treasurer, set about the arduous task of signing his name two thousand times. A witness recalled that every time Workman "dipped his pen in the ink-well he absently shook it towards the universe at large, to rid it of any spare ink that might cause a blot. By the time he had finished the two thousandth signature, the office, including a brand new carpet, presented a general polka dot effect." With the transaction at last completed and the money in the bank, Workman telegraphed his son to draw a warrant for $2 million to the order of the Los Angeles City Water Company. After endorsements by W. H. Perry, president, and S. H. Mott, secretary, the money was paid. The city at last owned its waterworks.[11]

Treasurer Workman received a hero's welcome when he stepped off the train in Los Angeles and heard the music of a welcoming brass band. Mathews, who also received high praise for his adroit dealings with the eastern money men and attorneys, remained in the East consulting with lawyers about the Hooker and Pomeroy condemnation case then before the Supreme Court. Several weeks later, on a Sunday afternoon, February 25, 1902, this self-effacing man quietly slipped back into town after having made a detour to his boyhood home in Maysville, Kentucky.[12]

Two weeks earlier, on February 6, in an event as plain and down-to-earth as Mathews's return to the city, Mayor Snyder and members of the council marched from City Hall to the old water office at Marchessault and Alameda. Upon entering the building, the mayor asked for the attention of all those present and then pronounced that he now took possession of the waterworks on behalf of the City of Los Angeles. All thirty-one employees of the old water company were to be retained, and William Mulholland was officially named the new superintendent. Mulholland would later say, "When the city bought the works, they bought me along with it."[13]

THE CITY'S NEW ACQUISITION

Before the bond election, a specially appointed committee had wrestled with problems of organization and questions concerning the new city water department's management and personnel (including inquiries to fifty cities with municipal water systems in order to examine their procedures). Both the committee and city council had determined that its management would be conducted under strict civil service rules and independent of the political body; therefore, a board of elected water commissioners would control the system. Debate immediately arose over the composition of the commission, but the council finally agreed to select seven temporary commissioners until regulars could be elected the following year. Fred Eaton was considered and rejected on the grounds that "his views as an engineer might clash on technical points with those of the superintendent, who must be an experienced engineer, according to the terms of the ordinance." (Eaton was, however, retained as a consulting engineer for the first three months after the takeover.)[14]

The committee also took up the matter of a new location for the water system's headquarters. The old office on Marchessault Street where Mulholland had once lived and worked was now in the heart of the tenderloin district. Because eliminating the expense of door-to-door collectors was soon to necessitate all water customers' paying at a central office, a more convenient and desirable location had to be established. The old office would remain as a storage center and maintenance yard.

Against this backdrop of activity and confusion as the city learned how to run its own water department, William Mulholland stepped out of the shadows into the public light. His name and opinions began to appear with regularity in the newspapers. The city fathers, some of whom called him the "grand old man" of the waterworks (he was forty-seven), agreed that he should continue as superintendent, although a few were reluctant to pay the $5,000 salary that he demanded. He had received $3,000 a year from the private water company, but as he explained to the council, he had also been able to take outside work. The previous year, he had received more than $8,000 from such jobs. Standard Oil Company, for example, had retained him for a few days at $500 a day. The city ordinance, however, required the superintendent to devote his entire time to the duties of his office, so that henceforth he would be unable to take such lucrative assignments.[15]

He now met regularly with the water commissioners, who in their first meeting on February 13, 1902, requested that he prepare for them a list of all the property formerly belonging to the water company. Mulholland in turn presented a preliminary report on the system's most needed extensions, enlargements, and repairs. He later recalled how much had been needed to expand a system "at least ten years behind the actual needs of the city," which itself was about to experience "a period of growth unprecedented in the annals of any considerable city of the country." He urged giving utmost importance to two future projects: first, the building of an infiltration gallery (in effect, a "submerged dam") for water storage at the Narrows and the Buena Vista pumping station—an installation that would secure each day 6.5 million more gallons of water that were currently flowing away unused and unseen underground; second (and more controversial), the adoption of the meter system of selling water.[16]

With monthly receipts of $43,000 and operating expenses of $5,000, the department's earnings were expected to finance these projects as well as pay off its bonded indebtedness. Along with promises of lower water rates, other reforms included shortening the work day from ten to eight hours for all employees and laborers in the water department. At the urging of Commissioner Toll, the board also agreed that laborers should be paid weekly rather than monthly.[17]

After Mulholland and City Engineer Stafford indicated that the grave hydraulic engineering problems on the infiltration gallery required a consulting engineer, the board employed Fred Eaton for three months. What else he did that spring of 1902 would not be fully known for several years, but with hindsight a clue appears in an account of an April meeting of the Engineers' and Architects' Society of Southern California in the Eaton home. Described as a "delightfully unconventional social affair" and not the usual "stag" party, it was hosted by Mrs. Eaton and several other ladies, who enhanced the evening with vocal offerings, one even playing a cornet solo. "Mr. Eaton," the report read, "was unexpectedly absent, plunging around in the mountains in search of a gold mine." The treasure he sought was, in fact, water, and the date marks the renewal of his serious investigations in Owens Valley. Later he was to say that although he had informed Mulholland of his searches, he did not reveal their locations at that time.[18]

As a public official, Mulholland's activities expanded into social spheres previously unvisited. In what was apparently a combination business-social weekend in early spring, Mulholland was a guest at Henry O'Melveny's mountain retreat, the Crags, in the San Gabriel Mountains. Also present was banker John Mackay Elliott of the newly appointed water commission. Although the outing seems to have been relaxed and friendly (Elliott's family was with him), surely water matters were foremost. Soon after that weekend, Mulholland became a member of the distinguished Sunset Club, doubtless under the aegis of O'Melveny and Elliott, who were charter members.[19]

WATCHDOGS OF WATER CONSERVATION

Wasting water ranked with the seven deadly sins in Mulholland's view, and because he was passionate about water meters as a means of curtailing overuse, he began campaigning for their installation almost as soon as he became superintendent. He also began to issue warnings about Los Angeles's limited water supply. "I will call your attention," he said to the water commissioners at the beginning of 1902, "to the rather startling fact that with the exception of the 12,000,000 or 14,000,000 gallons of water daily that was delivered to irrigators last summer, the water company was delivering to its consumers every available gallon of water that could be derived by the means of supply now in use from the watershed of the Los Angeles River." Urging that the first meters be placed with the excessive users, he concluded, "I am quite confident that with the use of even 1,000 meters, to be placed at random where extravagant use is reported, a saving of from 1,000,000 to 1,500,000 gallons daily would be effected."[20]

Persuaded by his arguments and those from other authoritative sources (especially cities pioneering the meter system such as Cleveland, Detroit, Minneapolis, and St. Louis), the water commission agreed to install meters selectively. Protests were not long in coming, and as complaints arose, the public got its first taste of Mulholland's rough side. His first adversary was ironically a lawyer whose legislation, the 1887 Wright Irrigation Act, had enabled communities to form irrigation districts that challenged the dominance of California's monopolistic land moguls. Formerly a senator from Modesto, C. C. Wright had in 1901 served as a trustee of the Los Angeles Bar Association and had been a member of the citizens' committee that had supported municipalizing water. He lived in Boyle Heights not far from the Mulhollands, and here, with rising indignation, Mulholland had observed his wanton use of precious city water on an expanse of greensward. Deciding to use Wright as an example, Mulholland, water commission president Herman Silver, and several workmen descended like avenging angels on Wright's place to install a meter. (The city's water ordinance allowed department employees to enter a private property for business purposes such as repairs and meter reading.) As work got under way, Wright appeared and threatened to kick them all into the road. At the next commission meeting, Wright acknowledged his heavy use of water. He attempted some placating remarks to Mulholland and Silver, saying he did not object to the idea of meters, but added, "I do object to anybody coming and digging on my premises, without so much as saying, 'good morning, sir,' and I will not permit it, until the courts shall have passed upon the subject."[21]

Mulholland next had his say. "For more than two years I have gone by Mr. Wright's place many times, and I never went by, either day or night, that sprinklers were not running. The collectors and inspectors have constantly made the same complaints, and the water has frequently been found running down the street from Wright's lawn, and everybody complained of the waste of water. . . . If everybody used water like he does," he continued, "only 3,000 consumers in the entire city would get water, and the other 21,000 would go without. The Hazard Reservoir, from which he is supplied, was down to two feet, and in a few hours would have been empty, unless all waste was stopped, and as his was the most flagrant case, I sent the men to put a meter on, and he threatened to kick the whole outfit into the street."

The next day, Wright got a restraining order against the City of Los Angeles, the commissioners, and Mulholland, charging that the water meter ordinance violated the Fourteenth Amendment. The commissioners felt they should support Mulholland for fear that his authority might subsequently be called into question, although privately some must have wished that he could have applied a slightly more velvet glove. Tact and diplomacy were never much in evidence when Mulholland thought he was right, and doubtless some of the enmities that piled up against him through the years resulted from his sometimes abrupt manner and blunt tongue. When one man tried to sell the city a private water pipeline, Mulholland told the commissioners the city had as much use for a wooden leg as it did for a mile of clay pipe. A year later at a water commission meeting, a delegation from Garvanza showed up to protest the abominable water they were getting and also to complain that the young man who was supposed to activate the pump each morning at 5:00 A.M. to assure delivery of water was not rousing himself until 8:00 A.M., so that Garvanzans found themselves much distressed and incommoded. Mulholland did not offer much comfort about the quality of water and told them that lack of funds prevented any immediate action on cleaning the system, but he did assure them something would be done about the slug-abed youth at the pumphouse. One of the committee then piped up to suggest a possible replacement: "I know a good old man . . ." Mulholland cut him short: "I'm not here to investigate the merits or demerits of old men. I'll get someone that can run that pump." One so rudely dismissed was not apt to harbor warm feelings towards Mulholland.[22]

As guardian of the domestic water supply for Los Angeles, Mulholland knew the limits of its resources. He also had a kind of rough-hewn populist social philosophy about urban water use, which is perhaps best captured in a statement he made at the time of the meter uproar. "Owing to peculiar climatic conditions we can never expect Los Angeles to rank among the cities of small water-consumption for the reason that the semi-leisure class is attracted here by the adaptability of both soil and climate for building up beautiful homes by reason of the long intervals of almost absolute cessation of rainfall." But, he concluded, that was no reason "why the privilege of using water for this purpose should be given on the present unbusiness-like basis, which compels the careful and frugal to pay for the carelessness and extravagance of others. . . . Water bills, where meters have been applied, have frequently been reduced one-half, without apparent detriment to the lawns or grounds. In my judgment, meters should be applied, and additional inspectors employed."[23]

The summer of 1902 began with Mayor Snyder's proclamation restricting water use. With the meter system under way, certain owners, especially those with lawns and large gardens, protested the limitation of six hours each day for sprinkling. The commissioners were assailed with complaints, and President Silver reported that one caller to his office had grown so abusive that he had to order him out. The beleaguered Silver said he contemplated making a requisition from the water fund for a bed and mattress in the office, as he had been called out at midnight and four o'clock in the morning "to come out to Stickety-stick Street and stop a leak." Other customers were wily in their ruses to beat the system. The hired man of oil magnate E. L. Doheny allowed the water department to put a meter on a service pipe at his employer's estate but failed to mention that there were two service pipes. After the department had installed a meter on one pipe, the hired man merely hooked up the meterless pipe and merrily continued his unlimited consumption of water. Self-styled experts began to publish figures to show that water was in fact ample and that meters were simply an unnecessary expense. When the *Evening Express* accused the commission of favoring certain big businesses with cheap rates, the board quickly rebutted, pointing out that those establishments' low rates resulted from their use of zanja, rather than domestic, water—a practice that was soon to stop.[24]

ENLARGING THE WORKS

Superintendent Mulholland did not only attend meetings but was often to be found in the field, as when a reporter caught up with him in May 1902, at the Buena Vista work site. After donning rubber boots and a sou'wester, the reporter had the thrill of riding in a tin bucket with Mulholland 112 feet down a shaft eleven and a half feet in diameter to the site where tunnel work for the new infiltration gallery was under way. Down this hole where lay the city's hopes for more water, the reporter found his footing on the muddy bottom, noticed water oozing from the tunnel walls, and observed that the sky seemed very far away. In darkness relieved only by a string of electric globes and candles in wire frames attached to the tunnel walls, he could faintly make out a "husky fellow" hard at it with a pick as his companion loaded the broken shale, dirt, and mud into baskets and buckets sent to the surface by a windlass run with a small stationary engine. The tunnel work was a hazardous around-the-clock operation, and as only one man could work in the heading, three shifts of two men each laboriously dug and hauled with pick and shovel. Mulholland explained that it was hard to get good experienced men to handle the pick at the bottom of the shaft, but that he was satisfied with their progress. These toilers—the Pat Harkinses and Handsome Bradys—were never far from Mulholland's mind when he inveighed against water-wasters. He knew the cost in human terms at which their water was bought. Although completing the tunnel would take two years, Mulholland hoped that by summer the water from the wells they planned to sink and pipe to Buena Vista Reservoir by means of a new large and modern pump would supply an additional 2 million gallons a day. When the tunnel was completed, 6 million gallons a day could be expected. Having seen enough, the reporter climbed into the bucket and Mulholland sent him flying to the surface with a pull of the cord. Once again in the sunshine, the reporter concluded that one descent had been enough.[25]

In addition to proposing construction of a second reservoir near Ivanhoe on a 110-acre tract of city-owned land, Mulholland in June asked attorney Mathews to start proceedings against the owners of two pumping plants near the Pomeroy and Hooker ranch near Burbank. The river ran through the lands of two ranchers, and although the private water company had left them undisturbed, now Mulholland wanted to secure the rights for Los Angeles. Mathews in the meantime created a new charter amendment (adopted by the people in the December election) by which the water commissioners alone were to administer the water plant and collect revenues, out of which operating costs would be defrayed while the surplus was applied to the interest and sinking fund on the bonds. Now officially known as the Water Department, its future commissioners (reduced from seven to five) were to be appointed by the mayor and be subject to confirmation by the council. Members would serve gratis, although the president of the commission (or board) was to receive a salary of $3,000 a year. The board was to maintain an office accessible to the public and was to meet once a week.

All in all, the first year of the new municipal waterworks went surprisingly well. Rates by the end of the year had been reduced 10 percent, and between the first of February and the end of November, water revenues amounted to $455,469.13. "Actual Gold Mine," crowed the *Los Angeles Times*. In his semiannual report, Mulholland expressed satisfaction with the tunnel work near the Buena Vista pumping station and announced that six wells had been completed, promising to add 500 inches of water to the supply. Yet beneath this optimism lay his continued worry that the dry cycle of the last decade might continue while the city's population grew. He knew he could not rely solely on admonitions to the people to conserve, and he feared having to seek water in the heavy gravel beds south of the city, a process that would be expensive. "Since the summer of 1893," he wrote, "there has not been a season that has not shown a decrease in the flow of the stream over that of the preceding year . . . until in the present year the diminution . . . amounts to considerable over 50 percent from that of 1893."[26]

CHAPTER 9

New Regime for a Booming Town

1903–1904

"A SPLENDID BODY OF BUSINESSMEN"

For all the congratulatory talk about having removed the water system from politics, it never altogether escaped the controversies and power struggles centered in City Hall. Although Democrat Meredith Snyder became mayor again at the end of 1902 with a plurality of 2,700 after winning every precinct in the city, the majority of city officers and councilmen remained Republican. In selecting the new five-member board of water commissioners, Snyder reflected this balance by choosing two Republicans, one Democrat who voted Republican, and two Democrats. During this board's tenure, the Los Angeles water system would be revolutionized. All the players were assembled—heroes, villains, and simple walk-ons—for a drama that would play out in the decade ahead. The city council's reaction to the mayor's selections for membership in these new organizations reflected the growing power of white, conservative Anglo-Americans who trusted businessmen, feared labor, and equated progress with economic growth and patriotism. Their epitome became General Harrison Gray Otis, whose voice would grow louder and stronger in the decade ahead. Mayor Snyder's choices for the reorganized five-member water commission received full council approval, demonstrating its unabashed faith in capitalists and a disregard for engineer James C. Kays's suggestion that a well-paid superintendent, auditor, and engineer named by the mayor would manage the waterworks far better than a commission of businessmen. For the department now to be under the supervision of two new governmental commissions, water and civil service, the mayor named five wealthy men: two bankers, a real estate man, an electric rail magnate, and a building contractor with special ties to the Santa Fe Railroad Company. No doctors, lawyers, or representatives of labor, science, and education seem to have been considered, an indication that water affairs would be conducted with attitudes and methods not unlike those of the old water company. Indeed, within the year, such charges were being made.[1]

The first water commission apparently gave Mulholland no qualms, for he later commended its makeup ("a splendid body of business men"), especially praising the two who had served as directors with the old water company and with whom he already had congenial working relations: John M. Elliott, president of the First National Bank, and J. J. Fay, former president of Citizens Bank. Fay became the first president of the water commission, a full-time job with a salary of $3,000 a year. The others served without compensation other than a per diem of $10. A third commissioner, William Mead, had been involved in Los Angeles real estate since 1886, while the last two represented bank and rail interests. Lewis A. Grant, who served only briefly as he died the following year, was a contractor for the Santa Fe Railroad; Moses H. Sherman was vice president of the Los Angeles–Pacific Railway Company. Both were directors of the Bank of California, and Sherman was a founding stockholder. Of the five commissioners, only Sherman would become controversial and problematic in the water story.[2]

Whereas not a word arose in the city council over Snyder's choice of water commissioners, a hubbub erupted over one of his candidates for the newly formed civil service commission, Charles Dwight Willard. A civic booster and Progressive Republican who voted Democratic and had been prominent as secretary of the chamber of commerce in the fight for the harbor at San Pedro, Willard was, at the time of his appointment, secretary of the reform-minded Municipal League and also of the Jobbers' Association. He had old-guard enemies in City Hall, and his confirmation was contested because he was already a paid secretary of another organization (such fine points of conflict of interest had not disturbed the civic conscience in choosing members for the water commission). The conservative Republican councilman backed by railroad interests, Frank Nofziger (grandfather of Ronald Reagan's consultant Lynn Nofziger), branded Willard "an extremist." To avoid a showdown, Willard sent the mayor a graceful letter of withdrawal in which he said, "Like the average American citizen, I dislike to seem to retreat under fire, but if the fight is to result in endangering a reform for which thousands of the best men of the city have worked faithfully, then there is nothing for me to do but yield good-naturedly to the inevitable." Mayor Snyder, angry at the council's refusal of his candidate, unhappily accepted Willard's departure. By March, all of Snyder's appointments had been confirmed, and when as if freshly anointed he entertained his new official family with a banquet, Henry O'Melveny of the civil service sat at his right hand, J. J. Fay and J. M. Elliott of the water commission at his left. After the sumptuous feast and toasts with Mumm's Extra Dry, the mayor thanked all thirty new commissioners for their service to the municipality.[3]

HOW TO MEET WATER DEMANDS

At its first meeting, the new water commission reappointed William Mulholland as superintendent; James P. Vroman, secretary; L. M. Anderson, auditor; Niles Knickerbocker, cashier; and George D. Pessell, water overseer. Throughout the spring of 1903, water affairs advanced smoothly as the commission dealt chiefly with minor matters and began to consider bids for a new department headquarters building on city-owned property at Second and Central Avenue. Rains at the first of the year seemed to have relieved the threat of drought, but when he reported an annual rainfall of 10.26 inches in March, Mulholland was moved to tell the board, "One of the trials of my life is to make people believe we have not had a very wet year. We can't meet the demand with less than fourteen inches." A week after those words, the city was drenched with almost an inch of rain.[4]

Two large and costly projects preoccupied Mulholland in the spring of 1903: replacing the domestic water service's main conduit north of the city limits with an enlarged duct, and completing the high-gravity reservoir in Elysian Park west of the Buena Vista Reservoir. The latter, as Mulholland had explained in his annual report, was undertaken to secure greater water storage because of the growing city's increasing demands and the alarming depletion of ground supplies from agricultural use. "It may be urged that in the event of a wet winter, the river will supply all the water needed by the city for all purposes, but it is a well-known fact that the river makes no sudden response to a single year of abundant rainfall."[5]

Mulholland fretted about the expanding city he served. How would water be delivered if builders insisted on higher skyscrapers? "I don't know what we'll do if they keep on climbing skyward," he confided to a reporter. "It will not be possible to put on enough pressure to supply them, even if we were inclined to try it." He pointed out that some eastern cities had ordered a five-story limit; those who built higher had to provide their own pumping facilities. Domestic users continued to demand better water pressure, which, when provided, often resulted in bursting mains, especially among the older services. In Boyle Heights, after greater pressure had been provided, some of the old pipes, said Mulholland, "had revolted."[6]

A third major engineering project involved the manufacture and installation of two large pumps for the infiltration gallery at the Buena Vista Pumping Station. By midyear, impatient with progress on the pump ordered from the Risdon Iron and Locomotive Works in San Francisco, Mulholland traveled north several times in the spring of 1903 with his associate engineer, Fred Fischer, to consult with the company's mechanical engineer and his good friend, David Dorward. Mulholland's ten-year-old son, Perry, accompanied the men on one of their junkets and later remembered that they arrived just as the celebrations for the completion of the Pacific Cable began, a revolutionary event that meant a message now could be sent around the world in twelve minutes. Amid the sounds of gunfire and cannon salutes on the waterfront, the ten-year-old boy thought the Spanish-American War had resumed.[7]

Mulholland returned home to confront a threat to the city's water supply by an oil refinery on the banks of the Arroyo Seco. In the 1890s, oil discoveries within the city by E. L. Doheny and his partner had set off such a frenzy of drilling that, by the time Fred Eaton became mayor, Los Angeles was in danger of being permanently defaced by a landscape of rough wooden derrick towers and drilling equipment. Accusations and complaints of pollution and odors were constant, especially near the mushrooming refineries. Two weeks after Mulholland's return from San Francisco, on July 17, 1903, the department of public works ordered him and Dr. Powers of the health department to study a court ruling resulting from property owners' complaints against the Union Consolidated Refining Company on the south bank of the Arroyo Seco between Avenues 22 and 23. One hundred thirty-five feet below the sands on which the refinery was situated lay the infiltration tunnel then under construction for the city's increased water supply. After investigating the refinery, Mulholland reported that the crude oil posed no menace, as it was too heavy to percolate down into the soil, but the refined oil and liquid runoffs from the plant would endanger the water supply. He considered "the presence of the refinery in its present location as being a most decided menace to the water supply of the City," and he proposed that "all the tanks containing refined oil might be set in a concrete basin of sufficient capacity to hold all the oil in case it should escape from the tanks." Should a large fire occur, then all the oil would be caught and could not penetrate the soil. Although the manager of the plant indicated a willingness to make this correction, nearby owners continued to insist that the whole plant be removed, and so the matter went to the courts.[8]

LOCAL SCANDALS

While the first of the big pumps in the new infiltration gallery was about to be activated at the end of September, Mulholland was shocked by two scandals affecting men he knew. On September 4, the man who gave Griffith Park to the city, Colonel Griffith J. Griffith, shot and maimed his wife. Eleven days later, former mayor Fred Eaton divorced his. Mulholland later appeared as a character witness at the highly publicized Griffith trial, for which defense attorney Earl Rogers devised a new defense of "alcoholic insanity." Although Eaton's divorce may not have come as a surprise to Mulholland (the Eatons had been maintaining separate domiciles in Santa Monica), the fact that a distraught Mrs. Eaton blurted to a reporter that she could explain the breakup in one word— "whiskey"—would have struck him as an unfortunate public laundering of dirty linen. Helen Eaton now became a poignant figure living alone with her aged mother as Fred secured custody of the adult children, a curious business as by then his daughter was a married woman.[9]

Eaton listed his residence as the California Club. Apparently energized by the dramatic change in his life that included a romance with a woman twenty years his junior, he renewed his pursuit of a great water system for Los Angeles. For over ten years Eaton had been possessed of the vision that, by his own account, had come the summer of 1892 as he looked over the prospects of an irrigation project in Owens Valley, Inyo County. Finding the project economically unworkable but still intrigued with the possibility of supplying Los Angeles with the abundant water he found there, Eaton spent $10,000 "on a gamble that surveys would show it feasible." He had apparently spoken of the grandiose scheme at times to his engineering colleagues, who dismissed it as a pipe dream. Although continuing his local engineering and real estate activities, Eaton renewed his Owens Valley endeavors, especially after learning that the United States Government Reclamation Service had begun to consider the area as a possible site for an irrigation district.[10]

THE BACTERIA PROBLEM

In September, Dr. Powers announced the bacteria count was too high in tests of river water. Because of the increased number of typhoid cases in the city, he declared the supply from that source would have to be cut off. "Good drinking water should not contain more than 500 bacteria to a cubic centimeter," he said. The river was testing 6,000. Powers hastened to reassure the public that their chief source of drinking water from Crystal Springs tested less than 50. Notices listing punishable violations were now posted along the river, along with announcements that changes would have to be made along the river banks, and pigeon and livestock keepers were issued warnings.[11]

At this time a new member who would play a curious role in the coming aqueduct story joined Dr. Powers's staff. Miss Ethel L. Leonard, described as a "lady bacteriologist," was a graduate of the medical department of the University of Southern California. After advanced studies at Johns Hopkins University, she had been hired by the city to fight bubonic plague and other contagious diseases. The board of health appointed her city bacteriologist at a salary of $75 a month, jocosely announcing that the choice could not be regarded as political as she was unable to vote. Characterized as young and ambitious, she would one day become one of Mulholland's virulent enemies.[12]

"THE WATER IS YOURS. ENJOY IT BUT DON'T WASTE IT."

At the end of the rainless summer of 1903, word went out that householders were to have first claim on the domestic water supply. When asked, "How about the irrigators, Mr. Mulholland?" the superintendent shot back, "Oh, they're dead." Explaining that no water was left for irrigation after the domestic supply was taken out, he signaled his intent in the coming year to close the zanja system, which had outlived its usefulness. Would the parks suffer when the zanjas dried up? Would they receive city water? Yes, Mulholland replied with a burst of lyricism, "Make the parks blossom as the rose; make 'em fresh and green and beautiful, but—" Here the lyric mode ceased as he uttered next what was to be his essential policy and message to the city: "The water is yours. Enjoy it but don't waste it."[13]

Water commission meetings were often taken up with petitioners from outlying and sparsely settled sections leveling charges of unfair treatment. A group from the highlands northwest of the city repeatedly demanded that a special pump be installed to provide water on their properties. After each demand they were told that their properties were 100 feet or more above the level to which the city system could supply water and that they must create their own water plant. Then, they were told, when they had gained enough consumers to produce a revenue equal to 10 percent of the investment, the city would be willing to buy it. The commission explained that because it could not comply with the demands of each small group that wanted special service, it based its policy on performing the greatest good for the greatest number. This meant they could not supply water to the city's sparsely inhabited areas. All this had been repeated many times, but on December 1, the group reappeared at a commission meeting led by one Mrs. Scott, who carried a large umbrella that she used as a means of emphasizing her message. Repeatedly whacking it on the table before the impassive faces of the water board, she launched her tirade. "If you people were ordinary mortals and not bankers, we'd have a better chance. The trouble with you men is that you count water like money. You show no justice nor fairness to us." Declaring that a break in the Angeleno Heights Reservoir the week before was "a judgment" sent on them, she threatened legal action, whacked the table one more time and departed, leaving behind a room of silent men, with only Commissioner Elliott muttering, "Humph." Breaking the silence, Mulholland reported that the damage in the reservoir break would not exceed $600 or $700, and that the repair work had already begun.[14]

Although the commissioners persisted in pointing out that the city charter strictly prohibited the delivery of water beyond the city limits, unhappy hill dwellers continued to appear. They included former mayor Henry T. Hazard, who insisted that he receive water on his property, which lay outside the city limits. When denied, he left in high dudgeon, muttering about "usurpation" and "confiscation." With the increasing demand for water, Mulholland and the commission began to voice their opposition to annexations to the city. In his annual report for 1903, Mulholland cited the dubious wisdom of having admitted the suburb of Garvanza, where the city had spent "not less than ten times more per capita to properly serve that small addition than was spent for the balance of the city, and the end is not yet." Although the Hollywood area boasted that its supply, provided by Union Hollywood Water Company, could provide for a city of 10,000, in fact part of its water came from a company about to be purchased by the City of Los Angeles.[15]

At year's end, complaints notwithstanding, the city's waterworks had earned general approval, improved services, and reduced rates to the consumer. Gross revenues of $614,264.92 for the fiscal year had equaled 30 percent of the purchase price; the department had laid over forty miles of mains and installed 4,002 taps; the flat rate to consumers had been reduced 10 percent, and the metered rate, 50 percent. An editorial in the *Los Angeles Herald* applauded the commission for its service and management and Mulholland "for his sound judgment and efficient supervision." It concluded, "The wisdom of taking the department out of politics is amply vindicated. The water board is composed of business and professional men who made considerable sacrifices in accepting the responsibilities thrust upon them, and the result is a credit both to their citizenship and to their ability. Nor should it be forgotten that the board attributes, in large degree, the high standard of efficiency maintained by the water force, to the fostering influence of the civil service."[16]

SEEDS OF FUTURE TROUBLE

Two events during the period from 1902 to 1903 created little stir at the time, but certain chroniclers later came to regard them as having portentous—possibly even sinister—significance in the city's water story. One was Moses H. Sherman's appointment to the water commission; the second was the formation of a syndicate that opened Whitley Heights in Hollywood and next participated in a land deal involving George K. Porter's ranch in the San Fernando Valley. In years to come, some would see the figures enmeshed in those events as conspirators in a great plot to dupe the city into paying for a costly water system devised to render their land deals profitable.[17]

Whatever qualities Mayor Snyder may have been looking for when he named Moses Hazeltine Sherman to the first water commission, idealism and devotion to municipally owned waterworks could not have counted among them. For all his undoubted intelligence, capabilities, and business acumen, a dark side lurked in Sherman, who practiced a ruthless brand of laissez-faire capitalism and had mastered the art of growing rich with other men's money. He never went to jail and he rarely lost a lawsuit, but he skirted both. A native of Vermont, he came as a young schoolteacher to Arizona Territory, where his ability and ambition soon put him in the forefront of public affairs. He shortly abandoned the classroom for a career of land acquisition, speculation, banking, and, most important, the development of transportation systems. He briefly served as Arizona's adjutant general in 1883, and afterward used the honorific "General," thus creating an interesting confusion with General William Tecumseh Sherman of Civil War fame.

Moses Sherman had early engaged in politics (Republican) and water development and in 1883 was involved in an irrigation project known as the Arizona Canal. By the time of his selection as a water commissioner in Los Angeles, he had for many years been vice president and a major shareholder in the Phoenix Water Company, which at the end of 1903 was threatened by a public that wanted to hold a bond election in order to acquire its own municipal system. Sherman announced that he would fight the attempt all the way to the Supreme Court, and in the spring of 1904 he brought suit against the municipality to stop the sale of bonds for the proposed waterworks.[18]

Accounts of the boom lured Sherman to Los Angeles in 1889, and by 1891, with his partner and brother-in-law, Eli P. Clark, he had created the first electric rail system between Los Angeles and Pasadena. After selling it to Henry E. Huntington, the brothers-in-law built lines towards Santa Monica and other ocean points. This system, sold to E. H. Harriman and expanded in 1907, was taken over by Huntington in 1910 and became property of the Southern Pacific—a network of interurban lines popularly known as the Big Red Cars that interconnected far-flung areas to central Los Angeles.[19]

In the 1890s, with their hard times and business panics, Sherman was often embroiled in legal battles that earned him enemies and a reputation for tough-minded wiliness. In the early nineties, he had figured in the case of *San Diego v. the San Diego and Los Angeles Railroad Company.* San Diego had granted 5,000 acres of pueblo land to the rail company for development of a transit system, and the suit was brought when Sherman, one of the two trustees acting for the city, proved to be a stockholder in and a director of the railroad company. Based on the general principle that no man can faithfully serve two masters, the court found that he had violated the strictures surrounding conflict of interest, even though his honesty and impartiality were unquestioned.[20]

In 1894, a San Francisco banker doing jail time after the debacle and collapse of his father's Pacific Bank accused Sherman of having helped to break that bank. Through demands, intimidation, and threats of blackmail, according to the imprisoned banker, Sherman had exacted a loan of $165,000 to convert a horse car line in Phoenix, Arizona, into an electric road. He had bullied the bank into making the loan it could ill afford by threatening to reveal its shaky financial condition to the banking commission. Then he had subsequently been unwilling to repay the loan in a timely fashion. Sherman, the banker accused, had contributed to the demise of his and his father's bank. Sherman denied everything.[21]

A year later, stockholders in the by then defunct Los Angeles Consolidated Electric Railway accused Sherman, who as founder and president had held most of its stock, of having seized control of all the assets. In the sale and reorganization, they charged, he gave them no part of the stock but instead retained it all in his own name. Four years later, in December 1899, the Pacific Bank brought an action against Sherman asking for a judgment of $250,000. Believing that Sherman had manipulated its funds so as to pay no dividends, the bank now asked for an accounting, especially in regard to 25,500 shares of stock in the Los Angeles Consolidated Electric Railway, which Sherman and the bank had held as equal owners but now had vanished into a financial maze devised by Sherman and Clark. Whatever the truth about these machinations, Sherman had earned the dislike and distrust of the *San Francisco Examiner,* and when William Randolph Hearst founded the *Los Angeles Examiner* at the end of 1903, that paper would be the first to launch an attack against Sherman in Los Angeles.[22]

By 1903, Sherman and Clark were masters of a successful and burgeoning electric railway company as well as recognized leaders in Los Angeles financial and banking circles. Their connections and business associations now included membership in land syndicates involving General Harrison Gray Otis and Harry Chandler, general manager of the *Times,* who, with various other associates, had embarked on a program of massive land acquisitions. In April, Sherman and a number of these associates participated in an event that, although apparently unconnected with Mulholland and water, did involve men who would one day be seen as having conspired in events to come. While Mulholland and the water commissioners wrestled with ways to improve the city's water system, a group of civic leaders and promoters celebrated the simultaneous opening of Whitley Heights in Hollywood and a new Los Angeles–Pacific Railway line leading there from downtown Los Angeles. Water Commissioner Sherman was one of the new road's builders. On the gala day, in his private parlor car, "Mermaid," he led a jolly crowd to the outlying district of Hollywood. As they rattled along, Sherman told amusing stories and pointed out the extensive work being done on Sunset Boulevard, the avenue that would connect Hollywood to Los Angeles. After a day of picnicking, tallyho rides, races with newfangled automobiles, visits to the grounds of the new Hollywood Hotel and to the Outpost, the nearby home of General and Mrs. Harrison Gray Otis (who also entertained with an Arbor Day tree planting on their estate), the climax arrived on Whitley Heights with a ceremony of flag raising and speeches. Amid the paeans to progress, Mayor Snyder praised new developments and loosely borrowed from John Keats's poetry when he rhapsodized that "a good road is a thing of beauty and a joy forever."[23]

While this group of self-congratulating capitalists celebrated their advancement of civilization into the Hollywood hills, back in town a strike against Sherman and Clark's rail line had just been broken up. After the labor movement's weakening in the late 1890s, an unprecedented "surge of unionism" between 1900 and 1904 had invigorated workers to take action regarding their grievances. When the strike proved of short duration, the anti-union *Los Angeles Times* jeered, "There are still laborers who call themselves strikers, but they are only men out of work." When President Theodore Roosevelt came to town a week later, local strifes were temporarily set aside, as everyone, including the Council of Labor, turned out for a great parade with brass bands and a marching group known as "Teddy's Terrors" to cheer a travel-worn president as he proceeded rumpled and unshaven from the train station to the Westminster Hotel, where he was to address a luncheon meeting.[24]

The September 1903 sale of George K. Porter's San Fernando Valley ranch land to a syndicate whose membership included General Otis was no secret; it was, in fact, trumpeted in the newspapers. The investors, including Porter himself, were E. H. Harriman, H. E. Huntington, A. B. Hammond, W. G. Kerckhoff, General H. G. Otis, J. F. Sartori, George C. Hunt, and E. T. Earl. The holding comprised one-third of the northern half of the San Fernando Valley, with the east-west Roscoe Boulevard as the approximate dividing line. The 16,450 acres sold for $575,750, or $35 an acre. During the Southern Pacific's construction of the San Fernando Tunnel in 1874 and 1875, the north half of the 175,000-acre valley had been acquired by San Francisco boot and shoe wholesalers Ben F. Porter and George K. Porter and by Senator Charles Maclay, then living in Los Angeles. Maclay's lands lay east of the Southern Pacific tracks. In 1874 he had platted lots and farmlands and had established the town site of San Fernando near the mission. The west section, owned by Ben F. Porter, began at Aliso Canyon and extended to the Santa Susana Pass. Between these two tracts (which included the west end of the town of San Fernando) lay George K. Porter's land. As earlier recounted, during the boom Fred Eaton had attempted a water project for Ben Porter near the fledgling town site of Chatsworth Park. After its dam failed, the land had remained vacant aside from a few sales and some dry farming of grain crops.

With the quarrying of rock in the Chatsworth hills for the breakwater in San Pedro and the commencement of the building of the Chatsworth Tunnel in 1898, the little settlement livened up to a degree, but during the 1890s, hard times and squatters in the valley had especially plagued George K. Porter's holding. In the spring of 1901, he began to negotiate with the syndicate through L. C. Brand, a leader in Glendale's development, who acted as agent and trustee for the parties. The sale was publicized, extravagant claims were made for the land's future development, and the usual assurances were offered that the purchase was not for speculation, "but for the purpose of holding and developing the property." Only as events unfolded did it begin to seem that some aspects of the purchase were compromised and that perhaps Sherman's presence on the water commission had made him privy to confidential information about future water plans that influenced the deal.[25]

At the end of 1903, less than half an inch of rain had fallen, and the United States Department of Agriculture warned of a grain shortage in Southern California for the coming season. Hard, dry north winds swept the land in early December, fanning brush fires in the canyons. The severest occurred along thirty miles of sea coast and into the chaparral-covered Santa Monica mountains, where the mansion of Malibu Ranch owner Frederick Rindge was reduced to ash. In the city, nine days of wind created a pestilence of dust that caused both a health problem and a transportation crisis. With the city choking, the Chamber of Commerce warned that tourists were being driven away. Health officers cautioned that the diphtheria epidemic then raging was due in part to dust-borne germs, while the street superintendent complained of the streetcars' air brakes' blowing clouds of dust onto people in the streets. When an angry city council demanded that the transit companies sprinkle the streets adjacent to the tracks, the companies protested the expense and said it was the city's job. Water users were warned to husband supplies as protection against a possible drought, while Henry O'Melveny, scrupulous in his rainfall entries, noted at the end of 1903 that aside from .46 inch in September, none had fallen since April. On Christmas Day he remarked on the dilapidated look of the plant life around him and wrote, "Driest I have ever known."[26]

CHAPTER 10

Desperate Remedies in a Dry Season

1904

A WATER CRISIS

As dry conditions continued through the winter of 1903–1904, railroad officials were announcing that they expected 10,000 colonists to arrive in California in 1904, and builders were anticipating a boom. Meanwhile, thousands of cattle were starving in the Antelope Valley for lack of rain, and returning hunters reported that Lake Elizabeth had disappeared, leaving only a mud flat. Field crop growers announced that between winter frosts and drought, shipments of vegetables from Southern California had fallen several hundred carloads below estimate. In Los Angeles, pine trees in Elysian Park were turning brown from lack of water, and on January 10, the city's clergymen called for all the churches on the coming Sabbath to pray for rain.[1]

As water demands besieged the department, Mulholland scrambled to meet the needs. Not only was the population growing but its hygienic practices were changing. When the principal of one grammar school produced estimates that only 23 percent of American homes had bathtubs, she prevailed upon the school superintendent to have a bath house built on the school grounds so the children could bathe. Although some parents were indignant at the inference that their offspring might need ablutions, the program became so successful that the superintendent began to install bathtubs and showers in other city schools. New homes with improved plumbing also increased demands for water and put a greater

burden on a sewer system that was already in an alarming state of deterioration and by summer would produce a crisis.[2]

In addition to the looming water shortage, Mulholland and the water
commissioners had to cut back on expenditures for improvements in order to raise funds for upcoming payments on the bonds. They had spent
all of the recent revenues on improvements to the water plant, instead
of putting money into the sinking fund. Now they would be forced to
save incoming revenues for the rest of the year and reduce by at least half
construction work for the next five months. The commissioners therefore suspended work on the main supply conduit from the headworks
until August, which made Dr. Powers unhappy as he had long urged closing the tunnel in the interests of delivering a supply of pure drinking water
to the city.[3]

Fred Eaton, at work on Mulholland's municipal distribution plan,
added his opposition to the annexation of lands to the City of Los Angeles because of the difficulty in supplying water to them. As both
Cahuenga Valley and Belvedere (about 500 acres east of the city) clam-
ored for admission to the corporate limits of the city, Eaton argued that
Los Angeles was already big enough, with its existing area of 44 square
miles making it the fifth or sixth largest city in the United States. He also
voiced fears that annexations could jeopardize pending court decisions
regarding the city's paramount rights to the waters of the Los Angeles
River. Cahuenga Valley, if annexed, would be entitled to city water at a
time when the city was already arguing that it needed all available water.[4]

In June, completion of new projects promised relief as Mulholland
announced that "we have relieved most of the famine today." A large
new pump near Elysian Park and the new high-service Beaudry Reservoir promised to lower water anxieties, although, as the reservoir filled,
warnings went out to Bunker Hill residents that the new service with its
added 60 pounds of pressure might well burst some of the tired old pipes.
At this juncture, the water commissioners, citing the pressure that the
superintendent had been under since the first of the year, granted Mulholland a two-week vacation to be taken at his pleasure. He turned it
down, saying that he felt the need of a rest but no more than did the men
who worked under him. He praised their great endurance as they worked
day and night for the city, and added that he could not take time off just
then. A week later, he set off a debate in the city council when he announced that the city must abandon and discard the old sprinkling cars
and begin to lay the dust on streets with oil. Charging that people were

still wasting water, he also announced his intention to put more inspectors on patrol to stop excessive irrigation. By the end of July, 150 violators had been caught citywide, mostly using water outside of the legal hours (lawn-sprinkling hours were from six to nine o'clock in the morning and from five to eight o'clock in the evening).[5]

When Mulholland finally did leave town at the end of summer, it was not for a vacation but for a trip that would alter his destiny and the city's. His refusal to leave the city earlier had stemmed from his deep concern over water supplies and his sense of urgency about completing current projects. What is more, he was overseeing the installation of the second, larger, pump for the infiltration gallery at the Buena Vista pumping station. As it was about to be activated, Mulholland was described as one who had been "sleeplessly watching over the great system he has brought up from its swaddling clothes . . . not the man to be satisfied with letting well enough alone." This new iron monster with its gauges staring out like shiny eyes bore the complex description "Cross Compound Condensing Crank and Fly Wheel Direct Action Pumping Engine." Dwarfing the old equipment, it had been manufactured at the Snow Steam Pump Company in Buffalo, New York, for a contract price of $24,000 (The figure was ridiculously low, said Mulholland, because the company had been so anxious to beat Risdon Iron Works in San Francisco that it underbid the job. The freight alone on the new pump had been $4,000.) Now, every twenty-four hours, the new marvel promised to raise 6 million gallons of water with a lift of 240 feet to supplement the first pump installed the year before. Brought up from the underground dam 125 feet below, the water would supply the downtown business section, with its overflow going into the old Buena Vista Dam. One reporter felt he had witnessed a historic occasion when he watched the great wheel begin to revolve as "Superintendent Mulholland and a corps of assistants ran eagerly about and crawled into dangerous positions to squirt oil into cracks or pound it with a hammer and in other ways nurse it into action. For hours this process was kept up until all the parts worked together and the monster, as the ship in Kipling's story, had 'found itself.'"[6]

Only one large city water project remained this year, and by the end of summer, if all financial arrangements were successful, Mulholland intended to have in operation a Corliss pumping plant at Los Feliz Point on the Griffith Ranch near Tropico. This installation promised 400 miner's inches of water to the main conduit. These additions to the city's water system offered hope that a water famine might be averted.[7]

The celebrated new pump at the Buena Vista station soon produced a perturbing result. At the end of July, Mulholland noted that the city's water consumption for one twenty-four-hour period had been 40 million gallons, exactly the amount the water system was able to produce in the same time period. He wrote to city officials that in the week ending July 25 "the rate of water consumption had aggregated 16 million gallons in excess of supply." He also warned that should that rate be kept up, the city would be in a very serious state. Two weeks earlier, consumption had been only 33 million gallons, and Mulholland could not account for the sudden jump. More alarmingly, he also observed that one reservoir had failed to rise to its normal twelve feet during the night. Somewhere, he realized, a terrible waste was occurring, and at the present rate, the system was stretched dangerously to its limit.[8]

Seeking the cooperation of the newspapers to alert the citizens to the importance of conserving water, he set about to study the situation. A week later, on August 3, he discovered a shocking situation. NINE MILLION GALLONS OF WATER ARE WASTED read the headline in the *Los Angeles Herald*. Leaks in the outfall sewer had allowed water to flow in from the powerful new pump at the Buena Vista infiltration gallery. The water for which so much effort had been expended was simply draining out to sea in the old sewer line. "This is an outrage," Mulholland declared. With a current-meter placed on the suspected sewer line for twenty-four hours, he calculated that 5 million gallons of pure water had been lost to the leaks in the sewer line. Another 2 million gallons, he estimated, were being lost to the sewer that drained East Los Angeles and Boyle Heights. The rest he ascribed to varieties of wasteful usage such as leaky fixtures and excessive yard watering. Voicing discouragement, he spoke of the cure that must come: "The little meter that never goes to sleep will cure it; we are putting them in as fast as possible and will continue until all the water goes through meters." He then thanked the daily papers for their help in publicizing the crisis. The meter plan met with resistance. When an officer of the Los Angeles Railway Company complained that its high bill must be because the meter was not in good order, Mulholland retorted that if the meter were not in good order, it would not register at all. He then invited the officer to come to the shop where the meters were tested; there he would discover that their mechanical construction made it "*absolutely impossible* to register more than passes through them."[9]

On August 15, in a freak of nature, a wind and electric storm dumped .13 inch of rain on Los Angeles—scarcely enough to lay the dust. As the reservoirs began to resume their accustomed levels, Mulholland gave

credit not to the brief sprinkles but rather to the economies of cooperative water-users. Later, it became an article of faith among antiaqueduct
critics that water was intentionally dumped with accompanying threats
of scarcity so as to frighten and coerce citizens into voting for water and
aqueduct bonds. In view of contemporary accounts, however, that
charge lacks credence. In fact, the old sewer systems had long been neg-
lected for lack of funds and were giving way under the pressures of a
growing population. Mulholland and the city engineers had been warning of the problem and offering solutions that remained unattended until the situation blew up into a municipal scandal in 1906.[10]

The water loss had been alarming, however, and led Mulholland and
the water commissioners to act decisively to establish more completely
the paramount rights of the City of Los Angeles to the waters of the Los
Angeles River. To do this, City Attorney Mathews brought an injunction
suit restraining every owner in the San Fernando Valley from taking water
from beneath his lands. Howls of protest arose, so that Mathews quickly
had to explain that the action did not mean every landowner in the valley. In fact, he said, most of the 163 persons named in the suit were
landowners near Tropico, Glendale, and Burbank, where heavy pumping
of river water was occurring and where so many earlier dissensions had
occurred. Furious, however, the valley ranchers organized, levied themselves each a dollar, and retained two legal firms to fight their case. Mathews and Mulholland were adamant. "From our standpoint," said Mathews, "there is no equity in this case." Mulholland amplified, "To grant
this contention of the owners of the ranches in the San Fernando Valley
would be preposterous. If they can take any part of our water, they can
take all of it, and our great conduit would be a dusty run-way for squir-
rels and coyotes, and our great filtration gallery which crosses under the
river at the Buena Vista station would soon be dry enough for a railway
tunnel." Many argued against this unpopular action, however, as lacking
a moral right even though the city might have a legal right to the water.[11]

TWO FRIENDS MAKE A TREK

On September 18, an inconspicuous item in the *Los Angeles Herald* noted
that William Mulholland was to be gone on vacation for about three
weeks. It appeared two days after a spirited election in which a councilman had been voted out in the first recall ballot in the history of the United
States, a triumph for labor, the Progressives, and the recall's author, Dr.
John Randolph Haynes, a reformer who would later also play a large

role in the water story. Overshadowed by election news, the obscure item noted that in addition to taking a rest, Mulholland was also to inspect several of the large water systems in the north. He was, in fact, about to see the great water supply of which Eaton had so long boasted.[12]

The day before the water commissioners granted Mulholland his leave of absence, Fred Eaton was about to leave for New York in an effort to secure funds for purchasing the Long Valley site on the Rickey Ranch in Owens Valley. At Mulholland's request, Eaton revised his plans, and the two set out on a trek that was to alter the history of Los Angeles and Southern California. On a buckboard with a team of mules, they made their way to the Owens River along the route that Eaton had determined, while Mulholland made notes and a sketch of the plan.[13]

After exploring other water resources in the upper Owens Valley, the two "sold the team and journeyed to San Francisco by rail. From there, Eaton and his daughter, who was waiting for him, left for New York. Before parting, Mulholland asked Eaton if it would be all right to seek legal advice to see if it would be possible to acquire such a water supply." Eaton consented and, just before leaving for New York, received a telegram from Mulholland asking him to name a date when he could meet Mr. Mathews at a certain hotel in that city.[14]

This took some scrambling on Mulholland's part, as Mathews was about to leave on October 3 for Washington, D.C., where he would argue two cases before the Supreme Court concerning redistricting the gas works' operation outside the city limits. On the very eve of his departure, Mathews agreed to rendezvous with Eaton in the East. He spent a day in New York with Eaton at the law firm of Dillon and Hubbard, which had earlier helped with the bond issue for the city's purchase of the private water company. After the attorneys decided the city could go out of the county for a water supply, Mathews said that he wished to deal directly with Eaton rather than a syndicate in securing land options. Although Eaton at first demurred, he finally consented, at Dillon's urging. In short, Eaton was to act as sole agent in the Owens Valley for the City of Los Angeles.[15]

THE THIRD MAN

The third engineer in this venture, Joseph Barlow Lippincott (1864–1942), was a hydrographer-engineer with the National Geological Survey. An enthusiastic resident of Los Angeles since 1891, he was by 1903 an employee of the National Reclamation Service, whose mission was to locate and survey sites for irrigation projects and dams in the West. As supervising engineer, Lippincott worked under two highly principled officers of the service, Chief Engineer Frederick H. Newell in Washington, D.C., and Engineer Arthur Powell Davis in California. Davis had been Lippincott's partner in an earlier private water venture.[16]

A key figure in the Los Angeles–Owens Valley story, Lippincott is thought by some to have been duped by Fred Eaton, while others have accused him of duplicity on behalf of Los Angeles's municipal water interests. His role in Owens Valley began on April 29, 1903—over a year before Eaton took Mulholland there—when Newell wrote from Washington to ask if Lippincott had ever considered, with a view to a possible irrigation project, "an examination of Owens River Valley and the desirability of segregating public lands." Newell suggested that if Lippincott as supervising engineer concurred, then he should send "a suitable man . . . and have a reconnaissance quietly made, with the idea of withdrawing lands pending survey." Lippincott promptly gave the assignment to Jacob C. Clausen, a twenty-seven-year-old California native and graduate of the University of California, Berkeley. By early July, Clausen had completed his mission and wired Lippincott, "Have finished reconnaissance large reservoir site, all patents for dam site. Private parties have all water, sixty thousand public, fifty thousand private land irrigable." Lippincott in turn reported back to Newell in Washington that prospects looked good for an irrigation project but that private power interests were also checking possibilities. Still, Lippincott felt that the two groups could proceed "without mutual interference." With a continent separating them, Newell gave Lippincott the authority to make his own decision, offering the guideline that "If there is an opportunity for Government reclamation on a large scale, I think that we should not let this opportunity go by."[17]

Lippincott now made his own inspection of Owens Valley, where he found large tracts of good public land and local settlers enthusiastic over the prospect of a large irrigation project. Although concerned about possible conflicts with private irrigation and power interests, on August 6, 1903, he nonetheless recommended to Newell that "all the remaining public lands in Owens Valley should be withdrawn pending further examination."

When Fred Eaton got wind of this development, he set to laying the foundation for the project he had long dreamed of in Owens Valley and had heard promulgated by an engineer during special Senate committee hearings in 1889. In 1892, he and Frank Austin had investigated the possibilities of an irrigation project in the Owens Valley but abandoned it "as an unprofitable venture on account of the transportation facilities." (Ironically, Austin's younger brother, Stafford Austin, along with his wife, the noted author Mary Hunter Austin, would become outspoken enemies of Los Angeles and its water engineers.) Impressed by the quantities of water he had seen, Eaton had continued his investigations with a survey made by Joseph Seely, former surveyor of Inyo County, for the purpose of moving Owens River water out of its shed into Indian Wells Valley. Further research ("engineering data from Civil Engineer Brooks, war maps and Southern Pacific Railway Surveys . . . and the help of a couple of good aneroids") convinced him that conveying water to Los Angeles was feasible. Now in 1903, with the Reclamation Service showing interest in the water for an irrigation district, Eaton decided to act, and thus began the complicated drama that would one day tarnish both his and Lippincott's reputations with suspicions of conflict of interest and unprofessional conduct.[18]

Lippincott was among those whom irrigation enthusiast William E. Smythe called "Uncle Sam's Young Men"—a group of talented engineers assembled in 1902 as consultants in the newly organized United States Reclamation Service. A native of Scranton, Pennsylvania, Lippincott was the son of a distinguished minister and educator. After early training at Dickinson College, where his father taught mathematics, he earned a degree in civil engineering at the University of Kansas in either 1886 or 1887 (sources vary); worked for the Santa Fe Railway; was a topographer with the United States Geological Survey in New Mexico and California; and then worked for private irrigation companies in Arizona and California. Married in 1890 to Josephine Cook, he came to Los Angeles the following year with his wife and a baby girl, his only daughter, Rose Lippincott. As a member of the United States Geological Society, he was to serve as assistant to another of Uncle Sam's Young Men, topographer Arthur P. Davis, in mapping Southern California.[19]

At the end of a year, Lippincott left his government job and undertook several private irrigation endeavors in Southern California, but the depressed years of the early 1890s weighed against success. Drought and hard times undid various projects, including a partnership with Davis in planning a waterworks in the Antelope Valley. He returned to government service in June 1895, as state hydrographer with the U.S. Geological Survey. Because government salaries were inadequate for his family, he also secured an understanding that the survey would allow him to do some private work.[20]

Throughout the 1890s, Lippincott was active in the regional engineering fraternity: expert witness in the later phases of the Hooker-
Pomeroy case and member of a panel of experts in the city's suit against
the Crystal Springs Land and Water Company and the City Water Company in February 1898. Among his fellow panelists were veterans of the
local water scene James D. Schuyler, A. H. Koebig, and Fred Eaton; if he
had not yet met Mulholland, he would have encountered him when they
testified on opposing sides regarding questions of water flows and infiltration pipes.[21]

During Eaton's mayoralty and campaign for the municipal ownership of water, Lippincott stood squarely behind him in public support
of the bonds. Not only did he offer his services in preparing precinct
maps, he spoke at meetings and rallies and declared that it seemed foolish "to give up this chance for municipal ownership and leave the water
supply of the city in the hands of a grasping corporation." Lippincott's
public utterances echoed Eaton's animus against the private water company, and certainly by the summer of 1899 the two were more than casual acquaintances.[22]

Lippincott remained active in both city and Geological Survey affairs
during Eaton's administration. He reported on the progress of the survey's plans to conserve the state's water in "a period of the worst drouth
ever recorded in the State." With other members of the survey, he further explored the Los Angeles River to study percolation rates through
various soils. Then, with Elwood Mead (later chief engineer of Boulder
Dam), City Engineer Frank Olmstead (now Lippincott's business partner), and survey member Homer Hamlin, he investigated water conditions in the San Fernando Valley. In a lengthy summary of the water situation prepared for the city engineer's annual report, he concluded, "If
the comparative growth of the city during the last ten years be projected
into the future for ten years more, it will indicate a population of 200,000
people at the expiration of a decade. At the rate at which we are now
using our water it would appear that the natural supply would be exhausted in four and one-half years. At the termination of this period,
methods will have to be devised to meet the situation. This will indicate
from a physical standpoint alone, the necessity of a remedy of the situation."[23] By the autumn of 1902, as supervising engineer for California in the Reclamation Service, Lippincott was third in command under his old partner, Arthur P. Davis, and his former chief, F. H. Newell.
Ten months later, he received the telegram from Newell regarding
Owens Valley.[24]

BEHIND THE SCENES

After his first inspection of Owens Valley in September 1903, Lippincott proposed to Governor George C. Pardee a study for a reservoir site in Owens Valley. In December he reported that further studies were needed, especially in the matter of a storage dam. For this, he recommended a Long Valley site on property owned by a local land baron, Thomas B. Rickey. Rickey Land and Water Company was a cattle spread of 22,380 acres in Mono and Inyo Counties, and although Rickey's claim to some of the land was dubious, he was considered a tough customer who ran his fiefdom in the old ways of the roughshod West. He opposed reclamation projects, so obtaining any part of his land would require skillful negotiations.

In a disputed incident the following April, Eaton and Lippincott are said to have encountered each other in Owens Valley while Lippincott was waiting for the arrival of a drill to test the bedrock at the Long Valley dam site. Eaton by now had established his son in Independence, and the two were scouting riparian sites along the Owens River with a view to acquisition. Witnesses remembered seeing the two together frequently, but Lippincott later denied that Eaton made any mention of his interest there. For his part, Eaton denied even being in Owens Valley during April 1904.[25]

At this juncture, Newell, aware that Lippincott and his engineering partner, O. K. Parker, were involved in a number of private water projects, suggested that Lippincott's continued private practice was not acceptable for one in government service. Lippincott defended his outside work and argued that Parker had taken charge of all their private business, which was mostly with public agencies. He further agreed to avoid private work, including court appearances as an expert witness. Given this assurance, Newell approved a salary raise for Lippincott in June 1904, and plans for the Owens Valley project proceeded.[26]

In June and July 1904, Lippincott was much in the public eye in Los Angeles and keeping up an exhausting schedule. As well as being in Owens Valley in April, he had also gone on an inspection trip to Baja California and discussed irrigation problems along the Colorado River in connection with the Yuma reclamation project. In Yuma a large group of engineers had met, including Thomas H. Means, who had just returned from an inspection tour of irrigating systems in Egypt and was about to go to Owens Valley to make soil tests. In May, Lippincott appeared at the California River Convention meeting at San Francisco's Palace Hotel, where he spoke on the Geological Survey's investigations of the Sacramento Basin. Then, on June 15, he appeared before the Los Angeles Park Commission with reforestation proposals for Griffith Park. (On the eve of a trip back to Washington, D.C., the previous December, he had consulted with Henry O'Melveny over the possibility of a plant experimental station at the park and promised to bring the matter to the attention of Chief Forester Gifford Pinchot.) Lippincott was also appointed to the city's civil service commission headed by Dr. John R. Haynes, and on July 27 Mayor Snyder complimented his service to the city, citing his role in helping to purchase the properties of the West Side Water Company. Lippincott, he claimed, had worked for "a comparatively small salary" when he could have gone to the other side and earned much more. Praising his faithfulness to the city, the mayor said that Lippincott, in addition to the work at Griffith Park, was also eager to see a better road constructed through the Providencia Ranch (the Glendale area) to connect with the Cahuenga Pass road.[27]

Given this crowded life with city, state, and federal projects, a vacation seemed warranted in the late summer of 1904, but the Lippincott family's camping trip to Yosemite in August would be remembered as something more than a mere pleasant outing. The Lippincotts invited several friends to join them and their two small children (a baby boy, Joseph Reading Lippincott, had been born in 1901), and the party included Fred Eaton and artist Fernand Lungren, who was to sketch nature scenes. After camping in Yosemite, the group made its way from Tuolumne Meadows down the precipitate Tioga Pass into Bishop, where they bought supplies and met more friends, among them, Jacob Clausen and Thomas Means of the Reclamation Service. Because Clausen had done the Owens River study and was therefore the most knowledgeable about the country, he guided a tour that included the reservoir site at Long Valley.[28]

Lippincott, along with other members of the group, later claimed that none of the party suspected Eaton's interest in the place at the time, but the upshot of the camping trip was Eaton's return to Los Angeles to tell Mulholland of the Reclamation Service's intentions in Owens Valley and to express fears that the city might miss its chance. Hearing of this turn of events, Mulholland decided it was time to learn about Owens River, and so the two set out on their momentous survey.

Events now moved rapidly. Lippincott returned from his vacation and, with full knowledge of Eaton's plans, on September 17, wrote to inform Newell in Washington of the city's interest in the Owens River for domestic use. Newell agreed to come west and meet with all the parties on November 22 to discuss the matter. By now, however, he was also receiving petitions on behalf of an irrigation project from enthusiastic Owens Valley residents, as well as reports recommending the project from his department engineers, Clausen and Means. These interests were colliding at a time when the Reclamation Bureau itself faced a budget crisis. The $30 million set aside for reclamation projects had by now been largely committed to other undertakings such as those on the Yuma and Klamath Rivers, and Newell realized that his bureau could not undertake all of its desired projects in the West at this time. In the November meeting, Newell conceded the city's need for Owens River water, but insisted that the project would have to be "an exclusively municipal one." That meant Fred Eaton would have to abandon his dream of profiting in a joint venture with the city. Reluctantly Eaton agreed.[29]

For the next three months, the city conducted reconnaissance work on the Owens River project, so that by the beginning of 1905, a decision was forming. As Mulholland later wrote, "The superintendent reported favorably on the adequacy of the water supply and the feasibility of constructing a canal to bring it to the City, and the Board of Water Commissioners then asked him to make a preliminary estimate of the probable cost of such an enterprise, with a view to getting data on which to base a bond issue for the purchase of the Eaton water rights." The dry language of an engineering report scarcely conveys Mulholland's enthusiasm for the project. He had returned from Owens Valley fired with the belief that the Owens River would solve chronic water shortages in Los Angeles. Keeping silent proved difficult, however, for on October 21, when he read "The Water Supply of Southern California," his first long paper to the Sunset Club, he could not refrain from hinting at a grand solution that at present would seem only "visionary and chimerical."[30]

CHAPTER 11

A Plan Revealed

1905

> Some people appear to be objecting to the scheme. They say we
> worked in the dark. In fact, we worked in the light, while they were
> in the dark, for if some of the objectors had been "on" to what was
> happening, there would have been a migration to the Owens Valley,
> and we never could have obtained the water for anything like the
> price we are to pay.
>
> WILLIAM MULHOLLAND, 1905

A SECRET POORLY KEPT

Months before the proposal to acquire Owens River water for Los Angeles was finally made public on July 29, 1905, hints and rumors circulated around town. In December 1904, hardly able to contain his secret or enthusiasm, Mulholland gave a statement to the city's newest morning newspaper, Hearst's year-old *Los Angeles Examiner*, which had urged the city to solve its chronic water shortage. He assured the public it had no need to panic at the present population but warned that growth beyond 225,000 would cause a problem—unless, he slyly suggested, a way were found to kill Frank Wiggins, perennial civic booster and spokesman for the Los Angeles Chamber of Commerce. Then, seemingly out of the blue, Mulholland commented that if a gigantic project were to be undertaken, it would require large expenditures. "Hence," he went on, "it would be the part of wisdom to have appointed a commission composed of good business men, together with, say, two or three hydraulic engineers of standing, whose residence and practice here have been long enough to acquaint them thoroughly with hydrographic conditions in Southern California." Mulholland also advised the city to plan ahead and not wait until it found itself short, for "it will require the work of years to guarantee against the future, and we should begin the task at once." Thus in general terms, as if preparing the public for the coming specifics, he spoke of great undertakings.[1]

COPING WITH THE PRESENT

If people in Los Angeles were largely in the dark at the beginning of 1905, those in Owens Valley had seen glimmers of some great change during 1904 as surveyors and engineers became active in their territory. While optimists foresaw a federal reclamation project for their valley, others sold their land or granted options to, among others, the apparently land-hungry Fred Eaton. By January 1905, Mulholland was corresponding with local engineer-surveyors in and around Owens Valley. As letters and money orders for work and supplies arrived there from the water department of Los Angeles, not everyone in Owens Valley could have been in the dark about the city's involvement, later disclaimers notwithstanding.[2]

Mulholland, though excited by the prospects of this magnificent and challenging project, also recognized that even if it were to materialize, the city would not enjoy the bounty of its water for years. His immediate task was to wrestle with the problems of the city's present supply, and though above-average amounts of rain fell in the winter of 1904–1905 (19.52 inches, over 3.0 inches above normal), water demands continued to threaten to exceed supply.

Discontent arose in April when fifty prominent building contractors filed a protest with the city against what they maintained were exorbitant costs for tapping mains, claiming that voters had expected these costs to go down under municipal ownership. Criticism intensified as private water promoters hatched plans to supplant the city's works. A rumor surfaced that tycoon Henry E. Huntington had a plan to supply the city with water from the Santa Clara River at a point near Newhall with a proposed aqueduct modeled on the one built to bring water to Boston, Massachusetts, from Lake Winnipesaukee one hundred miles away. Word also circulated that Frederick Rindge, owner of Malibu Ranch, had taken over the Maclay waterworks in the San Fernando Valley and intended to sell its water. (This scheme came to nothing in August, when just a week before the election that approved the Owens River water bonds, Rindge died suddenly in Yreka, California.)[3]

Lippincott was committed to aiding the City of Los Angeles with its water problem, but he also was a federal employee. At the beginning of 1905, an emergency had required him to bring a crew of reclamation workers from Owens Valley to Imperial Valley, where the Salton Sea had begun to fill and flood as the result of the Colorado River's changing its course. With rail traffic severely impeded, Lippincott's crew arrived with others to study and remedy the problem. By this time, Lippincott's involvement with the City of Los Angeles was so widely recognized that the *Imperial Valley News* even suggested that both he and his chief, Frederick H. Newell, might be under the influence of Otis and the *Los Angeles Times*.[4]

Lippincott's focus was still on the Owens River, however, as indicated in a letter he wrote to Mulholland at the end of February. Touching upon Reclamation Service activities in Owens Valley, he advised that in the event "this project be turned over to the city of Los Angeles, then the city should repay the Service for expenses incurred in surveys and drillings for bed rock at the Long Valley dam site." Soon, however, his juggling of city and Reclamation Service projects raised such serious ethical questions in Washington, D.C., that an investigation forced his separation from Reclamation in 1906.[5]

In March, after Mulholland and Eaton took their stand against wooden pipe for an Oakland sewer bond election, they participated with Lippincott in the Southern California Irrigation Congress, which was attended by most of the engineers who were to be actively involved in planning and building the Owens River project. For all the ink that has been spilled over tales of conspiracies and devious plots in the Owens River project, hardly a drop has been given to the large group of imaginative, opinionated, and articulate engineers who not only knew one another but often intermeshed at this time in a variety of water projects in the West. A collegiality existed among them as they met at each other's homes, exchanged ideas on outings and camping trips, and gathered at professional conferences such as this. Mulholland's first address to this body, "Water Waste," emphasized how the meter system had greatly reduced waste of the water supply in Los Angeles. Lippincott read a paper, "Stream Characteristics of Southern California," as well as joining W. C. Mendenhall, also of the United States Reclamation Service, in a discussion, "Forestry and the Supply of Water." While the veteran western engineer James D. Schuyler spoke on "The Impounding of Flood Waters," rain began to fall, pouring down a torrential 3.49 inches on the city. The Los Angeles River went on a rampage, tore out the Seventh Street Bridge, swept away two young men to their deaths, and caused the sewer at Fourth Street to overflow. As if to mock the gathering of engineers and irrigationists who had been discussing water scarcity and conservation, local rainmaker and "Wizard of Esperanza" Charles Hatfield took credit for causing the deluge with a secret chemical process that he claimed produced an "affinity" with rain.[6]

As the engineers concluded their conference, City Attorney Mathews hastened to Sacramento with a delegation backed by the Chamber of Commerce to fight legislation that would have threatened any possibility of an Owens River project for Los Angeles. Known as the Pendleton Eminent Domain Bill, it would have allowed a county's inhabitants to condemn for their own use any water stored or flowing therein intended for use in another county. Ironically, its author was a Los Angeles man, about whom the *Herald* said, "it would be a stretch of charity to say that he was an innocent tool of schemers who had important personal or corporate interests to subserve." Urging Governor Pardee to veto the bill, Mathews minced no words. "It means that if we are forced to go outside of Los Angeles County to develop water and bring it into the city by means of pipes and tunnels at tremendous expense that should a small town situated in the county in which the water was developed desire to use some of the water they would have the right to it."[7]

THE CAT OUT OF THE BAG

When the Owens River project was finally announced on July 29, 1905, the cat may not have been altogether out of the bag, but its nose and whiskers had certainly been visible. During the five months after Mulholland's and Eaton's first trip together to Owens Valley, both men had made many quiet returns, Eaton on a regular basis to secure land options and Mulholland five times to investigate and consult with the surveyors mapping the dam sites and route of the future aqueduct. City officials masquerading either as park developers or cattlemen (accounts differ) had inspected the area in April and consulted with Eaton regarding his proposal to sell his land options and contracts to the city. In early May, Mayor Owen McAleer was granted a ten days' leave and disappeared from the city with attorney Mathews. No one seemed to know exactly what they were up to. The *Herald* reported that they had gone to San Francisco, ostensibly to attend the hearings of a suit against Rancho Bartolo Water Company, which, rumor had it, the City of Los Angeles might buy to increase its water supply. (One old-timer who doubted the story remarked that "Johnny" Mott's scheme to sell water from Rancho Paso de Bartolo was old enough to vote.) The *Times* featured the puzzle of the missing mayor with a cartoon and headline reading, GONE A FISHING, IS IT FOR WATER?[8]

   While Mulholland and his crews struggled to implement service lines and fend off citizen complaints about poor water service, voices against municipal ownership rose again. Grievances piled up at City Hall until by mid-July a group of businessmen demanded an investigation of the water commission. Local attorney Oscar Lawler, who represented private electric interests, announced that $3 million had been raised to begin construction of a huge dam across Big Tujunga Canyon. Mulholland, not unaware of this scheme, was quick to point out that the Big Tujunga Wash was part of the watershed of the San Fernando Valley, whose water rights belonged to the city. As these events threatened the municipal water system's advance, one councilman, Edward Kern, raised his voice against the various water schemes being brought to the council. "I shall fight with all my might any proposition to put it back into the hands of private corporations," he declared.[9]

This rising opposition to municipal water by citizens and private interests, along with the more urgent need to secure money by October 1 to pay for Fred Eaton's options in Owens Valley, prodded the water commissioners to spring their surprise announcement in the middle of summer. In a torrent of headlines and articles the story washed over the city: BIG DEAL IN WATER. WATER SUPPLY FOR 2,000,000 PEOPLE. A river of pure mountain water in the Sierra was to be transported to the thirsty dwellers on the plains below. At almost 240 miles, the proposed aqueduct would be second in length only to the Coolgardie in New South Wales, Australia, which ran 307. The public revelation of the Owens River plan seized everyone's attention, and then, because of journalistic rivalry, immediately provoked a controversy.

When news of the project had earlier begun to leak, city officials met with the editors of the major dailies, who agreed to remain silent and make a simultaneous announcement. The *Times,* however, in its usual bullyboy manner, jumped the gun and published a day early (July 29 instead of July 30, as agreed upon by the other papers). The scoop resulted in editorial bad feelings, especially with the rival morning newspapers, the *Examiner* and the *Herald.* (Mayor McAleer next day published a statement in the *Examiner* deploring the breach of faith by "another paper.") This furor in part reflected the circulation war between the *Times* and the *Examiner.* Published since December 12, 1903, the latter was a relative newcomer to Los Angeles, although its sister newspaper, the *San Francisco Examiner,* had long been familiar in the south. The animus between Otis and Hearst—and Henry A. Loewenthal, the editor of Hearst's *Los Angeles Examiner*—was intense but probably had less to do initially with the water question than with competition, profits, and political differences. In a personal letter to Lippincott, Mulholland blamed an engineer with the Edison Electric Company as the one "inspiring malicious communications to the *Examiner* newspaper." Despite a period of editorial opposition, the *Examiner* generally covered the water story well, and in fact, the differences among the six leading dailies on the Owens River question were minimal. Only later in the year did the *Evening News*, created specifically to oppose the water plan under the editorship of Samuel Travers Clover, grow truly scurrilous in its attacks upon the Owens River project and its architects.[10]

Alternative water proposals published in the *Examiner* came from self-interested parties such as the private owners of the water supply at Piru Creek, who reported to the city council that they could supply the city with water for $3.3 million instead of the exorbitant $23 million estimated for the Owens River project. Oscar Lawler, whose group wished to secure the water power of the Big Tujunga for lighting, warned that the Owens River plan probably would cost nearly $50 million and cautioned that the lighting companies were preparing to fight the bond election because it raised the specter of a municipal lighting plant. One Dr. Adelbert Feynes, of Pasadena, described as a physician and traveler, claimed he had personally examined the water of Owens River and found it unfit to drink; moreover, typhoid fever was endemic year-round in Owens Valley. One H. C. Morse, who claimed to pay taxes on $200,000 worth of local property, declared the plan a swindle, for in the 1870s when he had been a road master around Owens Lake, he had found its waters not fit for a dog to drink—nothing but alkali and borax—and as for the river, why, its waters moved like the hour hand on a clock. He predicted that "the city is going to get up a tree if they take that property." Mulholland laughed off the most absurd proposals and seriously answered the others. Of Piru Creek, he said, "That water would not be worth 30¢ to Los Angeles. I know all about that water shed. I owned an orange ranch on the edge of it for several years. I sold it because there was not enough water to raise a crop." He spoke of the amount of study that had gone into the proposal. "If there are any people in Los Angeles who think we have gone into this proposition like a lot of schoolboys, with a whoop and a hurrah, they should come in and look over a few of the maps we have made in this last year."[11]

Before the bond election that would decide the issue, Mulholland assessed the local scene for Lippincott, then working and vacationing at Klamath Falls, Oregon. Mulholland wanted Lippincott to return to Los Angeles to help in the bond campaign, but Lippincott in his ambiguous situation expressed considerable hesitancy about entering into a public discussion of the matter. Finding the chief opposition among engineers representing private power interests, Mulholland singled out Frederick C. Finkle, who was to become a leading adversary of the water plan. "Our worthy friend, Finkle," he wrote, "implies that he should have been employed on account of his large experience in construction work, the claim being set forth that neither you nor I have had any experience in this line."[12]

In August, when it came to a vote in City Hall to approve a $1.5 million bond election, Councilman Arthur D. "Doc" Houghton, who had replaced the councilman recalled the previous year, stood out as the lone opponent. Houghton had been hailed not only as a friend of the unions but also as a champion of free institutions and good government responsive to the will of the people. Something of a maverick (some said a "crank"), he proved pesky. The previous November he had so angered one political opponent with innuendoes of bribery that the man knocked him unconscious in an encounter at Second and Spring Streets, and he had to be hospitalized. Because of his prolabor stands, he was favored by the *Examiner* and disdained by the *Times*, which routinely referred to him as "'Spook' Howton." (He was rumored to have once conducted seances in Chicago.) The *Times* declared him a Hearst hireling (meaning prounion). The *Herald* remained content to call him simply an obstructionist, the "Honorable Misrepresentative of the Sixth Ward."[13]

OPPOSING VOICES

On August 15, before the city council's final vote to set the date for the bond election, Houghton delayed and insisted that Mulholland be summoned for questioning. Busy in a meeting with the water commissioners, Mulholland finally appeared. Although he had been patient in earlier encounters, this time he let loose when Houghton badgered him about the veracity of the chemical analysis of Owens River water. "I have been in my present position as superintendent of the water works almost thirty years and am not in the habit of deceiving the people. I have never done it yet. For five months I have examined the Owens River and valley and it looks better to me each time I go back. The mean flow of the river is 20,000 miner's inches and the water is remarkable for its purity." Undeterred, Houghton next asked if he had ever "built anything like a $23,000,000 water aqueduct, or had any personal knowledge of such an undertaking?" To this, Mulholland rounded with "Such a thing has never been done. This will be one of the greatest engineering achievements in the world."[14]

The need for haste in the matter, he explained, was his understanding that if the bonds were issued immediately and moneys paid by January 1, the city could save $45,000. Moreover, a payment of $50,000 was due on the land and water options by October 1. Houghton dismissed the $45,000 as "nothing" and next asked if a two weeks' delay would imperil the project while he personally inspected the Owens Valley area. Mulholland answered that he knew little about the time required for a bond issue and that Eaton could better answer that. Getting an admission from Mulholland that another twenty-four hours' delay while contacting Eaton would not hurt the project, Houghton moved to adjourn until the following Monday morning. Because of his gadfly performance, however, he was simply overridden, and the council approved plans for a bond election on September 7. At this point, the *Examiner*'s anti-aqueduct editor, Henry Loewenthal, blasted the city fathers. "Appearances could not have been worse had the Council been voting a $22,000,000 contract to a private corporation in which the members had an individual interest of something like $100,000 each. As it was, there could be no charges of graft."[15]

In defense of the city council, which represented a diverse group (although some critics have insisted they were all Southern Pacific hirelings), their near unanimity suggests a very real agreement about the Owens River proposal. Mulholland expressed his pleasure when he wrote to tell Lippincott (still at Klamath Falls) that the city council had approved a bond election for September 7 and that he had no doubt of its ultimate success. He renewed his opinion about most of the opposition's source. "Finkle . . . for the Edison Electric Co., is making a scurrilous and dirty fight in opposition thereto, by inspiring malicious communications to the Examiner newspaper. This, you will remember, is a pleasing occupation to him, as to my certain knowledge he has attempted to inflict his presence as an engineer on every project of importance in this country." He also cited two other disgruntled engineers, "Purcell with the Kern River project and Hawgood with the Mojave," who, on behalf of their clients "give utterance to vagrant statements that while not being particularly mendacious are at least misleading." Urging Lippincott to return soon in order to participate in the coming campaign, Mulholland closed by expressing his regret that Lippincott would not be on hand that night at the Municipal League banquet, where he was slated to speak.[16]

Although overridden, Houghton had nonetheless made telling points to which the councilmen might well have given more consideration as they pursued the enterprise through the years. When he questioned the precipitate haste of approving a project that would cost the voters at least $22 million, he made an accusation that was to have a long life. "It almost looks," he declared, "as if some of these men whose character and integrity are above reproach had been let in on this deal three or four months ago, had purchased arid lands and are in haste to have them made valuable by this water project." The San Fernando Valley lands to which he referred would in the following year become the focus of accusations and suspicions that were not to fade away.[17]

MULHOLLAND MAKES A SPEECH

The Municipal League banquet was held on August 15, after the council's approval of the Owens River plan. Sponsored by the Municipal League in order to lay before its membership a presentation of the giant undertaking the city had assumed, the affair drew one hundred and forty of Los Angeles's most prominent and influential citizens. Guests included the mayor, along with members of the city council and water department. Mulholland and Eaton spoke at length, and their combined speeches constituted a concise history of the city's water story. When Mulholland was introduced with the words "What can I say of him except that he is Will Mulholland," cheers shook the room. He demurred, "It is rather a poor return for this repast to have to ask you to swallow a few chestnuts." One reporter commented that the speech was long, but that "Mr. Mulholland has a rugged, vigorous way of putting things that is more convincing than oratory." When asked about the magnitude of the project, he replied, "The engineering project is a big one. But it is a simple one. The man who has made one brick can make two bricks. That is the bigness of this engineering problem. It is big, but it is simply big."[18]

With the aid of maps, Mulholland outlined the city's past, present, and future water needs; spoke of the Los Angeles River and its sources and its limitations; recounted his explorations of other sources with Eaton and Lippincott; and finally, detailed the investigations in Owens Valley and the reports provided by F. H. Newell and Jacob Clausen of the Reclamation Service. He referred to himself as having been "a kind of stepmother to the Los Angeles River," as for the past thirty years he had worked during storms, in gumshoes and gum coat, to keep mud out of the reservoirs so that the people would not have turbid water "such as the people of St. Louis drink the whole year round." He spoke of Lippincott's studies and explorations for water in this southern country, and of Eaton, he said, "Mr. Eaton had talked to me about Owens River for thirteen years; and would twit me with the fact that sooner or later the city of Los Angeles would go to the Owens River country to get an additional water supply. When he first broached the thing to me I thought it was so absurd that I just fairly laughed in his face." Admitting he had been a pessimist, Mulholland confessed he had thought he would never live to see the day when the city would have 100,000 people.

Eaton told of his early experiences in Owens Valley and confirmed that Mulholland was "never so enthusiastic in the future of Southern California as I was." He spoke of their trip the previous September; of Mathews's insistence that Eaton act as the sole purchasing agent for the city in the Owens Valley, along with the water commissioners' assistance; and of his success in securing the Rickey lands. He too vouched for the purity of the water and touched upon some of the engineering difficulties that would be encountered.

Water Commissioner John Elliott next explained in detail the necessity for secrecy and haste: how the water department urgently needed the funds that it had already invested in the project; how the city had to meet the payment of $50,000 on October 1 or lose its land options, which would then allow private interests to move in and take them up. "If the city votes $1,500,000 in bonds, the money can be used so that the city will absolutely own this proposition. After that, you can vote the money necessary to bring the water here. If you do not do this, the water can be sold to others. Mr. Eaton agrees to take it off your hands and pay for it." He spoke of his trust in Mulholland and said that in their thirteen years of association, he "worked within his estimates and never went over them." (This produced applause from the gathering.) After speaking of journeying to Owens Valley with a group of engineers and city officials and seeing for himself the snow-covered mountains, Elliott quoted John Muir, who, when he had drunk from the headwaters of the Owens River twenty-five years earlier, praised its taste as the best he had ever had and likened it to "unstimulating champagne."[19]

Mathews followed with his support of the plan and the need for an early bond election. He deprecated his own role, claiming that "the handling of the matter has really revolved around the prime minister of the water department—Mr. Mulholland—his practical experience and his full wisdom being consulted by every one at every step." Mathews said the city should take pride in the ownership of its waterworks, adding that when a proposal had lately been made to lease it to a private corporation, Mulholland had said, "Huh! You may as well suggest to a man that he lease his wife."

In a year crowded with events both challenging and saddening, this evening stood as a triumph for Mulholland, with his peers' recognition of his years of unswerving devotion to the city. Yet within a few days, a terrible and unsettling experience at the new filtration plant at Burbank confronted him again with the caprices of fortune. As he talked to a workman, C. F. Helsey, a rope broke on a derrick that was hoisting a heavy pipe. A falling block struck Helsey's head ("Mulholland fairly felt the wind of it") and fractured his skull. He died an hour later. Shaken by this first fatality or serious accident he had ever had on a job, Mulholland mused, "I have worked thousands of men . . . but it was the other man that was called. My time had not come."[20]

THE DARK SIDE OF THE MATTER

In the three weeks between the night of the Municipal League banquet and the bond election on September 7, several issues threatened the enterprise: questions about its undue haste; the role of Fred Eaton; and growing rumbles of anger and discontent from Owens Valley. Commissioner Elliott had been candid at the Municipal League banquet in admitting that the commission had spent money from the water fund on land options in Owens Valley without consulting anyone. He defended the action on the grounds that it had saved the city money by heading off speculators who would have driven up the land prices; therefore, the bond campaign's haste was plainly due to the urgency of raising funds to meet "a $50,000 payment which we have not got money to pay for." As events proved, few seemed to care about the action's moral niceties. Even though they had been kept in the dark about its beginnings, the citizenry, who had long put up with a water system that at its best was merely adequate, did not boggle at the means by which an improved water supply was to be secured. Any strict accounting must concede that the enterprise involved subterfuge. Had it been a military operation, it would have earned high marks for adroit stratagem, but being a civic matter, some found much that was dubious. Initially, however, the most unforgiving and censorious were those with the strongest economic motives for wishing the project to fail, those whom Mulholland called "arrant schemers."[21]

Eaton's land deals in the Owens Valley have always seemed troublesome to some and even today resonate with echoes of Mark Twain's *The Man That Corrupted Hadleyburg*, a tale of a stranger who seems to offer a possibility of riches that turn out to be quite otherwise. Eaton, the big city man, had arrived in a remote area and announced that he was going into the cattle business in a big way. Hearing of his desire to buy land, hard-pressed settlers saw a chance to bail out of their marginal existences. (Although Eaton was later accused of having misled the people, it is true that "the trickster never works alone. His audience works with him." Certainly no one was forced to sell his land. For some, the city's price was simply right.) With the revelation that the true owner of the land and water rights was to be the City of Los Angeles, the storm broke, as Eaton commented, "I used to be the best fellow in the world among those people, but now they think I am the Prince of Devils."[22]

For Owens Valleyites, the final disappointment came with the news that the Reclamation Service would not be building a dam in Long Valley, for in order to do so, it would have had to condemn land on the Rickey Ranch now held by Los Angeles (and Fred Eaton); nor did the federal government have the power to take water intended for domestic purposes. Thus, what seemed sweet to Los Angeles turned to gall in Owens Valley, whose dwellers now understood Eaton's land sales.

Eaton escaped the valley and spent a few days in a hospital in San Francisco before returning to Los Angeles on August 4, "drawn and limping with rheumatism," but ready to defend his actions. Expecting to remain in town "until things quiet down up there," he explained, "Some of those people think I sold them out in taking the water out of the valley. It will probably mean moving the county seat of Inyo County from Independence to Bishop. You know, we have practically bought Independence." On the same day Eaton spoke to the press, surveyor J. A. Killian wrote to Mulholland from Bishop, "Bishop is in a state of excitement at the present. They think Los Angeles is going to turn the place into a desert. Had a mass meeting here last night and denounced everybody connected with the scheme." Eaton tried to palliate his deeds by explaining that he had acted largely for the city rather than himself and told of an encounter in San Francisco with "old man Rickey," who chewed him out for not going in on a deal with him. They could have sold to private interests, Rickey told him, and made half a million. Nor did Eaton underestimate the rage in Owens Valley. "They say I sold them out, sold them out, and the government, too; that I shall never take the water out of the valley; that when I go back for my cattle, they will drown me in the river."[23]

Mulholland, who had not yet faced the direct fury of Owens Valley folk and was still buoyed by the euphoria of success, spoke exuberantly, if not always judiciously, of their accomplishment. "We have corralled everything upon each side of the river," he cheered, while dismissing the land around Independence as being of little value. He praised Eaton as the only one who could have pulled off the land deals without being found out; only on the last visit had "a canny old Scotch woman who owns a little piece of property south of the lake" solved the mystery. Privately, Mulholland conveyed his optimism to Lippincott:

> As I suppose you have already heard, there was a holy row raised at a meeting at Bishop in which we were all designated as scoundrels, etc. Happily this phase of the situation, while making some annoyance, tends at the same time to discount the claims a few of the knockers make, that there is no water to be had in Owens River Valley, the point being that if we take nothing, what in the world are those fellows up there making such a row about? I have no doubt that on a proper investigation by the Reclamation Department and the publication of such investigation, you will be cleared from the charge of any treacherous work to the inhabitants of that valley.[24]

The *Examiner* was not long in accusing Eaton of profiteering at the city's expense on land and cattle deals. FORMER MAYOR HAS GOLDEN KEY, blazed the headline. "Since May," the article accused, "the former mayor has been busy getting these options and at the same time getting rich." In an interview the next day, Eaton was allowed to rebut the charges. "There is no graft," he said. "I have made money but no city official gets one cent. I would rather have a moderate sum and many friends than a big sum and no friends. I'm no cattle king yet, but I have hopes of being." Eaton then gave his account of having owned land in Owens Valley since 1893, of his earlier attempts to develop water there, of his trip to New York, and of his decision finally to do business with the city after securing an option on the Rickey Ranch. According to Eaton, cattle came into the picture because owner T. B. Rickey agreed to sell only if he could "take my money and step from the ranch into a railroad train. He didn't want to be bothered with cattle, any piece of land or anything else. It must be a clean sale or nothing." The City of Los Angeles, having no desire or use for cattle, had let Eaton have them as a commission for his services. Mulholland defended his friend as one "who never made a dirty dollar in his life and never will." Attorney Mathews said Eaton's only profit was on the Rickey Ranch land; the city had paid him ten dollars a day for his services as confidential agent in securing land options along the Owens River. Thus, on the eve of a great enterprise, Eaton's character was impugned. Yet for later detractors to paint him simply as a self-seeking manipulator and exploiter is unfair, for he had demonstrated more than once in the past that he loved his native city. Ultimately he was perhaps hoist on his own petard of conflicting desires to enrich himself and to supply his homeland with abundant water.[25]

THE CITY VOTES

A week before the bond election, temperatures soared into the hundreds, and in the heat wave, city reservoirs sank with increased use. Days before the election, the Municipal League, the Chamber of Commerce, and the Merchants and Manufacturers Association, after an investigation of the project, declared their support and recommended inviting a delegation from Owens Valley to Los Angeles for a conference in an attempt to "convert antipathy into friendliness." On September 7, the public went to the polls and voted fourteen to one in favor: 10,693 for, 754 against. Even opponent Houghton's ward voted 1,879 in favor and 149 against. In an untypical outburst of "Let me tell you how I feel. I'm intoxicated, drunk with delight. I want to whoop and yell like a kid," Mulholland exulted that he would leave the next day for San Francisco to purchase equipment for six gangs of surveyors who would go into the field within fifteen days. Eaton set out for Owens Valley to attend the city's business there, and Mathews began to arrange the sale of the bonds. The great enterprise was at last under way. Four days later found Mulholland busy in San Francisco while, in the company of family and friends, he celebrated his fiftieth birthday and prepared to be drawn onto a broader canvas of history that would bring him fame and great reputation but also great calumny.[26]

Preparations for an Aqueduct and a Trip to Washington, D.C.

1906

EARLY SKIRMISHES

Even though the overwhelming event of 1906 for California was the earthquake and fire in San Francisco, the year was pivotal for Los Angeles in that it saw not only the establishment of the city's right to import water from distant places but also marked the beginnings of the open shop's triumph over organized labor and the rise of the Progressive movement in politics. In combination, these developments produced great civic turbulence and change, beginning with a turmoil of debate on the Owens Valley question as water men continued to lay ground for the massive undertaking.

As the city pressed the federal government to turn over public lands in Owens Valley and stop all public works there, the people of Owens Valley demanded that their irrigation needs be considered. Pushed from both sides, Secretary of the Interior Ethan A. Hitchcock delayed his decision as he sought more counsel from C. E. Grunsky, city engineer of San Francisco, and also a consulting engineer and advisor on reclamation matters for Interior. Grunsky had completed a tour of western reclamation projects the year before and had already announced the previous September that Interior had no plans for a project in Owens Valley because if it proceeded with work at Klamath and Yuma no further funds would be available. Grunsky also defended Lippincott, whose work in Owens Valley, he stated, had not favored Los Angeles and whose findings were public property "accessible to all." Now Grunsky's reply to

Hitchcock on January 4, 1906, was noncommittal on the conflict between Owens Valley and Los Angeles, focusing instead on the project's
engineering feasibility. He concluded that if Los Angeles were to take
Owens River water for municipal use, then the proposed irrigation project
in Owens Valley would not be possible.[1]

Information and opinions about Owens Valley traveled among western engineers. Grunsky, for example, worked at City Hall in San Francisco, as did Mulholland's old friend and colleague J. Henry "Doc"
Dockweiler, formerly a Los Angeles city engineer but now a consulting
engineer in the San Francisco city attorney's office for the Tuolumne
River proposal. Mulholland and Dockweiler regularly shared technical
information about each other's city water systems, and shortly after
Grunsky sent his report to Hitchcock, Dockweiler asked Mulholland to
send Grunsky a copy of the last year's annual report. Then on January
5, 1906, Mulholland asked Dockweiler for a list of fifteen or twenty
names of "eminent hydraulic engineers" for the process of selecting a
board of engineers to study the plan and cost of the Owens River enterprise. (The water commissioners ultimately would be responsible for
choosing the panel but looked to experts like Mulholland for advice.)
He wanted to choose from a larger pool than those whose names he
knew, especially, he wrote, "men who have not been connected with the
booming of the cost of engineering work, as there is a very apparent effort being made on the part of local power companies here to depreci-
ate the value of the power, and to exaggerate the probable cost of carrying through this enterprise." He was referring to recent critical articles
in the new *Evening News,* as well as to former city engineer Frank L.
Olmstead, who "had lent himself to this purpose in the fool report he
submitted a week or two ago." (Olmstead had submitted a sixty-three-
page report to the city council on how the aqueduct should be built. In
it he found all of Mulholland's estimates too low—altogether almost
$15 million too low!)[2]

An embattled Lippincott was still with Reclamation at the beginning
of 1906, still defending his assistance to the city while an employee of a
federal agency. A meeting with Newell the previous November 22 had
produced an agreement that the city could move ahead with its plans,
but by then he had come under such heavy fire for his putative unethical behavior in Owens Valley that he invited an investigation to clear his
name—only to discover that one was already under way. Notwithstanding, Mulholland, energetically laying groundwork for the aqueduct,
solicited Lippincott's help in securing power rights for the city on Cot-

tonwood Creek in Inyo County, urging him to emphasize that "the power to be derived from this stream will be of great importance to the city in the prosecution of the stupendous undertaking it is about to begin." Mathews also wired a Senate lobbyist in Washington, instructing him to take "map and letter of November 2nd to Newell, concerning City's water project" and also to inform both Hitchcock and Frank Flint, the Republican senator from Southern California who would fight for the Owens River project in Washington.[3]

By mid-February Mulholland was expecting Fred Eaton back from Owens Valley, where ditch work had begun below Charley's Butte for the aqueduct's intake. Eaton, who had spent the first six weeks of 1906 overseeing some of the preliminary survey work, now found himself balked in making further land acquisitions while a debate raged in the city council over allocating any further funds to him. Mulholland was also stalled in his plans to take the newly chosen board of public works on a tour of Owens Valley because Councilman Houghton withheld approval of the new water board on grounds that it lacked labor representation and that it had concocted a scheme whereby the aqueduct would be constructed with "alien labor." While waiting for the arrival of new machinery for a big conduit for the city works, Mulholland was asked about the wrangling in City Hall and replied with what became his well-known paradox: "If Los Angeles does not secure the Owens Valley water supply, she will never need it."[4]

THE CITY FATHERS IN OWENS VALLEY

At last, on February 20, Mulholland wrote Surveyor T. W. Young in Independence that Eaton had secured the board's approval "with regard to hasty procurement of the right of way over all the private lands in the valley" and alerted him that he would soon lead the board of public works ("when it is appointed") on an inspection of the route. They planned to go by auto as far as Haiwee, where Young was to meet them with a rig in which they would ride for the balance of the journey ("your big wagon with spring seats and four animals"). In March Mulholland alerted Young to get the spare beds ready at the Rickey Ranch and to round up enough bedding for four or five people.[5]

A trip to Owens Valley from Los Angeles was always arduous, and this one proved no exception. On a rainy Tuesday, March 20, Mayor McAleer with members of the water commission and the board of public works began their inspection tour under Mulholland's guidance. Part of the group left the city in three White steam automobiles, while three others took the night train to Mojave. They encountered flood conditions in Soledad Canyon, where the autos became mired in quicksand, washed-out roads, and torrents of water. With the three cars pulling each other out of the mud and sometimes using block and tackle snubbed to a tree, they limped into Mojave—two cars with broken springs and several of the passengers water soaked. After patching up the cars, the men proceeded the next day to Haiwee. Along the way, Mulholland pointed out the "fool plan" Olmstead had proposed, which would have taken the conduit east of Indian Wells into low-lying land, a route, he assured them, that he had never contemplated and that was "utterly impracticable." Instead, if the added cost proved acceptable, he proposed to run the line across one 400-foot depression by means of an inverted siphon.[6]

They spent the night at the Orr Ranch at Haiwee Meadows, where a number of them had to sleep out in the barn because Mrs. Orr lacked beds for the entire group. (Mira E. "Mother" Orr had sold land to the city.) As prearranged, engineer Young met them with the wagon, and the next morning they set out towards Owens Lake, where the roads became too sandy for auto travel. At Cottonwood Creek, they saw the first water that was to come to the city and were told of the barren soil at the southern end of Owens Valley, which produced little even when irrigated. Proceeding to the oasis settlement of Lone Pine and thence eighteen miles north to Independence, they were met by Fred Eaton, who had arrived by rail and was to lead them on to Big Pine, Bishop, and the Rickey Ranch.

Upon arrival in Bishop on Sunday, they dodged a conference with townspeople on the plea that they were there only to look and had no special authority to speak. The locals saw the evasion as a snub and said it was another instance of Eaton's giving them the back of his hand. The reporter covering the junket thought the delegation might have helped to allay "the apprehensions of Bishop" had they prolonged their visit. Instead the men from the big city left, still suspect and with animosities unrelieved, especially towards Eaton and Lippincott.

The return trip was equally eventful. The group traveled from Bishop to Big Pine by carriage, then by rail to Keeler on the northeastern shore of Owens Lake, and finally by wagon to Haiwee, where they picked up the automobiles and two new guests: a sheriff of Inyo and an editor from Independence, Irving Mulholland (no relation to William), who had already sold property to Los Angeles. This was the sheriff's first ride in an automobile, and he became an instant enthusiast when they accomplished the 44-mile run from Haiwee to Coyote Wells in a dashing two hours and twenty minutes. Luck ran out, however, when one of the cars developed engine trouble and had to be towed by Mulholland's, so that the next stretch from Coyote Wells to Mojave—45 miles—took a tortoise-like four hours. At Mojave they put the crippled car on a train along with the rest of the party, while Mulholland and two board members stayed with the two remaining automobiles. Although they were rewarded with a spectacular spring display of desert wildflowers as they motored back to the city through Antelope Valley, Elizabeth Lake, and San Francisquito Canyon, the 91-mile trip from Mojave to Los Angeles took eight hours because of rain and mud.

EARTHQUAKE WORRIES

The water board did not publish its official report on the Owens River project until June, and in the interim, the San Francisco earthquake and fire had pushed the Owens River affair to the back pages. Two days before the earthquake, Mulholland had been studying recent communications from engineer Young that included the sketch of a contour line for a ditch from Haiwee Reservoir along with specifications for a portable cookhouse. When he answered Young two days later to assure him that the cook wagon was nearly completed and that a cook and flunky were on their way with two pairs of mules, he also mentioned that one of the men who had intended to work in San Francisco "will probably be able to return to your camp by reason of failure to secure the employment he expected, due to the frightful San Francisco catastrophe."[7]

Recalling that Inyo County had suffered a similarly severe quake in 1872, Harry Brooks, assistant editor of the *Times,* wrote Mulholland immediately after the quake to express concern about the safety of the cement pipes proposed for the Owens River project. Responding promptly with a three-page discussion of damage to waterworks structures by earthquakes, Mulholland declared the topic had engaged the attention of many West Coast engineers. Noting that a full study had yet to be made, he admitted that "possibly over fifty per cent of the property loss due to the recent catastrophe in San Francisco is to be accounted for by the failure of the water supply, yet it will be found that the damage to the water works will, in all probability, prove, when full examination is made, to be less than to any other extensive structure in the fated town." He explained that the pipelines, being almost all substructural (buried), could not move and shake as freely as if they had been above ground.

All of the dams, both earth and concrete, in San Francisco's Spring Valley system had held, and all had been full at the time of the earthquake and thus subject to maximum strain. Moreover, the main trunk line at Millbrae-Belmont had held; otherwise, he concluded, "the city would be entirely deprived of water."

As to the Owens Valley project, Mulholland assured Brooks that because the proposed conduit would be almost wholly buried in the ground, "little need be feared as to any irreparable destruction of it due to seismic shock." He added that he had studied "the effect of the great quake of 1872 near Lone Pine, as evidenced by the faulted condition of the ground along the crack that then occurred and the evidence of which is still as freshly apparent almost as the day it happened." Admitting that damage could occur, he contended it would be confined to local breakage here and there and probably would not be "beyond the possibility of repair in reasonable time and at moderate cost." He concluded with an upbeat statement about the brave people of Los Angeles, who would go ahead with "this great work," willing to take "their chances on earthquakes or other abnormal though seemingly inevitable happenings, rather than see the welfare of this fair country languish from lack of water."[8]

A CEMENT MAN

Shortly before the earthquake, Mulholland had been attempting without success to secure the services of engineer-geologist Edwin Duryea, Jr., to explore the possibilities of the city's manufacturing its own cement on the Owens River project. Duryea, a cement expert from San Francisco, was then in charge of the cement plant for Roosevelt Dam in Arizona. When Mulholland requested Duryea's services to examine lime deposits near the route of the aqueduct with a view to their use in cement making, Chief Engineer Newell of the Reclamation Bureau responded, "It is not legal for any regular employee of the Reclamation Service to undertake outside work." Mulholland, both aggressive and tenacious in seeking the best talents for the job, enticed Duryea with the proposal that if Duryea were to find sufficient available deposits for the project, then "we could employ you permanently under probably better conditions than the Government offers you." In response Duryea suggested taking a leave of absence from Reclamation, unofficially and without pay, to "make a recreation trip to the Owens River, say in June, and look over the ground and materials." The resulting knowledgeable report that he submitted July 1 resulted in an arrangement whereby the Department of the Interior allowed him to devote one-half of his time to the City of Los Angeles.[9]

THEODORE ROOSEVELT WRITES A LETTER

Although Mulholland was to make many trips to the nation's capital on behalf of his city's water supply, the first, in June 1906, remained memorable not only for its momentous outcome but also because he first saw Congress in action. He would later regale his children with tales of the colorful and immensely popular Republican Speaker of the House, Joseph "Uncle Joe" Cannon of Indiana. Cannon's forceful style and wit made a deep impression on Mulholland, as did the fact that he helped expedite the water bill through Congress. Then being spoken of as a possible presidential candidate, the Speaker had once ascribed his success to having been "an average man . . . one of the great army of mediocrity which constitutes the majority." The Californians arrived in Washington as Congress was scrambling to wind up its current session. In view of the impending big battles over bills for pure food, meat inspection, and railroad rates, the California water issue did not loom large on the national agenda.[10]

Shortly before the Los Angeles group left for Washington, the water commissioners released their official report, hoping to clear up public misapprehensions about the water plan. They told again the familiar story of the growing city's need for more water, of Eaton's, Lippincott's, and Mulholland's Owens River investigations and explorations, and of the decision to proceed with the project. In Washington, by mid-June the two opposing representatives from Southern and Central California, James MacLachlan of Pasadena and Sylvester C. Smith of Bakersfield and Inyo, had led the debate in the House on the Flint-McLachlan Bill, which granted right-of-way over the land of the aqueduct route: "the proposed sale of the right of way from Inyo county to the city of Los Angeles for a municipal water supply." By the time the Angelenos arrived, Smith and attorneys for the private power interests seemed about to defeat the scheme, which Smith declared to be chimerical on account of its cost. During two days of impassioned discussions that included a confrontation with a resistant secretary of the interior, Mulholland explained the project and its probable cost while Mathews addressed the legal issues. Secretary Hitchcock wanted to preclude using the water for irrigation and thus restrict the city's use to domestic purposes only. Fearful of such an outcome, MacLachlan went to President Theodore Roosevelt, who agreed to an interview with the principals.[11]

Like a god from the machine, on June 25, 1906, Roosevelt listened to all of the arguments, then retired and dictated a decisive and now famous letter to the secretary of the interior. It began, "As I think it is best that there should be a record of our attitude in the Los Angeles water supply matter, I am dictating this letter to you in your presence and that of Senator [Frank] Flint on behalf of the California delegation, of Director [Charles D.] Walcott of the Geological Survey and of Chief Forester [Gifford] Pinchot. The question is whether the city of Los Angeles should be prohibited from using the water it will obtain under this bill for irrigation purposes."

Arguing that Los Angeles sought to provide its water supply for the next half century and would have surpluses in the beginning, Roosevelt decided the city could divert those surpluses for irrigation. He further noted:

> I am also impressed by the fact that the chief opposition to this bill, aside from the opposition of a few settlers in Owens Valley (whose interest is genuine, but whose interest must unfortunately be disregarded in view of the infinitely greater interest to be served by putting the water in Los Angeles) comes from certain private power companies whose object evidently is for their own pecuniary interest to prevent the municipality from furnishing its own water.
>
> The people at the head of these power companies are doubtless respectable citizens, nevertheless, their opposition seems to me to afford one of the strongest arguments for passing the law, inasmuch as it ought not to be within the power of private individuals to control such a necessary of life as against the municipality itself.
>
> Under the circumstances I decide, in accordance with the recommendations of the director of the geological survey and the chief of the forestry service, that the bill be approved, with the prohibition against the use of water by municipality for irrigation, struck out.
>
> I request, however, that there be put in the bill a prohibition against the city of Los Angeles ever selling or letting to any corporation or individual except a municipality, the right for that corporation or that individual itself to sell or sublet the water given to it or him for irrigation purposes. [12]

After finding that everyone agreed with his statements, Roosevelt added that he submitted it "with a more satisfied heart than when I started to dictate this letter." Flush with success, MacLachlan next received Speaker Cannon's assurance that the amendment to the Flint-MacLachlan Bill would be called up quickly. Before noon of the following day, the House unanimously consented to the amended bill, which would give Los Angeles the right to take an unlimited amount of water from the Owens River for both domestic and irrigation purposes. With equal speed, Senator Flint secured Senate approval on June 28, and the bill went to the president for his signature. The victorious California delegation immediately left for New York to discuss with financiers the question of floating bonds to construct the Owens River Aqueduct.

Events moved quickly. A week later, Lippincott resigned from his Reclamation job to become Mulholland's assistant engineer on the aqueduct, and in August, Mathews became the attorney for the aqueduct's legal department. While the Los Angeles dailies applauded the victory in Washington, only the *News* warned of the project's extravagance, declaring, "The taxpayers are being bunkoed." Eaton had stayed home, but nonetheless managed to create a stir of his own just as the Flint-MacLachlan Bill triumphed in Congress by marrying Alice Slosson, whom he had known for three years. The former secretary of attorney Mathews, she was described as "a charming stenographer . . . who knew almost as much about legal forms as Mr. Mathews himself." Mulholland immediately sent good wishes to his old friend and, mindful of his bibulous propensities, added the comradely hope that "the moral restraint will be a great benefit to you and will largely make up for the many days in which you must have been somewhat unhappy."[13]

A BOUQUET AND A FEW BRICKS

Soon after returning from Washington, Mulholland set out with Lippincott in the faithful White Steamer to tour the aqueduct's route and to make an important stop to investigate the actions of George Chaffey, a prominent water and land developer whose alleged appropriations of water and power rights on Cottonwood Creek threatened to impede the project. Mathews had already sent a protest to Washington against approving Chaffey's filings, but by the end of the year a decision had gone against the city, thus launching a struggle not to be resolved until 1912. More happily for the city, however, the Department of the Interior withdrew all public lands along the surveyed line of the Owens River Aqueduct.[14]

On August 15, the Chamber of Commerce presented a formal proclamation of thanks to each of those who had been in Washington on the city's behalf. After three years of struggle, turmoil, and controversy, the City Council of Los Angeles, on August 23, 1906, confirmed the appointment of William Mulholland as chief engineer of the Owens River

Aqueduct. On the same day, the board of public works confirmed the appointment of three eastern engineers noted for their achievements in hydraulic engineering to investigate and report on the Owens River project: J. R. Freeman, F. P. Stearns, and J. D. Schuyler. The *News* lost no time in attacking the choice of Schuyler, claiming that among other shortcomings he had built a defective dam in Oregon. When Schuyler wrote Mulholland on August 31 to express his gratification at being chosen, he added that he had seen the articles and commented, "It is perhaps idle to notice such slanders, as it is well known that the reservoirs I built are all in use." He then explained that earth movement had caused the trouble with the Oregon dam.[15]

By the end of summer, the *News* had made charges against Mulholland's character that have never died. One was that Mulholland concocted water shortages to bully voters into complying with his requests for water bond issues. Changing conditions did sometimes contrive to make him appear a liar, as in June, when before going to Washington, D.C., he had assured the president of the Chamber of Commerce that Los Angeles currently enjoyed an ample water supply because of two successive years of above average rainfall. While he was in Washington, however, the Geological Survey published Walter Mendenhall's report on the groundwater resources of the coastal plain region of Southern California, and its findings put Mulholland on alert. Because of the past ten years' low rainfall and the large drafts upon the area's underground waters, the report stated that a shortage threatened in the near future. Although Mendenhall did not see an immediate crisis, he recommended prudence and restraint, especially in irrigating crops. Thus, in the annual report for 1906, Mulholland heeded Mendenhall, and after reiterating that rainfall had been abundant in the past two years, acknowledged that the Los Angeles River's flow was down 40 percent, which he attributed to pumping by San Fernando Valley ranchers.[16]

With his mandate to plan ahead for the city's needs, in early August he reluctantly invoked the city's right to shut down the pumps of certain ranchers in the San Fernando Valley (mostly those near the river in today's Burbank and Glendale areas; the western half of the valley was not involved). When he ordered a stoppage in late August, the ranchers' resistance made headlines not only at home but also in the *San Francisco Chronicle*: "THREATENED BY USERS OF WATER. Los Angeles Superintendent Says He Does Not Fear for His Life." Mulholland dismissed the anonymous threats as "the vaporings of a few crazy and disgruntled water users."[17]

THE EXPERTS INSPECT

On October 22, shortly before the formal survey of the aqueduct project was to begin, Mulholland and Lippincott made an informal survey trip to Owens Valley with Schuyler, who had just returned from Mexico. Frederick Newell, chief engineer of Reclamation, came through town on his way to Yuma from Sacramento and expressed public surprise that there should be any controversy over the project. "It doesn't seem to me to be a question of feasibility, but rather of cash and nerve," he said, adding that he had always believed the people of Los Angeles had plenty of the latter.[18]

As the city council authorized more purchases of land for the Owens River project and the *News* beat the drums for its currently favored water project on the Mojave River near Victorville, the other two eastern experts arrived with their wives on November 13. Mulholland and Lippincott escorted them from the station to the Alexandria Hotel, then considered the last word in deluxe accommodation. Both experts enjoyed outstanding reputations as hydraulic engineers. Mulholland and Lippincott had especially sought John R. Freeman because of his experience in evaluating the water systems of large cities in Massachusetts and New York. He had done a massive survey of New York City's water supply, claimed to be the most elaborate waterworks report ever made by one engineer and, according to his peers, free of any biases of local pressures or prejudices. Equally distinguished was Frederick P. Stearns, then president of the American Society of Civil Engineers and a member of the Isthmian Canal Association. He was then serving also on the water commission in charge of New York's $160 million Catskills project. Of the three experts, Schuyler had the greatest familiarity with the West. Builder of the Sweetwater Dam in Oregon (the one the *News* claimed was defective), he also had constructed the highest masonry dam in the West at Hemet, California.

All three had already studied reports of the Owens River project, and after a day's survey of the San Fernando Valley on November 14, began a trek complicated by severe winter weather: windstorms, snow, and a blizzard. From Red Rock Canyon to Haiwee, the ferocious winds continually blew out the White steam auto's fire. When it finally had to be towed, Mulholland predicted that it would prove its worth later in the trip. At Haiwee they found shelter but no warmth with Mother Orr, as the wind had blown away her chimney and she could not risk burning her house down with a fire. The weather did not abate as they strug-

Hugh Mulholland (1829–1885), Dublin.

Ellen Deakers Mulholland (1834–1862), with a daughter on lap and an unidentified relative beside her, Dublin, circa 1859.

Jane Smith Mulholland (1835–1901), with Mary Mulholland, only daughter of Hugh and Jane, Dublin, circa 1876.

First known likeness of William Mulholland, with brother, Hugh
Patrick (*seated*), Los Angeles, circa 1878.

Mulholland (*at right*) with the Deakers family at 15 San Pedro Street, Los Angeles, 1880s. His cousin, Ella, and his uncle, Richard Deakers, are seated.

William Mulholland about the time of his marriage, 1890.

Lillie Ferguson (1868–1915)
before her marriage to
Mulholland, Los Angeles,
circa 1888.

Mulholland home from 1894 to 1921, at Sixth and Cummings Streets,
Boyle Heights, circa 1898. Children and friends are on porch. Designed by
Mulholland, the house was demolished for the construction of the Santa Ana
Freeway in the 1950s.

Family outing on Mulholland's fiftieth birthday with friends and associates, on board the moored British ship *Hyderabad* in Sausalito, California, September 10, 1905. Mulholland crouches in front, gazing at baby. His wife, Lillie, with large hat, stands at left between her niece Frances Mitchell at left and oldest daughter, Rose, to the right. His sons, Perry and Tom, sit side by side on the stairs. Because aqueduct bonds had just been approved, Mulholland was also in the Bay Area to order and procure supplies for the great undertaking.

First water supply system for Los Angeles, 1864. An early flume and water-wheel to carry water to a ditch flowing to the reservoir near the plaza of Los Angeles.

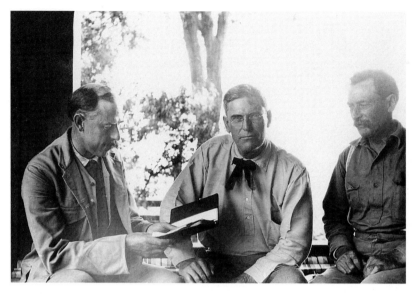

The "fathers" of the Owens River project. *Left to right:* J. B. Lippincott, Fred Eaton, William Mulholland, 1905–1906. Photograph by Andrew A. Forbes.

William B. Mathews (1865–1932), an attorney whose long, untiring efforts secured municipally owned water and power systems for Los Angeles.

Anti-aqueduct cartoon portraying Mulholland as a behind-the-scenes manipulator, *Los Angeles Evening News*, September 24, 1906.

Consulting engineers during inspection of aqueduct line, 1905. *Left to right:* John R. Freeman, James D. Schuyler, J. B. Lippincott, Frederick P. Stearns, William Mulholland. Photograph by Bledsoe. Courtesy of the Los Angeles Department of Water and Power.

Fred Eaton on muleback during a camping trip in the Sierra
Nevada and the Kings River area, circa 1902. This photograph
and the one on the facing page are from the J. B. Lippincott
Collection (LIPP 139: 62, 63). Used with permission of the Water
Resources Center Archives, University of California, Berkeley.

J. B. Lippincott, taken on camping trip with Fred Eaton, circa 1902.

Lone Pine Lake, Owens Valley. Photograph by Andrew A. Forbes.

Snowstorm during consulting engineers' inspection tour, 1905. Photograph by Andrew A. Forbes.

City-owned freighting outfit hauling aqueduct material on the desert. Photograph by Bledsoe. Courtesy of the Los Angeles Department of Water and Power.

Building roads in the Jawbone Division. Photographs on this and facing page are by Bledsoe. Courtesy of the Los Angeles Department of Water and Power.

Dredge No. 1, working in Owens Valley.

Tunnel No. 71, Antelope Division.

Lining the aqueduct with concrete, Mojave Division.

Workers standing by one of the twenty-three inverted siphons constructed along the aqueduct line.

Owens River near the intake for the aqueduct. Photograph by Andrew A. Forbes.

The Deluge.

Undated clipping from a scrapbook of William Mulholland's.

Opening-day ceremony for aqueduct, November 5, 1913. *Left to right:*
General Harrison Gray Otis, owner-editor of the *Los Angeles Times;* Ellen
"Lark Ellen" Beach Yaw, singer; and William Mulholland. His daughter
Rose stands behind him.

William Mulholland with daughters, Rose and Lucile, November 5, 1913. Peering over his shoulder is Mrs. D. L. Reaburn, wife of an aqueduct engineer who would later lay out Mulholland Highway.

Last photograph of Lillie Mulholland, 1914–1915.

Mulholland's residence from 1921 until his death in 1935, 426 South Saint Andrews Place, Los Angeles. It was demolished in the 1970s to make way for apartment buildings.

Stalwarts of the Los Angeles Water Department, early 1920s. *Back row, left to right:* George Read, Roderick McKay, L. M. Anderson; *front:* Frederick J. Fischer, William Mulholland, Thomas Brooks. These men worked all their lives on behalf of city water.

A gathering of city bigwigs for a preview of Mulholland Highway, March 27, 1924. *Left to right:* William Mulholland, Moses H. Sherman, D. L. Reaburn, Harry Chandler, and three members of the water commission.

Subject—Bill Mulholland.

Trade or Occupation—Chief Engineer of the Aqueduct.

Duties—Competing with Jupiter Pluvius.

Pet·Aversion—Afternoon teas.

Greatest Ambition—To meet Mayor Cryer face to face.

Favorite Fowl—Aqua Ducks.

Favorite Philosophy—Work.

Favorite Book—The family album.

Favorite Song—"Waltz Me Around Again, Willie"—as sung by Fred Eaton.

Most Famous Speech—"There it is. Take it!"—When the water first gushed through the Aqueduct.

Favorite Virtue—Brusqueness.

Favorite Vice—Receiving guests in his bathrobe.

Hobby—Collecting cuss-words.

Religion—The Golden Rule.

Favorite Maxim—"When you buy a hog you don't have to eat the bristles."

Motto—Dammit!

Remarks—Bill Mulholland wasn't born. He's a self-made man, he admits. He began life as a ditch-digger. The last ditch he dug took him five years to dig it. That ditch was the Los Angeles Aqueduct. Mr. Mulholland achieved additional fame recently by having his name tacked onto a road or a street or something up in the mountains.

Cartoon of William Mulholland, *Los Angeles Times*, February 22, 1925.

William Mulholland (*right*) and Harvey Van Norman
leaning against a boat alongside the Colorado River during
a conference on Boulder Dam, 1925.

William Mulholland and Harvey Van Norman amid the wreckage of the failed Saint Francis Dam, March 13, 1928. Photograph courtesy of the Los Angeles Department of Water and Power.

Mulholland with his three grandchildren at the Mulholland Ranch in the San Fernando Valley shortly after the dam disaster, Easter 1928. *To his right:* Lillian Sloan; *at left:* Richard Mulholland; *in front:* Catherine Mulholland.

William Mulholland and his son Perry on a trip to Ensenada, Mexico, 1929.

Mulholland with engineers and politicians gathered for a Metropolitan Water District project, the spreading of the upper Santa Ana River, San Bernardino County, February 17, 1932.

Last photograph of William Mulholland in the Los Angeles Water Department, March 1933. He holds a memorial vial of Owens River water from opening-day ceremonies in 1913.

gled all next day to reach Independence. When they arrived there late that night, a worried Eaton met them, fearful of what might have happened to them in such a storm.

Stearns and Mulholland must have been the least comfortable members of the group. Stearns, evidently sold on California's clement weather by Schuyler, had worn only a khaki suit and light rain coat, in which he shivered stoically. At one point, however, as the wind howled about them, he turned to Schuyler and sang a line from an old Swiss song: "You speak of sunny skies to me, of orange groves and bowers/Of winds that make soft melody through leaf and blooming flowers." Mulholland's discomfort began at Independence when he bit into a savory Inyo quail pie prepared by Eaton's daughter-in-law and wedged a pellet of shot between his teeth. Attempts to dig it out only lodged it further, so that biting was agony. To console him, the company around the table joked about dynamiting it out. Weather and personal discomforts aside, in the almost two weeks of travel and study, they visited all the necessary sites along the proposed aqueduct's route, concluding with Bishop and a visit to the proposed site of the Long Valley reservoir.[19]

Freeman, Stearns, and Schuyler returned to Los Angeles and, without comment, closeted themselves on the eleventh floor of the Union Trust Building with their mass of data, plans, and maps. "When the engineers want us, we will go to them," reported Mulholland. "I shan't go near them until they send for me. They have a pile of plans three feet high to wade through. After these are digested they will go up the Valley again. Stearns and Freeman are old campaigners—Freeman knows a great deal about that country. No engineer, with the possible exception of Lippincott, knows more about the rainfall than he does." When pressed for details about alternate routes, the Chief replied, "We want these men to figure this out themselves. I can tell you this, that we can make the route 201 miles, or 211 miles or 221 miles. The idea is not particularly to lessen the cost. The consideration of the route by the engineers would include the safety of the line."[20]

NEW WORKS AT HOME

Mulholland's immediate duties at home included supervising construction of two important and interrelated city reservoirs: the more northerly Ivanhoe, begun in 1905, and Silver Lake, begun in August 1906. Located in Ivanhoe Valley in the hills between Elysian Park and Hollywood, the first had a capacity of 50 million gallons and held all the water from the main supply conduit, which headed on the Hooker and Pomeroy tract, as well as from an area called the high gravity system. It fed a distribution point near Sixth Street and Wilshire Boulevard. The second, an impounding reservoir to be named for the old champion of municipal water, Herman Silver, anticipated a capacity of 773 million gallons. With its completion expected in February 1907, the two dams would hold the equivalent of a twenty-day supply (820 million gallons) for the entire city at its current rate of use, thus insuring against summer shortages.[21]

Because Silver Lake would be poised in the hills above the city where a break could cause a disaster not unlike the recent Johnstown flood, Mulholland did not design the usual earthen dam. Instead, its core was a concrete wall three feet thick, and at its center a continuous watertight wall of riveted steel plates extended from bedrock to water level. He also introduced an application of hydraulic sluicing that threw up the mud being dredged from the bed onto the dam that was to create the reservoir. This so-called innovation created a stir in engineering circles. At a meeting of the American Society of Civil Engineers, one member declared the method impracticable because water pressure could not force heavy material uphill through pipes, while Stearns defended the procedure, saying it was often used in hydraulic gold dredging. Mulholland added that it was all a matter of pressure. "Put on the power," he said, "and you can send anvils and flatirons through the pipe. Nothing new in it; it is done every day, and I'm surprised that any one should question so obvious a fact." The method aroused the interest of the Isthmian Canal Commission, which sent one of its engineers to observe the process. He was favorably impressed not only with the sluicing method but also with a centrifugal pump designed by Mulholland. Similar hydraulic sluicing was later used on the difficult Culebra (now Gaillard) Cut of the Panama Canal and eventually on similar projects in the Northwest.[22]

GEARING UP

All of Mulholland's organizational skills were now put to the test as he oversaw the myriad tasks necessary to put the immense project into operation. In a gigantic juggling act, he dealt with endless detail as well as matters of materiel and personnel. Shortly after his return from Washington, he told a job seeker that he was receiving an average of fifteen applications a week from engineers seeking work on the Owens River project. Fortunately, with the civil service commission recently instituted, he was spared the task of judging the applicants' qualifications. Each of them, be he engineer, surveyor, instrument man, chain man or rod-man, was told that he would have to qualify through the civil service commission.[23]

At year's end the grand jury investigating the Owens River project issued a terse but favorable report. "An investigation of lengthy duration was made into the matters of criticism appearing in the public press in connection with the Owens river project for Los Angeles city. Nothing was found justifying public censure by this grand jury. On the other hand, this valuable source of water supply was obtained by methods showing commendable business sense and economy on the part of those who represented the city's interests in these transactions."[24]

The final good news was Freeman, Schuyler, and Stearns's fifteen-page report, which concluded:

1. The project was feasible.
2. The Owens River and its tributaries could deliver a supply of about 400 cubic feet of good quality water to the city.
3. The cost, excluding the cost of the future Long Valley Reservoir or those to be built in the San Fernando Valley or structures related to the development of power, would be about $24.5 million.
4. The water conveyed through the aqueduct could develop sufficient electricity to supply 49,000 horsepower continuously, twenty-four hours per day "if portions of it are used only during ordinary working hours."

The report closed, "We find the project admirable in conception and outline and full of promise for the continued prosperity of Los Angeles."[25]

Although opponents were quick to point out the experts' changes in Mulholland's original plan, Schuyler spoke to the press before he left town and said that even they had been surprised at how close their estimates came to those of the original. One significant difference was their recommendation for more tunneling than Mulholland planned. Moreover, they altered his route somewhat and adopted different price units. Yet Schuyler concluded the overall report must be considered a thorough endorsement of "Mr. Mulholland's judgment and his natural engineering insight and skill which have come from long practice." He also exhorted the citizens of Los Angeles to realize the grandness of the project and the magnificence of the setting from which the water would come. Lastly, he urged the city to develop hydroelectric power, as the subsequent revenues could pay for the entire project.[26]

All of the daily newspapers applauded the report. Even the *News* and *Examiner* wrote grudgingly favorable editorials, although both continued to express skepticism about the cost and amount of water that would be available while gloating that Mulholland's original plans had been "knocked into a cocked hat." Scripps's prolabor *Record* concluded that municipal power would make money for the city, pointing out that the Edison Electric Company "is paying almost as much as the estimated cost of the Owens river aqueduct for its Kern river power works, and it is bringing down electricity alone, whereas the city will have both the water and the electricity." The *Record* did warn, however, against the pitfall of politics, proclaiming in boldface type, "Mayor-elect Harper may make or ruin the Owens river project." [27]

CHAPTER 13

The Big Job Begins

1907

A NEW MAYOR AND ENGINEERING WORRIES

The year 1907 ushered in a new mayor and a political debate that did not subside until after the noisy and spirited springtime campaign for the passage of the $24 million Owens River bond issue. At the end of 1906 the mayoral campaign's four candidates had reflected the divisions within the city. Democrat Arthur G. Harper won by a slender margin after the Republicans, fearful of losing to one of the nonparty Progressive or Labor candidates, had thrown their support to him. Harper was allied to the city's old-guard political machine, with ties to Southern Pacific interests. A genial but pliant man, well connected to the town's wealthy families, Harper, along with his new administration, was feted at a banquet hosted by the reform-minded Municipal League on January 4.

With 200 of their 625 members in attendance, the municipal reformers created a formidable presence for the city's newly elected officials. One reporter likened them to the British in India "who invited the hill princes and their retinues to a grand powwow. There, ringed by troops of red coats with glittering bayonets, the guests were peaceably but forcefully made aware of the raj." After a few jocular words, Mayor Harper produced a paper from his coat and then tucked it back in, saying he had decided not to lay his plans before them at this time but promised "the best business administration I know how." When the Hon. Frank G. Tyrrell of the League next rose and grew eloquent on the need for municipal virtue, he turned directly to the mayor-elect. "Mr. Harper. It has been said that you were elected by a class of citizens that hope for and expect at last a lax administration, a wide-open town, a yielding to quasi-criminal elements. . . ." After a pause to allow a sort of mental gasp to sweep the room, he then extended the olive branch, declaring, "I don't believe it." Yet he exhorted Harper to steer the city towards a heroic age when officials would be "unpurchasable, wise, firm and true." The ovation of the evening went to Mulholland, who declared the Owens River project now beyond the talking stage and urged directing all possible energy toward its accomplishment.[1]

On January 5, Lippincott and Mathews left Los Angeles for Chicago, where they spent two days with railroad executives discussing the possibilities of building a line on the desert from Mojave to Owens Valley. Both men continued east, where Mathews was to meet with bond financiers to discover whether authorizing the entire $23 million bond issue in one election would be legal and feasible. Both men spent several days in Washington, D.C., working out right-of-way matters in the land department and seeking reassurances that the power companies would not interfere in the city's water project. In anticipation of the Owens River bond issue's passage, Lippincott next began to investigate the capacities of eastern manufacturers of steel and machines to construct and deliver material and equipment for the project. This advance work was intended to prevent unnecessary delays in orders from mills, which were then running at full capacity. While on his assignment, Lippincott received news of the death of his father, Dr. J. A. Lippincott, the former chancellor of the University of Kansas. By now the aqueduct's planning so dominated its builders' lives that after attending the funeral in Kansas City, Lippincott spoke to local reporters not to eulogize his father but to praise the Owens River project. When completed, he told them, the water supply would be sufficient for one million people as well as for irrigating 100,000 acres of suburban land. It would be, he illustrated, as if an aqueduct were to bring water from the Mississippi River to Kansas City.[2]

Mathews meanwhile had returned from the East only to become embattled in legal wrangles in Sacramento that threatened the very life of the enterprise. The first proved a minor scuffle after the state supreme court disallowed the applications for certain Owens Valley lands made by an Oregonian claiming preemptive rights. The second, however, seriously threatened the city's plans. Two years earlier the Edison Electric Company had advanced the McCartney Bill, which proposed that any city contemplating municipal ownership of heating, lighting, or water systems would first have to buy, or offer to buy, the existing private plants.

Map 2. Los Angeles Aqueduct and adjacent territory with divisions, October 1908 (Los Angeles Department of Water and Power).

Now backed by private power interests, the bill had resurfaced. As its passage would drive up costs and impede municipalization, the state's progressive forces, led by the California League of Municipalities, went into action against the measure. Mathews hastened to seek Governor Pardee's veto of the bill, while City Attorney Leslie Hewitt also traveled north to protest to the legislature. In an adroit and controversial move before leaving Los Angeles, Mathews instructed the city auditor, W. C. Mushet, to withhold from the power companies' attorney all access to contracts, records, and files pertaining to the Owens River water project. Such an outcry arose throughout the state over what was understood to be a power grab by the utility companies that the bill was withdrawn by the end of January.[3]

Mulholland meantime was absorbed in directing five parties of fifteen men each deployed along the aqueduct's route. This early phase of preliminary construction involved setting up work camps and delivering supplies. But for its larger scope, it was not unlike the many smaller projects Mulholland had supervised along the Los Angeles River. For communication with their Chief in Los Angeles, the men in the field relied on letters. At the beginning of 1907, for instance, John Gray, a veteran mining engineer who would achieve acclaim as the aqueduct's champion tunnel man, was preparing pipe for the diversion of water at Cottonwood as well as keeping Mulholland informed of George Chaffey's activities. (At this juncture Chaffey had served notice that the city had no title to any of the water rights on Cottonwood Creek and was to stop all work there.) Above all, Gray was concerned that an insufficiency of cement was delaying his work. Mulholland, always with an eagle eye on keeping expenses within bounds, ordered the hydrographer at Cottonwood, George Shuey, to avoid the expense of measuring the whole high flow of streams but simply to get a fairly correct measurement when streams were low. When R. H. Sawyer, headquartered at Mojave, needed more livestock, Mulholland answered that he was looking but found "so far nothing that can be had within reason." Learning that thieves had been busy stealing supplies at Mojave, Mulholland urged Sawyer to spare no pains seeking out the culprits, "as we are but just at the beginning of our enterprise and it stands us in hand to be strict with such pirates."[4]

NEW PERSONNEL

In the midst of these preparations for one of the world's great engineering undertakings, the chief engineer, at the age of fifty-one, received a piece of paper that must have seemed, if not tardy, somewhat superfluous. It was a diploma from the American Society of Civil Engineers certifying that he, William Mulholland, had become, as of February 6, 1907, a member in good standing. Although doubtless gratifying as a professional validation, it also would serve to rebut those who sneered at his lack of formal training.

Two engineers who were to become major players now joined the water department. The first, Ezra F. Scattergood (1871–1947), was an electrical engineer whose career and fight for municipal power will be discussed later. The second, Harvey Van Norman (1878–1954), would become not only one of Mulholland's best-loved associates but also his successor as chief of the water department. Texas-born "Van" came with his family to Los Angeles in 1882 when he was four years old. Largely self-educated in engineering like Mulholland, he began his career as a stationary engineer at a pumping plant near Yuma, Arizona. After stints as a steam engineer with the Los Angeles Railway and a construction superintendent with the Los Angeles Gas and Electric Company, he went to the Philippine Islands on a construction job during the Spanish-American War. Towering over the average man at a height of 6 feet, 5 inches, this boyish-faced giant was an affable fellow who could bend an elbow with the most roistering of men at the sometimes rowdy, always rough, construction camps. Yet when occasion demanded, he could also be sober and resolute. He had begun work for the water department in February 1907, superintending the construction of buildings and installation of equipment at the Slauson and Headworks pumping plants. By year's end, however, he was sent to Owens Valley to complete work on the Division Creek and Cottonwood hydroelectric plants that would supply power for construction work along the aqueduct from the intake to Mojave.[5]

Van Norman later recalled his excitement at the opportunity to be part of the great enterprise, even though his first trip to Owens Valley took him aback when he viewed the desolation of the country and tried to conceive of millions of gallons of water being transported through all that aridity. "For the final part of my trip," he once remembered, "the only means of transportation was a stage coach. As we crossed burning, desolate stretches of desert and laboriously crawled over bleak, forbidding mountain passes, I would close my eyes and try to visualize an aqueduct crossing that same kind of country."

Adding to his discouragement was the absence of his beautiful young wife, Bessie, whom he had married only three weeks before and had had to leave behind in Los Angeles. Bessie eventually joined him to become one of that rare number of women who not only endured the hardships of living on the aqueduct's construction areas but managed to surmount them. Our family often told the story of how she hung dotted Swiss curtains at the windows of her cabin and planted geraniums in window boxes. When the wind destroyed them, she stoically remarked, "I just started all over again." An expert seamstress in Independence remembered that Mrs. Van Norman had once asked her to help select a new hat for Easter. Taken aback as she knew of no millinery shops in Independence, the seamstress still dressed for an afternoon of shopping and knocked on the Van Normans' door. To her surprise, she was welcomed in, served tea, and then spent the afternoon with her hostess making a selection from mail order catalogs.[6]

SUSPICIONS OF SUBVERSION AT CITY HALL

Although Mayor Harper had publicly lauded the water enterprise, in late March both the *Examiner* and the *Record* revealed that he and certain councilmen had secretly inspected well sites near Long Beach, a privately owned spring in the Big Tujunga reported to have 2,000 inches of water, and a stream near Palmdale called Big Rock Creek. Moreover, after consulting an engineer whose identity they refused to reveal, this group also proposed a plan to begin work on the aqueduct at the city's end rather than at the planned intake on the Owens River. The *Examiner,* still ambivalent about the city's water plans, was quick to play up the drama of the new mayor's going around the backs of Mulholland, Lippincott, Mathews, and the board of public works. When interviewed, Mathews said he thought such projects unnecessary, but Mulholland, obviously angered by the maneuver, declared the effort a useless waste of money, and then vented his exasperation. "I want to say this. I have been working for this city since 1878, and I know I have been a faithful servant. I have worked for the Owens River scheme because I know it is the only permanent solution of the water supply. But if after all of my work the people of Los Angeles should see fit to defeat the project by voting down the bonds I would not lose one night's sleep over the matter." Assuring that water supplies would be adequate for the next few years, he silenced some of his critics a week later with the March 31 issuance of the *First Annual Report of the Los Angeles Aqueduct,* a comprehensive, clearly written account of the activities surrounding the Owens River project since its inception.[7]

Only the *News* objected to the report on the grounds that it failed to state the amounts already laid out on the project. This was a sensitive area because a few weeks before the report's release City Auditor W. G. Mushet had discovered two forged signatures on demands for payment of land in Owens Valley. Although the demands proved regular and the amounts properly due the parties to whom they were paid, the discovery set in motion a reform in the auditor's office to introduce a system already used by the aqueduct department that required strict checks on purchases and payments. By May 25, criticism was quashed when the aqueduct disbursement officer issued a statement of expenditures from the start of the Owens River project to April 1, 1907. It revealed that of the $1.5 million bond issue of 1905, $1,294,251.02 had been expended. With those funds, the city had purchased 76,581 acres of land, opened and graded 5 miles of canals in Owens Valley, built 6 miles of wagon roads, done more than 700 miles of surveys and studies of route conditions, purchased a partial right of way, and acquired necessary machinery, equipment and tools. The total of $1,035,073.77 spent on real estate and water rights included $13,014.90 in commissions to Fred Eaton and B. A. Vollmer, who had acted as land agents for the city. (Eaton had received $10,666.15.)[8]

Disturbed by indications of subversive activity at City Hall, Mulholland, Mathews, and J. A. Anderson, head of the board of public works, made an informal call on Mayor Harper the morning of April 1. They proceeded to sound out his plans regarding the Big Rock Creek scheme, his intentions to call a date for the special water bond election, and his plans for an inspection trip to Owens Valley. Harper temporized but indicated that he would travel to Owens Valley without any water officials, as he wished to spend time with ranchers and leaders of Inyo County in order to gather information that would help him to gauge the attitudes of residents there. Two days after this interview, in a night session lasting from eight until midnight, these same men, along with council members and the city attorney, agreed that the council should set a date for the Owens River bond election, which, although at first set for May 15, eventually took place June 12.[9]

Harper's plan to visit Owens Valley without water officials fell by the board. On April 12, Mulholland wrote the chief engineer of Southern Pacific, with whom he and Lippincott were conferring over the proposed railway to serve the aqueduct, that he would have to postpone their meeting in San Francisco because either he or Lippincott "has got to accompany the Mayor and Council on a contemplated trip to Owens River." As it turned out, not only Mulholland and Lippincott but J. Henry Dock-

weiler as well took part in a tour comprising eighteen city fathers. Mulholland stayed only long enough to ride with the mayor from Mojave to
Owens Valley and point out the route of the conduit. He then returned
to the city with a lone councilman, who, despite the usual quota of mo-
tor breakdowns, failed to lose his enthusiasm for what he had seen: water
in such abundance, he related, that it could moisten Los Angeles for the
next hundred years. When Mayor Harper and his party returned two
days later under Dockweiler's guidance, they too had been converted to
the cause of building the Owens River Aqueduct as rapidly as possible.[10]

THE OPPOSITION FINDS A VOICE

On May 8, the mayor gathered the council in executive session to discuss how best to rouse public interest in the upcoming bond election. On
the eighteenth, less than a month before the election, a campaign committee was formed. Sam Clover's *News* had begun its fight against the
aqueduct bonds a month earlier when it began publishing a series of letters over the signature "Veritas." The letters, which eventually would
run from April 18 to June 8, attacked current water policies and rehashed
old grievances against the city harking back to the Hooker and Pomeroy
case. Veritas proved to be an old enemy of the city's water establishment,
William T. Spilman. In the 1890s, while promoting his Spilman Suburban Water Company near the Hooker-Pomeroy lands in the settlement
of Tropico (merged with Glendale in 1918), Spilman had almost succeeded in swindling the city of water rights along the Los Angeles River
in a crafty scheme too lengthy to recount here. His subsequent bankruptcy and personal scandals had turned him into an embittered, obsessive person who held the city's water men responsible for his Tropico
land scheme's failure in 1894. Now Spilman renewed his vendetta, beginning with a virulent attack on Mulholland, who, he charged, had been
responsible for a water famine at a time when the city had secured an
abundance of water by condemning a tract of land north of West Glendale but then failed to develop. This would have included not only the
Hooker and Pomeroy land, but also Spilman's failed land and water company. He also accused Mulholland of building, for reasons not made clear,
a "fake tunnel" near Elysian Park and, while doing so, depriving people
of water. The supposed results were horrific. "Throughout the city the
lawns were all turned brown or entirely destroyed while no proper fire
protection was to be had, and the lakes in our city parks were so stagnant that the fish were drying and decaying, while the winds were car-

rying the death-dealing vapors and stenches from the sewers as well as from the lakes, . . . causing sickness and death especially among small children and infants—a fact that many a mother can testify to."[11]

L. M. Anderson, auditor of the water department, delivered a strong rebuttal. "You've read the truthful (?) *News* about Mulholland's 'dry tunnel,'" wrote Anderson. "The fact is this tunnel today supplies the greater part of the water used on Boyle Heights and the East Side. . . . They won't tell the truth when they know it," he continued. "They come to our office for information, which has never been refused, and though we told them, it was no use to give them the figures, as they lie about the facts." He also added that Mulholland did not care "so long as he knows he's right," but Lippincott was rather thin-skinned and had finally refused to give them anything, so that they now also considered him a rascal.[12]

Each Veritas letter piled up more charges: Mathews's injunction against the San Fernando ranchers was a meaningless exercise because Mulholland had simply been withholding water to create the impression of a water famine and deceive the people into agreeing with Eaton's and Lippincott's selfish schemes in Owens Valley. Mulholland lied about the amount of flow from the Los Angeles River. Southern California had ample water in the San Gabriel and Santa Ana Rivers, for example, without having to bring brackish and alkaline water great distances at enormous expense from Owens Valley in order to benefit the pockets of "promoter Eaton." Veritas linked Mulholland to the *Los Angeles Times* with repeated use of such phrases as "his chief organ" and "his boosting organ." The *Times* in turn called Veritas Sam Clover's "assistant Ananias" and a "sneaking coyote," asking if any sane man in Los Angeles believed that Mulholland was a liar and a thief.[13]

According to the *News*, Mulholland's alkali bond folly not only was going to bilk the good taxpayers of Los Angeles but also would end up giving them water worse than they already had. When Harry Brooks of the *Times* sent Mulholland a sample of these accusations and asked if he could provide information about the limestone content of water in eastern cities, Mulholland responded with a three-page letter, in which he commented that "the screed you enclosed is but another emanation from a source absolutely ignorant of the true conditions that obtain in the Owens River Valley." He had been unable at short notice to obtain information about eastern cities, he replied, but could say that many middle and southern states had water "more impregnated with carbonate of lime and alkaline salts than the waters of the Los Angeles River or the

Owens River at its very worst." He outlined various government laboratory studies that indicated water from the Owens River project would
be "about twice as pure as the water we are now consuming." Moreover, concluded Mulholland, "Our enemies are as conversant with these
facts as we are, but persist in the reiteration of assertions to the contrary
in general terms, and display in greatest eagerness the screeds of igno-
rances, such as the one you mailed me."[14]

However unwelcome these attacks, the water men were fortunate that
their opposition was concentrated so largely in one journal, for in the
coming years other anti-aqueduct voices would diffuse and confuse the
slanders. Attorney Job Harriman of the Socialist Labor Party, for example, in fighting the aqueduct bonds, claimed that the aqueduct promoters were robbing the workingman and that after their project had
bankrupted the city they would sell out to the private power companies.
Mulholland, however, enjoyed support from many workers. One, at the
time of the bond campaign, said he would vote for Bill Mulholland "even
if he ran for the office of town pump." When Mulholland spoke to 250
iron workers at Baker's Iron Works, a follow-up straw vote for the water
bonds garnered 245 in favor and 15 against. Similar success followed
him in other gatherings.[15]

Throughout the city, interest and approval greeted campaigners as they
addressed political groups, women's clubs, labor organizations, and
church groups. Campaign organizers feared complacency about the outcome would keep voters from the polls, so in the two weeks before the
election, the water men campaigned indefatigably, sometimes speaking
to several groups in one day. Lippincott made polished presentations with
maps, charts, stereopticon views, and a moving picture to illustrate the
project. At one gathering when a persistent fly continued to obscure the
screen with its enlarged image, the chairman of the event proclaimed to
great laughter and applause that it depicted "the only microbe ever found
in Owens Valley water." Mulholland later remembered the public speaking as the least pleasant part of his job, saying he would rather skin dead
dogs than make speeches. He said he was like the Irishman who got a
job deep-sea diving and after one submersion in the diving suit declared
that he did not like the job. "The machine works all right," he said, "but
I can't spit on me hands."[16]

Boosts for the aqueduct came from what today would be unexpected
places. Naturalist John Muir, visiting with friends in Pasadena, offered
a testimonial to the Owens River water's purity and seemed unopposed
to Los Angeles's designs. "The purest on earth," he pronounced. "The

river above the basin, with its pure and sparkling flow, will be tapped
for the fluid which will go into the conduit for the future water supply
of Los Angeles." Two days before the election, Arthur P. Davis, Lippincott's old partner and chief engineer of Reclamation, arrived en route to
Yuma to inspect a reclamation project and expressed his admiration for
"the pluck of Los Angeles in going after Owens River water." He praised
Lippincott "as honest and as capable as any man I ever knew." As to the
project's cost, he found it cheap, certainly no more than New York spent
to acquire its supply.[17]

Pamphlets on the aqueduct appeared. First, an Owens Valley primer
with its catechism of questions and answers:

What is the proposed Los Angeles Aqueduct?

It is an undertaking by the city to construct, own and operate an aqueduct, two hundred and twenty-five miles long with a daily capacity of
260,000,000 gallons, to bring to Los Angeles a water supply from the high
Sierras. (The present consumption of the city of 40,000,000 gallons daily.)

Elsewhere, an anti-aqueduct primer disputed every point:

What is the proposed Los Angeles Aqueduct?

It is a piece of gigantic folly that will cost the taxpayers fifty millions of
dollars, or more, increasing their taxes three times the present rate.[18]

Cartoonists kept pens busy for their respective papers. One curiosity is
a cartoon by George Herriman, soon to be famous as the creator of *Krazy
Kat* but then a staff artist for the *Examiner*. His drawing simply showed
a stern-visaged and mustachioed man with his finger pointed at the viewer
over the admonishment, "It Is Your Duty to Vote Today for Owens River
Bonds." The *Times* announced a contest with three hundred dollars in
prizes for the closest estimate of the voting's outcome.[19]

Four days before the election, an acrimonious session took place at a
rally in Simpson's Auditorium at Hope Street near Seventh. The *News*
had touted the event as an occasion when Job Harriman and other aqueduct opponents would face down Mulholland and Lippincott in public
debate. Mulholland and Lippincott, however, claimed they had never
agreed to appear and were speaking at other gatherings. In their place
were Judge R. M. Widney and political leader Meyer Lissner of the Municipal League (also president of the city's public utilities board). Harriman immediately challenged Widney's right to speak as a private citizen in favor of the bonds: "if you are not a committee representative, we

don't want to hear from you." The audience began to applaud, so Widney was allowed to make his case for the city's need of water. Self-described engineer R. S. Watt, who had impugned Mulholland's and Eaton's veracity, followed. As he reiterated the now-familiar charge that the two men had once testified that 20,000 inches of water was running waste in the San Fernando Valley, Lissner challenged him from the floor to demonstrate where, in any court transcript, either Eaton or Mulholland had given such testimony. Unable to do so, a flustered Watt tried to cite Finkle. "No, no," interrupted Lissner. "Finkle does not count. Finkle is an engineer who was hired by Mr. Pomeroy and Mr. Hooker to testify in their suit against the city. This same John G. Hooker is the man who tried to sell his land to the city for $1,500,000 and was awarded by a court of condemnation only $30,000. Hooker hired Finkle, and Finkle's statements and testimony have been utterly discredited by every unbiased engineer."[20]

The final rally at Simpson's brought forth an estimated audience of 2,000 and a full complement of dignitaries: Mayor Harper, Mulholland, Lippincott, and special guest Arthur P. Davis. Three other rallies took place the eve of the election: one in the chapel at the University of Southern California where Mulholland and Lippincott gave their final speeches; the second at a midtown location where councilmen spoke; and the third, conducted in French and Spanish, outdoors at the plaza.[21]

On election morning, a light and rare June rain dampened the city. Some saw it as a fair omen. Mulholland rose early and, possessed with the calm confidence of Mark Twain's Christian holding five aces, set out for the polls, which opened at 6:00 A.M. On his way, he instructed his driver to pick up a neighbor, Erastus Root, a ninety-seven-year-old resident of the Hollenbeck Home for the Aged. At their mutual polling place they became the seventh and eighth men to vote. (Early voting proved the order of the day; half of the 24,000 voters had gone to the polls by 9:00 A.M.) Thus assured of at least two proaqueduct votes, Mulholland next drove across town to escort Fred Eaton's octogenarian father, Judge Benjamin S. Eaton, to the polls. After that, there was nothing to do but wait—and dictate a letter instructing one of the engineers at Independence to go up to the Rickey Ranch "near Division Creek and size up a locust grove . . . with a view to cutting and peeling poles for the power line that we will have to construct within a month or so."[22]

The final tally gave the bonds a 10.71 to 1 margin of victory: 21,918 for and 2,128 against. Although the *Times* had hoped for a 20 to 1 margin and the total was over 7,000 votes fewer than were cast in the previous mayoral election, the vote was still the largest ever in the city for a special election. It represented a solid validation of the city's water plans, as well as the citizens' willingness to incur a large debt to build the system. Aqueduct enemies momentarily receded from view. Old opponent Doc Houghton, who remained opposed to the end, had to endure the embarrassment of his ward's producing the heaviest pro vote of any in the city (4,315 for, 485 against). The *News* swiftly acknowledged defeat and asked that the hatchet be buried. Whatever his private thoughts about the *News* and Clover, Mulholland had no time for public grudge matches. He declared, "There is no soreness on my part. . . . It was a square fight and the people won. I was made the scapegoat and things were said about me that should not have been printed, but it is past now. If I had made the fight and got licked I would have worn the beefsteak on my eye and taken my medicine, as the *Evening News* is doing." Mathews declared Clover's statement "a manly declaration," but the *Times* granted no such absolution and published a rehash of every dubious statement the *News* (and sometimes the *Examiner*) had made during the campaign. Losing advertising revenue because of its unpopular stand on the water question, the *News* was soon to go under, but the anti-aqueduct material it had disseminated would have a long life.[23]

Nationally, the Los Angeles water story received a modicum of attention, only to be upstaged a week later by New York City, whose work on the great Peekskill Aqueduct was about to begin. To be larger than all of the Roman aqueducts combined, its cost when completed would be $161 million, and it would provide 500 million gallons of water to the city every twenty-four hours. It would become part of the Croton system, for which twenty-seven villages would eventually be condemned and lost in order to supply water to the metropolis, the entire project not to be completed until 1930.[24]

THE CHIEF RECEIVES A GO-AHEAD

On July 1, 1907, a water department purchase order authorized Mulholland "to make such trips as necessary in connection with your duties as an executive of the Los Angeles Aqueduct during the month of July." This may have been a roundabout way of granting the Chief a respite, for the bond campaign had exhausted him. Even his arch critic, Sam Clover of the *Evening News,* remarked that his face showed "the ordeal through which he has passed during the late campaign." Although Mulholland took an occasional Saturday afternoon off to watch a baseball

game with his boys and friends (especially Mathews), he seemed consti-
tutionally unable to take extended absences from his work. In mid-July,
however, he took two friends and his sons on a high Sierra camping and
hunting trip that became an annual July event during the years of aqueduct construction.[25]

To flee the city and get out on the line was always a welcome change,
especially when freed from the duties of acting as a tour guide for visiting dignitaries. The surviving photographs of that 1907 outing reveal
scenes of unspoiled forests and campsites by pure streams alive with fish.
Sons Perry and Tom, fourteen and twelve, would learn the finer points
of rod, reel, and gun from the zealous Nimrod and fisherman, George
Read, head of the city's water meter department. Also with them was
Allen Kelly of the *Times,* who had just written a profile of Mulholland
for his paper and whose account of their outing began with a memory
of his own Sierra visits years before when "there were few trails and no
maps." Remembering "the solitude of the mountains," Kelly commented
ruefully on the toll progress would take on the wilderness, as the building of a railway to Owens Valley would bring sightseers and vacation-
ers; then, "the woods shall be infested by the summer tourist, and the si-
lences and the solitude of the wilderness shall be no more." Yet, he
concluded, the Sierra forests that thousands would come to know and
enjoy could provide "a boon to the greater number that even the most
selfish seekers of solitude cannot begrudge."[26]

The group left their automobile in Round Valley, rode by mule team
to Long Valley, where they saw the bounty of water running in McGee
Creek and, further on, in the lakes of the Mammoth basin. The old mining camp of Mammoth was now "a picturesque ruin," a ghost town
where the sign on a decaying building proclaimed that it had once been
the "Windy City Hotel." North of Mammoth, they stood amid snow
banks on the crest of the Sierra, with the Owens River on one side and
the San Joaquin on the other. Across the San Joaquin gorge rose "the
sharp spires of the Minarets and the pyramid peak of Mount Lyell, clad
in snow and glacial ice." At this lonely, splendid height of 10,000 feet,
Mulholland, whose thoughts dwelt on matters other than mountain sub-
limity, turned to Kelly and said, "And there are pinheads in Los Angeles who did their measly damndest to keep that water from the city."
Musing that the city was lucky not to have paid $5 million for the water
rights, he added that they would have been worth it even at that price.[27]

Back at his desk at the end of July, Mulholland confronted a pile of
duties, problems and confusions. An engineer from the Panama Canal

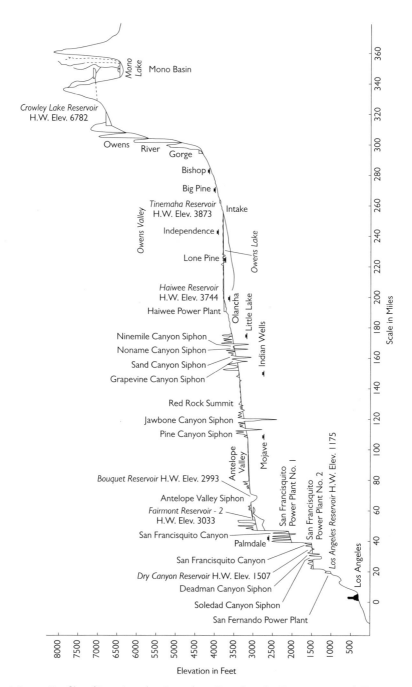

Map 3. Profile of Los Angeles Aqueduct (Los Angeles Department of Water and Power).

Commission had arrived in town to observe Silver Lake Reservoir and its hydraulic method of dam building. Less pleasantly, in Mulholland's absence, the city auditor had jeopardized aqueduct affairs by refusing to honor certain requisitions that he claimed had not been properly authorized. Hence, a grading crew about to begin work at Cottonwood had attached the equipment when it learned its payroll had not been met. More alarmingly, because the auditor had questioned its method of billing, the Southern Pacific was threatening to withdraw favorable freight rates for aqueduct materiel unless it received immediate payment.[28]

Lippincott and the field engineers kept Mulholland informed about activities and mishaps along the line: the progress on trenches and spillways; the cost of clearing up Cottonwood Ranch; the amount of pipe now at Haiwee; the eighteen sacks of cement that negligent workers left lying in the rain; the stolen lumber; and the generally poor quality of local labor in Owens Valley. Both Lippincott and Mulholland complained that the civil service board had created another vexatious labor problem by sending inexperienced "schoolboys" to work as chain men, young men who had crammed for the test but knew nothing of the nature of the work and who, after a summer out of doors, would leave and return to school. A showdown with the civil service board was about to erupt.[29]

In view of labor's turbulent history in Los Angeles during this period, the aqueduct in its first years had surprisingly little labor-management conflict, while the city itself was entering a strife-torn era as organized labor gradually lost ground to the onslaught of open shop proponents and practices. The panic of October 1907, however, created an economic slump that produced serious unemployment. Estimates of the jobless in Los Angeles by the beginning of 1908 varied from 10,000 to 20,000. While the city instituted a program to employ 400 men with families to construct a boulevard connecting Elysian to Griffith Park, the prospect of jobs on the aqueduct also promised some relief. As a municipal enterprise, the project could employ only American citizens and non-Orientals, but as labor recruitment expanded for this vast undertaking, exploiters popped up. Learning that a *Denver Post* advertisement promising aqueduct employment for 5,000 men and 1,000 teams had required applicants to pay from one to five dollars for enrollment, Mulholland shot off a letter to the editor. He explained that the city did its own hiring and had no dealings with any employment agencies. "A simple fake is being perpetrated on a class of men who can afford it least," he wrote, adding that the matter was being taken up with postal authorities "in an effort to stop the swindle," which he had learned was being worked in several cities. The *Post* promptly agreed to refuse such future advertising.[30]

Harmonious relations between Mulholland and the board of public works proved beneficial to the planning of the project, especially in dealing with the city council. In one instance, when he and Commissioner A. A. Hubbard (former owner and operator of an important brick works in Los Angeles) advertised for bids for eight hundred miles of copper wire (four hundred for the transmission of electric power on the aqueduct and the other four hundred for a municipal telephone service along the waterway) and demanded that bids be submitted within the week, certain city councilmen objected to the short notice and questioned the great quantity being purchased. The two explained that they intended to make one large purchase and had been watching and waiting for a bear market in copper. They made the interval brief to avoid being caught with a possible price rise that would raise the city's cost. The council approved the strategy.[31]

Equally cooperative were relations with the board chairman, attorney James A. Anderson (also an active member of the progressive Municipal League), who accompanied Mulholland and City Engineer Homer Hamlin for ten days along the aqueduct line in early December. The Chief had technical questions for Hamlin, a respected western geologist, regarding certain rock formations affecting the construction. Although they returned to the city on the thirteenth with the good news that 35,000 inches of water was flowing into the city's streams, for Hamlin the outing's high point had been his discovery of two fossil remains on the desert that he believed to be a new species of saurian.[32]

Before Mulholland left on the Owens Valley trip, his second annual report of the aqueduct appeared on November 30 with a reassuring account of the past year's progress along with future expectations: an arrangement secured with Southern Pacific for reduced freight rates as well as the company's assurance that it would build a railroad into Owens Valley; two reservoir sites chosen, one at Fairmount and one in the San Fernando Valley; two power plant sites selected, one at Cottonwood and one in San Francisquito Canyon; and a cement plant planned for Tehachapi. Although a group of private capitalists were touting their own plans for a cement factory at Tehachapi with claims that the city intended to purchase Portland cement from them, at the end of 1907 the board announced that the city would construct its own cement plant under Duryea's direction. He predicted they would be in operation within nine months. Work had also begun at the south portal of the tunnel near Elizabeth Lake, and twenty miles of road had been built in Division No. 2. At year's end, the report concluded, 327 men and 180 head of stock were at work on the aqueduct.[33]

Just before Christmas, Lippincott wrote from Mojave to suggest a general meeting in Los Angeles of all the aqueduct engineers and members of the general accounting office, the board of public works, and the auditor to discuss a broad array of subjects. One item on the agenda would certainly have been money; rosy reports notwithstanding, the aqueduct project was low on funds. With its banks in good shape, Los Angeles ultimately squeaked through the Panic of 1907 by declaring bank holidays and issuing scrip, but hard times were not to abate until the middle of the following year. In December, the city lacked funds to pay police and firemen's salaries until January 1908. Although the first of the water bonds had been put out for sale in August, no money had yet been realized, so that by the end of November, just at Thanksgiving, the aqueduct department found itself short. The board of public works wanted to transfer $10,000 from some other department, but the auditor objected that it could lead to vicious financial practices. After a tortuous debate, the city council finally granted permission to move funds from the water department to the aqueduct department, reasoning that the risk of losing track of the money would be less likely.

On a cheerier note, at Christmastime Van Norman wrote from Division Creek to thank Mulholland for arranging matters so that his wife could be with him over the holidays. Engineer John Gray wrote from Cottonwood that work was going well. The best holiday gift, however, came on December 27 when Mayor Harper signed the first issue of aqueduct bonds for $510,000 and Mathews delivered it to Sacramento. Now work could truly proceed.[34]

CHAPTER 14

The Chief and the General

1908

ENTER THE GENERAL

Mulholland had told Allen Kelly that he knew what building the aqueduct would entail. "I'm going into this as a man in the army goes into war, because it would be cowardly to quit. It will take the life out of me and if I stay to the end I'll come out a rickety old man, tied together with baling wire. But if you think I'm going to wear myself out for a lot of political jobbers, you can think again." This outburst was not without cause, as since the election of Mayor Harper and the passage of the water bonds, Mulholland's files had begun to fill with letters from job seekers or petitioners for friends and acquaintances of the mayor. Nor was his military analogy inapt as the organization needed to achieve this mighty task resembled a military campaign. When it began to appear that political favoritism and unwieldy red tape might subvert a clean operation, help arrived in the shape of an old army man.[1]

Although the Progressive reform group fought to retain the retiring chairman of the board of public works, J. A. Anderson, an authority on water law who had proven both able and fair handed, Mayor Harper was prevailed upon to name an aging military hero and friend of General Otis, Lieutenant General Adna Romanza Chaffee (1842–1914). General Chaffee, a great bear of a man with piercing eyes, had recently retired with his family to Los Angeles after a long, distinguished military career. He had been cited for conspicuous bravery at Gettysburg as a cavalry officer in the Civil War; he had fought Indian wars in Texas, New

Mexico, and Arizona; and he had commanded victorious troops in the Philippines during the Spanish-American War. He had also led troops into Peking to relieve the American delegation during the Boxer Rebellion in 1900, and for several years before his retirement, he had been the chief of staff of the United States Army. He enjoyed the admiration of the city and the unbounding enthusiasm of General Otis, whose esteem had more to do with his military stature than his political beliefs.[2]

As the *Times* beat the drums for his selection, a few expressed fears that the sixty-five-year-old Chaffee was too old for the job. The only serious protest, however, came from E. T. Earl's *Express*, whose Progressive editor, Edward Dickson, not only defended the departing Anderson but may have assumed the general shared Otis's anti-Progressive philosophy. That fear proved groundless after the apolitical old militarist revealed that he had never cast a vote until the presidential election of 1908. When asked then how he intended to vote, he told the reporter "to go to—Mojave!"—that even his wife did not know the answer to that.[3]

Chaffee's appointment was generally popular, and at the end of January 1908, Mulholland, Mathews, and the two other board members conferred with the general in order to acquaint him with the scope and duties of the public works board. (A new city charter effected in January 1906 had created this board, which was to consist of three men appointed by the mayor and confirmed by the council.) When Chaffee in turn told them that his greatest interest lay in the aqueduct project, they decided to name him chairman of the advisory aqueduct board rather than chairman of the board of public works. Because of his friendship with Progressives who opposed Chaffee, Mulholland initially may have harbored a certain ambivalence about the appointment, but Chaffee, with his experience supervising engineering as well as military projects, soon demonstrated his ability to improve the aqueduct operation's logistics. Within a few months, Mulholland would write Allen Kelly that "Chaffee is proving himself a very able executive." Among the few clippings saved in Mulholland's personal scrapbook is a column from the *Record* that apparently echoed the consensus of approval for General Chaffee with a cartoon of Chaffee and Mulholland sweating and breaking rock with pick and shovel as Chaffee declares, "We'll dig it, Bill."[4]

Two urgent matters confronted the board of public works: whether to accept an offer to sell water rights in Mono Lake and Owens Valley from a power company that had opposed the aqueduct; and how to deal with unexpectedly high new bids for freight rates from the Southern Pacific. The water rights offer came from Silver Lake Power and Irrigation Company, with which the city already had contended over its claimed water rights in those locations. The German-owned company's president was the son of a millionaire brewer, while its chief engineer, A. H. Koebig, was a well-known foe of the aqueduct who since 1899 had championed a Mojave River water project for Los Angeles. Koebig now proposed to convey all of Silver Lake's water rights in Mono and Inyo Counties and drop all pending lawsuits against the city for $50,000, half of the $100,000 the company claimed to have already spent on its various projects. After Mulholland inspected the site while on tour with Chaffee and Harper, and upon subsequent consultation with attorneys who felt the company's technical holdings were not of great value, the board declined the offer. It also rejected the Southern Pacific's bid for carrying freight along the aqueduct, but that was simply one move in a complicated bargaining process with the railroad.[5]

At the end of February, General Chaffee, Mayor Harper, water board member J. H. Norton, and Mulholland set out for an inspection tour of the aqueduct and Owens Valley. The entire operation consisted of eleven sections, or divisions, the first beginning at the far north in Long Valley and the eleventh in the south as it terminated near San Fernando. The group first visited the tunnel under construction at the tenth division near Elizabeth Lake. In the three months since work had begun, more than 1,000 feet of the bore had been driven at a cost of $50 a foot. Hopes rose for a completion earlier than estimated with an accompanying cost reduction of $700,000 (the original estimate had been $75 a foot) once electric power came. The city was to purchase the power from the Edison Company, and three crews were working overtime to rush lines from Castaic to the south portal of the tunnel. Then "the real work will begin," Mulholland informed them, for two mining crews would thereupon be able to excavate 600 feet of tunnel a month.[6]

As they neared the construction site, the visitors were told of the difficulties in finding horses able to haul the big freighting wagons up to the Lake Elizabeth area's 2,900-foot elevation. After viewing the camp nestled like a small village in the mountains near the mouth of the tunnel where 200 workers lived, each member of the party was handed a lighted candle and invited to enter the tunnel, 13 feet wide and 14 feet high, with little timbering for it was in solid rock. When they emerged, Mulholland picked up a piece of blue-ribbed rock from a nearby pile and said to the engineer in charge, "This is gneiss rock all right. I do not believe we shall encounter much real granite." The mayor, in an effort to be agreeable, echoed, "Very nice rock." Mulholland smiled and explained, "This nice is spelled g-n-e-i-s-s, Mayor. Striated granite and much easier to tunnel than granite." In fact, he added, if granite were found only in the ribs, it could mean a saving of at least $500,000 to the city. Very nice rock indeed.[7]

While the mayor had his geology lesson, Chaffee had spied an injured worker, his foot wrapped in towels with not a doctor in sight. An accident in the tunnel that morning had mashed the miner's toes. On the return trip, Chaffee inquired about him and was told he was recovering, but the general announced that a physician should be on the spot to take care of everyone. "If the city puts 500 men out there in the wilderness, it must send a physician along to look after them." His subsequent report to the board included the directive that "there shall be immediately organized for the Aqueduct a Medical Department; and for this purpose shall be erected at the south and north portal of the Elizabeth Tunnel, and at the cement [plant] a small hospital each sufficient to accommodate six beds, a small dispensary, and sleeping quarters for a hospital steward."[8]

By mid-May, three young doctors had received contracts to organize the medical department on the aqueduct project. To maintain it, each employee who earned forty dollars or more a month was to be assessed one dollar a month; those earning less, fifty cents. The assessments would pay the physicians, while the city was to provide field hospitals and pay for their attendants and maintenance. Patients with severe injuries and sicknesses were sent on to the California Hospital in Los Angeles. As only 400 men were employed on the aqueduct at the outset, the three physicians received a very modest recompense, but when the workforce swelled to 4,000, their financial picture improved considerably.[9]

A CIVIL SERVICE SNARL

For all his sympathy with many of the Progressive movement's aims and his approval of civil service as a means of avoiding political graft and favoritism, Mulholland was fundamentally a pragmatist, impatient with red tape, who demanded a free hand in certain decisions. He had asked the civil service commission to exempt certain workers on the aqueduct from examination because of their proven abilities. This request had included the existing staff of the city's water department, as well as Mathews and his assistant attorneys. Among others to be exempted were tunnel engineers, miners, carpenters, team bosses, blacksmiths, harriers, and certain men with specialized skills. Mulholland and Lippincott had already complained of inexperienced boys sent out to work on the line simply because they had been able to pass an examination, but neither could have imagined that their differences with the commission in 1908 would culminate in Lippincott's being threatened with discharge from his aqueduct post unless he himself took the civil service examination.

This absurdity came about in part because of a civil service shakeup when one of the city's leading Progressives, Dr. John R. Haynes, was ousted as president of the commission because he allegedly tolerated laxness and misdoing by one of the examiners. Due to what it considered dereliction under Haynes's regime, the new commission decided to institute a policy of investigating complaints in person rather than simply relying on written evidence. Thus, in late May an examiner disguised as a worker was sent to investigate complaints in the aqueduct camps. His cover was blown at the first camp when he was recognized by workers who had taken the examination under him in Los Angeles. On his return, the examiner recommended that the commission refuse to exempt the position of tunnel engineer from civil service. As this meant dismissing one of the two engineers in charge of the Elizabeth Lake tunnel and putting an untried man in his place, Mulholland and Lippincott, both outraged, came forth with personal appeals to retain a man who, they said, was doing an excellent job and should not be replaced.[10]

To resolve this quasi war between civil service and the aqueduct men, General Chaffee wrote a report proposing that the board of public works should direct all of the aqueduct affairs and that the civil service commission should deal through the board and not, as it previously had, directly with the employee. The commission's response to General Chaffee's blunt and somewhat tactless communiqué included the stinger that engineer Lippincott was illegally employed by the city and must take the civil service examination. When Lippincott's case came before the commission, Chaffee and Mulholland both argued for his exemption on the grounds that his knowledge of hydrographic conditions in Owens Valley was unmatched, as were his two years' experience as assistant chief engineer of the aqueduct. As to a civil service examination, Mulholland warned, "There is always danger that he might not stand first, . . . and his loss to the aqueduct would be a great one. He knows what he is doing from the ground up, and if an examination were held he would have to compete with some of the best engineers who, though they might best him in an examination, would be vastly inferior in knowledge of the work in hand." The board took the matter under advisement, but before it reached any decision Mayor Harper had resigned from office; his successor, George Alexander, the Good Government candidate, had renamed Haynes to the civil service commission; and Lippincott remained unscathed.[11]

A SHORTAGE OF FUNDS AND OTHER WORRIES

Of grave concern in 1908 was the growing need for money as the aqueduct project moved towards its next stage, entailing the beginning of work on the Jawbone Division. Bids had been coming in since early in the year, and Mulholland estimated the division would cost almost $2 million, most of which would pay for labor. As funds from the first bond issue were almost exhausted, new sales had to begin at once or work on the project would have to stop. Selling did not prove easy because the lingering slump from the Panic of 1907 kept investors wary, and there were no takers for the bonds at 4.0 percent. Mathews reported from New York that a sale could be arranged at 4.5 percent. As that required the city council's approval, a wrangle over whether to approve the issue arose in early July. Proponents pointed out that San Francisco and New York were paying 5.0 percent on their current public works bonds, but opponents wanted to wait until other offers materialized. Hostility against Mathews flared, but when all the dust had settled, a unanimous vote approved a contract to market $21 million of aqueduct bonds at 4.5 percent, of which $4 million was an outright purchase by the syndicate Kountze Brothers and Leach and Company of New York. The president of the council remarked that it was the greatest bond sale Los Angeles had ever made and expressed his confidence in the New York bankers while also asserting his belief that the question of financing the aqueduct was finally settled. An hour after the approval, the board of public works awarded contracts for $50,000 worth of machinery to be used on the aqueduct, while two much relieved men, Mulholland and Chaffee, predicted that Owens Valley water would be flowing into the San Fernando Valley by July 1912.[12]

Work on the formidable Jawbone Division could now proceed. Even today this section of the aqueduct stands out as the most impressive achievement of the entire undertaking with its gigantic mile-and-a-half-long siphon accomplished by the dramatic use of fifty-two-mule teams to haul the pipe up the canyon. Miners had named the canyon because its steep walls rising from the desert floor resembled a jutting lower jaw. When engineer John R. Freeman first viewed these badlands, he had told Mulholland they looked like a tough place for canal digging. Mulholland agreed that it was rough on top, explaining that he planned to take the aqueduct underground. He added, "When you buy a piece of pork, you don't have to eat the bristles." Over twelve miles of tunnel were to be bored across this desolate landscape where temperatures could soar to 120°F in the summer and drop to freezing in the winter. In a terrain without water, without trees, without any feature whatsoever to furnish sustenance and comfort to the workers or supplies for fuel or construction, a mighty work requiring an army of men, animals, and machines was about to be undertaken.[13]

Two years of preliminary study had preceded Mulholland's final approval, during which four surveys were conducted, leading the locating engineer, E. A. Bayley, to decide that the "old man" never would be satisfied. Crucial to the endeavor was a supply of potable water, for when the first surveying party began its work near Red Rock Canyon in 1906, the water there had made the men sick and Mulholland had shipped them bottled Puritas water from Los Angeles, an expense that would have been prohibitive for a large workforce. A supply of good water for the north end of the division was established twenty-two miles away in Water Canyon, where at an elevation of 4,000 feet, a water line of four-inch steel pipe was laid along trackless wilderness. To supply the south end of the division a second pipeline was run from city-owned wells in Tehachapi.[14]

The problems of transportation were no less daunting, as an estimated 350,000 tons of freight were expected to be delivered. Bids for hauling had involved months of conferences and discussions until the Southern Pacific received the contract to build eighteen miles of road that would lead almost to the mouth of Jawbone Canyon. From there northward to Red Rock Canyon the city would build a spur line of eight and a half miles. Roads for teams and trails had to be constructed; telephone lines strung; and the all-important power for the powerhouses sent from the new hydroelectric plant at Cottonwood, built under the supervision of electrical engineer Ezra F. Scattergood.

Living and sleeping quarters for 1,000 men had to be provided, as well as cook, mess, and medical facilities. Mail service for the workers was important, given their isolation, and a lively correspondence and controversy ensued over appropriate locations for post offices. When one person in the settlement of Ricardo near Red Rock Canyon applied for a station, Mulholland argued for a site at Jawbone. Ricardo, he wrote, was "only a small grocery store and a saloon," so that a post office there would serve not more than a half dozen persons. His chief objection to Ricardo, however, was that its saloon would draw workers. "As employees of the Aque-

duct in this locality will be required to work under unusual climatic conditions and where free access to intoxicants will impair their efficiency it
is the desire of Aqueduct officials to keep the men as far as possible from
the desert saloon." He took equally strong objection to a postmaster at
Haiwee who was rumored to have been run out of Oakland, California,
for practicing dentistry without a license and who also stood suspected
of writing bum checks. The postmaster's reputation in the community,
according to Mulholland, was "decidedly unsavory." Although the den-
tist-postmaster was ultimately replaced, good mail service remained elusive along the aqueduct line during the construction years.[15]

A DEBATE ON THE CONTRACT SYSTEM

In early July, Mulholland retreated with his two sons into the Sierra
Nevada, which, as he later wrote his friend, David Dorward, was enjoyable, although the pilgrimage through the desert heat had been rough.
When he returned, a letter awaited him from Allen Kelly, now editor of
the *Imperial Valley Press,* whom Harry Chandler had asked to write a
progress report on the aqueduct for the *Times.* Could he join Mulholland on a trip along the aqueduct? Mulholland responded promptly on
July 28 that he would be going along the line about August 10. He also
confided that as the bids on the Jawbone section were coming in "somewhat over our estimates," he thought the city might do its own work.
Three days later the announcement came that the city would do work on
the Jawbone Division by day labor or force account, which would result
in a savings of several hundred thousand dollars.[16]

Because tunneling represented the major portion of the work on the
Jawbone, the board, upon the aqueduct advisory commission's recommendation, announced that it would adopt a bonus system for tunnel
crews. A bonus was to be paid for completing more than an "average
day's work" in twenty-four hours. The engineering department defined
an average day's work in the tunnel as six feet in twenty-four hours where
timbering was necessary and eight feet in twenty-four hours where it was
not. Shift bosses, miners, muckers, and motormen also qualified for
bonuses. Each man on a crew received forty cents for every foot in excess of the average day's work. "After paying this bonus the city will still
save several dollars on each foot completed in excess of the work of the
average day," Mulholland announced.

Because of high bids from private contractors, Mulholland had prevailed over Chaffee and the board, who had hoped private contracts

would give the city's engineers more time for other aspects of the work. The Chief, however, maintained that the "day's work" system had been tried and always worked admirably in his experience. Dr. Taylor in his memoir remembered that Chaffee advocated letting contracts for work, while Mulholland "was confident that the city could run its own camps and do its own construction work more cheaply than by contract, and he felt they would probably get a better job." One large private contract was let, however, for construction in the Antelope Division later that year, but for the most part, the city did its own work. Chaffee prevailed in having outside contractors for food and medicine, which yielded mixed results, for although the medical crew acquitted itself well, the food contractor created a large-scale ruckus in 1910 that led to the most serious labor dispute on the aqueduct. On the other hand, Mulholland's day labor and bonus system produced prodigious results with record-breaking speeds while keeping well within—sometimes even below—both time estimates and budget.[17]

Although the relative merits of the contract and day labor systems stirred controversy among engineer-contractors at that time, neither system would have satisfied organized labor. Because of the city's high unemployment and labor's weakened organization, little argument arose over these matters, especially as the Progressive reformers were always more intent on political reform in municipal affairs than in the advancement of organized labor. Organized labor had, however, long opposed the contract system with the employers' not uncommon practice of overcharging workers for inferior accommodations at boarding camps. In 1892, the People's Party in Los Angeles had agitated for prohibition of contract work on public works and, in later years, although the labor council had taken a more aggressive stand against contracting, it had not succeeded in having it banned from public works. Another dilemma for labor and the Socialists in 1908 was their support of municipal ownership of public utilities, which the water project represented, along with their opposition to both the contract and day labor systems by which it was to be built.[18]

WORKERS AND NEW MACHINES

In the hope that aqueduct families would provide a more stable environment during construction and offset the roughhouse and vagrant ways of single men in construction camps, Mulholland announced, "Any man of family in Los Angeles who desires work at manual labor for $2 a day can secure a place." Modest homes were under construction and a one-room public school opened at the south portal of Elizabeth Lake Tunnel. Others followed at key points along the aqueduct.

New equipment and machinery appeared: a dredger invented by Mulholland that the men called "Big Bill" (both for the Chief and, depending on one's politics, presidential nominees William Howard Taft or William Jennings Bryan) proved an enormous success on a site between Black Rock Springs and the Alabama Hills. A stenographer in the aqueduct office was quoted as saying, "Mr. Mulholland thinks as much of that dredger as though it were his baby." More spectacular than Big Bill, however, was a newfangled traction engine that Benjamin Holt had developed for use in the peat bogs of Stockton, California, then being cultivated for agriculture. One amazing feature of this machine was its ability to climb hills through mud and loose gravel. Mulholland is said to have exclaimed when he first watched it maneuvering up an impossible slope, "The damn thing looks like a caterpillar," and has thus been credited with naming the Caterpillar tractor. Apocryphal or not, the new wonder did make its debut during the building of the aqueduct, where, unfortunately, it did not prove out. Other new equipment also disappointed, as in the case of an excavator whose malfunctioning sent one of the department's engineers to consult with its Chicago manufacturer in early June. As the engineer's absence extended throughout the summer, a frustrated Mulholland fumed at the delay. Not until December did the returned excavator begin to tear up ground for the conduit six miles south of Mojave.[19]

New machinery notwithstanding, certain work was entrusted to one of the great work animals of all time, the mule. When the city council received the unusual request from the board of public works to purchase 1,000 tons of hay at no more than $20 a ton, speculation broke out as to who or what would eat that mountain of hay. All became clear with the next request for the purchase of 200 mules. One councilman wondered if the mules should be subject to civil service examination. Wondering why the board wanted to make these purchases on the open market, the councilmen were told it would rather trust Mulholland's judgment on mules and hay than rely on so-called experts. After a certain amount of jocularity imagining Mulholland in the corrals inspecting animals bearing labels ("Take me home for $199.99"), the council learned that Mulholland had made a small contract on the ton-mile basis for hay, and even if the city fathers were not too clear about that, they authorized $60,000 for mules and hay. In the year to come, they would better understand the good use to which the money had been put.[20]

A QUESTION OF LAND SALES

The Eatons remained active in 1908, securing land deals both for themselves and the city. In May, Eaton's son, Harold, offered to sell the city eighty acres of riparian land near Citrus for $25 an acre. Mulholland wrote him that the board turned down the offer because it found the price unreasonable as the land had no improvements and no rights in any ditch or other means of irrigation. Then he questioned the ethics of such a deal. "Since your father was acting as Agent for the City in the purchasing of lands at the time that you contracted with the State for this land, such contract was made in view of having the City in prospect as an ultimate purchaser and that your price, in honor, should be scaled accordingly." Mulholland's increasing disenchantment with some of Eaton's real estate dealings dates from this time, especially when it appeared that Eaton was attempting to take advantage of the city in order to profit his children.

O'Melveny's journals offer another glimpse of the Eatons' activities when, on November 4, 1908, a day after Taft had defeated Bryan for the presidency and the attorney sat in his office bemoaning the election results ("hopelessly Republican"), Eaton had appeared with his son-in-law and a map. As they consulted the map, Eaton told O'Melveny that he would be selling the land to the city at actual cost and that he wanted O'Melveny to draw up the offer. The following day Eaton and his son-in-law returned to the attorney's office, looked over the offer for a sale of property in the Owens Valley to the City of Los Angeles, said it was satisfactory, and left, taking the document with them. Twelve days later, however, on November 17, O'Melveny noted that in the matter of Fred Eaton, Big Pine, and Owens River, he had met Mathews and left him the offer, but that same morning as he prepared to make a formal presentation, Mulholland informed him that "after inspection, the matter had taken a radical change and could only be settled with Eaton present." This episode was to lead to turbulent consequences in the 1920s.[21]

CONSTRUCTION "APPALLING IN ITS MAGNITUDE AND EXPENSE"

In the third annual report, released at the end of November, Mulholland explained that actual construction of the aqueduct commenced in October 1908 and that the preliminary work "necessary to enable construction to begin" had been "appalling in its magnitude and expense."

Yet it would prove justified, he continued, for engineers have long
known in such projects that "Well begun is half done." He reviewed what
had been accomplished: "the building of a great cement factory at
Tehachapi; the laying of scores of miles of water pipe to convey water
for construction and domestic purposes over the long stretches of arid
desert traversed by the Aqueduct; the building of power plants and transmission lines for the development and conveyance of electrical energy to
be used in construction; the building of roads, trails, and telephone lines
and the erection of camps for the housing of workmen,—all these things
required large expenditures of money and diligent effort." He then predicted rapid progress in the year to come, beginning in March: an ac-
celeration in the rate of advance from the current six hundred feet per
day to nine hundred. By November 1909, he forecast, an added 58 miles
of aqueduct would have been constructed at a cost of $4,633,618. Nor
did he see any reason why the work should not be completed well within
its time schedules and cost estimates.[22]

The demands on Mulholland's time and energies were immense. The
day after Christmas, Harry Brooks of the *Times* wrote to ask him about
reports that polluted well water was causing unusual amounts of sickness in the Vernon area. Brooks expressed his regret that, because of the
demands of putting out the annual midwinter supplement to the newspaper, he had missed the Sunset Club Christmas party. Mulholland
replied, assuring Brooks that another source would have to be sought
for Vernon's troubles as its district was receiving water from the same
source as other parts of the city where no such incidence of illness was
occurring. He added, "I too, through stress of work, found it impossible to be with fellow Sunsetters Saturday night and regretted the fact
not a little."[23]

CHAPTER 15

Building the Aqueduct: The Best Year

1909

THE WICKEDEST TOWN IN THE WEST

In most ways, 1909 was the best of all the seven years of aqueduct construction. Ample funds were available, work advanced on schedule, and crews set new world records for speed in tunnel drilling. Nor did the city's uproar as it threatened to become the first in the nation to recall its mayor much affect work. In early February 1909, Mulholland wrote his friend and colleague Henry Dockweiler, who was helping San Francisco to prepare a brief in the Spring Valley water case as well as to fix rates for San Rafael, Oakland, and San Francisco. Doc had asked Bill for some specifications and plans and, not having received them, wrote again. Mulholland explained that not only was the department's auditor moving into larger quarters so that things were all torn up, but "as you can imagine, the work is keeping us all very busy these days, with a working force of over 3,000 men, 40 camps, and 230 miles of line to get over about ever so often. During the first ten days of last month we drove 2,456 feet of tunnel on the Jawbone section which brought the total up to 18,400 feet since we began in October."

When Dockweiler received the materials a week later, he wrote a note of thanks, adding that he hoped the good progress on the aqueduct would quiet those who believed a city could not do work as well as a private corporation. "I have become tired of listening," he went on, "to the objections that have been set forth, that this city [San Francisco] will never be able to accomplish anything in the way of building a water works.

The Aqueduct will be a standing refutation to that argument." As Los Angeles became a pacesetter in the municipalization and management of water, other cities looked to it as a model; Omaha and Denver sought advice in their campaigns for municipal water during 1909, while Oakland asked for help with its plans to meter its water.[1]

Even though progress on the aqueduct was excellent, hitches on a project of its magnitude were inevitable, and predictably, as the labor force increased, so did the problems. The first came when a group of aqueduct workers were involved in a fracas on the streets of Mojave and landed in jail. By now Mojave was being called "the wickedest town in the West," although in the early stages of aqueduct planning, the chief complaints against it had been climatic. In October 1905, surveying engineer T. W. Young had written to Mulholland about the Mojave wind—so strong that no work could be done and so wild that all he and his crew could do was hold onto their tents. "I braced and guyed every way, but the wind came every way also." After failing to find either a house or boxcar for shelter, they were forced to weather it out. "Prospects of cheese and crackers and sleep on the ground," wrote Young, "but I am not in the least discouraged." When the wind snapped the ridgepole of his tent the following night, he discovered the nature of the desert town, for there was "not enough lumber in the place to make a new pole, so I must send to L. A." Eventually he found an old room measuring 25 feet by 50 feet, rented it for fifty cents a day, and moved in the crew. When Mulholland wrote back, he thanked Young for the "Weather Bureau reports with regard to the climatology of Mojave," adding that "Mojave enjoys special privileges in the way of weather, for which she has reason to be proud."[2]

Pronounced *Mo-harvy* by old-time railroad men, the settlement had been a rail center since 1876 and was the jumping-off place to Owens Valley. For thousands of aqueduct workers, it also became the place where one went to blow one's pay. Surrounded by desert and edged on its west by railroad track, Mojave consisted of about a thousand feet of business frontage—a string of low, one-story wooden structures whose facades would be instantly recognizable to anyone who has ever watched a western movie. The largest building and chief reputable enterprise was Asher's general merchandise store, which drew among its respectable patrons the neighboring ranchers, and miners, along with their wives and children. Straggling off the main drag down a few side blocks stood less genteel establishments that lured men from the nearby mines and construction camps: the saloons, dance halls, fancy houses and gambling

joints that earned Mojave its notorious reputation. Everyone agreed that
the best and cleanest hostelry in town was the Harvey House alongside
the railroad tracks. Erwin W. Widney, fresh out of high school in 1908,
remembered his first impressions of Mojave when he had traveled north
from Los Angeles that summer to a job with the Southern Pacific, then
building along the line of the aqueduct. When he first stepped off the
train just before dawn and stood on the station platform, he wrote, "I saw
lights in every saloon, dance hall and gambling room, men passing in
and out, some voluntarily, some propelled, some head first, some feet
first. I heard a dozen different tunes being played on a dozen different
pianos and phonographs; women's laughter, harsh and mirthless; men's
voices expressing all sorts of emotions. It was 4:30 in the morning. I wondered at such activity, but I soon discovered that it was a pay day on the
aqueduct and railroad, and hundreds, yes, thousands of men had come
to town to give vent to pent-up emotions and be separated from their
wages."[3] Mulholland's sons had vivid boyhood memories of Mojave—
the noise and drunkenness and confusion as they left the train and walked
with their father through the dirt streets to the lodging where they would
spend the night. They laughingly remembered that "Dad" always first
checked for bed bugs; little else of what they heard and saw was much
repeated in polite company. What they managed to convey was their
shock and delight at finding themselves in such an outlaw world. Once,
with Harvey Van Norman, they reminisced about a gambler and pimp,
who moved along the route of the aqueduct with his lady in a horse-
drawn wagon tricked out as a dual-purpose brothel and gambling hall.
His end came after he was suspected of cheating at faro and was later
found buried head down in a canyon, with only his boot heels pointing
to the sky.

The gamblers and layabouts of Los Angeles increasingly lit out for
Mojave, their exodus coinciding conveniently with one of the city's periodic convulsions of civic virtue. This time the Progressives led the push
to rid the city of its liquor and vice interests, along with its mayor, whom
they suspected of cozy relations with these low associates. Crime began
to rise along the aqueduct. Raids on cookhouses depleted supplies while
holdup men lurking in the rocks and brush as paydays neared made it
unsafe to walk from an aqueduct camp into town at night. Still, the men
could not resist the lure of Mojave. After all, in that wilderness, what
else was there? The first serious trouble occurred at a dance hall one Saturday night when a group of drinking aqueduct employees traded insults
that led to blows. Some local men entered the brawl in an attempt to

break it up, but they were set upon in turn. In the melee, one aqueduct foreman drew a gun but did not fire. The aqueduct men were overpowered and handcuffed by the locals who turned out to be Mojave police, although they had worn no identifying stars. Among those thrown in jail were a hospital steward and several foremen who had been attempting to stop the fighting. When Mulholland received news of this trouble, he was on the point of leaving to file the official aqueduct survey at the United States land office in Independence. While he was securing the council's approval of the survey, he and the other members of the aqueduct commission took the opportunity to request support of pending legislation that would forbid the sale of alcohol within four miles of any public work. The threat of drunkenness and brawling delaying work on the aqueduct demonstrated more than ever the need for controls over the "Mojave peril."[4]

TUNNEL DRILLERS AND MULE SKINNERS

Complaints about working conditions on the aqueduct began to drift back to the city in early 1909. In one instance, Mulholland's secretary, Burt Heinly, directly contacted an employee who had complained to the press, asking him to come in and discuss the matter with the Chief. Next, a representative from the machinists' union appeared before the board of public works to complain that not a man on the aqueduct received more than $3.50 a day, while the Southern Pacific was paying machinists $3.96 for a day of nine hours. The chairman answered that the aqueduct men worked an eight-hour day as approved by the labor council, and that the Southern Pacific's added $.44 would amount to $3.52 for an eight-hour day. The aqueduct, therefore, was $.02 behind, and the chairman told the representative to submit the complaint in writing if he wished to continue it. A more serious threat to the aqueduct budget was a measure before the legislature setting a minimum wage of $2.50 a day on all public works in California. Mulholland, who estimated that 20 percent of the aqueduct's cost was labor, grew alarmed that this bill would add $3.5 million to the aqueduct's cost and overrun his estimates. Because the state was still in a depression and unemployment remained high, the legislature, as it had already done in previous years, voted the measure down.[5]

By March 1909, 3,000 men were on the aqueduct, half the gamblers of the West had shown up to ply their trade, and 400 handpicked mules were about to appear. The city had been renting mules at $20 a head per month at a total cost of $100,000 a year, but the aqueduct men decided the city could maintain its own mules for less and would be able to recover the original cost when work ended. Mulholland, who admired the mule for its sturdiness and stability of character, had seriously considered taking time out from his busy life to choose them himself, until he learned that the law required bidding on the contract to furnish the mules. Therefore, two councilmen expert in mule matters were sent to Kansas City for the finest in the land. The 261 chosen were loaded onto fourteen stock cars, and their arrival in Los Angeles created a memorable scene as they were released into pens for a two-day rest before moving on to Mojave. Only one was lost on the journey, and an enthusiastic councilman declared that they were "the best lot of mules ever brought across the Rockies."[6]

The mules had to be good, for they faced a task that became the stuff of legend among the water men: hauling pipe for the great Jawbone Siphon. Twenty-mule teams and tractors were already in use along the aqueduct, but neither was up to this labor, which a singular use of fifty-two-mule teams was about to solve. To haul 36-foot sections of 7½-foot-diameter pipe weighing around 26 tons each from the station at Cinco 4 miles up to Jawbone Canyon, Harvey Van Norman devised an ingenious arrangement of massive wagons with flat beds on steel wheels with tires 2 feet wide. Two of these powerful wagons were then drawn in tandem by fifty-two mules controlled by three jerklines: eight rows of six animals abreast, two "wheelers" at the tongue, and a lead pair at the head.[7]

To propel this unwieldy and cumbersome arrangement of metal and beasts required the skill of a supremely gifted mule skinner, and although run-of-the-mill skinners were not hard to come by in that land of mines and desert, a gifted one was rare. Van Norman first engaged a man called Wilson, whose success on his first run from Cinco so overcame him that he picked a fight with a corral wrangler, whomped him on the head with a whip handle, and for his pains was canned and sent packing. Van Norman (a two-fisted drinker himself in those days) went down to Mojave in search of another skinner and while quenching his thirst in a local saloon overheard an old geezer at the bar bragging about how many mules he could drive. "Yeah," called Van Norman. "How many can you drive?" After a silent stare and a squirt of tobacco juice, the old man replied, "I can drive 'em as far as I can see 'em." Thus entered the legendary "Whistling Dick," who could work the jerklines as well as Itzhak Perlman can play the violin and who delivered the giant pipe from Cinco to Jawbone. At least, he did until almost at the end of the job when, for reasons unknown, he fell from his mount and was crushed beneath the wagon's steel wheels.[8]

Mules were not the only hard workers on the aqueduct. Tunnel-drilling crews began to break records for rapid hard rock tunnel excavation. They shattered two on the south portal of the Elizabeth Tunnel under the leadership of W. C. Aston, the "difficult" foreman of whom the civil service commission had earlier wished to dispose; at the north portal, John Gray, tough and capable with years of mining experience behind him, led his crew to even more record breakers. One, a run of 166 feet in thirty-one days using three shifts, bested the government's Gunnison Tunnel by 16 feet. Up on the Jawbone, where the rock was softer but the conditions severe, prodigies of speed occurred when A. C. Hansen, who had successfully built the city's latest outfall sewer, oversaw an army of one thousand men amid dust and dynamite explosions to two runs of 370 feet in record time. When Mulholland inspected the line in April, he said, "Don't think all the good men are at work on the Elizabeth Tunnel because two American records have been broken there. I don't know what the record is for two shifts, but in this contest which is going on between the tunnel men I believe the Jawbone men, with 370 feet to their credit, have surpassed anything done on the aqueduct so far. The rock in which they worked is practically the same as that encountered in the Elizabeth Tunnel, and the other conditions are about the same."[9]

Two international records fell in a contest between American and Swiss tunnel drillers. In June 1909, the men in the Saugus Division north of Newhall overtook a record established in 1903 in the Ricken Tunnel, Switzerland. Then, in August, under the direction of Tom Flanigan, a redheaded Irishman who had previously worked in the city and earned Mulholland's high regard because of his ability to handle men and get work done fast, the crew at Tunnel 17-M in a soft sandstone at the head of the Red Rock Canyon excavated from two headings a 10,596-foot-long tunnel in seven months. They then completely lined it in eight months. In other words, they drove and lined this two-mile tunnel in a year and a quarter.[10]

POLITICS AND THE AQUEDUCT: A MAYOR BOWS OUT

At the time of these exploits, journalist Allen Kelly made one of his periodic treks along the aqueduct. He noted that the Owens Valley settlers who had feared the loss of all their water seemed relieved because groundwater in the valley had risen from artesian wells since the digging of the canals. Kelly also reported that anti-aqueduct talk seemed to have died down and that the city was now leasing land to local ranchers. Impressed by the progress, he described the Chief's ability to delegate authority and his capacity for soaring above a morass of detail. Mulholland sometimes replaced elaborate notes and blueprints with mere stick scratches in the sand as he instructed an engineer to go ahead and do it "your way." Choose the right man and then give him his head, Mulholland told Kelly. Associates attested to his prodigious memory and powers of observation, recalling that although his sketches and notes on the first survey had been bare-bones by academic standards (made simply with a pocket compass and an aneroid barometer), the overarching plan and vision were clearly in his head. Remembering those earlier days, Mulholland told Kelly that the man who drove the buckboard on that occasion had thought he was "a locoed prospector hunting for a lost mine." Musing that Mulholland might have made a great general or military engineer, Kelly concluded that then he would have been responsible for "prodigies of destruction instead of construction."[11]

Accompanying this group was J. Waldo Smith, chief engineer of the Catskill aqueduct project, described as "a blown-in-the-bottle New Yorker" who "regarded everything west of the Hudson as unexplored territory peopled by semi-civilized tribes addicted to big talk." After his survey, however, Smith declared himself amazed: amazed by the courage of men who went into the desert to find water; amazed by a municipality willing to do its own work rather than contract it; and amazed that the leaders had been able to keep out the politicians and grafters. "No hint of Tammany here!" he declared.

Mulholland always credited the bonus system for the success of the tunnel work. "The men in a bonus crew themselves eliminated the drones and did not tolerate loafing." Having devised the system used on the aqueduct, he was devoted to it, but it ran into difficulties in June when the city auditor decided that the Chief's computations were too generous. Securing the board's approval of his calculations, the auditor cut bonuses 56 percent. When the payroll was delayed in order to make the changes, two hundred men walked off the job. The former system was quickly restored as General Chaffee explained that Mulholland had thought they should try the auditor's plan "to see how it would work," adding sardonically that now they had found out. With a revised system reinstated, the men returned to work, but in the following year, organized labor would raise further opposition.[12]

Los Angeles had no Tammany Hall, but its politics did impinge on aqueduct affairs, especially after Mayor Harper retired from his office in March rather than face the divisiveness and humiliation of a recall. The progressive Democratic League had backed Harper's successor, George Alexander, and almost immediately after Alexander's installation, league secretary M. G. Yoakum reintroduced the San Fernando Valley "land grab" issue in an attempt to unseat Moses Sherman from the water board. That matter had remained quiescent until Yoakum wrote letters to both the new acting mayor and the city council demanding an investigation and renewing the familiar accusations made in 1906 by the *Examiner* and *Evening News* that the funds for the aqueduct would pay for the project only as far as the head of the San Fernando Valley; that the additional land and rights-of-way needed to bring the Owens River water across the valley to the City of Los Angeles would have to be purchased from the San Fernando Mission Land Company in order to complete the work; and that Sherman was a participant in that land company.[13]

The new mayor handed this hot potato to Mulholland, admitting at the time that he did not know what the Democratic League meant by its communication. He soon found out when the water board, Mulholland, and Sherman each responded with letters dismissing the charges in the strongest terms. The board pointed out that the land company had purchased its valley holding in 1903, two years before aqueduct plans were made public. L. C. Brand, who had originated the purchase and acted as trustee for the company, also declared that he had originally feared the aqueduct project would swamp their land. When he was assured that the reservoirs would prevent such damage, he had given the city 200 acres for a reservoir and sold 155 acres more at $75 an acre. Speaking on his own behalf, Sherman acknowledged that he had once owned a one-tenth interest in the Mission Land Company as well as interests at Mojave, in the San Fernando Valley, and in Hollywood. Moreover, he regretted that he no longer held them, as they would be of greater value today than when he had bought them. This statement was somewhat disingenuous, for he omitted to say that he and some of his former associates in the Mission Land Company were now in the midst of negotiating a deal to purchase the entire southern half of the San Fernando Valley, a body of land unconnected to the Mission Land Company but which some writers have later mistakenly merged into the conspiracy theory. Mulholland, just returned from an official inspection of the aqueduct on which a group of city officials had accompanied him, wrote a sharp letter that the mayor did not make public, saying only that Mulholland's word was good enough for him and that no more was to be said on the matter.[14]

PROGRESS ACCOMPANIED BY A RUMBLE OF DISCONTENT

Between trips along the aqueduct line, Mulholland oversaw plans for the local water supply. He reported to the water commissioners in April that the old conduit at Crystal Springs should be replaced. Recalling that it had been built piecemeal between 1886 and 1891 and without a proper anticipation of how the city would grow, he now proposed a new conduit of about 9,000 feet from the Crystal Springs gatehouse in Griffith Park to the head of the Bellevue Reservoir branch line in the Ivanhoe subdivision. For the work, he recommended the purchase of a steam shovel and a gravel-loading device estimated at $65,000. By September, one hundred men and one steam shovel had completed a mile and a half of the work.[15]

Although the aqueduct was Mulholland's overwhelming concern, sometimes a lesser comedy of errors could require his attention. When the *Examiner* printed an article claiming that the city, upon the suggestion and authorization of Mulholland and Chief Forester Gifford Pinchot, was about to plant a large acreage of eucalyptus in the Owens Valley, his office was barraged with inquiries from eastern agents and investors wishing to do business with the city. Explaining to one New Yorker that "it was a story made out of the whole cloth as is so often the case these days with newspaper stories," Mulholland wrote that a eucalyptus enthusiast named Webb had appeared at the board of public works to extol the tree's virtues. The board, of course, was already familiar with the tree, as California was then in the midst of a eucalyptus boom after it had been falsely touted as a hardwood. (The boom eventually went bust, but not before the eucalyptus became almost as widespread in the Southern California landscape as the palm would later.) Once it was known that the tree could never thrive in the harsh winters and elevations of Owens Valley, the eager inquiries ceased.[16]

At midyear, Mulholland reported good progress on all aspects of the work, as did visitors returning from aqueduct tours. The once faultfinding City Auditor Mushet returned from his first visit full of enthusiasm and praise. "I wish every citizen of Los Angeles could see just what I had seen. . . . the genius of this enterprise is doing more for Los Angeles than this generation will ever dream of. . . . I take off my hat to him evermore." Dr. Luther Powers of Public Health pronounced Owens River water sweet and pure. "Any man who knocks this enterprise is a fool. He will speak without knowledge because if he saw what is being done and how it is being done, he would be ashamed of himself." Although Mulholland was encouraged to say that the aqueduct could be completed a year earlier than originally estimated, he wrote otherwise to his friend Charles Dwight Willard. Willard, former leader in the Municipal League and editor of its magazine, *Municipal Affairs,* had been sidelined by his "ancient enemy," tuberculosis. While convalescing, he had undertaken a new weekly publication, *Pacific Outlook,* in which he wanted either Mulholland or his secretary, Burt Heinly, to write a weekly account of progress on the aqueduct. When Mulholland explained that the constraints of time and work would not permit such a task, Willard then asked for a signed article about estimated times for the aqueduct's completion. Mulholland hedged with the reply that although it now looked as if it were going ahead faster than expected, he was reluctant to put that in writing, even though if "I thought that we were going to have to ask for more money and take a couple of extra years on this work, I wouldn't be able to sleep nights. As it is, my slumber is as peaceful as a baby's."[17]

Almost as he wrote those lines, trouble erupted over the food at the fifty-five camps. General Chaffee promptly left to investigate and upon return reported that he found conditions satisfactory, although he promised to seek improvement in the general sanitary conditions at the camps. Of the food, however, he warned that "one cannot expect to get things as good as at home." He had found the quality varied from camp to camp; moreover, good cooks were in short supply and providing fresh foods without refrigeration was difficult in desert areas.[18]

Until August 1908, the aqueduct had maintained its own commissary department. Each meal had cost 25¢, and the diet had been based upon what the United States Geological Survey then used. Then General Chaffee had persuaded the board that letting out the food concession to contract would simplify their burden of work and allow the enterprise to run more smoothly. The concessionaire, Daniel Joseph "Joe" Desmond, was the son and namesake of a pioneer Los Angeles hatter-haberdasher whose family Mulholland had known since his earliest times in California. Born in Los Angeles in 1875, Desmond began his career as a food contractor in his thirties when he and his partner, E. S. Shattuck, had run boardinghouses in connection with railroad construction. Their reputation grew after they set up soup kitchens in various permanent camps in San Francisco after the 1906 earthquake. Although initially praised and commended by army officers, complaints subsequently arose over the food, and five months after the disaster, Shattuck and Desmond were given notice that a local relief corporation was to replace them. As they were then serving 600 people three meals a day at 15¢ per meal, each of which cost about 7½¢ to provide, they were understandably reluctant to lose the arrangement.[19]

His partnership with Shattuck dissolved, Desmond received the aqueduct contract in July 1908, but soon discovered that some men were arranging their own private messes because of dissatisfaction with the food. In the Cinco Division, he reported that the official mess tent was almost empty. Therefore, on June 21, 1909, when an order went out along the line that all aqueduct workers were to get subsistence from the restaurants of D. J. Desmond and that they were to pay 70¢ a day whether they ate there or not, the workers' response was hostile. Chaffee acknowledged that the situation was trying, yet he also insisted that without an official subsistence organization the whole operation would degenerate.[20]

Workers reported that they moved on because of the poor food, probably only a partial truth, for many of the aqueduct laborers were men whom Mulholland called "short-stakers," those who worked from place to place, staying only long enough to collect a grubstake before moving on. A payroll for May 1909 provided 3,200 positions yet contained more than 7,000 names, indicating that over half the men remained only a few days. In October, the labor council sounded an ominous tone when it informed the city council that it had failed to secure satisfaction from either the aqueduct commission or Mayor Alexander and now requested the council to "investigate the question of wages and food conditions." Because some felt that behind this demand lay the desire to open an inquiry on "the whole question of aqueduct management," creating charges of "political trickery" at great extra expense, the council decided the whole matter must remain in the aqueduct commission's jurisdiction. Two weeks later, the commissioners traveled on the line with Mulholland and returned with a report that while the food was "not all the best in the world" and keeping fresh eatables on the desert was difficult, the bad spots were few.[21]

A YEAR OF GOOD WORK

By the end of summer, progress on the aqueduct was so well advanced that the board appointed Ezra F. Scattergood chief electrical engineer. At a salary of $5,000 a year, Scattergood was to conduct the affairs of the new power bureau, whose facilities would provide needed revenues for the enterprise. The board also voted to raise Mulholland's salary from $10,000 to $15,000 a year. More good news came in October when light broke through the mile-long Tunnel No. 35 on the Jawbone Division and jubilant crews began to celebrate its "holing." Now only a mile and a half remained to complete the twelve miles of tunnel on the Jawbone, and Mulholland commented to a friend in San Francisco that the remarkable way in which the men were "tearing up the ground" gave him cause for rejoicing. Indeed, before a meeting of city officials at year's end, he set aside the reticence he had shown with Willard and announced that the project would be completed early and under budget.[22]

As he left for his final inspection tour of 1909, Mulholland learned of the Supreme Court decision granting the City of Los Angeles the subterranean water rights of the San Fernando Valley. He and the water commissioners were quick to reassure the valley ranchers that with the coming of Owens River water they would not assert those rights. In fact, with an anticipated 20,000 miner's inches of Owens River water, they would face the problem of what to do with the excess. One municipality eager to secure some of it was Pasadena, but a great deal of discussion about consolidation and annexation would have to precede that decision.[23]

Back home a week before Christmas, the Chief described a sudden storm that had rendered Independence snowbound, with one of its canals frozen under a foot of ice. Yet, he added, only a few miles south, 2,500 men worked without interruption. The issues of labor, food, the contract system, the disposal of excess water, and San Fernando Valley land deals seemed to be receding. But as the following years would demonstrate, they had been mere forewarnings of storms to come.[24]

CHAPTER 16

Troubles and Interruptions

1910

SHAKE-UP AT CITY HALL

In an apparent attempt to keep his campaign promise of fairness and justice for all groups, incoming Mayor George Alexander shook up the city commissions with surprising additions and removals. He appointed the first union man ever to serve on a municipal commission, Ben C. Wilson of the Typographical Union, to the fire commission and restored Dr. John Randolph Haynes, a Progressive, to head the civil service commission. More controversial were his naming Lippincott to the park commission and removing Sherman from the water board. When Lippincott, with his penchant for controversial behavior, accepted the appointment, some saw a dangerous precedent in allowing one man to hold two important public offices at the same time, questioning too how he could do justice to the new post while also serving as assistant chief engineer of the aqueduct, for which he was paid a salary of $500 a month. The mayor argued that he wanted an engineer on parks, and although some wondered why some other able engineer could not be found to fill the post, Lippincott was still confirmed.[1]

Sherman's removal proved more controversial, but the Municipal League and one of its leaders, Meyer Lissner, were pressuring the mayor to force the resignation. Their charge against Sherman had been that he held stock in a downtown office building where the board of public works leased offices for the aqueduct department. As the city charter provided that no city official should have any direct or indirect interest in any contract with the city, the city attorney brought suit. Sherman's supporters were quick to point out that by that strict standard a number of other businessmen holding elective and appointive offices would also be ineligible (including two current members of the water commission who were bankers). Others, however, suggested that the chief ethical grounds for Sherman's disqualification were his ties to the Southern Pacific and the city's largest utility company. While Sherman's attorneys delayed, the Municipal League met with city council members and decided to offer him the opportunity to resign. With the same mixture of moral righteousness and defiance he had manifested regarding his conflicting interests in Arizona, San Francisco, and San Diego, he dismissed the charges as simply "technical" and refused to resign. The mayor, with council approval, then proceeded to remove him. The *Times* was predictably outraged while the Progressives savored the victory that Lissner had helped to achieve. [2]

To serve out Sherman's unexpired term and to act as president of the water commission Alexander named attorney and former mayor of Los Angeles William D. Stephens. Later in this politically volatile year that would see the election of Hiram Johnson to the governorship of California, Stephens became one of California's three successful Progressive candidates for Congress. His appointment to the $3,000 a year salaried post of water board president brought an end to J. J. Fay's eight-year tenure. The other appointment went to an old legal warrior from the days of the city's battles with the private water company, Henry T. Lee. The three remaining members included two bankers, Major John Norton and General John R. Mathews, along with Mayor Harper's last appointee, the genial and noncontroversial Democrat Reginaldo del Valle. This shakeup of the water commission also derived from Progressive opposition to the earlier commission's plans to build a four-story water department office at Fifth and Olive. Questions had been raised about the commission's power to spend water revenues on such a building, but after wrangles and accusations that the commissioners were "czars," the debate ended when the city attorney found that the city charter gave the water commission the right to build with its own funds. [3]

"THE GOOSE HANGS HIGH"

Work advanced on the aqueduct as the biggest concrete pipeline in the world (a record interior diameter of 120 inches running 955 feet) was being installed southeast of Newhall: a reinforced concrete siphon designed to operate under a head of 65 feet. In early March, the teams at the Elizabeth Tunnel under John Gray and William Aston broke yet more records amid estimates that at their present rate they would bring in the work a year early with a resultant savings of $119,000.[4]

That January, Mulholland and Mathews testified at a hearing in Independence before the United States Land Office about restoring to entry certain federal lands needed to preserve the purity of the water sent to Los Angeles. At this time Mulholland publicly addressed the local antagonisms in Owens Valley that had arisen over misunderstandings of the city's intentions and said that after all the evidence had been presented many fears had been allayed. An Inyo resident who attended all the proceedings lamented to the *Inyo Register* the absence of locals and their apparent indifference to "what is probably the most important case Inyo ever had or ever will have." He also noted that the Los Angeles men who testified presented a striking contrast to the "'tin horn' politicians and reporters who first came through the valley on earlier so-called tours of inspection." Especially impressed with Mulholland's testimony and clear recital of the history of Los Angeles's search for water in Owens Valley, he ruefully added, "If Inyo had had a Bill Mulholland to look out for her interests, in the intelligent and patriotic way he does for Los Angeles we would be in a different position today." On March 3, Senator Frank Flint wrote Mulholland that the secretaries of interior and agriculture had each agreed not to take any action without first notifying Flint. Finally, on April 27, Representative McLachlan entered a bill in the House giving the City of Los Angeles authority to a strip of land not more than 250 feet wide over public lands and forest reservations in Inyo, Kern, and Los Angeles Counties.[5]

While Mulholland spent early March on the aqueduct and in Owens Valley, the new water commissioner, William Stephens, arrived for a tour. Regardless of political affiliation, everyone who traveled the line with the Chief returned to the city a convert and enthusiast. Stephens was impressed by the quantity of water he saw, and he found the construction camps efficient, comfortable, and clean. As to the food, he allowed that a man who boarded regularly at the California Club might fault the lack of napkins and tablecloths, but compared to other construction camps, those along the aqueduct seemed clean and adequate. Another favorable report came from S. T. Henry, engineer and associate editor of *The Engineering Record of New York*. Struck by the spirit of organization and teamwork he had found along the line, he declared the food superior to any he had ever eaten at any railroad camp. Part of the current problem, he suggested, might stem from the fact that many of the men, especially those building the tunnels, were "highly paid, high class workmen who expected to be served banquets."[6]

Sanguine about affairs along the aqueduct that spring, Mulholland wrote Henry Dockweiler on March 15 that the "goose hangs high. . . . Returned from Independence Sunday night," he commented, "and have never seen things looking better than they did on this trip." He now turned his attention to the city's campaign for the passage of harbor and power bonds. A panel of experts had made a preliminary report finding that the 400-feet-per-second average flow in the aqueduct could deliver an average of 64,000 horsepower to the city and achieve a peak load of 120,000 horsepower. The proposed power bonds would finance the power plants' construction, one in San Francisquito Canyon where topographical studies by Scattergood and his assistant, Stanley Dunham, were already under way. Although not an active campaigner as he had been for the aqueduct, Mulholland issued a statement urging support for the power bonds. The project, he explained, was more of an investment than an improvement, for it would produce revenue once it was in operation. As civic sentiment seemed fairly united for passage of the bonds, the question generated little heat until almost the eve of the election when an anti-bond circular appeared. It prophesied that these bonds would cripple the city's credit and consequently hinder the aqueduct's completion. City attorneys Mathews and Hewitt assured voters that the city was well within the limits of its bonded indebtedness and retorted that the accusations smacked of a bad-faith effort that came too late in the campaign for adequate rebuttal. The voters evidently agreed, as they continued to support the city's policies for continued growth and on April 19 voted nine to one in favor of the bonds.[7]

A FORCED LAYOFF

As 3,600 men "tore up the ground" at a wonderfully rapid pace along the aqueduct, their very success—and the machinations of the eastern bond syndicate—were about to trip up the aqueduct builders. The work forged ahead until mid-May, when 2,700 men were abruptly laid off. The layoff's havoc and the emotion Mulholland must have felt were masked in the laconic engineering report he wrote months later. "This disorganization, coupled with the fact that it is naturally difficult to retain labor on the desert during the summer months, has seriously interfered with the progress schedule and the cost estimates."[8]

Because the accelerated pace of construction in 1909 had increased monthly expenditures as much as $600,000 a month, available funds by the end of May 1910 were reduced to $160,000 a month, and the workforce had to be reduced to 1,100 men. Difficulties intensified when the bond syndicate suddenly refused to make advance deliveries as it had the year before, declaring the bonds now had no buyers. The delay from its refusal to release its options on the bonds threatened to raise the cost of the project. To the argument that advancing the date of completion would bring the entire bond indebtedness to full issue in 1911 instead of 1913, Mulholland replied that an early completion would also bring equalizing benefits as the income from sales of water would also begin a year early. Faced with the necessity of raising $250,000 in additional taxes to pay the interest that would accrue a year earlier because of advancing the program one year, the city council agreed to invest $50,000 of sinking fund money in aqueduct bonds maturing from 1911 to 1918. To seek relief from the bond syndicate's hard terms and to head off a disastrous shutdown on the aqueduct, Mulholland and Mathews by the end of April prepared to go East.[9]

As this crisis mounted, attorney Henry O'Melveny persuaded Mulholland to take time out to visit the Dominguez Rancho where he had once dug artesian wells for old Manuel Dominguez. Now the heirs wished to develop the land and sought advice from Mulholland, who, after one tour over several tracts of the family's holdings, was overtaken by more urgent events so that he was not able to present a preliminary plan until the following October.[10]

A VISIT TO THE HALLS OF MAMMON

In May, Mulholland and Mathews, along with W. J. Washburn, chairman of the city council finance committee, spent three discouraging weeks in New York at the Hotel Belmont while they negotiated with the bond syndicate. Finding only a difficult market and apparently no buyers, Mulholland left Mathews to pursue the problem while he returned alone to take up aqueduct affairs. To anxious Angelenos, all he could offer was hope that things would improve. By late June, with two-thirds of the aqueduct work curtailed, Burt Heinly wrote his friend S. T. Henry, editor of *The Engineering Record,* that the cutbacks were heartbreaking. "Mr. Mulholland is wonderfully courageous," he went on. "He is the only one of the whole bunch who says nothing, but I am with him enough to know that he is thinking a great deal."[11]

While in New York, Mulholland visited his friend and associate J. Waldo Smith, chief engineer of New York City's board of water supply and of the New York Catskill Aqueduct, which would not be completed until 1917. Back in Los Angeles, he wrote to thank Smith for his hospitality and the tour of the Catskill project ("your great work"), also expressing regret that he had been unable to see him again because he had spent his last two days in the hotel with "a severe cold." It must have been a grim two days, for he wrote Smith of "your New York financiers pretty hard games." He described a moment of insight as he had stood on the steps of one of the banks. "I noticed in looking up . . . that the halls of Mammon were fully ten stories higher than the cross of Christ on the steeple of the little church across the way,—a fact which would indicate a degree of degradation that might easily exercise malign and potent influence on the habitues of that region."[12]

After a discouraged Mathews failed to find a buyer for the bonds in the East, he came home and found that civic support was about to rally. First the banker Marco H. Hellman offered to purchase $500,000 of the bonds on behalf of the New York Life Insurance Company. Hellman said he had initiated the sale after a broker came into his bank and badmouthed Los Angeles's credit standing. Next, the *Examiner* jumped in, boasting that it had secured a similar offer from Metropolitan Life. As lawyers and city council members huddled to see if they could legally transact a sale without first securing a release from their contract with the eastern bond company, a journal called *Spectator* sounded a sour note, wondering who had muddled affairs by making a contract with an eastern outfit that made "mutts" out of the city. The *Herald* meanwhile engaged in dark talk about the power trust that was thwarting bond sales in its determination to head off Los Angeles's plans to generate municipal electricity from Owens River water.[13]

As local offers to buy bonds came in, a July 11 message to the city council from Mayor Alexander surprised everyone by repeating the *Herald*'s accusation that the power companies were indeed holding up bond sales in the East, but that through a Los Angeles representative other eastern interests had offered to buy $5 million worth of the bonds. He then threw down the gauntlet and served notice on the syndicate that by July 31 it must either buy the bonds or terminate the option. A week later, the crisis ended when the syndicate agreed to sell to the two big insurance companies and also agreed to take up another $530,000 itself. Although this would not be the end of money woes, the aqueduct was back in business for now with $300,000 a month to draw upon. Mulholland hastened to recruit 2,000 men to get the work under way once more. Unfortunately, during the hiatus, many of the miners and mechanics had drifted off to find work in Arizona and Colorado, but as miners were to be paid $3 a day plus bonus for extra accomplishment, many returned, and the Chief remained publicly optimistic that the work could be completed by 1912.[14]

LABOR DISCONTENT

At the end of July, Mulholland and his sons took a brief vacation in the Sierras with a group of men that included Henry O'Melveny and his sons, Van Norman, and Major Henry Lee of the water board. The camping trip over, Mulholland next guided William Humphreys, latest member of the board of public works, over the project just as a dispute broke out over Joe Desmond's demand for an increase in the price of meals to twenty-five cents. Because Humphreys and Chaffee opposed the rise, the aqueduct board denied the request, but the issue was far from resolved. More disquieting to Mulholland, however, were reports of labor troubles at the south portal of the Elizabeth Tunnel, where the miners and muckers were threatening to strike unless the board met their demands for a pay raise. Then, the first week in August, the miners struck. Fifteen walked off, were paid their time, and left camp, while 250 others waited for orders from union headquarters in Denver. Two patrolmen were quickly dispatched from Los Angeles to guard the powder and dynamite stores at the site.[15]

The previous spring, when Mulholland returned from his failed New York mission reflecting on the halls of Mammon and the cross of Christ on Wall Street, the Merchants and Manufacturers' Association (M&M) in his own city had met to pass a resolution favoring the open shop. Shortly thereafter, amid growing tensions between labor and management, the city council unanimously passed a stringent antipicketing ordinance and thus created an obstacle against which previously squabbling unions could unite. The action also demonstrated that the Progressives, or Goo Goos (for good government), were not necessarily good friends of organized labor, for all had supported the ordinance. Although the stiffening attitudes and tensions surrounding labor issues inevitably affected the aqueduct, nothing during its construction equaled the infamous bombing of the *Los Angeles Times* building in October 1910.[16]

It is fair to say that vested private interests did more to impede the aqueduct than labor problems did. For one thing, aqueduct employees worked a union-approved eight-hour day on a public works project that promised to benefit all the dwellers of the city. In the beginning, at least, the bonus system was not unpopular with the workers; although it involved extra, speeded-up work, its reward of extra pay was a palliative. Moreover, the inaccessibility of the work camps stretched out many miles from each other hindered organizers, while the almost-military surveillance on the line tended to catch anyone suspected of agitating. Yet aqueduct construction always held the potential for labor disputes. Its skilled workers—especially the miners and tunnel men—had a strong union organization, the Western Federation of Miners, while the pipe and steel manufacturers without whose products no aqueduct could be built were notorious enemies of the closed shop and the metal-trades unions. Although General Otis may have been the dominant local voice and symbol of antiunionism, most of the city's leading capitalists and manufacturers shared his stance. Prominent among those affected by the increasing labor hostilities in 1910 were local metal manufacturers and suppliers such as Fred Baker, of Baker Iron Works; John Llewellyn, of Llewellyn Iron Works; and William Lacy, of Lacy Manufacturing Company. After strikes and walkouts in their plants, they became outspoken supporters of the antipicketing ordinance, and in the wake of the shocking *Times* explosion that killed twenty-three workers, both the Baker and Llewellyn works were subjected to less destructive dynamite attempts.

MORE TROUBLE ON THE LINE

With the city still absorbing the seismic shock of the *Times* bombing, the miners on the aqueduct struck a month later after the price of meals increased a nickel to thirty cents and the board failed to authorize a corresponding rise in wages. With dynamite dominating people's thoughts, the aqueduct strike made little news except in the pro-labor *Record*, which called it crippling and devoted a large space to the event. (The *Inyo Register* in Owens Valley also took note.) Not surprisingly, the *Times* gave it withering attention. "Preferring loafing to working, several hundred laborers, mostly miners, on the aqueduct, have quit their jobs, giving as a reason that they would not pay the increased price of mess in the camps." Mulholland, returning from a tour of the aqueduct with Mayor Alexander, made light of the business, saying it was not unusual for men to quit with the approach of cold weather and that 3,000 men were still at work along the line. The mayor said he had heard talk of a strike but had not seen much evidence of one. The *Examiner* investigated and found it "the most harmless strike that ever happened and there are no evidences of it."[17]

The *Record,* however, reported that members of the strike committee had come to Mulholland and told him they had proof that in the mad haste of construction, faulty work had been done, and that he, Mulholland, had accepted worthless work. His reply to them was direct. "All right. Prove it." Rumors of faulty construction had long circulated, especially after one section of concrete along the line had to be replaced because it had frozen before it could set. Mulholland had discussed the problem in his fifth annual report, but the sight of the discarded concrete chunks lying like boulders along several miles of the line had given rise to talk of faulty work. Perhaps to quiet the story, Mulholland challenged newspapermen, "Come on out and look it over. They say there's a lot of bum work . . . I've looked for it and I can't find it. If it's there I want to know. Come out and find it for me."[18]

The *Record* sent its City Hall reporter, Robert E. Rinehart, to cover the story. In his two informative articles on the state of aqueduct construction at that time, he had found Mulholland unduly optimistic, describing him as "persistently cheerful." While he did not deny the strike or conceal its extent, "in his heart he must regret the breaking of his wonderful working organization," wrote Rinehart. "All his division engineers do," he added. With 250 veteran miners and muckers gone, the tunnel work had dwindled, and not a single division on the aqueduct had escaped losses. At Haiwee, almost every veteran had left and been replaced with raw recruits for engineer Phil Wintz to struggle with and get back on line. Desmond's kitchens, however, were doing well, and Rinehart found the food acceptable as did most of the men he interviewed, although one workman told him that "the cook had spread himself for our coming." Finally, after days of probing and interviewing, Rinehart came away with the conclusion that only "a lynx-eyed caviller" could pick a flaw in the building of the aqueduct.[19]

A FESTIVE TREK TO OWENS VALLEY

In the month before the strike, on October 29, another junket to Owens Valley had taken place under the auspices of the *Times* and the Los Angeles Chamber of Commerce. Originally scheduled to coincide with the driving of the silver spike at Owenyo on October 18 to celebrate the almost-completed California-Nevada branch of the transcontinental Southern Pacific line that traversed Owens Valley as far as Owenyo on its way to Los Angeles, the excursion was delayed because of the *Times* bombing and Mulholland's heavy schedule. Lippincott had substituted for the Chief on the platform for dignitaries in Owenyo that day, and editor Chalfant of the *Inyo Register* later described him as a "betrayer of the reclamation project" and complained that he had been granted "a recognition to which he is not entitled."[20]

On October 29, Mulholland joined the delayed excursion, which comprised one hundred of Los Angeles's leading citizens, including at the last minute Mayor Alexander, who suddenly announced that he had never toured the aqueduct and wanted to join. Thus, on a cloudy Saturday morning, the mayor and Mulholland, with their driver, led a fleet of twenty-five automobiles out of town. One of the thrills that day was to drive through the empty aqueduct tunnels that would soon be filled with water destined for the city. After inspection stops at the south and north portals of Elizabeth Tunnel, where General Chaffee joined them, the cars pulled into Mojave by six that evening, the rapid travel time an indication of the improvements in both autos and roads since 1905. Along the rail sidings awaited sleeping cars for the night's rest. At dinner, Mulholland, now something of a cynosure, was overwhelmed by the chant of "What's the matter with Mulholland? . . . He's all right!" After a night spent listening to the clangings and crashings of train movements and shuntings in the yard, they advanced to Haiwee. Greeting them that evening were Fred Eaton, who had taken the newly completed train down from Owens Valley; Joe Desmond, in charge of their food for the weekend; and Lippincott, who assisted in explaining the engineering technicalities of the aqueduct.[21]

Earlier in the day, as they had passed Vasquez Rock, old-timers in the group were stirred to recall stories of Tiburcio Vasquez, who had used the landmark as his vantage point when ambushing miners descending from the Cerro Gordo mines with their bullion. (Among the touring group was former sheriff Uncle Billy Rowland, who had led the posse that captured Vasquez.) That night in Haiwee, after Mulholland had spoken of the challenges of building the Jawbone section and Fred Eaton had told of how he had confided his conception of the aqueduct to the Chief, a small group including Mulholland and former mayor Hazard retired to the aqueduct office and, perched on cracker barrels before bedtime, spun yarns that a captivated reporter described as the "unwritten history of Los Angeles." (Fred Eaton had slipped away on the night train to Independence to help arrange a chicken dinner for the crowd, which would arrive the following evening.) Among the tales told that night was Rowland's rambling account of how Mulholland as a young man had barely escaped being shot for a cattle thief. While riding across a stretch of dry river bed, Mulholland had come upon a well-known Los Angeles character suspected of horse and cattle rustling. The bad man and his associates were busy skinning a black cow. As Mulholland recognized both the men and the cow, he feigned indifference and simply passed by with a "Hello, boys." At nightfall, however, after leaving a lamp lighted in his window to give the appearance of being in his cabin, he struck out for Sheriff Rowland. The thieves had left by the time sheriff and posse arrived but were soon spied over towards Elysian Park, headed in the direction of the San Fernando Valley. As Mulholland followed the pursuit, a shot caused his little mare to bolt, and unable to stop her, he found himself in the cross fire. Stretching out beneath her neck, he clung to her as the bullets whizzed until finally one of the posse shot the thief dead. The reporter concluded from the yarn: "Discretion even in his younger days was part of the Mulholland."[22]

The third day, October 31, the travelers saw the steam shovels at work (still a novel sight for many) and visited the power plant at Cottonwood, where work in that section had been completed. Mulholland was constantly surrounded and barraged with questions. When asked if there were really a bug on the desert that destroyed cement walls, he replied, "Yes. I know all about that bug. Its generic name is the Crocus Knockeritis." After lunch at the hotel in Lone Pine, Mulholland and Chaffee agreed that for the best fried chicken, hot biscuits, and white gravy in town you had to go to "Mother" Green's cottage, a noted local character who had lived in Lone Pine thirty-four years. Their stayover in Independence that night so strained sleeping facilities in the town of 1,500 that several gentlemen slept in the county jail and pronounced it the best accommodations of the trip. A festive Halloween spirit developed when several wives in the party sang a concert on the hotel porch and became so enlivened that they marched to the jailhouse to serenade the sleeping men with such numbers as "Where Is My Wandering Boy Tonight?" and "Locked in the Stable with the Sheep." When they decided to find Mulholland, they entered the garden of the house where he was supposed to be and broke into the strains of "Has Anybody Here Seen Billy, Billy of the Aqueduct?" Doors suddenly opened to reveal a group of townspeople gathered for a Halloween card party. Then "Billy of the Aqueduct" revealed that he had been marching unseen behind the marauding singers, who, in a final burst of bacchanal, proceeded to march down the main street of Independence singing "Hot Time in the Old Town Tonight." Certainly in the

annals of Independence, this evening must rank as one of its odder social occasions.[23]

After a quick trip to Bishop and a visit to Eaton's ambitious chicken
ranch, Mulholland and Mayor Alexander caught a night train out of Mojave. Upon their arrival in the city next morning after a five-day, 650-mile
journey, the sunburned, enthusiastic Mayor Alexander declared he could
hardly find words to express his approval. He had seen the water with
Mulholland and been made a believer. The project was one of the biggest
things ever attempted, and "the man who laid out the line is a great genius. It is a mystery to me how human ingenuity can do such things."[24]

WORK RESUMES WITH NEW
UNDERCURRENTS OF COMPLAINT

This euphoria perhaps strengthened Alexander's resolve to reject the bond
syndicate's offer for the further sale of aqueduct bonds. The city council had been about to agree to a sale that would have cost the city $62,000
in lost premiums, but the mayor vetoed the measure. He was vindicated
in mid-December, when the bond syndicate capitulated to the terms.
Meantime, these matters did not immediately affect work on the aqueduct. Money was sufficient for the coming year; most of the hardest work
had been completed, except for fourteen miles of siphons; and Mulholland was devising new ways to cut costs. The bond strictures did, however, cause a lack of funds to purchase steel pipe for the siphons, which
had to be ordered a year in advance. All of these problems would extend
into the coming year, in addition to grave new ones. Feeling the increasing
pressures, Mulholland wrote Dockweiler in early December that he would
not be able to come north to serve in an important Contra Costa water
case. He expressed his interest in the matter but felt at present, "I would
neither do credit to myself nor be of substantial assistance to my client."
He expanded, "Now problems have arisen here which again precipitate
me into the thick of the fray; namely, the disposal of the surplus waters
of Owens River. Already, I have been charged, by innuendo and all manner of sinister hints, with a desire to favor owners of large tracts of land
in the San Fernando Valley, the instigators of these charges well knowing that inevitably large quantities of the water will be used there, and
an attempt will hence be made to imply that it was the result of undue
influence."[25]

Open sessions on the all-important question of what to do with the
surplus water from Owens River had begun in September. After the se-

crecy and closed-door planning that led to building the aqueduct, the citizens who had paid for the project would now be heard, as would those entities anxious to receive the water, such as the City of Pasadena. At the opening session the night of September 22, Mulholland presented his memorandum of proposals, which he called only "a brief treatment of a very large subject." His central principle was that the City of Los Angeles must have no thought of parting with its rights to the water. He opposed taking in other cities but suggested what he called a bonus system, by which Los Angeles would receive a premium for putting water on the land and also collect an annual rental. These ideas led to a stream of questions and objections as the sessions continued for a week, constituting only an opening exercise in a matter that had no easy solutions. Mulholland was still pondering the question on November 23, when he wrote to ask Frederic Stearns about the proceedings used in organizing Boston's metropolitan water board. Later thanking Stearns for the information he had sent, Mulholland acknowledged that Boston's conditions were very different from those of Los Angeles, which had, in addition to its domestic supply, 135,000 acres of irrigation districts where the water could be used until the domestic need increased. One point he made clear to Stearns: "It is not desired, and it is not probable that the City would ever consent to the sale of the right to a single inch of Owens River water."[26]

CHAPTER 17

Aqueduct Progress and Political Fireworks

1911

A WORK DELAYED

Having maneuvered the shoals of the previous year, Mulholland remained optimistic about the aqueduct's progress in 1911. The city demonstrated its continued faith by offering to purchase $500,000 of its own bonds in order to advance funds when the foot-dragging New York syndicate was reluctant to sell its 1911 subscription. With money available, the work could advance. Only 1,295 feet of granite separated the two Elizabeth Tunnel crews digging and blasting their way through the mountain to the anticipated meeting; the steam shovels, drillers, and concrete workers were progressing across the desert at a rate of five or six miles a month; and the Haiwee Dam was shaping up rapidly. When only the last 86 miles of the aqueduct's 235-mile stretch remained to be completed, a reporter suggested that Mulholland could turn to authorship and compose a treatise describing all the innovative machinery and engineering that the project had introduced and employed. Instead, by year's end, he found himself embroiled in the very brand of politics he had hoped to avoid.

Questions about the electric power to be developed from Owens River water now gained public attention. Was this enterprise to be completely municipal or would private companies (that is, investor-owned utilities) be allowed to coexist? The city's chief electrical engineer, Ezra Scattergood, was adamant that the project be completely municipal, but the private companies, especially California Edison, pushed to come in, and public debate grew heated. Some of the Progressives, including political leader

Meyer Lissner, who had enthusiastically supported the city's water leaders and policies since 1905, did not oppose private power; indeed, they argued that the city should entertain private offers to see if a proposition might benefit and profit the city. The Progressive and pro-labor *Record,* however, had championed publicly owned power since the earliest days of the aqueduct and now urged a straw vote on the issue in an upcoming election on charter amendments. Mayor Alexander agreed, and with the city council, called for its inclusion on the March 6 ballot. The results produced a victory for the amendments and a ten-to-one approval of municipal ownership of power (11,149 to 2,214).[1]

When Mulholland submitted his sixth annual aqueduct report in mid-July 1911, he acknowledged that the suspension of work in the past fiscal year had proven "a very expensive experience" and implicitly abandoned his dream of completion in 1912 but expressed the hope that it would be finished at the time of the original estimate, spring 1913. He could not have predicted the social turmoils that were to culminate in a nasty mayoral campaign during which his reputation was so impugned that he asked for an investigation into the building of the aqueduct.

The costly work stoppage on the aqueduct in 1910 crippled the enterprise so that even when full activity resumed, it had lost its momentum, coinciding with an increasingly unsettled economic and political climate in the city. The labor-connected bombings and deaths in 1910 had hardened lines between labor and management. Symptomatic of the strife's effect on the aqueduct was a letter that Mayor Alexander forwarded to Mulholland at the beginning of the year from a Western Federation of Mines organizer requesting a permit to visit the aqueduct camps and see if any of his members were working there. He already had been refused admittance at several camps, and he questioned their right to keep him out. He also wondered why, if the mayor approved of arbitration, he did not seek it in the "boarding-house grievance" (Desmond's food services). The mayor passed the note along to Mulholland, remarking that he "would not care to interfere in a matter of which I have no personal knowledge." A month later, after miners and other skilled laborers were denied a wage increase of fifteen cents a day to pay for the five-cent increase granted to Desmond, the steam shovel men walked off. As machinists and members of the Western Federation of Mines, they had asked for $4.00 a day and an increase in meal allowance. Mulholland argued that aqueduct workers were already better paid than private employees nearby. For a ten-hour day aqueduct laborers received $3.00 (for either wet or dry work) and $1.00 a day for board; miners received $3.50

for an eight-hour day when they worked in wet ground and $.90 a day
for board. With bonuses they could increase their wages from 10 to 40
percent. The mayor, loath to interfere in aqueduct matters, made no
protest when the aqueduct board turned down the workers' demands,
and unfortunately for the workers, the strike came too late to significantly
dent aqueduct construction. Moreover, Mulholland, anticipating trouble, had already deployed other steam shovel men to take over the work.
The ill feelings generated among certain workers, however, would feed
events later in the year.[2]

GETTING DAYLIGHT

The strike was almost obscured, however, in the jubilation over the Elizabeth Lake Tunnel's completion. Its breakthrough, or "getting daylight,"
occurred toward noon of February 27, when a candle fluttering in the
north section told the men that air was coming from the other side and
that the wall was about to be pierced. Their foreman scrambled up out
of the water in which they were standing to the top of a nearby granite
boulder and shouted, "Hey!" Suddenly the drilling on the other side
stopped, and there came an answering "Hello!" Each foreman, holding
a candle, moved forward until one said, "I can see your nose. Can you
see mine?" Amid the calls and congratulations, arguments began over
which side broke through first. With the final blast of dynamite, Superintendent John Gray said, "If it goes through, it will end the biggest thing
of its kind ever undertaken." When someone reminded him that the Gunnison Tunnel was longer, Gray returned, "Longer, but not so big and not
anywhere near as difficult."[3]

   The Elizabeth Lake Tunnel's completion made national news, described in superlatives even by the deliberate *Christian Science Monitor* as "an engineering feat without parallel for low cost and the short
time employed." Begun October 1907, the work had gone on day and
night for almost four and a half years as men, drills, and dynamite tun-
neled through 5.09 miles of granite. It was a marvel of precision, as its
final alignment proved to be out only two and a quarter inches and the
grade only seven-thousandths of a foot. For finishing almost a year ahead
of schedule (the board of engineering experts had estimated five years)
and $411,800 under estimate, great credit went to its two supervisors,
John Gray and William Aston. Gray was next deployed to supervise concrete work at San Francisquito Canyon, while Aston, the man whose abilities the civil service board had once questioned, moved on with four of

his top foremen to superintend the Hilo tunnel about to be constructed across the island of Hawaii.[4]

CHANGES AT CITY HALL

Among the city charter amendments that triumphed at the polls in March was one that abolished the old water board and reorganized it into a new agency, the public service commission. Both Good Government and labor observers had questioned some of the old board's actions, such as Sherman's questionable behavior, and the *Record* had also begun to show signs of disaffection, especially when it discovered that, contrary to the provisions of the city charter, the water commission had since 1908 been allowing the Los Angeles Gas and Electric Company to place settling vats along the west bank of the Los Angeles River. Although the commission swiftly responded by ordering the gas company to vacate, the *Record* still questioned how good a job the water commission was doing in safeguarding the "interests of ALL THE PEOPLE ALL THE TIME."[5]

Members of the old board prepared a survey of its history for the new commissioners, claiming it was a record to be envied by any public agency. Since its original organization in 1902, the board had received $10,134,455.52 and had expended $9,289,402.51 for current expenses and betterments; had turned over to the aqueduct board $580,893.83; and still had $264,159.18 to its credit in the city's water revenue fund. During this same period water service had increased from 23,180 to 66,379 deliveries, and the annual income from $614,264 in 1903 to $1,102,589 in 1910. Beginning with 29 employees, including inspectors and collectors, their numbers had grown to 76 office employees. Of the original 29, 24 were still with the service; 2 had died and 3 resigned. Perhaps of greatest pride to the old-timers was that although receipts in the past year were 79 percent higher than in the administration's first year, the cost of water to consumers was now about 58 percent lower. Moreover, per capita consumption had decreased from 306 to 140 gallons a day. These changes were largely because of an increase in population and the installation of meters.[6]

A week after the new public service organization had celebrated with its first annual banquet, the mayor asked it to organize a power and light bureau headed by Scattergood. (Each of these bureaus, water and power, would operate autonomously under Scattergood's and Mulholland's leadership.) Mulholland meanwhile prepared to lead new members of both the commission and city council on yet another guided tour over the aqueduct. Highlights on this one included a trolley ride through the five-mile length of the Elizabeth Tunnel on which the cement work was about to begin and one councilman's discovery of a fossil oyster more than nine inches long amid a pile of material excavated for the aqueduct in Dry Rock Canyon.[7]

The new public service commission began its mission by addressing the vexing and complex question of irrigation and disposal of excess water from Owens River. Experts chosen for the panel of consulting engineers included Homer Hamlin, city engineer; John H. Quinton, an old hand from the United States Reclamation Service who was regarded as the dean of American irrigation engineers; and William H. Code, new to Los Angeles but noted as chief inspector of Indian reservation irrigation. A leery Mulholland noted that the panel was the board's idea—not his—but acknowledged that they were all experts and "we may learn something from them." Pointing out that more land adjacent to the city needed water than the city could supply, he asserted, "The supply is nowhere equal to the demand. Those who believe that we will have more water than we know what to do with and later will get it cheaper are badly mistaken. No one will get it any cheaper than those who have mortgaged their homes to bring it here."[8]

Submitted in July, the consultants' report contained three major conclusions: (1) much of the excess water should be reserved in the underground San Fernando reservoir; (2) districts allotted excess water must be annexed to the city; (3) these districts would have to pay in advance the cost of their main distribution conduits. Those disappointed in their hopes for the water were Pasadena, South Pasadena, and Alhambra and, in the eastern San Gabriel Valley, Covina, Azusa, and Glendora. Mulholland argued that as they lay higher than the terminus of the aqueduct, the added work of tunneling and piping would make the cost impracticable. This decision stirred controversy and spawned hostility towards Mulholland in what came to be known as the high-line fight led by S. C. Graham, a Progressive opponent of annexation and a proponent of consolidation who advocated carrying water to the east on a "high line." His critics derided the plan with the old country joke that you can compel water to run uphill—but it will cost you money to do it. Graham argued in turn for a selective system of high water rates to insure the city a good financial return. While some areas were angered that under the existing plan only ranchers in the San Fernando Valley could hope to irrigate with Owens River water, Mulholland was also cautioning that reserving water for power would make less available to outlying districts anxious to receive it. Because the promise of water for the San Fernando Valley coincided with the opening sales promotion of the old Lankershim–Van Nuys lands and the founding of the new town of Van Nuys, earlier accusations of a capitalist conspiracy revived with added plausibility. The *Tribune,* recently acquired by Otis's enemy, E. T. Earl, was among the first to raise the issue in an editorial questioning the right of "certain rich men" to profit in land sales based on their speculations in Owens River water. Land worth $50 an acre, it charged, was selling at over $500 an acre on the assurance that it would get water.[9]

At the mayor's request, Mulholland had assembled a water department report, which, in addition to enumerating the trunk-line mains being laid in growing sections of the city, announced the building of a 40-million-gallon reservoir at Ivanhoe to store future Owens River water and also to serve the Hollywood region. Moreover, the creation of the San Fernando Dam would mark a new epoch in the city's water history, he declared, as it would form part of "a very capacious system, which will permit a sustained flow through the Aqueduct during the winter when the consumption is less and the water is not needed, thereby not only serving to perpetuate the flow through the Aqueduct for power purposes, but also providing a greater quantity of water for summer use." By summer, in his sixth annual report, he also anticipated the aqueduct's completion in the spring of 1913. Many of these matters were soon to become grist for the mill of one of Los Angeles's most notorious mayoral campaigns.[10]

FALLOUT FROM THE *TIMES* BOMBING: THE RISE OF JOB HARRIMAN

Labor remained in upheaval throughout 1911 as fresh disputes produced strikes against a candy company, a brewery, and cigar makers. Although the Progressives had achieved political victories with the election in 1910 of Hiram Johnson as governor of California and a Progressive majority in both houses of the legislature, labor found its strongest ally in the Socialist Party. Among the speakers on April 15 at a large labor rally to celebrate the passage of the eight-hour day for women workers was labor attorney Job Harriman, who by year's end, as a candidate for mayor of Los Angeles, was to launch a full-scale attack against Mulholland and his associates. Also in April came the arrest of the McNamara brothers for complicity in the *Times* bombing, and in May, carpenters, other building trades workers, and bakers had gone out on strike. Political collaboration between Socialists and labor increased as Stanley Wilson, editor of the labor newspaper, the *Citizen*, joined the Socialist Party, while Job Harriman, now a member of the McNamaras' defense team, became the Socialist candidate for mayor.[11]

The city's mayoral campaigns were animated and short, but because of increasingly splintered class attitudes in the city, this one became highly acrimonious and drew Mulholland deep into its brambles. On August 6, as the McNamara brothers' trial approached, the Socialist Party staged a kickoff rally at which Harriman laid out their objectives for the city. His major issues were the aqueduct, the harbor, and what he claimed was the unsavory record of the present administration. He intended to prevent Owens River water from being placed on San Fernando Valley lands because it would enhance their value to $1,000 an acre and enrich its owners; he would see the water taken through the city, in sewers and septic tanks if necessary, for its use on a great area that the city would buy and sell and thereby make enough to pay off the aqueduct debt. The Socialist platform promised "to abolish graft in construction of the aqueduct from the Owens River and to extend the municipally owned water system." As there had been no charges of graft from any quarter up to this point, this insinuation smacked of a straw man strategy. Yet because the complexities of the water issue rarely yielded simple or easy explanations, the tactic was effective. Was there graft on the aqueduct? No one had suspected it, but now it became a possibility. Would valley lands sell for $1,000 an acre? Though none did until almost World War II, many believed Harriman's claim. The Socialist campaign pamphlet "The Coming Victory" contained charges so scurrilous and various against the water project that the board of public works prepared a long documented rebuttal.[12]

Many believed Harriman and the Socialists simply because they were uninformed on the subject, knew little or nothing about the San Fernando Valley, and found his theme of the haves exploiting the have-nots plausible because of rising class and economic divisions in the city. Sometimes called "the era of the successful entrepreneur," this period also could have been characterized as the era of the land-grabber, for the people accused of conspiring with the city's water men to enrich their San Fernando Valley lands with Owens River water had been equally assiduous in acquiring land unrelated to the aqueduct project. Since 1901, during the first subdivision of Hollywood, these same men (who included Otis, Chandler, Sherman, Brant, and Whitley) acquired vast tracts in Kings County where they laid out the town of Corcoran; in Kern County where they purchased the 270,000-acre Rancho El Tejon; and along the California-Mexican border where they controlled the C&M Company, a spread of almost a million acres.[13]

Much of what Job Harriman charged was based upon past files of Clover's *Evening News* and the writings of W. T. Spilman. Harriman mocked Mulholland's popularity, called him "Saint Mulholland" or "the sainted Mulholland," essentially called him a liar, and pointed out that he owned 160 acres in the San Fernando Valley, which, "if supplied with water, will become worth $1000 an acre." In the same breath that he complained of graft in the present municipally owned water department he extolled municipal ownership of all public utilities as a panacea. Because he was an attractive and forceful campaigner who drew many to his cause, in September Samuel Gompers visited Los Angeles to urge support of Harriman. On October 31, a Halloween in sharp contrast to the previous year's when Mulholland had been courted and serenaded in the streets of Independence, voters went to the polls and gave Harriman a plurality. Of 45,500 votes cast, Harriman received slightly over 20,000; Alexander, 16,800; and Mushet, Republican and former auditor, 7,500. The final election on December 5 promised to be memorable, for not only would the city's women cast their first votes but a Socialist candidate might well prevail.[14]

Although some writers have dismissed Mayor Alexander as an aging nonentity, he was far from a ninny. At seventy-two, he was a sharp and vigorous administrator who had earlier served two terms on the county board of supervisors. A canny Scotsman from Iowa who referred to himself as "Uncle Aleck" (he sported a goatee for which Harriman accused him of trying to resemble Uncle Sam!), he had fought in the Civil War and settled afterwards in Los Angeles with his wife and daughter. He was a modest landholder-farmer whose subsequent actions vindicated the Progressives' faith in him. He favored women's suffrage and opposed the railroad's high freight rates, even though he was stuck with the bargain former mayor Harper had struck with the Southern Pacific. On the water and power question, he was unequivocal. He considered it the principal issue in the campaign, asserting that the city must distribute light and power at inexpensive rates. "But we are not going to succeed," he warned, "unless we are mighty sharp. The light and power corporations are not going to let us, if they can prevent it." On another hot issue, he protested, "They say I am to 'come through' for some real estate speculators in the San Fernando Valley. Come through with what?" he asked. The city charter, he pointed out, required that "the distribution of water and power must be approved of by two-thirds of the voters," so how could he give away the water?[15]

With the increased possibility of Harriman's victory in December, the *Express* worried editorially, along with most of the business community, that if he were mayor, the city might become anathema to the eastern bond market and be unable to sell its current issues. The *Citizen* rebutted with statements from New York bond dealers who declared Harriman's election would make no difference in their continued business with the city, while an anti-Alexander voice pointed out that the City of Berkeley, which had just elected the state's first Socialist mayor, did not anticipate problems with bond sales. Of the coming election, Lincoln Steffens, in town to cover the McNamara trial, claimed that Harriman's opponents were "atremble" at the possibility of his triumph.[16]

Paralleling the mayoral campaign in November and attracting national attention was the McNamara trial, with famed attorney Clarence Darrow acting for the defense. In this febrile and tense atmosphere, Steffens launched a mission that today seems quixotic: namely, he intended to defuse the labor war and class struggle by bringing together the warring factions and persuading them to be led by the Christian ethic of the Golden Rule. This meant that the General Otises and Samuel Gomperses of the world were somehow to effect a reconciliation by focusing not on blame but on the causes of the social ills that confronted and divided them. Steffens saw the situation in Los Angeles as ideal for testing his theory and, if he is to be believed, persuaded Harry Chandler, and Chandler in turn, General Otis, to consider a settlement of the McNamara case in which the bombers would escape hanging and labor would be let off the hook. On Wednesday, November 29, twenty of the city's business leaders, both conservative and progressive, met to discuss the proposition. As they seemed to find some virtue in his ideas, Steffens gathered together the next day a few other leading citizens whom he considered "insiders." Included among them were Mulholland, Lippincott, Mathews, and C. D. Willard, but as Steffens later related, although they all favored the idea, "they were too public-spirited to count big in my experiment as an experiment."[17]

THE CHIEF TILTS WITH HARRIMAN

Five days before the election, on December 1, the McNamara brothers confessed to bombing the *Times* building. Establishment figures breathed more easily, but Harriman's followers were grief-stricken and angry over the reversal of fortunes. Amid the tears and gloom of campaigners in the Labor Temple, an angry group felt that the McNamaras had betrayed their cause while the most dedicated believed them simply martyrs of the class struggle. The day after the McNamara confession, Mulholland was scheduled to defend his position against Harriman's accusations at a City Club luncheon. Instead of a somber affair, a spirited crowd of three hundred gave three cheers when Meyer Lissner made the introduction. "I want to present the biggest man in Los Angeles—Bill Mulholland." In the spirit of the occasion, the Chief had brought with him a demijohn of Owens River water left over from ceremonies the previous October when President William Howard Taft had dedicated the Buena Vista Bridge. Offering it around to those sitting at his table, he asserted its purity by declaring that it was as sweet now as then. His speech was long and repeated many of the points he had already presented to an audience of six hundred women on November 27. He said he was before them "as parliamentarians say, on a question of personal privilege." He did not intend a campaign speech but wished to elucidate "some matters that were falsely presented to the public. Not only he, but the present administration, his associates, and the work of the aqueduct had been maligned and their acts distorted."[18]

He began with Harriman's charge that Mulholland had put a valuation of $3 million on the private waterworks in 1901. Not true, he protested, going through the old valuations presented long ago at the arbitration hearings and recalling that his had been $1,732,541. He had heard that Mr. Harriman referred to him as Saint Mulholland. "Well," he mused, "I got to looking at myself in the glass and I couldn't see much semblance to a saint, a man past middle age, with a tendency to corpulence and all the other features that a man of my time of life who has lived an active life usually presents." But, he explained, after the laughter died down, "I found he is addicted to that sort of thing. I can excuse him for his representations of me being a saintly man, because he refers to himself in the placards all over the city as the modern Abraham Lincoln." This brought down the house, as Mulholland proceeded to answer more Harriman accusations. He said a famine was created "not by God all Mighty who controls the rain . . . but by the Board of Water Commissioners of the City of Los Angeles and the saintly William Mulholland." After refuting various charges with a battery of figures for rainfall and water consumption, he apologized for the length of his speech but then continued with documentation of water use, pointing out that Los Angeles goes eight or nine months each year without rain, and that because of its beautification (lawns, trees, plants, flowers) and because its streets "require constant sprinkling under the aridity of our climate and the wind that blows here in the afternoon," consumption of 300 gallons and over was not unusual.

He touched on the old canard about water being run into the outfall sewer, reviewed the history of the aqueduct's construction, and explained why it should terminate in the San Fernando Valley: "Because it is the logical geographical spot." He pretended to puzzle over the title of Harriman's campaign pamphlet, "The Coming Victory." "Oh, what was it called? 'The Coming Calamity?'" *(Laughter and applause.)*

As to releasing water in the San Fernando Valley, the chief announced that he would just "as leave think of turning a band of wild steers down Main Street here as of turning that water loose across the San Fernando. To run 20,000 inches of water to the Los Angeles River would create 'something appalling.'" Nowhere did an official document exist that even hinted of such an intent, he insisted. Yet the rumor persisted. "Why, my telephone is almost worn out by people asking me about turning the water across the San Fernando Valley." He said even his wife had taken to complaining about his speaking of it so often and wondered why he did not just publish a denial in the newspapers.

Harriman had declared he would not allow a drop of Owens River water in the San Fernando Valley, but he also chastised the city's water men for depriving the valley people of their water. Mulholland reviewed the legal struggles over the city's right to the Los Angeles River waters and then turned to the accusation that the city had colluded with the land syndicates. Now he spoke his piece on his relationship with General Harrison Gray Otis:

> It may astonish you, gentlemen, when you know that I have been in public life here for over a quarter of a century, occupying a position with a fair degree of prominence and in the public eye a great deal, and yet I have never met General Harrison Gray Otis but twice in all that time to speak to him; and if he walked into this room and I wasn't on this platform and his attention not specially called to me, I know he wouldn't know me. I pass him dozens of times on the streets without even the ignorant off-hand nod that you read of in the magazines, not a sign of recognition. I don't know him myself at all. I have spoken to him twice; once on official business and the other time on a matter of indifference. I met him in a picture store, by the way, one Christmas Eve. That is the extent of my acquaintance with Gen. Otis. He has lambasted me good and hard on the back, possibly when I deserved it, but par-

ticularly with reference to the suits against the people of the San Fernando Valley using water of the Los Angeles River.

E. T. Earl, he said, happened to be the owner of the building where the aqueduct offices were housed, but his encounters with him also had been only few and casual. They met occasionally in the elevator and Earl sometimes asked him how the aqueduct was getting along, but that was the extent of the acquaintance. With some of the land syndicate, he admitted to unfriendly relations, but named only L. C. Brand, whom Mulholland had angered in a water contest.

Then he rounded back to the question of the aqueduct's terminus. Not only was the northern point in the San Fernando Valley a logical site in the direction toward Los Angeles, but it was also at the proper elevation. At 1,450 feet above sea level, it enjoyed "a commanding position to take the water wherever we can find customers." He acknowledged that he owned land in the San Fernando Valley, "a pretty good dry land proposition. It is away up in the west end of the valley. That land has been open for years and there is lots of it there yet to be bought by anybody. It is no crime to buy it, no sedition against this city to buy a piece of land there." He pointed out that Harriman owned land in the San Gabriel Valley, that many owned land in Southern California. In fact, did anybody know of any land that somebody didn't own? They all needed water, but the city did not intend to make a present of it. The people, those "who have gone down in their jeans to pay for it, need not fear that the water would be wrested from them." For "the law is so fixed" that this could never happen.

Finally, he understood that he might be discredited if he were to say that "the aqueduct will last as long as the pyramids of Egypt or the Parthenon of Athens . . . that would sound as though I was trying to be grandiloquent or something like that. But I will tell you that the aqueduct will at least endure until Job Harriman is elected Mayor of the City of Los Angeles." (*Great applause.*)

Three days later, almost 137,000 of Los Angeles's 180,000 eligible voters went to the polls and gave Mayor Alexander a comfortable majority of slightly more than 34,000 votes. Yet with all the twists, turns, and reversals of fortune, Harriman still managed to receive 51,423 votes, a constituency that would underpin labor's continued bitter struggle. A week after the election, to counter the serious charges against himself and the aqueduct in the heat of the campaign, the Chief recommended, with the board of public works' support, that the city council create a committee to investigate the aqueduct project. In turn, the defeated Socialists planned to retaliate during the investigation. At their December convention, on Harriman's suggestion, they demanded representation on the investigating committee proportional to the election results (two Socialists on a committee of five), and they listed twelve questions to be answered, covering much the same ground as Mulholland had in his speech.[19]

CHAPTER 18

The Investigation

1912

A SEA OF TROUBLES

If 1909 can be reckoned as the year when everything went right during the building of the aqueduct, 1912 should be remembered as the one when everything went wrong: the year when Mulholland's old dream of keeping the city's water affairs out of politics was shattered in the bitter aftermath of the *Times* bombing and the deeply divisive 1911 mayoral campaign. Given the amount of sniping and insinuation aimed at the aqueduct during the campaign of 1911, Mulholland and the aqueduct advisory board probably had no choice but to request an investigation, even though the process opened a Pandora's box from which flew a cloud of spiteful and cantankerous imps. No absurdist drama by Ionesco surpasses the aqueduct investigation board's gyrations, from its preliminary skirmishes to its final conclusion that, although it found no significant fault or malfeasance on the aqueduct project, opportunities for graft did exist, and if more time (and money) had been granted, it might have unearthed something.

After the Socialists demanded that the aqueduct investigation board (hereafter, AIB) have five members, with two Socialists to reflect the party's share of the vote in the previous election, the council opted for a panel of three engineers. The angered Socialists made good their threat to submit the matter as an initiative measure in a special election at the end of May. Until May, when the voters finally approved by a margin of 867 votes an investigation along the lines the Socialists proposed, little was accomplished other than raising hackles and spreading innuendo.

The conflict reflected the shifts in city government as certain Good Government proponents allied themselves with the Socialist-labor bloc while others briefly coalesced with conservative elements to combat what they regarded as the socialist menace, the extremism of the Harriman forces, and the discontents of labor. Not surprisingly, because the aqueduct was the largest public works project the city had ever undertaken, it also became the logical focus for controversy.[1]

After a flurry of fact-finding by detectives sent to gather data along the aqueduct and look for evidence of faulty construction or other grounds for criticizing the project, an initial report yielded only picayune faults (some mismanaged warehouses and theft, but no graft) while Mulholland himself had already documented the larger problems in his 1911 annual report (poor concrete construction, not from improper engineering but from "bad fortune"; the $140,000 spent on Caterpillar tractors that had proved inadequate on the rough terrain and had been abandoned in favor of mules). Other charges proved without merit, fostered by prejudiced parties living in the vicinity: that the main dam at Haiwee did not go down to bedrock, and that the water was not fit for use. With such meager and inconclusive testimony, board member Charles E. Warner announced that the committee would have to begin to subpoena persons alleged to have important information concerning the aqueduct work.[2]

Warner, who became the leading board member in the investigation, was an electrical engineer who had come to Los Angeles in 1908 after work in Vancouver, B. C.; Nova Scotia; and San Juan, Puerto Rico. Hired to inspect metal work and wiring in the city's newly completed Hall of Records, he afterwards become a confidential advisor to Mayor Alexander in an examination of telephone and electric light rates. Although identified as a member of Good Government, he had tangled with another Good Government man, Meyer Lissner, during the phone and light rate evaluations. Before setting out on an inspection tour of the aqueduct with two fellow investigators (engineers of an older and more conservative stripe), Warner not inconspicuously signaled his departure by being photographed in the get-up he was going to wear along the aqueduct: hobnailed boots, puttees, work pants, and a red flannel shirt. "Warner to Probe Aqueduct Disguised as Laborer," proclaimed the *Times*.[3]

SHARP WORDS AND INSOMNIA

When Arthur P. Davis of the Reclamation Service returned at this time from an aqueduct tour and acknowledged that no doubt mistakes had been made but it was "the best piece of work of a big project I have ever seen," Mulholland must have appreciated the generous words, for the stress of the job and the increasing dissension on all fronts was beginning to take its toll. (At home, too, his wife had begun her struggle with the cancer that eventually took her life.) He had consulted Dr. Powers about his insomnia and had been advised, "Rest and forget the existence of the aqueduct." Mulholland's idea of a "cure," however, was to wander through City Hall visiting old and new acquaintances, to whom he would confess, "The strain and the responsibility have shattered my health." He looked forward, he said, to a long rest.[4]

Mulholland's temper had grown shorter and his tongue sharper. In a long-standing disagreement, members of the San Fernando Mission Land Company, led by L. C. Brand, contended that the site of the San Fernando Reservoir had jeopardized certain of their lands and made claims against the city for flood damages sustained after heavy spring rains. The Chief, who was frequently at the dam site overseeing work, blew up in a denial of the charges and later wrote a note of apology to the company's agent, John Wilson, for his immoderate language. At the same time, in answering those who believed that the aqueduct had been built for favored land syndicates in the San Fernando Valley, after conceding that the land had been gobbled up, that the capitalists had captured the unearned increment, and that price hikes would slow the country's growth for the next twenty years, he made a wildly exaggerated claim during the Harriman campaign, often quoted as evidence that untold millions were made in the San Fernando Valley's so-called land grab. "Arable lands," he lashed out, "which should be selling at about $100 an acre have been seized by a few capitalists who have forced the prices to $1000 an acre." In fact, no record exists that any land in the San Fernando Valley then sold for that amount. Top prices for lots in the fledgling towns of Van Nuys and Owensmouth (Canoga Park) ranged from $250 to $500.[5]

The uncertainties of financing the aqueduct also exacerbated Mulholland's insomnia as Mathews again traveled to New York in February to find bond buyers. The New York bond syndicate, having noted the many municipal projects under way in Los Angeles (harbor, municipal railway, power distribution system, and park extensions), had refused its option to buy more aqueduct bonds until the city set a debt limit. By early April, however, the untiring attorney had succeeded in selling what bonds were necessary for continued progress on harbor and aqueduct construction, as well as for the development of electrical power.[6]

THE INVESTIGATORS COMMENCE

While the AIB was on its ten-day inspection tour of the aqueduct, Mulholland submitted his plans for distributing Owens River water, a sixty-page report that outlined delivery to the City of Los Angeles from the San Fernando reservoirs. It described the trunk lines that would carry the water and named the outlying cities that would also be served—altogether an area of 195,000 acres. A week later, while the council and other officials pondered this document of charts and complexities, the investigating committee returned from its tour a day early. Despite encountering snowstorms and mud, they had learned a great deal, but they would not make any statements until they had written their report.[7]

Within the week, however, Warner, with his showboat tendencies at full throttle and much against the wishes of his two colleagues, who considered the action premature, issued his own report, which focused on bad food and the need for better wages, ground already covered by the Socialists. After indicting Desmond, the report concluded with the gratuitous suggestion that humans should at least be treated as well as mules. The mayor, who had been his chief supporter, now accused Warner of impugning Mulholland's ability and integrity. Warner replied that he had never mentioned Mulholland's name, but "Uncle Aleck" labeled that mere sophistry and answered that as chief engineer of the project Mulholland was inevitably maligned by implication in such an assault. Meyer Lissner, now thoroughly hostile to Warner, had the *Tribune* reprint a piece he had written lauding Mulholland for *The American Magazine*. A week later, the division engineer and foreman at Grapevine and Sand Canyon sent Mulholland a report denouncing Warner's criticisms, which he felt were motivated by some animus rather than a plain desire to obtain facts. Warner had been in camp for one night, he claimed, had dined with him at the private club in the canyon, and never saw the mess rooms at meal times. (Warner rebutted this, saying he did not have to eat in the mess, as he already had testimony from workingmen who had.)[8]

Mulholland reserved his opinion of Warner for a later date, although he did complain at the time that the statements were unjust and seriously reflected upon his own management and reputation. General Chaffee, however, responded swiftly. First, he criticized Warner for issuing the report without consulting either him or Mulholland; next, he peremptorily renewed Desmond's contract with the aqueduct and awarded him a new one for the power bureau construction camps in San Francisquito Canyon. With battle lines drawn for a full-scale showdown, Warner, who had taken to his bed with rheumatism after the rigors of the first Owens Valley trip, offered to resign from public service. Rallying, however, he promised to fight back with a full store of ammunition. After a spirited debate, the city council approved Desmond's contracts with only one dissenting vote from a councilman sympathetic to Warner.[9]

As the AIB prepared to leave town for its second tour in early April, Warner defended himself in an appearance before the Alembic Club, a reform-minded organization whose membership included Socialists and Progressives such as Dr. John R. Haynes. Warner declared that he had been a Good Government man and that for years he had heard nothing but good about the aqueduct, had even remained skeptical about the Socialists' bad reports in the recent political campaign. Now, however, his experiences on the investigating committee had persuaded him otherwise. His chief barbs were for Chaffee and Desmond, as he insisted that no private contracts should have been granted on the aqueduct. Yet upon his return from a second inspection tour on April 17, he moderated his stance and reported that food conditions were somewhat improved.[10]

A CONSPIRACY THEORY

In the midst of this furor, Major Henry T. Lee of the public service commission died at seventy-one after a brief illness. He and Mulholland had been fellow partisans for the city since the days of the private water company, and his death not only meant the loss of a friend and ally but created a second vacancy on the public service board, which the mayor's new appointments were about to wrench with conflict. The two new members, both Good Government men (that is, Progressives), were soon to clash with Mulholland over proposals for distributing surplus aqueduct waters. Within weeks, another member of the commission resigned in disgust over the board's disharmony, and the mayor then made the unpopular move of naming his private secretary to the board, who by voting for himself, was able to become president of the commission, thus pushing out old-timer del Valle. This loss of the old with the emergence of new, not always congenial, associates who lacked their predecessors' knowledge and background soon proved another thorn in Mulholland's side.[11]

During these springtime turmoils, a seventy-one-page pamphlet began to circulate around town, doubtless calculated to influence the voters' decision at the May election on whether to continue the aqueduct investigation. The *Municipal News* (itself a new venture in Good Government journalism) announced in April that the Alembic Club had just printed a booklet on the aqueduct controversy entitled *The Conspiracy: An Exposure of the Owens River Water and San Fernando Valley Land Frauds*. Its author was none other than that ancient adversary of the city's water establishment, W. T. Spilman. As an effective propaganda instrument, it proved durable. Beginning in the factual manner of an engineering report, it sets out to establish that Los Angeles has ample nearby water resources but then gradually heightens an attack against the power structure of Los Angeles—government, business, industry, press, and engineers—claiming a collusion against a hard-pressed tax-paying citizenry in order to profit certain capitalists and land specula-tors. It repeats old charges of an artificial water famine and the unnec-essary secrecy of the Owens River scheme from Spilman's "Veritas" letters of 1907. As the language grows increasingly melodramatic with references to "dark and vile recesses," Spilman charges that the news-papers constitute a great combine that lies to the people, suppresses in-formation, and ruins reputations so that a few wealthy gentlemen can enjoy their millions. The tract ends with a small photograph of one for-lorn billboard standing amid scrub weeds and brush against a moun-tain background. Its caption, END OF THE LOS ANGELES AQUEDUCT, is accompanied by the following text:

> Thirty miles from Los Angeles, a dismal hole in the hill, strung about with debris and wreckage, lonely, deserted and desolate, marks the end of the Owens River Aqueduct. The signboard shown above was erected by the en-gineers. This stands a living monument, a confession of the conspirators that they deceived the people of Los Angeles when they drew such glowing word pictures of the pure water coming down from the base of the snowclad Sier-ras piped into their home. . . . The end of the Aqueduct is miles away. The in-vestigation is far from its end. It has but begun. There will be no signboard marking the end of the genuine investigation until the mask shall be torn from the faces of the exploiting hypocrites who pose as public benefactors.[12]

Mulholland received an early copy of *The Conspiracy* and sent his eval-uation to the AIB on April 16. After dismissing the publication as "too frantic and hysterical to require any notice whatsoever," he addressed only one point in which Spilman, in order to demonstrate that the aque-duct was unnecessary, contended that the local water supply from win-ter rainfall in the San Fernando Valley was greater than either Mulhol-land or Lippincott had claimed; that, indeed, it amounted to "almost double the capacity of the Croton Aqueduct which supplies New York with water, the capacity of which is 300,000,000 gallons daily." Mul-holland's refutation follows:

By turning to page 10 where the document attempts to deal with the origin of the water supply of the city of Los Angeles, it will be noticed that by the method of computing the run-off, all of which the writer of the pamphlet claims to be available for use by the City of Los Angeles, he takes the total rainfall over the whole watershed and assumes it to be without waste either for evaporation, plant life or any other source of loss and resolves it into a continuous stream of even flow throughout the year. Manifestly this reasoning will deceive no one, for even if it were assumed that the whole watershed were roofed with tin or other impervious material, the resulting stream would come no where near aggregating the total volume of the rainfall.

There are very few watersheds in Southern California with our meagre rainfall that will yield ten per cent of the volume of precipitation on an average. In fact we have occasional years here—we have experienced several of them in succession—when the runoff of some of our watersheds reaches the vanishing point.

I am prepared in a single day's examination to show Your Board both by physical observation, oral testimony of men who are familiar with all the flow of the San Fernando Basin and by documentary data relating to gaugings and extending over long periods of time that the winter sources of the Basin were long since fully utilized. Also; I am prepared to show that the Narrows Tunnel, which the author of this document declares to be useless, recovers practically all of the sub-flow passing down the Valley at that point.

I present this statement, apologizing to Your Board for the implied discounting of your intelligence by even this brief reference to the document.[13]

Another longtime bugbear, Frederick Finkle, now reappeared to demand an investigation of the quality of cement produced by the city's plant at Tehachapi. His group claimed to have been retained by the American Portland Cement Company to test the city's cement, but after they charged that they had been denied test samples, Mulholland exploded, declaring that their request was made in bad faith and that they had gone along the aqueduct in "a skulking manner": "They never came near my office to ask for permission to get the samples desired," he accused, "but sneaked up there [to Monolith] and at one place represented themselves as members of the city's investigating committee, and at another as reclamation engineers." He also accused Finkle of being "a professional disturber."[14]

WHERE WILL OWENS RIVER WATER GO?

By mid-May, only twenty-six miles of aqueduct remained uncompleted and hopes were expressed for water by the beginning of 1913, yet the question of distributing surplus water remained unsettled. Of the 20,000 inches of water that the aqueduct would soon deliver, the city, presently needed only 2,000. To decide how the overage should be distributed, three general questions had to be settled:

1. What districts should be served? Should Los Angeles insist upon annexation of cities needing water?
2. Who should pay for the distributing system? Should Los Angeles own all pipe lines?
3. What price should Los Angeles charge for the water?[15]

For the next two months Mulholland attended meeting after meeting addressed to these questions. He listened to groups from Pasadena, Santa Monica, Glendale, Long Beach, and the San Fernando Valley clamor for aqueduct water. He heard Pasadena object to annexation because Los Angeles had saloons, heard Santa Monica conversely complain that the city closed saloons on Sunday so that "a man had to buy a meal in order to obtain a glass of beer." He had to explain that San Pedro, in the midst of a water famine, had tied its own hands by signing a thirty-year franchise with the private Terminal Island Water Company, about which he was later to quip that to buy it would be like "accepting a present of a case of the itch." He was often attacked, sometimes treated to insults. During one harangue, a reporter described him as keeping his eyes glued to the ceiling throughout the diatribe.[16]

He remained adamant that any city or town that received aqueduct water should pay for its own distribution system. "Los Angeles should not spend one dollar on a distribution system," he declared, to which the new water commissioner, S. C. Graham, took issue, citing a report in April that argued the city should lay mains and pipes in order to supply maximum amounts to outlying territories, thereby insuring a steady market, keen competition, and by maintaining water running at full capacity, the production of electric power. Graham especially wanted to see delivery to the eastern San Gabriel Valley on what became known as the high line. This policy drew support from none other than Mulholland's special antagonist, Frederick Finkle, who declared he had severed his connections with Edison Company but remained a foe of the city's power plans and leaders. Also soon to clash with Mulholland was another Graham ally on the public service commission, Good Government appointee attorney Charles Wellborn.

Although the commission in mid-May acceded to Mulholland's plan to create the Franklin Canyon Dam and Tunnel through the Hollywood hills as part of the trunk line into the city, they had agreed upon nothing

Map 4. Annexations to the City of Los Angeles, 1899–1944 (Bureau of Governmental Research, University of California at Los Angeles).

else and Mulholland's patience was wearing thin. It snapped during a night session at the end of May when Wellborn remarked that after reading the reports, he doubted if Los Angeles needed Owens River water then or ever. Mulholland angrily rounded, "I am sorry that I ever had anything to do with the aqueduct. At the beginning there was a lot of you fellows pushing the aqueduct proposition along and you are now trying to delay things. We are holding these conferences night after night and getting nowhere. There are but two things to be done. Find out what territory you are going to sell the surplus water to and how much you are going to charge for it." This outburst seems to have settled down the committee to a serious policy discussion, during which Mulholland repeated his opposition to Graham's idea of demanding high prices for water. "All this talk about charging thirty, forty, and fifty dollars an acre for water is ridiculous," he insisted. "If you charge more than $10 an acre, there will be an interference with the prosperity march that is attracting so many strangers to the beautiful Southland." Commissioner Davidson voiced his belief that any municipality that wanted water should annex itself to Los Angeles, but no one seemed interested in dealing with that issue.[17]

After the stormy night session, a partial compromise was effected after attorney Mathews agreed with Wellborn and Henderson on a contract plan that combined Mulholland's insistence that each district receiving water should pay for its own distribution system and Graham's desire to put the water where it would pay the most. Fifteen-year contracts were to be issued for each inch of available surplus water (that is, 18,000 contracts) at ten dollars an acre. As one inch of water could irrigate seven and a half acres (based on a miner's inch, which was equivalent to almost 13,000 gallons of water every twenty-four hours), an owner could estimate the number of contracts he would need for his particular acreage. Tentative estimates of the proposed fees indicated that the method would be a money-maker for the city, but the city charter required a majority vote of the citizens before such a system could be put in place.[18]

Announcement of the contract plan provoked public debate, Finkle being among the first to offer opinions that bore a powerful resemblance to Graham's and Wellborn's (whom he had doubtless influenced). At a public lecture, he announced that he did not believe the city would ever use aqueduct water for general municipal service, and therefore the system of distribution (the high line) that he recommended would foil the designs of the land speculators and exploiters in the San Fernando Valley to seize the water. If the city charged high rates for the water (which Mulholland opposed), land profiteers would have to pay, and the city would profit accordingly. His argument proved to be a siren song to voters later in the year.[19]

The water commission's affairs seemed to unravel after another resignation left del Valle the solitary "old man" among a Good Government majority. In the meantime, Warner returned from yet another tour conveniently timed to coincide with the impending election, when voters would decide whether to continue the aqueduct investigation. Accompanying him was a reporter from the *Record* who published a bleak account of profiteering doctors and terrible, overpriced food managed by the careless Desmond. After voters approved continuing the investigation, the *Record* insisted upon calling the exercise the "People's Aqueduct Investigation" as it continued to denigrate the city's water establishment.[20]

SOME COMPLETIONS AND A MISHAP

At the end of May, plans began for the first stage of the aqueduct distribution system, the Franklin Tunnel between the San Fernando Valley and Franklin Canyon Reservoir, which would deliver water to Hollywood, Inglewood, Redondo Beach, and the areas west and southwest of the city. Even with the end in sight, between 2,000 and 3,000 men remained employed on the aqueduct at over forty work camps. On June 1, $2.5 million remained for the aqueduct's completion, and General Chaffee announced that if no accidents occurred the work would be finished with that amount on June 1, 1913. By now great salvage sales were disposing of equipment and material from the aqueduct, and discussions began over whether to sell the cement plant. The good news that the giant siphons at Jawbone and Soledad had been completed and were being tested came against the counterpoint of AIB charges that aqueduct mules were being improperly fed with hay containing foxtails. Although a flood at Cottonwood had destroyed an embankment, Mulholland estimated that the damage would not exceed $1,000, and in his seventh annual report (the last before the final report in 1916), he described the year along the aqueduct as one of "quiet industry." Still, the continuing attacks and accusations in the city had eroded morale, so that on June 14, as a sign of support, Mulholland and the advisory board sent letters of endorsement, praise, and approval to the engineers, officials, and workers along the aqueduct.[21]

To acknowledge the good work and to counteract some of the bad press resulting from the investigation and squabbles over water distribution, the Chamber of Commerce announced an evening smoker on June 18 to hear the latest progress reports on the aqueduct. It promised to be a grand affair in Agricultural Park, where a new art-glass ceiling portraying scenes of California's history was to be illuminated for the first time with power lights. Twelve hundred guests were expected, but the AIB struck a discordant note when, to demonstrate its independence from such doings, it issued a letter the day before the affair announcing that it was leaving on yet another tour of inspection, this one without two of the original committee members, who had refused to join them.[22]

These sparrings were suddenly pushed to the back pages when on early Sunday morning, June 16, the worst accident in the aqueduct's construction occurred. A dynamite explosion in the Clearwater Tunnel caved in the tunnel roof. Three men were killed instantly, while four others, badly injured, had to dig and claw their way to freedom. Many of the crew, largely Russian, who were timbering farther down the tunnel were also hurt by falling rock and debris. One mule survived and could be heard bawling within the dark earthen tomb from which it was rescued the following day. It was a sad ending for Superintendent John Gray after his record-breaking performance on the Elizabeth Tunnel, especially as one of the severely injured was his own son, Louis. The coroner's jury returned a verdict of "accidental powder explosion from causes unknown." A month later, more violence occurred in the same tunnel when a Russian named Boronoff and a Mexican named Morias fought a duel almost to the death with their miners' picks. Morias, the larger, had been bullying Boronoff for weeks, according to John Gray, and although savagely wounded by the enraged Russian, survived after a week in the hospital.[23]

Death and mayhem notwithstanding, the AIB continued its inspection tour while, according to which paper one read, a crowd of either 1,500 (*Examiner*), 2,500 (*Express*), or 3,000 (*Tribune*) gathered at the Exposition Building in Agricultural Park to greet Lieutenant Governor A. J. Wallace and to give a standing ovation to the man of the hour, William Mulholland. Wallace praised the city's water project and compared it to New York's, which was costing $160 million to bring water ninety miles to an already moist region, while Los Angeles's was costing only $24 million to bring half as much water 240 miles, mostly through an arid waste. He congratulated the people of Los Angeles on having a man who had accomplished this remarkable feat of engineering sagacity. Mulholland in turn revealed that when he first came to Los Angeles and was puzzling over what to do with his life, he heard a Spaniard say, "*El agua es la sangre de la tierra*" (Water is the blood of the soil). Struck by the phrase, he began his study of hydrography. Then, aided by a stereopticon, he presented views of the aqueduct, tunnels, lakes, and mountains to accompany his story. The *Record* sounded its sour note with an editorial column questioning Mulholland's candor, raising doubts about the purity of Owens River water, and marveling that men who probably considered themselves hardheaded businessmen could have sat and listened to an evening of such dubious statements.[24]

As a kind of rebuttal, Mulholland submitted a progress report to the advisory board stating that only twenty-two and a half miles of aqueduct remained to be completed. He spoke of the tunnel accident, saying that while such an occurrence was not unusual in this type of work, someone on the job doubtless had been careless or inadvertent. A rule now in place prohibited placing a cap on the fuse at the site where the powder was placed.[25]

MULHOLLAND ON THE HOT SEAT

How divided opinions about the aqueduct had become may be gauged by noting that a day after the *Record*'s attack on Mulholland, the main speaker at the Los Angeles High School commencement exercises, Colonel J. J. Steadman of the board of education, singled him out as an example of a man with a vision—not a visionary, he added—but one who was willing to see the bigness of things without losing sight of the practicalities involved in achieving the goals. The aqueduct and the Panama Canal both figured in his oration, which predicted a bright future for the city and urged those about to enter its life as young adults not to be afraid of work. Among those graduating was Mulholland's son Perry, who later sailed to San Francisco with his father, who was to consult with engineers over his and Lippincott's report earlier that year concerning the development of groundwaters in the Livermore Valley, as well as his latest report on the proposed Calaveras Creek Dam. Afterward, they took the Shasta Limited to Seattle to attend a session of the American Society of Civil Engineers, where Mulholland delivered an address on the aqueduct. After this busman's holiday, he was back at his desk on July 5, replying to a letter from former senator Frank Flint, who as a property owner in La Cañada wanted to know when the proposed high line would be built.[26]

Mulholland's answer to Flint must have reminded Mulholland of what lay ahead, as he politely explained that the board would have to make

the decision on the high line. Still, he could not suppress his own opposition to the plan as he warned that the construction would be slow, expensive, and that considerable time would elapse before such a pipeline
could be made ready for the water. "One single item of the survey as it
now stands is a tunnel with a length a little over four miles," he explained.
"This would be comparable only with the five-mile Elizabeth tunnel of
the Aqueduct by which the Owens River is to be carried under the crest
of the Coast Range, and which it has taken us about four years to ex-
cavate and line."[27]

Mulholland spent much of July giving evidence, beginning with the
AIB on July 10. A spirit of vindictiveness pervaded the hearings from the
outset, even in the manner by which Mulholland and General Chaffee
were summoned to appear. While riding together in a July 9 parade to
celebrate the departments of municipal government, they were accosted
and slapped with subpoenas. Mulholland, who had seen the most difficult parts of his master work accomplished in good shape, who had
weathered the economic crisis of 1910, and who had received the general approbation of the engineering fraternity, was now to have his competence and integrity challenged in a hearing that at times resembled a
kangaroo court and at others sank into a morass of insinuations and accusations. An *Express* reporter commented that during Mulholland's first
appearance "the attitude of the investigators was rather as if they were
trying to show that the city had acted crookedly or ruthlessly . . . or as
if the investigators were attorneys for the persons who lost to the city in
the contests decided by the United States land office in those contests over
water rights and water-bearing lands." He concluded that the controlling members of the board seemed more politically motivated and hostile to city government, past and present, than actually concerned with
the quality of the aqueduct. Rumors circulated that the committee was
acting under orders from the Socialist Party, and one disgruntled engineer claimed Warner had made a deal with the Socialists for their support in a future mayoral race, a charge that he denied.[28]

In the midst of the several days of Mulholland's testimony, two of
the original committee resigned and submitted a twenty-five-page report that approved the aqueduct project and protested the manner of
the investigation. This bombshell raised the question of the remaining
committee's legitimacy, but the court quickly validated it, and the investigation proceeded. Mulholland soldiered on with the process he himself had set in motion. At one session he blurted that the aqueduct was
worth $100 million to the city, and as if to fight fire with fire—or per-

haps even to lighten the tone with the Socialist committeemen—declared it the biggest socialistic proposition in Los Angeles, as it was being built for the entire community. His inquisitors remained implacable and humorless as they interrogated him for minute details on technical water data in the San Fernando Valley. At one point, when asked what percentage of rains ran off from the surface of all portions of the watershed having an elevation of 2,500 feet, Mulholland responded, "What kind of a memory do you think I have?"

"You've been making a study of these things for years, you say, and yet you can't answer that question?" sneered his questioner.

Mulholland retorted, "You've been studying law for years but you couldn't give me a citation without going to a book and looking at it."[29]

Asked about rumors that Fred Eaton had robbed the city by obtaining land in Owens Valley, Mulholland replied, "God bless him! I'd like to see a monument a mile high in his honor when the aqueduct is done. I've known him intimately ever since he was a boy. There isn't a straighter man on God's footstool in money matters. I'd trust him with carloads of money." Only once towards the end of his time on the hot seat did Mulholland seem to inject a personal note: "I've wanted to turn over to Los Angeles a magnificent heritage. If I couldn't see ahead five or six or seven years, the reward of approbation that will surely come when the aqueduct is done and the people realize what they have, I wouldn't be here, I couldn't go on with the work. I'm worn out—worn out." Yet he continued to cooperate with the committee and fulfilled his promise to provide it with any information it desired. A few days after his last appearance, he sent written answers to eight questions that Warner had submitted, the most absurd of which was, "What is the total water delivered to consumers unmetered?" Answer: "It is of course impossible to answer this question."[30]

After his stint before the AIB, Mulholland was called on July 24 to testify in a libel suit against General Otis; Harry Chandler; and the editor of the *Times*, Harry Andrews, brought by Frank Henderson, president of the public service commission. The suit had been provoked by a *Times* editorial accusing the mayor of politicizing the public service commission by naming the "spoils hunter" Graham and enabling the mayor's "little creature, Henderson" to become the head of the board. Otis, resplendent in his familiar white flannel suit and Panama hat, arrived in court accompanied by his less conspicuous son-in-law, Harry Chandler, and the almost nondescript Andrews. On the proceedings' third day, July 25, after a jury selection complicated by the veniremen's strong opin-

ions about Otis, Mulholland was called early to the witness stand to allow him to begin a scheduled inspection trip over the aqueduct later in
the day. Testifying for the prosecution, Mulholland was asked about the
editorial statement that Graham was out "to get Mulholland's scalp."
He denied the allegation, stating he and Graham were on good terms,
but under cross-examination by the *Times*'s attorney, he admitted that
between himself and Graham "a radical and insurmountable difference
exists and always will remain because I am strenuously opposed to
spreading water over one acre more than the supply warrants. Mr. Graham's plan includes 50,000 or 60,000 acres more than can be covered
by the water which will be available."[31]

His closely reasoned criticism of the Graham plan caused one reporter
to remark that "the examination brought out a large amount of interesting aqueduct history not pertinent to the matter in hand." Under oath,
Mulholland explained that not only did the Graham plan take the water
farther east than he thought financially reasonable, but it also covered
more land with the expectation of getting higher prices and greater revenues. He amplified his objection to such a scheme. "I look farther. I have
gone through one water famine and I don't want to see a repetition of
that. This is the essential and radical difference between Mr. Graham and
myself and I always freely and forcibly express it." To take water east of
Glendora would not be good policy, he explained, because that would
supply a territory not contiguous to the city. Moreover, Graham's plan
would entail an expense of millions, and did not make clear who would
do the distribution work. Mulholland proposed that a group of incorporated cities—Pasadena, Alhambra, Monrovia, and others—band together, arrange a bond issue, and carry the water there themselves. He
also stated his belief that landowners should bear the burden of paying
for distribution works, a matter the Graham plan left unclear. In conclusion, however, he repeated that he and Graham were amicable.[32]

Throughout the *Times* libel trial and on into the dog days of August,
the AIB continued to hear a parade of witnesses: Chaffee, Lippincott,
Mathews, and Van Norman. Eaton was summoned but indicated he was
unable to come and instead sent a letter describing how he had shown
Mulholland the water supply in Owens Valley in 1904 and how he had
secured the original option on the Rickey lands. E. T. Earl was queried
about his land deals in the San Fernando Valley, and former managing
editor of the *Los Angeles Examiner* Henry Loewenthal was trotted out
to repeat all of his 1905–1906 charges against the city, Mulholland, and

the San Fernando Valley land deals. In anticipation of similar questioning, Otis printed a long article in the *Times* about his land activities in
the San Fernando Valley.[33]

By the end of August, committee funds were depleted, and the city
council refused to grant more. One opponent, Martin Betkouski, declared, "I wouldn't trust these fellows with more money if they spend it
like they have the $10,000 they have had." The council also denied a re-
quest to publish 50,000 copies of the board's eight-volume report. What
finally appeared in January 1913 was an abridged version of 163 pages
in a hard-to-read tabloid format of four columns to a page. But the committee itself had already released many of its findings and conclusions to
the press almost before the hearings were over, its most sensational being a recommendation to take legal action against Fred Eaton for recovery
of property he had retained in his land dealings with the people. To be
included as defendants in the threatened suit were those who had engaged in those deals on behalf of the city: Mathews, Mulholland, and
members of the water board. The committee also reported a long list of
deficiencies and assertions: the aqueduct project had been unnecessary
because local water supplies had not been thoroughly developed; the city
lost over $2 million in its dealing with the New York bondsmen; the dam
at Owens River gorge should be 140 instead of 100 feet; the workmen
were neither well paid nor well fed. Then, with an air of regret, the committee reported that it had been unable to find any graft on the aqueduct, although it might have, given more time. With this conflicted and
unresolved conclusion, the investigation closed, but its effect was to perpetuate the divisive opinions about Los Angeles's water story; or, as Abraham Hoffman has understated, "its dual view of the aqueduct would
prove most irritatingly enduring."[34]

The mayor lost no time condemning the report, which Warner later
accused him of not having even read. While other city officials joined in
general disapprobation, Mulholland asked for a review by unbiased citizens and engineers. He impugned Warner indirectly when he spoke of
newcomers and upstarts who had attacked men grown gray in their service to the city, to which Warner snapped back that "Boss" Tweed had
also grown gray during his years exploiting New York. Mulholland did
not respond. To have seven years of complete dedication to a project end
with one's competence and integrity thus questioned had worn him out,
or as he remarked to his sons, "I can take the shit. It's the farts that wear
me down."[35]

THE END IN SIGHT

The issue of Graham's high line was to be decided in the November election along with a new city charter and an amendment to permit horse racing. Lippincott and Mathews took to the hustings to fight the Graham plan, but Mulholland, who had spoken his mind so often on the subject, fell silent. On November 6, when Woodrow Wilson was elected president of the United States, Los Angeles voters approved the Graham plan by almost two to one and banned horse racing by the same ratio. The AIB's findings against the "old guard" in water policy may have influenced many, but probably more convincing to the electorate was the Graham plan's promise that it would be a big revenue producer for the city.[36]

Mulholland continued silent as various aqueduct matters absorbed him at the end of 1912. Tunnel construction began on the Franklin Canyon line in the Hollywood hills. A labor shortage threatened, as growing troubles in the Balkans caused workers from those countries to leave and join the fight. Serbs, Greeks, Montenegrins, and Austrians—1,500 of them— had left the aqueduct by mid-December, and Mulholland feared their departure would delay completion. "They were among the best laborers on the Aqueduct," he said, "and we found some difficulty in replacing them." There being then little unemployment in Southern California, labor was in short supply.[37]

The Graham plan was about to get under way when a hitch arose. Although landowners along the San Gabriel Valley had raised funds to finance the tunnel construction, City Attorney Shenk and water attorney Mathews reported that two weeks of legal study had established that the water board by law could not accept such advance money but must finance the project with a bond issue. That stopped everything until the city fathers gathered the day after Christmas and set a date of February 11, 1913, for a bond election that would include the Graham plan. A photograph from the *Express* shows city leaders gathered around Mayor Alexander to ponder that news, and although it is usually not wise to read much into the expressions on faces in photographs, Mulholland, his curly hair bushier than usual, stands behind a phalanx of dignitaries including Mathews and del Valle looking for all the world like the cat that ate the canary. His silence about the Graham plan during the recent bond election had not been because he had nothing to say about it.[38]

As the year came to an end and the aqueduct increasingly became a reality, human interest stories and interviews with the Chief began to crop up in the papers: his views on duck-hunting ("I like ducks . . . especially roasted, with a touch of garlic"); his escape from Dame Fortune ("What do I want with a million? I wouldn't have it. I never wanted to be wealthy. All I did want was work. A job. And I guess I have it, at last."); and on the aqueduct ("When I get through working, and it's time for me to die and give some other fellow a turn at it, I want them to put this on my monument—just this—*that I helped to build the aqueduct*.").[39]

At year's end, on December 30, 1912, the mayor and the aqueduct men gathered downtown at the Richelieu cafe to honor General Chaffee's retirement from public works. Mulholland presented the general with a hammered brass desk set. "May the ink flowing from that stand ever make as an indelible mark as your justice and good example has on our hearts," he blarneyed. Toasts and tributes went round the table, including a welcome to Chaffee's successor, newcomer Edward Johnson, the engineer who had earlier resigned from the AIB in protest after becoming convinced of its bias.[40]

CHAPTER 19

The Completion of the Aqueduct

1913

WINDING DOWN

Many old-timers of Los Angeles would long remember 1913 not as the year that saw the completion of the Owens River Aqueduct but as the year of the Big Freeze. A cold wave the first week of January produced one of the worst freezes ever in Southern California. Eighty percent of crops were destroyed and the citrus industry crippled. One land developer who surveyed the damage from Pasadena to Monrovia reported that "things are so badly frozen that it is impossible to try and clean them up." Work on the aqueduct halted when the temperature dipped to 8°F at Haiwee and water froze in the pipes to the north. Lippincott reported that in Owens Valley the winter was the most severe in memory and that work and water stoppages would delay filling Haiwee Reservoir until April or May.[1]

Although only one mile remained to complete the aqueduct, problems great and small still arose. A mule had left with an unpaid board bill of $70.50. The advisory board thought that because Desmond had sometimes worked the animal he should pay the bill, but Van Norman thought the mule had done enough work to warrant the city's paying his tab. A mule owner renting to the city demanded recompense for a twenty-year-old mule he claimed had been returned physically unfit for work. He also put in a $250 claim for a $200 mule killed in a train accident. When Mulholland heard this, along with the information that the city had been paying $10.00 a month rent and $1.50 a month pasturage, he recommended, "Don't pay it; we never guaranteed immortality to rented mules." At this same time a mysterious theft of 120,000 sacks of cement at the city's Monolith plant was reported. As the advisory board pondered this peculiar loss that had yielded no clues as to the thieves, a January 17 flare-up fire on the Jawbone Division killed three men. A cigarette or pipe was believed to have been lit while the men were painting the inside of the siphon with a coal tar preparation mixed with distillate; or perhaps one of the candles that illuminated the interior had ignited the explosive mix. The victims, burnt beyond recognition, were simply described in the newspapers as "two Mexicans and an Irishman." The accident was especially sad coming as it did so near the end of a great project and not many months after the fatal dynamite explosion at Clearwater. Even with these tragic mishaps, however, the aqueduct's safety record remained remarkably good in view of the amount of high-hazard digging, blasting, and tunneling. About five million pounds of powder had been used in driving the tunnels, yet only five fatalities had resulted from explosions.[2]

Among the various challenges and uncertainties was a threatened suit from Natural Soda Products Company, whose owners included members of a pioneer Owens Valley family, the Wattersons, leaders in subsequent battles against Los Angeles. The company had initiated a suit in Inyo County against the city to prevent it from taking any water from Owens Valley, claiming that its prior riparian rights on Owens River took precedence over the city's claims. Although some believed it to be another attempt by the "power trust" to thwart the city's plans for distributing its own power, Mathews prepared for yet another legal action. Locally, the city council reluctantly issued the AIB report, in which opponents found a new source of ammunition for a continued attack on the city's water men. Circulars began to appear with a list of questions such as, "Do you want to know how the aqueduct money was spent?" Answers included allegations that the amount of water from Owens River would be less than promised; that the cost of the project would be much greater than projected; that taxpayers would be paying for the aqueduct until 1927; and that city water was being allowed to go free to private corporations while citizens' money was spent on the aqueduct.[3]

Of greater urgency to Mulholland, however, was his participation in a campaign against Graham's high line, which Mayor Alexander had included in the upcoming February bond election. On January 9, before a joint gathering of civic bodies to discuss and debate the issue, Mulholland minced no words, declaring that he had promised the people that they would not have to bear such costs. "If I build a house in this city I must pay to have the water carried to it. That is the right principle and I contend it should apply in this instance. If the orange growers and ranchers along the high line want the water," he advised, "let them dig into their pockets and pay for their system."[4]

MULHOLLAND FOR MAYOR?

To complicate Mulholland's already crowded life, Progressive leaders E. T. Earl, Meyer Lissner, and Charles Dwight Willard proposed at the end of January that he run for mayor, as Earl's newspapers, the *Express* and *Tribune,* had begun to urge his candidacy. He answered each with a polite refusal, but Earl, in a confidential letter to Lissner, insisted that the matter be pursued, feeling that Mulholland's refusal was not unequivocal, that "there is no other man in sight to solve some of the big problems that now confront the city," and that, moreover, he was the only man around who was electable. Publicly, Mulholland declared his devotion to the city but rejected the idea of running for mayor, saying that his first loyalty to the city was with the water department, where he had worked for thirty-two years.[5]

A week earlier, however, he had also written his old friend Willard a more complete explanation of his refusal as well as a candid self-analysis more revealing than any on record. Willard, still fighting tuberculosis and rusticating in the foothills of Pasadena, had during the holiday season composed a circular Christmas letter explaining that after four years of illness and the loss of his home by fire, he was still reasonably happy but hoped that his friends out in the "step-lively" world would feel disposed to send him a word or two, which he intended to put in a scrapbook to be labeled "Christmas 1912." Mulholland, because of his crowded schedule, managed to answer only after he himself was felled by a winter illness. While convalescing, he wrote on January 24, 1913, to express his admiration for Willard's "heroic spiritual resignation" in his struggle with a disease that had taken so many of Mulholland's own family. Then he tackled the question of running for mayor:

> I feel, however, that there is but one way for me to deal with this matter and that is to recognize my temperamental unfitness for the position of Mayor. It is not generally known but it is nevertheless a fact that in the execution of my work I have tendencies that are absolutely autocratic and at times unreasonably domineering. But I am also gifted with the skill of concealing this trait from those who serve with me. This I could not do, of course, in the position

of Mayor of this City where events move so rapidly that my impetuosity under necessarily quick action would reveal my weakness.

It has always been a great pride with me that I have been able to secure
and retain the loyal devotion of my co-workers, if not to myself personally, at
least to the projects I had in hand, but I feel quite certain that in the discharge
of the multifarious duties of Mayor I would utterly fail in this particular.[6]

With that subject seemingly put to rest, two weeks later a restored Mulholland attended the ceremonial turning on of water at the aqueduct intake above Independence. With a small party of engineers and city dignitaries, he and his associates turned the wheels to open the water gates
as Van Norman's wife, Bessie, broke a bottle of champagne on the simple
concrete structure that was to divert the Owens River waters to the City
of Los Angeles. Even today one is struck by the simplicity and undra-
matic aspect of the lonely weir whose purpose would animate such an
epic struggle in the years ahead. One onlooker that day remarked that
it seemed to him that "the source, the fountain of the great waterway
should be marked with a towering arch or some other fitting monument."
Just as the long-sought water at last began to run in the pipes, a torrential rain flooded part of Los Angeles, causing a high-spirited Mulholland
to jest that it was only "evaporation from Haiwee."[7]

TURNING ON THE FIRST FLOW

Mulholland's opponents, always on the scent for some possible misdeed,
seem to have either missed or overlooked the Chief's consulting work at
the Dominguez Rancho during this time. While Scattergood was being
criticized for taking work as a private consultant, Mulholland continued serving unremarked on the Dominguez Land Company's board of
directors. Upon his return from the intake and after the heavy rains of
February, he accompanied the foreman of the estate to view flood damage and make recommendations. Pressures of public life, however, soon
brought this activity to a halt and on February 28, he met with O'Melveny to settle accounts. They agreed on $400,000 as the cost of his part
of the work, for which Mulholland would receive 2.5 percent, or
$10,000. He had already received $3,000 in cash and agreed to accept
bonds of the Dominguez Land Company for the balance. The two men
proceeded to the bank, where he received seven bonds in full payment
for services.[8]

Mulholland's preoccupation was now with overseeing the aqueduct's
completion and the orderly closing down of construction. Although crit-

icisms continued (the *South Pasadena Record* ran a letter that claimed the aqueduct line was leaking and that Owens River water was unfit to drink), Mulholland returned in mid-March after inspecting the intake to report that water flowing into Haiwee had already created a lake two miles long by a quarter of a mile wide with a maximum depth of 35 feet. He admitted that some water had leaked from an inconsequential break in the line that had been quickly repaired, but all told, he declared, there had not been "two-bits worth of damage" since the water had been turned on. A few days later, he returned to the intake and turned the full flow of the Owens River into the first sixty-five miles of the aqueduct.[9]

Engineers Lippincott and Roderick McKay were meanwhile supervising the appraisal and sale of equipment, machinery, materials and supplies from the construction of the aqueduct. Everything from chisels, hammers, and lanterns to steam shovels and mules was on the block, and offers to buy came from Canada, the Midwest, and even Honolulu. Purchases at this municipal second-hand store required cash and all sales were final. The estimated inventory was $500,000, and by June 1913, over $300,000 worth of material had been sold. Negotiations were also afoot to sell the cement mill and excess lands, evaluated at $550,000.[10]

Aqueduct engineers also began to disperse. Because the project's fame had spread over the world, calls for its veterans' services and know-how came from South America, Mexico, and the Orient. Through Mulholland's recommendations and negotiations with a major engineering company in London, John Gray, after six years on the aqueduct and with a growing reputation because of his record-breaking work on the Elizabeth Tunnel, left with two of his foremen for Barcelona, Spain, where he took over the completion of a mile-long tramway tunnel that had run into construction difficulties. Also bound for Spain was J. S. "Jack" Taney, who began as a chain man in 1906 under E. A. Bayley, had advanced through the ranks—building the Grapevine and Jawbone Division roads—and now for the next four years was to oversee a Spanish irrigation and power project. He later wrote that the first man he met on the new job in Spain had been an aqueduct laborer at Mojave. De-Witt Reaburn, of the Saugus Division, went to Argentina as a locating engineer for a railway running to Chile but returned to Los Angeles in time to participate in the aqueduct celebrations in 1913 and later became the engineer of Mulholland Highway in the Hollywood hills. William C. Aston, as earlier mentioned, went to the Hawaiian Islands after completing the Elizabeth Tunnel; T. F. "Tommie" Flanigan, who "had everything in his noodle about a tunnel that he ought to know," and who had broken a record at Red Rock Canyon, went on to the Catskill Aqueduct; and Phil Wintz, builder of the Haiwee Dam, retired to his home in the West Adams section of Los Angeles. Others found their way to Japan, the Philippines, Brazil, Bolivia, and various sites on the Pacific Coast. Not only had the aqueduct proven a training ground for beginners and a graduate school for experienced professionals, its successful completion in record time had also enhanced its builders' reputations.[11]

Mulholland was later to say of all the thousands who had worked on the great project, who dug ditches, skinned mules, and drilled tunnels, his greatest sorrow was that "the millions of dollars that were spent for labor did the men who toiled on the aqueduct so little permanent good." He praised many of them as brave, loyal, and generous and others as "a roving, happy-go-lucky lot, who, even though many earned $5 or $6 or $7 a day, spent it all." In the midst of the satisfaction surrounding the aqueduct's completion, he paid them the following tribute:

> My sympathy is alive for these men, and most of the time raw and bleeding, to think that they do so much to so little purpose. I know this type of man; in my early life as a sailor I worked with them and slept with them, and I would rather be with them, to sit around camp with them, than to be in a circle of lawyers and doctors and bankers. Professional men are trained to conceal their thoughts, but these men are frank, blunt and human and a man gets more real insight into human life and affairs with them than with the other type. They were a grand lot, they did their work and took their chances in the tunnels, dry or wet, safe or indifferent, with gas or free from it, and in other dangerous jobs, and they spent their money like sailors ashore, and that is the one thing that saddens me today.[12]

CONTENTIOUS PARTIES

Throughout the spring, Los Angeles was caught up in a series of four contentious city elections that reflected the increasing complexity of the rapidly growing city. A new charter amendment had revamped election procedures that thereby legislated the entire current administration out of office six months early. The flurry of campaigning that ensued created a rift in the Progressive Party from which it was not to recover. With Job Harriman once more a mayoral candidate and their own party deeply divided, certain Progressive leaders, anxious to thwart a Socialist victory, revived the idea of running Mulholland for mayor. Nominally a Democrat but sympathetic to many of the Progressives' aims, especially municipal ownership of water and power, he seemed an ideal coalition candidate. He was also a popular and familiar public figure.

Earl and his editor, Edward Dickson, renewed their boom for Mulholland as mayor in the *Express* and *Tribune*, while the *Times*, which represented the most conservative voice of the Republican Party, immediately opposed, saying Mulholland should remain where he was. Although Earl's papers later blamed a "reactionary alliance" for Mulholland's elimination as a prospective candidate, the truth is that Mulholland dealt himself out. Even though he is remembered for having said that he would rather give birth to a porcupine backward than be mayor of Los Angeles, he had also been momentarily beguiled by the flattery, compliments and urgings, especially when a delegation of civic leaders arrived at his home one night to persuade him to run. His two oldest children, Rose and Perry, later recalled that when he had shown signs of weakening, Lillie Mulholland entered the parlor to register her opposition. The newspapers next day reported that Mulholland had buried his own political boom, while one eyewitness commented that Mrs. Mulholland was "very much opposed to his entering the political fight."[13]

Mulholland's next effort was to defeat Graham's high line in the April bond election, which asked voters to decide on eight projects affecting the city's future. In part because of his and Lippincott's well-publicized attacks on Graham's water plan (Mulholland called it "audacious rapacity"), voters trounced the high-line bonds two to one. General Otis expressed his pleasure in a rare note to Mulholland. "The pertinence and force of your arguments and the clarity of your sentences appeal to me strongly, as one who professes to know a little about the English language," blandished the general, adding in a postscript, "It was a glorious victory, and the advocates of the 'high line' canal tumbled off their perch in so sudden and violent a manner as to inflict deserved bruises upon their impotent carcasses."[14]

Although the water bonds to complete the aqueduct trunk line overwhelmingly won approval, the power bonds to develop municipal electricity fell 5,000 votes short of a two-thirds majority. Mulholland's efforts on behalf of power, however, evoked no praise from General Otis, whose *Times*, after championing municipal water development, opposed municipal power on the grounds that private power companies were already functioning in the city. Earl's *Tribune* blamed the defeat on Hearst, Otis, and the power trust for their unremitting attack against municipal power, but also questioned if voters had understood when they originally voted for the $23 million bond issue for the aqueduct and the preliminary $1.5 million for surveys and land purchases that they had in effect pledged themselves to vote future funds necessary to develop and distribute aqueduct power. Mulholland felt voters had been confused because the issue had not been presented clearly or precisely. He believed that if the ballot had been drafted with separate votes for development and distribution, voters would have approved the plan for generating power even if they might have rejected the distribution plan.[15]

THE SAND CANYON MISFORTUNE

Of major concern at this time were construction problems on the last of the great siphons in Sand Canyon, sixty miles north of Mojave and twenty-five miles south of the Haiwee Reservoir. This was an inverted siphon, or airtight pipe, by which the water was made to drop into the canyon below the grade level of the aqueduct and rise back out. Experimental and unique to the project, it comprised two underground tunnels, one down each side of the canyon and connected across by a steel pipe. Because the canyon seemed to be massive granite, the engineering experts had thought inclined pressure tunnels could accomplish a great savings. At the end of March, however, as water began to fill the pipes and pressure tests were applied, some seepage and leakage was observed. With increased pressure, blowouts began to occur. The first, at the end of March, tore away part of the siphon's north side. As the pressure was boosted, other breaks occurred. One on Sunday, April 20, only five days after the bond election, tore out part of the south side. After inspecting the damage, a frustrated Mulholland returned to the city with the announcement that the completion of the aqueduct probably would be delayed ninety days. All testing ended a month later, between May 18 and 20, when the final blowout convinced the Chief that the project had failed and must be replaced with a steel siphon.[16]

The siphon blowout at Sand Canyon was the single largest failure on the aqueduct, and Mulholland had had his doubts about its construction from the beginning. Because rock siphons of this type had been used on the New York Aqueduct and because of technical literature extolling them, the original consulting engineers tended to favor them over steel siphons. Mulholland, with his knowledge of seismic activity in California, had been dubious, but the eastern experts had overridden him. He had agreed to this one because the span was to be short and because the rock seemed to be solid. Now sadly vindicated by this costly failure, he announced that he was through with experiments, had wired orders for the necessary pipe, and would install a steel siphon. As the work camp at Sand Canyon was intact and the necessary equipment at hand, sixty men were immediately deployed under Van Norman to build a new, all-steel, aboveground siphon in another location across the canyon. The added cost was under $40,000, which Mulholland defended as representing only ⅛ of 1 percent of the total cost of the project. He also expressed the belief that the people of the city would not feel sorry for themselves because of this failed experiment. "We were all desirous of turning over this project to the city without a single accident, of course, but when we wished for that, we wished for a miracle." Optimists and boomers such as Frank Wiggins of the Chamber of Commerce used the delay as an opportunity to expand and embellish plans for an aqueduct celebration, while opponents such as the *Record* made dire predictions that the loss would come to $80,000. Setbacks notwithstanding, work on the aqueduct was coming to an end. On May 10, the board of public works announced that it would transfer all affairs of the aqueduct bureau to the control of the public service commission; Mulholland was to remain as head of the water department, while Lippincott would simply be paid $20 a day for time actually employed in helping Mulholland complete the report on the aqueduct.[17]

NEW FACES IN CITY POLITICS

The spring mayoral campaign kicked off with Job Harriman avowing "to lay bare the Aqueduct frame-up." Because he was no longer in contention as a candidate, Mulholland for the first time in his life campaigned for a friend, John W. Shenk, whose plurality had forced Harriman out of the race in the primary. Shenk finally lost by 8,000 votes after Harriman backers, organized labor, and Hearst's pro-labor *Examiner* threw their support to the primary candidate who had come in second, Henry Howard Rose, a somewhat unpredictable Republican. The new mayor was also an Episcopalian, a Mason, and an Elk who had come from Wisconsin to Los Angeles in 1888 and served in various legal capacities for the city since 1903. A police judge since 1905, he promised to fight vice and prostitution, strongly appealing to women who had only begun to vote and at a time when police corruption was still rife in a wide open city. Los Angeles had just witnessed a sensational morals trial involving a deputy district attorney accused of contributing to the delinquency of a sixteen-year-old girl. Further indicating this election's blurred political divisions and party lines is that while Socialists had supported Rose as an alternative to Shenk, whom they saw as representing conservative forces, non-Socialists helped elect to city council Fred Wheeler, who thereby became the first Socialist in Los Angeles history to win an elective position in city government.[18]

Because he had a busy schedule and also had been offended by the new mayor's labeling Shenk a puppet of conservative Progressives, Mulholland did not meet with Rose until two months after his election. Before that, however, a new set of charges forced the Chief to appear before the city council to defend himself against possible censure for having barred certain "people's representatives" from a trip to the aqueduct. After the election, while Mulholland and Lippincott were preparing the final annual aqueduct report, the Socialist members of the former AIB pursued their goals of wresting the Owens River project from its present managers and reclaiming from Fred Eaton certain of his Owens Valley lands. Working with an organization devised for these purposes, the Independent Civic League, former AIB investigator Henry A. Hart and his allies began to file nuisance suits against the city, beginning with one claiming that city residents were being cheated with "used water" from Owens Valley. When that had failed to generate much political heat, they turned to Fred Eaton and his Long Valley lands. Deciding to inspect the lands, they went before the city council to announce their need for funds to make the journey. Receiving the money, they next accused Mulholland of barring them from taking the trip and called for his censure. When he appeared in his own defense, he spoke at length; praised the aqueduct and the men who built it; called it "the big thing in my life," and vouched for its integrity, knowing that the project was "clean, straight, honest." Yet he also acknowledged that the continued attacks by innuendo and unsubstantiated charges had hurt the enterprise as well as himself. "I have not lost caste with my profession nor with the part of the community that knows," he declared, but he foresaw that "if you repeat a lie often enough those who do not know begin to accept it as truth."[19]

Of the suggested suit against Fred Eaton, he said, "I want to see the suit brought against Fred Eaton for which the enemies of the aqueduct have been clamoring, attacking on behalf of the city his right to the 4200 acres of Owens Valley lands which he retained when he turned the option for lands and water rights over to the city." He found it "a heartbreaking thing to have these charges scattered broadcast. They say Fred Eaton made a million dollars out of the deal. He is really a comparatively poor man, with his 4200 acres of grazing land of small value, while the city got 34,000 acres of valley land."

As for denying transportation to the investigators, Mulholland wryly acknowledged that if it had been possible and had they given him enough time, he would have hired a hearse, if it had been necessary, to take them along. As it was, he had received late notice on the afternoon of his and attorney Stephens's departure for Mojave. He had been in a water board meeting at the time and had no idea he was supposed to make travel arrangements for them. As for affronting the council, he wondered if the council had not affronted him in asking him "to act as nurse-maid to these men who have been persistent enemies of the Aqueduct."

He ended by praising progress on the aqueduct, which had just come through an epic desert cloudburst and flood that piled gravel and boulders in places over the line with only a few ribs of pipeline showing signs of cracking. Assigning September 12 as the projected completion date for the Sand Canyon siphon, he explained, "I have some sentiment on that score, as I left for my first trip over the route of the proposed aqueduct on that date, my birthday, and I told the boys on the job that I wanted the new steel siphon done by that time." After his peroration, even the lone councilman who had first voted to censure Mulholland abandoned his attempt as the entire council rejected sending the investigating party to the aqueduct and declared the incident closed. Eaton later filed a denial that he had taken aqueduct cement to make improvements on his ranch in Long Valley, and the city council formally exonerated him of this charge on December 18, 1913. The Independent Civic League waited to spring its next ambush in the weeks preceding the celebration of the aqueduct opening.[20]

A TIMELY COMPLETION

A week after his defense before the city council, Mulholland met Mayor Rose in an encounter described as "brief and cordial." Since taking office, Rose had honored his pledge to support the city's water and power projects, nor could his overhaul of the board of public works have displeased the Chief. He had replaced high-line defenders Graham and Henderson and two other Alexander appointees with longtime water loyalists and Democrats: banker Boyle Workman and former mayor Meredith "Pinkie" Snyder. Reginaldo del Valle, the only survivor from the old board, was at last elected president of the commission.[21]

On June 23, Mulholland submitted the report on the completion of the aqueduct, whose $24.6 million cost had met the original estimate. The city auditor later reported that after examining the books he gave high marks to the accounting on the aqueduct project although he had found certain discrepancies largely attributable to the inefficiency of some of the clerical force and some negligence on the part of division engineers to account properly for all the material used. His other cavil was that further savings could have been effected had other railroads than the Southern Pacific been given a chance to compete for the transcontinental freight. One item of mystery was $15,000 in unclaimed laborers' checks; about 5,000 checks had accumulated since 1907 and still awaited distribution in 1913.[22]

On the eve of the aqueduct's completion, questions of water distribution, annexation, and rate schedules continued to perplex the citizenry. Areas served by private companies were anxious to have aqueduct water, but not all wished to annex to Los Angeles. In the San Fernando Valley meetings were held amid sharp debate. Ranchers who had developed wells and used limited irrigation opposed annexation. Others, who wanted more irrigated agriculture and larger towns, favored it.[23]

On Friday, June 13, the city broke its record for water consumption when it used 69.4 million gallons, over 10 million more than the previous ten days' average. At this rate, worried the Chief, the supply would be exhausted in a year, even though by then aqueduct water would have arrived and the city's troubles would be over. By late September, however, a dry hot spell, a large downtown fire, and an outbreak of fires in the hills and mountains north of La Cañada and Tujunga made draws on the water supply that almost emptied Buena Vista Reservoir. Mulholland asked the people of the city to curtail watering gardens and to use water frugally. "I am not an alarmist. I am not in the habit of crying wolf. But in this case I want to say to the water users of the city that prodigality in the use of water for the next day or so may cost us dearly. The reservoirs are low and the consumption is higher than it has ever been in the history of the city water department." He reported that although the supply would be replenished in a few days, it would be drawing from underground basins in the San Fernando Valley that were being conserved for use a year hence. In short, as time drew near for the completion of the aqueduct, the city found itself dipping deep into its existing water capital.[24]

AQUEDUCT EUPHORIA

On September 1, a group of city fathers traveled to the north end of the San Fernando Valley to stand at the terminus of the aqueduct and witness the first flow of water down the spillway that Mulholland had named the Cascade. Days later, he left on the night train to Mojave for his last end-to-end inspection before the project's completion. Accompanying him were city councilman Martin F. Betkouski, city building inspector J. J. Backus, and journalist Alan Kelly, who had just completed an official history of the aqueduct. At Independence they were to meet Fred Eaton, who was then to guide Betkouski on a tour of Long Valley. Mayor Rose, planning to meet the group in Owens Valley, had set out earlier in the day with his chauffeur to travel alone by automobile. Ten days later, when Rose returned from his inspection tour, he commented that as far as he could determine, "criticism of the aqueduct is captious." He had seen an astonishing supply of pure sweet water, found Haiwee Reservoir filling up, and not, as had been rumored in the city, afloat with dead cattle and drowned varmints. Betkouski reaffirmed the mayor's findings and also spoke of the great surplus of water ("twice as much as the aqueduct will carry") and the need in future for a storage reservoir at Long Valley. A satisfied Mulholland reported that the rumored leak at Haiwee was water percolating through a lava formation that had holes in it like a Swiss cheese. When asked if he were worried about the "leak," he replied, "About as much as I am that the sun won't come up tomorrow. We'll get in there when we get ready and stop the percolation. But there's no hurry." (The stoppage was not accomplished until 1919.)[25]

Ten days later, on September 24, the Chief traveled along the line to see if the Sand Canyon siphon were ready to begin receiving water. After it had withstood its test and water flowed on its way to Fairmont Reservoir, he exulted that only an act of God could stop it now. For the next five days, with engineers McKay and Van Norman, he oversaw the 135-mile stretch of ditch and tunnel between Haiwee and Fairmont. Asked if there had been any ceremony when the gates were opened at Haiwee, he replied there was none. He had been thirty miles south of the reservoir and, after phoning the dam keeper to open the gates, simply waited overnight for the water's first appearance. "Perhaps we did start the water going without much hurrah," he amplified, "but there never has been much sentiment about the aqueduct—it has been a plain business proposition from start to finish, but a mighty big proposition." Reflecting that everything that could be said about the immensity of the work had been said a hundred times before, he asked that one fact be considered. "There are fifty-three miles of tunnel in the 217 miles of aqueduct's length. Just imagine riding at a good smart clip in an automobile for two or two and a half hours in total darkness through them, if it could be done, and you will have some idea of the mountainous character of the country traversed by the project."[26]

Excitement heightened all through October as the public was informed of the Owens River water's progress. On October 1, Mayor Rose opened the gates at Fairmont Reservoir along with Councilman Betkouski and the Chief. They made so many toasts to the city with water samples that Mulholland remarked that he was gratified for the sake of Los Angeles's reputation that it was water they were imbibing. The general spirit and expansiveness of celebration were enhanced by the mayor's proclamation to celebrate on October 10 the completion of the Culebra Cut on the Panama Canal, which would create the meeting of the waters of the Atlantic and Pacific Oceans and herald the promise of an unimaginable expansion of trade and traffic on the Pacific Coast. Flags were to be flown, bells rung, and schoolchildren told of this important day in the world's history.[27]

Civic spirits rose as each increment of the aqueduct line proved sound, but elsewhere voices of doom tolled their plaints of failure and wrongdoing. From Owens Valley came predictions that the project would prove to be a blunder; that the intake was in the wrong place and to receive pure water it would have to be relocated higher in the valley; and that city officials recently seen in Owens Valley with Fred Eaton may well have had more than mere sociability on their minds. Days after he had opened the gates at Fairmont and prepared to celebrate the blowing-out of the Culebra Cut, Mayor Rose was presented with a long document from the Independent Civic League requesting detailed information about the alleged secret conferences between city officials and Owens Valley representatives concerning water rights in the valley. The mayor replied that there had been only one meeting with Fred Eaton, on September 4 in the office of the public service commission. Accompanying Eaton, now chairman of an Owens Valley committee of water users of Big Pine Creek, was his fellow member, S. E. Vermilyea. The aim of the meeting had been "to bring about a better and clearer understanding of the water rights of the city and the owners in the Owens River Valley, thereby making it possible to better protect the city from encroachment by outside power companies and other interests." Rose also explained that neither Eaton's holdings on the Rickey lands in Long Valley nor any monetary amounts had been discussed.[28]

The sour notes were muted as the city prepared to receive its long-awaited water with an opening-day ceremony of cannon booms, fireworks, steam whistles, car horns, and a great banquet in the evening. The second day of festivity was to begin with a mammoth parade celebrating the city's industrial might, followed in the afternoon with ceremonies for the official opening of the County Museum of History, Science and Art at Exposition Park. As invitations went out, letters of congratulations came in from all over North America. By mid-October, Mulholland, water officials, and members of the celebration committee readied the spectacle to take place on November 5. They had turned on a head of between 8,000 and 9,000 inches of water to test the effect of the tumbling liquid, which at full capacity would roar down the spillway in a 20,000-inch cataract. "The big job is finished," Mulholland declared, "thanks to the faith of the people of Los Angeles, the loyalty and intelligence of the aqueduct workers, and to the cooperation and wise advisory course pursued by city officials. Nothing remains now but to shoot off a few firecrackers, turn on the water and tackle the next big job."[29]

As he knew, water issues never took a holiday, and the eve of the celebrations found Lippincott presenting a brief to the Colorado River Commission then in Los Angeles to hear Southwest arguments against four upper-Colorado diversion schemes, a topic that would increasingly dominate engineering interests once the aqueduct was complete. Meanwhile, Scattergood, head of the power bureau, was active in the current debate over whether to approve a $6.5 million power-bond election in mid-November. Most immediate, however, were the unresolved complexities of the city's relationships with parties in Owens Valley, especially those who had pending litigations over water and power rights in Inyo County. On October 19, a delegation from Inyo County met with Mayor Rose to seek ways to cooperate and set mutual goals. The mayor suggested that improved rail and highway connections would bring the two areas closer, but the Owens Valley Defense Association, which included large Inyo landholders, sought permanent stipulation of rights to the waters of the Owens River Valley. Still others attempted to adjudicate their differences over power development at the Owens River gorge. The ground for future battles was also being laid at this time, as the city began to consider claiming the water that fed the creeks at Mono Lake, a move that would bring increased conflict with private power companies such as Silver Lake Power Company.[30]

A few days before the official aqueduct opening, Mulholland and Mathews hastened to Independence for a day in court as the Natural Soda Products Company's suit got under way. With top western legal talent appearing for each side, the case generated a good deal of interest, some considering it the greatest water rights case ever tried in the West. The soda company contended that Owens Lake possessed at least

70 million tons of soda (some said the largest deposit anywhere in the world) and that removing the river's water would dry up and ruin the deposit (and the soda industry). On Saturday, November 1, after hearing the soda company's affidavits concerning its operations at Owens Lake, Mathews asked for, and was denied, a continuance so the city might better prepare its case. Mulholland once again testified as to the aqueduct's conception and history, while Mathews, who was later asked if it were not true that at least 80 percent of Owens River water would be used for irrigation in Southern California, refused to answer.[31]

"THERE IT IS. TAKE IT."

As Los Angeles geared up for its big day, the daily newspapers provided schedules and details of the coming ceremonials, as well as human interest items such as Mulholland's discovery while rooting in his closet for his formal wear that the family cat had lodged her new litter in his top hat; that moths had perforated his dress suit; and that his long-unused dress shirt had turned the shade of tufa cement. He thought the suit could be salvaged and a new shirt was not out of the question, but the hat he decided to leave to the cat and her kittens, declaring that in all the years he had owned the thing, he had worn it only twice—both times to funerals, and this occasion was to be no funeral. Mingling with the levity and jubilation, however, was the uncertainty of his wife's well-being. Only days before the crowning moment of his professional life, Lillie Mulholland had been forced to undergo critical surgery for uterine cancer. With her fate in doubt, daughters Rose and Lucile took her place at the opening ceremonies, during which they received word that she had "passed the danger line." A measure of the day's giddiness may be read in the story's headline: WATER CURES SICK WOMAN.[32]

Fred Eaton did not attend the ceremonies because he claimed the water tumbling down the Cascade that day would not be truly from Owens River but simply stored rainwater. This rather lame explanation, however, must have masked a tumult of warring emotions. Even though Mulholland publicly continued to champion and defend his old friend and certainly Eaton was everywhere credited with conceiving the idea of bringing Owens River water to Los Angeles, the two men's conflicting goals were driving them apart. Still determined to profit from his land deals in Owens Valley, Eaton had just consummated a sale of 6,000 acres in Long Valley to the Symon brothers, local landowners, for a reputed

$60,000 As chairman of a ditch-owners group, he also had produced an engineering report for water use on Big Pine Creek. Both activities were prelude to events that would explode in the 1920s.[33]

The city had never seen anything like the celebration of the aqueduct's completion. The intricate logistics of the two-day carnival had fallen largely to the Chamber of Commerce, which could later congratulate itself on a job well done. Crews from ships of the United States fleet that were in harbor were granted leave to join in the merriment; the Shriners were in town for a convention; and two nights before the big event, the San Fernando Valley received its first night illumination when the developers of the new towns of Van Nuys, Owensmouth (Canoga Park), and Marian (Reseda) turned on street lights along the recently completed Sherman Way. On Wednesday, November 5, at least 30,000 people (some said 50,000) converged at the site near present-day Sylmar in the San Fernando Valley to watch the water come down. They had traveled from the city and surrounding territories by car, buckboard, buggy, and special trains. Some made it a family outing with picnic lunches. One valley old-timer remembered in 1977 how "Dad put us all in that old Ford and we went up there and watched that water come down."

The weather was perfect: fair and sunny. The popular Catalina Island band played for the first hour as the crowd settled in around the open area below the Cascade and along the channel through which the released water would make its way across the San Fernando Valley towards the city. In the prevailing festive mood, cheers went up as dignitaries took their places on a grandstand erected for the occasion just below the Cascade. First to speak was Congressman William Stephens, followed by General Otis, resplendent in full dress as he paid tribute to his favorite hometown singer, Ellen Beach Yaw, who had composed an anthem for the occasion. Undaunted by gusting canyon breezes that blew the ostrich plumes of her elegant chapeau across her face and threatened to muffle her voice as well, "Lark Ellen" sang "California—Hail the Waters!"— "Lift your voices in gratitude/A river now is here."

Former governor George C. Pardee next delivered a classic oration with allusions to the ancient Romans and their aqueducts. History, he declared, tended to remember those who had destroyed human life—the conquerors—but the aqueduct that day, bringing pure water to the inhabitants of a great city, "ranks higher than the bloody accomplishments of all the Caesars; sets high among the great men of the world those whose genius has made it possible, and records among the great people of the earth the Californians who commanded that it should be built."

After the band played "I Love You, California," Mulholland was introduced—"the man who built the aqueduct." Amid the cheers, as one reporter described, a "slow, silent, tired man" came forward. Without notes and apparently unprepared, he made a brief, heartfelt speech. He thanked all those who had worked in partnership with him in the great enterprise and acknowledged the importance of the celebration not only to those present but to the entire municipality. As a steward of the people, he wished to render his account. He then sketched the reasons for building the aqueduct and paid homage to Fred Eaton, the pioneer of the project. "I am sorry that the man whom I consider the father of the aqueduct is not here, former Mayor Eaton. To him all the honor is due. He planned it—we simply put together the bricks and the mortar." Then, reverting to the imagery and language of the faith he had long ago abandoned, he concluded, "This rude platform is an altar, and on it we are consecrating this water supply and dedicating this aqueduct to you and your children and your children's children—for all time." He stopped then, as if pausing to collect his thoughts for another utterance, but instead brusquely said, "That's all," and went back to his seat.

The Chamber of Commerce then made a "surprise" presentation of handsome silver loving cups to Mulholland and Lippincott, the latter speaking in tribute to colleagues and workers, singling out for praise the work of General Chaffee. Chaffee, with four of the aqueduct engineers (Roderick McKay, D. L. Reaburn, A. C. Hansen, and H. A. Van Norman), stood above, manning the wheels that would open the gates. At the grand climax, Mulholland, the central figure in the scene, unfurled the Stars and Stripes as a signal to release the water.

> A stream of water began to trickle from beneath the big iron gates set in the concrete frame on the hillside. The gates ascended with painful slowness. The man at the flagpole stood inert, hearing nothing, noticing nothing, seeing nothing of the jubilant confusion about him.
>
> The stream grew into a flood, the flood into a torrent, the water boiled and seethed down the steep incline laid for it. It topped the rise immediately above the grandstand and came rushing over, pell-mell.
>
> Then, as he watched this miracle, the grizzled man sat down with a sigh that had a sob in it. For just a moment he closed his eyes. A smile replaced his drawn look, his shoulders straightened, his head was thrown back and he laughed—laughed like a boy.
>
> "Well, it's finished!" he said simply.[34]

In the happy confusion of aerial bombs and gun salutes that followed, the crowd moved forward to see and sample their new water. The program called for Mulholland to make a formal presentation of the project to the city, but amid the noisy, festive stampede and after his daughters had thrown their arms around him with expressions of love and pride, all he could manage to call out to Mayor Rose was, "There it is. Take it." Praised later as the greatest short speech ever made, it also became the best remembered moment of the occasion. The mayor could only reply, "Thank you," as he assured those around him that his prepared acceptance would be printed in the afternoon newspapers.

As Mulholland mingled afterwards and prepared to attend a celebratory luncheon party in nearby San Fernando, he found himself standing by a man watching the swiftly rushing aqueduct waters. "I wonder," mused the man, "how fast that water travels." Suddenly his hat—a Tyrolean felt adorned with a peacock feather—dropped off his head into the water and as he watched it sail away, Mulholland answered, "You'll find it at the dam in seven minutes."[35]

Two hundred dignitaries attended the lunch at Fred L. Boruff's San Fernando ranch. Boruff, who had married Ben Porter's widow, had been one of the valley's chief boosters for the aqueduct. After another round of tributes to Mulholland, Boruff presented him with a set of nested silver cups, each engraved with a scene from the aqueduct: the intake, Owens River, Haiwee Reservoir, and others. Again Mulholland praised those he had worked with, this time singling out for special commendation the mayors and General Chaffee. Even a bad city administration (Mayor Harper's), he declared, had produced the appointment of Chaffee, of whom he said, "Failure cannot come to anything that Southern California undertakes with such citizens. We are undoubtedly a people doomed to success."[36]

The banquet that night at the Alexandria Hotel was crowded with dignitaries and awash with oratory and more gifts as Chaffee acted as toastmaster. Like ancient Danes in their mead-hall celebrating and presenting gifts to a hero returned from a successful voyage, they feted and gifted Mulholland the Chief again at the end of the long exhausting day. Lippincott in his address, "He Who Goes to the Mountain Goes to His Mother," predicted that other communities of Southern California would again go to the eastern Sierra for water. The Engineers and Architects Association presented a scroll with a depiction of a Roman aqueduct, while a large bronze medallion came from the engineers of the Spring Valley Water Company ("From San Francisco Friends in Token of their appreciation of his worth as a man and his ability as an engineer"). Inscribed below a handsome bas relief of a crouching Native American holding a bowl up to a freshet of water flowing from a cleft stone were the words "He hath compassed the waters, with Bounds, until the day and night comes to an end."

By the time Mulholland rose to give the last speech, he must have been pixilated by the long day's overwhelming events, for he whimsically referred to his heritage with an account of an old Irish mate who had once advised him when he was debating whether to leave his life at sea. The mate had warned him that the reason the Irish did not succeed was that they lacked frugality and prudence. So, Mulholland explained, "I sort of figured that I would have to grow whiskers and wait for the restoration of the Democratic party to power, and then I would get a job as a policeman." Instead, he visited an uncle in Pittsburgh who was in the dry goods business and where he "tore off calico by the yard for about three months." His uncle (given the fictitious name of Duffy) lived where the coal trains went by and soon he learned, after hearing a thundering clatter above, that "Uncle Duffy" kept a goat tied on the tin roof of the house. Each time a train came by, the fireman on the train threw a lump of coal at the goat, which as his uncle explained, was how he laid in his winter supply of fuel. And so from that, Mulholland concluded his apocryphal tale, "I learned that even an Irishman may turn things to his account in unexpected ways and being more encouraged I came West."

Having delivered this curious preamble, he talked about the aqueduct, describing how in 1902 and 1903, the city had found itself in dire straits ("we were at our wits' end for water"). He spoke of Eaton; how he had proposed that they get water from the Sierras; how he had been up there on his own account, "with the purpose of exploiting that great water supply and had succeeded in getting options on a great deal of land." He admitted that he knew from the first they would have to buy Eaton out and praised the old water board that had been willing to gamble on the scheme ("it had red blood in its veins"). He applauded Mathews and his adroit management of aqueduct affairs ("there has never been a sacrifice of the city's interests") and admitted that although the criticism of the project was annoying, he kept much too busy to become nervous over it, knowing that when the water was finally delivered, all would bless its coming.[37]

What was so momentous in Los Angeles rated only a mention in San Francisco, then battling to create its own controversial Hetch Hetchy water project. Buried on the fifth page of the *San Francisco Chronicle* was a brief item headlined OWENS WATER IN HUGE AQUEDUCT. The front page of the *New York Times* heralded its own city's latest expansion of the Catskill Water Project by proclaiming its importance as an engineering feat second only to the Panama Canal—a claim Los Angeles was also making for its aqueduct. Back on page six was the Los Angeles story, headed PIPES WATER 250 MILES. The few lines devoted to the subject mentioned only General Chaffee by name. The *Boston Globe,* however, acknowledged editorially that the aqueduct was "one of the monumental engineering achievements of all ages, and of all lands." It had, moreover, been built without graft and for the benefit of the people and the municipality.[38]

CHAPTER 20

After the Aqueduct

1914–1919

IN THE WAKE: CRITICS AND ADMIRERS

Mulholland's pace did not slacken after the aqueduct hoopla. Five days later he was back in Independence for the soda works case. Shortly after he testified that Fred Eaton's water appropriations were on behalf of the City of Los Angeles and that work on the surveys and preliminary construction had begun one year before the city had voted its first bonds for the project, a writ of prohibition stopped the hearings. A change of venue had been requested, claiming conflict of interest as presiding Judge William D. Dehy was a riparian owner of Owens River property, and now an appellate court had enjoined Dehy from proceeding. Days later, Mulholland confronted the board of public works over its recent purchase of electrical machinery with aqueduct funds needed for tunnel building in San Francisquito Canyon. The resulting delay, he told them, would hinder the ultimate completion of the aqueduct. The next day, after receiving the silk flag he had unfurled at the opening ceremonies (purchased by a subscription of the office force) and expressing his pleasure and appreciation for the gift, he left on a night train to San Francisco, where he was scheduled to appear November 24 as an expert in a lawsuit between the fledgling East Bay Water Company and the City of Oakland. When asked during the deposition what difficulties he had encountered in the construction of the aqueduct, he replied, "The real difficulties of the Aqueduct were not the physical difficulties. They were human difficulties."[1]

Celebrations aside, the aqueduct would not be pronounced finished until the end of June 1914, when the trunk line across the San Fernando Valley and through Franklin Canyon began to deliver Owens River water to Los Angeles. As construction work continued through the winter, naysayers kept up their attacks, establishing a theme that would be heard in the years ahead as the city attempted to establish its municipal power system. Only three days after the civic celebration at the Cascade, Frederick Finkle published a long letter in the *Examiner* calling the celebration premature, the project incomplete, and the aqueduct's construction flawed. Predicting cost overruns and expressing doubts that the system would ever be able to deliver 20,000 inches of water as promised, he concluded the city would never receive more from Owens River than its leavings or wastewater because of prior claims to the upper reaches of the stream. "History," he prophesied, "will no doubt record that no one was benefitted by the celebration, except those having real estate for sale in the San Fernando Valley." The *Record* chimed in to report that "the monster Haiwee Reservoir" was leaking and insisted that Mulholland's $15,000 salary should be slashed by $5,000.[2]

Finkle was correct on one score: the great work could not be considered completed until both water and electric power had been brought to Los Angeles under municipal control, and this proved a long and difficult task. Whereas the city's business interests had fairly unanimously supported a municipal water system, opinion divided sharply on the power question, especially in the manner of its distribution, which had been under the control of private power companies now wanting to buy at wholesale the coming city system's power. The power companies delayed a decision to lease and/or sell their private distributing systems to the city as it pushed to resubmit to the voters the lately defeated $6.5 million power bond issue. Without funds to continue the project, aqueduct water would go unused for the production of power, and some warned that the aqueduct could prove to be a white elephant, or as one headline put it, AQUE-DUCT WATERS AT REST GATHER NO REVENUES. After a long and stormy session on March 1, the city council agreed to call a bond election in May.[3]

Mathews at this point announced his retirement as water bureau counsel to make his transition to the public service commission, where he began his long fight for city power. At the banquet in his honor, he was presented with a silver loving cup, and among the praises from his associates was Mulholland's. "I don't know how good a lawyer Mathews is, but I know he was always valuable in extricating us from difficulties into which we were continually falling. We would go to him and tell him we were in trouble again about something and he would get down Jones on torts and Smith on polygamy and go off there to the City Hall and fix it up somehow." He also used the occasion to take a swipe at the old city charter. "I don't know who was the author of the city charter we used to have, but I think I discerned from its literary style that it was written by the man who invented reinforced concrete. We used to be violating something that the charter prohibited all the time, but I may say that Mathews never failed to get us out of our scrapes." (In after years, Mulholland sometimes joked, "I did the work, but Mathews kept me out of jail.")[4]

A week after Mathews's "retirement" banquet, Charles "Charlie" Dwight Willard lost his long battle with tuberculosis. His funeral, held under the auspices of the Sunset Club, of which he had been a founder, lasted all afternoon. While an army of friends paid their final respects to one of the city's most ardent boosters, a driving rain developed into the fiercest storm Southern California had experienced since the aqueduct project began. (The season proved wet—23.31 inches—and its damage to Southern California led later in the year to the famous Reagan Report on flood control.) When word came from those who patrolled the aqueduct line that sand and debris had washed into the open conduit in Owens Valley and that boulders and trees had broken some concrete slabs and caused minor damage to a temporary dam near San Francisquito Creek, Mulholland left to inspect and oversee the repairs. Although damage proved slight, continued rainfall was to test the system further.[5]

The rains' most dramatic and publicized result was the collapse of about two hundred feet of siphon in the Antelope Valley when two concrete piers supporting it washed out. This gave Finkle new ammunition with which to attack Mulholland's competence, and in a trade journal, *The Contractor*, he wrote on March 7 that the mishap had been far more serious than the earlier failure at Sand Canyon and that these breakdowns stood in stark contrast to the excellence of the Edison plants, which had withstood the storm's onslaughts. Mulholland ignored the bad-mouthing and proceeded to repair the pipe just as he said he would. Introducing water at full pressure restored the siphon's original shape—as good as if it had never been damaged. The negative reports spurred Mayor Rose to an inspection tour of the aqueduct, but upon return in early April, he pronounced the horror stories of faulty construction "all bosh and invented by people who want to hurt the aqueduct." Earlier in March, J. Waldo Smith, of the Catskill Aqueduct, had also toured the system and pronounced it one of the greatest municipal accomplishments of mod-

ern history, giving high praise to its chief engineer who had achieved the
work "without suspicion of graft."[6]

With the spring campaign for power bonds came oddly assorted opposition from Finkle; the Independent Civic League; the *Record;* the Socialist journal *The Gopher;* the Building Trades Council; and the conservative *Los Angeles Times*. Not only did *The Gopher* ("Goes to the
roots" was its motto) accuse Mulholland of being in league with private
water and power companies; it also concocted a fiction that he was an
engineer of dubious, even sinister, character who took a huge salary from
the city while also receiving money for acting on behalf of a private water
company as well as for a power corporation owned by E. T. Earl that
had power rights on the Feather River. He was also later accused of ill-
treating labor on the aqueduct, while the Building Trades Council headlined him as a "Corporation Hireling on the City Payroll." The Chamber of Commerce remained divided on the power question, but even some
of its conservative leaders deplored Otis's "brazen aspersions" against
municipal power and, under the spirited influence of Dr. John Randolph
Haynes and his Progressive allies, finally gave its approval for the bonds.
Organized labor was split: the Central Labor Council approved passage
of the bonds; the Building Trades Council did not and was suspected of
receiving secret financing from the private power companies. In a vigorous and noisy campaign that again sent Scattergood and Mulholland
to the hustings, municipal power triumphed on May 8 when voters gave
a generous excess (56,183 for; 23,164 against) over the two-thirds vote
required for the bonds' passage.[7]

In a triumphant mood, Mulholland left the city to participate in a
happy event when, on May 12, the University of California at Berkeley
awarded him an honorary doctorate during its commencement exercises.
Two years earlier, Meyer Lissner had recommended the honor to Governor Johnson ("upon suggestion of one of Mulholland's most ardent
admirers in the engineering profession"). "The University would not
[only] honor the man but would honor itself by showing that it appreciated true achievements, whether coming from a college man or from a
man who has attained prominence through self-education, and it would
be thoroughly appreciated I assure you by the people in this end of the
state." Also honored were George Washington Goethals, chief engineer
of the Panama Canal, and David Starr Jordan, educator and president
of Stanford University. For a man who had never studied a day at any
university, it was a rare and deeply satisfying moment to march in academic procession to the Greek Theatre and receive this prize from the

hands of the university's president, Benjamin Ide Wheeler. As a prelude (and probably also to validate him professionally as he had no academic degrees), he was also granted membership into the largest engineering society in America, Tau Beta Pi.[8]

Five days later, Mulholland was back guiding a group of city officials and the new public service commission along the system, many of whom had never seen it. Shortly after, on May 27, the city council heard the Independent Civic League's demand to reduce Mulholland's salary from $15,000 to $7,000 and to dismiss Scattergood. The council denied both items, while one member declared, "I believe that if we paid Mulholland ten times his present salary, and he lived to draw it 150 years, we would still owe him a great deal." During this busy spring, the Chief wedged in an agreeable if somewhat quirky encounter with the builder of Egypt's Aswan Dam, Sir William Willcocks. The federal government had retained Willcocks, a world authority on irrigation and water systems, to inspect and report on reclamation projects in the West and Southwest. When the two Williams met, Sir William said, "I take my hat off to you," to which plain Bill replied, "Mine is already off to you." A tiny but vigorous octogenarian who insisted on taking a morning constitutional before embarking on a day of touring the southern end of the aqueduct, Willcocks must have impressed Mulholland favorably, for the Chief prevailed upon his ailing wife to make a rare appearance in his office that he might introduce her to the distinguished visitor. Both men spoke that night at a banquet in Willcocks's honor. Some attendees left disappointed when neither addressed serious questions of engineering and instead told stories of experiences in their work. Mulholland set the informal tone for the evening when he announced, "In England they have a custom of knighting men who distinguish themselves in their professions. In America it is the custom to roast them."[9]

THE CHIEF DEFENDS HIS WORK

With honors and distinguished visitors behind him, Mulholland began a project he had wished to see undertaken for the past ten years: the laying of a filtration bed to purify the water drawn from the Los Angeles River. Located at the Narrows on the old Hooker-Pomeroy land, the installation would free the surface water of impurities and also wash out the clay particles that discolored and muddied the present water supply. The system was to be used until aqueduct water was completely connected with the city water system, a process that would take several years.

A week later, Mulholland announced that the first delivery of aqueduct water to city mains from the Franklin Canyon pipeline had been completed. The system could now deliver 40 million gallons of water a day, yielding to the city a revenue of $200,000 a year. By the end of July, residents west of Western Avenue who had long complained of poor water service now reported that the water from Owens River was proving "softer and purer" than that to which they had been accustomed.[10]

Ironically, at this moment of success, a particularly malicious attack on the aqueduct began and would result in a long trial the following year. The familiar Socialist participants of the Aqueduct Investigation Board, H. A. Hart and attorney Ingle Carpenter, led the onslaught with a court appearance before Judge John D. Works in mid-August, at which they filed a petition for an injunction against the further use of aqueduct water on the grounds that it was a menace to public health. They produced depositions from city health officers and chemists questioning the sanitary conditions along the aqueduct's route. The *Record*, which had never ceased its anti-Otis attacks and accusations against San Fernando Valley millionaire profiteers with their links to Owens River water, jumped into the fray by printing sections of one report with the scare front-page headline AQUEDUCT WATER IS POISON. The subheadline, "Owens River Unfit For Humans Says Bacteriologist," was followed by a description of the filth and unsanitary conditions along the aqueduct. Three days later the second report was headlined AQUEDUCT WATER IS LIQUID MANURE.[11]

Mulholland protested, "The claim that Owens River water is not fit for human consumption is too preposterous to talk about—it is too outrageously ridiculous to even consider. I have had thousands of men working on the aqueduct, all drinking the water, and not a single instance of ill effect. Since the aqueduct water has been turned into the city mains I have had hundreds of letters congratulating me on its excellent quality." He branded the attempt "one of the most mendacious outrages that has been perpetrated on this city," an effort "to create public hysteria to promote private ends." He clinched his response with two hard questions. "Where are you going to get pure water if we haven't it in the Owens River Valley? If it isn't pure in the Sierras, where is it pure? There is not a water supply to any city of any size in the country that is as pure and free from contamination. The city of London draws its supply from a watershed where the inhabitation is 400 to the square mile, as against 1¼ per square mile in the Owens River Valley."[12]

The author of this alarmist report was Dr. Ethel Leonard, who, although currently residing in Chicago, had a long history of activity in the medical and health affairs of Los Angeles. Of remarkable accomplishment, Ethel Langdon Leonard, a native of Chicago, had graduated from medical school at the University of Southern California and done postgraduate work at Johns Hopkins, as well as further studies in England, Germany, and Canada. In 1903, under the city health officer, Dr. L. M. Powers, she became city bacteriologist and, in an age newly aware of the need for better hygiene and sanitation, seems to have been a zealous microbe hunter.[13]

Leonard's motives in lending her talents to attacking the aqueduct remain obscure. She later testified in court that she did not know her report would be published, although a posed newspaper photograph of her at work in her laboratory suggests she could not have been altogether innocent of the *Record*'s interest in her. Moreover, while working on a project in Chicago, she had been highly vocal to reporters there about the abominable condition of Owens River water, and in her report she wrote a pious self-justification. "Poisoning or polluting the wells is one of the most outrageous crimes known to history . . . and yet in Los Angeles we have the spectacle of a city government itself deliberately poisoning the entire water supply of the whole population. They are committing one of the worst offenses in all the category of crimes known to man. And the facts in my report prove it." In spite of these dire utterances, however, when she was requested to appear at the first court hearing in the fall, she declared she was too busy in Chicago to come west, although she indicated that she would be available for a payment of $1,000 and a round-trip railway ticket. Her terms denied and the hearing delayed, she did not appear in court until she was subpoenaed to the trial at the beginning of the following year.[14]

The city fathers closed ranks to defend the safety of the water while several leading bacteriologists and chemical engineers of impeccable credentials also vouched for its purity. At a preliminary hearing in September Mathews wondered who was financing this costly attack, and although guesses included the private power companies, bottled water suppliers, and the private Hollywood Union Water Company, denials arose from all quarters and the matter remained undetermined. Mulholland began to hear from engineers around the country who had received in the mail a small booklet containing Hart's and Carpenter's charges against the aqueduct water. Deploring the attempt to blacken his work and the city's reputation ("a most treasonable thing," he raged), the Chief continued to insist that it was the work of the power interests.[15]

Whatever the complexities of his life, Mulholland remained focused on engineering matters. While sitting home one evening "with nothing to do" during this post-aqueduct period he thought of a new (and better) method of concreting tunnels. Instead of the usual way of mixing concrete outside the tunnel and loading it onto cars and shoveling it out, he devised a system of forcing cement through pipes against the walls of the tunnel. When it was tried in the power tunnels at San Francisquito Canyon, it not only proved successful but reduced the expense by half.[16]

IS THE WATER PURE?

The trial to restrain Owens River water from Los Angeles took forty days in court during the first three months of 1915. While his wife was dying at home, Mulholland sat in court as Mathews defended the aqueduct. Among the early deponents and witnesses for the plaintiff were Owens Valley men who testified to the polluting presence of dead cattle and corral drainages into the creeks in the Owens River Valley. (One of these was George Watterson of the Watterson clan, later to play a prominent role in the valley's opposition to Mulholland and Los Angeles.) After Mathews attempted early on to discover who was behind the suit, the court ruled that the only issue to be considered was the purity of the water. Leonard reported her bacteriological findings but under cross-examination admitted that they were "of no value." At the end of January, Mulholland spent a day testifying and refuting the statements of a San Francisco bacteriologist who claimed that the canyon winds in Owens Valley moved the water too rapidly to allow for the devitalization of bacteria. When Mulholland set out to explain how water became purified in Haiwee Reservoir, he was challenged about his fitness to testify as an expert witness on geological matters, to which he replied, "I have been a student of geology for the last thirty years. I at first took it up as a sort of fad because I liked it, but soon found that it was useful to me in my profession as an engineer. Since then I have become familiar with the works of practically all the well-known authorities on the subject of geology, and on one occasion I qualified as an expert witness on geology." With the objection overruled, Mulholland spent the rest of the day on the stand explaining the principles of purification at work in a storage reservoir, explaining also that Haiwee is not properly a storage reservoir, as the water rushes through it from ingress to egress. He declared sanitary conditions along the Owens River and the aqueduct superior to those along the streams and watersheds of San Francisco, Oakland, Cincinnati, and many other cities. His testimony also provided a seminar on the winds of that area based on his years of observation. When he next appeared a few days later, he produced some moments of mirth as his patience wore thin with attorney Ingle Carpenter's unremittingly hostile objections and questions. When Carpenter asked, "Mr. Mulholland, how fast does water flow through a reservoir?" he shot back, "What's the use of answering a question like that? That's about as silly as how big is a piece of chalk? How do I know?"

When next goaded to comment on the "grossly polluted condition of the water as it enters Haiwee reservoir," Mulholland roared, "What do you mean by grossly? None of that water's polluted—let alone being grossly." He then proceeded to explain that it would take a drop of water from three to four years to flow from the intake at Owens River to the city's water mains. From Haiwee it would take sixty to seventy days, not the two or three contended by the plaintiff. The Haiwee itself is the purifier, he explained, and in comparing the amount of organic matter lying in its depth to that in the Catskill Reservoir supplying the City of New York, he declared, "The Haiwee is as a painted lily compared to that." He explained that on the site of the Catskill Reservoir had once stood four towns whose organic matter existed below to a depth of between thirty and forty feet.[17]

The heaviest blows to the plaintiff's case came when subsequent testimony by distinguished scientists corroborated Mulholland's claims. One of the world's leading bacteriologists, Dr. Edwin O. Jordan of the University of Chicago, whom the plaintiffs had frequently cited as an authority, undermined their contentions when he inspected the aqueduct and concluded that the "water at the effluent of the Haiwee reservoir is potable and safe for human consumption." The next powerful endorsement of the water's purity came with the testimony of Professor Charles Gilman Hyde, engineer for the state board of health and engineering professor at the University of California, Berkeley. He declared that if the waters of the Mississippi or Missouri Rivers in their most polluted state should be emptied into the upper reaches of the Los Angeles Aqueduct, Haiwee Reservoir would render the water wholesome and pure, so great was its capacity as a purifying agent. Del Valle of the water board remarked at the time that he wished the city's schoolchildren could have attended the hearings, for they would have received a liberal education in several of the sciences from leading authorities in their field.[18]

Finally, in the late afternoon of March 19, 1915, Judge Works announced his decision to deny the injunction and allow the city judgment for its costs in defending its water system. Mulholland stood with Mathews and upon hearing that they had prevailed, jubilantly exclaimed, "It's all said, you old tar heel, and I knew it ten years ago. Let's go drink some of that 'polluted stuff' they say comes from up the valley, just to show them how good it is." Mathews agreed that the aqueduct had just been put to the severest possible test and not been found wanting. The decision was appealed, however, and not until 1919 did the state supreme court make a final decision for the city. By then, it was academic, for as the president of the public service commission remarked at the time, "The aqueduct water has long ago been proved to be healthful and pure, and the fact that the city has the aqueduct supply to fall back on proves the wisdom of the project." In fact, in a ten-year period, cases of typhoid in Los Angeles had decreased from 20 per 100,000 in 1909 to 3 per 100,000 in 1919.[19]

Throughout the trial, Mulholland kept busy with other urgent water matters for the city. One weekend in late February, he traveled to Alameda to work out a sale of steam shovels as part of the aqueduct salvage program. As the San Fernando Reservoir, completed on January 22, began to fill with Owens River water and water lines were rapidly being extended to expand water service in the city, two vexing issues remained unresolved: annexation and buying up the remaining private water companies. After months of negotiation and debate, the Hollywood Union Company at last sold to the city, and on March 20, eligible voters of the sparsely settled San Fernando Valley chose almost unanimously to annex: 681 for and 25 against. As the next step was an election on May 4 to secure the city's approval, opposition to annexation arose from certain groups advocating the building of S. C. Graham's high line. When Graham argued his case in the city council, Mulholland rebutted by citing statistics showing that Graham, despite all his efforts, had not signed up as many users for water along the high line as were already prepared and anxious for aqueduct water in the San Fernando Valley.[20]

A DEATH AND NEW CHALLENGES

In early April 1915, with councilmen Betkouski and Wheeler, Mulholland escorted a party of Socialist office seekers along the aqueduct line in the valley in an attempt to win them to the cause of valley annexation. He had also planned to escort the same group to San Francisquito Canyon at the end of April, but instead remained with his wife, who was to die of cancer on April 28 at the age of forty-seven. The day of her funeral, the executive offices of the water department remained closed. (Even the collection offices were briefly shut.) All of the pallbearers were the Chief's close friends and water associates so that in death as in life, Lillie Mulholland was overshadowed by the events and men surrounding her husband.[21]

Now a widower with five grown but unmarried children, Mulholland increasingly allowed work and public life to dominate his existence. Two days after the funeral, he was back in his office, where, on April 30, he issued a public statement to the citizens of Los Angeles, recommending that they vote yes on annexation in the May 4 election. After a fiercely argued campaign, the annexation measures prevailed but were eclipsed by the amazing mayoral victory of the currently suspended chief of police, C. E. Sebastian, whose chief recommendation for office seems to have been his good looks. At the time of the election, Sebastian faced a felony charge of sexual misconduct; although acquitted of the immorality charges, he was forced to resign a year later in the wake of accusations of municipal corruption.[22]

For the next four or five years, Mulholland constantly improved and refined the city's water system. The long-awaited filtration gallery for purifying Los Angeles River water, for instance, went into operation in 1915. He occasionally acted as a troubleshooter as well. When he heard that ranchers and residents in the Zelzah area (today, Northridge) were stealing water from the Zelzah Ditch by secretly diverting it at night from the land to which it was being ditched, he went immediately to straighten the matter out in a powwow with valley ranchers. He sometimes found time for lesser projects as when, for the Panama-Pacific Exposition (1915–1916) and an annual meeting of the American Society of Civil Engineers where he was to read a paper on the aqueduct, he devised a scale relief map of the Owens River Aqueduct with a process he invented using layered vulcanized pasteboard to reproduce topographical surveys. (Subsequently the United States government adopted the method for making relief maps.) Because he understood that the average city-dweller had little idea of the magnitude of the project, he urged them to come and see an accurate replica at the department offices in the Knickerbocker Building at Olive near Seventh. "There is nothing like it in the whole world," he assured them.[23]

He continued to act as guide and diplomat along the aqueduct to a passing parade of politicians, officials, dignitaries, and visitors, many out west from Washington, D.C., to view reclamation projects, flood control plans, and aqueduct construction. Above all in the post-aqueduct years, he jousted with councilmen and mayors. Mayor Sebastian, who was supported (and possibly coerced) by the Municipal League, which had become stridently opposed to public power, tried to put through a cost-cutting budget by insisting upon the city's need for $500,000 from the water department. He succeeded in strong-arming the public service commission into conceding that it could spare $225,000 without injuring the progress of its expansion plans for water and power, but the power bureau, desperate for funds, requested and on August 29 received from the council $38,000 from its reserve fund for development work in the Owens River Gorge and Long Valley region. With this amount, work could continue until April 1917, when, the bureau hoped, the power bonds would be voted and approved. Part of the urgency was to hold off incursions from the private power companies: "The city of Los Angeles has some valuable holdings in the Long Valley region and the Owens River Gorge. . . . Certain private power interests are trying to get a foothold in the Owens River Gorge, but the city so far has been winning the fight."[24]

Scandal-ridden Mayor Sebastian retired in 1916 "for reasons of health," and the council replaced him with Frederic Thomas Woodman, a New England attorney who had come to California in 1908 because of his wife's delicate health and who, as a member of the harbor commission, had worked to quiet title and recover all the tide lands at the harbor. A civic booster and student of the administration of police affairs (an area of city government sorely in need of reform), Woodman, a staid conservative and somewhat colorless Republican and Mason, epitomized the white, Protestant male who now dominated the city's politics. The new mayor immediately announced that he could make no decisions on the power matter until he had toured the aqueduct. When he told Mulholland to go with him, he received a curt response. "Is that your order?"

To which the mayor replied, "That is my order."

"Then I will go," rejoined Mulholland.[25]

After four days along the line, Mayor Woodman returned to the city declaring his commitment to developing municipal power and a willingness to mediate the disputes with the private power companies. During his administration, however, the water and power men suffered defeat when voters trounced the important 1917 bond measure. It was to have funded the completion of generating facilities at what would become Power House No. 2 in San Francisquito Canyon and to have paid for land and rights for future development along the Owens River Gorge. The combined opposition of the *Times* and *Record*, of various business groups (including the revived Committee of 1000, largely the creature of the Edison Company), of parties that hinted the city was secretly in league with private power and intended ultimately to sell to the power trust—all these foes of varying persuasions, as well as general resistance to an increased tax load, handed the water and power establishment one of its worst defeats. A 40 percent turnout delivered a vote of 33,370 for and 51,267 against the power bonds. Labor, which had supported municipal power, also found itself a heavy loser, as bond passage would have resulted in jobs for members of its local unions. The defeat at the polls also reflected the waning of progressivism and the ascendancy of conservatism in an increasingly business-minded and open-shop city. The bonds did not succeed until after World War I, when in June 1919, they passed with 4,000 more votes than needed for a two-thirds majority, 46,656 for and 21,248 against. At that time, voters also swept Woodman out of office and replaced him with former mayor Meredith "Pinky" Snyder.[26]

During the successful campaign against municipal power in 1917, while the *Times* decried public power as a Socialist plot, the *Record* expressed its opposition to the water-power establishment with a series of clever, albeit vicious, cartoons portraying Mulholland and Scattergood as a pair of broken-down vaudeville comedians, Mul and Skat, constantly harried in their attempts to nurse back to health a strange-looking creature known as Acqua-Duck, or Bill's Ducky. Ducky resembled the Tik-Tok man of Oz, a spherical duck-billed creature of iron-plated patchwork possessed of an insatiable appetite for taxpayer dollars, which its desperate caretakers attempted to satisfy by bilking taxpayers of their hard-earned money. A more serious note was struck when warnings of a dynamiting plot at Haiwee forced the city to place extra guards along the aqueduct. At this same time, the Owens Valley newspaper, the *Inyo Register,* began to reprint the *Record*'s attacks amid reports of increasing resistance in the north to the city's plans for municipal power.[27]

BLOWOUTS AND RUMORS OF RETIREMENT

On July 11, shortly after the disastrous bond election and a heat wave that produced record-breaking drains on the water supply, an Owens Valley earthquake cracked a piece of the aqueduct in the Alabama hills. At the time, Mulholland was overseeing the installation of filtration galleries to purify irrigation water for domestic use in the Boyle Heights district and preparing to begin work on the Chatsworth Reservoir. Hastening to the scene, Mulholland promised immediate repair, but later, on Sunday, July 15, at one o'clock in the afternoon, he received word at home that two new blowouts had occurred along the aqueduct: one near Neenach in the Antelope Valley, the other near Little Lake south of Haiwee. He set out immediately for Neenach, while Van Norman hurried down from Haiwee to Little Lake. Mayor Woodman blurted that he suspected dynamitings, which produced headlines along with his declaration that he would place added guards along the aqueduct and near reservoirs with orders of "Shoot to Kill." Mulholland deplored disseminating such alarmist information without verification and, after an inspection of the break near Neenach, phoned a more cautious statement to his secretary, Burt Heinly. "Two widely separated and serious breaks occurred in the Los Angeles Aqueduct early this morning. I have investigated one of them and can say that there are circumstances which make me suspicious as to the agency responsible. I do not want to charge that some outside agency is responsible for what has happened. A most thorough inquiry will be made to learn just what happened and just why the breaks occurred."[28] What Mulholland had discovered near Neenach was a sixty-foot break in the line, which he estimated would require three days to repair. Van Norman reported more extensive destruction near Little Lake, where the damaged tunnel had blocked water flow and caused flooding that washed out two hundred feet of rail track and weakened the supports of a bridge so that a southbound freight train partially derailed when it crossed the weakened structure. The water engineers at first observed that both breaks had in common a proximity to manholes that, although securely covered, could have been easily opened so that an explosive could be dropped into the conduit. After a week of inspection, however, Mulholland concluded that the break near Little Lake resulted from earthquake. He remained suspicious of the Neenach break, however, and extra surveillance along that stretch of the line produced the arrest of one man after he had been observed loitering for four days in the vicinity of Fairmont Dam. Suspicions increased when he turned out to be an employee of the city's foe, the Los Angeles Gas and Electric Corporation, especially after he could not account for his presence there. Although taken into custody, he was later released.[29]

Mulholland and Van Norman spent the remainder of July examining and overseeing repairs, while down in the city, the *Record* used the blowouts as a pretext to renew its attack on Mulholland's competence. These attacks against the water and power establishment sufficiently swayed Mayor Woodman that at the end of summer he requested a complete audit of the public service commission by a disinterested accountant, with the results to be made public. Woodman also defended his public statements about dynamitings, saying he thought the public should be informed and that Mulholland's silence on the matter presented an appearance of secrecy. After accusing him and Scattergood of "too much of the star chamber idea in their methods," the mayor declared his intention to make changes on the water board, adding that although good engineers, the two leaders were not successes as executives.[30]

With gossip about Woodman's possible shake-up of the public service commission rife in City Hall, four members handed in their resignations, while the *Record* crowed that it alone was responsible for defeating "Invisible Government," "Earlism," and "the schemes of Bill Mulholland." Through all these flaps, Mulholland remained silent. He had seen mayors and administrations come and go while he remained a fixture on the civic landscape. At sixty-two, he had learned to control his temper most of the time, and he remained clear about one of his missions: to keep whoever was mayor on the path of supporting municipal water and power. Private concerns took much of his time and energy in 1918, which led to rumors of his retirement, but the hopes of those who wished to see him disappear were dashed in January 1919, when he announced that he had no thought of retiring.[31]

A GROWING CITY DURING WORLD WAR I

In spite of crises and interruptions, by the end of the decade, Los Angeles had created a reliable water supply for its population of 533,535 (which now outstripped its northern rival, San Francisco, with 471,023). Growth, however, meant the need to convince citizens to vote funds for a continued expansion of water and power services and to familiarize them with issues often complex, unclear, and usually to a layman, matters of indifference. As World War I ended with its lifting of domestic restrictions, plans and hopes for municipal power quickened. When construction began on cottages and facilities in San Francisquito Canyon, even the unfriendly *Los Angeles Times* printed a Sunday feature piece on construction there of Power Plant No. 2 with the headline CITY REARS NEW TEMPLE OF THOR. With unabated growth and bustle in the city, as well as continued annexation (Sawtelle came in, and the Dominguez and Palos Verdes Ranchos planned to join in the near future), concern for increased demands on water supplies continued. By March 1919, only 6.07 inches of rain had fallen (the season's total would be 8.62 inches), so that by midsummer, when San Fernando Valley ranchers were at the peak of their irrigation season and Mulholland expected them to use one-third more than they had the year before, he cautioned them to organize, to learn to take their turns, and in some cases, to rely on night irrigation. Planning ahead for a possible drought, he directed Van Norman to begin drilling 100 wells in Owens Valley as a precautionary measure, while in August, work began on the large reservoir known as San Fernando No. 1, north of No. 2. Repairs to the leak that had long plagued Haiwee Dam finally became possible when its lowered water level revealed the problem to be a crevasse in the side of the canyon near the dam.[32]

Shortly before Christmas 1919, as a harbinger to the turbulent decade ahead, word came from Washington, D.C., that the all-important power right-of-way bill was in trouble. Nine large power companies, along with Inyo-Kern power and irrigation project advocates, had blocked this legislation that would have cleared up titles to the aqueduct's power line rights-of-way. Mathews, just back from the capital, was forced to turn around and return, while Mulholland was alerted that he would probably be needed to testify in the Senate early in the new year.[33]

CHAPTER 21

A Stormy Decade Begins

1920–1923

THOUGHTS OF BOULDER DAM

The fight for municipal power in Los Angeles and the later campaign to build the federal project of Boulder Dam occurred during the politically reactionary years of the Harding, Coolidge, and Hoover administrations and produced some of the ugliest political hate campaigns in the history of the West. Permanent scars yet remain on the reputations of those who battled in those wars, for the private interests proved almost insuperable adversaries against the advocates of public ownership. Not until 1936, a year after Mulholland's death, would the municipalization of power in Los Angeles be fully realized, nor did the Chief live to see the completion of Boulder Dam and the Colorado River Aqueduct. In those years of struggle when hopes rose only to be dashed, skillfully crafted propaganda campaigns against the city's aims so artfully manipulated public sentiment and made such deep inroads into the popular psyche that many of the spurious charges not only were believed but have long since grown entrenched. As Tom Sitton has written in his biography of municipal power champion John Randolph Haynes, "The legacy of this struggle is a never-ending parade of historical accounts, some expounding conspiracy theories and others staunchly defending Los Angeles in its quest for Owens Valley water."[1]

In early April 1920, Mulholland left for Washington, D.C., with Scattergood, Mathews, and the president of city council, Ralph Criswell, to appeal to the Senate for passage of the aqueduct right-of-way bill. At the time, Mulholland and his family were in the throes of settling into a new home at 426 South Saint Andrews Place in the recently opened Windsor Square Tract after leaving Boyle Heights, where they had lived for twenty-five years. Daughter Rose recalled that after "Papa" had assured her he was all packed for the trip, she investigated the Gladstone bag he always carried and discovered its entire contents to consist of two clean collars and a bottle of whiskey. The passage of the important amendment was to insure the city against encroachments from private power companies in Inyo County, but within two weeks of their arrival in Washington, the attorney for the Southern Sierra and Nevada-California Power Companies made a surprise attack, challenging the city's power right-of-way for the Owens River Gorge below the Long Valley Reservoir. The city, he argued, had water rights but not power rights in the land it had acquired. If upheld, the claim would have thrown the city into years of litigation. Mathews and Mulholland argued otherwise and ultimately prevailed when the bill was approved June 5, but similar land mines threatened each step on the long tortuous path.[2]

SOME PENALTIES OF RAPID GROWTH

By 1920, Los Angeles had in part fallen victim to its own success, which in many quarters excited hostility, not to say envy and its counterpart, derision. It was now the tenth most populous city in the United States (estimated at 730,000); its aqueduct was a triumph, as was its harbor; agriculture in the San Fernando Valley had earned $13 million in 1919; and a thriving movie industry was gaining worldwide fame and popularity. When Mulholland participated in a panel at the Sunset Club in 1921 to discuss "Some of the Penalties of Rapid Growth in Los Angeles," he must have cited as one penalty the increasing need for resources that others were loath to share or part with. As the statewide competition for water supplies grew through the decade, so would animosities.

The city's success was predicated on an efficient municipal water organization's providing an adequate supply at low rates, along with a growing power system able to produce low-priced electricity in competition with existing private systems. In the spring of 1920, for example, when the state railroad commission granted Edison Electric Company a 27 percent rate increase, the city's power bureau announced that it would not raise light rates. Later in the year, when Mulholland announced the need to increase water rates, he countered protests by pointing out that Los Angeles's metered rates were lower than the average

Map 5. Greater Los Angeles, 1925 (adapted from Lester S. Ready, J. O. Marsh, and Richard Sachse, *Joint Report on Street Railway Survey, City of Los Angeles to the Railroad Commission of the State of California* [Los Angeles, 1925], Los Angeles Department of Public Utilities).

maximum and minimum rates for the forty-nine largest cities in the United States.[3]

As the city pressed its cause in Washington for additional water rights to ensure a greater production of hydroelectric power, a statewide flurry of protests arose. The previous winter (1919–1920) had been dry. Much of California suffered from drought, and by late summer, such acute power shortages occurred in the north that San Francisco had to curtail commercial sign and window lighting. Yet with Haiwee Dam full and other storage areas in good supply, Los Angeles was not severely affected. Neighboring communities, however, did not applaud this success. Bakersfield was suffering, and one of its editors, remarking on Los Angeles's recent victory in Congress allowing it to purchase water rights in Mono Basin, warned that "Los Angeles has its eyes on Mono lake waters and if she can freeze out a few homesteaders she will be without just that much opposition in the final grab." When San Francisco city officials learned that Los Angeles had made preliminary filings for possible power plants on both the Tuolumne and Merced Rivers as well as Yosemite Creek, they threatened action along with the Sierra Club. Mathews hastened to assure all parties that Los Angeles would undertake no project that would conflict with any San Francisco plan, but headlines in Bakersfield and Owens Valley papers quickly protested the city's "mad grab of all water and hydro-electric rights in Southern and Central California." The *Bakersfield Californian* condemned Los Angeles as a "water hog" and described its public service commission as "a group of radicals and public ownership faddists," while an Owens Valley paper declared BISHOP WILL ASSIST IN CURBING L. A. At a town meeting held in Bishop in July 1920, one lone dissenter dared to say he thought the local hysteria was a movement "favored by the Southern Sierras Power Company."[4]

The Bakersfield editor also acknowledged that his information about Los Angeles and Owens Valley came largely from the Los Angeles *Record,* which, acting as the exchange editor, was supplying material about "the outrage of smaller communities over L. A.'s water-grabbing." The *Record* also resumed its old vendetta against Mulholland, now referring to him as "Aqueduct Bill" and portraying him as an intractable curmudgeon. According to the *Record,* when Aqueduct Bill offered an opinion, he never "spoke" or "uttered"; instead, he "grunted" or "wrathfully charged." Scare headlines warned of possible water famine and polluted aqueduct water under Aqueduct Bill's mismanagement, while cartoons of "Bill's Acqua-Duck" ridiculed both his engineering and business ability.[5]

Map 6. Southern California water supply, 1925 (Los Angeles Department of Water and Power).

Against this backdrop of negative comment appeared an increasing number of articles couching the city's behavior in terms of theft, rape, and exploitation. An August 3, 1921, editorial in the conservative *Bakersfield Californian* forcefully struck the theme. "Los Angeles, preoccupied in the task of working out its splendid destiny, has long failed to realize that there are penalties attached to ruthless aggression and disregard of the rights of others." As this campaign expanded through the state, a story evolved to resonate with the sentimental fiction of the Old West and wring the hearts of all who champion the underdog. Written and rewritten in many places throughout the decade, it became an enduring tale of the sad fate of decent, modest pioneer folk betrayed and skinned by highbinders and money boys from the city. Other than an occasional grumbling comment throughout the war years, Owens Valley newspapers had said little about Los Angeles. The aqueduct builders' and workers' presence in Owens Valley seemed no longer noteworthy, and although certain locals harbored animosity, relationships overall had been peaceful. Then abruptly, in 1920, seven years after the aqueduct had been completed and fifteen since the whole enterprise began, many valley residents and land owners, as if long in deep slumber, awakened and began to describe themselves as victims of a great oppressor, Mulholland, and those who did his bidding, the public service commission of Los Angeles. A harsh new tone arose as local journalists heightened their rhetoric and flailed out with reckless and malicious accusations of the city's wicked destruction of Owens Valley.

This outpouring of exposé stories—a veritable renaissance of muckraking journalism—appears, in retrospect, orchestrated rather than spontaneous. Between 1920 and 1924, the number of articles attacking Los Angeles quadrupled in the three Owens Valley newspapers, two of which were in part underwritten (or at least in debt to) the two major factions of opposing landowners in Owens Valley. Devoted to unmasking the city's villainy, the *Owens Valley Herald* was edited by Harry A. Glasscock, nephew of one of the paper's founders, and copublished by a Watterson in-law, newspaperman Court E. Kunze. Its accusations against the city became so virulent and false that at one point the public service commission debated suing for slander. The second journal, the *Bishop Index,* edited by local attorney Leicester C. Hall, was sponsored by a rival group who were considered pro–Los Angeles. The *Bishop Index* seemed dedicated to opposing the *Owens Valley Herald* and denouncing Fred Eaton. The third (most respectable, independent, and almost certainly, least subsidized) was the venerable journalistic voice of the *Inyo Register,* owned and edited by an honorable descendant of Owens Valley journalist-printers, William A. Chalfant. Chalfant had always been anti–Los Angeles, but in the 1920s as the verbal abuse against the city and its representatives intensified, even he sometimes was a voice of moderation. During some of the most abusive attacks, he pointed out that the city did after all pay county taxes on all the land it had acquired in Owens Valley and thus provided needed revenues to Inyo County.[6]

Mulholland had long been accused of an unfeeling disregard for the people of Owens Valley, and by the 1920s, this may well have appeared true as Owens Valley affairs by then drew only a fraction of his professional attention. Unlike Goethals, who after completing the Panama Canal, left Panama and never returned, Mulholland, a man who rarely took a day off, remained devoted to his adopted city, became ever more deeply involved in civic affairs, and with Scattergood, began to consider the Colorado River as a source of hydroelectric power. In early 1921, they made an exploratory trip to study possible dam sites there, which resulted in a later decision to send survey parties to continue the work. Since his wife's death, Mulholland seemed to find it difficult to turn down requests, so that when his old associate, G. E. Elliott, chief engineer of the Spring Valley Water Company, asked him to take on the additional task of serving on an advisory committee on storage and distribution of water for the state department of public works, he found himself unable to refuse. (Also serving were George Goethals and Arthur P. Davis.) Thus, during many of the major negotiations and confrontations in Owens Valley during the 1920s, longtime coworkers Ed Leahey and Harvey Van Norman served as the city's representatives, both having worked, lived, and established good relationships with many people in the valley.[7]

To imagine that Mulholland was unaware and uncaring of the people of Owens Valley is to misread the man. Of course, he knew that irrevocable change would occur with the removal of Owens River water and the purchase of lands. Years before he had acknowledged Mary Austin's Cassandra-like prophecies, but as an engineer, he was allied to those who believed their technical skills contributed to civilization's advance. He also understood that Roosevelt's Benthamite utilitarian principle of "the greatest good for the greatest number" would not necessarily lead to the "greatest good for *all*"; that the contradiction in this philosophy that could logically lead to either complete bureaucracy or complete anarchy would inevitably injure some in this region of seven thousand souls. As a pragmatist, he did not believe that the interests of the valley people had been stinted. The city had paid fair prices to those who willingly sold their land, while those who remained had enough water to serve their needs. The Owens Valley, after all, had not been vacated and drowned as upstate villages had been in the New York Aqueduct project, where even the dead had been removed from their burial sites. Nor was this so-called ruthlessness directed against small landowners and townspeople but against those few who wished to profit at the expense of the city, the private interests that he believed thwarted "the greatest good" by blocking its intentions. Here he could be fierce. Even such a city partisan as public service commissioner William Paul Whitsett once commented that when it came to the city's interest, Mulholland drove a hard bargain, and no one in Owens Valley knew this better than his old friend and associate Fred Eaton.[8]

THE LONG VALLEY QUESTION

The issue of the Long Valley dam site had never gone away, and in the 1920s Eaton and certain Owens Valley landowners were to use it as a lever in their attempt to wrest concessions from Los Angeles and get top prices for their land. Mulholland's frugality with the expenditure of public moneys was one of his virtues as a public administrator, so that when Eaton years before had asked a price for his Long Valley lands that Mulholland judged too high, the Chief set aside the original plan to build a 140-foot dam on the site and declared it only "possibly necessary" at some future date. Since that standoff, Eaton no longer dealt directly with Mulholland on city matters. Mathews, for example, sought Scattergood's help when he wished Eaton to adjudicate among the protesting parties in Mono County during the contention over the power rights-of-way legislation in Washington, D.C., in 1919.[9]

Eaton and his wife divided their time between Los Angeles and Owens Valley, where his older son, Harold, now also with a second wife, lived and managed many of their land and ranching operations. Although Eaton continued to use the California Club as his city address and spend time in Santa Monica, his principal interests centered on his Long Valley ranch (the former Rickey Ranch was now the Eaton Land and Cattle Company, with an area devoted to chicken growing called the Owens River Poultry Corporation). By 1923, when Eaton was encountering financial difficulties and arranging for a mortgage loan, the holding was thus described: "May 16—Eaton Land & Cattle Co. Fred Eaton, Pres. Report from THE MERCANTILE AGENCY, Bishop, Inyo County. Incorporated under Calif. law with a capital of $300,000 and has between

2,000 and 3,000 head of cattle. Well managed, has good holdings, pays bills promptly, and 'no one is found who is familiar with the details of the company.'"[10]

Eaton and his son had joined a group of leading Owens Valley owners and businessmen to form an irrigation district after the city's success in Congress over the right-of-way matter not only promised that it could take water from the Mono Basin but indicated that it would probably have to build the Long Valley Reservoir to impound the flows from above. By pooling their holdings, this group intended to be better able to drive a hard bargain with the city when it came to selling. Called the Owens Valley Property Owners Protective Association, it was dominated by two brothers of the prolific pioneering Watterson family, Wilfred W. and the younger Mark Q. Another member of their large clan was brother-in-law J. C. "Jake" Clausen, who had long ago written the report recommending building the Long Valley Reservoir as a Reclamation Bureau project. By 1922, the Watterson brothers had created a banking monopoly with their ownership of all five valley banks, which, along with their many local interests and business connections, assured their financial dominance in Owens Valley.[11]

The Protective Association comprised major owners of irrigation ditches at the northern end of Owens Valley above the aqueduct intake. Claiming that the city's piecemeal buying amounted to a divide-and-conquer acquisition of water-bearing valley lands, they intended to press the city into buying land en bloc. The city answered this charge through its land agents, John Martin and George Shuey (the latter having been on the Owens Valley scene since 1903). The city, they acknowledged, had always bargained for the lowest prices it could get, a practice Chalfant scornfully characterized as "peaceful assimilation."[12]

Of the other three most important ditch companies expressing opposition to any diversion of waters in the upper valley, one, the Owens River Canal Company, was considered friendlier to the city than the Eaton-Watterson group, which feared that the former's selling to the city would almost certainly undermine their goal. After the Canal Company had negotiated with the city in the spring of 1921 and gained assurances that its members would continue to receive adequate irrigation water during the growing season, the Eaton Land and Cattle Company brought suit against the Canal Company in July to establish riparian claims along certain creek tributaries to Owens River. This infighting between two ditch-owning groups was complicated by the presence in the rival group of Wilfred and Mark Watterson's uncle, George Watterson, secretary of the

Bishop Creek Ditch. Assisting him was Bishop attorney Leicester C. Hall, also editor of the *Bishop Index* and treasurer of the Owens River Canal Company. The third participant consisted of McNally Ditch owners (known as the Associated group) whose president was William Symons. Attorney-editor Hall editorialized for his group while Harry Glasscock, owner-editor of the *Owens Valley Herald,* did the same for the Watterson-Eaton group.[13]

Six months after Eaton had filed his action against the Owens River Canal Company, on January 20, 1922, Ed Leahey, the city's chief representative in Owens Valley since 1919, wrote Van Norman concerning Eaton's activities. He included clippings from the *Owens Valley Herald* that, he had been told, were the work of Fred Eaton and in which he was sure Van Norman would recognize Eaton's "fine Italian hand." The articles proclaimed that "the Owens Valley is standing together" against the depredations of Los Angeles, and to this end, Eaton had gone to San Francisco to retain some of the top legal talent of California. Throughout the year, attack pieces appeared featuring horror stories of the city's egregious misuse of water. "We suppose you are aware that waters of Owens River flowing down the aqueduct for municipal purposes are used in irrigating lands in the San Fernando Valley owned by Mulholland, Van Norman, McKay—then flowing through Beverly Hills and Benedict Canyon to the ocean and lost." The reality of the 130,000 acres the city had already purchased at the southern end of Owens Valley provoked wrenching descriptions of ruined farmlands, dead orchards, and alfalfa fields reverting to sagebrush. These accounts helped fuel local passions against the city so that they approved the creation of an irrigation district in a December 1922 election, followed on August 7, 1923, by the passage of over a million dollars in bonds for the acquisition of its waters and for new facilities and improvements. Although touted as a measure to save Owens Valley, this new irrigation district ultimately created nothing other than a convenient governmental instrument for bargaining with the city. All future contentions with the city centered on top prices for land sales, demands for reparations for past injuries, and the question of whether a dam would be built in Long Valley.[14]

On June 1, 1923, as Los Angeles focused on an election that, among other items, would determine the passage of a $35 million bond measure for Boulder Dam (it was defeated by 11,790 votes), a small notice in the Los Angeles *Express* announced that the city had just paid a million dollars for almost 12,000 acres of rich farmlands in the Owens Valley. The purchases had been made over a long time by land agent John T.

Martin and had been done in secrecy "for the purpose of protecting the city's water rights in the valley." It would add 10,000 miner's inches to the present supply and be adequate for the needs of 3 million persons. The city now owned 80 percent of the McNally Ditch interests, and this purchase confirmed to the Watterson-Eaton Protective Association that the rival Watterson-Hall-Symon Associated group were sellouts to the city. The *Inyo Register* accused the city of getting its land at bargain prices and claimed owners "had been panicked into selling all the rewards that should have been theirs for the years of work they have put in." A month later, in early July, Mathews and Mulholland met with the rival Protective Association (Watterson, Clausen, and others) at a public service commission meeting in Los Angeles to hammer out a tentative agreement over water and pumping rights, but nothing definitive was decided.[15]

Mulholland spent a busy July in the city. A magazine article about him that month claimed, "Even now, at more than 67, he is still a tremendous worker." He attended meetings on flood control plans for the Los Angeles River, which under the Reagan Plan was about to be riprapped; discussed with Goethals what type of dam would best withstand earthquakes at Boulder Canyon (both favored a rock-filled dam); and after a big earthquake shook the southland on Sunday night, July 22, spoke publicly with a geologist about the phenomenon of seismic movement and the need for further study in order to guard against serious results and loss of life. He also noted the continuing attacks of the *Los Angeles Times* against the power bureau over its so-called wanton expenditures in the recent election and refuted the false charges that he had created an artificial water famine in the San Fernando Valley. By the end of the month, he also learned that Fred Eaton, on behalf of the Eaton Land and Cattle Company, had filed a temporary injunction against Los Angeles to prohibit the construction of a dam 150 feet high in Long Valley. Two weeks later, on August 17, after city workers had cleared brush and begun to dig a diversion ditch on its recently acquired property along Big Pine Ditch, a troop of armed ranchers mounted guard over the headgate of Big Pine Ditch and halted the work. Four days later, a Bridgeport court began hearing a suit brought by the Eaton Land and Cattle Company against the City of Los Angeles for damages inflicted by its agents on the claimant's dams and ditches. Harold Eaton testified in protest of their actions, while Ed Leahey, representing the city, said the action had been taken at the directive of Mulholland and Scattergood. These events set the stage for what came to be known as the Owens Valley Water War.[16]

LOS ANGELES, THE WATER HOG

Opposition to Los Angeles was not confined to Owens Valley. At the end of 1920, during a League of Municipalities banquet in Bakersfield, that town's mayor had remarked in a backhanded jesting compliment to the mayor of Los Angeles, "You stole our water, gas and power while our eyes were shut to our own opportunities." Amid laughter, he added, "Next thing you know, they will want to use the Vernal Falls at Yosemite." Mayor Snyder of Los Angeles gave a wan smile and jested back that in spite of his city's glories, its city hall and jail were nothing to be proud of. While Mayor Snyder caught flak from fellow mayors in Bakersfield over the city's greediness, Mulholland, seeking new solutions embracing a broader vision of water and power regulation for California, attended a banquet in Los Angeles with Elwood Mead and other water gurus to discuss Colonel Robert Marshall's irrigation plan for the San Joaquin Valley. In September, he already had attended a similar meeting at Sacramento to consider Marshall's plan to use California's rivers to irrigate 12 million acres of San Joaquin Valley land, and at that time, both he and Colonel M. M. O'Shaughnessy, engineer of the Hetch Hetchy project, viewed it with favor. Some of this plan later merged into the Water and Power Act, a proposed constitutional amendment created in 1921 by Progressive forces for state regulation of water and electrical power. Mulholland threw the weight of his not inconsiderable prestige behind the measure. (In April 1921, the American Association of Engineers had just named him one of the top engineers in the world, placing him in company with Goethals, Steinmetz, and Orville Wright.) He served on the executive board of the Water and Power Act campaign along with its two chief financial supporters, Dr. John R. Haynes, of Los Angeles, and Rudolph Spreckels, of San Francisco; and leading Progressives, William Kent, of Kentfield, and Louis Bartlett, mayor of Berkeley. The proposal, opposed by the private power companies (it was later said they had spent $500,000 to defeat it) and the conservative press, went down to defeat in the reactionary flood of 1922 that swept Warren G. ("Back to Normalcy") Harding into the White House.[17]

Among those rejoicing in the Water and Power Act's defeat was Harry Chandler, whose *Times* had predictably deplored the proposed amendment and afterward insulted Mulholland's motives and intelligence by apologizing for him with the suggestion that "demagogues and socialists" had duped him. The proponents of the defeated amendment, determined to continue the fight, warned of the propaganda being used against Los Angeles in its municipal ownership projects. Spreckels accused the *Times* of making people believe that its municipal power project was a failure, while local public service commissioner John Kemp declared, "Nearly every day some article attacking the Public Service Commission appears in an opposition paper [the *Record* or the *Times*]."[18]

The election of 1922 also brought to Sacramento one of the dreariest, most backward-looking governors the state has ever had, Friend Richardson, who proved to be mostly a friend to vested interests. Of his term from 1922 to 1926, Mowry has written that the "new California conservatism was mainly interested in lower taxes for corporations and in legislation granting long term franchises to electric power companies and other public utility corporations." An early example of Richardson's bias was his unsuccessful attempt to remove one of the city's leading Progressives and champions of public power ownership, Dr. John R. Haynes, from the board of regents of the University of California. Thus, in this political climate and amid waning Progressive influence, the battle was waged for the creation of Boulder Dam and the Colorado River Aqueduct, projects on which Mulholland pinned his hopes as the answer to the city's ever-growing needs for water and power.[19]

In his annual report for 1922, Mulholland noted that the population of Los Angeles had more than tripled since 1905 and, foreseeing increased water problems, warned the city to curtail its wholesale annexation of territory and expressed concern that the San Fernando Valley was fast becoming a residential center rather than an agricultural one. Elsewhere he began to urge the development of all possible hydroelectric power as he raised the specter of the depletion of the nation's oil reserves in the foreseeable future. He admonished that "what nature took millions and millions of years to store and conserve, man would use up in less than one century." So persuaded was he by the truth of this idea that at a San Joaquin League of Municipalities dinner, he warned that the United States had already used one-quarter of its oil supplies in twenty-five years, and that at the present rate, it could not be sentimental about turning to hydroelectric power, even if it meant using water in the national parks. Eventually, he declared, the power of the Yellowstone Falls would have to be utilized just as that of Niagara Falls was about to be. Later critics of Mulholland have taken such statements to demonstrate that he was an antienvironmentalist, which in itself is an anachronism, as the environment had not emerged as a powerful issue in his day. Such opinions on oil and hydroelectric power were current among men of science. Thomas Edison expounded them, and when Charles Steinmetz, the electrical wizard of

General Electric, spoke at the Los Angeles Electric Club the following year, he also urged harnessing rivers for electric power.[20]

Much of Harry Chandler's reputation as the "boss" of Los Angeles dates from this period, yet as one Progressive Republican congressman of the 1920s later observed (citing items in which Chandler had an interest such as ship subsidies, airmail contracts, national parks, and protection from governmental interference in the formation of power monopolies), when it came to "Big Business in Politics" Chandler was "no more than a field general in a far-off province who must take orders from the titanic dinosaurs and who must deliver the goods in the form of subservient Congressmen from his province if he desired to share in the profits of invisible government." Making this assessment was Joe Crail, who had begun his political career in 1916 as Hiram Johnson's campaign manager in Southern California during the latter's initial run for the Senate and who, by the early 1920s, after becoming active in supporting Boulder Dam and public power, announced his intention to run for Congress. Seeking support from the *Times*, he was granted an interview with Chandler soon after his announcement. Led before the presence (accompanied by the chairman of the Republican Congressional Committee), Crail was quickly told that the city's plans for the Colorado River were not correct from either an engineering or an economic standpoint. Then, according to Crail, Chandler imparted startling information. "There is a secret agreement between the city on the one hand and the Southern California Edison Company on the other, by which they will jointly file application to the Federal Power Board for authority to develop power from the Colorado River. The city will get all of the water it needs, or wants, through long trenches in the sand which will filter out the silt." Whether Chandler believed this fantasy is moot, but after Crail answered that he supported the Colorado plans as well as the All-American Canal, an angered Chandler declared that if his judgment was that poor, then he would not support him for Congress. In the end, however, party loyalty prevailed, and the *Times* recommended Crail, who won by a large margin and went on to Washington, where he worked on behalf of the Boulder Dam bill.[21]

Political tensions and hostilities sometimes took a toll on the water and power warriors. In March 1923, Scattergood, while in an elevator with Mulholland and Van Norman, had crumpled to the floor in a state of collapse. His "nervous breakdown," as it was called, came two months before the bitterly contested and crucial $35 million power bond election, which was narrowly defeated. The *Times* subsequently gloated and accused the power bureau of having spent $50,000 on campaign posters, letters, and (horrors!) "JAZZ BANDS." Yet the vote was sufficiently close that success seemed possible at a future election, and two months later a recovered Scattergood was back in the fray as he reported that Power Plant No. 1 at San Francisquito had begun to generate power. At the same time he informed the public that the city was still forced to purchase 30 percent of its power for consumers at more than twice the cost per kilowatt hour as the city's own production.[22]

Continued drought prompted Mulholland to warn people to be frugal with water, and when the leading Los Angeles golf clubs complained of high water rates and brought suit against the city to secure lower costs, Mulholland suggested in the ensuing hearing that "If the golfers threaten to leave town, let 'em. We don't want 'em." He continued the ban against reservoir fishing and criticized the big mess a film crew left around Chatsworth while shooting Mary Pickford's *Tess of the Storm Country.* Even though four more dams were in various stages of planning and construction in Weid (Hollywood) Canyon, Stone Canyon, Encino, and San Francisquito, worry remained constant over how to provide the ever-growing city with water and power.[23]

THE FLOURISHING OF THE CHIEF

Amid these contentious public issues in the early 1920s, Mulholland's reputation as a successful leader in a dynamic city flourished, his opinions sought and valued in many quarters. Perhaps to reassert his Irish origins, he assumed the presidency of the Celtic Club in 1922, continued his participation in the Sunset Club, where he spoke that year on the Boulder Canyon Dam project, and served on the executive committee of the Southwest Museum under the leadership of Charles Lummis. He even had a brief moment as a movie actor when he performed in a municipal film production, *Into the Future,* to boost Los Angeles's water and power establishment. This venture led to a suit by private power interests accusing the city of having wasted public funds for political purposes. At the hearing, Mulholland testified that he had played "a sort of Bill Hart of the aqueduct," and testified that he had found the life of a film star hard. With Scattergood and a delegation of Los Angeles leaders he spoke at a major conference in Phoenix at which Herbert Hoover presided. Given an ovation, he addressed the flood threat to Imperial Valley and urged the dam project, exhorting, "Let's build now and settle the quibbles later."[24]

In early 1923, Mulholland and Scattergood attended an important irrigation conference in Fresno. The two engineers had endorsed the Pine
Flat project to provide water and power for the Fresno area and assured
the thirty-seven districts present that Los Angeles wanted harmony with
the San Joaquin Valley and not one ounce of their irrigation water. Days
after returning home, Mulholland received a singular distinction, the
naming of a highway in his honor. On February 9, he stood with the
mayor to watch the first turning of earth for a ridge route that he had
long ago proposed to run from Hollywood to the sea. To inaugurate the
future Mulholland Scenic Highway, William Gibbs McAdoo (soon to be
a Democratic contender for the presidency and later a United States senator) ceremonially buried a casket with the three flags that had flown
over California: Spanish, Mexican, and United States.[25]

Mulholland and Scattergood's efforts to create a municipal power system drew increasing recognition. One article from the *Dearborn Independent* (later reprinted in the *Rochester, New York Times-Union*) applauded the city's willingness to fight its powerful foes, while nearer home
the *Sacramento Bee* cited Los Angeles as a model of the wisdom of public ownership of hydroelectric service. In all comparisons of consumer
rates with those of Edison, it asserted, the city's had proven lower, and
at less cost. Further accolades came from Senator George N. Norris of
Nebraska, then fighting Henry Ford's attempt to take over Muscle Shoals
as well as seeking governmental support for Boulder Dam, while Carl
Hayden of Arizona declared that Los Angeles was now the best lighted
city in the world, with the cheapest manufacturing power. Locally, P. D.
Noel of the Sierra Club and the Central Labor Council warned that "a
desperate effort is being made by selfish private power companies, their
financial allies and their Los Angeles morning newspaper mouthpiece to
wreck and discredit this city's notably successful Municipal Bureau of
Power and Light."[26]

A TOUR ON THE COLORADO RIVER

After sailing down the Colorado in November on a five-day observation
tour with Van Norman and a group of engineers, Mulholland announced
that the trip had confirmed his studies and observations of the past ten
years; that the project of bringing Colorado River water to Los Angeles
was feasible; and that the dam site should be in Boulder Canyon. He hoped
shortly to resume the voyage from Parker, Arizona, but important business had brought him home. He was to be a chief speaker at a major Boul-

der Dam Association conference in Santa Ana as well as a witness in a suit brought against the city by one Volney Craig on behalf of a few disgruntled irrigators in the San Fernando Valley who claimed they were being deprived of water. The judge subsequently denied the injunction (in 1924), declaring the principle that the Los Angeles Aqueduct should be used primarily to satisfy the needs of water consumers and only secondarily to generate hydroelectric energy.[27]

Days after Mulholland's return from the Colorado came news that San Franciscans had voted for the Hetch Hetchy project, which represented yet another triumph over private interests. As the boring of the Hetch Hetchy Tunnel began in the north, Mulholland began construction on the dam in Weid Canyon that he promised would be completed in two years and should be called Hollywood Reservoir. In 1924, however, the public service commission voted to call it Mulholland Dam.[28]

CHAPTER 22

Boulder Dam and Dynamite

1924

THE SWING-JOHNSON BILL AND TROUBLING RUMORS

Controversy over Boulder Dam and the second Swing-Johnson bill (a bill to provide for the protection and development of the lower Colorado River Basin) dominated the news in Los Angeles during the fifteen months after armed ranchers had mounted the Big Pine Ditch and stopped work on the city's proposed diversion ditch in the summer of 1923. At the beginning of 1924, the discontents in Owens Valley were somewhat muted, and with a continued drought in the state, Mulholland's most critical concern was planning future water and power supplies in his burgeoning city. To maintain the power system, he felt it urgent to complete the dams in Weid and San Francisquito Canyons and to continue the campaign for the Boulder Dam project. Owens Valley water could supply current needs, but because he was responsible for future supplies and forced to look ten years ahead, he deemed that with the city's present rate of growth, only the Colorado River could supply those needs, especially for hydroelectric power. Concerned about the present supply's limits, however, he deplored some of the annexations and distant subdivisions being developed far in advance of need while land lay idle well within the existing city limits.[1]

Joining in the Boulder Dam promotion was Arthur P. Davis, who in a political play had been relieved of his Reclamation post as chief engineer of the Boulder project and replaced by Frank Weymouth. Secretary of the Interior Hubert Work claimed the project needed an administrator rather than an engineer, but Davis believed his support of public power had led to his removal. Quickly hired as a consultant for the city, Davis claimed that a dam in Boulder Canyon could be built for less than $50 million and that electricity could be generated three to four years after work started. He found Mulholland's plans for getting Colorado water to the city physically possible but questioned their magnitude and cost. As the campaign for public water and power continued, former senator James Phelan of San Francisco attended a public service commission meeting in Los Angeles with Mulholland and Scattergood, at which he declared that San Francisco's fight with private power interests was exactly similar to Los Angeles's. The two cities were bound together by a common enemy and should join forces to protect the rights of consumers. At the end of January, Mulholland and a delegation of Southern Californians that included Mathews, Scattergood, electrical engineer W. F. Durand, and several mayors of Southern California cities set out for Washington, D.C., to throw their support behind the second Swing-Johnson bill for Boulder Dam.[2]

After two weeks of conferences with members of the secretary of the interior's staff and members of the arid lands committee, during which, according to columnist Joseph Timmons, Mulholland's eloquence opened their eyes to the undercover opposition and falsehoods being disseminated by "a Los Angeles morning paper" (the *Times*), the aging Chief stood up in Congress on February 15 and dropped the bombshell that Congressman Phil Swing, coauthor of the bill, had feared would further complicate the already tangled fight over Colorado River waters but that he later decided had helped the cause along. "I am here," Mulholland declared, "in the interest of a domestic water supply for the City of Los Angeles, and that injects a new phase into this whole matter."[3]

Mulholland testified for two days, insisting that Boulder Dam would fit well with the city's plan to build an aqueduct connecting the Colorado River to Los Angeles. He predicted that the Boulder project would produce more power than all the oil fields in California and argued against creating the Topoc Dam being touted by private interests. Calling it the Poppycock Dam, he joked that its chief virtue was that, although it would hold water, it would produce no power. When probed to name the power companies and other organizations fighting the Swing-Johnson bill, he sidestepped by saying most of the activity was covert but that everybody recognized it. "It is a good deal like a mole," he described. "You know the mole is there; you see where he has made the hole and the hump in the ground where he has crawled; but if you try to jab a snickersnee into

him he may not be there. We had the same sort of opposition to building the Aqueduct." He concluded with the observation that there are
"some men whose religion it is to be against public ownership of every
kind," but when pressed to identify corporations active in this fight, he
named only the Southern California Edison Company, which, he claimed,
had filings for power on the entire river. He added that he had heard one
of its vice presidents, R. H. Ballard, declare their intention to develop it
all—to create, in short, a monopoly. He admitted that he had thought
the Owens Valley Aqueduct would supply Los Angeles for forty or fifty
years, but the city's surprising population increase had proven him wrong.
Drought had forced that project, he recalled, just as the current drought
forced this one. "You must understand," he told the House Committee
on Irrigation and Reclamation, "that the very salubrity of our climate
brings about aridity."[4]

After an afternoon of cross-examination by Representative Carl Hayden of Arizona and others over the Colorado project's flood control aspects, Mulholland concluded his testimony and left for the West Coast,
leaving behind a hearing that was to drag on into spring. After months
of stalling, Harry Chandler finally made a bland appearance, imparting
the impression that he had never in his life heard of such a thing as a
power grab by private interests. Hiram Johnson, one of the bill's authors,
was so infuriated by the performance that he called Harry Chandler a
greater enemy to California than the Southern Pacific railroad octopus
had ever been. The bill failed to get out of committee before the session
adjourned, and a disappointed Phil Swing returned to California to face
a hard fight for reelection.[5]

When Mulholland arrived home on February 19, he brought optimistic words that the Teapot Dome scandal's eruption had created an
atmosphere of support for the people's cause and one of embarrassment
for the opposing private interests. Adding that the people of Los Angeles should thank Providence for the aqueduct ("It is such a protection in
this enormously destructive drought"), he cautioned that even with that
blessing they must look ahead and go to the Colorado River for a future
water supply.[6]

Meanwhile, with the snowpack in the Sierras only 10 inches deep
against a 65-inch average, the drought showed no sign of abating. Other
disturbing reports also came to the returning Mulholland as the ditch
owners in Owens Valley pursued their plans to press the city. One ominous note was the repetition of a September 1923 warning by Catholic

priest John J. Crowley, who, on February 12, in an open letter to the citizens of Inyo County, again deplored the presence in their midst of a Ku Klux Klan organizer, one M. B. Haver, who, he avowed, had arrived not for religious reasons but rather to make "a misguided attempt to solve our water situation." The priest, whose later efforts to reconcile Owens Valley with Los Angeles were honored by the naming of Lake Crowley, also noted that although the *Inyo Register* had printed his first warning against this organization of "bigotry and ignorance," the *Owens Valley Herald* had refused.[7]

Another more immediate mischief afoot in Owens Valley prompted Mulholland on February 27 to wire Mathews, who was still at the Boulder hearings:

> Longyear group of banker owners Owens Valley lands are trying to stir up rebellion amongst farmers San Fernando Valley representing that they have plenty of water that city must buy STOP Streams are now so low quite satisfied they will see contrary in month or two STOP Hope you may return and press Eaton matter otherwise we will be completely deprived of all benefit of our efforts of past year to obtain water STOP Condition our reservoirs and review of our prospects for year indicate safe margin for domestic use and permanent tree growth in Fernando Valley This of course implies complete exhaustion of stores of water by first of November STOP Come soon[8]

William Douglas Longyear was a prominent member of the Los Angeles banking-investor fraternity as well as an associate of the San Fernando land syndicate headed by General Otis, Harry Chandler, Otto F. Brant, and H. J. Whitley, which had acquired in 1909–1910 the southern half of the San Fernando Valley. Longyear's holdings centered around present-day Sherman Oaks. In 1917, Longyear and his son, David, obtained land southwest of Bishop, where the latter now lived and purportedly ranched. The Longyears, active members of the ditch owners' Owens Valley Protective Association, were not only involved with the small group of irrigators in the San Fernando Valley who in the spring of 1924 went to Owens Valley in a scheme to buy irrigation water direct from the ditch owners; they also played a hand in the later land-selling controversy in which the Watterson-Eaton faction attempted to sell their holdings at what the city considered exorbitant rates. (Although much has been written about the Eaton-Mulholland feud as the chief impediment to the city's purchasing of land at high prices, absentee owners and sellers trying to gouge the city were equally salient.) A month after receiving Mulholland's admonitory wire, Mathews managed an apparent coup by securing the services of William Symons, head of the rival McNally's Ditch group, to take on commission all of the options he could arrange with that ditch's property owners. Some observers later believed this development triggered the subsequent water war.[9]

By spring, with an impending primary election on May 6, fierce debate arose over two issues: power bonds for the city and approving the Boulder Dam project. Power issues were intensely fought, with both labor and Progressive forces in favor while conservatives (with powerful backing from the *Los Angeles Times*) opposed. In retrospect, several marvelous coincidences militated against passage of a pro-public power bond issue. First, under protest from public power interests, a $35 million bond issue for flood control in the San Gabriel Mountains was suddenly forced on the ballot to compete with other costly municipal items. Not surprisingly, the *Times* piously touted the need for flood control over the need for public power and urged a no vote on the latter. When all the dust had settled, the voters had passed the flood control measure and approved the Boulder Dam power project but resoundingly defeated the city power bonds. On the eve of the election, councilman Wheeler declared, "For twenty years I have been active on behalf of municipal ownership and I will say in the present campaign we have had more lies per square inch than in all the rest of the campaigns put together." Feelings were so inflamed that when a camp of water department workers from the Encino Reservoir came to vote in Encino, a woman on the election board announced, "I'm not going to let that riffraff vote. They're all employed by the water department and are going to vote for the bonds." It took a call to the registrar of voters before they were allowed to cast their ballots.[10]

OWENS VALLEY FIGHTS BACK

The second apparently coincidental preelection event was the appearance, beginning in late March and concluding one week before the primary election, of a series of twelve articles in the *San Francisco Call* by staff writer Court E. Kunze, Watterson brother-in-law and coeditor of the *Owens Valley Herald*. Kunze's sketches of Los Angeles's nefarious behavior against the poor, embattled Owens Valley dwellers were artful contrivances and effective propaganda, as they oversimplified complex issues and reduced the players to villain and victim. Kunze compared "the tragedy of Owens Valley" to *Evangeline* and declared that because Los Angeles was deaf to all pleas, it had created "a valley of broken hearts."

Much praised in Owens Valley and reprinted throughout the state, this series, by shading the truth, went far to confirm the increasing impression of a victimized people under the foot of an uncaring tyrant, namely, Mulholland. Implied was the proposition that if only the city were to build a dam at Long Valley, many hearts in Owens Valley would be healed. Whatever else may be said, these pieces without a doubt helped whip up the outrage that led on May 21, 1924, at 1:30 A.M., to the first dynamiting of the aqueduct.[11]

The explosion occurred twenty-two miles north of Haiwee and blasted away a section of concrete canal and part of the hill slope where the dynamite had been placed. From Independence, engineer Roderick McKay called Mulholland, who proceeded immediately to City Hall to announce the news. "We had heard of threats from disgruntled persons," he told the council, "but going on the theory that barking dogs do not bite, we did not pay any attention to them. Last night they bit."[12]

After the council voted to appropriate a $10,000 reward for the capture of the perpetrators, Mulholland left to investigate the damage and to personally superintend the repairs. He was asked before leaving about a possible motivation. Considering that his masterpiece had been seriously tampered with, his remarks seem moderate, although in the frenzied spirit of hatred and resentment now loose in Owens Valley, even they were construed malevolent. "Dissatisfaction in the valley?" he asked rhetorically. "Yes, a lot of it. Dissatisfaction is a sort of condition that prevails there, like the hoof-and-mouth disease. You can't tell where the infection is until it breaks out, and it keeps breaking out in new spots." As if that were not enough to incite fury in Owens Valley, he added, "There are those in the valley like Tam O'Shanter's wife who nursed her wrath to keep it warm."[13]

Everybody had a theory. The *Times* accused the Kunze articles of fanning the flames of dissension; city detectives in the police department's radical bureau suspected the IWW and set out to look for Wobblies. When the fragment of a love letter on the back of a movie theater program from Bishop was discovered near the scene, hopes rose that it would provide a lead. In fact, the malefactors were apparently well known to most of the valley, and it was generally acknowledged that in the Klan-like fashion of nightriders, at least forty men had set out from Bishop on the night of the deed in a caravan of cars that had been observed by the inhabitants of the little towns along their southerly route. Throughout the ensuing investigation, the valleyites were unrepentant, even gleeful, at the stir. Ed Leahey received veiled threats on his life when he appeared in Bishop, and Fred Eaton made a pallid defense of valley people's being "law-abiding citizens" who did not countenance violence. At last, ran local sentiment, we have gotten the attention we have been looking for. In the midst of this hullabaloo, Los Angeles mayor George Cryer (who had replaced Snyder in June 1921) left town with his wife for a three-week vacation in the East while a Los Angeles businessman announced he was going to build a new $80,000 hotel in Bishop. Reginaldo del Valle, the longest serving member of the public service commission, stated that in the past eighteen months, the city had expended $3,684,969 to purchase water lands in Owens Valley. "Greed," he concluded, "prompting its possessors to attempt to wring exorbitant prices from Los Angeles for water lands in Owens Valley, is at the root of all the trouble which led up to and follows the dynamiting of the Aqueduct near Lone Pine."[14]

Because of the aroused passions in Owens Valley, the hearings on the dynamiting eventually were moved to remote northern Alpine County. As negotiations between city officials and Owens Valley men began, the incident might have been minimized if not for certain of the press. The debate over Boulder Dam continued to dominate the news in Los Angeles, but in Owens Valley, all other issues were suppressed in order to keep anger over the city's villainy alive. Mulholland was excoriated ("King of Home Destroyers") and compared to Albert Fall, the corrupt secretary of the interior who was about to be indicted for giving away federal oil lands to private oil men led by Edward Doheny. As summer wore on, a Los Angeles dry goods merchant showed up in Bishop and told a complete fabrication to the *Inyo Register*: Mulholland was interested in Owens Valley land deals to enrich some privileged few just as he had done in the San Fernando Valley. Even two local suicides were blamed on the city's heartlessness toward the benighted settlers.[15]

DYNAMITE AND "PEACE" MEETINGS

A month after the explosion, the publisher of the *Record,* B. H. Canfield, arrived in Owens Valley with four of his staff to ascertain the "truth." The locals hailed him as the only man to publish the truth in Los Angeles since Sam Clover had once dared to oppose "the controlling ring and political interests." (Unmentioned, however, was Sam Clover's current editorship of a Los Angeles periodical, *Saturday Night,* for which he composed laudatory profiles of such former enemies as Henry Huntington,

Harry Chandler, and William Mulholland, collected and published as *Constructive Californians* in 1926.)[16]

The *Record* began a series of exposés recounting Los Angeles's perfidy to Owens Valley. So wanton were some press attacks against Los Angeles and its water establishment that by the end of summer the *Fresno Republican* published an editorial warning the city's enemies to exercise restraint. Unheeded at the time, it proved shrewdly prophetic as the final drama played itself out in the following years. To the city's attackers, the Fresno editor offered a parable from the Old Testament story of Ahab, the king of Israel, who desired the vineyard of Naboth. When Naboth denied Ahab, he found himself at the mercy of Jezebel and was slain. (Here, by the editor's own admission, the analogy became a bit strained as he asked, "Is there a Jezebel?") Likening the Owens Valley dwellers to Naboth, he described the current scene:

> Naboth is in revolt. And he is doing some very irregular things. He is blowing up the property of Ahab. And he is going out "nightriding" to the discomfort of Ahab's plants. In due time Naboth will be sorry for these things. He will be arrested and indicted, and shown the error of his ways. While he is in jail, his crops will perish for want of attention as well as for water. And he will sell his depreciated acres for the cost of hiring an attorney in a vain attempt to show that he had a right to take a sideswipe at Ahab. The sale will turn out to be one more good turn for Ahab.
>
> Naboth was stoned to death. We do it differently these days.[17]

A month before this editorial appeared, Mulholland had begun construction of the dam in Weid Canyon, even as he announced that water supplies were holding but that conservation should be continued in this driest spell in fifty years. When Lippincott and two other engineers who had been exploring Los Angeles's water resources reported to the Chief that all sources were exhausted, he stepped up his argument that the city must look to the Colorado River for a solution. Then a crisis flared that caused him to threaten his resignation. Home from his vacation, Mayor Cryer had gone to Owens Valley with his secretary at the end of July. After two days of being shown around and listening to local ranchers and businessmen, he returned home persuaded that the city should meet the landowners' demands to buy them out and, moreover, to pay their prices. When Cryer referred to antagonism in the valley towards "certain Aqueduct officials," Mulholland erupted at what he considered a public undercutting of his policies. "I would resign right now rather than have such charges left unanswered," he flared. "I have no defense to make and I don't intend, after forty-odd years in the work of this department, to have my service assailed in this way without meeting it in the most emphatic manner possible." With that, he spent the next day writing a statement rebutting each of Cryer's charges as del Valle and councilman Criswell echoed equal outrage. Cryer responded to this barrage by fleeing to San Bernardino on the excuse that he had to fetch his children home from summer camp. The city council next attacked him, while banker J. A. Graves took time out from his vacation in Bohemian Grove to send a wire calling the mayor "spineless" and asserting of Mulholland, "No man has ever charged him with a dishonest act." Only the *Record* applauded the mayor and questioned both Mulholland's competence and integrity.[18]

In the next two weeks, the public service commission announced Owens Valley purchases of the Manzanar Tract (4,958 acres) and the McNally Ditch (2,031 acres). To further protect the city's water supply, Mulholland also initiated irrigation restraints against the San Fernando Valley bean growers. He continued to defend his land acquisition policy, which was to buy Owens Valley land only as needed. "I will not stand for any wholesale purchases," he declared, "especially at figures ranging from $4,000,000 to $8,000,000."[19]

Two weeks after the uproar, on August 14, Cryer and Mulholland met at a luncheon for city employees and shook hands, thus disappointing those who expected fireworks. As a Progressive who supported public power and the Boulder project, and in view of the all-important city power bond issue coming up on August 26, Cryer's lapse could be overlooked, especially as it had been so generally disapproved. Although only 25 percent of voters turned out, they approved the city power bonds this time by a ratio of eight to one, while Phil Swing, by retaining his congressional seat, also insured that the Boulder project would retain its California supporter.[20]

In Owens Valley, however, news of the city's latest land purchases spurred new responses, and on the heels of the primary election came word that a gang of Bishop men had snatched from a local restaurant attorney-editor L. C. Hall (one of the Watterson-Symons group), whom they had roughed up and later released on condition that he leave Owens Valley. They suspected Hall of having bought up water rights for the city behind the backs of the group that had pooled its holdings. Also threatened were the lives of George Watterson, Symons, and others accused of being in league with Los Angeles. Mulholland, about to leave on a "peace tour" to Owens Valley, remarked that Hall had not been engaged in any capacity for Los Angeles in several months and that the legal services he had rendered in the past were not of sufficient importance to warrant the Bishop crowd's drastic measures. Ed Leahey also had been threatened as word went out for Mulholland to stay out of the valley. Revealing then that he had received at least a dozen anonymous letters from Owens Valley threatening his life, Mulholland left undeterred on September 2, in a car with Van Norman, while other city dignitaries followed by rail. Valley nerves had become so edgy that when two strange men on motorcycles accosted and beat up a foreman on the Eaton Ranch, instant suspicion fell on Los Angeles agents. As ranchers fanned out into the hills in search of the enemy, the attackers were apprehended, one of whom proved to be an ex-pugilist from San Francisco, evidently pursuing some grudge against the foreman.[21]

The peace meetings at Haiwee, which included W. W. Watterson, resulted in guarded optimism about a future harmony between the city and Owens Valley. The Big Pine Chamber of Commerce hosted a luncheon at which Mulholland received a generous ovation when he rose to speak. Soon after, however, local businessmen asked the city to reimburse them for the losses and depreciations of their property resulting from the loss of water on the city-owned ranch lands. The Los Angeles men acknowledged the merit of their requests and indicated the city's willingness to pay for such damage. Mulholland said, "The people are entitled to justice, and justice they shall have." Some felt, however, that while the city had kept strictly within its legal rights, it had also incurred a moral obligation that it had not met. When Mulholland urged them to back the Swing-Johnson bill and stated his belief that the ultimate solution would come with the development of Colorado River water, their response was emotional. "You have ruined our community. We are bankrupt. Something must be done for us now, and not at some future date." Out of this session, agreement was reached that the Big Pine Committee should come to Los Angeles to present its case to city representatives. A bit of public relations was also arranged at Big Pine with a reunion of Mathews, Mulholland, and their old Lone Pine landlady of aqueduct days, "Mother" Green, whose company and hospitality the two men had always enjoyed as well as her memorable line, "Us akeyducks has got to stick together." In comparing the newspaper photo in 1924 with one taken almost twenty years earlier that showed Mathews and a jaunty Mulholland with his arm around Mrs. Green (then jocularly referred to as "the Bride of the Aqueduct"), one notes that although time had taken its toll, they all looked to be even yet three tough old birds.[22]

As the delegation moved up the valley, one of the newest members of the public service commission, William Paul Whitsett, chief founder and developer of Van Nuys in the San Fernando Valley and long an enthusiast of the beauty and grandeur of the Sierras, extolled the area's possibilities as an American Alps. He had been to Switzerland and studied its tourist resources after being struck by the similarities he had found between the two magnificent mountain regions. Now he proposed Owens Valley as a great mountain playground and park. "All you need is publicity," he declared. "When tourists learn what you have here there will not be enough hotels to contain them." Whitsett, a new and younger voice who did not prevail against Mulholland and his older colleagues, recalled in later years how he had argued on the commission for the purchase and annexation of the Owens Valley towns to the city in order to create a park not unlike the Rocky Mountain park of Denver. The plan, he reasoned, would have been not unlike the shoestring annexation employed by the city for the creation of its harbor, but Mulholland and del Valle, he remembered, had disagreed.[23]

The entire town of Bishop turned out to meet with its city visitors at the high school auditorium on September 5. Chairing the event, W. W. Watterson announced that this was to be a business meeting and that there should be no hisses or applause, then read a position paper from the Bishop landowners to the members of the public service commission seated at a table in front with him. In the front row, Mathews and Mulholland, who did not speak, listened to those on the stage. Earlier in the day, however, a rough patch had arisen that augured ill for future peace. In the morning, on a tour of an area near Big Pine where earlier city construction work had been halted, Watterson and Fred Eaton urged the need to construct the Long Valley Dam. After hearing them out, Mulholland, with Van Norman's backing , rejected outright any notion of doing so, citing the porous volcanic formation that would cause leakage problems were such a structure to be placed there. His refusal provoked an ominous statement from Fred Eaton about city water officials endangering water sources for the aqueduct and warning that unless there were a change in attitude, its entire water supply might find itself in jeopardy. Then he resorted to an ad hominem rebuke. "The main difficulty, as far as I can determine, is Bill Mulholland's animosity towards me. Petty personalities should not be permitted to enter into a matter like this that vitally affects the life of two communities."[24]

This remark, delivered at a moment when all sides were attempting to remain civil, was gratuitous. What was not then public knowledge was that an increasingly bitter Eaton was falling into serious financial difficulties. By the time of the peace conference, he and another ditch owner, Frank Butler, had begun to receive duns from the public service commission in Los Angeles for unpaid rentals on cattle grazing lands on the city's Crooked Creek property. Moreover, Eaton had been unable to get his price for the Long Valley lands in ongoing behind-the-scenes negotiations with Ed Leahey. His old friend may have made a convenient scapegoat, but Mulholland was in no way the author of all of Fred Eaton's woes.[25]

An unresponding Mulholland returned to the city with Van Norman and commissioners Clarence Dykstra and Haynes, saying simply of the conference, "There is unquestionably, an economic, or if you prefer, a sociological side to the question, an equity difficult to appraise, but nevertheless existent, of which the board will undoubtedly take cognizance." If that statement was a bit murky, there was nothing vague about the land-buying policy from which he refused to retreat, concluding that "there is no sense in buying land to acquire water that can't be delivered." Much has been made of the Eaton-Mulholland feud, almost all of it emanating from Fred Eaton and Owens Valley defenders. Mulholland never made a public remark about it in his life, and certain of his family members believed that Mulholland, although silent, had been deeply hurt by Eaton's remarks.[26]

If not exactly a love feast, the conference did seem to move towards conciliation, as the public service commission promised to begin a study to ameliorate conditions and make good on a pledge to expedite building a good highway from Mojave to Bishop. Yet almost before Mulholland and company had left the valley, cries of dissatisfaction sounded in its local newspapers. The only creature in California larger than the Oakland Mole, mocked the *Owens Valley Herald,* was the Los Angeles Bull. Mulholland was a "cruel heartless destructionist," and "the Czar of L. A." A cartoon portrayed him in the guise of the sleepy little boy in pajamas from a famous automobile tire advertisement whose legend was "Time to Retire." New fuel for the fire arrived with the start of the grand jury hearing on the May aqueduct bombing and the L. C. Hall kidnapping. Fortunately it fizzled. Although everyone in Owens Valley apparently knew who was responsible, no one was inclined to speak, while Hall had been allowed to flee to Mexico after promising not to identify his kidnappers. Two weeks later, back from Baja California, he was es-

tablished at a Glendale address and gave Mulholland as a credit reference in applying for a charge account at the May Company. Mulholland
recommended him by stating that from what he knew of Hall as an employee, "he is steady and reliable and it would be my personal opinion
that he would be fully able to take care of his obligations up to a reasonable amount."[27]

THE TAKING OF THE ALABAMA GATES

Mulholland was honored on his sixty-ninth birthday with an observance
of the twentieth anniversary of the 1904 aqueduct survey when he and
a nameless Scottish cook had spent forty days in the desert surveying the
route for an aqueduct that now served a city of almost a million people
and whose accomplishment had brought to its builder much satisfaction
but little rest. At the end of September, he also received a gold service
badge for thirty-eight years as chief engineer of the municipal waterworks. Then, after preparing a speech for a large Boulder Dam conference in Pasadena that his assistant, W. W. Hurlbut, read in his absence
and which Van Norman reinforced with more material, Mulholland left
for the East Bay area to report on his recent survey of the water resources
of Oakland, Alameda, and Berkeley, where his friend and associate,
Arthur P. Davis, was about to become head of the East Bay Municipal
Utility District (EBMUD).[28]

Trouble stirred again in October in Owens Valley. Although the public service commission had followed through with a petition to the state
for a highway from Mojave to Bishop, it also decided to comply with
Mulholland's policy and announced it would make no blanket land purchases. Amid valley charges of "insincere" and "unfair," Mathews declared that those crying loudest were the members of an irrigation district association "which does not own an inch of water or an acre of land
in the valley." The board further announced at this time that it would
lease land for orchards in Owens Valley.[29]

With Owens Valley matters unresolved, Mulholland left town November 6 to escort a group of officials from a number of Southern California towns on a five-day inspection trip to the Colorado River region,
while Mathews and Van Norman began a series of conferences with
Owens Valley ranchers. Although the Colorado junket went well and secured the enthusiastic support of Mayor Cryer, who accompanied them,
the Chief must have been feeling the weight of the year's tumultuous
events. As he stood above the river in Boulder Canyon on an autumn

day, he dropped his usual confident front and before an assemblage of dignitaries "mused his thoughts aloud," as one reporter described it. After reflecting that he believed the Boulder project to be historic, he added, "For myself, I should prefer to see Los Angeles get its water elsewhere. I'm growing to be an old man; in a few months I shall pass three score and ten, the allotted span. Before I slip into the wooden overcoat I should prefer for myself a few years of rest and peace. For me, this enterprise means only more strife and fatigue in a life that has been filled with both. I can hardly hope to see it accomplished—but my desire is not for myself."[30] He returned home to more bad news. The conference in Owens Valley had not gone well. Nothing had been settled. Certain ranchers now accused one of their own, George B. Warren, of treason for selling what was called "a worthless piece of property" for $46,000 in exchange for becoming a city partisan. Warren had also reported favorably on the city's plan to set aside 30,000 acres for agricultural development around the greater Bishop area, based on the recommendation of Mathews, Van Norman, Lee, and Louis G. Hill, a member of the special Owens Valley committee. After listening to Warren, who was their president, the Associated Chambers of Commerce in Owens Valley framed a resolution to remove him from the presidency. An *Owens Valley Herald* column ridiculed the city's proposal to plant orchards as "a utopian dream of making the country bloom again, but everyone knows it is the bunk, coming from the City's agents as it does." Watterson's group, now calling itself the Big Pine Property Owners' Association, rejected the city's proposal, which provoked Van Norman to declare, "Although I have been in close touch with Owens Valley for more than fifteen years, I never knew until this morning that there existed an organization known as the 'Big Pine Property Owners' Association.'"[31]

Then, on Sunday, November 16, all hell broke loose up in Owens Valley. Over a hundred residents of Inyo County, led by Mark Q. Watterson, seized a part of the aqueduct, opened the Alabama gates about four miles north of Lone Pine, and let the water flood out on the land. The leaders proclaimed their intention to remain until the city met their demands. Mulholland refused to deal, declaring that the seventy-five or one hundred men responsible for the deed "were not representative of the people of Owens Valley." The incident became a media event, a high-profile act that seized everyone's attention and brought to a climax the drama that had been building throughout recent years. With local feeling against Los Angeles at fever pitch, a crowd of more than one hundred local ranchers in a spirit combining the features of an outdoor frolic and a lynching bee, seized, opened, and held for five days the headgates as precious water intended for Los Angeles flowed instead out onto desert lands. It became a community spree as housewives arrived with food for the rebels and newsmen swarmed to photograph and interview them. Tom Mix, the cowboy film star who happened to be shooting a western in the Alabama hills, provided a Hollywood touch with incidental western music. Mix's presence cannot be reckoned as a political statement, however, for a month later, he starred in a rodeo at Calabasas as part of the entertainment he and Cecil B. DeMille planned and produced for the festivities to celebrate the Mulholland Highway's December opening.[32]

Governor Richardson denied the local sheriff's request for help by refusing to call in the militia, saying he found it strange that the aggressors should be asking for troops while the injured parties asked for nothing. The presence of troops, he believed, would only create another opportunity for more "yellow journalism." The whole matter, he declared, should be settled in the courts. City officials, apparently in agreement, announced they would bring suits against Inyo County for the loss of their water, estimated at $15,000 a day. When the sheriff served injunction papers on the rebels, they greeted him with merriment and told him they would love to keep them as souvenirs. The governor sent state engineer W. S. McClure as his emissary to investigate the Inyo County matter, but McClure's report in 1925 was to result only in further obfuscation. The *Fresno Bee* rationally called the Inyo action a tempest in a teapot, while Los Angeles papers understandably covered the event at length, expressing outrage over its lawlessness. Certain human interest pieces, however, recognized that injuries had been sustained in the valley, while the *Record* predictably issued warnings of possible bloodshed and civil war and urged Mulholland's removal.[33]

When W. W. Watterson appeared before the Los Angeles Clearing House Association to urge appointing a commission of disinterested men to adjust the differences over water rights between the Owens Valley ranchers and the city, J. A. Graves, president of Farmers' and Merchants' Bank and chairman of the association, agreed to undertake the commission, but only if the mob would retire from the headgates and allow the courts to decide. Graves also stipulated that all Owens Valley claims must be presented to the clearing house in writing. This agreed to, the crowd surrendered the gates but before going home held a final barbecue to finish off all the food they had accumulated against the long siege they were prepared to maintain against the city. One worldly Los Angeles reporter saw overtones of a Wild West drama and, as he watched the rebels pack up and depart, remarked that the "producers of the 'Battle of Lone Pine' have not yet announced when the next installment of their serial will be released."[34]

By December 3, Watterson had handed the clearing house committee a document demanding that the city pay the valley's ranchers $5.3 million in reparations for the Owens River's diversion into the aqueduct and offering to sell their land en bloc to the city for $12 million. Graves responded to this wish list with some hard questions. First, what damages, if any, had the farmers of Owens Valley suffered by reason of any acts of the city? Evidence would be needed, as a mere unsupported statement could not be the basis for such a claim. Second, if damages had been incurred, was the city liable, either in law or in equity? Graves further asked,

> Another question which would have great weight with me is this: Whether any moneys which the city would agree to pay are to be divided among the farmers of the valley, or whether the lion's share thereof would go to a junta of Los Angeles and Bishop capitalists who do their farming through the newspapers, who are reported to have bought both lands and water rights at a low figure, and for which they now want from the city millions?
>
> It would appear that all the propaganda going on and, I imagine, much of the trouble and dissatisfaction created in the minds of the people of the Owens River Valley, has been fomented by this junta.[35]

MULHOLLAND HIGHWAY

As the turbulent year came to an end, Los Angeles celebrated the Mulholland Highway's opening. Private land developers had underwritten a million-dollar bond issue for its construction, calling it a gift to the city from the owners of 10,000 acres of land along the route. Its engineer, DeWitt L. Reaburn, had been an associate of Mulholland on the aqueduct, and the gala opening, months in planning, extended all the way from Hollywood Boulevard to Calabasas, as its promoters promised the new roadway would create yet another link between isolated parts of the expanding metropolis. On the morning of December 27, standing at a floral gate with a golden key, Mulholland dedicated the roadway with a bottle of aqueduct water. (This was Prohibition; no champagne!) With the symbolic gate to the highway unlocked, the crowd next moved on to a rodeo in the fields of Calabasas with the omnipresent Tom Mix and his cowboys, a depiction of a wild and woolly forty-niners' mining camp staged by Universal Studios, and an exhibition of daredevil stunt flying. An automotive caravan then advanced to the Hollywood Bowl for a second program produced by Cecil B. DeMille, where Mayor Cryer and Mulholland were principal speakers followed by dignitaries and film stars introduced for the occasion. A parade through Hollywood was followed by a street carnival and open-air dance on Vine Street with thousands of participants and strolling bands. When rumors of renewed attacks on the aqueduct and threats against Mulholland spread during the celebration, the unfailingly hostile *Record* reported that they had emanated solely from Mulholland himself.[36]

CHAPTER 23

More Dynamite

1925–1927

WHY NOT BUY ALL OF OWENS VALLEY?

Although no further acts of violence against the aqueduct occurred in 1925, the war of words persisted, especially after state engineer W. F. Mc-Clure in January released his report on the Owens Valley–Los Angeles controversy to the state legislature in Sacramento. McClure, who had once lived in Owens Valley and was friendly to its people, produced a wildly one-sided document, almost as if he were an attorney preparing a brief for his client. Freighted with reprints of editorials from the Owens Valley–San Joaquin Valley newspapers and reports from the major ditch companies, the "letter of transmittal" offered little for the Los Angeles side other than selected snippets from the first annual aqueduct report to prove that Mulholland had once approved building Long Valley Dam, along with an editorial from the *Los Angeles Times* urging peace and moderation among all parties after the Alabama Gates incident. The city was indignant, citing a bias against Los Angeles in Sacramento. On the basis of the report, the senate nonetheless formed a committee to investigate the matter. After they had chosen four members, however, sentiments became so divided that the legislators could not agree on a fifth member and the probe stalled.[1]

The public service commission denounced the McClure Report, rebutted with its own pamphlet, and rejected the proposal to pay reparations and buy the ranchers' lands en bloc. The Clearing House Association now announced its withdrawal from the controversy, citing as impediments to an adequate investigation a lack of facts and "too many cooks." Its chairman, banker Jackson A. Graves, would also later cite financial irregularities he had noted in the Watterson records. The Wattersons remained indefatigable, however, and next appeared in Sacramento with a committee of ranchers to ask the legislature "to right the grievous wrong which is being done to the business interests of this valley." The legislature answered that it had no power to prevent the purchase of as much land as owners wished to sell, "particularly as in this case, when such purchase is done solely from a desire to peacefully settle a controversy." Thwarted, the group turned its efforts to combat a bill from Los Angeles that would make it a felony to injure water systems owned by a municipality. By the end of the legislative session, it had also successfully lobbied for the passage of a reparations act that would make municipal corporations such as Los Angeles liable for damages caused by the "acquisition of a water supply, or taking, diverting and transporting of water from a watershed." In response to valley demands for reparations, the public service commission demurred, replying that it wished to have the courts test the bill's legality before making any payments.[2]

Some writers have criticized Mulholland for intransigence in his dealings with the Owens Valley ditch owners. Why not buy up Owens Valley, as Mayor Cryer had been willing to consider, pay the high prices, and be done with it? Such a policy might have avoided trouble, but Mulholland, schooled in an older, sterner system, believed he had pledged his word to the taxpayers of Los Angeles to deliver their waterworks at the amounts they had agreed to pay for through their bond elections. Having already been falsely accused of conspiring with vested interests in the San Fernando Valley in building the aqueduct, he was gun-shy when it came to making overly generous arrangements with apparently wealthy landholders who were using images of embattled pioneers and victimized smallholders as their ammunition against Los Angeles. He was privately convinced, too, that some in the Owens Valley group simply saw Los Angeles as a gold mine. He knew that some of the city's bankers and moneyed men held interests in Owens Valley, and, moreover, as he had pointed out in his report to Mayor Cryer, the city's land purchases of 1923 had brought the city very little additional water, "as the remaining owners in the valley contest the right of the city to take the water she purchased with that land out of the valley." His attitude toward profiteering is best expressed in an anecdote he liked to tell his sons about a man he admired and often saw downtown—a hauler of fat and renderings. Passing him one hot day, with his wagon stinking and dripping with the greasy leavings from restaurants and markets, Mulholland had called out, "That's a dirty job you've got there, Sal." Sal called back, "Yes, Bill. But the money's clean."

His behavior fits Ortega y Gasset's description of the man with a clear head "who can perceive under the chaos presented by every vital situation the hidden anatomy of the movement"; the man, in a word, who does not lose himself in life is "the man with the really clear head." This clarity, perceived by some as ruthlessness, accompanies "the inevitable sternness with which anyone who has his life fixed on some undertaking must bear himself. When we are really going to do something and have dedicated ourselves to a purpose, we cannot be expected to be ready at hand to look after every passer-by and to lend ourselves to every chance display of altruism." If Mulholland sometimes failed in "displays of altruism," he also avoided the pitfalls of corruption, cheating, favoritism, and failure. The man with a clear head is not always lovable.[3]

In an effort to satisfy grievances, the city undertook more land purchases in 1925 and by August had acquired about 16,000 more acres, bringing the total of city-owned acres in Owens Valley to 189,000. This left approximately 11,000 acres of remaining arable land to be purchased. These constituted a compact parcel in the general contour of a half-moon west of Bishop along the west bank of the Owens River. This acreage led to the next phase of the water war.

WATER EXPANSIONS

The Owens Valley controversy rode tandem with the ongoing struggle for the Colorado River project. The boom years of the 1920s had produced similar controversies throughout the nation. Because of its rapid growth, Chicago was currently in conflict with Canada over the amounts of water the Chicago Drainage Canal was taking from the Great Lakes. Other water and power struggles in California included San Francisco's with Hetch Hetchy; Fresno's with Pine Flat Dam; and the Edison Company's water fight with owners along the San Joaquin River. Greatest of all and involving all the states along the Colorado River was the Boulder Dam proposal. When the McClure Report on Owens Valley was issued, Mulholland was preoccupied with a bill in Sacramento providing for a huge water district in Southern California that would allow the formation of a Colorado River domestic water district. It would comprise thirty or more cities and towns in the southern part of the state supplied by a giant aqueduct. The legislature defeated the bill in the first round, amid strong opposition from Harry Chandler's *Times* and the Los Angeles Chamber of Commerce, but it finally passed a second bill organizing the Metropolitan Water District at the beginning of 1927.[4]

On Saint Patrick's Day 1925, in homage to Mulholland's Irish origins, the board of the public service commission declared a day of celebration for the dedication of Mulholland Dam in Weid Canyon. Standing by the most romantic and scenic of all his dams, the Chief praised his codesigner and engineer, H. L. Jacques, for his work with the department since 1910. Self-deprecating, he said that his associates often twitted him on the appearance of his work. "They say it looks like an old woman's apron—an object of utility, but not of beauty." Then he made a rare smile as he pointed towards the graceful curve of the concrete wall. "But in this job," he added, "I think I may take a little pardonable pride." He recalled the man for whom the canyon had been named, Ivar Weid, a wine gauger who had lived in the canyon at the present site of the dam and whom he remembered from 1882. At the time, Mulholland had been quarrying rock in the canyon for the city jail. He jested that he was happy to have outlived the ignominy of that and to have his name now identified with a structure more in keeping with the spirit of Los Angeles. He also took the occasion to encourage support for the upcoming water bond issue with a bit of blarney and fatherly instruction. "I am glad there is such a large and intelligent audience here because the people have been greatly misinformed concerning their water supply. For your telephone talks you are paying two and one-half the times the cost of your water supply, or a little more than a third of what it costs other cities of similar size."[5]

Mayor Cryer, in the midst of a hot mayoral campaign, limited his remarks to a gracious appreciation of Mulholland's service to the city. "Long may he live and prosper!" Six weeks later, the mayor prevailed over his opponent, Judge Benjamin F. Bledsoe, an ally of Harry Chandler in the fight against municipal ownership of power. The removal of three of the five assemblymen who had voted against the Metropolitan Water District Act further manifested favorable public attitudes toward municipal water and power. After actively campaigning throughout May for Boulder Dam and water bonds mostly to fund the land purchases in Owens Valley, Mulholland and Scattergood were gratified by the wide margins favoring both issues.[6]

THOUGHTS ON MORTALITY
AND THE DEATH OF A FRIEND

At the end of June, torrential rains in the Tehachapis and high desert (the worst in fifteen years) washed out rail communication north of Mojave and shattered 400 feet of the aqueduct at locations near Jawbone, Sand Canyon, and Dove Springs, south of Little Lake. Tons of debris and silt clogged the damaged sections and stopped the flow from Haiwee. Mulholland went immediately to consult with Roderick McKay, who was desperately working with crews to open the line. For the next ten days, he remained to help supervise repairs before he set out on an unusual expedition with his associate and fellow engineer E. A. Bayley. They journeyed to the Gros Ventre country north of Jackson, Wyoming, to study a giant landslide that had removed part of Sheep Mountain into the path of a river and thus created a lake behind it. Bayley took photographs while Mulholland pondered the work of nature to see what hints it might provide for a man-made lake. Could the towering canyon walls at Boulder perhaps be toppled into the abyss at their base with a titanic dynamite blast? Mulholland cheerfully reported that Mother Nature had done a bang-up job. "Never saw a better job in my life. The dam is a typical earth and rock fill structure and when I saw it, it was tight as a trivet. Of course, it won't stand. Nature made no provisions for a spillway and, in time, the water will cut a new channel to its old level." Back in town, he immediately set out again with Van Norman to inspect the repair work on the aqueduct.[7]

Two weeks later, just as fears of brewing trouble and possible violence in Owens Valley had led the city to increase its police guard along the aqueduct, Roderick McKay, one of the Chief's closest associates since joining the water bureau in 1907, collapsed and died while rushing repairs on the line. The stress and urgency of the demanding work had proven too much for the sixty-two-year-old Scotsman, whom del Valle eulogized by saying that he had given his life in service to his city.[8]

Days after McKay's death, Mulholland requested that Van Norman return to the water bureau to serve as the Chief's assistant. For the past two years, he had been loaned out to the department of public works to oversee the completion of the outfall sewer and then had been named city engineer. As Van Norman would take over the active detailed work of the department, the board directed Mulholland to take the vacation that he had earned, but he demurred by repeating his old story of spending an afternoon at Long Beach once and becoming so bored that he showed up for work next morning. To reporter Joseph Timmons, who reminded him that he would soon be seventy, Mulholland spoke bluntly. "I may die some day. Nothing is more certain than that. I may go as suddenly as McKay. But I am not thinking of retiring." The truth emerged; he loved his work. "If I knew of anything that would afford me as much amusement and entertainment as the constructive work in this job, I would retire and do it." He did not intend to quit unless God called him or "some of those who wish I would retire can induce the Water and Power Commission to get rid of the old codger."[9]

He had decisions to make, he told Timmons, about the tunnel that would carry Colorado River water through San Gorgonio Pass. Should it be dug through sandstone or granite? Should it be swung towards the Yucaipa side through sandstone or toward the San Jacinto side and be granite-walled? He sometimes rode across the desert in his limousine—which he referred to as his hearse—simply to contemplate the work ahead. He was awed by it, he said, but not scared. Then he spoke of an early experience at sea.

> Soon after I went to sea at 14, I had a task to do on the quarterdeck. An old sailor named Jack, for whom I had formed a liking, was at the wheel. I had often edged up to him and let my hand rest on the wheel, while I watched the sails with him, getting the instinct for steering by the wind. This day as I stood there he remarked that he wished he had his sou'wester, as spray was wetting him. I said, "Why don't you go get it? I'll take the wheel." He did it, without stopping for second thought and, as I stood there with the rolling ship responding to my touch as I held her to the right course, with wind abeam, I felt an elation, an exultation that cannot be described. I felt like Jove.

He concluded, "That is the way one feels at 70 at the wheel of an organization like this, and a task like the building of the Colorado aqueduct ahead. I am awed, as I was then by the majestic harmony of ship and sea and sail and wind, but I wasn't afraid then, and I'm not now."[10]

For his seventieth birthday on September 11, he took a week off but not for recreation. Instead, he headed for Oakland and Berkeley to consult over plans for a new $35 million East Bay water project, after which he proceeded to Sacramento for more consultations and inspection tours. Before he left, he also moved his office into new quarters at the end of August when the water and power bureaus moved into a thirteen-story building with a seven-story annex on the south side of Second Street between Broadway and Hill Streets. The move produced another burst of reminiscence as he recalled the early days of the water company when he and Tom Brooks had lived over the office at Alameda and Marchessault Streets.[11]

TESTIFYING FOR BOULDER DAM

By October, two large work camps along the Colorado River were doing preliminary surveys and road building near San Gorgonio. The end of the month found the Chief at the top of his form, doing battle with an Arizona senator who wanted to abandon plans for a high dam at Boulder Canyon and substitute a low dam proposed by a rival engineer, C. A. LaRue. Mulholland laid into the plan, called it "an atrociously preposterous pipe dream." As the interchanges grew hot, some of Mulholland's answers evoked merriment among the crowd of three hundred in the ballroom of the Biltmore Hotel, where the hearing was held. "Do you mind me asking these questions?" Senator Ashurst asked at one point. "No," countered Mulholland. "Pitch right in. They give me a rest."[12]

The hearings continued at Las Vegas with an inspection of Boulder Dam, during which Arthur P. Davis, Frank E. Weymouth, and Mulholland all spoke to the project's engineering feasibility. State engineer McClure, who had condemned Los Angeles's water activities in his report, now accompanied the Los Angeles engineers (who included Mulholland, Lippincott, Van Norman, and E. A. Bayley) on an eight-day inspection tour along Mulholland's proposed route of the Colorado River Aqueduct. Unfortunately, no reports of their conversations seem to have survived.[13]

THE PLOT THICKENS IN OWENS VALLEY

Owens Valley dwellers had done a lot of sniping through their local newspapers in 1925. They described the guards at Haiwee Reservoir, for instance, as an "armed invasion of Los Angeles hirelings." But the area remained peaceful until the announcement of the city's August purchase of the Longyear holdings for $300,000. With credit given to William Lacy, president of the Los Angeles Chamber of Commerce, and Harvey Van Norman for their services in resolving the negotiation, Longyear declared that he had sold low because he wanted an amicable settlement between Owens Valley and the city. The sale meant that the city now owned all of the improved water-bearing land in that portion of northern Owens Valley except the so-called Keough pool (4,482 acres), which was under the sway of Carl Keough and W. W. Watterson. The city had offered them

$1.25 million (or 4.6 times the assessed value), but the owners turned it down, demanding $2.1 million.[14]

Some of this group saw in the Longyear sale evidence of George Watterson's influence, so in mid-September, when the only recent violence in Owens Valley had been rifle shots during deer season, and while W. W. Watterson was recuperating from an appendectomy in Glendale (in the same hospital with his wife, who months earlier had suffered a general breakdown and been hospitalized), three of his rancher allies visited Uncle George and told him to get out of Bishop until the land and water matters with the city had been resolved. The threatening men claimed they represented 80 percent of northern Inyo County ranchers who wanted him out because they thought he was the cause of lower land prices. An indignant Watterson declared he had no intention of leaving the place where he had lived for thirty-five years and complained to the justice of the peace, who fined the men fifty dollars apiece for offensive conduct and disturbing the peace.[15]

Other Owens Valley owners were suing the city, claiming their ranches had been rendered arid by nearby wells that the city had drilled during the drought. Geologists shot down these claims in court, demonstrating that the rock strata precluded the wells, which had been drilled at some distance away, from affecting the ranches. Amid these contentions, the city announced that since the valley had refused to accept the public service commission's plan to leave 30,000 acres of the best land in the district under private ownership and permanent cultivation, it now intended to maintain the best sections of the city-owned land for agriculture and grazing and began to encourage bids for their use. Since 1923, the city had expended $8 million on land purchases in Owens Valley, and the current acquisitions amounted to $4 million more, which satisfied many in Los Angeles that the water and power commission had dealt generously and expeditiously with Owens Valley residents while also protecting the city's interests.[16]

Throughout 1925, various city representatives, mainly Mathews and Van Norman, had dealt with Fred Eaton as attorneys and associates plugged along, trying to reach an agreement on the Long Valley matter. (Duns for Eaton's unpaid grazing rentals piled up in the water department's files until, after four years, attempts at collecting seem to have been abandoned.) At one point in May, Eaton, with his associates and attorneys, indicated a willingness "to play ball" with the city, but the Eaton Land and Cattle Company now had a number of shareholders who were apparently not of one mind, so that time ran out for an agreement.[17]

At the beginning of 1926, Eaton suffered a stroke. Van Norman wired the news to Mathews, then in Washington, where he would remain for the next six months to attend the congressional hearings for the third Swing-Johnson bill. Eaton's son, Harold, and an associate of Eaton now requested that the Eaton properties in Long Valley be appraised the same as those lands "of same character lately purchased in Owens Valley." According to Van Norman, Mulholland was agreeable, and Leahey had been instructed to get the appraisal committee right on it. He also informed Mathews in the same wire that Longyear had sold his cattle to Hearst and was ready to close the deal and that the "water situation looks good with prospect of above deals and other deals pending on Owens River Canal."[18]

Two weeks later, Mathews wired Mulholland via the Chief's private secretary, Eve H. Shoemaker. "My home advises Fred Eaton seriously ill and anxious about my return Please get from him or those caring for him any message he may wish sent me Also convey to him my affectionate regard and earnest hope for early recovery." A week later, on March 11, when Van Norman wired Mathews for advice on matters before the public service commission, he added that Harold Eaton was pressing for the sale of the Eaton property. Van Norman suggested a deal for 12,000 acres at $40 an acre ($480,000) might be possible. Harold, however, had "intimated that the deal could be closed for sixty-six per acre" ($792,000). The younger Eaton also reported that his father's associate, banker John E. Fishburn, was forming a syndicate "to tie up property for five years with option to purchase at end of this time." After Van Norman and Mulholland decided the latter development was probably a bluff, Mulholland indicated he was reluctant to have anything to do with it. Van Norman then consulted with Mathews over a proper price, also informing him that he was heading for Owens Valley to investigate and concluded with the good news that forty feet of water was now in the "new St. Francis."[19]

With the city's refusal to pay their price, the Eatons arranged a mortgage with Watterson Bros., Inc., for $200,000, to consist of forty promissory notes of $5,000 each, payable on or before five years after date, with interest of 8 percent per annum, payable semiannually. By year's end, Wilfred Watterson was deeply involved in Eaton's holdings, as he requested abstracts of the Long Valley property and clarification of documents regarding lands near Haiwee that Eaton had previously sold to the city. Because Eaton and his wife were living in Los Angeles-Santa Monica during his recovery, and because Eaton's right side had been partially paralyzed so that he now had to use his left hand to sign his name, his wife, Alice, acted as his amanuensis for his business correspondence.[20]

In the spring of 1926, while the dealings with Fred Eaton remained unresolved, a well was mysteriously dynamited on property that W. W. Watterson had sold to the city a year before. Dynamite caps were found in the automobile of Carl Keough, president of the Owens River Canal Company, that was still holding out on a sale to the city and in which Watterson also had an interest. Leahey traveled down to Los Angeles to report the incident, but it was not a matter of grave concern. More newsworthy were the water and power board's threat to sue the editor of the *Owens Valley Herald*, Harry Glasscock, for libel, and plans to celebrate the opening in early May of a new highway between Los Angeles and Bishop. (The first 104 miles to Mojave were all concrete, while the next stretch to Bishop was a graded dirt roadway.) Weeks later, however, another blast ripped a ten-foot hole in the aqueduct about four miles from Lone Pine, near the Alabama Hills. Again, the blast was linked to the Keough group but Mulholland declared it "simply a gesture to get our attention. . . . They do it now and then up that way," he explained. "Then they make reparation claims. The dynamite is set off one night and we get a boxful of reparations claims the next morning. . . . That," he concluded, "tells the whole story." Again, repairs on the line were quickly made.[21]

On July 1, a third blast ushered in the Fourth of July by blowing up a construction shack northeast of Bishop, but in Los Angeles it scarcely rated a notice amid the celebration of Mathews's return from Washington, D.C., after six months of work on behalf of the Boulder Dam Act. Mulholland paid his old friend high tribute, saying that without him the aqueduct could not have been built and that now he was equally invaluable in the Boulder fight. Politicking took up much of the summer until the primary election on August 31 approved the much-needed water and power bonds. Voters also selected candidates for the November election who would usher out Richardson and bring to office a strong pro-Boulder candidate, former lieutenant-governor C. C. Young.[22]

WATTERSON TAKES CHARGE

On December 31, 1926, W. W. Watterson wrote a less than jolly New Year's letter to Fred Eaton as he slowly recovered from his stroke. After speaking of certain problems finding accurate records for the Long Valley property, he indicated that if Eaton's deal for a sale to the city did not materialize, he believed they could work something out for him "in connection with other plans we have." The same day, Watterson wrote

with great candor to his brother-in-law, J. C. "Jake" Clausen, then living in Los Angeles and in almost daily contact with Eaton. Acknowledging that he was glad "we have the mortgage and have it duly recorded
and under our control since you have told us of his [Eaton's] mental attitude towards the situation. Reminds me of old Charlie Summers for
whom we have done more than almost any other man in the country
and he is one of our nastiest enemies." (Summers, hard-boiled and cantankerous, was one of the old-time Owens Valley cattlemen and, probably because of depressed market prices during this period, must have
been encumbered with mortgages at the Watterson banks.)[23]

Watterson outlined to Clausen various strategies for successful land
deals in Owens Valley. One was to put the squeeze on Eaton for an option on his Long Valley land; the other was "to get a big lot of property
under pool—this of course quite confidentially—and then make an effort to sell it to the City. I can't give you in this letter the details of our
plan but I am satisfied it will work out just as successfull [sic] as our efforts to sell Round Valley and West Bishop did," that is, their earlier campaign that involved forming the Big Pine Property Owners Association
and ousting George Warren from the presidency of the Associated Chambers of Commerce in Owens Valley.

What Watterson also saw fit to include in this letter were instructions
on wangling an option on Eaton's Long Valley land, as "I am satisfied
that if we had that we would accomplish more for Eaton than anything
he will be able to do for himself." He cautioned about Eaton's lack of
trust in anybody else's ability to achieve successful dealings with the city
but argued that he could point out to him their success in Round Valley
and West Bishop, "where the sales amounted to over a million dollars"
and "we sold every piece of property placed in our hands at the price
the farmer named and did not in any instance have to reduce the price a
single dollar."

EATON HOLDS OUT

With the beginning of 1927, Los Angeles continued its fight for Boulder
Dam, sending off a team headed by veteran attorney Mathews to Washington, D.C. At home the stalemate on Long Valley continued as Harold
Eaton asked for $800,000 while the city agreed to $600,000. Mulholland's response to the stalemate was to authorize a dam at the Tinemaha
site and secure agreements with the railway to begin moving its rail sites
to the west side of the valley from Owenyo to Laws.[24]

In precarious health and with no good economic news, Eaton held out for his price of $2.1 million. He next received a blockbuster letter from W. W. Watterson. Written February 6, 1927, it announced without preamble that none of Eaton's strategies for selling had succeeded nor ever would; that none of his city friends had been of help to him; that they (the Wattersons) had carried him along as a friend, but "after three years of fruitless effort" on the Long Valley property, it was time to yield and follow their advice. Soon, Watterson continued, the city would have acquired "all of the properties in this watershed except those belonging to two or three men to whom they feel antagonistic like yourself, Longyear, and the Crowell Zombro interests." (J. Crowell and Sumter F. Zombro were Los Angeles financiers.)[25]

After detailing his plans for cleaning up land sales in Owens Valley, Watterson informed Eaton of their dealings with the city:

> Senator Joe Inman, our attorney in Sacramento, has been active lately in making arrangements to sell to the City the remaining lands here. We are encouraging the movement because it seems to be the most feasible channel through which to get all the remaining interests consolidated. Inman is working with Jess Hession [district attorney of Inyo County], and if they get enough property under option so that it will be worthwhile to carry on a proper campaign to make a sale to the City of the same, and also that there will be enough of the property to insure proper compensation to Inman and his group, it will go through. We are giving Inman an option on our ranch holdings and town property along with many other people who are doing the same, and we feel that you should join us in this movement and do so immediately. The sooner it is done, the sooner something can be accomplished in the way of working out our program.

Watterson instructed Eaton to put his price as "the net amount that you are to get out of it, leaving it so that Hession and Inman will have to depend on the raise in price above your option for their compensation." He also advised Eaton not to think of what the property is worth to the city but rather "what a given amount of money is worth to you now and to your families after you are gone. . . . You should not," he warned, "under any circumstances gamble with the property at this time. A reasonable amount now, and safety, is the only path you should follow in arriving at a price to set on the property." Reminding him that for several years the Wattersons had been providing funds to carry him along but now seeing no hope of future improvement ("the indebtedness is growing steadily"), he warned that Eaton could not expect future help unless he accepted a one-year option.

Silence followed this hard-nosed letter until ten days later, when Clausen reported to Watterson that he surmised Eaton had been "put out," having heard nothing from the man who customarily called him almost every day. Eaton's daughter-in-law, Mrs. Burdick Eaton, had told Clausen that he felt "very badly" and warned him to stay away for a while. Eaton's brother-in-law also informed Clausen that "Mr. Eaton was much peeved," declared he did not know who Inman was and was sure he could not do anything anyway, and wondered if "Wilfred was trying to make some money out of the situation." Clausen confided that in his opinion, "Fred is mentally impossible to deal with—He is suspicious of everybody—and you will surely get into difficulties with him if you attempt to carry out any cooperation plan—no matter how advantageous to him."[26]

While Watterson worked on Eaton, Van Norman was writing his concerns to Mathews. On February 3, he included the annual report of the Owens Valley Irrigation District (dominated by the Wattersons) and noted that its costs and salaries came to $12,000, of which the city paid 80 percent. "This money is being used by the officers of the district in promoting law suits and propaganda against the city." Was there no way to stop it, he wondered. He also spoke of problems dealing with the Inyo County banks, all Watterson-owned: "like pulling teeth to get the documents out" (mortgages, land titles, and such). In some cases, Van Norman complained, "the City's money has been in the bank as long as six months for the satisfaction of a mortgage before the bank would complete transactions; there being no reason other than that the bank has held the money to use as long as possible." Citing other difficulties, he concluded, "We do not feel safe in depositing large sums of money there under the present conditions and if another bank is opened in the Valley, it will go a long ways towards solving our problem." More positively, he reported that the Lone Pine Chamber of Commerce had written a letter of thanks to the public service commission for its attitude toward the valley, "especially in the matter of advertising last year; the movement . . . to get the railroad broad-gauged; and its assistance in building roads into the mountains." He also indicated that similar letters of appreciation would be forthcoming from other chambers in the valley.[27]

THE LAST ROUND OF "SHOOTING THE DUCK"

Fighting words preceded the dynamitings in the second phase of the water war. After the Big Pine Property Owners Association met in February, the *Owens Valley Herald* heightened the event by likening it to the well-known statue of a defeated Indian warrior on his horse, *The End of the Trail*. As Senator Inman began his fight for the reparations act in Sacramento, a powerful propaganda barrage against Los Angeles began. Various legislators were invited to view the havoc wrought in Owens Valley. Frederick Faulkner, editor of the *Sacramento Union,* arrived and subsequently wrote a series entitled *Owens Valley: Where the Trail of the Wrecker Runs* (March 28 to April 2). The columns coincided with the attempt to push through the reparations act. Los Angeles rebutted with Don Kinsey's pamphlet, *The Owens Valley Dispute.* Then, on April 6, the *Owens Valley Herald* announced that a fistfight between a Los Angeles deputy sheriff and an Owens Valley Property Owners Protective Association officer had drawn first blood. Magnifying this scuffle outside a pool hall into a portent of the Los Angeles Aqueduct's running red with human blood, the paper began to report each dead creature found in a local creek (a deer, a mountain lion) as victims of the aqueduct and a reminder to the people of the south that the water they drank and imagined to be pure was, because of the dead bodies it sometimes contained, "a kind of a cannibal soup, flavored with the carcasses of the lower animals."[28]

Journalist C. E. Kunze and his wife next arrived in Bishop to rewrite and reprint in pamphlet form his successful series, *The Valley of Broken Hearts,* which was now to be distributed throughout the United States along with 10,000 mailers of Faulkner's pieces. (Watterson's later claim that he had spent $30,000 on these efforts seems to confirm Van Norman's accusation that Los Angeles was subsidizing attacks against itself.) After two months of widely disseminated assaults against the city and mounting anger in Owens Valley as the reparations bill neared a vote, the senate tabled the reparations resolution on April 27. A pleased Mulholland branded the Owens Valley charges false and was further elated a week later when Governor Young signed the Metropolitan Water District Act. Ten days hence, however, the disappointed Owens Valleyites renewed their sport of "shooting the duck." Between May and July seven dynamitings shook the aqueduct.[29]

The first two explosions occurred only days apart on May 20 and 28, destroying the No Name Siphon and 475 feet of aqueduct as well as the penstock of the Big Pine powerhouse. As guards and police rushed to the scene from Los Angeles to protect against further depredations, the board of water and power commissioners condemned the deeds, as did the city council. Mulholland, with Van Norman, hastened north to meet with Leahey and W. J. Clark, a former deputy district attorney of Los Angeles now delegated to investigate the sabotage. After viewing the damage, Mulholland expressed his outrage but also, as he had done so many times before when the water supply appeared threatened, reassured the city that the destruction would not cause a water shortage. Both he and Scattergood cited the recent completion of the Saint Francis Dam as providential in the crisis because its current capacity would help the city to avoid serious power shortages.[30]

Having done what he could, Mulholland left in a chauffeured car and returned safely to Los Angeles. His colleagues, however, following later in a large and speeding touring sedan, missed a sharp turn on a mountain road in Mint Canyon about twenty miles north of Saugus. The back brakes locked and the car plunged down an embankment, turning over several times. Although all fortunately escaped death, at this moment of crisis two of Mulholland's most valuable coworkers, Van Norman and Leahey, lay in the hospital with severe injuries.[31]

Five days after the car accident, a June 6 dynamiting crippled a section of the aqueduct near the Cottonwood powerhouse; two more damaging blasts followed two weeks later. Amid growing consternation and the city's demands to bring in state troops, Governor Young refused, speaking vaguely of the need for arbitration, a proposal promptly shot down by Owens Valleyites. On July 6, Mulholland made an urgent request to the Federal Radio Commission for permits and licenses for shortwave radio transmitters between Owens Valley and Los Angeles. "Due to extreme dangers and threats to life and property along Los Angeles Aqueduct System, it is vitally necessary to establish an emergency means of communication between Headquarters of the Department of Water and Power in Los Angeles and its Lone Pine, California, maintenance branch at the source of its water supply." Citing "recent depredations" that had destroyed both telephone and telegraph lines, the message declared it "imperative to have an emergency source of intelligence that Radio alone can supply."[32]

A week after Mulholland sent that wire, another section of the aqueduct north of Independence was blown out July 15. A blast that followed the next day proved to be the last. The city's efforts to quell the destruction and round up the culprits had met with some success, but the violence finally ended because Owens Valley events and plots unraveled on their own. First, an ex-major, C. Percy Watson, was found with a cache of dynamite and arrested as a principal in the dynamitings. (Later, to the surprise of many, he was exonerated.) Then amid this atmosphere of increasing lawlessness that threatened a serious disruption of water and power supplies, a turn worthy of Greek tragedy produced a reversal of fortunes. Bank examiners, discovering irregularities in the five Watterson banks, ordered their closure and charged the brothers with embezzlement and fraud. One million dollars could not be accounted for, and by the end of August, the Wattersons had been arraigned.[33]

What ensued was a sorry saga of local betrayals and a further deepening of hatreds, as what had been portrayed as the Valley of Broken Hearts due to predatory water men from the big city truly became a place of heartbreak and loss at the hands of its own. As costly and demoralizing as the dynamitings had been to the city—damage to the aqueduct was estimated at $250,000, to say nothing of the lost water and interrupted power service in Los Angeles—they paled beside Owens Valley's emotional and financial losses as it grew clear that Los Angeles had prevailed and loomed now as a permanent overlord. In the propaganda war, however, Owens Valley triumphed, for its charges and insinuations have long since been woven into the tapestry of myths depicting Los Angeles as a water stealer and exploiter. Just as later writers have credulously used the many undocumented charges of that time, so today do some Owens Valleyites remain as intransigent towards the city as unreconstructed Southerners towards the Yankee North. Fifty years after the dynamitings, a woman who had been a young mother at the time of the Alabama Gates incident remained unyielding in her opinion. "Had the men who owned the bank had a chance they could have made every dime good. The two men went to prison. The Water & Power was behind it all. My father lost what money he had and so did my father-in-law." As the Fresno editor had prophesied, Naboth had met his doom.[34]

THE PLAYING OUT OF A SAD SAGA

With attention focused on the upcoming and highly emotional Watterson trial, Mulholland observed his seventy-second birthday. By then, Leahey and Van Norman were sufficiently recovered from their injuries to return to work and oversee the continuing aqueduct repairs while Los Angeles and Owens Valley civic leaders attempted to find grounds for reconciliation. The public service commission announced it would buy Longyear's and Zombro's lands at prices the Los Angeles bankers had earlier refused. Other appeals for the city to buy lands now flooded in with the vain hope that it might save the ailing banks, but as Mulholland pointed out, "If we should proceed to buy the remaining ranches, mighty little of the money we paid would be thrown into the pot by the ranch owners to save the banks. The Wattersons long ago sold us their ranches and turned their attention to trying to force us to pay millions in reparations to the townspeople. The banks have mortgages on some of the ranches we have not bought and a part of the money, if we bought them now, would go to the banks, but not enough to re-establish the banks."[35]

Amid the valley's misfortunes, Harry Glasscock of the *Owens Valley Herald* maintained an unrepentant bravado and continued to blame the valley's woes on the city. With uncertainty, anger, and the threat of violence palpable throughout the valley, and after more explosives were discovered near the aqueduct around Lone Pine, the city purchased sixteen Thompson machine guns to beef up security along the line. To compound the confusion, cloudbursts and an earthquake clogged a portion of the aqueduct with debris, so that crews rushed in to clear away the rocks and dirt.[36]

The unremitting strain and worry of the strife between Los Angeles and Owens Valley had taken an unimaginable toll on all the players in this saga. On September 11, Mulholland's birthday, Ben Leete, president of the Owens Valley Protective Association, a close associate of the Wattersons and one of the leaders in the fight against Los Angeles, dropped dead of a heart attack. Later, editor Glasscock would commit suicide. With the approach of the explosive Watterson trial and continued anonymous threats against Mulholland's life, his family and friends insisted that he absent himself from the city and take a genuine vacation. Even though his extraordinary vigor had allowed him to maintain a pace arduous for a man of any age, intimations of mortality had begun to encroach. Increasingly his name appeared as an honorary pallbearer at the funerals of old associates, while McKay's sudden death, old friend and contemporary Eaton's afflictions, and the recent auto accident that had almost cost the lives of two of his most valued (and younger) friends and coworkers crowded in to demonstrate life's uncertainties. The Chief continued to dismiss threats against him as pure bluff but at last succumbed to the wishes of his concerned family.[37]

The day the Watterson trial began in Owens Valley, October 31, 1927, Mulholland, with his son and daughter-in-law, Perry and Addie Mulholland, sailed on the SS *Mongolia* of the Panama Pacific Line for a cruise to New York via the Panama Canal. He was about to see firsthand the engineering marvel that rivaled his own. Fifty years had passed since he last saw what was then the precanal Isthmus of Panama, hiking across it with his brother. Now he sailed out of San Pedro as a world-renowned engineer on a swift modern steamer under the command of one Captain H. A. T. Candy. Quartered in a first-class cabin and seated at the captain's table, Mulholland enjoyed the status of an honored guest. "They made a big fuss over Dad," Addie later recalled. One week out and on the eve of their November 8 arrival at Balboa, she wrote her sister-in-law, Rose Mulholland, that the honor of the captain's table was proving a dubious pleasure, for Captain Candy was "inclined to be rather obstinate." She explained, "He and Dad have had several very heated discussions but I hope they are through for the trip." She thought, however, that he was enjoying the cruise, for he "generally finds some one interesting to talk to and if he doesn't he sleeps." The day before, he had spent the afternoon with "an *Examiner* man named Talbert." On other days, he and Perry had spent "a great deal of time looking at the scenery which consists *principally* of salt water." He had not, she reported, opened a book on the trip.[38]

Mulholland returned from vacation a month later with renewed hope that matters might be resolved in Owens Valley. During his absence, the Wattersons had been found guilty and sentenced to ten years in San Quentin. Negotiations between the city and Owens Valley inched along, and after five months of work, Tinemaha Dam was half finished under the supervision of engineer Stanley Dunham, who had built the Saint Francis Dam in 1926. An earth-fill structure south of Big Pine, Tinemaha was intended as a holding basin in the event of trouble between itself and Haiwee.[39]

With the focus once more on the Boulder Dam proposal that was about to be argued yet again in Congress, Mulholland left for Washington, D.C., in early January 1928, with Van Norman and Mathews, to testify on behalf of the third Swing-Johnson bill. Upon returning from his Panama trip, he had made a strong public statement in favor of the upcoming bill and expressed his impatience with the years of foot-dragging since 1923–24. Even Senators Swing and Johnson were beginning to feel discouraged about its chances of passage.[40]

Hearings were to have begun January 6, 1928, but by the tenth, Mulholland wrote to Rose from his hotel in Washington, D.C., "I imagined that by this time I could give you some idea of the time of my return but it still is uncertain. . . . I had a bad attack of neuritis for two days but am all right now." He never testified, and as congressmen, engineers, and lobbyists for the Colorado River states continued to tilt over the bill, he and Van Norman departed on January 16, leaving Representative Evans of Glendale to enter into the *Congressional Record* Mulholland's report arguing Los Angeles's need for Boulder Dam and asserting that at the current rate of growth, its present water supply would be inadequate by 1947. Back in Los Angeles, Mulholland announced his belief that the long-contested Swing-Johnson bill would ultimately pass, but by the time it had, on December 28, 1928, Mulholland's world had irrevocably broken.[41]

MULHOLLAND VISITS EATON

Soon after his return from Washington, Mulholland visited Fred Eaton. Van Norman in turn reported by wire to Mathews on February 13: "Fred is in about same frame of mind respecting property as he has always been." Since the Watterson debacle, the Eaton Land and Cattle Company had gone into receivership. Van Norman, hoping to persuade him to sell to the city, asked Eaton's old friend and associate, G. J. Kuhrts, former city engineer and now general manager of the Los Angeles Railway Company, to intercede. Mulholland reported the results of that mission in a long letter to Mathews:

> Burdick Eaton's wife called me last Friday to come and see Fred. I was somewhat alarmed by the urgency of her call and responded at once, but found when I got there that he was merely in a talkative mood, due to a recent visit of George Kuhrts. He wanted to prod me up about his affairs. He doesn't seem to me to be ailing any more than he did a couple of months ago when he called here at my office, but seems to realize that the time is getting short to urge his case in the land matter on the Board.
>
> This morning George Kuhrts called on me, and having accomplished nothing with Fred,—as he refrained from telling me anything about what he expected to get from the land, in spite of my inquiry,—Van and I put it directly up to Kuhrts. He seemed shy about revealing to us anything in regard to what Eaton expected, but started in with a million dollars, and finally worked down to the point where he said he understood we would give $800,000. I thought I would let you know this so that you might be informed of what took place here.
>
> Kuhrts is quite sure that Eaton won't accept this figure, but Van was in a mood to test him out anyway and find out really what was in the back of his head. We have not had the matter up with anyone since we left you in Washington. In fact, as you know, I am keeping clear of it altogether myself, except when urged to talk about it, as I was on my visit to Eaton, but I avoided discussion of the matter as much as I could. I told him he would have to take it up with the proper committee. The Board has not approached the subject in my presence at any time within the last three or four months, or at any

time since you left here. My purpose in writing you this is, as I stated, so as to let you know how things stand as far as anything we have done here is concerned.

In closing, Mulholland said that nothing new was going on, but that the winter was dry. "We are now twenty per cent shy of the normal, and snow falls so far have been very light." Expressing a hope for rain, he also gave thanks that the storage supply was better than it had ever been because of the "excessive precipitation of the last two years." He closed by saying that he hoped to hear good news soon about the Boulder bill. A month later, his career was in ruins.[42]

CHAPTER 24

The Saint Francis Dam Disaster and After

1928–1935

AN ILL-STARRED DAM

Great human defeats are never forgotten. They pass into the annals of history and myth, even enter our racial memory as the Achilles' heels of human aspirations: the sinking of the *Titanic*, the explosion of the *Graf* zeppelin, the failure of the space ship *Challenger*, and the collapse of the Saint Francis Dam. Rose Mulholland remembered how the horrible news came to their home in the middle of the night. When the upstairs telephone rang sometime after midnight in the hallway just outside her father's bedroom door, she took the call. It was Van Norman, who told her the dam had gone out. She went to her father's bed and awakened him with the news. As he rose and stumbled toward the phone, she heard him repeat over and over, "Please, God. Don't let people be killed."

The day before, on March 12, he and Van Norman had inspected the dam and declared it sound, although there had been talk and concern for some time about leakage at its west abutment. Mulholland remained unworried, said such leakage was typical of concrete dams and not significant. But less than twelve hours later, sometime after midnight, the dam had given way and released an ocean of impounded water to cut a destructive swath to the sea. In those roiling waters, more than four hundred people lost their lives in what became the greatest man-made disaster in the history of California and the greatest American civil engineering failure in the twentieth century.[1]

Construction of the Saint Francis Dam grew out of the California drought of the 1920s, the apparently unending growth of Los Angeles, and the need to store additional water acquired since the city's most recent purchases in Owens Valley. The specter of a water dearth always haunted the city's water men. To forestall that possibility and provide storage for a year's supply of water for Los Angeles, they built nine new reservoirs during that decade, the largest of which was the Saint Francis Dam.[2] Its site in the picturesque San Francisquito Canyon was a second choice for Mulholland, whose first had been nearer the city in Tujunga Canyon. When landowners in that area began to inflate their prices, however, he decided that rather than meet their expensive demands or wait for lengthy condemnation proceedings, he would turn to the canyon site where the city already generated its electric energy at two power plants. Under the supervision of Stanley Dunham, who would later supervise construction of Tinemaha Dam, the Saint Francis was begun in August 1924. The work proceeded without incident except for nearby ranchers and growers who expressed concern over the city's designs on their water from San Francisquito Creek. The city assured them that it did not intend to impound the San Francisquito Creek's waters. On March 12, 1926, as the attention of the city's water men focused on the fight for Boulder Dam and passage of the Swing-Johnson bill, the Saint Francis Dam began to fill with water. Then, two years later to the day, it failed.[3]

The story of this ill-starred dam has been told in many places and the causes of its failure remain controversial. Geologists had long recognized the site's problematic nature because of potentially unstable mica schist on its southeastern canyon wall, but its topography also offered an ideal location for a dam. Caught by the urgency to impound waters and maintain hydroelectric power generation, Mulholland recognized geological difficulties in San Francisquito Canyon yet still believed it to be safe and decided to build there. Instead of the usual hydraulic fill dam such as the South Haiwee and Fairmont, the Saint Francis was modeled after the city's first concrete gravity arch dam structure, the Hollywood Reservoir. Because of the increasing annual use of water in Los Angeles and the desire to achieve maximum storage capacity, the Saint Francis was built 20 vertical feet higher than planned without substantially widening its base. These elements, along with the state of engineering at that time, which did not yet appreciate certain technical knowledge available today such as the destabilizing effects of uplift pressures, may all have contributed to the dam's failure.[4]

Even as water rose for the first time in the reservoir, cracks had appeared on the face of the main structure. They were filled, cemented, and sealed to prevent further seepage. Then, during spring runoff in January 1928, with the dam at full capacity (32,000 acre feets), new leaks appeared on both abutments. For these Mulholland ordered corrective measures. By March, however, the leaking water had turned muddy, suggesting that the ground beneath the west abutment was giving way. Locals, especially those who lived below the dam and had long entertained anxieties about the amount of seepage and leakage they had observed, began to jest in a kind of gallows humor about the imminent collapse of the dam. One, in leaving a companion, had joshed, "Well, good-bye, Ed, I will see you again if the dam don't break." A rancher who survived the disaster would later not forget the last words he had heard from the assistant dam keeper, Jack Ely, two days before the dam went out. As they stood observing the leaks on the west abutment, the rancher twitted him, "Ely, what are you sons-of-guns going to do here, going to flood us out down below?" to which Ely joked back, "We expect this dam to break any minute!"[5]

Minutes before midnight, on March 12, ground gave way on the east side, and the force of the onrushing water collapsed the abutment. Moments later the west side fell, as an overwhelming mountain of water roared down the canyon to run its annihilating course along the bed of the Santa Clara River to the Pacific Ocean. As the monster cataract made its crushing way, it overwhelmed Castaic Junction in a sixty-foot tide. Eleven miles further on, it inundated a construction camp of Southern California Edison Company workers, killing 84 of the 140 people then sleeping there. Next, it began its destructive path across the Santa Clara Valley, as those in the little towns of Piru, Fillmore, and Santa Paula were alerted to the impending juggernaut.[6]

"AFTER THE FIRST DEATH THERE IS NO OTHER"

The horror of any catastrophe has many faces. How can one tell all the stories of that terrible time? Tales of heroism and courage (the young telephone operator in Santa Paula who risked her life by remaining at her post in the path of the coming waters in order to warn people) and tales of shame (looters in the flood-torn little towns). A profusion of records and testimony exists in official papers, engineering reports, and especially, the transcription of the Los Angeles County's coroner's report at the inquest over victims of the Saint Francis Dam disaster. For those with the stomach to look, there are morgue photographs of corpses recovered from the mud, rock, and sand in which the flooding waters churned and mauled their victims. There is the stark dead look of Mulholland, photographed with Van Norman as they stood in the nightmare of every engineer: to have been responsible for a structure that not only failed but killed. There is the progression of his words as at first he said some terrific earth movement (not an earthquake) must have caused the collapse. Then in testimony at the coroner's inquest, after hinting at the possibility of sabotage, with tears coursing down his face and at the point of breaking down, he said he envied the dead.[7]

Endless stories are told of that terrible time, but as Dylan Thomas wrote in "A Refusal to Mourn," his elegy to a child killed in a London fire raid early in World War II, "After the first death there is no other." So let here stand one letter for the many lost on that appalling night. Its author, Daisy Shaw Orton, lived with her family in Fillmore. Her husband, Lucius R. "Luce" (pronounced *Loosh*) Orton, a former undersheriff of Ventura County, was managing the Ventura Distributing Company, which sold and delivered the Ventura Refining Company's gasoline and oil. Anxious to let family in the San Fernando Valley know that they had survived, Daisy wrote the following day:

FILLMORE
MARCH 14, 1928

Dear Folks.

Ever since yesterday morning we have had calls into all our relations to tell that "all is well" with us—and the only call I have succeeded in getting thru was to my folks and as we were limited to three minutes I didn't have brains enough to ask them to relay messages for me to all of you.

For us right here in Fillmore there haven't been so many missing. With very few exceptions all are safe. The bodies that are being found here some 50 in number are from further up toward Castaic.

I don't believe I will ever forget that terrible night we went thru. The fire bell at 2-o'cl. woke us & we could keep hearing an awful roar. Luce dressed and started out and when he got out the door the neighbor man was just going out and told him what had happened. He came back and told us—the children were all awakened by the bell ringing—and then he went to the river to see just where the water was. In just a few minutes more the phone rang—calling more men out—and that the water was at Ventura St. Just the block below us. We then all dressed. 2 A.M.—no lights but my lovely red ornamental candles. I put some clothes for the children in a suitcase and when Luce got back he said the water was going down. We didn't go back to bed but built a fire in the fireplace and stayed up. It was sure a terrible night and I don't believe I will ever forget that awful roar of the water. Who would ever have thot that such a calamity could have overtaken us here.

The Bridge at Bardsdale is completely gone, taken by the water and debris. The river is absolutely clean of trees. Not a willow in sight. All of the houses on the Bardsdale side just off the Bridge are moved—some gone. This side what few were near the river are moved onto the street.

Luce has been gone all day yesterday and into the night and again today. The men here have organized searching parties and have recovered some 50 bodies. Luce says they were not drowned—but battered and bruised [sic]—but don't show anguish—so that probably they were taken in their sleep and didn't know what had happened.

Santa Paula's lower street—River St—had houses moved and twisted. Their lovely new school filled with water—many people left homeless. There is lots of outside aid coming in and as far as we can hear—everything is being done that can possibly be done. There are hundreds of your high powered—blue uniformed—Los Angeles police up here.

I understand from our truck drivers today that they are stopping everyone at the Saticoy crossing—The only way at present that you could get over here would be that way—But I imagine in a couple of days everything will be normal. All companies concerned are clearing roads—building bridges—putting up light and telephone lines. The only ones who they let thru must have *urgent* business. There were hundreds of sight-seeers yesterday—and Luce says that they have hindered men that were working trying to get things in shape. Will Bland was here from Lompoc. Got thru by knowing one of the cops on duty. He said that John was coming down but don't suppose they can get thru.

Gragg was here today. Had gotten *pinched* and had to come to court. Since I have started this your bookkeeper has phoned. So glad. Understand the mail was going out today. No trains—only from Ventura here. No further as yet, but think you will get this all right.

Daisy[8]

WHAT WENT WRONG?

Everyone had an explanation or surmise. Official response was immediate, sometimes surprisingly so. Within three days of the failure, Governor Young ordered a state investigation after the state engineer made the rapid and facile judgment that foundation weaknesses in the dam's abutments were responsible for the collapse and therefore declared "the responsibility rests with the Los Angeles city engineering authorities who built the dam." Mulholland had already asserted that if there were human error, it was his and his alone, which earned him praise and respect in many quarters as he went on to say, "We must have overlooked something." Newspapers throughout America headlined the story and editorially praised the old engineer's courage and honesty in assuming responsibility.

The city was quick to acknowledge its responsibility for the disaster, and within days, a committee under the leadership of George Eastman, president of the Los Angeles Chamber of Commerce, met with Ventura County leaders not only to take care of emergency relief but also to provide for permanent reconstruction. This arbitration committee would work for the next two years to achieve rehabilitation and restitution. Money from the city's general fund was quickly forthcoming after Eastman called on the city council to approve $1 million to begin reconstruction, while engineers from the Los Angeles Department of Water and Power supervised cleaning up the devastation, an enormous job that took three months and involved thousands of laborers, hundreds of tractors, and other heavy equipment. Ultimately, the city paid all claims established by the various committees—a total of $15 million. Charles Collins Teague, the Santa Paula area's leading citrus and walnut grower and owner of the immense Limoneira Ranch, was later to write, "Never before in the history of the world, as far as I am able to learn, was complete and equitable restitution and rehabilitation made by a great metropolitan people to a rural people, where damage had been done and where large sums of money were involved, without recourse to court action. In fact, these settlements were made on the broad ground of moral responsibility without the legal responsibility having been previously determined by the courts."[9]

Investigations followed swiftly upon the dam failure. First, on March 14, engineers for the state arrived, and within a day, one had declared that the dam had been built on a faulty site. Their later report to Governor C. C. Young, today regarded by most engineers as cursory and inadequate, concluded that "the manner in which the dam failed" had not been determined but that there were foundation weaknesses at the abutments, and, finally, that "the responsibility rests with the Los Angeles city engineering authorities who built the dam." Thus, the state washed its hands although the state board of inquiry's recommendation that plans for all future dams should be subject to outside consultants led to pioneer legislation afterward adopted by other states. All but federally sponsored dams and reservoirs would subsequently be subject to state review.[10]

Various city agencies now called for investigations and reports: district attorney Asa Keys called a group; the Los Angeles County Board of Supervisors retained J. B. Lippincott to write a report; and the city council appointed a committee of engineers headed by Elwood Mead (later, chief engineer of Boulder Dam), which reported on April 10 that a defective foundation had failed on the west wall. Most powerful of all the hearings, however, was the inquest of the Los Angeles coroner that began on

March 21 in the Hall of Justice, ten days after the disaster. Technically, the inquest would be for the sixty-five flood victims found in Los Angeles County, while a later inquest was to be held for those found in Ventura County. In a room crammed with spectators, Mulholland took the witness stand, where he testified at length concerning the details of building the Saint Francis Dam. He declared that he had personally supervised the building of the dam, had inspected it often, and had not regarded the leaks as serious: "All dams have leaks." When asked if he knew what caused the dam to go, he replied, "I have a suspicion but I do not want to say." When asked to clarify, he would only state that he would not build there again, that "there is a hoodoo on it." Asked to explain, he would only allow, "Well, it was vulnerable." To what, he would not say, but because of the recent Owens Valley dynamitings, suspicions had inevitably turned to the possibility of sabotage. (Today, most scholars believe that the failure resulted from geological problems rather than human wrongdoing.) Later, in his testimony, he accepted the responsibility for what had happened when, almost breaking down, he declared, "Fasten it on me if there was any error of judgment—human judgment!"[11]

Because the dam failed on the eve of the passage of the Swing-Johnson bill in Washington, opponents of Boulder Dam swooped like vultures to indict the break. To express his sorrow, Mathews hurried back from Washington, where he had been working as a member of California's Colorado River Commission. "Our hearts have been broken by this awful loss of life," he declared. The *Wall Street Journal,* however, editorially viewed the catastrophe not only as a refutation of the value of municipal ownership but as a warning to curtail the Boulder project. The *Los Angeles Examiner* damned the editorial, saying, "it is hard to remember a more ghoulish and contemptible use of public calamity to serve private interests." The bill did finally pass on December 14, 1928.[12]

Other political fallout included renewed questions about the safety of every dam and reservoir in the city's system. The Mulholland Dam especially, although nestled in the Hollywood hills and aesthetically the loveliest of Mulholland's dams, nevertheless shared its design with the Saint Francis, so that, understandably after the disaster, people living nearby were apprehensive. As one of his last acts as chief, Mulholland prudently ordered the water lowered in the Hollywood Reservoir, which, according to engineer Rogers, likely saved the dam, for subsequent studies found its base also lacked sufficient width to "withstand uplift and earthquake loading, or against basal sliding," elements that may have contributed to the failure of the Saint Francis. After engineering recommendations in 1931, the dam was closed down in 1932 for two years of massive retrofitting. Today the structure stands as a peaceful oasis in the Hollywood hills.[13]

Engineers have long studied and debated the causes of the dam's failure without arriving at agreement. Recently the widely published consulting geological engineer J. David Rogers, after years of research, has created renewed interest in the subject with his findings. His investigation, which began with a low regard for Mulholland's character and engineering skills, ultimately led to a reconsideration. "I am of the opinion that we should be so lucky as to have any men with just half his character, integrity, imagination and leadership today."

THE AFTERMATH

Had I but died an hour before this chance
I had lived a blessed time; for, from this instant,
There's nothing serious in mortality,
All is but toys; renown and grace is dead,
The wine of life is drawn, and the mere lees
Is left this vault to brag of.

Macbeth

Lillian Darrow, a native of Newark, New Jersey, had come to California in 1921 and as a young woman in her early twenties worked for the Department of Water and Power in the right-of-way and land department. At the time of the dam failure, she was in the legal department dealing with belongings of the victims. Her memory years later of sorting out clothes and other possessions evoked the remark, "Some of the things I saw were pitiful." She also recalled that Mulholland before the tragedy had been "such a sweet man," who had always greeted her pleasantly whenever they met, but afterward "He went down. His face aged twenty years."[14]

Those who hated Mulholland (or just the idea of him) now had reason to hate him even more. Threats were made against his life, and he lived with an armed guard around his home. He requested a leave of absence, not wishing to embarrass the water board with his presence during the investigation, and although the commission refused to grant it, he knew he could no longer be effective. Even as he accepted responsibility, he remained puzzled. "This expert testimony is all very good," he was heard to say during the coroner's inquest. "But I wish I knew why the St. Francis Dam went out." One reporter noted that "the testimony of the numerous experts did not seem to satisfy him. He shook his head occasionally and a puzzled look came over his face." Fifty years later, his nephew and namesake, William Bodine Mulholland, said his uncle had never been satisfied. "With the knowledge that was available—and he had as much knowledge of those kinds of things as anybody in the world, and he used every bit of the knowledge that was available, and it [the dam] didn't stay there."[15]

Be that as it may, Mulholland's time was over, and in March 1929, Van Norman became chief engineer and general manager of a newly unified organization to be known henceforth as the Department of Water and Power (Scattergood, head of the formerly separate power bureau, became the chief electrical engineer, while Frank E. Weymouth, the hydraulic engineer formerly with the United States Reclamation Service, became assistant to Van Norman in the water bureau). Somewhat in the manner of a professor emeritus, the old Chief was retained as a consultant with an office in the department at a salary of five hundred dollars a month. Even this stipend after a lifetime of service to his city provoked the relentless *Record* to print a letter declaring it preposterous for "a man who had practically acknowledged his responsibility in connection with the Saint Francis tragedy and its sacrifice of over 400 lives, to continue to hold a position of such prestige."[16]

Public opprobrium was one thing; Mulholland had had a lifetime of it mingled with praise and adulation. But certain private hurts cut deep. One mechanical engineer who had worked with him since the days of the old private water company in the 1890s; who had traveled with him on business trips to San Francisco and Owens Valley; had lunched with him almost daily when the two were at the department—now, whether out of disapproval or from an inability to face the Chief—quit speaking to him. One of Mulholland's nephews still puzzled over it years later. "After having been that close to him all that time, he *shunned* him. It was the craziest thing I ever heard of."[17]

A month after the shutdown of the Mulholland Dam for retrofit in December 1931, the Chief suffered another hurtful loss with the sudden and unexpected death after abdominal surgery of his old "partner in crime," attorney W. B. Mathews. No law man in the history of Los Angeles had fought more legal battles for the public good. Eight months after the Saint Francis disaster, he had witnessed the White House signing of the Swing-Johnson bill, and almost to the time of his death, he continued to combat the ongoing threats against the Boulder project. He also lived to see the final approval of the Metropolitan Water District Act, for whose passage he had worked so long and hard. Lake Mathews in Riverside County remains a fitting memorial for the man whose intelligence and imagination are in part responsible for its very existence.

LAST YEARS

It has become a cliché to say that Mulholland was broken by the failure of the dam, and it is true that not unlike the American poet Ezra Pound, incarcerated in a madhouse for treason after World War II, Mulholland sought ever greater refuge in silence. Yet even after all the investigations and studies and speculations about the failure of the Saint Francis Dam, he remained unconvinced that an ultimate explanation had been reached. In accepting responsibility, he did not thereby consider himself to blame for something that had occurred beyond his power. Still, his cup was bitter as he and his family, having endured years of public controversy over water issues, drew further inward. He visited more frequently at the ranch in the San Fernando Valley, where, between 1910 and 1916, he had eventually acquired 640 acres on which his son, Perry, developed and managed the Mulholland Orchard Company, a family partnership. On the old Chief's seventy-fifth birthday in 1930, friends, family, and associates gathered for a private banquet at the ranch, but there were no public announcements or observances. He accompanied his children and grandchildren more frequently on outings and excursions: a day riding the cable car up Mount Lowe, a weekend cruise to Ensenada.[18]

One vivid recollection is of a trip to El Centro and Palm Springs in either 1930 or 1931, part of whose purpose was doubtless to view waterworks in connection with Imperial Valley and the Colorado River. (Among the men of our family, viewing waterworks was considered recreational in the way that museums, amusement parks, or zoos might be to others.) The family car was a dark green 1927 LaSalle touring sedan with a commodious interior. We stayed one night at the Barbara Worth Hotel in El Centro, where the lobby mural of Barbara Worth in the desert captured my imagination. (Years later I discovered in my grandfather's library a copy of *The Winning of Barbara Worth* [1911] by Harold Bell Wright. A best-selling romance celebrating engineers, water, the desert, and an orphan heroine, it upheld the virtues of westerners over materialistic easterners. Pasted in the book was a letter from Wright thanking Mulholland for the tour of the aqueduct and "his kindness in the days when I was collecting material for this story.")

As we motored towards Palm Springs at the end of the next day, discussion arose as to where we would stay the night. (In those days, one could make such impromptu arrangements for lodgings.) Approaching the elegant and newly opened Desert Inn, someone suggested that we ask about accommodations there. My father went in and returned to the car with the information that rooms were available, but rates began at $10.00 a night. Rates at the Barbara Worth Hotel the night before had ranged from $3.50 to $5.00. Grandpa, who had been semidozing up to then, came suddenly to life. "Did you tell them we didn't want to buy the place?" he protested.

We motored on, and instead of the Desert Inn, ended up in decidedly downscale tourist cabins. Next morning, some now long-forgotten exchange arose between my father and grandfather, one of those tense moments which the enforced intimacy of car travel seems to stimulate; perhaps it concerned how best to arrange the luggage in the car. Whatever it was, my agitated father backed over a water hydrant outside the cabin. From the broken pipe spouted a geyser of water, and as both men clambered out of the car, the rest of us emerged from our cabins ready to depart. Water spewed everywhere, and as my father went for help at the front office, I saw my grandfather alone beside the jetting stream. Only the excitement and confusion of the scene registered on me then, but now, years later, the memory of that old man who had been one of the world's leading hydraulic engineers standing helpless by a broken water pipe outside a tourist cabin in the desert strikes me as one of those consummately ironic moments when the gods play their Olympian jokes and laugh in heartless derision at us mere mortals.

GOING OUT

In his iconoclastic study of Los Angeles, *City of Quartz,* Mike Davis has with some justice called Mulholland a Promethean figure. Certainly he was not granted an easy end. He kept his old habits, went to the office where he was no longer in charge and could be of no further public use in the Boulder fight. His name vanished from the newspapers and except for family, close friends and associates, he receded from view. He attended some public events and received small honors from well-wishers. In 1931, on National Hospital Day (to honor the birth of Florence Nightingale, mother of nursing from the time of the Crimean War), old friends and associates of the Chief gathered in the boardroom of the Water and Power Commission, where once he had been the power on the throne and watched as dignitaries from the Florence Nightingale Institute of Honorables awarded him a certificate of honor for public service as "an individual whose forward-looking vision contributed infinitely to enhance the happiness, prosperity and progress of multitudes of human beings by enabling you to conceive and execute methods for producing a supply of water in the City of Los Angeles adequate for the uses of a population calculated on an unprecedentedly rapid basis of increase." He responded graciously, remembered that he had been born at the time of the Crimean War and that some of his people had fought in it. Florence Nightingale, he said, had been a household word in his family, and he had never dreamed that any of her humanitarian work would ever be associated with any honor that might come to him. He held up the plaque for a photograph, and although his expression was kindly, the eyes looking towards the camera seem to be staring into the void.[19]

Yet even with a blasted life, he kept his equanimity. When the powerful and destructive 1933 Long Beach earthquake shook his home at five o'clock in the afternoon, he was reading the evening paper in the den. Daughter Rose rushed to him from the kitchen, calling, "Get under a door, Dad. It's an earthquake!"

"Oh! Is that what it is," he replied without looking up from his paper. "I thought that physic I took this morning had begun to work."

Fred Eaton died March 11, 1934, and not long after, Mulholland told Rose that he had dreamed of Fred. They were walking together—young and virile as both had once been—but he recognized in the dream that they both were dead. During August of that year, Rose often drove him to visit the ramshackle beach house in Santa Monica that my family had rented for the month to escape the valley heat. By a bay window in a chintz-covered overstuffed chair, he sat muffled in his dark suit and gazed out to sea. When we children waved to him from the surf, he did not wave back. In October, he fell and broke his arm, a harbinger of the major stroke in December that paralyzed not only his body but his throat, so that he could neither speak nor take solid food. Although the death certificate later stated cause of death as arteriosclerosis and apoplexy, his nurses agreed that he had simply starved to death. Stretched like an old hulk on a hospital bed in his own bedroom and ministered to by a doughty day nurse with rust-colored hair and an apt name—Miss Ironsides—the tough old man's durable body resisted death for six months. The end came on July 22, 1935, at 9:45 A.M. Flags in the city hung at half-staff. On July 24, his body lay in state in the rotunda of Los Angeles City Hall as mourners passed and civic leaders eulogized. During later private ser-

vices at Forest Lawn, all work on the Colorado River Aqueduct ceased
for a minute of silence in tribute to his memory while the waters at Haiwee Dam were also stopped in their flow to the city. Robert V. Phillips,
then a teenaged lad, happened to be with his father, J. E. Phillips, head
of the aqueduct division. Amid the noise and clangor of men, engines,
and equipment, he remembered when the silence began. It went on and
on, he said—that silence on the desert—tribute to the man who had
meant so much to all of them and also to Southern California. No more
fitting tribute could have been paid to the man who long ago had said,
"I want it written on my monument that I helped to build the Aqueduct."

Map 7. Major water distribution facilities, City of Los Angeles (Los Angeles Department of Water and Power).

Afterword

In 1989, a filmmaking group for public television asked me to participate in a documentary video film, *Mulholland: The Dream-Builder* (part of the Los Angeles History Project series for KCET). One of the shoots took place April 28 in San Francisquito Canyon, where I had not been since I was five years old when my shaken father had taken me the day after the disaster to view the wreckage. Sixty years later, although trepid about visiting what still seemed haunted and forbidden grounds, I hiked with the crew on a warm sunny day to the former dam site where few traces of the tragedy remain. (The standing portion of dam wall had been blasted away in 1929.) Perched on a boulder in the riverbed of the canyon, I spoke before camera of the devastation that overtook so many in this place, including my grandfather.

Afterwards, Richard Callison, one of the young Department of Water and Power engineers who had escorted us, drove me up to Power House One and beyond to see the employees' quarters, which, being above the dam, had been untouched by its failure. In this idyllic spot in the quiet of the canyon where ancient native sycamores shade the ground stood vintage wooden bungalows recalling the Southern California of my childhood. Callison told me the department engineers enjoyed duty there because of the beauty and quiet of the place, and then he said he would like to give me something. We proceeded to his garage, where after rummaging about in a carton, he brought forth a small water glass of lavender tint.

"We explore down there where the dam went out," he explained, "and sometimes we find things. This glass came from the area where the old cookhouse was washed away." He held it out to me. "Would you like it?" he asked.

Moved, I expressed my appreciation and taking the small tumbler, remarked on its opalescent hue and said I had seen glass that had turned this shade in old houses.

"The action of the sun and weather on old glass," he went on to explain. It had lain in the riverbed for over half a century.

As we headed back to join the others, he turned and spoke. "You know what you said about the dam. That was a terrible thing, I know, but it was only one part of a whole. The only part which failed. The rest has held." Then to make his meaning clear, he repeated, "The whole system has held. Because it has integrity."

I thought then, and I think today, that those words could very well stand as an epitaph for William Mulholland. On a shelf in my home, that little water glass stands beside another memento from a thoughtful acquaintance, a small vial containing Owens River water, a souvenir handed out by the San Fernando Chamber of Commerce on the opening day of the Owens River Aqueduct in 1913. The whole story abides for me in those two objects: water as blessing, water as curse; water as life giver and destroyer. The clear little bottle holds the life-giving water that enabled a great city to grow, while the lavender glass speaks of the darker consequences of man's efforts to master a world he ultimately never fully comprehends or controls.

Notes

The titles of Los Angeles newspapers will appear in abbreviated form—for example, *Times* for *Los Angeles Times*. All out-of-town papers are cited with full title, such as *San Francisco Chronicle*.

The following works will be cited by author's last name only:

Hoffman, Abraham, *Vision or Villainy*

Kahrl, William, *Water and Power*

Nadeau, Remi, *The Water Seekers*

Ostrom, Vincent, *Water and Politics*

Many of Mulholland's office files came to light in the late 1980s. The chance circumstances of one discovery are best described by Elizabeth Wimmer, retired Department of Water and Power special projects officer. "William Mulholland's office file material was received from Russell A. Majors of Valley Generating Station, who said he received it from a painter who bought an old file from salvage and found the papers inside it." Wimmer to C. Mulholland, January 1991.

Not so fortunate is the fate of the wonderful collection of clippings books kept by the Department of Water and Power since 1903. In the course of microfilming them in the late 1990s, a foolish decision was made to destroy some of the originals, thus degrading the possibility of making good-quality reproductions for future publication from the many interesting cartoons contained there.

CHAPTER 1: THE LONG JOURNEY
FROM DUBLIN TO LOS ANGELES, 1855–1876

1. John Omicinski, "Modern Times," September 13, 1990, Gannett News Service, Washington.

2. John Russell McCarthy, "Water: The Saga of Bill Mulholland," *Pacific Saturday Night*, March 26, 1938, p. 5; Phil L.Snyder, ed., *Detachment and the Writing of History* (Ithaca, New York: Cornell University Press, 1958), p. 19.

3. "Mulholland is almost exclusive to Ulster, where it is most common in Counties Antrim, Down, and Derry. The name is in Gaelic ó Maolchalann, 'son of the devotee of St. Calann.' Although there was a sept of Mulhollands in Co. Donegall, most of the name descend from the Mulhollands of Loughinsholin in Co. Derry. They are famous for having been, with the Mallons, the hereditary keepers of St. Patrick's bell, the Bell of the Testament. From the fourteenth century the family spread into the western and southern part of Massereene in Co. Antrim, in which barony the name is seventh most numerous" (Bell, *The Book of Ulster Surnames*, p.198).

4. F. S. L. Lyons, *Ireland Since the Famine* (London: Fontana Press, 1971), p. 87.

5. Edmund Valel, *The Mail Coach Men of the Late Eighteenth Century* (London: Cassell, 1960), p. 49.

6. Lyons, op. cit., p. 47.

7. Classification of Studies, School Registry No. 4, O'Connell School, Dublin.

8. John deCourcy Ireland, *Ireland and the Irish in Maritime History* (Dublin: The Glendale Press, 1986), pp. 237–77.

9. Lloyd's Register of Shipping, 1869. The *Gleniffer* was rated as "a vessel well and sufficiently found." Built in 1866 in Glasgow, she was typical of many small ships of the era that carried small cargoes great distances. Her destination on Mulholland's first voyage was Montreal, and her shipmaster was S. J. Coffey, who left his command the same year that Mulholland came ashore.

10. Bancroft, "History of California," vol. 7, p. 704.

CHAPTER 2: THE CITY OF ANGELS, 1877

1. H. Raitt and C. Wayne, *We Three Came West: A True Chronicle* (San Diego: Tofua Press, 1974), pp. 30–31.

2. *Evening Express*, January 8, 11, 1877; *Star*, February 3, 6, 9, 25, 1877; March 2; April 14; May 2, 1877. The four daily newspapers of the 1870s were the *Los Angeles Express*, the *Los Angeles Star*, the *Evening Express*, and the *Daily Herald*. A weekly, the *Los Angeles Mirror*, became the *Times* after Harrison Gray Otis purchased it from his partner, H. H. Boyce, in 1886.

3. Bell, *On the Old West Coast*, pp. 164–65.

4. *Star*, January 8; August 9, 23, 1878.

5. *Herald*, August 31, 1878; September 17, 26; October 6, 1878.

6. Spriggs, *History of Domestic Water Supply*, p. 67; *Times*, July 7, 1907; undated clipping, Mulholland scrapbook, probably 1911–12.

7. *First Annual Report of the Los Angeles Aqueduct*, p. 3. Layne, *Water and*

Power for a Great City (1957), presents a detailed account as do Hoffman and Stern's undated paper, "The Zanjas" (DWP). Background information may also be found in the writings of Horace Bell, J. M. Guinn, Harris Newmark, and William A. Spalding, as well as those of Fogelson, Ostrom, and Starr.

8. The term *zanja* originated in Cuba, according to F. de Santamaria, *Diccionario de Mejicanismos* (1959), to denote a person who digs *zanjas* (ditches, canals or drains) or *acequias*, a synonym deriving from the Arabic. As late as the 1960s, ranchers in Southern California used the anglicized term *sanky* for the district water manager to whom they addressed their orders for irrigation water.

9. Bell, op. cit., p. 251. Turner was mayor in 1869–70.

10. Layne, op. cit., p. 41.

11. Mulholland, "Municipal Ownership of Public Utilities," speech to the Sunset Club, 1905. Mulholland, office files, WP04-22:24 . Much about the old water company is unverifiable, as its records and books have been either lost or destroyed.

12. The promise must have been poorly kept, for when city chronicler W. A. Spalding got his reporting job at the *Los Angeles Herald* in 1874, his first piece addressed the dilapidated appearance of the plaza and its fountain "reminiscent of Hood's 'The fountain was a-dry—neglect and time/Has marred the work of artisan and mason.'" (*History and Reminiscences*, pp. 15–16). Nor had matters improved by the 1880s when Helen Hunt Jackson visited the city, for she found the plaza "a dusty and dismal little place with a parsimonious fountain in the centre . . ." (*Glimpses of Three Coasts* [1886], p. 111).

13. Layne, op. cit., p. 47, and Spalding, *History of Los Angeles*, vol. 1, p. 203.

14. Layne, op. cit., p. 48.

CHAPTER 3: THE PRIVATE WATER COMPANY AND ITS OWNERS, 1878–1879

1. Spriggs, pp. 70–71.

2. *Times*, March 3, 1898.

3. *Herald*, July 12, 1878; July 9, August 16, October 31, 1879. Attorney Frank H. Howard, who argued for the city in 1878, was later greatly admired by Mulholland. The *Herald* commented then that no member of the bar was more knowledgeable about water rights than he, and that because he was an accomplished linguist, he had "all the good concerning irrigation that is contained in the laws of the Romans, the French, of Spain, Italy and Mexico."

4. Brooks, "Notes"; Layne, pp. 51–52; *Times*, January 15, 1882.

5. Bell, op. cit., pp. 75, 80–81; *Herald*, Sept. 28, 1881; Brooks, "Notes."

6. *Evening Express*, July 23–27, 1877.

7. Mulholland, Speech, Sunset Club, 1905, p. 5; Brooks, "Notes."

8. W. A. Spalding, *History of Los Angeles City and County*, vol. 1, p. 171.

9. Hayes, *Pioneer Notes*, p. 167; *Illustrated History of Los Angeles County*, pp. 462–63; John Steven McGroarty, vol. 3, p. 482.

10. In consultation with Miles, Fred Eaton's father undertook a similar project in Pasadena to bring water from Devil's Gate in the Arroyo Seco to a reservoir site at the present intersection of Colorado Street and Orange Grove Avenue.

Miles also organized and became the chief engineer of the first volunteer fire brigade, created when the Los Angeles Water Company, in 1872–73, installed a few fire hydrants about the town (young Eaton being one of the first volunteers). In the 1880s, Miles also served as county recorder. Once described as "popular and sometimes festive," his festiveness ended in 1885, when he was arrested for embezzling $12,000. Charges were dismissed when he paid back the money, but he was still ousted from office. Fellow employees, however, continued to hold him in esteem as he had been an effective worker. McGroarty, *History of Los Angeles County*, vol. 3, p. 482; Layne, p. 39; Page, *Pasadena: Its Early Years*, p. 39; Hine, *Spalding*, p. 20.

CHAPTER 4: ADVANCING IN THE WATER BUSINESS, 1880–1886

1. Spriggs, pp. 68–69; *Intake*, Dept. of Water and Power, January 1933.
2. Layne, *Water and Power*, p. 99. Layne interviewed J. B. Campbell on December 10, 1947.
3. *Evening Express*, June 20, 1884; *Porcupine*, October 8, 1892.
4. *Express*, August 4, 1884.
5. Mary Foy, member of the pioneer Macy-Foy clan, attended Los Angeles High School and got her library post in 1880 by simply going to the mayor and each member of the city council and telling them that she could do a good job. *Herald*, October 7, 1881; *Times*, November 16, 1947.
6. *Herald*, January 7, 1881; *Times*, March 18, 1882. Also assuming office in the IOOF with Eaton and Mulholland was Moses L. Wicks, prominent land boomer and water developer. For his activities, see Dumke, *The Boom of the Eighties*, pp. 210–211.
7. In 1883 the Water Works Company consisted of S. B. Caswell, collector and bookkeeper; Fred Eaton, superintendent and engineer; Tom Burns, assistant; Thomas Brooks, assistant to Burns; four laborers plus two ditch and reservoir keepers. The directors were W. H. Perry, president of the board; S. H. Mott, secretary and treasurer; William Ferguson; Solomon Lazard; Charles Ducommon; and W. J. Broderick (Brooks, "Notes").
8. *Herald*, May 16, 1879; *Evening Express*, March 15, 1884.
9. *Times*, February 10, 1882.
10. *Times*, November 18, 1882; Brooks, "Notes."
11. Reagan Report, vol. 2, pp. 536, 553.
12. City Council Proceedings, V.XIV, pp. 729–30; V.XVIII, pp. 341, 353, September 29, 1883. Eaton and Mulholland bid for construction of a sewer line on Seventh Street. Rejected. Bids were M. S. Baker & Co., "to make fire hydrants at $45 each; S. M. Perry, ten at $75 each; William Mulholland, five or ten at $92 each. Referred to Committee on Fire and Water." The *Evening Express*, August 9, 1884. Also Council Proceedings, December 2, 1884, Los Angeles Water Company Time Book (1884–85), Public Affairs Division, Dept. of Water and Power.
13. William Perry participated in the founding of Fillmore, California, in 1887. The year before, during the height of the boom, he and a group of Los Angeles businessmen purchased 3,400 acres of Rancho Sespe. Then, for $25,000, they

secured water rights on Sespe Creek from a man named Dye, and in April 1886, they incorporated as the Sespe Land and Water Company (Freeman, pp. 24–25); *Express,* January 17, 1917.

14. *Times,* December 16, 1886.

15. Mulholland, Eaton, et al., pamphlet, "Wooden Pipes a Failure"(1905), Huntington Library.

CHAPTER 5: THE NEW SUPERINTENDENT, 1887–1892

1. Spalding, vol. 1, p. 263; *Evening Express,* January, February, 1887.

2. *Times,* April 15, 26, 1887.

3. *Times,* November 9; December 13, 1887.

4. *Times,* December 21, 1887.

5. Reagan Report, II, p. 545; Schuyler, Papers, Nos. 30, 31; *Times,* October 8, 1888. Eaton's dam was probably near Twin Lakes. Engineer James D. Schuyler measured water flows for this project in May 1888. The development coincided with a proposed railroad linking Ventura to Los Angeles via the Simi and Santa Susana Pass. Tradition has it that Chatsworth was named by someone with ties to (or knowledge of) the estate of the duke of Devonshire in England. As the overseer of the water project was a man named Forbes, who had built many dams in England, he likely named it. Much about the enterprise is murky. In the original plat, one of the streets was named Ben Porter Avenue, and probably Porter still held title to much of the land in question, for after the failure, a great deal of the tract reverted to the Porter Estate, and no further development occurred until 1893. The Porter Land and Water Company, with a firm hold on the north half of the San Fernando Valley, also had begun to create a water system west of San Fernando in conjunction with opening tracts for sale in the Mission area for citrus growing. The company boasted that it was spending fifty thousand dollars for a waterworks and offered land at $150 an acre, "with plenty of pure free water piped to each tract."

6. *Times,* May 11, 1888.

7. *Times,* March 8; May 12, 27, 1888.

8. *Times,* May 27, 1888.

9. Thomas Brooks, "Notes." Mulholland's later friend and associate, Joseph B. Lippincott, once described G. F. Fanning's treatise on water supply engineering as the hydraulic engineer's bible. *Herald,* January 31, 1892.

10. *Times,* July 16, 18, 1890. The gold watch remains in the Mulholland family.

11. Crystal Springs could supply daily 15,000,000 gallons of clear pure water, the amount needed to fill Buena Vista Reservoir. Steam dredgers were brought in to dig trenches down to ten and fifteen feet until they reached a layer of gravel "in which innumerable springs have their source." Large pipes from 14 to 24 inches in diameter were then laid to receive the water percolating through the gravel. To prevent damage and washouts such as had been previously experienced, a tunnel three-quarters of a mile was dug into one of the western hills and pipe was run through it to connect ultimately with Buena Vista Reservoir. In addition, a wooden flume was constructed around the hill as a backup system in

the event that trouble arose in the tunnel. It was a major undertaking, estimated at $200,000, but it would assure water without sediment or sand. *Evening Express,* August 19, 1890.

12. Spalding, vol. 1, p. 266. "Ivanhoe was situated on the Los Feliz Rancho, comprising the eatern portion of the Lick Tract; it was recorded June 2, 1887, and consisted of 700 acres divided into 1,300 lots, ranging in size from one-hundred-foot frontages to five acres and in price from $150 to $750. A free carriage went to the tract daily" (Dumke, *The Boom of the Eighties,* p. 188).

13. McGroarty, vol. 3, pp. 482–85; Spalding, vol. 1, pp. 167, 198, 402; *Herald,* June 22, 1890. Inquiries to the Eaton family have been met with silence. In 1988 during the official celebration of the seventy-fifth anniversary of the completion of the Owens River Aqueduct, descendants of both Eaton and Mulholland attended, but the *Los Angeles Times* (November 18, 1988) reported only the words of an Eaton, who in response to a question about her ancestor, replied, "They were all crooks."

14. *Herald,* June 7, 1890; *Evening Express,* July 23, 1890.

15. *Evening Express,* "Review of the City," December 31, 1889.

16. *Illustrated History of Los Angeles County,* pp. 462–63.

17. After designers had completed a new dado in the entry halls of the Perry residence, the following description appeared in the *Times,* March 5, 1892: "In the old Empire style, the walls had been finished in marron flake, highlighted in gold, copper and green bronze. The newel in the lower hall was carved in the shape of a Moor holding in his hand a three-light candelabra, which Mr. Perry had imported from Italy at a cost of $380. The 'aerial blue' ceilings of the upper halls were graced with painted cupids."

CHAPTER 6: WATER PLOTS AND POLITICS, 1893–1895

1. *Times,* October 5, 1898; Mulholland, *First Annual Report,* Board of Water Commissioners, 1902, p.13. Material for this chapter chiefly derives from newspaper reports, which often gave fuller accounts than city council records. For more generalized accounts (although not always accurate in details), see Fogelson, pp. 94–96; Ostrom, pp. 44–46; Kahrl, pp. 12–13.

2. *Times,* July 30, October 12, December 16, 1886. Ostrom (p. 45) and Kahrl (p. 11) both describe this work as surreptitious, yet reports of its progress appeared in the daily press.

3. Layne, pp. 53–46; Ostrom, p. 96.

4. *Herald,* April 11, 1890; *Times,* August 22, 26, 28; September 6, 8, 1890; *Evening Express,* December 29, 30, 1891.

5. *Herald,* February 2, 16, 17, 21, 25, 26, 1892; *Times,* February 2, 1892.

6. *Herald,* January 11, 1892; *Times,* January 1, 11, 13, 1892.

7. *Herald, Times,* February 21, 22, 1892.

8. *Times,* January 1, 1892; April 21, 1892; *Herald,* April 21, 1892. The *Herald* was partially subsidized by the water company, although its editor, W. A. Spalding, who was in favor of public ownership, wrote that no one ever interfered with his editorial stands. "Had the *Herald* . . . , known to be the property

of the water magnates, urged some settlement unfair to the city . . . , it would have raised such a storm as to more than negative [sic] all our efforts, and would have been fatal to the paper besides" (Hine, *Spalding,* pp. 141–142).

9. *Times,* June 22, 1893.

10. *Times,* September 30, October 10, November 14, 1893.

11. *Times,* November 14, 21, 1893.

12. Layne, p. 67; Ostrom, p. 34.

13. *Times,* May 27, 1893; *The Porcupine,* October 29, 1892. A small notice appeared in the latter over the name "Wm. Mulholland" for proposals from pump manufacturers for "one four-million gallon high duty pumping engine." The engine was "to pump water for domestic use to the hill portions of the city of Los Angeles."

14. *Times,* May 30, 1893.

15. See Ostrom, chapter 6. As a result of the court decision, Garvanza and Highland Park voted to annex to the City of Los Angeles, while Vernon rejected annexation. According to Ostrom, "this wave of annexation added 14.05 square miles to the area of the city giving it a total area of 43.26 square miles at the turn of the century"(p. 146).

16. Spalding, vol. 1, p. 315; Mulholland, *Owensmouth Baby,* pp. 19, 67; *Who's Who in the Pacific Southwest,* p. 295.

17. *Times,* June 9, 1893. The newspaper printed the opinion verbatim.

18. *Times,* September 15, 1896.

19. *Times,* September 15, 17; November 10, 1896; Ostrom, p. 147.

20. *Times,* November 3, 1894.

21. Brooks, "Notes"; *Times,* November 8, 1894.

22. *Times,* August 18, 1895; Mulholland, "Municipal Ownership of Public Utilities," speech to Sunset Club, 1905. The photographs of *El Almuerzo* always hung in Mulholland's home, and his children often mentioned the occasion as memorable to their father.

23. Mulholland, "Municipal Ownership of Public Utilities," op. cit.; *Times,* February 18, 1896; June 2, 1898.

24. Mulholland, "Municipal Ownership of Public Utilities," op. cit.

25. Steffens, *Autobiography,* pp. 572–574; Sitton, *Haynes,* pp. 79–80.

CHAPTER 7: THE YEARS OF MAYOR EATON, 1898–1900

1. *Times,* January 1, 1898; Layne, p. 65; Spalding, vol. 1, pp. 319–320; Spriggs, pp. 50–52. Mulholland's children remembered their father's discussions of the conflict he underwent during those years. For an analysis of the political climate of 1890s Los Angeles and the rise of Progressivism, see Fogelson, pp. 210–12.

2. Spriggs, p. 53; *Times,* March 1, 17, 1898; Hine, *Spalding,* p. 145. W. A. Spalding, editor of the respected *Herald,* then owned by certain members of the water company, wrote of the trial, "I got through the ordeal without taking partizan ground for the water company, and there was no complaint or remonstrance from our backers."

3. Hine, op. cit., p. 133; Gottlieb and Wolt, *Thinking Big,* p. 123. On June 5,

1894, Chandler, a widower and then circulation manager of the *Times,* had married Otis's second daughter, Marion Otis. She was, according to Spalding, a much respected member of her father's business staff.

4. *Times,* May 24, June 1, 1898; Layne, p. 66; Spriggs, pp. 54–56.

5. *Times,* June 22, 25, 1898.

6. *Times,* September 29, 1898.

7. *Times,* November 26, 27, 1898.

8. Lippincott, pp. 161–62; *Times,* November 23, 24, 26, 27; December 1, 8, 1898.

9. O'Melveny, Journals, December 25, 1898.

10. Election returns suggest the tenuous nature of Eaton's victory, which the *Times* had whooped up as a great triumph for the Republicans ("Democratic City Ticket Goes Down Like a Spanish Fleet in a Fight"). Eaton's plurality over Snyder was only 580 votes (8,273 to 7,693), while Socialist candidate Henning Hansen received 510 votes. In the next mayoral election, Snyder overwhelmed his Republican opponent, Herman Silver, with a plurality of 3,131 votes. *Times,* December 6, 1898; *Herald,* December 6, 1900.

11. L. M. Powers, M.D., born 1853 in North Carolina, came to Los Angeles in 1887 and entered private practice. He received his M.D. at Washington University and trained at Bellevue and College of Physicians and Surgeons in New York (1877–1885). In Los Angeles, he introduced new systems of quarantining persons with certain contagious diseases and improved sanitation in waste disposal, slaughterhouse practices, and water usage. He also introduced the new diphtheria antitoxin and inaugurated milk testing and meat inspection. In the Municipal Reform organization of 1900 he was also a member of the Committee of One Hundred (*Who's Who In the Pacific Southwest,* p. 302; *Times,* November 8, 1890).

12. *Times,* January 5, 18, 1899.

13. Layne, p. 66; Mulholland, address to Sunset Club, 1904.

14. *Times,* April 3, June 1, 1899.

15. *Times,* May 6, 1899.

16. *Times,* July 3, 18, 20, 1899.

17. O'Melveny, July 22, 1899; *Times,* August 4, 5, 6, 10, 26, 1899. Was the threat of a disruption in water supply during the neediest time of the year and only two weeks before a bond election to fund a municipally owned system an accident or a contrived coincidence? No one raised a public doubt at the time, but similar suggestions of collusion by later weavers of conspiracy theories would become a stock element in future accusations that the city's water men created artificial water famines to frighten citizens into voting for proposed waterworks.

18. *Times,* August 5, 1899.

19. *Times,* August 5, 6, 7, 1899.

20. Layne, p. 57; *Times,* August 22, 29, 1899.

21. *Times,* November 16, 1899; December 16, 1900.

22. *Times,* January 24, 27, 1900; Stimson, *Rise of Labor Movement in Los Angeles,* p. 203.

23. *Times,* February 20, 21, 1900.

24. *Times,* February 7, 1900.

25. *Times,* March 23, 1900.

26. *Herald,* May 23, 29, 1900; *Times,* April 17, May 26, June 15, 1900.

27. The United States had recently appropriated $25,000 for such a study. Further indication of how the dry years and increased population had heightened interest in water projects was a recently completed report by Professor Frank Soulé, University of California, Berkeley, regarding water rights and litigations along the San Joaquin River. At the end of July, Soulé planned to conduct further studies north of Fresno. *Times,* July 10, 1900.

28. *Times,* September 29; November 25, 1900.

29. *Times,* November 23, 29, 1900.

30. *Times,* December 4, 1900; January 6, 1901. Eaton may have been scheming to lay the ground for his plan of an Owens River project, as Kahrl suggests in *Water and Power* (p. 47), but certainly nothing of a concrete nature occurred during his mayoralty. Whatever his private designs, his dislike of the water company seems to have been powerful and personal, and there is no proof that his belief in municipal ownership of water was insincere.

31. *Times,* October 7, 1900; January 6, 7, 1901; September 18, 1903.

CHAPTER 8: THE CITY'S VICTORY OVER THE "GRAND MONOPOLY," 1901–1902

1. *Times,* May 18, July 19, 1901. Two months later, a chief stockholder in the Mountain Water Company sought an injunction against the directors, charging that they had conspired to defraud him.

2. *Times,* May 20, 21, 1901.

3. *Times,* April 19, 1901.

4. Spriggs, p. 58; Mulholland, Office Files, WP04–22:13. Speech prepared for the Board of Trade, City of Pasadena, April 6, 1904; "Municipal Ownership of Public Utilities," speech to the Sunset Club, April 1905.

5. *Times,* August 2, 1901.

6. *Times,* August 11, 15, 1901.

7. *Times,* August 23, 25, 27, 1901; Workman, pp. 297, 462–63.
The senior Waldron owned thirty-five acres on the southwest corner of Main and Washington Streets that he had developed into a popular pleasure resort, Washington (later, Chutes) Park. By using zanja water, he kept his water bill low. Other opposition leaders were John R. Newberry, successful merchant whose Newberry variety stores were widespread in Southern California (Newmark, p. 551); Joseph Mesmer, businessman and philanthropist, whose father had come to Los Angeles in 1858 (Newmark, p. 644); Sherman Page, attorney, whose family had come to Los Angeles when he was seven. He apprenticed under C. C. Wright, expert on water law who created the Wright Irrigation Act, and was also the son-in-law of Judge R. H. F. Variel (*Who's Who in the Pacific Southwest,* p. 283).

8. *Times,* August 27, 28, 29, 1901.

9. *Times,* August 29, 30, 1901.

10. *Times,* October 22, 1901. Elliott provided the public a lengthy and rational explanation of bond market conditions in the East.

11. Workman, p. 297.

12. *Times,* February 5, 26, 1902. Workman, who had forgone a planned visit to his birthplace in Booneville, Missouri, in order to return to Los Angeles to celebrate, later received a bill from the city council for $1,100 for his expenses during his two-month stay in New York and Washington. Accused of extravagance, Workman defended his expenditures by explaining that on the advice of eastern attorneys, he had been forced to move about lest the defaulting company attempt to serve papers on him that could involve the water bonds in litigation. Such moving had proved expensive, as had his time in Washington, D.C., where he had lobbied members of Congress for appropriations for the harbor and a new post office. "Why, sir, my God! I had to keep up the reputation of the town," expostulated Uncle Billy." I couldn't go around with those men and be entertained and not reciprocate." Upon the advice of attorney Mathews, who had feared such criticism, he had unhappily stayed at "a second-rate hotel" (the Hoffman House instead of the Waldorf-Astoria), and moveover, had spent $400 of his own money on cigars, treats, and the like, so as not to appear cheap before those with whom he was dealing (*Times,* May 10, 1902).

13. Layne, *Water and Power for a Great City,* pp. 69–70. The day before this event, Mayor Snyder had presented an ordinance to the council, which it then voted to accept. Layne's account derives from an interview with L. M. Anderson, who was present that day and who, shortly after, became auditor of the new water department, a position he held his entire working life.

The new civil service requirement was waived because of the men's known qualifications. Anderson's list of the thirty-one men then employed with the old water company on a monthly salary in 1902 named William Mulholland, A. W. Ryan, Niles Knickerbocker, L. M. Anderson, Edward Leake, T. G. Haines, George H. Kimball, C. L. Brimhall, H. H. Gibbs, George T. Gilmore, J. W. Bullas, Charles E. Brown, John Horner, F. W. Parker, W. S. Reavis, Charles W. Clark, F. R. Cady, J. W. Gillette, J. O. Bradbury, W. H. Carter, John Herlihy, W. M. Hughes, E. Ihm, A. P. Stevenson, J. A. Osgood, J. P. Vroman, F. W. Cook, Thomas Brooks, F. J. Fischer, and George Read.

14. *Times,* March 18, 1902. Ostrom, p. 69; Annual Report, Board of Water Commissioners, 1902, p. 5. Members of the first water commission were Herman Silver, president; Henry T. Lee; James M. Elliott; Charles H. Toll; F. W. King; L. A. Grant; and J. C. Drake.

15. *Times,* February 7, 1902.

16. Mulholland, Speech to Sunset Club, 1905; *Times,* February 14, 1902; Brooks, "Notes on Los Angeles Water Supply."

Also on the agenda were completion of work at the Angeleno Heights Reservoir, construction of several new water lines along Alameda Street and Central Avenue as far south as Ninth Street, and the purchase of 1,000 tons of four- and six-inch pipe for replacements and extensions. As the new policy required that no water main of a diameter less than four inches was to be laid, many old two-inch mains were about to be replaced. As Mulholland noted, with 337 miles of water pipe in the city streets, the system was "a marvel of attenuation alongside of which Barnum's living skeleton would be considered the very embodiment of unwieldy corpulence" (Annual Report of Water Commissioners, 1902, p. 30).

17. *Times,* February 16, 1902.

18. *Times,* April 25, 1902; McGroarty, *History of Los Angeles County,* vol. 3, p. 483.

19. O'Melveny, Journals, April 5, 1902. The Sunset Club was organized in 1895.

20. *Times,* May 18, 1902; Annual Report of Water Commissioners, 1902, pp. 6–9. Brooks, "Notes." Tom Brooks had installed the first meter in Los Angeles's domestic water system on August 16, 1889, at Charles Stern's Winery on Macy Street west of Mission Road. It was a two-inch Worthington piston type. Other meters were later installed at various business and manufacturing organizations. Slightly over 1 percent of water-users were metered in Los Angeles in 1902.

21. *Times,* May 13, 14, 1902; Robinson, *Lawyers of Los Angeles,* p. 315. For analyses of the Wright Act and its mixed consequences, see Cooper, *Aqueduct Empire,* pp. 94–97; Hundley, *The Great Thirst,* pp. 98–100; Reisner, *Cadillac Desert,* pp. 113–14; Starr, *Material Dreams,* p. 14.

22. *Los Angeles Times,* June 17, August 18, 1903. Mulholland could also be brutal with the humorless and self-important. His daughter, Rose, remembered her mingled embarrassment and amusement when shopping once with her father at Barker Brothers (a leading furniture store). An officious young salesman insisted that a library table they were examining was solid mahogany. Mulholland, who prided himself on his knowledge of woods, said it was veneer. When contradicted, Mulholland took out his penknife and scratched a side to reveal the veneer, saying as he did so, "I knew about woods before your head was the size of a cranberry."

23. *Los Angeles Times,* May 18, 1902.

24. *Times,* June 3, 1902. When W. T. Spilman became a leading propagandist for the antiaqueduct forces, he charged that the people of the city had been hornswoggled by Mulholland's lies about daily water consumption and that "it is difficult for the average mind to understand how meters could make any material saving when the people were already restricted as to the amount of water they used." Out of this spurious argument, he evolved the conclusion that the water department was secretly disposing of the water in order to create a water shortage for "a designing purpose" (Spilman, *The Conspiracy,* pp. 20–21).

25. *Times,* May 18, 1902.

26. Mulholland, Office Files, WP04–22:5, Mulholland to Willard, August 30, 1902. *Times,* May 18; September 6, 18; October 21; November 30, 1902. Mulholland's semiannual summary of local water conditions in May 1902: present water available, 25,000,000 gallons daily; present water consumption, 23,000,000; probable supply from present sources in July, 23,500,000; highest demand in 1901, 24,100,000; probable highest demand in 1902, based on increase in population, 26,765,000; shortage to be supplied, 3,264,000. Of this shortage, 2,000,000 was expected to be filled from the new work and the balance from the main supply ditch. The estimated per capita daily consumption: 267 gallons.

CHAPTER 9: NEW REGIME FOR A BOOMING TOWN, 1903–1904

1. *Times,* February 3, 4, 6, 1903; Layne, p. 69; Ostrom, pp. 52–53; Workman, p. 298. In September 1995, Robert V. Phillips, a former general manager of the Department of Water and Power, commented to me, "Although technically the DWP is still an independent department the fact is that over the years the council has increasingly destroyed its independence until now it is almost completely politicized. The people who first established the DWP as an independent agency, free of political misuse (and they tried desperately to accomplish this) were absolutely right in their intent."

2. *Times,* February 4, 6, 1903; Layne, p. 74; McGroarty, vol. 2, p. 159; *Who's Who in the Pacific Southwest,* p. 252.

3. *Times,* February 3, 11; March 8, 1903. Willard was among those committed to cleansing government of corruption and corporate control. He believed that democracy should be a positive moral force and challenged Theodore Roosevelt's characterization of democracy as merely a means to an end. "It is a soul-satisfying thing," he wrote the president (Mowry, *The California Progressives,* p. 99).

4. *Times,* March 17, 1903.

5. Annual Report of the Board of Water Commissioners, 1902, p. 28; *Times,* January 20; April 14, 1903.

6. *Times,* June 28, 1903. One fan letter to Mulholland came from East Los Angeles from one William Holgate, proprietor of a furniture store on Downey Avenue. Along with other Eastside neighbors, Downey wrote their thanks "for your success in giting [*sic*] us water so that we do not have to stay up nights this summer to get even a drink of water." He added, "You have done what *you promised you would do—years ago* if they would only give you a show . . . LA has got the Right man in the Right place" (Mulholland, Office Files, WP04–21:22, May 4, 1903).

7. Mulholland, Office Files, WP04–22:15.

8. *Times,* July 18, 1903; Mulholland, Office Files, WP04–21:7, Mulholland to City Council, July 29, 1903.

9. *Los Angeles Times,* September 18, 1903.

10. McGroarty, *History of Los Angeles County,* p. 483. The first annual report of the aqueduct by the chief engineer in 1907 gives the date as 1893.

An intriguing item in Mulholland Office Files is a letter dated July 15, 1903, from Mulholland to J. D. Fredericks, district attorney of Los Angeles County. Responding to Frederick's request for road conditions from Mojave to Bishop, Mulholland supplies careful details of mileage and conditions. For example, "Haiwee Meadows to Olancha, 9 miles, road is slow and for 3 miles midway between the two points is exceedingly heavy. This part of the trip will fully test the power of any machine of less gauge than 59 inches (standard gauge of auto is 55" to 56")." The letter gives no indication of why Fredericks desired this information, and as Mulholland supposedly had never been to Owens Valley, experienced travelers to the area such as Eaton or Lippincott would have been the logical choices to consult (Mulholland, Office Files, WP04–21:19).

11. *Times,* September 20, 1903.

12. *Times,* October 2, 1903.

13. *Times,* July 26; August 24, 1903.

14. *Times,* December 1, 1903.

15. *Times,* December 1, 1903; *Herald,* December 15, 1903.

16. *Herald,* December 15, 1903.

17. Writers who either espouse or lend credence to the "San Fernando Valley land grab" story include Bonelli, Caughey, Gottlieb and Wolt, Kahrl, McWilliams, and Walton.

18. *Herald,* December 13, 1903; April 3, 1904. Mulholland, *Owensmouth Baby,* pp. 7–8. Hendricks, *M. H. Sherman,* provides a good account of Sherman's early life.

19. Spalding, *History,* vol. 1, p. 303.

20. This case (44 Cal. 16) was cited as an authority in another water suit in 1895, *Santa Ana Water Company v. the Town of San Buenaventura* (56 Fed. Rep. 339), an action involving the rights of an incorporated town to establish water rates. Judge Ross of the United States Circuit Court had found that a trustee for the city was also treasurer of the water company. He quoted from the prior case in which Sherman's role had been questioned: "We do not doubt that a majority of the trustees might execute the power, but the question is, whether Sherman, who was a stockholder and director of the railroad company, could be one of that majority. When he entered upon the duties of trustee, his relations to the city became those of an agent to his principal, or of a trustee to his cestui que trust, and while holding the office he could do nothing inconsistent with those relations. This is clear upon principle, and rests upon abundant authority" (*Times,* January 15, 1895).

21. *Times,* May 10, 11, 1894. The story was first carried in the *San Francisco Examiner* and later picked up by the *Times.*

22. *Times,* December 14, 1895; January 25, 1899.

23. *Times,* April 25, 1903.

24. Stimson, *Rise of Labor,* pp. 205–15; *Times,* April 26, 1903.

25. *Times,* October 23, 1903; Hoffman, p. 126.

26. O'Melveny, Journals, December 25, 1903; *Herald,* December 15, 27, 30, 1903; *Times,* December 6, 29, 1903. City Attorney Mathews, who took a hard line against the transit companies, prevailed in bringing suit for their failure to perform their contracted duties. Among those cited was M. H. Sherman's partner, E. P. Clark, president of the Pacific Electric Line.

CHAPTER 10: DESPERATE REMEDIES IN A DRY SEASON, 1904

1. *Herald,* January 17, 27; February 3, 1904; *Times,* January 22, 24; February 27; March 11, 1904; National Weather Service, WeatherData, Inc. With great pains and dubious evidence, Kahrl accuses Mulholland of having created a mythical drought and cites what he calls "the perfectly average" rainfall of 11.88 inches in 1903–1904 to confirm that the dearth was fabricated as a scare tactic to stampede voters later to support the aqueduct bonds (Kahrl, pp. 83–86).

Contemporary accounts of arid conditions run counter to Kahrl's conspiracy charges, as do those of modern researchers. See Freeman, *People-Land-Water,* pp.

168–69. Engineer-hydrologist Robert V. Phillips has rebutted Kahrl by pointing out that the "mean annual rainfall in Los Angeles was 15 inches a year. . . . If it drops to a 'perfectly average' 11.88," he has written, "we are in deep trouble."

Using the hydrologic measurement of years from October 1 to September 30, Phillips establishes the following annual rainfall average from 1898 to 1904:

1898–1899—5.5"

1899–1900—7.5"

1900–1901—16.5"

1901–1902—11.0"

1902–1903—19.0"

1903–1904—8.0"

Average—11.25"

2. *Herald,* January 12, 17, 23, 27, 28; February 4, 1904; *Times,* January 14, 1904.

3. *Herald,* March 10, April 8, 1904; *Times,* March 10, 1904.

4. *Herald,* January 5, 1904.

5. *Herald,* June 5, 1904; *Times,* May 23; June 3, 14, 1904.

6. Layne, pp. 76–77; *Herald,* June 6, 1904; *Times,* June 12, 1904.

7. Layne, p. 77; Brooks, "Notes."

8. Mulholland, Office Files, WP04–22:2, Mulholland to Lee and Scott, July 25, 1904; *Herald,* July 28, 1904.

9. Mulholland, Office Files, WP04–22:3; *Herald,* July 28; August 2, 1904; *Times,* August 4, 1904.

10. *Herald,* August 16, 1904.

11. *Times,* August 16, 1904.

12. *Herald,* September 17, 18, 1904; Nadeau, pp. 22–23; Sitton, p. 49.

13. Hoffman, p. 60; Kahrl, p. 49; McGroarty, vol. 2, pp. 483–84; Nadeau, pp. 21–24. The Progressive editor (and strong temperance man), E. T. Earl, testified in 1912 before the Aqueduct Investigation Board (p. 46 of their report) that aqueduct workers joked about the trail of liquor bottles they followed to mark their way. Mulholland always told his children that he and Fred made the trip with "a mule team, a buckboard, and a demijohn of whiskey." In view of the ultimate productive outcome of the trip, the idea of two sots on a spree is improbable, but the story has been happily retold by many antagonists who seem unaware that beans and whiskey had been stock trail fare since the days of the forty-niners.

14. McGroarty, vol. 2, pp. 483–84; Nadeau, p. 23.

15. McGroarty, vol. 2, pp. 483–84; *Herald,* October 4, 1904.

16. Hoffman, pp. 19–24, gives a good summary of Lippincott's first years in the Southwest. *Who's Who in the Pacific Southwest,* pp. 228–29.

17. Hoffman, pp. 51–59. Hoffman gives the best and clearest account of Lippincott's tangled relations with the federal government and the City of Los Angeles. Kahrl's is detailed but less lucid. Both consulted primary documents from Bureau of Reclamation files, and I am indebted to their research.

18. McGroarty, vol. 2, pp. 483–84. U.S. Congress, Senate Report 928, Part 3, Vol. 2. The use of the Owens River to irrigate the Antelope Valley had been proposed to the Senate Committee hearing on Arid Lands by M. A. Knapp.

19. Freeman, *People-Land-Water,* p. 42; Smythe, *The Conquest of the Arid West,* p. 297. Arthur P. Davis was the nephew of John Wesley Powell, leader of the National Geological Survey, surveyor of the Colorado River, and powerful critic of national land policies.

20. Hoffman, pp. 50–51.

21. *Times,* November 7, 1897.

22. *Times,* August 18, 1899.

23. *Times,* November 22, 25; December 24, 1899.

24. Hoffman, p. 51.

25. *Herald,* April 3; May 18, 1904; Kahrl, p. 48; O'Melveny, Journals, March 7, 22, 1904. Eaton may have been telling the truth, because he maintained a busy schedule in Los Angeles in the spring of 1904. In March Henry O'Melveny retained him as a referee in setting land valuations in *City of Los Angeles v. Rowland and Van Nuys,* and in April, he served with Charles D. Willard on a special committee with the board of supervisors for harbor improvements at San Pedro. None of this precludes his presence in Owens Valley, but neither does any hard evidence prove it.

26. Hoffman, op. cit., pp. 56–58; Kahrl, op. cit., pp. 47–48. Kahrl ascribes the most cynical motives to Eaton based mostly on a letter from Arthur Davis in 1905. I would want more evidence than that before indicting the man.

27. *Herald,* April 20, July 27, 1904.

28. Hoffman, pp. 58–59.

29. Hoffman, p. 60; *First Annual Report of the Los Angeles Aqueduct,* p. 18; Layne, p. 99.

30. *First Annual Report,* p. 18; Mulholland, Office Files, WP04–24, "Water Supply of Southern California," speech to the Sunset Club, Dec. 1904. Mulholland joined the Sunset Club in 1904, served as its president in 1919, and remained a member for the rest of his life, saying that it had been for him "a sanctum of peaceful communion," as he likened it to the biblical "Shadow of a Great Rock in a Weary Land." The Sunset Club, patterned after the original in Chicago, was founded in 1895 by Charles D. Willard, W. C. Patterson, Charles F. Lummis, Burt Estes Howard, and Fred L. Alles. Meetings were held on the last Friday of each month at sunset in a popular restaurant for two hours of dining and conversation; then, at eight, after the topic for discussion was announced, a principal paper was read, followed by two shorter ones and a discussion. Its members played an important role in the intellectual and political life of the city at the turn of the century.

CHAPTER 11: A PLAN REVEALED, 1905

1. *Examiner,* December 4, 16, 17, 1904. A few days after these articles appeared, the Los Angeles Chamber of Commerce met on December 21 and named a committee of Mulholland, Lippincott, and H. Hawgood to take up the question of a water supply for Los Angeles "outside of the present one." Mulholland

responded December 28 with a preliminary report with statistics indicating that current consumption, if unabated, would continue to exceed the city's supply. Of this report, Mulholland wrote shortly afterward to Lippincott, who was in Washington, D.C., "I wrote the document myself and as you will notice from its tenor it is somewhat of a standoff as I did not altogether approve of taking up the investigation in your absence, especially with Hawgood, as I understand from outside sources he is back of a project to promote the sale of some alleged rights to the Mojave River to the City of Los Angeles" (Mulholland, Office Files, WP04–21:16 and 22:4). For a good discussion of this period, see Hoffman, pp. 79–86.

2. Mulholland, Office Files, WP04–21:6, January, March–June, 1905.

3. *Herald,* April 23, August 30, 1905.

4. *Imperial Valley News,* February 10, 1905. A syndicate of capitalists headed by H. G. Otis, Harry Chandler, and O. F. Brant of the Title Insurance and Trust Company had acquired the Colorado River Land Company, consisting of about 800,000 acres in the Mexicali Valley and, on the American side, another 1,000 acres in the Imperial Valley. The enormous holding along part of the Colorado Delta aroused the suspicions and enmities of locals, who also suspected that the Reclamation Service, with its Yuma project under way, might be in cahoots with the syndicate. The editorial that questioned Lippincott's allegiances concluded with a rallying cry of "Let's defeat Otis!" For a full account, see Stowe, "Pioneering Land Development," *California Historical Society Quarterly* 47, No. 1 (1968), pp. 16–39. Also, Gottlieb and Wolt, *Thinking Big,* pp. 165–68.

5. Mulholland, Office Files, WP04–22:4, Lippincott to Mulholland, February 20, 1905. The conflict of interest problem was brewing in January 1905, when Lippincott's chief at Reclamation in Washington, D.C., Arthur P. Davis, denied Mulholland's request to allow Lippincott and government geologist W. C. Mendenhall to appear as witnesses for Los Angeles in a case attempting to establish water rights in the San Fernando Valley. Davis later gave provisional consent because of the men's previous studies of the Los Angeles River and "because we wish to be of service to the City of Los Angeles" (Mulholland, Office Files, WP04–21:17, Davis to Mulholland, January 25, 1905).

6. *Herald,* March 10–15, 1905.

7. *Herald,* March 16, 17, 1905.

8. *Herald,* May 3, July 22, 1905; *Times,* May 3, 1905. During this period Mulholland was also enduring with his family the anguish of losing their youngest child to spinal meningitis. Born in 1903, Richard James Mulholland died on May 15, 1905. Weeks later, Mulholland wrote his friend J. Henry Dockweiler, former Los Angeles engineer-attorney but now a consulting engineer and city attorney in San Francisco, to explain why he would not be able to testify in the valuation hearings of the Spring Valley Water Company. "I confess I am still as much in the dark as ever as things are developing very rapidly here on the scheme for increased water supply for the City of Los Angeles and my presence in consequence is required about constantly. I have had to give up the idea of a Portland trip I had promised to take with my wife who is much worn out since the death of our little boy about six or seven weeks ago" (Mulholland, Office Files, WP04–21:17, Mulholland to Dockweiler, June 26, 1905).

9. *Herald,* July 22, 1905. In "The Straight of the Owens River Deal," Mulholland wrote, "All through the period with which our investigations proceeded, the Commission was beseiged by schemers with all kinds of propositions to furnish water to the city, until one would think that the whole country was crisscrossed with roaring torrents of water. It is from these parties, some of whom are simply deluded individuals while others are arrant schemers, that we expect our greatest opposition to the Owens River scheme" (*Graphic,* September 1905).

10. Mulholland, Office Files, WP04–22:4, Mulholland to Lippincott, August 15, 1905. Nadeau, pp.32–33; Kahrl, pp. 91 ff. Both Nadeau and Kahrl discuss the newspapers' rivalry without emphasizing the fierce circulation war or the chronically inflamed rhetoric then characteristic of the *Times,* when the mildest dissent from its opinions became a pretext for outrage. A careful reading of the six dailies in the six weeks after the Owens Valley announcement demonstrates that they all gave extensive and largely supportive coverage to the plan. Although the *Examiner* later wrote hard-hitting and hostile editorials, its news coverage remained comprehensive, and its editorial of July 31, 1905, had given enthusiastic support, pointing out its earlier "agitation for an adequate and unfailing supply of water for the needs of Los Angeles." For a good account of the *Examiner*'s entry into Los Angeles, see Stimson, *Rise of the Labor Movement in Los Angeles,* pp. 270–80. Begun as a pro-labor voice against the *Times*'s open shop policy, the *Examiner* failed to buck the power of the *Times*'s moneyed interests and by 1906 had begun to back off from its pro-labor stance.

The short-lived *Evening News* (October 2, 1905, to April 18, 1908) would have been only a transient curiosity in the history of Los Angeles journalism had it not been produced by the talented newspaperman Samuel "Alkali Sammy" Clover. All denials to the contrary, the paper was almost certainly bankrolled by special interests: local old-guard opponents and private electric power companies. An attractive small paper, it is chiefly remembered for having become an *omnium gatherum* of aqueduct opponents, ranging from Progressives such as John R. Haynes and Councilman Arthur D. Houghton to dissenting engineers, private water and electric interests, and certain pipe manufacturers.

11. *Examiner,* August 2, 3, and 6, 1905; *Times,* August 1–6, 1905; *Herald,* August 1–6, 1905.

12. Mulholland, Office Files, WP04–22:4, Mulholland to Lippincott, August 11 and 15, 1905.

13. Stimson, pp. 284–85; *Herald,* September 1, November 29, 1904; *Times,* October 30, 1904; August 10, 1905.

14. *Herald,* August 15, 1905. Two days earlier, when Mulholland learned that Dr. Houghton intended to visit Owens Valley with culture tubes to test the purity of the water, he had scoffed, "It is all nonsense in my opinion. At this time of the year cattle will be found wading in the water. The water has been analyzed and found to be purer in some respects than our present city water" (*Examiner,* August 13, 1905).

15. *Examiner,* August 15, 1905.

16. Mulholland, Office Files, WP04–22:4, August 15, 1905. Frederick Cecil Finkle came to Los Angeles from his native Wisconsin in 1887 and was associated with irrigation and water developments in San Bernardino and Riverside

Counties. In 1897, he became the chief hydraulic engineer for Southern California Edison Company and from 1906 was a consultant for a number of western hydroelectric companies. He had extensive commercial landholdings in Southern California and, according to *Who's Who in the Pacific Southwest* (1913), claimed interest in "reforms which will benefit the working classes." Finkle remained a bugbear in Mulholland's life and was unceasing in his disparagement of Mulholland's engineering abilities.

17. *Examiner*, August 15, 1905.

18. *Examiner*, August 16, 1905. Major Henry T. Lee, attorney and special counsel in water litigation for Los Angeles (1895–1907), was chairman of the evening and described Mulholland as "Bill Mulholland, water superintendent, true as steel, straight as a string, and saturated with knowledge of the needs of the city" (*Times*, August 16, 1905).

19. Elliott did not mention that the group, as reported in the *Times*, had posed as a party interested in inspecting Mount Whitney with a view to developing a summer resort area. (Other versions claimed that they represented themselves as cattlemen to avoid local suspicions.) Nor did he reveal that the journey's rigors had almost undone him, for he fell ill before they reached Independence and had to be taken out of the valley by J. J. Fay, president of the water commission, on the little narrow-gauge Reno and Carson Railway into Nevada and thence into San Francisco, where he spent the next three weeks in the hospital (*Times*, July 29, August 16, 1905).

20. *Times*, August 23, 1905.

21. My father, Perry Mulholland, used to cite to me as a parallel case Franklin Roosevelt's decision in 1940—when America was officially neutral—to aid England in its fight against Germany by slipping old World War I destroyers to the British Navy. To do so, he had to circumvent a suspicious Congress by an exchange of boats for leases of naval bases on British territory. Because the bases could be regarded as strengthening America's defense, Roosevelt, as commander in chief, could act without Congress. When the transfer became public, isolationists claimed the deed bordered on treason, but the public at large was sufficiently pro-British and anti-Nazi to find the matter of minor import. In like manner, the Los Angeles waterseekers' activities would have been viewed more critically had there not been powerful public sentiment favoring their goals.

22. *Times*, July 29, 1905; *Herald*, August 1, 1905. The "trickster" observation is by magician James Randi ("Secrets of the Psychic," *Nova*, PBS,1993).

23. *Examiner*, July 30, 1905; *Times*, August 3, 5, 1905; Mulholland, Office Files, WP04–2:11, August 3, 1905.

24. Mulholland, Office Files, WP04–22:4, Mulholland to Lippincott, August 15, 1905.

25. *Examiner*, August 3, 1905.

26. *Times*, September 8, 1905; *Herald*, September 2, 9, 1905. The *Times* boasted that this lopsided vote was the greatest majority ever given at a bond election in Los Angeles. Kahrl discredits the returns as a scanty vote reflecting voter indifference and cites returns double that size in a previous municipal election in 1904 and one on an antisaloon proposal in 1905 (p. 103). What he omits are comparisons to analogous water bond elections. The returns on the acquisi-

tion of the West Side Water Company in April 1904 had yielded a total of only 1,121 votes, while even the crucial and long-debated decision to acquire the private water company in 1901 produced a mere 7,551 votes. Voter turnout was historically light for water and sewer bonds, perhaps because, as it was said in 1901, when it came to those issues, there was "no dough out there to hustle the vote." When voters made the big decision to approve the $23 million bond issue to build the aqueduct the following year, however, more than 24,000 cast votes, a ratio of over ten to one in favor of the aqueduct. The accusation by historians such as Carey McWilliams (*Southern California Country,* p. 189) and John Caughey (*California,* p. 369) that capitalistic interests bilked the voters into bankrolling a water project for the former's interest is not only a slur on voter intelligence but also a failure to concede the average consumer's realistic desire for good and abundant water.

CHAPTER 12: PREPARATIONS FOR AN AQUEDUCT AND A TRIP TO WASHINGTON, D.C., 1906

1. *San Francisco Chronicle,* September 13, 1905; Hoffman, p. 123; Kahrl, pp. 134–35.

2. Mulholland, Office Files, WP04–21:16, 17, January 6, 1905; January 13, 15, 1906. *Times,* December 27, 1905. See also note 8, chapter 11.

3. Mulholland, Office Files, WP04–22:4, Jan. 9, 1906; Hoffman, pp. 104–5.

4. *Times,* February 7, 1906. Houghton also objected to John J. Fay's reappointment to the water board. So obstreperous did he become during this period that by March he and Mayor McAleer almost came to blows after the mayor accused Houghton of graft in granting favors to the Santa Fe Railway. When Houghton in turn accused the mayor of having formed a company to make pipe for the Owens River conduit, McAleer lunged at him, shouting, "You have lied about me as no man ever dared lie before." Thinking better of it, however, he struck no blow (*Times,* March 16, 1906).

5. Mulholland, Office Files, WP04–22:6, Mulholland to Young, March 9, 1906.

6. *Times,* March 30, 1906. The following account derives from an unsigned article, most likely by Allen Kelly (see note 19). Of local sentiment in Owens Valley, the column opined, "The kickers don't like Eaton a little bit, but their animosity is mild compared to their hostility to Engineer Lippincott. They say something serious would happen to Lippincott if he should venture to visit Bishop, and they say it in a way that can be interpreted only as a threat of personal violence."

7. Mulholland, Office Files, WP04–23:6, Mulholland to Young, April 20, 1906.

8. Mulholland, Office Files, WP04–21:7, Mulholland to Brooks, April 20, 1906. A similar correspondence occurred between Mulholland and the editor of the Pasadena *Evening Star,* WP04–22:8, May 15, 1906.

9. Mulholland, Office Files, WP04–21:12, Mulholland to Duryea, March 30 to July 14, 1906. *First Annual Report,* p. 55.

10. According to Cannon's biographer, President Theodore Roosevelt's great-

est concern about California at the time was its Japanese population. After Japan's victory at Mukden in the Russo-Japanese War the year before, Roosevelt's fears of a Japanese threat resulted in increased expenditures for the defense of Pearl Harbor in what were then called the Sandwich Islands; a large appropriation for battleships and torpedo boats; and in 1907, the barring of Japanese immigrants into the United States (Busbey, *Uncle Joe Cannon,* pp. 224–228).

11. For a full discussion, see Hoffman, *Vision or Villainy?* pp. 128–35. *San Francisco Chronicle,* June 16, 22, 1906; *Times,* June 23, 1906. *Times* columnist Harry Carr castigated Hitchcock's behavior in the Owens River matter, but acknowledged that from Mulholland Hitchcock had received "some of the plainest, most dynamic English ever hurled at the head of a Cabinet officer" and that some of the California delegates had feared lest Mulholland's "vigorous talk" should alienate him. (Carr elsewhere claimed that Mulholland's tongue "could scrape barnacles off a ship bottom.") Eight months later, however, when Roosevelt requested Hitchcock's "retirement," Carr allowed that the secretary was an honest man even though "irascible, obstinate and domineering," and that he could be unbearably insulting to those with whom he did business (*Times,* July 29, 1906; March 10, 1907).

12. Mulholland, *First Annual Report of the Los Angeles Aqueduct,* pp. 26–27. Members of the committee chosen by the Los Angeles Chamber of Commerce were W. J. Washburn and J. O. Koepfli, of the chamber; Wm. Mulholland, department of water; and W. B. Mathews, city attorney. Also attending were Chas. D. Walcott, director of the Geological Survey; F. H. Newell, chief engineer of the Reclamation Service; Gifford Pinchot, chief forester; and Senator F. Flint.

13. *Times,* June 24, 27; October 12, 1906; Mulholland, Office Files, WP04–21:19, Mulholland to Eaton, July 14, 1906.

14. *Times,* July 30 and 31, 1906. Some writers (notably Kahrl) have portrayed George Chaffey as a wronged victim of grasping, water-greedy Los Angeles while maligning Eaton for his secret manipulations on behalf of the city. Yet the two men shared striking similarities. Both were pioneer developers of water systems in Southern California in the 1880s and '90s; both were land promoters and equally well connected in financial circles, as well as in rail and transportation. Each was a clever strategist, and to imagine that Chaffey's motives were higher than Eaton's is, at the least, ingenuous. Many private money interests were active in Owens Valley at this time, and Chaffey aimed not merely to create an idyllic community (Manzanar) but also to secure water rights for private electric companies (see Burdette, *American Biography,* vol. 1, pp. 74–81; Cooper, *Aqueduct Empire,* pp. 70–71; Robert Glass Cleland and Osgood Hardy, "The March of Industry," *California,* pp. 213, 353–54; Jackson Graves, *My Seventy Years in California,* pp. 247–48; Clipping Book, Department of Water and Power, vol. 3, 1906; Mulholland, Office Files, WP04–22, Mulholland to Lippincott, June 29, 1909).

15. Copies of the chamber's proclamation were given to Senator Frank Flint, Representative James MacLachlan, William Mulholland, William B. Mathews, and chamber members W. J. Washburn and J. O. Koepfli. Among various other expressions of gratitude, the document states, "You indignantly rejected all the invidious conditions and trammels which if accepted would have prevented the

City from using its own waters as it may see fit in every lawful ways [*sic*] for the benefit of this municipality and surrounding territory." It continued, "You accomplished these great things for us during the last days of the session of Congress in the face of most determined opposition both from private and official sources, which to men of a lesser loyalty and pluck would have seemed and would have been insurmountable." Mulholland's copy of this tribute, executed in graceful calligraphy, hung in his home for the rest of his life. Mulholland, Office Files, WP04–22:17, Schuyler to Mulholland, August 31, 1906. James D. Schuyler's engineering skills were further vindicated in 1908, when an English syndicate appointed him to a commission to report on the construction of a plant that would power street railways in Tokyo and Yokohama as well as supply current for electric lighting and various industrial enterprises in Japan. The first installation would cost $5 million and would be the greatest of its kind ever attempted in Japan (*Times*, March 13, 1908).

   16. *Fifth Annual Report of the Board of Water Commissioners*, p.7.

   17. *San Francisco Chronicle*, August 29, 1906.

   18. *Examiner*, October 29, 1906.

   19. Details here derive from a long account by Allen Kelly, *Times*, December 2, 1902. Kelly's accounts of these early trips to Owens Valley are sharply observed. On this trip, he noted a "remarkable change in the attitude of Bishop towards the city's project . . . none of the wild talk I heard a year ago." He also attacked speculators buying up property, claiming they followed Eaton around to discover his movements and then rushed in with options to buy. He singled out A. H. Koebig, water system engineer and entrepreneur with ties to power corporations. "He wants nothing until the city needs it. And behind Koebig, the jackal engineer, is a power company using the money it makes out of Los Angeles to prevent the city from obtaining Owens Valley water. . . ." He also named Frederick Finkle and the Edison Company. Doubtless, Kelly reflected the opinions of Mulholland and Lippincott, but at the same time, the *Record*, a prolabor Scripps' newspaper with little sympathy for either the *Times* or the *Examiner*, also editorialized against men such as Chaffey and Koebig, calling them moneygrubbers with no civic pride (*Record*, December 13, 1906).

   Writers who dismiss Kelly as no more than an apologist for the *Times* and the aqueduct forces seem unaware of his earlier journalistic career. A veteran reporter who had observed and written of New York politics under Boss Tweed, he had a reputation for being a social reformer with a knack for sizing up people. Ten years earlier, while with the *San Francisco Examiner*, he was described as "a small, slight, dark, nervous-looking chap who affects good clothes and large canes" and whose only mark of unconventionality was a black slouch hat. A crack shot who was known as "the man who is looking for something to be afraid of," he was sent by the *Examiner* in 1889 to capture a grizzly bear and write about it. He went missing in the wilds for five months, and just as the newspaper was about to give up on him, he returned with a bear (Arthur McEwen, "Allen Kelly, the Journalist and Grizzly Catcher," *Los Angeles Evening Express*, July 19, 1890).

   20. *Evening News*, November 27, 1906. The *News* suggested that Mulholland had demonstrated his incompetence by indicating a route later altered by

experts, but others, including reporter Kelly, argued that the route was deliberately fudged to some degree to keep speculators from buying.

21. Mulholland's use of an oil lining on Ivanhoe Reservoir prompted a query about its success from the distinguished professor of irrigation at the University of California, Berkeley, B. A. Etcheverry. Mulholland replied that it had proved out except for a southern embankment "on which the work was but very poorly and hastily done." Strong north winds had raised waves high enough to spray over the bank, and after twenty-four hours unabated, cut holes in the slopes. Still, Mulholland maintained that with proper application the method would prove "a complete success" (Mulholland, Office Files, WP04–21:19, Mulholland to Etcheverry, December 11, 20, 1906). The Ivanhoe, completed in 1906, was subsequently plagued with algae and "larva and mulluscan growths," so that in 1907, both it and Bellevue Reservoir had to be roofed with timber supported by reinforced concrete girders and posts. The wooden posts erected in 1896 to support the Bellevue's previous roof had rotted and collapsed. Mulholland, ever alert to possible charges of extravagance, reported that the greater portion of the lumber had been saved and was being used again in reconstruction (*Sixth Annual Report of the Board of Water Commissioners*, pp. 6–7).

22. Mulholland, Office Files, WP04–21:7, May 9, 1906; Spriggs, pp. 40–41; Layne, p. 85; *Times*, November 26, 1906; July 31, 1907. Anthony Chabot's construction of Lake Temescal and Lake Chabot in the Oakland area during the 1870s had already used sluicing techniques derived from California mining practices (Burgess, *The Water King*, pp. 126–130).

23. Mulholland, Office Files, WP04–21:7, Mulholland to C. D. Brown, July 9, 1906.

24. *Evening News, Times*, December 20, 1906.

25. *First Annual Report of the Los Angeles Aqueduct*, Appendix E, pp. 117–132; J. D. Schuyler et al., "Report of the Consulting Engineers on the Project of the Los Angeles Aqueduct from Owens River to San Fernando Valley," December 22, 1906; *Examiner*, December 23, 1906; *News*, December 22, 1906.

26. *Express*, December 26, 27, 1906.

27. *Evening News*, December 25, 1906; *Examiner*, December 26, 1906; *Record*, December 31, 1906. Earlier in the year a scandal had occurred over undone work recommended by Mulholland on the outfall sewer. When City Engineer Harry Stafford was found dead by gas asphyxiation in August with his records hopelessly disordered, suspicions arose that shady deals with outside contractors had been made out of his office. Stafford had been appointed by previous City Engineer Frank Olmstead, who was now with the San Gabriel Electric Company. With this recent scandal in mind, the *Record* feared that the new mayor's possible connections to some of the suspects, especially the Southern Pacific "Nofziger-Stansbury & Powell crowd," could taint the Owens River works and turn the people against it.

CHAPTER 13: THE BIG JOB BEGINS, 1907

1. Spalding, *History of Los Angeles City and County*, vol. 1, p. 348. For a fuller discussion, see Mowry, *The California Progressives*, pp. 40–45.

2. *Herald,* January 13, 1907; *Times,* January 30, 1907.

3. On January 3, 1907, the board of public works, and later the city council, voted to approve Mathews as special legal adviser to the Los Angeles Aqueduct. His salary jumped from $3,000 a year as city attorney to $6,000 a year, and his office was moved to the Union Trust Building, closer to Mulholland. The precedent for such acts stemmed from the earlier litigations with private water companies when the city employed a special attorney. Under the special contract, either Mathews or the city could terminate the appointment by giving sixty days' notice. *Herald,* January 4, 5, 31, 1907; *Examiner,* January 4, 1907; *Evening News,* January 5, 1907; *Times,* January 31, 1907.

4. Mulholland, Office Files, WP04–22:13, "Chaffee Appropriations," September 21, 1906; WP04–21:21, Gray-Mulholland correspondence, 1907–1908; WP04–22:20, Shuey-Mulholland correspondence, 1907.

5. *Intake,* September, 1944, pp. 5–9.

6. Ibid.; *Saga of Inyo,* p. 216.

7. *Examiner,* March 25, 27, 31, 1907; *Record,* March 25, 1907; *Times,* March 28, 1907.

8. *Herald,* May 26, 1907. The auditor, W. M. Nelson, had been a traveling auditor with the Southern Pacific. When he joined the aqueduct staff, he introduced the railroad's system of accounting and financial management—a system that the Interstate Commerce Commission had mandated for all railways. Already in use for work on the Panama Canal, the system included a voucher system of payment, timekeepers placed under bond to guard against irregularities and overpayments, and competitive bidding for all purchases.

9. Mulholland, Office Files, WP04–21:19, April 2, 1907; *News,* April 1, 1907; *Examiner,* April 3, 1907.

10. Mulholland, Office Files, WP04–21:22, April 12, 1907; *News,* April 18, 19, 1907; *Times,* April 23, 27, 1907.

11. *Evening News,* April 22, 1907. The fourteen "Veritas" letters appeared on April 18, 20, 22, 23, 24, 25, 29; May 10, 22, 27, 29, 30, 31; and June 1, 1907. Entries in city directories suggest that W. T. Spilman's affairs had not prospered since his business and domestic failures in the 1890s. The 1905 directory listed him as a contractor living in rooms at 315 West Sixth; those from 1907 to 1911, as a machinist at 343 North Main.

12. *Times,* June 7, 1907.

13. *Times,* May 23, 1907.

14. Mulholland, Office Files, WP04–21:7, Mulholland to Brooks, May 17, 1907.

15. *Evening News,* June 8, 1907; *Herald,* June 4, 1907.

16. *Express,* June 10, 1907; *Times,* July 28, 1907. Clipping Book, DWP, May–June 1907.

17. *Express,* June 7, 10, 1907.

18. Clipping Book, DWP, "Owens River: Questions Answered"; *Evening News,* June 8, 1907.

19. *Times,* May 22, 1907; *Examiner,* June 12, 1907. Herriman lived much of his life in Los Angeles and at one time was a neighbor of Mary Mulholland (a niece of William) on the Arroyo Seco. One of Mary's brothers remembered stand-

ing with Herriman after a winter flood had taken out thirteen houses along the wash. While "99 percent of the people were out having a Roman holiday . . . the cartoonist soberly remarked, 'Nature can be terrible'" (William "Bill" Mulholland, interview by author, 1978).

20. *Express,* June 8, 1907.

21. *Express,* June 8, 11, 1907; *Times,* June 11, 1907.

22. *Herald,* June 23, 1907; Mulholland, Office Files, WP04–22:13, Mulholland to Shuey, June 12, 1907.

23. *Examiner, Herald, News, Times,* June 13, 1907.

24. *Record,* June 20, 1907; *Express,* June 20, 1907.

25. *Evening News,* June 13, 1907; Mulholland, Office Files, WP04–22:11, July 1, 1907.

26. *Times,* July 7,28, 1907.

27. *Times,* July 28, 1907.

28. *Times,* July 28, 31, 1907.

29. Mulholland, Office Files, WP04–22:20, Shuey-Lippincott-Mulholland correspondence, August 3, 6, 7, 1907; WP04–21:6, Mulholland to Bailey, August 15, 1907. *Times,* July 31, 1907.

30. Stimson, *Rise of Labor Movement in Los Angeles,* p. 318; Mulholland, Office Files, WP04–22:2, Mulholland to Editor, *Denver Post,* September 12, 1907.

31. *Times,* November 1, 1907.

32. *Times,* December 14, 1907. Hamlin had already supplied the Smithsonian Institution with fossils found while building the new outfall sewer, some of which the institution believed might be a new variety of camel from the Pleistocene. Of these finds, Hamlin had commented, "Looks as though we drove the outfall through a zoölogical garden."

33. *Times,* October 1; November 1, 1907.

34. Mulholland, Office Files, WP04–22:4, Gray to Mulholland, December 21, 1907; 22:26, Van Norman to Mulholland, December 26, 1907. Stimson, *Rise of the Labor Movement in Los Angeles,* p. 318; *Los Angeles Times,* November 27; December 1, 27, 1907.

CHAPTER 14: THE CHIEF AND THE GENERAL, 1908

1. Mulholland, Office Files, WP04–21:23, Harper; *Los Angeles Times,* July 7 and 31, 1907.

2. *Who's Who in the Pacific Southwest,* p. 81; Layne, pp. 111–112; *Times,* February 11, 1908. In 1906, Chaffee had refused the police commissionership of New York (*San Francisco Chronicle,* April 6, 1906).

3. Rumors about Otis's pressuring Mayor Harper to name Chaffee persisted, however, and a year later, as the campaign to recall Harper was under way, Otis published in the *Times* a letter of denial to Major Henry T. Lee, in which he claimed to have spoken only twice to Harper on the matter. Harper in turn told Otis he felt undue pressure was being put upon him to reappoint Anderson, and Otis charged the Municipal League with insincerity and trouble-making in driving Harper out of office (*Times,* October 10, 1908; February 19, 28, 1909; see also Ostrom, pp. 93–94, and Sitton, *Haynes,* p. 82).

4. Spalding, *History of Los Angeles City and County,* vol. 3, pp. 428–29; *Record,* March 25, 1908; Mulholland, Office Files, WP04–22:2, July 28, 1908; Mulholland Scrapbook, undated clipping.

5. Layne, pp. 108–9; *Times,* February 21, 26, and March 19, 1908. A year later, shortly after the inauguration of President William Howard Taft, Mulholland wrote W. C. Mendenhall of the United States Geological Survey expressing his concern over an Interior Department appointment proposed for Koebig's attorney, Oscar Lawler. "Lawler has been the attorney of the Koebig Silver Lake crowd and in his capacity as U.S. District Attorney for this District gave us considerable annoyance here. His appointment, no doubt, was dictated by machine influences opposed to us and I believe that our good friend [Representative] Smith had some intimation of what was coming as in our interview with him in [Representative] McLachlan's office he hinted very broadly of changed conditions under the incoming administration." (Mulholland, Office Files, WP04–22:5, Mulholland to Mendenhall, March 26, 1909; see also note 19, chapter 12.) Lawler had been appointed United States attorney to the Southern California District; in 1909, he was appointed assistant to the attorney general of the United States (Spalding, vol. 1, pp. 348, 358).

6. *Times,* February 26, March 10, 1908.

7. *Times,* March 10, 1908.

8. Taylor, *Men, Medicine and Water: The Building of the Los Aqueduct,* p. 22.

9. Taylor, *Men, Medicine and Water,* p. 23; *Times,* May 15, 1908.

10. The engineer in question was W. C. Aston, who, according to Dr. Taylor's aforementioned memoir (p. 25), was never "very friendly; in fact, he was rather belligerent in all his dealings with us." Although Taylor eventually found a way to get along with the difficult engineer, apparently the civil service examiner did not. Aston was, in fact, a graduate mining engineer from Ohio State University with thirteen years' experience in the mines of Colorado. He had gained a certain fame there for having driven what was then known as the Joker Tunnel, which drained for seven miles (*Times,* May 29, June 3, 1908; March 12, 1911).

11. *Times,* January 13, 1909; Sitton, *Haynes,* pp. 78–79.

12. Mulholland, Office Files, WP04–22:2, July 28, 1908; *Complete Report—Aqueduct Construction,* pp. 267–68; *Los Angeles Times,* June 23, July 9, 10, 11, 1908.

13. *Complete Report—Aqueduct Construction,* pp. 194–97; Layne, pp. 135–137.

14. *Times,* July 21, 1908; September 12, 1909. Mulholland maintained an Argus-like alertness at his work. His sons remembered that while others might drowse during monotonous stretches along the aqueduct, their father remained observant. After one inspection tour, he wrote to one of his chief surveyors stationed near Freeman, Kern County, "On my way home, in looking up at the mountain side running southerly from your work, I think if you have a laborer to take pick and shovel and blaze marks in the hill where the grade line runs, say every two or three hundred feet, the line will show up perfectly from the road . . . and will be a great aid in finding the stakes while traversing that rough country" (Mulholland, Office Files, WP04–21:6, July 12, 1906).

15. Mulholland, Office Files, WP04–22:10, October 3, 1908. Subsequent events seemed to vindicate Mulholland's suspicions about the Haiwee postmaster, for in 1911, the same "Doctor" Merritt was convicted and sentenced in San Francisco for fraudulent use of the mails in an oil scam called the Haiwee–Pacific Oil Company (*Express*, April 13, 1911).

16. Mulholland, Office Files, WP04–22:2, July 28, 1908; *Complete Report— Aqueduct Construction*, p. 259.

17. Taylor, p. 22; *Times*, December 13, 1908; *Engineering-Contracting: A Weekly "Methods and Costs" Journal for Civil Engineers and Contractors*, October 20, 1909, p. 325. The editor of this Chicago journal conceded that for the first time in his long editorial life, he was acknowledging that economical tunnel work had been done by the day labor method on the Los Angeles Aqueduct. He also credited the bonus system: "*Make sub-contractors out of all your foremen and workmen by paying them a bonus for work performed in excess of a stipulated minimum daily output.*" He questioned, however, the practicality of such a method in municipalities because of graft: "Imagine a Tammany applying a bonus system to streetcleaning!" he mused. Yet he also conceded that the bonus system stimulated achievement. This debate flourished in technical engineering and contracting publications of the time and remains unresolved. The bonus system prevailed in 1994 after the Northridge Earthquake in Los Angeles, when the severely damaged Santa Monica Freeway was repaired ahead of schedule and its contractor given a bonus of $4 million. The day labor method on public works received an added boost in 1908 when, after local private contractors sought injunctions against the city on both the aqueduct and sewer projects, a court upheld the city's right. The court did, however, question whether in an age of keen competition, public works could be built to the best advantage on these terms (*Pacific Outlook*, December 11, 1909).

18. Stimson, *Rise of Labor Movement in Los Angeles*, pp. 95, 147, 203, and 324; *Times*, June 12, 1908.

19. Mulholland, Office Files, WP04–21:17, June 30–September 8, 1908.

20. *Times*, December 1, 1908.

21. Mulholland, Office Files, WP04–21:19; O'Melveny, Journals, November 4, 17, 1908. Harold Eaton was having marital difficulties and in the following year separated from his wife, who charged him with nonsupport (*Times*, November 23, 1909).

22. Mulholland, Office Files, WP04–21:9, November, 1908; *Third Annual Report; Times*, December 3, 1908.

23. Mulholland, Office Files, WP04–21:7, Mulholland to Brooks, December 26 and 29, 1908.

CHAPTER 15: BUILDING THE AQUEDUCT: THE BEST YEAR, 1909

1. Mulholland, Office Files, WP04–21:17, Dockweiler-Mulholland correspondence, January 30, February 3 and 9, 1909; WP04–22:7, March 4, 1909.

2. Mulholland, Office Files, WP04–23:6, Mulholland-Young correspondence, October 7 and 12, 1905.

3. Widney, "We Build a Railroad," *Touring Topics*, March 1931, p. 36. See also Taylor, *Men, Medicine and Water*, pp. 28–29.

4. Hoffman, *Vision or Villainy*, pp. 150–151; *Times*, January 19, 20, 23; February 2, 1909.

5. Mulholland, Office Files, WP04-21:17, February 6 and May 3, 1909; *Times*, February 4 and 10, 1909.

6. *Times*, February 19; April 17, 20, 1909.

7. *Complete Report—Aqueduct Construction*, p. 219.

8. Layne, *Water and Power for a Great City*, p. 136; Nadeau, pp. 37–38; personal recollections of Van Norman and my father, Perry Mulholland, reminiscing about aqueduct days and "Whistling Dick."

9. *Times*, April 4, 1909.

10. In August 1909, Flanigan's crew drove 1,061.6 feet, a world record for fast tunnel driving for one month's run. The Swiss at Loetchberg Tunnel, working in limestone, had held the record with 1,013 feet. They had used compressed-air-driven machine drills, however, while the Americans used only hand drills. *Complete Report—Aqueduct Construction*, p. 156. *Express*, September 3, 1909; *Herald*, September 12, 1909; *Times*, September 2, 1909.

11. *Times*, September 12, 1909.

12. *Complete Report—Aqueduct Construction*, p. 151; *Times*, April 5, June 5, 1909.

13. For a good account of the mayoral campaign, see Sitton, *Haynes*, pp. 81–83. Upon his election, Alexander was reported to want all the city's commissioners ousted to fulfill the Democratic League's recommendations. He especially singled out a man on the water board "inimical to the interests of the city" (*Times*, April 23, 1909).

14. Mulholland, Office Files, WP04-21:1, undated and unlabeled news clipping, "Yoakum's Bombshell Failed to Explode," April 1909; *Times*, May 1, 1909.

15. Mulholland, Office Files, WP04-21:8, April 19, 1909.

16. Mulholland, Office Files, WP04-21:20, November 1, 1909; *Examiner*, September 21, 1909.

17. Mulholland, Office Files, WP04-22:26, Mulholland-Willard correspondence, June 5; July 17, 18, 1909; *Times*, May 2, June 11, 1909; *Times*, December 2, 1909.

18. *Times*, June 29, July 1, 1909.

19. Taylor, pp. 165–66; *San Francisco Chronicle*, September 28, 1906; *Examiner*, December 26, 1909. Members of the Desmond family had been passengers aboard the ship on which Mulholland and his brother had stowed away from New York to Panama in 1876 and had befriended their aunt, Catherine Deakers, during her trials on that voyage.

20. Taylor, pp. 112–13; *Times*, July 1, 3, 13, 1909.

21. *Times*, November 16, 1909.

22. Mulholland, Office Files, WP04-21:6, October 20, 1909. *Times*, December 2, 1909.

23. *Times*, November 30, December 14, 1909.

24. *Times*, October 27, November 16, December 17, 1909.

CHAPTER 16: TROUBLES AND INTERRUPTIONS, 1910

1. Hoffman, p. 149; *Times,* January 1, 11, 1910.

2. *Graphic,* January 24, 1910; *Pacific Outlook,* January 29, 1910; *Times,* January 20, 1910; Kahrl, pp. 172–73. Kahrl denigrates the differences between the Progressives and the old guard (and dismisses Mayor Alexander as a fumbler) in his assertion that an oligarchy of business interests controlled the city. For a more even-handed and accurate estimate of the Progressive efforts to modernize city government and restructure political power in Los Angeles, see Sitton, pp. 106–8.

3. *Graphic,* January 29, 1910; *Pacific Outlook,* January 29, 1910; *Examiner,* February 16, 1910; *Express,* February 15, 1910; *Herald,* February 15, 16, 1910; *Times,* January 11, 17, 20, 1910; February 15, 1910.

4. *Fifth Annual Report,* pp. 14–15; *Examiner,* February 11, 1910.

5. Mulholland, Office Files, WP04–21:19, March 3, 1910; *Examiner,* April 28, 1910; *Inyo Register,* January 13, 20, 27, 1910; June 9, 1910. The editor of the *Inyo Register,* W. A. Chalfont, had earlier alerted Owens Valley people to gather their forces for the land hearing (Sept. 9, 1909).

6. *Express,* March 20, 1910; *Examiner,* March 20, 1910; *Herald,* March 22, 1910.

7. Mulholland, Office Files, WP04–21:17, March 17, 1910; *Fifth Annual Report,* pp. 27–8; *Los Angeles Times,* March 5, 1910; *Los Angeles Examiner,* April 11, 1910; Clipping Book, Department of Water and Power, vol. 4, April 1910.

8. *Tenth Annual Report,* p. 21.

9. *Examiner,* May 9, 27, 1910.

10. For a full account of this enterprise, see Grenier, *California Legacy: The Watson Family,* pp. 326–332. O'Melveny, Journals, April 9, 21; October 15, 31; November 30; December 14, 1910.

11. *Final Report—Aqueduct,* pp. 268–69; Mulholland, Office Files, WP04–21:19, June 17, 19, 1910. The bond syndicate was Kountze Bros. and A. B. Leach and Company of New York.

12. Mulholland, Office Files, WP04–22:17, Mulholland to Smith, June 1, 1910; *Examiner,* May 9, 25, 27; June 3, 1910; *Herald,* May 23, 1910.

13. *Examiner,* June 25, 26; July 5, 9, 10, 11, 12, 1910; *Express,* July 9, 11, 12, 13, 1910; *Herald,* July 12, 13, 15, 16, 1910; *Record,* July 11, 13, 1910; *Spectator,* July 13, 16, 1910; *Times,* June 26, 1910; All above clippings from Scrapbook, Department of Water and Power, vol. 4, 1910. For a negative interpretation, see Kahrl, pp. 165–67. He writes, "Precipitate haste had been a hallmark of the city's handling of water bonds ever since the first issue to pay the costs of buying up the works of the Los Angeles Water Company." He rejects the possibility that the private electric power companies could have had a hand in the matter, although every newspaper in the city suspected as much.

14. *Examiner,* July 20, 21, 1910; *Express,* July 20, 1910; *Herald,* July 20, 1910; *Times,* July 21, 1910.

15. *Examiner,* July 29, 30; August 8, 1910; O'Melveny, Journals, July 1910. Mulholland spoke of his sons (then eighteen and sixteen) to a reporter. "They are good boys, right good boys, but they can't take their father as anything but

a huge joke. They read what the papers publish about me like they read about Buster Brown [a popular comic strip character]" (*Record,* July 21, 1910).

16. *Times,* June 1, 1910; Stimson, pp. 340–344. Many historians and journalists have written of the *Times* bombing, the most remembered event of labor conflict in Los Angeles. Notable among them are Louis Adamic, "The McNamara Affair," *Dynamite* (1931); Grace Stimson, "Crime of the Century," *Rise of the Labor Movement in Los Angeles* (1955); and Gottlieb and Wolt, "The Bombing of the Times' Building," *Thinking Big* (1972).

17. *Examiner,* November 21, 1910; *Express,* November 2, 21, 1910; *Herald,* November 4, 1910; *Inyo Register,* November 24, 1910; *Record,* November 11, 1910. Stimson, p. 351.

J. Desmond had threatened the city with a suit to reclaim his alleged losses on the aqueduct concession and received the increase after insuring that the quality of the food would improve. Years later, Dr. Taylor recalled that General Chaffee asked how much he and Desmond had made on the aqueduct job. After Taylor, who had headed the aqueduct medical department, said he had made about $6,000 a year for the five years, or $30,000, Desmond said, "I made about a quarter of a million," at which Chaffee exploded. "Damn it, Joe, you made too much and the doctor didn't make enough" (Taylor, *Men, Medicine and Water,* p. 157).

18. *Record,* November 22, 1910. The *Inyo Register* had reported earlier in March that "improper mixing of cement" had caused cave-ins, and that scores of aqueduct workers were leaving for the Bakersfield oil fields (March 24, 1910).

19. *Fifth Annual Report,* p. 7; *Times,* November 16, 1910; *Herald,* November 4, 1910; *Record,* November 7, 11, 21, and 22, 1910; *Examiner,* November 21, 1910. At the end of 1911, Rinehart left the *Record* to become a press association's state correspondent in Sacramento; he returned to Los Angeles in 1912 to manage and edit the new but short-lived Progressive experiment, the *Municipal News.* A Woodrow Wilson Democrat, he believed in municipal ownership and felt Mayor Alexander to be "a better Socialist than Harriman" (*Times,* February 14, 1912).

20. Chalfant, *Story of Inyo,* p. 213; *Inyo Register,* October 20, 1910. The impact of expanded transportation facilities during the years of aqueduct construction upon Owens Valley has been inadequately remarked. A month before the silver spike ceremony, a California governor had visited Inyo County for the first time in its history. Under the auspices of the Good Roads Committee, Governor James Norris Gillett visited the valley towns with speeches extolling the beauties of the area, which, he predicted, with better roads and increased access, would be visited and admired as were the Alps in Europe. Hopes for a bright future stirred in Owens Valley, for which some credited the influence of Los Angeles and the aqueduct, which might prove a blessing in disguise. Others, like Chalfant, doubted—although conceding that the railroad would improve their lives (*Inyo Register,* September 1, 15, 1910; *Times,* September 7, 1910).

21. *Express,* November 4, 1910; *Herald,* November 4, 1910; *Pacific Outlook,* November 5, 1910; *Times,* October 30, November 3, 5, 1910.

22. *Times,* October 21, 23; November 5, 1910.

23. *Express,* November 4, 1910; *Times,* November 5, 1910.

24. *Express,* November 4, 1910; *Herald,* November 4, 1910.

25. Mulholland, Office Files, WP04–21:16, December 2, 1910; *Examiner,* November 18, 1910; *Express,* November 25, 1910; *Herald,* November 22, 1910; *Times,* November 28, 1910.

26. Mulholland, Office Files, WP04–22:17, Mulholland-Stearns correspondence, November 23; December 6, 1910. *Express,* September 29, 1910; *Examiner,* September 24, 28, 29, 1910; *Herald,* September 28, 30, 1910; *Times,* September 23, 28, 1910.

CHAPTER 17: AQUEDUCT PROGRESS
AND POLITICAL FIREWORKS, 1911

1. *Herald,* March 7, 8, 1911. Years later, Scattergood recalled that Mayor Alexander had buttonholed him after the election to exhort, "Get ready to manufacture, distribute and sell to the people of Los Angeles, the power you say you can develop from the aqueduct." He also credited the mayor with instilling in him his idealism about municipal ownership (*Herald-Express,* July 10, 1940). On the other hand, Progressive Lissner and three other members of the public utilities commission resigned after the election in disapproval of the mayor's power policies. Calling the post "a thankless task," Lissner refused further public support of Alexander although he kept "hands off" the subsequent mayoral campaign (Meyer L. Lissner Papers, Box 3, Folders 42, 43, June 30 and July 17, 1911). For discussion of the municipal ownership movement, see Fogelson, *Fragmented Metropolis,* Chapter 11; and Sitton, *Haynes,* Chapter 5.

2. Mulholland, Office Files, WP04–21:11, Alexander to Mulholland, January 5, 6, 1911; *Herald,* February 10, 1911; *Record,* February 16, 1911.

3. *Examiner,* February 26, 27, 28, 1910; *Express,* February 25, 1910.

4. *Sixth Annual Report of the Aqueduct, 1911,* pp. 38–41; *Christian Science Monitor,* March 1, 1911; *Examiner,* March 21, 1911; *Times,* March 12, 1911.

5. Ostrom, p. 96; *Los Angeles Record,* January 30, 31, 1911.

6. Ostrom, pp. 95–96; *Express,* April 7, 1911; *Examiner,* March 26, 28; April 16, 1911; *Herald,* March 23, 26, 1911; *Times,* March 26; April 7, 16, 1911.

7. Ostrom, pp. 96–97; *Herald,* May 3, 1911; *Times,* April 19, 1911.

8. Ostrom, pp. 148–50; *Herald,* March 16, 1911; *Examiner,* March 16, July 4, 1911; *Times,* March 26, 1911.

9. Hoffman, pp. 156–58; Kahrl, pp. 182–83; Ostrom, pp. 150–52; *Times,* August 4, 10, 1911; *Tribune,* August 23, 1911. Earl was then under grand jury investigation for stealing a wireless message relating to the *Times* bombing and publishing it in his papers. Otis in turn attacked Earl in the harshest terms as a "friend of dynamiters." By 1914, Earl had a court case pending against Otis for libel.

10. *Sixth Annual Report—Aqueduct,* pp. 7–8; *Examiner,* July 16, 18, 1911; *Herald,* July 16, 1911.

11. Stimson, *Rise of the Labor Movement in Los Angeles,* pp. 331 ff.

12. Mulholland, Office Files, WP04–22:23, Statement by Public Service Commission, November 17, 1911; *The Citizen,* December 3, 1911; *Times,* September 29, 1911; *Tribune,* October, 23, 25, 1911. The unnamed district Harriman

intended the city should buy for water storage was probably near Redondo Beach, according to Mellie A. Calvert, who once worked as Harriman's secretary. The daughter of Midwestern Socialists, she had settled with her family in the utopian Socialist colony of Llano, later married, and taught biology and physiology at Canoga Park High School from 1932 until her retirement in the 1950s. Regrettably, she was never interviewed for an oral history; but she was my teacher, and I had several conversations with her in the late 1970s about Socialist attitudes towards the Owens River project.

13. For a more detailed account of this group's activities in the San Fernando Valley, see my *Owensmouth Baby*, Chapter 1, pp. 3 ff. Also, Fogelson, pp. 104–5; Hundley, *The Great Thirst*, pp. 158–60.

14. Fogelson, pp. 214–15; Mowry, pp. 50–52; Sitton, pp.110–12; *Examiner*, October 24, 1911; *Tribune*, October 23, 25, 1911.

15. Burdette, *American Biography*, pp. 274–76; *Times*, October 15, 1911; *Tribune*, October 25, 1911. In his memoirs, *Sixty Years in Southern California*, Harris Newmark, expressing the most conservative view of the time, held Alexander responsible for the success of the Progressive Party whose "Socialistic policies" he deplored (p. 639).

16. *The Citizen*, December 3, 1911; *California Outlook*, December 2, 1911; *Express*, December 1, 2, 3, 1911; *Times*, November 19, 25, 26, 28, 1911; *Tribune*, November 28, 1911.

17. Steffens, *Autobiography*, pp. 670–89; *Pacific Outlook*, December 2, 1911. C. D. Willard, editor of the *Outlook*, published Steffens's November 25 speech to the City Club, "How to Beat the Socialists." "By facing the social problem," said Steffens, one then secures the participation of "bad" men (that is, Otis, Chandler, and the others) in the experiment.

18. *Express*, November 4, 1911; *The Citizen*, December 2, 3, 1911; Mulholland, Office Files, WP04–22:24, Statements and Speeches of William Mulholland, City Club, December 2,1911. The twenty-seven-page, double-spaced, unpaginated typescript includes Meyer Lissner's introduction and the questions and answers after the speech. Following paragraphs in this text derive from that document (also, *Times*, December 2, 1911). Lissner, although silent about Mayor Alexander, was an important backer of Hiram Johnson in Southern California and during this period had sought Mulholland's recommendations for candidates to the state engineer's office. In forwarding one such recommendation to the governor, Lissner wrote, "I know of no man in the state of California whose opinion I would rather have on a question of this sort than Mulholland" (Lissner Papers, Box 3, Folder 45, Lissner to H. Johnson, October 18, 1911).

19. *Examiner*, December 23, 1911; *Tribune*, December 18, 23, 1911.

CHAPTER 18: THE INVESTIGATION, 1912

1. *Express, Herald*, March 25, 26, 1912. Ostrom, pp. 56–59. For a detailed chronological account of the formation of the AIB, see Abraham Hoffman, "The Los Angeles Aqueduct Investigation Board of 1912: A Reappraisal," *Southern California Quarterly*, vol. 62, No. 4, (1980), pp. 329–60.

2. *Sixth Annual Report of Los Angeles Aqueduct*, 1911, pp. 34–36; *Herald*,

January 6, 16, 1912; *Record,* February 16, 1912; *Times,* February 20, 1912; *Tribune,* February 15, 1912.

3. *Times,* January 13, March 3, 1912.

4. *Record,* March 11, 1912; *Examiner,* March 22, 1912.

5. Mulholland, Office Files, WP04–22:18, Mulholland to John Wilson, March 12, 1912; *Record,* March 22, 1912; Hoffman, *Vision or Villainy,* pp. 125–128; Mulholland, *Owensmouth Baby,* pp. 73–74.

6. *Complete Report—Aqueduct Construction,* pp. 208–9; *Examiner,* January 25, 1912; *Times,* February 3, 1912.

7. *Examiner, Express, Tribune,* March 20, 21, 22, 1912; *Record,* March 21, 22, 1912; *Times,* March 21, 24, 1912.

8. *Express, Record,* and *Times,* March 29, 1912; *Examiner,* March 30, 31, 1912; *Tribune,* March 31, 1912.

9. *Examiner,* March 30, 31; April 1, 1912; *Tribune,* March 31, April 1, 1912.

10. *Record,* April 1, 4, 12, 1912; *Times,* April 3, 1912.

11. *Express,* April 4, 1912; *Times,* April 4, 1912; *Record,* April 5, 6, 1912.

12. Spilman, *The Conspiracy,* p. 71.

13. Mulholland, Office Files, WP04–21:5, Mulholland to Board of Investigation, April 16, 1912.

14. *Times,* April 27, 1912; *Tribune,* May 2, 1912.

15. *Tribune,* April 18 and May 14, 1912; *Municipal News,* May 5, 1912.

16. *Express,* April 17, 24, 1912; *Municipal News,* January 22, 1913; *Record,* April 25, 1912; *Times,* April 26, 1912.

17. *Examiner,* May 21, 1912; *Record,* May 21, 1912.

18. *Express* and *Record,* April 12, 1912; *Examiner,* May 2, 21, and 22, 1912; *Herald,* May 22, 1912; *Municipal News,* May 22, 1912.

19. *Examiner,* May 22, 1912; *Record,* June 4, 1912; *San Fernando Democrat,* May 30, 1912.

20. *Record,* May 25, 31; June 1, 1912.

21. *Seventh Annual Report—Aqueduct,* 1912, p. 8; *Los Angeles Times,* May 29, 1912.

22. *Express,* June 17, 1912; *Herald,* June 14, 1912; *Record,* June 5, 1912; *Tribune,* June 7, 1912.

23. *Express,* June 14, 17, 1912; *Times,* June 17, 1912; *Examiner,* June 20, 1912; *Herald,* July 5, 1912.

24. *Examiner, Express, Tribune,* June 19, 1912; *Record,* June 20, 21, 1912.

25. *Times,* June 22, 1912.

26. *Times,* June 22, 1912. Family letters in author's possession: Perry Mulholland to Lillie and Rose Mulholland, June 25 and July 1, 1912. *Tribune,* July 6, 1912. In February 1912, Mulholland and Lippincott had written for the Spring Valley Water Company a groundwater study for a proposed catchment on Alameda Creek. On this trip they consulted with both F. C. Herrman, chief engineer, and S. P. Eastman, vice president and manager of Spring Valley Water. Between 1910 and 1913, Mulholland was also a consultant on Calaveras Creek Dam along with engineers John R. Freeman and Samuel Storrow and geologists Andrew Lawson of the University of California, Berkeley, and John Caspar Brauner of Stanford. In his report, Mulholland reverted to sea imagery in de-

scribing how water surrounding the outlet tower for the dam would "dampen the effect of an earthquake on the tower," just as, he wrote, "in a ship the vibrations from the machinery may be plainly felt when the hand is placed against the side above the water line, but not below the water line." He recommended the sluicing method used on Silver Lake, Dry Canyon, and Haiwee Dams. The Calaveras Dam failed during construction (March 24, 1918) when the soft core mud flowed out at the footing. Investigating engineers found that the "fine core material over the extended interior of the dam had remained mobile as near-liquid," yet concluded that the sluicing method was acceptable if properly controlled. Some later critics have cited the dam's failure as evidence that Mulholland was not a good engineer. Derleth Papers, Reports on the Calaveras Dam.

27. Mulholland, Office Files, WP04–21:19, Mulholland to Flint, July 5, 1912.

28. *Examiner*, July 6, 10, 1912; *Express*, July 10, 1912; *Municipal News*, July 10, 1912; *Record*, July 3, 8, 10, 1912; *Tribune*, July 10, 1912.

29. *Express, Herald, Record, Tribune*, July 16, 17, 1912.

30. *Examiner*, July 11, 1912; *Express*, July 16, 1912; *Herald*, July 11, 1912; *Record*, July 11, 12, 1912. Warner's zeal to demonstrate Mulholland's incompetence included writing to the British admiralty to verify a statement the chief had made to answer the criticism of "certain engineers" that the steel siphons had not been painted until rust had accumulated. He was alleged to have said that it was a practice in Britain to send vessels to sea in order that the hulls might become rusty before being painted. Warner was happy to learn from the admiralty that such was not the case, and the *Record* headlined the finding BRITISH ADMIRALTY FAILS TO SUPPORT MULHOLLAND THEORY (*Record*, August 27, 1912).

31. *Express*, July 25, 26, 1912; *Times*, July 26, 1912.

32. *Examiner*, July 18, 19, 1912; *Express*, July 23, 24, 25, 1912; *Record*, July 20, 23, 24, 25, 1912; *Times*, April 24; July 17, 23, 24, 25, 1912; *Tribune*, July 23, 24, 25, 1912. E. T. Earl's *Express*, in its apparent glee over Otis's discomfiture, reported only Mulholland's denial of friction on the board and omitted his opposition to Graham's plan. The trial ended with a verdict of not guilty (*Times*, July 31, 1912).

33. *Record*, August 1, 8, 15, 16, 19, 1912; *Times*, August 25, 1912.

34. *Municipal News*, August 28, 1912; *Record*, August 22, 29, 1912; September 3, 1912. See also Hoffman, pp. 352–56.

35. *Examiner*, September 2, 3, 1912; *Record*, September 3, 1912; *Times*, August 27, 1912.

36. *Examiner*, October 27; November 6, 13, 1912; *Express*, October 8, 1912; *Times*, September 26; October 27, 31, 1912.

37. *Express*, December 6, 7, 1912; *Tribune*, December 11, 12, 1912.

38. *Express*, December 26, 1912; *Record*, December 11, 1912; *Tribune*, December 31, 1912.

39. *Tribune*, October 26, December 31, 1912; *Express*, December 7, 1912; Los Angeles Aqueduct and Water Company, Press Clippings, vol. 7, 1912.

40. *Tribune*, December 31, 1912. A year before, Mulholland had recommended Johnson for the office of state engineer (Lissner Papers, Box 3, Folder 45, Meyer Lissner to Hiram Johnson, October 18, 1911).

CHAPTER 19: THE COMPLETION OF THE AQUEDUCT, 1913

1. *Municipal News,* January 8, 1913; Mulholland, *Owensmouth Baby,* pp. 58–60; O'Melveny, Journals, January 4, 5, 6, 1913.

2. *Examiner,* January 19, 1912; *Express, Tribune,* January 18, 1912; *Municipal News,* February 5, 1913.

3. Department of Water and Power, Clipping Book, vol. 8, 1913, No.1; *Examiner,* January 1, 1913; *Inyo Register,* January 7, 1913; *Record,* January 1, 1913.

4. *Herald,* January 10, 1913; *Tribune,* January 5, 1913.

5. *Express, Tribune,* January 22, 23, 27, 1913; *Examiner, Times,* January 23, 1913; Meyer Lissner Papers, Box 15, Folder 314, Mulholland to M. Lissner, January 30, 1913; E. T. Earl to M. Lissner, January 31, 1913. In the letter to Lissner, Mulholland also expressed his regret for his differences with the new public service commissioners ("I found myself outside the pale of concert of action"), but he also insisted that his opinions had been long held, and, he concluded, "consistency is a jewel."

6. C. D. Willard Papers, Mulholland to Willard, January 24, 1913.

7. *Examiner,* February 9, 16, 1913; *Express,* February 13, 1918; *Herald,* February 13, 1913; *Inyo Register,* February 20, 1913; *Municipal News,* February 26, 1913; *Times,* February 14, 1912; *Final Report—Aqueduct Construction,* p. 111.

8. O'Melveny, Journals, January 30, 1913; February 28, 1913.

9. *Inyo Register,* February 20, 27, 1913; *Times,* March 11, 1913; *Tribune,* February 23, 1913.

10. Department of Water and Power, Clipping Book, vol. 8, 1913, No. 1; *Pasadena Record,* March 9, 1913; *Times,* March 2, 13, 1913; *Final Report,* pp. 270–271.

11. *Tribune,* March 14, 1913; undated clipping, Mulholland Scrapbook.

12. *Examiner,* November 5, 1913.

13. *Express,* April 1, 1913; *Times,* March 31, 1913; *Municipal News,* April 2, 1912; *Tribune,* March 29, 1913; Mowry, *The California Progressives,* pp. 196–97. For a recent evaluation of the 1913 municipal election, see Sitton, *Haynes,* pp. 118–19. Mowry is inaccurate when he states that Earl's choice of Mulholland reflected the former's rift with the other leading Progressive, Meyer Lissner. In fact, Lissner's papers reveal that both Earl and Lissner sought Mulholland and only after his unequivocal refusal to run did they chose the nonpartisan candidate John W. Shenk (E. T. Earl to M. Lissner, January 31, 1913, Meyer Lissner Papers, Stanford). Mowry also errs in dismissing Shenk (misspelled "Schenk," pp. 206 ff.) as an "honest but otherwise undistinguished conservative." Unmentioned is Shenk's able service as assistant, and later, city attorney (elected in 1911 with a majority of 34,663), when he successfully led the city's fight against the Pacific Electric and the Southern Pacific for valuable tide and submerged lands around San Pedro. A political independent who had worked with Mathews on a number of water cases and also helped to create an early roadblock for Graham's high line, Shenk was well liked by Mulholland, who at the time was working with him and Mathews on arriving at amicable settlements

with private water companies in Owens Valley (*Inyo Register*, April 10, 1913). Shenk, in his failed run for mayor, was the only political candidate Mulholland ever openly campaigned for in his entire public career (*Who's Who in the Pacific Southwest*, p.337; Robinson, *Lawyers of Los Angeles*, pp. 124–25).

14. Mulholland Scrapbook, Otis to Mulholland, April 17, 1913; *Examiner*, April 16, 1913; *Times*, April 10, 14, 15, 1913.

15. *Examiner*, April 15, 16, 1913; *Tribune*, April 22, 1913.

16. *Final Report—Aqueduct Construction*, pp. 227–34; *Examiner*, April 21, 1913.

17. *Final Report—Aqueduct Construction*, pp. 227–235; *Examiner*, May 1, 1913; *Herald, Times*, May 21, 1913; *Tribune*, April 21, May 22, 1913; *Record*, May 26, 1913.

18. *Examiner, Times*, May 1, 5, 1913; Department of Water and Power, Clipping Book, vol. 8, No. 2; Fogelson, pp. 216–17. Shenk resumed his duties as city attorney and soon left for Sacramento to fight the Inman Bill, legislation designed to prevent municipalities from disposing of surplus water to outside districts and thus thwart the city's present plans for water distribution. Soon after, Shenk became a superior court judge where he served until 1924, at which time he was advanced to the Supreme Court of California, where he served until his death in 1959 (Robinson, pp. 320, 341).

19. Department of Water and Power, Clipping Book, vol. 8, No. 2, 1913; *Examiner*, August 7, 8, 9 ,11, 12, 1913; *Express*, July 8; August 6, 1913; *Record*, August 6, 7, 1913; *Times*, August 9, 1913. The following paragraphs derive from the above sources.

20. *Times*, December 19, 1913.

21. *Examiner*, July 16, 1912; *Express*, July 8, 1913; *Tribune*, July 8, 27, 1913; *Times*, August 6, 1913. Sitton points out that although Rose unseated Progressives, he still retained some reformers on city commissions, so that he did not put the quietus on Progressivism (p. 119).

22. *Final Report—Aqueduct Construction*, p. 270; *Examiner*, July 4, 1913; *Times*, June 19, 1913; *Tribune*, June 22, 1913. City auditor Myers had initiated legal action against the Southern Pacific when the Santa Fe had made a bid that would have saved $40,000 on the total cost of hauling aqueduct steel. The Southern Pacific had originally offered to meet any bid that was made, but after the Santa Fe withdrew its offer, the Southern Pacific refused to equal it. Myers then withheld the difference until the city attorney held they did not have sufficient grounds for a legal action, even though a moral obligation was implied (*Times*, September 18, 1913).

23. Mulholland, *Owensmouth Baby*, pp. 64–68; *Examiner*, June 21, 1913; *Express*, August 19, 20, 1913; *Times*, August 20, 1913.

24. *Examiner*, July 11, September 12, 1913; *Express*, July 11, 1913.

25. Los Angeles Aqueduct and Water Department, Clipping Book, vol. 9, 1913–14. *Examiner*, August 17, 1913; *Tribune*, July 9; August 1, 17, 1913; *Express*, October 11, 1919.

26. *Times*, September 26, 1913; *Tribune*, September 28, 29, 1913.

27. Department of Water and Power, Clipping Book, vol. 9, 1913–1914; *Times*, October 2, 1913.

28. *Record,* October 7, 1913; *Express,* October 7, 1913; *Inyo Register,* September 26, October 30, 1913; *Times,* October 8, 1913.

29. *Examiner,* October 17, November 5, 1913; *Express,* October 14, 1913; *Tribune,* October 15, 1913.

30. *Times,* October 3, 19, 21, 1913; *Examiner,* October 19, 1913; *Express,* October 13, 1913; *Inyo Register,* October 30, 31, 1913.

31. *Examiner,* October 31, November 1, 1913; *Inyo Register,* November 6, 1913; *San Francisco Chronicle,* November 1, 2, 1913.

32. Department of Water and Power, Clipping Book, vol. 9, 1913–14; *Examiner,* November 4, 1913; *Times,* November 4, 5, 6, 1913.

33. Hoffman, p. 172; Nadeau, pp. 66–67; *Inyo Register,* October 13, 30, 1913. The rift between Eaton and Mulholland has been oft-told and oversimplified. In 1913, the Eaton and Mulholland men remained on good terms. Perry Mulholland, William's oldest son, worked that year with the United States Geological Survey on its first survey of the White Mountains. In July he wrote from Bishop that at the hotel he had met Fred Eaton's son, Harold, who reported that he was "running the chicken ranch and says he is doing well" (Mulholland Family Papers).

34. *Tribune,* November 6, 1913. The preceding description of opening ceremonies is derived from the Los Angeles newspapers' many accounts.

35. *Examiner,* November 6, 1913.

36. *Examiner,* November 6, 1913.

37. *Examiner,* November 6, 1913.

38. Department of Water and Power, Clipping Book, vol. 9, 1913; *San Francisco Chronicle,* November 6, 1913; *New York Times,* November 6, 1913; *Boston Globe,* November 7, 1913.

CHAPTER 20: AFTER THE AQUEDUCT, 1914–1919

1. *Examiner,* November 19, 1913; *Herald,* November 11, 1913; *Inyo Register,* November 13, 1913; *San Francisco Chronicle,* December 9, 1913; *Tribune,* November 12, 19, 29, 1913. Mulholland, Testimony, November 24, 1913. I am indebted to J. David Rogers for having lately provided me with a partial copy of the deposition in which Mulholland's sworn testimony happily corroborates my own account.

2. *Examiner,* November 9, 1913; *Municipal News,* January 16, 1914; *Times* and *Record,* January 17, 1914. Finkle was also embroiled in a row over Mayor Rose's removal of a public utilities commissioner. During the ensuing controversy, Finkle was accused of "having grown rich in the employ of public service corporations as expert" (*Times,* November 26, 1913).

3. *Examiner,* February 6, 1914; *Tribune,* February 13, 14, 17, 1914.

4. Mulholland, Office Files, WP04–22:6, B. Heinley to John R. Mathews, January 14, 1914; *Examiner,* January 18, June 12, 1914.

5. O'Melveny, Journals, January 24, February 18, 1914; *Express,* January 29, 1914.

6. Department of Water and Power, Clipping Book, vol. 9, 1913–14; *Exam-*

iner, March 30, 1914; *Express,* March 24, 1914; *Herald,* March 24, 26, 1914; *Record,* March 26, 1914; *Times,* March 25, 1914.

7. Department of Water and Power, Clipping Book, vol. 10, April–May 1914; *Examiner,* April 8; May 2, 4, 5, 1914; *Municipal News,* May 18, 25, 1914; *Record,* April 8, 1914. For a discussion of the Progressives in the campaign, see Sitton, *Haynes,* pp. 120–121. A split between the Socialist Party and organized labor came as labor perceived the Socialists as more interested in political goals than in economic objectives. Even Fred Wheeler, the first Socialist elected to the city council, fell afoul of his own party when he sided with the labor cause (Perry and Perry, *History of the Los Angeles Labor Movement,* pp. 118–119).

8. Meyer Lissner Papers, Stanford University, Box 3, Folders 56, 57, M. Lissner to H. Johnson, March 13, 1912; M. Lissner to J. B. Lippincott, March 29, 1912; Box 43, Folder 744. *Examiner,* May 1, 1914. Apparently Lippincott was responsible for having suggested Mulholland to Lissner for such an honor. Henry O'Melveny also recommended it. Both diplomas remain with Mulholland's family.

9. *Examiner,* May 24, 1914; *Express,* May 27, 5, 1914; *Tribune,* May 14, June, 6, 1914.

10. *Examiner,* July 15, 28, 1914; *Herald,* June 18, 1914; *Record,* July 7, 1914. One of the long-standing canards against the water establishment has been that when it wanted to influence the public to achieve its selfish ends, it wasted water by allowing it to run to the sea. (This alleged practice was one of the evils portrayed in the motion picture *Chinatown.*) The opening of the Franklin Canyon conduit demonstrates that engineers had more rational and practical motives for letting water run. Before the conduit was activated, a wastegate allowed water from Owens River to run for two days down through Ballona to the ocean in order to clear the Franklin Canyon pipes of mud.

11. *Record,* August 1, 15, 17, 18, 19, 1914; *Examiner,* August 18, 1914.

12. *Express,* August 22, 1914; *Examiner,* August 16, 1914; *Record,* August 20, 1914.

13. *Who's Who in the Pacific Southwest,* p. 224; *Times,* September 7, 21, 25, 1904; *Herald,* January 19, 1905; January 19, 1907. Leonard is mentioned in passing in an essay detailing the development of clinical laboratories in Los Angeles in the early twentieth century (James Howard Cremin, "The Los Angeles Clinical Laboratory Medical Group," *Southern California Quarterly* 67, No. 4 [1985], pp. 395–96).

14. *Examiner,* August 21, 1913; *Herald,* August 20, 1914; *Record,* August 18, 19, 1914. Kahrl, pp. 217–18. Kahrl ascribes Leonard's behavior simply to her gullibility in accepting horror stories about bad water from Owens Valley locals, but this seems much too simplistic in view of her training and background. There is some hint of her socialist sympathies but nothing well documented.

15. *Examiner,* August 25, 26, 30, 1914; *Express,* August 25, 1914; *Inyo Register,* August 20, 1914; *Record,* August 22, 1914.

16. *Examiner,* December 16, 1914.

17. The paragraphs above derive from Department of Water and Power, Clipping Book, vol. 10, 1914–15, especially the following: *Examiner,* January 6,

28, 29; February 3, 19, 1914; *Express,* January 5, 28, 1914; *Express,* January 5, 1914; *Tribune,* January 8, 29, 30; February 3, 1914; *Times,* January 6, 8, 23, 29, 1914. Engineer Robert V. Phillips has criticized Kahrl's flawed knowledge concerning the aqueduct, citing as one flagrant example his dismissal of Haiwee Reservoir as "a small settling reservoir the city proposed to build at Haiwee Point" (*Water and Power,* pp. 156, 200). The Haiwee (there is no Haiwee Point, Phillips points out) was from the beginning "a major and keystone element of the Aqueduct," constructed "in order to equate the variable flow from the north to the constant flow south." Built in a long narrow gorge, the reservoir stretches seven miles and when built had a capacity of 63,000 acre feet, "by far the largest reservoir in the Los Angeles water system until Long Valley Dam was finished in 1940." Phillips adds that although the Haiwee does provide a clarification function, that is "the icing on the cake—not the cake," so that Kahrl's misapprehension leads him to "attack Mulholland for failing to provide the very function Haiwee Reservoir was designed to—and does—provide" (Phillips, "Water and Power—Wm. Kahrl").

18. *Examiner,* February 17, 19, 24, 1914; *Express,* February 20, 24, 1914; *Times,* February 24; March 6, 1914; *Tribune,* February 11, 24, 1914.

19. *Examiner,* September 15, 1919; *Express,* August 12, 1919. Mulholland was to remain ever after touchy on the subject of the purity of aqueduct water. The daughter-in-law of Haiwee engineer Phil Wintz recalled that one hot day when she and her husband, Homer Wintz, were ranching in the San Fernando Valley in the 1930s she had spied from her house "Mr. Mulholland sitting in a car while [his son] Perry and [Wintz's son] Homer stood on the road discussing farm matters." Thinking that the old fellow looked warm and uncomfortable, she carried a glass of water out to him from her olla in the kitchen. One sip, however, and he spit it out, gave her one of his famous glares, and said, "This is bottled water!" (Lucy Wintz Allen, interview by author, Woodland Hills, California, April 15, 1983).

20. Fogelson, pp. 221–28; Ostrom, pp. 156–58; *Examiner,* February 28; March 20, 22, 1915; *Times,* March 3; April 1, 1915; *Tribune,* February 21; March 21, 1915.

21. *Examiner,* April 20, 29, 1915; *Times,* April 25, 1915; *Tribune,* April 24, 29, 1914.

22. Sitton, *Haynes,* pp. 124–25; Department of Water and Power, Clipping Book, vol. 11, May 1915. For an entertaining, albeit unreliable, account of Sebastian as mayor, see Adela Rogers St. Johns, *Final Verdict* (New York: Doubleday, 1962), pp. 487 ff.

23. *Examiner,* July 17, 1915; *Herald,* June 1, 1915; *Times,* May 6, June 10, July 17, 1915; *Tribune,* June 2, 9; July 17, 26, 1915. For the eighty-fifth anniversary of the aqueduct in 1998, Linda Colton, civil engineer with the Department of Water and Power, located the map in storage, cleaned it, and supervised its installation beneath a portrait of Mulholland on the executive floor of department headquarters.

24. *Examiner,* August 29, 1916.

25. Spalding, *History of Los Angeles,* vol. 3, pp. 177–78; *Times,* September 3, 5, 22, 1916; *Examiner,* September 21, 1916.

26. Department of Water and Power, Clipping Book, vol. 12, 1916–17; Ostrom, pp. 59–60; Perry and Perry, *History of the Los Angeles Labor Movement,* pp. 119–20; *Examiner,* September 21, 1916; *Express, Herald,* June 4, 1919.

27. Kahrl, pp. 234–36. Kahrl outlines a not altogether accurate version of the struggle for municipal power. His statement that "Mulholland's lack of expertise in the field of hydroelectric generation" was "politically convenient for him" (p. 235), while Scattergood was left to take the flak, is simply not borne out by the literature of the period. For a more accurate account, see Ostrom, pp. 63–64. *Record,* January 13, 30; February 1; March 30, 1917; *Times,* January 8, April 2, 1917; *Inyo Register,* February 1, 22, 1917; *Tribune,* March 30, 1917. Space limitations prevent a more detailed account of the struggle for municipal power, but it should be noted that a subtext to the controversy was the animus among various owners of city newspapers which resulted in varying treatments of the same story. Hearst's *Examiner* remained a champion of municipal ownership, while Otis-Chandler's *Times* favored only municipal water and opposed power. The *Record* (suspected at this time of being subsidized by the Los Angeles Gas and Electric Corporation, a leader of opposition to municipal water and power) constantly attacked an "invisible government" that seemed to consist mostly of those connected with the Progressives, especially E. T. Earl and his allies. The other dailies supported municipal ownership.

28. Department of Water and Power, Clipping Book, Box PR-56–886, June 2, 1917 to November 18, 1917; *Examiner,* June 17; July 8, 16, 1917; *Herald,* July 16, 1917; *Inyo Register,* July 16, 1917; *Record,* June 16, 18; July 16, 1917; *Times,* June 16, July 11, 1917; *Tribune,* July 15, 1917. Wartime jitters doubtless played a role in the summer tensions of 1917, as a rash of violent events punctuated the season. At the same time as the aqueduct blowouts, a fire in Mojave at dawn on Sunday, July 15, wiped out a good part of the town, destroying the press office (where the fire began), the Miners' Union Hall, a general store, a dance hall, and the Postal Telegraph Building. Suspicions fell on the International Workers of the World ("Wobblies"), whose activities in Southern California had turned them into the easiest scapegoat when violence occurred. (They were at this time also suspected in two recent mysterious emptyings of Santa Monica's high-line reservoir.) Added anxiety about possible sabotage by the German enemy was heightened in mid-August when an unidentified airplane was discovered on a field in Lancaster (*Examiner,* August 11, 1917).

29. *Examiner,* July 17, 1917; *Tribune,* July 17, 1917. The proximity of the breaks to manholes raises an interesting speculation over a small squib in the *Record* (May 29, 1917) that reported Mulholland had ordered manholes with removable covers installed along the route so that desert dwellers and passersby could drop down a bucket on a rope and get a drink, but the pull of the stream was such that it could also pull in the bucket and the holder of the rope. After hearing a desert rancher say that when one tried to get water from the aqueduct it was "good bye, bucket," Mulholland had locked the manholes and installed hand pumps on top of them—perhaps also to forestall exactly the kind of violence that was to come.

30. *Record,* July 19, 24; August 11, 1917; *Express,* September 8, 1917. The *Record's* intemperate rhetoric subsided slightly the following year, after its edi-

tor of the previous two years, Dana Sleeth, had the misfortune of driving under the influence on Main Street the night of December 7 and colliding with the automobile of an attorney whose wife was injured in the accident. A suit against Sleeth resulted in his resignation from the *Record* in mid-December (*Record*, December 17, 1917; *Tribune*, January 24, 1918).

31. *Examiner*, January 8, 1919. Details of Mulholland's private life have been largely omitted here. It should be remarked, however, that between 1915 (the year of his wife's death) and 1921, his family underwent many turmoils and changes. His daughter Lucile made two rash and fleeting marriages, marrying her third (and last) husband in 1921. Her only child, Mulholland's first grandchild, was Lillian Sloan (born 1917), over whom a brief custody battle was settled amicably in 1920–21. Also in 1917 William's beloved brother, Hugh Mulholland, died after a long struggle with cancer. Oldest son, Perry, began to farm his father's San Fernando Valley acreage in 1916 and married Addie Haas, a descendant of valley pioneers, in 1921. William's second son, Thomas, fought on the front with the American Expeditionary Force in 1918, was gassed during the Battle of Argonne, and returned home at the end of 1919. Youngest daughter, Ruth, had a failed marriage in 1922 and eventually lived most of her adult life in New York. Rose, the oldest, remained at home and kept house for her father and brother, Tom. For brief vignettes of the domestic Mulholland, see my "Recollections of a Valley Past," in *California Childhood* (Berkeley: Creative Arts Book Company, 1988), pp. 179 ff., and *Owensmouth Baby*, pp. 170–71.

32. *Public Service*, DWP, vol. 1, Nos. 4, 5, 6, 1917; *Examiner*, February 14, 1919; *Express*, July 25, 26, 1919; *Herald*, July 26, 1919; *Times*, March 2; July 24, 26, October 11, 1919; *Record*, July 26, 1919.

33. *Times*, December 21, 1919.

CHAPTER 21: A STORMY DECADE BEGINS, 1920–1923

1. Sitton, *Haynes*, p. 170.

2. *Examiner*, May 13, 1920; *Express*, April 26, May 4, June 2, 1920; *Herald*, April 6, 20, 1920; *Times*, April 6, 22, 1920.

3. *Examiner*, May 9, 12, 1920; *Herald*, April 1, 1920.

4. *Examiner*, August 10, 1920; *Bishop Index*, July 24, 29, 1920; *Bakersfield Californian*, August 3, 5, 1920.

5. Chief author of these articles was R. W. "Rube" Borough, whose managing editor, Bruce Knisely, along with B. H. Canfield (head of the board of directors of the Record Publishing Company), were later revealed to have heavy involvements in financial dealings with leading Owens Valley banker-businessmen (the Wattersons) in their fight against the city (See *Municipal League of Los Angeles Bulletin*, vol. 5, no. 3, October 31, 1927; Haynes Papers, Box 124, Folder 30, Knisely to Haynes, July 31, 1926). This connection helps to explain the sometimes baffling and contradictory positions the newspaper took on water and power issues; for instance, while attacking the city's alleged depredations against Owens Valley, it remained in favor of public power. Recognized as an advocacy paper that provided a countervoice to the major dailies in offering different perspectives on timely issues, the *Record* sometimes found itself in anomalous

stances, as when it supported the state Water and Power Act in 1922–23 but never mentioned that Mulholland was actively campaigning for it. As an exchange editorial, the *Record* also disseminated slanderous material that sometimes took circuitous routes. A charge that Mulholland planned to steal water from Owens Valley ranchers simply to supply Japanese gardeners in the south first appeared in the Tonopah *Daily News,* June 21, 1921, followed by its next appearance in the Bishop *Index,* July 8, 1921.

6. *Saga of Inyo,* p. 21; Chalfant, *Story of Inyo,* p. 373. One former Owens Valley landowner, George B. Warren, later stated his belief that the city had paid liberal prices and that many had been eager to sell. In 1933, now a resident of Los Angeles, he complained, "The city owns about 90% or better, of all town and ranch property in Valley, and I do not believe it has 2% influence politically. This is bad. The people of the [Owens] Valley vote for county purposes, and the City pays the taxes" (Haynes Papers, Box 124, Folder 1–24, G. B. Warren to Haynes, August 20, 1933).

7. Mulholland, Office Files, No. 1-File "E"—Elliott to Mulholland, May 2, 1922; Mulholland to Elliott, May 9, 1922; *Herald, Times,* February 26, 1921.

8. Even San Fernando land developers who were supposed to be benefiting from aqueduct water confirmed Mulholland's toughmindedness on the city's behalf. When H. J. Whitley, head of the L. A. Suburban Land Development Co., tried to get the city to bear some of the cost of connecting water lines to new services for recent land purchases in the southern half of the San Fernando Valley, he was refused and wrote in his journal of Mulholland and Scattergood, "The Scotchman Mulholland was sometimes mistaken for a Scotsman because of a slight trace of burr then remaining in his speech] and the man from Mr. Chandler's state, where they sell wooden nutmegs, are certainly the limit. They want someone else to pay the bills" (H. J. Whitley Papers, Box 16, Minutes of the Board Meeting, March 6, 1914). Whitley erred again; Scattergood was born in New Jersey; Harry Chandler in New Hampshire.

9. *Examiner,* January 9, 15, 1919; *Times,* February 13, 1919. Leading the rival groups were George Watterson and Edson F. Adams, attorney for private power companies. Mathews had wired, "If Eaton available and would not feel embarrassed in relations with friends neighbors in valley think his presence here advisable to secure harmonious adjustment hearing next Friday morning ten o' clock" (Mathews, WP01–70:13, W. B. Mathews to E. F. Scattergood, Feb. 1, 1919).

10. Mulholland, Office Files, WP06–1:8, May 15, 1923.

11. Hoffman, pp. 178–79; Kahrl, pp. 274–75; Layne, pp. 153–54.

12. *Inyo Register,* August 1, 18, 1923; *Owens Valley Herald,* August 1, 1923.

13. Owens Valley Historical Records, WP06–2:11, *Eaton Land and Cattle Co. vs. Owens River Canal Co.,* Mono Cty. *Bishop Index,* June 17, July 8, December 9, 1921; *Inyo Register,* July 19, 1922; *Owens Valley Herald,* September 21, November 30, December 7, 1921.

14. Mulholland, Office Files, WP06–2:11, January 20, 1922; *Owens Valley Herald,* March 29, 1922; *Inyo Register,* August 1, 18, 1923. For various versions and interpretations of these three groups, see Hoffman, pp. 178–80; Kahrl, pp. 278–81; Layne, pp. 158–59.

15. *Express,* June 1, 1923; *Inyo Enterprise,* July 26, 1923; *Owens Valley Herald,* July 12, 1923.

16. Mulholland Office Files, WP06-2:11; Lloyd Hampton, "An Irishman Moves West," *Success Magazine,* August 1923; *Owens Valley Herald,* July 12, 1923; *Examiner,* July 17, 22, 1923; *Herald,* July 23, 1923; *Inyo Register,* July 26, 1923. The issue of the dam site at Long Valley remains a bone of contention among various commentators (Hoffman, pp. 178, 193; Kahrl, pp. 245–52; Layne, pp. 212–13). R. V. Phillips has commented, ". . . the Long Valley reservoir was never an essential part of Mulholland's aqueduct plan. He recognized it was a good reservoir site and might be useful in the future and he would have liked to tie up the land for it at the beginning. Negotiations with Eaton, owner of the site, failed, so that when the Long Valley Reservoir and dam [Crowley Lake] were completed, both men were dead." Harvey Van Norman later oversaw construction of the 100-foot contour dam originally planned by Mulholland. It was dedicated to Fr. John J. Crowley, who had served as a peacemaker and advocate for the people of Owens Velley (Karl, pp. 361–66; Hoffman, pp. 261–62; Nadeau, pp. 132–33).

17. Bakersfield *Morning Echo,* March 5; December 16, 20, 1920; *Bakersfield Californian,* September 15; December 4, 16, 1920; *Herald,* December 21, 1920. For a good account of the Water and Power Act campaign, see Sitton, *Haynes,* pp. 164–65.

18. *Examiner,* December 12, 1922. For a discussion of Hearst's support of the Progressives' efforts for municipal ownership, see Sitton, *Haynes,* p. 167.

19. Mowry, pp. 289–90; Sitton, pp. 152–53.

20. *Examiner,* December 16, 1922; *Express,* December 20, 1922; September, 17, 1923; *Herald,* July 21, 1920; *Times,* February 25, 1921; Bakersfield *Morning Echo,* February 23, 1921. In 1924, Thomas Edison prophesied that "when man has exhausted the possibilities of oil as a fuel, and of water power as a source of energy, he will learn how to harness the sun, the winds, tides and growing vegetables, and to generate from them energy sufficient for all his needs" (*Record,* February 19, 1924).

21. Crail, *My Twin Joe,* pp. 354–56. In articles decrying the building of Boulder Dam, the *Times* skirted Mulholland's support of the project by directing its chief barbs at Mathews and Scattergood. The *Examiner,* enthusiastic about Boulder Dam and municipal power, ran frequent informative interviews with Mulholland by veteran journalist Joseph Timmons.

22. *Examiner,* June 12, 1923; *Herald,* June 11, 1923; *Times,* June 7, 1923.

23. *Examiner,* March 11, 1923; *Times,* March 23, April 10, 1923.

24. Mulholland, Office Files, 1–1923; *Examiner,* March 13, July 9, August 17, 1922; *Express,* January 30, 1922; *Herald,* March 15, 17, 25, 1922.

25. *Fresno Herald,* February 5, 1923; *Herald,* January 3, 13, 1923; *Times,* February 9, 1923. Actual construction on Mulholland Highway began in December, after voters approved a $1 million bond four to one in a tiny vote of 398 for, 89 against (*Examiner,* October 9, 1923).

26. *Examiner,* March 12, October 21, 1923; *Rochester, N.Y. Times-Union,* January 27, 1922; *Sacramento Bee,* October 18, 1923.

27. *History and First Annual Report,* Metropolitan Water District of Southern California, pp. 35–36. The Volney Craig case seems to have been yet another

attempt to stifle the development of municipal hydroelectric power. Representing himself as the head of a taxpayers' association, Craig had published a series of twelve letters in 1923 charging Mulholland with various incompetencies, among them the creation of a water famine, which also included the old chestnut about wasting good water into the ocean. These ran variously in the *Owens Valley Herald, Record,* and *Los Angeles Times.* In denying Craig's charges, Mulholland wondered aloud, ". . . as his only taxable property is a house and lot in Pasadena, it is hard to understand what his interest is." For two days, Mulholland testified that most valley ranchers were satisfied with the city's handling of irrigation water, and that so much aqueduct water had been used in the San Fernando Valley that the water plane had been raised to the point that the soil was saturated in many places. One reporter observed that although Mulholland raised a few smiles with his spirited replies, interest in the trial was minor, as one lone spectator observed besides the newsmen (*Express,* November 21, 22, 1923; *Times,* January 11, 1924).

28. *Examiner,* November 6, 1923; *Times,* January 11, 1924.

CHAPTER 22: BOULDER DAM AND DYNAMITE, 1924

1. Moeller, *Phil Swing and Boulder Dam,* p. 30; *Daily News,* January 5, 1924; *Examiner,* January 5, 11, 1924; *Herald,* January 5, 1924.

2. Department of Water and Power, Clipping Book, 1923–24; Hoffman, p. 245; *Daily News,* January 3, 11, 1924; *Examiner,* December 13, 21, 23, 27, 28, 1923; January 5, 11, 1924; *Herald,* December 20, 1923; January 8, 24, 25, 1924; *Record,* January 4, 1924.

3. Moeller, pp. 48–54, 154; *Examiner,* February 15, 1924; *Record,* February 15, 1924; *Daily News,* February 19, 1924.

4. Moeller, pp. 50–51; *Daily News,* February 19, 1924; *Examiner, Herald, Times,* February 16, 1914. For a good review of the Boulder Dam controversy, see Hundley, *The Great Thirst,* pp. 203–20.

5. Moeller, pp. 48–54, 157; Los Angeles Board of Public Service Commission, Clipping Scrap Book, February 18 to August 2, 1924, especially, *Daily News,* May 8, 1924; *Examiner,* February 16, 21; May 10, 1924; *Herald,* February 16, 21, 1924; *Times,* May 8, 1924.

6. *Examiner, Herald, Record,* February 21, 1924.

7. Los Angeles Department of Water and Power, Scrap Book, File No. PR 56–883: Crowley, "Open Letter to Citizens of Inyo," February 12, 1924; Layne, pp. 159–60. In expressing his sorrow that the Klan had come to Inyo, Father Crowley wrote, "No one knows better than the writer that the real reason for the coming of the Klan to this county was not religious, but rather a misguided attempt to solve the water situation, yet no one knows better than the writer either that many have joined the local Klan with full approval of its anti-Catholic platform." Some latter-day Owens Valley proponents have denied any Klan activity in the valley, but if there were none, why would the only Catholic priest in the area have bothered to sound such an alarm?

8. Mulholland, Office Files, WP06–3:12, 1922–1930. Mulholland to Mathews, February 27, 1924.

9. Layne, pp. 158–59; Mulholland, *Owensmouth Baby,* pp. 20, 175; *Inyo Register,* June 28, 1917; *Owens Valley Herald,* December 7, 1921; August 1, 1923; April 4, 1924. The Longyear property four miles southwest of Bishop consisted of 2,110 acres of land with 1,550 shares of stock in Bishop Creek and Rawson Ditches. A basin area, the land was heavily saturated with water. Longyear was asking $250 an acre, or $527,000. He sold to the city in August 1925, for $300,000 (J. R. Haynes Collection, Box 124, especially Folder 2–22).

10. *Record,* May 5, 1924; *Examiner,* May 7, 1924. The director of publicity for the public service commission had warned that the election would be bitter, even suggesting that it might be necessary "to directly charge a conspiracy of Power Barons against Los Angeles" (Haynes Papers, MacGillivray to Public Service Commission, March 7, 1924, Box 113, Folder 45).

11. *San Francisco Call,* March 20; April 1, 2, 19, 20, 22, 24, 26, 27, 29; May 1, 3, 1924. Kunze was evidently long active in public affairs in Owens Valley, for in December 1911, he had written Meyer Lissner in Los Angeles requesting his help in appointing "a progressive Postmaster in Bishop." Lissner had replied that he did not interfere in matters of this kind and suggested that Kunze seek help from Senator Works (M. Lissner Papers, Box 3, Folder 48, M. Lissner to C.E. Kunze, December 11, 1911).

12. *Express, Herald, Record,* May 21, 1923.

13. *Express,* May 22, 1923; *Times,* May 22, 1923.

14. Los Angeles Board of Public Service Commission, Newspaper Clippings, May 2 to August 19, 1924. *Daily News,* May 30, 1924; *Examiner,* May 25, 30, 1924.

15. Department of Water and Power, Clipping Book, PR-56–884. "Re. Owens Valley Settlers' Controversy," 1921–1928. *Inyo Register,* June 5, 19, 1924; *Owens Valley Herald,* June 5, 18, 1924.

16. *Inyo Register,* June 5, 1924; *Owens Valley Herald,* June 4, 18, 21, 1924.

17. *Fresno Republican,* September 1, 1924. The editorial was most probably the work of Progressive editor Chester Rowell.

18. *Examiner,* July 23 and August 1, 2, 1924; *Owens Valley Herald,* July 30, 1924; *Express,* July 30 and August 2, 1924; *Record,* August 4, 1924.

19. *Daily Journal,* August 7, 1924; *Examiner,* August 7, 13, 1924; *Times,* August 6, 13, 1924; *Record,* August 13, 15, 1924.

20. *Examiner, Herald, Times,* August 27, 1924.

21. *Examiner,* August 29, September 2, 1924; *Fresno Bee, Fresno Republican, Bakersfield Echo,* August 28, 1924; *Times,* September 2, 1924; *Record* and *Herald,* September 1, 2, 1924; *Herald,* September 2, 1924.

22. *Examiner,* September 2, 1924; *Fresno Republican,* September 6, 1924; *Herald,* September 8, 1924; *Inyo Register,* September 11, 1924; *Owens Valley Herald,* September 3, 10, 1924; *Record,* September 6, 1924.

23. *Times,* September 4, 1924; *Examiner,* September 7, 1924; Whitsett, *Success Is No Accident,* pp. 130–31.

24. *Examiner, Record,* September 5, 6, 7, 1924; *Herald,* September 6, 1924; *Owens Valley Herald,* September 10, 1924.

25. Mulholland, Office Files, WP06–1:8, February 23, 1924; March 3, 1925; *Times,* September 9, 1924; *Herald,* September 8, 1924.

26. *Herald,* September 8, 1924; *Times,* September 11, 1924.

27. Mulholland, Office Files, No. 1, September 25, 1924; *Owens Valley Herald,* September 10, 17, 1924; *Inyo Register,* September 11, 1924.

28. Mulholland, Office Files, No. 1, Mulholland to W. Mayo Newhall, September 27, 1924. *Express,* September 24, 1924; *Herald,* September 10, 1924.

29. *Examiner,* October 18, 1924; *Herald,* October 18, 23, 1924; *Times,* October 5, 1924.

30. *Times,* November 16, 1924.

31. *Owens Valley Herald,* November 12, 1924; *Times, Record, Herald, Examiner, Herald,* December 10, 12, 1924.

32. Hoffman, p. 185; Kahrl, pp. 292–93; Nadeau, pp. 85–90. *Owens Valley Herald,* November 19, 20, 1924; *Record,* November 18, 20, 1924. This oft-told episode may be found in many writings, of which the above are only a sample.

33. *Fresno Bee,* November 22, 1914; *Record, Examiner, Times,* November 19, 1924.

34. *Express,* November 20, 1924; *Record,* December 3, 1924.

35. Kahrl, p. 294; *Herald,* December 3, 1924; *Examiner,* December 4, 1924.

36. *Daily News,* December 28, 1924; *Examiner,* December 28, 1924; *Express,* December 26, 1924; *Record,* December 28, 1924; *Times,* December 27, 1924.

CHAPTER 23: MORE DYNAMITE, 1925–1927

1. McClure, "Letter of Transmittal," January 9, 1925; *Daily News,* January 21, 1925; *Examiner,* January 13, 1925; *Express,* February 3, 1925; *Fresno Californian,* January 19, 23, 24, 1925; *Inyo Register,* January 22, 1925; *Herald,* January 30, 1925; *Times,* February 3, 1925.

2. Department of Water and Power, "Facts Concerning the Owens Valley Reparations Claims," undated pamphlet; *Examiner,* January 11, March 26, 1924; *Express,* January 10, February 3, 1925; *Herald,* January 9, 1925; *Daily News,* January 10, 1925; *Fresno Californian,* January 19, 1925; *Inyo Register,* January 9, 1925; *Owens Valley Herald,* January 9, 1925; *Times,* January 9, 11, 20, 1925.

3. Ortega y Gasset, *The Revolt of the Masses,* authorized translation (New York: W. W. Norton, 1932), pp. 105, 115.

4. Hundley, *The Great Thirst,* pp. 214–15; *Examiner,* January 30, 1925; *Express,* February 3, 1925.

5. *Examiner, Herald, Times,* March 18, 1925.

6. Gottlieb and Wolt, *Thinking Big,* pp. 198–99; *Examiner,* June 2, 1925; *Record,* March 8, April 9, 1925; *Times,* May 5, 6, 1925.

7. *Herald,* July 20, 25, 1925; *Times,* June 30, 1925. E. A. Bayley had been a locating engineer for the Salt Lake Railroad and the aqueduct. In recommending him for the job of state engineer in 1911, Mulholland had described him as "a mathematical genius" (M. Lissner Papers, Box 3, Folder 45, Lissner to Hiram Johnson, October 14, 1911).

8. *Herald, Times, Record,* August 6, 1925; *Daily News,* August 7, 1925; *Examiner,* August 6, 9, 1925.

9. *Examiner,* August 12, 14, 1925; *Record,* August 14, 1925; *Times,* August 12, 1925.

10. *Examiner,* August 14, 1925.

11. *Express,* August 26, 1925; *Herald, Times,* September 15, 1925.

12. *Examiner,* October 25, 1925; *Herald,* October 27, 1925.

13. *Times,* December 6, 1925.

14. See note 9, chapter 22; *Express, Herald, Owens Valley Herald, Record,* August 5, 1925; *Examiner, Record, Times,* August 12, 1925. The *Owens Valley Herald* described the Longyear sale as "another chapter to the disgraceful story of how the City of Los Angeles is forcing the ruination of Owens Valley . . ."

15. *Daily News, Examiner, Herald, Record, Times,* September 1, 5, 18, 1925.

16. *Daily News,* August 23, 1925; *Examiner,* August 22, 1925; *Times,* August 16, 1925.

17. Mulholland, Office Files, WP06–1:8, Jas. Vroman to Van Norman, October 23, 29, 1924; Chas. H. Lee to Van Norman, October 30, 1925; Geo. Young to Mathews, December 15, 1925.

18. Mulholland, Office Files, WP06–1:8, Van Norman to Mathews, January 15, 1926.

19. Mulholland, Office Files, WP06–1:8, Van Norman to Mathews, January 15, 1926; Mathews to Shoemaker, March 3, 1926; Van Norman to Mathews, March 11, 1926.

20. Owens Valley Historical Records, WP06–2:11, April 6, 1926. Mortgage recorded May 8, 1926.

21. *Examiner,* April 6, May 13, 1926; *Express,* May 10, 13, 1926; *Daily News,* May 13, 1926.

22. *Daily News,* July 1, 1926; *Examiner,* July 1, 2, 1926; *Herald,* July 1, 1926; *Record,* July 1, 1926. In its continuing attack against the city's water men, the *Record* was the only local paper to report the relatively inconsequential blasting of the construction shed. An interesting letter in the Haynes papers further reveals that the connections between the *Record* and Owens Valley property owners were more than casual. In what is apparently a transcript of a conversation between Haynes and B. Knisely (editor and close associate of the *Record*'s publisher, B. H. Canfield), Knisely outlines the *Record*'s willingness to support the bonds in the upcoming city election if the board would agree to use the money ($600,000) to clear up "the purchase of remaining ranch land." Haynes Papers, Box 124, Folder 30, July 31, 1926.

23. Owens Valley Historical Records, DWP, WP06–5:9, Watterson to Eaton, December 31, 1926; *Saga of Inyo,* p. 124.

24. Owens Valley Historical Records, WP06–1:8, Van Norman to Mathews, January 10, 1927.

25. Owens Valley Historical Records, DWP, Watterson to Eaton, February 6, 1927.

26. Owens Valley Historical Records, DWP, Clausen to Watterson, February 16, 1927.

27. Owens Valley Historical Records, DWP, WP06–2:12, Van Norman to Mathews, February 3, 1927.

28. *Owens Valley Herald,* April 6, 1927.

29. Don J. Kinsey, *The Owens Valley Dispute* (Los Angeles: Department of Water and Power, 1927); *Big Pine Citizen,* March 12, 1927; *Examiner,* April 27,

1927; *Inyo Register,* March 31, April 7, 1927; *Owens Valley Herald,* March 9, 16, 23; April 6; May 4, 11, 1927; *Sacramento Union,* March 23–April 2, 1927. By year's end, an exchange of letters between Burton Knisely, editor of the *Record,* and W. W. Watterson came to light, further substantiating the connection between the newspaper and Owens Valley interests. Those implicated were not only B. H. Canfield, president of the board of directors of the Record Publishing Company, but stockholders W. D. Longyear and Andrae Nordskog, later a vociferous attacker of the city's water establishment (*Municipal League Bulletin,* vol. 5, no. 3, October 1927).

30. Department of Water and Power, Clippings Scrap Book, "Owens Valley Dynamitings," 1927; Department of Water and Power, Clippings Scrap Book, DWP, PR, 56–884, Out of Town Articles, 1927. For samples of the increasingly intemperate language emanating from Owens Valley, see the *Owens Valley Herald,* May and June 1927; the *Record* often reprinted these inflamed attacks.

31. *Daily News, Examiner, Express, Times,* June 1, 1927.

32. DWP, File No. 450–55, Mulholland to Federal Radio Commission, July 6, 1927.

33. Department of Water and Power, Clippings Scrapbook, DWP, July–August, 1927; *Examiner,* July 17; August 5, 13, 24; September 28, 1927; *Spartan News,* August 18, 1927.

34. *The Saga of Inyo,* p. 66.

35. *Daily News, Herald,* August 6, 1927; *Examiner,* August 13, 1927.

36. *Times,* September 2, 1927; *Examiner,* September 17, 18, 1927; Office Files, DWP, telegram from Haiwee to Hurlbut, September 22, 1927. The wire gives the sixteen machine guns' serial numbers.

37. *Examiner,* September 11, 1927. The most visible evidences of Mulholland's advancing age were hand tremors and a shuffled gait. Described in other writings as Parkinson's disease, it was never so diagnosed by his personal physicians. His maternal uncle, Richard Deakers, as well as his sons, Perry and Tom, suffered the same involuntary hand tremor, which our family unmedically referred to as "the Deakers Shake." Stress aggravated the trembling, yet my father recalled that his own dad could so control his unsteady hand that in executing a sketch, he was able, painstakingly and with tiny strokes, to draw a straight line that showed no sign of interruption. His later handwriting, however, with its wavering lines, betrays the condition, and I remember from childhood observing him shakily—yet deftly—carving a joint or roast fowl at family dinners. Until he suffered his first stroke in 1934, he always stood with his snickersnee in hand, ready, as a true Victorian paterfamilias, to do the honors of the table.

38. Addie Mulholland to Rose Mulholland, November 8, 1927. Letter in author's possession.

39. According to Robert V. Phillips, at 16,500 acre feet, Tinemaha Dam and Reservoir was less than one-tenth the proposed Long Valley Reservoir's capacity and was never intended as an alternative to Long Valley. As its purpose is operational, its normal condition is empty or near-empty (conversation, September 13, 1995).

40. Moeller, p.105; *Times,* December 9, 1927.

41. Mulholland to Rose Mulholland, January 10, 1928. Letter in author's possession.

42. Owens Valley Historical File, WP06–1:8, Mulholland to Mathews, February 13, 1928. The Long Valley matter was not resolved until 1933, when the city authorized the purchase of the Eaton property in Long Valley for $650,000 (see above file, November 7, 1932, January 13, 1933).

CHAPTER 24: THE SAINT FRANCIS DAM
DISASTER AND AFTER, 1928–1935

1. Parts of this chapter appeared in different form in my essay, "Mulholland and the St. Francis Dam," from Nunis, *The St. Francis Dam Disaster Revisited*, pp. 111–37.

2. The other reservoirs were Lower Franklin, Stone Canyon, Upper and Lower San Fernando, Encino, Sawtelle, Ascot, and Hollywood.

3. Layne, p. 186; Nadeau, p. 116; Rogers, "A Man, a Dam, and a Disaster: Mulholland and the St. Francis Dam," *The St. Francis Dam Disaster Revisited*, pp. 20–21.

4. Rogers, pp. 26–28. Rogers's discussion of geology and dam construction and his analysis of uplift theory and advanced methods of dam building since Mulholland's day are not detailed here, not only because of space limitations but because he has already covered them masterfully in his own writings. When recently challenged for his apparent vindication of Mulholland in an article by journalist Kermit Patterson ("Why Did the Dam Burst?" *American Heritage of Invention & Technology*, Summer 1998, pp. 23–31), Rogers commented, "That non-scientifically-trained historians can pass judgment on historic standard-of-care in civil engineering seems incredulous [*sic*] to me, but that's the world we live in" (Rogers to C. Mulholland, February 24, 1998).

Also invaluable to this subject is Charles Outland's pioneer study *Manmade Disaster*. Charles Outland was a Santa Paula native who as a youth had lived through the experience and devoted years to his study. See also Abraham Hoffman's critique of Outland's work in *The St. Francis Dam Disaster Revisited*, pp. 165–76. Of additional interest is the long narrative poem, "The Death of the Dam," by Charles H. Lawrance (privately printed, Santa Barbara, 1971, 1995). Lawrance, a consulting engineer, wrote this ambitious literary work before Rogers's work had been published. Since reading Rogers, he has remarked, "Someday I might even add 5 or 6 verses to the poem to recognize this aspect" (Lawrance to C. Mulholland, April 24, 1998).

An effective video recording on famous American floods (the Johnstown, the Saint Francis, and the inundations on the upper Mississippi in 1993) is "The Wrath of God: Torrents of Death" (Tower Productions, 1997.)

5. Nadeau, pp. 116–17; Outland, pp. 52–53.

6. For excellent and vivid accounts, see Nadeau, pp. 117–22 and Outland, chapters 6 to 10, pp. 79–139.

7. Clippings Scrapbook, DWP, "St. Francis Dam, 1928." Los Angeles County Coroner, Transcript and Verdict of the Coroner's Jury in the Inquest over Victims of the St. Franics Dam Disaster: Book 26902.

8. I am indebted to an old family friend, Raymond Orton, for having provided me with this eyewitness document. Orton, at this writing in his nineties and living in Upland, California, explained, "When the San Francisquito Dam failed . . . Daisy Shaw Orton sent a letter to my parents in Owensmouth [pioneer settlers in what is now Canoga Park in the San Fernando Valley] telling them of the tragic event. Mother sent the letter on to me and I have kept it in my files ever since." Raymond, a recent graduate of UC Berkeley, was living and working in San Francisco at the time. Orton to C. Mulholland, August 8, 1993.

9. Layne, pp.199–200; Nadeau, p. 122; Outland, pp. 178–79; Teague, *Fifty Years a Rancher,* pp. 182–85; *Times,* March 17; April 5, 1928; April 18, 1929. The city paid for the flood damages through a tax increase to its property owners (*Daily News,* August 29, 1928).

10. Rogers, *A Man, a Dam, and a Disaster,* pp. 83–84.

11. *Examiner,* April 20, 21, 22, 1928.

12. Moeller, *Phil Swing and Boulder Dam,* p. 111. *Examiner,* March 23, 1928.

13. Rogers, pp. 85–86. In September 1928, a motion picture director, David Horsely, fueled flood fears when he began to issue a weekly sheet, *Hollyood Dam News,* that called into question Mulholland's work and featured horror stories about cracks in concrete, other dam failures, and anti–Boulder Dam propaganda.

14. Telephone conversation with Lillian Darrow, 1988.

15. Plainfield, New Jersey, *Courier,* April 7, 1928; interview, William B. Mulholland, March 7, 1978.

16. *Examiner,* March 13, 20, 1929; *Record,* March 20, 1929.

17. William B. Mulholland, interview, March 7, 1978.

18. Mulholland, "Recollections of a Valley Past," *California Childhood,* pp. 179 ff; *Owensmouth Baby,* pp. 73–75. Such were the passions aroused by the Mulholland name that on the rare occasions when my mother and father traveled into Owens Valley and the high desert area they registered under my mother's maiden name in hotels or tourist accommodations. We children were never taken there, and my first visit was shortly after my marriage in 1949, when I was in my mid-twenties and had the protection of a new surname.

19. *Daily News,* May 12, 1931.

Bibliography

The following includes chief sources and influences. Further bibliographic material and commentary are to be found in the back notes.

BOOKS

Adamic, Louis. *Dynamite: The Story of Class Violence in America*. New York: Viking Press, 1931.

Annals of the Sunset Club of Los Angeles. Vols. 2 and 3. Privately printed, Los Angeles, 1927.

Armitage, Merle. *Success Is No Accident: The Biography of William Paul Whitsett*. Yucca Valley, California: The Manzanita Press, 1959.

Austin, Mary. *Earth Horizon: Autobiography*. New York: The Literary Guild, 1932.

Bancroft, Hubert Howe. *Works*. San Francisco: The History Company Publishers, 1890.

Baur, John E. *The Health Seekers of Southern California*. San Marino, California: The Huntington Library, 1959.

Bell, Horace. *On the Old West Coast*. New York: Wm. Morrow & Co., 1930.

Bell, Robert. *The Book of Ulster Surnames*. Belfast and St. Paul, Minnesota: The Blackstaff Press, 1988.

Bixby, Sarah. *Adobe Days*. Cedar Rapids, Iowa: The Torch Press, 1926.

Bonelli, William G. *Billion Dollar Blackjack*. Beverly Hills: Civic Research Press, 1954.

Brewer, William H. *Up and Down California in 1860–1864*. Ed. Francis P. Farquhar. New edition. Berkeley and Los Angeles: University of California Press, 1966.

Burdette, Robert J. *American Biography and Genealogy*. 2 vols. Chicago: The Lewis Publishing Company, [1907–1908?].

Burgess, Sherwood D. *The Water King: Anthony Chabot, His Life and Times.* Davis, California: Panorama West Publishing, 1992.

Busbey, L. White. *Uncle Joe Cannon.* New York: Henry Holt and Company, 1927.

Carr, Harry. *Los Angeles: City of Dreams.* New York: Grosset and Dunlap Publishers, 1935.

Caughey, John W. *California: A Remarkable State's Life History.* Englewood Cliffs, N.J.: Prentice Hall, 1970.

Chalfant, W. A. *The Story of Inyo.* Rev. ed. Privately printed, Bishop, California, 1933.

Chatterton, E. Keble. *Seamen All.* Boston: Little, Brown and Co., 1924.

Cleland, Robert Graves, and Osgood Hardy. *March of Industry.* Los Angeles: Powell, 1929.

Cooper, Erwin. *Aqueduct Empire: A Guide to Water in California: Its Turbulent History, Its Management Today.* Glendale, California: Arthur Clark Company, 1968.

Crail, Charles S. *My Twin Joe: A Romantic Biography.* Garden City, New York: Country Life Press, 1932.

Dumke, Glenn S. *The Boom of the Eighties in Southern California.* San Marino, California: Huntington Library, 1970.

Dunbar, Robert G. *Forging New Rights in Western Waters.* Lincoln: University of Nebraska Press, 1983.

Engh, Michael E., S.J. *Frontier Faiths: Church, Temple, and Synagogue in Los Angeles, 1846–1888.* Albuquerque: University of New Mexico Press, 1992.

First Annual Report of the Chief Engineer of the Los Angeles Aqueduct to the Board of Public Works, March 15, 1907. Los Angeles, California, 1907.

Fogelson, Robert M. *The Fragmented Metropolis: Los Angeles 1850–1930.* Cambridge, Massachusetts: Harvard University Press, 1967.

Freeman, Vernon M. *People-Land-Water: Santa Clara Valley and Oxnard Plain, Ventura County, California.* Los Angeles: Lorrin L. Morrison, 1968.

Gottlieb, Robert, and Irene Wolt. *Thinking Big: The Story of the Los Angeles Times, Its Publishers and Their Influence on Southern California.* New York: G. P. Putnam's Son, 1977.

Graves, Jackson A. *My Seventy Years in California, 1857–1927.* Los Angeles: Times-Mirror Press, 1927.

Grenier, Judson A., with Robert C. Gillingham. *California Legacy: The Watson Family.* N.P.: Watson Land Company, 1987.

Guinn, J. M. *A History of California and an Extended History of Its Southern Coast Counties.* Vols. 1 and 2. Los Angeles: Historic Record Company, 1907.

Hancock, Ralph. *Fabulous Boulevard.* New York: Funk and Wagnalls Company, 1949.

Hayes, Benjamin. *Pioneer Notes from the Diaries of Benjamin Hayes, 1849–1875.* Privately printed, Los Angeles, 1929.

Hine, Robert V., ed. *William Andrew Spalding: Los Angeles Newspaper Man.* San Marino, California: The Huntington Library, 1961.

Historical Record and Souvenir of the Los Angeles County Pioneer Society. Los Angeles: Times-Mirror Press, 1923.

Hoffman, Abraham. *Vision or Villainy: Origins of the Owens Valley-Los Angeles Water Controversy.* College Station: Texas A&M University Press, 1981.

Hundley, Norris, Jr. *Water and the West: The Colorado River Compact and the Politics of Water in the American West.* Berkeley and Los Angeles: University of California Press, 1975.

———. *The Great Thirst: Californians and Water, 1770s-1990s.* Berkeley and Los Angeles: University of California Press, 1992.

An Illustrated History of Los Angeles County. Chicago: The Lewis Publishing Company, 1889.

Kahrl, William L. *Water and Power.* Berkeley and Los Angeles: University of California Press, 1982.

King, Clarence. *Mountaineering in the Sierra Nevada.* New York: Charles Scribner's Sons, 1905.

Lavender, David. *California: Land of New Beginnings.* New York: Harper & Row, 1972.

Lloyd's Register of Shipping, 1870–1876.

Los Angeles Board of Public Service Commissioners. *Complete Report on Construction of the Los Angeles Aqueduct.* Los Angeles: Department of Public Service, 1916.

McGroarty, John Steven. *History of Los Angeles County.* 3 vols. Chicago: The American Historical Society, 1923.

McWilliams, Carey. *Southern California Country: An Island on the Land.* New York: Duell, Sloan and Pearce, 1946.

Matson, Robert Mayson. *William Mulholland: A Forgotten Forefather.* Stockton, California: Pacific Center for Western Studies, University of the Pacific, 1976.

Moeller, Beverley Bowen. *Phil Swing and Boulder Dam.* Berkeley and Los Angeles: University of California Press, 1971.

Mowry, George E. *The California Progressives.* Berkeley and Los Angeles: University of California Press, 1951.

Mulholland, Catherine. *Owensmouth Baby: The Making of a San Fernando Valley Town.* Northridge, Calif.: Santa Susana Press, 1987.

Myers, William A., and Ira L. Swett. *Trolleys to the Surf: The Story of the Los Angeles Pacific Railway.* Glendale, California: Interurban Publications, 1976.

Nadeau, Remi. *The Water Seekers.* Garden City, New York: Doubleday and Company, 1950.

Newmark, Harris. *Sixty Years in Southern California, 1853–1913.* New York: The Knickerbocker Press, 1916.

Nunis, Doyce B., Jr., ed. *The St. Francis Dam Disaster Revisited.* Los Angeles: Historical Society of Southern California; Ventura: Ventura County Museum of History of Art, 1995.

Ostrom, Vincent. *Water and Politics: A Study of Water Policies and Administration in the Development of Los Angeles.* Los Angeles: The Haynes Foundation, 1953.

Outland, Charles. *Man-Made Disaster: The Story of St. Francis Dam.* Glendale, Calif.: Arthur H. Clark, 1977.

Page, Henry Markham. *Pasadena: Its Early Years.* Los Angeles: Lorrin L. Morrison, 1964.

Perry, Richard B., and Louis S. Perry. *A History of the Los Angeles Labor Movement, 1911–1941.* Berkeley and Los Angeles: University of California Press, 1963.

Reagan, James W. *Report of J. W. Reagan, upon the Control of Flood Waters in the Los Angeles Flood Control District.* Los Angeles: Los Angeles County Flood Control District, 1917.

Robinson, W. W. *Lawyers of Los Angeles: A History of the Los Angeles Bar Association and of the Bar of Los Angeles County.* Los Angeles: Los Angeles Bar Association, 1959.

Sauder, Robert A. *The Lost Frontier: Water Diversion in the Growth and Destruction of Owens Valley Agriculture:* Tucson: University of Arizona Press, 1994.

Sitton, Tom. *John Randolph Haynes: California Progressive.* Stanford, California: Stanford University Press, 1992.

Smith, Henry Nash. *Virgin Land: The American West as Symbol and Myth.* Cambridge, Massachusetts: Harvard University Press, 1950.

Smythe, William E. *The Conquest of Arid America.* Rev. ed. Seattle: The University of Washington Press, 1969.

Somerville-Large, Peter. *Dublin.* London: Hamish Hamilton, 1979; London: Granada, 1981.

Southern Inyo American Association of Retired Persons, Chapter 183. *Saga of Inyo County.* Covina, Calif.: Taylor Publishing Co., 1977.

Spalding, William A. *History and Reminiscences: Los Angeles City and County California.* 3 vols. Los Angeles: J. R. Finnell & Sons Publishing Company, 1929.

Starr, Kevin. *Material Dreams: Southern California Through the 1920s.* New York: Oxford University Press, 1990.

Steffens, Lincoln. *The Autobiography of Lincoln Steffens.* New York: Harcourt, Brace and Co., 1931.

Stimson, Grace Heilman. *Rise of the Labor Movement in Los Angeles.* Berkeley and Los Angeles: University of California Press, 1955.

Taylor, Raymond G. *Men, Medicine and Water: The Building of the Los Angeles Aqueduct, 1908–1913, a Physician's Recollections.* Edited, with a prologue and epilogue by Doyce B. Nunis, Jr. Los Angeles: Friends of the LACMA Library with the assistance of Los Angeles Department of Water and Power, 1982.

Teague, Charles Collins. *Fifty Years a Rancher: The Recollections of Half a Century Devoted to the Citrus and Walnut Industries of California and to Furthering the Cooperative Movement in Agriculture.* Los Angeles: The Ward Ritchie Press, 1944.

U.S. Congress. Senate Report 928, Part 3 of the Special Committee of the United States Senate on the Irrigation and Reclamation of Arid Lands. Vol. 2, The Great Basin Region and California. Washington, D.C., 1900.

United States Patent Office Records, 1891.

Walton, John. *Western Times and Water Wars: State, Culture, and Rebellion in California.* Berkeley and Los Angeles: University of California Press, 1992.

Who's Who in the Pacific Southwest. Los Angeles: The Times-Mirror Printing & Binding House, 1913.

Wood, J. W. *Pasadena, California: Historical and Personal, a Complete History of the Organization of the Indiana Colony.* Privately printed, 1917.

Wood, Richard Coke. *The Owens Valley and the Los Angeles Water Controversy: Owens Valley as I Knew It.* Stockton, California: Pacific Center for Western Historical Studies, University of the Pacific, 1973.

Workman, Boyle. *The City That Grew, 1840–1936.* Los Angeles: Southland Publishing Co., 1936.

PAMPHLETS, THESES, ARTICLES,
AND UNPUBLISHED MATERIALS

Blake, Donal S. "The Christian Brothers and Education in Nineteenth-Century Ireland." Unpublished master's thesis, University College, Cork; National University of Ireland, 1977. Program Library.

Brooks, Thomas. "Notes on Los Angeles Water Supply," 1938, typescript, Los Angeles Department of Water and Power Historical Records, Program Library, Ephemera Collection, Box II:8.

Davenport, Robert W. "Weird Note for the Vox Populi: The Los Angeles *Municipal News.*" *California Historical Society Quarterly* 44 (March 1965), pp. 3–15.

Derleth, Charles. Calaveras Creek Dam. Reports, Water Resources Center Archives. University of California, Berkeley.

Eaton, Mulholland, et al. "Wood Pipes a Failure." Pamphlet for Oakland Bond Election, 1905. Huntington Library, San Marino, California.

"Facts Concerning the Owens Valley Reparations Claims for the Information of the People of California." Los Angeles Department of Water and Power, 1926.

Hendricks, William O. *M. H. Sherman, a Pioneer of the Southwest.* Corona del Mar, California: The Sherman Foundation, 1973.

Hoffman, Abraham. "Joseph Barlow Lippincott and the Owens Valley Controversy: Time for Revision." *Southern California Quarterly* 54, No. 3 (Fall 1972), pp. 239–54.

———. "The Los Angeles Aqueduct Investigation Board of 1912: A Reappraisal." *Southern California Quarterly* 62, no. 4 (1980): 329–60.

Hoffman, Abraham, and Teena Stern. "The Zanjas: Pioneer Water System," undated, typescript, Los Angeles Department of Water and Power.

Layne, J. Gregg. "Water and Power for a Great City," 1957, typescript, Los Angeles Department of Water and Power.

———. "William Mulholland—Engineer, Pioneer, Raconteur," parts 1 and 2, *Civil Engineering* 2 (February and March 1941).

Los Angeles City Council Minutes. Los Angeles Archives.

McCarthy, John Russell. "Water: The Story of Bill Mulholland." *Los Angeles Saturday Night,* October 30, 1938.

McClure, W. F. "Letter of Transmittal Concerning the Owens Valley–Los Angeles Controversy." Senate, California Legislature, Sacramento, California, 1925.

McCorkle, Julia Norton. "A History of Los Angeles Journalism." *Annual Pub-*

lications: *Historical Society of Southern California, 1915–16,* vol. 10. Los Angeles, 1916, pp. 24–43.

Mulholland, William. "The Water Supply of Southern California." *Proceedings of the Engineers and Architects Association of Southern California.* Vol. 2. Los Angeles: Engineers and Architects Association of Southern California, 1907.

Phillips, Robert V. "Water and Power—Wm. Kahrl," typescript, November 18, 1997.

Pratt, Lowell Clark. "Theodore Roosevelt 'Discovers' California." *Journal of the West* 3, no. 1 (January 1964), pp. 40–46.

Rodriguez, Mary Louise Bine. *The Earthquake of 1906.* Privately printed, San Francisco, 1951.

Spilman, W. T. *The Conspiracy: An Exposure of the Owens River Water and San Fernando Land Frauds.* Los Angeles: The Alembic Club, 1912.

Spriggs, Elizabeth Mathieu. "The History of the Domestic Water Supply of Los Angeles." Master's thesis, University of Southern California, 1931.

Stowe, Noel J. "Pioneering Land Development in the Californias: An Interview with David Otto Brant." *California Historical Society Quarterly* 47 (1968), pp. 15–39, 141–55, 237–50.

Van Norman, H. A. "Memoir of William Mulholland." *Transactions of the American Society of Civil Engineers* 62, No. 8 (1936).

Wayte, Beverly. "Linda Vista Revisited." *Southern California Quarterly* 73 (Summer 1991), pp. 125–56.

Widney, Erwin W. "We Build a Railroad." *Touring Topics,* March 1931, pp. 36–41, 52–53.

MANUSCRIPT COLLECTIONS

Haynes, John Randolph. Papers. University of California, Los Angeles.

Lippincott, Joseph B. Papers. Water Resources Center Archives. University of California, Berkeley.

Lissner, Meyer. Papers. Stanford University.

Means, Thomas H. Papers. Water Resources Center Archives. University of California, Berkeley.

Mulholland, William. Office Files. 1902–1914. Also, Owens Valley Historical Documents. Los Angeles Department of Water and Power.

O'Melveny, Henry W. Journals. Huntington Library. San Marino, California.

Schuyler, James Dix. Papers. Water Resources Center Archives. University of California, Berkeley.

Sherman, Moses Hazeltine. Papers. Sherman Foundation Library. Corona del Mar, California.

Whitley, Hobart Johnstone. Papers. University of California, Los Angeles.

Willard, Charles Dwight. Papers. Huntington Library. San Marino, California.

NEWSPAPERS

Press Clipping Books, 1902–1942. Los Angeles Department of Water and Power.
Inyo Independent
Inyo Register
Los Angeles Evening Express
Los Angeles Examiner
Los Angeles Herald
Los Angeles Record
Los Angeles Times
San Francisco Chronicle
San Francisco Examiner

INTERVIEWS

(CASSETTES IN AUTHOR'S POSSESSION)

Mitchell, Frances. June 16, 1976, Berkeley, California; April 17, 1981, Fairhope, Alabama.
Mulholland, Joseph. April 16, 1978, Thousand Oaks, California.
Mulholland, William Bodine. March 7, 1978, Van Nuys, California.
Waith, Margaret Deakers. February 23, 1978, Los Angeles, California.

Index

AFL. *See* American Federation of Labor

Agricultural Park (*now* University of Southern California campus), 25, 220

Aguilar, Don Cristobal, 20–21, 26

AIB (aqueduct investigation board), 229; creation of, 207–8, 209; findings of, 210, 212–13, 225; Mulholland's testimony before, 222–23, 367n30; witnesses before, 224–25

Alabama Gates incident, 295–96, 314

Alembic Club, 213

Alexander, George, 178; aqueduct tour of, 192, 194; in bond sales negotiations, 188, 194; Harriman's loss to, 207; municipal appointments by, 164, 183, 184; on water and power issues, 197, 203–4, 361n13, 364n1, 365n15

Alhambra, 200

Allen, Lucy Wintz, 372n19

Alles, Fred L., 349n30

El Almuerzo de la Cabeza Tatemada (The Lunch of the Roasted Head), 58, 341n22

American Federation of Labor (AFL), 78–79

American Forestry Service conference (1899), 68

The American Magazine, 212

American Society of Civil Engineers, 136, 138, 145, 221

Anderson, James A., 51–52, 157, 159, 160

Anderson, L. M., 90, 149, 344n13

Andrews, Harry, 223–24, 367n32

Angeleno Heights Reservoir, 94, 344–45n16

Annexations: Eaton on, 101; map of, 217 fig.; Mulholland on, 94; Owens Valley proposed as, 292; of San Fernando Valley, 239, 258, 259; for use of water, 55, 200, 216, 263, 341n15

Antelope Division, 167

Antelope Valley, 107, 349n18

Antipicketing ordinance (1910), 189

Aqueduct. *See* Los Angeles Acqueduct; Owens River Project

Aqueduct bonds: and bond-selling difficulties, 164, 187, 188–89, 204, 211, 362n13; disbursements from, 147; election campaigns for, 118–19, 121, 122, 141, 150–52; voter approval of, 125, 152–53, 352–53n26

Aqueduct distribution system: compromise proposal for, 218–19; experts' recommendations for, 200; Harriman on, 202–3, 364n12; high line issue of, 200–201, 216, 222, 229–30, 258; Mulholland on, 194–95, 206, 224, 234; municipal power issue of, 250; Otis on, 234; voter's decision on, 226

Aqueduct investigation board. *See* AIB

Aqueduct right-of-way bill. *See* Power right-of-way bill

Ashurst (senator), 305
Aston, William C., 176, 185, 198, 232, 359n10
Austin, Frank, 106–7
Austin, Mary Hunter, 107, 271
Austin, Stafford, 107
Ayers, J. J., xv, 58
Azusa, 200

Backus, J. J., 240
Baker, Fred, 190
Baker Iron Works, 150, 190
Bakersfield, 268, 276
Bakersfield Californian, 268, 270
Baldwin, Leon, 25
Ballard, R. H., 284
Bancroft, Hubert Howe, 12
Bandini, Juan, 58
Barbara Worth Hotel (El Centro), 328, 329
Barker Brothers (furniture store), 345n22
Barnard brothers, 20
Bartlett, Louis, 276
Bayley, E. A., 165, 232, 303, 305, 379n7
Beaudry, Prudent, 54–55; private water venture of, 19–22
Beaudry, Victor, 19
Beaudry's High Reservoir (Reservoir No. 4), 20, 22, 25, 38, 101
Becker, Carl, 5
Bell, Horace, xv, 15, 19, 26, 31, 46, 49, 58
Bellevue Reservoir, 57, 356n21
Bellevue Terrace, 19–20
Belvedere, 101
Betkousky, Martin, 225, 240, 258
"Big Bill" dredger, 168
Big Freeze (1913), 228
Big Pine Creek, 241, 244
Big Pine Ditch, 282
Big Pine Property Owners' Association, 295, 309, 311–12
Big Red Cars (trolley cars), 45, 96
Big Rock Creek scheme, 146, 147
Big Tujunga Wash, 38, 56–57, 77–78, 116–17
Bishop: highway from Mojave to, 293, 294; Longyear's property in, 378n9; Mulholland's peace tour to, 292–93; reaction to Eaton in, 122–24, 129, 353n6
Bishop Index, 270, 274, 374–75n5
Bledsoe, Benjamin F., 302
Board of Public Works: Chaffee's appointment to, 160, 358n3; engineering appointments by, 135; Mulholland's relations with, 157; Owens Valley tour of, 128–30; and

Silver Lake's water rights, 160–61, 359n5
Boddy, Manchester, xv
Bonds. *See* Aqueduct bonds; Power bond elections; Water bonds
Bonus system, 166–67, 177, 190, 198, 360n17
Borough, R. W., 374–75n5
Boruff, Fred L., 246
Boston Globe, 248
Boulder Dam project, xvi, 274; Crail's support of, 278; Davis's support of, 282–83; inspection tour of, 294–95, 305; Mulholland's campaign for, 279, 280–81, 282, 283–84, 301–2, 308, 316–17; newspapers' positions on, 376n21; Swing-Johnson bill on, 282, 283, 291, 316–17, 325; type of construction for, 275; voter approval of, 286
Boyce, H. H., 336n2
Boyle Heights, 5, 38, 73, 91, 103
Bradbury, J. O., 344n13
Brady, Handsome, 37, 86
Brand, L. C., 99, 178, 207, 211
Brant, O. F., 350n4
Brauner, John Caspar, 366–67n26
Brimhall, C. L., 344n13
Broderick, William J., 27, 338n7
Brooks, Harry, 130, 131, 149, 170
Brooks, Thomas, 305, 344n13; Jenkins's clash with, 26–27; meter installation by, 345n20; on Mulholland, 42, 46–47; on Water Company, 28, 33; Water Company position of, 37, 338n7
Brown, Charles E., 344n13
Browne, J. Ross, 15
Brown's Canyon, 40
Bryan, William Jennings, 73, 168, 169
Buena Vista Pumping Station, 54, 87; infiltration gallery at, 82, 86, 91, 102–3
Buena Vista Reservoir, 22, 24, 25; capacity of, 67, 339–40n11; improvement projects at, 29, 31–32, 34–35, 40, 43, 339–40n11; 1913 draws on, 239
Building Trades Council, 252
Bullas, J. W., 344n13
Bunker Hill, 101
Burdick, Horace, 51
Burdick Block (commerical building), 45
Burns, Tom, 26, 338n7
Butler, Frank, 293

Cadillac Desert (Reisner), xiv
Cady, F. R., 344n13
Cahuenga Mining and Water Company, 56

Cahuenga Valley, 16, 56–57, 101
Calaveras Creek Dam, 221, 366–67n26
California Edison. *See* Edison Electric Company
California Hospital (Los Angeles), 162
California League of Municipalities, 144
California River Convention (1904, San Francisco), 109–10
California Supreme Court: on Pomeroy and Hooker case, 67; on river water rights, 55–56; on Water Company's contract, 67–68
California Water and Power Act (1921), 276–77, 374–75n5
Callison, Richard, 333–34
Calvert, Mellie A., 364n12
Campbell, J. H., 31
Camp tours. *See* Construction camp tours
Candy, H. A. T., 316
Canfield, B. H., 288, 374–75n5, 380–81n29
Cannon, Joseph, 132, 133
Carpenter, Ingle, 254, 257
Carr, Harry, 354n11
Carter, W. H., 344n13
Cast iron pipeline, 29, 337–38n10
Caswell, S. B., 41, 338n7
Caterpillar tractors, 168, 210
Catskill Water Project, xv, 136, 188, 248, 257
Caughey, John, 352–53n26
Celtic Club, 279
Cement: city's plant for, 157; Duryea's expertise in, 131–32; and faulty construction, 191, 363n18; Finkle on, 215; for substructural pipeline, 130–31; theft of, at Monolith, 229
Central Labor Council, 252
Chabot, Anthony, 356n22
Chaffee, Adna Romanza, 224, 248; on aqueduct completion date, 219; at aqueduct opening, 245, 246; aqueduct tour of, 192, 193; background of, 159–60, 358n2; on civil service requirements, 163; on contracts system, 166–67; on Desmond's earnings, 363n17; on food quality, 180, 181; on medical care, 162; municipal board positions of, 160, 358n3; retirement of, 227; and Warner, 212
Chaffey, George, 134, 144, 354n14, 355n19
Chalfant, William A., 192, 271, 273, 362n5, 363n20
Chamber of Commerce: and dam

disaster, 324; on Metropolitan Water District, 302; on municipal power, 252; opening festivities by, 244–47; tribute to aqueduct delegation from, 134, 354–55n15; water supply report to, 349–50n1
Chandler, Harry, xv, xvi, 166; on Boulder Dam issue, 278, 284; Henderson's suit against, 223–24, 367n32; land syndicates of, 97, 285, 350n4; marriage to Marion Otis, 341–42n3; on state regulation bill, 276–77; in Steffens's experiment, 204
Chandler, Marion Otis, 341–42n3
Charles Stern's Winery, 345n20
Charley's Butte (Owens Valley), 128
Chatsworth reservoirs, 40, 98–99, 261, 339n5
Chatsworth Tunnel, 99
Chinatown (film), 4
Chinese Massacre in Nigger Alley (1871), 15
Christian Brothers Schools, 8–9
Christian Science Monitor, 198
The Citizen (labor newspaper), 202, 204
Citizens' Water Company, 49, 54
City council: on commissioner appointees, 88–90; Mulholland's hearing before, 237–38; municipal waterworks proposals of, 51–52, 53–54; and Owens River project, 118, 119, 134–35, 146–48, 181; on Pirtle Cut, 56–57; purchase offers to Water Company by, 75–77; recalled member of, 104–5; Water Company investigation by, 27–28; Water Company's ties to, 21, 46; water lease agreement of, 19, 20–22, 61, 337n11; in water rates battles, 34, 59, 63, 70–71
City of Los Angeles v. Rowland and Van Nuys, 349n25
City of Los Angeles v. the Los Angeles Water Company, 48
City of Quartz (Davis), 329
Civil Service Commission, 89–90, 110
Civil Service Examination, 138–39, 156, 162–64
Civil War, 26
Clark, Charles W., 344n13
Clark, Eli P., 45, 96, 97
Clark, W. J., 312–13
Clausen, Jacob C., 106, 110, 111, 120; and Eaton's land deal, 273, 309, 311
Clearwater Tunnel accident, 220, 229
Clover, Samuel Travers, 117, 148, 153, 288–89, 351n10
C&M Company, 203

Code, William H., 200
Coffey, S. J., 336n9
Colorado River, 17, 242; domestic water
    district of, 302; exploratory trips to,
    271, 280–81; for hydroelectric power,
    282–83. *See also* Boulder Dam project
Colorado River Commission, 242
Colorado River Land Company, 350n4
Colton, Linda, 372n23
"The Coming Victory" (Socialist Party
    pamphlet), 202, 206
Committee of One Hundred, 69, 342n11
*The Conspiracy: An Exposure of the
    Owens River Water and San Fernando
    Valley Land Frauds* (Spilman), 214–15
Construction camp tours, 161–62,
    180–81, 185–86. *See also* Workers,
    aqueduct
Constructive Californians (Clover), 289
Contract labor, 70, 166–67
The Contractor (journal), 251
Cook, F. W., 344n13
Coolgardie Aqueduct (New South
    Wales), 116
Corcoran (Kings County), 202
Coronel, Antonio, 55
Cottonwood Creek (Inyo County), 129,
    219; Chaffey's appropriations on,
    134, 144; dynamiting incident at, 313;
    power plant site at, 127–28, 157, 165,
    193
Covina, 200
Crags, the (mountain retreat), 82
Craig, Volney, 281, 376n27
Crail, Joe, 278
Crescent City of Liverpool (ship), 12
Criswell, Ralph, 265, 290
Croton Aqueduct (New York), 31, 214
Crow, George F., 40
Crowell, J., 310
Crowley, Father John J., 285, 376n16,
    377n7
Cryer, George, 288, 289–90, 294, 298,
    300, 302
Crystal Springs, 23; bacteria count
    in, 93; collapsed tunnel at, 68–69,
    342n17; conduit system for, 36–37,
    49, 179, 340n2; legal controversy
    over, 24, 48–49, 61–62, 63, 71–72,
    341n2; percolation pipes project at,
    43, 339–40n11; Water Company's
    claims to, 24, 49
Crystal Springs Land and Water
    Company, 62, 63, 68, 71, 108;
    formation of, 24, 49
Culebra Cut of Panama Canal, 138, 241
Culver, J. P., 36–37

Dalton, E. H., 55
Darrow, Clarence, 204
Darrow, Lillian, 326
Davis, Arthur P., 152, 271, 294, 349n19;
    in Boulder Dam campaign, 282–83,
    305; and Lippincott, 106, 107, 108,
    350n5; on Owens River project, 151,
    210–11
Davis, Margaret Leslie, xvi–xvii
Davis, Mike, 329
Day labor system, 166–67, 360n17
Deakers, Catherine (née Thorpe), 12–13,
    361n19
Deakers, Ella (Mulholland's cousin), 13
Deakers, Richard, Jr. (Mulholland's
    uncle), 7–8, 12, 381n37
Dearborn Independent, 280
Dehy, William D., 249
Del Valle, Reginaldo, 58, 184, 213, 219,
    238, 257, 288, 290, 303
DeMille, Cecil B., 296, 298
Democratic League, 178, 361n13
Denver Post, 156–57
Desmond, Daniel Joseph, 180–81, 189,
    191, 197, 212, 361n19, 363n17
Dewey, George, 62
Dickson, Edward, xv, 160, 234
Dillon and Hubbard (New York law
    firm), 105
Diptheria epidemic (1903), 99
Dockweiler, J. Henry: Mulholland's
    correspondence with, 127, 186, 194,
    350n8; and Owens River project, 147–
    48; on San Francisco waterworks,
    171–72; on Water Company's value,
    53, 67
Doheny, Edward, 85, 91–92, 288
Domestic water: citizen complaints about,
    27–28, 31, 39, 54; city council's lease
    of, 20–22; controversial source of,
    24, 49, 61–62; metering of, 83–86,
    345nn20,24; oil refineries' threat to,
    91–92; private ownership schemes
    for, 19–20; water pressure demands
    on, 90–91, 346n6
Dominguez, Manuel, 17, 187
Dominguez Rancho, 187, 231
Dorward, David, 91, 166
Downey, John, 22
Drake, J. C., 344n14
Dredger invention, 168
Drought: of 1870s, 15, 16, 30–31; as
    mythical, 214, 347–48n1; and night
    sprinkling, 15; of 1903–1904, 99, 100
Dublin (Ireland), 8, 10
Ducommon, Charles, 338n7
Dunham, Stanley, 186, 316, 320

Durand, W. F., 283
Duryea, Edwin, Jr., 131–32
Dykstra, Clarence, 293

Earl, Edwin T., xv, 207; AIB testimony
of, 348n13; land syndicate of, 98, 224;
and Mulholland's mayoral prospects,
230, 234, 368–69n13; and municipal
power, 252; and Otis, 201, 364n9
Earthquakes, 261–62, 275, 330; safety
of pipes in, 130–31
East Bay Water Company (Oakland),
249, 370n1
Eastman, George, 324
Eastman, S. P., 366–67n26
East Side Springs Water Company, 49
Eaton, Alice (née Slosson), 134, 307
Eaton, Benjamin S., 24, 29, 30–31, 152
Eaton, Frederick, 32, 34, 77, 240;
and AIB investigation, 224, 225;
on annexations, 101; aqueduct tour
of, 192; background of, 29; Chaffey
compared to, 354n14; character traits
of, 44, 73–74; Chatsworth Park reservoirs of, 40, 98–99, 339n5; as city
surveyor, 38–39; civic/political activities of, 44–45; condemned profiteering
of, 122–24, 129, 353n6; critical of
Water Company, 35, 37, 61, 64, 71;
death of, 330; divorce of, 74, 92; on
dynamiting incident, 288; and Independent Civic League, 237, 238, 241;
and Lippincott, 108, 109, 110; Long
Valley land deals of, 169, 243–44, 272,
293, 306–7, 308–9, 310–11, 317–18,
382n42; marriage to Alice Slosson,
134; as mayor, 63–66, 342n10; Mulholland on, 223, 237, 245, 247; Mulholland's rift with, 169, 243–44, 292–
93, 370n33; at Municipal League
banquet, 120–21; municipal waterworks goal of, 51, 66, 69–70, 71–72,
73, 108, 343n30; Owens Valley interests of, 30–31, 82, 92, 105, 106–7,
113, 115, 348n13, 349n25; at Owens
Valley peace conference, 292–93;
in power right-of-way battles, 272,
273–75, 375n9; real estate commissions to, 147; San Joaquin Valley
expedition of, 72, 343n27; Water
Company role of, 26, 38–39, 338n7;
Water Department role of, 81
Eaton, George, 31
Eaton, Harold, 169, 272, 307, 360n21,
370n33
Eaton, Helena (née Hayes), 29, 92
Eaton, Mrs. Burdick, 311

Eaton Land and Cattle Company (formerly Rickey Ranch), 272–73, 275,
306, 317
Edison, Thomas, 277–78, 376n20
Edison Electric Company, 140, 161,
196, 355n19; city's rates versus,
266, 280; Colorado River interests
of, 284; McCartney bill of, 142, 144
Egan, Richard, 44
Elizabeth Lake Tunnel, 163, 168, 196;
completion of, 198; drilling records at,
176, 185; inspection tour of, 161–62;
miners strike at, 189
Elliott, G. E., 271
Elliott, John M., 82–83; Owens Valley
trip of, 121, 352n19; on Waldron
litigation, 79–80, 343n10; on water
commission, 89, 90, 344n14
Ely, Jack, 321
Elysian Park: reservoir project in, 90,
101; waterworks structures in, 50 fig.
Engineers: recruitment of, 127, 131–32,
135, 136, 138–39, 145; relocation of,
232–33. See also Workers, aqueduct
Engineers' and Architects' Society of
Southern California (1902), 82
Etcheverry, B. A., 356n21
Eucalyptus trees, 179
Evans (Glendale congressman), 317
Exposition Park, County Museum at, 242

Fairmount Reservoir, 157, 240, 241
Fall, Albert, 288
Fanning, G. F., 339n9
Faulkner, Frederick, 312
Fay, John J., 89, 90, 184, 352n19, 353n4
Federal Radio Commission, 313
Feliz Ditch, 20, 24
Feliz Rancho, 20, 24
Ferguson, James, 43
Ferguson, Lillie. See Mulholland, Lillie
Ferguson, William, 338n7
Feynes, Adelbert, 117
Fillmore, 36, 338–39n13
Finkle, Frederick C.: critical of aqueduct,
118, 119, 215, 250, 251, 355n19,
370n2; and Hooker-Pomeroy suit,
152; on municipal power, 250, 252;
professional background of, 351–
52n16; on surplus water issue, 216,
218–19
Fire hydrants, 34, 58–59, 67, 337–38n10
Fischer, Fred. J., 91, 344n13
Fishburn, John E., 307
Flanigan, T. F., 176, 232–33, 361n10
Flint, Frank, 128, 133, 134, 221,
354–55n15

Flint-MacLachlan Bill, 132–34, 354n12
Florence Nightingale Institute of Honorables, 330
Food concessions: concessionaire of, 180; food quality from, 185–86, 191, 212, 213; prices of meals at, 180–81, 189, 190, 197; total earnings of, 363n17
Forbes (engineer), 339n5
Ford, Henry, 280
Forster, Don Marco, 44, 45
Fountains: in Los Angeles plaza, 21–22, 337n12; Mulholland's Memorial, 23
Foy, Mary, 32, 338n5
Franklin Canyon, 216, 219, 226, 254, 371n10
Fredericks, J. D., 346n10
Freeman, John R., 135, 136–37, 139–40, 164, 366–67n26
Frémont, John Charles, 16
Fresno Bee, 296
Fresno Republican, 289, 378n17

Garvanza (Arroyo Seco), 49, 84–85, 341n15
Gasset, Ortega y, 301
Geronimo (Apache chief), 17
Gibbs, H. H., 344n13
Gillett, James Norris, 363n20
Gillette, J. W., 344n13
Gilmore, George T., 344n13
Glasnevin cemetery (Dublin), 7
Glasscock, Harry A., 270, 274, 308, 315
Glendale, 216
Glendora, 200
Gleniffer (ship), 10, 336n9
Goethals, George Washington, 252, 271, 275
Gompers, Samuel, 203
Good Government. See Progressives
The Gopher (journal), 252
Graham, Margaret Collier, 14
Graham, S. C., 200, 216, 218, 224, 226, 238, 258
Grant, Lewis A., 89, 344n14
Graves, J. A., 290, 296, 297
Gray, John, 144, 158, 176, 185, 198, 220, 232
Gray, Louis, 220
The Great Thirst (Hundley), xiv
Greeley, Horace, 28
Green, "Mother," 291
Griffin, John S., 19–22, 24, 26, 29
Griffin, Louise (née Hayes), 29
Griffith, Griffith J., 92
Griffith Park, 36–37, 92, 110, 179
Grunsky, C. E., 126–27
Guaranty Trust Company (New York), 80

Haines, T. G., 344n13
Haiwee postmaster, 166, 360n15
Haiwee Reservoir, 130, 191; in Big Freeze, 228; leakage at, 240, 250, 264; Mulholland tribute at, 331; water purification in, 256, 257, 371n17
Hall, Leicester C., 270, 274, 290–91, 293–94
Hamlin, Homer, 108, 157, 200, 358n32
Hammond, A. B., 98
Hanna, George, 55–57
Hanna, Phil Townsend, 46
Hansen, A. C., 176, 245
Hansen, George, 19, 20
Hansen, Henning, 342n10
Harding, Warren G., 276
Harkins, Pat, 37, 86
Harper, Arthur G., 140, 152, 158; appointment of Chaffee by, 159–60, 358n3; aqueduct schemes of, 146; at Elizabeth Tunnel site, 161–62; mayoral election of, 141–42; Owens River trip of, 147–48; resignation of, 163–64, 178
Harper's Weekly, 15
Harriman, E. H., 98
Harriman, Job, 150, 151, 201, 233; in mayoral race, 236; Mulholland's refutation of, 205–7; Socialist Party platform of, 202, 203, 364n12
Harrison, Benjamin, 44
Hart, Henry A., 237, 254
Harvey House (Mojave), 173
Hasker, Thomas, 7
Hatfield, Charles, 114
Hawgood, Harry, 57, 67, 349–50n1
Hayden, Carl, 280, 284
Hayes, Benjamin J., 29
Hayes, Helena, 29
Hayes, Louisa, 29
Haynes, John R., 213, 265, 293, 351n10, 380n22; on civil service commission, 110, 163, 164, 183; on municipal power, 252, 276, 277; and recall election, 104–5
Hazard, Henry T., 49, 94, 192
Hearst, William Randolph, xv, 116
Heinly, Burt, 174, 180, 187, 262
Hellman, H. W., 58
Hellman, I. W., 52, 58, 76
Hellman, Marco H., 188
Helsey, C. F., 122
Henderson, Frank, 218, 223, 238
Henry, S. T., 185–86, 187
Herlihy, John, 344n13
Herriman, George, 151, 357–58n19
Herrman, F. C., 366–67n26

Hession, Jess, 310
Hetch Hetchy project (San Francisco), 247, 281
Hewitt, Leslie, 144, 186
Hicknell, F. T., 72, 343n27
Highland Park, 341n15
Highland Water Company, 49
High line distribution, 216, 258; contract plan for, 218–19; Mulholland's opposition to, 218, 221–22, 224, 229–30, 234; voter approval of, 226
Hill, Louis G., 295
Hitchcock, Ethan A., 126–27, 128, 132, 354n11
Hittell, John S., 18
Hobson, Uncle (relative of Deakers family), 12
Hoffman, Abraham, xiv, 348n17
Holgate, William, 346n6
Hollenbeck Park (Boyle Heights), 73
Hollister, William Welles, 28
Hollywood, 94, 97–98
Hollywood Dam News (weekly sheet), 383n13
Hollywood Reservoir, 320, 325
Hollywood Union Water Company, 255, 258
Holt, Benjamin, 168
Holt, L. M., 16
Hooker, J. D., 53, 152
Hooker and Pomeroy case, 53–54, 67, 80, 108, 148, 152
Hoover, Herbert, 279
Horner, John, 344n13
Horsely, David, 383n13
Houghton, Arthur D., 125, 153, 351n10; and McAleer, 353n4; on Owens River project, 118–20, 128, 351n14
Howard, Burt Estes, 349n30
Howard, Frank H., 337n3
"How to Beat the Socialists" (Steffens), 365n17
Hubbard, A. A., 157
Hughes, W. M., 344n13
Humphreys, William, 189
Hundley, Norris, xiv
Hunt, George C., 98
Huntington, Henry E., 45, 96, 98, 113
Hurlbut, W. W., 294
Hyde, Charles Gilman, 257
Hydraulic sluicing innovation, 138, 156, 356n22, 366–67n26
Hydroelectric power: from Colorado River, 271, 282–83; at Cottonwood site, 127–28, 157, 165, 193; debate on ownership of, 196–97, 252, 260, 364n1, 371n7; Mulholland's support

of, 277–78; from Owens River project, 139, 140, 186, 196–97. See also Municipal power
Hygiene practices. See Public health

Ihm, E., 344n13
Imperial Valley, 113, 350n4
Imperial Valley News, 114
Imperial Valley Press, 166
"The Impounding of Flood Waters" (Schuyler), 114
Independence (Inyo County), 123, 193–94, 231
Independent Civic League, 237–38, 241, 252, 253
Indianapolis Journal, 53
Infiltration gallery, 82, 86, 91–92, 102–3
Inman, Joe, 310, 311, 312
International Order of Odd Fellows (IOOF), 32, 338n6
International Workers of the World (IWW), 287, 373n28
"Into the Future" (municipal film), 279
Inyo County taxes, 271, 375n6
Inyo Register, 185, 190, 192, 261, 270–71, 275, 285
IOOF (International Order of Odd Fellows), 32, 338n6
Ireland: Mulholland's ancestors in, 6–8, 336n3; Mulholland's boyhood in, 8–10
Irrigation water: extra-municipal petitions for, 55–56, 93–94; municipal control of, 24, 55–57; Owens River as source of, 132–34; theft of, 24–25, 56–57; Water Company's depletion of, 76
Isthmian Canal Commission, 138
Ivanhoe (real estate tract), 43, 340n12; reservoir project of, 137–38, 201, 356n21
IWW (International Workers of the World), 287, 373n28

Jackson, Helen Hunt, 337n12
Jacques, H. L., 302
Japanese immigrants, 353–54n10
Jawbone Division, 219; cost of, 164; day labor system of, 166–67; fatal accident on, 229; mule teams of, 175–76; 1909 progress on, 171; obstacles to, 164–66; tunnel drilling on, 176, 181–82
Jenkins, Charles, 26–27
Jenkins, William, 27
Jenner vaccine, 14
Johnson, Edward, 227, 367n40

Johnson, Hiram, 184, 201, 278, 284
Jordan, David Starr, 252
Jordan, Edwin O., 257
Joyce, James, 7, 9, 10
Joyce, John, 9

Kahrl, William, xiv, 340n2, 348n17, 351n10; on Eaton's post-mayoral plans, 343n30; on Haiwee Reservoir, 371n17; on municipal power, 373n27; on mythical drought, 347–48n1; on 1905 bond election, 352–53n26; on 1910 bond sales, 362n13; on role of Progressives, 352n2
Kays, James C., 88
Kelley, W. J., 35, 37
Kelly, Allen, 160, 240, 353n6; on Mulholland's abilities, 177; on Owens River project, 154, 176–77, 355n19, 355–56n20; professional background of, 355n19
Kemp, John, 277
Kenealy, John, 58
Kenilworth (real estate tract), 43
Kent, William, 276
Keough, Carl, 305, 308
Kerckhoff, W. G., 98
Kern, Edward, 116
Kester Ranch fire (1878), 16
Keys, Asa, 324
Killian, J. A., 123
Kimball, George H., 344n13
King, A. J., 21
King, F. W., 344n14
Kings River Valley, 72, 343n27
Kinsey, Don, 312
Knapp, M. A., 349n18
Knickerbocker, Niles, 90, 344n13
Knisely, Bruce, 374–75n5, 380nn22,29
Knox, George C., 39
Koebig, A. H., 108, 161, 355n19
Koepfli, J. O., 354nn12,15
Kountze Brothers (New York), 164
Kuhrts, G. J., 317
Kuhrts Street Bridge, 39
Ku Klux Klan, 285, 377n7
Kunze, Court E., 270, 286–87, 312, 378n11

Labor, organized, 126; on aqueduct bonds, 150; and miners' strike, 189, 190–91, 197–98; on municipal power, 252, 261; on municipal water, 78–79; and railway strike, 98; Socialist Party's ties to, 201–2, 371n7; Times versus Examiner on, 118, 351n10
Lacy, William, 190, 305

Lacy Manufacturing Company, 190
LaRue, C. A., 305
Lawler, Oscar, 116, 117, 359n5
Lawrance, Charles H., 382n4
Lawson, Andrew, 366–67n26
Lazard, Solomon, 19–22, 338n7
Leach and Company (New York), 164
Leahey, Ed, 312; in car accident, 313; as emissary to Owens Valley, 271, 274, 275; threats against, 287–88, 291
Leake, Edward, 344n13
LeConte, Joseph, 17
Lee, Henry T., 184, 189, 213, 295, 352n18, 358n3
Leete, Ben, 315
Leonard, Ethel Langdon, 93, 254–55, 256, 371nn13,14
Life (magazine), 4
Limoneira Ranch (Santa Paula), 323
Lincoln, Abraham, 9
Lippincott, J. A., 142
Lippincott, Joseph B., xvi, 77, 120, 221, 224, 236, 339n9, 366–67n26; at aqueduct opening, 245, 246; aqueduct tour of, 192; Bishop's condemnation of, 129, 353n6; civil service examination of, 163–64; and Colorado River project, 242, 305; commissioner appointment of, 183; conflicting allegiances of, 113–14, 117, 127–28, 183, 350n5; and dam disaster, 324; and federal reclamation prospects, 106, 109, 110, 126; Mulholland's correspondence with, 119, 124, 127–28, 349–50n1; and Mulholland's honorary award, 371n8; on municipal water, 69; and Owens River project, 134, 136–37, 142, 147–48, 150, 232; professional background of, 105–6, 107–8; San Fernando Valley surveys by, 67, 71; San Joaquin Valley expedition of, 72, 343n27; at silver spike ceremony, 192; at Simpson Auditorium rally, 152; on timber laws, 68
Lippincott, Josephine (née Cook), 107
Lippincott, Joseph Reading, 110
Lippincott, Rose, 107
Lissner, Meyer: and Kunze, 378n11; on municipal power, 151–52, 197, 364n1; and Sherman's removal, 183–84; supportive of Mulholland, 205, 230, 252, 365n18, 368nn5,13, 371n8; and Warner, 210, 212
Little Lake break (1917), 262, 373n29
Llewellyn, John, 190
Llewellyn, William, 58

Llewellyn Iron Works, 190
Lodging House Association, 70
Loetchberg Tunnel (Switzerland), 361n10
Loewenthal, Henry A., 116, 119, 224–25
Lone Pine earthquake (1872), 131
Long Beach, 216
Long Valley (Owens Valley), 105; Eaton's
land deals in, 243–44, 272, 293, 306–
7, 308–9, 310–11, 317–18, 382n42;
federal government's interest in, 109,
110, 114; reservoir construction issue
in, 123, 240, 272, 273–74, 275, 287,
292, 376n16
Longyear, David, 285
Longyear, William D., 285, 380–81n29;
land sale of, 305–6, 314, 378n9,
380n14
Lopez, Don Antonio, 77
Los Angeles: annexations to, map of, 217
fig.; Big Freeze of 1913 in, 228; Con-
federate sentiments of, 26; drought
problems of, 15, 16, 30–31, 99, 100;
dust in, 34; Eaton's suit against, 275;
first land boom in, 38; first metered
water of, 345n20; heterogenous cultures of, 16, 32–33; Inyo County taxes
on, 271, 375n6; in land purchase controversy, 243–44, 274–75, 285–86,
290, 299–300, 305–6, 305–9, 310–
11, 317–18, 380n14, 382n42; and
Long Valley dam issue, 240, 272,
273–74, 275, 287, 292, 376n16; Los
Angeles River water rights of, 24,
55–57, 104, 206; map of Greater, 267
fig.; Mulholland's journey to, 12–13;
Owens Valley media attacks on, 268,
270–71, 274, 286–87; Panic of 1907
in, 156, 158; plaza fountain of, 21–22,
337n12; San Fernando Valley water
rights of, 182; surplus water rights
of, 194–95, 200–201, 206, 215–16,
218–19; Tujunga Wash stragegy of,
77–78; Water Company purchased
by, 76–80; Water Company sued by,
48, 49, 75, 108; water consumption
record in, 239; water distribution
facilities in, 332 fig.; Wattersons's suit
against, 229. See also Annexations
Los Angeles Aqueduct: Alabama Gates
incident at, 295–97; construction
inventory from, 232; and demand for
reparations, 297, 300, 312; dynamite
attacks on, 287–88, 289, 308, 312–
13, 314, 380n22; Finkle's criticism of,
250, 251; maps of, 143 fig., 155 fig.;
Mulholland's relief map of, 259,
372n23; newspaper coverage of,

247–48; 1917 blowouts on, 261–63,
373n28; opening ceremonies of, 231,
241–42, 243–47; rains' damage to,
251, 303; security directives for, 313,
315; seventy-fifth anniversary of,
340n13; terminus of, 206, 207. See
also Aqueduct bonds; Aqueduct
distribution system; Owens River
project; Workers, aqueduct
Los Angeles Canal and Reservoir
Company, 20, 24
Los Angeles City Water Company. See
Water Company
Los Angeles City Water Department. See
Water Department
Los Angeles Clearing House Association,
296–97, 299–300
Los Angeles Consolidated Electric
Railway, 97
Los Angeles Daily Herald, 336n2
Los Angeles Daily Star, 14
Los Angeles Department of Water
and Power, xvii, 327. See also Water
Department
Los Angeles Evening Express, 34, 85–86,
336n2, 338n12
Los Angeles Evening News, 203; anti-
aqueduct stance of, 117, 127, 134,
136, 140, 153; attacks on Mulholland
in, 135, 148–49, 150, 355–56n20,
357n11; financial backers of, 351n10;
on Schuyler's appointment, 135; on
Simpson Auditorium debate, 151
Los Angeles Examiner: on Boulder Dam
project, 325, 376n21; on Eaton, 124;
eucalyptus article in, 179; Finkle's
letter in, 250; on Harper, 146; on
Harriman, 204; on Houghton, 118;
on miners' strike, 190–91; on municipal ownership, 373n27; in newspaper
rivalries, 116; on 1910 bond sales,
188; on Owens River project, 112,
117, 119, 140, 351n10
Los Angeles Express, 160, 222, 226,
234, 274, 336n2
Los Angeles Gas and Electric Company,
199, 262
Los Angeles Herald: on Buena Vista
leaks, 103; on Houghton, 118; on
Howard, 337n3; on Jenkins, 27; on
Mulholland's vacation, 104–5; in
newspaper rivalries, 116; on 1910
bond sales, 188; on Pendleton bill,
115; on sale of Water Company, 52,
340–41n8; on Moses Sherman, 97;
on water commission, 95
Los Angeles Mirror, 336n2

Los Angeles–Pacific Railway Company, 89, 97, 103

Los Angeles Record: on Alabama Gates incident, 296; on aqueduct investigation, 219, 367n30; contradictory positions of, 374–75n5; critical of aqueduct, 236, 262–63, 289, 370n2, 373–74n30; critical of Mulholland, 160, 261, 268, 327, 367n30; on Harper, 140, 146, 356n27; on land speculators, 355n19; on miners' strike, 190, 191; on municipal power, 140, 197, 252, 260–61, 373n27; on Owens River water, 232, 254; Owens Valley ties of, 380nn22,29; on water commission, 199

Los Angeles River, 275; bacteria count in, 93; city's legal rights to, 24, 55–57, 104, 206; Crystal Springs waters of, 24, 48–49, 61–62; origin and watershed of, 24; salt content explorations of, 71; theft of water from, 24–25, 56–57; zanja system of, 18. *See also* Zanja system

Los Angeles Star, 336n2

Los Angeles Times, 51; on Beaudry, 55; bombed building of, 189, 201, 363n16, 364n9; on Boulder Dam project, 278, 376n21; on Clover, 149; on dynamiting incident, 287; on Eaton, 63, 64, 74, 342n10; on Eaton family, 340n13; Henderson's suit against, 223–24, 367n32; on Houghton, 118; on Metropolitan Water District, 302; on miners' strike, 190; *Mirror* becomes, 336n2; on Mulholland as mayor, 234; on municipal power, 252, 260–61, 276–77, 278–79, 286, 373n27; in newspaper rivalries, 116, 351n10; on Owens River project, 115, 116, 152–53, 352–53n26, 354n11; on Perry residence, 340n17; on railway strikers, 98; on Sherman's removal, 184; on Waldron litigation, 79; on Water Department, 87

Los Angeles Tribune, 212, 234

Los Feliz Ditch, 20, 24

Los Feliz Point, 102

Los Feliz Rancho, 20, 24

The Lost Frontier (Sauder), xiv

Lummis, Charles F., 279, 349n30

Lungren, Fernand, 110

Lynch, J. D., xv

Macedo, Lillian Sloan (Mulholland's granddaughter), 32, 374n31

MacLachlan, James, 132, 133, 354–55n15

Maclay, Charles, 98

Maclay waterworks, 113

Mail service, 165–66

Mammoth (Mono County), 154

Manhole covers, 262, 373n29

Manzanar Tract, 290

Markham, Edwin C., 58

Marshall, Robert, 276

Martin, John T., 273, 274–75

Massarene, viscount, 6

Mathews, John R., 184

Mathews, William B., 153, 224, 294, 295, 354n12, 368–69n13; as aqueduct's legal adviser, 134, 357n3; bond-selling missions of, 80, 187, 211; in Boulder Dam campaign, 283, 309, 316, 380; death of, 327–28; and Eaton's land deal, 306, 307, 317–18; on Eaton's land profit, 124; lawsuits by, as city attorney, 86–87, 104, 347n26; Mulholland on, 247, 250–51; and municipal ownership, 75, 76, 186, 265–66, 268; and Owens River project, 105, 115, 121, 128, 134, 142, 144; Owens Valley peace tour of, 291, 292; on Pendleton Eminent Domain Bill, 115; and right-of-way bill, 272, 375n9; at Soda Company's trial, 242–43; and Water Department's administration, 87; at water purity trial, 256, 258

Matson, Robert, xvi

McAdoo, William Gibbs, 280

McAleer, Owen, 115, 128–30, 353n4

McCarthy, John Russell, 4–5

McCartney bill, 142, 144

McClure, W. S., 296, 299, 305

McClure Report (1925), 296, 299, 301, 305

McGregor, D., 35

McKay, Roderick, 232, 240, 245, 287, 303, 315

McKinley, William, 62, 73, 79

McNally Ditch, 274–75, 286, 290

McNamara trial, 201, 202, 204–5

McWilliams, Carey, 352–53n26

Mead, Elwood, 108, 276, 324

Mead, William, 89

Means, Thomas H., 71, 109, 110, 111

Medical department, 162, 167, 363n17

Mendenhall, Walter C., 114, 135, 350n5, 359n5

Merchants and Manufacturers' Association, 78, 189

Mesmer, Joseph, 343n7

Meters: on Buena Vista sewer lines, 103; first installation of, 345n20; Mulholland's proposal of, 82, 83–85; opposition to, 85–86, 345n24; "Water Waste" paper on, 114

Metropolitan Life Insurance Company, 188

Metropolitan Water District Act, 302, 312

Miles, Charles E., 29, 337–38n10

Miners' strike, 189, 190–91, 197–98

Mission Land Company, 178

Mix, Tom, 296, 297–98

Mojave: climate of, 172; disreputable establishments of, 172–74; highway from, to Bishop, 293, 294; livestock needs of, 144; 1917 fire in, 373n28

Mojave River, 136, 161, 349–50n1

Mono County, right-of-way battle in, 242, 268, 272, 375n9

Morse, H. C., 117

Mosher, Ed, 31

Mott, S. H., 53, 80, 338n7

Mountain Water Company, 49, 75

Mowry, George E., 277, 368–69n13

Muir, John, 121, 150–51

Mules, 168, 174–76, 219, 228–29

Mulholland, Addie (née Haas), 315–16, 374n31

Mulholland, Ellen (née Deakers, Mulholland's mother), 6, 7, 8

Mulholland, Hugh (Mulholland's father), 6–7, 8

Mulholland, Hugh Patrick (Mulholland's brother), 6, 10, 11–13, 17, 31–32, 374n31

Mulholland, Irving (newspaper editor), 129

Mulholland, Jane (née Smith, Mulholland's stepmother), 9

Mulholland, Joseph (Mulholland's stepbrother), 9

Mulholland, Lillie (née Ferguson, Mulholland's wife), 5, 42–43, 234, 243, 258–59

Mulholland, Lucile (Mulholland's daughter), 5, 243, 374n31

Mulholland, Mary (Mulholland's niece), 357–58n19

Mulholland, Mary (Mulholland's stepsister), 9

Mulholland, Michael (Mulholland's stepbrother), 9

Mulholland, Patrick (Mulholland's grandfather), 6

Mulholland, Richard James (Mulholland's son), 350n8

Mulholland, Rose Ellen (Mulholland's daughter), 11, 234, 266, 316, 374n31; at aqueduct ceremonies, 243; birth of, 43; on dam disaster, 319; in Mulholland's last years, 5, 330; on Mulholland's traits, 266, 345n22

Mulholland, Ruth (Mulholland's daughter), 374n31

Mulholland: The Dream-Builder (documentary film), 333

Mulholland, Thomas (Mulholland's brother), 6, 8–9

Mulholland, Thomas Ferguson (Mulholland's son), 43, 154, 374n31, 381n37

Mulholland, William: ancestry/origins of, 6–8, 44, 336n6; awards/recognitions of, 4, 23, 42, 134–35, 144–45, 245, 246–47, 252–53, 276, 280, 294, 302, 330, 354–55n15, 371n8, 376n25; boyhood of, 8–10; in British Merchant Marine, 10–11; with Deakers family, 11–12; death of, 330–31; and death of son, 350n8; and death of wife, 258–59; Eaton's rift with, 169, 243–44, 292–93, 370n33; family dwellings of, 5, 266; family members of, 1915–1921, 374n31; geology interest of, 17, 256; at Highway opening, 297–98; in human interest stories, 226–27, 243; as independent contractor, 35, 37, 338n12; insomnia of, 211; inventions/innovations of, 45, 138, 168, 256; lasting notoriety of, 383n18; in last years, 328–30; in logging accident, 11; marriage to Lillie Ferguson, 5, 42–43; and mayoral prospects, 230–31, 233–34; Memorial Fountain to, 23; as movie actor, 279; naturalization of, 37; odd jobs of, 11, 17; on Otis, 206–7; papers of, 111, 114, 266; Parkinson's disease of, 381n37; Perry's influence on, 28, 46–47; Pittsburgh to Los Angeles trip of, 12–13; in professional associations, 83, 279, 349n30; reading choices of, 17, 42, 339n9; at Rowland's breakfast, 58, 341n22; Sespe Creek project of, 36; vacations of, 154, 189, 315–16

Mulholland, William, character traits of, 5; alertness, 41, 359n14; autocratic/domineering, 230–31; avid reader, 32, 42, 339n9; bluntness, 84–85, 120, 211, 345n22, 352n18, 354n11; clarity of purpose, 301; discretion, 33; fair-mindedness, 64–65; frugality, 272; hygiene notions, 66; prodigious memory, 64, 177; public speaking disinclination, 150

Mulholland, William, as Chief of Owens River project: at Agricultural Park festivities, 220–21; at AIB hearing, 222–23, 367n30; annual reports of, 146–47, 158, 169–70, 191, 197, 201, 219; aqueduct map of, 259, 372n23; at aqueduct opening, 231, 243, 245–46, 247; aqueduct tours of, 161–62, 192–94, 199–200, 239–40; and board of public works, 157–58; in bond campaign, 150, 152–53; on civil service requirements, 162–63; on completion date, 179–80, 182, 187, 189, 197, 201, 235; confirmed appointment of, 134–35; on earthquake safety, 130–31; on Eaton's land purchases, 123–24, 169, 352n21; enemies' attacks on, 202–3, 205–7, 237–38, 368n18; grand jury's endorsement of, 139–40; and Harper's subversion, 146, 147–48; on high line, 218, 221–22, 224, 229–30, 234; investigatory trips of, 105, 110–11, 115, 136–37, 348n13, 355n19; on Jawbone digging, 164–65; on labor recruitment schemes, 156; labor system of, 166–67, 177, 360n17; Long Valley dam plans of, 272, 292, 376n16; on Mathews, 247, 250–51; military analogy of, 159; at Municipal League banquet, 120–22, 352n18; at Owens Valley land hearing, 185–86, 362n5; pipeline route of, 137, 139, 355–56n20; on post office locations, 165–66, 360n15; in preliminary construction phase, 144; recruitment of engineers by, 127, 131–32, 135, 136, 138–39; salary of, 181, 250, 253; on San Fernando Valley land grab, 178, 211; on Spilman's *Conspiracy,* 214–15; on surplus water distribution, 194–95, 200–201, 206, 218, 224, 226; at *Times* libel trial, 223–24, 367n32; at U.S. Congressional hearing, 132–33, 354nn11,12; on water quality, 118, 149–50, 254, 256–58, 351n14, 372n19

Mulholland, William, as city water superintendent: abandonment of zanja system by, 18, 93; on annexations, 94; appointment of, 80, 90; Boulder Dam campaign of, 279, 280–81, 282, 283–84, 294–95, 301–2, 305, 308, 316–17; city focus of, 271–72, 375n8; and Cryer incident, 289–90; and dynamiting incidents, 261–63, 287, 288, 308, 312–13; on hydroelectric power, 277–78; improvement projects of, 82,

86, 90, 101, 102–3, 137–38, 138, 179, 259, 344–45n16, 356n21; irrigation patrols of, 102; land purchase policy of, 169, 290, 300–301, 314–15, 317–18; meter system of, 82, 83–85, 103; and municipal power issue, 186, 261, 264, 265–66, 276–77, 373n27; at new Water and Power Department, 327; 1902 water condition summary of, 345n26; on oil refinery threat, 91–92; Owens Valley peace tour of, 290–93; on Saint Francis Dam collapse, 319, 322, 323, 325, 326–27, 328; salary of, 81; Spilman's attack on, 148–49, 150, 214–15; on water pressure demands, 90–91; on water shortages, 83, 84, 87, 101–2, 112, 135, 349–50n1

Mulholland, William, at Water Company: as deputy zanjero, 23–24, 25; gold watch for, 42; and main tunnel crisis, 68–69, 342n17; promotions of, 30, 32, 37–38; in purchase offer negotiations, 76–77; on rate increase, 70–71; San Joaquin Valley trip of, 72, 343n27; tunnel/pipeline projects of, 35, 37, 39–40, 43, 49, 54, 57; at water arbitration hearings, 62, 64–65, 67; on Water Company policies, 58–59, 62

Mulholland, William Bodine (Mulholland's nephew), 33, 327

Mulholland, William Perry (Mulholland's son), 234, 352n21, 361n8; birth of, 43; on Eaton, 370n33; hand tremors of, 381n37; high school graduation of, 221; marriage to Addie Haas, 374n31; at Panama Canal, 315–16; ranch of, 328; on trips with Mulholland, 91, 154

Mulholland Dam (*formerly* Weid Canyon Dam), 281, 282, 289, 302, 325–26, 383n13

Mulholland Highway, 280, 296, 297–98, 376n25

Municipal Affairs (magazine), 180

Municipal League: and Harper's election, 141–42; on municipal power, 260; and Owens River project, 120–22, 352n18

The Municipal News, 213–14

Municipal power: bond campaigns for, 186, 234–35, 252, 260–61, 278–79, 286, 290, 378n10; Craig lawsuit and, 281, 376–77n27; distribution issue of, 250; divisive stands on, 196–97, 252, 260, 265, 364n1, 371n7; newspapers' treatment of, 234–35, 276–77, 280, 373n27; 1936 realization of, 265; and

Water and Power Act campaign, 276.
  See also Hydroelectric power
Municipal waterworks: city's proposals
  for, in 1890s, 51–52, 53–54; Eaton's
  support of, 51, 66, 69–70, 71–72, 73,
  108, 343n30; Lippincott on, 108; and
  McCartney bill, 142, 144; Mulholland's support of, 59–60; 1901 bond
  election on, 77, 78–79; opposition to,
  78, 113, 115–16, 117, 343n7, 351n9.
  See also Water Department
Mushet, W. C., 144, 147, 179, 203
Myers (city auditor), 369n22

Nadeau, Remi, xiii, 351n10
Narrows, the, 82, 215, 253
National Bank of California (Los
  Angeles), 44
National Geological Survey, 107, 108,
  349n19
National Reclamation Service. *See* U.S.
  Reclamation Service
Natural Soda Products Company, 229,
  242–43
Neenach break (1917), 262, 373n29
Nelson, W. M., 357n8
Nevada-California Power Company, 266
Newberry, John R., 343n7
Newell, Frederick H., 108, 120, 131,
  354n12; at American Forestry Service
  conference, 68; and Otis, 114; and
  Owens Valley project, 106, 108, 109,
  110–11, 127, 128, 136; San Joaquin
  Valley expedition of, 72, 343n27
Newmark, Harris, 365n15
New York Life Insurance Company, 188
New York Times, 4, 247–48
Noel, P. D., 280
Nofziger, Frank, 89
Nordskog, Andrae, 380–81n29
Norris, George N., 280
Northridge (*formerly* Zelzah), 259
Norton, John, 184

O'Connell, Daniel, 7
O'Connell School (Dublin), 8–9
Oil, 91–92, 277, 376n20
Olmstead, Frank L., 67, 70, 73, 108,
  127, 129
Olvera Street plaza, 18
O'Melveny, Henry, xvi, 65, 90, 371n8;
  and Dominguez Rancho, 187, 231;
  and Eaton, 169, 349n25; and Lippin-
  cott, 110; Mulholland's social ties to,
  82–83, 189; rainfall records of, 73, 99
Orr, Mira E., 129, 136
Orton, Daisy Shaw, 322–23, 383n8

Orton, Lucius R., 322–23
Orton, Raymond, 383n8
Osgood, J. A., 344n13
O'Shaughnessy, M. M., 276
Ostrom, Vincent, xiii–xiv, 340n2,
  341n15
Otis, Harrison Gray, xv, 88, 225; at
  aqueduct opening, 244; and Chaffee's
  appointment, 159–60, 358n3; and
  Earl, 201, 364n9; Henderson's suit
  against, 223–24, 367n32; on high line,
  234; home of, 98; land syndicates of,
  97, 98, 285, 350n4; Mulholland on,
  206–7; on municipal power, 234,
  252; in newspaper rivalries, 116; at
  Rowland's breakfast, 58; in Spanish-
  American War, 62; in Steffens's
  experiment, 204
Outland, Charles, 382n4
Owens Lake, soda content of, 242–43
Owens River Canal Company, 273, 274
Owens River project: accounting system
  for, 147, 357n8; AIB's investigation of,
  207–8, 209–10, 212, 222–23, 224–25,
  367n30; announcement of, 116–17,
  351n10, 355n19; annual reports on,
  146–47, 158, 169–70, 191, 197, 201,
  219; cement needs of, 131–32, 144,
  157; city auditor's report on, 238–
  39, 369n22; city council's role in,
  119, 134–35, 146–48; civil service
  employees on, 156, 162–63; cost
  estimates of, 127, 139, 238; earthquake safety of, 130–31; equipment/
  machinery for, 168; failed rock siphon
  of, 235–36; fatal accidents on, 220,
  221, 229; and faulty construction
  rumors, 191, 363n18; funding difficulties of, 158, 164, 187, 188–89,
  204, 211, 362n13; grand jury's
  approval of, 139–40; Harriman's
  attacks on, 202–3, 205–6, 207; hydroelectric power from, 139, 140, 186,
  196–97; inspection tours of, 192–94,
  239–40; Interior's decision on, 126–
  27; as irrigation resource, 132–34;
  Jawbone Division of, 164–66; labor
  problems on, 189, 190–91, 197–98;
  labor system of, 166–67, 177, 190,
  198, 360n17; and McCartney bill,
  142, 144; medical department for,
  162, 167, 363n17; mules for, 168,
  174–76, 219, 228–29; Municipal
  League banquet for, 120–22, 352n18;
  1909 progress on, 171, 179–80, 181–
  82; preliminary construction of, 144;
  private opposition to, 117–20, 148–

Owens River project (*continued*)
49, 150, 214–15, 351nn14,16;
recruitment of engineers for, 127,
131–32, 135, 136, 138–39, 145;
route of pipeline for, 137, 355–56n20;
rumors of, in *Examiner*, 112, 349–
50n1; tunnel drilling in, 161–62, 176,
181–82. *See also* Aqueduct bonds;
Aqueduct distribution system; Los
Angeles Aqueduct; Workers, aqueduct
Owens River water: alarmist report on,
254–55, 371n14; Muir on, 121, 150–
51; Mulholland on, 118, 149–50, 254,
258, 351n14, 372n19; trial on purity
of, 256–58
Owens Valley: and Alabama Gates incident, 295–97; California governor
in, 363n20; city's inspection tour of,
128–30; Cryer's response to, 289–90;
and dynamiting incidents, 287–88,
289, 308, 312–13, 380n22; earthquake in, 261–62; Eaton's interest in,
30–31, 82, 92, 105, 106–7, 113, 115,
122–25, 169, 348n13, 349n25; federal
government's interest in, 106, 107,
109, 110–11, 349n18; Ku Klux Klan
in, 285, 377n7; land purchase controversy in, 243–44, 274–75, 285–86,
290, 299–301, 305–9, 310–11, 317–
18, 380n14, 382n42; Long Valley dam
issue of, 240, 272, 273–74, 275, 287,
292, 376n16; McClure report on, 296,
299, 301; Mulholland's investigations
in, 105, 110–11, 115, 136–37, 348n13,
355n19; Mulholland's peace tour to,
290–93; orchards proposal for, 294,
295; proposed annexation of, 292;
reaction of, to aqueduct, 122–24, 185,
362n5; reparation demands by, 297,
300, 312; road conditions in, 346n10;
water rights issue in, 241, 242–43,
268, 270–71, 274; well drilling in,
264, 306
*Owens Valley: Where the Trail of the
Wrecker Runs* (Faulkner), 312
Owens Valley Defense Association, 242
The Owens Valley Dispute (Kinsey), 312
Owens Valley Herald, 270, 274, 285,
293, 295, 311–12, 315
Owens Valley Irrigation District, 92,
106–7; costs of, to city, 311; formation of, 273, 274
Owens Valley Property Owners
Protective Association, 273, 275, 285,
312
Owenyo, silver spike ceremony at, 191–
92, 363n20

Pacific Bank, 96–97
Pacific Electric Railway, 45
Pacific Outlook (magazine), 180
Page, Sherman, 343n7
Panama Canal, 138, 241, 315–16
Panama-Pacific Exposition (1915–1916),
259
Panic of 1907, 156, 158, 164
Pardee, George C., 109, 115, 144, 244
Parker, F. W., 344n13
Parker, O. K., 67, 109
Pasadena, 29, 76–77, 182, 195, 216,
337–38n10
Patterson, Kermit, 382n4
Patterson, W. C., 349n30
Peekskill Aqueduct (New York City),
153
Pendleton Eminent Domain Bill, 115
People's Party, 167
Perry, Florence, 47
Perry, Mamie, 47
Perry, William Hayes, 80; background
of, 28; and Eaton, 35; and Mulhol-
land, 28, 42, 46–47; Sespe Creek
project of, 36, 338–39n13; sewer line
bid of, 338n12; social status of, 47,
340n17, 349n17; Water Company
position of, 21, 46, 338n7; on Water
Company's value, 51, 78
Perry, Woodworth & Co., 28
Pessell, George D., 90
Phelan, James, 283
Phillips, J. E., 331
Phillips, Robert V., 331, 346n1, 347–
48n1, 371n17, 376n16
Phoenix Water Company, 96
Pico, Pio, 62
Pinchot, Gifford, 68, 110, 133, 179,
354n12
Pipeline, cast iron, 29, 337–38n10
Pirtle, John A., 55–57
Pirtle Cut, 56–57
Piru Creek, 117
Pomeroy, A. E., 53, 54, 152. *See also*
Hooker and Pomeroy case
Porcupine (weekly newspaper), 15, 31,
46, 54, 341n13
Porter, Benjamin F., 40, 98–99, 339n5
Porter, George K., 98–99
Porter Land and Water Company, 339n5
Potts, J. W., 55
Powell, John Wesley, 349n19
Power bond elections: of 1910, 186; of
1913, 234–35; of 1914, 252; of 1917,
260–61; of 1919, 261; of 1923, 278–
79; of 1924, 286, 290, 378n10. *See
also* Municipal power

Power right-of-way bill, 264, 265–66, 272, 273–74, 375n9

Powers, Luther Milton, 101, 211; on bacteria count, 93; and Ethel Leonard, 255; and oil refinery investigation, 91–92; on Owens River project, 179; public health contributions of, 66, 342n11

Progressives (Good Government), 126; on antipicketing ordinance, 189; on Chaffee's appointment, 160; on Mojave perils, 173; and Mulholland's mayoral prospects, 230–31, 233–34, 368–69n13; on municipal power, 196–97; political allies of, 210; and Governor Richardson, 277; and Mayor Rose, 369n21; on surplus waters issue, 213; victorious candidates of, 184, 201; and water commission upheaval, 183–84, 362n2

Providencia Rancho Company, 53

Public health, 14, 66, 93, 100, 342n11

Public service commission (*formerly* water commission): aqueduct bureau under, 236; establishment of, 199; on McClure Report, 299; 1912 turnover in, 213, 219; Owens Valley peace tour of, 291–93; Owens Valley policy decisions of, 294; Rose's overhaul of, 238, 369n21; suit against *Times* by, 223–24; on surplus water issue, 200–201, 216, 218–19; Woodman's audit of, 263. *See also* Water commission

Quinton, John H., 200

Railways: civilizing impact of, 15; Eaton's ventures in, 45, 89; from Los Angeles to Hollywood, 97–98; Sherman's ventures in, 45, 96–98; water sprinkling duty of, 99, 347n26. *See also* Southern Pacific Railroad

Rainfall: damage to aqueduct from, 251, 303; in 1883–1884, 35; in 1887, 38; in 1898–1904, 347–48n1; in 1903–1904, 99, 100; in 1919, 263–64; O'Melveny's records of, 73, 99

Ramirez, Juan R., 58

Rancho Bartolo Water Company, 115

Rancho El Tejon, 203

Reaburn, DeWitt L., 232, 245, 297–98

Read, George, 154, 344n13

Reagan Report, 251, 275

Reavis, W. S., 344n13

Red Rock Canyon, 165, 176

Reisner, Marc, xiv

Republican Party, 63, 88

Reservoir No. 4. *See* Beaudry's High Reservoir

The Resources of California (Hittell), 18

Ricardo settlement, 165–66

Richardson, Friend, 277, 296

Ricken Tunnel (Switzerland), 176

Rickey, Thomas B., 109, 123, 124

Rickey Ranch (*later* Eaton Land and Cattle Company), 109, 123, 124, 272. *See also* Eaton Land and Cattle Company

Rindge, Frederick, 99, 113

Rinehart, Robert E., 191, 363n19

Riparian rights, doctrine of, 52

Risdon Iron and Locomotive Works (San Francisco), 91, 102

Rivers in the Desert (Davis), xvi–xvii

Rochester, New York Times-Union, 280

Rogers, Earl, 92

Rogers, J. David, 325, 326, 370n1, 382n4

Rogers, Ralph, 49

Roosevelt, Franklin D., 352n21

Roosevelt, Theodore, 79, 98, 133, 353–54n10

Root, Erastus, 152

Rose, Henry Howard, 251; at aqueduct opening, 241, 246; final inspection tour of, 240; 1913 mayoral election of, 236; overhaul of city commissions by, 238, 369n21, 370n2; and Owens Valley project, 241, 242

Ross (U.S. Circuit Court judge), 347n20

Rowell, Chester, 378n17

Rowena Reservoir, 43

Rowland, William, 58, 192–93

Royal British Mail, 6–7

Royal British Navy, 10

Ryan, A. W., 344n13

Sacramento Bee, 280

Sacramento Union, 312

Saint Francis Dam, 313; collapse of, 319, 320–21; construction methods for, 320, 382n4; geology of site for, 320

Saint Francis Dam disaster, 4; city's response to, 323–24; Coroner's inquest into, 324–25; lives lost from, 319, 321; Mulholland's reaction to, 319, 322, 323, 325, 326–27, 328; possible causes of, 320, 324, 325, 326, 382n4; survivor's letter on, 322–23, 383n8

Salaries/wages: of aqueduct workers, 174, 197–98; and bonuses, 166, 177, 190, 198, 360n17; of city zanjero, 26; of Lippincott, 183, 236; of Matthews,

Salaries/wages (*continued*)
357n3; of Mulholland, 35, 37, 81,
181, 250, 253, 327; of water commissioners, 87; of Water Company
workers, 26, 35, 37
Saloons, 65–66, 216
Sand Canyon siphon, 235–36, 238, 240
*San Diego v. the San Diego and Los
Angeles Railroad Company,* 96,
347n20
San Fernando (city), 98
San Fernando Dam, 201, 211
San Fernando Mission Land Company,
211
San Fernando Tunnel, 98
San Fernando Valley: annexation of, 239,
258, 259; aqueduct's terminus in, 206,
207; city's suit against, 104; city's
water rights in, 182; Craig lawsuit for,
281, 376n27; first nighttime illumination in, 244; land grab issue in, 98–99,
178, 211; Lippincott's surveys of, 67,
71; Longyear's role in, 285; 1919
agricultural earnings in, 266; 1906
water usage in, 135; and surplus water
issue, 200–201, 202, 203, 206, 216;
watershed of, 214–15
San Fernando Valley Water Company, 40
San Francisco: municipal power issue in,
283; 1906 earthquake in, 126, 130–
31; soup kitchens of, 180–81; in water
rights dispute, 268; waterworks
project in, 171–72
San Francisco Call, 286–87
San Francisco Chronicle, 135, 247
San Francisco Examiner, 97, 116,
355n19
San Francisquito Canyon, 282; power
plant site at, 157, 186, 212, 260, 263,
279; Saint Francis Dam site at, 320,
333; tunnel building in, 249
San Francisquito Creek, 320
San Gabriel Valley, 16, 216, 226
San Joaquin Valley, 72, 276, 280,
343n27
San Juan-by-the-Sea, 44–45
Sanky (term), 337n8
San Pedro, 216
*Santa Ana Water Company v. the Town
of San Buenaventura,* 347n20
Santa Clara River, 113
Santa Fe Railroad, 89, 369n22
Santa Monica, 216
Santa Paula, 321, 324
Sartori, J. F., 98
Saturday Night (periodical), 288
Sauder, John, xiv

Sawyer, R. H., 144
Scattergood, Ezra F., 145, 165, 181, 186,
253; collapse of, 278; and Colorado
River project, 271, 283; criticism of,
263, 375n8; on dynamiting incident,
313; and municipal power issue, 196,
279, 280, 364n1, 373n27; power
bureau role of, 199, 242; *Record*'s
cartoon of, 261; at Water and Power
Department, 327
Schuyler, James D., 108, 114, 339n5;
engineering skills of, 135, 354–55n15;
and Owens River project, 136–37,
139–40
Sebastian, C. E., 259, 260
Seely, Joseph, 107
Sepulveda, Ygnacio, 58
Sespe Land and Water Company, 36,
338–39n13
Shattuck, E. S., 180–81
Shaw, George Bernard, 8
Shaw, Lucien, 55
Sheep Mountain (Wyoming), 303
Shenk, John W., 226, 236, 368–69n13,
369n18
Sherman, Moses Hazeltine, 45, 89;
business background of, 95–97,
347n20; and Porter Ranch deal, 98–
99; removed from water board, 178,
183–84
Sherman, William Tecumseh, 16, 96
Shoemaker, Eve H., 307
Shuey, George, 144, 273
Sierra Club, 268, 280
Silver, Herman, 72, 83–84, 85, 138,
342n10, 344n14
Silver Lake Power and Irrigation Com-
pany, 160–61, 242, 359n5
Silver Lake Reservoir, 20, 138, 156
Simpson Auditorium rally, 151–52
Siphons, rock versus steel, 235–36
Sisters of Charity, 14
Sitton, Tom, 265, 369n21
Slauson, James, 43
Sleeth, Dana, 373–74n30
Smallpox epidemic, 14
Smith, J. Waldo, 177, 188, 251–52
Smith, Sylvester C., 132
Smythe, William E., 107
Snow Steam Pump Company (Buffalo,
New York), 102
Snyder, Meredith P., 65, 72, 238, 261,
342n10; at Bakersfield banquet, 276;
on Lippincott, 110; on Los Angeles-
to-Hollywood railway, 98; municipal
appointments by, 88–89, 95; and mu-
nicipal waterworks, 79, 80

Socialist Party, 79; AIB role of, 208, 209, 222, 237; anti-aqueduct stance of, 202–3, 364–65n12; on municipal power, 252; political allies of, 201–2, 210, 371n7

"Some of the Penalties of Rapid Growth in Los Angeles" (Mulholland), 266

Southern California Edison Company. *See* Edison Electric Company

Southern California Irrigation Congress (1905), 114

Southern California water supply, 269 fig.

Southern Pacific Railroad, 96; aqueduct's contract with, 165, 239, 369n22; civilizing impact of, 15; freight rates of, 156, 157, 161; silver spike ceremony of, 191–92, 363n20; wages on, 174; Water Company's ties to, 61

Southern Sierra Power Company, 266

South Pasadena, 200

Spalding, W. A., 337n12, 340–41n8, 341n2

Spanish-American War (1898), 62

Spectator (journal), 188

Spilman, William T., 203; on meter system, 345n24; Mulholland's response to, 149–50, 214–15; on Owens River project, 148–49, 214, 357n11

Spilman Suburban Water Company, 148

Spreckels, Rudolph, 276, 277

Spring Valley Water Company (San Francisco), 64, 271, 350n8, 366–67n26

Stafford, Harry, 82, 356n27

Standard Oil Company, 81

Steadman, J. J., 221

Stearns, Frederick P., 135, 136–37, 138, 139–40, 195

Steffens, Lincoln, 60, 204, 365n17

Stegner, Wallace, xiv

Steinmetz, Charles, 277–78

Stephens, William D., 184, 185, 244

Stevenson, A. P., 344n13

Storrow, Samuel, 366–67n26

"Stream Characteristics of Southern California" (Lippincott), 114

Strikes, 201; miners', 189, 190–91, 197–98; railway, 98

Sullivan, Mark, xv–xvi

Summers, Charlie, 309

Sunset Club, 83, 170, 266, 349n30

Surplus waters. *See* Aqueduct distribution system

Sweetwater Dam (Oregon), 136

Swing, Phil, 283, 284, 290

Swing-Johnson bill, 282, 283, 291, 307, 316–17, 325

Symon brothers, 243–44

Symons, William, 274, 286, 290

Taft, William Howard, 168, 169, 205

Taney, J. S., 232

Taylor, Raymond G., 167, 359n10, 363n17

Teague, Charles Collins, 323

Teddy's Terrors (marching group), 98

Tehachapi, 165; cement plant at, 157, 170, 215

Terminal Island Water Company, 216

Tess of the Storm Country (film), 279

Third Street Tunnel, 70

Timmons, Joseph, 283, 304, 376n21

Tinemaha Dam, 309, 316, 320, 381n39

Toll, Charles H., 71, 82, 344n14

Tonopah Daily News, 374–75n5

Topoc Dam project, 283

Transit companies. *See* Railways

Trolley cars, 45, 96

Tropico land scheme, 148

Truman, Benjamin, xv, 58

Tujunga Wash. *See* Big Tujunga Wash

Tunnel drilling: broken records in, 176, 361n10; at Buena Vista infiltration gallery, 86; at Elizabeth Lake, 161–62, 163, 168, 176; at Jawbone, 176, 181–82

Tunnel 17-M (Red Rock Canyon), 176

Turner, Joel H., 19

Typhoid fever, 93, 117

Union Consolidated Refining Company, 91–92

Union Hollywood Water Company, 94

Union Labor News, 78

Union League Club, 44

Unions. *See* Labor, organized

University of California at Berkeley, 4, 252

U.S. Congress: and Boulder Dam testimony, 283–84; and Flint-McLachlan Bill, 132–34, 354n12

U.S. Department of Agriculture, 99

U.S. Geological Survey, 107, 108, 349n19

U.S. Land Office hearing (1910), 185, 362n5

U.S. Reclamation Service: Duryea with, 131–32; financial difficulties of, 111; Lippincott with, 105–6, 113–14, 127–28, 350n5; and Otis, 350n4;

U.S. Reclamation Service (*continued*)
Owens Valley interests of, 92, 106,
107, 109, 110–11, 349n18
U.S. Supreme Court decision, 71–72

The Valley of Broken Hearts (Kunze),
286–87, 312
Van Norman, Bessie, 145–46, 231
Van Norman, Harvey, xvi, 173, 189,
224, 264, 303; at aqueduct's opening,
245; background of, 145; and Boulder
Dam project, 305, 316; in car accident,
313; and dam disaster, 319; final
inspection tour of, 240; and Little
Lake blowout, 262; mule teams of,
175, 228, 361n8; in Owens Valley
negotiations, 274, 291, 292, 294, 295,
307, 311, 317–18; steel siphon project
of, 236; at Water and Power Department,
327
Van Nuys, 201
Variel, R. H. F., 343n7
Vasquez, Tiburcio, 16, 58, 192
Veritas letters (Spilman), 148, 149, 214,
357n11; Mulholland's response to,
149–50
Vermilyea, S. E., 241
Vernon, 55–56, 341n15
*Vernon Irrigation Company v. City of
Los Angeles,* 55–56
Victorio (Apache chief), 17
*Vision or Villainy: Origins of the Owens
Valley–Los Angeles Water Controversy*
(Hoffman), xiv
Vollmer, B. A., 147
Vroman, J. P., 90, 344n13

Wages. *See* Salaries/wages
Walcott, Charles D., 133, 354n12
Waldron, David V., 78, 79–80, 343n7
Waldron, S. A., 78
Wallace, A. J., 220
Wall Street Journal, 325
Walton, John, xiv
Warner, Charles W., 210; aqueduct
investigation by, 212, 213, 222, 223,
225, 367n30
Warren, George B., 295, 309, 375n6
Washburn, W. J., 354nn12,15
Washington Park (*later* Chutes Park),
343n7
*Water and Politics: A Study of Water
Policies and Administration in the
Development of Los Angeles*
(Ostrom), xiii–xiv
Water and Power (Kahrl), xiv
Water and the West (Hundley), xiv

Water bonds: Eaton's campaign for,
69–70; funding payments on, 101;
1901 election on, 77, 78–79; ruled
invalid, 76; sale of, 80; Waldron's
litigation against, 79–80, 343n10.
See also Municipal waterworks
Water Canyon, 165
Water commission (*later* public service
commission): announcement of
aqueduct by, 116; financial record
of, 199; *Herald* on, 95; membership
of, 81, 88–89, 344n14, 346n1; 1910
upheaval in, 183–84; 1911 reorganization
of, 199; Owens Valley tour of,
128–30; salaries of, 87, 89; on serving
outlying areas, 93–94; Water Department
appointments by, 90. *See also*
Public service commission
Water Company: asking price of, 76, 77;
city council's ties to, 21, 46; city's
lawsuits against, 48, 49, 75, 108;
city's purchase of, 76–80; and Crystal
Springs controversy, 24, 49, 61–62,
63, 64–65, 67–68, 341n2; directors
of, 28, 338n7; Eaton's criticism of, 35,
37, 61, 64, 71; estimated revenues of,
78; estimated value of, 67; fire hydrants
of, 34, 58–59, 67, 337n6, 341n10; leased
water rights of, 20–22, 61, 337n11;
Mulholland on, 58–59, 76–77; new
headquarters for, 41; personnel of,
26, 338n7; primitive equipment of,
26, 33; quality of water from, 27–28,
31, 39, 54; reservoir projects of, 22,
57; retained employees from, 344n13;
salaries at, 26, 35, 37; sale of, to Indianapolis
syndicate, 51, 52–53; in water
rates battles, 34, 59, 63, 70–71, 72;
zanjero's clashes with, 26–27, 76
Water Department: first commissioners
of, 81, 88–89, 344n14, 346n1; funds
from, for aqueduct, 158; headquarters
of, 81; improvements/reforms by, 82,
344n16; private schemes against, 113,
115–16, 117, 351n9; rates of, 87, 95,
266, 268; revenues of, 87, 95. *See
also* Municipal waterworks; Water
commission
Water pressure demands, 90–91, 101,
346n6
Water rates: Water Company's battles
over, 34, 59, 63, 70–71, 72; of Water
Department, 87, 95, 266, 268
The Water Seekers (Nadeau), xiii
"The Water Steal" (flier), 78
"The Water Supply of Southern
California" (Mulholland), 111

"Water Waste" (Mulholland), 114
Watson, C. Percy, 313
Watt, R. S., 152
Watterson, George, 256, 273–74, 290, 306, 314, 316
Watterson, Mark Q., 256, 314, 316
Watterson, Wilfred W., 291; and Eaton's land deal, 307, 308–9, 310–11; fraud trial of, 314, 316; and Longyear sale, 305–6; in water rights dispute, 229, 256, 292, 296–97
Weid, Ivar, 302
Weid Canyon Dam. See Mulholland Dam
Wellborn, Charles, 216, 218
Western Federation of Miners, 190, 197
Western Times and Water Wars (Walton), xiv
West Los Angeles Water Company, 56–57
West Side Water Company, 67, 78, 110, 352–53n26
Weymouth, Frank, 282, 305, 327
Wheeler, Fred, 236–37, 258, 286, 371n7
"Whistling Dick" (mule skinner), 175–76, 361n8
White, Stephen M., 58, 65
White Steamer automobiles, 129–30, 136
Whitley, H. J., 285, 375n8
Whitley Heights (Hollywood), 97–98
Whitsett, William Paul, 272, 292
Wicks, Moses L., 49, 338n6
Widney, Erwin W., 173
Widney, R. M., 151–52
Wiggins, Frank, 112, 236
Wilde, Oscar, 8
Willard, Charles Dwight, xvi, 346n3, 349nn25,30; death of, 251; Mulholland to, on completion date, 180; Mulholland to, on mayoralty, 230–31; as water commissioner, 89–90
Willcocks, Sir William, 253
William Mulholland: A Forgotten Forefather (Matson), xvi
William Mulholland Memorial Fountain, 23
Wilson (mule skinner), 175
Wilson, Ben C., 183

Wilson, John, 211
Wilson, Stanley, 202
Wilson, Woodrow, 226
Wintz, Homer, 372n19
Wintz, Philip, 36, 191, 233
Woodard, J. H., 51, 52, 53
Woodman, Frederic Thomas, 260, 262–63
Woolen Ditch Dam. See Beaudry's High Reservoir
Work, Hubert, 282–83
Workers, aqueduct: bonus system of, 166–67, 177, 190, 198, 360n17; civil service requirements of, 162–63; with families, 167–68; labor unrest of, 186–87, 189–91; mail service for, 165–66; meals for, 180–81, 185–86, 189, 190, 212, 363n17; medical care for, 162; Mojave's lure for, 172–74; number of, 171, 174, 181, 219; potable water for, 165; recruitment of, 156; relocation of, 232–33; wages of, 174, 197–98. See also Engineers
Workman, Boyle, 78, 238
Workman, William, 39, 40, 58, 80, 343n12
Works, John D., 254, 257–58, 378n11
Wright, C. C., 83–84, 343n7
Wright, Harold Bell, 328
Wright Irrigation Act, 83

Yaw, Ellen Beach, 244
Yoakum, M. G., 178
Young, C. C., 312, 313, 323, 324
Young, T. W., 128, 129, 130, 172
Yuma reclamation project, 109, 111

Zanja (term), 337n8; anglicization of, 31
Zanja Madre (Mother Ditch), 18, 69
Zanja Madre Tunnel, 35
Zanja system: abandonment of, 18, 93; described, 18; equipment of, 26; headed by Jenkins, 26–27; low-cost water from, 78, 86, 343n7; management of, 19
Zanjero (water steward), 19, 26–27, 31, 76
Zelzah (now Northridge), 259
Zombro, Sumter F., 310, 314

Compositor:	Integrated Composition Systems
Text:	10/13 Sabon
Display:	Bodoni
Printer and Binder:	Data Reproductions Corporation